Lecture Notes in Computer Science 3767

Commenced Publication in 1973
Founding and Former Series Editors:
Gerhard Goos, Juris Hartmanis, and Jan van Leeuwen

Editorial Board

David Hutchison
  Lancaster University, UK
Takeo Kanade
  Carnegie Mellon University, Pittsburgh, PA, USA
Josef Kittler
  University of Surrey, Guildford, UK
Jon M. Kleinberg
  Cornell University, Ithaca, NY, USA
Friedemann Mattern
  ETH Zurich, Switzerland
John C. Mitchell
  Stanford University, CA, USA
Moni Naor
  Weizmann Institute of Science, Rehovot, Israel
Oscar Nierstrasz
  University of Bern, Switzerland
C. Pandu Rangan
  Indian Institute of Technology, Madras, India
Bernhard Steffen
  University of Dortmund, Germany
Madhu Sudan
  Massachusetts Institute of Technology, MA, USA
Demetri Terzopoulos
  New York University, NY, USA
Doug Tygar
  University of California, Berkeley, CA, USA
Moshe Y. Vardi
  Rice University, Houston, TX, USA
Gerhard Weikum
  Max-Planck Institute of Computer Science, Saarbruecken, Germany

Lecture Notes in Computer Science

Commenced Publication in 1973
Founding and Former Series Editors:
Gerhard Goos, Juris Hartmanis, and Jan van Leeuwen

Editorial Board

David Hutchison
 Lancaster University, UK
Takeo Kanade
 Carnegie Mellon University, Pittsburgh, PA, USA
Josef Kittler
 University of Surrey, Guildford, UK
Jon M. Kleinberg
 Cornell University, Ithaca, NY, USA
Friedemann Mattern
 ETH Zurich, Switzerland
John C. Mitchell
 Stanford University, CA, USA
Moni Naor
 Weizmann Institute of Science, Rehovot, Israel
Oscar Nierstrasz
 University of Bern, Switzerland
C. Pandu Rangan
 Indian Institute of Technology, Madras, India
Bernhard Steffen
 University of Dortmund, Germany
Madhu Sudan
 Massachusetts Institute of Technology, MA, USA
Demetri Terzopoulos
 New York University, NY, USA
Doug Tygar
 University of California, Berkeley, CA, USA
Moshe Y. Vardi
 Rice University, Houston, TX, USA
Gerhard Weikum
 Max-Planck Institute of Computer Science, Saarbruecken, Germany

Yo-Sung Ho   Hyoung Joong Kim (Eds.)

Advances in Multimedia Information Processing – PCM 2005

6th Pacific-Rim Conference on Multimedia
Jeju Island, Korea, November 13-16, 2005
Proceedings, Part I

Springer

Volume Editors

Yo-Sung Ho
Gwangju Institute of Science and Technology (GIST)
1 Oryong-dong buk-gu, Gwangju, 500-712, Korea
E-mail: hoyo@gist.ac.kr

Hyoung Joong Kim
Kangwon National University
Department of Control and Instrumentation Engineering
Kangwondaehakgil, Chunchon, Kangwondo, 200-701, Korea
E-mail: khj@kangwon.ac.kr

Library of Congress Control Number: 2005935481

CR Subject Classification (1998): H.5.1, H.3, H.5, C.2, H.4, I.3, K.6, I.7, I.4

ISSN   0302-9743
ISBN-10   3-540-30027-9 Springer Berlin Heidelberg New York
ISBN-13   978-3-540-30027-4 Springer Berlin Heidelberg New York

This work is subject to copyright. All rights are reserved, whether the whole or part of the material is concerned, specifically the rights of translation, reprinting, re-use of illustrations, recitation, broadcasting, reproduction on microfilms or in any other way, and storage in data banks. Duplication of this publication or parts thereof is permitted only under the provisions of the German Copyright Law of September 9, 1965, in its current version, and permission for use must always be obtained from Springer. Violations are liable to prosecution under the German Copyright Law.

Springer is a part of Springer Science+Business Media

springeronline.com

© Springer-Verlag Berlin Heidelberg 2005
Printed in Germany

Typesetting: Camera-ready by author, data conversion by Scientific Publishing Services, Chennai, India
Printed on acid-free paper   SPIN: 11581772   06/3142   5 4 3 2 1 0

Preface

We are delighted to welcome readers to the proceedings of the 6th Pacific-Rim Conference on Multimedia (PCM). The first PCM was held in Sydney, Australia, in 2000. Since then, it has been hosted successfully by Beijing, China, in 2001, Hsinchu, Taiwan, in 2002, Singapore in 2003, and Tokyo, Japan, in 2004, and finally Jeju, one of the most beautiful and fantastic islands in Korea.

This year, we accepted 181 papers out of 570 submissions including regular and special session papers. The acceptance rate of 32% indicates our commitment to ensuring a very high-quality conference. This would not be possible without the full support of the excellent Technical Committee and anonymous reviewers that provided timely and insightful reviews. We would therefore like to thank the Program Committee and all reviewers.

The program of this year reflects the current interests of the PCM's. The accepted papers cover a range of topics, including, all aspects of multimedia, both technical and artistic perspectives and both theoretical and practical issues. The PCM 2005 program covers tutorial sessions and plenary lectures as well as regular presentations in three tracks of oral sessions and a poster session in a single track. We have tried to expand the scope of PCM to the artistic papers which need not to be strictly technical. Since we are living in the age of convergence, we believe that convergence of technology and art is also highly needed. However, we realize that bridging the gap between them has not been easy due to the lack of mutual understanding and lack of fair evaluation criteria. Of course, a few papers widen the horizon of the PCM 2005. Traditional topics of multimedia, such as multimedia communications, audio-visual compressions, multimedia security, image and signal processing techniques, multimedia data processing, and other important works are balanced in the PCM 2005.

We give a special thanks to Prof. Jae-Kyoon Kim, General Chair, for his brilliant leadership in organizing this conference. This was an important work which was dealt with very efficiently and harmoniously. Our thanks must go to all the Organizing Committee members for their precious time and enthusiasm. They did their best in financing, publicity, proceedings, registration, Web and local arrangement. We cannot forget Victoria Kim for her professionalism in managing and assisting us as a Conference Secretary. We express our thanks to the sponsors including the Ministry of Information and Communication, the Institute of Information Technology Assessment, Korea National Tourism Organization, and Korea Society of Broadcast Engineers.

Yo-Sung Ho
Hyoung Joong Kim

Committee List

Technical Program Committee Members

Masao Aizu (Canon, Japan)
John Apostolopoulos (Hewlett-Packard, USA)
Yasuo Ariki (Kobe University, Japan)
Goh Wooi Boon (Nanyang Technological University, Singapore)
Nozha Boujemaa (INRIA Rocquencourt, France)
Hye Ran Byun (Yonsei University, Korea)
Long-Wen Chang (National Tsing Hua University, Taiwan)
Yung-Chang Chen (National Tsing Hua University, Taiwan)
Liang-Tien Chia (Nanyang Technological University, Singapore)
Yoon Sik Choe (Yonsei University, Korea)
Song Chong (KAIST, Korea)
Alberto Del Bimbo (University of Florence, Italy)
Chabane Djeraba (Laboratoire d' Informatique Fondamentale de Lille, France)
Toshiaki Fujii (Nagoya University, Japan)
Patrick Gioia (France Telecom R&D, France)
Yihong Gong (NEC Laboratories America, USA)
Patrick Gros (IRISA-CNRS, France)
William Grosky (University of Michigan - Dearborn, USA)
Irene H. Y. Gu (Chalmers, Sweden)
Ling Guan (Ryerson University, Canada)
Anthony T. S. Ho (Nanyang Technological University, Singapore)
Yo-Sung Ho (GIST, Korea)
Min Cheol Hong (Soongsil University, Korea)
Xian-Sheng Hua (Microsoft, China)
Jenq-Nenq Hwang (University of Washington, USA)
Ichiro Ide (Nagoya University, Japan)
Alejandro Jaimes (FX Pal Japan, Fuji Xerox, USA)
R. C. Jain (Birla Institute of Science and Technology, India)
Kyeong Hoon Jung (Kookmin University, Korea)
Mohan S. Kankanhalli (National University of Singapore, Singapore)
Aggelos Katsaggelos (Northwestern University, USA)
Jiro Katto (Waseda University, Japan)
Roichi Kawada (KDDI R&D Laboratories Inc., Japan)
Dong In Kim (Simon Fraser University, Canada)
Hae Kwang Kim (Sejong University, Korea)
Hae Yong Kim (University of São Paulo, Brazil)
Hong Kook Kim (GIST, Korea)

Hyoung Joong Kim (Kangwon National University, Korea)
Jong Won Kim (GIST, Korea)
Man Bae Kim (Kangwon National University, Korea)
Asanobu Kitamoto (National Institute of Informatics, Japan)
Hitoshi Kiya (Tokyo Metropolitan University, Japan)
Sung-Jea Ko (Korea University, Korea)
Ki Ryong Kwon (Pusan University of Foreign Studies, Korea)
Chil Woo Lee (Chonnam National University, Korea)
Jeong A. Lee (Chosun University, Korea)
Jong Weon Lee (Sejong University, Korea)
Kwan Heng Lee (GIST, Korea)
Yoon Joon Lee (KAIST, Korea)
Yung Lyul Lee (Sejong University, Korea)
Riccardo Leonardi (Università degli Studi di Brescia, Italy)
Jin Jang Leou (National Chung Cheng University, Taiwan)
Michael Lew (University of Leiden, The Netherlands)
Chung Sheng Li (IBM, USA)
Kin Li (Microsoft, USA)
Mingjing Li (Microsoft Research Asia, China)
Rainer Lienhart (University of Augsburg, Germany)
Chia Wen Lin (National Chung Cheng University, Taiwan)
David Lin (National Chiao Tung University, Taiwan)
Weisi Lin (Agency for Science, Technology and Research, Singapore)
Wanquan Liu (Curtin University of Technology, Australia)
Kai Kuang Ma (Nanyang Technological University, Singapore)
Wei Ying Ma (Microsoft Research Asia, China)
Young Shik Moon (Hanyang University, Korea)
Chong Wah Ngo (City University of Hong Kong, Hong Kong)
Vincent Oria (New Jersey Institute of Technology, USA)
Rae Hong Park (Sogang University, Korea)
Peter Pyun (Hewlett-Packard, USA)
Anthony Reeves (Cornell University, USA)
Kang Hyeon Rhee (Chosun University, Korea)
Takahiro Saito (Kanagawa University, Japan)
Philippe Salembier (Universitat Politècnica de Catalunya, Spain)
Peter Schelkens (Vrije Universiteit Brussel, Belgium)
Nicu Sebe (University of Amsterdam, The Netherlands)
Timothy K. Shih (Tamkang University, Taiwan)
Dong Gyu Sim (Kwangwoon University, Korea)
John R. Smith (IBM T. J. Watson Research Center, USA)
Lifeng Sun (Tsinghua University, China)
Luis Torres (Universitat Politècnica de Catalunya, Spain)
Hsiao-Rong Tyan (Chung Yuan Christian University, Taiwan)
Shekhar Verma (Indian Institute of Information Technology, India)
Chee Sun Won (Dongguk University, Korea)

You Jip Won (Hanyang University, Korea)
Lingda Wu (National University of Defense Technology, China)
Changsheng Xu (Agency for Science, Technology and Research, Singapore)
Youngjun Francis Yoo (Texas Instruments, USA)
Lu Yu (Zhe Jiang University, China)
Ley Zhang (Microsoft Research Asia, China)
Xiao-Ping Zhang (Ryerson University, Canada)

Additional Reviewer List

Jeong-Hwan Ahn (Samsung AIT, Korea)
Hee Jun An (Seoul National University of Technology, Korea)
Jaakko Astola (Tampere University of Technology, Finland)
Marcos Avilés Rodrigálvarez (Universidad Politécnica de Madrid, Spain)
Konsung Bae (Kyungpook National University, Korea)
Joong-Hwan Baek (Hankuk Aviation University, Korea)
Hyokyung Bahn (Ewha Womans University, Korea)
Raphaèle Balter (France Telecom R&D, France)
Gaspard Breton (France Telecom R&D, France)
David Cailliere (France Telecom R&D, France)
Kyung-Ae Cha (Daegu University, Korea)
Ching-Han Chen (I-Shou University, Taiwan)
Adrian David Cheok (National University of Singapore, Singapore)
Hoyong Choi (Chungbuk National University, Korea)
Jong-Soo Choi (Chung-Ang University, Korea)
Sumi Choi (Sejong University, Korea)
Ho-Yong Choi (Chungbuk National University, Korea)
Ki Dong Chung (Pusan National University, Korea)
Thomas Di Giacomo (University of Geneva, Switzerland)
Jean-Pierre Evain (European Broadcasting Union, France)
Víctor Fernández (UAM (ES), Spain)
Masaaki Fujiyoshi (Tokyo Metropolitan University, Japan)
Wen Gao (Joint Research & Development Laboratory, China)
Takayuki Hamamoto (Tokyo University of Science, Japan)
JungHyun Han (Korea University, Korea)
Mahnjin Han (Samsung AIT, Korea)
Dongsoo Har (GIST, Korea)
Jun Heo (Konkuk University, Korea)
HyunKi Hong (Chung-Ang University, Korea)
Jin-Woo Hong (ETRI, Korea)
Ki-Sang Hong (POSTECH, Korea)
Eenjun Hwang (Korea University, Korea)
Euee S. Jang (Hanyang University, Korea)
Ju-wook Jang (Sogang University, Korea)
Byeungwoo Jeon (Sung Kyun Kwan University, Korea)

Jechang Jeong (Hanyang University, Korea)
Xiaoyue Jiang (Northwestern Polytechnical University, China)
Xiaogang Jin (Zhejiang University, China)
Nam Ik Joe (Seoul National University, Korea)
Inwhee Joe (Hanyang University, Korea)
Jae Hak Jung (Inha University, Korea)
Soon Ki Jung (Kyungpook National University, Korea)
Sung-Hwan Jung (Changwon National University, Korea)
Dong Wook Kang (Kookmin University, Korea)
Hong-Goo Kang (Yonsei University, Korea)
Hyun-Soo Kang (Chungbuk National University, Korea)
Mun Gi Kang (Yonsei University, Korea)
Sooyong Kang (Hanyang University, Korea)
Mohan Kankanhalli (National University of Singapore, Singapore)
Hirokazu Kato (Osaka University, Japan)
Stefan Katzenbeisser (Technische Universität München, Germany)
Bo Yon Kim (Kangwon National University, Korea)
Chong-kwon Kim (Seoul National University, Korea)
Changick Kim (ICU, Korea)
Doh-Suk Kim (Lucent Technologies, USA)
Gerard Jounghyun Kim (POSTECH, Korea)
HyungJun Kim (Korea University, Korea)
Jaejoon Kim (Daegu University, Korea)
Jong-Nam Kim (Pukyong National University, Korea)
JongWeon Kim (Sangmyung University, Korea)
Keunho Kim (Samsung AIT, Korea)
Laehyun Kim (KIST, Korea)
Mun Chul Kim (ICU, Korea)
Sangwook Kim (Kyungpook National University, Korea)
Sang-Wook Kim (Samsung AIT, Korea)
Weon-Goo Kim (Kunsan National University, Korea)
Whoi-Yul Yura Kim (Hanyang University, Korea)
Won-Ha Kim (Kyung Hee University, Korea)
Wook-Joong Kim (ETRI, Korea)
Yong Kuk Kim (Sejong University, Korea)
Young Yong Kim (Yonsei University, Korea)
Youngseop Kim (Dankook University, Korea)
Hideaki Kimata (NTT Advanced Technology, Japan)
Lisimachos P. Kondi (State University of New York, USA)
Alex C. Kot (Nanyang Technological University, Singapore)
Sunil Kumar (Clarkson University, USA)
No-Yoon Kwak (Cheonan University, Korea)
Gauthier Lafruit (IMEC-DESICS-Multimedia, Belgium)
Chulhee Lee (Yonsei University, Korea)
Haeyoung Lee (Hongik University, Korea)

Heung-Kyu Lee (KAIST, Korea)
Jeong-Gun Lee (University of Cambridge, UK)
MeeSuk Lee (ETRI, Korea)
Minkyu Lee (Lucent Technologies, USA)
Sang Hwa Lee (Seoul National University, Korea)
Sang Wook Lee (Sogang University, Korea)
Sangyoun Lee (Yonsei University, Korea)
Seok-Pil Lee (KETI, Korea)
Seong-Won Lee (Kangwon National University, Korea)
Si-Woong Lee (Hanbat National University, Korea)
Suk-Hwan Lee (Tongmyong University, Korea)
Yugyung Lee (University of Missouri, USA)
Igor Lemberski (Transport and Telecommunication Institute, Latvia)
Jae Hyuck Lim (Yonsei University, Korea)
B. S. Manjunath (University of Califormnia Santa Barbara, USA)
Yannick Maret (École Polytechnique Fédérale de Lausanne, Switzerland)
Jeonghoon Mo (ICU, Korea)
Sang Man Mo (Chosun University, Korea)
Francisco Morán Burgos (Universidad Politécnica de Madrid, Spain)
Hiroaki Morino (Shibaura Institute of Technology, Japan)
Hiroshi Murase (Nagoya University, Japan)
Jae Yul Nam (Keimyung University, Korea)
Jeho Nam (ETRI, Korea)
Yang-Hee Nam (Ewha Womans University, Korea)
Tobias Oelbaum (Technische Universität München, Germany)
Seoung-Jun Oh (Kangwon National University, Korea)
Joonki Paik (Chung-Ang University, Korea)
Sung Bum Pan (Chosun Universirty, Korea)
Zhigeng Pan (Zhejiang University, China)
Raveendran Paramesran (University of Malaya, Malaysia)
Changhan Park (Chung-Ang University, Korea)
Changhoon Park (University of Tokyo, Japan)
Dong-Kwon Park (Ubix System Inc., Korea)
HyunWook Park (KAIST, Korea)
Jong-Il Park (Hanyang University, Korea)
Seung Kwon Park (Hanyang University, Korea)
In Kyu Park (Inha University, Korea)
Fernando Pereira (IST(PT), Portugal)
Sylvain Prat (France Telecom R&D, France)
Marius Preda (Institut National des Télécommunications, France)
Safavi-Naini Rei (University of Wollongong, Australia)
Kyung Hyune Rhee (PuKyong National University, Korea)
Yong Man Ro (ICU, Korea)
Yeonseung Ryu (Myongji University, Korea)
Shin'ichi Satoh (National Institute of Informatics, Japan)

Yong Duk Seo (Sogang University, Korea)
Jaehong Shim (Chosun University, Korea)
Seokjoo Shin (Chosun University, Korea)
Jitae Shin (Sungkyunkwan University, Korea)
Yoan Shin (Soongsil University, Korea)
Kwang-Hoon Son (Yonsei University, Korea)
Sung-Hoon Son (Sangmyung University, Korea)
Wookho Son (ETRI, Korea)
Hwangjun Song (POSTECH, Korea)
Junehwa Song (KAIST, Korea)
Po-Chyi Su (National Central University, Taiwan)
Doug Young Suh (KyungHee University, Korea)
Sanghoon Sull (Korea University, Korea)
Huifang Sun (Mitsubishi Electric Research Labs, USA)
Seyoon Tak (Samsung AIT, Korea)
Tomokazu Takahashi (Nagoya University, Japan)
Rin-ichiro Taniguchi (Kyushu University, Japan)
Ronald M. Tol (Philips Applied Technologies, The Netherlands)
Chun-Jen Tsai (National Chiao Tung University, Taiwan)
Gi-Mun Um (ETRI, Korea)
S. Verma (Indian Institute of Information Technology and Management, India)
Semyung Wang (GIST, Korea)
Lin Weisi (Institute for Infocomm Research, Singapore)
Duminda Wijesekera (George Mason University, USA)
Woontack Woo (GIST, Korea)
Jeong-Hyu Yang (LG Electronics, Korea)
Jianjun Ye (Harbin Institute of Technology, China)
Changhoon Yim (Konkuk University, Korea)
Naokazu Yokoya (Nara Institute of Science and Technology, Japan)
Chuck Yoo (Korea University, Korea)
Hui Zhang (Samsung AIT, China)

Table of Contents – I

New Panoramic Image Generation Based on Modeling of Vignetting
and Illumination Effects
   Dong-Gyu Sim 1

Virtual Object Placement in Video for Augmented Reality
   Jong-Seung Park, Mee Young Sung, Sung-Ryul Noh 13

Realtime Control for Motion Creation of 3D Avatars
   Dong Hoon Kim, Mee Young Sung, Jong-Seung Park, Kyungkoo Jun,
   Sang-Rak Lee 25

Environment Matting of Transparent Objects Based on
Frequency-Domain Analysis
   I-Cheng Chang, Tian-Lin Yang, Chung-Ling Huang 37

Adaptation of Quadric Metric Simplification to MPEG-4 Animated
Object
   Marius Preda, Son Tran, Françoise Prêteux 49

Progressive Lower Trees of Wavelet Coefficients: Efficient Spatial and
SNR Scalable Coding of 3D Models
   Marcos Avilés, Francisco Morán, Narciso García 61

An Adaptive Quantization Scheme for Efficient Texture Coordinate
Compression in MPEG 3DMC
   Sunyoung Lee, Byeongwook Min, Daiyong Kim, Eun-Young Chang,
   Namho Hur, Soo In Lee, Euee S. Jang 73

Special Effects: Efficient and Scalable Encoding of the 3D
Metamorphosis Animation with MESHGRID
   Ioan Alexandru Salomie, Rudi Deklerck, Dan Cernea,
   Aneta Markova, Adrian Munteanu, Peter Schelkens, Jan Cornelis ... 84

Hardware Accelerated Image-Based Rendering with Compressed
Surface Light Fields and Multiresolution Geometry
   Masaki Kitahara, Shinya Shimizu, Kazuto Kamikura,
   Yashima Yoshiyuki 96

Adaptive Vertex Chasing for the Lossless Geometry Coding of 3D
Meshes
   Haeyoung Lee, Sujin Park 108

Analysis and Performance Evaluation of Flexible Marcoblock Ordering
for H.264 Video Transmission over Packet-Lossy Networks
Changhoon Yim, Wonjung Kim, Hyesook Lim 120

Motion Perception Based Adaptive Quantization for Video Coding
Chih-Wei Tang 132

Hybrid Deblocking Algorithm for Block-Based Low Bit Rate Coded
Images
Kee-Koo Kwon, In-Su Jeon, Dong-Sun Lim 144

A Cross-Resolution Leaky Prediction Scheme for In-Band Wavelet
Video Coding with Spatial Scalability
*Dongdong Zhang, Jizheng Xu, Feng Wu, Wenjun Zhang,
Hongkai Xiong* 156

Efficient Intra Prediction Mode Decision for H.264 Video
Seong Soo Chun, Ja-Cheon Yoon, Sanghoon Sull 168

Optimum Quantization Parameters for Mode Decision in Scalable
Extension of H.264/AVC Video Codec
Seung-Hwan Kim, Yo-Sung Ho 179

A Metadata Model for Event Notification on Interactive Broadcasting
Service
Kyunghee Ji, Nammee Moon, Jungwon Kang 191

Target Advertisement Service Using TV Viewers' Profile Inference
Munjo Kim, Sanggil Kang, Munchurl Kim, Jaegon Kim 202

Personalized TV Services and T-Learning Based on TV-Anytime
Metadata
HeeKyung Lee, Seung-Jun Yang, Han-Kyu Lee, Jinwoo Hong 212

Metadata Generation and Distribution for Live Programs on
Broadcasting-Telecommunication Linkage Services
*Yuko Kon'ya, Hidetaka Kuwano, Tomokazu Yamada,
Masahito Kawamori, Katsuhiko Kawazoe* 224

Data Broadcast Metadata Based on PMCP for Open Interface to a
DTV Data Server
Minsik Park, Yong Ho Kim, Jin Soo Choi, Jin Woo Hong 234

Super-resolution Sharpening-Demosaicking with Spatially Adaptive
Total-Variation Image Regularization
Takahiro Saito, Takashi Komatsu 246

Gradient Based Image Completion by Solving Poisson Equation
  Jianbing Shen, Xiaogang Jin, Chuan Zhou 257

Predictive Directional Rectangular Zonal Search for Digital Multimedia Processor
  Soon-Tak Lee, Joong-Hwan Baek................................ 269

Motion Field Refinement and Region-Based Motion Segmentation
  Sun-Kyoo Hwang, Whoi-Yul Kim 280

Motion Adaptive De-interlacing with Horizontal and Vertical Motions Detection
  Chung-Chi Lin, Ming-Hwa Sheu, Huann-Keng Chiang, Chishyan Liaw 291

All-in-Focus Image Generation by Merging Multiple Differently Focused Images in Three-Dimensional Frequency Domain
  Kazuya Kodama, Hiroshi Mo, Akira Kubota 303

Free-Hand Stroke Based NURBS Surface for Sketching and Deforming 3D Contents
  Jung-hoon Kwon, Han-wool Choi, Jeong-in Lee, Young-Ho Chai 315

Redeeming Valleys and Ridges for Line-Drawing
  Kyung Gun Na, Moon Ryul Jung, Jongwan Lee, Changgeun Song ... 327

Interactive Rembrandt Lighting Design
  Hongmi Joe, Kyoung Chin Seo, Sang Wook Lee................... 339

Image-Based Generation of Facial Skin Texture with Make-Up
  Sang Min Kim, Kyoung Chin Seo, Sang Wook Lee 350

Responsive Multimedia System for Virtual Storytelling
  Youngho Lee, Sejin Oh, Youngmin Park, Beom-Chan Lee, Jeung-Chul Park, Yoo Rhee Oh, Seokhee Lee, Han Oh, Jeha Ryu, Kwan H. Lee, Hong Kook Kim, Yong-Gu Lee, JongWon Kim, Yo-Sung Ho, Woontack Woo 361

Communication and Control of a Home Robot Using a Mobile Phone
  Kuniya Shinozaki, Hajime Sakamoto, Takaho Tanaka, Ryohei Nakatsu.. 373

Real-Time Stereo Using Foreground Segmentation and Hierarchical Disparity Estimation
  Hansung Kim, Dong Bo Min, Kwanghoon Sohn.................... 384

Multi-view Video Coding Using Illumination Change-Adaptive Motion
Estimation and 2-D Direct Mode
  Yung-Lyul Lee, Yung-Ki Lee, Dae-Yeon Kim 396

Fast Ray-Space Interpolation with Depth Discontinuity Preserving for
Free Viewpoint Video System
  *Gangyi Jiang, Liangzhong Fan, Mei Yu, Xien Ye, Rangding Wang,
  Yong-Deak Kim* 408

Haptic Interaction with Depth Video Media
  *Jongeun Cha, Seung-man Kim, Ian Oakley, Jeha Ryu,
  Kwan H. Lee* 420

A Framework for Multi-view Video Coding Using Layered Depth
Images
  Seung-Uk Yoon, Eun-Kyung Lee, Sung-Yeol Kim, Yo-Sung Ho 431

A Proxy-Based Distributed Approach for Reliable Content Sharing
Among UPnP-Enabled Home Networks
  HyunRyong Lee, JongWon Kim 443

Adaptive Distributed Video Coding for Video Applications in Ad-Hoc
Networks
  Ke Liang, Lifeng Sun, Yuzhuo Zhong 455

High Speed JPEG Coder Based on Modularized and Pipelined
Architecture with Distributed Control
  *Fahad Ali Mujahid, Eun-Gu Jung, Dong-Soo Har, Jun-Hee Hong,
  Hoi-Jeong Lim* 466

Efficient Distribution of Feature Parameters for Speech Recognition in
Network Environments
  Jae Sam Yoon, Gil Ho Lee, Hong Kook Kim 477

Magnitude-Sign Split Quantization for Bandwidth Scalable Wideband
Speech Codec
  *Ji-Hyuk You, Chul-Man Park, Jung-Il Lee, Chang-Beom Ahn,
  Seoung-Jun Oh, Hochong Park* 489

Self-timed Interconnect with Layered Interface Based on Distributed
and Modularized Control for Multimedia SoCs
  *Eun-Gu Jung, Eon-Pyo Hong, Kyoung-Son Jhang, Jeong-A Lee,
  Dong-Soo Har* 500

Enhanced Downhill Simplex Search for Fast Video Motion Estimation
  Hwai-Chung Fei, Chun-Jen Chen, Shang-Hong Lai 512

Camera Motion Detection in Video Sequences Using Motion Cooccurrences
Hyun-Ho Jeon, Andrea Basso, Peter F. Driessen 524

A Hybrid Motion Compensated 3-D Video Coding System for Blocking Artifacts Reduction
Cho-Chun Cheng, Wen-Liang Hwang, Zuowei Shen, Tao Xia 535

Fast Panoramic Image Generation Method Using Morphological Corner Detection
Jungho Lee, Woongho Lee, Ikhwan Cho, Dongseok Jeong 547

Generation of 3D Building Model Using 3D Line Detection Scheme Based on Line Fitting of Elevation Data
Dong-Min Woo, Seung-Soo Han, Young-Kee Jung, Kyu-Won Lee ... 559

Segmentation of the Liver Using the Deformable Contour Method on CT Images
Seong-Jae Lim, Yong-Yeon Jeong, Yo-Sung Ho 570

Radial Projection: A Feature Extraction Method for Topographical Shapes
Yong-Il Kwon, Ho-Hyun Park, Jixue Liu, Mario A. Nascimento 582

A Robust Text Segmentation Approach in Complex Background Based on Multiple Constraints
Libo Fu, Weiqiang Wang, Yaowen Zhan 594

Specularity-Free Projection on Nonplanar Surface
Hanhoon Park, Moon-Hyun Lee, Sang-Jun Kim, Jong-Il Park 606

Salient Feature Selection for Visual Concept Learning
Feng Xu, Lei Zhang, Yu-Jin Zhang, Wei-Ying Ma 617

Contourlet Image Coding Based on Adjusted SPIHT
Haohao Song, Songyu Yu, Li Song, Hongkai Xiong 629

Using Bitstream Structure Descriptions for the Exploitation of Multi-layered Temporal Scalability in H.264/AVC's Base Specification
Wesley De Neve, Davy Van Deursen, Davy De Schrijver, Koen De Wolf, Rik Van de Walle 641

Efficient Control for the Distortion Incurred by Dropping DCT Coefficients in Compressed Domain
Jin-Soo Kim, Jae-Gon Kim 653

Kalman Filter Based Error Resilience for H.264 Motion Vector Recovery
  Ki-Hong Ko, Seong-Whan Kim 664

High Efficient Context-Based Variable Length Coding with Parallel Orientation
  Qiang Wang, Debin Zhao, Wen Gao, Siwei Ma 675

Texture Coordinate Compression for 3-D Mesh Models Using Texture Image Rearrangement
  Sung-Yeol Kim, Young-Suk Yoon, Seung-Man Kim, Kwan-Heng Lee, Yo-Sung Ho 687

Classification of Audio Signals Using Gradient-Based Fuzzy c-Means Algorithm with Divergence Measure
  Dong-Chul Park, Duc-Hoai Nguyen, Seung-Hwa Beack, Sancho Park 698

Variable Bit Quantization for Virtual Source Location Information in Spatial Audio Coding
  Sang Bae Chon, In Yong Choi, Jeongil Seo, Koeng-Mo Sung 709

The Realtime Method Based on Audio Scenegraph for 3D Sound Rendering
  Jeong-Seon Yi, Suk-Jeong Seong, Yang-Hee Nam 720

Dual-Domain Quantization for Transform Coding of Speech and Audio Signals
  Jun-Seong Hong, Jong-Hyun Choi, Chang-Beom Ahn, Chae-Bong Sohn, Seoung-Jun Oh, Hochong Park 731

A Multi-channel Audio Compression Method with Virtual Source Location Information
  Han-gil Moon, Jeong-il Seo, Seungkwon Beak, Koeng-Mo Sung 742

A System for Detecting and Tracking Internet News Event
  Zhen Lei, Ling-da Wu, Ying Zhang, Yu-chi Liu 754

A Video Summarization Method for Basketball Game
  Eui-Jin Kim, Gwang-Gook Lee, Cheolkon Jung, Sang-Kyun Kim, Ji-Yeun Kim, Whoi-Yul Kim 765

Improvement of Commercial Boundary Detection Using Audiovisual Features
  Jun-Cheng Chen, Jen-Hao Yeh, Wei-Ta Chu, Jin-Hau Kuo, Ja-Ling Wu 776

Automatic Dissolve Detection Scheme Based on Visual Rhythm
Spectrum
  *Seong Jun Park, Kwang-Deok Seo, Jae-Gon Kim,
  Samuel Moon-Ho Song* 787

A Study on the Relation Between the Frame Pruning and the Robust
Speaker Identification with Multivariate t-Distribution
  Younjeong Lee, Joohun Lee, Hernsoo Hahn 799

Auto-summarization of Multimedia Meeting Records Based on
Accessing Log
  Weisheng He, Yuanchun Shi, Xin Xiao 809

Towards a High-Level Audio Framework for Video Retrieval Combining
Conceptual Descriptions and Fully-Automated Processes
  Mbarek Charhad, Mohammed Belkhatir 820

A New Concept of Security Camera Monitoring with Privacy Protection
by Masking Moving Objects
  Kenichi Yabuta, Hitoshi Kitazawa, Toshihisa Tanaka 831

Feature Fusion-Based Multiple People Tracking
  *Junhaeng Lee, Sangjin Kim, Daehee Kim, Jeongho Shin,
  Joonki Paik* 843

Extracting the Movement of Lip and Tongue During Articulation
  *Hanhoon Park, Seung-Wook Hong, Jong-Il Park, Sung-Kyun Moon,
  Hyeongseok Ko* 854

A Scheme for Ball Detection and Tracking in Broadcast Soccer Video
  Dawei Liang, Yang Liu, Qingming Huang, Wen Gao 864

A Shape-Based Retrieval Scheme for Leaf Images
  Yunyoung Nam, Eenjun Hwang 876

Lung Detection by Using Geodesic Active Contour Model Based on
Characteristics of Lung Parenchyma Region
  Chul-Ho Won, Seung-Ik Lee, Dong-Hun Kim, Jin-Ho Cho 888

Improved Automatic Liver Segmentation of a Contrast Enhanced CT
Image
  Kyung-Sik Seo, Jong-An Park 899

Automated Detection of Tumors in Mammograms Using Two Segments
for Classification
  Mahmoud R. Hejazi, Yo-Sung Ho 910

Registration of Brain MR Images Using Feature Information of
Structural Elements
  Jeong-Sook Chae, Hyung-Jea Cho 922

Cyber Surgery: Parameterized Mesh for Multi-modal Surgery
Simulation
  Qiang Liu, Edmond C. Prakash 934

Image Retrieval Based on Co-occurrence Matrix Using Block
Classification Characteristics
  Tae-Su Kim, Seung-Jin Kim, Kuhn-Il Lee 946

Automatic Generation of the Initial Query Set for CBIR on the Mobile
Web
  Deok Hwan Kim, Chan Young Kim, Yoon Ho Cho 957

Classification of MPEG Video Content Using Divergence Measure with
Data Covariance
  Dong-Chul Park, Chung-Nguyen Tran, Yunsik Lee 969

Image Retrieval Using Spatial Color and Edge Detection
  Chin-Chen Chang, Yung-Chen Chou, Wen-Chuan Wu 981

Understanding Multimedia Document Semantics for Cross-Media
Retrieval
  Fei Wu, Yi Yang, Yueting Zhuang, Yunhe Pan 993

Multimedia Retrieval from a Large Number of Sources in a Ubiquitous
Environment
  Gamhewage C. de Silva, T. Yamasaki, K. Aizawa 1005

Author Index 1017

Table of Contents – II

Efficient Cache Management for QoS Adaptive Multimedia Streaming Services
   Taeseok Kim, Hyokyung Bahn, Kern Koh 1

An Effective Failure Recovery Mechanism with Pipeline Computing in Clustered-Based VOD Servers
   Dongmahn Seo, Joahyoung Lee, Dongkook Kim, Yoon Kim, Inbum Jung 12

Dynamic and Scalable Caching Algorithm of Proxy Server for Multiple Videos
   Hyung Rai Oh, Hwangjun Song 24

Dynamic Adaptive Architecture for Self-adaptation in VideoConferencing System
   Chulho Jung, Sanghee Lee, Eunseok Lee 36

Scalable and Reliable Overlay Multicast Network for Live Media Streaming
   Eunyong Park, Sunyoung Han, Sangjoon Ahn, Hyunje Park, Sangchul Shin 48

Apollon : File System Level Support for QoS Augmented I/O
   Taeseok Kim, Youjip Won, Doohan Kim, Kern Koh, Yong H. Shin .. 59

Seamless Video Streaming for Video on Demand Services in Vertical Handoff
   Jae-Won Kim, Hye-Soo Kim, Jae-Woong Yun, Hyeong-Min Nam, Sung-Jea Ko 71

MPEG-4 FGS Video Traffic Model and Its Application in Simulations for Layered Video Multicast
   Hui Wang, Jichang Sha, Xiao Sun, Jun Tao, Wei He 83

Dynamic Voltage Scaling for Real-Time Scheduling of Multimedia Tasks
   Yeong Rak Seong, Min-Sik Gong, Ha Ryoung Oh, Cheol-Hoon Lee 94

Class Renegotiating Mechanism for Guaranteed End-to-End QoS over DiffServ Networks
   Dai-Boong Lee, Hwangjun Song 105

Secure and Efficient ID-Based Group Key Agreement Fitted for Pay-TV
Hyunjue Kim, Junghyun Nam, Seungjoo Kim, Dongho Won 117

A Method of Generating Table of Contents for Educational Videos
Gwang-Gook Lee, Eui-Jin Kim, Jung Won Kang, Jae-Gon Kim, Whoi-Yul Kim 129

Study of Inter-effect and Behavior of Multimedia Traffic in a QoS-Enabled Communication Network
Nashwa Abdel-Baki, Hans Peter Großmann 141

Broadcast Synchronizing System Using Audio Watermark
DongHwan Shin, JongWeon Kim, JongUk Choi 153

Realistic Broadcasting Using Multi-modal Immersive Media
Sung-Yeol Kim, Seung-Uk Yoon, Yo-Sung Ho 164

Client System for Realistic Broadcasting: A First Prototype
Jongeun Cha, Seung-Man Kim, Sung-Yeol Kim, Sehwan Kim, Seung-Uk Yoon, Ian Oakley, Jeha Ryu, Kwan H. Lee, Woontack Woo, Yo-Sung Ho 176

Proposal of Cooperative Transmission for the Uplink of TDD-CDMA Systems
Ho Van Khuong, Hyung-Yun Kong 187

A Novel Scheduler for 1xEV-DO Type System Supporting Diverse Multimedia Traffics
Shan Guo Quan, Jeong-Jun Suh, Tae Chul Hong, Young Yong Kim . 200

Proposal of Space-Time Block Coded Cooperative Wireless Transmission in Rayleigh Fading Channels
Ho Van Khuong, Hyung-Yun Kong 212

Downlink Packet Scheduling Based on Channel Condition for Multimedia Services of Mobile Users in OFDMA-TDD
Ryong Oh, Se-Jin Kim, Hyong-Woo Lee, Choong-Ho Cho 224

An Efficient Channel Tracking Method for OFDM Based High Mobility Wireless Multimedia System
Kwanghoon Kim, Haelyong Kim, Hyuncheol Park 235

A Novel Key Management and Distribution Solution for Secure Video Multicast
Hao Yin, Xiaowen Chu, Chuang Lin, Feng Qiu, Geyong Min 246

A Robust Method for Data Hiding in Color Images
  Mohsen Ashourian, Peyman Moallem, Yo-Sung Ho 258

A Color Image Encryption Algorithm Based on Magic Cube
Transformation and Modular Arithmetic Operation
  Jianbing Shen, Xiaogang Jin, Chuan Zhou 270

Selective Video Encryption Based on Advanced Video Coding
  Shiguo Lian, Zhongxuan Liu, Zhen Ren, Zhiquan Wang 281

Key Frame Extraction Based on Shot Coverage and Distortion
  *Ki Tae Park, Joong Yong Lee, Kee Wook Rim,
  Young Shik Moon* 291

Secret Message Location Steganalysis Based on Local Coherences of Hue
  Xiang-Wei Kong, Wen-Feng Liu, Xin-Gang You 301

Feature-Based Image Watermarking Method Using Scale-Invariant
Keypoints
  *Hae-Yeoun Lee, Choong-hoon Lee, Heung-Kyu Lee,
  Jeho Nam* 312

Watermarking NURBS Surfaces
  Zhigeng Pan, Shusen Sun, Mingmin Zhang, Daxing Zhang 325

Digital Watermarking Based on Three-Dimensional Wavelet Transform
for Video Data
  *Seung-Jin Kim, Tae-Su Kim, Ki-Ryong Kwon, Sang-Ho Ahn,
  Kuhn-Il Lee* 337

Using Space-Time Coding for Watermarking of Three-Dimensional
Triangle Mesh
  Mohsen Ashourian, Keyvan Mohebbi 349

Perceptually Tuned Auto-correlation Based Video Watermarking Using
Independent Component Analysis
  Seong-Whan Kim, Hyun-Sung Sung 360

Invertible Watermarking Scheme for Authentication and Integrity
  Kil-Sang Yoo, Mi-Ae Kim, Won-Hyung Lee 371

Adaptive Congestion Control Scheme Based on DCCP for
Wireless/Mobile Access Networks
  Si-Yong Park, Sung-Min Kim, Tae-Hoon Lee, Ki-Dong Chung 382

SARS : A Linear Source Model Based Adaptive Rate-Control Scheme
for TCP-Friendly Real-Time MPEG-4 Video Streaming
Eric Hsiao-Kuang Wu, Ming-I Hsieh, Chung-Yuan Knight Chang ... 394

Evaluation of a Crossover Router Based QoS Mechanism in Fast Mobile
IPv6 Networks*
*Zheng Wan, Zhengyou Wang, Zhijun Fang, Weiming Zeng,
Shiqian Wu* 405

Adaptive and QoS Downlink Multimedia Packet Scheduling for
Broadband Wireless Systems
Seungwan Ryu, Byunghan Ryu, Hyunhwa Seo 417

A Practical Multicast Transmission Control Method for Multi-channel
HDTV IP Broadcasting System
*Kazuhiro Kamimura, Teruyuki Hasegawa, Haruo Hoshino,
Shigehiro Ano, Toru Hasegawa* 429

MEET : Multicast Debugging Toolkit with End-to-End Packet Trace
Jinyong Jo, Jaiseung Kwak, Okhwan Byeon 441

Traffic Management for Video Streaming Service over Diff-Serv
Sang-Hyun Park, Jeong-Sik Park, Jae-Young Pyun 453

Scalable and Adaptive QoS Mapping Control Framework for Packet
Video Delivery
Gooyoun Hwang, Jitae Shin, JongWon Kim 465

A Frame-Layer Rate Control Algorithm for H.264 Using Rate-
Dependent Mode Selection
Jun-Yup Kim, Seung-Hwan Kim, Yo-Sung Ho 477

TCP-Friendly Congestion Control over Heterogeneous Wired/Wireless
IP Network
*Jae-Young Pyun, Jong An Park, Seung Jo Han, Yoon Kim,
Sang-Hyun Park* 489

A Balanced Revenue-Based Resource Sharing Scheme for Advance and
Immediate Reservations
Dong-Hoon Yi, JongWon Kim 501

Sequential Mesh Coding Using Wave Partitioning
Tae-Wan Kim, Kyoung Won Min, Byeong Ho Choi, Yo-Sung Ho ... 514

Dimension-Reduction Technique for MPEG-7 Audio Descriptors
Jui-Yu Lee, Shingchern D. You 526

Design of an Asynchronous Switch Based on Butterfly Fat-Tree for
Network-on-Chip Applications
Min-Chang Kang, Eun-Gu Jung, Dong-Soo Har 538

Adaptive Deinterlacing for Real-Time Applications
*Qian Huang, Wen Gao, Debin Zhao,
Huifang Sun* 550

Adaptive MAP High-Resolution Image Reconstruction Algorithm Using
Local Statistics
Kyung-Ho Kim, Yoan Shin, Min-Cheol Hong 561

Energy-Efficient Cooperative Image Processing in Video Sensor
Networks
Dan Tao, Huadong Ma, Yonghe Liu 572

Mathematical PSNR Prediction Model Between Compressed Normal
Maps and Rendered 3D Images
Toshihiko Yamasaki, Kazuya Hayase, Kiyoharu Aizawa 584

Fast Adaptive Skin Detection in JPEG Images
Qing-Fang Zheng, Wen Gao 595

Effective Blocking Artifact Reduction Using Classification of Block
Boundary Area
Jung-Youp Suk, Gun-Woo Lee, Kuhn-Il Lee 606

Adaptive Rate-Distortion Optimization for H.264
Kwan-Jung Oh, Yo-Sung Ho 617

Directional Lifting-Based Wavelet Transform for Multiple Description
Image Coding with Quincunx Segmentation
Nan Zhang, Yan Lu, Feng Wu, Baocai Yin 629

Non-periodic Frame Refreshment Based on the Uncertainty Models of
the Reference Frames
*Yong Tae Kim, Youngil Yoo, Dong Wook Kang, Kyeong Hoon Jung,
Ki-Doo Kim, Seung-Jun Lee* 641

Color Quantization of Digital Images
Xin Zhang, Zuman Song, Yunli Wang, Hui Wang 653

Directional Feature Detection and Correspondence
Wen-Hao Wang, Fu-Jen Hsiao, Tsuhan Chen 665

An Improvement of Dead Reckoning Algorithm Using Kalman Filter
for Minimizing Network Traffic of 3D On-Line Games
  Hyon-Gook Kim, Seong-Whan Kim 676

IRED Gun: Infrared LED Tracking System for Game Interface
  *SeongHo Baek, TaeYong Kim, JongSu Kim,
  ChaSeop Im, Chan Lim*.. 688

On the Implementation of Gentle Phone's Function Based on PSOLA
Algorithm
  JongKuk Kim, MyungJin Bae 700

A Novel Blind Equalizer Based on Dual-Mode MCMA and DD
Algorithm
  *Seokho Yoon, Sang Won Choi, Jumi Lee, Hyoungmoon Kwon,
  Iickho Song* 711

Robust Secret Key Based Authentication Scheme Using Smart Cards
  Eun-Jun Yoon, Kee-Young Yoo 723

A Dynamically Configurable Multimedia Middleware
  Hendry, Munchurl Kim 735

Adaptive VoIP Smoothing of Pareto Traffic Based on Optimal E-Model
Quality
  Shyh-Fang Huang, Eric Hsiao-Kuang Wu, Pao-Chi Chang 747

Indoor Scene Reconstruction Using a Projection-Based Registration
Technique of Multi-view Depth Images
  Sehwan Kim, Woontack Woo.................................... 759

Image-Based Relighting in Dynamic Scenes
  Yong-Ho Hwang, Hyun-Ki Hong, Jun-Sik Kwon 772

Stippling Technique Based on Color Analysis
  Seok Jang, Hyun-Ki Hong 782

Photometry Data Coding for Three-Dimensional Mesh Models Using
Connectivity and Geometry Information
  Young-Suk Yoon, Sung-Yeol Kim, Yo-Sung Ho.................... 794

Adaptation of MPEG-4 BIFS Scenes into MPEG-4 LASeR Scenes in
MPEG-21 DIA Framework
  Qonita M. Shahab, Munchurl Kim 806

Performance Evaluation of H.264 Mapping Strategies over IEEE
802.11e WLAN for Robust Video Streaming
  Umar Iqbal Choudhry, JongWon Kim 818

Reducing Spatial Resolution for MPEG-2 to H.264/AVC Transcoding
  Bo Hu, Peng Zhang, Qingming Huang, Wen Gao 830

Low-Bitrate Video Quality Enhancement by Frame Rate Up-Conversion
and Adaptive Frame Encoding
  Ya-Ting Yang, Yi-Shin Tung, Ja-Ling Wu, Chung-Yi Weng 841

Face Recognition Using Neighborhood Preserving Projections
  Yanwei Pang, Nenghai Yu, Houqiang Li, Rong Zhang, Zhengkai Liu . 854

An Efficient Virtual Aesthetic Surgery Model Based on 2D Color
Photograph
  Hyun Park, Kee Wook Rim, Young Shik Moon 865

Automatic Photo Indexing Based on Person Identity
  *Seungji Yang, Kyong Sok Seo, Sang Kyun Kim, Yong Man Ro,
  Ji-Yeon Kim, Yang Suk Seo* 877

Bayesian Colorization Using MRF Color Image Modeling
  Hideki Noda, Hitoshi Korekuni, Nobuteru Takao, Michiharu Niimi .. 889

An Efficient Player for MPEG-4 Contents on a Mobile Device
  Sangwook Kim, Kyungdeok Kim 900

Conversion Mechanism of XMT into SMIL in MPEG-4 System
  Heesun Kim 912

Two-Channel-Based Noise Reduction in a Complex Spectrum Plane for
Hands-Free Communication System
  Toshiya Ohkubo, Tetsuya Takiguchi, Yasuo Ariki 923

An Efficient Classifier Fusion for Face Recognition Including Varying
Illumination
  Mi Young Nam, Jo Hyung Yoo, Phill Kyu Rhee 935

Illumination Invariant Feature Selection for Face Recognition
  Yazhou Liu, Hongxun Yao, Wen Gao, Debin Zhao 946

Specular Removal Using CL-Projection
  Joung Wook Park, Jae Doug Yoo, Kwan H. Lee 958

Oriental Color-Ink Model Based Painterly Rendering for Realtime Application
  Crystal S. Oh, Yang-Hee Nam 970

An Adjusted-Q Digital Graphic Equalizer Employing Opposite Filters
  Yonghee Lee, Rinchul Kim, Googchun Cho, Seong Jong Choi 981

Interactive Transfer of Human Facial Color
  Kyoung Chin Seo, Giroo Shin, Sang Wook Lee 993

Panoramic Mesh Model Generation from Multiple Range Data for Indoor Scene Reconstruction
  Wonwoo Lee, Woontack Woo 1004

A Novel Low Latency Packet Scheduling Scheme for Broadband Networks
  Eric Hsiao-Kuang Wu, Ming-I Hsieh, Hsu-Te Lai 1015

Creative Cartoon Face Synthesis System for Mobile Entertainment
  Junfa Liu, Yiqiang Chen, Wen Gao, Rong Fu, Renqin Zhou 1027

Concept and Construction of the Caddy Robot
  Florent Servillat, Ryohei Nakatsu, Xiao-feng Wu, Kazuo Itoh .. 1039

Rapid Algorithms for MPEG-2 to H.264 Transcoding
  Xiaoming Sun, Pin Tao 1049

A New Method for Controlling Smoke's Shape
  Yongxia Zhou, Jiaoying Shi, Jiarong Yu 1060

A Scene Change Detection in H.264/AVC Compression Domain
  Sung Min Kim, Ju Wan Byun, Chee Sun Won 1072

Author Index 1083

New Panoramic Image Generation Based on Modeling of Vignetting and Illumination Effects

Dong-Gyu Sim

Image Processing Systems Laboratory,
Dept. of Computer Engineering, Kwangwoon University,
447-1, Wolgye-dong, Nowon-gu,
Seoul 139-701, Korea
dgsim@kw.ac.kr
http://ipsl.kw.ac.kr

Abstract. In this paper, a new panoramic image generation algorithm is proposed based on more realistic image formation processes. Perspective projection, lens distortion, vignetting and illumination effects are incorporated into the proposed panoramic modeling. Intrinsic and extrinsic camera parameters are estimated by the proposed stable camera parameter estimation algorithm derived from panning camera constraints. This paper shows that accurate panoramic images can be reconstructed based on the proposed camera modeling and parameters estimation. The effectiveness of the proposed algorithm is also shown with several image sequences in terms of reconstruction error from the generated panoramic image.

1 Introduction

Panoramic image generation from multiple images can be widely used for computer graphics, video coding, object tracking, and omni-directional video representation [1][2]. In particular, this is possible with an extension of the planar 2D images to a spherical or cylindrical image plane for wide view representation. The representation can be used for the visualization of 2D images at a certain viewpoint into every direction. The technology can be applied to broadcasting and multimedia storage applications. Furthermore, the accurate panoramic modeling can be utilized in many emerging applications such as immersive video representation and surveillance camera systems [3][4]. However, several algorithms based on their individual camera modeling have been proposed that suffer from inaccuracy of panoramic image generation caused by improper camera modeling and unstable parameter estimation.

In this paper, more realistic camera modeling and estimation method are proposed. For the camera modeling, we employ not only the perspective projection and lens distortion but also vignetting and illumination change effects. Additionally, we present a stable camera parameter estimation algorithm based on panning camera constraints. In this paper, the effectiveness of the proposed panoramic image generation is shown with several video sequences acquired under diverse conditions.

2 Camera Model for Panoramic Imaging

Images acquired from a camera depend on intrinsic and extrinsic camera parameters. Thus, image analysis incorporating an accurate model based on image formation process would yield better results [5]. In this paper, we consider the perspective projection imaging, lens distortion, illumination and vignetting effects as shown in Fig. 1. Lens distortion of an inexpensive wide FOV camera would not be negligible. In cases of high lens distortion, a straight line will be shown as a curved line in the acquired image. The radial lens distortion removing terms higher than the fifth order [6][7] can be denoted by

$$\begin{aligned} x_u &= x_d \{1 + K_1(x_d^2 + y_d^2) + K_2(x_d^2 + y_d^2)^2\} \\ y_u &= y_d \{1 + K_1(x_d^2 + y_d^2) + K_2(x_d^2 + y_d^2)^2\} \end{aligned}, \quad (1)$$

where (x_d, y_d) and (x_u, y_u) represent the distorted and undistorted image coordinates, respectively. We have two parameters (K_1 and K_2) to be estimated during initialization. Furthermore, we introduce the illumination and vignetting effects by

$$I'(x_d, y_d) = \frac{L^0 I(x_d, y_d) + L^1}{V \cos^4\left(\arctan\left(\frac{\Delta\sqrt{x_d^2 + y_d^2}}{f}\right)\right) + 1 - V}, \quad (2)$$

where L^1 and L^0 are the illumination parameters and V is the vignetting parameter, Δ denotes pixel spacing between two neighboring pixels, and f is a camera focal length. Illumination changes are caused by external lighting conditions, and vignetting is the gradual fading into the surrounding image, caused by the obstruction of incoming light at a wide angle.

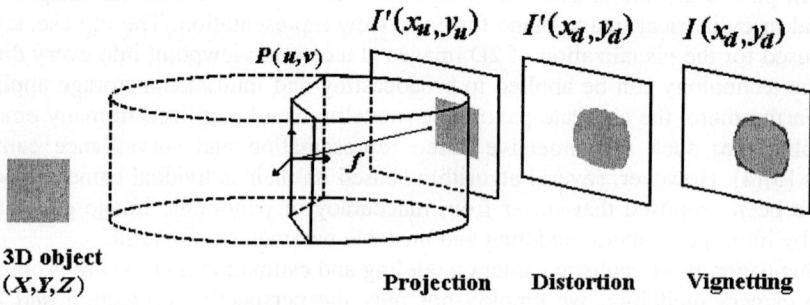

Fig. 1. Image formation processes

3 Camera Calibration

Several camera calibration algorithms have been proposed to compute many unknown variables simultaneously [6][7][8]. However, camera parameter estimation with a high degree of freedom could result in instability. We propose a new calibration method for panoramic imaging. By assuming that input images are acquired with a panning camera, we only need to estimate the focal length and lens distortion.

We estimate the focal length based on the planar perspective relationship between two consecutive images. A planar perspective transformation that has eight parameters is used to model the images acquired with a moving camera;

$$\begin{bmatrix} x' \\ y' \\ 1 \end{bmatrix} = \alpha \begin{bmatrix} m_0 & m_1 & m_2 \\ m_3 & m_4 & m_5 \\ m_6 & m_7 & 1 \end{bmatrix} \begin{bmatrix} x \\ y \\ 1 \end{bmatrix}, \qquad (3)$$

where $(x',y',1)^T$ and $(x,y,1)^T$ represent the pixel positions in the two images for the same object point in 3D space. This relation can be rewritten into

$$x' = \frac{m_0 x + m_1 y + m_2}{m_6 x + m_7 y + 1}, \quad y' = \frac{m_3 x + m_4 y + m_5}{m_6 x + m_7 y + 1}. \qquad (4)$$

With the panning camera assumption, the equations can be simplified into
$x' = m_0 x + m_2, \quad y' = y$.

We can compute m_0 and m_2 by a linear regression method with more than two correspondence points, which are detected by block matching.

On the other hand, a point (p) in 3D space is projected by

$$x' \sim PRp \text{ and } x \sim Pp, \qquad (5)$$

onto the two images acquired with a rotating camera. Here, the rotation and projection matrices are defined by

$$R = \begin{bmatrix} r_{00} & r_{01} & r_{02} \\ r_{10} & r_{11} & r_{12} \\ r_{20} & r_{21} & r_{22} \end{bmatrix}$$

$$P = \begin{bmatrix} f & 0 & 0 \\ 0 & f & 0 \\ 0 & 0 & 1 \end{bmatrix}, \qquad (6)$$

respectively. Eqs. (3) and (5) can be combined into $x' \sim VRV^{-1}x$ and we have

$$\begin{bmatrix} m_0 & 0 & m_2 \\ 0 & 1 & 0 \\ 0 & 0 & 1 \end{bmatrix} \cong \begin{bmatrix} r_{00} & r_{01} & r_{02}f \\ r_{10} & r_{11} & r_{12}f \\ r_{20}/f & r_{21}/f & r_{22} \end{bmatrix}. \tag{7}$$

The first two rows (columns) of the rotation matrix should have the same norm and be orthogonal so that we obtain get the following relationship,

$$f^2 = \frac{m_2^2}{1 - m_0^2}. \tag{8}$$

To estimate lens distortion, we make use of the fact that straight lines in 3D space should appear as straight lines in the undistorted 2D space. Let (x_{dj}^i, y_{dj}^i) and (x_{uj}^i, y_{uj}^i) be the jth point on the ith arbitrarily chosen line in the distorted and undistorted images, respectively. Then, both points should satisfy Eq. (1). Since each line should be straight, the straightness error can be expressed with

$$e_{Lj}^i = [(x_{u j-1}^i - x_{u j-2}^i)(y_{u j}^i - y_{u j-1}^i) - (x_{u j}^i - x_{u j-1}^i)(y_{u j-1}^i - y_{u j-2}^i)]. \tag{9}$$

We can obtain the lens distortion parameters, K_1 and K_2, by minimizing the cost function,

$$E = \sum_i^I \sum_j^{J_i - 1} \{e_{Lj}^i\}^2, \tag{10}$$

where I and J_i represent the number of lines and the number of points on the ith line, respectively. The parameters of the cost function are estimated by a gradient descent method suitable for non-quadratic functions.

4 Panoramic Image Generation

Figure 2 shows the process used in panoramic image generation from multiple images acquired with a camera panning on its focal point. Input images (IV_m) undergo not only perspective projection and cylindrical mapping, but also suffer from lens distortion. The relationship between the panoramic image coordinates (u,v) and the undistorted coordinates (x_u, y_u) shown in Fig. 1 can be denoted by

$$x_u = \tan(\frac{u}{f}), \quad y_u = v/\cos(\frac{u}{f}). \tag{11}$$

Given (u,v), the associated distorted coordinates (x_d, y_d) can be obtained by combining Eqs. (1) and (11). Eq. (1) is a fifth-order polynomial, thus we need a high-order root finder. However, in cases where the lens has barrel distortion, K_1 is positive. If K_2 is set to zero, we have one explicit real solution and two imaginary solutions. The real solution of x_d can be obtained by

$$Q_x = -\frac{x_u^2}{3K_1(x_u^2+y_u^2)}, \quad R_x = \frac{x_u^3}{2K_1(x_u^2+y_u^2)}$$

$$A_x = \begin{cases} -(R_x+\sqrt{R_x^2-Q_x^3}), & R_x > 0 \\ (-R_x+\sqrt{R_x^2-Q_x^3}), & \text{otherwise} \end{cases} \tag{12}$$

$$x_d = \begin{cases} A_x + \dfrac{Q_x}{A_x}, & A_x \neq 0 \\ 0, & \text{otherwise} \end{cases}$$

y_d can be computed in the same way as x_d. For the panoramic image generation, a backward warping is used to generate the cylindrical image, $P_m(u,v)$, from the m-th distorted image, IV_m, by using a quadratic interpolation.

As shown in Fig. 2(b), the next step is to register all the cylindrical images before stitching them to produce a panoramic image. In registration, one feature point is detected by finding a 32×32 window having the maximum variance over an overlapped region. The overlapped region is estimated by considering the speed of camera movement and the number of frames over one scanning period. For the detected feature point, we can obtain the corresponding point in the next cylindrical image based on block-based matching. Before blending the registered cylindrical images, the vignetting effect needs to be estimated and compensated. We can compute the vignetting parameter (V_p) by minimizing the cost function,

$$E_P = \sum_{u_m,v_m}^{\text{overlapped area}} e_P^2(u_m, v_m)$$

$$e_P(u_m, v_m) = \frac{P_m(u_m, v_m)}{V_p \cos^4\left(\arctan\left(\dfrac{\Delta\sqrt{u_m^2+v_m^2}}{f}\right)\right)+1-V_p}$$

$$- \frac{P_{m+1}(u_{m+1}, v_{m+1})}{V_p \cos^4\left(\arctan\left(\dfrac{\Delta\sqrt{u_{m+1}^2+v_{m+1}^2}}{f}\right)\right)+1-V_p} \tag{13}$$

$$u_m = u_{m+1}+\Delta u_m, \quad v_m = v_{m+1}+\Delta v_m,$$

where (Δu_m, Δv_m) is a displacement vector. Here, it is assumed that the same vignetting parameter is applied to all the frames that are used in generating the panoramic image. Lighting conditions are also assumed to be identical in all the frames so that the illumination parameters do not need to be considered. To obtain one stitched panoramic image shown in Fig. 2(a), an alpha blending method is applied to each consecutive image pair. To make the generated panoramic image rectangular, the padding algorithm used in MPEG-4's arbitrary shape coding is employed.

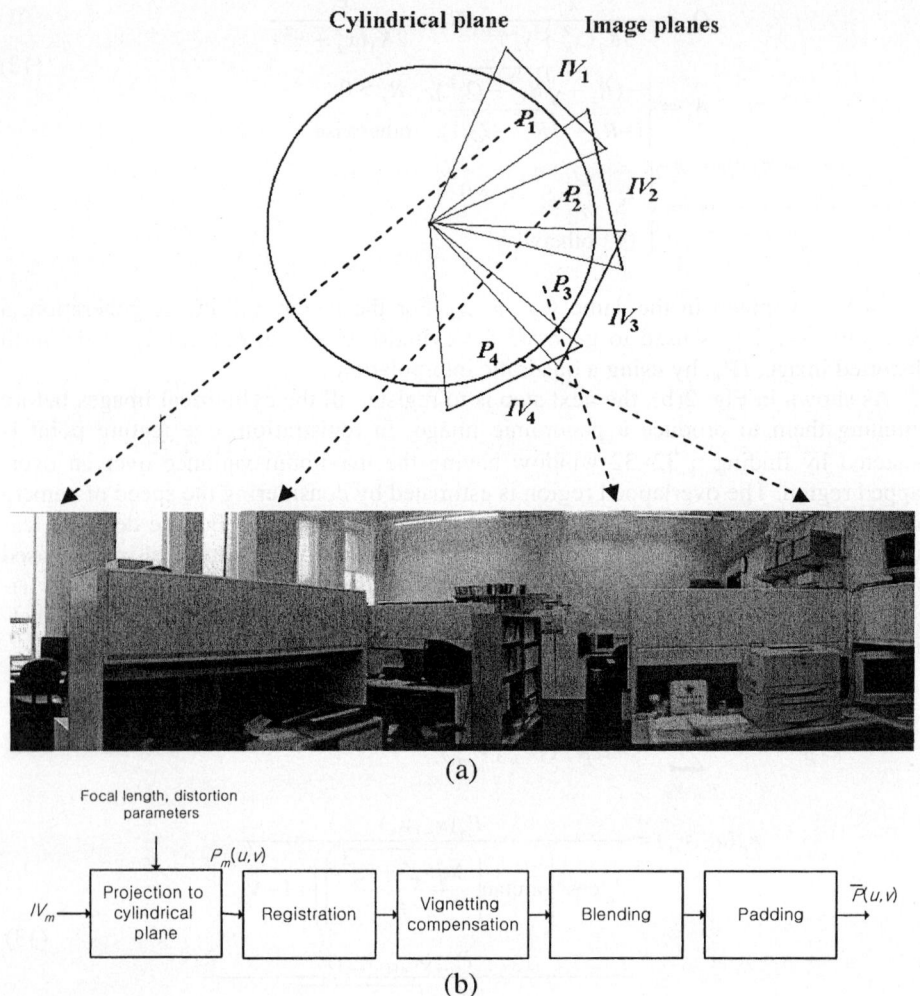

Fig. 2. Panoramic image generation. (a) Cylindrical mapping and (b) block diagram for panoramic image generation.

5 Parameter Estimation and Background Reconstruction

Once the panoramic image has been generated, an incoming input image, $I_n(x_d, y_d)$, can be generated with several parameters such as illumination and vignetting parameters and one correspondence point with respect to the panoramic image. First, the input image is projected onto the cylindrical plane, resulting in $P_n(u,v)$. The projection is performed in the same way and with the same parameters used in panoramic image generation. A camera's panning is represented as translational displacements in the cylindrical plane. The correspondence point (T_{nx}, T_{ny}) is estimated by minimizing the cost function:

$$E = \sum_{all\,u,v\,in\,P_n(u,v)} \delta_T \left(P_n(u,v) - P(u - T_{nx}, v - T_{ny}) \right), \quad (14)$$

where $\delta_T(x)$ is 0 when x is smaller than T and 1 when x is larger than or equal to T. T is the standard deviation of e_P in Eq. (13). The cost function can be interpreted as the number of pixels considered as background. We do not use the conventional absolute error nor square error because they are very sensitive to outliers. In background estimation, the moving object regions would behave as outliers, and the estimates would deteriorate [9][10]. The input image size and the search space for the correspondence point over the panoramic image are quite large. For efficient computing, the correspondence point is estimated by using a three-level pyramid structure in minimizing the cost function.

Estimation for illumination and vignetting parameters and background is performed. A back-projection is performed to convert a part of $P_n(u,v)$ in the cylindrical coordinate corresponding to the input image into an uncompensated background image, $B_n'(x_d, y_d)$, in the distorted image plane. The back-projection is carried out with the inverse of the projection used in panoramic image generation by using Eqs. (1) and (11). A background image, $B_n(x_d, y_d)$, is estimated by compensating for the illumination and vignetting effects on the uncompensated background as follows:

$$B_n(x_d, y_d) = \frac{B_n'(x_d, y_d) \cdot \left\{ V_n \cos^4\left(\arctan\left(\frac{\Delta\sqrt{x_d^2 + y_d^2}}{f} \right) \right) + 1 - V_n \right\} - L_n^1}{L_n^0}. \quad (15)$$

V_n, L_n^0, and L_n^1 are estimated by optimizing the following energy function:

$$E = \sum \rho(I_n - B_n) = \sum \rho \left(I_n - \frac{B_n'(x_d, y_d) \cdot \left\{ V_n \cos^4\left(\arctan\left(\frac{\Delta\sqrt{x_d^2 + y_d^2}}{f} \right) \right) + 1 - V_n \right\} - L_n^1}{L_n^0} \right), \quad (16)$$

where the cost function is defined by

$$\rho(x) = \frac{(x/a)^2}{1 + (x/a)^2}. \quad (17)$$

This cost function is introduced for robust estimation against those moving objects functioning as outliers. The threshold a can be set to the standard deviation of

$$e_P(u_m, v_m) \times V_p \cos^4\left(\arctan\left(\frac{\Delta\sqrt{u_{m+1}^2 + v_{m+1}^2}}{f}\right)\right) + 1 - V_p \qquad (18)$$

assuming that the error characteristics in input image parametric modeling is similar to those in panoramic image generation.

6 Experiment Results

The representation capability of the proposed system was evaluated with multiple video sequences by comparing with JPEG-2000 [11] and MPEG-4 [12] coding. Table I lists the video sequences used in our evaluation, which were captured with a Sony camcoder and an Intel USB camera. They include indoor and outdoor scenes to test the robustness regarding various input sequence characteristics. The evaluation was performed by turning the automatic control for white balance and exposure time on and off. Two sequences were acquired by disabling the automatic mode, leading to fixed exposure time and no white balance. The others were captured with the automatic mode enabled. Automatic control resulted in better quality images. We compared the proposed algorithm, JPEG-2000 and MPEG-4 in terms of PSNR and the number of bits used in coding. In the case of MPEG-4, the performance was measured with respect to different frame rates due to the fact that MPEG takes advantage of temporal redundancy. Furthermore, a low frame rate is commonly used for video communication and surveillance purpose.

Table 1. Input video sequences

Sequence	Size	Acquisition	Contents	Camera parameters	Number of frames
Sequence 1	360x240	Camcorder	Indoor	Auto	157
Sequence 2	360x240	Camcorder	Indoor	Fixed	170
Sequence 3	320x240	USB camera	Indoor	Auto	212
Sequence 4	360x240	Camcorder	Outdoor	Auto	169

Fig. 3. Panoramic background image obtained after cylindrical mapping

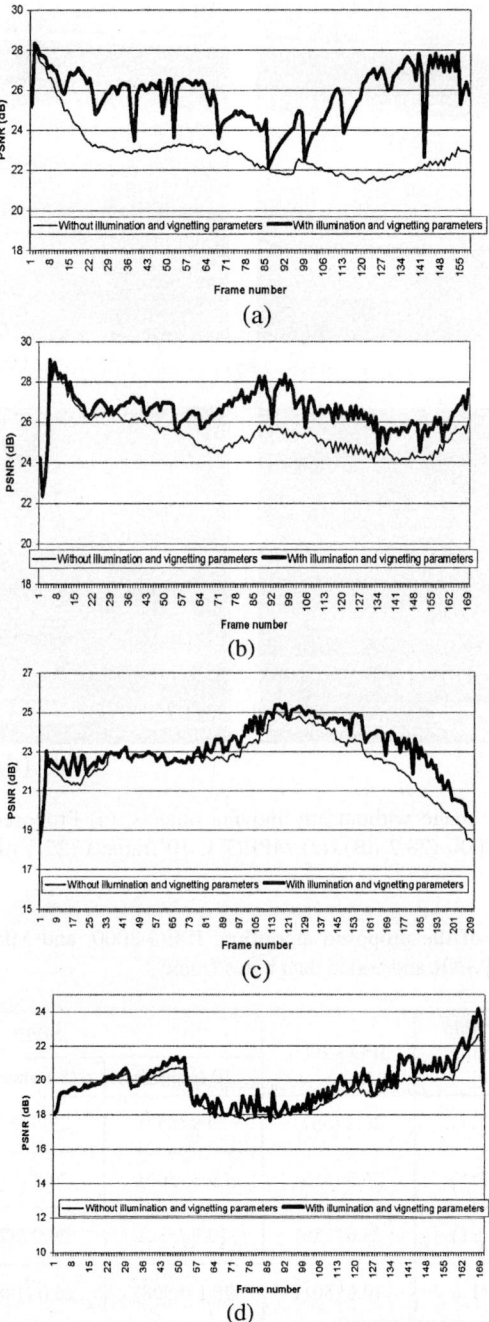

Fig. 4. PSNR of video sequences with and without the illumination and vignetting parameters. (a) Sequence 1, (b) sequence 2, (c) sequence 3 and (d) sequence 4.

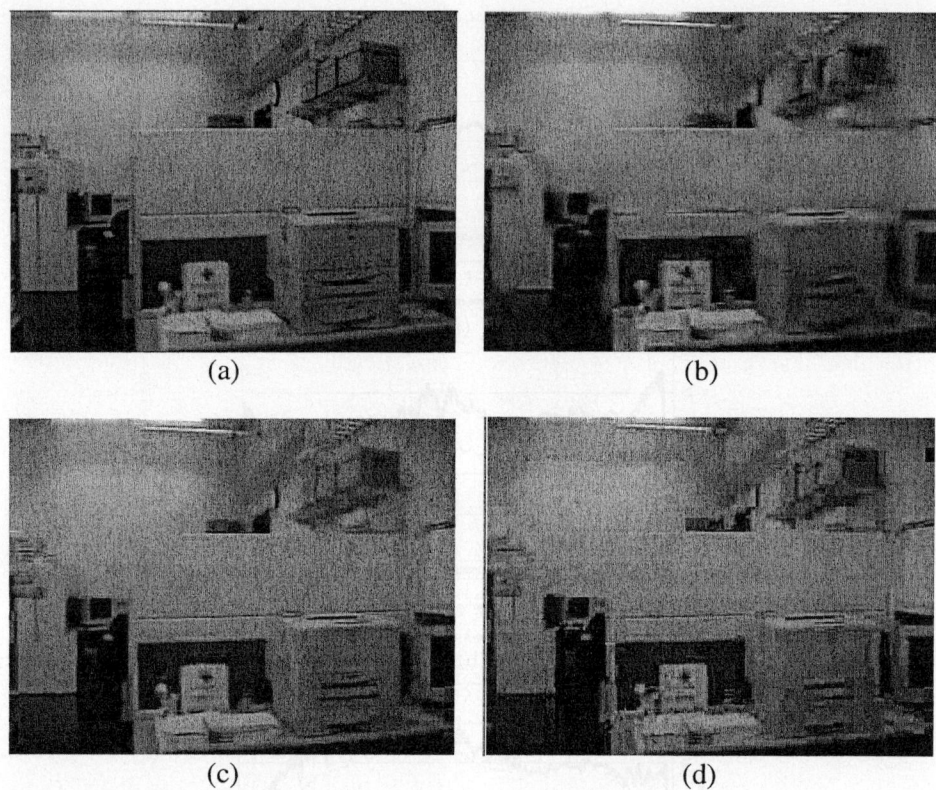

Fig. 5. Reconstructed image without any moving objects. (a) Proposed panoramic modeling (28.3 dB), (b) JPEG-2000 (28.2 dB), (c) MPEG-4, 10 frame/s (29.5 dB) and (d) MPEG-4, 1 frame/s (28.4 dB).

Table 2. Comparison of the proposed algorithm, JPEG-2000, and MPEG-4 with four video sequences in terms of PSNR and coded data bytes/frame

	Panoramic modeling only	JPEG-2000	MPEG-4		
			10 frames/s	5 frames/s	1 frame/s
Sequence 1	26.6 (11)	26.2 (587)	29.9 (557)	29.5 (658)	27.9 (1854)
Sequence 2	25.7 (11)	25.3 (455)	29.8 (560)	29.3 (714)	28.2 (1872)
Sequence 3	23.2 (11)	23.6 (389)	29.9 (534)	29.9 (570)	28.5 (1819)
Sequence 4	19.8 (11)	19.6 (501)	26.1 (1598)	26.0 (1882)	25.2 (5899)

Figure 3 shows a panoramic background image generated by the proposed algorithm for sequence 1. A seamless panoramic image has been obtained by following the steps in Fig. 2(b). This background image can be now coded with JPEG-2000 and transferred to the decoder side.

Table II compares the proposed algorithm, JPEG-2000, and MPEG-4 in terms of PSNR and the number of bytes/frame with four video sequences. The panoramic modeling alone leads to moderate PSNRs with as small as 11 bytes. Thus, compared with JPEG-2000, our algorithm is quite effective in those sequences with no moving objects. The performance of MPEG-4 deteriorates as the frame rate decreases due to its reliance on temporal redundancy.

Figure 4 shows the PSNR using our algorithm with and without the illumination and vignetting parameters. Employing these parameters improves the image quality by 1-2 dB. As shown Fig. 5, the subjective image quality of the proposed algorithm is better than that of conventional algorithms, even though they have all similar PSNR values. There are no blocky or ringing artifacts in the proposed panoramic representation.

7 Conclusion

In this paper, a new panoramic image generation algorithm is proposed based on more realistic image formation processes. Perspective projection, lens distortion, vignetting and illumination effects are incorporated into the proposed panoramic modeling. Intrinsic and extrinsic camera parameters are estimated by the proposed stable camera parameter estimation algorithm derived from panning camera constraints. It is shown that the proposed algorithm is effective to generate a panoramic image from acquired images in terms of objective and subjective assessments. Further study will be focused on application of the proposed algorithm to surveillance systems.

Acknowledgement

The present research has been conducted by the Research Grant of Kwangwoon University in 2005.

References

1. Burt, P.J., Irani, M., Hsu, A.C., Anadan, P., Hansen, M.W.: Method and apparatus for performing mosaic based image compression. United State Patent 5,991,444, Nov. 1999.
2. Shum, H.-Y., Szeliski, R.:Construction and refinement of panoramic mosaics with global and local alignment. Proc. Conf. Computer Vision (1998) 953-956
3. Pavlidis, I., Morellas, V., Tsiamyrtzis, P., Harp, S.: Urban surveillance systems: From the laboratory to the commercial world. Proceedings of IEEE, vol. 89 (2001) 1478-1497
4. Atzpadin, N., Kauff, P., Schreer, O.: Stereo analysis by hybrid recursive matching for real-time immersive video conferencing. IEEE Trans. on CSVT, vol. 14 (2004) 321-334
5. Altunbasak, Y., Mersereau, R. M., Patti, A. J.: A fast parametric motion estimation algorithm with illumination and lens distortion correction. IEEE Trans. Image Processing, vol. 12 (2003) 395-408

6. Zhang, Z.: On the epipolar geometry between two images with lens distortions. Proc. Int. Conf. Pattern Recognition, vol. 1 (1996) 407-411
7. Stein, G.: Lens distortion calibration using point correspondences. Proc. IEEE Conf. Computer Vision and Pattern Recognition (1997) 602-608
8. Asada, N., Amano, A., Baba, M.: Photometric calibration of zoom lens systems. Proc. Int. Conf. Pattern Recognition (1996) 186-190
9. Black, M.J., Anandan, P.: The robust estimation of multiple motions. Computer Vision and Image Understanding, vol. 63 (1996) 75-104
10. Sim, D.-G., Park, R.-H.: Robust reweighted MAP motion estimation. IEEE Trans. Pattern Analysis and Machine Intelligence, vol. 21 (1998) 353-365
11. Adams, M. D., Kossentini, F.: Jasper: a software-based JPEG-2000 codec implementation. Int. Conf. Image Processing, vol. 2 (2000) 53-56
12. ISO/IEC 14496-2: Information technology-Coding of audio-visual object, Part-2

Virtual Object Placement in Video for Augmented Reality

Jong-Seung Park[1], Mee Young Sung[1], and Sung-Ryul Noh[2]

[1] Department of Computer Science & Engineering, University of Incheon,
177 Dohwa-dong, Nam-gu, Incheon 402-749, Republic of Korea
{jong, mysung}@incheon.ac.kr
[2] SIRIUS, IVC 3F, 169-1 Juan-dong, Nam-gu, Incheon 402-201, Republic of Korea
noh@sirius.co.kr

Abstract. This article describes a method to insert virtual objects into a real video stream based on feature tracking and camera pose estimation from a set of single-camera video frames. To insert or modify 3D shapes to target video frames, the transformation from the 3D objects to the projection of the objects onto the video frames should be revealed. It is shown that, without a camera calibration process, the 3D reconstruction is possible using multiple images from a single camera under the fixed internal camera parameters. The proposed approach is based on the simplification of the camera matrix of intrinsic parameters and the use of projective geometry. The method is particularly useful for augmented reality applications to insert or modify models to a real video stream. Several experimental results are presented on real-world video streams, demonstrating the usefulness of our method for the augmented reality applications.

Keywords: video editing, metric reconstruction, texture blending, feature tracking.

1 Introduction

A flexible synthesis of real environments with virtual objects is interested in wide range of augmented reality applications. Methods of virtual view generation can be classified into two categories: In the first category, a full 3D structure of the scene is constructed and then reprojected in order to generate a virtual view[1]. The main issue in this approach is the problem of generating a full 3D model from 2D information. Though several novel methods have been presented based on multiple view geometry[2], the 3D reconstruction problem is still an ill posed problem. In the second category, virtual views are directly generated without having to estimate the scene structure[3]. This approach reconstructs virtual views from a set of reference views without concerning the geometric structure. However, these approaches require a considerable amount of computational cost to compute dense correspondences and also to generate virtual views from a moving user-defined viewpoint.

This paper describes a method to generate real-time virtual views in which real objects observed by a camera are replaced with virtual objects. Our approach to the virtual view generation falls into the first category which requires relatively cheap computational cost. To avoid numerical instability of 3D reconstruction, our method finds and tracks only a moderate number of apparent feature points.

Two main subtasks are camera pose estimation relative to the real object and seamless video blending. Camera pose estimation is to find the camera positions and orientations relative to the target object. In typical augmented reality applications, there are two types of camera pose estimation: marker-based approaches and motion-based approaches: Marker-based approaches utilize a simple black and white marker for easy detection and tracking of the marker area[4][5]. In these kind of applications, the marker plays a key role for the camera pose estimation. On the other hand, motion-based approaches track many feature points and recover camera motion parameters from the point correspondences [1]. The current state of the art technology provides solutions that can be applied only under strict conditions. A common constraint is to assume that all the images are taken by exactly the same camera, without change of focus or zoom. Existing theory and algorithms have been restricted to constant camera parameters. The image axes can be assumed orthogonal and often the aspect ratio is known.

In the past few years some preliminary research results have been presented on the 3D construction using single-camera images. Recently, Kahl [6] presented a method to model smoothness constraints about the random camera motion such as the motion of hand-held video cameras. With developing a maximum a posteriori (MAP) estimator, a way to estimate both Euclidean structure and motion was proposed. Heyden [7] proposed a method to improve the estimation quality of the absolute quadric refined by a nonlinear technique and more accurate Euclidean reconstruction.

A video blending task is related to the overlay of virtual objects, replacing real objects with virtual objects, or removing real objects[8]. Blending approaches should consider the scene depth structure in composition to become accepted the real and virtual objects for augmented reality applications [9]. Moreover, it is preferred to figure out and reconfigure the illumination conditions so that the virtual objects and the real objects share a common lighting environment. Though there have been some works on the geometry of the light sources[10], determining reflectance and light position is still a difficult problem in the image analysis field.

Our 3D reconstruction system consists of three steps: feature tracking, metric reconstruction, and object insertion. Fig. 1 illustrates the overall steps of our method. First, good features are selected and tracked for input video frames. Good features include most corner points of real objects and any other points that can be reliably tracked. Second, camera poses are estimated using the feature correspondences. Finally, virtual objects are inserted to target positions according to the camera poses. The target positions are identified from the user initialization of object corners at the first frame.

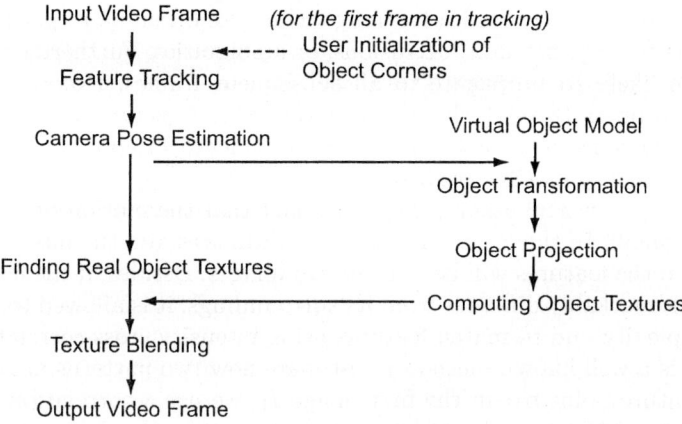

Fig. 1. Steps of our video synthesis system

This paper is organized as follows. A feature tracking and camera parameter estimation method is described and the algorithm for 3D reconstruction is detailed in Section 2. In Section 3, we explain the object insertion and texture blending process. The last two sections give experimental results and conclusion.

2 Object Pose Estimation

The video analysis process to insert a virtual object into a video stream is one of formidable tasks in augmented reality applications. The difficulty comes mainly from the fact that little information is available at the beginning process. Except for a few restrict assumptions such as a basic pinhole camera model, rigid scene, and diffuse reflectance characteristics of the surface, neither the world geometry nor the camera geometry is known.

To insert a virtual object, we must know where the real world objects lies. The camera pose tracking is a problem of obtaining the relative camera-to-object position and orientation. With a prior knowledge of model geometry, it can be done by simply tracking feature points. In our approach, the model geometry is assumed to be unknown. The tracking features do not have to lie on a specific real object. The only assumption is that initial reference positions are assigned by the user at the first image frame to indicate the target place of object insertion. For each frame, the camera pose is computed only from feature correspondences without using any model geometry.

2.1 Feature Tracking

We compute the object pose relative to the camera coordinate system using feature correspondences between two images. However, reliable pixel correspondences are difficult to obtain, especially over a long sequence of images: Region tracking using motion segmentation methods often fails to detect the motions of low textured region[11]. Feature-tracking techniques often fail to produce correct matches due to large motions, occlusions, or ambiguities. Furthermore, errors in a frame are likely to propagate to all subsequent frames. However, there are some clues to break through the difficulties. Outlier rejection techniques can reduce these problems. Knowledge of camera parameters or epipolar geometry can simplify the correspondence problem.

A valid and powerful assumption is the fact that the motion between frames is generally small. In this case, the feature coordinates and the intensity distribution around the features will be alike in two images. Besides, if the feature to be matched is remarkably different from its surroundings, it is allowed to reduce the search complexity and to match features using intensity cross correlation. Cross correlation is a well known method to estimate how two patterns are correlated. For each feature point $\mathbf{m}_1$ in the first image I_1, we use a correlation window of size $(2N+1) \times (2M+1)$ and perform a correlation operation between $\mathbf{m}_1$ and all features $\mathbf{m}_2$ lying within a search area in the second image I_2. The correlation score is evaluated as

$$s(\mathbf{m}_1, \mathbf{m}_2) = \sum_{i=-N}^{N} \sum_{j=-M}^{M} \left[g_{ij}(\mathbf{m}_1) - \bar{g}(\mathbf{m}_1) \right] \left[g_{ij}(\mathbf{m}_2) - \bar{g}(\mathbf{m}_2) \right] / d \qquad (1)$$

where $d = (2N+1)(2M+1)\sqrt{\sigma^2(\mathbf{m}_1)\sigma^2(\mathbf{m}_2)}$, $g_{ij}(\mathbf{m}_k)$ is the intensity at point $\mathbf{m}_k + (i, j)$ in image I_k, $\bar{g}(\mathbf{m}_k)$ is the average intensity at point $\mathbf{m}_k$ of I_k, and $\sigma(\mathbf{m}_k)$ is the standard deviation of I_k in the neighborhood of $\mathbf{m}_k$. Based on the correlation score and spatial consistency, we obtain a large enough number of accurate feature correspondences between two consecutive image frames.

2.2 Obtaining Camera Parameters

When a camera moves, the camera coordinates of scene points are also changed [2]. A camera movement causes unknown camera extrinsic parameters to be considered: R for camera rotation and t for camera translation. The reconstruction problem is directly related to the computation of these camera parameters. When all the parameters of the camera are given, the reconstruction is straightforward. Many of the previous works assume that the intrinsic camera parameters are known. Computing camera motion with known intrinsic parameters is the well-known relative orientation problem and several effective methods are available[12]. In many practical augmented reality applications, however, assuming fixed intrinsic parameters or off-line calibration is not suitable. Hence, we are going to focus on the case of a single camera with unknown intrinsic parameters and unknown motion. The only available information is the video sequence.

Before computing metric calibration, an affine calibration is computed first, or equivalently, the plane at infinity is located first in the projective space, which is observed to be the most difficult step. Armstrong et al. [13] obtained the affine calibration using some views of pure translations. With additional views of general motions, a metric calibration can be easily obtained. Hartley [14] proposed an algorithm by using dense search. Pollefeys and Gool [15] show a nonlinear algorithm based on modulus provides one polynomial equation of degree four in the coefficients of the infinity plane.

A 3D point M is projected into an image point m which is the intersection of the retinal plane with the line passing M and the optical center. Let $\mathbf{X} = (X, Y, Z)$ be the coordinates of M in the world coordinate system and $\mathbf{x} = (u, v)$ the pixel coordinates of m. Let $\tilde{\mathbf{X}}$ and $\tilde{\mathbf{x}}$ be the homogeneous notations of $\mathbf{X}$ and $\mathbf{x}$, respectively. Then, the transformation from $\tilde{\mathbf{X}}$ to $\tilde{\mathbf{x}}$ is given by $\lambda\tilde{\mathbf{x}} = \tilde{P}\tilde{\mathbf{X}}$ where λ is an arbitrary nonzero scalar. The 3×4 matrix $\tilde{P}$ is called the *camera matrix*. Using a QR factorization, the camera matrix $\tilde{P}$ can be decomposed into the product form: $\tilde{P} = K[R|t]$. The 3×3 matrix K has five unknowns: the focal lengths in two image directions (α_x and α_y), the principal point in terms of pixel dimensions (x_0 and y_0), and the skew parameter (s) which is close to zero in most cases. The matrix K depends on the intrinsic parameters only. The extrinsic parameters represent the rigid transformation that aligns the camera reference frame and the world reference frame and they are encoded by the rotation matrix R and the translation t.

Auto-calibration is the process of determining both internal parameters and external parameters directly from multiple uncalibrated images. The general approach has two steps: First obtain a projective reconstruction (P^i, X^j). Then determine a rectifying homography H from auto-calibration constraints, and transform to a metric reconstruction $(P^i H, H^{-1} X^j)$. We assume that there are m cameras with projection matrices P_M^i, $i = 1, \ldots, m$. The coordinates of 3D points in Euclidean world frame are denoted by X_M^j, $i = 1, \ldots, n$. Then, the i'th camera projects X_M^j to an image point $x^i = P_M^i X_M^j$. The calibrated cameras may be written as $P_M^i = K^i[R^i|t^i]$ for $i = 1, \ldots, m$. The projective cameras P^i are related to P_M^i by $P_M^i = P^i H$ where H is an unknown homography. The absolute dual quadric Ω^* is the symmetric 4×4 rank 3 matrix. In a Euclidean frame, Ω^* has the form $\tilde{I} = \mathrm{diag}(1, 1, 1, 0)$ and, in a projective frame, Ω^* has the form $\Omega^* = H\tilde{I}H^T$. The absolute dual quadric Ω^* projects to the dual image of the absolute conic ω^{*i} and we have $\omega^{*i} = P^i \Omega^* P^{iT}$ [2]. The matrix Ω^* may be determined in the projective reconstruction from constraints on intrinsic parameters. Then the homography H is also determined by decomposing Ω^* as $H\tilde{I}H^T$. Since Ω^* is a real symmetric matrix a decomposition of Ω^* is easily computed using Jacobi's eigenvalue decomposition algorithm. H^{-1} is a homography that takes the projective frame to a Euclidean frame. We get a metric reconstruction by applying H^{-1} to the points and H to the cameras.

2.3 Metric Reconstruction

With some constraints on intrinsic parameters we can obtain an initial guess by a linear method. Assume that the principal point is known. We change the image coordinates so that the origin corresponds to the principal point: $x_0 = y_0 = 0$. Moreover we assume that the skew is zero: $s = 0$. These two constraints significantly simplify the problem. The dual image of the absolute conic becomes $\omega^* = \mathrm{diag}(\alpha_x^2, \alpha_y^2, 1)$ and the three equations follows from the zero entries:

$$(P^i \Omega^* P^{iT})_{1,2} = 0, (P^i \Omega^* P^{iT})_{1,3} = 0, (P^i \Omega^* P^{iT})_{2,3} = 0 \qquad (2)$$

For m views, there are $3m$ constraints. The estimation of Ω^* is a problem of the linear system. Since the matrix is symmetric, it is parametrized linearly by a 10D vector $\mathbf{x}$:

$$\mathbf{x} = [q_{11}, q_{12}, q_{13}, q_{14}, q_{22}, q_{23}, q_{24}, q_{33}, q_{34}, q_{44}]^T$$

Rearranging (2) into a matrix equation of the form $A\mathbf{x} = \mathbf{0}$ where A is a $3m \times 10$ coefficient matrix from P^i, we get a usual linear system. A least-squares solution of $A\mathbf{x} = \mathbf{0}$ is obtained using the SVD. From three images 12 equations are available and a least-squares solution is obtained.

The homography H is obtained by decomposing Ω^*. Then, by applying H^{-1} to the points and H to the cameras, we get a metric reconstruction. The rank 3 constraint does not be enforced and the absolute dual quadric Ω^* computed by the linear method will not be rank 3 in general. A rank 3 matrix can be obtained by setting the smallest eigenvalue to zero in the eigenvalue decomposition. The rank 3 matrix can be used as an initial value for an iterative method.

The calibration matrix K^i of each camera may be computed directly by computing $\omega^{*i} = P^i \Omega^* P^{iT}$ and by Cholesky factorization from the equation $\omega^{*i} = K^i K^{iT}$. However, there is a difficulty in enforcing the condition that Ω^* is positive semi-definite. If Ω^* is not positive semi-definite, ω^* would not be positive-definite and ω^* cannot be decomposed using Cholesky factorization to compute the calibration matrix.

3 Object Image Blending

Once we recover the scene structures and camera parameters using the method described in the previous section, it is possible to insert virtual objects into the video frames. Since virtual objects are provided with their local coordinates and the recovered scene is represented with world coordinates, we should transform the virtual objects to the world coordinate system. A user manually assigns four corresponding points of a virtual object and the recovered scene structure by clicking their image points. Using the correspondences, the local to world transformation matrix is computed. The texture blending process is shown in Fig. 2. Now the virtual object is projected to each video frame using the recovered camera projection matrix and the image regions for the object are found. For each projected face, the texture pixels are computed from the textures of the virtual object. For each inner position (x, y) of the projected face, the color $f'(x, y)$ of the pixel is determined by the color $f(u, v)$ at the input frame and and also by the color $t(x, y)$ at the virtual 3D object. The weight for $t(x, y)$ is increased when the position is close to a face edge.

To make the blended view photo-realistic, we fully implemented the entire steps of transformations and texture mapping. For the visible faces, the corresponding textures are projected to the image space with a suitable interpolation scheme. For the fast rendering, we trace the projected area on the frames and determine the pixel color for each pixel position.

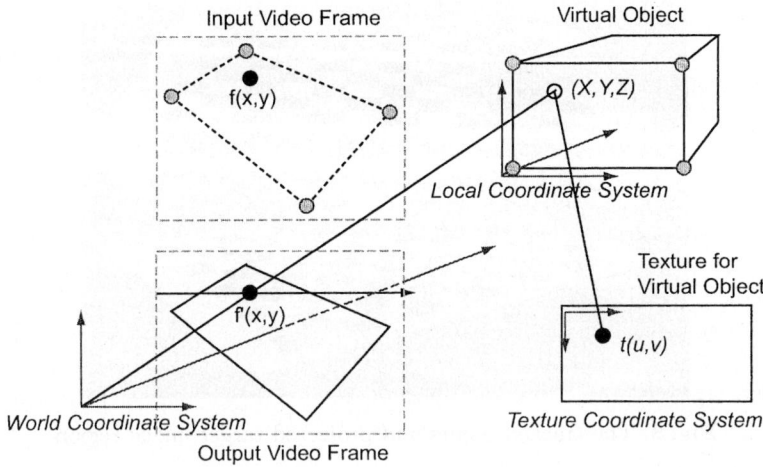

Fig. 2. Computation of target pixel colors for the object placement

Texture fusion process should consider the two important aspects: edge blending and illumination changes. The blended textures should change accordantly across the projected edges. Abrupt changes cause seams which make unnatural blending. To replace the original frame textures into virtual object textures without seams, near edge pixels should reflect original frame colors. Though the illumination of the virtual object textures and that of the real frame textures could possibly be significantly different, adjusting overall brightness of virtual object textures to that of the real frame textures decreases the difference of the illumination and hence increases the output quality.

4 Experimental Results

The proposed feature tracking and 3D recovery method has been implemented and experiments have been performed on a desktop computer. For an initial frame, a number of corner points are extracted. Among them, the user selects target positions which indicate the locations of corresponding corners of a virtual object to be inserted. The feature tracker tracks all the extracted corner points including the selected points. Using tracking results metric reconstruction is performed. The features should be tracked along at least three consecutive frames. The target virtual object is projected to each frame using the reconstructed camera projection matrix. There would be small errors between the tracked points and the projected points. Fig. 3 shows an example of such errors. The black circles are the user clicked positions and the red lines are the projection of a rectangle of the recovered structure. From the four selected corner positions, we obtained stable tracking and reconstruction results which are shown in Fig. 4. For each position, the reprojection error was at most 3 pixels. The tracking accuracy is very critical since the metric reconstruction is directly influenced by

Fig. 3. The tracked points and projected target image region

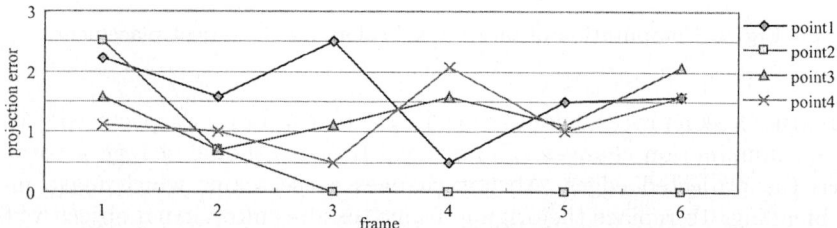

Fig. 4. Distances between projection points and tracked points

Fig. 5. Test images from the house frames (upper) and the village frames (lower)

the tracking accuracy. Fig. 5 and Fig. 6 show two test results of metric reconstruction. The actual size of the structure needs not be considered since only the relative depths of object faces are used in the blending stage. Once a metric structure is available, a wide range of video synthesis applications are possible.

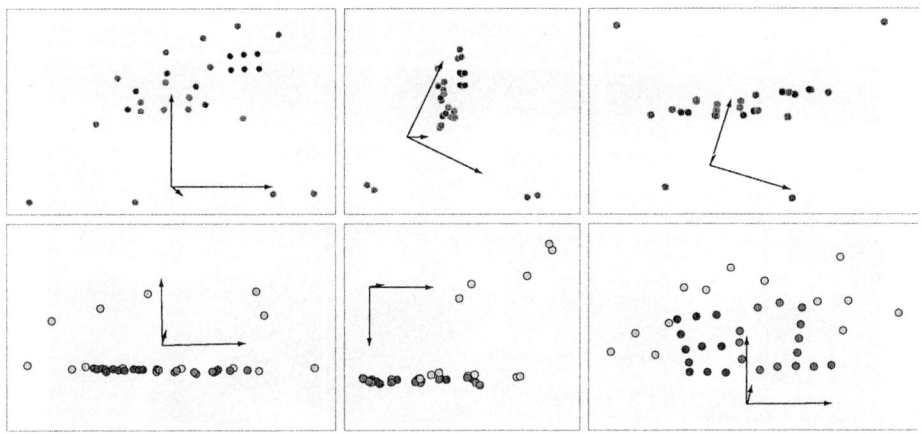

Fig. 6. The recovered structures from the house frames (upper) and from the village frames (lower)

Fig. 7. The chessboard frames (upper) and the blended frames (lower)

Fig. 7 shows the input video frames with tracked points and the modified video frames using a simple external texture. The gab between the projected boundary and the region of the checkerboard rectangle is indistinguishable. In Fig. 8, a virtual desktop calendar is placed at the real desktop calendar. The tracking of the corners is robust and the virtual calendar is not oscillated even when the camera moves or rotates abruptly. Fig. 9 shows results of seamless edge blending applied to the desktop calendar test set. The upper left figure is an input frame. We placed a rectangular object using a simple texture replacement (upper middle) and using a seamless edge blending (upper right). The lower figures show the magnified views of the upper right corner areas. Similar textures could be replaced to give better image quality or to enhance the visibility. In Fig. 10, a used tissue box (upper) is replaced by a new tissue box with a brighter texture.

Fig. 8. The calendar frames (upper) and the blended frames (lower)

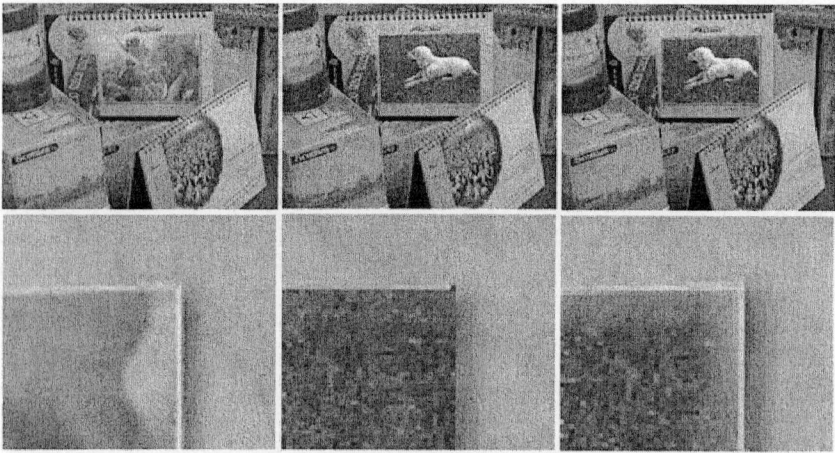

Fig. 9. Comparison of a simple texture blending and a seamless edge blending

Several other experiments also verified that our system works well for real video streams in which objects are static and the motion of the camera is dominant.

5 Conclusion

We proposed a method of 3D structure reconstruction and blending using a single-camera video stream. Our approach is based on a simplification of camera parameters and the use of projective geometry without camera calibration.

The proposed method can be applied to many practical applications. For examples, the method can be used as a core module for reconstruction systems of

Fig. 10. Three sample images from the tissue box video frames(upper) and the blended video frames (lower)

architecture buildings, real-world environment modelers from videos, measurement applications, camera pose control systems, and other applications. The method is particularly useful to augmented reality applications to insert virtual 3D objects to a real video stream.

Future work still remains. It has been not an easy problem to detect occlusion and fill the holes on the reconstructed surfaces. The high order surface equations should be approximated to substitute appropriate surface patches. Noisy points prohibit accurate estimation of structure geometry and we need to develop a more reliable method which is robust to outliers.

Acknowledgement. This work was supported by the Ministry of Commerce, Industry and Energy (MOCIE) through the Incheon IT Promotion Agency (IIT).

References

1. Cornelis, K., Pollefeys, M., Vergauwen, M., Gool, L.V.: Augmented reality using uncalibrated video sequences. In: Proceedings 2nd European workshop on 3D structure from multiple images of large-scale environments - SMILE. Volume 2018., Springer Verlag (2000) 144–160
2. Hartley, R., A.Zisserman: Multiple View Geometry in Computer Vision, 2nd ed. Cambridge University Press (2003)
3. Chang, N.L., Zakhor, A.: View generation for three-dimensional scenes from video sequences. IEEE Trans. Image Processing **6(4)** (1997) 584–598
4. Azuma, R.T.: A survey of augmented reality. Presence: Teleoperators and Virtual Environments **6** (1997) 355–385
5. Kato, H., Poupyrev, M.B.I., Imamoto, K., Tachibana, K.: Virtual object manipulation on a table-top ar environment. In: proceedings of the International Symposium on Augmented Reality (ISAR 2000), Munich, Germany. (2000) 111–119

6. Kahl, F., Heyden, A.: Euclidean reconstruction and auto-calibration from continuous motion. In: Proc. 8th International Conference on Computer Vision. (2001) 572–577
7. Heyden, A., Huynh, D.: Auto-calibration via the absolute quadric and scene constraints. In: Proc. 16th International Conference on Pattern Recognition. (2002) 631–634
8. Zhang, Y., Xiao, J., Shah, M.: Region completion in a single image. In: EuroGraphics, Grenoble, France. (2004)
9. Rehg, M., Kang, S.B., Cham, T.J.: Video editing using figure tracking and image-based rendering. In: International Conference on Image Processing. (2000) 17–20
10. Fournier, A.: Illumination problems in computer augmented reality. Journee Analyse/Synthèse d'Images (JASI) (1994) 1–21
11. Aguiar, P.M.Q., Moura, J.M.F.: Maximum likelihood estimation of the template of a rigid moving object. In: EMMCVPR. (2001) 34–49
12. Huang, T., Netravali, A.: Motion and structure from feature correspondences: A review. In: Proceedings of IEEE. Volume 82(2). (1994) 252–268
13. Armstrong, M., Zisserman, A., Beardsley, P.: Euclidean reconstruction from uncalibrated images. In: Proc. 5th British Machine Vision Conference. (1994) 509–518
14. Hartley, R., Hayman, E., de Agapito, L., Reid, I.: Camera calibration and the search for infinity. In: Proc. 7th International Conference on Computer Vision. (1999) 510–517
15. Pollefeys, M., Gool, L.: Stratified self-calibration with the modulus constraint. IEEE Transactions on Pattern Analysis and Machine Intelligence **21(8)** (1999) 707–724

Realtime Control for Motion Creation of 3D Avatars

Dong Hoon Kim, Mee Young Sung, Jong-Seung Park, Kyungkoo Jun,
and Sang-Rak Lee

Department of Computer Science & Engineering, University of Incheon,
177 Dowhadong, Namgu, 402-749 Incheon, South Korea
{dinoman, mysung, jong, kjun, srlee}@incheon.ac.kr

Abstract. In this paper, we are proposing a new mechanism for controlling 3D (three dimensional) avatars to create user-designed peculiar motions of avatars in real-time using general interfaces, such as a mouse, a keyboard, or a joystick. The main idea is based on the new way of interactive control that is the combined usage of keyboard and mouse simultaneously. In order to generate natural human motions of avatars, we adopted the center line concept of art drawing and some influencing physics algorithms which developed intensively in the field of biped humanoid robot research. We demonstrate that user-designed motions of avatar can be created in real-time using proposed interaction method with keyboard and mouse. Also, we show that a rich set of peculiar behaviors can be generated from a ready-made motion with motion capture data or created and stored in our system. Note that the generated peculiar motions can be more natural if we appropriately apply our center line concept and physics algorithms.

Keywords: Human motion creation, 3D avatars, Real-time interactive control, Interface.

1 Introduction

As the virtual life closer resembles the real life, we tend to spend more time on the networked virtual world we call the Internet. In consequence, the desire to express ourselves using virtual avatars increases and development in this area is inevitable. In addition, the popularity of 3D (three dimensional) computer games with human characters has demonstrated that the real-time control of avatars is an important objective.

Real-time control of 3D avatars is important in the context of computer games and virtual environments. Two difficulties arise in animating and controlling avatars: designing a rich set of behaviors for the avatar, and giving the user control over those behaviors. Designing a set of behaviors for an avatar is difficult primarily due to real-time constraints. Providing the user with an intuitive interface to control the avatar's motion is difficult because the character's motion is highly dimensional and most of the available input devices are not.

Motions of avatars created by 3D authoring tools or motion capture devices allow only for playing the motions as they designed, and do not allow to be controlled in the middle of motions. We study the real-time motion controls of 3D avatars to overcome this limitation. Like human bodies, an avatar can be made of the articulations of bones. Therefore, an avatar can move its body as human beings by controlling its articulations of bones.

We can model the structure of bones of an avatar and calculate the corresponding matrix values by modeling the hierarchy of articulations of human body. Diverse kinematics algorithms (such as forward kinematics and inverse kinematics) can be used to calculate the position of bones at given degrees of articulations. On the other hand, many of the ongoing studies on biped humanoid robots have been interested in the pattern generation and the walking control with the precise knowledge of robot dynamics including mass, center of gravity, and inertia of each link to prepare walking patterns. This research adopts the ZMP based approach [1], [2].

Recently, the methodologies for representing human being in 3D have developed a lot along with the popularity of computer games such as FPS (First Person Shooter) games. Many of the applications envisioned for avatars have involved interpersonal communication. As a result, much of the research has focused on the subtle aspects of the avatar's appearance and motion that are essential for communication: facial expressions, speech, eye gaze direction, and emotional expression. Also, many techniques concerning the motion capture and physics engines have been introduced for creating more natural human body movement. Because our focus is on applications in which whole body actions are required and subtle communication is not, we need to create an environment that allows the characters to move freely, and where the users can define the motions of these characters. Therefore, we are proposing an interactive control method for allowing users to create user-designed motion of 3D avatars, along with some appropriate interaction methods and interfaces. We will use common interfaces such as keyboards and joysticks to interact with an avatar. Eventually, we will study the development of a more comfortable control interface for interacting with an avatar.

The purpose of this study is to develop a system for creating natural human motions of avatars in allowing users to control the motion of 3D avatars in real-time using simple interactions. In this paper, we show that a rich set of peculiar behaviors can be created from extended real-time avatar control using a variety of input combinations from the keyboard and mouse. A unique aspect of our approach is that the original motion data and the interactively created motion data can be blended in real-time with respect to the physics algorithms concerning the human body movements.

The related work presented in the next section describes some of the animation techniques that have influenced our work. In the third section, some existing control systems are examined. Our ideas about human avatar control are then described in section four. These ideas lead to the new interactive control for peculiar motion editing described in section five, concluding our work.

2 Related Works

The behaviors required for animating virtual humans range from very subtle motions such as a slight smile to highly dynamic motions such as diving or running. Our focus is on applications in which whole body actions are required. Thus, we review only the research related to whole body human motion. Animated human figures have been driven by key framed motion techniques, rule-based systems [3], control systems, dynamics [4], and of course, motion capture data. Motion capture data is the most common technique in commercial systems because many of the subtle details of human motion are naturally present in the data rather than having to be introduced via domain knowledge. Most research on handling motion capture data has focused on techniques for modifying and varying existing motions [5]. This need may be partially obviated by the growing availability of significant quantities of data.

However, adaptation techniques will still be required for interactive applications in which the required motions cannot be precisely or completely predicted in advance. A number of researchers have shared our goal of creating new motions for a controllable avatar from a set of examples. For simple behaviors like reaching and pointing the current set of motions may be adequate. This section presents some existing concepts already developed in the area of computer animation and influenced a lot our work: they are Kinematics, ZMP, and Skin Mesh.

2.1 Forward and Inverse Kinematics

Kinematics is the study of motion without regard to the forces that cause those motions. Forward kinematics is a method for finding the end-effector given the joint positions and angles. Inverse kinematics is a method for finding the original joint positions and angles of the robot arm given a goal position. Advantage of forward kinematics comes from its easiness for implementation. However, it is difficult to calculate the desired position of end-effector if it involves many joints. On the contrary, inverse kinematics is advantageous in the cases of many joints, because the calculation starts from the end-effector. The disadvantage of inverse kinematics is that the solution is often non-deterministic, even infinitive or not existing. For example, as shown in Fig.1 we could obtain three different solutions and it is difficult to select an appropriate solution [6]. However, this problem can be resolved by restricting the degrees of joint rotations, as human joints cannot rotate 360 degrees. Note also that applying the Jacobian matrix is helpful to reduce the amount of calculations of inverse kinematics.

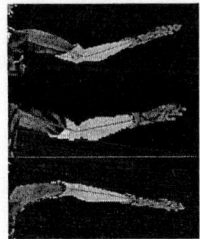

The elbow joint is rotated to the direction of X-axis

The elbow joint is rotated to the direction of Z-axis

The elbow joint is rotated to the direction of Y-axis

Fig. 1. Three different solutions of joint movements calculated using inverse kinematics

Kinematic control, either forward or inverse, has proven to be a powerful technique for the interactive positioning and the animation of complex articulated figures [7]. Until now, cooperation of both techniques has been widely studied in motion design.

2.2 ZMP

Extensive research has been done on the control of biped humanoid robots. Among these, the most influencing method is the ZMP proposed by Miomir Vukobratovich. The ZMP is the point on the ground where the tipping moment acting on the biped, due to gravity and inertia forces, equals zero. The tipping moment being defined as the term of the moment that is tangential to the supporting surface. ZMP is not a perfectly exact expression because the normal term of the moment generated by the inertia forces acting on the biped is not necessarily zero. If we bear in mind, however, that ZMP abridges the exact expression "zero tipping moment point," then the term becomes perfectly acceptable. ZMP corresponds to the point of balance in a support polygon. For example, if a robot stands on one foot, the support polygon corresponds exactly to the shape of robot's foot. ZMP is the dynamically changing center of gravity. The basis of robot walking is to control robot's movement while keeping ZMP is inside the support polygon.

2.3 Skin Mesh

Skinning is a popular method for doing deformations of characters and objects in many 3D games. Skinning is the process of binding a skeleton hierarchy to a single mesh object. This is done by assigning one or more influencing joints (ie: bones) to each vertex of the mesh, each with an associated weighting value. The weight value defines how much a specific bone influences the vertex in the deformation process. Skeletons in a 3D character animation have a direct correlation to a human skeleton: they consist of articulated joints and bones, and they can be used as a controlling mechanism to deform attached mesh data via "skinning". Skinning deformation is the process of deforming the mesh as the skeleton is animated or moved. As the skeleton of bones is moved or animated, a matrix association with the vertices of the mesh causes them to deform in a weighted manner.

The following formulas allows for calculating the world coordinate of a vertex that is influenced by two bones.

$$Vw = Vm \times M_1 \times w + Vm \times M_2 \times (1-w)$$

Vw = coordinate of a vetex in world coordinate

Vm = coordinate of a vertex in local coordinate

Mi = transform matrix of ith bones

w = weight (the sum of weghts is less than 1)

3 Control Interfaces

The objective of this study is to develop a system for creating natural human motions of avatars in allowing users to control the motion of 3D avatars in real-time using simple interactions. We would like to present some existing control systems relevant to our study and some general control interfaces in this section.

Control interfaces for user interactions are usually developed for unique uses in their own systems. Some control systems for interaction for games and Scientific Fiction simulation games are interesting to examine: they are the control system of a mechanic action game Virtual-On, that of Mech Warrior, and the controller of home-use walking robot Nuvo.

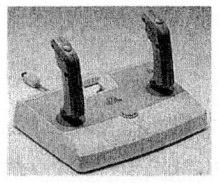

(a) Controller of Virtual-On   (b) Mech Warrior   (c) Nuvo

Fig. 2. Existing control systems relevant to our study

- Virtual-On

Sega developed CYBER TROOPERS: VIRTUAL-ON which is an action shooting game and is high-speed mobile battles in virtual 3-D world with gigantic robots (Virtuaroids). Its direct operations, its high quality and the stylish VR design are combined to give it a high reputation. Sega also developed a double stick controller for Virtual-On. This model allows users to command diverse operations using its 2 sticks rotating 8 directions and 4 buttons. This controller is a simple and intuitive interface with various operations. However, it does not provide the capability for detailed control of movement and equipping the interfacing device (controller) can be expensive.

- Mech Warrior

This is a robot simulation game developed by Microsoft which uses almost all keys of a keyboard to control mechanical robots. Every key is mapped to a specific action, such as key "c" which corresponds to the action "sit down" or "stand up". The user interface of this system provides a variety of operations without any extra expense for equipping it. However, it is difficult to memorize the functions of all keys described in the manual of Mech Warrior.

- Nuvo

Creating a humanoid robot has been a recurring dream for mankind for quite some time and humanoid technologies are rapidly developing now. Robots are generally controlled remotely from PCs. Recently robots which can be controlled from PDAs and cellular phones. Nuvo developed by TOKYO – ZMP Inc., which stands 39cm tall and weighs 2.5kg, can stand up, walk, dance and perform other movements, responding to voice commands or signals from a remote control. The robot can also be operated remotely from a cellular phone. With this function, users can check their homes while they are out – viewing images captured by the robot's built-in camera on their cell phones. Nuvo's core technology was developed by ZMP (refer to Section 2.2).

4 Some Ideas About Human Avatar Control

Providing the user with an intuitive interface to control the avatar's motion is difficult because the character's motion is highly dimensional and most of the available input devices are not. The nature of human motions is characterized by intentional movements of body parts and the tendency for balancing the whole body. In this section, we would like to examine the nature of human motions in order to define how to control avatar's body for creating natural human motions.

4.1 Control Structure

Among the movements of the human body, the movement of the arms, the legs, the head, the rotation of the torso, and walking are the most important. If we could control these parts of a 3D avatar freely, then the avatar would be able to move freely in a virtual space. But how can the body parts of an avatar be controlled in this fashion? That's the question.

The arms and the legs each use 2 joints excluding the movements of the wrists and ankles. Thus, there are 4 pivots in the movements of arms and legs, and there is a limitation in the rotation angle around each pivot. In the control scheme of marionette dolls, the movement of the fingertips and the tiptoes can create the motion of a marionette without any consideration about the pivots of arms and legs. If we control just the fingertips and the tiptoes, we have 4 positions for control. These 4 positions are moving in 3D coordinates and are limited by the length of the arms and the legs, and the limited angles of the related joints.

The torso rotation is fixed by the vertebra. The vertebra consists of the cervical vertebra (7 units), the thoracic vertebra (12 units), and the lumber vertebra (5 units). The cervical vertebra influences the movement of the neck. The thoracic vertebra influences the bending and straightening of the chest and the back. The lumber vertebra influences the movement of the rotation of the whole torso. As far as we are concerned, we need not consider the cervical vertebra because it is related to the movement of the head. Thus, we have 2 pivots related to the movement of the torso.

Walking is influenced by the stride and pace, and the angle of the land surface. Users need not control the influence of the land surface's angle as this can be resolved by some interpolation methods proposed in several other studies. Therefore, the only parameters we must consider for the users control are the stride and the pace of walking.

Consequently, we should consider the movements of head and shoulders. We exclude the control of the shoulders, because their rotation angle is quite small and their movements can be calculated from the movements of other related parts – such as the arms. Also, we must consider the diversity of walking patterns. This can be resolved by using the motion capture technique. However, motion capturing is not in the scope of this study and we do not discuss the walking patterns in this paper.

4.2 Balancing Structure

As we examined the control aspect in the previous section, let's turn to the balancing aspect. If the movement of human body is not balanced, motions are not natural.

Natural human motions can be obtained if human motions are balanced. The balanced state of human body is the state where the body weight is distributed equally. If a human body is inclined to one side, the hand or the foot stretches to the opposite side to balance its weight. If a human stands on one foot, the body weight is balanced as a top spins. In this case, the body status can be compared to an inverted triangle. If a human stands on two feet, the status can be compared to that of a rectangle.

It is certain that human motion looks more natural if the human body is distributed equally on the left part and the right part of the center line in the body polygon. Fig. 3 illustrates some examples of center lines which pass through the center of the body polygon (a triangle or a rectangle) of human motion [8]. The balancing mechanism of any human body follows the principles of mechanical movements of rigid objects [9].

Fig. 3. Center lines in human body movement

The weights of human body segments have been calculated through many studies and experiments [8]. Table 1 summarizes the mean weight of each body segment relative to the weight of whole body.

Table 1. Ratio of the weight of each Segment to the weight of whole body

Head and Trunk	Upper arm	Forearm and hand	Thigh	Calves and foot
55.9%	5.80% (2.90% each)	4.60% (2.30% each)	21.5% (0.72% each)	12.2% (6.1% each)

The center of gravity in the human body, denoted by M can be calculated using the following equation, where each Wi denotes the ratio of the weight of each segment to the weight of the whole body and each of xi, yi, and zi denotes the coordinates of its position on the x-axis, y-axis, and z-axis respectively:

$$M(x, y, z) = \frac{W_1(x_1, y_1, z_1) + W_2(x_2, y_2, z_2) + \cdots + W_9(x_9, y_9, z_9)}{W_1 + W_2 + \cdots + W_9}$$

If there are some supporting points on the ground surface, we can draw a geometrical figure (a triangle, a rectangle, or a polyhedron) by connecting the supporting points on the ground surface and extending the supporting polygon until the top of the head. We can estimate that the avatar is balanced if its center of gravity exists with in the geometrical figure.

5 Suggestion of a New Interactive Control

The Avatar of our system is actively in pursuit of mimicking human motions as similarly as possible; therefore our avatar's bones and joints should resemble that of human. The relationship between the representation of the avatar's bones and the kinematics are discussed in this section.

5.1 Skeleton Hierarchy and Kinematics

As shown in Fig. 4, A good skeleton building technique is to place the pelvis at the root, make the abdomen (corresponds to the pelvis) and thighs children of the pelvis, then make the torso a child of the abdomen, then make the biceps and neck children of the torso, and so on.

When adding bones, you are defining the hierarchy (called a skeleton), indicating which connections should be kinematics chains, and specifying the local space of each bone. Before adding a bone, you first select its parent (if no bone is selected, the new bone is added at the root). The skeleton can be adjusted later by using drag drop in the Project Workspace tree. A parent bone passes its translation, rotation, and scale on to its children.

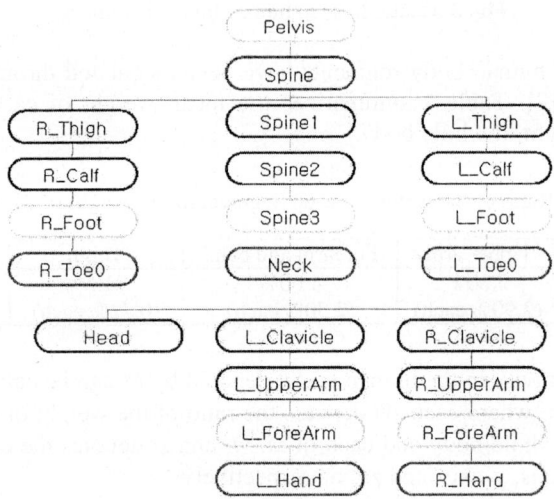

Fig. 4. Skeleton hierarchy of human body

For inverse kinematics, add nulls at the root of the hierarchy for use with hand and feet constraints. The nulls can have a hierarchy of their own to ease in moving them together. For example, you can have a null that is the parent of all nulls, one that is the parent of the lower body nulls, the left leg nulls, etc. Reordering the bones in the Project Workspace tree with drag and drop can easily modify the skeleton. Rearranging the skeleton also changes the inverse kinematics.

The orientation of a bone defines its local frame of reference. Along the length of the bone defines the local Z-axis; the roll handle is the bone's local Y-axis, and the local X-axis is perpendicular to both the bone and the roll handle. This is the coordinate system that scale, rotate, and translate uses when animating. Two models that are to share actions require the bones to have the same names and same basic hierarchical relationship. In addition, the bones and the roll handles should be placed into the model in the same way. If the roll handle points to the back on one model, then it should point the same way on the other model. However, if one character is modeled with its arms out and another with its arms down, then the actions can still be shared.

Kinematics, either forward or inverse, can be applied to calculate the position of bones given the joint positions and angles in this skeleton hierarchy. Now, we should decide which kinematics will be used to create motions. In the case of walking motion, as the foot is an end-effector, the inverse kinematics is desirable for calculating the joints from the foot to the pelvis. If forward kinematics is used, it could be complicated to create movement sequentially from the pelvis to the foot, and the foot may position below or above the earth surface. Therefore, time-wasting adjustment of foot positions may occur. However, if we calculate the positions of the upper arm or the fore arm according to the rotation of the pelvis or the shoulder, then forward kinematics is more advantageous than inverse kinematics. The selection of the more efficient kinematics control depends on the situation and it requires the appropriate and well-timed decision. In summary, it is recommended that inverse kinematics be used for calculating joint positions in the upward direction of the pelvis of the skeleton hierarchy from the moving joint, while the forward kinematics is useful for calculating joint positions in the downward direction to the joint from the pelvis [10].

5.2 Control Interface

Nowadays, the user interfaces are wide-ranging from keyboards, mouse, and joysticks, to human iris, human eye movements, human brain waves, etc. However, we would like to focus on only the very common general interfacing devices, such as keyboards, mouse, joysticks, etc. We adopt the keyboard and mouse as the user interface for commanding our 3D avatar into action. The combined usage of keyboard and mouse can provide a rich set of control commands. However, it is also necessary for user to provide an easy way of simultaneous usage of keys and mouse.

In addition, human body acts and reacts in order to put his or her center of gravity at the position where the body can balance itself [11]. The position corresponds to the ZMP; Zero Moment Position. Therefore, we can consider a 3D avatar as a sort of rigid body with mass which always tries to balance itself with respect to gravity [10]. Supposing a 3D avatar is a rigid body, we propose two control mechanisms: there is one method using only the keyboard, and another method using both the keyboard and mouse.

- Method 1: Using keyboard only (like marionette)

This control method originates from the way of controlling marionette dolls. Each of 5 direction keys corresponds to the left hand, the right hand, the left leg, the right leg, and the head, respectively. The left-shift key gives effect to lower the string, and the release of left-shift key gives effect to lift up the string upward. Each of W, A, S, D keys gives effect to move to the 4 directions: left, right, up, down. Once, one of the W, A, S, D keys is activated, the string movement is deactivated. Table 1 illustrates the key allocations and the operations of combined usage of keys. Those keys in the table 1 can be used in multiple and simultaneously. This control method is intuitive and advantageous because avatar motions can be created using simple key controls and multiple parts of avatar body can be manipulated at the same time. However, very subtle delicate motions may not be controlled with this marionette method.

Table 2. Key allocation table for method 1: Using keyboard only (like marionette)

	Num 1	Num 3	Num 4	Num 6
None	Raise the left foot	Raise the right foot	Raise the left hand	Raise the right hand
+ Left-Shift	Put down the left foot	Put down the right foot	Put down the left hand	Put down the right hand

	Num 1	Num 3	Num 4	Num 6	Num 5
W	Put up the left foot	Put up the right foot	Put up left hand	Put up the right foot	Put up the head
S	Put down the left foot	Put down the right foot	Put down the left hand	Put down the right foot	Put down the left foot
A	Put left the left foot	Put left the right foot	Put left the left hand	Put left the right hand	Put left the head
D	Put right the left foot	Put right the right foot	Put right the left hand	Put right the right hand	Put right the head

- Method 2: Using keyboard and mouse simultaneously

The Second method needs both of keyboard and mouse. Main control is performed by the mouse and the keyboard is used in assistance. Mouse resembles the joysticks is a device which has 2 sticks and 1~6 buttons. The reason why we choose mouse as interface is that the speed of movement is more controllable than joysticks. Mouse takes charge of the rotations of screens, the rotation of characters, and the rotations of joints. The Microsoft mouse has 2 buttons and a wheel and it is sufficient to be used in our second control method. This control method is advantageous as it allows user to control the speed of movement with mouse. However, it still remains the problem of making natural movements because it still uses the 2-dimentional control for movement of 3D avatars. Fig.5 illustrates some examples of new motions created by using method 2.

Table 3. Key allocation table for method 2: Using keyboard and mouse

	Mouse left button	Mouse right button	A	S	Z	X
+ Mouse	Camera translation	Character rotation	Left hand translation	Right hand translation	Left foot translation	Right foot translation

D	G	R	F
Walking to the left	Walking to the right	Walking Forward	Walking Backward

Fig. 5. Examples of new motion creation: kicking and saluting

6 Conclusion

For allowing users to express freely their intention and emotion through an avatar in diverse immersive virtual environments, we proposed a new interaction mechanism for controlling 3D avatars.

Many current studies on the motion creation are biased to the retreating of motion capture data for generating more natural human motions. Working on motion capture data should confront the limitation of the diversity of motions, because we could not capture all kind of human motions with the limited equipments and manpower. In order to overcome this limitation, we developed a prototype system that allows users to create new motions not existing before, using a general and intuitive control mechanism. Our prototype system corresponds to an interactive real-time editor of 3D avatar's motion and it demonstrates an extensible real-time motion creation of 3D avatars. Some experiments using our system lead us to conclude that our method can provide the capability of repeatedly creating some new human actions by editing concurrently the playing animation. The playing animation can be a ready-made motion generated from motion captures databases or created and stored in our system.

Our study will contribute a method of creating diverse services using avatars, which can act like human beings without any limitation of motion. Some simulation tools for motion of human bodies can also be developed based on our study. Some new genres of games can be explored from our study. The results of our study can be integrated into any existing 3D avatar services such as online games and avatar chatting for expressing their action and emotion freely. Existing game engines or rendering engines can include the result of our study for allowing their avatars to move as users interactions controls.

Note that the generated peculiar motions can be more natural if we appropriately apply the center line concept and physics algorithms. In the future, we will investigate the optimized algorithms for applying the center line concept physics algorithms for making generated motions more natural.

Acknowledgement. This work was supported by the Ministry of Commerce, Industry and Energy (MOCIE) through the Incheon IT Promotion Agency (IIT) and the Multimedia Research Center (MRC) at the University of Incheon.

References

[1] Hirai, K., Hirose, M., Haikawa, Y., Takenaka, T.: The development of honda humanoid robot. In Proc. IEEE Int'l Conf. on Robotics and Automation (ICRA'98), pages 1321--1326, May 1998
[2] Sardain P., Dessonnet, G.: Forces Actinf on a Biped Robot. Center of Pressure-Zero Moment Point. IEEE TRANSACTIONS ON SYSTEMS, MAN, AND CYBERNETICS—PART A: SYSTEMS AND HUMANS, VOL. 34, NO. 5, SEPTEMBER 2004
[3] Bruderlin, A., Calvert, T. W.: Goal-directed, dynamic animation of human walking. In Computer Graphics (Proceedings of SIGGRAPH 89), vol. 23, 233–242
[4] Hodgins, J. K., Wooten, W. L., Brogan, D. C., and O'Brien, J. F.: Animating human athletics. In Proceedings of SIGGRAPH 95, 71–78
[5] Gleighcher, M.: Comparing constraint-based motion editing methods. Graphical Models 63, 2, 107–123, 2001
[6] Spong, M.W., Vidyasagar, M.: Robot Dynamics and Control. John Wiley & Sons, page 74~149, 1989
[7] Boulic, R., Thalmann, D.: Combined direct and inverse kinematics control for articulated figures motion editing. Computer Graphics Forum, 11(4):189-202, 1992
[8] Chung, H. K., Bae, S. S.: Study of the Center of Gravity in the Human Body and each Segment. Korean Soci. Of Phys. Ther., Vol. 5, No. 1, June, 1993
[9] Silva, F.M., Machado, J.A.T.: Kinematic Aspects of Robotic Biped Locomotion Systems. Proc. IEEE Int. Conf. on Intelligent Robots and Systems, IROS' 97, Vol.1, pages 266-271, 8-13 1997
[10] Animation Foundation http://www.animfound.com/
[11] Boulic, R., Mas, R., Thalmann, D.: A robust approach for the center of mass postion control with inverse kinetics. Journal of Computers and Graphics, 20(5), 1996

Environment Matting of Transparent Objects Based on Frequency-Domain Analysis

I-Cheng Chang[1], Tian-Lin Yang[2], and Chung-Ling Huang[2]

[1] Department of Computer Science and Information Engineering,
National Dong Hwa University, Hualein, Taiwan
`icchang@mail.ndhu.edu.tw`
[2] Department of Electrical Engineering, National Ting Hua University, Hsin Chu, Taiwan

Abstract. The paper proposed a new environment matting algorithm to model the appearance of transparent object under different background. We used the frequency response to compute the relationship between the area of foreground object and background image. Moreover, the Kaczmarz method was applied to obtain more accurate weight matrices. In the experiments, we demonstrated that the algorithm can effectively improve the quality of compositing picture and has higher PSNR than the previous method. Besides, we also showed that the proposed algorithm can maintain the quality even the high threshold is set to reduce the computation time.

1 Introduction

Digital compositing is a quite important and practical topic in the field of computer graphics and image processing. Many relevant researches focus on how to come up with a good method to make people be unable to differentiate the real and composite images. According to the kind of the materials and the lighting reflective characteristics, foreground objects can be classified into two major categories: opaque and transparent. It needs quite different approaches to model the two kinds of objects. The modeling of opaque objects usually adopt the method of BRDF(Bidirectional Reflectance Distribution Function) or IBR(Imag-based Rendering). In the paper, we are dealing with the compositing of transparent object. Two kinds of approaches are proposed in the previous researches, one is based on spatial-domain analysis and the other frequency-domain analysis. The main difference between them is the design of the lighting pattern. Spatial-domain analysis examines the variation of the lighting pattern in the spatial domain. However, frequency-domain analysis inspects the variations of the lighting pattern in both the spatial and the frequency domain. When we acquire the images, some unexpected noises may be introduced, for example, environmental light, light of the monitor, etc. The noises will influence the accuracy while we analyze the object model. The design of frequency-domain analysis is to allocate different frequency information related to different position of the light source plane, so one can separate noises from the original image series. Therefore, the compositing image can get more accurate result.

Zongker *et al.* [1] used coarse-to-fine images as backdrops to be displayed in CRT screen. The object is placed in front of the CRT screen, and camera records the change in different backdrops. They optimized the positions of light source in the background corresponding to each pixel of the imaging plane of camera. If several light sources of the background contribute to one pixel, this algorithm can only find out the largest light source position among them. In [2] [3], the authors use stripes of one-dimensional Gaussian as the sweep line. The camera captures the variation of the color when the stripes shift at a regular step. Finally, they use Levenburg-Marquardt optimization procedure to find out the matting model in the form of 2D Gaussian.

Wexler et al.[4] proposed an algorithm that does not need to know the content of backdrops in advance. They move the object in front of a fixed background picture, and use geometric registration to find out the characteristics of light refraction and the relative position between the object and the background. Peers and Dutre[5] adoptd the wavelet patterns as the backdrop. When the backdrop changes in the acquisition process, the algorithm computes the contribution of the wavelet pattern corresponding to each level.

Zhu and Yang[6] first adopted the frequency response as the basis to get the matting model. They use the row-based and column-based stripe patterns, where each stripe corresponds to different frequency. Then DFT is used to analyze the contributions of different frequency. The matting model of the object is computed from the contribution of row-based area and column-based area.

We proposed a new algorithm which extends the method of frequency-domain analysis described in [6]. The proposed algorithm uses simultaneous equations that represent the distribution of the light source to derive more correct model of the object. The experiments demonstrated that our method can improve the quality of the compositing image and has higher PSNR than Zhu's method. Besides, we compute the transformation matrix between the world and camera coordinates in advance. Therefore, one can obtain the new background of the compositing image by the transformation matrix, and need not recapture the background of the new image.

The paper is organized as follows. In section 2, we describe the proposed environment matting equation. Section 3 describes how to extract the foreground object area. In section4, we explain the generation of background patterns. Section 5 describes the computation of weight matrices is stated in section 5. The experimental results are demonstrated in Section 6.

2 Environment Matting Equation

In the traditional matting equation[9], the compositing image C can be described as the compound of a foreground image F and a background image B with alpha channel α,

$$C = \alpha F + (1-\alpha)B. \tag{1}$$

The alpha channel plays a dual role: it is simultaneously used to represent both the coverage of a pixel by a foreground element, and the opacity of this foreground element. In generally image compositing, the foreground element can be thought of as a synthesis of two different components: the emissive component come from foreground element itself and the reflection or refraction come from light sources of the environment.

We propose a new structure to describe how light in an environment is reflected and refracted by a foreground element. The definition of new environment matting equation as follows:

$$C = \alpha F + (1-\alpha)R\hat{B}_g + \alpha\Phi. \tag{2}$$

where C represents the result of recorded image in the imaging plane, F represents emissive component come from foreground element itself, and α represents background whether is covered by foreground element or not. If $\alpha = 0$, then the corresponding pixel belongs to the background. On the contrary, if $\alpha = 1$, then it means that the pixel belongs to the foreground. B_g represents the background image of $n \times m$ pixels in world coordinate and $\hat{B}_g$ represents the image of $n' \times m'$ pixels in the camera coordinate. R represents the attenuation from the position of the light source to the camera. R_R, R_G, R_B represent the attenuation of RGB channel separately. Φ depicts the contribution of the light which comes from the environment and pass through the foreground element.

The light received by the camera comes from the light sources in the environment. So the total amount Φ_p of light received by point p in the imaging plane can be described as an integral over area of all light from the environment that contributes to point p.

$$\Phi_p = \int W(\lambda)E(\lambda)d\lambda. \tag{3}$$

where λ is the position of light source and $E(\lambda)$ is the distribution of the lighting condition.

We divide background B_g into $S \times T$ pieces of axis-aligned region, and express the average of every axis-aligned region as $B_g(s,t)$. Because Φ is a set of all pixel of foreground element in the imaging plane, Φ can be written as follows:

$$\Phi = \sum_{s=1,t=1}^{s=S,t=T} W(s,t)B_g(s,t). \tag{4}$$

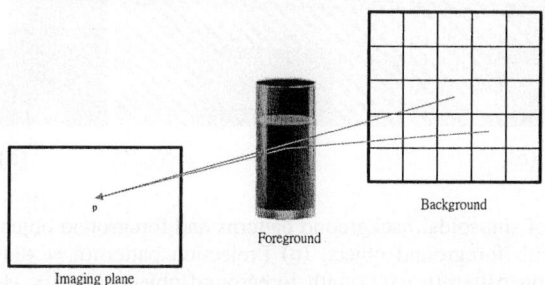

Fig. 1. Description of the environment matting. The light from several different postions may be received by position p in image plane.

where $W(s,t)$ represents the attenuation of axis-aligned region $B_g(s,t)$ from the position of light source to the camera. **Fig.1** describes the relationship between image plane and background.

Thus, our environment matting equation is described as follows:

$$C = \alpha F + (1-\alpha)R\hat{B}_g + \alpha \sum_{s=1,t=1}^{s=S,t=T} W(s,t)B_g(s,t). \tag{5}$$

3 Extraction of Foreground Object Area

While analyzing environment matting, we divide imaging plane into two areas: covered area and uncovered area. We adopt different image synthetic methods in these two areas because the covered area is overlayed with foreground element and the uncovered area contains only the backdrop. We adopt sinusoidal background patterns ([6]) to sample foreground element area. The following equation tells the assignment of pixel value of the projection patterns:

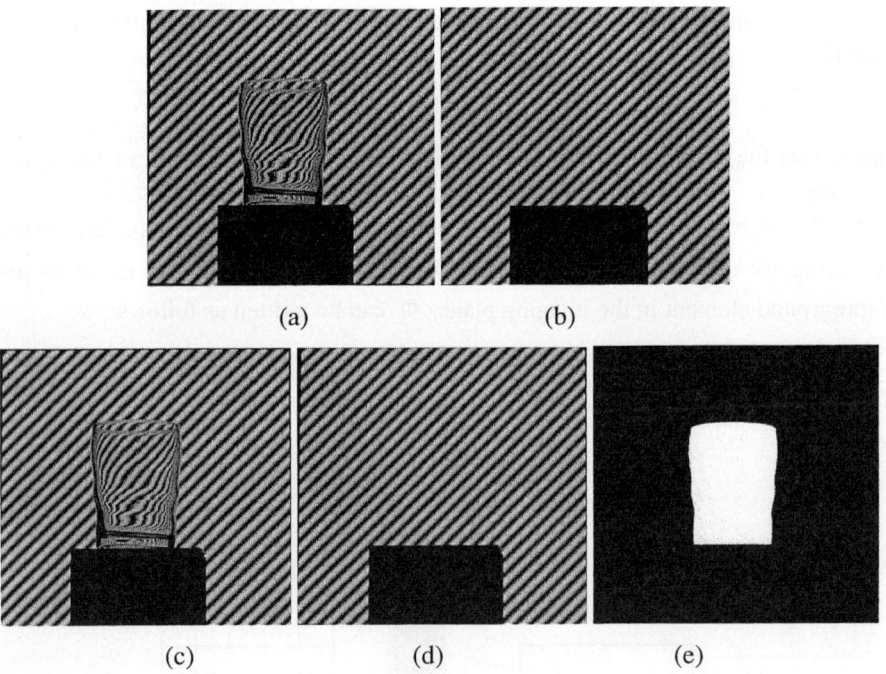

Fig. 2. Projection of sinusoidal background patterns and foreground object area. (a) Projection pattern(n = +1) with foreground object, (b) Projection pattern(n = +1) without foreground object,.(c) Projection pattern(n = -1) with foreground object, (d) n = -1 without foreground object, and (e) foreground object area.

$$C_i(x,y,n) = (1+n\sin(\frac{2\pi(x+y)}{\lambda}+i\frac{\pi}{3}))\times 127. \quad (6)$$

where i=0,1,2 for R,G,B domain and n=-1 or 1. $C_i(x,y,n)$ is the intensity of color channel i at pixel location (x, y). To maximize the per-pixel difference between the two background patterns, we shift the pattern by phase 180° (n=-1 or 1). The user can define the period of the sinusoidal stripes with the parameter λ. Here we set $\lambda = 50$ and capture 4 images of $n = \pm 1$, with and without object. After the image substraction and post processing, we can get the foreground object area. Fig.2 shows the resultsof the process.

4 Generation of the Background Patterns

We adopt the method of column-based and row-based background patterns proposed in [6]. Every column-base and row-base area is assigned a regular frequency, and the pixel values $B(f_c,t)$ of every area of background patterns are stated as follows.

$$B(f_c,t) = \rho(1+\cos(2\pi \cdot f_c \cdot \frac{t}{N})) \quad (7)$$

where f_c is the frequency of this area and N depicts number of sample of cosine function in time domain. Besides, in order to prevent the results of DFT from aliasing phenomenon, N should be selected to satisfy the Nyquist theorem. The range of values of cosine function varies in [-1,1], and we set ρ be equal 127.5 in order to let the range of pixel values be [0,255].

5 Computation of the Weight Matrix

5.1 Initial Value Computation

By the spectrum of Fourier transform of column-based background patterns, one can obtain the attenuation ($W_c(1)$, $W_c(2)$, ... , $W_c(S)$) and ($W_r(1)$, $W_r(2)$, ... , $W_r(T)$) of these light sources which contribute to some position of the imaging plane. Next, we normalize the column-base weights ($W_c(1)$, $W_c(2)$, ..., $W_c(S)$) and row-base weights ($W_r(1)$, $W_r(2)$, ..., $W_r(t)$) respectively. The normalized results are $W_c'(1)$, $W_c'(2)$, ... , $W_c'(S)$ and $W_r'(1)$, $W_r'(2)$, ... , $W_r'(T)$. The contribution weight of every axis-aligned region is computed as follows.

First, we calculate normal weight of every axis-aligned region as,

$$W'(s,t) = W_c'(s)W_r'(t), \quad s = 1, 2, ... , S \quad t = 1, 2, ... , T. \quad (8)$$

After executing the de-normalization process, one can obtain weight of every axis-aligned region.

$$W(s,t) = W'(s,t)\frac{W_c(s)}{W_c'(s)}, \quad s = 1, 2, ... , S \quad t = 1, 2, ... , T. \quad (9)$$

Every position of the imaging plane can obtain a set of weights of all axis-aligned region, and the set of weights is called "weight matrix". If the imaging plane has $n \times m$ positions, the size of the weight matrix is also $n \times m$. Fig. 3 (a) and (b) show the distribution that the contribution weight of each column and row of the background, and (c) shows the contribution weight corresponding to each axis-aligned region.

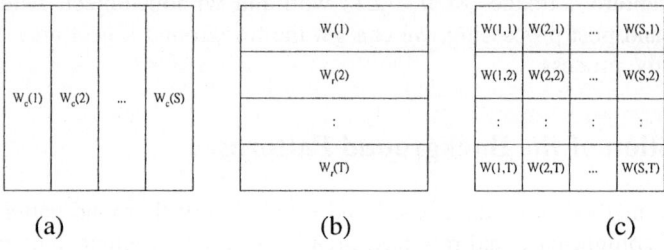

(a) (b) (c)

Fig. 3. (a) The contribution weight of every column position of the background. (b) The contribution weight of each row position of the background (c) The contribution weight of each axis-aligned region of the background.

5.2 Projection Operation

In the section, we will explain how to refine the weight matrix by using the Kaczmarz method([7][8]). Let's start with an algebraic equation:

$$B_{11}W_1 + B_{12}W_2 + B_{13}W_3 + \ldots + B_{1N}W_N = R_1. \qquad (10)$$

where B_{11}, B_{12}, B_{13}, $\cdots$, B_{1N} and R_1 are known values, and W_1, W_2, W_3, $\cdots$, W_N are unknown. After the computation process, the parameters can be described as

$$W_j^{(i)} = W_j^{(i)} + \frac{R_i - Q_i}{\sum_{k=1}^{N} B_{ik}^2} B_{ij} . \qquad (11)$$

We compute the coefficients by using the pixel value $B(f_c, t)$ of column-based and row-based background patterns, and the value R_n represents the value corresponding to the n-th background pattern in the imaging plane. We can describe the relationship as:

$$\sum_{s=1,t=1}^{s=S,t=T} B(s,n)W(s,t) = R_n . \qquad (12)$$

where $B(s,n)$ represents the pixel value $B(f_c, t)$ of column-based and row-based background patterns. Then these equations can be transformed to simultaneous equations as follows.

$$\begin{cases} B(1,1)W(1,1)+B(2,1)W(2,1)+\cdots+B(S,1)W(S,1)+ \\ B(1,1)W(1,2)+B(2,1)W(2,2)+\cdots+B(S,1)W(S,2)+\cdots+ \\ B(1,1)W(1,T)+B(2,1)W(2,T)+\cdots+B(S,1)W(S,T)=R_1 \\ \\ B(1,2)W(1,1)+B(2,2)W(2,1)+\cdots+B(S,2)W(S,1)+ \\ B(1,2)W(1,2)+B(2,2)W(2,2)+\cdots+B(S,2)W(S,1)+\cdots+ \\ B(1,2)W(1,T)+B(2,2)W(2,T)+\cdots+B(S,2)W(S,T)=R_2 \\ \vdots \\ B(1,N)W(1,1)+B(2,N)W(2,1)+\cdots+B(S,N)W(S,1)+ \\ B(1,N)W(1,2)+B(2,N)W(2,2)+\cdots+B(S,N)W(S,2)+\cdots+ \\ B(1,N)W(1,T)+B(2,N)W(2,T)+\cdots+B(S,N)W(S,T)=R_N \end{cases} \quad (13)$$

$$\begin{cases} B(1,1)W(1,1)+B(1,1)W(2,1)+\cdots+B(1,1)W(S,1)+ \\ B(2,1)W(1,2)+B(2,1)W(2,2)+\cdots+B(2,1)W(S,2)+\cdots+ \\ B(T,1)W(1,T)+B(T,1)W(2,T)+\cdots+B(T,1)W(S,T)=R_1 \\ \\ B(1,2)W(1,1)+B(1,2)W(2,1)+\cdots+B(1,2)W(S,1)+ \\ B(2,2)W(1,2)+B(2,2)W(2,2)+\cdots+B(2,2)W(S,1)+\cdots+ \\ B(T,2)W(1,T)+B(T,2)W(2,T)+\cdots+B(T,2)W(S,T)=R_2 \\ \vdots \\ B(1,N)W(1,1)+B(1,N)W(2,1)+\cdots+B(1,N)W(S,1)+ \\ B(2,N)W(1,2)+B(2,N)W(2,2)+\cdots+B(2,N)W(S,2)+\cdots+ \\ B(T,N)W(1,T)+B(T,N)W(2,T)+\cdots+B(T,N)W(S,T)=R_N \end{cases} \quad (14)$$

where $B(1,1), B(1,2), \cdots, B(S,N), \cdots, B(T,N)$ are the sampling result of $B(f_c, t)$, $R_1, R_2, \cdots R_N$ are the pixel values of the different captured frame, $W(1,1), W(1,2), \cdots, W(S,T)$ are the parameters of the weight matrix. We apply iteration processing to (13) and (14) to get the coefficients of weight matrices.

6 Experimental Results

In the section, we will demonstrate two experiments to verify the proposed algorithm. We use Canon EOS D60 as our acquisition device, P4-2.4G CPU together with 1G byte RAM, and windows XP as our operating system. LCD monitor is used to project the background patterns. The digital camera records the variation respond of each backdrop pattern, and it costs about 17 seconds to capture all the images. The size of backdrop pattern is set 960×960 pixels, and the size of axis-aligned region is set 4×4 pixels.

After getting information of all images, we investigate the spectrum of every pixel of the imaging plane and compute the weight matrix. Meanwhile, we set up a threshold to find out the largest magnitude from spectrum of every pixel, and only reserve these magnitudes that larger than threshold. So we only have to calculate the weights of these light source position with larger contribution, and the position of the other light source set as zero. We set 7 kinds of different threshold (max/k, k=2、4、8、16、32、64、128) to analyze and compare their PSNR.

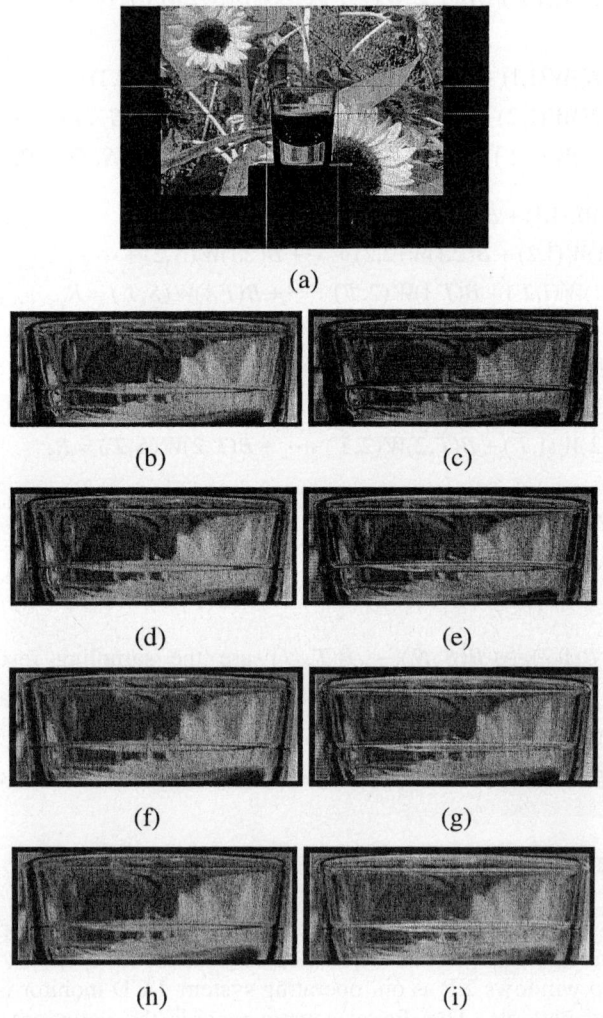

Fig. 4. Sixth background images (a) Real picture with new background and object. (b) (d) (f) (h) are the results by using the proposed method and (c)(e)(g)(i) by using Zhu's method. The thresholds are max/2, max/4, max/8 and max/16, respectively.

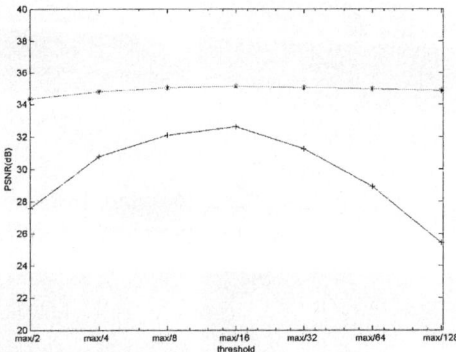

Fig. 5. PSNR Comparison. '*' represents the result of the proposed method, '+' represents the result of Zhu's method.

Firstly, we demonstrate our propose algorithm can improve the quality of the compositing image. We compare the results by using our proposed method and Zhu's method, and compute the corresponding PSNR. Fig.4 (b)(d)(f)(h) show the compositing image by using the proposed algorithm and (c)(e)(g)(i) are the results from the Zhu's method. The visual performance of the proposed algorithm is obviously better than the other.

And we compare the PSNR between the two algorithms. Fig.5 shows the PSNR vs. threshold curves corresponding to the two algorithms. The new algorithm maintains the PSNR at the level between 34 and 35, however, the PSNR corresponding to the previous algorithm is below 32.

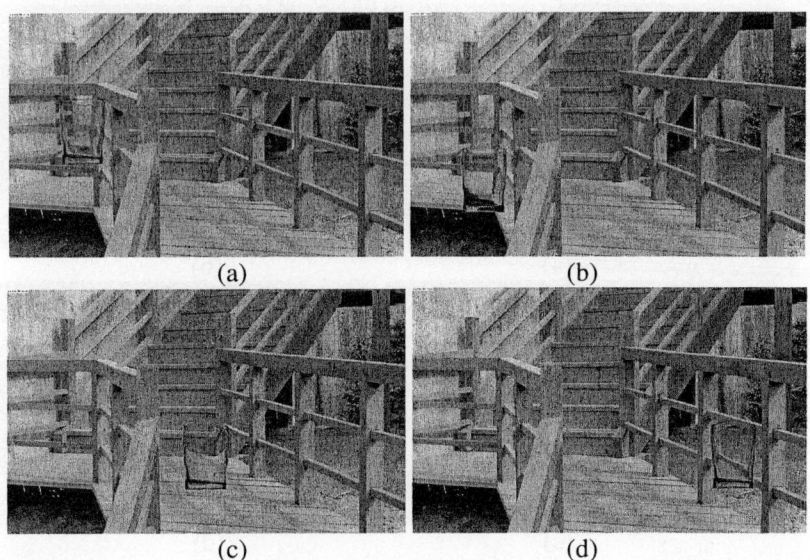

Fig. 6. Motion video images

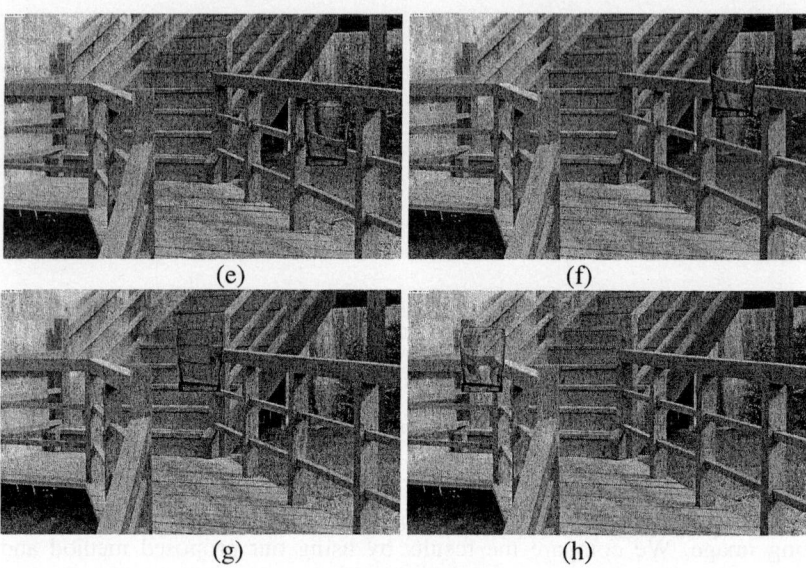

Fig. 6. (*Continued*)

We find that the PNSR is lower when the threshold is high (for example: max/2). The reason is that contribution of the light source is only limited to at most a few positions. However, it would cause noise on FFT analysis if we select the lower threshold (for example: max/128). The noise from LCD screen or the digital camera will influence PSNR if the threshold is set to low value.

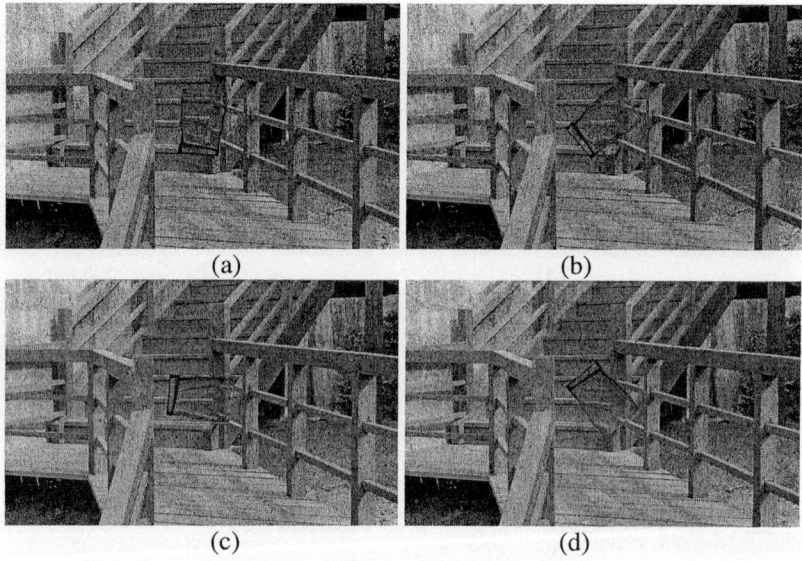

Fig. 7. Rotation video images

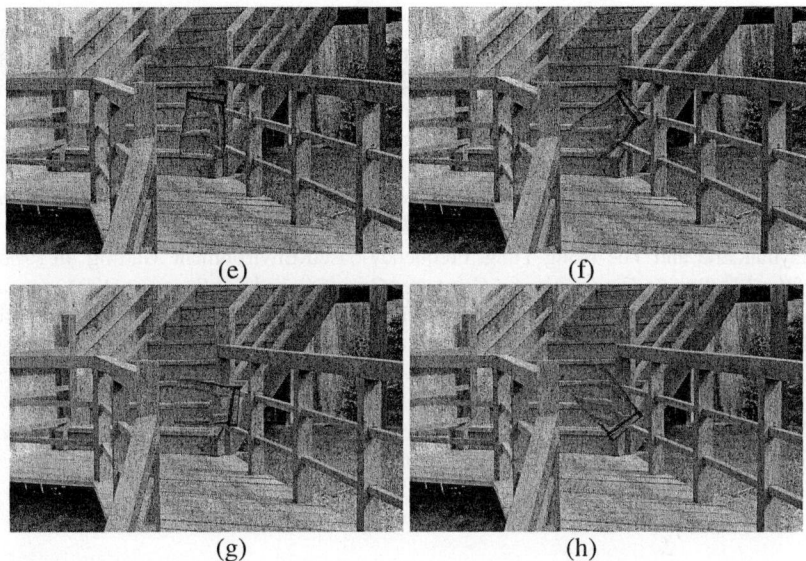

(e) (f)

(g) (h)

Fig. 7. (*Continued*)

Secondly, we simulate two compositing results of the transparent model in video sequence. Fig.6 shows the results of object motion, and Fig.7 is the compositing of object rotation.

7 Conclusion

In the research, we propose a new frequency-domain method to improve the compositing image by refinding the weight matrices. The propose algorithm can generate the result pictures with good quality and has higher PSNR than previous method. Furthermore, we can maintain the quality while setting the high threshold to reduce the computation time. The experiments demonstrate that the compositing result is good even the threshold is set to be max/2. At present, we need to capture the photos of more than 1,000 for single view, so enormous photos are needed if we want to compute a multi-view model. Therefore, one important issue of future work is to how reduce the number of needed images and develop a faster algorithm to let user obtain the model easily.

References

1. Douglas E. Zongker, Dawn M. Werner, Brian Curless, and David H. Salesin. Environment matting and compositing. In *Proceedings of ACM SIGGRAPH 1999*, pages 205–214, 1999.
2. Yung-Yu Chuang, Douglas E. Zongker, Joel Hindorff, Brian Curless, David H. Salesin, and Richard Szeliski. Environment matting extensions: Towards higher accuracy and real-time capture. In *Proceedings of ACM SIGGRAPH 2000*, pages 121–130, July 2000.

3. Wojciech Matusik, Hanspeter Pfister, Remo Ziegler, Addy Ngan, and Leonard McMillan. Acquisition and rendering of transparent and refractive objects. In *Thirteenth Eurographics Workshop on Rendering*, pages 267–277, 2002.
4. Yonatan Wexler, Andrew W. Fitzgibbon, and Andrew Zisserman. Image-based environment matting. In *Proceedings of EuroGraphics Workshop on Rendering 2002*, pages 289–299, June 26–28 2002.
5. Pieter Peers and Philip Dutre. Wavelet environment matting. In *Proceedings of Eurographics workshop on Rendering 2003*, pages 157–166, 2003.
6. Jiayuan Zhu and Yee-Hong Yang. Frequency-based Environment Matting. In *Proceedings of the 12th Pacific Conference on Computer Graphics and Applications*, 2004.
7. Avinash C. Kak and Malcolm Slaney. Principles of Computerized Tomographic Imaging. IEEE Press, New York, 1988.
8. K. Tanabe. Projection method for solving a singular system of linear equation and applications. In *Numerical Mathematics*, volume 17, pages 203-214, 1971.
9. Thomas Porter and Tom Duff. Compositing Digital Images. In *Computer Graphics*, volume 18, number 3, pages 253-259, July 1984.

Adaptation of Quadric Metric Simplification to MPEG-4 Animated Object

Marius Preda, Son Tran, and Françoise Prêteux

ARTEMIS Project Unit, GET-INT, 9 rue Charles Fourier, 91011 Evry, France
{marius.preda, son.tran, françoise.preteux}@int-evry.fr
http://www-artemis.int-evry.fr

Abstract. Our work focuses on the simplification of MPEG-4 avatar models. Similar to other general purposed 3D models, these avatars often claim complex, highly detailed presentation to maintain a convincing level of realism. However, the full complexity of such models is not always required, especially when a client terminal — for the reason of portability and cost reduction — cannot or does not necessarily support high complex presentation. First, we deploy the well-known 3D simplification based on quadric error metric to create a simplified version of the avatar in question, taking into account that the avatar is also a 3D model based on manifold mesh. Within this general scope, we introduce a new weight factor to overcome an uncertainty in choosing target for decimation. Next, exploiting the biomechanical characteristic of avatars — having the underlying skeleton structure — we propose an adaptation of the simplifying technique to avatars. The concept of bones is taken into account as either a boundary constraint or a cost-component for the quadric error. Encouraging results can be obtained with these modified procedures.

1 Introduction

Many applications in 3D computer graphics can benefit from automatic simplification of complex polygonal surface models. That is because applications are often confronted with either very densely over-sampled surfaces or models too complex to maintain a convincing level of realism. However, due to the diverse configuration of client-terminal, the full complexity of such models is not always required, and since the computational cost of using a model is directly related to its complexity, it is useful to have simpler version of complex models. In recent years, the problem of surface simplification, and the more general problem of multiresolution modeling, has received increasing attention. The most relevant algorithms, which target the simplification of triangle-based polygonal models — the most general of representing 3D object — can be broadly categorized into 3 classes [6]. The *Vertex Decimation* algorithm iteratively selects a vertex for removal, removes all adjacent faces, and retriangulates the resulting holes. In *Vertex Clustering* technique, several vertices sharing a same volumetric cell are clustered together into a single vertex, and the model faces are updated accordingly. The *Iterative Edge Contraction* can be considered as a compromised solution between the previous twos. By merging only 2 vertices at a time, *i.e.* collapsing one edge, the algorithm still inherits the speed of the *Vertex Clustering* but also improves the robustness of the *Vertex Decimation* technique. The surface simplification based on quadric error metric (QEM) [1, 2, 3] is based on the iterative contraction of vertex pairs. It differs most substantially from other related methods in the way of choosing an edge to contract. By introduction of the quadric error metric Q, which closely interprets the surface curvature of a 3D model, the algorithm is claimed to be a fast and high quality one [3]. When an edge is decided to be contracted, two primary policies for choosing the target position can be considered. With *Subset Placement* — one of the endpoints of the origin edge, which has smaller Q — will be the combined vertex. The *Optimal Placement* can produce better approximations by trying to find the point such that it minimizes the local function Q constructed by the edge in question. Hereafter, we will use SPQ and OPQ to refer to the first and the second strategy respectively. Although the SPQ strategy does not minimize the cost while processing edge collapse, it does not create new set of vertices in comparison with the origin, high resolution model. Therefore, there is no need of informing the coordinates as well as the associated attributes of the new vertices.

The emergence of the recent MPEG-4 standard is aimed to satisfy the new requirements of the multimedia era: efficiently storing / transmitting various types of media data for sophisticated presentation, easily composing / manipulating the data to build a complex multimedia platform. Among many others, the support of 3D mesh objects and the specification of Animation Framework eXtension [4, 5] (AFX – pronounced 'effects') are the new considerate features, which make the MPEG-4 completely different from the predecessors. MPEG-4 provides a suite of tools for coding 3D polygonal meshes, including technologies to compress the connectivity, geometry, and properties such as shading normals, colors and texture coordinates of 3D polygonal meshes of interest. The AFX provides an integrated toolbox for building attractive and powerful synthetic MPEG-4 environments. The framework defines a collection of interoperable tool categories that collaborate to produce a reusable architecture for interactive animated contents. With the assistance of a skeleton, *i.e.* a joint structure of bones, the movements and the actions of the living organisms can be easily and naturally applied to the 3D models in AFX. Similar to other general 3D models, these models sometimes become too cumbersome to render at some resource limited terminals. Even though general simplification algorithm can be exploited, some special consideration should be taken into account while dealing with AFX based models. The collapsing process should take the skeleton of the 3D target into account to ensure the correlation between the skeleton and the resulting truncated model, safely maintaining the animation of the newly created model using the old skeleton.

Taking the aforementioned observations into account, our work here addresses the adaptation of simplifying algorithm QEM to the model animated with the assistance of skeleton scheme. In the next section, the origin algorithm will be summarized briefly. Our experience related to the implementation of the algorithm is then discussed. Section 3 describes how we combine the bone information into the simplifying process. Section 4 evaluates the performance of technique through simulation. We close our paper with conclusion and perspectives for future works in the last section.

2 Case Study on the 3D Mesh Simplification Based on QEM

The key technique of the QEM is to define a cost associated to each vertex of the 3D model. For vertex v with an associated set of planes P (they are all incident to the vertex v), the error at that vertex can be defined as the sum of squared distances of the vertex to all the planes in the corresponding set as following:

$$E_{plane}(v) = \sum_{i}^{i \in P} D_i^2(v) = Q(v) \qquad (1)$$

where i is the index of a plane in the set P. We refer readers to 2 for the detailed deduction of the function Q — a symmetric 4x4 matrix. For a given contraction $(v_1, v_2) \to \bar{v}$, the new position also possesses its own matrix $\bar{Q}$, where $\bar{Q} = Q_1 + Q_2$. The additive rule here can be interpreted as constructing a new set of planes, which is the union of the two plane sets $P_1 \cup P_2$. To see how this error metric might work in practice, consider the 2D example in Fig. 1, where planes are degenerated to line-segments. The vertices v_1, v_2 have associated sets of lines $P_1=\{A,C\}$ and $P_2=\{B,C\}$ respectively. Upon contracting this pair, the new union of lines becomes $\bar{P} = P_1 \cup P_2 = \{A,B,C\}$. Then the costs of the vertices v_1, v_2 to $\bar{P}$ will be $\bar{Q}(v_1) = b_1^2$ and $\bar{Q}(v_2) = a_2^2$ respectively. In the case of SPQ, the vertex with smaller $\bar{Q}(v)$ will be merged to the other. With OPQ strategy, the optimal position, where $\bar{Q}(\bar{v}) = min(\bar{Q}(v)) = a_{12}^2 + b_{12}^2 + c_{12}^2$, will be detected.

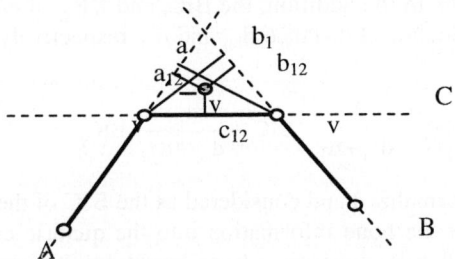

Fig. 1. Measuring contracting cost in 2D prototype

The full algorithm QEM itself can be shortly summarized as follows:

1. Compute the Q matrices for all the initial vertices.
2. For each valid pair (v_1, v_2), compute the union matrix (Q_1+Q_2) and the optimal contraction target $\bar{v}$ ($\bar{v}$ can be coincident to either v_1 of v_2 in the case of SPQ). The error $(Q_1+Q_2)(\bar{v})$ is considered as the cost of contracting that pair.
3. Place all the pairs in a heap keyed on cost with the minimum cost pair at the top.
4. Iteratively remove the pair (v_1, v_2) of the least cost from the heap, contract this pair, and update the costs of all valid pairs involving v_1, v_2 (in the case of SPQ, only pairs that are incident to the removed vertex must be recomputed).

3 Deployment of QEM to MPEG-4 Avatar Framework

Without considering the bone information while simplifying AFX based 3D model, the simplification can lead to undesirable results. For instance, at high level of simplification, the output mesh no longer contains the detailed components, which may have some small associated bones. Currently, we are dealing only with the lossless simplification of the skeleton. In other words, each bone and its effects on the skin must be retained in the simplified mesh. Removing all the vertices corresponding to a detailed bone means that we implicitly remove its skin and therefore the influence of that bone on the resulting model, which is unwilling.

The vertices on the skin of a virtual character can be classified into two categories: they can be affected by either one or more bones. Hereafter, we use S_{lb} and S_{nb} to refer to these two categories respectively. Vertices in the former category concentrate on the body of a bone, while those in the latter are found at the joints of the skeleton. The complete skin model of the skeleton is the union of the two categories, that is $S = S_{lb} \cup S_{nb}$. When the model is animated, the rigid motion of the skeleton is transferred to the corresponding skin by means of weighed transformations. Obviously, a vertex S_{lb} has one while a vertex S_{nb} has a set of influences which correspond to the affect exposed by bone(s) on that vertex. From now on, we refer to the set of influences in the latter case as the bone-based influent configuration (BIC). In some case, for instance when we use OPQ to collapse vertices, the BIC_{ij} of the newly created vertex must be deduced from its parents BIC_i and BIC_j. The BICs of the two origin vertices can be added together as two N dimensional vectors (N is the number all bones in the 3D model). In the addition, the BIC_i and BIC_j of each component vector are weighed with its Euclidean distance $d_{i,ij}$ and $d_{j,ij}$ respectively to the new vertex as following:

$$BIC_{ij} = \frac{d_{i,ij}}{d_{i,ij}+d_{j,ij}} \cdot BIC_i + \frac{d_{j,ij}}{d_{i,ij}+d_{j,ij}} \cdot BIC_j \qquad (2)$$

The resulting BIC is normalized and considered as the BIC of the new target vertex.

The introduction of the bone information into the quadric error metric technique can be subdivided into two categories: bone-based constraints and bone-based removal, which correspond to the degree of their intervention on the conventional simplifying technique.

3.1 Bone-Based Constraints

We introduced two new constraints to the decimating step of the QEM as follows:

1. To explicitly force the lossless of the skin for any bone, we defined a minimum number of vertices per bone, which can be adjustable on demand. The decimating step processes the vertex removal as usual until it finds that the candidate for the current removal violates the threshold for certain bone. That candidate is then skipped, and the process proceeds on the next possible candidate from the heap.
2. To directly keep the extremities of the virtual character (ends of fingers, top of the head, *etc.*), a special type of vertices S_e should be taken into account in step 4. We define vertices S_e as follows. For each extreme bone — a bone that has no children — we arrange all the vertices S_{lb} of this bone in the order of the distance from the center of the bone to that vertex itself. The vertices S_e of that extreme bone are the farthest n vertices, where n is a settable parameter in accordance with the requirement of the given application. A vertex S_e is not be collapsed if it is se-

lected from the heap as the next removal vertex. Then, the decimating step simply jumps to the next candidate in the heap.

3.2 Bone-Based Removal

The bone-based removal technique actually affects the operation of not only step 4 but all the steps of the origin QEM algorithm. We proposed here two approaches to intensively involve bone information into the simplifying process. In the *removal with truncated model* scheme, only the vertices S_{lb} are involved in the QEM as if the vertices S_{nb} do not exist in the current 3D model. The purpose of this technique is to maintain the animation effect of bones at the joints of the avatar. The *removal with bone cost* scheme considers bone information as an additional attribute of vertex. Then the extended simplification algorithm based on quadric error metric [3] can be exploited.

3.2.1 Removal with Truncated Model
If an application requires a perfect animation at all joints of the avatar model, the simplifying process should not remove any vertices S_{nb}. That means only vertices S_{lb} can be considered as candidates for the collapsing process. However, we can expand the set of vertices S_{lb}, that is to increase the collapsing capability, by adding some "virtual" S_{lb} vertices. Virtual S_{lb} vertices are vertices S_{nb}, which are forced to be treated as if they were in S_{lb}. The process to reorder the vertices S_{nb} to S_{lb} is the followings:

1. We define a "center" BIC (CBIC) for a given vertex S_{nb}, which has the same number of influences as the origin BIC, but the weight is equally distributed among the affecting bones.
2. Application should decide a threshold, a level for reordering vertex from S_{nb} to S_{lb}. In fact, if we consider BIC as an N dimensional vector (N is the number of influences in that BIC), the selected threshold t outlines a globe with radius t around the endpoint of the BIC vector in the N dimensional coordinate system.
3. If the Euclidean distance between the endpoint of a BIC vector and that of its CBIC vector is larger than the threshold t — it falls outside the aforementioned globe — then the associated vertex can be rearranged to the set S_{lb} of the bone, who has the most dominant influence in its BIC. Fig. 2 demonstrates the geometric meaning of this rearrangement.

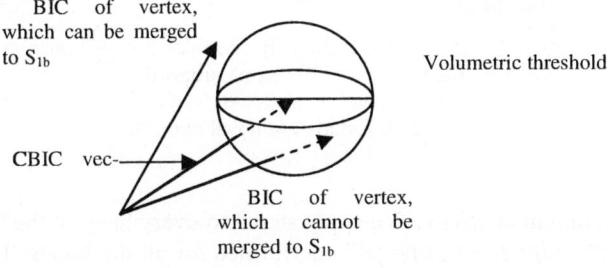

Fig. 2. Extension of S_{1b}

The above reclassification aims to letting the simplifying process remove even the vertices S_{nb} toward (but not including) those that are exactly on the joint level, equally influenced by several bones.

After identifying all vertices from the set S_{1b} (extended S_{1b}), we process the first two steps of QEM to these vertices. Step 3 is carried out locally for each bone. In other word, we have as many heaps as the number of bones in the avatar. Then we can use two strategies to process the step 4 as follows:

- **Absolute removal strategy.** We first apply step 4 to the heap of the bone, which has the most number of vertices. Vertices will be removed only from this heap until the associated bone has no longer the most number of vertices. Then step 4 will be processed on the new heap, whose associated bone just becomes the one having the most number of vertices. The process runs over and over again until the number of removed vertices is achieved. This strategy ensures that the skin of the bone having the least number of vertices will not be removed until the skin of all other bones are reduced to have the same number of vertices. Fig 3. graphically outlines the operations of the absolute removal strategy for a skeleton of 4 bones (4 heaps).

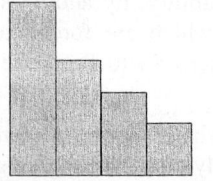 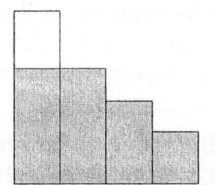 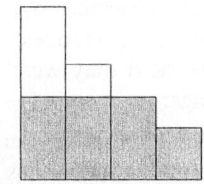

A. The bones are ordered with respect to the number of vertices each one affects.

B. The removal of vertices affected by the first bone continues until their number becomes equal to the second bone.

C. The removal of the vertices affected by the first two bones continues until their number becomes equal to the third bone.

Fig. 3. Absolute removal algorithm

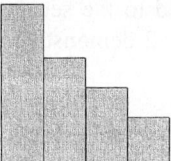 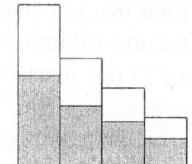

A. The bones are ordered with respect to the number of vertices each one affects.

B. Vertices for all bones are removed in the same proportion.

Fig. 4. Relative removal algorithm

- **Relative removal strategy.** We apply step 4 to every heap of the bone, so that the same local percentage L_p of removal is performed for all the bones. The amount L_p is computed from the global percentage G_p demanded by user as follow:

$$L_p = \frac{G_p \cdot N(S)}{N(S_{lb})} \tag{3}$$

where $N(S)$, $N(S_{lb})$ and $N(S_{nb})$ are the number of vertices of the set S, S_{lb} and S_{nb} respectively. The strategy ensures the same amount of vertex collapse for all bones of the avatar. Fig. 4 illustrates the ration of removed vertices for a skeleton having also 4 bones (4 heaps).

3.2.2 Removal with Bone Cost

Bone information can be considered as a discrete attribute of a vertex, therefore it can be directly involved into the calculation of cost occurring when a vertex is collapsed. We expanded the cost of every vertex V_i with new component bone cost $C_B(V_i)$. This type of cost can be weighed with a settable coefficient to adjust its effect on the overall cost. The bone cost $C_B(V_i)$ is defined as followings:

1. It is equal to zero, if the vertex belongs to S_{lb}.
2. It is inversely proportional to the sum of the deviation between each coefficient in BIC and its average, if the vertex belongs to S_{nb}.

Mathematically, the bone cost $C_B(V_i)$ can be written as following:

$$C_B(V_i) = \begin{cases} 0 & if\ V_i \in S_{lb} \\ 1 - \sum_{j \in M} \left| w_j - \frac{1}{M} \right| & if\ V_i \in S_{Nb} \end{cases} \tag{4}$$

where w_j is the jth coefficient in BIC of the vertex V_i, which has M coefficients. The overall bone cost will become $(Q_1+Q_2)(\overline{v}) + C_B(\overline{v})$. By choosing the bone cost function as above, we implicitly ensure that the vertices S_{nb} always has greater cost than S_{lb} even they provide the same geometry information. Furthermore, for the same vertices S_{nb}, the one having more equal distribution of BIC possesses a higher cost than those having high fluctuation in BIC.

4 Simulation and Results

The simplification algorithms discussed above were applied to several small- (number of faces $N < 15000$) and medium-size ($N=15000-150000$) models to evaluate their performance. Besides the evaluation based on the subjective visualization of simplified models, we also derived the Hausdorff distances to gain a more precise understanding of approximation. We used here the asymmetric version of the Hausdorff distance to speed up its calculation. It is the distance d from a vertex v of the original model to the closest vertex w in the simplified model. The approximation error E is then defined as the average of these distances computed for all vertices of the origin model.

$$E = Avg(d) = Avg(\min_{w \in P(M)} \|v - w\|) \tag{5}$$

Fig. 5 illustrates the performance of bone based constraints applied to the avatar Fig. 5-A. By explicitly ensuring the minimum number of vertices per bone as well as keeping certain number of the extreme vertex for the extreme bones, we have a better visual appearance of the fingers at slightly increased E. Hence, the animation of the finger-bones will deduces better effect on the skin area of the hands.

Fig. 6 denotes the capability and the performance of removal with truncated model. Each variation of this technique is marked with 3 letters. The first two letters, which can be *KJ* or *SJ*, stands for *Keep Joints* or *Simplify Joints* respectively; the third letter — either *A* or *R* — represents *Absolute* or *Relative* strategy. For SJ technique, where the candidates for collapse are from the set of virtual S_{lb} (see Section 3.2.1), we also specify the threshold for simplification after the third letter.

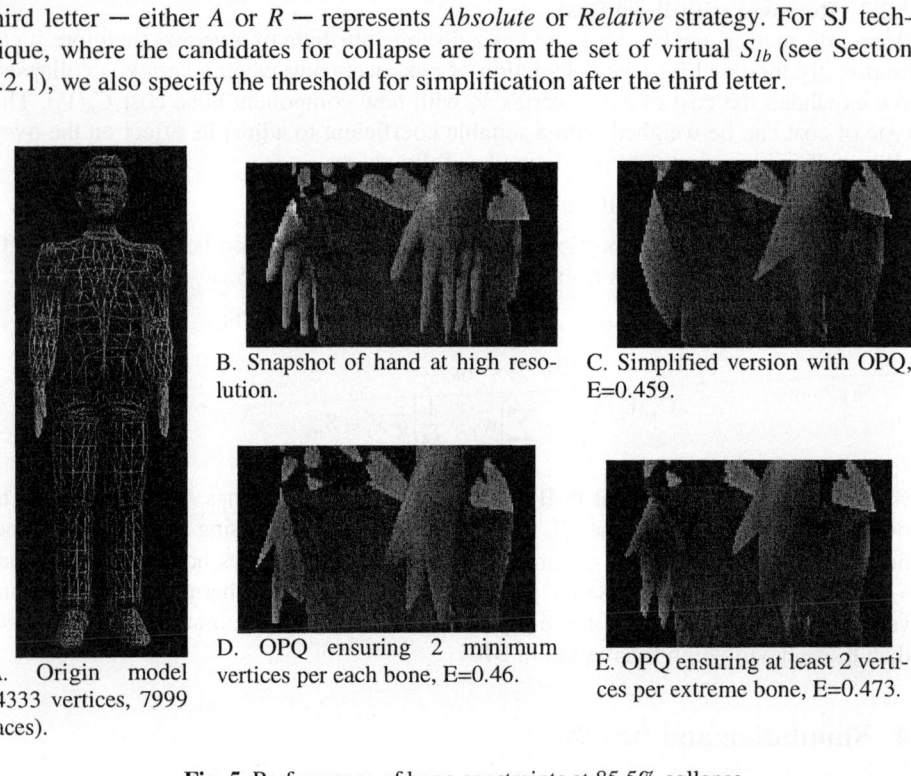

A. Origin model (4333 vertices, 7999 faces).
B. Snapshot of hand at high resolution.
C. Simplified version with OPQ, E=0.459.
D. OPQ ensuring 2 minimum vertices per each bone, E=0.46.
E. OPQ ensuring at least 2 vertices per extreme bone, E=0.473.

Fig. 5. Performance of bone constraints at 85,5% collapse

For the complex 3D model in Fig. 8-A, collapsing only the vertices from the pure S_{lb} (Fig. 6-A) can reduce small number of vertices. The resulting model contain minimum 887 vertices (over 1151 vertices as in the complete model) in order to reproduce exactly the effect of the joints of bones. We can undergo this boundary by extending the S_{lb}, using some thresholds as in Fig. 6-B. With threshold 0.9, we can archive the lowest model at 316 vertices. Then both strategies *SJA0.9* and *SJR0.9* converge at the point having about 23 approximation error, where all the virtual S_{lb} are already removed (Fig. 6-B). It can be seen that for the dragon model in Fig. 8-A, the strategy *SJA* gives a better results in approximation than *SJR* in general (Fig. 6-B).

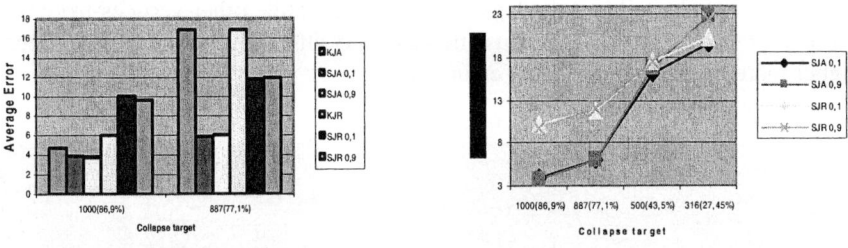

A. Limit of the KJ method   B. Limit of the SJ method with threshold 0.9

Fig. 6. Performance up to some specific limit of the removal with truncated model algorithm

It does mean that the bone having the most number of vertices (we refer as bone-based redundancy) in this model also has the most number of redundant vertices in the geometrical meaning. Obviously, these two factors are not necessarily coincident. In such case, the strategy *SJR* will perform better. Also from Fig. 6-B, we can see that lower threshold will give better approximation error for all level of collapse. The fact that larger set of removed candidates is provided by lower threshold, will improves the possibility of the coincidence between the bone- and geometry-based redundancies.

Fig. 7 puts all the techniques for avatar simplification together for comparison. In the meaning of approximation error, the SPQ takes the lowest boundary. The strategy *SJA* and *SJR* trade this error for better bone-based animation of the avatar. The bone cost removing techniques create a transition state, filling the gap between these boundaries.

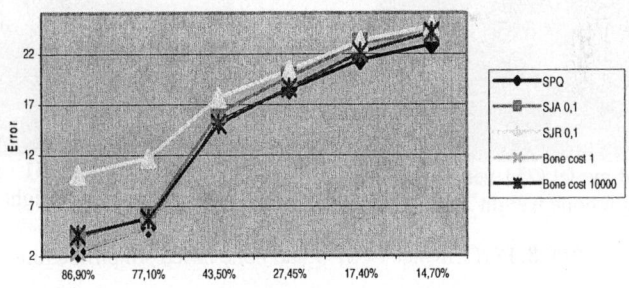

Fig. 7. High collapsing techniques based on bone information

Fig. 8 and Fig. 9 visualize some snapshots of the removal with truncated model as well as the bone-base removal. Fig. 8-B and Fig. 8-D show two distinct levels of involving bone cost into collapsing process: bone cost has no effect at all in the former, and it has dominant contribution in the latter. When bone cost plays an important role in the overall cost (its weight is 50000 as in Fig. 8-D) more vertices at the joints are kept (along the tail and the legs of the dragon) while other vertices from the body, from the head of the dragon must be removed although these latter vertices cause higher increase in approximation error.

A. Origin dragon model (1151 vertices 2102 faces)

B. Simplified model (251 vertices): SPQ algorithm

C. Simplified model (251 vertices): SPQ algorithm with bone weight 1

D. Simplified model (251 vertices): SPQ algorithm with bone weight 50000

Fig. 8. Performance of SPQ and bone based simplifications

Fig. 9 demonstrates the compromise between removal with the truncated model and the conventional SPQ. The strategy *SJA* intensively searches for removed candidates from head bone (Fig. 9-B), which contains the highest density of vertices, while the strategy *SJR* distributes equally the candidates among the bones (Fig. 9-C). Therefore the distortion is spread out. By combining the *SJR* with ensuring 2 extreme vertices for each extreme bone, we can obtain more pleasure appearance as in Fig. 9-D.

A. Simplified model (491 vertices) with SPQ

B. Simplified model (496 vertices) with SJA strategy, threshold = 0.9

C. Simplified model (497 vertices) with SJR strategy, threshold = 0.9

D. Simplified model (497 vertices) with SJR strategy, threshold = 0.9, ensuring 2 vertices for extreme bone.

Fig. 9. Performance of removal with truncated model versus SPQ

5 Conclusion

The theme topic of our work is the simplification of 3D models. The famous algorithm for simplification based on quadric error metrics is comprehensively studied. An additional cost component is proposed to overcome the ambiguity of choosing the merging target in certain situation. Going further than that, we restructure the algorithm so that the simplification can be applied to 3D avatar models, which are actually the 3D models but associated with bone skeleton in order to easily simulate the biological actions of live world. We integrate the bone information into the conventional algorithm throughout several steps. It can be involved as a boundary constraint or a key factor in the collapsing process. These techniques create several compromises between simplifying a volumetric geometry and retaining the effects of skeleton on it.

It offers service-providers a set of tools for choosing the best one, which fits the most to a given application.

As a perspective of the future work, we are working on the more robust tool for simplifying avatar model. Some faster general purposed algorithms such as face-based can be involved. Even the model of the skeleton can be also simplified. As a result, avatar models are efficiently provided with high flexibility in displaying and animation over the strongly diverse environment of multimedia terminals available at the client-side.

Acknowledgement

This work has been partially supported by the 6th Framework Programme of the European Commission, within its research project FP6-IST-1-507926: On-Line GAming (OLGA).

References

1. M. Garland and P. S. Heckbert, "Surface Simplification Using Quadric Error Metrics", ACM SIGGRAPH 97 conference proceedings, p. 209-216, August 1997.
2. H. Hoppe, "New Quadric Metric for Simplifying Meshes with Appearance Attributes", IEEE Conference on Visualization, San Francisco, USA, p. 59-66, October 1999.
3. M. Garland, "Quadric-based Polygonal Surface Simplification", PhD. Thesis, May 1999.
4. M. B. Severnier, "An introduction to MPEG-4 animation framework extension (AFX)", International Conference on Image Processing, Rochester, USA, September 2002.
5. MPEG (Moving Picture Experts Group, formally ISO/IEC JTC1/SC29/WG11): "ISO/IEC 14496-16:2004 Information technology — Coding of audio-visual objects — Part 16: Animation Framework eXtension (AFX)", *ISO/IEC standard*, December 2002.
6. M. Franc, Methods for Polygonal Mesh Simplification, Technical Report No. DCSR:TR-2002-01, January, 2002.

Progressive Lower Trees of Wavelet Coefficients: Efficient Spatial and SNR Scalable Coding of 3D Models

Marcos Avilés, Francisco Morán, and Narciso García

Grupo de Tratamiento de Imágenes, Universidad Politécnica de Madrid,
E.T.S. Ing. Telecomunicación — 28040 Madrid, Spain
{mar, fmb, ngs}@gti.ssr.upm.es

Abstract. We perform an in-depth analysis of current state-of-the-art wavelet-based 3D model coding techniques and then present a new one that outperforms them in terms of compression efficiency and, more importantly, provides full spatial and SNR scalability: PLTW (Progressive Lower Tree Wavelet) coding. As all SNR scalable bit-streams, ours can be used in heterogeneous networks with a wide range of terminals, both in terms of processing power and bandwidth. But because of being spatially scalable, the PLTW bit-stream does not impose on the less powerful terminals the need of building detail trees as deep as required by the maximum LOD, because the wavelet coefficients are sent on a per-LOD basis, thus achieving a "local" SNR scalability within a "global" spatial scalability. In particular, we show that our technique provides a substantial advantage over the only similar one in a current ISO standard (MPEG-4), and thus suggest that PLTW be considered for its future versions.

1 Introduction

Traditional coding algorithms have only focussed on efficient compression, with the sole objective of optimizing data size for a given reconstruction quality. However, due to the growth of the Internet and networking technology, users with different processing capabilities and network bandwidth can easily communicate. As a result, efficient compression alone is not enough. A new challenge appears: providing a single flexible bit-stream that can be consumed by multiple users with different terminal capabilities and network resources. Scalable coding is the response to this challenge. A scalable coder produces a bit-stream containing embedded subsets, each of which represents increasingly better versions of the original data, either in terms of resolution or distortion. Different parts of the bit-stream can then be selected and decoded by the terminal to meet certain requirements. Low performance terminals will only decode a small portion of the bit-stream and reconstruct a low quality and/or resolution version of the source, whereas higher performance decoders will take advantage of the reception of bigger portions to achieve higher quality and/or resolution.

Two different types of scalability can be typically applied to 3D geometry coding, exactly as in the better known case of image coding: SNR (Signal to Noise Ratio) scalability and spatial scalability. SNR scalability refers to the possibility of having different terminals decode the 3D model (or image) with the same spatial resolution but with different fidelity. On the other hand, spatial scalability is the feature in the bit-stream that allows to decode the 3D model (or image) with different spatial resolutions, i.e., number of vertices/facets (or pixels).

Both scalability types are desirable, and so is progressiveness in the bit-stream, especially in the case of streaming scenarios where bandwidth is a limiting factor and it is important to be able to receive and display a coarse version of the media as soon as possible, and later refine it gradually, as more data are transmitted. However, for terminals with low processing power, both in terms of CPU and RAM, and with low resolution screens, as is the case of cell phones (and to a lesser extent that of PDAs), perhaps the most important kind of scalability is the spatial one. There is little point in encoding a 3D mesh so that may be progressively refined to have 100000 triangles if the cell phone that must render it can barely handle hundreds. And there is even less point in doing so if the decoding process that must take place prior to the rendering one will completely eat up all the cell phone resources. And even less if, anyway, nobody will be able to tell the difference between a 100 triangle mesh and a 1000 triangle one when rendered on a screen of 200x200 pixels!

In this paper we review the scalability of current state-of-the-art WSS (Wavelet Subdivision Surface) coders [3] and then present a new algorithm that outperforms previous techniques in terms of compression efficiency and, more importantly, provides full spatial and SNR scalability. We have chosen the WSS modelling/coding paradigm for its adequacy to approximating and manipulating 3D surfaces at different LODs (Levels Of Detail). The successive control meshes yielded along the subdivision process, usually called LODs themselves, are pyramidally nested, and inherently define a multi-resolution model of the limit 3D surface, which is most appropriate to address spatial scalability — without forgetting the SNR scalability, which comes naturally from using wavelet coefficients.

The rest of this paper is organized as follows. Section 2 reviews the SPIHT algorithm [6] and analyses both its scalability and the extra benefits of entropy coding its output. In Section 3, we present our PLTW coder and describe the proposed modifications to the LTW algorithm [5] to achieve both SNR and spatial scalability. Section 4 compares the rate-distortion performance of the proposed coder with other SPIHT-based coders. Finally, Section 5 concludes our presentation.

2 Analysis of SPIHT-Based Coders

For almost a decade already, the SPIHT algorithm [6] has been the reference against which to compare other coding techniques based on the wavelet transform. It was originally designed to code scalar wavelet coefficients, but this has been no obstacle for extending it to handle 3D coefficients, such as the ones resulting from colour images or 3D surfaces modelled thanks to WSSs [2][3][4]. Typically, a coordinate transform is applied to the coefficients coming from the RGB pixels or XYZ detail vectors, so that their three components are decorrelated, and then the SPIHT algorithm is run on each of the three transformed components, yielding three independent bit-streams whose bits are interleaved in some sensible way.

2.1 Scalability

Due to the coefficient ordering and bit-plane encoding achieved by the SPIHT algorithm, the resulting bit-stream is inherently SNR scalable: every bit contributes to reduce the reconstruction error as much as possible for the number of already read bits. This feature allows the decoder to simply stop reading from the bit-stream at any point and have the best possible reconstructed model for that number of decoded bits. Typical rate-distortion curves for a geometry coder based on the SPIHT algorithm are shown in Fig. 1. The horizontal axis reflects the number of bits per vertex while the vertical one shows the PSNR, defined as PSNR = 20 $\log_{10}(bbox/d)$, where $bbox$ is the bounding box diagonal, and d is the L^2 distance between the original and reconstructed meshes, measured with MESH [1].

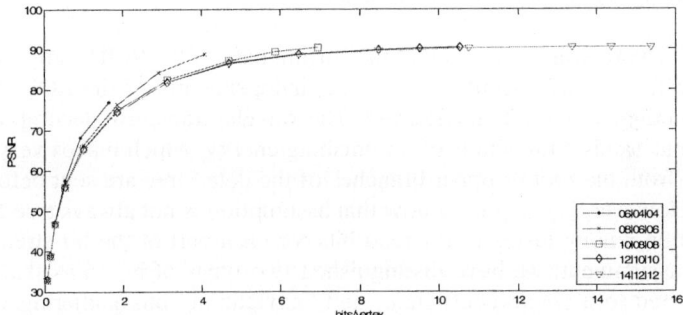

Fig. 1. Rate-distortion curves for different quantization schemes

Besides, as the generated bit-stream is fully embedded, it can also be truncated at a given size in case the target file size is a restriction. However, one might wonder whether it is better to cut the (long) bit-stream produced by running the coder over finely quantized coefficients, or to consume the whole (shorter) bit-stream resulting from coarsely quantized coefficients. Fig. 1 shows the rate distortion curves obtained for bit-streams produced with different sets of quantization values. In all the cases, coefficients have been expressed using local frames to decorrelate energy and save bits by quantizing each of the tangential components four times more coarsely (i.e., with two bits less) than the normal one [2][3]. The three values in each of the entries of the legend reflect the number of bits assigned to the normal and two tangential components, respectively: $nbits_N|nbits_{T1}|nbits_{T2}$. It can be seen how, for a given target size S, the best option is to choose the values $nbits_N$, $nbits_{T1}$ and $nbits_{T2}$ (note that there is only one variable if one sets $nbits_{T1} = nbits_{T2} = nbits_N - 2$) so that the resulting bit-stream is slightly larger than S, and then truncate it to S. In fact, quantization sets of high values (e.g., 14|12|12) hardly contribute to lessen the reconstruction error compared to sets with lower values (08|06|06 or 10|08|08), even though the generated bit-stream is substantially larger.

Nevertheless, although the SPIHT coder is fully SNR scalable, it does not support spatial scalability and does not yield a bit-stream that can be easily parsed according to a given maximum resolution (i.e., number of subdivisions or LODs) imposed by

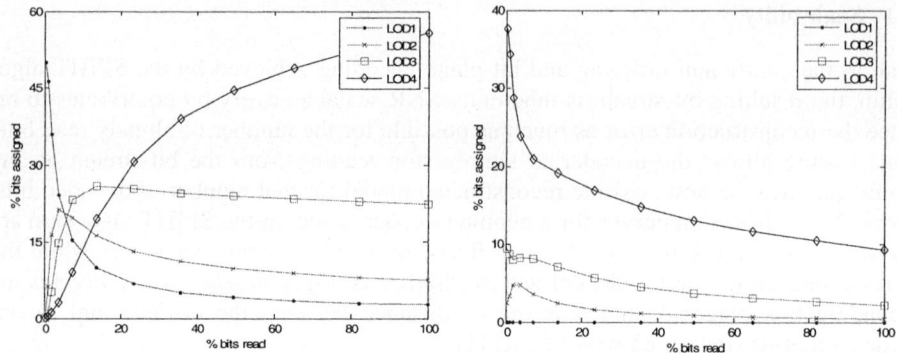

Fig. 2. Bit-stream distribution among different LOD's for the venus model: coefficient (left) and navigation (right) bits assigned to each LOD

the decoder. The reason for this is that the sorting pass of the SPIHT algorithm groups together coefficients with similar magnitude, independently of the LOD they belong to, and then outputs their bits interleaved. The wavelet transform decomposes the initial model into bands with details of diminishing energy, which makes very likely that coefficients from the root or upper branches of the detail tree are sent before those of the leaves. However, Fig. 2 proves how that assumption is not always true by showing the distribution among levels of the read bits for each part of the bit-stream. For this bit-to-level assignment, we have distinguished two types of bits: bits that can be directly attributed to a single coefficient; and "navigation" bits gathering information from multiple coefficients (which are the descendants of some other), which are used to guide the algorithm through the different stages. The assignment of the first ones is straightforward and it is depicted in Fig. 2 (left). For the second ones, we have decided to split each bit between all the coefficients involved and impute them only a fraction of that bit. For instance, let us call *nsubdiv* the total number of subdivisions (in Fig. 2, *nsubdiv* = 4), and consider one of the navigation bits that must be output to reflect the significance, with respect to the current bit-plane, of the descendants of a given coefficient of LOD *nsubdiv* − 2. As such a coefficient has (in general) four sons and sixteen grandsons, 4/20 bits will be imputed to LOD *nsubdiv* − 1 and 16/20 to LOD *nsubdiv*. The fraction of navigation bits vs. the fraction of read bits is plotted in Fig. 2 (right). As it is shown, at any stage of the bit-stream, the bit contribution comes from all levels, and even at its beginning, where almost all the coefficient bits come from lower LODs, the amount of navigation bits from LOD 4 is especially high — which is not at all desirable if a terminal can only handle, say, LOD 2, as it may already be obvious, but explained further in Section 4.

2.2 Entropy Coding

Even though the SPIHT algorithm is very efficient at exploiting the correlations between the detail of a parent and those of its descendants, its output can be further compressed by using entropy coding. In this respect, arithmetic coding [8] is probably the best choice, as it allows to use a fractional number of bits per symbol, although at the expense of larger (de)coding complexity.

As already stated in the original SPIHT paper [6], there is little gain by entropy coding coefficient signs or bits output during the refinement pass. However, significance bits are not uniformly distributed: for early bit-planes, most coefficients are insignificant, resulting in zeroes, whereas for later bit-planes, many coefficients become significant, resulting in ones. Besides, there is also a statistical dependence between the significance of a coefficient and those of its descendants, and between spatially close coefficients.

We have then implemented arithmetic coding of the coefficients using two approaches. The first one consists in using an adaptive model for each type of bit (significance, sign, refinement and so on) sent to the output, reflecting the fact that some symbols tend to be grouped. The second approach takes also advantage of the spatial correlation between coefficients by grouping the significance bits of the children of a detail and coding them as a single symbol [6].

Table 1 shows the efficiency gain obtained by using arithmetic coding. There is a benefit of around 6% when the first approach (row "AC") is followed and around 8% when the more complex modelling (row "AC++") is considered. In a typical asymmetric scenario where one encoder runs as an off-line process on a much more powerful machine than the ones used by the many decoders, so encoder complexity is not as big an issue as decoder complexity is. The ultimate decision of whether to use entropy coding or not is then a compromise between compression and decoder complexity. Nevertheless, notice that the second approach is hardly preferable to the first one, as it only provides a very slight compression improvement, whereas the complexity of its decoder (especially in terms of memory) is considerably larger.

Table 1. Effect of arithmetic coding of the SPIHT bit-stream for some models

model	venus	bunny	horse	dinosaur
no AC	1414885	646111	662048	1466663
AC	1326293	603238	621358	1381779
AC++	1298064	590795	607414	1353311

3 Proposed Technique: Progressive Lower Tree Wavelet Coder

The proposed technique builds upon the work described in [5] for still image coding, which represents a low complexity alternative to traditional wavelet coders, like SPIHT [6] and EBCOT [7], with a higher compression performance and featuring spatial scalability. As a counterpart, it does not provide full SNR scalability due to the fixed, sequential traversal of the coefficients. To achieve both spatial and SNR scalability, we have introduced bit-plane encoding of the coefficients for each LOD.

3.1 Algorithm

In this algorithm, the quantization process is performed by following two strategies: a scalar uniform quantization of the coefficients with *nbits* bits is applied prior to the encoding itself; later on, once the algorithm is executed, the *rplanes* least significant

> 0. INITIALIZATION
>   **output** *nbits*
>   **output** *rplanes*
> 1. CALCULATE LABELS
>   scan the bottom-most detail level in blocks B of coefficients within the same tree
>   for each $d \in B$
>   if $d < 2^{rplanes}\ \forall d \in B$
> $d := LOWER\_COMPONENT\ \forall d \in B$
>   else
>   for each $d \in B$
>   if $d < 2^{rplanes}$
> $d := LOWER$
>   scan the rest of levels from bottom to top in blocks B of coefficients within the tree (top level details will be arranged in groups of 4)
>   for each $d \in B$
>   if $d < 2^{rplanes} \wedge d' = LOWER\_COMPONENT\ \forall d \in B,\ \forall d' \in O(d)$
> $d := LOWER\_COMPONENT\ \forall d \in B$
>   else
>   for each $d \in B$
>   if $d < 2^{rplanes} \wedge d' = LOWER\_COMPONENT\ \forall d' \in O(d)$
> $d := LOWER$
>   if $d < 2^{rplanes} \wedge d' \neq LOWER\_COMPONENT\ \forall d' \in O(d)$
> $d := ISOLATED\_LOWER$
> 2. OUTPUT COEFFICIENTS
>   scan the detail levels from top to bottom
> $LIC := LSC := \emptyset$
>   Add all the details not labeled as *LOWER_COMPONENT* to the *LIC*
>   **output** *nbb* (number of bits needed to code the largest coefficient in the LOD)
>   set $n := nbb$
>   while $n > rplanes$
>   for each $d \in LIC$
>   **output** $b := n^{th}$ bit of d
>   if b = 1
>   **output** sgn(d)
>   if $O(d) \neq \emptyset$
>   **output** $b := (d' \neq LOWER\_COMPONENT)\ \forall d' \in O(d)$
>   move d to the *LSC*
>   for each $d \in LSC$ (excluding entries just appended in this same pass)
>   **output** $b := n^{th}$ bit of d
>   for each $d \in LIC$
>   **output** the label of d (can only be *LOWER* or *ISOLATED_LOWER*)
>   decrement n by one

Fig. 3. Proposed encoding algorithm

bit-planes of the coefficient are removed. As it can be seen in Fig. 3, the final algorithm has two main stages.

During the first step, the coefficient trees are scanned from the leaves (bottom) to the root (top) to try and grow subtrees of what we call "irrelevant" coefficients, i.e., lower than $2^{rplanes}$. A node whose descendants (represented as $O(d)$ in Fig. 3) are all irrelevant is labelled as *LOWER_COMPONENT*. To start, all coefficients of the bottom-most level (i.e., LOD *nsubdiv*) sharing the same parent (of LOD *nsubdiv* − 1) are checked for irrelevance, and hopefully labelled all as *LOWER_COMPONENT*. Later on, if an upper level node N is irrelevant and all its sons are labelled as *LOWER_COMPONENT*, then N is a good candidate to be tagged itself as *LOWER_COMPONENT*, yielding a new, larger lower-tree, providing that all its siblings are also candidates to be tagged as *LOWER_COMPONENT*. However, if any of the sons of a node N is relevant, the lower-tree cannot continue growing upwards. In that case, those irrelevant sons of N having all their sons labelled as *LOWER_COMPONENT* will be tagged as *LOWER*, while other irrelevant sons of N will be tagged as *ISOLATED_LOWER* (see Fig. 3).

Notice that some nodes are not labelled at all, and that no extra space is needed to store these four labels (∅, *LOWER*, *LOWER_COMPONENT*, *ISOLATED_LOWER*), since the lower *rplanes* bits of the coefficient are not coded, which allows to encode them as codewords in the range [0, 3] as long as $rplanes \geq 2$.

In the second stage, which is our main contribution, the coefficients are sequentially scanned in LODs starting from the top-most one and moving downwards. Coefficients are bit-plane encoded with the help of two lists, *LIC* (List of Insignificant Coefficients) and *LSC* (List of Significant Coefficients), used to keep track of their significance with respect to the current bit-plane. In each bit-plane pass n, all the coefficients in the *LIC* are tested: those having the nth most significant bit set are moved to the *LSC*. Then, the coefficients in the *LSC* are processed sequentially and the nth bit of each of them is output. The last step before moving to the next LOD consists in encoding the labels of the remaining coefficients, which are still kept in the *LIC*. These symbols do not contribute to lower the reconstruction error as they only provide information for the next LODs, and could even be skipped if the decoder will not decode further LODs.

3.2 Scalability

The hierarchical traversal of the coefficients, scanned in LODs, naturally produces a spatially scalable bit-stream. This way, the decoder first receives all the coefficients corresponding to a LOD and, only when it has finished reading them, it proceeds (if it has enough resources) with those from the next. Besides, with the introduction of bit-plane encoding, bits from each LOD are ordered in such a way that the first to arrive are the ones that contribute more to lower the reconstruction error, while bits from negligible coefficients arrive last. Fig. 4 shows renderings of the bunny model at different stages of the decoding process. First, LOD 1 is progressively reconstructed (second row). Once all coefficients of LOD 1 have been decoded, the mesh is subdivided and details in LOD 2 are processed (third row). LOD 3 (fourth row) and forthcoming levels are sequentially decoded until the whole bit-stream is read.

Fig. 5 shows the rate distortion curves for both the original LTW coder and our technique. The leap between LODs is clearly reflected in the curve discontinuities, which are the result of applying a subdivision scheme with a smoothing stage, such as

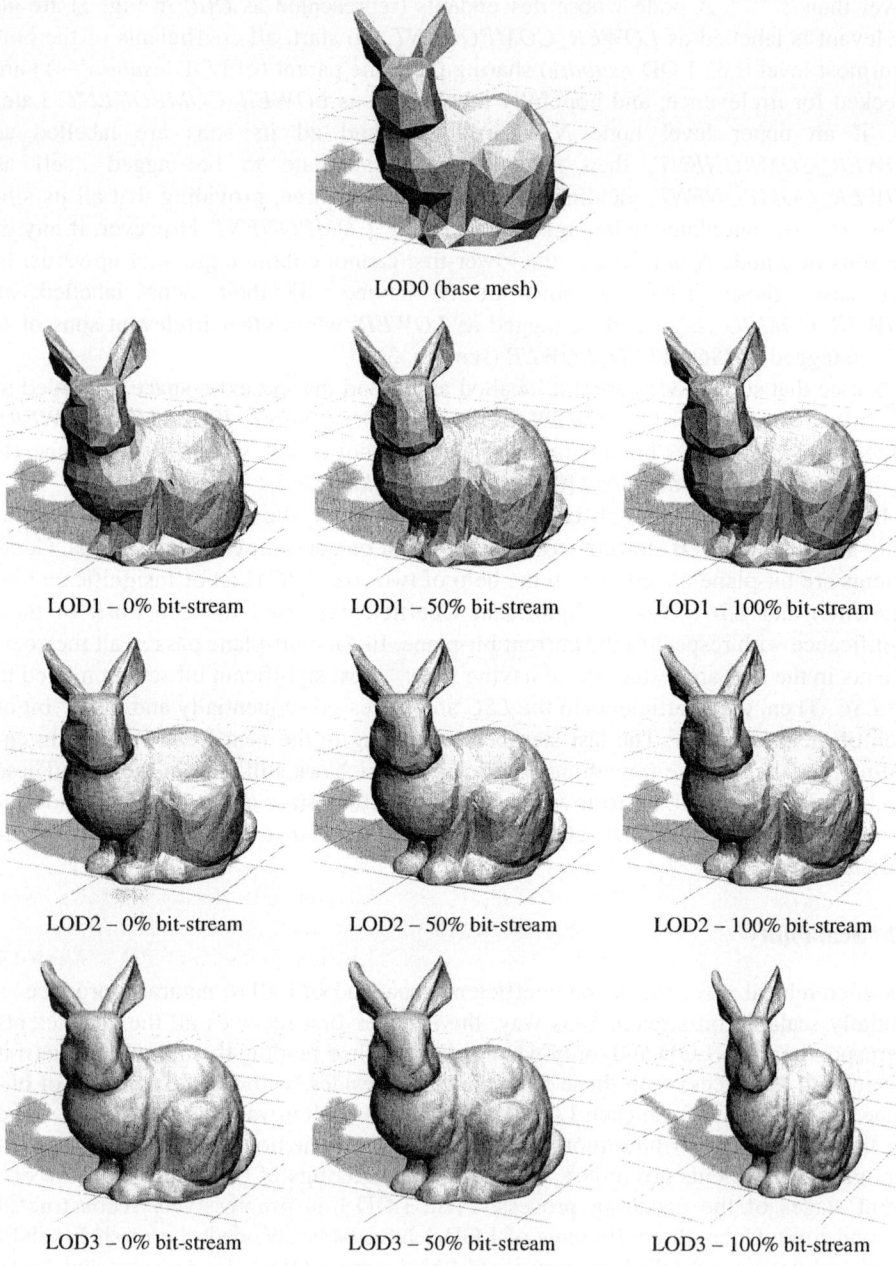

Fig. 4. Progressive reconstruction of the bunny model from a PLTW bit-stream

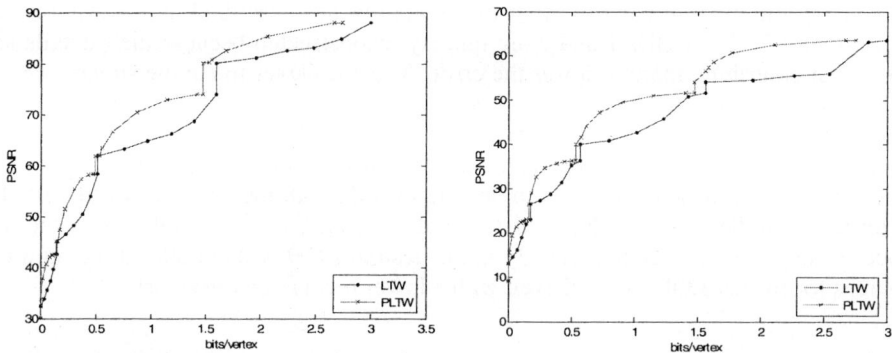

Fig. 5. Scalability of the original LTW algorithm and our PLTW technique for the venus (left) and bunny (right) models

Butterfly or Loop. This means that just by moving from a given LOD n to LOD $n + 1$, the reconstruction error is reduced (this effect will not occur for Midpoint subdivision, which only consists of an upsampling stage). Because of the sequential scanning of the coefficients in the LTW algorithm, the distortion curves between levels are arbitrarily shaped, although monotonically increasing, as they depend on the also arbitrary distribution of coefficients. In contrast, the curves for the PLTW coder demonstrate how bits with larger contribution are sent first whereas unimportant ones are output at the end. Note that the whole curve is not globally smooth, as in the SPIHT algorithm (see Fig. 1), because the bit-plane encoding is only performed on a per-level basis, while the SPIHT algorithm considers coefficients from all levels at the same time.

3.3 Entropy Coding

We have also analysed the gain obtained by entropy coding the PLTW bit-stream. Table 2 shows there is around a 46% benefit (42% in the worst case, for all the models we tested) when adding an arithmetic coder. Therefore, the PLTW algorithm is not as efficient as the SPIHT coder at exploiting relations between coefficients and the use of an entropy coder is almost required. However, the number of adaptive models needed in the arithmetic coder is still low, reducing the complexity and requirements of both the encoder and the decoder.

Table 2. Arithmetic coding of the PLTW bit-stream

model	venus	bunny	horse	dinosaur
no AC	1681701	825543	879696	1945907
AC	970636	441077	454124	1006442

4 PLTW vs. SPIHT

We now compare the PLTW coder with other SPIHT-based coders. Fig. 6 (top) shows the rate distortion curves for the PLTW coder and the arithmetic coded version of the

SPIHT algorithm (following the first of the approaches described in Subsection 2.2) for different LODs. LODs 1 and 2 are quickly reconstructed because their details are those that contribute more to lower the error. It seems clever to cut the stream or stop decoding after some point (e.g., 0,75 b/v for LOD 1 or 1,5 b/v for LOD 2) if only interested in coarser LODs, as the bits to come will hardly increase the PSNR. However, even in those cases, the decoder needs to build the whole detail tree (including finer LODs than those of interest) to be able to follow all the branches of the SPIHT algorithm. On the contrary, due to the spatial scalability of the PLTW coder, the decoder is able to stop decoding exactly at the desired LOD without allocating extra resources for further LODs — and even with a lower reconstruction error!

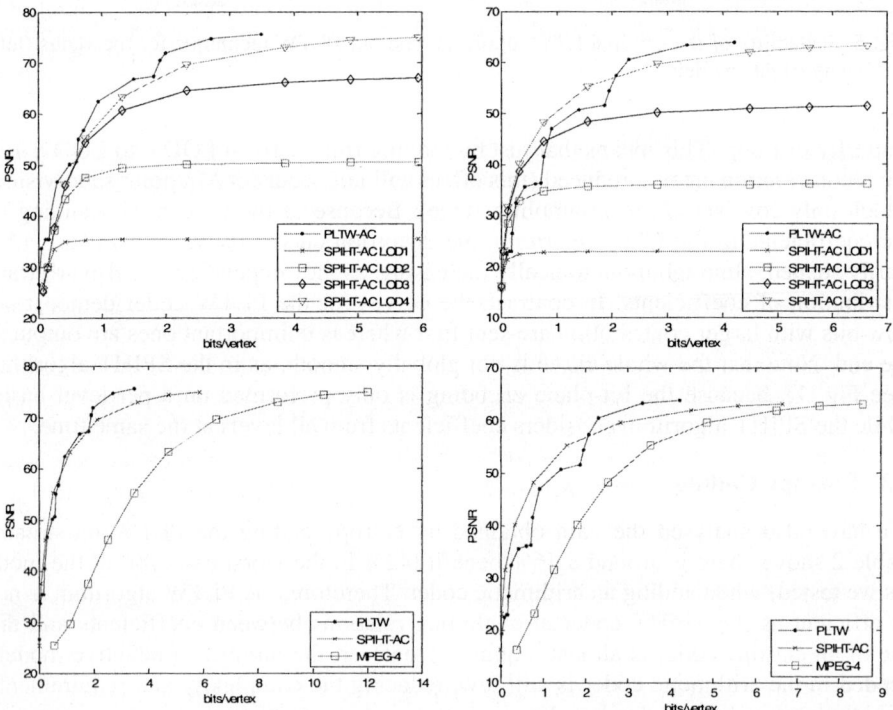

Fig. 6. PLTW vs. SPIHT: Per-LOD comparison (top) and overall compression (bottom) for the Max-Planck (left) and bunny (right) models

Fig. 6 (bottom) compares the overall compression performance of our technique with the SPIHT-AC algorithm and the WSS tool of MPEG-4's AFX (Animation Framework eXtension) [4], which also uses the SPIHT, but without AC. Except at very low rates, where the PLTW is still reconstructing upper LODs and does not benefit from the smoothing effect of subdivision (while its competitors do), our technique always results in higher PSNRs for the same bitrate. It is also noticeable how none of the SPIHT-based coders is able to reach the same PSNR as the PLTW coder even employing 160% (SPIHT-AC) or 330% (MPEG-4) of the bits used by PLTW for the same quantization set of values. The poor results of the MPEG-4 coder are due to the overhead introduced to support view-dependent transmission of coefficient trees.

5 Conclusion

After an in-depth analysis of current state-of-the-art techniques for the hierarchical coding of 3D models with WSSs, we have proposed ours, the PLTW (Progressive Lower Tree Wavelet) coder, which achieves higher compression ratios and features both spatial and SNR scalability. Thanks to this, the same compact and scalable bit-stream can be used in heterogeneous networks with a wide range of terminals, both in terms of processing power and bandwidth. Our bit-stream does not impose on the less computationally powerful terminals the need of building detail trees as deep as required by the maximum LOD to follow the logical branching of the SPIHT algorithm, because the wavelet coefficients are sent on a per-LOD basis, thus achieving a "local" SNR scalability within a "global" spatial scalability.

Entropy coding has also been studied as a post-processing solution, and proven to provide an important benefit in compression efficiency, especially in the PLTW algorithm, compared to the additional complexity added to the decoder.

In particular, we have shown how our PLTW technique provides a substantial advantage over MPEG-4's WSS tool, which is the only similar one in a current ISO standard. We therefore believe that our technique should be considered for future versions of MPEG-4's AFX toolset, especially if one of its targets will be 3D Graphics applications for mobile terminals, in which the view-dependence offered by its current WSS tool would be much less important than the computational complexity and bandwidth savings offered by PLTW.

Finally, we would like to stress that, although we have developed our technique within the field of 3D model coding, it should yield the same excellent results when applied to image coding, or to any other problem addressable with the SPIHT algorithm.

Acknowledgments

This work has been partially supported by the 6th Framework Programme of the European Commission, within its research project FP6-IST-1-507926: On-Line GAming (OLGA). Datasets are courtesy of Cyberware, Max-Planck Institut für Informatik and Stanford Computer Graphics Laboratory.

References

1. N. Aspert, D. Santa Cruz, and T. Ebrahimi, "MESH: Measuring Errors between Surfaces using the Hausdorff Distance," *Proceedings of the IEEE International Conference on Multimedia and Expo*, 705–708, August 2002.
2. A. Khodakovsky, P. Schröder, and W. Sweldens, "Progressive Geometry Compression," *Proceedings of the ACM SIGGRAPH Conference*, 271–278, July 2000.

3. F. Morán and N. García, "Comparison of Wavelet-Based Three-Dimensional Model Coding Techniques," *IEEE Transactions on Circuits and Systems for Video Technology*, **14**-7, 937–949, July 2004.
4. MPEG: "ISO/IEC 14496 (MPEG-4) Part 16: Animation Framework eXtension (AFX)", ISO/IEC, April 2003 (International Standard status).
5. J. Oliver and M. P. Malumbres, "Fast and Efficient Spatial Scalable Image Compression using Wavelet Lower Trees," *Proceedings of the IEEE Data Compression Conference*, 133–142, March 2003.
6. A. Said and A. Pearlman, "A New, Fast and Efficient Image Codec Based on Set Partitioning in Hierarchical Trees," *IEEE Transactions on Circuits and Systems for Video Technology*, **6**-3, 243–250, June 1996.
7. D. Taubman, "High Performance Scalable Image Compression with EBCOT," *IEEE Transactions on Image Processing*, **9**-7, 1158–1170, July 2000.
8. I. H. Witten, R. M. Neal, and J. G. Cleary, "Arithmetic Coding for Data Compression," *Communications of the ACM*, **30**-6, 520–540, June 1987.

An Adaptive Quantization Scheme for Efficient Texture Coordinate Compression in MPEG 3DMC

Sunyoung Lee[1], Byeongwook Min[1], Daiyong Kim[1], Eun-Young Chang[2], Namho Hur[2], Soo In Lee[2], and Euee S. Jang[1]

[1] Digital Media Lab., College of Information and Communications, Hanyang University,
17 Haengdang-dong, Seongdong-gu, Seoul 133-791, Korea
sunnykr@ihanyang.ac.kr, esjang@hanyang.ac.kr
[2] Digital Broadcasting Research Division, Broadcasting System Research Group,
Electronics and Telecommunications Research Institute,
161 Gajeong-dong, Yuseong-gu, Daejeon 305-350, Korea

Abstract. Graphic models represented by 3D polygonal mesh (with geometry, color, normal vector, and texture coordinate information) are now heavily used in interactive multimedia applications. As an international standard, MPEG-4 3D mesh coding (3DMC) is a compression tool for 3D mesh models. Texture mapping on a 3D mesh model is now getting popular, since it can produce high quality reconstruction even with small number of polygons used. Texture coordinates (TCs) play an important role in texture mapping. In compressing TCs using 3DMC, we found that the lossless compression is not guaranteed, which jeopardizes the texture mapping due to the precision error between the original and reconstructed TC values. In this paper, we proposed an adaptive quantization scheme for efficient TC compression in 3DMC. By adaptively choosing the step size for quantization, the proposed method can guarantee the lossless compression.

1 Introduction

3D polygonal mesh models are now heavily used in interactive multimedia applications. To maintain a convincing level of realism, many applications require highly detailed complex models. However, such models demand broad bandwidth and much storage capacity to transmit and store. To address these problems, many 3-D mesh compression algorithms have been proposed by reducing the size of 3-D models.

As one of the well-known conventional algorithms, 3D mesh coding (3DMC) introduced in MPEG-4 Visual Version 2 [M4V2] can typically compress VRML data 1 40 to 50 times without noticeable visual degradation 23. Moreover, other than compression, incremental rendering, error resilience, support of nonmanifold models, and hierarchical buildup functionalities are supported by 3DMC 23.

A 3D mesh model is described by geometry information, connectivity information, and other properties, such as colors, normal vectors, and texture coordinates. 3DMC compresses all information and properties of the 3D mesh model, where texture coordinate (TC) values are also compressed 4.

The more the number of polygons used, the better the quality of the rendered 3D model is. However, this increases the complexity of rendering. Another popular way is to use a small number of polygons with high quality texture with texture mapping. This helps accelerating the rendering process by decreasing the number of polygons.

TCs play an important role in mapping a texture on top of the 3D geometry of a model. Using 3DMC, we found that TC may be coded lossy, which means that the original value may not be preserved after compression. The precision error of a TC value can cause a serious texture mapping distortion 5. And lossless compression of 3D meshes is clearly identified as mandatory functionalities in MPEG 6.

There have been quite a few papers on geometry compression of 3D meshes thus far 7-10. It, however, should be noted that many existing researches overlooked the importance of lossless compression of texture coordinate information.

In this paper, we proposed an adaptive quantization scheme for efficient TC compression in 3DMC. The proposed scheme is to enable lossless compression of TC values (possibly) with better compression efficiency.

The remainder of this paper is as follows. Section 2 describes the TC compression and the proposed methods in 3DMC. In the Section 3, experimental results are given. Finally, we summarize this paper in Section 4.

2 Adaptive Texture Coordinate Quantization Scheme

2.1 Texture Mapping and Mapping Distortion

In order to map a texture on a polygon of 3D mesh, TCs are used to map vertices of the polygon to the corresponding texture. TCs are originally represented by integer numbers, since they indicate the pixel locations. However, TCs are described as real numbers between 0 and 1 in many textual descriptions for convenience.

Precision error by converting from integer to real may have an impact on rendered image. This precision error is not a critical problem, when compared to the quantization error caused by any compression algorithm. Since most mesh compression algorithm is lossy, there is no guarantee to losslessly represent TC values.

Fig. 1 shows an example of texture mapping distortion due to the lossy compression using 3DMC. The mapping distortion happens in the quantization process, where each real value is quantized, which no longer represents the original integer value.

2.2 Proposed Adaptive Quantization Scheme

In order to solve this distortion problem caused by quantization, we proposed to use an adaptive quantization scheme that adaptively chooses the quantization step size (QSS). Originally, the quantization step size is determined by bits per texture coordinates (bpt) given by the encoder input. However, in order to minimize the impact of quantization error, one can exploit two factors: 1) inverse of the texture image size and 2) interval of TCs.

If the QSS is set to be one pixel width (by choosing 1/texture image size), the quantization error can be minimized. We also found that (ordered) TC values are quite often evenly spaced with a regular interval. In this case, the QSS value can be set to be the found regular interval of ordered TC values (in pixels). Finally, the value of QSS can be one of the following values as shown in Equation (1).

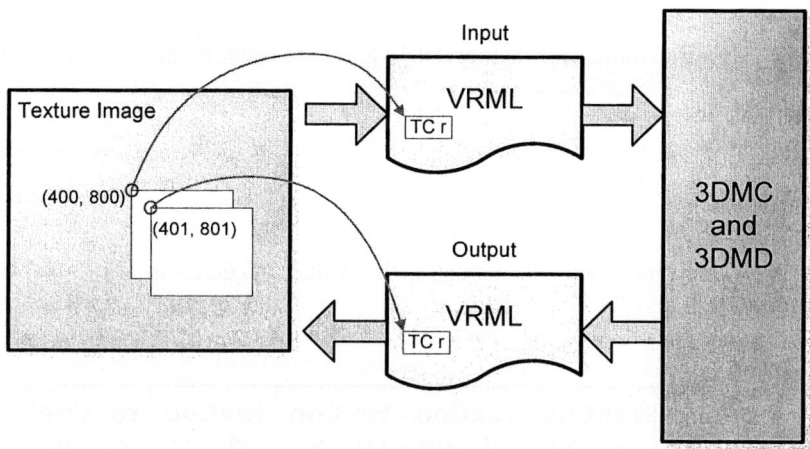

Fig. 1. Mapping distortion from quantization error

TC values are quantized by a step size in three cases. In (1-a), we used *bpt* of the conventional 3DMC as the quantization step size that never considers the value of TC. However, QSS1 or QSS2 may be a divisor of TC values, where further reduction of bits is expected.

$$QTC_i = TC_i / step\_size$$

$step\_size : 2^{-bpt}$ (1-a) 3DMC

$: texture\_size^{-1}$ (1-b) QSS1

$: regular\_interval$ (1-c) QSS2

where, $step\_size \leq 2^{-bpt}$ and $0 \leq QTC_i \leq 2^{bpt} - 1$.

The major reason for further reduction in compression of TC values is that the QSS (in 3DMC) value is normally larger than QSS1 or QSS2. Otherwise, a lossless texture compression cannot be guaranteed. For instance if an image size is 500 x 500, the encore is likely to use the QSS value of 9 ($2^9 = 512 > 500$). If we choose QSS to be 1/500 (instead of 1/512), we are saving unnecessary 12 quantization steps (with more compression) and (hence) increasing the fidelity of TC values. If there is a regular interval that is larger than one-pel width, one can expect more bit savings.

2.3 Bit-Stream Syntax and Semantics

In order to house this change in the coder-decoder structure of 3DMC, we have to add a signal to indicate the usage of adaptive QSS as shown in Fig. 2. If QSS_flag is 'ON', QSS_u and QSS_v are available in bit-stream. Their semantics are as follows.

- QSS_flag

This boolean value indicates whether delta values are used or not.

- QSS_u

This 16-bit unsigned integer indicates the value of delta in direction u(x) for quantization.

- QSS_v

This 16-bit unsigned integer indicates the value of delta in direction v(y) for quantization.

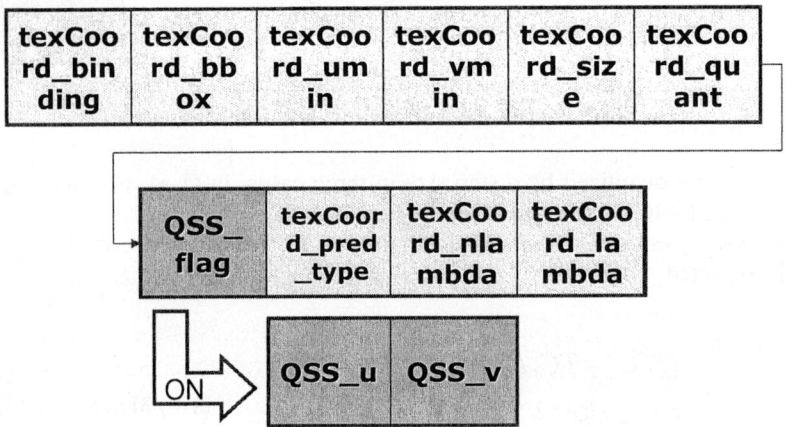

Fig. 2. Bit-stream syntax with QSS

3 Experimental Results

3.1 Test Conditions

We have used a few models with TCs which are available in SNHC homepage. The used test models are listed in Table 1. To evaluate the lossless coding performance, we have used three methods: 1) 3DMC, 2) QSS1, and 3) QSS2.

For evaluation of lossless performance of the methods, we computed mean square error (MSE), compared bit rates, and counted the number of losslessly encoded coordinates. In addition to the objective measures, we have compared the test results subjectively and attached some of the results.

3.2 Error Estimation and Overhead Bits in Original and Fixed VRML Files

Objective performance evaluation on the reference method (3DMC) and the proposed methods are given in Tables 2 and 3. We have used the term 'original VRML' to indicate the original test models, whereas the term 'fixed VRML' is used when the input file to 3DMC is filtered first before encoding. The filtering process is to avoid multiple (different) real values that indicate the same integer texture coordinate. Therefore, the 'fixed' VRML files can guarantee one-to-one mapping in data type conversion from real to integer even after compression.

Table 1. Image size for test models

VRML	Image	Image size
batteryD.wrl	battery.jpg	600*400
earth.wrl	earth.jpg	800*400
nefert131b.wrl	nefert131.jpg	512*512
vase131b.wrl	vase131.jpg	512*512
vase212b.wrl	vase212.jpg	512*512

If losslessly compressed, the value of MSE is zero and the lossless count is 100. To estimate compressed TC bits, we use TC bits of 3DMC as a reference. From the table, one can clearly see that the proposed methods can support lossless compression with better compression efficiency. TC bits of QSS1 and QSS2 are about 10 percent less than those of 3DMC with 'original VRML'. In 'fixed VRML', QSS1 and QSS2 have 10 ~ 40 percent better compression efficiency than 3DMC with lossless coding.

From Table 2, it should be noted that selection of QSS may lead to different compression results with the same *bpt* value. For example, the tested model *batteryD* was compressed more and better using the QSS1 method than the 3DMC method. It means that the *bpt* value simply indicates that the encoder will choose the number of quantization steps from 1 to $2^{bpt}-1$.

3.3 Error Estimation and Overhead Bits with the Same BPT and Maximum BPT

In Table 4, we analyzed the performance of the coding methods at the same bpt. The results clearly indicated that the proposed method meets the lossless coding requirement with better compression efficiency. We also evaluated the best-effort performance of 3DMC to reach its best effort to support lossless compression at the maximum bpt (16) which leads to the fact that 3DMC was not able to support lossless compression in Table 5.

Table 2. Objective evaluation with original VRML

	Method	MSE	Lossless count (%)	TC bits (%)	bpt
batteryD	3DMC	0.8073	26.97	100.00	10
	QSS1	0.0000	100.00	89.83	10
	QSS2	0.0000	100.00	253.83	24
earth	3DMC	0.9937	14.69	100.00	10
	QSS1	0.0000	100.00	94.48	10
	QSS2	0.0000	100.00	59.55	7
nefert131b	3DMC	0.8420	26.52	100.00	10
	QSS1	0.0000	100.00	90.48	9
	QSS2	0.8253	27.00	90.40	9
vase131b	3DMC	0.8422	26.32	100.00	10
	QSS1	0.0000	100.00	90.52	9
	QSS2	0.8468	25.49	90.46	9
vase212b	3DMC	0.8410	26.74	100.00	10
	QSS1	0.0000	100.00	90.47	9
	QSS2	0.8996	21.74	90.55	9

Table 3. Objective evaluation with fixed VRML

	Method	MSE	Lossless count (%)	TC bits (%)	bpt
batteryD	3DMC	0.8002	24.82	100.00	10
	QSS1	0.0000	100.00	93.68	10
	QSS2	0.0000	100.00	93.68	10
earth	3DMC	0.9422	12.24	100.00	10
	QSS1	0.0000	100.00	94.43	10
	QSS2	0.0000	100.00	59.52	7
nefert131b	3DMC	0.8426	25.56	100.00	10
	QSS1	0.0000	100.00	90.48	9
	QSS2	0.0000	100.00	90.48	9
vase131b	3DMC	0.8441	25.65	100.00	10
	QSS1	0.0000	100.00	90.52	9
	QSS2	0.0000	100.00	90.52	9
vase212b	3DMC	0.8264	27.72	100.00	10
	QSS1	0.0000	100.00	90.47	9
	QSS2	0.0000	100.00	90.47	9

Table 4. Objective evaluation compared with the same bpt

	Method	MSE	Lossless count (%)	TC bits (%)	bpt
batteryD	3DMC	0.8073	**26.97**	100.00	10
	QSS1	0.0000	**100.00**	89.83	10
earth	3DMC	7.1106	**0.00**	100.00	7
	QSS2	0.0000	**100.00**	82.86	7
nefert131b	3DMC	1.5963	**10.95**	100.00	9
	QSS1	0.0000	**100.00**	100.11	9
vase131b	3DMC	1.5685	**9.17**	100.00	9
	QSS1	0.0000	**100.00**	100.06	9
vase212b	3DMC	1.4167	**0.07**	100.00	9
	QSS1	0.0000	**100.00**	100.02	9

Table 5. Objective evaluation compared with maximum bpt (16)

	Method	MSE	Lossless count (%)	TC bits (%)	bpt
batteryD	3DMC	0.0125	98.75	**100.00**	16
	QSS1	0.0000	100.00	**50.45**	10
earth	3DMC	0.0303	96.98	**100.00**	16
	QSS2	0.0000	100.00	**34.88**	7
nefert131b	3DMC	0.0211	97.90	**100.00**	16
	QSS1	0.0000	100.00	**57.37**	9
vase131b	3DMC	0.0220	97.80	**100.00**	16
	QSS1	0.0000	100.00	**57.58**	9
vase212b	3DMC	0.0386	96.15	**100.00**	16
	QSS1	0.0000	100.00	**57.49**	9

3.4 Subjective Quality

The original *nefert131b* model before compression is showed in Fig. 3. In Fig. 4, we provided some snapshots of rendered images of the three coding methods for comparison. We used 10 bpt for (a) 3DMC and 9 bpt for (b) QSS1 and (c) QSS2.

The original *vase212b* model before compression is also showed in Fig. 5. Some snapshots of rendered images of the three coding methods are presented in Fig. 6. We also used 10 bpt for (a) 3DMC and 9 bpt for (b) QSS1 and (c) QSS2. From the snapshots, one can clearly see the mapping distortion from 3DMC.

Fig. 3. Rendered model before coding (nefert131b)

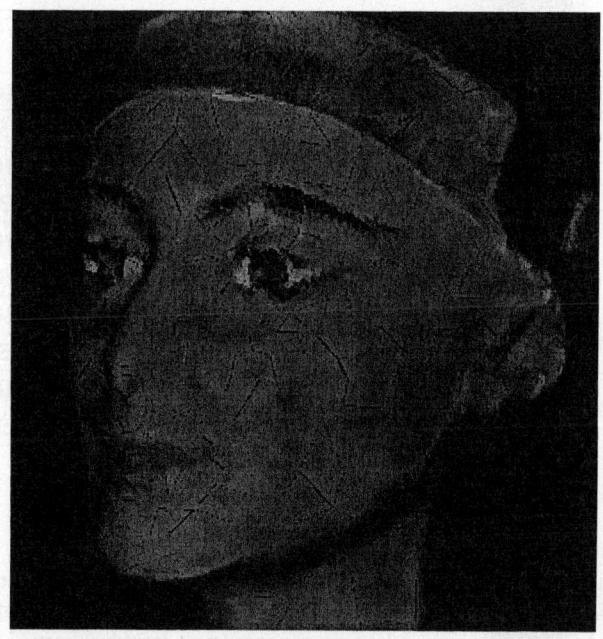

(a) 3DMC (MSE: 0.8420 Lossless count: 26.52% TC bits: 100% bpt: 10)

Fig. 4. Subjective quality (nefert131b)

(b) QSS1 (MSE: 0.0 Lossless count: 100% TC bits: 90.48% bpt: 9)

(c) QSS2 (MSE: 0.8253 Lossless count: 27.0% TC bits: 90.4% bpt: 9)

Fig. 4. (*Continued*)

Fig. 5. Rendered model before coding (vase212b)

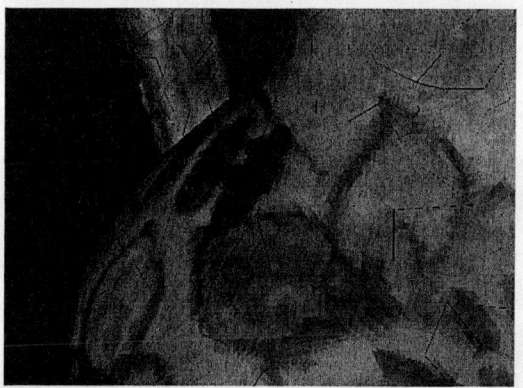

(a) 3DMC (MSE: 0.8410 Lossless count: 26.74% TC bits: 100% bpt: 10)

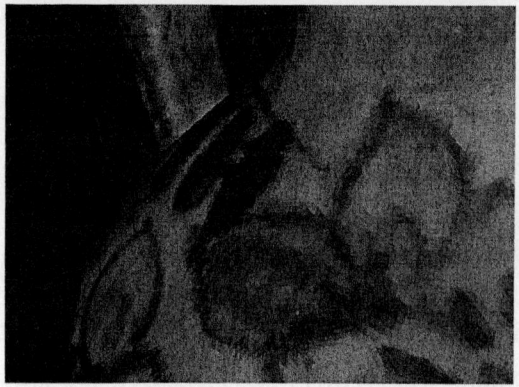

(b) QSS1 (MSE: 0.0 Lossless count: 100% TC bits: 90.47% bpt: 9)

Fig. 6. Subjective quality (vase212b)

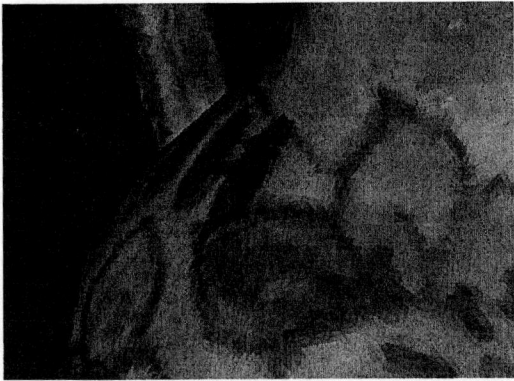

(c) QSS2 (MSE: 0.8996 Lossless count: 21.74% TC bits: 90.55% bpt: 9)

Fig. 6. (*Continued*)

4 Conclusions

Texture mapping is an important method to realistically present 3D mesh model, which is highly dependent upon TC accuracy. For the lossless compression of TC, we proposed an adaptive quantization scheme in 3DMC. By adaptively choosing the step size for quantization, the proposed method can guarantee the lossless compression. Efficiently estimating regular interval in TC values would be one of the future directions that we intend to research.

References

1. A. Nadeau, VRML 2.0 Sourcebook, Wiley, 1997.
2. Fernando Pereira and Touradj Ebrahimi, The MPEG-4 Book, Prentice Hall, 2002
3. Aaron E. Walsh and Mikael Bourges-Sevenier, MPEG-4 Jump-Start, Prentice Hall, 2002
4. "Information Technology - Coding of Audio-Visual Objects - Part2: Visual", ISO/IEC JTC1/SC29/WG11 N5546, Mar. 2003, Pattaya, Thailand
5. Sunyoung Lee, Daiyong Kim, Byeongwook Min, Eun-Young Chang, Namho Hur, Soo In Lee, and Euee S. Jang, "Efficient texture coordinate compression based on 3DMC", ISO/IEC JTC1/SC29/WG11, M11933, Apr. 2005, Busan, Korea.
6. "MPEG-4 requirements, version 18", ISO/IEC JTC1/SC29/WG11 N5866, Jul. 2003, Trondheim, Norway
7. G. Taubin and J. Rossignac, "Geometric compression through topological surgery", ACM Transactions on Graphics, 1998.
8. M. Isenburg and J.Snoeyink, "Mesh collapse compression", In Proceedings of SIBGRAPI'99 - 12th Brazilian Symposium on Computer Graphics and Image Processing, 1999.
9. M. Isenburg, "Triangle Fixer: Edge-based Connectivity Compression", 16th European Workshop Comput. Geom., 2000.
10. Eun-Young Chang, Daiyong Kim, Byeongwook Min, Sunyoung Lee, Namho Hur, Soo In Lee, and Euee S. Jang, "3DMC Extension for the Efficient Animation Support", ISO/IEC JTC1/SC29/WG11 M11938, April, 2005, Busan, Korea

Special Effects: Efficient and Scalable Encoding of the 3D Metamorphosis Animation with MESHGRID

Ioan Alexandru Salomie, Rudi Deklerck, Dan Cernea, Aneta Markova,
Adrian Munteanu*, Peter Schelkens*, and Jan Cornelis

Vrije Universiteit Brussel, Dept. ETRO, Pleinlaan 2, 1050 Brussels, Belgium
{iasalomi, rpdekler, cdcostin, amarkova, acmuntea,
pschelke, jpcornel}@etro.vub.ac.be

Abstract. Metamorphosis or morphing is a technique to accomplish a gradual shape transformation between a source object and a target object. This technique is usually used for animation, i.e., to create some special effects, but it can be also employed as a modeling tool where some existing shapes are combined in order to obtain new shapes. Several interactive or automatic morphing techniques were designed in the past but always with a specific object representation in mind. In this paper we propose a generic framework for 3D morphing, that allows multi-resolution surface extraction and provides a hybrid (surface-volume) dynamic representation which is suitable for encoding the static models, for supporting different morphing methods, and for encoding the intermediate 3D frames (generated during the morphing process) in a MPEG-4 stream.

1 Introduction

Morphing is a computer animation method to blend shapes, which has been successfully used for the generation of special effects in movies, TV advertisements, and computer games. It also finds applications in 3D medical image analysis and visualization, in industrial applications (CAD, CAM), scientific modeling and visualization. According to [1], some more concrete example applications are: visualization during cranio-facial surgery; anthropological studies on the evolution of the shape of the skulls of primates and humans; study of environmental changes on sea level and forest cover; continental drift or erosion; and study of the biological processes such as plant growth and fetal development. Given the diversity of applications morphing has not only taken an important place in the computer graphics world, but also in other scientific fields.

Some principles to achieve "good" morphing results, such as topology preservation, feature preservation, rigidity preservation, smoothness and monotonicity, are mentioned in [2]. But not all of these principles are always valid since they are strongly application dependent, e.g., in special-effects industry sometimes artificial shape transformations are more impressive than physically correct transformations, which however would be mandatory in some technical applications.

---

* This work was supported by DWTC – Belgium (TAP Tracing project). P. Schelkens and A. Munteanu have post-doctoral fellowships with the Fund for Scientific Research – Flanders (FWO), Egmontstraat 5, B-1000 Brussels, Belgium.

Morphing techniques are in general strongly dependent on the object representation, i.e. on the way one describes the models. A detailed survey of the various morphing approaches classified according to object representation is given in [3]. The object representations suited for morphing can be coarsely classified into 3 groups: boundary, volumetric and elevation models.

Boundary morphing is the process of metamorphosis where the source and target are objects described by a set of polygons. One of the important characteristics of a mesh model is that it describes the topology of the model. Therefore, several packages support model creation in this format, and several mesh morphing methods have been developed for the entertainment industry. One of the key problems in boundary morphing is the correspondence problem, i.e., to establish an appropriate parametrization correspondence between the source and one or more destination 3D meshes. Gregory et al. [4] and Kanai et al. [5] successfully solved this problem by embedding the input 3D meshes into a sphere or a disk and then finding the parametrization correspondence there. Further, Lee et al. [6] used multiresolution analysis in order to solve the correspondence problem via coarse-to-fine parametrization matching. However, these methods are limited to cases in which 3D source meshes need to be morphed to topologically equivalent (i.e., homeomorphic) destination meshes.

Morphing a source mesh to a topologically different destination mesh (e.g. morphing a sphere into a torus) without, or with minimal, user interaction, is still a challenge. A possible approach is using Reeb graphs [7] to detect the critical points where the changes in topology occur. The Reeb graph (which defines the topological skeleton of an object) together with the contours of the object represent the entire 3D object. By using this method, the metamorphosis can be seen as a sequence of transitions between the different topology types. Additionally, there are some interactive solutions [8] which insert *key-frames* to link two distinct surface topological types during a topological transition. Nevertheless, complex topologies are time-consuming to morph especially if they require constant user interaction.

Algorithms are however a bit more straightforward when using volumetric representations. Within a volumetric representation the object is described by an entity that provides a value at each point in 3D space, e.g., by evaluating an analytically expressed function or by retrieving the value from discrete samples stored in a 3D grid. While volumetric approaches are not as popular as polygonal formats for the entertainment industry, volumetric approaches are free of restrictions on topology and geometries: they can easily morph objects of different genus (e.g., a sphere with a torus), are typically not burdened with the difficult vertex/edge/face bookkeeping of surface methods and surfaces cannot pass through each other. Most volumetric algorithms do not need a bijective mapping between the vertices of the source and target formats like mesh morphing techniques. In addition, volumetric morphing can easily be applied to meshes by converting them to volumetric data or implicit surfaces [9], while the reverse operation may result in topologies that are difficult to morph.

Several volumetric approaches have been designed. The simplest method to morph is to linearly interpolate between the source and the target volume, but this approach doesn't produce a natural and smooth morphing. Therefore, Hughes in [10] suggests not to interpolate volumes directly, but in the frequency domain. His approach is based on the observation that high-frequency components of the volumetric model represent usually small details, while the low-frequency components represent the general shape of the object. The interpolation of details seems unimportant compared to the interpolation of the general shape. So Hughes suggests to gradually remove the high frequencies of the source model, interpolate towards the low frequencies of the second model, and then blend in the high frequencies of the second model. He et al. [11] takes the idea further by morphing in the wavelet domain. Since a wavelet transform is localized in both the frequency domain and the spatial domain, the problems of high frequency distortion encountered in [10] and unsmooth transformation can be alleviated simultaneously. Breen et. al [12] takes another approach; they employ an active deformable surface which starts from the source shape and smoothly changes it into the target shape. This deformation process is described by the optimization of an objective function that measures the similarity between the target and the deforming surface. They represent the deformable surface as a level set (iso-surface) of a densely sampled scalar 3D function, and derive surface movements from changes in the grayscale values of the volume, computed via the narrow-band method. Semval et al. [1] uses the concept of cellular automata to perform morphing, which is a dynamic system where an N dimensional space is created with each cell containing a value which changes according to pre-determined rules depending on the neighborhood. From this simple local concept, complex global patterns and behavior emerge as the morphing animation considers the response of all the cells within the lattice. Yet, although volumetric approaches offer many advantages, an important drawback when processing high resolution volumetric data is the large memory requirements. Therefore, to support the morphing approaches in a memory efficient way, a scalable representation allowing to perform the processing on a region of interest (ROI) basis is needed.

In this paper we will explain how the MPEG-4 MESHGRID object representation ([13], [14], [15], [16]), can be used to represent the source and destination models, to support different morphing methods, and to encode the 3D morphing sequence as a scalable MPEG-4 stream so that it can be played back as a free-viewpoint interactive 3D animation. In the next section MESHGRID will be described in more detail and we will see that it is accompanied by a surface extraction method called TRISCAN ([14], [16]), which can be used to extract multi-resolution surfaces of the shape underlying the volumetric or implicit surface representation. It will be shown that MESHGRID is a hybrid representation, which works on a ROI basis, and which preserves both the volumetric description of the scene and the surface description of the objects within the scene. In section 3 it is illustrated that MESHGRID can be employed for performing morphing and for encoding the morphing sequence.

2 Hybrid Object Description, Representation and Encoding

TRISCAN is a new surface extraction algorithm that generates multi-resolution object descriptions from 3D scalar fields in the MPEG-4 MESHGRID representation [13] Contrary to other surface representation methods that perform the contouring in one direction only [17], or those which directly target the computation of the surface polygons [18], TRISCAN aims a "global description" of the object's surface. The strategy followed by TRISCAN is, in a first step, to perform the contouring of the object in three sets of reference surfaces $\{S_U, S_V, S_W\}$ (colored in red, green, blue in Fig. 1(b)), defining the reference system of the object. The intersection of $\{S_U, S_V, S_W\}$ defines the reference-grid points. In a second step the connectivity-wireframe (CW) is built as the result of the union of the object's contours, whose vertices are defined with respect to the discrete positions of the reference-grid (RG) points inside each reference-surface (RS). The discrete position (u,v,w) of each RG point represents the indices of the RSs $\{S_U, S_V, S_W\}$ intersecting in that point, while the coordinates (x,y,z) of the RG point are equal to the coordinates of the computed intersection point. In the general case, the RSs are not planar, but curvilinear and non-equidistant.

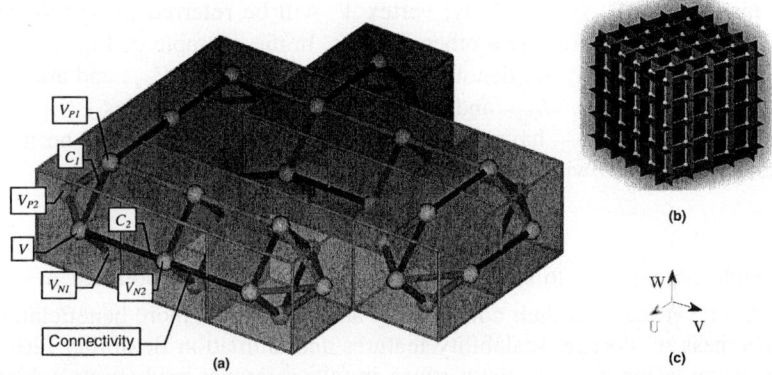

Fig. 1. (a) A 3D view of a connectivity-wireframe derived for a discrete object (i.e., the transparent set of cubes); (b) three sets of reference surfaces $\{S_U, S_V, S_W\}$ and (c) their axes

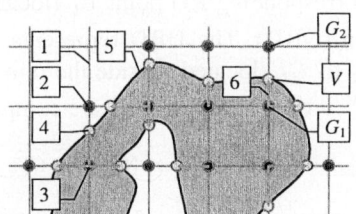

Fig. 2. Relationship between the vertices and the RG points shown in a cross-section through a 3D object (displayed in grey color)

To perform the contouring in each RS from the defined reference-system $\{S_U, S_V, S_W\}$, TRISCAN employs a boundary-tracking algorithm similar to the mid-crack algorithm described in [19]. An example of a contour obtained inside a RS intersecting the object, and the relationship between the contour's vertices and the RG points is shown in Fig. 2. Each contour vertex belonging to the CW is located on a line (curve) l (label 1), resulting from the intersection between two RSs, belonging to two different sets. The line (curve) l, called the RG line, passes implicitly through the series of RG points (labels 2, 3) resulting from its intersection with the RS belonging to the third set. The absolute coordinates $C_{x,y,z}^V$ of each vertex V (label 4) on the RG line l are given by the intersection point of line l with the object's surface.

A reference-grid line might intersect the surface of the object at different positions; hence in each intersection point a different vertex must be considered.

An intuitive example illustrating the structure of the connectivity-wireframe, exemplified for a discrete object of one slice thickness, is shown in Fig. 1(a), where the cubes represent the voxels. Since a vertex V is located on a RG line, which in its turn is defined by the intersection of two RSs S_1 and S_2 from two different sets, there will be two connectivity-vectors ($-L_{N1}$- and $-L_{N2}$-) going from vertex V to other vertices (*outgoing*): one connectivity vector is located inside the RS S_1, while the other one is located inside the RS S_2. Similarly, vertex V will be referred to by two *incoming* links ($-L_{P1}$- and $-L_{P2}$-) from two other vertices. In the example of Fig. 1(a), the four neighboring vertices of V are denoted as V_{P1}, V_{P2}, V_{N1} and V_{N2}, and are connected with V via $-L_{P1}$-, $-L_{P2}$-, $-L_{N1}$- and $-L_{N2}$- respectively. The indices $i \in \{1,2\}$ for the connectivity vectors $-L_{Ni}$- have been chosen in such a way that the normal vector computed with the following equation points outwards the surface:

$$\vec{N} = (L_{N1} - L_{P1}) \times (L_{N2} - L_{P2}). \tag{1}$$

Although it is possible to store the CW as standalone, since both the (x,y,z) coordinates of the vertices and their connectivity are known, it is more beneficial, in terms of compactness of storage, scalability features and animation flexibility [20], to preserve the relationship between the vertices and the reference-grid points, which represents the basic idea of the MESHGRID representation – hence MESHGRID is a hybrid object representation preserving both the surface and volumetric description.

In MESHGRID, a vertex V within the CW stores, instead of the coordinates (x,y,z), the indices (u,v,w) of the corresponding RG point G_1 (located inside the object), and the discrete border direction (DBD). The DBD represents the orientation along the RG line l pointing from G_1 to G_2 (located outside the object) – see Fig. 2. This implies that the coordinates $C^V_{x,y,z}$ of vertex $V(u,v,w)$ are computed as:

$$C^V_{x,y,z} = C^{G_1}_{x,y,z} + \text{offset} \cdot (C^{G_2}_{x,y,z} - C^{G_1}_{x,y,z}), \tag{2}$$

where *offset* (label 6) is a scalar in the range $[0,1)$. The coordinates of V are updated each time the *offset* or one of the coordinates of G_1 and G_2 change, e.g. during the animation.

The decomposition of a MESHGRID object into its components is illustrated in Fig. 3 for a hierarchical cuboid model with three resolution levels, obtained by applying the TRISCAN method on a composite implicit function definition. Fig. 3(a) shows the MESHGRID representation of the model, which consists of the hierarchical CW (Fig. 3(b)) and the hierarchical RG (Fig. 3(c)). The RG is defined by a hierarchical reference-system that can be decomposed into three reference-systems, each consisting of three sets of reference-surfaces $\{S_U, S_V, S_W\}$, as shown in Fig. 3(d). For readability purposes the reference-surfaces (Fig. 3(d)) from each set are shown planar and equidistant, while the reference-surfaces from the different sets are reciprocally perpendicular. In general however, the reference-surfaces are curvilinear and non-equidistant, in order to allow an adaptive triangulation according to the topology or usability purposes of the model – the RG should have a higher density in high curvature areas (Fig. 3(a)) or where the mesh is supposed to change during the animation (e.g., humanoid's knees from Fig. 7) or morphing. Note that MESHGRID is not limited to surfaces obtained with the TRISCAN approach, it can be used for closed or open quadrilateral meshes defined in cylindrical, spherical or toroidal coordinates [14].

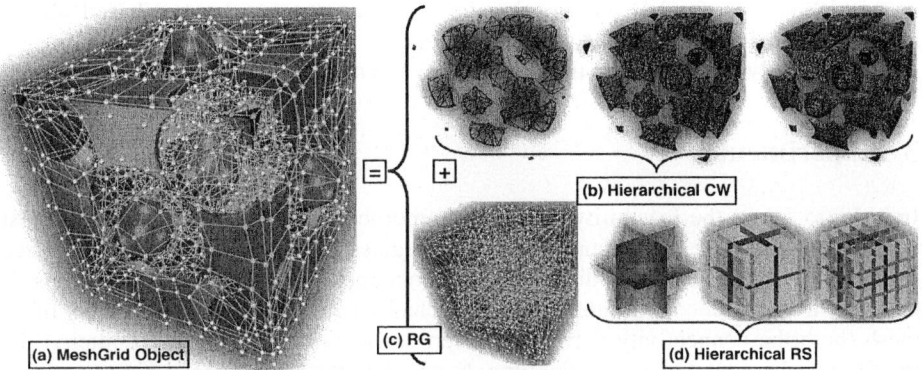

Fig. 3. The components of the MESHGRID representation

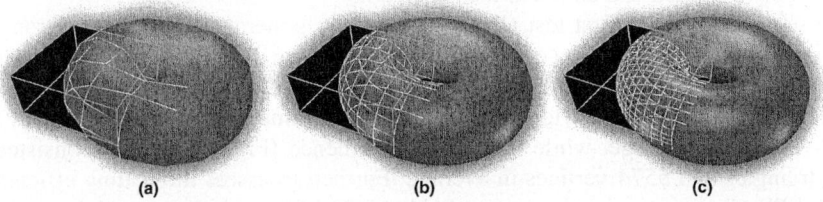

Fig. 4. Splitting the model at different resolution levels into ROIs for surface extraction, processing or encoding

2.1 MESHGRID Encoding

The MESHGRID stream consists in general of three parts: (1) a *connectivity-wireframe description*, (2) a *reference-grid description*, and (3) a *vertices-refinement description* (VR). This last part contains the offsets needed for refining the position of the vertices relative to the reference-grid (eq. (2)). All these three parts can be encoded at each resolution level either as one entity or in separate *region of interests* (ROIs) for memory efficient decoding. Due to its regular nature, as shown by the green box from Fig. 4, it is straightforward to divide the reference-grid at each resolution level into ROIs, and to encode for each ROI the corresponding descriptions (CW, RG and VR) independently. The encoding of a multi-resolution CW is done at each resolution level and for each ROI independently, but takes as well into account the outgoing connectivity-vectors pointing to the neighbor ROIs (see the red and blue lines from Fig. 4). Therefore, when randomly decoding the ROIs, the mesh from adjacent ROIs will perfectly stitch together due to the connectivity-vectors which reciprocally point to the places that need to be connected. The encoding of the CW is done using a new type of 3-D extension of Freeman chain-code that considers the RG points as (u,v,w) reference positions in space. Since the RG is a smooth vector field $(x(u,v,w),$ $y(u,v,w),$ $z(u,v,w))$ defined on the regular discrete 3-D space (u,v,w), each component is coded separately on a ROI basis using a multi-resolution progressive coding algorithm based on a combination of a 3-D wavelet transform and an intra-band octree-based wavelet coder [13], [14]. Uniformly distributed grids can be compressed very efficiently since in this case only the corners of the grid need to be coded.

3 Experiments

In order to assess the feasibility of encoding morphing sequences three types of tests were performed. The first group of tests has targeted the least compact encoding scenario where for each intermediate 3D frame obtained during the metamorphosis the CW had to be re-encoded due to dramatic changes in the topology or genus of the mesh (both the connectivity between the vertices and their number were altered) but the RG was kept unchanged all the time. Even when the CW changes from one frame to another, the transition is smooth and natural (Fig. 5). To generate the animation bitstream, the first frame was fully encoded, while for each following frame only the CW has been encoded and added to the bitstream.

The sequences of the first test (Fig. 5) have been generated by applying transformations in the time domain to composite implicit surface descriptions. The 3D frames were obtained from these composite implicit surface descriptions using TRISCAN. The "MeltPlast" sequence (Fig. 5(top)) consists of 249 frames with 16000 triangles and 32000 vertices in average, while the "Blobs" sequence (Fig. 5(bottom)) consisted of 11136 triangles and 5574 vertices in average. Further, to assess the coding efficiency, the "MeltPlast" sequence has been encoded lossy at different bitrates, and the decoded 3D frames were compared with the non-compressed 3D frames by measuring the Hausdorf distance [21] between the surfaces of the corresponding 3D frames. Since for this model the reference-grid is distributed uniformly, the bit-rates are specified by imposing different values for the number of bitplanes used to quantise the vertices' offsets (bpo) [13], [14], [16]. Note that the total number of bits per vertex (bpv) is computed as 4 + bpo, where 4 are the number of bpv used to encode the connectivity (which is fixed). The coding efficiency can be followed in Fig. 6. for three different bitrates, i.e. 5, 7 and 9 bpv. The first row shows the decoded 3D frame, wile the second row illustrates the distribution of the errors.

The second test aimed to explore the coding performance of MESHGRID by taking into account the inter-frame similarities. This time the CW was kept the same for the entire animation and only the vertices' coordinates were modified. Since the vertices are attached to the RG and their coordinates are derived according to eq. (2) from the coordinates of the RG points, it is possible to move the RG points instead of the vertices and yield the same morphing result. Therefore this time only the RG points were moved. In the animation bitstream, the full model, i.e. the mesh connectivity and the reference-grid, was encoded only once (i.e. for the first frame), while for each of the following frames only the changes in the RG with respect to its previous frame were encoded.

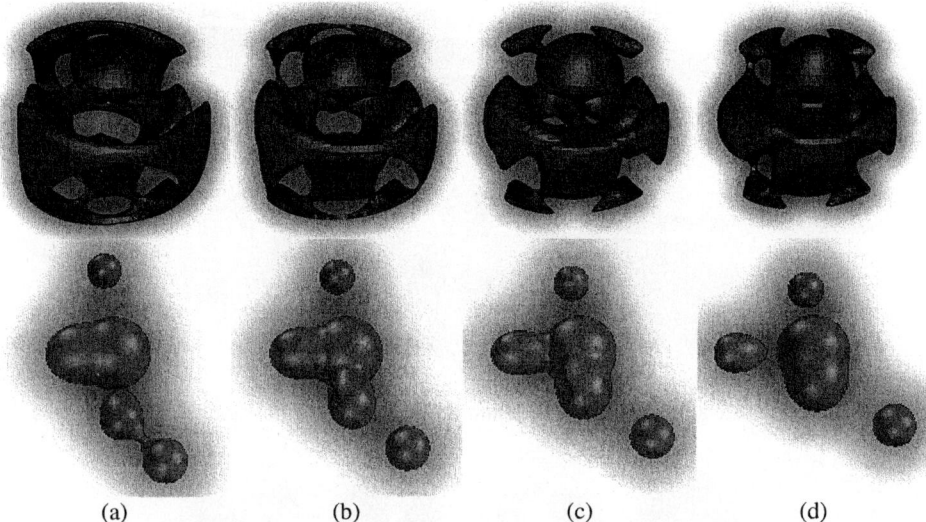

Fig. 5. Frames ((a) to (d)) from a morphing sequence simulating: Top – dynamic (MeltPlast) sequence of melting plastic objects (two consecutive images are at 10 frames distance). Bottom – five bouncing blobs (two consecutive images are at 5 frames distance).

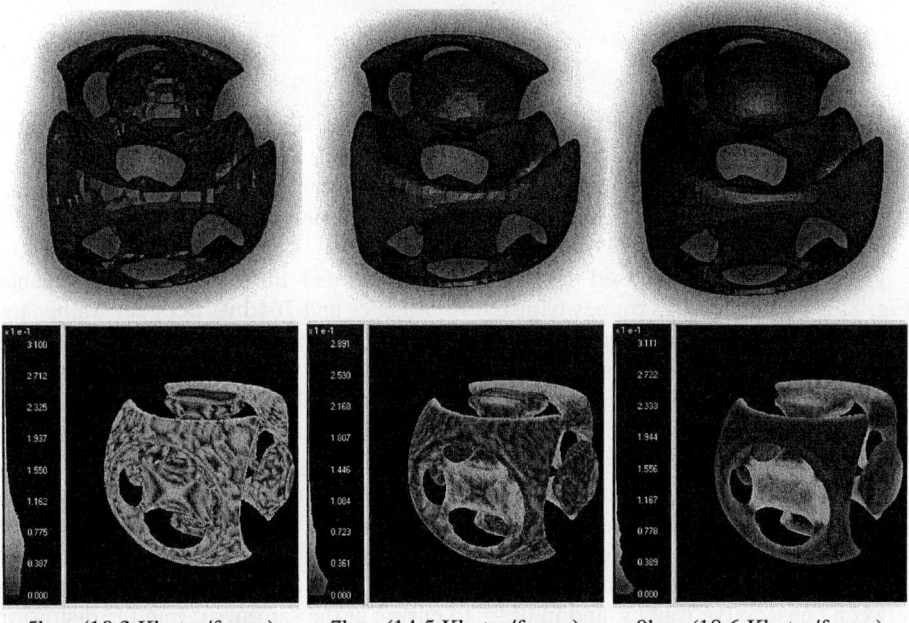

5bpv (10.3 Kbytes/frame) 7bpv (14.5 Kbytes/frame) 9bpv (18.6 Kbytes/frame)

Fig. 6. Coding efficiency at 5, 7 and 9 bpv for the "MeltPlast" sequence: Top – a decoded 3D frame; Bottom – the distribution on the surface and the histogram (left) of the errors with respect to the non-compressed 3D frame (Hausdorff distance)

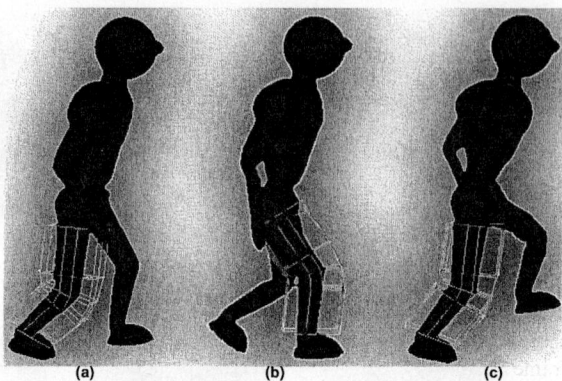

Fig. 7. Volumetric animation of a "Humanoid" by altering the positions of the RG points

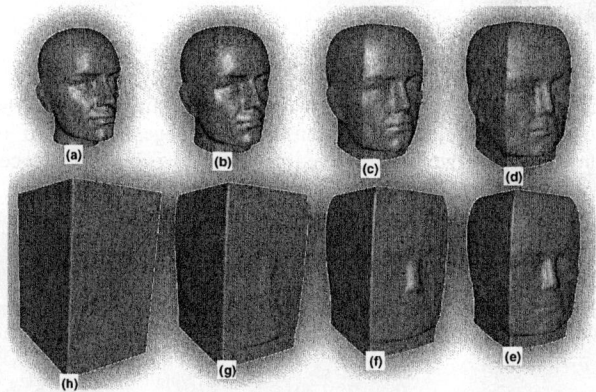

Fig. 8. Morphing the "Head" model to a box

Two sequences were used for the second test: (1) the "Humanoid" sequence (Fig. 7) consisting of 152 frames with 15196 triangles and 7646 vertices per frame, and (2) the "Head" sequence (Fig. 8) consisting of 100 frames with 82108 triangles and 32000 vertices per frame. For the "Humanoid" sequence, the TRISCAN approach was used only once to generate the initial Humanoid model, which further was morphed by means of the RG. The "Head" model has been imported to MESHGRID as a quadrilateral mesh, which was initially generated by a structured light scanner technique[1].

Similarly, to assess the coding efficiency of the second test, the "Humanoid" sequence has been encoded lossy at different bitrates (Fig. 9), and the Hausdorf distance [21] has been used again to compare the decoded 3D frames with the corresponding non-compressed ones. In order to optimally encode in a lossy way the differences between consecutive frames, and in order to ensure at the same time that the distortion of the model does not exceed an imposed maximum error, an optimal truncation algorithm of the wavelet coefficients bitplanes has been applied [22].

---

[1] We thank Eyetronics (HQ, Heverlee, Belgium) for providing the "Head" model (www.eyetronics.com).

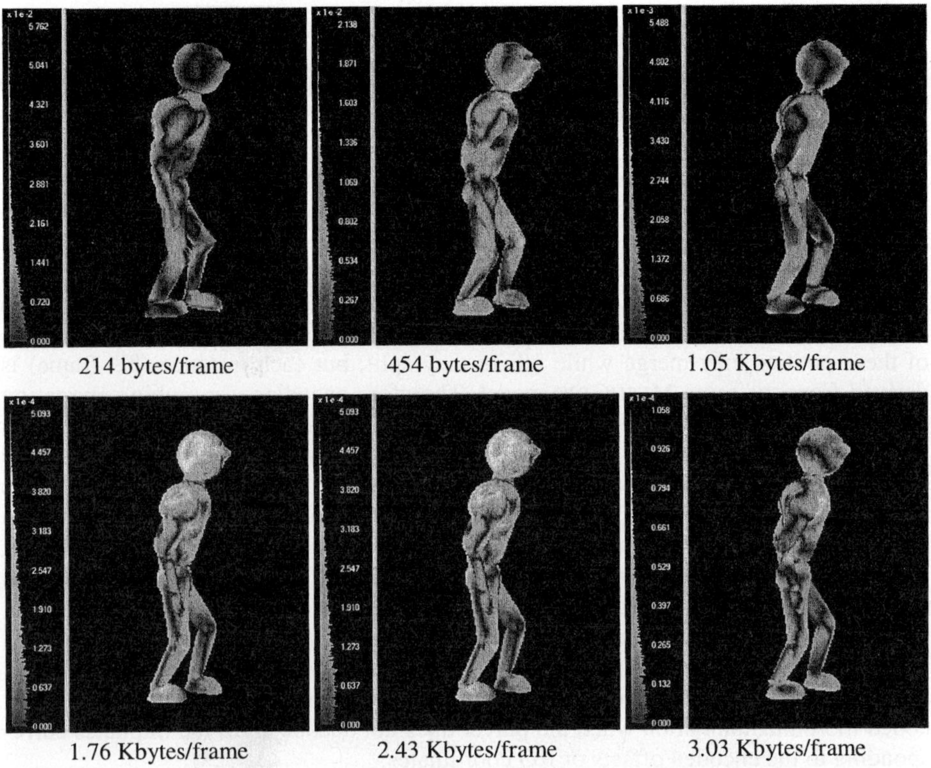

Special Effects: Efficient and Scalable Encoding of the 3D Metamorphosis Animation

| 214 bytes/frame | 454 bytes/frame | 1.05 Kbytes/frame |
| 1.76 Kbytes/frame | 2.43 Kbytes/frame | 3.03 Kbytes/frame |

Fig. 9. "Humanoid" sequence: distribution on the surface (right) and the histogram (left) of the coding errors with respect to the non-compressed 3D frame at different bitrates measured with the Hausdorff distance

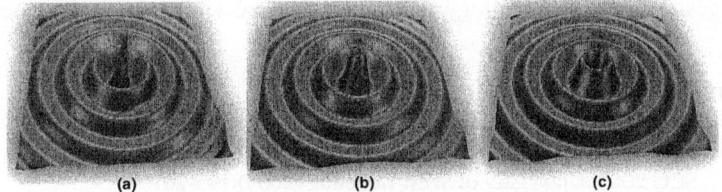

Fig. 10. A morphing example accomplished by modifying the vertices' offsets

The third test looks at the possibility to encode low amplitude or oscillating animations, such as, ripple or wave effects. In this case the differences between successive frames can be encoded at the level of the vertices' offsets, which is very compact because an offset is only a scalar value. When decoding, any changes in the offsets will trigger, according to eq. (2), an update of the vertices' coordinates. The morphing example from Fig. 10 simulates the propagation of a wave. It is a typical morphing example of an elevation model.

4 Conclusions

A MESHGRID object comprises one or several surface layers (CW) attached to and located within a volumetric grid (RG), where the RG samples the 3D space uniformly or non-uniformly depending on the shape and usage purposes of the object. Any deformation performed to the volume is transferred to the surface and vice versa. In addition, one MESHGRID model can be split into ROIs to optimize the memory usage. Since each ROI can be seen as an independent MESHGRID model, any operation that would need to be performed on the entire volume can be performed on each ROI separately. Moreover, a MESHGRID object encodes the information within a certain 3D space, which may contain several non-connected entities. During morphing some of these entities may merge while others may split, but each instance (3D frame) is derived from the same MESHGRID model. Therefore encoding a morphing animation with MESHGRID is rather straightforward: the first 3D frame needs to be encoded fully (as done for a static model), while for each subsequent morphed 3D frame one needs to identify for each ROI what changes occurred (if any) with respect to the previous frame and encode those differences. Usually lossy transformations are accepted in order to target a more compact stream. Based on a quality measure [22], for each ROI one may choose the most compact way to encode the differences: encode the CW and choose a uniformly distributed RG for which only its 8 corners need to be encoded, update the vertices offsets, keep the same CW but update the RG, or some combination of these 3. One might consider at certain time intervals to encode the 3D frames fully and not only difference frames, in order to prevent the degradation of the decoded morphing animation when the player does not decode all of the bitplanes corresponding to the encoded offsets or RG coordinates.

The paper demonstrates that MESHGRID can be used to efficiently represent the models for morphing purposes and to encode the sequence in a scalable and compact way. Since MESHGRID allows to subdivide the space into ROIs, memory efficient algorithms can be implemented. Moreover, the generated MPEG-4 stream [13] copes with changes in the mesh' topology and allows for free-viewpoint reconstruction.

References

1. Semwal, S., K., Chandrashekhar, K.: Cellular Automata for 3D Morphing of Volume Data. WSCG 2005, University of West Bohemia (2005) 195-201
2. Gomes, J., Darsa, L., Costa, B., Velho, L.: Morphing and Warping of Graphical Objects. Morgan Kaufmann (1999)
3. Lazarus, F., Verroust, A.: Three-dimensional metamorphosis: a survey. The Visual Computer, Vol. 14, Issue 8 - 9 (1998) 373 – 389
4. Gregory, A., State, A., Lin, M., Monocha, D., Livingston, M.: Feature-based surface decomposition for correspondence and morphing between polyhedra. In Computer Animation '98. IEEE Computer Society Press (1998) 64-71
5. Kanai, T., Suzuki, H., Kimura, F.: Metamorphosis of arbitrary triangular meshes. IEEE Computer Graphics and Applications, 20(2), (2000) 62-75
6. Lee, A. W. E, Dobkin, D., Sweldens, W., Schroder, P.: Multiresolution mesh morphing. In Computer Graphics (Proceedings Siggraph '99), (1999) 343-350
7. Attene, M., Biasotti, S., Spagnuolo, M.: Re-Meshing Techniques for Topological Analysis. International Conference on Shape Modeling; Applications May 07 -11 (2001)

8. Takahashi, S., Kokojima, Y., Ohbuchi, R.: Explicit Control of Topological Transitions in Morphing Shapes of 3D Meshes. Proceedings of the Pacific Graphics (2001) 70-79, Tokyo, Japan, Oct.16-18 (2001)
9. Yngve, G. Turk, G.: Robust Creation of Implicit Surfaces from Polygonal Meshes, IEEE Transactions on Visualization and Computer Graphics, Vol. 8, No 4, October-December (2002)
10. Hughes, J., F.: Scheduled Fourier Volume Morphing, SIGGRAPH '92: Proceedings of the 19th annual conference on Computer graphics and interactive techniques, (1992) 43-46.
11. He, T., Wang, S., Kaufman, A.: Wavelet-Based Volume Morphing. Proc. IEEE Visualization (1994) 85-92
12. Breen, D., E., Whitaker, R., T.: A Level-Set Approach for the Metamorphosis of Solid Models. IEEE Transactions on Visualization and Computer Graphics, Vol. 7, No 2, April-June (2001)
13. ISO/IEC 14496-16:2003, Information technology — Coding of audio-visual objects — Part 16: Animation Framework eXtension (AFX) (2000)
14. Salomie, I., A.: Extraction, Hierarchical Representation and Flexible Compression of Surface Meshes derived from 3D Data. Ph.D. Thesis, Dept. ETRO-IRIS, Vrije Universiteit Brussel, January (2005), http://www.etro.vub.ac.be/Members/SALOMIE.Ioan/Thesis.htm
15. Salomie, I., A., Deklerck R., Cornelis J.: System and method to obtain surface structures of multidimensional objects, and to represent those surface structures for animation, transmission and display, Ref. No. US 60/260,006 / US 60/303,680 / GB 01171578
16. Salomie, I., A., Munteanu, A., Gavrilescu, A., Lafruit, G., Schelkens, P., Deklerck, R., Cornelis, J.: MESHGRID — A Compact, Multi-Scalable and Animation-Friendly Surface Representation. Special issue of the IEEE CSVT journal on MPEG-4 SNHC, July (2004)
17. Bajaj, C., Coyle, E., Lin K.: Arbitrary Topology Shape Reconstruction from Planar Cross Sections. Graphical Models and Image Processing, Vol. 58, no. 6, (1996) 524-543
18. Lorensen, W., E., Cline, H., E.: Marching Cubes: A high resolution 3D surface construction algorithm. Comp. Graphics (SIGGRAPH '87), Vol. 21, (1987) 163-169
19. Shih, F., Y., Wong, W.: A new single-pass algorithm for extracting the mid-crack codes of multiple regions. Journal of Visual Communication and Image Representation, Vol. 3, no. 3, Sep. (1992) 217-224
20. Preda, M., Salomie, I., A., Preteux, F., Lafruit, G.: Virtual Character Definition and Animation within the MPEG-4 Standard. In M. Strintzis, N. Sarris (Ed.), 3-D Modeling and Animation: Synthesis and Analysis Techniques for the Human Body, chap. 2, Idea Group Inc., Hershey, PA, USA, Aug. (2003)
21. Aspert, N., Santa-Cruz, D., Ebrahimi, T.: MESH: Measuring Error between Surfaces using the Hausdorff distance. Proceedings of the IEEE International Conference on Multimedia and Expo (2002) (ICME), vol. I, 705-708. http://mesh.berlios.de.
22. Cernea, C., D., Salomie, I., A., Alecu, A., Schelkens, P., Munteanu, A.: Wavelet-based Scalable L-Iinfinite-Oriented Coding of MPEG-4 MeshGrid Surface Models. Accepted at the SPIE Symposium on Optics East, Boston, Massachusetts USA, 23-26 October (2005)

Hardware Accelerated Image-Based Rendering with Compressed Surface Light Fields and Multiresolution Geometry

Masaki Kitahara, Shinya Shimizu, Kazuto Kamikura, and Yashima Yoshiyuki

NTT Cyber Space Laboratories, NTT Corporation,
1-1, Hikari-no-oka, Yokosuka 239-0847, Japan
kitahara.masaki@lab.ntt.co.jp

Abstract. Surface Light Fields(SLF) are light fields parameterized to the surface of a geometric model. Past research in this area has explored the use of parameterization of aquired geometric model to the base mesh, in the context of rendering from compressed representation of the SLF. We further extend this aproach to enable hardware-accelerated SLF rendering. We show that our aproach enables hardware-accelerated, scalable rendering with commodity graphics hardware.

1 Introduction

Image-based rendering (IBR) methods render images of arbitrary views using captured rays aquired by multiple cameras. The surface light field (SLF) method[1] is one of the methods in the IBR framework, which use rays parameterized to the surface of a geometric model that approximates the scene/object, to render images of novel views. Such collection of rays are called SLF.

Since the amount of data of SLF is very large, many reseach related to SLF in the past has dealt with compression. In [2] and [3], methods to render images of novel views directly from a compressed representation by interpolating factorized (compressed) data, which is equivalent to performing interpolation of approximated SLF rays, were proposed. Since these methods do not decompress all the SLF rays prior to rendering, and perform decompression "on-the-fly" (we will refer to this type of reconstruction as "on-the-fly rendering"), the amount of memory used to store the data stays small. Functionality that allows on-the-fly rendering can be considered as one of the most important functionalities for a IBR-based compression method.

Graphics hardware optimized for various 3D rendering acceleration (we will refer to this type of hardware as "GPU") is available in the market for high-end to even low-end personal computers. Many hardware accelerated rendering algorithms that utilize such GPUs have been proposed for the purpose of realistic computer graphics and IBR. Chen et. al.[3] has proposed such method for SLF rendering.

On the other hand, Wood et. al.[2] has proposed a framework for SLF rendering that parameterize SLF to the base mesh[4], [5] that approximates the original geometric model, to enable fast rendering. Further more, they also introduce a view-dependent geometry refinement aproach to SLF rendering by utilizing such parameterization. Although on-the-fly rendering is possible, there are no known ways to perform interpolation of the SLF rays for rendering novel views with existing GPUs.

It is easy to see that, another effective way to use such parameterization is to use multiresolution geometry for SLF rendering. Remeshing methods such as the one proposed by Lee et. al.[5] can be used to generate a hierarchy of meshes for such purpose. Since rendering speed highly depends of the complexity of the geometric model, such scalable geometry should be effectively utilized to enable a more flexible rendering.

In this paper, we further extend the aproach in [2] to enable hardware accelerated, scalable, on-the-fly rendering. Based on our representation, interpolation of SLF rays can be performed directly from the compressed representation, completely with commodity GPUs. Furthermore, multiresolution representation of geometry is used to enable complexity scalable rendering. We present some experimental results based on our implementation to show the rendering perfomace and characteristics of our aproach.

2 Compressed Representation of SLF

2.1 Parameterization of SLF to the Base Mesh

In the SLF method, a geometic model that approximates the surface of the scene or the object must be acquired. Denoting u as the 3D coordinate on the surface of the geometric model, and w as direction of the ray, SLF can be defined as a function that maps (u, w) to the color of the ray (eg. RGB intensity values). In this paper, we denote SLF as $L(u, w)$. In other words, $L(u, w)$ can be interpreted as a value of the ray that originates from the point u on the surface of the geometric model, and points to direction w. In this section, we give a brief summary of the aproach proposed by Wood et. al.[2], mainly about the parameterization and the compressed representation.

In Woods' aproach, SLF is approximated by a weighted sum of K basis functions $v(w, k)$, $k = 0, 1, .., K - 1$ as expressed in the folowing equation.

$$L(u, w) \approx d(u) + \sum_{k=0}^{K-1} s(u, k) v(w, k) \qquad (1)$$

$d(u)$ is called a "diffuse" map, and represents a median value of the SLF rays with respect to a single point u. On the other hand, $s(u, k)$, $k = 0, 1, .., K-1$ are functions that represent the weights for the sum, which we refer to as weighting functions. In practice, discretely sampled values of SLF with respect to u and w is used to interpolate the SLF values for the whole surface and direction.

On the other hand, a parameterization that maps the original geometric model to the base mesh[4] is derived with methods such as one proposed in [5].

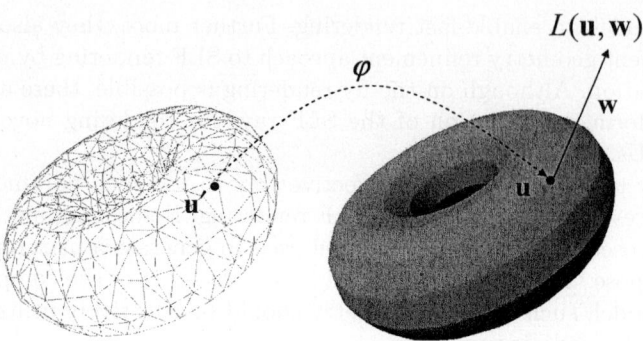

Fig. 1. SLF representation on parameterized geometry

To be precise, a one-to-one mapping $\varphi()$ that maps every point $\acute{u}$ on the surface of the base mesh to a point $u = \varphi(\acute{u})$ on surface of the original geometric model is derived. This concept is described in figure 1. If we view every base mesh triangle as 2D texture domains, texture mapping is defined for the original geometric model by the map $\varphi()$[7]. In Woods' aproach, SLF $L(u, w)$ is discretely sampled with respect to u on the points that the texels are mapped by the map $\varphi()$, as described in figure 2.

As for the sampling with respect to direction w, directions originating from the center of a spherical mesh generated by subdividing an octahedron, towards the vertices of the spherical mesh is used. One important remark is that direction w is defined in different coordinate systems depending on the sampling points u_i, $i = 0, 1, 2, .., I - 1$ on the geometric model. To be precise, relations between the global coordinate system $A_l, l = 0, 1, 2$ and the coordinate system $A_{l,i}, l = 0, 1, 2$ of the point u_i with normal n_i is given as follows.

$$A_{l,i} = 2(n_i^T A_l)n_i - A_l \qquad (2)$$

Although values for SLF rays that point inside the geometric model can not be defined to have any physical meaning, together with the transformation (2) and extrapolation for such rays, approximation of SLF with small numbers of basis functions is possible. See [2] for more details.

2.2 The Proposed Representation

There have been reports on hardware accelerated rendering with separable decompositions similar to equation (1)[3], [6]. In these methods, both basis and weighting functions are represented as 2D texture maps to enable hardware accelerated rendering.

As explained earlier, if the base mesh is parameterized to 2D texture domains, texture mapping can be applied to a mesh that is parameterized to the base mesh[7].

On the other hand, if the direction w is defined for the whole sphere, a 2D parameterization can be realized by spherical mapping (parameterization

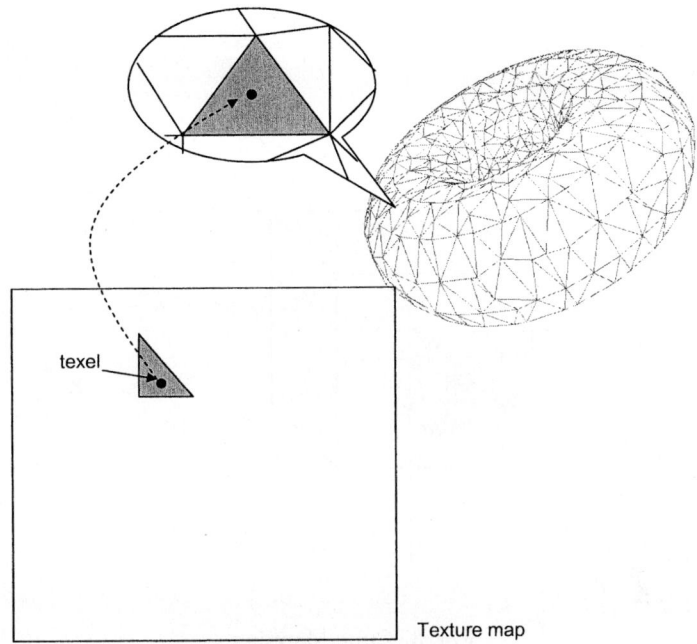

Fig. 2. Surface sampling by texture mapping to the base mesh

to (θ, ϕ)). The problem with this parameterization is that the distribution of sampling points on the sphere will be highly ununiform, and there are many complications for high quality rendering [8]. Regarding these facts, we propose to use cube mapping[8]. Cube mapping is one kind of texture mapping method that is often used for environment mapping, and is implemented in many recent commodity GPUs. Consider 3 vectors $\dot{\boldsymbol{w}}_0$, $\dot{\boldsymbol{w}}_1$, $\dot{\boldsymbol{w}}_2$ which represents directions assigned to the 3 vertices of a triangle in a (triangular) mesh. As described in figure 3,in cube mapping, the area formed by intersection of $\dot{\boldsymbol{w}}_0$, $\dot{\boldsymbol{w}}_1$, $\dot{\boldsymbol{w}}_2$ to the cube, is mapped to the triangle in the mesh.

In order to use cube mapping, the sampling of directions $\boldsymbol{w}$ for $L(\boldsymbol{u}, \boldsymbol{w})$ is given as follows. In the coordinate system $\boldsymbol{A}_{l,i}$, $l = 0, 1, 2$ of $\boldsymbol{u}_i$, consider a cube with all 6 faces perpendicular to each axix. As described in figure 4, directions $\boldsymbol{w}_j$, $j = 0, 1, 2, .., J - 1$ are sampled as vectors that originates from the origin to the square shaped cells formed by regular grids on each of the faces (these cells correspond to texels in a cube map).

As for sampling of the surface of the geometric model, we use the same kind of parameterization as [5]. In addition, we use a "hierarchy of meshes" with "subdivision connectivity"[4] constructed by remeshing the original geometric model with the parameterization $\varphi()$[5]. This type of remeshing generates N meshes which we denote M_n, $n = 0, 1, 2, .., N - 1$, where M_n is derived by applying midpoint subdivision uniformly to the base mesh n times, and perturbing the vertex $\boldsymbol{p}$ of n-times subdivided base mesh to $\varphi(\boldsymbol{p})$. The remeshing process is described

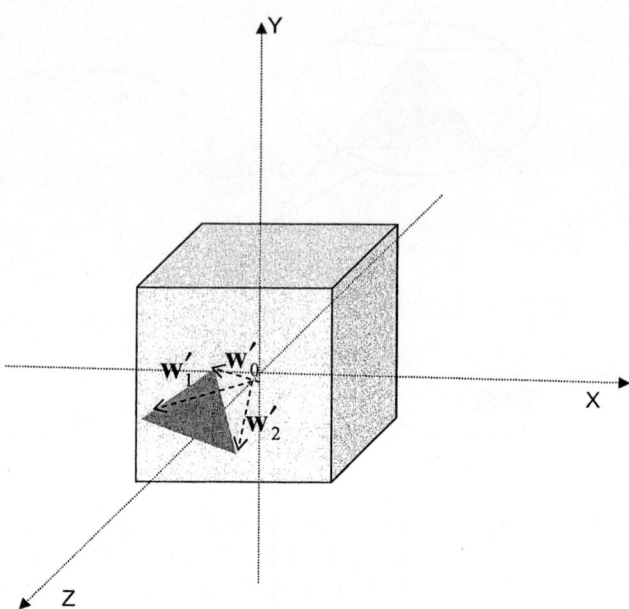

Fig. 3. Cube Mapping

in figure 5. Since mesh $M_{\acute{n}}$ is embedded in mesh M_n where $\acute{n} < n$, an appropriate mesh can be selected from hierarchy of meshes M_n, $n = 0, 1, 2, .., N-1$ depending on the rendering environment to render with efficient speed. It is obvious that if we consider a map $\varphi_n()$, that is $\varphi_n(\boldsymbol{p}) = \varphi(\boldsymbol{p})$ at the vertices, and is piecewise linear at other areas, mesh M_n for each level in the hierarchy has consistent parameterization to the base mesh. In other words, a texel in the 2D texture map which the base mesh is parameterized to, can be mapped to a surface point on the mesh M_n by $\varphi_n()$, for all levels $n = 0, 1, 2, .., N-1$. More importantly, hardware texture mapping works exactly the same as the maps $\varphi_n()$, $n = 0, 1, 2, .., N-1$. Thus, for mesh M_n in the hierarchy, we define the sampling points to be at the point where the texels are mapped, according to $\varphi_n()$.

Since the coordinate values of the sampling points $\boldsymbol{u}_i^n$, $i = 0, 1, 2, .., I-1$ generated on the mesh of each level n are different (ie. $\boldsymbol{u}_i^n \neq \boldsymbol{u}_i^{\acute{n}}$, if $n \neq \acute{n}$), for the best rendering result, different SLF rays should be sampled for each level n according to the coordinate values of the sampling points. However, the data size will be large. In our current proposal, we choose to aquire SLF with the most dense mesh (ie. mesh M_{N-1}), and map the same ray to other meshes M_n, $n = 0, 1, 2, .., N-2$. Although this aproach may induce some artifacts for meshes $M_n C n = 0, 1, 2, .., N-2$, artifacts are expected to be fairly small, since the remeshing and the parameterization methods such as the one described in [5] are designed to generate good approximations between meshes of different levels in the hierarchy.

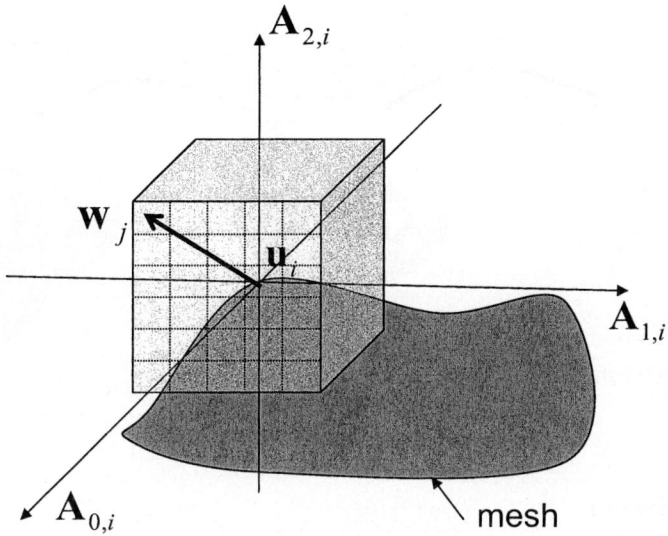

Fig. 4. Direction sampling

Rays are sampled from the input images to obtain values for the SLF representation described above, and compressed to yield the representation in equation (1). For this purpose, factorization methods that can deal with rays that point inside the mesh as "missing values" can be used, such as methods described in [2] and [9]. By using this kind of method, minimization of approximation errors with respect to the values that are "not missing" (ie. rays that point outside the mesh) can be conducted.

3 Rendering and Implementation

3.1 Texture Maps

For texture maps for the diffuse map and the weighting functions, the texture is decomposed to square block areas, and the right-angled triangle using the lower left area of the block is asigned to each of the base mesh, leaving the upper right area unused. This is described in figure 6.Since most GPUs support bilinear interpolation of texture maps, if the texels in upper right area are padded with zeros or any other values that are negligent of the values in the corresponding lower left area, discontinuities will be visible in the rendered images. Thus, values corresponding to the base mesh triangle that shares the edge with the base mesh triangle corresponding to the lower left corner of the block, is padded to the upper right area. As for texture maps for the basis functions, 2D textures corresponding to each of the cube map face are obtained.

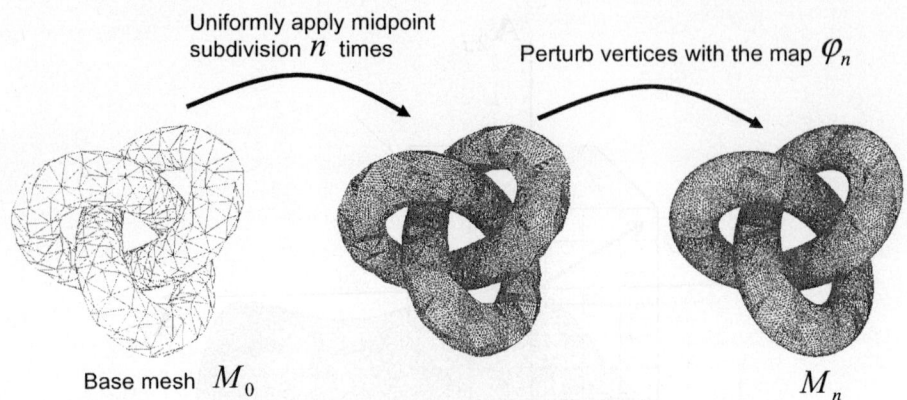

Fig. 5. Remeshing process for M_n

3.2 Rendering

Here, we describe a hardware accelerated, on-the-fly rendering algorithm that perform interpolation of rays. By "on-the-fly" rendering, we mean the following computation. Consider a ray that originates from the mesh M_n at a point u and intersects the image plane of the virtual camera, and has direction w. Denote n as the normal at u, and consider the reflected vector $\hat{w}$ derived by the equation below (Note that this reflection computation is needed to take account for coordinate system transformation in equation (2)).

$$\hat{w} = 2(n^T w)n - w \qquad (3)$$

$d(u)$, $s(u)$, and $v(\hat{w})$ is computed by interpolation in the texture domain (ie. diffuse map texture, basis function textures, and weighting function textures) with nearby texels, and $L(u, \hat{w})$ is computed by equation (1). An important remark is that none of the original SLF ray values are explicitly reconstructed in advance, where a naive aproach would reconstruct all SLF rays offline and place them in the memory prior to rendering. It is easy to see that above on-the-fly rendering is equvalent to interpolating the actual SLF rays, but keeps the memory consumption minimal.

A multi-pass rendering approach similar to methods described in [6] and [3] is implemented. We use one rendering pass to render the mesh with the diffuse map texture (corresponding to $d(u)$ in equation (1)), and two rendering passes to render the mesh with multiplication of the weighting function texture and the basis function texture(corresponding to $s(u,k)v(w,k)$ in equation (1)) per one approximation term, and resulting images of all rendering passes are blended together. This results in $2K+1$ rendering passes for SLF with K approximation terms. This rendering routine is executed every time the view point or the view direction of the virtual camera is changed.

As for rendering with diffuse texture maps, rendering can be done with the usual OpenGL or DirectX based implementations. On the other hand, for rendering the multiplication of the weighting function texture and the basis function

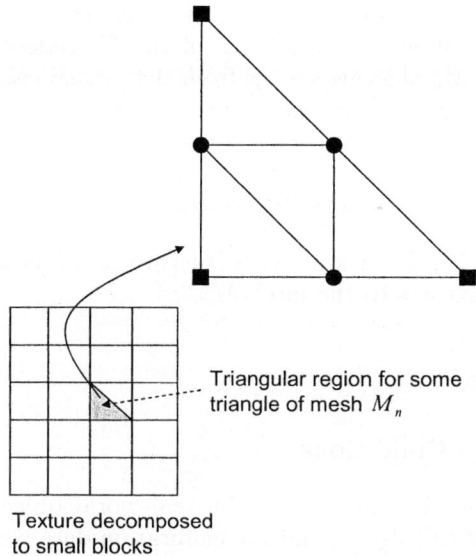

Fig. 6. Hierarchical structure of the texture coordinates

texture, texel values with negative signs and extended dynamic range must be dealt with. For such purpose, Nvidia GPUs with Register Combiner extention or ATI GPUs with Fragment Shader extension can be used. When using Register Combiner extension for example, if we attempt to compute $s(\boldsymbol{u},k)v(\boldsymbol{w},k)$ with one pass, negative values of $s(\boldsymbol{u},k)v(\boldsymbol{w},k)$ are clipped to zero. The same method as described in [3] is used here. Consider $s^+(\boldsymbol{u},k)$ as $s(\boldsymbol{u},k)$ with negative values clipped to zero, and $s^-(\boldsymbol{u},k)$ as $-s(\boldsymbol{u},k)$ with negative values clipped to zero. One pass is used to render $s^+(\boldsymbol{u},k)v(\boldsymbol{w},k)$, and another pass is rendered with $s^-(\boldsymbol{u},k)v(\boldsymbol{w},k)$, with the latter pass used for subtraction in the blending. This results in rendering $s^+(\boldsymbol{u},k)v(\boldsymbol{w},k) - s^-(\boldsymbol{u},k)v(\boldsymbol{w},k)$ with two passes.

When rendering with textures using the above approach, texture coordinates must be assigned for each 3-vertices of each triangle in the mesh M_n used for rendering. For the diffuse map and the weighting function textures, thanks to the map $\varphi_n()$, different texture coordinates for mesh of each level n do not have to be stored. To be precise, texture coordinates for mesh M_n is a subset of the texture coordinates for M_{n+1}. In other words, if texture coordinates for the most dense mesh M_{N-1} is available, texture coordinates for the mesh of any level n can be obtained, by selecting the appropriate subset. The hierarchical strucure of the texture coordinates is described in figure 6, where texture coordinates for vertices of mesh M_n is illustrated as squares, and texture coordinates for vertices of mesh M_{n+1} is illustrated as squares and circles.

On the other hand, the texture coordinates for the basis function textures depends on the view point/direction of the virtual camera, and must be dynamically calculated each time the view point/direction of the virtual camera is changed. Consider e_p, $p = 0, 1, 2, .., P-1$ as normalized vectors that point the direction of the virtual camera from each of the P vertices, which correspond to triangles of mesh M_n that are visible from the virtual camera. A vector r_p is computed by reflecting e_p with respect to the normal n_p at vertex indexed p. This can be computed by the following equation.

$$r_p = 2(n_p^T e_p) n_p - e_p \qquad (4)$$

Vectors r_p, $p = 0, 1, 2, .., P-1$ are used as texture coordinates for cube mapping the basis function textures to the mesh M_n.

4 Experiments

4.1 Experimental Conditions

SLF rays were acquired from images of a real world object. The geometrical model, the images of the object, and the calibration data was provided by Intel [10]. One example image is shown in figure 7.

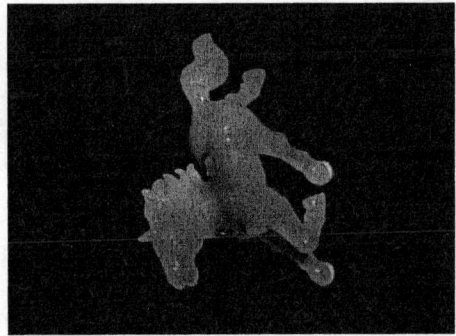

Fig. 7. One example of the image used for the experiments

The base mesh, the parameterization $\varphi()$, and the remeshed meshes were derived with the algorithm described in [5], resulting in a 3-level hierarchy of meshes ($N = 3$). The number of triangles for the mesh M_2 is 22976, M_1 is 5744, and M_0 is 1436. The number of sampling points I, with respect to u is $I = 45954$. On the other hand, number of sampling points with respect to w is $J = 384$, where the resolution of each cube map face is 8×8.

The mesh M_2 was projected on to each input images, and bilinear filtered value with the direction that the angle with w_j was the smallest, was used as the SLF ray value of w_j. The diffuse map was computed as the average of the SLF rays with respect to j for each u_i. The basis functions and the weighting functions were derived from the residual data using the principal component analysis method described in [9], treating rays that point outwards of the mesh M_2 as missing values.

The viewer was implemented using the C++ language, and was compiled using the compiler of Visual C++ .net. Register Combiner extension was used to implement the texture multiplication.

The following results were obtained on a PC with 1GB main memory and a Pentium4 3.4GHz CPU, with a Nvidia GeForce 6800 Ultra GPU.

4.2 Results

Figure 8 shows some examples of rendered images. In these examples, $K = 5$ approximation terms were used. This results in approximately 16:1000 compression compared to the discretely sampled SLF rays (these rays include ones that point inside the mesh), where the texture maps are in RGB 24bits and approximately 4.7 MBytes in total (with padded values). We do not disscuss about the

Fig. 8. Rendered images(left: M_2, middle: M_1, right: M_0)

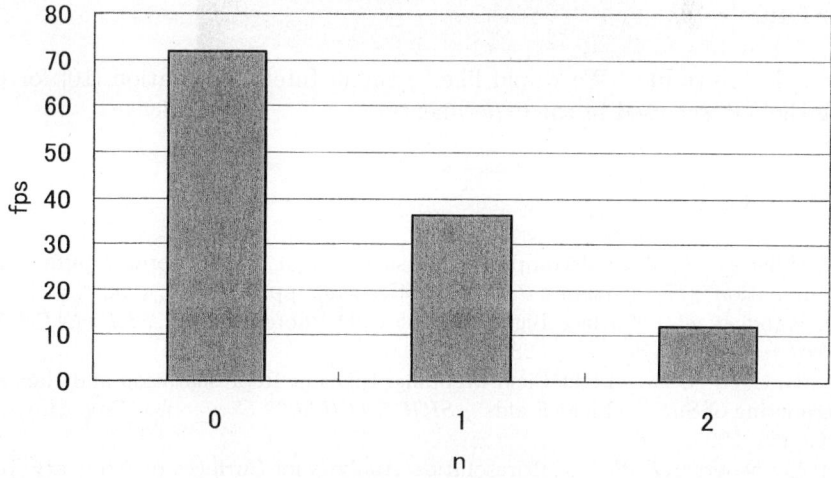

Fig. 9. Rendering speed vs mesh resolution

amount of approximation errors here, since the approximation error depends on the optimization method used to derive the basis functions and the weighting functions, and this is not the main point of our proposal. For example, using Woods' Principal Function Analysis method [2] instead of method in [9] should result in a similar approximation result that they provided.

Figure 9 shows the frame rate in fps (frames per second), corresponding to figure 8. In order to compute these fps values, an average value of results from rendering 100 times was evaluated.

As can be seen from figure 9, by reducing the level of the mesh by one level, the rendering speed can be faster two to three times. On the other hand, we can see from figure 8, although artifacts at the contours can be visible by reducing the level n, it is not significant since the remeshing does not induce significant differences between the shape of the meshes M_n, $n = 0, 1, 2$.

5 Conclusions

In this paper, we proposed a compressed representation of SLF that fully utilizes the multiresolution representation of the geometrical model, and rendering can be conducted directly from the compressed representation using commodity GPUs.

The main point of our paper was to propose a compressed representation of SLF that enable scalable (in terms of mesh resolution), hardware-accelerated rendering, and we did not discuss about the relation between the approximation error and the rendering speed. This time, we used a fairly naive optimization method to derive the basis functions and weighting functions due to implementation reasons. We suspect that an improvement can be achieved by using a more appropriate method in terms of approximation errors. We plan to develop such implementation, and compare with other methods to further assess our method in our future work.

Acknowledgements. We would like to thank Intel Corporation [10] for providing the dataset used in the experiments.

References

1. G. Miller et. al., "Lazy decompression of surface light fields for precomputed global illumination", *Eurographics Rendering Workshop*, pp. 281–292, 1998.
2. D. Wood et. al., "Surface Light Fields for 3D Photography", *SIGGRAPH 2000 Conference Proceedings*, pp. 287–296, 2000.
3. W. C. Chen et. al., "Light Field Mapping: Efficient Representation and Hardware Rendering of Surface Light Fields", *SIGGRAPH 2002 Conference Proceedings*, pp. 447–456, 2005.
4. M. Lounsberry et. al., "Multiresolution Analysis for Surfaces of Arbitrary Topological Type", *SPIE ACM Transactions on Graphics*, Vol 16, No.1, pp. 34–73, 1997.

5. W. Lee et. al., "Maps: Multiresolution adaptive parameterization of surfaces", *SIGGRAPH 1998 Conference Proceedings*, pp. 95–104, 1998.
6. J. Kautz et. al., "Interactive Rendering with Arbitrary BRDFs using Separable Approximations", *Eurographics Rendering Workshop*, pp. 247–260, 1999.
7. A. Certain et. al., "Interactive Multiresolution Surface Viewing", *SIGGRAPH 1996 Conference Proceedings*, pp. 91–98, 1996.
8. D. Voorhies et. al., "Reflection vector shading hardware", *SIGGRAPH 1994 Conference Proceedings*, pp. 163–166, 1994.
9. B. Grung et. al., "Missing values in principal component analysis", *Chemometrics and Intelligent Laboratory Systems*, pp. 125–139, 1998.
10. http://www.intel.com

Adaptive Vertex Chasing for the Lossless Geometry Coding of 3D Meshes

Haeyoung Lee and Sujin Park

Hongik University, Dept. of Computer Engineering,
72-1 Sangsoodong Mapogu, Seoul, Korea 121-791
{leeh, parks}@cs.hongik.ac.kr

Abstract. We present a new lossless geometry coding method for 3D triangle-quad meshes, Adaptive Vertex Chasing. Previous localized geometry coding methods have demonstrated better compression ratios than the global approach but they are considered hard to use in practice. It is because a proper linear quantization of the local range with three inputs is time-consuming, totally dependent on a user's trials and errors. Our new localized scheme replaces this quantization with an adaptive subdivision of the range with only one input, a subdivision level. The deeper level a user choose, the closer to the original the mesh will be restored. We also present a connectivity coder improved upon the current leading Angle-Analyzer's with a context-modeling. Without losing the current level of efficiency, our new coder provides simple and systematic way to control the balance between distortions and the bit-rates.

1 Introduction

Due to the technological advances in 3D sensing and scanning, highly detailed 3D models can be created easily. The huge size of these refined models has motivated active researches into 3D mesh compression. Many 3D mesh compression methods for single-rate [3], [4], [8], [9] and progressive transmission [6], [12], [15] have been introduced. While the low compression rate has been considered the most sought-after feature, other features such as resiliency, a small memory footprint [16], and random accessibility [11] are also important. Especially in practice with a high-speed network, simple and systematic algorithms can be more meaningful than complex algorithms with lower bit-rates depending on the applications.

Recently the localized approaches for the geometry coding in single-rate [9] and progressive transmissions [13], [12], [10] have demonstrated the lower rates than the most widely used Touma-Gotsman's global quantization method [3]. However the localized geometry coding is considered hard to use in practice because a proper quantization and the control of the balance between the bit-rates and distortions are time-consuming, totally dependent on a user's trials and errors.

In this paper, we present a new localized geometry coder which is simple and reliable without losing the current level of efficiency (see Figure 1, 2, and Table 2).

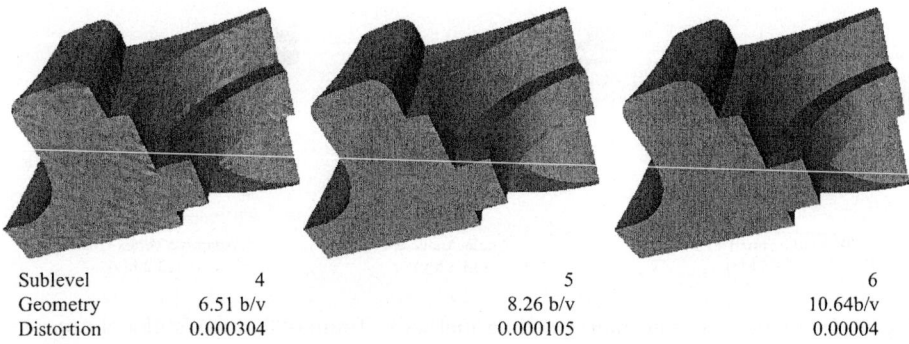

Sublevel	4	5	6
Geometry	6.51 b/v	8.26 b/v	10.64b/v
Distortion	0.000304	0.000105	0.00004

Fig. 1. A result by our adaptive vertex chasing (Fandisk model): Without losing efficiency, our Adaptive Vertex Chasing can control the balance between distortions and the bit-rates with a subdivision level. 10.64b/v by ours is still lowest than 11.66b/v by the Angle-Analyzer's [9] and 13.79b/v by the Touma-Gotsman's [3] with the same level of distortion. The distortions are measured by Metro [20].

We also improves the current leading Angle-Analyzer's connectivity coder [9] by a context-modeling. As a matter of fact, our Adaptive Vertex Chasing can be used with any of the connectivity coders in single-rate [8] or progressive transmissions [13], [12], [10].

1.1 Related Work

Geometry Coding. Since Deering's [1] first work on 3D triangle strips compression, several geometry coding methods have been suggested. Touma-Gotsman's global quantization with the linear prediction [3] has been the most widely used one. Recently the localized approaches were introduced with lower bit-rates for single-rate [9] and progressive transmission [13], [12], [10].

While the global approach uses a uniform quantization, mostly from 8 to 12 bit for global x, y, and z ranges, the localized approaches allow a non-uniform quantization of the smaller ranges (see Figure 2). The non-uniform quantizations contributed to lower rates but required 3 inputs for localized x, y, and z ranges, whose values are hard to find by trials and errors only. As a result, it is not easy to balance between the bit-rates and distortions.

Connectivity Coding. Regarding the connectivity coding, there has been active researches with theoretical studies. Typically the connectivity coding decides the type of compression, single-rate [3], [4], [8], [9] or progressive transmission [6], [12], [15]. Previous works are mostly concentrated on triangle meshes but [7], [14], [9], [15] are for quad or polygon meshes.

Context-Modeling. The concept of context-modeling is from 2D image processing [19]. A context is a helper to approximate next code by building conditional probabilities for codes. Recently context-modelings to the single-rate [17] and the progressive [10] were presented with better compression ratios.

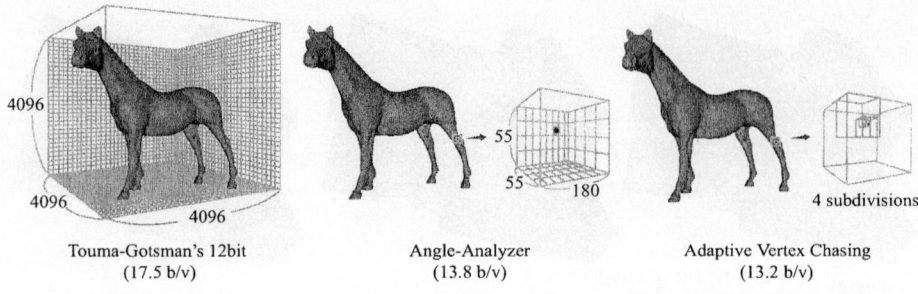

Fig. 2. Comparisons of geometry coding methods: Touma-Gotsman's global approach uses a simple uniform quantization (i.e., 12bit) but results in high bit-rates. Angle-Analyzer allows a non-uniform quantization (55 X 55 X 180) for low bit-rates but requires time-consuming trials and errors. With still low bit-rates, our Adaptive Vertex Chasing uses a simple adaptive subdivision.

During the last summer, we were trying to build a 3D website with Angle-Analyzer, known the best coder so far. There is an international standard, MPEG-4 3D mesh coding(3DMC), which adapted [2]. For connectivity and geometry coding, Touma-Gotsman's algorithm already showed about 60% better compression ratios than 3DMC and Angle-Analyzer about 20% better then Touma-Gotsman's. However we spent a lot of time to find proper quantizations rather than programming and making the website. Therefore, our goal was to create a new geometry coder which provides a simple and reliable control between the bit-rates and distortions while keeping low bit-rates.

1.2 Overview of Our Algorithm

We starts from the current leading coder, Angle-Analyzer [9], a connectivity-driven two-pass algorithm: While traversing the mesh, connectivity is coded first and then geometry is coded only if necessary. A gate as an oriented edge

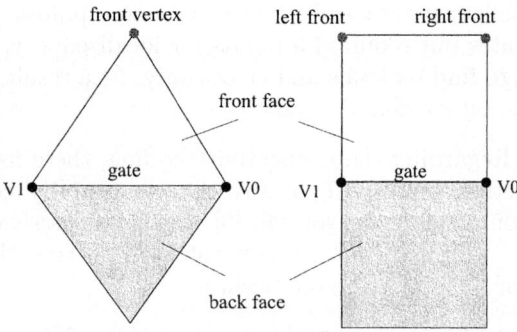

Fig. 3. Local gate configuration for a triangle and a quad mesh. A gate is an oriented edge from V0 to V1. The back face is visited and the front face is the next to be visited.

(see Figure 3) is required to traverse a mesh. Gates are organized in ordered lists, and a stack of gate lists are also needed to manage gate lists. The encoding is processed as follows:

Pseudo-Code:

```
repeat
        init
                pick the next uncoded connected component
                        1.pick a seed face (degree 3 or 4)
                        2.store its gates in ordered list
                        3.put the list on top of the stack of lists
        mesh traversal
                repeat
                        pop the first ordered list off the stack
                        repeat
                                1.pick the best gate in the ordered list
                                2.if the front face is unprocessed,
                                  -encode connectivity (triangle or quad)
                                  -store the resulting gates in ordered list
                                  -if new front vertex, encode geometry (*)
                                3. remove processed gate from the list
                        until the list is empty
                until the stack is empty
        until no more connected component
```

The 1st pass is to build a range containing all the localized vertices so the minimum and maximum of localized x, y, z coordinates are measured in the part marked by (*). In the 2nd pass the actual geometry encoding is performed with the found range. The decoding is a reverse process of the encoding.

Our new coder has the same process as the above except that a different method is applied for geometry encoding marked by (*) during the 2nd pass. The key idea of our new geometry encoding is to modify the range found according to each vertex position, adjust the level of subdivisions, and then subdivide the modified range while generating subcell numbers to encode (see Figure 2, 4). Only one input (i.e., an initial subdivision level) from the user is enough, instead of three inputs for linear quantizations for the Angle-Analyzer (see Table 2). The deeper we subdivide the range, the less distortion the restored has as shown in Figure 1. Now the control between distortions and the bit-rates by our new method becomes systematic and reliable. We also simulates the non-uniformity of the Angle-Analyzer by introducing a non-uniform subdivision for the range. For our connectivity encoding, a context-modeling using intrinsic properties is applied to Angle-Analyzer's [9]and reduces the bit-rates further.

As a result, our new single-rate coder can produce competitive bit-rates as shown in Table 2 in a much simpler and more systematic way than Angle-Analyzer [9].

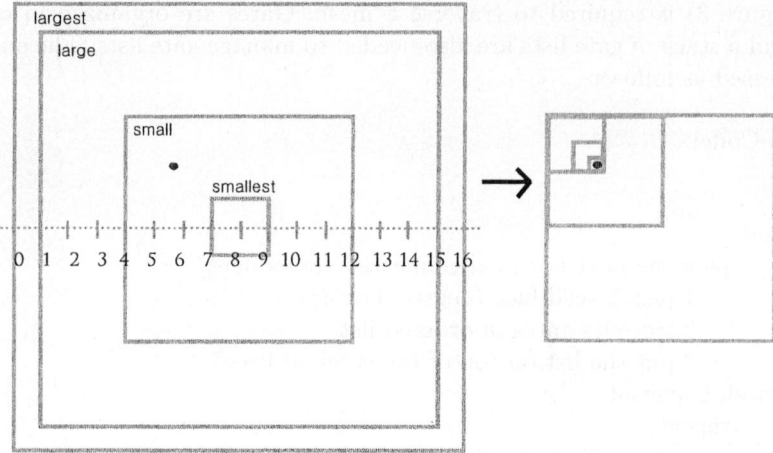

Fig. 4. The local range classification example: The local range is adjusted to one of 4 subranges based on each vertex position. The 4 subranges are the largest (the original local range), the large, the small, and the smallest. The number of subdivisions is decreased by one from the largest with a given depth. With a given depth 6, the red vertex belongs to the small so 4 subdivisions will be actually executed.

2 Angle-Analyzer Revisited

Angle-Analyzer(AA) [9] can compress triangle, quad, and hybrid of triangle-quad meshes in a single or multi-component forms. In this paper we will concentrate on triangle meshes because the basic idea is same for quad meshes. The pseudo code in Section 1.2 shows the overall process.

2.1 AA's Connectivity Coding

Connectivity is coded by 5 descriptors for triangle meshes 5, 8 descriptors for quad meshes, and 12 descriptors for hybrid of triangle-quad meshes. If the front vertex is not processed, C(Create) is coded and geometry coding for this vertex follows. Two new gates from the front face replace the current gate in the ordered gatelist. If the front vertex is already processed, Clockwise(CW) or counterclockwise(CCW) turning around the gate can locate the front vertex. one new gate from the front face replaces the current gate and the next(CW) or previous gate(CCW) in the ordered gatlist. If no front vertex, S(Skip) is coded. If the visited front vertex can not be found, J(Join) occurs with an offset. The offset is an index of the array of visited vertices, sorted by the Euclidean distance to V1 of the gate. The decoder will use the offset to locate the front vertex from the same array of sorted vertices. If the front vertex belongs to the current gatelist, splitting the current gatelist into two gatelists occurs. If not, merging the current gatelist and the gatelist with the front vertex occurs. Since the code J requires an offset and additional processing, minimizing the occurrences of J is important for low bit-rates and fast processing.

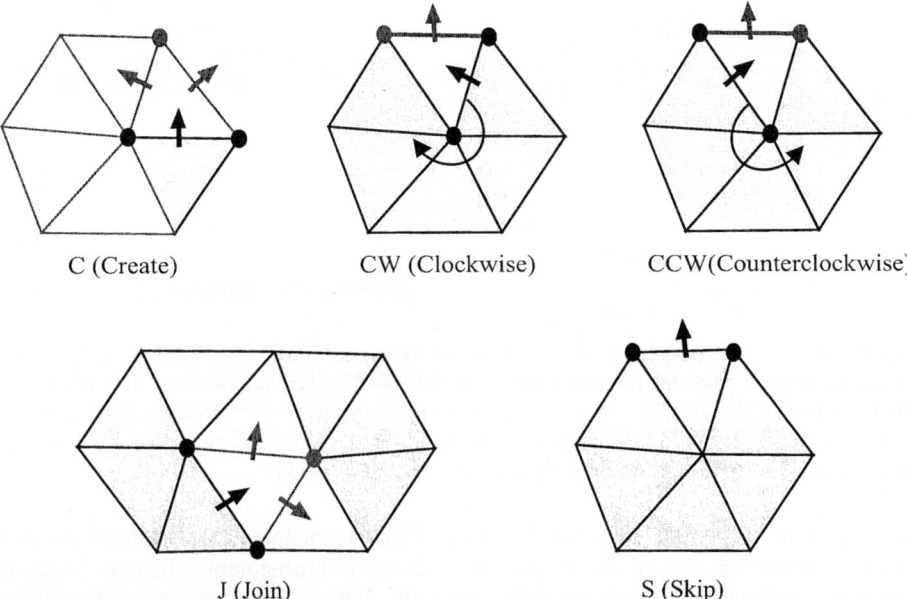

Fig. 5. 5 descriptors for connectivity of triangle meshes:C for new front vertex. CW or CCW for already processed front vertex, which can be found by either clockwise or counterclockwise turning around the gate, S for no front vertex. J for processed but impossible to locate the position by turning.

The adaptive traversal of the mesh plays a role to avoid J. AA chooses a gate having the minimum angle with the following gate as for the best gate to visit next. The choice of the gate based on the intrinsic mesh property consequently forces to visit the concave area of the gatelist first generatng CW or CCW, reduces the occurrences of J, and results in low bit-rates.

The three vertices of a seed face in a header file will be passed to the decoder. The decoder will process the same adaptive traversal of the mesh by building the same gatelists with the same minimum-angle rule and restore connectivity with decoded descriptors.

2.2 AA's Geometry Coding

To locate the vertex position, AA suggested two approaches. One is a localized approach and the other is an angle-based approach. Since our new geometry coding method is improved upon the localized approach, we will explain the localized approach in this paper. For the angle-based geometry coding, please refer to [9].

As shown in Figure 6, the local coordinate system is defined on each front face. The current gate will be the localized x-axis. The rotation of the x-axis around the normal of the back face by -90 degree will give the localized y-axis. The localized z-axis can be found either by cross product of the x-axis and

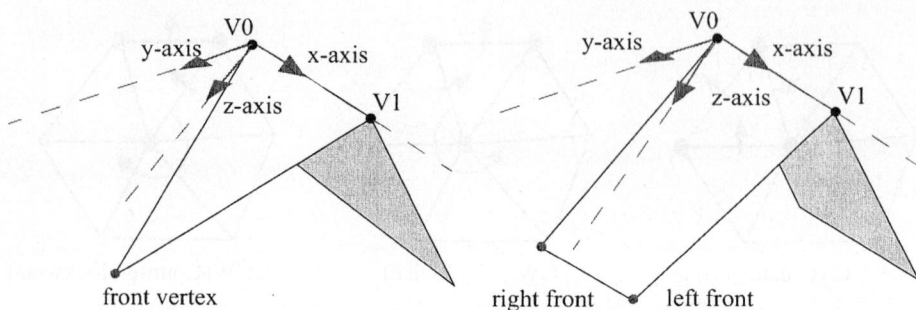

Fig. 6. AA's localized coordinate system on the front face. The current gate is the localized x-axis. The -90 degree rotated of the localized x-axis around the normal of the back face is the localized y-axis. The cross product of the localized x-axis and y-axis is the z-axis. The global coordinates of the front vertex is transformed to this localized coordinate system and then linearly quantized and encoded.

the y-axis or the reversed normal vector of the back face. For triangle meshes, the global coordinates of the front vertex is to be transformed to this local coordinate system. For quad meshes, both the left and the right front vertices will be transformed to the local coordinate system. During the 1st pass, a local bounding range containing every vertex will be calculated. In the 2nd pass, the vertex position is quantized linearly and encoded. A decoding simulation is processed to infer the decoded position of the front vertex. The encoder uses this updated position in the following computation to synchronize with the decoder.

Geometry decoding is also symmetric to encoding. After finding the unit vectors on the local coordinate axis, the decoded local coordinates are transformed to the global coordinates for the restored front vertex.

Discussion. Contrary to the global quantization method [3], AA's localized geometry coding restricts the bounding box of the mesh to just local coordinates. With quantization number relatively small to the one used in global quantization (see Figure 2, it could specify the vertex position more accurately. However, to find the proper quantization numbers for each localized x, y, and z range, there is no systematic way but a user's trials and errors with different sets of numbers. As shown in Table 2, various numbers depending on models (i.e., 50 - 110 for x and y ranges and 90 - 300 for z range) are found for the same distortion of the 12-bit global quantization.

3 Our New Geometry Coding: Adaptive Vertex Chasing

The localized geometry coding methods have demonstrated better bit-rates than the global approach. Especially a non-uniform quantization in [13], [9], [10] showed the lowest geometry bit-rates so far. Every localized geometry coding has the following steps:

- Define a localized coordinate system
- Transform the global coordinates to the local coordinates
- Quantize localized coordinate values into symbols (*)
- Encode the generated sequences of symbols

However in the 3rd step marked by (*) it is very hard and time-consuming to find a proper set of quantization numbers for acceptable bit-rates with low distortions: From 50 to 110 for x and y ranges and from 90 to 300 for z range depending on models (see the Table 2). A user should keep trying different sets of numbers, restore the decompressed, measure the distortions, and repeat the process again until proper bit-rates with tolerable distortions. Our adaptive vertex chasing replaces this quantization step marked by (*) in the above with an adaptive subdivision of the local range. Instead of three different quantization numbers, our method only requires one input, a depth of subdivisions (Figure 2). The deeper a user choose, the closer to the original the restored model will be.

Table 1. Distribution of geometry in the localized range: The local range is classified into 4 types based on each vertex position as shown in Figure 4: largest, large, small, smallest. The number of vertices in each range are shown. The last column shows the rate of the number of vertices in the largest over the total number of vertices. Only a few belong to the largest and the most vertices belong to one type so low entropy in the sequence of types are resulted in.

Model	No. of Vertices	largest	large	small	smallest	% of largest
fandisk	6475	27	587	5717	141	0.4%
horse	19851	3	8929	10884	38	0.02%
maxpl.	25445	26	9230	16020	166	0.1%
tf2	14169	8	11326	2734	98	0.05%
dino	14070	4	3054	10974	35	0.03%
feline	19864	11	1812	46037	2001	0.05%
venus	8268	29	984	7180	72	0.35%

We notice that we can classify this local range into 4 types based on each vertex position as shown in Table 1 and Figure 4. Only a few, about 0.14% on average of the total vertices belong to the largest of the range, which requires more subdivisions. Therefore we adjust the given depth further based on the classified range each vertex belongs. The size of the smallest range is 1/8 of the largest range so 3 subdivisions from the largest can be saved. We simply decrement the depth by one from the largest to each smaller range. For example, with a given depth 6, we actually apply 5, 4, and 3 to the large, the small, and the smallest. Notice also that the most vertices of each model belong to one type, the small or the large, which results in a low entropy in the sequence of types and hence contributes to low bit-rates.

To simulate the non-uniform quantization of previous geometry coding, we apply a non-uniform subdivision to this adjusted local range such as 2 X 2 X 4

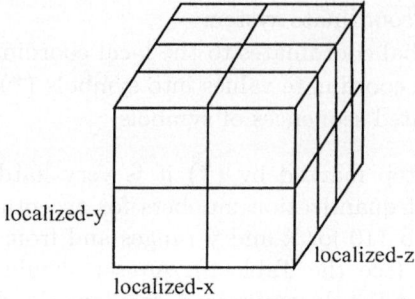

Fig. 7. Non-uniform subdivision of the range: 2 X 2 X 4 for x X y X z. To simulate the non-uniform quantization of previous geometry coding, a non-uniform subdivision of the range is introduced.

(see Figure 7). Various patterns for non-uniformity can also be practiced but 2 X 2 X 4 is already enough for lower bit-rates than Angle-Analyzer.

Therefore, by our new geometry coding, a type of the local range and subcell numbers tracing each vertex position will be generated. With the size of the local range and a given depth for subdivisions from the encoder, the decoder can restore the vertex position in reverse.

As a result, our adaptive vertex chasing provides simple and intuitive control between distortions and the bit-rates as shown in Figure 1 and still keep efficiency as shown in Table 2.

4 Context-Modeling for Geometry and Connectivity Coding

An entropy-based arithmetic coder [18] is used to code sequences of symbols generated for both geometry and connectivity coding. Recently, the context-modeling, originated from 2D image processing [19], has been suggested for better compression ratios in isosurface compressions [17] and [10]. Therefore we experiment a context-modeling for both geometry and connectivity coding of 3D meshes.

Context for Connectivity Coding. The Angle-Analyzer choose the next gate to traverse based on angles between gates in succession. We notice that these angles are related to the connectivity codes. If the angle is small (less than 60 degrees), a CW(clockwise) usually occurs. If the angle is large (more than 200 degrees), a C(create) usually occurs. Therefore we choose to use context 3: the previous angle, the previous code, and the current angle. Since the range of the angles in floating point format is wide, we simply classified them into 4 groups and used 4 codes for the angles. Our context simply reduces on average 19% bit-rates lower than Angle-Analyzer, as shown in the Table 2.

Context for Geometry Coding. We also apply a context-modeling to geometry coding. 3 parent subcell numbers in succession as for context 3 produces the best

Table 2. Results: Con. for connectiviy bit-rates. Geo. for geometry bit-rates. The unit is b/v. AA means by Angle-Analyzer [9] while AVC by our method. The bit-rates by two methods have the same level of distortions (i.e., 12-bit global quantization) by Metro [20]. Our new method shows competitive ratios with depth as one input while AA requires various sets of quantization numbers as three inputs.

Model	No. of Vertices	Con. AA	Geo. AA	Quantization AA (x,y,z)	Con. AVC	Geo. AVC	Depth AVC
fandisk	6475	1.2	11.9	(50,50,280)	0.95	10.6	6
bunny	35947	0.9	12.3	(80,80,160)	0.8	11.3	6
horse	19851	1.4	12.5	(55,55,180)	0.94	12.2	6
maxplanck	25445	1.4	13.8	(50,50,90)	1.21	15.1	6
tf2	14169	1.0	11.5	(60,60,120)	0.6	12.4	6
dinosaur	14070	1.7	17.0	(100,100,200)	1.38	18.2	7
feline	19864	1.5	13.8	(60,60,120)	1.21	13.9	6
venus	8268	2.0	19.6	(110,110,300)	1.75	18.5	7

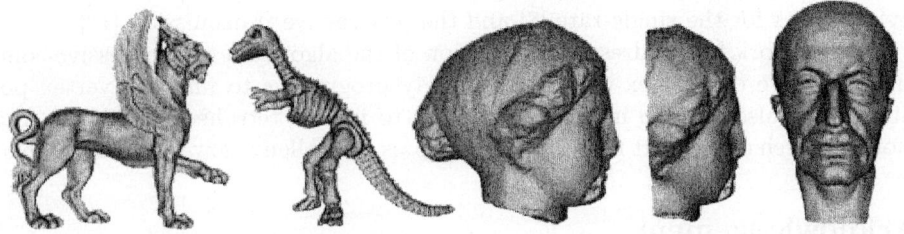

Fig. 8. Triangle meshes we tested

bit-rates among our trials. There seems a pattern to chase the vertex position during subdivisions.

5 Results

Our Adaptive Vertex Chasing produces a little better geometry coding than Angle-Analyzer [9], the current leading geometry coder so far (see Table 2). Even if the efficiency of our Adaptive Vertex Chasing is improved a little, the simplicity and the reliability of our algorithm is much better than Angle-Analyzer. A user simply starts with a same depth for every model and if intolerable distortions in the decompressed, then choose a deeper level to subdivide. In this way, the balance between distortions and the bit-rates can be systematically controlled as shown in Figure 1. Our connectivity coding with a context-modeling also produces better ratios than the original connectivity. Our Adaptive Vertex Chasing can handle geometry coding of quad meshes in the same way as for triangle meshes.

6 Conclusion and Future Work

We have presented a new localized geometry coding, Adaptive Vertex Chasing with a connectivity coding improved upon Angle-Analyzer's [9]. Our new single-rate coder can handle triangle, quad, hybrid of triangle-quad meshes and deal with high genus and multi-components as Angle-Analyzer did.

The popularity of the global quantization by [3] comes mostly from simple and intuitive control of the bit-rates and distortions. Our goal is to design a simple and intuitive coding method while keeping the efficiency of localized geometry coding, which is better than the global approach. With insights in the distribution of vertex positions in the local range, we introduces an adaptive subdivision to replace impractical quantization of Angle-Analyzer's geometry coding. Furthermore to simulate non-uniform quantization, non-uniform subdivisions are practiced.

As a result, like the simple global geometry coding, with one input our Adaptive Vertex Chasing can control the balance between the bit-rates and distortions. Our Adaptive Vertex Chasing can be used with any of previous connectivity coders for the single-rate [8] and the progressive transmission [12].

Future work will address the extension of the algorithm to progressive compression since our vertex chasing is already progressive to find the vertex positions. We also plan to improve our coder to handle tetrahedral meshes. And more research on context modeling will help us to challenge low bit-rates further.

Acknowledgement

This work was supported by grant No. R01-2005-000-10120-0 from Korea Science and Engineering Foundation in Ministry of Science & Technology.

References

1. Deering M.: "Geometry Compression", Siggraph 95 Conference Proceedings, 1995.
2. Taubin G., Rossignac J.: "Geometric compression through topological surgery", Research Report RC-20340, IBM Research Division, 1996.
3. Touma C., Gotsman C.: "Triangle Mesh Compression", Graphics Interface 98 Conference Proceedings, 1998.
4. Rossignac J.: "EdgeBreaker: Connectivity Compression for Triangle Meshes", IEEE Transactions on Visualization and Computer Graphics, 1999.
5. Devillers O., Gandoin P-M.: "Geometric Compression for Interactive Transmission", Visualization 2000 Conference Proceedings, 2000.
6. Hoppe H.: "Progressive Meshes", Siggraph 96 Conference Proceedings, 1996.
7. Isenburg M., Snoeyink J.: "Face Fixer: Compressing Polygon Meshes With Properties", ACM SIGGRAPH 2000 Conference Proceedings, 2000.
8. Alliez P., Desbrun M.: "Valence-Driven Connectivity Encoding of 3D Meshes", Computer Graphics Forum (Proc. Eurographics'01), 2001.
9. Lee H., Alliez P., Desbrun M.: "Angle-Analyzer: A Triangle-Quad Mesh Codec", Computer Graphics Forum (Proc. Eurographics'02), 2002.

10. Lee H., Desbrun M., Schröder P.: "Progressive Encoding of Complex Isosurfaces", ACM Transactions on Graphics (Proc. Siggraphics'03), 2003.
11. Choe S., Kim J., Lee H., Lee S., Seidel H.-P.: "Mesh Compression with Random Accessibility", The 5th Korea-Israel Bi-National Conference on Geometric Modeling and Computer Graphics, 2004.
12. Pierre A., Desbrun M.: "Progressive Encoding for Lossless Transmission of 3D Meshes", ACM Siggraph Conference Proc, 2001.
13. Khodakovsky A., Schröder P., Sweldens W.: "Progressive Geometry Compression", ACM Siggraph Conference Proceedings, 2000.
14. Khodakovsky A., Alliez P., Desbrun M., Schröder P.: "Near-Optimal Connectivity Encoding of 2-Manifold Polygon Meshes", Special Issue of Graphical Model, 2002.
15. Gandoin P-M., Devillers O.: "Progressive Lossless Compression of Arbitrary Simplicial Complexes", ACM Trans. on Graphics, Vol. 21(3), 2002.
16. Isenburg M., Gumhold S.: "Out-of-core compression for gigantic polygon meshes", ACM Transactions on Graphics, Vol. 22(3), 2003.
17. Taubin G.: "BLIC: Bi-Level Isosurface Compression", Proc. of IEEE Visualization, 2002.
18. Wheeler F.: Adaptive Arithmetic Coding Source Code, http://www.cipr.rpi.edu/~wheeler/ac, 1996.
19. Pennebaker W. B., Mitchell J. L.: "JPEG: Still Image Date Data Compression Standard", Van Nostrand Reinhold, 1993.
20. Cignoni P., Rocchini C., Scopigno R.: "Metro: Measuring Error on Simplified Surfaces", Computer Graphics Forum, Vol. 17(2), 1998.

Analysis and Performance Evaluation of Flexible Marcoblock Ordering for H.264 Video Transmission over Packet-Lossy Networks

Changhoon Yim[1,*], Wonjung Kim[2], and Hyesook Lim[2]

[1] Konkuk University, Seoul 143-701, Korea
cyim@konkuk.ac.kr
[2] Ewha W. University, Seoul 120-750, Korea
hlim@ewha.ac.kr

Abstract. Flexible macroblock ordering (FMO) is an error resilience feature of H.264 for video transmission over packet-lossy networks. Error concealment (EC) provides a basic error resilience tool for decoder to recover lost information and to reduce error propagation effect. This paper presents an analysis on the dependency of EC performance on FMO modes through the investigation of the expected number of correctly received neighboring macroblocks for a lost macroblock. We present simulation results and performance evaluation of FMO with different encoding parameters in various packet loss rates in the context of EC performance. Simulation results show that FMO provides an effective feature for PSNR improvement in environments with high packet loss rates, especially when intra-frame period is large.

1 Introduction

H.264 is the most recent international video coding standard of the ITU-T Video Coding Experts Group (VCEG) and ISO/IEC Moving Pictures Experts Group (MPEG) [1]. The goals of H.264 include improved coding efficiency and improved network adaptation [2], [3]. The need for location-independent and fast access to multimedia services on Internet and wireless networks has been steadily increased. Internet protocol (IP) and most current and future wireless networks provide multimedia services through packet-switched transmission modes. Three major applications exist in IP-based networks: download type, streaming, and conversational applications [2]. In download type applications, video streams can be transmistted without timing constraints, and whole packets can be delivered with reliable Transmission Control Protocol (TCP). In TCP, packet delivery can be gauranteed with retransmission mechanism. However in streaming and conversational applications, video streams need to be transmitted in real-time with timing constraints. Current IP-based networks cannot provide gauranteed delivery in real-time. Hence packet loss is inevitable in real-time video transmission over IP networks. For real-time video transmission in packet-switched networks,

---

[*] This paper was supported by Konkuk University in 2005.

unreliable User Datagram Protocol (UDP) is normally adopted as transport protocol which does not perform retransmission for lost packets.

Usually two kinds of errors exist in packet-switched transmission over wireless networks: bit inversion errors and packet losses [3], [4], [5]. Bit-inversion errors would result in bit-errorneous packets if the number of bit inversion in a packet is greater than the correction capability of forward error correction (FEC). In the standardization of H.264 for reference software development, bit-errorneous packets are assumed to be discarded [3]. Hence in packet-switched H.264 video transmission, packet losses occur quite often for real-time applications.

In previous video compression standards, the following error resilience features were used: picture segmentation, intra placement, reference picture selection, and data partioning. H.264 introduces three new error resilience features: parameter sets, redundant slices (RS), flexible macroblock ordering (FMO) [2], [3]. Parameter sets include crucial information to start decoding, and can be sent out-of-band using reliable transmission protocol. In the same bit-stream, one or more redundant representation can exist with RS feature. It might be effective in highly error-prone environments, but it would require quite amount of extra bits to be effective when the packet loss rate becomes high.

Macroblock order can be different from the raster scan order in FMO. FMO can be quite effective for the improvement of error concealment performance in packet-lossy networks. There are several modes in FMO, and the best mode would be dependent on packet loss rates. Other encoding parameters including intra-frame period may also affect the performance of error concealment for lost slices.

In this paper, we present analysis and performance evaluation of FMO feature for H.264 video transmission over packet-lossy networks. This work would provide a useful guideline for the selection of FMO mode in different encoding paramters including intra-frame period and in various packet loss rates.

2   FMO in H.264

This section presents mathematical formulation of FMO modes in H.264. Let $f(i,j)$ be the intensity value at pixel coordinate (i,j) in current frame. Let K and L be the number of macroblocks in vertical and in horizontal direction, respectively. Let x and y be the macroblock (MB) coordinate in vertical and in horizontal derection, respectively, with $0 \leq x < K$ and $0 \leq y < L$. Let $mb(x,y)$ represent the MB at macroblock coordinate (x,y). If $N \times N$ is the MB size, N is 16 and 8 for luminance and chrominance components, respectively. The macroblock $mb(x,y)$ is composed of pixels with coordinates (i,j) such that $(N-1)x \leq i < Nx$ and $(N-1)y \leq j < Ny$.

Slice is a set of macroblocks. In this paper, two slices per frame case is presented for comparison with and without FMO. Other cases can be similarly defined and compared.

Let S_0 and S_1 represent slice 0 and 1, respectively. If (x_0, y_0) is the last macroblock coordinate of slice 0 in raster scan order, the macroblock coordinates of S_0 and S_1 can be represented as follows.

$$S_0 = \{mb(x,y) : 0 \leq x < x_0, 0 \leq y < L\} \cup \{mb(x,y) : x = x_0, 0 \leq y \leq y_0\},$$

$$S_1 = \{mb(x,y) : x_0 < x < K, 0 < y < L\} \cup \{mb(x,y) : x = x_0, y_0 < y < L\}.$$

When FMO is not used, it is simply called as raster scan mode.

When FMO is used, a set of macroblocks is called slice group. Let S_0^i and S_1^i represent slice group 0 and 1, respectively, when interleaved mode FMO is used. Then S_0^i and S_1^i can be represented as a set of macroblocks:

$$S_0^i = \{mb(2x, y) : 0 \leq x < K/2, 0 \leq y < L\},$$

$$S_1^i = \{mb(2x+1, y) : 0 \leq x < K/2, 0 \leq y < L\}.$$

Let S_0^d and S_1^d represent slice group 0 and 1, respectively, when dispersed mode FMO is used. Then S_0^d and S_1^d can be represented as:

$$S_0^d = \{mb(2x, 2y) \cup mb(2x+1, 2y+1) : 0 \leq x < K/2, 0 \leq y < L/2\},$$

$$S_1^d = \{mb(2x, 2y+1) \cup mb(2x+1, 2y) : 0 \leq x < K/2, 0 \leq y < L/2\}.$$

3 Error Concealment in H.264

In current H.264 decoder reference software [8], intra- and inter-frame error concealment (EC) algorithms are implemented as a non-normative feature.

Intra-frame EC algorithm is based on weighted pixel averaging [3], [6]. If $mb(x,y)$ is lost, it is concealed from pixel values of four spatial neighboring MBs: $mb(x-1,y)$, $mb(x+1,y)$, $mb(x,y-1)$, $mb(x,y+1)$. If the lost MB has at least two correctly received neighboring MBs, only these neighboring MBs are used in the concealment process. Otherwise, previously concealed neighboring MBs are used for spatial EC. If previously concealed neighboring MBs are used for EC, spatial error propagation would occur and the performance of EC would be worse compared to the case just using correctly received neighboring MBs. Hence when a MB is lost, the performance of EC would depend on the number of correctly received MBs among four neighboring MBs.

Inter-frame EC uses motion vector recovery algorithm based on boundary matching [3], [6], [7]. The motion activity of correctly received slices of current frame is investigated first. If the average length of motion vector (MV) is smaller than a pre-defined threshold, all lost MBs are simply concealed by copying the spatially corresponding MBs in the reference frame. Otherwise, motion vector recovery algorithm is invoked for motion-compensated error concealment.

Let $v(x,y)$ represent motion vector of macroblock $mb(x,y)$. If $mb(x,y)$ is lost, then $v(x,y)$ is selected (concealed) among motion vectors of neighboring macroblocks and zero motion vector. Let $C_v(x,y)$ represent the set of candidate motion vectors to be selected as $v(x,y)$.

$$C_v(x,y) = \{v(x-1,y), v(x+1,y), v(x,y-1), v(x,y+1), v_0\} \quad (1)$$

where v_0 is the zero motion vector. Let $\hat{f}(i,j)$ represent the intensity value at coordinate (i,j) in reference frame. Let d_x and d_y represent the vertical and horizontal component of candidate motion vector, respectively. Let D_L, D_R, D_T, and D_B represent side matching distortion of concealed macroblock $mb(x,y)$ and neighboring MBs in left, right, top, and bottom directions, respectively. Then

$$D_L = \sum_{i=(N-1)x}^{Nx-1} |\hat{f}(i+d_x,(N-1)y+d_y) - f(i,(N-1)y-1)|,$$

$$D_R = \sum_{i=(N-1)x}^{Nx-1} |\hat{f}(i+d_x,Ny-1+d_y) - f(i,Ny)|,$$

$$D_T = \sum_{j=(N-1)y}^{Ny-1} |\hat{f}((N-1)x+d_x,j+d_y) - f((N-1)x-1,j)|,$$

$$D_B = \sum_{j=(N-1)y}^{Ny-1} |\hat{f}(Nx-1+d_x,j+d_y) - f(Nx,j)|.$$

Let D represent the boundary matching distortion for motion vector selection. When correctly received neighboring macroblock exist, the boundary matching distortion is calculated only over them. For example, if top and bottom MBs, i.e., $mb(x-1,y)$ and $mb(x+1,y)$, are correctly received, then only D_T and D_B are included in the calculation of D, i.e., $D = D_T + D_B$. If there is no correctly received MB, then concealed neighboring MBs are included in the calculation of D. In this case, inter-frame EC performance would be degradaded. The motion vector which gives minimal boundary matching distortion is selected among candidate motion vector as:

$$\arg\min_{(d_x,d_y)\in C_v(x,y)} D. \qquad (2)$$

The accuracy of boundary matching would depend on the number of correctly received neighboring MBs, and the performance of inter-frame EC would also depend on the number of correctly received neighboring MBs. When a slice or slice group is lost in a frame, some errors would remain even though EC is performed, and these errors would propagate in temporal direction to the following frames until the next I frame. Hence the decoded PSNR including EC would be also dependent on the intra-frame period due to temporal error prapagation.

4 Analysis of EC Performance Dependency on FMO

As explained in Section 3, both intra- and inter-frame EC operations depend on the number of correctly received neighboring MBs. The number of correctly received neighboring MBs would be dependent on the FMO mode. This section presents theoretical analysis on the expected number of correctly received MBs given packet loss rate for each FMO mode. The analysis would show the performance of EC is closely related to the FMO mode.

Let $n^r(x,y)$, $n^i(x,y)$, and $n^d(x,y)$ represent the number of correctly received neighboring MBs when raster scan, interleaved, and dispersed mode FMO is used, respectively. Let p_l represent the probability of packet loss. We assume that one slice becomes one packet in encoded bitstream. If a slice is lost, then the probability that the other slice in the same frame is correctly received is $1-p_l$. Let $E[n^r]$, $E[n^i]$, and $E[n^d]$ represent the expected number of correctly received neighboring MBs for a lost MB when raster scan, interleaved, and dispersed mode FMO is used, respectively.

Firstly consider when raster scan mode is used. For simplicity, we assume that new slice begins at the first MB in a row, i.e., $y_0 = L-1$. If $mb(x,y)$ in S_0 is lost and S_1 is received, then

$$n^r(x,y) = \begin{cases} 1, x = x_0 \\ 0, \text{otherwise.} \end{cases} \quad (3)$$

$E[n^r]$ can be calculated as

$$E[n^r] = \frac{1-p_l}{x_0+1} \sum_{x=0}^{x_0} n^r(x,y). \quad (4)$$

When $mb(x,y)$ in S_1 is lost and S_0 is received, $n^r(x,y)$ and $E[n^r]$ can be similarly represented and calculated as (3) and (4).

Secondly consider when interleaved mode FMO is used. If $mb(x,y)$ in S_0^i is lost and S_1^i is received, then

$$n^i(x,y) = \begin{cases} 1, x = 0 \\ 2, \text{otherwise.} \end{cases} \quad (5)$$

$E[n^i]$ can be calculated as

$$E[n^i] = \frac{2(1-p_l)}{K} \sum_{x=0}^{K/2} n^i(x,y). \quad (6)$$

$E[n^i]$ value would be the same as (6) when $mb(x,y)$ in S_1^i is lost and S_0^i is received.

Thirdly consider when dispersed mode FMO is used. If $mb(x,y)$ in S_0^d is lost and S_1^d is received,

$$n^d(x,y) = \begin{cases} 3, x = 0 \\ 4, \text{otherwise.} \end{cases} \quad (7)$$

$E[n^d]$ can be calculated as

$$E[n^d] = \frac{2(1-p_l)}{K} \sum_{x=0}^{K/2} n^d(x,y). \quad (8)$$

$E[n^d]$ value would be the same as (8) when $mb(x,y)$ in S_1^d is lost and S_0^d is received.

Now consider the following case as an example for the expected number of correctly received neighboring MBs. When luminance component of common intermedia format (CIF) video sequence is considered, $K = 22$ and $L = 18$. If the packet loss rate is 10%, $p_l = 0.1$. If we assume that the slice size is the same in raster scan mode, $x_0 = 10$. From (4), (6), and (8), $E[n^r] = 0.082$, $E[n^i] = 1.72$, and $E[n^d] = 3.52$, in this case.

This analysis shows that the expected number of correctly received neighboring MBs becomes larger in FMO modes than in raster scan mode, and dispersed mode gives larger expected number than interleaved mode. From this analysis, we can expect that the performance of EC would be better in FMO modes than in raster scan mode, and the dispersed mode would give better EC performance than interleaved mode.

5 Simulation Results and Performance Evaluation

We performed simulations using JM9.3 H.264 reference software [8]. Real-time Transport Protocol (RTP) packet mode is selected as output file mode. Packet loss simulator is implemented by modifying the C code in [9], [10]. Arbitrary packets can be dropped (lost) from encoded bitstream file composed of RTP packets, and new bitstream file is composed without dropped packets.

Simulations are performed using 'Foreman' and 'Mobile' CIF video sequence with 0%, 3%, 5%, 10%, and 20% packet loss rate. Fig. 1 shows the PSNR performance with several packet loss rate when the intra-frame period is 1, i.e.,

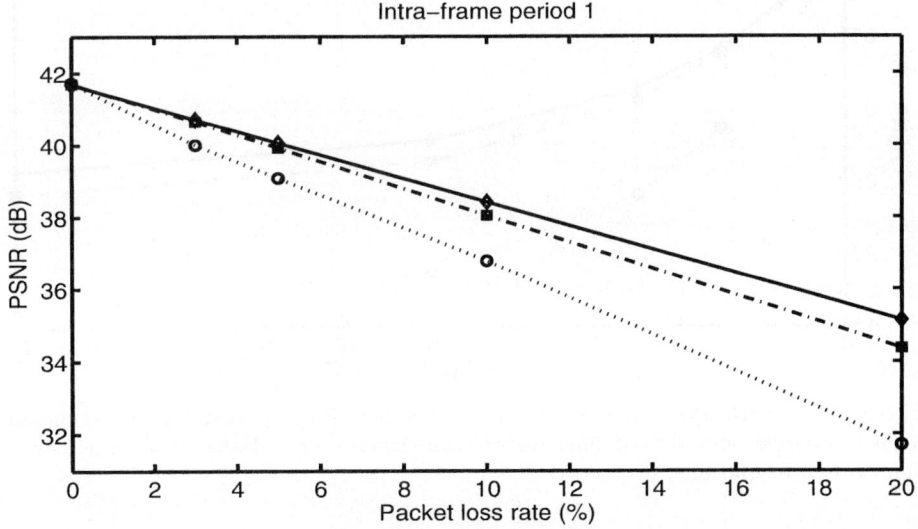

Fig. 1. PSNR with several packet loss rates when intra-frame period is 1 for 'Foreman' sequence (circle with dotted line: raster scan, square with dashed line: interleaved, diamond with solid line: dispersed)

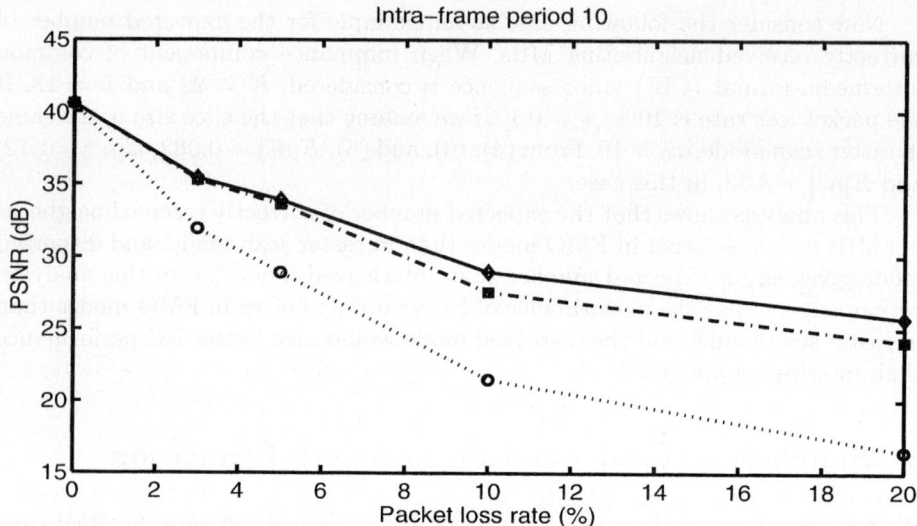

Fig. 2. PSNR with several packet loss rates when intra-frame period is 10 for 'Foreman' sequence (circle with dotted line: raster scan, square with dashed line: interleaved, diamond with solid line: dispersed)

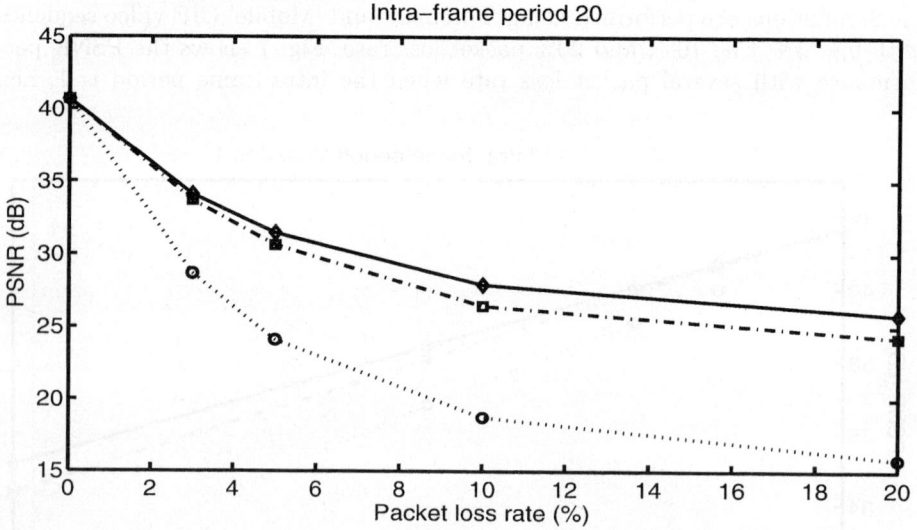

Fig. 3. PSNR with several packet loss rates when intra-frame period is 20 for 'Foreman' sequence (circle with dotted line: raster scan, square with dashed line: interleaved, diamond with solid line: dispersed)

intra-frame only case for 'Foreman' sequence. From this result, we can see that the PSNR performance is very close at 0% packet loss rate, and interleaved and dispersed FMO modes give better PSNR than raster scan mode as the packet loss rate becomes larger. At 20% packet loss rate, both FMO modes give about

3 ~ 4dB higher PSNR than raster scan mode, and dispersed mode gives slightly higher PSNR than interleaved mode.

Fig. 2 and Fig. 3 show the PSNR with several packet loss rates when the intra-frame period is 10 and 20, respectively, for 'Foreman' sequence. The overall tendency is similar, but we can observe that the PSNR difference becomes larger as the intra-frame period becomes larger. When the intra-frame period is 20 in Fig. 3, dispersed mode FMO gives about 10dB higher PSNR than raster scan mode, which is much larger difference compared to the intra-frame period 1 case in Fig. 1. As the intra-frame period becomes larger, the temporal error propagation effect becomes more severe and the FMO modes affect more on the decoded PSNR including EC.

Fig. 4 shows the PSNR performance at several bit rates when the packet loss rate is 0% and intra-frame period is 1 for 'Mobile' sequence. In this case, the raster scan mode gives the best result, while the dispersed mode FMO gives the worst result. The raster scan mode gives about 2dB higher PSNR than the dispersed mode FMO. Since no intra-frame prediction is performed across slice or slice group boundaries in encoding, raster scan mode gives the best result, while the dispersed mode gives the worst result. When dispersed mode FMO is used, there would be no horizontal and vertical neighboring MB in the same slice group for intra-frame prediction in encoding.

Fig. 5 shows the PSNR at several bit rates when the packet loss rate is 20% and intra-frame period is 1 for 'Mobile' sequence. In this case, the raster scan gives the worst result, while interleaved and dispersed mode FMO gives similar

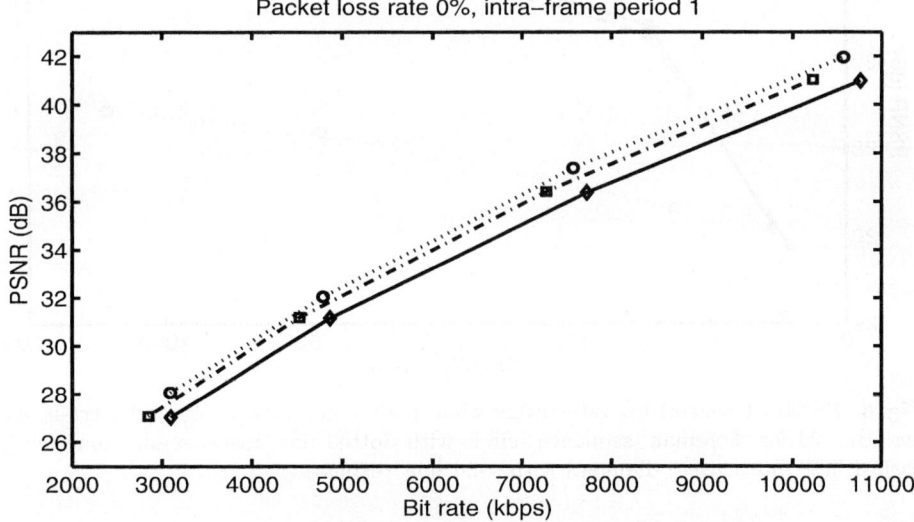

Fig. 4. PSNR at several bit rates rate when packet loss rate is 0% and intra-frame period is 1 for 'Mobile' sequence (circle with dotted line: raster scan, square with dashed line: interleaved, diamond with solid line: dispersed)

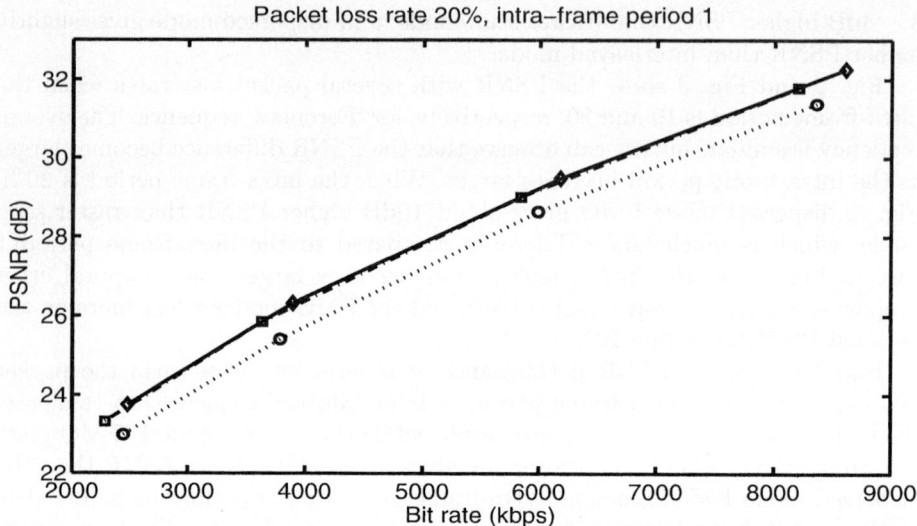

Fig. 5. PSNR at several bit rates rates when packet loss rate is 20% and intra-frame period is 1 for 'Mobile' sequence (circle with dotted line: raster scan, square with dashed line: interleaved, diamond with solid line: dispersed)

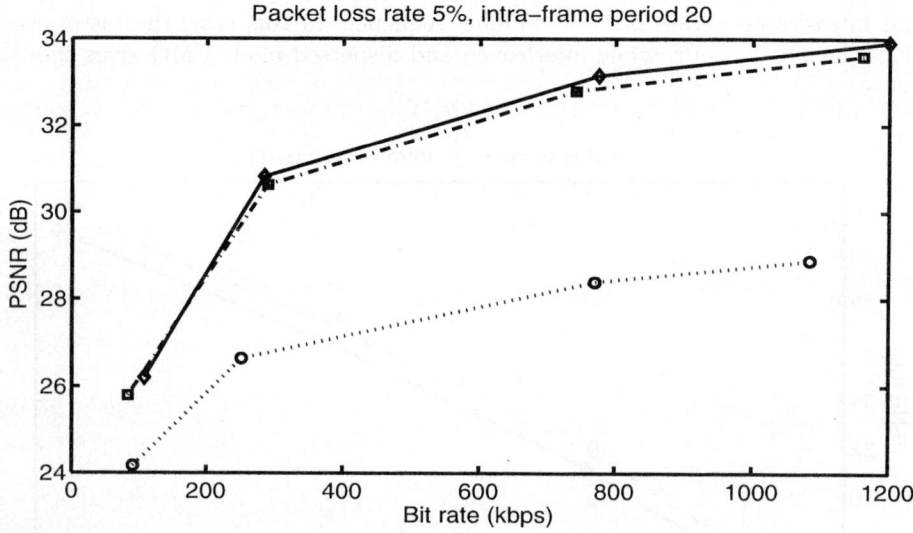

Fig. 6. PSNR at several bit rates rates when packet loss rate is 5% and intra-frame period is 20 for 'Foreman' sequence (circle with dotted line: raster scan, square with dashed line: interleaved, diamond with solid line: dispersed)

performance. FMO gives about 1 ∼ 2dB better performance than raster scan mode. As the packet loss rate becomes higher, the performance of EC becomes more important for higher PSNR. As explained in Section 2, the expected number of correctly received neighboring MBs is much larger in FMO modes than in raster scan mode, and the performance of intra-frame EC is better in FMO modes than in raster scan mode.

Fig. 6 shows the PSNR at several bit rates when the packet loss rate is 5% and the intra-frame period is 20 for 'Foreman' sequence. In this case, interleaved and

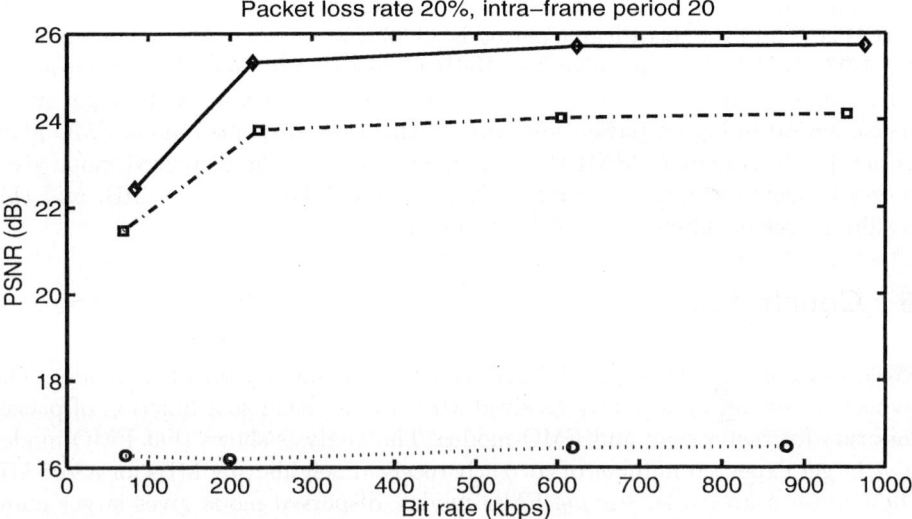

Fig. 7. PSNR at several bit rates rate when packet loss rate is 20% and intra-frame period is 20 for 'Foreman' sequence (circle with dotted line: raster scan, square with dashed line: interleaved, diamond with solid line: dispersed)

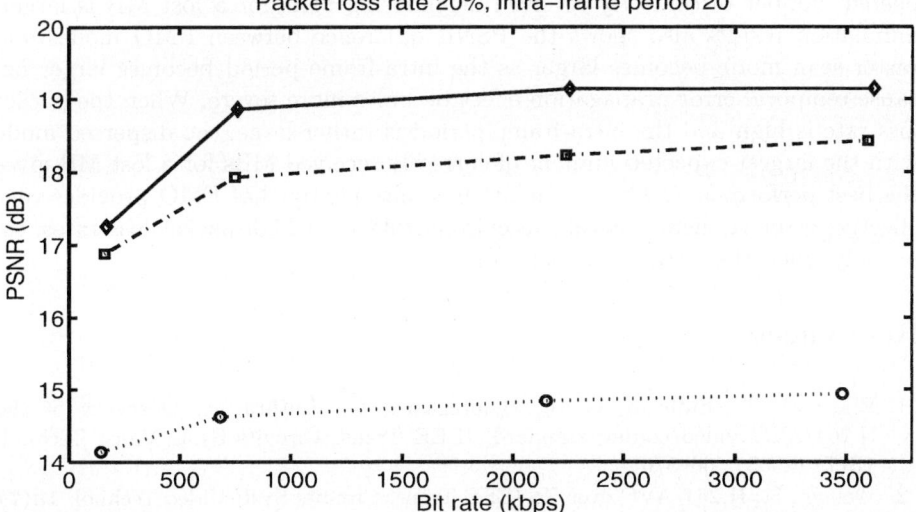

Fig. 8. PSNR at several bit rates rate when packet loss rate is 20% and intra-frame period is 20 for 'Mobile' sequence (circle with dotted line: raster scan, square with dashed line: interleaved, diamond with solid line: dispersed)

dispersed FMO modes show similar performance, and FMO modes show about 4 ∼ 5dB higher PSNR than raster scan mode. The PSNR of raster scan mode is lower in raster scan mode because the inter-frame EC performance is worse and temporal error prapagation effect becomes more severe as the intra-frame period is larger.

Fig. 7 and Fig. 8 show the PSNR at several bit rates when the packet loss rate is 20% and the intra-frame period is 20 for 'Foreman' and 'Mobile' sequence, respectively. FMO modes give 4 ∼ 10dB higher PSNR than raster scan mode. The temporal error propagation effect becomes more severe with larger intra-frame period in higher packet loss rate. In this case, dispersed mode FMO gives about 1 ∼ 2dB higher PSNR than interleaved mode. The dispersed mode gives larger expected number of received neighboring MBs for a lost MB, and this results in better inter-frame EC performance.

6 Conclusion

We presented an anlaysis on EC performance dependency on FMO modes. The expected number of correctly received MBs are modeled as a function of packet loss rate for raster scan and FMO modes. The analysis shows that FMO modes give larger expected number of correctly received neighboring MBs for a lost MB than raster scan mode. Among FMO modes, dispersed mode gives larger number than interleaved mode. Simulation results show that PSNR is slightly higher in raster scan mode than in dispersed mode when there is no packet loss since no EC needs to be performed. However as the packet loss rate becomes higher, the performance of EC becomes more important for decoded PSNR. When the packet loss rate becomes higher, FMO modes give larger PSNR since the expected number of correctly received neighboring MBs for a lost MB is larger. Simulation results also shows the PSNR difference between FMO modes and raster scan mode becomes larger as the intra-frame period becomes larger because temporal error prapagation effect becomes more severe. When the packet loss rate is high and the intra-frame period is rather large, the dispersed mode with the largest expected number of correctly received MBs for a lost MB gives the best performance. These simulation results justify that FMO provides very effective error resilience feature in evironments with high packet loss rates, especially when the intra-frame period is large.

References

1. Wiegand, T., Sullivan, G. J., Bjøntegaard, G., Luthra, A: Overview of the H.264/AVC video coding standard. IEEE Trans. Circuits Syst. Video Technol. **13(7)** (2003) 560–576
2. Wenger, S.: H.264/AVC over IP. IEEE Trans. Circuits Syst. Video Technol. **13(7)** (2003) 645–656
3. Sockhammer, T., Hannuksela, M. M., Wiegand, T.: H.264/AVC in wireless environments. IEEE Trans. Circuits Syst. Video Technol. **13(7)** (2003) 657–673

4. Sockhammer, T., Wiegand, T., Wenger, S.: Optimized transmission of H.26L/JVT coded video over paket-lossy networks. Proc. IEEE Int. Conf. Image Processing, (2002)
5. Sockhammer, T., Wiegand, T., Oelbaum, T., Obermeier, F.: Video coding and transport layer techniques for H.264/AVC-based transmission over paket-lossy networks. Proc. IEEE Int. Conf. Image Processing, (2003)
6. Wang, Y.-K., Hannuksela, M. M., Varsa, V., Hourunranta, A., Gabbouj. M.: The error concealment feature in the H.26L test model. Proc. IEEE Int. Conf. Image Processing, **2** (2002), 729-733
7. Lam, W.-M., Reibman, A. R., Liu, B.: Recovery of lost or erroneously received motion vectors. Proc. IEEE Int. Conf. Acoust. Speech Signal Proc., **5** (1993), 417-420
8. H.264/AVC software coordination. http://bs.hhi.de/~suehring/
9. Wenger, S.: Common conditions for wire-line, low delay IP/UDP/RTP packet loss resilient testing. ITU-T SG16 Doc. VCEG-N79r1, (2001)
10. Luttrell, M., Wenger, S., Gallant, M.: New versions of packet loss environment and pseudomux tools. http://www.stewe.org/contrib.htm, Q15-I-09.zip, (1999)

Motion Perception Based Adaptive Quantization for Video Coding

Chih-Wei Tang

chihwei.ee88g@nctu.edu.tw

Abstract. A visual measure for the purpose of video compressions is proposed in this paper. The novelty of the proposed scheme relies on combining three human perception models: motion attention model, eye movement based spatiotemporal visual sensitivity function, and visual masking model. With the aid of spatiotemporal visual sensitivity function, the visual sensitivities to DCT coefficients on less attended macroblocks are evaluated. The spatiotemporal distortion masking measures at macroblock level are then estimated based on the visual masking thresholds of the DCT coefficients with low sensitivities. Accordingly, macroblocks that can hide more distortions are assigned larger quantization parameters. Experiments conducted on the basis of H.264 demonstrate that this scheme effectively improves coding efficiency without picture quality degradation.

1 Introduction

With target bit allocation and adaptive quantization, rate control modules of the video encoders optimize the perceived picture quality and achieves a given constant average bit rate. The performance of adaptive quantization is deeply affected by activity measures of macroblocks, such MAD in rate control module of JM9.0 for H.264 [1]. However, one problem with such measure is its mismatch for the sensitivity property of human visual system.

Various coding techniques have been investigated to enhance visual quality. For instance, a substitute strategy for the perceptually weighted distortion measure is the priority coding policy. Video coders are guided by the distance between the location to be encoded and the visually salient location [2]-[5]. Fewer bits are allocated to visually less attended regions that are predicted by pre-analysis [3] or color contrast, intensity, orientation, flicker and motion intensity information [2].

Human visual sensitivity varies with spatial frequencies of image patterns. This property has been extensively utilized to design optimal quantization matrices. Visual sensitivity also changes with the moving velocity of the eye-tracking target. Coding efficiencies can be improved by employing the spatiotemporal visual sensitivity function [6] to reduce psychophysical redundancy [7]. It is noted that the loss of visual sensitivity might be compensated by smooth pursuit eye movement. Thus, by considering both the visual attention model and the eye movement based spatiotemporal contrast sensitivity function [8], a rendering method is devised to accelerate global illumination computation in [9].

Visual masking denotes that the visibility of a signal is changed due to the existence of other signals. In addition to visual attention and visual sensitivity, visual masking gives another important cue to efficiently compress video data. Constant quality across images can be achieved by adapting quantization parameters to texture masking energies of image blocks [10][11].

In this paper, a novel adaptive quantization scheme is accomplished by adopting the visual attention model, eye movement based spatiotemporal contrast sensitivity function, and visual masking model. The attended regions are identified based on motion intensities and motion directions since motion information is usually stronger predictors of human saccades than static image features [12]. Next, for DCT coefficients on less attended regions, coefficients with low sensitivities are identified according to spatial frequencies and moving velocities of their corresponding blocks. Spatiotemporal distortion masking measures are then estimated on the basis of the visual masking thresholds of these coefficients. Finally, rate reduction without visual degradation is achieved by adapting quantization parameters to local image contents.

The rest of this paper is organized as follows. Section 2 describes the proposed motion attention model. The employed eye movement based spatiotemporal sensitivity function and visual masking model are given in Section 3. Based on these analyses, Section 4 presents an adaptive quantization scheme. The performance of the proposed scheme is illustrated in Section 5. Finally, Section 6 concludes this paper.

2 The Motion Attention Model

The strategy that biological vision systems serially process the incoming information is referred as selective attention or focal attention [13]. The psychophysical, neurophysiological and computational approaches research into this theory in different ways. Visual attention includes bottom-up and top-down processes. Bottom-up attention consists of static attention and motion attention. This paper focuses on the latter since motion and temporal change are usually stronger predictors of human saccades than static image features [12]. An example of the computational motion attention model builds motion conspicuity maps based on multiscale Gaussian pyramids of motion intensities for image rendering [9]. Another model utilizing both motion intensities and motion directions but disusing camera motion estimation and object tracking is devised for video skimming [14].

Regarding block-based video coders, the translational rigid motion model may lead to coding inefficiency in case of regions with complex motions. Nevertheless, such regions often receive more visual attentions and hence human visions are more sensitive to the coding error in these regions. Thus, this section proposes a motion attention model for the purpose of video coding.

This motion attention model is revised from [14]. It is made up of three inductors: intensity inductor, spatial coherence inductor, and contrast coherence inductor. Each inductor ranges from zero to one. Let the motion vector of the macroblock indexed by (i,j) of the nth frame be (Vx_{nij}, Vy_{nij}). The intensity inductor for this macroblock is

$$I_{nij} = \sqrt{Vx_{nij}^2 + Vy_{nij}^2} / \max I, \tag{1}$$

where $\max I$ is the maximal motion intensity in the nth frame. The spatial coherence inductor derived from the entropy of the directions of motion vectors, inside a spatial window containing $w_1 \times w_1$ macroblocks, is

$$Cs_{nij} = -\sum_{b=1}^{n_s} p_n(b)\log(p_n(b)), \quad (2)$$

where $p_n(b)$ is the probability of occurrence of bth bin and n_s is the number of histogram bins. Next, we define the contrast coherence inductor as

$$Cv_{nij} = \begin{cases} 1 - N_{nij}/I_{nij}, & \text{if } I_{nij} >= N_{nij}. \\ 1 - I_{nij}/N_{nij}, & \text{otherwise.} \end{cases} \quad (3)$$

$$N_{nij} = (\sum_{u=-(w_2-1)/2}^{(w_2-1)/2} \sum_{v=-(w_2-1)/2}^{(w_2-1)/2} I_{nuv})/(w_2 \times w_2), \text{u} \neq \text{i and v} \neq \text{j}. \quad (4)$$

It estimates the contrast between I_{nij} and the mean of $(w_2 \times w_2 - 1)$ motion intensities in the neighborhood.

Fig. 1. (a) Frame 119 in STEFAN (b) motion attention map for (a) (c) Frame 16 in FOOTBALL (d) motion attention map for (c). The maps are magnified by a factor of 255.

Intensity inductors of blocks in the background are possibly larger than those in the foreground. Thus, motion attended regions cannot be simply identified based on intensity inductors. On the other hand, since moving objects in the foreground are with either dissimilar motion directions or dissimilar motion intensities to those in the background, blocks with larger spatial coherence inductors or contrast coherence inductors might suggest that they contain or are close to the borders of moving objects. Thus, the motion attention index for the macroblock indexed by (i,j) is defined as

$$M_{nij} = Cv_{nij} + I_{nij} \times Cs_{nij}. \quad (5)$$

Examples of motion attention maps are shown in Figs. 1(a) and 1(b) for STEFAN and FOOTBALL, respectively.

Attended regions are predicted on a bottom-up basis. However, the fixation point is likely on the less attended regions since the final decision is controlled by human brains. Regarding static features, there is a strong connection between region smoothness and visibility of coding errors. The coding efficiency can be improved by reducing psychovisual redundancy in regions with high spatial frequencies and/or high temporal frequencies where more coding errors can be hidden. Thus, next section further introduces a spatiotemporal distortion masking measure for content dependent adaptive quantization on less attended regions.

3 The Visual Sensitivity Model and the Visual Masking Model

In this section, the visual sensitivity model and visual masking model cooperate to reduce the spatial and temporal perception redundancy. Human visions lose sensitivity to high spatial frequency patterns with rapid moving velocities in video scenes. Nevertheless, smooth pursuit eye movement is capable of reducing retinal velocities of eye-tracking targets and thus compensates for the loss of visual sensitivity [8]. This paper employs an eye movement incorporated spatiotemporal contrast sensitivity function to evaluate visual sensitivities of DCT coefficients at different spatial frequencies on less attended blocks. For the DCT coefficients with low spatiotemporal sensitivities, their capabilities for visual masking are further concerned based on a two-dimensional visual masking model.

At first, the image plane velocity v_I is converted into the retinal velocity v_R by [8]

$$v_E = \min\lfloor (g_{SP} \cdot v_T) + v_{MIN}, v_{MAX} \rfloor, \tag{6}$$

$$v_R = v_I - v_E, \tag{7}$$

where v_E is the eye velocity and v_T is the target velocity (v_T is set as v_I in the following). All velocities are in deg/sec. g_{sp} is 0.82 (the gain of smooth pursuit eye movement). v_{min} is 0.15. v_{max} is 80. v_I at location (x,y) in pixel-domain is [10]

$$v_I(x, y) = \frac{\Delta P(x,y) \times f_r}{f_s}, \tag{8}$$

where $\Delta P(x,y)$ is the pixel displacement between two consecutive frames, f_r is frame rate in frame/sec and f_s is sampling density in pel/deg that relies on viewing distance.

Before estimating the sensitivity for the 2-D DCT coefficient c_{uvk} on a DCT block that has retinal velocity v_R ((u,v) indexes the coefficient and k indexes this $N\times N$ DCT block), the normalized spatial frequency $f_d(u,v)$ in cy/pel has to be converted to spatial frequency $f(u,v)$ in cy/deg of c_{uvk} by [15]

$$f(u,v) = f_d(u,v) \times f_s, \tag{9}$$

$$f_d(i, j) = \frac{\sqrt{u^2 + v^2}}{2N}, \quad u,v = 0,1,..,N-1. \tag{10}$$

The eye movement incorporated spatiovelocity sensitivity [8] is then evaluated by introducing v_R into Kelly's CSF [6]

$$CSF(\rho, v_R) = k \cdot c_0 \cdot c_2 \cdot v_R \cdot (c_1 2\pi\rho)^2 \exp\left(-\frac{c_1 4\pi\rho}{\rho_{\max}}\right), \quad (11)$$

$$k = s_1 + s_2 \cdot |\log(c_2 v_R / 3)|^3, \quad (12)$$

$$\rho_{\max} = p_1 / (c_2 v_R + 2), \quad (13)$$

where ρ is the spatial frequency in cy/deg, s_1 is 6.1, s_2 is 7.3 and p_1 is 45.9. The parameters settings that c_0 is 1.14, c_1 is 0.67 and c_2 is 1.7 are suggested by Daly [8].

For the coefficients that have low visual sensitivities (smaller than a given threshold α), their capabilities of visual masking are further concerned. Visual masking refers to the reduction of visibility of a signal due to the existence of other signals. For the purpose of video coders, this property is quite important since rate reduction can be achieved without perceptual degradation by allocating fewer bits to regions that can mask more coding distortions. In [10], the term "texture masking energy" is defined based on the DCT-domain sensitivity function that varies with spatial frequencies. Instead of the sensitivity function, Watson's DCT-domain contrast masking model [16] is adopted here to estimate masking energies. The masking threshold of the DCT coefficient c_{uvk} is given by

$$e_{uvk} = \max[t_{uvk}, |c_{uvk}|^{w_{uv}} \cdot t_{uvk}^{1-w_{uv}}], \quad (14)$$

where t_{uvk} is the luminance masking threshold, w_{00} is 0 and w_{uv} is 0.7 for $(u,v) \neq (0,0)$. Based on this, the coding distortion tolerance index T_{nij} for the mth macroblock is proposed in this paper, and, it is defined as

$$T_{nij} = (\sum_{k=1}^{(16\times 16)/(N\times N)} \sum_{u=1}^{N} \sum_{v=1}^{N} e_{uvk}^{\beta})^{1/\beta} \quad (15)$$

where β is a parameter and is experimentally determined. Please note that the contrast sensitivities and visual masking thresholds of the DC coefficients are not evaluated in the proposed scheme. The AC coefficients with significant contrast sensitivities (larger than a given threshold α) are also excluded from the evaluation of (15).

4 The Adaptive Quantization Scheme

In the proposed scheme, the quantization parameters at macroblock level are adjusted based on motion attention indexes and coding distortion tolerance indexes. A region is judged to be whether attended by

$$M'_{nij} = \begin{cases} 1, & \text{if } M_{nij} > \gamma. \\ 0, & \text{otherwise.} \end{cases} \quad (16)$$

where γ is a given threshold between 0 and 1. The coding bits allocated to attended regions are unaltered. Since the predicted image saliency only provides the candidates of saccade locations [12], the quantization parameters assigned to different attended regions are identical. Note that allocating more bits will give rise to the issues of the control of bit-rate increase and the gracefully visual degradation between attended and unattended regions.

Finally, rate reduction is achieved by allocating fewer bits to less attended regions according to T_{nij}. One example is

$$QP'_{nij} = QP_{nij} + \Delta QP_{nij} \qquad (17)$$

$$\Delta QP_{nij} = \begin{cases} q_1, & \text{if } T_{nij} \leq \gamma_1 \\ q_2, & \text{if } \gamma_1 < T_{nij} < \gamma_2 \\ q_3, & \text{if } \gamma_1 < T_{nij} < \gamma_3 \\ q_4, & \text{otherwise} \end{cases} \qquad (18)$$

where QP_{nij} is the initial quantization parameter. Parameters γ_1, γ_2 and γ_3 classify contents into different classes for visual masking: low, medium, high, and very high. According to the experiment results, the parameters are $\gamma_1 = 15$, $\gamma_2 = 30$, and $\gamma_3 = 50$. q_1, q_2, q_3 and q_4 are nonnegative integers. A conservative policy for settings q_1, q_2, q_3, and q_4 are $q_1 = 0$, $q_2 = 1$, $q_3 = 2$, and $q_4 = 4$.

5 Experimental Results

This section demonstrates the performance of the proposed scheme by utilizing the spatiotemporal distortion masking measure to guide JM 9.0 of H.264. The encoder configuration is as follows. ProfileIDC is 77. RDO mode, CABAC, and loop filter are enabled. No B frame is inserted. Intra modes for non I-slices are enabled. Fast motion estimation is disabled. Due to the limited space, the results are shown for sequences STEFAN and FOOTBALL at CIF resolution at 30 fps. STEFAN contains 300 frames and FOOTBALL contains 260 frames. The parameter settings are $N=4$, $\alpha=1$, $w_1 = 5$, $w_2 = 3$, $n_s = 16$, and $\gamma=0.15$. Viewing distance is 3 picture heights. The test sequences are presented on a Samsung SyncMaster 770 TFT display. The motion vectors used for constructing attention saliency map are generated by full search block matching. The image plane velocities for 16 4×4 2-D DCT block within the same macroblock are represented by the macroblock velocity.

By disabling rate control module, the comparisons of the coding performance between H.264 with fixed quantization scheme and H.264 with adaptive quantization scheme (the proposed scheme) are exhibited in Figs. 2(a) and 2(b). Rates and distortions corresponding to six initial QPs, including 22, 26, 30, 32, 40, and 44, are measured for both schemes. Rate reduction ranges from 13% to 23% for STEFAN sequences and from 3% to 8% for FOOTBALL sequences.

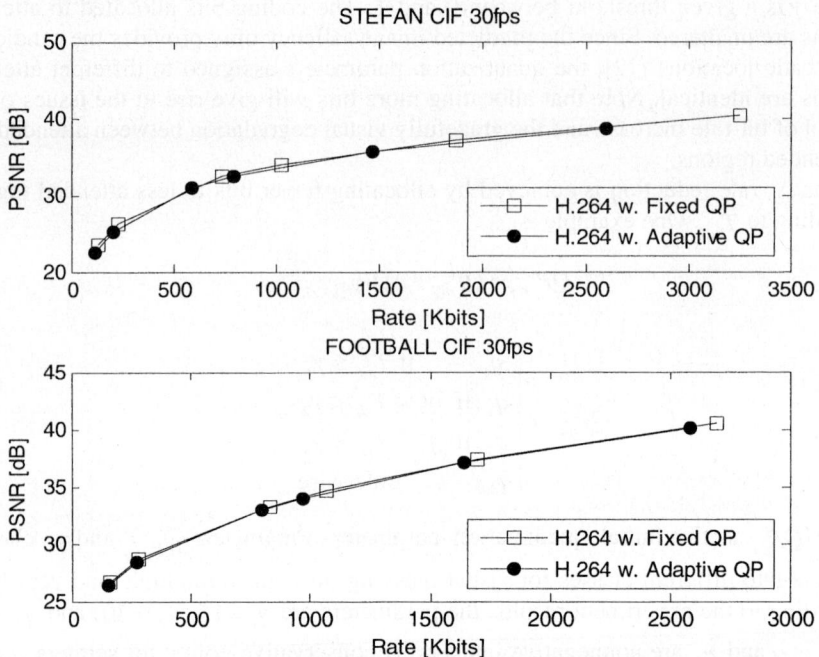

Fig. 2. The comparisons of coding performance between two different schemes for STEFAN and FOOTBALL, respectively. Each figure contains two curves. Each curve is created based on initial QP: 22, 26, 30, 32, 40, and 44.

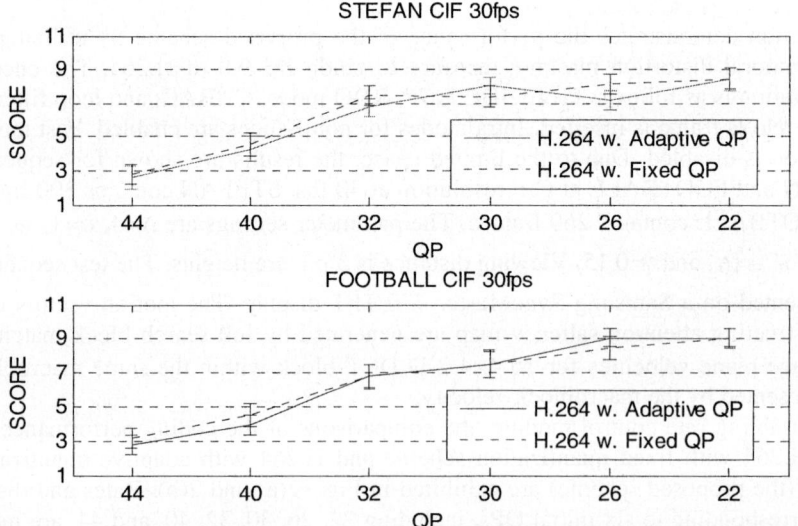

Fig. 3. The comparisons of subjective visual tests between two different quantization schemes for STEFAN and FOOTBALL, respectively. The confidence interval (CI) is 90%. Each figure contains two curves. Each curve is created based on initial QP: 22, 26, 30, 32, 40, and 44.

(a)

(b)

Fig. 4. Comparisons between different quantization schemes for frame 282 in STEFAN (Initial QP=22): (a) Fixed QP (PSNR= 39.71 dB) and (b) adaptive QP (PSNR=36.87dB)

(a)

(b)

Fig. 5. Comparisons between different quantization schemes for frame 281 in STEFAN (Initial QP=26): (a) Fixed QP (PSNR= 36.29 dB) and (b) adaptive QP (PSNR=33.54dB)

Fig. 6. Comparisons between different quantization schemes for frame 123 in FOOTBALL (Initial QP=22): (a) Fixed QP (PSNR= 39.60 dB) and (b) adaptive QP (PSNR=38.76dB)

The comparisons of the subjective visual tests between H.264 with fixed quantization scheme and H.264 with adaptive quantization scheme (the proposed scheme) are shown in Figs. 3(a) and 3(b). Fifteen non-expert subjects take part in this test. The testing procedure is based on single stimulus method (SS) [17]. The 11-grade quality scale ranges from 1 to 11. The test sequences are presented in random order. The confidence interval revealed in Figs. 3(a) and 3(b) is 90%. Although the overall PSNR drops are all less than 1.6dB for STEFAN and 0.5 dB for FOOTBALL, there is no perceptual degradation since the proposed coding scheme is directed by a perceptual measure. Figures 4 to 6 show the side by side comparisons for reconstructed frames in STEFAN and FOOTBALL. Please note that the PSNR difference between two reconstructed frames in Figs. 4(a) and 4(b) is 2.84 dB and it is 2.75 dB between Figs. 5(a) and 5(b). However, since most regions are with fast motions and there are large regions with high spatial frequencies, i.e. audience, in 281th frame and 282th frame in STEFAN, large T_{nij} values in (15) are resulted. This indicates that larger coding distortions can be covered up in these frames.

6 Conclusions

This paper proposes a motion perception measure combining visual attention, eye movement based spatiotemporal visual sensitivity, and visual masking. This measure can be incorporated with the existing coders to facilitate an efficiently perceptual coder. Future work will focus on the model refinement and extensive tests.

References

1. H.264/AVC Software, "http://iphome.hhi.de/suehring/tml".
2. L. Itti: Automatic Foveation for Video Compression Using a Neurobiological Model of Visual Attention. IEEE Trans. Image Processing, Vol. 13, No. 10 (2004) 1304-1318
3. D. Agrafiotis, N. Canagarajah, D.R. Bull, and M. Dye: Perceptually Optimized Sign Language Video Coding Based on Eye Tracking Analysis. IEE Electronics Letters, Vol. 39, No. 2 (November 2003) 1703-1705
4. Z. Wang, L. Lu and A. C. Bovik: Foveation Scalable Video Coding with Automatic Fixation Selection. IEEE Trans. Image Processing, Vol. 12, No. 2 (February 2003) 243-254
5. A. Basu and K. Wiebe: Videoconferencing Using Spatially Varying Sensing with Multiple and Moving Foveas. Proc. IEEE Intl. Conference on Pattern Recognition (October 1994)
6. D. H. Kelly: Motion and Vision II. Stabilized Spatio-Temporal Threshold Surface. J. Opt. Soc. Amer., Vol. 69, No. 10 (October 1979) 1340-1349
7. S.-C. Pei and C.-L. Lai: Very Low Bit-Rate Coding Algorithm for Stereo Video with Spatiotemporal HVS Model and Binary Correlation Disparity Estimator. IEEE Journal on Selected Areas in Communications, Vol. 16, No. 1 (January 1998) 98-107
8. S. Daly: Engineering Observations from Spatiovelocity and Spatiotemporal Visual Models. IS&T/SPIE Conference on Human Vision and Electronic and Electronic Imaging IV, Vol. 3644 (1999) 162-166
9. H. Yee, S. Pattanaik, and D. P. Greenberg: Spatiotemporal Sensitivity and Visual Attention for Efficient Rendering of Dynamic Environments. ACM 2001 Trans. Computer Graphics, Vol. 20(1) (January 2001) 39-65
10. S. H. Tan, K. K. Pang, and K. N. Ngan: Classified Perceptual Coding with Adaptive Quantization. IEEE Trans. Circuits and Systems for Video Technology, Vol. 6, No. 4 (August 1996) 375-388

11. C.-W. Tang, C.-H. Chen, Y.-H. Yu, and C.-J. Tsai: Visual Sensitivity Guided Bit Allocation for Video Coding. Accepted by IEEE Trans. Multimedia (2005)
12. L. Itti: Quantifying the Contribution of Low-Level Saliency to Human Eye Movements in Dynamic Scenes. Visual Cognition (2005)
13. C. Koch: Biological Models of Motion Perception: Spatio-Temporal Energy Models and Electrophysiology (2004)
14. Y.-F. Ma, and H.-J. Zhang: A Model of Motion Attention for Video Skimming. Proc. Int. Conf. Image Processing, Vol. 1 (2002) I-129-132
15. B. Chitprasert and K. R. Rao: Human Visual Weighted Progressive Image Transmission. IEEE Trans. Communication, Vol. 38 (July 1990) 1040-1944
16. A. B. Watson: Visual Optimization of DCT Quantization Matrices for Individual Images. Proc. AIAA Computing in Aerospace 9, San Diego, CA, American Institute of Aeronautics and Astronautics (1993) 286-291
17. F. Pereira and T. Ebrahimi: The MPEG-4 Book (2002) 669-675

Hybrid Deblocking Algorithm for Block-Based Low Bit Rate Coded Images

Kee-Koo Kwon[1], In-Su Jeon[2], and Dong-Sun Lim[1]

[1] Embedded S/W Research Division, ETRI,
161 Gajeong-dong, Yuseong-gu, Daejeon 305-350, Korea
{kwonkk, dslim}@etri.re.kr

[2] Telecommunication Network Business, Samsung Electronics Co., LTD,
Gongdan 2-dong, Gumi-si, Gyeongsangbuk-do 730-736, Korea
is7680.jeon@samsung.com

Abstract. In this paper, we propose a hybrid deblocking algorithm to improve the visual quality of block-based low bit rate coded images, those are processed both spatial and wavelet domains. The proposed algorithm reduces the blocking artifacts using the statistical characteristics of block discontinuity as well as the lipschitz regularity along the behavior of wavelet coefficients across scales. In this algorithm, detection of blocking artifacts and block boundary classification is performed in spatial domain to reduce the computational complexity for performing the wavelet transform and inverse wavelet transform for all image, and adaptive filtering is processed in spatial or wavelet domains. Spatial adaptive filtering is processed to reduce the blocking artifacts in smooth region with the blocking artifacts. For complex or mixed region, the Lipschitz regularity is obtained to analyze the evolution of the local maxima of the wavelet transform modulus across scales and these irregular singularities are adaptively removed in wavelet domain. Experimental results show that the proposed algorithm produced better results than those of conventional algorithms both PSNR and visual quality.

1 Introduction

Block DCT-based video coding technique is widely used the video coding standard such as H.263 [1] and MPEG-4 [2]-[4]. However the drawback of this method is the lossy quantization stage which leads to quantization noise. Moreover, this noise makes serious degradation called blocking and ringing artifacts at low bit rates. To reduce these artifacts, a variety of post-processing algorithms have been studied [1]-[12]. A variety of post-processing schemes to reduce the blocking and ringing artifacts have already been proposed to improve the visual quality of block-based coded images in the decoder, such as adaptive filtering methods in spatial domain [1]-[4], the projections onto convex sets (POCS)-based method [7], estimating the lost DCT coefficients in the transform domain [8], and wavelet transform based method [9]-[12]. The POCS-based method has produced good results, however, since it is based on an iterative approach, it is computationally expensive and time consuming.

In MPEG-4 committee draft, the blocking and ringing artifacts are reduced using the verification model (VM) post-filter, deblocking filter and deringing filter [2]-[4]. The MPEG-4 deblocking algorithm which operates in two modes: DC offset mode for low activity blocks and default mode. Block activity is determined according to the amount of changes in the pixels near the block boundaries. All modes apply a one-dimensional (1-D) filter in a separable way. The default mode filter uses the DCT coefficients of the pixels being processed and the DC offset mode uses a 1-D filter. Although this algorithm can conserve the complex regions, it is unable to eliminate the blocking artifacts in complex regions efficiently.

Ramamurthi's algorithm [5] classifies each block as either monotone or an edge area, then 2-D filter is performed to remove grid noise from the monotone areas, then 1-D filter is performed to remove staircase noise from the edge areas. However, this algorithm is unable to accurately classify monotone and edge blocks. Qui's algorithm [6] used a feedforward neural network. In this algorithm, the useful features extracted from the decompressed image are used as the input to a feedforward neural network. Yet, since the neural network is applied to all block boundaries, the edge components are blurred. And since this algorithm processes only two pixels near the block boundary, other blocking artifacts are occurred to the inner regions of the block.

Recently, the discrete wavelet transform (DWT) has attracted considerable attention because the wavelet transform provides good localization in both spatial and spectral domains, allowing noise removal and edge preservation. Several approaches also have been proposed to reduce the blocking and ringing artifacts [9]-[12]. The wavelet transform modulus maxima (WTMM) representation was used to characterize a signal based on the Lipschitz exponents [11], [14], [15]. It enables local and effective operations on multiscale edges. Xiong et al. [10] proposed an approach to deblocking of JPEG compressed images using overcomplete wavelet representations. However, this algorithm is unable to accurately classify smooth regions and edge regions. Hsung et al. [11] proposed the WTMM approach for JPEG images deblocking. Since this algorithm included segmentation process to identify the texture regions and the POCS technique to reconstruct the processed image, it is computationally expensive and time consuming. In Kim's method [12], the blocking artifacts were described as an impulse in the first scale wavelet domain and a dispersed impulse in the second scale wavelet domain. Using 1-D DWT, blocking artifacts are reduced by median filtering. However, this method only reduces the blocking artifacts without consideration of the ringing artifacts.

Accordingly, we propose a hybrid deblocking algorithm that can remove blocking and ringing artifacts from signals by spatial adaptive filtering and estimating the Lipschitz regularity in wavelet domain. The proposed method classifies the block boundary into smooth region, complex region, and mixed region in spatial domain and detects the blocky region which includes the blocking artifacts in smooth region. Because there exists the regions those are not exist the blocking artifacts in smooth region, the existence of blocking artifacts is detected and then adaptive filtering is processed to reduce the computational complexity.

That is, spatial adaptive filtering is processed to reduce the blocking artifacts in smooth region with the blocking artifacts. For complex or mixed region, the Lipschitz regularity is obtained to analyze the evolution of the local maxima of the wavelet transform modulus across scales [14], [15] and this value is used to extract irregular singularities due to blocking and ringing artifacts from the multiscales in a signal. These irregular singularities are adaptively removed according to two types of region, a complex region and mixed region. Because the proposed method transforms only the complex or mixed region, computational complexity is less than conventional 1-D DWT-based methods.

Experimental results confirmed that the proposed algorithm can reduce the blocking and ringing artifacts efficiently and preserve the image details.

2 Singularity Detection Using Overcomplete Wavelet Representations

2.1 Discrete Dyadic Wavelet Transform

In this section we briefly summarize the discrete dyadic wavelet transform used in our deblocking algorithm, as introduced by Mallat *et al.* [14], [15]. The discrete dyadic wavelet transform of 1-D signal $f(x)$ is defined as $\{S_{2^J}f(x), (W_{2^j}f(x))_{1 \leq j \leq J}\}$ where $f(x) \in L^2(R)$. Each component is obtained by the convolution of $f(x)$ with the scaling function and dilated wavelet: $S_{2^J}f(x) = f(x) * \phi_{2^J}(x)$, $W_{2^j}f(x) = f(x) * \psi_{2^j}(x)$. The wavelet $\psi(x)$ is designed to be the derivative of a smoothing function. That is, $\psi(x) = d\theta(x)/dx$ where $\theta(x)$ is a smoothing function whose integral is equal to 1 and that converges to 0 at infinity, and $\psi_{2^j}(x) = 1/2^j \psi(x/2^j)$ denotes the dilation of $\psi(x)$ by a factor 2^j. The wavelet transform $W_{2^j}f(x)$ is proportional respectively to the first derivative of $f(x)$ smoothed by $\theta(x)$. A local maxima is thus any point x_0 such that $|W_{2^j}f(x)| < |W_{2^j}f(x_0)|$ when x belongs to either the right or left neighborhood of x_0, and $|W_{2^j}f(x)| \leq |W_{2^j}f(x_0)|$ when x belongs to the other side of the neighborhood of x_0.

2.2 Estimation of Lipschitz Regularity

To characterize the singular structure of a signal, it is necessary to quantify local regularities precisely. Lipschitz exponents provide not only uniform regularity measurements over time intervals, but also pointwise Lipschitz regularity at any point ν of a signal. The following theorem explains how to use the local maxima to estimate the Lipschitz regularity. Suppose that wavelet $\psi(x)$ has a compact support, first-time continuously differentiable, and the first derivative of a smoothing function.

Theorem [15]; Let $f(x)$ be a tempered distribution whose wavelet transform is well defined over $[a, b]$, and let $x_0 \in [a, b]$. We suppose that there exists a scale 2^j and a constant C, all the modulus maxima of $W_{2^j}f(x)$ belong to a cone defined by $|x - x_0| \leq 2^j C$. Then, at all points $x_1 \in [a, b]$, $x_1 \neq x_0$, $f(x)$ is uniformly

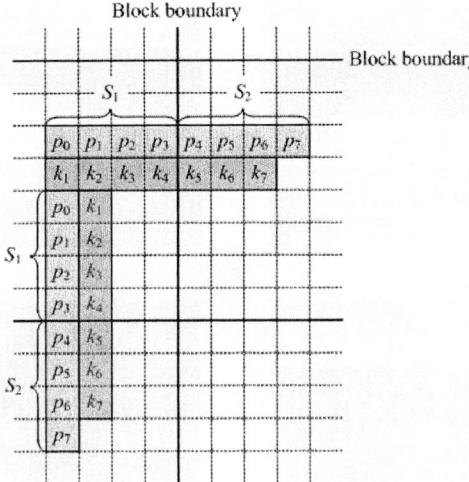

Fig. 1. The eight pixels used for block boundary classification and smooth region filtering

Lipschitz in a neighborhood of x_1. Let $\alpha < n$ be a non-integer. The function $f(x)$ is Lipschitz α at x_0 if and only if there exists a constant A such that at each local maximum $(2^j, x)$ in the cone

$$|W_{2^j} f(x)| \leq A 2^{j\alpha} \qquad (1)$$

that is equivalent to

$$\log |W_{2^j} f(x)| \leq \log(A) + \alpha \log(2^j) \qquad (2)$$

If the local maxima satisfy the cone distribution imposed by the theorem, (2) proves that the Lipschitz regularity at x_0 is the maximum slope of the straight lines that remain above $\log |W_{2^j} f(x)|$ on a logarithmic scale. The local maxima are only detected along a dyadic sequence of scales $(2^j)_{j \in Z}$. For each scale 2^j, the position of the local maxima of $|W_{2^j} f(x)|$ is recorded along with the value of $W_{2^j} f(x)$ at the corresponding position. The Lipschitz regularity of a function is characterized by the decay across the dyadic scales of the local modulus.

3 Proposed Deblocking Algorithm

3.1 Detection of Blocking Artifacts and Block Boundary Classification

Each block boundary is classified into smooth or complex sub-region using the statistical characteristics of four pixels within a block boundary. And then we classify the region into smooth region, complex region, and mixed region. This classification is performed depending on the condition of pixel values around

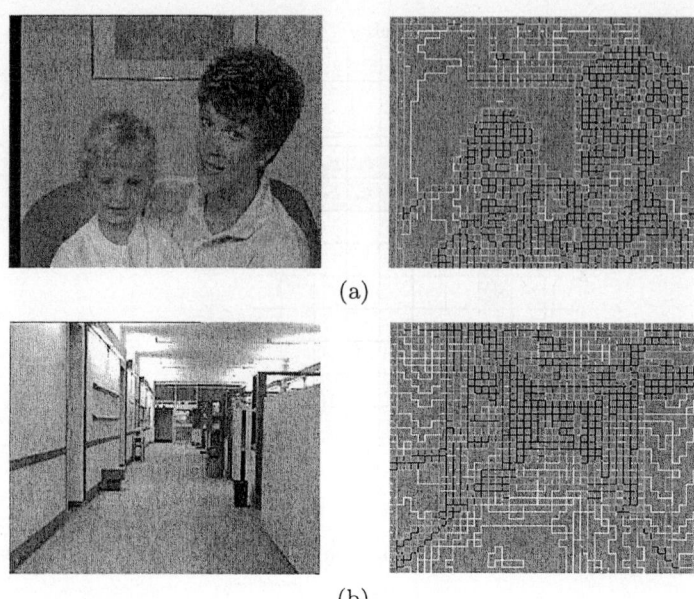

Fig. 2. Sequences with CIF decoded by MPEG-4 and results of block boundary classification for each sequence: (a) Mother and daughter Foreman (QP=10); (b) Hall monitor (QP=12)

block boundary. The pixel values and their mean value in each sub-region S_1 and S_2 are used to classify the region as shown in Fig. 1. If the differences of the pixel values and their mean value in sub-region are less than T_s, the sub-region is decided to smooth sub-region. Otherwise the sub-region is decided to complex sub-region. The threshold value $T_s = 0.5 \times$ QP, and QP is a quantization parameter.

If both sub-regions are decided to smooth sub-region, the region is classified into smooth region. And if both sub-regions are decided to complex sub-region, the region is classified into complex region. And if both sub-regions are not decided to same region, the region is classified into mixed region. Then we detect whether the blocking artifacts are appeared or not in smooth region. If the difference of the pixel values at block boundary is less than T_m, we decide that the blocking artifacts are appeared at block boundary. The threshold T_m is determined using Weber's law. Weber's law states that the ratio of the increment threshold to the background intensity is a constant in $10 \sim 10^3 cd/m^2$ intensity range. That is, $\triangle L/L \approx 0.02$, where, $\triangle L$ is the increment of illumination and L is the background intensity. So the threshold T_m is determined considering the intensity variation of mid-range intensity 127 in 8 bit and filtering complexity.

The proposed block boundary classification method classifies efficiently for various bit rates decoded images. Fig. 2 shows that the results of the proposed block boundary classification method. In this figure, white line indicate the smooth region blcok boundaries, gray lines indicate the mixed region block boundaries, and black lines indicate the complex region blcok boundaries.

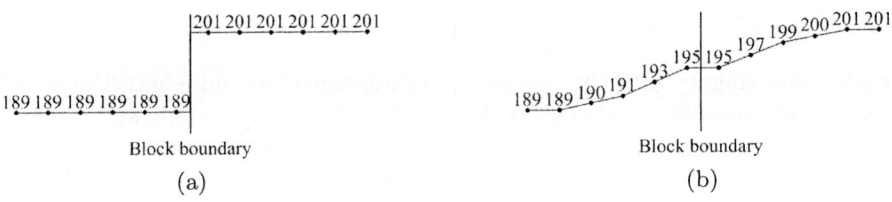

Fig. 3. (a) Examples of blocking artifacts in smooth region and (b) results after proposed filtering

3.2 Deblocking in Smooth Region

Based on the above classification scheme, a novel post-filtering method using simple spatial adaptive filter is proposed. For smooth regions with the blocking artifacts, 1-D 8-tap spatial adaptive filter is used to process the block boundary as shown in Fig. 1. The outputs of the deblocking filter are formed as

$$\widehat{p}_n = p_n + sign(B_s)\frac{B_s}{\alpha_n}, n = 0, 1, \cdots, 7 \qquad (3)$$

where, $B_s = |P_3 - P_4|$, $\alpha_n = \{8, 6, 3, 2, -2, -3, -6, -8\}$. The results of blocking artifacts reduction method in smooth regions is shown in Fig. 3. In smooth regions, the blocking artifacts seem a step-wise function, so the blocking artifacts can be reduced by above simple scheme.

3.3 Deblocking in Complex Region

In conventional wavelet-based deblocking algorithms, all image is transformed using 1-D or 2-D DWT. But we use 8-tap 1-D DWT so as to reduce the computational complexity. That is, 1-D DWT is performed in eight pixels near block boundary as shown in Fig. 1.

Blocking artifacts appear as periodical discontinuities in each block boundary. The local maxima in the first scale detect all singularities in the signals including the blocking artifacts, which are then propagated to the second scale within the cone of influence. The Lipschitz regularity is obtained to analyze the evolution of the local maxima of the wavelet transform modulus across scales and this value is used to extract irregular singularities due to blocking artifacts. That is, it has been theoretically established that the irregular structure of a blocking artifacts has a negative Lipschitz regularity whose modulus values increase when the scale decreases. As such, wavelet transform modulus with a negative Lipschitz regularity is adaptively removed using soft-thresholding method [9]. The soft-thresholding is defined as

$$T(W_{2^1}f(x)) = \begin{cases} W_{2^1}f(x), & W_{2^1}f(x) > thr_1 \\ 0, & |W_{2^1}f(x)| \leq thr_1 \\ W_{2^1}f(x), & W_{2^1}f(x) < -thr_1 \end{cases} \qquad (4)$$

The threshold value $thr_1 = 0.75 \times \text{QP}$.

3.4 Deblocking and Deringing in Mixed Region

Because the ringing artifacts are generally appeared around edges, the ringing artifacts are generated between smooth sub-region and complex sub-region. If there are no edges in complex sub-region out of mixed region, complex sub-region can be regarded as containing the ringing artifacts. So not only the blocking artifacts but also the ringing artifacts are reduced together in case of mixed region.

The blocking artifacts in mixed region are reduced in a similar manner in complex region. And ringing artifacts are reduced by adjusting the first scale all wavelet coefficients with a negative Lipschitz regularity as follows.

If the ith wavelet coefficient of the first scale is adjusted by the mth filter tap coefficient k_m, $m \in [1,7]$ as shown in Fig. 1, the wavelet coefficient of before adjustment and expected wavelet coefficient of after adjustment is given as followed equation by high pass filter (HPF) tap coefficients which are used for inverse wavelet transform.

$$\begin{aligned}
\tilde{p}_{i-2} &= p_{i-2} - 0.012(1-k_m)(p_i - p_{i+1}) \\
\tilde{p}_{i-1} &= p_{i-1} - 0.11(1-k_m)(p_i - p_{i+1}) \\
\tilde{p}_i &= 0.66p_i + 0.34p_{i+1} + 0.34k_m(p_i - p_{i+1}) \\
\tilde{p}_{i+1} &= 0.66p_{i+1} + 0.34p_i - 0.34k_m(p_i - p_{i+1}) \\
\tilde{p}_{i+2} &= p_{i+2} + 0.11(1-k_m)(p_i - p_{i+1}) \\
\tilde{p}_{i+3} &= p_{i+3} + 0.012(1-k_m)(p_i - p_{i+1})
\end{aligned} \tag{5}$$

The six pixel values are affected by adjusting one wavelet coefficient of the first scale, but the other pixel values are little affected except the ith and $i+1$th pixel value. From the relation of the ith and $i+1$th pixel values, therefore, relational equation of wavelet coefficients can be derived about k_m. And k_m can be obtained by setting the expected wavelet coefficient $\tilde{W}_{2^1}$ as (8).

$$\tilde{v}_i - \tilde{v}_{i+1} = 0.32(v_i - v_{i+1}) + 0.68k_m(v_i - v_{i+1}) \tag{6}$$

$$\tilde{W}_{2^1} = 0.32W_{2^1} + 0.68k_m W_{2^1} \tag{7}$$

$$k_m = \frac{\tilde{W}_{2^1}f(x) - 0.32 \times W_{2^1}f(x)}{0.68 \times W_{2^1}f(x)} \tag{8}$$

After obtaining k_m, the wavelet coefficients are adjusted using (9).

$$\hat{W}_{2^1}f(x) = k_m \times W_{2^1}f(x) \tag{9}$$

(9) is represented the relation of expected the pixel values after adjustment and the pixel values before adjustment. Adjustment of wavelet coefficients is generally done at block boundary when the amplitude of $W_{2^1}f(x)$ is less than thr_2. That is, if the amplitude of $W_{2^1}f(x)$ is more than thr_2, there will be no adjustment of wavelet coefficient. The thr_2 is an experimental value which is changing according to QP. In (9), $\tilde{W}_{2^1}f(x) = 0.5 \times thr_2$.

Table 1. Experimental results for MPEG-4 decoded sequences

Bit rates, frame rates	Sequences	QP	Average PSNR [dB]			
			MPEG-4 decoded	VM-18 post filter	Kim's method	Proposed method
48 kbps, 7.5 Hz	News	18	31.26	31.37	31.31	31.43
	Moth. & daugh.	10	36.10	36.01	36.17	36.32
	Hall monitor	12	33.60	33.60	33.79	33.98
112 kbps, 15 Hz	News	11	34.16	34.27	33.94	34.37
	Foreman	30	28.43	28.53	28.57	28.53
	Coastguard	29	26.53	26.37	26.57	26.53

4 Experimental Results

To evaluate the performance of the proposed method, computer simulations were performed using MPEG-4 VM-18 coder [2]. Each video sequence is CIF in size, 300 frames, and compressed at various bit rates. The coding mode was IPPP···, i.e. all frames of a sequence were coded in inter frame mode except for the first frame which was coded as I-picture. To arrive at a certain bit rate, an appropriate quantization parameter was chosen and kept constant throughout the sequence, and H.263 quantization method was used.

To compare the proposed algorithm with conventional algorithms [2], [12], the PSNR performances are presented in Table 1, Table 2, Fig. 4, and Fig. 5. In Table 1, the proposed algorithm produced the maximum 0.38 PSNR improvement than those of decoded sequence. In Table 2, the proposed algorithm produced the maximum 0.81 PSNR improvement than those of decoded sequence. And in Fig. 4 and Fig. 5, the proposed algorithm produces better results than the performances of the VM-18 post-filter for all frames.

Table 2. Experimental results for MPEG-4 decoded infra frame sequences

Bit rates, frame rates	Sequences	QP	Infra frame PSNR [dB]			
			MPEG-4 decoded	VM-18 post filter	Kim's method	Proposed method
48 kbps, 7.5 Hz	News	18	31.78	32.23	32.20	32.26
	Moth. & daugh.	10	36.68	36.91	37.19	37.24
	Hall monitor	12	34.86	34.80	35.31	35.44
112 kbps, 15 Hz	News	11	34.85	35.25	35.07	35.34
	Foreman	30	28.98	29.78	29.75	29.79
	Coastguard	29	27.11	27.44	27.44	27.40

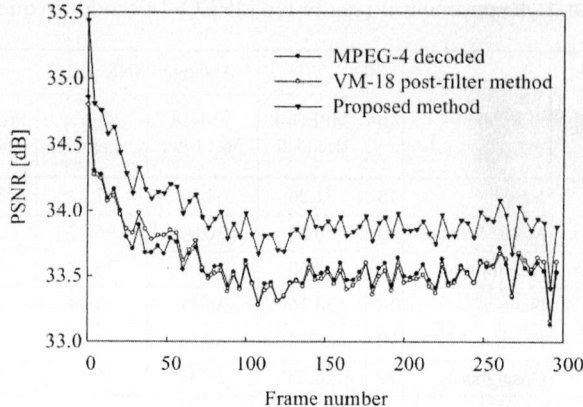

Fig. 4. Experimental results by VM-18 post-filter and proposed post-filter method for Hall monitor sequence decoded by MPEG-4 with CIF, 48 kbps, 7.5 Hz, QP=12

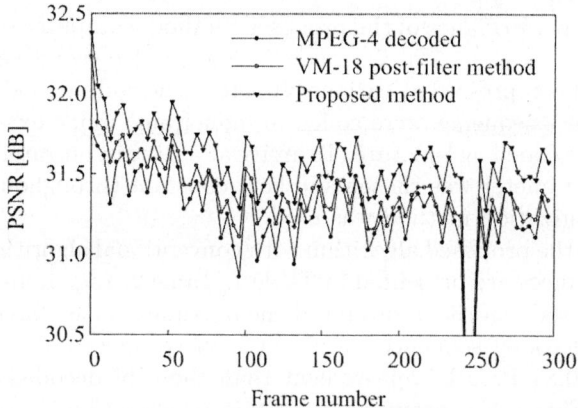

Fig. 5. Experimental results by VM-18 post-filter and proposed post-filter method for News sequence decoded by MPEG-4 with CIF, 48 kbps, 7.5 Hz, QP=18

The Hall monitor sequence decoded by MPEG-4 with 48 kbps, 7.5 Hz, QP=12, and the post-processed sequences are shown in Fig. 6. The proposed algorithm effectively reduced the blocking artifacts and preserved the original high-frequency components. And we showed that the post-processed image by using VM-18 post-filter [2], has the most subjective quality among the conventional methods. But the blocking artifacts in complex regions and the ringing artifacts near the edges are still remained.

And the Foreman sequence decoded by MPEG-4 with 112 kbps, 15 Hz, QP=30, and the post-processed sequences are shown in Fig. 7. The proposed algorithm effectively reduced the blocking artifacts and preserved the original high-frequency components, such as edges. But, VM-18 post-filter reduced the blocking artifacts in smooth regions, but the blocking artifacts in complex regions are still remained.

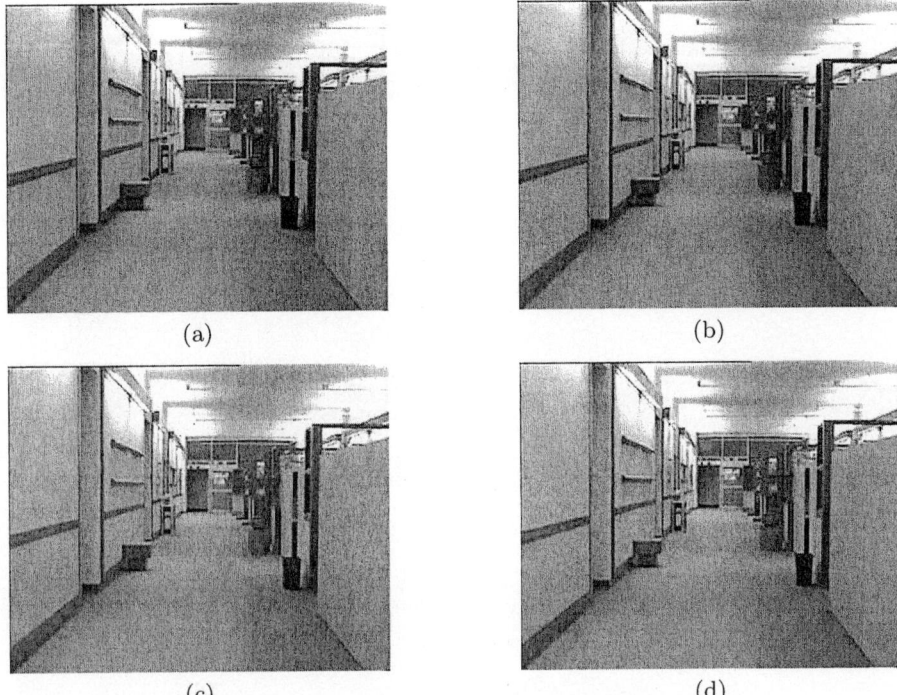

Fig. 6. (a) The Hall monitor sequence decoded by MPEG-4 with 48 kbps, 7.5 Hz, QP=12, and post-processed sequences by (b) VM-18 deblocking filter method, (c) VM-18 deblocking and deringing filter method, and (d) proposed method

5 Conclusions

We propose a hybrid deblocking algorithm that can remove blocking and ringing artifacts from signals by spatial adaptive filtering and estimating the Lipschitz regularity in wavelet domain. The proposed method classifies the block boundary into smooth region, complex region, and mixed region in spatial domain and detects the blocky region which includes the blocking artifacts in smooth region. Spatial adaptive filtering is processed to reduce the blocking artifacts in smooth region with the blocking artifacts. For complex or mixed region, the Lipschitz regularity is obtained to analyze the evolution of the local maxima of the wavelet transform modulus across scales and this value is used to extract irregular singularities due to blocking and ringing artifacts from the multiscales in a signal. These irregular singularities are adaptively removed. Experimental results confirmed that the proposed algorithm can reduce the presence of artifacts and preserve the edge details.

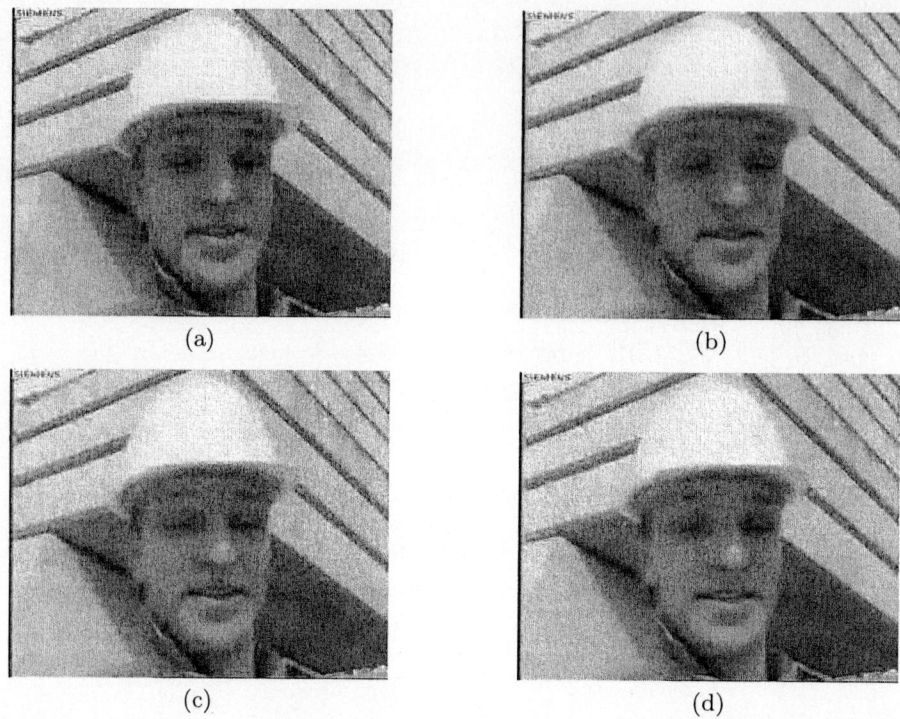

Fig. 7. (a) The Foreman sequence decoded by MPEG-4 with 112 kbps, 15 Hz, QP=30, and post-processed sequences by (b) VM-18 deblocking filter method, (c) VM-18 deblocking and deringing filter method, and (d) proposed method

References

1. ITU-T Recommendation H. 263 Version 2: Video Coding for Low Bit Rate Communication. Draft (1998)
2. MPEG Video Group: MPEG-4 video verification model version 18.0. ISO/IEC JTC1/SC29/WG11 N3908 (2001)
3. Kim, S. M., Park, J. H., Park, S. M., Koo, B. T., Shin, K. S., Suh, K. B., Kim, I. K., Eum, N. W., and Kim, K. S.: Hardware-software implementation of MPEG-4 video codec. ETRI Journal. 25 (2003) 489-502
4. Kim, S. D., Yi, J. Y., Kim, H. M., and Ra, J. B.: A deblocking filter with two separate modes in block-based video coding. IEEE Trans. Circuits Systems Video Technol. 9 (1999) 156-160
5. Ramamurthi, B. and Gersho, A.: Nonlinear space-variant postprocessing of block coded images. IEEE Trans. Acoustics, Speech, Signal Processing, 34 (1986) 1258–1268
6. Qui, G.: MLP for adaptive postprocessing block-coded images. IEEE Trans. Circuits Syst. Video Technol. 10 (2000) 1450–1454
7. Yang, Y., Galatsanos, N., and Katsagelos, A.: Projection-based spatially adaptive reconstruction of block-transform compressed images. IEEE Trans. Image Processing. 4 (1995) 896-908

8. Paek, H., Kim, R. C., and Lee, S. U.: A DCT-based spatially adaptive post-processing technique to reduce the blocking artifacts in transform coded images. IEEE Trans. Circuits Syst. Video Technol. 10 (2000) 36-41
9. Donoho, D. L.: De-noising by soft-thresholding. IEEE Trans. Inform. Theory. 41 (1995) 613-627
10. Xiong, Z., Orchard, M. T., and Zhang, Y. Q.: A deblocking algorithm for JPEG compressed images using overcomplete wavelet representations. IEEE Trans. Circuits Syst. Video Technol. 7 (1997) 433-437
11. Hsung, T. C., Lun, D. P. K., and Siu, W. C.: A deblocking technique for block-transform compressed image using wavelet transform modulus maxima. IEEE Trans. Image Process-ing. 7 (1998) 1488-1496
12. Kim, N. C., Jang, I. H., Kim, D. H., and Hong, W. H.: Reduction of blocking artifact in block-coded images using wavelet transform. IEEE Trans. Circuits Syst. Video Technol. 8 (1998) 253-257
13. Jaffard, S.: Pointwise smoothness, two micro localisation and wavelet coefficients. Publica-tions Mathematiques. 35 (1991)
14. Mallat, S. and Zhong, S.: Characterization of signals from multiscale edges. IEEE Trans. Pattern Anal. Machine Intell. 14 (1992) 710-732
15. Mallat, S. and Hwang, W. L.: Singularity detection and processing with wavelet. IEEE Trans. Inform. Theory. 38 (1992) 617-643

A Cross-Resolution Leaky Prediction Scheme for In-Band Wavelet Video Coding with Spatial Scalability

Dongdong Zhang[1,*], Jizheng Xu[2], Feng Wu[2], Wenjun Zhang[1], and Hongkai Xiong[1]

[1] Image Communication Institute, Shanghai Jiao Tong Univ., Haoran Hi-tech Building, No1954 Huashan Road, Shanghai 200030, China
{cessy, zhangwenjun, xionghongkai}@sjtu.edu.cn
[2] Microsoft Research Asia, 3F Sigma, No49 Zhichun Road, Haidian, Beijing 100080, China
{jzxu, fengwu}@microsoft.com

Abstract. In in-band wavelet video coding schemes, motion prediction is applied in the spatial subband domain. Compared to motion prediction in full-resolution image domain, in-band schemes suffer coding performance loss at full resolution. One reason is that signals of the subband at low resolution are predicted from the reference frames at low resolution, which has comparatively low quality. However, if signals of the subband at high resolution are involved in the prediction of signals at low resolution, mismatch will occur in decoding low-resolution video when the corresponding signals of high resolution are not available at the decoder. This paper first analyzes the mismatch error propagation when low-resolution video is decoded. Then based on the analysis we propose a frame-based cross-resolution leaky prediction scheme for in-band wavelet video coding to make a good trade-off between reducing mismatch error of low resolution and improving coding performance of high resolution. Experimental results show that, the proposed scheme can dramatically reduce the mismatch error by about 0.3~2.5dB at different bit rates for the low resolution, while for the high resolution, the performance loss is marginal.

1 Introduction

As many video communication applications take place in heterogeneous environment, the scalability of a video codec becomes an important feature besides coding efficiency. The video bitstream generated by the encoder should adapt to various bitrates, spatial resolutions and frame-rates according to the bandwidth of the network, storage and computation capability of a specific device.

3D wavelet video coding schemes with lifting-based motion compensated temporal filtering (MCTF) have been investigated by many scholars because its inherent scalable property as well as the embedded entropy coding technique can readily achieve spatial, temporal and SNR scalabilities simultaneously. Generally speaking, these schemes can be divided into two categories. The first is to perform MCTF on the input video sequence directly in full-resolution spatial domain before spatial

---

[*] This work has been done while the author is with Microsoft Research Asia.

transform, which is often referred as spatial domain MCTF (SDMCTF) [1], [2], [3], [4]. The second is to perform MCTF in subband domain after spatial transform, which is often referred as in-band MCTF (IBMCTF) [6], [7], [8], [9], [10]. SDMCTF scheme generally has high coding performance at full resolution. But it is not very suitable for spatial scalability. This is because the temporal transform in SDMCTF is applied in image domain at the encoder, while the inverse temporal transform is applied in subband domain when decoding low-resolution video. This mismatch keeps the quality of decoded low-resolution video from further improvement. Recently, IBMCTF scheme have attracted more attention because of direct support of spatial scalability and flexible coding framework.

Fig.1(a) shows the generalized block diagram of in-band wavelet video coding schemes. The spatial wavelet transform is firstly applied to original video sequence, which generates multiple spatial bands. Fig.1(b) illustrates the case of one-level spatial transform, where L/H means low-pass/high-pass band. Then temporal transform is used to exploit the temporal correlation within each spatial band. For each temporal band of a certain spatial band, the spatial transform can be further employed to exploit the spatial correlation. In the process of entropy coding, the residual coefficients of each spatio-temporal band are coded independently so that the server can easily drop unnecessary spatio-temporal bands according to the spatio-temporal resolution requested by the client. For example, spatial scalability can be achieved by just decoding LL band and dropping other three bands.

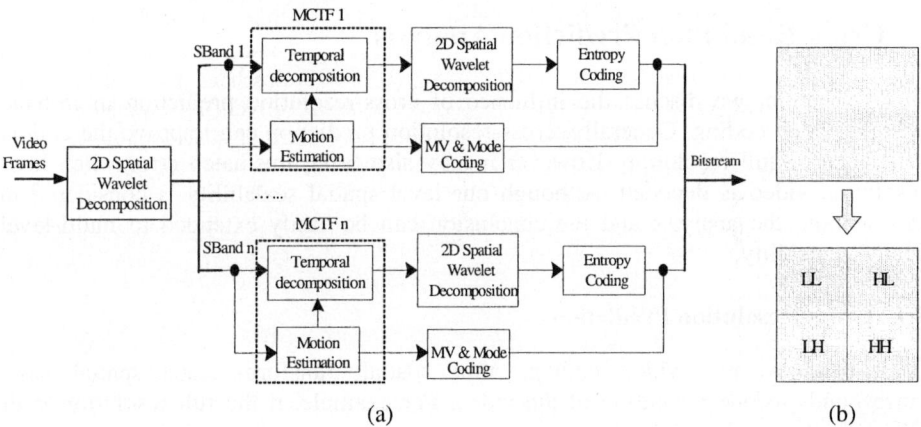

Fig. 1. (a) In-band wavelet video coding scheme (b) one level 2D spatial wavelet transform

Although IBMCTF scheme can easily support spatial scalability, its coding performance is inferior to SDMCTF scheme at full resolution. One reason is that the motion estimation/compensation (ME/MC) in subband domain is not as efficient as that in original image domain because of the shift-variance of wavelet transform. To solve this problem, Park and Kim proposed low band shift method (LBS), which can do the ME/MC more efficiently with the over-complete form of reference frames [5]. Based on LBS method, Schaar et al employed the interleaving algorithm for the over-complete wavelet coefficients of the references to get an optimized sub-pixel interpolated references for in-band motion estimation and motion compensation, which leads to a similar full-resolution performance to SDMCTF schemes[7], [8]. These technologies enable cross-band dependency to be used. In [5], [6], [7], [8], [10], the predictions of HL, LH, HH bands are performed with LL band. And [9] shows that HL, LH, HH bands can also involved in the prediction of LL band.

The coding efficiency of each spatial band can be improved with over-complete in-band ME/MC. However, if the temporal filtering in the spatial low-pass band does use data from the spatial high-pass bands, it will bring serious mismatch error when decoding low-resolution video since the corresponding high-pass bands are not available at the decoder. In this paper, we first analyze the mismatch error propagation along the lifting structure when low-resolution video is decoded. Then based on the analysis we propose a frame-based cross-resolution leaky prediction scheme for in-band wavelet video coding to make a good trade-off between the low-resolution mismatch error and the full-resolution coding performance. Different from [9], we use a frame-based scheme which is simple but effective, and the tradeoff is different for different level of temporal transform based on our analysis.

The rest of this paper is organized as follows. In section 2, we analyze the influence of cross-resolution prediction in in-band wavelet video coding and discuss its pros and cons. Section 3 introduces the proposed cross-resolution leaky prediction scheme for in-band wavelet video coding. In section 4, experimental results will be presented and discussed. Section 5 concludes this paper.

2 Cross-Resolution Prediction Analysis

In this section, we discuss the influence of cross-resolution prediction in in-band wavelet video coding. Generally, cross-resolution prediction can improve the coding efficiency of full resolution. However it may also bring mismatch error when low-resolution video is decoded. Although one-level spatial scalability is considered in this section, the analysis and the conclusion can be easily extended to multi-level spatial scalability.

2.1 Cross-Resolution Prediction

In in-band wavelet video coding, after spatial transform, each spatial band corresponds to one resolution of the video. For example, if the full resolution is of CIF size, then in Fig. 1(b), LL band is at QCIF resolution. Other three bands are of QCIF size, but they are used for reconstruction of CIF resolution video, so we think they are at CIF resolution. After spatial transform, usually lifting-based MCTF is applied as the temporal transform, which has two steps: prediction and update. In prediction, spatial bands of neighboring frames are used to predict the bands of the current frame. Cross-resolution prediction means that when coding a spatial band, which belongs to a specific resolution, can use information from other resolution to form the prediction. It can be done by generation of the band's reference using over-complete wavelet video transform. Fig. 2(b) shows the process to generate LL band's reference with the information from LL, LH, HL, and HH bands. Here, IDWT and ODWT operation actually act as a half-pixel interpolation. By comparison, the process to generate LL band's reference without utilizing the other bands' information is shown in Fig. 2(a). In this paper, we also call the reference in Fig. 2(a) low quality reference and the one in Fig. 2(b) high quality reference because the quality of the reference can be improved much with other bands' information, which leads to the improved coding efficiency.

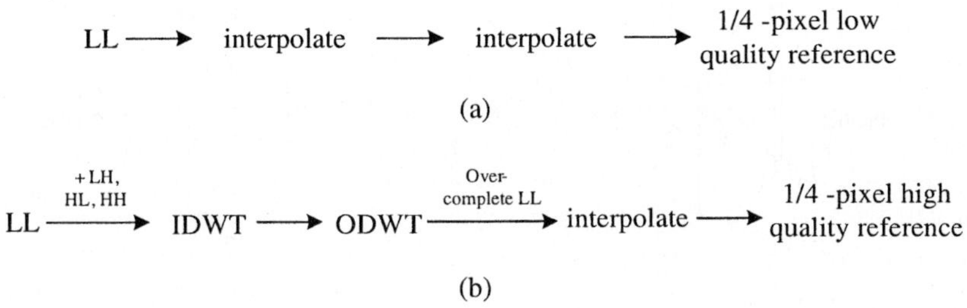

$$LL \longrightarrow interpolate \longrightarrow interpolate \longrightarrow \text{1/4 -pixel low quality reference}$$

(a)

$$LL \xrightarrow{+LH, HL, HH} IDWT \longrightarrow ODWT \xrightarrow{Over\text{-}complete\ LL} interpolate \longrightarrow \text{1/4 -pixel high quality reference}$$

(b)

Fig. 2. Generation of (a) low quality reference w/o cross-resolution prediction and (b) high quality reference w/ cross-resolution prediction, where IDWT and ODWT denote inverse discrete wavelet transform and over-complete discrete wavelet transform respectively

At the decoder, when low-resolution video is demanded, only LL band is obtained. So Fig. 2(a) is used to form the reference. If the encoder uses high quality reference for the prediction of LL band, there will be mismatch error when decoding low-resolution video. So basically using high quality reference for the LL band favors coding efficiency at full resolution, but it degrades low-resolution performance meanwhile.

For the HL, LH and HH bands, they can use other bands' information (e.g. LL band) to generate references without bringing any mismatch. Because when the decoder gets HL, LH and HH bands, it means that full resolution video is decoded. In this case all other bands should also available at the decoder. So our scheme always uses the method in Fig. 2(b) to generate references for spatial high-pass bands, both at the encoder and at the decoder.

2.2 Mismatch Error Propagation Along the Lifting Structure

In this sub-section we focus on the mismatch error propagation along the lifting structure for decoding video at the low resolution. As described above, when low-resolution video is decoded, using high quality reference for LL band's prediction brings mismatch error. Assume that N-level temporal filtering is used within each spatial band. Let $\{L_n^0\}$ denote the sequence of the LL band after one-level spatial transform. $\{L_n^i\}$ and $\{H_n^i\}$ denote the temporal low-pass sequence and high-pass sequence after i-level $(i=1,...,N)$ temporal filtering. $\{\tilde{L}_n^i\}$ and $\{\tilde{H}_n^i\}$ are the corresponding temporal reconstructed low-pass and high-pass sequences. Fig. 3 shows the lifting structure of the temporal filtering of LL band at the encoder and the decoder for low resolution with 5/3 filter. In the figure, the three joint blocks denote three high-pass bands used for the temporal filtering of LL band.

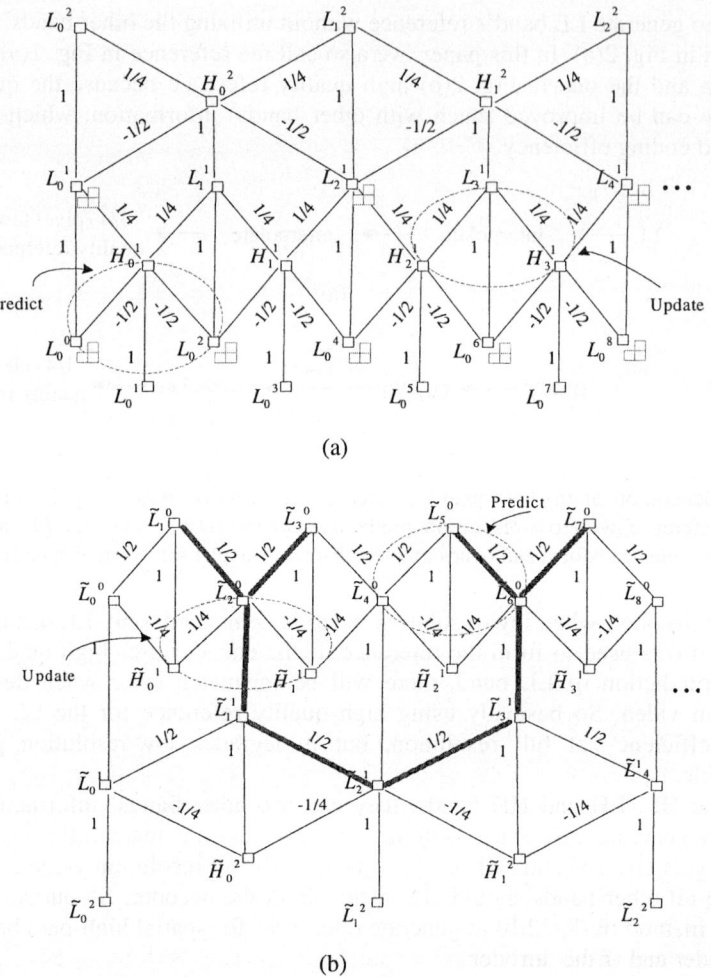

Fig. 3. The lifting structure of two-level temporal filtering for low resolution with 5/3 filter (a) is for the encoder and (b) is for the decoder

When decoding the low-resolution video, the decoding distortion consists of two parts - quantization error and mismtach error. Assume that quantization error and mismatch error are independent with each other. We can analyze the mismatch error independently at the decoder. Since the update step in the lifting has less effect on the MCTF of LL band compared with the predict step, the spatial high-pass bands are not used during the update step. So it does not bring the mismatch error. At the decoder, for each level of temporal synthesis, the update step is first used to reconstruct the frames with even index, followed by the predict step to reconstruct the frames with odd index. Because the mismatch error only comes from the predict step, after each temporal synthesis of LL band at the decoder, odd-index frames suffer more from the mismatch. When the reconstruction of the frame needs more prediction steps, the mismatch error of the reconstructed frame will be more and the quality of the reconstructed signal will be worse. The thick lines in Fig. 3 show the propagation of the mismatch error caused by the reference mismatch between the encoder and the decoder.

In the following, we analyze the propagation of the mismatch error which comes from the predict step along the lifting structure. When decoding low-resolution video, all three high-pass bands are not available at the decoder. At the decoder, after each level temporal synthesis, we have equations (1), (2) for decoding at low resolution and (1),(3) for decoding at full resolution.

$$\tilde{L}_{2n}^{i} = \tilde{L}_{n}^{i+1} - U(\tilde{H}_{n-1}^{i+1}, \tilde{H}_{n+1}^{i+1})$$
$$U(\tilde{H}_{n-1}^{i+1}, \tilde{H}_{n+1}^{i+1}) = \frac{1}{4}((MC(\tilde{H}_{n-1}^{i+1}, MV_{2n\to2n-1}) + MC(\tilde{H}_{n+1}^{i+1}, MV_{2n\to2n+1})) \quad i=0,\ldots,N-1 \quad (1)$$

$$\tilde{L}_{2n+1}^{i} = \tilde{H}_{n}^{i+1} + P(\tilde{L}_{2n}^{i}, \tilde{L}_{2n+2}^{i})$$
$$P(\tilde{L}_{2n}^{i}, \tilde{L}_{2n+2}^{i}) = \frac{1}{2}MC(R_{l}(\tilde{L}_{2n}^{i}), MV_{2n+1\to2n}) + \frac{1}{2}MC(R_{l}(\tilde{L}_{2n+2}^{i}), MV_{2n+1\to2n+2}) \quad i=0,\ldots,N-1 \quad (2)$$

$$\tilde{L}_{2n+1}^{i} = \tilde{H}_{n}^{i+1} + P(\tilde{L}_{2n}^{i}, \tilde{L}_{2n+2}^{i})$$
$$P(\tilde{L}_{2n}^{i}, \tilde{L}_{2n+2}^{i}) = \frac{1}{2}MC(R_{h}(\tilde{L}_{2n}^{i}), MV_{2n+1\to2n}) + \frac{1}{2}MC(R_{h}(\tilde{L}_{2n+2}^{i}), MV_{2n+1\to2n+2}) \quad i=0,\ldots,N-1 \quad (3)$$

Where, $P()$ and $U()$ denote the prediction and update step. $R_l()$ and $R_h()$ are the operations generating the low quality reference and the high quality reference respectively. $MC()$ means motion compensation process that generates the current frame's prediction from its consecutive frame. $MV_{2n\to2n-1}$ and $MV_{2n\to2n+1}$ are the sub-pixel motion vectors from an even frame to the forward and backward adjacent odd one.

We define the error between the high quality reference and the low quality reference as $\Delta_i(n) = R_l(L_h^i) - R_h(L_h^i), i=0,\ldots,N-1$. Assume that the errors $\Delta_i(n)$ $(n=1,2,\ldots;i=0,\ldots,N-1)$ are independent with each other. We can use linear combination of the variance $\sigma_i^2(n)$ of the error $\Delta_i(n)$ to describe the mismatch distortion of one given frame. Without considering the quantization error, the received sequences $\{\tilde{H}_n^i\}$ and $\{\tilde{L}_h^N\}$ at the decoder are the same as the coded sequences $\{H_n^i\}$ and $\{L_h^N\}$. So at the decoder the mismatch error for reconstructing the sequences $\{H_n^i\}$ and $\{L_h^N\}$ is equal to 0. According to the equation (1), (2) and (3), if low resolution video is decoded, the mismatch error for each level temporal synthesis can be recursively described as follows.

$$D_n^N = 0$$
$$D_{2n}^i = D_n^{i+1} \qquad i=0,...,N-1$$
$$D_{2n+1}^i = \frac{1}{4}(D_{2n}^i + \sigma_i^2(2n)) + \frac{1}{4}(D_{2n+2}^i + \sigma_i^2(2n+2)) \qquad i=0,...,N-1$$

Where, D_n^i denotes the mismatch distortion for reconstructing the frame L_n^i and in the derivation, we assume $MC(R_l(L_n^i) - R_h(L_n^i), MV) \approx R_l(L_n^i) - R_h(L_n^i)$.

The above equations show that the mismatch error at the higher temporal level will affect all of the lower level temporal synthesis when decoding the low resolution video. Considering the propagation of the error $\Delta_{N-1}(2n)$ at the $N-1$-temporal level, after one level temporal synthesis, this error will affect the quality of two reconstructed frames. After two-level synthesis, there would have six reconstructed frames affected by this error. After N-level synthesis, there will be $\sum_{j=0}^{N-1} 2^{(N-j)}$ reconstructed frames affected by the error. The total distortion caused by this error can be written as follow.

$$TotalD_{N-1}(2n) = \sum_{j=0}^{N-1} 2^{(N-j)} \times \left(\tfrac{1}{2}\right)^{2(N-j)} \sigma_{N-1}^2(2n) = \sum_{j=0}^{N-1} \left(\tfrac{1}{2}\right)^{N-j} \sigma_{N-1}^2(2n) \qquad (4)$$

Substitute $N-1$ with $m (0 < m \leq N-1)$ in the equation (4) and we can get the total mismatch distortion came from the error $\Delta_m(2n)$ at the mth temporal level as follow.

$$TotalD_m(2n) = \sum_{j=0}^{m} 2^{(m-j+1)} \times \left(\tfrac{1}{2}\right)^{2(m-j+1)} \sigma_m^2(2n) \quad 0 < m \leq N-1 \qquad (5)$$

From equation (5), we can see that the error at higher temporal level will deteriorate more reconstructed LL band frames' qualities and the total distortion caused by it will be more for decoding at the low resolution.

3 Cross-Resolution Leaky Prediction

For in-band wavelet video coding with spatial scalability, when spatial high-pass bands are used for the motion compensation of spatial low-pass band, the coding efficiency at full resolution can be improved. However, this will bring mismatch error for decoding low-resolution video. To make a good trade-off between reducing the mismatch error for decoding at low resolution and improving the coding efficiency at full resolution. We proposed a frame-based leaky motion compensation scheme for in-band wavelet video coding. Actually leaky prediction is an efficient technique for reducing mismatch errors. References [11], [12], [13], [14] have shown that leaky prediction is very useful in DCT-based SNR scalable video coding. In our scheme, when encoding the spatial LL band, the difference between the high quality reference and the low quality reference will be attenuated by a leaky factor. The high quality reference will be partly used to form a better reference frame of LL band. For spatial high-pass bands, the high quality references are always used for motion compensation at both encoder and decoder. Supposing that the N-level temporal filtering is used, the leaky motion compensation can be described as follow.

At the encoder we have equations (6) and (7):

$$H_n^{i+1} = L_{2n+1}^i - P(L_{2n}^i + L_{2n+2}^i)$$
$$P(L_{2n}^i, L_{2n+2}^i) = \frac{1}{2}MC((1-\alpha_i) \times R_l(L_{2n}^i) + \alpha_i \times R_h(L_{2n}^i), MV_{2n+1 \to 2n}) + \frac{1}{2}MC((1-\alpha_i) \times R_l(L_{2n+2}^i) + \alpha_i \times R_h(L_{2n+2}^i), MV_{2n+1 \to 2n+2}) \quad (6)$$
$$i = 0,...,N-1$$

$$L_n^{i+1} = L_{2n}^i + U(H_{n-1}^{i+1} + H_{n+1}^{i+1})$$
$$U(H_{n-1}^{i+1} + H_{n+1}^{i+1}) = \frac{1}{4}((MC(H_{n-1}^{i+1}, MV_{2n \to 2n-1}) + MC(H_{n+1}^{i+1}, MV_{2n \to 2n+1})) \quad i=0,...,N-1 \quad (7)$$

Where, $\alpha_i (0 \le \alpha_i \le 1)$ is the leaky factor for the ith level temporal filtering. At the decoder, we have equations (1), (2) for decoding low-resolution video and equation (1), (8) for decoding full-resolution video.

$$\tilde{L}_{2n+1}^i = \tilde{H}_n^{i+1} + P(\tilde{L}_{2n}^i + \tilde{L}_{2n+2}^i)$$
$$P(\tilde{L}_{2n}^i, \tilde{L}_{2n+2}^i) = \frac{1}{2}MC((1-\alpha_i) \times R_l(\tilde{L}_{2n}^i) + \alpha_i \times R_h(\tilde{L}_{2n}^i), MV_{2n+1 \to 2n}) + \frac{1}{2}MC((1-\alpha_i) \times R_l(\tilde{L}_{2n+2}^i) + \alpha_i \times R_h(\tilde{L}_{2n+2}^i), MV_{2n+1 \to 2n+2}) \quad (8)$$
$$i = 0,...,N-1$$

When the leaky motion compensation is used for the temporal filtering of LL band, the error $\Delta_i(2n)$ $(i=0,...,N-1)$ will be attenuated by the factor α_i. According to the analysis in section 2, when the multi-level temporal filtering is applied, the mismatch error of reconstructed signal will be greatly attenuated level by level. The total mismatch distortion came from the error $\Delta_m(2n)$ at the mth temporal level will be reduced as follow.

$$TotalD_m(2n) = \sum_{j=0}^{m} 2^{(m-j+1)} \times \left(\frac{1}{2}\right)^{2(m-j+1)} \cdot \alpha_j \cdots \alpha_{m-1} \cdot \sigma_m^2(2n) \quad 0 < m \le N-1 \quad (9)$$

The selection of each leak factor α_i is a critical issue to achieve a good tradeoff. If the value of α_i is close to 1, more information of high-pass band is used for a certain level temporal motion compensation of LL band, which leads to the best coding efficiency and on the same time, the less mismatch error reduction. On the other hand, for α_i that is close to zero, the mismatch error reduction is enhanced significantly at the cost of the reduced coding efficiency. According to the analysis in section 2, the error at the higher level temporal filtering will propagate to the lower level one. Meanwhile, for high level temporal filtering, the improvement of coding performance is not significant with the additional spatial high-pass bands because in such case, the subband frames to be decomposed have long time distance thus small dependency. So the leaky factor at the higher temporal level should be less than that at the lower temporal level. That is, at the higher temporal level, the less information of spatial high-pass bands is used for the motion compensation of LL band.

4 Experiment Results

Based on MPEG scalable video coding (SVC) reference software for wavelet ad-hoc group [15], [16], we test our proposed scheme. Fig. 4, 5 and 6 present the experiment results for foreman sequence (300 frames), bus sequence (150 frames) and mobile sequence (300 frames) in CIF format with different schemes. In the experiments, each sequence is first decomposed into four spatial bands with 9/7 filter and four-level temporal filtering with 5/3 filter is used with each spatial band. The high quality references are always applied to the motion compensation of three high-pass bands for all schemes. Scheme I denotes the scheme that the low quality interpolation reference is used for motion compensation of LL band. Scheme II denotes the scheme that the motion compensation of LL band is done with high quality interpolation reference. Scheme III and scheme IV are our proposed leaky motion compensation scheme with the different value of α_i. In these figures, the decoded sequence named "foreman_qcif_7.5Hz" means that the bit-stream of "foreman" sequence is decoded with image size of qcif at frame rate of 7.5 frames per second.

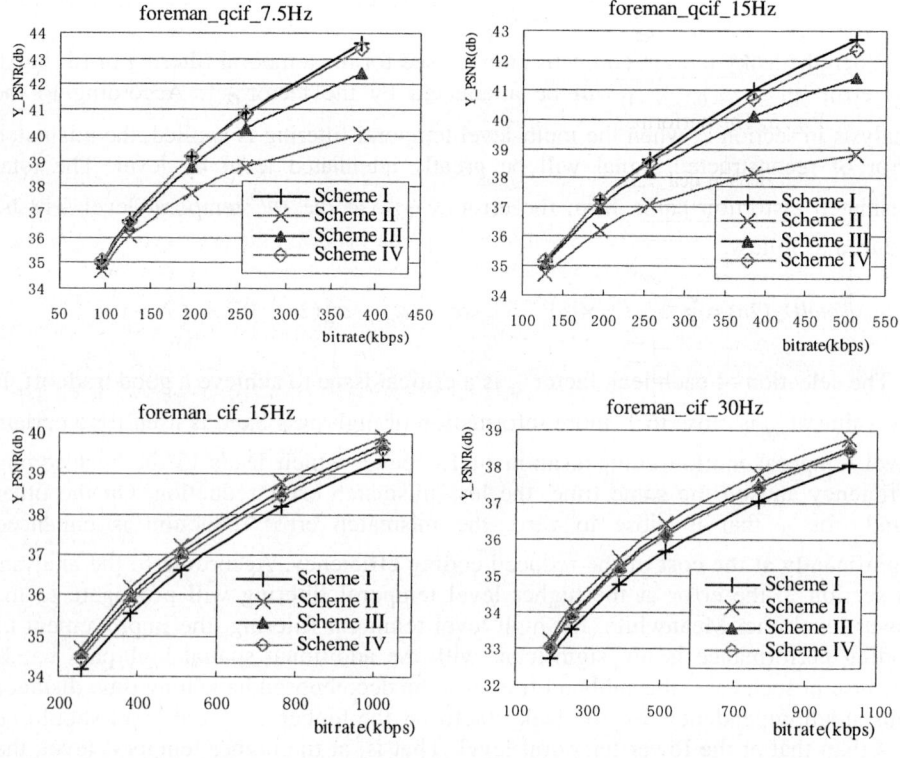

Fig. 4. The performance of the leaky motion compensation for foreman sequence

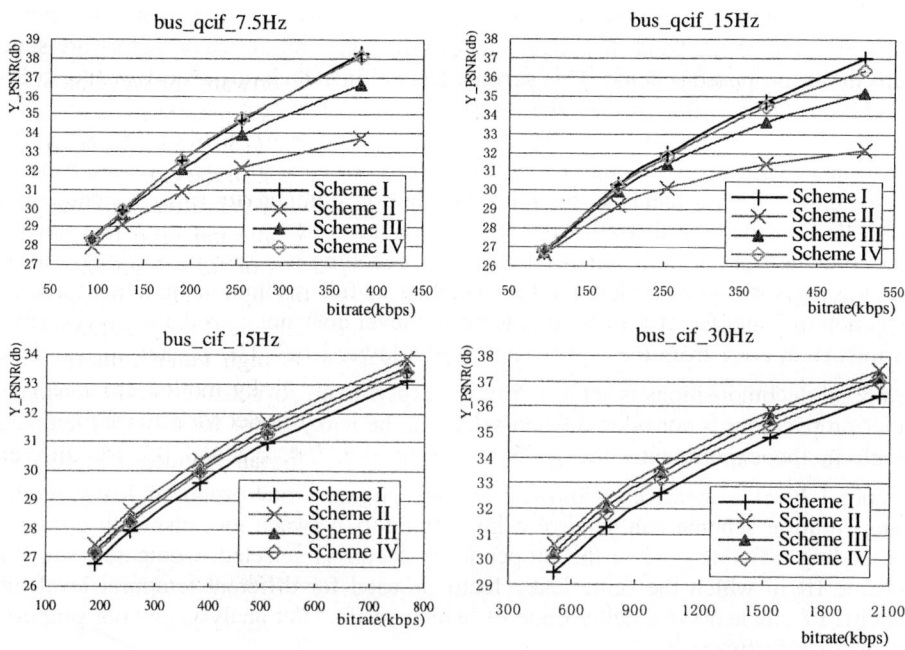

Fig. 5. The performance of the leaky motion compensation for bus sequence

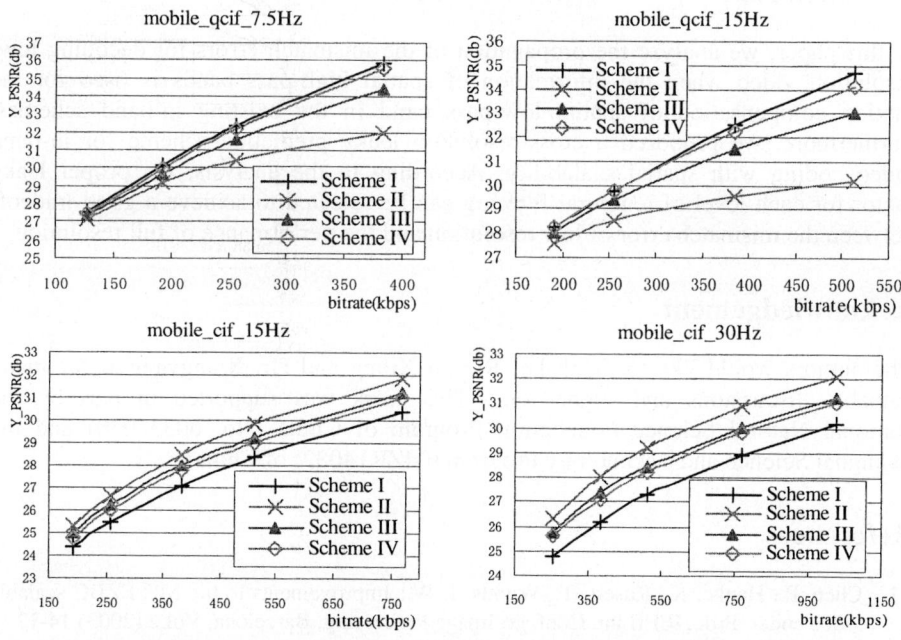

Fig. 6. The performance of the leaky motion compensation for mobile sequence

In scheme I, the high-pass band information is not used for the motion compensation of LL band. It is equivalent to the case that all leaky factors are set to zero in our proposed scheme. This scheme has no mismatch error for decoding at low resolution video while it has the lowest coding efficiency for decoding at full resolution. So in the figure, it is obvious that this scheme has the best low-resolution performance but the worst high resolution performance. In scheme II, the information of all the high-pass bands is used for the motion compensation of LL band. It is equivalent to the case that all leaky factors are set to unity in our proposed scheme. This scheme has the most mismatch error for decoding low-resolution video while it has the highest coding efficiency for decoding at full resolution. In scheme III, the selection of leaky factor for different temporal level does not consider the propagation of mismatch error from the higher level to the lower level. The α_i for all four level temporal decompositions is set as 0.5 in the experiments. In scheme IV, the mismatch error propagation is considered when selecting the leaky factor for different temporal level. In the experiments, the α_i is set to be 0.5, 0.4, 0.3 and 0.2 for different temporal level respectively. Showed in these figures, our proposed leaky motion compensation scheme can achieve a good tradeoff between the mismatch error and the coding efficiency when the proper leaky factor is selected. Compared with the scheme III in which the same leaky factor is used for different temporal level, the scheme IV can achieve a better tradeoff, which verifies our analysis and our proposed scheme's effectiveness.

5 Conclusion

In this paper, we analyze the propagation of the mismatch errors for decoding low-resolution video when the information of spatial high-pass bands is used for the motion compensation of spatial low-pass band in the existing in-band schemes. Furthermore, we proposed a cross-resolution leaky prediction scheme for in-band video coding with spatial scalability. According to the analysis, the proper leaky factor for each level of temporal filtering can be selected to achieve a good tradeoff between the mismatch error of low resolution and the performance of full resolution.

Acknowledgement

The authors would like to thank Dr. Ruiqin Xiong and Dr. Xiangyang Ji for many valuable discussions and suggestions. This work was supported in part by the National Natural Science Foundation Program of China (No. 60332030) and the Shanghai Science and Technology Program (04ZR14082) of China.

References

1. Chen, P., Hanke, K., Rusert, T., Woods, J. W.: Improvements to the MC-EZBC scalable video coder. Proc. IEEE Int. Conf. on Image Processing, Barcelona, Vol.2 (2003) 14-17
2. Xiong, R.Q., Wu, F., Li, S.P., Xiong, Z.X., Zhang, Y.Q.: Exploiting temporal correlation with adaptive block-size motion alignment for 3D wavelet coding. Proc. SPIE Visual Communications and Image Processing, San Jose, CA (2004) 144-155

3. Flierl, M., Girod, B.: Video coding with motion-compensated lifted wavelet transforms. EURASIP Signal Processing: Image Communication, Vol. 19 (2004) 561-575
4. Pau, G., Tillier, C., Pesquet-Popescu, B., Heijmans, H.: Motion compensation and scalability in lifting-based video coding. EURASIP Signal Processing: Image Communication, Vol. 19 (2004) 577-599
5. Park, H.W., Kim, H.S.: Motion Estimation Using Low-Band-Shift Method for Wavelet-Based Moving-Picture Coding. IEEE Trans. on Image Processing, Vol. 9 (2000) 577-587
6. Mehrseresht, N., Taubman, D. : An efficient content-adaptive MC 3D-DWT with enhanced spatial and temporal scalability. Proc. IEEE International Conference on Image Processing, Singapore, October (2004) 1329-1332
7. van der Schaar, M., Ye, J.C.: Adaptive Overcomplete Wavelet Video Coding with Spatial Transcaling. Proc. SPIE Video Communications and Image Processing (VCIP), Lugano Switzerland (2003) 489-500
8. Andreopoulos, Y., Munteanu, A., Barbarien, J., van der Schaar, M., Cornelis, J., Schelkens, P.: In-band motion compensated temporal filtering. EURASIP Signal Processing: Image Communication, Vol. 19 (2004) 653-673
9. Taubman, D., Mehrseresht, N., Leung, R.: SVC Technical Contribution: Overview of recent technology developments at UNSW. Int. Standards Org./Int.Electrotech. Comm.(ISO/IEC) ISO/IEC JTC1/SC29/WG11 Document M10868 (2004)
10. Li, X.: Scalable video compression via overcomplete motion compensated wavelet coding. EURASIP Signal Processing: Image Communication, Vol. 19 (2004) 637-651
11. Huang, H., Wang, C., Chiang, T.: A Robust Fine Granularity Scalability Using Trellis-Based Predictive Leak. IEEE trans. Circuits and Systems for Video Technology, Vol. 12 (2002) 372-385
12. Han, S., Girod, B.: Robust and Efficient Scalable Video Coding with Leaky Prediction. Proc. IEEE International Conference on Image Processing, Rochester NY (2002) 41-44
13. Liu, Y.X., Li, Z.. Salama, P., Delp, E.J.: A discussion of leaky prediction based scalable coding. Proc. IEEE International Conference on Multimedia and Expo, Vol 2 (2003) 565-568
14. Gao. Y.L.; Chau, L.P.: An efficient fine granularity scalable coding scheme using adaptive leaky prediction. Proc. Joint Conference of the Fourth International Conference on Information, Communications and Signal Processing and the Fourth Pacific Rim Conference on Multimedia, Vol. 1 (2003), 582-586
15. Xiong, R.Q., Ji, X.Y., Zhang, D.D., Xu, J.Z., Pau, G., Trocan, M., Bottreau, V.: Vidwav Wavelet Video Coding Specifications. Int. Standards Org./Int.Electrotech. Comm.(ISO/IEC) ISO/IEC JTC1/SC29/WG11 Document M12339 (2005)
16. Bottreau, V., Pau, G., Xu, J.Z.: Vidwav evaluation software manual, Int. Standards Org./Int.Electrotech. Comm.(ISO/IEC) ISO/IEC JTC1/SC29/WG11 Document M12176 (2005)

Efficient Intra Prediction Mode Decision for H.264 Video

Seong Soo Chun, Ja-Cheon Yoon, and Sanghoon Sull

Department of Electronics and Computer Engineering, Korea University, 5-1 Anam-dong,
Songbuk-gu, Seoul 136-701, Korea
{sschun, jcyoon, sull}@mpeg.korea.ac.kr

Abstract. In this paper, we propose an efficient 4×4 intra prediction mode decision method for the complexity reduction of H.264 video coding. Based on the observation that a good prediction could be achieved when local edge direction of a block is in the same direction as the intra prediction mode, local edge direction of block is obtained in transform domain to filter out majority of intra prediction modes. By filtering out majority of intra prediction modes, we only have to consider a candidate set of most highly probable 4×4 intra prediction modes for which the rate distortion optimization process should be performed. Experimental results show that the proposed method can achieve a considerable reduction of computation while maintaining similar PSNR and bit rate.

1 Introduction

1.1 Background

The H.264/AVC [1,2] is the newest video coding standard developed by ITU-T Video Coding Experts Group (VCEG) and ISO/IEC MPEG Video Group named Joint Video Group (JVT). H.264 is intended for use in a wide range of applications including high bitrate application such as HDTV broadcasting and low bitrate applications such as video delivery to mobile devices. The high coding efficiency of H.264, that gives perceptually equivalent video quality at much less bitrate compared to traditional video coding standards such as MPEG-2 [3], is expected to encourage TV and internet broadcasters to fast adopt the new H.264 video coding technology.

The dramatic bandwidth saving of H.264 is not a result of a single feature but a combination of various advanced features. Some advance features of H.264 include 4×4 integer DCT, intra prediction in I-frame coding, quarter-pixel motion compensation, multiple reference frames and multiple block size for P-frame. However, these advanced features makes H.264 video coding more complex and computationally heavy. Recently, various researches are currently being made to cope with these advanced features to develop efficient H.264 encoding systems. In order to optimize H.264 video coding, a number of researches have been made to explore fast algorithms in motion estimation known to be the most time consuming in H.264 encoding [4-7]. These algorithms achieve significant time saving with negligible loss of coding efficiency. In [7], a fast inter mode decision method is proposed by selecting a small number of inter modes subject to rate distortion optimization based on the homogeneity and stationarity of the video objects. Using the above fast motion estimation techniques to reduce the complexity, techniques for intra prediction can also contribute to a even less complex and computational encoding in H.264. In this paper, we propose a method for efficient intra prediction mode decision in transform domain for H.264.

1.2 Intra Prediction Mode Decision

The H.264 video coding standard supports intra prediction for various block sizes. In case of 4×4 luminance block, a total of nine prediction modes are defined using neighboring pixels of reconstructed blocks. The prediction block is calculated based on the samples labeled A-M as shown in Fig. 1.

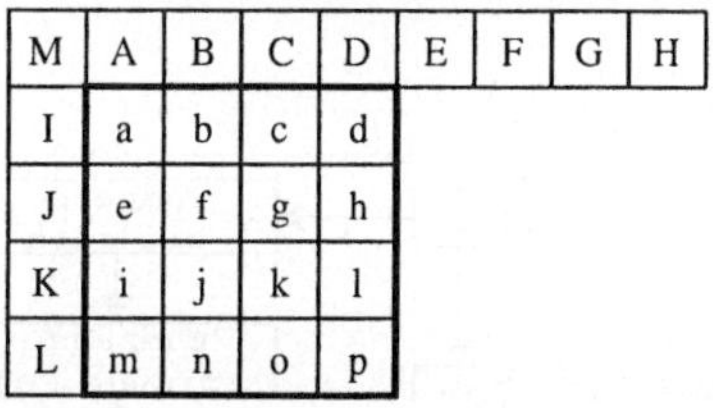

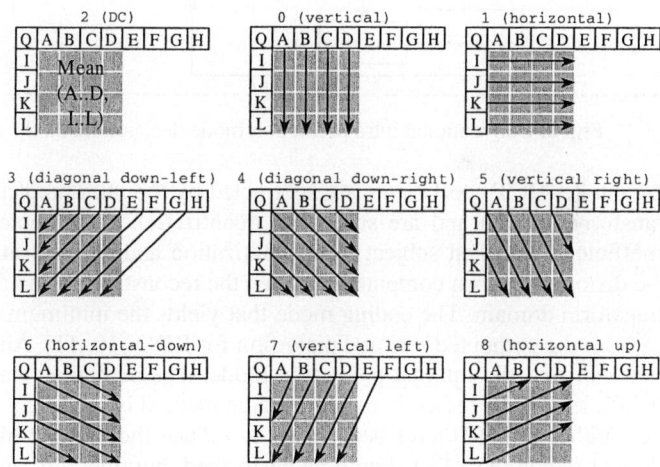

Fig. 1. Labeling of prediction samples

Fig. 2. Directions of intra prediction modes

For example, mode 2 is called DC prediction in which all pixels (labeled a to p) are predicted by $(A+B+C+D+I+J+K+L)/8$. The mode 0 specifies the vertical prediction mode in which pixels (labeled a, e, i and m) are predicted from A, and the pixels (labeled b, f, j and n) are predicted from B, and so on. The remaining modes are defined similarly according to the different directions as shown in Fig. 2. Note that in some cases, not all of the samples above and to the left are available within the current slice: in order to preserve independent decoding of slices, only samples within the current slice are available for prediction. DC prediction (mode 2) is modified depending on which samples A-M are available; the other modes (mode 1-8) may only be used if all of the required prediction samples are available (except when E, F, G and H are not available, their value is copied from sample D).

Fig. 3 illustrates the conventional transform domain intra prediction mode decision method for H.264 video coding [8, 9]. Although, the intra prediction process is by nature a pixel domain operation, computational savings can be achieved by performing the intra prediction process in transform domain by taking advantage of the fact the several intra prediction modes can be efficiently calculated. However, it resorts on using an exhaustive full search (FS) method to achieve rate-distortion optimization (RDO), which generates and encodes the video for all 9 intra prediction modes and selects the optimal prediction mode that minimizes the distortion and resulting bit rate at the same time.

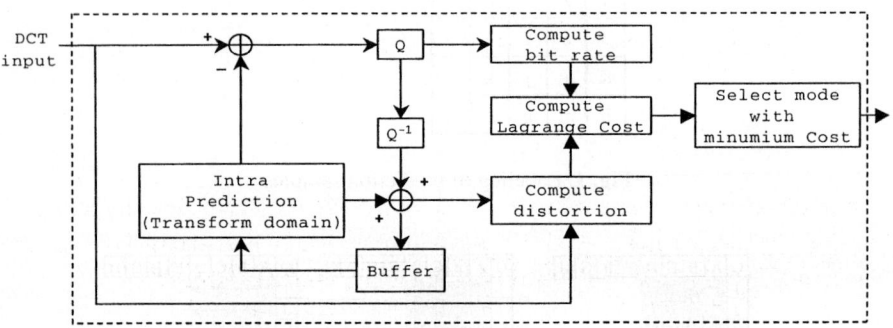

Fig. 3. Conventional intra prediction mode decision method

The H.264 integer DCT coefficients are subtracted by the intra predicted signal generated in transform domain and are subject to quantization to compute bit rate. The quantized coefficients are then subject to dequantization and compensation for reconstruction. The distortion is then computed between the reconstructed and the input block directly in transform domain. The coding mode that yields the minimum Lagrange cost then selected from the computed rate and distortion for RDO [10, 11]. Although the full search method can find the optimal prediction mode, it is computationally expensive. Therefore an efficient intra prediction mode decision method is needed.

Several researches [12, 13] have been made to reduce the number of possible prediction modes for which the RDO should be performed, but they rely on pixel domain operation and cannot be used in video transcoding systems [14, 15] conducted directly in transform domain. To our knowledge, no researches have yet been made in reducing the number of possible prediction modes directly in transform domain. In this paper, we propose a simple and yet effective intra prediction mode decision method based on local edge direction directly computed in transform domain. The proposed method filter outs the majority of intra prediction modes such that we only have to consider a candidate set of most probable 4×4 intra prediction modes for which the RDO should be performed.

The rest of this paper is organized as follows. Section 2 introduces our proposed intra prediction mode decision method. In order to show the effectiveness of the proposed method, the experimental results are provided in Section 3. In Section 4, the conclusions are drawn.

2 Proposed Intra Prediction Mode Decision

2.1 Local Edge Feature Extraction in Transform Domain

To compute the local edge direction of a 4×4 block, the block is divided into four non-overlapping 2×2 subblocks. Let us label the sub-blocks from 1 to 4 as in Fig. 4. Then the average luminance values A_k for the kth sub-block is computed.

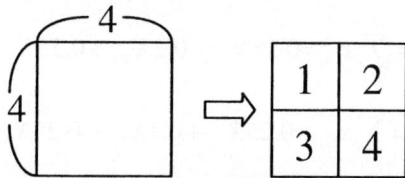

Fig. 4. Sub-blocks and their labeling

Using the average luminance values A_k (k=1,2,3,4), the local edge strength in the horizontal and vertical direction can be obtained using the horizontal edge feature E^{Hor} and vertical edge feature E^{Ver} defined as follows:

$$E^{Hor} = A_1 + A_2 - (A_3 + A_4),$$
$$E^{Ver} = A_1 + A_3 - (A_2 + A_4). \tag{1}$$

The equation (1) can be rewritten in terms of the pixel values as follows:

$$E^{Hor} = \sum_{i=1}^{2}\sum_{j=1}^{4}\left[x_{i,j} - x_{i+2,j}\right],$$
$$E^{Ver} = \sum_{j=1}^{2}\sum_{i=1}^{4}\left[x_{i,j} - x_{i,j+2}\right], \tag{2}$$

where $x_{i,j}$ denotes the pixel value at the ith row and j^{th} column of the block **x**.

In order to obtain E^{Hor} and E^{Ver} in transform domain, let us define the 2-D integer transform in H.264 as

$$\mathbf{X} = \mathbf{TxT^t}, \tag{3}$$

where

$$\mathbf{T} = \begin{bmatrix} 1 & 1 & 1 & 1 \\ 2 & 1 & -1 & -2 \\ 1 & -1 & -1 & 1 \\ 1 & -2 & 2 & -1 \end{bmatrix}. \tag{4}$$

From equation (2), we can derive the following equation

$$H = xT^t = T^{-1}X, \qquad (5)$$

where

$$T^{-1} = \begin{bmatrix} 0.25 & 0.2 & 0.25 & 0.1 \\ 0.25 & 0.1 & -0.25 & -0.2 \\ 0.25 & -0.1 & -0.25 & 0.2 \\ 0.25 & -0.2 & 0.25 & -0.1 \end{bmatrix}. \qquad (6)$$

Let us define H_i to be the value of the element at i^{th} row and first column of matrix H. Then, H_i (i=1, 2, 3, 4) can be represented as

$$H_1 = \sum_{j=1}^{4} x_{1,j} = 0.25X_{1,1} + 0.2X_{2,1} + 0.25X_{3,1} + 0.1X_{4,1}$$

$$H_2 = \sum_{j=1}^{4} x_{2,j} = 0.25X_{1,1} + 0.1X_{2,1} - 0.25X_{3,1} - 0.2X_{4,1}$$

$$H_3 = \sum_{j=1}^{4} x_{3,j} = 0.25X_{1,1} - 0.1X_{2,1} - 0.25X_{3,1} + 0.2X_{4,1}$$

$$H_4 = \sum_{j=1}^{4} x_{4,j} = 0.25X_{1,1} - 0.2X_{2,1} + 0.25X_{3,1} - 0.1X_{4,1}$$

$$(7)$$

where $X_{i,j}$ is the coefficient at the ith row and j^{th} column of X.

Using equation (7), the horizontal edge feature E^{Hor} in equation (2) can be rewritten as

$$E^{Hor} = \sum_{i=1}^{2} \sum_{j=1}^{4} \left[x_{i,j} - x_{i+2,j} \right]$$
$$= H_1 + H_2 - H_3 - H_4 = 0.6X_{2,1} - 0.2X_{4,1}. \qquad (8)$$

Similarly the vertical edge feature E^{Ver} may be computed by expressing equation (3) as

$$V = Tx = XT^{-t}, \qquad (9)$$

where

$$T^{-t} = \begin{bmatrix} 0.25 & 0.25 & 0.25 & 0.25 \\ 0.2 & 0.1 & -0.1 & -0.2 \\ 0.25 & -0.25 & -0.25 & 0.25 \\ 0.1 & -0.2 & 0.2 & -0.1 \end{bmatrix}. \qquad (10)$$

Let us define V_j to be the value of the element at first row and j^{th} column of the matrix V. Then, V_j (j=1, 2, 3, 4) can be represented as

$$V_1 = \sum_{i=1}^{4} x_{i,1} = 0.25X_{1,1} + 0.2X_{1,2} + 0.25X_{1,3} + 0.1X_{1,4}$$

$$V_2 = \sum_{i=1}^{4} x_{i,2} = 0.25X_{1,1} + 0.1X_{1,2} - 0.25X_{1,3} - 0.2X_{1,4}$$

$$V_3 = \sum_{i=1}^{4} x_{i,3} = 0.25X_{1,1} - 0.1X_{1,2} - 0.25X_{1,3} + 0.2X_{1,4}$$

$$V_4 = \sum_{i=1}^{4} x_{i,4} = 0.25X_{1,1} - 0.2X_{1,2} + 0.25X_{1,3} - 0.1X_{1,4}$$

(11)

where $X_{i,j}$ is the coefficient at the ith row and j^{th} column of $\mathbf{X}$.

Using equation (11), vertical edge feature E^{Ver} in equation (2) can be rewritten as

$$E^{Ver} = \sum_{j=1}^{2} \sum_{i=1}^{4} \left[x_{i,j} - x_{i,j+2} \right]$$
$$= V_1 + V_2 - V_3 - V_4 = 0.6X_{1,2} - 0.2X_{1,4}.$$

(12)

Therefore, the local horizontal edge feature E^{Hor} and vertical edge feature E^{Ver} can be computed directly in transform domain using equation (8) and (12). However, to avoid floating point operations, we use E^{Hor} and E^{Ver} value scaled by 5 since (8) and (12) can be rewritten as

$$E^{Hor} = 4X_{2,1} - X_{2,1} - X_{4,1},$$
$$E^{Ver} = 4X_{1,2} - X_{1,2} - X_{1,4},$$

(13)

and computed using only addition and shift operations.

2.2 Intra Prediction Mode Decision Using Local Edge Features

In order to achieve RDO, conventional transform domain intra prediction mode decision method, as previously shown in Fig. 3, uses full search (FS) method to evaluate the Lagrange cost of all nine 4×4 intra prediction modes and select the prediction mode that yields the minimum cost. Therefore, the computation of rate-distortion optimized intra prediction mode decision is computationally expensive. Fig. 5 illustrates the block diagram of our proposed method.

Compared to the conventional transform domain intra prediction mode decision method that uses full search (FS) method, our proposed method pre-selects a candidate set of most probable 4×4 intra prediction modes in transform domain such that fewer intra prediction modes are examined for RDO. Particularly, the most probable 4×4 intra prediction modes are selected based on observation that good prediction could be achieved when local edge direction of a block is in the same direction as the intra prediction mode. The edge direction of a 4×4 block is determined from the horizontal edge feature E^{Hor} and vertical edge feature E^{Ver} computed directly in transform domain from equation (13), and a candidate set of most probable intra prediction modes is selected depending upon each edge direction as summarized in Table 1, where *T* is an empirical threshold value.

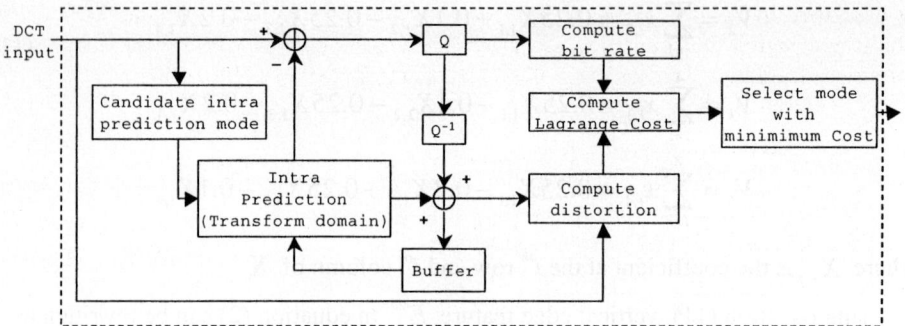

Fig. 5. Proposed intra prediction mode decision method

Table 1. Candidate modes for intra prediction based on E^{Hor} and E^{Ver}

Edge Direction		Condition	Candidate Modes
No Edge		$\left\|E^{Hor}\right\|<T, \left\|E^{Ver}\right\|<T$	2
Vertical		$\left\|E^{Hor}\right\|<T, \left\|E^{Ver}\right\|\geq T$	0,2
Horizontal		$\left\|E^{Hor}\right\|\geq T, \left\|E^{Ver}\right\|<T$	1,2
Diagonal down/left		$\left\|E^{Hor}\right\|-\left\|E^{Ver}\right\|\leq T, E^{Hor}\times E^{Ver}>0, \left\|E^{Hor}\right\|\geq T, \left\|E^{Ver}\right\|\geq T$	3,2
Diagonal down/right		$\left\|E^{Hor}\right\|-\left\|E^{Ver}\right\|\leq T, E^{Hor}\times E^{Ver}<0, \left\|E^{Hor}\right\|\geq T, \left\|E^{Ver}\right\|\geq T$	4,2
Horizontal dominant		$\left\|E^{Hor}\right\|-\left\|E^{Ver}\right\|>T, \left\|E^{Hor}\right\|\geq T, \left\|E^{Ver}\right\|\geq T$	4,6,1,8,3,2
Vertical dominant		$\left\|E^{Ver}\right\|-\left\|E^{Hor}\right\|>T, \left\|E^{Hor}\right\|\geq T, \left\|E^{Ver}\right\|\geq T$	3,7,0,5,4,2

In Table 1, the DC prediction mode 2 is considered in all cases, since it has higher possibility to be the best prediction mode than the other 8 modes due to the observation that a typical 4×4 block contains a smooth texture due to its small block size. In case of vertical, horizontal, diagonal down/left and diagonal down right edges, only the mode 0, mode 1 mode 3 and mode 4 are considered, respectively. In case of horizontal dominant edge, the modes 4, 6, 1, 8 and 3 that are directed in the horizontal direction are also considered. Similarly, modes 3, 7, 0, 5 and 4 that are directed in the vertical direction are also considered in case of vertical dominant edge.

Fig. 6 illustrates the flow chart of the proposed intra prediction mode decision method. For each block, the horizontal edge feature E^{Hor} and vertical edge feature E^{Ver} are obtained in transform domain to obtain the candidate intra prediction modes as described in Table 1. For each candidate intra prediction modes, we generate a 4×4 prediction signal and calculate the Lagrange cost. Then we choose the mode with minimum Lagrange cost within in the selected candidate intra prediction modes.

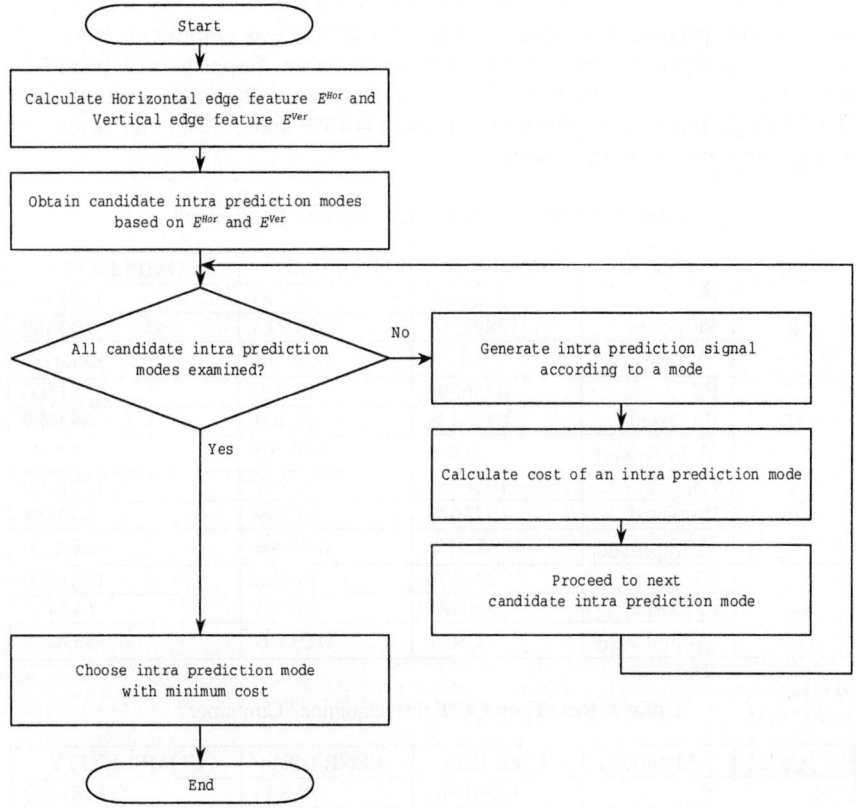

Fig. 6. Flow chart of proposed intra prediction mode decision method

3 Experimental Results

3.1 Environment of the Experiment

To evaluate the performance of the proposed method, our proposed method was implemented into H.264/AVC reference software JM9.4 [16] and tested with various Quantization Parameters Q_p. Four well known image sequences with different resolutions were used as test materials. Specifically, the image sequences "coastguard" and "container" in QCIF (176×144) resolution and image sequences "garden" and "football" in CIF (352×240) resolution were used. For each sequence, 100 frames were encoded with GOP structure of only I pictures and the threshold in Table 1 was set to $T=64$.

3.2 Performance Evaluation of the Proposed Method

Tables 2,3,4 and 5 show the tabulated performance comparison of our proposed with the full search method for different image sequences described above. In these tables, the total bits, average PSNR per frame, and the complexity, in terms of the total number of 4×4 intra prediction modes examined for RDO, was computed. Note that, the negative values in these tables show decrease in value. Experimental results of the proposed method show a significant reduction of computation in between 48.57% and 66.11%, a slight increase in bit rate in between 0.49% and 3.82%, and similar PSNR in comparison with full search method.

Table 2. Results on QCIF test sequence "Coastguard"

Q_p	Method	Total Bits	PSNR (dB)	COMPLEXITY
8	FS	13568704	52.715	1381500
	Proposed	13898992	52.713	643489
	Δ Improved	2.43%	0.00 dB	-53.42%
16	FS	8256896	45.710	1381500
	Proposed	8425438	45.704	643489
	Δ Improved	2.04%	-0.01 dB	-53.42%
32	FS	1906952	32.317	1381500
	Proposed	1972043	32.299	643489
	Δ Improved	3.41%	-0.02 dB	-53.42%
44	FS	370976	25.488	1381500
	Proposed	380488	25.483	643489
	Δ Improved	2.56%	0.01 dB	-53.42%

Table 3. Results on QCIF test sequence "Container"

Q_p	Method	Total Bits	PSNR (dB)	COMPLEXITY
8	FS	11501016	52.830	1381500
	Proposed	11784131	52.829	468253
	Δ Improved	2.46%	0.00 dB	-66.11%
16	FS	6691744	46.333	1381500
	Proposed	6794975	46.306	468253
	Δ Improved	1.54%	-0.03 dB	-66.11%
32	FS	1668184	34.170	1381500
	Proposed	1731955	34.182	468253
	Δ Improved	3.82%	0.01 dB	-66.11%
44	FS	470496	26.210	1381500
	Proposed	487768	26.171	468253
	Δ Improved	3.67%	-0.04 dB	-66.11%

Table 4. Results on CIF test sequence "Garden"

Q_p	Method	Total Bits	PSNR (dB)	COMPLEXITY
8	FS	84799088	52.733	4669500
	Proposed	85912782	52.731	2356845
	Δ Improved	1.31%	0.00 dB	-49.53%
16	FS	48544744	45.907	4669500
	Proposed	49401140	45.896	2356845
	Δ Improved	1.76%	-0.01 dB	-49.53%
32	FS	16379992	31.034	4669500
	Proposed	16655477	31.023	2356845
	Δ Improved	1.68%	-0.01 dB	-49.53%
44	FS	4482248	21.713	4669500
	Proposed	4504368	21.670	2356845
	Δ Improved	0.49%	-0.04 dB	-49.53%

Table 5. Results on CIF test sequence "Football"

Q_p	Method	Total Bits	PSNR (dB)	COMPLEXITY
8	FS	62409520	52.712	4669500
	Proposed	63658991	52.714	2401366
	Δ Improved	2.00%	0.00 dB	-48.57%
16	FS	37392088	45.680	4669500
	Proposed	37864040	45.674	2401366
	Δ Improved	1.26%	0.01 dB	-48.57%
32	FS	9232936	31.385	4669500
	Proposed	9422368	31.363	2401366
	Δ Improved	2.05%	-0.02 dB	-48.57%
44	FS	2028280	24.575	4669500
	Proposed	2080043	24.533	2401366
	Δ Improved	2.55%	-0.04 dB	-48.57%

4 Conclusion

In this paper, an efficient 4×4 intra prediction mode decision method for H.264 video is proposed based on the local edge direction of a block efficiently computed in transform domain. The proposed method filter outs the majority of intra prediction modes such that we only have to consider a candidate set of most probable 4×4 intra prediction modes for which the RDO should be performed. From the experimental results, we can see that the proposed method can achieve a considerable reduction of computation complexity while maintaining similar bit rate and PSNR. Our proposed method can also be applied to a transcoding system conducted in transform domain where the 4×4 transform coefficients of H.264 are directly computed from heterogeneous video coding formats. As future work, we are currently working on methods to extend our proposed method to 16×16 and 8×8 intra prediction modes.

References

1. ISO/IEC 14496-10, Information Technology - Coding of audio-visual objects - Part 10: Advanced Video Coding. ISO/IEC JTC1/SC29/WG11 (2004)
2. Wiegand, T., Sullivan, G., Bjontegaard, and G., Luthra, A.: Overview of H.264/AVC Video Coding Standard, IEEE Transactions on Circuits and System for Video Technology, Vol. 13 (2004) 560-576
3. ISO/IEC IS 13818, Information Technology - Generic coding of moving pictures and associated audio information, Part 2: Video. ISO/IEC JTC1/SC29/WG11 (2004)
4. Yang, L., Yu, K., Li, J., Li, S.: An effective variable block-size early termination algorithm for H.264 video coding. IEEE Transactions on Circuits and Systems for Video Technology, Vol. 15 (2005) 784-788
5. Chang, A., Wong, P.,Yeung, Y.M., Au, C.: Fast multi-block selection for H.264 video coding. IEEE International Symposium on Circuit and Systems, Vol. 3 (2004) 817-820
6. Fang, Z., Xudong, Z.: Fast macroblock mode decision in H.264, Vol. 2, IEEE International conference on Signal Processing, Vol. 2 (2004) 1183-1186
7. Wu, D., Pan, F., Lim, S., Wu, S., Li, G., Lin, X., Rahardja S., Ko. C.: Fast intermode decision in H.264/AVC video coding. IEEE Transctions on Circuits and Systems for Video Technology, Vol. 15 (2005) 953-958
8. Xin, J., Vetro, A., Sun, H.: Efficient macroblock coding-mode decision for H.264/AVC video coding. Picture Coding Symposium (2004)
9. Su, Y., Xin, J., Vetro, A., Sun, H.: Efficient MPEG-2 to H.264/AVC intra transcoding in transform-domain. IEEE international Symposium on Circuits and Systems (2005) 1234-1237
10. Sullivan, G.J., and Wiegend, T.: Rate-distortion optimization for video compression. IEEE Signal Processing Magazine, Vol. 15 (1998) 74-90
11. Wiegand, T., Schwarz, H., Joch, A., Kossentini, F. Sullivan, G.J.: Rate-constrained coder control and comparison of video coding standards. IEEE Transactions on Circuits and System for Video Technology, Vol. 13 (2003) 688-703
12. Pan, F., Lin, X., Rahardja, S., Lim, K.P., Li, Z.G.: A directional field based fast intra mode decision algorithm for H.264 video coding. IEEE International Conference on Multimedia and Expo, Vol. 2 (2003) 1147-1150
13. Meng, B., Au, O.C.: Fast intra-prediction mode selection for 4×4 blocks in H.264. IEEE conference on Acoustics, Speech, and Signal Processing, Vol. 3 (2003) 389-392
14. Xin, J., Vetro, A., Sun, H.: Converting DCT coefficients to H.264/AVC transform coefficients. Lecture Notes in Computer Science, Vol. 3332 (2004)
15. Chen, C., Wu, P.-H., and Chen, H.: MPEG-2 to H.264 Transcoding. Picture Coding Symposium (2004)
16. JVT Model reference software from http://iphome.hhi.de/suehring/tml/download/ old_jm/jm94.zip

Optimum Quantization Parameters for Mode Decision in Scalable Extension of H.264/AVC Video Codec

Seung-Hwan Kim and Yo-Sung Ho

Gwangju Institute of Science and Technology (GIST),
1 Oryong-dong Buk-gu, Gwangju 500-712, Korea
{kshkim, hoyo}@gist.ac.kr

Abstract. In the joint scalable video model (JSVM), selection of quantization parameters for mode decision (QPMD) and bit rate control (QPBC) is important for efficient coding performance. For quality (SNR) scalability, QPMD is adjusted only to the base layer QPBC in JSVM. Thus, it reduces coding efficiency in the enhancement layer. In this paper, we propose a new method for selecting optimum quantization parameters for mode decision (OQPMD) in order to improve coding efficiency for both the base and the enhancement layers. For the base layer, we propose optimum scaling factors in each decomposition stage. We also propose an offset quantization parameter for the enhancement layer. Experimental results show that the proposed method increases the average PSNR value up to 0.8dB.

Keywords: Scalable Video Coding, H.264, Quantization, Mode Decision.

1 Introduction

In recent years, scalable extension of the H.264/AVC video codec using motion-compensated temporal filtering (MCTF) has been investigated [1] [2]. The moving picture experts group (MPEG) of ISO/IEC and the video coding experts group (VCEG) of ITU-T agreed to jointly finalize the scalable video coding (SVC) project as an amendment of their H.264/AVC standard [3], and the scalable extension of H.264/AVC was selected as the first working draft [4]. The working draft provides a specification of the bit-stream syntax and the decoding process. The reference encoding process is described in the joint scalable video model (JSVM) [5].

The main idea of JSVM is to extend the hybrid video coding approach of H.264/AVC towards MCTF using a lifting framework [1]. Since the lifting structure is invertible without requiring invertible prediction and update steps, motion-compensated prediction using any possible motion model can be incorporated into the prediction and update steps. Using an efficient motion model of the H.264/AVC standard [1], both the prediction and update steps are processed as the motion-compensated prediction of B slices specified in the H.264/AVC standard.

Furthermore, the open-loop structure of the temporal subband representation enables us to incorporate temporal and quality (SNR) scalabilities efficiently [1].

The basic coding scheme for achieving spatio-temporal scalability and quality scalability can be classified as a layered video codec. The coding structure depends on the scalability space that is required by the application [6]. Figure 1 shows a block diagram for a typical scenario with three spatial layers. In each layer, an independent hierarchical motion-compensated prediction structure with motion parameters is employed. This hierarchical structure provides a temporal scalable representation of a sequence of input pictures and that structure is also suitable for efficiently incorporating spatial and quality scalability. Redundancy between different layers is exploited by inter-layer prediction that includes a prediction mechanism for motion parameters as well as texture data.

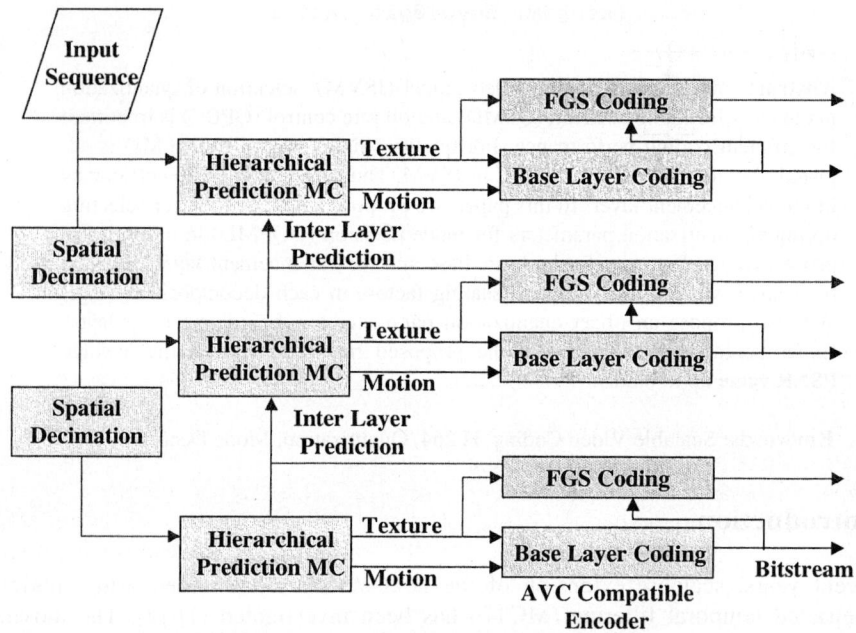

Fig. 1. Basic Structure for the Scalable Extension of H.264/AVC

A base representation of the input sequence in each layer is obtained by transform coding similar to that of H.264/AVC. In the H.264/AVC video coding standard, quantization parameters for mode decision (QPMD) and quantization parameters for bit rate control (QPBC) are always the same. However, in JSVM, QPMD and QPBC are often different in each decomposition stage. QPMD is also adjusted to the base layer QPBC. Therefore, these mismatches between QPMD and QPBC degrade the coding performance. In this paper, we propose a new method to select optimum quantization parameters for mode decision (OQPMD). Selection of OQPMD is achieved by improving coding efficiency for the base and enhancement layers.

This paper is organized as follows. After we introduce the lifting scheme for two-channel decomposition in Section 2, we describe fine granular scalability in Section 3. Then we explain two kinds of QPs in JSVM in Section 4, we propose a new method for optimum quantization parameter selection for mode decision in Section 5. After experimental results are presented in Section 6, we conclude this paper in Section 7.

2 Motion-Compensated Temporal Filtering (MCTF)

Figure 2 illustrates the lifting representation of the analysis-synthesis filter bank. At the analysis side, the odd samples $s[2k+1]$ of a given signal s are predicted by a linear combination of the even samples $s[2k]$ using a prediction operator $P(s[2k+1])$ and a high-pass signal $h[k]$ is formed by prediction residuals. A corresponding low-pass signal $l[k]$ is obtained by adding a linear combination of the prediction residuals $h[k]$ to the even samples $s[2k]$ of the input signal s using the update operator $U(s[2k])$ [7].

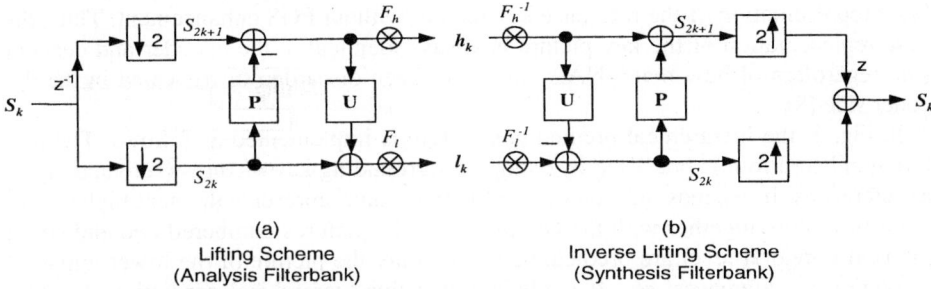

(a) Lifting Scheme (Analysis Filterbank)

(b) Inverse Lifting Scheme (Synthesis Filterbank)

Fig. 2. Lifting Representation of the Analysis-Synthesis Filter Bank

By repeating the analysis process in the lifting scheme, we have implemented the hierarchical prediction structure in JSVM. The hierarchical prediction structure can either be realized by the coding of hierarchical pictures, or by the generalized motion-compensated temporal filtering (MCTF). The MCTF process is composed of two separate operation; prediction and update. The prediction operation is very similar to the conventional motion compensation, except that it uses the original image as the reference frame. However, with update operation, we compensate the drift due to open-loop structure and improve the coding efficiency.

In Figure 3, an example of the hierarchical prediction structure for a group of eight pictures with dyadic temporal scalability is depicted. The first picture of a video sequence is intra-coded as the instantaneous decoder refresh (IDR) picture that is a kind of the key picture.

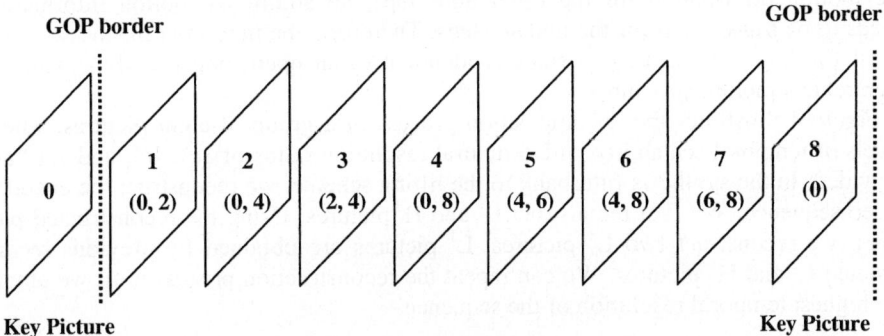

Fig. 3. The Hierarchical Prediction Structure

The key picture is located in regular or even irregular intervals. It also either intra-coded or inter-coded by using previous key picture as references for motion-compensated prediction. The sequence of the key picture is independent from any other pictures of the video sequence, and it generally represents the minimal temporal resolution that can be decoded. Furthermore, the key picture can be considered as re-synchronization points between encoder and decoder. For the other pictures, an open-loop encoder control can be used and the reference pictures including progressive refinement slices are used for motion-compensated prediction. However, the motion-compensated prediction signal for the key pictures is generated by using only the base layer representation of the reference key picture without FGS enhancement. Thus, the base representation of the key picture is always identical at the encoder and decoder side regardless of how many NAL units have been discarded or truncated in the decoder side [8].

In Fig. 3, the hierarchical prediction structure is implemented as follows. The picture numbered four is predicted by using the surrounding key pictures (zero and eight) as references. It depends only on the key pictures, and represents the next higher temporal resolution together with the key pictures. The pictures numbered two and six of the next temporal level are predicted by using only the picture of the lower temporal resolution as references, etc. It is obvious that this hierarchical prediction structure inherently provides temporal scalability; but it turned out that it also offers the possibility to efficiently integrating quality and spatial scalability [8].

The hierarchical picture coding can be extended to motion-compensated filtering. Motion-compensated update operations in MCTF are introduced in addition to the motion-compensated prediction. At the encoder side, the MCTF decomposition process starts at the highest temporal resolution. The group of pictures is partitioned into two groups: picture A and picture B. The picture B is predicted using the picture A and replaced by the motion-compensated prediction residuals. The prediction residual of the picture B is then again motion-compensated, but towards the picture A. The obtained motion-compensated prediction residual is added to the picture A, so that the picture A is replaced by a low-pass version that is effectively obtained by low-pass filtering along the motion information. These processes are iteratively applied to the set of low-pass pictures in each decomposition stage until a single low-pass picture is obtained as key picture [8].

Since the motion vectors for the motion-compensated update steps are derived from the motion information for the prediction steps, no additional motion information needs to be transmitted for the update steps. Therefore, the motion-compensated temporal filtering without update steps is identical to an open loop encoding with the hierarchical picture structure.

Figure 4 illustrates the decomposition process of a group of eight pictures, where levels of temporal scalability with temporal resolution ratios of 1/2, 1/4, and 1/12 are provided. In the synthesis filterbank in the lifting scheme, we reconstruct the encoded video sequence. We first reconstruct L^3 and H^3 pictures. Using the reconstructed pictures, we reconstruct two L^2 pictures. L^1 pictures are obtained by previous reconstructed L^2 and H^2 pictures. We can repeat the reconstruction process until we obtain the highest temporal resolution of the sequence.

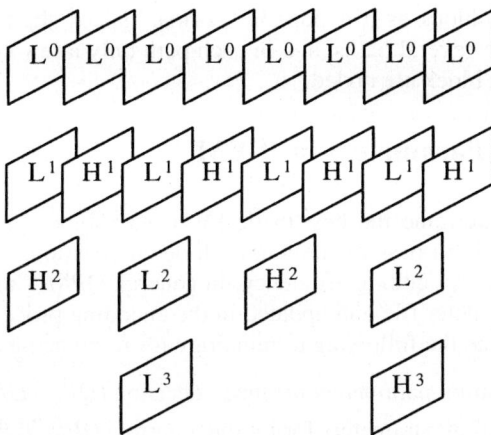

Fig. 4. Temporal Decomposition of a Group of Eight Pictures

3 Fine Granular Scalability

The fine granularity scalability (FGS) algorithm in the current JSVM encodes coefficients within an FGS slice in an order such that "more significant" coefficients are coded first. By arranging the bit stream in this way, the extraction process is biased so that a simple truncation is likely to retain those "more significant" coefficients, and therefore improve the reconstructed quality [8].

When FGS data is truncated, the decoder assumes the missing values to be zero. Consequently, coding zero values into the bit stream contributes nothing to the reconstruction, and coefficients with the greatest probability of being zero should be deferred until the end of the slice. Conversely, coefficients with the greatest probability of being non-zero should be coded first.

In cyclical block coding, unlike subband coding, the current scan position in a given coding pass will differ from one block to another. Furthermore, a correlation was observed between the scan position and probability of the next coefficient being non-zero. The function describing this correlation varies according to quantization parameter and sequence. Therefore, progressive refinement slices using cyclical block coding have been introduced in order to support fine granular quality scalability. A picture is generally represented by a non-scalable base representation, which includes all corresponding motion data as well as a "coarse" approximation of the intra and residual data, and zero or more quality scalable enhancement representations, which represent the residual between the original subband pictures and their reconstructed base representation.

Each enhancement representation contains a refinement signal that corresponds to a bisection of the quantization step size. The refinement signals are directly coded in the transform coefficient domain. Thus, at the decoder side, the inverse transform has to be performed only once for each transform block of a picture.

In order to provide quality enhancement layer NAL units that can be truncated at any arbitrary point, the coding order of transform coefficient levels has been modified for the progressive refinement slices. Instead of scanning the transform coefficients macroblock by macroblock as it is done in "normal" slices, the transform coefficient blocks are scanned in several paths, and in each path only a few coding symbols for a transform coefficient block are coded.

4 Quantization Parameters in JSVM

QPMD is used to determine the best mode for a macroblock and QPBC is used to encode low-pass and high-pass pictures in each decomposition stage. Thus, selection of QPMD is important for coding efficiency. In general, QPMD and QPBC are initialized in the input parameter file and updated in the encoding process [9] [10] [11]. For convenience, we define the following terminology for referencing different QPs.

QPMD: quantization parameters for mode decision (QP_{m1}, QP_{m2}, ... QP_{mn});
QPBC: quantization parameters for bit rate control (QP_{H1}, QP_{H2}, ... QP_{Hk});
QP_{mn}: QPMD for the n-th decomposition stage;
QP_{Hk}: QPBC for the high-pass pictures in the k-th decomposition stage;
QP_L: QPBC for the low-pass picture;

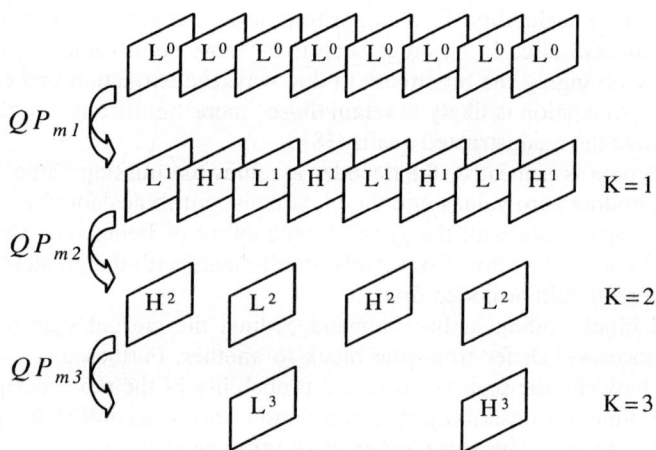

Fig. 5. Quantization Parameters in Each Decomposition Stage

Figure 5 graphically shows the function of QPMD and QPBC in each decomposition stage. For QPMD, QP_{m1}, QP_{m2}, and QP_{m3} are used to determine the best mode and to decompose two low-pass pictures in the previous stage into low-pass and high-pass pictures. For QPBC, the low-pass picture L^3 is quantized by QP_L and high-pass pictures, H^3, H^2, and H^1 are quantized by QP_{H3}, QP_{H2}, and QP_{H1}, respectively. Therefore, QP_L and QP_{Hk} are determined by

$$QP_L = \max(0, \min(51, Round(QP - 6\frac{\log_{10} SF_L}{\log_{10} 2}))) \quad (1)$$

$$QP_{Hk} = \max(0, \min(51, Round(QP - 6\frac{\log_{10} SF_{Hk}}{\log_{10} 2}))) \quad (2)$$

where SF_L is the scaling factor for low-pass picture. SF_{Hk} is the scaling factor for high-pass pictures in the k-th decomposition stage. The operator Round ( ) specifies rounding to the nearest integral number. QP represents the initialised quantization parameter in the input file. QPMD for the *k*-th decomposition stage, QP_{mn}, is obtained by

$$QP_{mn} = \max(0, \min(51, Round(QP - 6\frac{\log_{10} SF_{mn}}{\log_{10} 2}))) \quad (3)$$

where SF_{mn} is the scaling factor for quantization parameters for mode decision in the n-th decomposition stage. QP represents the initial quantization parameter for each decomposition stage. We have used the same QP for each decomposition stage.

5 Optimum Quantization Parameters for Mode Decision

In this section, we propose a new method for selecting optimum quantization parameters for mode decision (OQPMD). Proposed method is based on quality (SNR) scalability depicted in Figure 6.

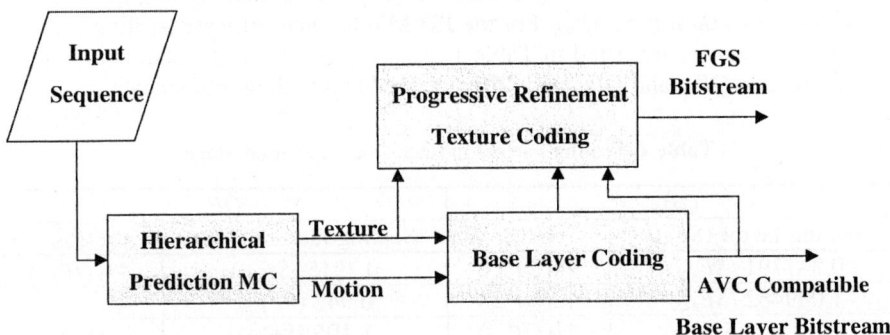

Fig. 6. Basic Structure for SNR Scalability

In the non-scalable video codec, such as the H.264/AVC video coding standard, quantization parameters for mode decision and bit rate control are the same. Hence, no error is caused by the mismatch between QPMD and QPBC. In JSVM using the motion-compensated temporal filtering technique, we should set QPMD and QPBC in each decomposition stage. If decomposition stages are independent of each other, each QPMD and QPBC would be set to the same value in the given decomposition stage. However, decomposition stages in MCTF have the hierarchical structure, as shown in Figure 4. Therefore, when we select QPMD in each decomposition stage, we need to consider the relationship between stages.

In order to find OQPMD, we first consider that decomposition processes in MCTF are implemented hierarchically and design a metric to measure errors caused by the mismatch between QPMD and QPBC in each decomposition stage. Based on this fact, we find the optimum scaling factor SF_{mn} in each stage. The errors caused by the mismatch between QP_{m1} and QP_{H1} are represented by

$$E = \alpha_1(QP_{m1} - QP_{H1}) \tag{4}$$

where α_1 represents the importance of the high-pass picture H_1. Since the decomposition process in MCTF has a hierarchical structure, the mode decision in the first stage influences pictures in the following stages, such as H_1, H_2, ... H_L, and L-pictures. Therefore, in order to find the total errors caused by QP_{m1}, we consider the mismatch among QP_{H1}, QP_{H2}, ... QP_{HL}, and QP_L. Hence, the total errors E_1 caused by QP_{m1} are represented by

$$E_1 = \sum_{k=1}^{L} \alpha_k (QP_{m1} - QP_{Hk}) + \alpha_L (QP_{m1} - QP_L) \tag{5}$$

where α_k and α_L represent the weighting factor of the high-pass picture in the k-th decomposition and the low-pass picture, respectively. For simplicity, these weighting factors are regarded as the corresponding scaling factors (SF_{Hk}, SF_L) of pictures in the decomposition stage. Based on Eq. (5), we can derive the total error E_t by

$$E_t = \sum_{k=1}^{L}\sum_{n=1}^{L} \alpha_k (QP_{mn} - QP_{Hk}) + \alpha_L (QP_{mn} - QP_L) \tag{6}$$

where L is the total number of stages. From Eq. (1), Eq. (2) and Eq. (3), the total error E_t is adjusted by controlling SF_{mn}. For the JSVM reference software, scaling factors in decomposition stages are listed in Table 1. As shown in Table 1, there is a large difference between QP_{m0} and QP_L, and difference reduces coding efficiency.

Table 1. Scaling Factors in Each Decomposition Stage

QP_m		QP_r	
Scaling factor (SF_{mn})	QP_{mn}	Scaling factor (SF_{Hk})	QP_{Hk}
0.847791 (SF_{m1})	44(QP_{m1})	0.7915 (SF_{H1})	44(QP_{H1})
1.009482 (SF_{m2})	42(QP_{m2})	0.942 (SF_{H2})	42(QP_{H2})
1.18386 (SF_{m3})	41(QP_{m3})	1.105 (SF_{H3})	41(QP_{H3})

* Scaling factor for low-pass frame (SF_L= 1.6062), QP_L=38, GOP=8

Therefore, we replace SF_{mn} by a weighted scaling factor WSF_{mn}.

$$WSF_{mn} = W_n \cdot SF_{mn} \tag{7}$$

where W_n represents the weighing factor of SF_{mn} which is determined by minimizing the total error E_t in Eq. (6). For simplicity, in our experiments, the weighing factors W_1, W_2, and W_3 are fixed to 2.5, 1.5, and 0.7, respectively.

In Figure 7, for quality (SNR) scalability, the difference between the original and reconstructed pictures in base layer is encoded with finer quantization parameters in the enhancement layer. For quality scalability, coding efficiency of the enhancement layer is much less than that of the base layer. From our intuition and extensive experiments, we find that the statistical distribution of the residual data is determined by

QPMD. Hence, coding efficiency in the base and enhancement layers can be adaptively controlled by QPMD.

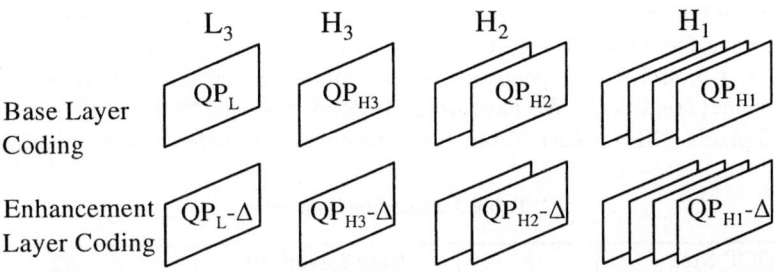

Fig. 7. Adjustment of Quantization Parameters for the Enhancement Layer

We also propose an offset quantization parameter Δ_m for mode decision to enhance coding efficiency of the enhancement layer. Coding efficiency in the base and enhancement layers is controlled by the proposed offset quantization parameter Δ_m for mode decision by which each QP_{mn} is equally shifted. Therefore, the optimal QPMD (OQPMD) is represented by

$$OQPMD = QP_{mn} - \Delta_m \qquad (8)$$

In Table 2, we compare the rate-distortion performance for various Δ_m which influences coding efficiency in the enhancement layer. We can regard the current JSVM reference software as the case of the offset value 0. Since the mode decision is only adjusted by quantization parameters for the base layer coding (QP_{H1}, QP_{H2}, ... QP_{HL}, and QP_L), the case of offset value 0 (JSVM) provides the best coding efficiency in the base layer but poor coding efficiency in the enhancement layer.

Table 2. Quantization Parameter Offset for Mode Decision

Offset Δ_m= 0		Offset Δ_m= -4		Offset Δ_m= 4	
Bit rate	PSNR	Bit rate	PSNR	Bit rate	PSNR
243(Base)	35.68	254(Base)	35.88	247(Base)	35.37
432	37.25	443	37.10	431	37.25
505	37.84	510	37.56	504	38.13
740	38.93	796	38.99	751	39.11
1117	40.19	1131	39.85	1119	40.82

If the offset value is four, though coding efficiency in the base layer is poor, coding efficiency in the enhancement layer is better than JSVM (Δ_m=0). By adjusting the offset value Δ_m, we can find the optimum offset value Δ_m without little reducing coding efficiency in the base layer. In our experiments, we use the offset value 2, which reduces coding efficiency but little in the base layer. According to the channel variation, we can adjust the offset value properly.

6 Experimental Results

In order to evaluate the efficiency of the proposed weighting factors and QP offset, we have implemented the OQPMD scheme in the JSVM reference software version 1.0. We have fixed the QP offset value to two and the weighing factors W_1, W_2, and W_3 to 2.5, 1.5, and 0.7, respectively. These values can be selected adaptively if we know channel conditions. We have used "FOREMAN" and "MOBILE" sequences of 352×288 pixels (CIF format). Table 3 lists encoding parameters in our experiment.

Table 3. Encoding Parameter

GOP Size	8	Base Layer QP	42
Resolution	352×288	Spatial Layers	1
Frame Rate	30	FGS Layers	0.5, 1, 1.5, 2

In Table 4 and Table 5, we compare PSNR values for different sizes of FGS layers. From Table 4 and Table 5, we observe that the proposed method provides slightly lower coding efficiency in the base layer, but much higher coding efficiency in the enhancement layer.

Table 4. PSNR Values Comparison ("FOREMAN")

FGS Layer	JSVM		Proposed Method	
	Bit rate (kbps)	PSNR	Bit rate (kbps)	PSNR
0	94	30.82	104	31.01
0.5	140	31.69	148	31.92
1	205	33.20	210	33.51
1.5	324	34.20	323	34.62
2	452	35.42	469	36.29

Table 5. PSNR Values Comparison ("MOBILE")

FGS Layer	JSVM		Proposed Method	
	Bit rate (kbps)	PSNR	Bit rate (kbps)	PSNR
0	200	26.27	209	26.37
0.5	351	27.66	357	27.79
1	535	29.32	536	29.52
1.5	845	30.49	821	30.65
2	1292	32.35	1295	32.85

Figure 8 displays rate-distortion curves for "MOBILE" and "FOREMAN" sequences. These curves have been obtained by changing the size of the FGS layer size by the unit of 0.5. For "FOREMAN" sequence, the PSNR value is enhanced up to 0.8dB. As the number of FGS layers increases, we note that the proposed method provides higher coding efficiency than JSVM.

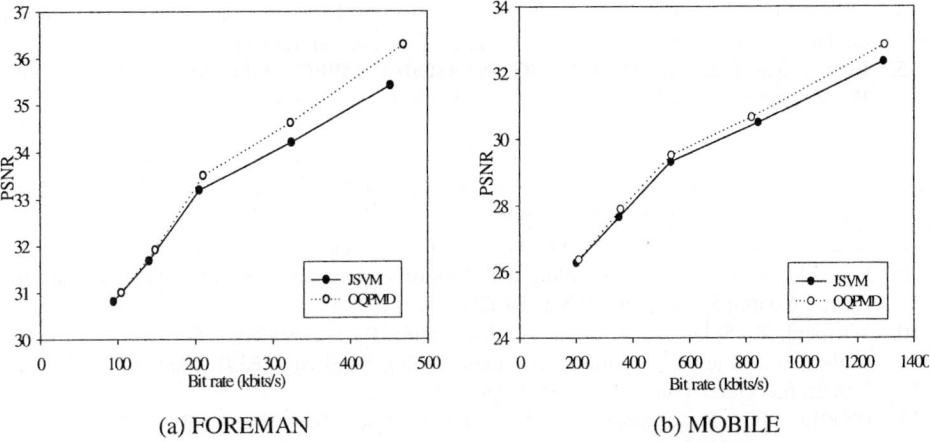

Fig. 8. PSNR Values for FOREMAN and MOBILE Sequences

7 Conclusions

In this paper, we proposed a new method to select optimum quantization parameters for mode decision (OQPMD) in order to improve coding efficiency for the base and enhancement layers. For the base layer, we proposed the optimum scaling factors for OQPMD in each decomposition stage. In order to find the optimum scaling factors, we designed a new metric to measure the error caused by the mismatch between quantization parameters for mode decision and bit rate control. We also proposed an offset quantization parameter for OQPMD to enhance coding efficiency in the enhancement layer. Using the proposed offset quantization parameter, we can efficiently control the coding efficiency in the base and enhancement layers. The proposed OQPMD is expected the efficiency in the video transmission under abruptly varying channel capacity. Experimental results represent that the proposed method increases the average PSNR value up to 0.8dB.

Acknowledgements. This work was supported in part by Gwangju Institute of Science and Technology (GIST), in part by the Ministry of Information and Communication (MIC) through the Realistic Broadcasting Research Center (RBRC), and in part by the Ministry of Education (MOE) through the Brain Korea 21 (BK21) project.

References

1. Schwarz, H., Hinz, T., Kirchhoffer, H., Marpe, D., and Wiegand, T.: Technical Description of the HHI proposal for SVC CE1: ISO/IEC JTC1/SC29/WG11, Document M11244, Palma de Mallorca, Spain, Oct. (2004)
2. ISO/IEC JTC1/SC29/WG11.: Scalable Video Model 3.0: ISO/IEC JTC1/SC29/WG11, Doc. N6716, Palma de Mallorca, Spain, Oct. (2004)
3. ITU-T Recommendation H.264 & ISO/IEC 14496-10 AVC.: Advanced Video Coding for Generic Audiovisual Services: version 3, (2005)

4. Joint Video Team of ITU-T VCEG and ISO/IEC MPEG.: Scalable Video Coding Working Draft 1: Joint Video Team, Document JVT-N020, Jan. (2005)
5. Joint Video Team of ITU-T VCEG and ISO/IEC MPEG.: Joint Scalable Video Model JSVM0: Joint Video Team, Document JVT-N021, Jan. (2005)
6. Taubman, D.: Successive Refinement of Video: Fundamental Issues, Past Efforts and New Directions. Proc. SPIE, Visual Communication and Image Processing (2003) 649-663
7. Schwarz, H., Marpe, D., and Wiegand, T.: Scalable Extension of H.264/AVC. ISO/IEC JTC1/WG11 Doc. M10569/SO3 (2004)
8. Scalable Extension of H.264/AVC: http://ip.hhi.de/imagecom_G1/ savce
9. Flierl, M., Girod, B.: Video Coding with Motion-Compensated Wavelet Transforms. Proc. Picture Coding Symposium (2003) 59-62
10. Wiegand, T., Schwarz, H., Joch, A., Kossentini, F., and Sullivan, G.: Rate-Constrained Coder Control and Comparison of Video Coding Sandards. IEEE Trans. on Circuit and System for Video Technology (2003) 688-703
11. ISO/IEC JTC1: Requirements and Application for Scalable Video Coding. ISO/IEC JTC1/WG11 Doc. N6025, Oct. (2003)

A Metadata Model for Event Notification on Interactive Broadcasting Service

Kyunghee Ji[1], Nammee Moon[1], and Jungwon Kang[2]

[1] Digital Media Dept., Seoul University of Venture and Information,
1603-54, Seocho-dong, Seocho-gu, Seoul, Korea
{everkyung, mnm}@suv.ac.kr
[2] Broadcasting Media Research Group, ETRI, 161 Gajeong-dong,
Yuseong-gu, Daejon, Korea
jungwon@etri.re.kr

Abstract. In this paper, we design the metadata model for Event notification that can be utilized for various commercial purposes on interactive broadcasting environment, and implement the testbed system based on the metadata model. The metadata model is based on the ISO/IEC 21000-15 and we extended some descriptions which have been adopted as ISO/IEC 21000-15 Committe Draft. Event notification service based on this metadata model achieves a step towards the healthy commercial future of interactive service by enabling target marketing, the audience rating analysis, user preference analysis, and monitoring illegal copies.

1 Introduction

Today, the advent of digital television allows the convergence of broadcasting and communication. The broadcasting environments become more complex to include diverse access devices on different networks. Access devices, with a large set of different terminal and network capabilities complementing the TV set, possess the functionality to be used in different locations and environments: anywhere and anytime. Broadcast content changes from the existing linear video-oriented program to rich multimedia contents including video, audio and additional data. In a digital television system, additional media content and interactive applications can be broadcasted, allowing the user to become involved and to change the classic linear program flow by interacting where desired. For example, user wants to get various interactive services like as commerce, game, e-learning while they are watching broadcast content instead of just watching the program in passive manner. Both content provider and user thus demand solutions that can deliver accessible and advanced multimedia creation and consumption on many platforms. These new content providers and the traditional media sources share a core set of concerns: access, delivery and management of content, repurposing content based on user preferences and device capabilities, protection of rights, and so on.

In this paper, we describe the metadata model for Event notification developed to support transparent and augmented use of multimedia contents on interactive broadcasting service. The model can be used for supporting contents commerce, contents protection, royalty calculation, and advertisement fee calculation in various commercial systems. In chapter 2, we introduce the overview of Event notification and present the abstract data model which has the power to describe the Event notification for interactive broadcasting service. In chapter 3, the foundations for realizing our metadata model based on established multimedia metadata language are described, and the implementation result taken to realize the model is presented. We close with conclusions in chapter 4.

2 A Metadata Model for Event Notification

Every interaction with multimedia contents in interactive broadcasting can be called an Event. Arising from an each Event, there is the opportunity to describe what occurred. However, there are a number of difficulties in providing an accurate report about an Event. Different observers of the Event may have vastly different perspectives, needs, and focuses. They may emphasize certain elements to the detriment of others, or they may describe an Event in a way that others may find confusing. Therefore, in this paper, we design the metadata model for Event notification based on existing standard ISO/IEC 21000-15: Event Reporting[1] to allow interoperability of the many components from different vendors found in a broadcasting system. These Event descriptions can be used for various kind of notification that includes monitoring of illegal copies, monitoring of performances, marketing information, copyright reports, proof of purchase, license purchase and delivery, network congestion, load balancing, and bandwidth usage and availability.

2.1 Concept of Event Notification

ISO/IEC 21000(MPEG-21) has identified the need for Event Reporting in its vision for an interoperable multimedia framework. Event Reporting is required within the MPEG-21 Multimedia Framework in order to provide a standardized means for sharing information about Events amongst Peer[1]s and Users.

The metadata model, outlined in Fig. 1, describes the key concept of Event notification based on ISO/IEC 21000. The Event notification service comprises of two components: Event Report Request(ER-R) and Event Report(ER). An ER-R is used to define the conditions or predicates under which an Event is deemed to have occurred. Events defined by ER-Rs trigger the creation of an associated ER, which contains information describing the Event, as specified in the associated ER-R. ER-R comprise of , at least, a description of the Event, the syntax/format of the ER, the recipient(s) of the ER and parameters related to delivery of ER. Upon the Event happening, an ER must be generated and delivered to the specified recipient(s) with requested information.

In the real world, examples of the need for Event notification are plentiful. One example relates to the monitoring of the usage of copyrighted material. The provider

---

[1] Devices or applications that compliantly processes digital contents.

offering Digital Item[2]s for download would specify in an Event Report Request that, whenever a Resource within a Digital Item is rendered (e.g. played), he would receive an Event Report enabling him to manage his royalties. Upon rendering, the Peer will generate an Event Report which will be delivered to the rights holder specified, in an Event Report Request, containing information about the Digital Item, the resource, and the conditions under which it has been rendered.

In another example, Event notifications are necessary for network nodes to know the exact connectivity condition between two Peers when trying to deliver Digital Items. While a network Peer may receive Digital Items from some Peers and forward them to other Peers in its network, the network Peer will monitor its load. When a critical threshold is reached, an Event Report may be created and sent to neighbouring network Peers who will in turn re-route their Digital Items to avoid the congested network Peer[1].

An ER-R is composed of three main items including ER-R Descriptor, ER Descriptor and Event Condition descriptor. An ER is composed of three main items including ER Descriptor, ER Data and Embedded ER-R. The detailed specifications for each item of ER-R and ER are described at the following sections.

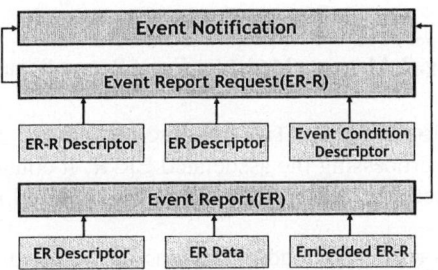

Fig. 1. Overview of the Metadata Model

2.2 Event Report Request Metadata Model

The purpose of ER-R is to describe the Event which is to be reported, and to indicate the data items that are to be included in such an Event Report and the parameters related to the delivery of the Event Report such as a recipient of ER, the delivery time of ER and the delivery mechanism. Fig. 2 shows the ER-R metadata model. We detail this model by introducing the underlying rational that leads to its development.

ER-R Descriptor. ERRDescriptor provides a description of the ER-R including aspects such as the lifetime, modifications and priority level of the ER-R. Lifetime is used to indicate a validity period for the specific ER-R. Modification is used to maintain the history of the ER-R. The priority level specifies the priority level for processing an ER-R. Event Report Requests can be processed according to their assigned priority. When two Event Report Requests have the same assigned priority, the Peer may make an arbitrary decision regarding the order in which they are processed.

---

[2] Structured digital object with a standard representation, identification and metadata within ISO/IEC 21000 framework.

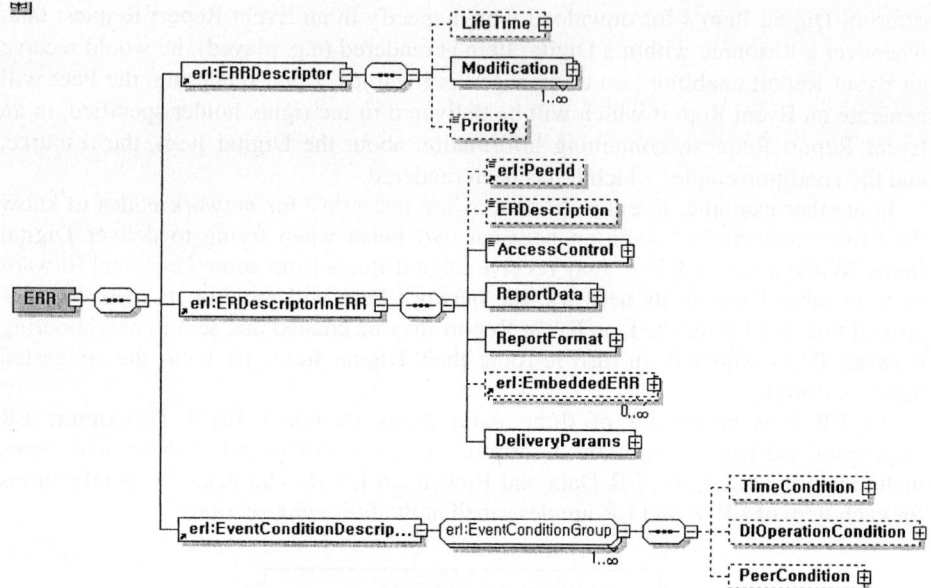

Fig. 2. Metadata Model for Event Report Request

ER Descriptor. `ERDescriptorInERR` describes Event Report(s) that will be created as the result of processing the associated ER-R. It contains aspects such as the data items to be reported, the format they should be reported in, delivery parameters and access control.

`ReportData` is to report payload data items to the recipient(s) when and ER is created as the result of an ER-R. The PeerId, UserId, DII, Related DII, Time and Location are optional sub-elements which can be requested to be sent when a specified Event occurs. When an ER is to be created, the format of the payload information needs to be known so that the ER's payload can be understood by the recipient peer(s). This is specified by the `ReportFormat`. The `DeliveryParams` associated with the recipient(s) for resulting ER, delivery time which indicates to the Peer when it is expected to deliver resulting ER's, and delivery mechanism(s) which describes the preferred transport service to be used by the Peer to deliver the Event Report to the recipient peer.

The delivery time of ER can be different from the Event occurrence time. Therefore we suggest the ISO/IEC 21000 to have the delivery time description of which indicates to the Peer when it is expected to deliver the resulting ER's as in Fig. 3[2][3] and it is adopted in the ISO/IEC 21000-15: Event Reporting Committee Draft. The `DeliveryTime`, indicating the delivery time of ER, can be specified in three different ways: "`SpecificTime`" that is a specific date and/or time, "`ElapsedTime`" that is expressed by a certain amount of elapsed time from the specific base, such as an Event, and "`PeriodicTime`" that occurs periodically as shown in Fig. 2. `SpecificTime` is classified into the specific time instant such as "Midnight of December 31 2004", before the specific time instant such as "before Midnight of December 31 2004", after the specific time instant such as "after

Midnight of December 31 2004", and from the specific time instant to the other specific time instant like as "from Midnight of December 31 2004 to Midnight of January 1 2005". ElapsedTime is represented as the elapsed time from a specific base time, which is classified into after the elapse, before the elapse, and after the elapse but before the other elapse. Examples include "1 hour after an Event occurs", "within 1 day after an Event occurs" and "1 hour after but before 2 hours after an Event occurs". PeriodicTime represents the repetitive time with a specific period. Examples include "every first Sunday of each month" and "from midnight to 1 o'clock of every 1st day of each month". The DeliveryTime is specified under the DeliveryParams element.

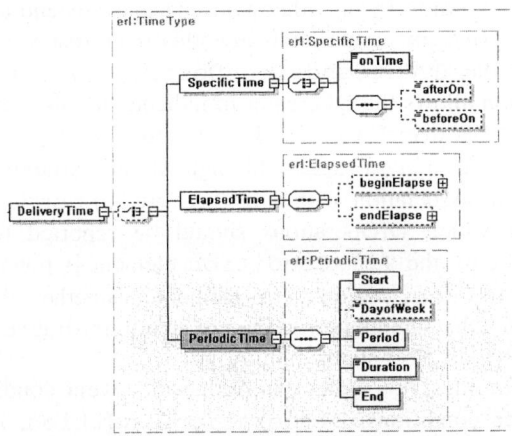

Fig. 3. *DeliveryTime* Description. *DeliveryTime* can be a choice among *SpecificTime*, which means a fixed date and/or time, *ElapsedTime*, which specifies a time "window" with start and end times being related to the time of the Event's occurrence, and *PeriodicTime*, which indicates a recurring time/date period.

Event Condition Descriptor. In order for a Peer to determine when a reportable Event has occurred, there is a need for the Digital Item creator to specify the conditions under which the Event is deemed to have occurred. This is achieved by specifying one or more conditions within the ER-R's EventConditionDescriptor element. Event Reporting within MPEG-21 provides a standardized means for "reportable events" to be specified, detected and acted upon. There two major classes of "reportable" Events: Events which are generated as a result of User-related-operations on a specific instance of a Digital Item(DIOperationCondition), and Events which are generated within a Peer that are related to internal Peer processes(PeerCondition)[4].

The most fundamental aspect of Event notification can be the ability to report on the usage of Digital Items by a User as they interact with Digital Items using a Peer using the DIOperationCondition. We can define a Peer's DI Operations with the 13 ActTypes in the MPEG-21 Rights Data Dictionary(RDD)[5]. These ActTypes are the basis on which all of the RDD terms are defined and include the following: Modify, Embed, Install, Enlarge, Play, Execute, Reduce, Print, Uninstall, Move,

Extract, Delete, and Adapt. Digital Item creators, through the use of a `DIOperationCondition`, can instruct a Peer to report when a downloaded application (e.g. a music album) is installed, uninstalled or executed. Similarly, when a Peer moves, adapts or plays a Digital Item, this event can also be reported.

A `PeerCondition` concerns events that are directly related to a Peer but not directly related to its handling of a Digital Item. The ability to specify conditions in an ER-R which take into account factors that are not related to DI manipulation is essential if Event notification is to be utilizable in a wide sphere of multimedia application domains. We extend the `PeerCondition` to be allowed to define a new Peer Event condition as necessary because it's impossible to define all kinds of Event conditions for various Users at this time. Therefore, this element is used to extend the Event condition from any other namespace. To extend the Event condition, using this element, define any condition in any other namespace.

We also extend the `EventConditionDescriptor` element to be able to specify time condition allows the DI creator to indicate that the condition depends on a date and/or time(`TimeCondition`). The structure of `TimeCondition` is the same as that of `DeliveryTime`. Although it is certainly possible to use `TimeCondition` in association with a `DIOperationCondition` to specify a time period within which DIOperations should be reported (e.g. with a super distributed Digital Item), the `TimeCondition` element is potentially more useful when coupled with the `PeerCondition` element. Together, they can be used to specify Peer attributes that should be reported to an administrative Peer on a periodic basis (perhaps for periodic Peer status monitoring).

We also extend the descriptor that can define the Event condition as a Boolean combination of three conditions, `DIOperationCondition`, `PeerCondition` or `TimeCondition` by having the descriptor Operator[6]. The `Operator` element is used to define the Boolean operator to combine `TimeCondition`, `DIOperationCondition` and/or `PeerCondition`. There are two kinds of Operator, `InternalOperator` and `ExternalOperator`. The `ExternalOperator` is used for specifying the operators among the Event conditions and it has the Boolean operators like as AND, OR, XOR, NOT and paranthesis. The `InternalOperator` specifies the operator used for PeerEvent to express the Peer's status such as, for example, NetworkCongestion >= 0.8. The `InternalOperator` consists of arithmetic operators.

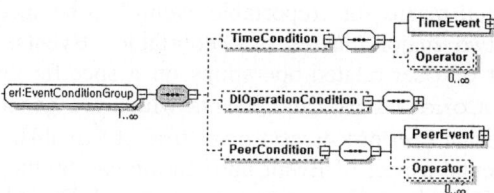

Fig. 4. Extended *EventConditionGroup* Description. The Event conditions may be defined as a Boolean combination of conditions, which can be any of three defined types: *DIOperationCondition*, *PeerCondition* or *TimeCondition*.

The extended `EventConditionDescriptor`, which is adopted in the ISO/IEC 21000-15 Committee Draft, is described in Fig. 4.

2.3 Event Report Metadata Model

As indicated previously, Events that need to be reported as specified by an ER-R are represented as an Event Report. ER consists of `ERDescriptor`, `ERData` and `EmbeddedERR` as shown in Fig. 5. The detailed description of each is as follows.

ER Descriptor. Describes ER itself. It consists of `Description`, for providing comments on a certain ER instance, `Status`, representing the completion status of the ER, `Modification`, indicating the history of creation and modification of ER, and `ERSource`, containing the original ER-R that created the ER.

ER Data. Provides a place for inclusion of "payload" data into an ER. This payload data corresponds to the report data items that were specified in the associated ER-R, which are formatted according to the format specification also included in the originating ER-R.

Embedded ER-R. This provides a simple mechanism that can be used to automate some quite powerful processes. When an ER is sent to a recipient, the ER may also contain an ER-R. Upon receipt of the ER, the Peer will parse and act upon the ER-R in the normal manner. This ER-R may specify, for instance that a new ER must be sent, perhaps as an acknowledgment of receipt for the ER in which it was embedded. Using this mechanism, the Peer that sent the original ER knows that its ER has been received and correctly parsed by its intended recipient. Additionally, the Embedded ER-R construct can also be used as a mechanism to enable automatic forwarding of ERs via a chain of pre-defined recipients. The Embedded ER-R may either be inline within an ER, or a reference to an external ER-R. We proposed this descriptor to ISO/IEC 21000[7] and it is also adopted in the ISO/IEC 21000-15 Committee Draft.

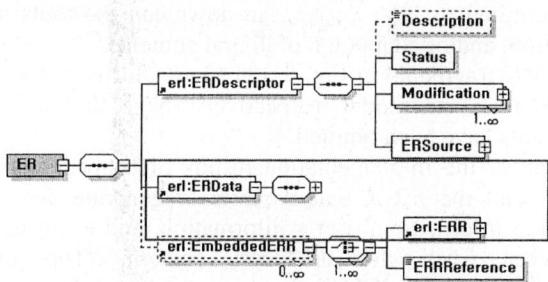

Fig. 5. Metadata Model for Event Report. It consists of *ERDescriptor*, *ERData* and *EmbeddedERR*. *EmbeddedERR* is used to request an acknowledgement of receipt for the ER or forwarding of ER.

3 Implementation

Based on the metadata model detailed in previous chapter, we implemented the testbed system comprising the Content Server, Terminal, Digital Item Adaptation(DIA) Server, and Tool Server on the convergence network of broadcasting and communication as described in Fig. 6.

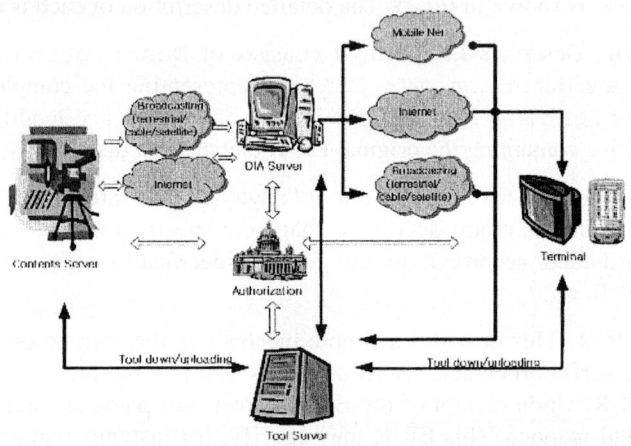

Fig. 6. Testbed System Supporting Interactive broadcasting service

There are two types of devices which create, save and consume the contents in testbed system: Content Server and Terminal. Content Server takes a role to create and deliver the broadcast multimedia content to the Terminal, and the Terminal, including broadcasting devices(e.g. TV) and communication devices(e.g. PC or PDA), consumes the content. Digital Item Adaptation Server adapts the Digital Item in compliance with the User's device environment and characteristics. The Content Server and Terminal exchange the digital contents directly or through DIA Server. Content Server, Terminal or DIA Server can download the tools necessary for the creation, consumption, and/or adaptation of digital contents.

The example XML fragments in Fig. 7 and Fig 8 illustrate the basic structure of our ER-R and ER metadata model, respectively. Note that for simplicity, some attributes and elements have been omitted.

Fig. 9 shows one of the implementation results of testbed system. The Content Server create and send the ER-R that requests to generate and send the content information, resource information, user's information, and event occurrence time to the contents server when the broadcast content "Top of English"(DII: urn:mpeg:mpeg21:DII:DI:0824108241) has been played or stopped at user's Terminal. The Terminal parses the ER-R when it receives the ER-R, monitors if the Event specified in the ER-R occurs. It makes the ER as specified in the associated ER-R and sends it to the recipient(in this case Content Server). This kind of implementation can be utilized for copyright management and marketing purposes.

```xml
<ERR>
  <ERRDescriptor>
    <LifeTime>
      <StartTime>2005-05-04T00:00:00</StartTime>
      <EndTime>2005-05-05T00:00:00</EndTime>
    </LifeTime>
    <Modification>...</Modification>
    <Priority>...</Priority>
  </ERRDescriptor>
  <ERDescriptorInERR>
    <AccessControl/>
    <ReportData>
      <PeerId/><UserId/><Time/><Location/><DII/><DIOperation/>
    </ReportData>
    <ReportFormat>
      <Ref> xmlns:xsi="http://www.w3.org/2001/XMLSchema-instance"</Ref>
    </ReportFormat>
    <DeliveryParams>
      <Recipient>
        <PeerId>MAC:00-08-E3-AE-1E-62</PeerId>
        <UserId> John </UserId>
      </Recipient>
      <DeliveryTime>
        <SpecificTime><beforeOn>2005-05-31T00:00:00</beforeOn>
        </SpecificTime>
      </DeliveryTime>
      <DITransportService>...</DITransportService>
    </DeliveryParams>
  </ERDescriptorInERR>
  <EventConditionDescriptor>
    <TimeCondition>
      <TimeEvent>
        <SpecificTime>
          <afterOn>2005-05-04T00:00:00</afterOn>
          <beforeOn>2005-05-06T00:00:00</beforeOn>
        </SpecificTme>
      </TimeEvent>
    </TimeCondition>
    <DIOperationCondition>
      <UserId>Kyunghee</UserId>
      <PeerId>GUID:1AC5-4527-A864-3EA2</PeerId>
      <Operation>urn:mpeg:mpeg21ra:RDD:156:735</Operation>
      <DII>urn:mpegra:mpeg21:DII:DI:0824108241</DII>
      <Operator kind="AND" location="perfeix"/>
    </DIOperationCondition>
  </EventConditionDescriptor>
</ERR>
```

Fig. 7. A Sample ER-R Instance of the Metadata Model. This ER-R requests to report user id, peer id, Event's occurrence time, user's location, DI's identifier and type of Event when *Kyunghee* plays the DI *"urn:mpegra:mpeg21:DII:DI:0824108241"* between May 4 2005 to May 6 2005 to the recipient *John* by using the format referenced as *"http://www.w3.org/2001/XMLSchema-instance"*. The ER generated by this ER-R should be sent by May 31 2005. And this ER-R is valid during May 4 2005.

```
<ER>
  <ERDescriptor>
    <Description>...</Description>
    <Status value="true"/>
    <Modification>
        <PeerId>GUID:1AC5-4527-A864-3EA2</PeerId>
        <UserId>Andrew</UserId>
        <Time>2005-05-04T12:31:00</Time>
    </Modification>
    <ERSource>
        <ERRReference>mpeg:mpeg21:dii:ERRID:001</ERRReference>
    </ERSource>
  </ERDescriptor>
  <ERData>
    <PeerId>GUID:1AC5-4527-A864-3EA2</PeerId>
    <UserId>Kyunghee</UserId>
    <Time>2005-05-04T12:30:00</Time>
    <Location>KR</Location>
    <DII>urn:mpeg:mpeg21:DII:DI:0824108241</DII>
    <DIOperation>urn:mpeg:mpeg21:ra:RDD:156:735</DIOperation>
  </ERData>
  <EmbeddedERR>
    <ERRReference>mpeg:mpeg21:dii:ERRID:010</ERRReference>
  </EmbeddedERR>
</ER>
```

Fig. 8. A Sample ER Instance of the Metadata Model. This ER generated by the ER-R in Fig. 7 specifies that *Kyunghee* played the DI "*urn:mpegra:mpeg21:DII:DI:0824108241*" at the Peer "*GUID:1AC5-4527-A864-3EA2*", Korea on May 4 12:30 2005, the completion status of this ER is true and there is an another ER-R being referenced by "*mpeg:mpeg21:dii:ERRID:010*". And the creator of this ER is *Andrew*, the corresponding Peer ID is "*GUID:1AC5-4527-A864-3EA2*" and the originating ER-R which triggers this ER is "*mpeg:mpeg21:dii:ERRID:001*".

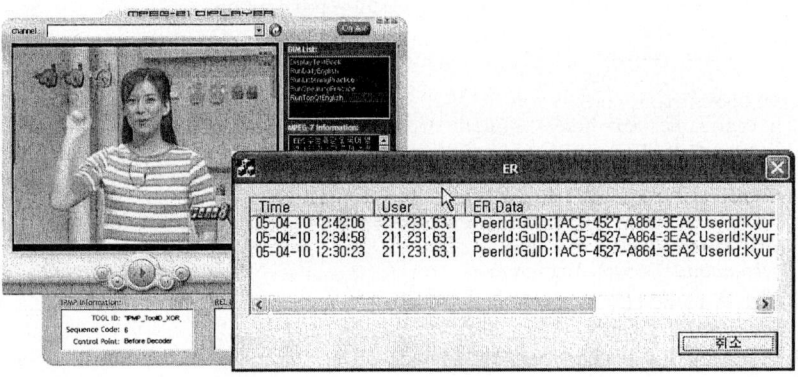

Fig. 9. Implementation Example of Event Notification on Interactive Broadcasting Environment

4 Conclusion

In this paper, we designed on metadata model for Event notification that can be utilized for various purposes on interactive broadcasting service. A realization of this model based on and extended from ISO/IEC 21000-15 has been described. Based on this, we implemented the testbed system. The metadata model we designed in this paper comprises of Event Report Request, which defines the conditions under which an Event is deemed to have occurred and requested information describing the Event, and Event Report, which is generated and delivered to the specified recipient(s) with requested information as specified in the associated Event Report Request.

The industry could release content onto the Internet and, in a trusted way, charge users for the content that they actually use rather than for an open-ended, free-use license by taking advantage of Event notification concepts. This is somewhat analogous to the distinction between buying and renting, where users only pay for what they use. By making event notification service a gateway to back-end accounting charging and billing systems, we can enable usage-based charging models. Similarly, industry could apply event notification concepts to pay-per-play charging models for games downloaded to a mobile device. If the game loses its interest, users could remove it and find a better one without paying any financial penalty. Therefore this Event notification service can be used for various kind of purpose that includes target marketing, personalized service by user's preference, t-Commerce, monitoring of illegal copies, proof of purchase, license purchase and delivery, monitoring of performances, network congestion, load balancing on interactive broadcasting.

We will do richer implementation using the metadata model and will keep on the study for extensible Event description that covers additional kind of Event Report Requests according to the increasing number of User preference and request.

References

1. MDS Group: ISO/IEC 21000 Event Reporting Committee Draft. ISO/IEC JTC1/SC29/WG11/N6783, Palma de Majorca (Oct. 2004)
2. Kyunghee Ji, Nammee Moon, YoungJoo Song, JinWoo Hong: Proposed Definition on Delivery Time and Recipient of MPEG-21 Event Reporting. ISO/IEC JTC1/SC29/WG11/m10619, Munich (March 2004)
3. Kyunghee Ji, Nammee Moon, Jaegon Kim: A Design on Time structure of MPEG-21 Event Reporting for Digital Contents over Multimedia Framework. Journal of Korea Multimedia Society, Vol.8, No.5. Korea (2005) 101-109
4. Requirements Group: Requirements for Event Reporting. ISO/IEC JTC1/SC29/WG11/N6279. Waikoloa (Dec. 2003)
5. Information Technology - Multimedia Framework, (MPEG-21)—Part 6: Rights Data Dictionary, ISO/IEC 21000-6(May 2004)
6. FX Nuttall, Youngjoo Song, Kyunghee Ji, A Tokmakoff, N Rump: Editor's Comments on MPEG-21 Event Reporting Committee Draft. ISO/IEC JTC1/SC29/WG11/m11639, Hong Kong (Jan. 2004)
7. Kyunghee Ji, Nammee Moon, YoungJoo Song, JinWoo Hong: Additional MPEG-21 Event Reporting Requirements. ISO/IEC JTC1/SC29/WG11/m10322, Hawaii (Dec. 2003)
8. Kyunghee Ji, Nammee Moon, Youngjoo Song,, Jaegon Kim: Implementation of MPEG-21 Event Reporting on Broadcasting and Communication Network, Proceeding of The Korean Society of Broadcast Engineers Summer Conference 2004, Korea (2004)110-12

Target Advertisement Service Using TV Viewers' Profile Inference

Munjo Kim[1], Sanggil Kang[2], Munchurl Kim[1], and Jaegon Kim[3]

[1] Laboratory for Multimedia Computing, Communications, and Broadcasting (MCCB Lab),
Information and Communications University (ICU)
{kimmj, mkim}@icu.ac.kr
[2] Department of Computer Science, College of Information and Technology,
The University of Suwon
sgkang@suwon.ac.kr
[3] Electronics and Telecommunications Research Institute (ETRI)
jgkim@etri.re.kr

Abstract. Due to the limitation of broadcasting service, in general, TV programs with commercial advertisements are scheduled to be broadcasted by demographics. The uniformly provided commercial can not draw many TV viewers' interest, which is not correspondent to the goal of the commercial. In order to solve the problem, a novel target advertisement technique is proposed in this paper. The target advertisement is a personalized advertisement according to TV viewers' profile such as their age, gender, occupation, etc. However, viewers are usually reluctant to inform their profile to the TV program provider or the advertisement company because their information can be used on some bad purpose by unknown people. Our target advertisement technique estimates a viewer's profile using Normalized Distance Sum and Inner product method. In the experiment, our method is evaluated for estimating the TV viewers' profile using TV usage history provided by AC Neilson Korea.

1 Introduction

Streaming service on the net such as internet broadcasting or web-casting [1] has been commonly used since a few years before, IPTV service [2] is also expected to be launched on the broadband network. Due to the invention and development of web-casting, the concept of the traditional broadcasting service is being refined. The traditional broadcasting service usually provides contents to unspecified individuals regardless of users' interests of the contents. For example, commercial advertisements are scheduled to be broadcasted by the demographic information such as TV program rating, age and gender group, and TV viewing time band. Unlike TV programs, the advertisements along with the programs are not selected by TV viewers' preference due to the limitation of the TV broadcasting environment. The randomly provided commercial can not draw many TV viewers' interest, which is not correspondent to the purpose of commercial advertisements: "providing advertisements to the right people in the right time." However, web-casting can allow users and content providers or servers to interact with one another by means of the bi-directional channels [3], which is the critical factor for providing personalized advertisement service. The personalized advertisement service targets the right commercials to the right users interested in them, and it is called target advertisement (TAD) in this paper.

To our best knowledge, not many researchers [4-6] have studied for developing target advertisement services. They usually cluster users and make groups according to similarity of their profiles and for a new-comer, find a group whose representative profile is close to the profile of the new-comer, to whom then the preferred advertisements of the group are provided to the new-comer. The clustering is done by collaborative filtering technique [7] based on users' profile. In their methods, TV viewers' profile such as gender, age, and occupation are explicitly informed to the TV content providers by personally inserting their information into the set-top box or the computer connected to the digital TV set. In general, people are reluctant to register their profile to the servers because of its improper use by unknown persons.

In order to serve TAD along with protecting users' privacy, we need to infer users' profile by analyzing users' implicit content consumption behaviors. In this paper, we introduce a novel method for inferring the users' profile with TV viewers' content consumption history such as TV watching day, time, and the preferred TV program genre. According to the target profiles for the inference, two different inference techniques are developed. One is for inferring a new viewer's age using a collaborative filtering technique. The technique groups TV viewers according to their ages, for a new viewer, find the age group whose preferred TV genre is similar to that of the new viewer's TV genre preference, and then provides the preferred commercial advertisements of the age group to the new viewer. The other is for inferring a new viewer's age and gender together using the look-up table method. In general, the more detail inference needs more TV viewers to increase the coverage of the cases of the inference. That is the reason why we use the look-up table for inferring age and gender together not using the collaborative filtering used in the age inference. Also, we design and model the prototype of our target advertisement system based on the inferred profile using the algorithms.

The remainder of this paper is organized as follows. Section 2 demonstrates the overall architecture of the target advertisement service. Section 3 describes our algorithms for inferring a viewer's profile. In Section 4, we show the experimental result of our algorithms using 2,000 TV viewers' TV program watching history and design and implement the prototype of the target advertisement service. We conclude our paper and propose future research work.

2 Overall Architecture of Target Advertisement Service

Fig. 1 illustrates the expected overall architecture of the target advertisement service in the condition that the interactive communication between content providers and TV viewers is possible by a web-casting scheme. There are three major users of the system such as content providers, advertisement companies, and TV viewers in the system. The content providers provide broadcasting contents with commercial advertisements to the TV or VOD (Video on Demand) viewers. The advertisement companies provide commercial items to the content providers. The target advertisement service system consists of three agents such as profiling agent (PA), interface agent

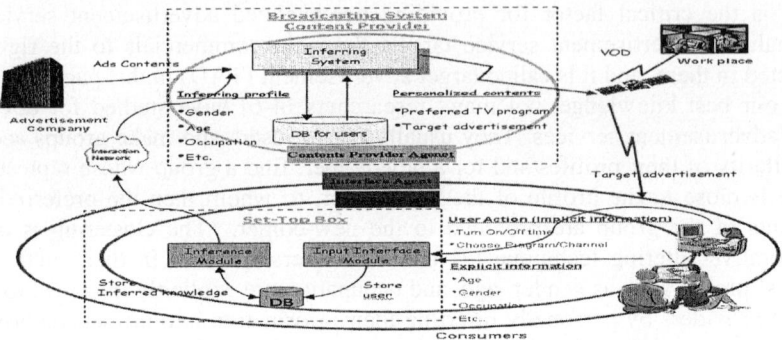

Fig. 1. The architecture of target advertisement service

(IA), and contents provider agent (CPA). The PA gathers the explicit information, e.g., TV viewers' profiles, directly input by TV viewers and the implicit information, e.g., content consumption behaviors such as TV program, viewing day, viewing time, and etc. The information is sent to the IA which is the graphic user interface (GUI) capable of the interaction between the PA and the CPA. The IA can be a set-top box connected to a TV set in viewers' house. The IA stores the received information into database through the input interface module. At the inference module in the IA, the stored viewer's consumption behavior data is analyzed for inferring his/her preferred TV genres and viewing day and time using any user's preference inference. The inferred knowledge (preferred TV genre in this paper) and the directly input profiles are sent to the CPA through the interactive network and stored into the database of viewers. Here, we assume that a restricted number of viewers sent their profiles to the CPA, e.g., around 10,000. The CPA analyzes the stored data and clusters the viewers according to the similarity of their profiles and the inferred information. For the viewers who are reluctant to send their profiles to the CPA, his/her profile can be inferred in the inference module using our proposed method which is explained in the next section. If an advertisement company requests the CPA to broadcast the commercial advertisements, the CPA provides the targeted viewers the commercial advertisements along with their preferred TV programs via the interactive networks.

In the following section, we describe our TV viewer profile inference method using the implicit information such as TV usage history.

3 TV Viewer Profile Inference

3.1 Age Inference System Using Normalized Distance Sum (NDS)

In general, the similarity of TV viewers' preferred genres can be characterized according to their age or gender. For instance, the documentary programs are usually popular favor for 30s and 40s man, while the show programs are for 10s and 20s. For each age group, the statistical preference of each genre can be calculated using Equation (1).

$$p_{i,k,a} = g_{i,k,a} / \sum_{i=1}^{I} g_{i,k,a} \qquad (1)$$

where $g_{i,k,a}$ is the frequency of watching genre i of a TV viewer k in his/her age group a during a predetermined period. Also, I is the total number of the genres. From the calculated values of the probabilities, the genres can be ordered from the highest ranked genre having the largest probability to the lowest ranked genre having the smallest probability. The ordered genres can be expressed with the vector form such as

$$V_{k,a} = \{R_{1,k,a} \ R_{2,k,a}, \cdots, R_{j,k,a}, \cdots, R_{I,k,a}\} \qquad (2)$$

where $R_{j,k,a}$ and $V_{k,a}$ is the jth ordered genre and the vector of the ordered genres of a TV viewer k in his/her age group a, respectively. For each viewer in group a in the database, the order of the preference of the genres can be various. If there are K number of viewers in the database in the content provider, the representative genre at $R_{j,k,a}$ can be decided by the frequencies of the consumption of the genres at the jth rank for viewer $k=1$ to $k=K$. At rank j, the genre having the largest frequency is considered as the representative genre, denoted as $\tilde{R}_{j,k,a}$. Also, the representative vector, denoted as $\tilde{V}_a$, for ages a can be denoted as

$$\tilde{V}_a = \{\tilde{R}_{1,k,a} \ \tilde{R}_{2,k,a}, \cdots, \tilde{R}_{j,k,a}, \cdots, \tilde{R}_{I,k,a}\} \qquad (3)$$

For a new (or test) TV viewer t, who has not been experienced by the content provider or has not input the viewer's profile to the interface agent, the vector of the order of the viewer's genre preference, denoted as V_t, can be obtained from his/her TV genre consumption behavior collected during a predetermined period and denoted as follows:

$$V_t = \{R_{1,t} \ R_{2,t}, \cdots, R_{j,t}, \cdots, R_{I,t}\} \qquad (4)$$

The measurement of the similarity of the new viewer and each age group can be obtained using NDS (Normalized Distance Sum) [8], one of image retrieval methods, and Vector correlation, measuring the similarity between two vectors. The NDS method provides the weights to the mismatch of order of genres according to the rank of the genres for measuring the similarity between two vectors $\tilde{V}_a$ and V_t. For example, if drama is the first ranked genre of a new viewer, the 3rd ranked for 20s, and the 2nd ranked for the 30s, then the degree of the mismatch of rank of drama between the new viewer and 20s and the new viewer and 30s. The degree of the mismatch for the ranks is called unsuitable distance in [8]. The unsuitable distances for all ranks can be normalized, which is used for the measurement of the similarity between vector $\tilde{V}_a$ and vector V_t as shown in Equation (5).

$$NDS(\tilde{V}_a, V_t) = \sum_j \{I - j + 1 \mid j: mismatched rank)\} / I(I+1)/2 \qquad (5)$$

For example, Table 1 shows an example of vector $\tilde{V}_a$ and vector V_t and the total number of genre, I, is 46. The mismatched genres of V_t are sports and comics to those of $\tilde{V}_a$ along with ranks 3 and 46. In Equation (5), the index j means the mismatched rank j in $\tilde{V}_a$. As the equation in the numerator of Equation (5), for the mismatched rank 3, the unsuitable distance is 44 (46-3+1=44) and for the mismatched rank 46, the unsuitable distance is 1 (46-46+1). From the numerical results, the penalty of the mismatch of higher ranked genre is given more than that of lower ranked genre. For all age groups, the NDSs of the new viewer can be computed using Equation (5), and the age band of the new viewer can be estimated the age band of the age group having the smallest value of NDS as denoted in Equation (6).

$$A\hat{g}es(t) = \min\{NDS(\tilde{V}_a, V_t \mid a \in A)\} \qquad (6)$$

where $A\hat{g}es(t)$ is the estimated age band of new viewer or test viewer t. By the estimated age band, the TV content provider can provide the commercials suitable for the age band. For example, if the new viewer's age band is estimated 10s, the advertisements related to electronic goods such as MP3, DVD, etc. can be provided. Fig. 2 is the schematic diagram for the NDS method, where G represents the age group such G1 (age 0~9), G2 (age 10~19), …., G7 (age over 60).

Table 1. An example of $\tilde{V}_a$ and V_t

Rank	1	2	3	…….	45	46
$\tilde{V}_a$	Drama	News	Sports	…….	Documentary	Comics
V_t	Drama	News	Comics	…….	Documentary	Sports

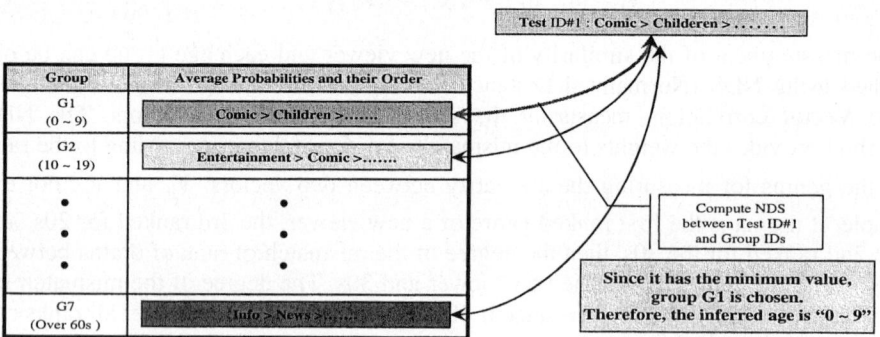

Fig. 2. The TV viewer's age inference using the NDS method

3.2 Age and Gender Inference System Using Vector Correlation

At the previous section, we demonstrated how to estimate a new viewer's age band using NDS technique. Sometime, more information about viewers' profile can increase the efficiency of the target advertisements. If the content providers know viewers' age and gender both, more detail commercial advertisement can be possible than they know viewers' age band. For example, if a viewer's age and gender are estimated 20 and woman, the content providers provide the advertisement of beauty goods such as cosmetics, accessories, etc.

As mentioned in the introduction section in this paper, in general, the more detail profile inference needs more TV viewers' consumption history which can increase the coverage of the cases of the inference. In order to take into the consideration for inferring a viewer's age and gender, we build the look-up table (LUT) of the order of the statistical preferences of genres for the viewers (reference viewers) in the database of the content providers as shown in Fig 3, where the value in the parenthesis next to the genres indicates their statistical preference.

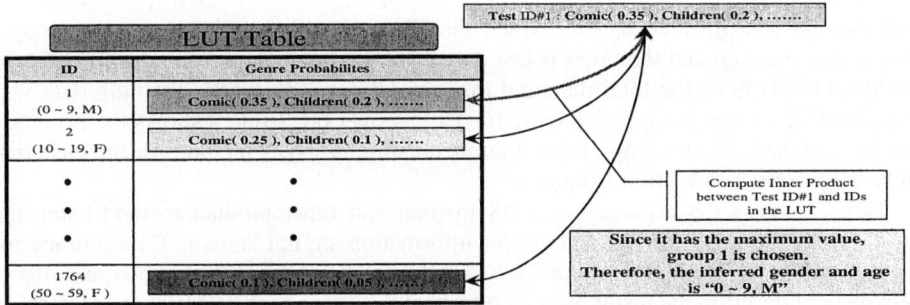

Fig. 3. Age and gender inference using LUT

When a new viewer comes, we can find the viewer in the reference viewers whose consumption behavior is very similar to that of the new viewer. The similarity between the vectors of the statistical preferences of the new viewer and each reference viewer can be calculated by the inner product between the vectors as shown in Equation (7).

$$Inn(V_{r_j}, V_t) = \cos\theta = V_{r_j} \cdot V_t / \|V_{r_j}\| \cdot \|V_t\| \qquad (7)$$

where $Inn(V_{r_j}, V_t)$ the inner product of V_{r_j} and V_t, which is the vector of the genre preference of jth reference viewer and the new viewer t, respectively. For all reference viewers, the inner product of the new viewer and each reference viewer can be computed using Equation (7), and the new viewer's age and gender can be estimated as the reference viewer's age and gender who having the maximum inner product as denoted in Equation (8).

$$\hat{g}a = \max\{Inn(V_{r_j}, V_t) \mid j \in J\} \qquad (8)$$

where J is the total number of reference viewers in the LUT. Fig 3 describes the schematic scheme of the vector inner product method of the reference viewers and the new viewer from the LUT.

4 Experimental Results and System Implementation

In this chapter, we show the accuracy of the proposed two profile inference methods using 2522 TV viewers' (Men: 1243, Women: 1279) usage history collected from Dec., 2002 to May, 2003. The NDS method is applied for inferring a viewer's age band when the content providers know the reference viewers' gender and the inner product method using the LUT is for a viewer's age and gender together when the content providers do not know the reference viewers' age and gender together. At the later section in this chapter, we show the implementation of the prototype of the target advertisement service system enabling target-oriented advertisement service based on our inference methods.

4.1 Accuracy of Our Profile Inference Methods

For the age band inference, we divided the TV usage history data into two groups; one is training data and the other is test data. The training data was randomly selected at 70% (1764) from the total data and the test data at 30% (758). Training data was classified into 7 age groups such 0~9, 10~19, ..., over 60. Table 2 shows the accuracy for the test data when our age band inference using the NDS method for the case that only the gender information is known.

Table 3 shows the accuracy of NDS method and Inner product method using the LUT for the case that the age and gender information are not known. The accuracy for the age inference method is about 77%. The accuracy of the ages for 30s and 40s is relatively high. From the result, we can infer that the range of their TV genre preference can not be wide, compared to the other age groups. In the mean while, the accuracy of the age of 20s is about 53%, which indicates that their TV genre preference can be wide.

Using NDS method, we can infer viewers' gender with the same way of inferring the age band. From Table 3, the Inner product method outperforms the NDS method when the reference viewers' age and gender are not known because the data sparseness happens when the NDS method is used for inferring more detail profile, as mentioned in the previous section. As seen in Table 3, we obtained 30.38% accuracy with NDS method and 39.42% accuracy for the men in 50s. With the Inner product method, we obtained average 67.4% accuracy and 89.37% accuracy for the women in 50s.

Table 2. The accuracy of the age band inference using the NDS method

Age Group	Accuracy (%)
0 ~ 9	66.90
10 ~ 19	77.60
20 ~ 29	53.53
30 ~ 39	89.05
40 ~ 49	89.08
50 ~ 59	77.34
60 ~	75.20
Total	**77.01**

Table 3. The accuracy of the age and gender using the Inner product method and NDS

Gender & Age Group	Accuracy (%)	
	NDS	Vector Correlation
0 ~ 9, M	37.81	62.14
0 ~ 9, F	36.11	84.15
10 ~ 19, M	31.73	55.53
10 ~ 19, F	34.44	79.57
20 ~ 29, M	30.36	58.01
20 ~ 29, F	30.03	75.60
30 ~ 39, M	34.27	50.79
30 ~ 39, F	18.75	78.93
40 ~ 49, M	31.54	54.14
40 ~ 49, F	26.25	79.81
50 ~ 59, M	39.42	56.25
50 ~ 59, F	20.26	89.37
60 ~ M	35.66	50.30
60 ~ F	30.38	67.65
Total	**30.38**	**67.40**

4.2 Prototype System of the Target Advertisement Service

In this section, we propose the result of prototype system of the target advertisement service based on the inference methods. As shown in Fig 4, the prototype system is consists of two parts, Client and Server. The server (Target advertisement Service Provider) contains a user profiling function and a broadcasting program delivering function. Client (User Interface) receives target advertisement contents. A user sends limited user's information to the prototype system, and the target advertisement service provider infers a TV viewers' profile based on the information and provides the target advertisement.

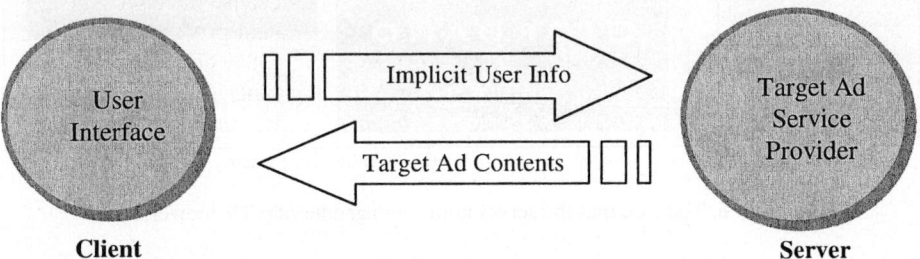

Fig. 4. Client and server in the target advertisement service

The experimental data for the prototype system of the target advertisement service used the free advertisement contents from NGTV (http://www.ngtv.net). We experimented with 28 advertisement contents and grouped those contents based on targeted ages and gender for the advertisement. When a client connects to a server, pop-up menu is displayed to receive the client's profile information. The pop-up menu enables 3 scenarios from Fig. 5 to Fig. 7. Fig. 5 (a) is the pop-up menu when the client connects to a server and provides nothing about ages and gender. Fig. 5 (b) is the result of prototype service. Since the client informs nothing about the client's profile, the server infers the client's gender and ages using vector correlation method and transmits the TAD contents to the client. The client user interface displays the received contents.

(a) Pop-Up Menu   (b) TAD Service Result

Fig. 5. The case that the server has no information about a TV viewer

We can see the inference result is women in 20s. The cell-phone advertisement for women in 20s is delivered to the client from the server. Fig 6 (a) is the pop-up menu when the client connects to a server and provides only the gender of a client. Fig 6 (b) is the result of prototype service. Since the client provides only about the client's gender, the server infers the client's ages using NDS method with the client's gender and TV usage history, and transmits the TAD contents to the client. The client user interface displays the received contents.

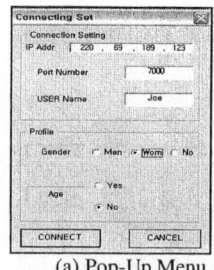 

(a) Pop-Up Menu   (b) TAD Service System

Fig. 6. The case that the server knows the gender of a TV viewer

Since the recommended ages is 20s, the server provides a fashion advertisement allocated for women in 20s. Fig 7 (a) is the pop-up menu when the client connects to a server and provides the gender (women) and age band (20s) of a client. Fig 7 (b) is the result of prototype service. Since the client informs about the client's gender and ages, the server does not have to infer the client's profile and transmits the TAD contents according to the client's given profile.

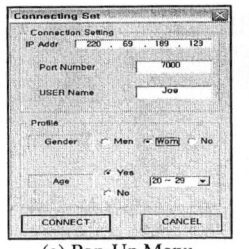 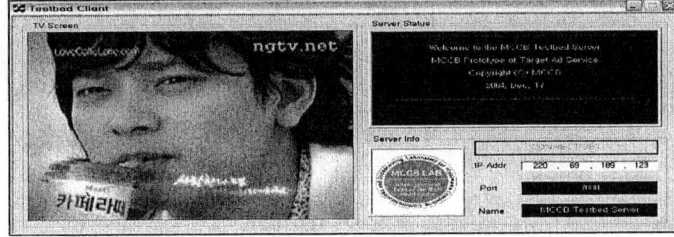

(a) Pop-Up Menu　　　　　　　　　　(b) TAD Service System

Fig. 7. The case that the server knows the gender and age band of a TV viewer

5 Conclusion

This paper proposed the target advertisement system using two TV viewers' profile inference methods; one is NDS method for inferring age band and the other is Inner product method for inferring age and gender together. In the experimental section, we implemented our method using real TV viewers' usage history and obtained about 70% accuracy when only gender information is known and about 77% accuracy when age and gender information is not known. The results are optimistic results for further studies about the target advertisement because only 1,764 viewers' usage history used for the training data is a too small data size. Also, we think our designed and implemented prototype of the target advertisement system can be the milestone for applying the system to practical use. For the future work, it is needed to improve our profile inference methods using larger size of the data than 1,764 viewers.

References

1. Marchese M., Ronchetti M.: New Models for Higher Educational Curricula. ITRE 2004. (21004) 69-73
2. Jennehag U., Zhang T.: Increasing Bandwidth Utilization In Next Generation Iptv Networks. International Conference of Image Processing. 3 (2004) 2075-2078
3. Katsaros D.,Manolopoulos Y.: Broadcast Program Generation for Webcasting. Source Data & Knowledge Engineering. Vol. 49, No. 1 (2004) 1-21
4. Bozios T., Lekakos G., Skoularidou V., Chorianopoulos K.: Advanced Techniques for Personalised Advertising in a Digital TV Environment: The iMEDIA System. Proceedings of the E-business and E-work Conference. (2001) 1025-1031
5. Miyahara K., Pazzani M. J.: Collaborative Filtering With the Simple Bayesian Classifier. Sixth Pacific-Rim International Conference on Artificial Intelligence. (2000) 230-237
6. Shahabi C., Faisal A., Kashani F.B., Faruque J.: INSITE: A Tool for Interpreting Users Interaction with a Web Space. International Conference on Very Large Data Bases (2000) 635-638
7. Terano T. , Murakami E.: Finding Users' Latent Interests for Recommendation by Learning Classifier Systems. Proceedings of Knowledge-Based Intelligent Engineering Systems and Allied Technologies. 2 (2000) 651-654
8. Suh C., Kim W.:A Novel Measurement for Retrieval Efficiency of Image Database Retrieval System. Journal The Korean Society of Broadcast Engineers. Vol. 5, No. 1 (2000) 68-81

Personalized TV Services and T-Learning Based on TV-Anytime Metadata

HeeKyung Lee, Seung-Jun Yang, Han-Kyu Lee, and Jinwoo Hong

ETRI, 161 Gajeong-Dong, Yuseong-gu, Daejeon 305-700, Korea
{lhk95, sjyang, hkl, jwhong}@etri.re.kr

Abstract. To support personalized broadcasting service and T-learning, we propose to use TV-Anytime standard. The TV-Anytime Forum is an association of organizations which seeks to develop specifications to enable audio-visual and other services based on mass-market high volume digital storage in consumer platforms such as a set-top box (STB). TV-Anytime standard is classified to Phase 1 and 2 according to its functionality. The former supports PVR-based applications in a uni-directional broadcast and the latter deals with the sharing and distribution of rich content among local storage devices and/or network digital recorders in home network environments. In this paper, we first overview TV-Anytime specifications, and secondly present an end-to-end prototype system for personalized broadcasting services based on TV-Anytime Phase 1 standard which consists of metadata authoring tool, transmission server, and set-top box. At the last, we propose the method to utilize content package in TV-Anytime Phase 2 to develop a T-learning environment.

1 Introduction

Digital broadcasting is evolving to a more complex and diverse consumption environment due to rapid increase of channels and content as well as various user devices and networks involved. In this new content consumption context, the personalized service that makes it allows for a user to more effectively access and select his/her preferred content at any time and/or in any place becomes increasingly important. To enable the personalized service, a PDR should be provided a rich set of metadata about content in addition to content itself.

In addition, nowadays it is hardly impossible to imagine learning without additional tools like computer-based training (CBT) and E-learning applications via the Internet. Nevertheless, these new training methods have problems as follows: First, delivery of video content with high bandwidth requirements is impossible. Second, video content in today's Internet learning applications lack true interactivity and it is not possible to easily browse and explore the video content. Finally, most learning content is fixed to general preferences and consuming environments. Therefore, we propose T-learning service that combines the usage of broadcast and optical disc media for high-quality content distribution and the usage of the internet for personalized content and interaction with the educational institute.

To support personalized broadcasting service and T-learning, we propose to use TV-Anytime standard. The TV-Anytime Forum is an association of organizations which seeks to develop specifications to enable audio-visual and other services based on mass-market high volume digital storage in consumer platforms such as a set-top box (STB). The TV-Anytime Forum's first specification series specify a set of metadata to be used for efficient and personalized access and browsing of broadcasting content [1], in a PDR-centric environment on a uni-directional broadcast. And recently, it wrapped up its work on Phase 2 including content package [6], which is an organic collection of various types of contents and can provide various interactive consumption experiences.

Therefore, in this paper, we first overview TV-Anytime specifications, and secondly present an end-to-end prototype system for personalized broadcasting services based on TV-Anytime Phase 1 standard which consists of metadata authoring tool, transmission server, and set-top box. At the last, we propose the method to utilize content package in TV-Anytime Phase 2 to develop a T-learning environment in which problems of new training methods are solved.

2 TV-Anytime System and Metadata

The TV-Anytime Forum is an association of organizations which seeks to develop specifications to enable audio-visual and other services based on mass-market high volume digital storage in consumer platforms such as a set-top box (STB). Especially, the Forum has developed specifications for applications that are independent of networks and delivery mechanisms such as Advanced Television Systems Committee (ATSC), Digital Video Broadcasting (DVB), Association of Radio Industries and Businesses (ARIB), and the Internet. At the end of 2002, the TV-Anytime Forum announced its first specification series for Phase 1 [2]-[5], which has been adopted into other industrial standard bodies such as DVB, ARIB and ETSI. And at June of 2005, TV-Anytime Forum also finished and announced its second specification series for Phase 2 [6]-[9], which was submitted to ETSI at July, 2005.

2.1 TV-Anytime Phase 1

The Phase 1 specifications enable one to search, select, acquire, and rightfully use content on local and/or remote storage both from broadcast and online sources. TV-Anytime metadata are instantiated as XML documents under a root element called "TVAMain." Each part of the metadata instances is associated together with the same AV program by the content referencing identification (CRID) as shown in Fig. 1 [3]. Content referencing is the process of associating a token to a piece of content that represents its location where the content can be acquired.

As shown in Fig. 1, the basic kinds of TV-Anytime metadata are content description metadata, instance description metadata, segmentation metadata and consumer metadata. Content description metadata are general information about a piece of content that does not change regardless of how the content is published or broadcasted. Instance description metadata describe a particular instance of a piece of content, including information such as the content location, usage rules, and delivery parameters (e.g., video format). Consumer metadata, borrowed from MPEG-7, include usage history data (logging data), annotation metadata, and user preferences for a personalized content service. Segmentation metadata describe a segment or groups of segments. A segment is a continuous portion of a piece of content. Segmentation metadata make it possible to repurpose programs, for example, video highlight, bookmark, and virtual program. Fig. 2 shows an example for virtual program which is reconstructed by a user with preference for tennis.

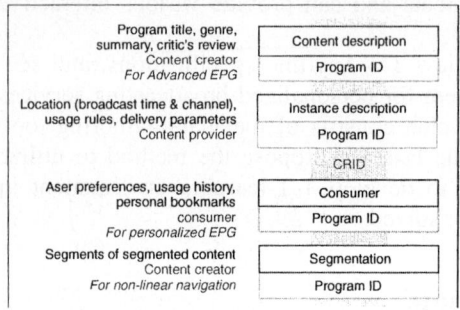

Fig. 1. TV-Anytime metadata and CRID

Fig. 2. Virtual program using segment metadata

2.2 TV-Anytime Phase 2

In addition to Phase 1, the TV-Anytime Forum has finished its work on Phase 2 [6]-[9], which mainly deals with the sharing and distribution of rich content among local storage devices and/or network digital recorders in home network environments. Especially, normative specifications of Phase 2 metadata include the following issues: packaging, e-flyer, interstitial, sharing, and remote programming.

First, content packaging is a collection of related content components as a unit of selection, and is an entry point for user 'experience'. These components can be various types of multimedia content such as video, audio, images, web pages, games, and applications [6]. The data model of a package adopts the multi-level structure of the MPEG-21 Digital Item Declaration (DID) [10], i.e., container-item-component, along with some refinements and extensions [6], [11], [12]. The key concepts related to packaging are as follows:

- Package and component identification: As a package is a unit of selection, the process is necessary to identify, select, and acquire a package.
- Targeting: Once a package is acquired, member components of the package are automatically matched and selected according to usage environment such as user, terminal, network, and nature [6]. To support targeting service, description for usage environment and description for interrelation between usage environment and components need to be provided.
- Content description for package & components: To help user's and/or agent's choice for package and components, descriptive metadata for attributes of them are supported in a package.
- Synchronization & rendering using relation: (Temporal & Spatial) Relation metadata among components is provided to indicate the exact order of components when they are consumed and the proper position of components where they are

rendered. Especially, synchronization is a timing service for intended operation such as multi-stream experience (multi-camera sport or alternative AV).

Fig. 3(a) shows a XML schema for package with multi-level structure of package-item-component, and Fig. 3(b) shows an exemplary package with two items: the introduction (as video or audio) and the first chapter of a course.

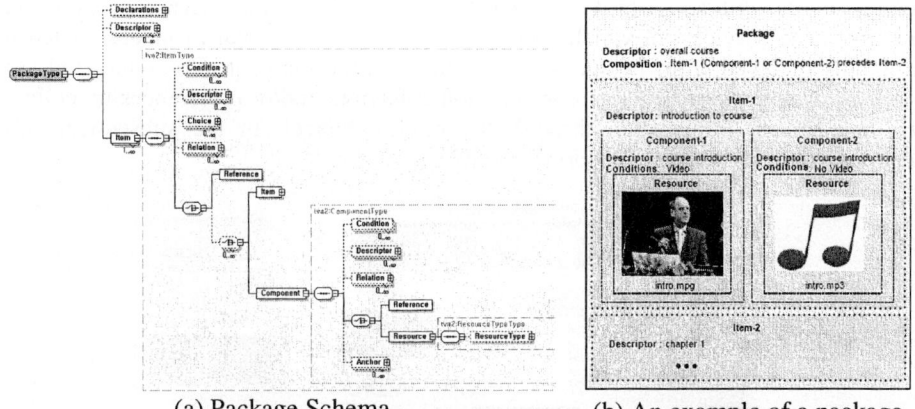

(a) Package Schema (b) An example of a package

Fig. 3. Package schema and an exemplary package

Second, E-flyer is an attractive metadata concerning business practices such as price, discounts, advertisements, subscription, promotion, coupon etc [6]. Third, Interstitial is an additional content that may be inserted within, at the start, or at the end of the primary content item. This additional content includes e.g. advertising spots, station indents, promos, and graphics. TV-Anytime Phase 2 target more advanced concepts such as interstitial replacement at playback time within a PDR device based on a number of criteria. The criteria to be used for the control of what content should be replaced, may be explicitly declared using the schema of RuleType [7]. Fourth, sharing (exchange of personal profiles) provides the method to exchange of user profiles in a secure environment. It offers a number of possible benefits to both consumers and service providers. For example, a personalized web-service in which a service provider provides the response of user's request using his consumer profile data, can offer the consumer a personally relevant content. Fifth, remote programming is remote control service for PDR and NDR. It defines protocols and functions to control the remote recording on PDR and NDR and to deliver the recorded contents and metadata to PDR and non-PDR remote device (ex. office PC, PDA, mobile phone) [9].

3 A Prototype System for Personalized Broadcasting Service

In this section, we present an end-to-end prototype system for personalized broadcasting services based on TV-Anytime Phase 1. Fig. 4 illustrates overall configuration of the system in a conceptual level. Metadata authored at the authoring tool are coded as a binary format (BiM), multiplexed with AV content (programs) into a MPEG-2

Transport Stream (TS), and then delivered to the client via unidirectional broadcasting channel. The client terminal (i.e., a PDR) is equipped with various kinds of functional modules for accessing, searching and browsing content, and enables users to consume the content in a personalized way. In home network environment, multiple devices (i.e., sub-PDR's like mobile devices) can also be connected with the main PDR. Then, content may need to be adapted, and delivered to diverse types of sub-PDR's according to their capabilities. A bi-directional return channel (i.e., the Internet) provides online metadata services, in which a user could acquire additional metadata related to programs received from broadcasting channel. Furthermore, it allows targeted services according to user content consumption behaviors and/or preferences by collecting user-centric information through the return channel. In the subsequent subsections, we describe each functional modules.

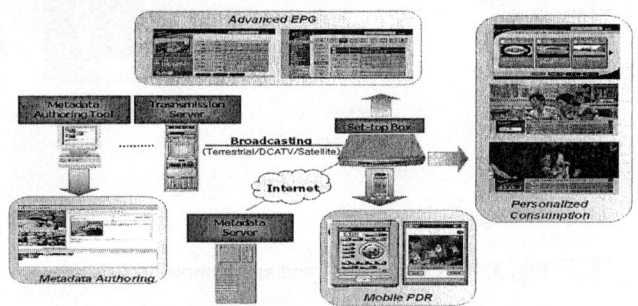

Fig. 4. Overall configuration of the prototype system

3.1 Authoring Tool

The TV-Anytime metadata authoring tool developed by ETRI, is to provide users visual and intuitive environment for authoring content descriptive metadata.

The over framework encompasses metadata visualization and editing, media access, and further several semi-automatic tools for authoring segment related metadata. First, we employed the extensible stylesheet language (XSL) transformation [13] for displaying the metadata. Each metadata element or attribute is converted to a visible or hidden component of the other document (i.e. HTML). The document is made editable by incorporating some extraneous interactive tools (e.g. forms, javascript), and may be communicated with the main application for the metadata updating and enhanced media handling operations. After the metadata are updated, re-visualization will happen in a sequence to keep the consistency between the underlying metadata content and the visualized one. The edited results will be saved as an XML document.

3.2 Transmission Server

This sub-section deals with metadata delivery including metadata encoding, encapsulation, and multiplexing. Especially, the architecture of developed BiM Codec and multiplexing scheme is presented. We basically follow the standard technologies for delivery of metadata: the MPEG-7 Systems for metadata encoding (BiM) [14]; the MPEG-2 Digital Storage Media Command and Control (DSM-CC) for metadata encapsulation as data carousel [15], and the MPEG-2 Systems AMD 1 for metadata multiplexing into a transport stream [16].

Metadata Coding:BiM Codec
For bandwidth efficiency, metadata which is in the form of XML document and need to be delivered are encoded as a binary format. In addition, in order to allow more flexible and efficient manipulation of metadata, they are decomposed into self-consistent units of data, called fragments. According to the MPEG-7 Systems [14], metadata are basically structured into a sequence of AUs. An AU is composed of one or more fragment update units (FUUs), each of which represents a small part of metadata description. The AU may convey updates for several distinct parts of the description simultaneously. Each FUU consists of a fragment update command (FU Command), a fragment update context (FU Context), and a fragment update payload (FU Payload) [14], [17], [18]. At first, the encoder generates DecoderInit (DI) initializing configuration parameters required for decoding a sequence of AUs such as identifiers of instantiated schema, an initial description. In a FUU encoder, each module generates respective FUU component referring to metadata and user parameters: FU command code word specifies a command to be executed on a description tree to be maintained at a BiM decoder; FU context specifies node of the description tree on which the FU Command should be executed; FU payload performs a task of compressing structural information of description and encoding each data type. Finally, FUU components are composed into a FU composer and passed to an AU queue.

Metadata Encapsulation and Multiplexing
To deliver metadata over broadcasting channel (here, terrestrial ATSC is assumed), we first encapsulate an encoded description stream as data carousel and carry it over a MPEG-2 transport stream [19] by multiplexing with main AV content according to the MPEG-2 Systems AMD 1 [16].

3.3 Set-Top Box

A prototype system of TV-Anytime compliant PDR consists of the following functional modules: metadata demultiplexer, metadata decoder, and metadata consumption. The PDR extracts metadata from the received ATSC stream by a series of processing steps of demodulation, demultiplexing of MPEG-2 TS, and decapsulation in real time. The metadata encoded as a format of BiM (binary format for metadata) is decoded into TeM (text format for metadata) format, and then the TeM format is finally decoded into an XML document. The TV-Anytime XML document is parsed and populated into a DB to be used for personalized content consumption services. The details will be given in the next Section.

Metadata De-multiplexing
The process of de-multiplexing is illustrated in Fig. 5. By analyzing Program Map Table (PMT) at first, the value of packet identifier (PID) [20] assigned to metadata and AV contents can be identified. By referring stream type included in the PMT, the protocol used for transporting metadata is identified. Finally, the metadata carried

over TS can be extracted by parsing the used protocol. Then, the extracted metadata are passed to the metadata decoder (In this case, BiM decoder). As well, AV content is passed to a MPEG-2 decoder.

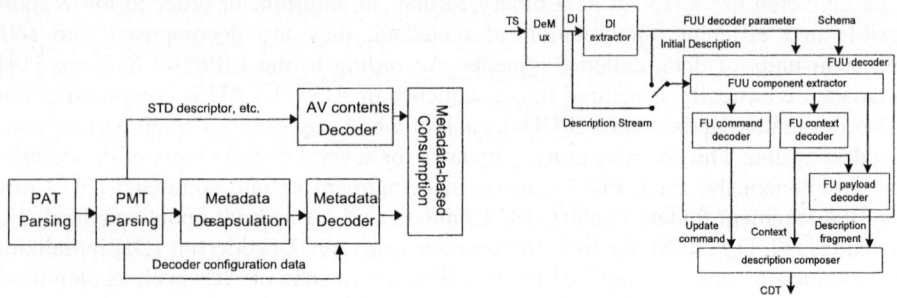

Fig. 5. The process of de-multiplexing

Fig. 6. BiM decoder architecture

Metadata Decoding

As illustrated in Fig. 6, the BiM decoder receives DecoderInit (DI) and metadata stream, and reconstructs delivered metadata. First, a Fragment Update Unit (FUU) decoder is initialized by initial parameters and schemas come from the DI. After initialization by the initial description, a description tree is updated by subsequent Access Units (AUs) from the description stream [21]. Then, each FUU component is extracted from a given AU in a FUU decoder. A FU command decoder refers to a simple look-up table to decode the update command, and passes it to a description composer. Decoded FU context information is passed to both of the description composer and a FU Payload decoder. Owing to the FU context information, a FU payload is decoded to a description fragment in the FU Payload decoder. The FU Payload is composed of a flag specifying certain decoding modes and a payload which can be either an element or a simple value. After an entire metadata is recomposed, they are saved in the metadata/media storage.

Personalized Content Consumption

In order to provide personalized services based on metadata, we have developed a metadata processing engine based on the TV-Anytime system model [6] emulating a STB, and built several personalized content access and browsing scenarios.

Metadata-Based Personalized Access and Browsing
– ACG (Advanced electronic Contents Guide)
When a large number of channels is available, ACG helps a user know where his/her wanted program is located in a broadcasting schedule in an efficient way. Fig. 7(a) shows the UI for ACG having a weekly timetable in which preferred programs can be represented by differently colored according to the degree of genre preference.

- ToC (Table of Contents) Browser
ToC-based browser provides non-linear navigation of interesting segments from selected program content. From the ToC, users could figure out overall story-structure of the underlying content and have access to the content in a segment level randomly.
- EbS (Event-based Summary) Browser
Event-based summary in Fig. 7(b) provides a function similar to the index of a book. Especially, news or sports video, where event is well defined (like news theme, sports event like goal, etc.), is quite suited for browsing with this way.
- Keyword-based search on segments
Fig. 7(c) shows the keyword-based search on programs and/or segments.

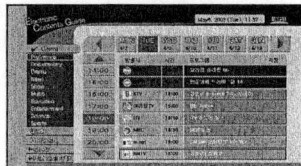

(a) Advanced electronic Contents Guide

(b) Event-based Summary

(c) Program/Segment Search

(d) Personal Program on PDA

Fig. 7. Personalizes service interface

Program Recommendation using User Preference: Personal Channel
Personal channel is a program rescheduling service according to various kinds of user preferences or life styles that happens dynamically in the PDR after the ACG information has been collected from a number of service providers.

Customized Consumption in Sub-PDRs: Personal Program
In home network environment where various kinds of devices are connected, to provide appropriate content multimedia information adaptively, we developed a personal program function that provides customized content according to user preferences and/or consuming conditions. Fig. 7(d) illustrates the consumption of adapted content in a PDA by using personal program function. In addition, remote control of main PDR by using a sub-PDR (PDA) is implemented.

4 T-Learning with TV-Anytime Through Packaging

Owing to the bandwidth limitation, today's learning systems like e-learning are not capable of some interesting learning concepts like multi-angle video or watching multiple streams simultaneously. Besides bandwidth issues, video in today's Web-based learning is plagued by two additional problems: lack of interactivity and lack of accessibility control [22]. Video on the Web doesn't have true interactivity, e.g., asking a question after a short video segment. It decreases the effect of education because limited interactivity makes it impossible for learners to actively participate in the education and to select preferable contents. Furthermore, although students have different user preferences and consuming environments, current learning applications are targeted on a certain platform, e.g., browser, and are not adjustable to user preferences. This really downgrades the quality of the learning system and the learning experience.

Therefore, to maximize the effect of education, the weakness of today's leaning systems need to be eliminated. To overcome the weakness, in this paper we propose the personalized educational contents service scenario through package which can provide preferable educational contents to each learner.

4.1 T-Learning Scenario

Fig. 8 shows overall operation scenario by the proposed personalized educational contents service through package. Details for each step are as followings:

1. First, the student attends or joins the course at university, college, or some other learning institute.
2. Second, the institute delivers the course on a disc, e.g., DVD or Blu-ray, which stores the basic learning package.
3. Third, the student studies the course at home using their personal devices and preferences.
    - The "PVR" gateway uses the user and terminal conditions to select the appropriate content, e.g., audio over video for a audio-only terminal, in order to target the package as closely as possible to the user preferences and consuming environment.
    - The "PVR" gateway handles the location resolution where a CRID resolves in the locator of contents that is locally available, e.g., on a disc or hard drive.
    - After the acquisition of contents using locator, learners can study.
4. Fourth, additional high-definition course material is delivered via a broadcast network, e.g., ATSC, DVB, or ARIB, and low-demanding material via Internet.
5. Finally, the Internet is used for personalized content and interaction with the institute.
    - At the location resolution step above, when content is not locally available, location resolution is delegated to the service provider, which then provides the locator.
    - Contents can be acquired from contents server on the Internet using locator, and then consumed.
    - Learners can acquire and consume various educational contents targeted to the capability, preference, and usage environment of learners using Internet.

By introducing disc and broadcast technology, it is possible to deliver high quality (e.g., high-definition) video to the student, and it relieves the student and learning application to download this content via the Internet. Now, the Internet can be utilized for personalized content, e.g., exercises on topics that the student doesn't master, and interaction with the institute, e.g., video conferencing with a teacher. To support these interactive educational services, it is most important to create a proper content. Package in TV-Anytime Phase 2 can be the most proper one, because it is an organic collection of various types of contents, so it can provide various interactive consumption experiences. The next sub-section presents an exemplary package instance for package-based T-learning.

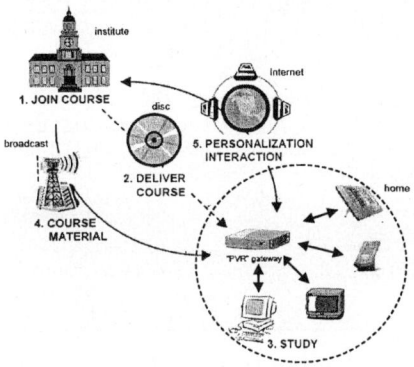

Fig. 8. Student learning scenario

4.2 Exemplary Package Instance for Package-Based T-Learning

The proposed package instance used for package-based T-learning is made for guitar lesson. The lesson consists of five levels as beginner / basic / intermediate I / intermediate II / Advanced. Each level has five one hour lessons. Each lesson is composed of 1 video clips (animated presentations), 1 audio clips and an application for test. Each lesson works as follows:

- Teaches each technique by showing video with synchronized audio
- Asks to practice with microphone on,.
- Listens to the practice and checks if the learner produces correct sound via application.
  - When there is a difference in sound, tells where the difference is and possible cause of the error.
  - If there is a significant difference, and if necessary, asks to go to the easier lesson and practice more.
  - If the practice sounds good, it tells to advance to the next lesson.

The xml snippet shows suitable component per each usage environment and relationship between item and/or component like contiguous.

```
<!--*************************************************************-->
<!--  Content for Intermediate Level 2 Lesson 5      -->
<!--*************************************************************  -->
<Item>
  <Condition require="Intermediate_II_5th"/>
  <Item>
    <Relation href="urn:tva:metadata:Phase2:cs:TemporalRelati-
onCS:2005-03" source="appl_I2_L5" target="video_I2_L5">
      <tva:Name>contiguous</tva:Name>
    </Relation>
    <Item item_id="audio_I2_L5">
      <Descriptor>  ......  </Descriptor>
      <Component>
        <Condition require="Audio_AAC"/>
        <Resource crid="crid://www.iebs.com/Guitar_Learning/
Intermediate_II_L5_Audio" imi="imi:GL_I2_L5_AAC1
imi:GL_I2_L5_AAC2"/>
      </Component>
      <Component>
        <Condition require="Audio_MP3"/>
        <Resource crid="crid://www.iebs.com/Guitar_Learning/
Intermediate_II_L5_Audio" imi="imi:GL_I2_L5_MP31
imi:GL_I2_L5_MP32"/>
      </Component>
    </Item>
    <Item item_id="video_I2_L5">  ......  </Item>
    <Item item_id="appl_I2_L5">   ......  </Item>
  </Item>
</Item>
```

5 Conclusion

In this paper, we give an outline of TV-Anytime specifications.

And we introduced a prototype system of PDR based on TV-Anytime metadata and system model. By extracting the instance of metadata description based on TV-Anytime specification, the proposed personalized services can be served between the TV-Anytime compatible devices. This technology can be applied to intelligent and customized digital TV broadcasting terminal and web-based customized services using user preference.

Subsequently the paper presented interactive and personalized T-learning services based on TV- Anytime metadata. These services combine the usage of broadcast and optical disc media for high- quality content distribution and the usage of the internet for personalized content and interaction with the educational institute. At the exemplary package instance for proposed package-based T-learning, selectable conditions based on various usage environments, suitable component per each condition, and relationship between components are shown.

Nowadays, we are working on designing and implementing a test-bed for validating package-based T-learning services.

References

1. The TV-Anytime, "TV-Anytime Forum," http://www.tv-anytime.org/, 2004.
2. S-2 (version 1.3: SP002v13), System Description, The TV-Anytime Forum, Feb. 2003. [Online]Available: ftp://tva:tva@ftp.bbc.co.uk/ pbu/Plenary/.

3. S-3 (version 1.3: SP003v13), Metadata, The TV-Anytime Forum, Dec. 2002.
4. S-4 (version 1.2: SP004v12), Content Referencing, The TV-Anytime Forum, June 2002.
5. S-6 (version 1.0: SP006v10), Metadata Services over a Bi-directional Network, The TV-Anytime Forum, Feb. 2003. Online]Available: ftp://tva:tva@ftp.bbc.co.uk/pbu/Plenary/.
6. ETSI TS 102 822-3-3 V1.1.1, Broadcast and On-line Services: Part 3: Metadata Sub-part 3: Phase 2 Extended Metadata Schemas, ETSI, Jul. 2005. [Online]Available: http://www.etsi.org.
7. ETSI TS 102 822-3-4 V1.1.1, Broadcast and On-line Services: Part 3: Metadata Sub-part 4: Phase 2 Interstitial Metadata, ETSI, Jul. 2005.
8. ETSI TS 102 822-6-3 V1.1.1, Broadcast and On-line Services: Part 6: Delivery of metadata over a bi-directional network Sub-part 3: Phase 2 Exchange of Personal Profiles, ETSI, Jul. 2005.
9. ETSI TS 102 822-9 V1.1.1, Broadcast and On-line Services: Part 9: Phase 2 Remote Programming, ETSI, Jul. 2005.
10. MPEG-21 Digital Item Declaration FDIS, ISO/IEC 2002-2 (N4813), May 2002, Fairvax, VA, USA.
11. TV-Anytime Forum, Working Document: Packaging and Targeting (2004, June). [Online]. Available: ftp://tva:tva@ftp.bbc.co.uk/pub/Plenary/WD997.zip.
12. Heekyung. L., Jae-Gon K., Jinsoo C., and Jinwoong K.: "Package Schema for Targeting & Synchronization," TV-Anytime Forum, AN602, March 2004. [Online]. Available: ftp://tva:tva@ftp.bbc.co.uk/pub/Contributions/
13. W3C, The extensible stylesheet language (XSL), Available [online] http://www.w3.org/Style/XSL.
14. Text of ISO/IEC 15938-1 Information Technology-Multimedia content Description Interface-part 1 Systems, ISO/IEC, 2002.
15. Text of ISO/IEC 13818-1 Information Technology- Generic Coding of Moving Pictures and Associated Audio Information - part 10 Digital Storage Media Command and Control (DSM-CC), ISO/IEC, 1998.
16. N5270, Text of ISO/IEC 13818-1:2000/PDAM1-Transport of Metadata, ISO/IEC JTC1/SC29/WG11 (MPEG), Nov. 2002.
17. Seung-Jun Y., Hyun Sung C., Young-tae K., Kyeongok K., and Nguyen N. T.: "Design of TeM Codec for Delivering MPEG-7 Descriptions," Proc. IEEE ICACT-2003, Jan. 2003, pp. 117-120.
18. AN 282, A Streamable XML Binary Encoding for TV-Anytime Metadata, The TV-Anytime Forum MD WG, June 2001.
19. Text of ISO/IEC 13818-1 Information Technology- Generic Coding of Moving Pictures and Associated Audio Information - part 1 Systems, ISO/IEC, 2002.
20. Hyun Sung C., and Kyeongok K.: "A Compressed Domain Scheme for Classifying Block Edge Patterns," accepted for the publication in IEEE Trans. Image Processing (Published in 2004).
21. W3C Recommendation 16, XSL Transformations (XSLT) Version 1.0., W3C, Nov. 1999.
22. Mike. F.: "Playback Media", Training Magazine, April 2004

Metadata Generation and Distribution for Live Programs on Broadcasting-Telecommunication Linkage Services

Yuko Kon'ya, Hidetaka Kuwano, Tomokazu Yamada, Masahito Kawamori, and Katsuhiko Kawazoe

NTT Cyber Solution Laboratories,
Yokosuka, Kanagawa 239-0847, Japan
{konya.yuko, kuwano.hidetaka, yamada.tomokazu,
kawamori.masahito, kawazoe.katsuhiko}@lab.ntt.co.jp

Abstract. This paper describes SceneCabinet/Live!, which is a system that generates real-time segment metadata using audio/video indexing and natural language processing to provide viewers with a continuously metadata update service of live programs. It significantly reduces the costs of generating segment metadata that is relevant to the viewer and reduces the time by about half. It enables metadata to be sent without delay in a metadata updateable service. We approached using audio/video recognition technologies to make index of the scene like a book because video programs are difficult to search scenes in. Segment metadata is used on broadcasting-telecommunication linkage services, affording a new way to view programs on optical and broadcast networks by supporting TV digests and videos from VoD services. These new metadata services are more convenient to use and more enjoyable to watch than conventional ones.

1 Introduction

In Japan, digital satellite and digital terrestrial broadcasting services are currently in use, and we are now investigating next generation broadcasting-telecommunication linkage services called server-based broadcasting.

Server-based broadcasting provides a new way of watching TV programs using metadata. For example, during baseball game broadcasts viewers can switch back and forth, search for and replay the most interesting scenes (e.g. homerun scene, hit scene), using Video on Demand (VoD) as shown in Figure 1.

In this service, we generate segment metadata that give a description of scenes of a program (title, synopsis, keywords, start-time, duration, key image, program-information, etc.) and the metadata is continuously updated during the program. Figure 2 shows an example scene metadata on baseball game. Audience can find the scene easily using it. However, generating segment metadata manually is difficult and costly, because few videos have indices like books. So it is difficult to find scenes in videos.

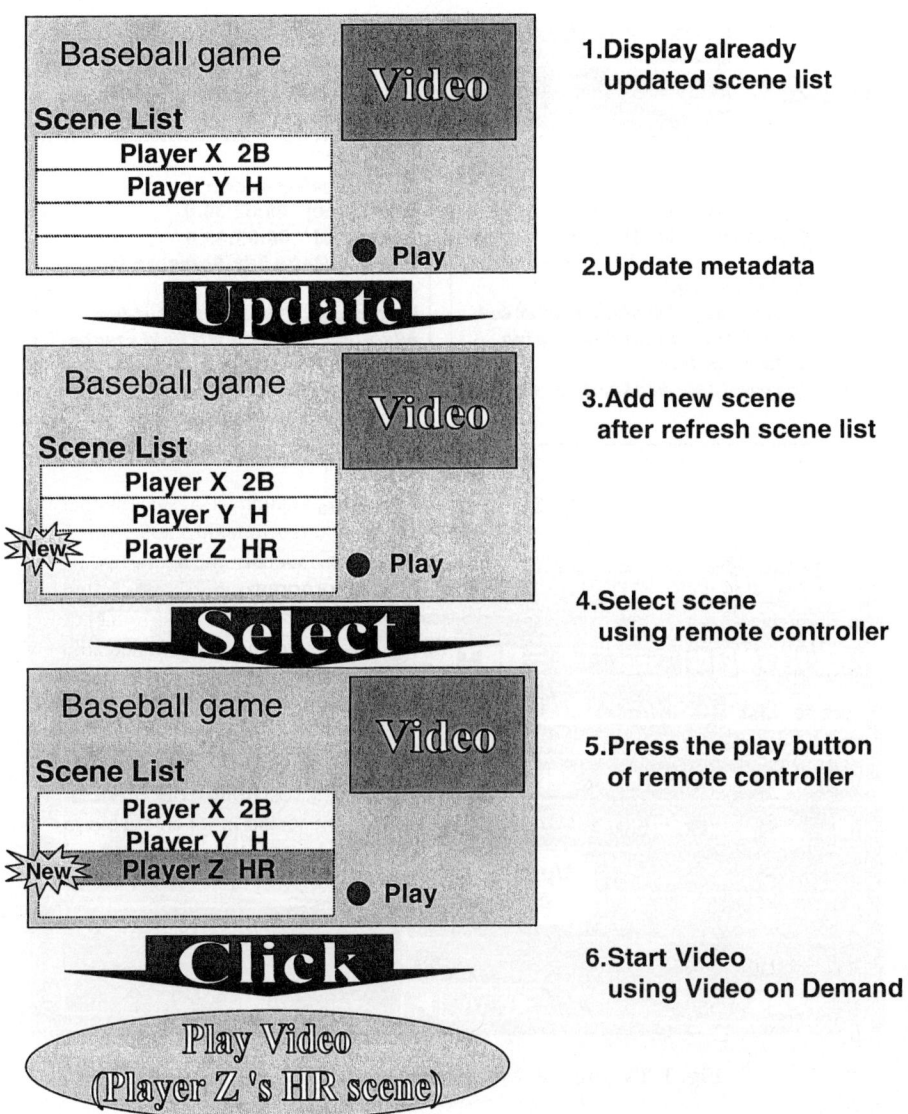

Fig. 1. Picture transition (continuously update metadata service)

After studying ways to reduce the cost of generating metadata for live programs, we developed SceneCabinet/Live!, which is cost effective and relatively easy to use. Metadata generated SceneCabinet/Live! is encoded in XML. Among the formats that SceneCabinet/Live! supports is the TV-Anytime metadata, the international standard metadata format for broadcasting, specified by the TV-Anytime Forum [4], and currently part of ETSI technical standards [2]. The TV-Anytime metadata can express a lot of information for broadcast contents and video contents.

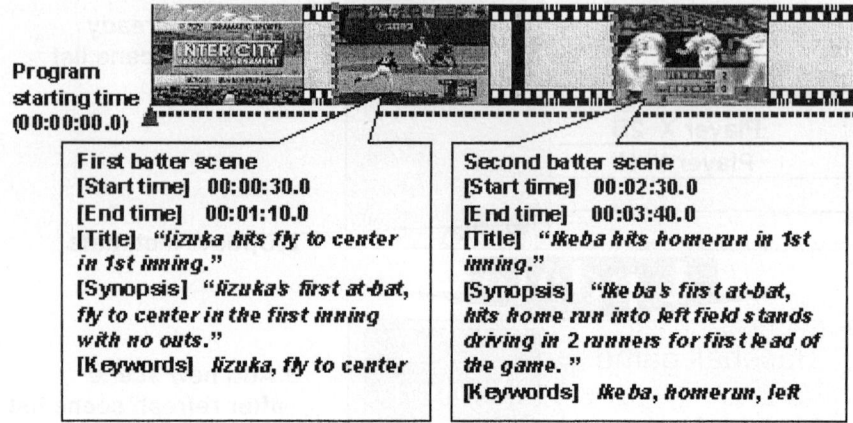

Fig. 2. Example of metadata

Fig. 3. TV screenshots (continuously update metadata)

On the other hand, a continuous metadata update service needs to send metadata to receiver. During a live program, metadata is continuously updated as the program progresses. Then the viewer is able to watch the action soon after it takes place. Therefore, it is essential that metadata transmission not be delayed

There are some ways of metadata distribution to receivers. One of the ways is using IP networks and another one is by DSM-CC data carousel which we use in this experiment; as shown in Figure 4, this sends metadata to receiver using a radio frequency (RF) network. We can view the scene metadata on receiver with a BML (Broadcast Markup Language) browser (see Figure 3), which is the standard markup language used in interactive digital data services for digital satellite and digital terrestrial broadcasting systems in Japan.

For the metadata update service, it is imperative that the delivery of metadata be timely. Timely delivery of updated metadata often hindered in practice by prohibitive cost of generating metadata and the bottlenecks in transmission. So we have studied the reduction in cost of metadata generation and verified if there is a bottleneck of the metadata transfer.

The remainder of this paper is organized as follows: Section 2 describes our approaches of metadata generation and metadata distribution. Experiments and results of metadata generation and metadata distribution for the continuously metadata update service are described in section 3 and we conclude the paper in section 4.

2 Our Approaches

2.1 Audio/Video Recognition

Scene Cabinet, which is described in a previous study [3], aggregates video analysis (scene changes, camera work, and subtitle recognition), speech recognition, and natural language processing techniques. It can automatically generate a key image list.

The key image browser that displays the results of video analysis and speech recognition with image, time point and recognition result (See Figure 5). It is effective for reducing the amount of work required to select a scene and generate segment metadata. The operator can replay scenes from a key image point. It creates a screen that looks like a table of contents for the video.

2.2 Creating a Synopsis Using Speech Recognition

To create text for a scene synopsis, the audio can be added verbally using a microphone and is automatically converted into text that is displayed on the user interface. Particularly during sporting events like baseball games, it is difficult to recognize voice of the sports commentator. In this case, we can use the voice of another person who gives orally the synopsis of the game. Speech recognition results are listed on the speech recognition results browser. And operator clicks on one of the results to replay video at the start time of the result.

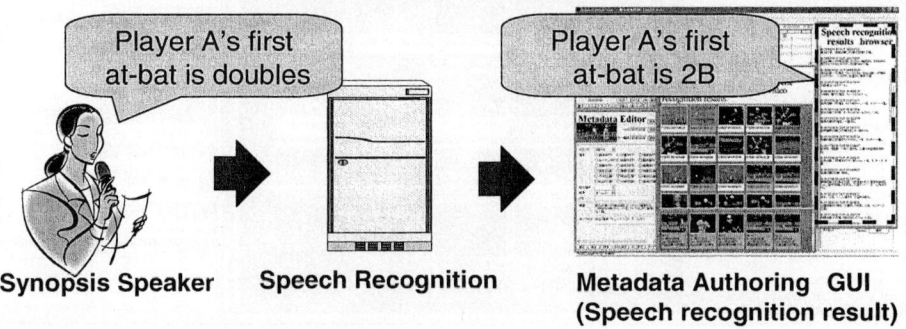

Fig. 4. Speech recognition workflow

One of the sentences, input to the recognition results browser as metadata corresponding to the scene, is selected and copied onto the metadata editor as the synopsis. It is difficult to search the target of result because the results queue up in time ascending order. If operator sets start time and end time at the metadata editor, SceneCabinet/Live! recommends the result between start time and end time by brightening the characters .

2.3 Automatic Keyword Generation Using Natural Language Processing

Keywords can be extracted automatically using natural language processing. This function was developed and described in our previous work, SceneCabinet. [3]

Keywords are generated by pressing the "keyword" button on the metadata editor. This activates natural language processing and keywords are automatically extracted from the title, thus creating a synopsis.

2.4 Metadata Generation Workflow Using SceneCabinet/Live!

Figure 5 shows metadata authoring GUI of Scene Cabinet/Live!. It is so designed that operator can obtain much information at a time. There are 5 panes (play back monitor, metadata editor, key image browser, timeline, and speech recognition result browser).

Fig. 5. SceneCabinet/Live! metadata authoring GUI

The following describes the work flow of metadata generation for baseball game. Some processes depend on the details of a program.

I. **Search scene from key image browser**
It is useful video analysis result of camera work and subtitle recognition in case of baseball game.

II. **Decide start time, end time and key image of the scene using Playback monitor and Metadata editor**
Click the key image and check the video on play back monitor. And set start and end time using fast-forward button and ±15seconds, ±1second or ±1 frame jump button under the Playback monitor.

III. **Generated title at metadata editor**
In this case, we customized the metadata editor for baseball game. It has radio buttons, check boxes, a pull-down menu and an input box. Operator can make scene title (innings, player's name, at-bat result) by only selecting from the menu.

IV. **Set synopsis at metadata editor** *(see Sect 2.2)*

V. **Set keyword at metadata editor** *(see Sect 2.3)*

VI. **Save scene metadata**
Press the save button under the metadata editor.

VII. **Upload the metadata to metadata transmission server** *(c.f. data carousel server).*

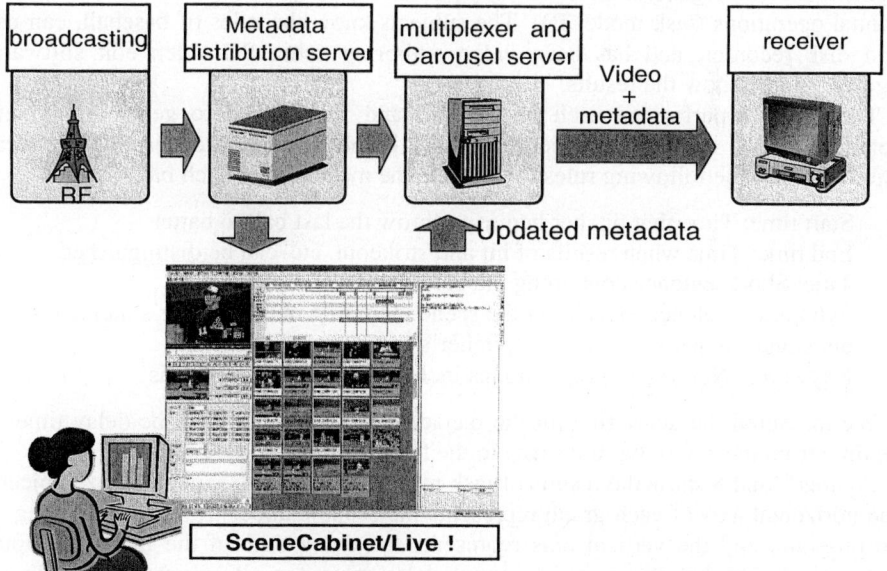

Fig. 6. Metadata distribution and update workflow

2.5 Real-Time Metadata Distribution

During a live program, metadata is continuously updated as the program progresses. The viewer is able to watch the action soon after it takes place. Therefore, it is essential that metadata transmission not be delayed.

Figure 6 shows metadata distribution and update work flow. Metadata is distributed from metadata distribution server and multiplexed by the multiplexer. After that, the data carousel server sends to receivers. The data carousel server transmission system executes everything from the delivery system to the receiver. [5] The processing time of metadata transfer is the key point of the service. If there is a bottleneck of the metadata transfer, this service is unachievable. Note that sending metadata by data carousel server is only one way to continuously metadata update service.

3 Experiments

In this section, we report on the experiments we conducted to verify our method.

3.1 Real-Time Metadata Generation

We conducted a series of experiments to compare the relative efficiency of generating segment metadata using SceneCabinet/Live! (task model A) and preparing the same segment metadata by manually operating the time-shift replay function, while recording the live baseball program on a hard disk recorder (task model B).

We asked six operators to take part in the experiments as subjects to compare segment metadata generation costs using SceneCabinet/Live! (Task model A) with manual operations (task model B). The subjects know the rules of baseball, can use hard disk recorder, and has been video authoring using PC video edit software. Figures 5 and 6 show the results.

The subjects performed each task model and were asked to generate segment metadata for all the batter scenes from one baseball game broadcast. They were required to use the following rules to generate the metadata for each batter scene.

- ➢ Start time: Time that pitcher begins to throw the last ball to batter
- ➢ End time: Time when results of hit and strikeout, etc. can be distinguished
- ➢ Title: Short sentence containing the batter's name, result, inning
- ➢ Synopsis: Sentence explaining the scene including inning, batter's name, results, out count, runner situation, and pitcher's name
- ➢ Keywords: Nouns and proper nouns included in title and synopsis

We measured the delay time of the metadata input. We defined the delay time as the time from the end of batting scene to the finished input at the end of the scene.

Figures 7 and 8 show the results of task models A and B, executed by six subjects. The horizontal axis of each graph represents the scene number from the beginning of the program, and the vertical axis represents the delay time of the metadata input. Figure 7 shows that the metadata input delay time for all subjects were almost constant, even as the program progressed, as in task model A. The maximum delay

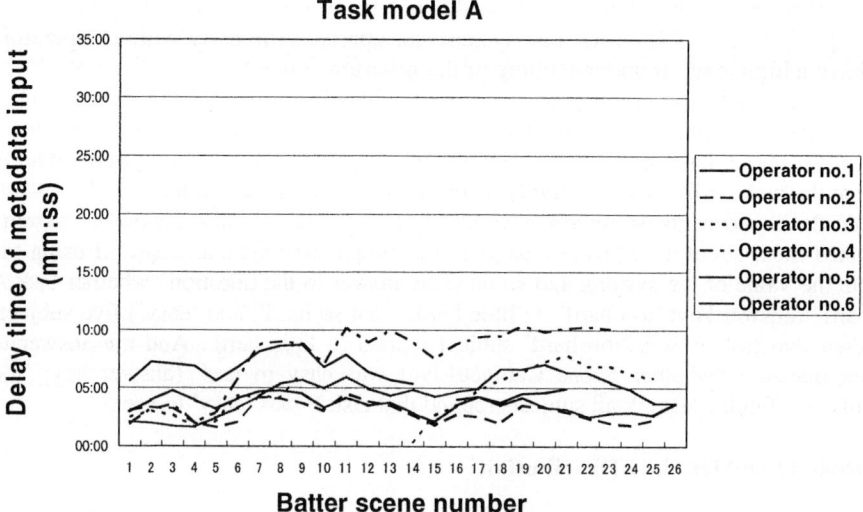

Fig. 7. Results of task model A

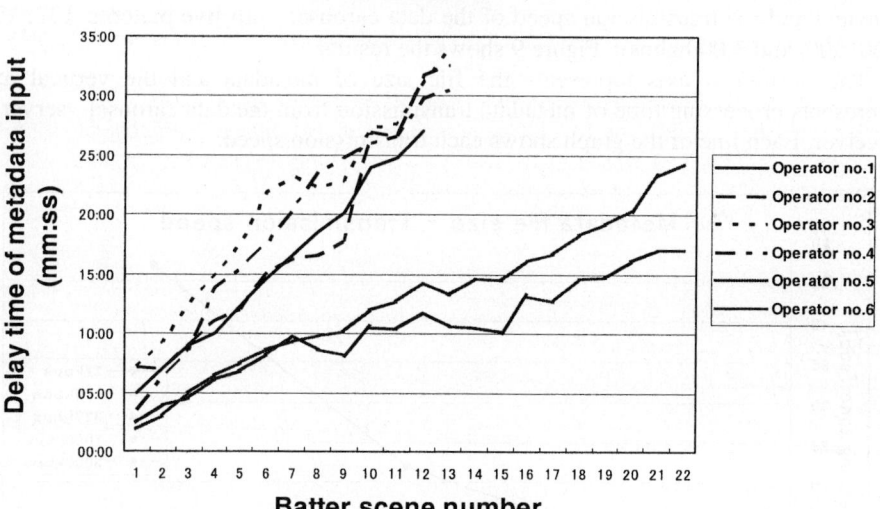

Fig. 8. Results of task model B

time was in ten minutes. On the other hand, in task model B, we noticed a tendency for the delay time to increase as the program progressed, as seen in Figure 8.

As a result, we verified that model A's task time using SceneCabinet/Live! was shorter than for task model B.

The fastest subject did not take as much time as the other subjects to create a detailed outline sentence or confirm the results. Therefore, there was a difference in work speed based on the subject's knowledge of the rules and understanding of the task.

However, these individual variations did not have a significant influence on the system performance. Therefore, this system can operate efficiently without operators who have a high level of understanding of the program content.

In task model B, the graph showed a significant difference between the oral input and the manual input. It depended heavily on the operator's skill and specialized knowledge about baseball, unlike task model A where the subjects were able to perform the task easily and effectively, even without specialized skills.

After the experiments we interviewed the subjects for their opinions about the system. We asked them about their level of fatigue, the comparative difficulty/ease of using the system, the value of the system, and so on. The answer to the question "whether task A was hard" (answer key; 'too hard', 'a little hard', 'not so hard', and 'easy') five subjects answered that task A was 'too hard' subject replied 'a little hard'. And the answer to another question "whether Scene Cabinet/Live! was easy to use" (answer key; 'too difficult', 'difficult', 'easy'), all subjects replied that task B was 'easy' to use.

3.2 Real-Time Metadata Distribution

In the metadata transmission experiment, we used the segment metadata update service during a live program to determine the optimal value and verified the data carousel transmission speed.

We changed the size of the metadata files into three patterns (17, 52, and 109 Kbytes) and the transmission speed of the data carousel into five patterns (32, 128, 320, 500, and 3,000 kbps). Figure 9 shows the results.

The horizontal axis represents the file size of metadata and the vertical axis represents processing time of metadata transmission from the data carousel server to receiver. Each line of the graph shows each transmission speed.

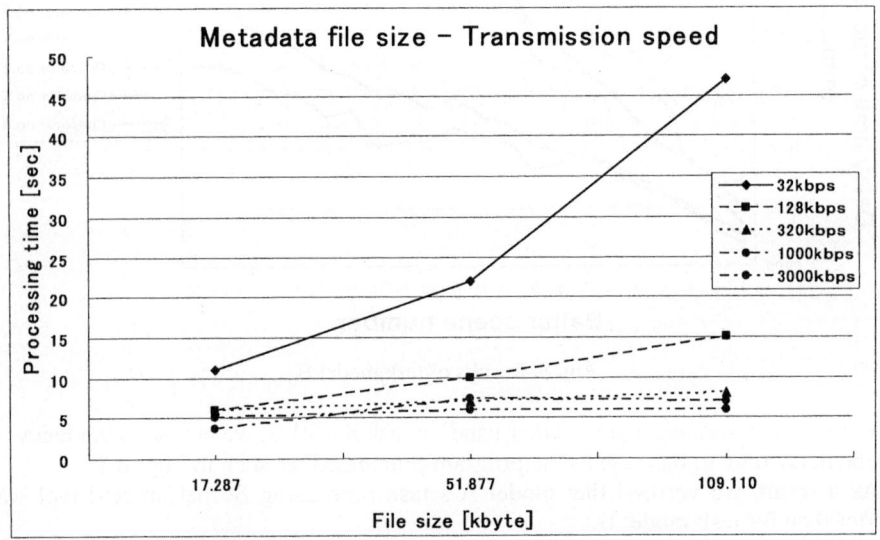

Fig. 9. Processing time of metadata distribution

This graph shows that when the metadata transmission speed was 32 kbps, the processing time was in proportion to the metadata size. Further, when the transmission speed was 128 kbps or more, it was almost horizontal, which is sufficient to support transmissions. The size of the file was 17 Kbytes, which means that the file includes segment metadata from each batting scene (about 30) in the two-hour baseball relay program.

In other words, 128 kbps is sufficient for transmitting six programs at the same time.

4 Conclusions

We described our design and implementation of Scene Cabinet/Live!, which generates segment metadata and provides a better transmission speed to enable faster distribution of live programs on broadcasting-telecommunication linkage services .

Scene Cabinet/Live! is useful for generating a continuously updated segment metadata service for live programs like baseball game. It can also reduce the costs of generating metadata to about half.

We proved the value of our program for efficiently generating metadata for live broadcasting. We therefore believe that SceneCabinet/Live! is one of the useful software for metadata generation.

We used this system for baseball game this time and our previous study Scene Cabinet for news archives. We will apply the system to other genres of video. We expect that it will become a useful system, by slight customization of its speech recognition dictionary and the metadata editor. These customizations are easy because they can be done by only changing property files.

This system, however, cannot make metadata without operator. So our future plans are to make scene metadata generation more automatic by using other recognition engines such as, for example, a motion recognition engine.

Acknowledgments

This work was carried out as a part of "Advanced Contents Distribution Trial" sponsored by the Ministry of Internal Affairs and Communications of Japan in 2004. We would like to thank all parties concerned with the trial for their contributions to this work.

References

1. The Association of Radio and Industies and Businesses, Japan. (ARIB). "Data Coding and Transmission Specification for Digital Broadcasting", ARIB-STD-B24.
2. European Telecommunications Standards Institute. "Broadcast and On-line Services: Search, select, and rightful use of content on personal storage systems ('TV-Anytime') ", ETSI TS 102 822.
3. H.Kuwano, Y.Matsuo and K.Kawazoe, "SceneCabinet: Semantic Metadata Extraction System combining Video/Audio Indexing and Natural Language Processing Techniques," Proc. of IBC2004, pp.458-466 (2004.9)
4. TV-*Anytime* Forum http://www.tv-anytime.org/
5. T.Yamaguchi, H.Matsumura, M.Kawamori and K.Kawazoe. "A Study on Acceleration of Metadata Distribution by Data Carousel Transmission" IEICE General Conference 2004.(in Japanese)

Data Broadcast Metadata Based on PMCP for Open Interface to a DTV Data Server

Minsik Park, Yong Ho Kim, Jin Soo Choi, and Jin Woo Hong

Electronics and Telecommunications Research Institute, 161 Gajeong-dong, Yuseong-gu,
Daejeon 305-700, Korea
{pms, solson, jschoi, jwhong}@etri.re.kr
http://www.etri.re.kr

Abstract. DTV data broadcasting offers broadcasters the new business model to acquire considerable revenue from digital broadcast. When the broadcasters integrate and maintain the data broadcast station system, they encounter the cost to be paid unnecessarily because there is no common interface specification among the equipments of DTV station system. This paper describes the flexible and open interface that will decrease the wasteful expenses in moving the transition to data broadcast station system.

1 Introduction

Data broadcasting has became to be an important role in providing users with multimedia data including rich information as the broadcasting environment is evolving from analog to digital. Data broadcasting provides users with the interactive and enhanced services by sending data elements in broadcast television transport. Data applications deliver the additional and useful information to viewers with a various type of media through a broadcast channel.

To provide data broadcast service, DTV broadcasters need several functional components to deliver data broadcast through DTV broadcast system. The most essential component is a so-called data server to encapsulate data elements into MPEG-2 transport stream. DTV broadcasters insert the data server into their DTV broadcast systems for supporting data broadcasting.

Although all the DTV broadcast systems utilize data server with same or similar function, they have each different interface between data server and other components because there is no common interface specification for DTV data broadcast system. Therefore, equipment manufactures and system integrator of data broadcasting should implement the interface specific to DTV broadcasters whenever they set up the data server to DTV data broadcast system. This is why that the integration work of data broadcast system not only decreases the flexibility of system extension but also increases the cost of system maintenance. The inoperability interface of DTV broadcast system may be a considerable obstacle when DTV broadcasters intend to change their DTV broadcast system to data broadcast system.

In recent years, ATSC(Advanced Television Systems Committee) has published PMCP(Programming Metadata Communication Protocol)[1] standard, the interface standard for exchanging PSIP(Program and System Information Protocol)[2] information among components of DTV broadcasts system. The ATSC PSIP standard, an essential element of the ATSC DTV system, provides a methodology for transporting digital television system information and electronic program guide data.

The PMCP specification will enable broadcasters and manufacturers to interconnect systems that process PSIP and other DTV metadata such as traffic, program management, listing service, automation, MPEG encoder, and PSIP generator. PMCP guarantees the interoperability among components that are required to exchange the PSIP information.

PMCP is based on XML (extensible markup language) message that is flexible and usable for various system architectures. ATSC, therefore, has a plan to extend PMCP to support ACAP(Advanced Common Application Platform)[3] data broadcasting, enhanced 8-VSB and non-PSIP metadata in the near future. ATSC has particularly decided to develop PMCP for data broadcasting in the first place. PMCP extension for data broadcasting can be developed by not only inserting data server into the PMCP reference system but also defining the new element of encapsulation, signaling and announcement for data broadcasting.

This paper describes the design of PMCP extension metadata to enable data server to transport ACAP data application in data broadcast system. The PMCP extension has interoperable interface for not only PSIP server but also data server if the PMCP extension metadata is standardized in ATSC.

2 Data Broadcast System

In order to provide content creators with the specification necessary to ensure their data to run on all kinds of receivers in equal performance, ATSC published DASE-1(DTV Application Software Environment-Level 1)[4] and ACAP[3] which define a software layer (middleware) that allows interactive and enhanced contents to run on receiver in a platform-independent manner. In particular, ACAP has been developed in need of the harmonization between DASE and OCAP (OpenCable Application Platform)[5] published by CableLabs.

In order to provide users with data broadcast through a broadcast channel, broadcasters need the emission station system to encode the data created according to the data broadcast standards [3,4]. ATSC DIWG(Data Implementation Working Group) recommends not only functional components but also physical interfaces in the emission station for data broadcasting emission. However, ATSC DIWG doesn't define the specific interface message so as to operate each functional component.

ATSC DIWG proposed the emission station environment for data broadcast in IS/151[6]. Fig. 1 shows the essential components of the emission station environments. The emission station consists of audio/video encoder, multiplexer manager, CA(Conditional Access) generator, PSIP server and data server. The emission station generates MPEG-2 transport streams containing compressed video and audio with encapsulated data and system information tables. Data server plays an important role in encapsulating data elements into MPEG-2 transport stream. Multiplexer manager sends PSIP information into PSIP server and data information into data server for operation. Data server needs to be inputted with encoding information so as to

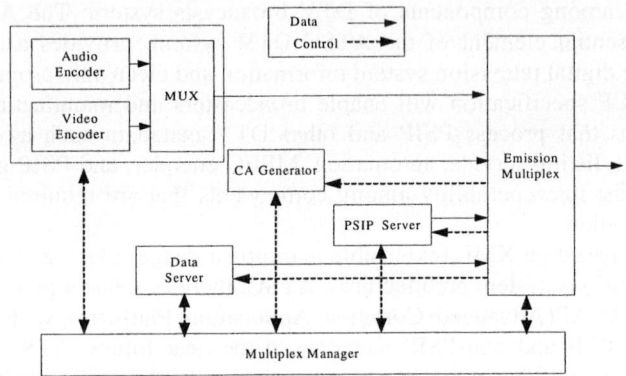

Fig. 1. Data broadcast station system

generate data stream according to the transport protocol defined in the data broadcast standard[3, 7-11].

The information of PSIP and data has been defined with various formats per broadcasters. In terms of PSIP information, PMCP provides the common interface specification between PSIP server and other components. However, there is no interface for data server with regards to data information.

In order to provide the interoperable interface between data server and other component of system, The PMCP schema should be extended for data broadcasting and data server should be added into PMCP reference system to encode data as well as to generate PSIP table.

Data server is connected into PMCP interface not only because data server needs to exchange the data information with PSIP server, but also because multiplex manager such as program management system, traffic system and automation system should control the operation of data server according to broadcast schedule. The following section describes the data broadcast metadata that data server should receive from other components.

3 Data Broadcast Metadata

The PMCP schema should be extended to describe the data information to enable data server to encode data application into transport stream. PMCP extension schema therefore should consider the following requirements:

- PMCP extension schema for data broadcasting should be backward compatible with PMCP schema so that conventional DTV station system based on PMCP schema can easily be implemented to data broadcast station system.
- PMCP extension schema should include the announcement information to create program and system table for data broadcasting.
- PMCP extension schema should describe the encapsulation information to encapsulate data into MPEG-2 transport stream.
- PMCP extension schema should contain the signaling information to generate system table into MPEG-2 transport stream.

Data information consists of announcement, encapsulation and signaling. ATSC defined data carousel [7], object carousel protocol [3] with respect to signaling and encapsulation for data broadcasting. ATSC also specified DET(Data Event Table) to announce data broadcast service in A/90 [7]. Although DET is not defined in ACAP, it may be used with announcement for ACAP in terrestrial data broadcasting.

3.1 PMCP Extension Schema for ACAP Announcement

Fig. 2-(a) shows PsipEvent element[1] that describes PSIP event related with audio and video excluding data. The PMCP schema for data broadcast, therefore, needs the new element to depict PSIP event with regard to data as shown in Fig. 2-(b).

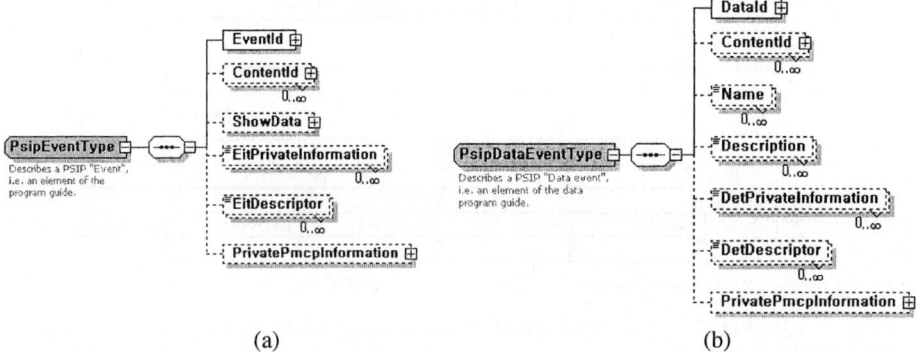

Fig. 2. Announcement Element (a) PsipEventType diagram (b) PsipDataEventType diagram

The new element can be named PsipDataEvent. PsipDataEventType is similar to PsipEventType in terms of schema structure. The "PsipDataEvent" element enables the PMCP schema to be extended for ACAP announcement.

There are four differences between PsipDataEventType and PsipEventType. First, PsipDataEventType has a "DataId" element instead of an "EventId", used to label or reference the event related to data. Second, PsipDataEventType contains more than one "ContentId" element because data contents are created and managed by means of the "ContentId" elements to be assigned apart from A/V content. Third, PsipDataEventType includes a "DetPrivateInformation" element and a "DetDescriptor" element instead of an "EitPrivateInformation" element and an "EitDescriptor" element, needed for generating PSIP DET[7]. Fourth, PsipDataEventType includes only the "Name" element and "Description" element among the children of "ShowData" element because Data Event Table don't have to carry the information related to the parental rating, audio service, caption service and redistribution control as Event Information Table. The "Name" element describes the data event title in the format of the Multiple String Structure and the "Description" element represents the detailed description of a data event.

3.2 PMCP Extension Schema for ACAP Encapsulation

The data and attributes of one U-U object in an object carousel are transmitted in one message. The message format is specified by the BIOP(Broadcast Inter ORB Protocol) and is referred to as the BIOP Generic Object Message format. BIOP Messages are carried in Modules of Data Carousels[12]. A module is composed of the one or more BIOP Message. Each object in the module is identified by the objectkey. According to the DSM-CC data carousel specification, each module is fragmented into one or more Blocks which are carried in a DownloadDataBlock message as shown in Fig. 3.

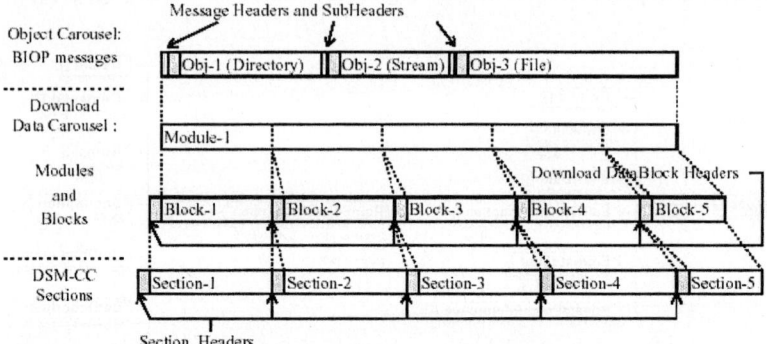

Fig. 3. Encapsulation and Fragmentation of BIOP Messages

The AcapObjectCarouselType is divided into two children element : "DataCarousel" element and "ObjectCarousel" element. "DataCarousel" element represents the information of data carousel that delivers the BIOP messages in modules, and the "ObectCarousel" element contains the information of BIOP messages of the object carousel.

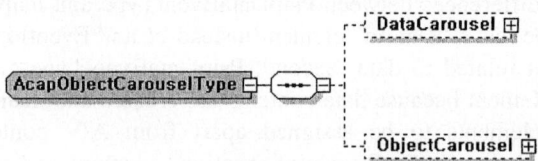

Fig. 4. AcapObjectCarouselType diagram

3.3 PMCP Extension Schema for ACAP Signaling

The signaling information enables receivers not only to identify applications associated with a service and their location from which to recover them. ACAP standard specifies PMT(Program Map Table) and AIT(Application Information Table) to signal data application into receiver. The PMCP extension schema for data broadcasting, therefore, should include the elements to describe the information relating to both AIT and PMT.

3.3.1 AcapApplicationType for ACAP Signaling

The Application Information Table describes applications and their associated information. Each Application Information Table includes one "common" descriptor loop at the top level for descriptors that are shared between application of that sub table and a loop of application. Each application in the application loop has an "application" descriptor loop containing the descriptors associated with that application. Fig. 5 illustrates the syntax structure of AIT defined in ACAP[3].

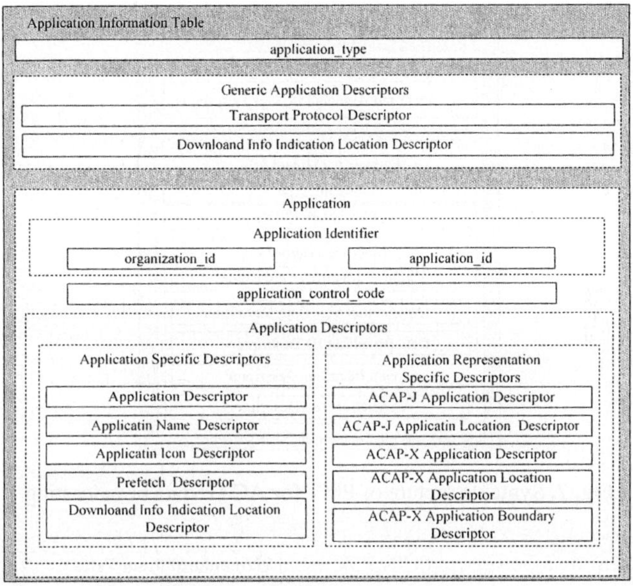

Fig. 5. Syntax structure of AIT

Descriptors of AIT are categorized into three parts: generic application descriptor, application specific descriptor and application representation specific descriptor. Generic application descriptors are included in common descriptor loop. The application specific descriptors also are specific to the application instance. Application representation specific descriptors are specific not only to application instance but also to application representation.

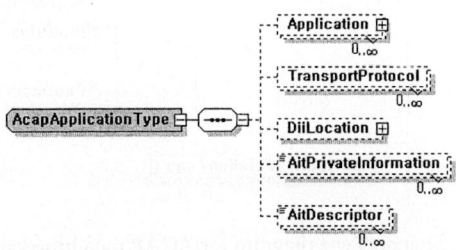

Fig. 6. AcapApplicationType diagram

The AIT and descriptors mentioned above can be represented with the schema as shown in Fig. 6.

The "TransportProtocol" and the "DiiLocation" describes the information of transport protocol descriptor and download info indication descriptor respectively. The "Application" element not only defines the organization_id, application_id and application_control_code with its attribute but also include the elements to describe the information of application descriptors of AIT.

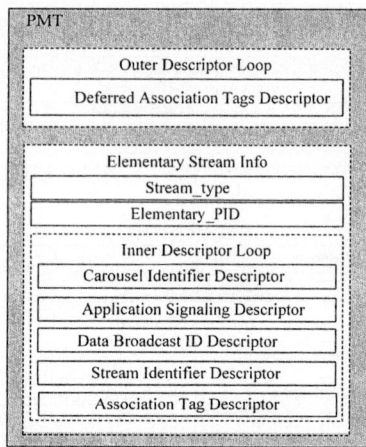

Fig. 7. Syntax structure of PMT for ACAP data broadcasting

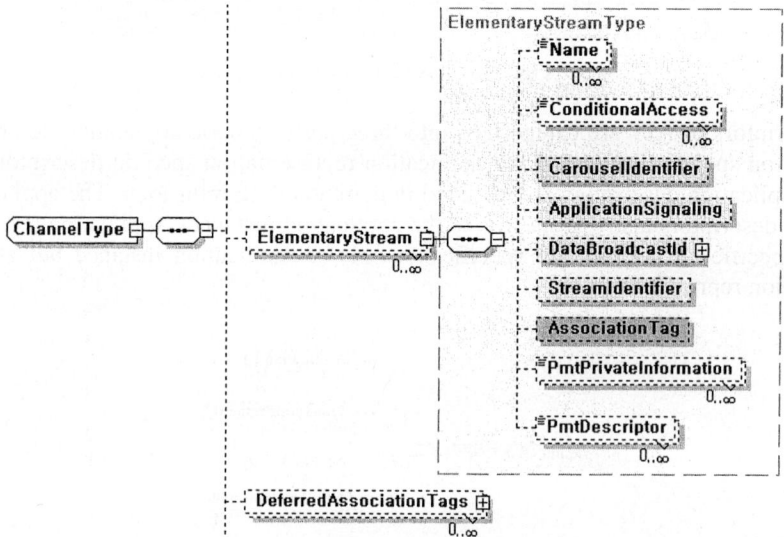

Fig. 8. ChannelType diagram for ACAP data broadcasting

3.3.2 ChannelType for PMT Signaling

In order to describe the elementary streams of the object carousel, The PMCP schema extended for ACAP data broadcasting should include the additional several elements to describe PMT descriptors. Fig. 7 represents the several PMT descriptors relating to data broadcasting. The first loop for PMT descriptor delivers deferred association tags descriptor; the second loop for PMT descriptor consists of carousel identifier descriptor, application signaling descriptor, data broadcast id descriptor, stream identifier descriptor and association tag descriptor.

Fig. 8 illustrates the schema of PMT descriptors for object carousel. New elements, which describes PMT descriptors for data broadcasting, can be added into "ElementaryStream" element of the ChannelType defined in PMCP[1] because "ElementaryStream" element plays a roll in describing the information of second loop descriptors for PMT.

3.4 PMCP Extension Schema for ACAP Data Broadcasting

Fig. 9 illustrates the AcapDataServiceType to define the information of encapsulation and signaling for data broadcasting. The AcapDataServiceType can be composed of the "ContentId" element, "AcapApplication" element and "AcapObjectCarousel" element.

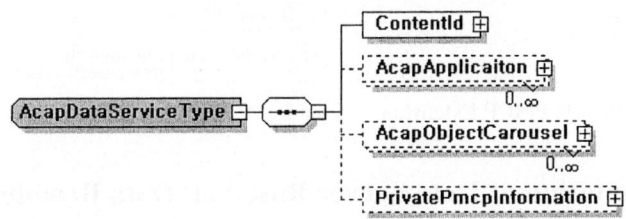

Fig. 9. AcapDataServiceType diagram for ACAP encapsulation and AIT signaling

The "ContentId" element provides the linkage between AcapDataServiceType and PsipEventType, or AcapDataService and PsipDataEventType. The linkage enables ACAP transport stream to obtain the schedule information from PsipEventType or PsipDataEventType that describes start time and duration with its attributes. Both the "AcapObjectCarousel" element in Section 3.2 and the "AcapApplication" element in Section 3.3.1 describe the encapsulation and the signalling information defined in ACAP[3].

The extended PMCP schema for data broadcasting has newly defined "PsipDataEvent" element for ACAP announcement in Section 3.1 and "AcapDataService" element for ACAP encapsulation and AIT signaling in Section 3.2 and 3.3.1, In addition, it has described the "Channel" element to be modified for PMT signaling specific to ACAP in Section 3.3.2. The "AcapDataService" element consists of three elements such as "ContentId" , "AcapObjectCarousel" and "AcapApplication". Both the "AcapObjectCarousel" and the "AcapApplication" should be combined with an "AcapDataService" element in that an ACAP data broadcast service is provided with the AIT and the object carousel that delivers applications and their signaling information respectively. The "AcapDataService" element contains "ContentId" element defined in the "PsipEvent" or the "PsipDataEvent" in the PMCP schema to associate an ACAP transport stream with a show event. The "ContentId" element enables "AcapDataService" element to identify the schedule information defined in "PsipEvent" element or "PsipDataEvent" element. The schedule information is used in controlling the delivery of the transport stream of ACAP data service.

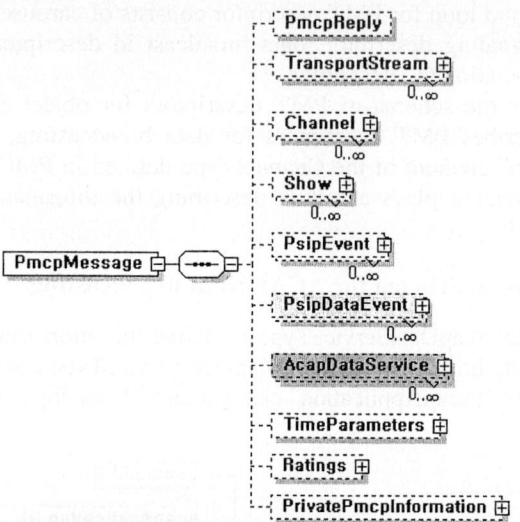

Fig. 10. PMCP Extension Schema for ACAP Data Broadcasting

4 Implementation of Data Server Based on Data Broadcast Metadata

ETRI has implemented ACAP data server to be operated through PMCP extension schema for data broadcasting as shown in Fig. 11. PMCP extension schema defines all the kinds of information needed for delivering data broadcast program. Data server

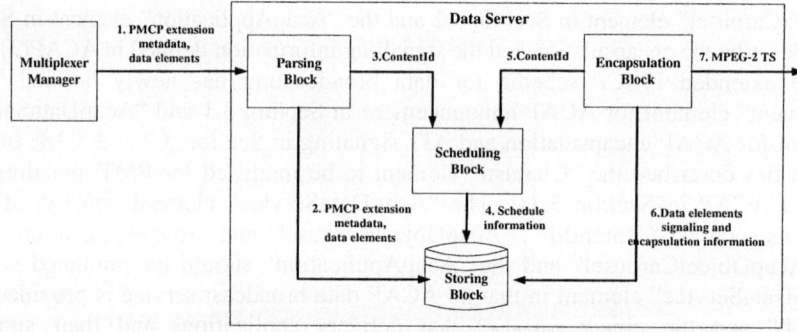

Fig. 11. Data server block structure based on PMCP extension metadata

first receives the data broadcast metadata from multiplexer manager. The data broadcast metadata is represented with XML message according to PMCP extension schema defined in Section 3.

Fig. 11 illustrates the structure of data server that has been implemented according to PMCP extension. Data server consists of parsing block, scheduling block, storing block, encapsulation block.

- **Parsing block** receives PMCP extension metadata and data broadcasting contents from multiplexer manager. It registers data broadcasting contents and system information, schedule information, encapsulation information extracted from PMCP extension metadata into storing block. It obtains the schedule information from the attribute of PSIP data event metadata and system (channel) information by using ContentId. It sends schedule researching information, ContentId into scheduling block.
- **Scheduling block** obtains the schedule information stored in the storing block by ContentId delivered from the parsing block. It checks out when data broadcast contents is delivered. It sends ContentId corresponding with data broadcast contents that should be delivered at a specific time into the encapsulation block.
- **Storing block** has the database for storing the scheduling, encapsulation information and data applications. Database is designed to be associated scheduling, encapsulation, data broadcast contents through the unique identifier, ContentId. Therefore, the scheduling block and encapsulation block could search data applications, scheduling, encapsulation by ContentId.
- **Encapsulation block** searches and obtains data applications, encapsulation and signaling information corresponding with the ContentId to be delivered from scheduling block. It encapsulates data applications into MPEG-2 transport stream according to the system and encapsulation information.

Fig. 12 illustrates the operation flow of data server as followings;

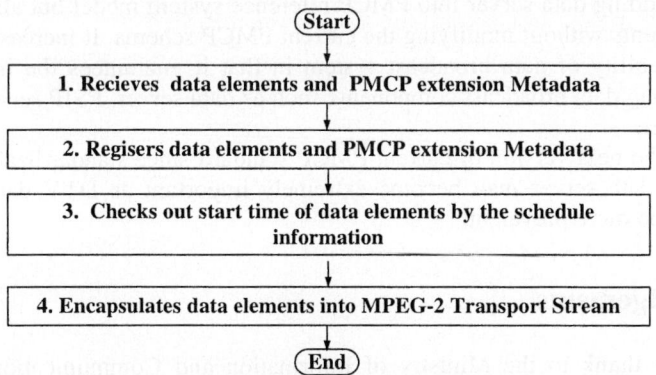

Fig. 12. The operation flow of data server

[Step 1] Data server receives data elements and PMCP extension metadata including system and encoding information such as data type, data location, encapsulation method and signaling information from Multiplexer Manager.
[Step 2] The parsing block obtains resisters data elements and system and encoding information into storing block.
[Step 3] The parsing block sends ContentId into scheduling block.
[Step 4] The scheduling block searches the schedule information stored in storing block by ContentId.
[Step 5] The scheduling block checks out start time of data elements by scheduling information to be acquired from storing block.
[Step 6] The scheduling block provides the encapsulation block with ContentId corresponding with data elements to be transported.
[Step 7] The scheduling block provides the encapsulation block with ContentId corresponding with data elements to be transported.
[Step 8] The encapsulation block acquires data elements and encoding information from the storing block.
[Step 9] The encapsulation block encodes data elements into MPEG-2 transport stream according to encoding information.

Data server encapsulates data application into DSM-CC object carousel and generates AIT table according to data broadcast metadata. And then the encapsulated data application and AIT is packetized with MPEG-2 transport stream. Data broadcast system combines both the multiplexed data and AIT transport stream delivered from data server and audio/video transport stream generated from A/V encoder into a MPEG-2 transport stream, which is transferred into receiver.

5 Conclusions

ETRI has designed the system interface to support data broadcasting by extending PMCP schema. The extension of PMCP for data broadcasting can be easily developed not only by adding data server into PMCP reference system model but also by defining new elements without modifying the current PMCP schema. It increases the flexibility and usability of data broadcast system in that it guarantees the interoperable interface among data broadcast components such as data server, PSIP server and multiplex manager.

It will be the next version of current PMCP standard since standardization of open interface for data server may become extremely important as DTV data broadcast system become more prevalent.

Acknowledgements

We faithfully thank to the Ministry of Information and Communication (MIC) of Korean government, who has supported our research under the title of "Development of data broadcasting technology in the interoperable networks of broadcasting and telecommunication".

References

1. Programming Metadata Communication Protocol Standard, A/76, ATSC
2. Program and System Information Protocol for Terrestrial Broadcast and Cable, A/65B, ATSC
3. Advanced Common Application Platform, Proposed Standard, ATSC
4. DTV Application Software Environment – Level 1 Standard, A/100, ATSC
5. OpenCable Application Platform Specification, OCAP 1.0, CableLabs
6. Implementation of Data Broadcasting in DTV Station, IS/151, ATSC
7. Data Broadcast Standard, A/90, ATSC
8. Delivery of IP Multicast Sessions over Data Broadcast Standard, A/92, ATSC
9. Synchronized/Asynchronous Trigger Standard, A/93, ATSC
10. Transport Stream File System Standard, A/95, ATSC
11. Software Download Protocol Standard, A/97, ATSC
12. Information Technology: Generic Coding of Moving Pictures and Associated Audio Information: Extensions for Digital Storage Media Command and Control, ISO 13818-6

Super-resolution Sharpening-Demosaicking with Spatially Adaptive Total-Variation Image Regularization

Takahiro Saito and Takashi Komatsu

Department of Electrical, Electronics and Information Engineering,
High-Tech Research Center, Kanagawa University, Yokohama 221-8686, Japan
{saitot01, komatt01}@kanagawa-u.ac.jp

Abstract. We previously presented a demosaicking method that simultaneously removes image blurs caused by an optical low-pass filter used in a digital color camera with the Bayer's RGB color filter array. Our prototypal sharpening-demosaicking method restored only spatial frequency components lower than the Nyquist frequency corresponding to the mosaicking pattern, but it often produced ringing artifacts near color edges. To overcome this difficulty, this paper introduces the super-resolution into the prototypal method. First, we formulate the recovery problem in the DFT domain, and then introduce the super-resolution by the total-variation (TV) image regularization into the sharpening-demosaicking approach. The TV-based super-resolution effectively demosaics sharp color images while preserving such image structures as intensity values are almost constant along edges, without producing ringing artifacts, but it tends to flatten signal variations excessively in texture image regions. To remedy the drawback, furthermore we introduce a spatially adaptive technique that controls the TV image regularization according to the saliency of color edges around a pixel.

1 Introduction

To suppress aliasing artifacts caused by the mosaicking, a digital camera uses an optical low-pass filter. This filter cannot sharply cut off high frequency components and hence images projected on the imaging surface are blurred. Most demosaicking methods try to interpolate intensity of non-observed color pixels, but do not try to remove image blurs caused by the optical low-pass filter [1]-[6]. To remove the image blurs, observed blurred color pixels as well as non-observed color pixels should be sharpened in the middle of the demosaicking. As a new demosaicking method, previously we presented the sharpening-demosaicking approach that simultaneously removes image blurs caused by the optical low-pass filter in the middle of the demosaicking [7]. Our previously presented sharpening-demosaicking method restored only spatial frequency components of color signals lower than the Nyquist frequency corresponding to the mosaicking pattern of each color filter, but it often produced visible ringing artifacts near sharp color edges.

To suppress ringing artifacts, this paper introduces the concept of the super-resolution into the sharpening-demosaicking approach. Recently, the total-variation

(TV) image regularization has been theoretically studied for the super-resolution by F. Malgouyres and F. Guichard [8]. They studied the deblurring-zooming problem for monochrome images from a theoretical viewpoint, and mathematically proved that some particular TV-based super-resolution approach can restore spatial frequency components higher than the Nyquist frequency from observed blurry spatial frequency components. Such a TV-based super-resolution approach can preserve image edges without producing ringing artifacts. Our super-resolution sharpening-demosaicking approach rests on these theoretical findings.

This paper reinforces our sharpening-demosaicking approach with the TV-based super-resolution, for the image sensor using the Bayer's RGB color filter array. First, this paper formulates the recovery problem in the DFT domain, and then introduces the super-resolution by the TV image regularization into the sharpening-demosaicking. The TV-based super-resolution makes it possible to restore spatial frequency components higher than the Nyquist frequency, and thus to demosaic and to sharpen color images effectively while preserving image edges without producing ringing artifacts. However, as side effects, the introduction of the TV image regularization influences frequency components lower than the Nyquist frequency, and if we excessively attach greater importance to the TV image regularization, it will tend to flatten original signal variations excessively in texture image regions, and hence fine textures will be degraded. To remedy the drawback, furthermore we introduce a spatially adaptive technique that controls the TV image regularization according to the saliency of color edges around a pixel.

This paper simulates a digital color camera with the Bayer's RGB color filter array through modeling the optical-physical behavior of the image sensor, and evaluates the restoration performance of our sharpening-demosaicking algorithms. While our prototypal sharpening-demosaicking algorithm produces faint but visible ringing-artifacts along thin color lines and/or fine color stripes, our new super-resolution sharpening-demosaicking algorithm with the spatially adaptive TV image regularization does not at all produce such ringing artifacts, and at the same time it does not at all degrade fine image textures.

2 Sharpening-Demosaicking Approach

2.1 Optical Low-Pass Filter

The actual optical low-pass filter is formed by combining two types of doubly refractive crystal device; the one separates its incident light into two traveling directions horizontally spaced each other by one pixel, and the other does vertically spaced by one pixel. Hence, on the imaging surface, the optical low-pass filter produces a blurred continuous image by summing up four shifted continuous images, namely the original continuous image and the horizontally, vertically and diagonally shifted images. Observed intensity of each pixel is given by the spatial integration of intensity within the four corresponding image portions of the four shifted continuous images. Assuming that each pixel has a 100% aperture, then the observed intensity of each pixel will be given by the spatial integration of intensity within the image portion of the size of vertically and horizontally twice the pixel interval.

The optical low-pass filter reduces the aliasing artifacts. However, it does not sharply cut off high frequency components, and it also reduces frequency components lower than the Nyquist frequency. Images projected on the imaging surface are blurred, and observed color pixels suffer from image blurs. To reconstruct a high-resolution color image, observed blurry color pixels as well as non-observed color pixels should be sharpened while the non-observed color pixels are interpolated through the demosaicking.

2.2 Formulation of Sharpening-Demosaicking in the DFT Domain

The imaging process consists of the optical low-pass filtering, the color-component separation, the hold process and the sub-sampling. The imaging process is irreversible, and hence our sharpening-demosaicking approach estimates the pseudo inverse operator of the imaging process containing image blurs caused by the optical low-pass filter [7]. The sharpening-demosaicking approach is formulated as the least square problem, but there exist multiple different least square solutions. To avoid the ambiguity, in the spatial-frequency domain we need to apply the pass-band limitation corresponding to the sub-sampling pattern of the mosaicking of color filters, to the blurring operator. Fig. 1 illustrates the frequency-band limitations. The introduction of the band-limitation allows us to formulate the recovery problem in the DFT domain explicitly.

We formulate the sharpening-demosaicking problem as the recovery problem that the original R-, G-, and B- images, each of which is composed of *2N x 2N* pixels, are recovered from the RGB-mosaicked color image of *2N x 2N* pixels. The mosaicked G-, R-, and B- signals are represented as the 2-D arrays, $g_{m,n}$, $r_{m,n}$, $b_{m,n}$, respectively.

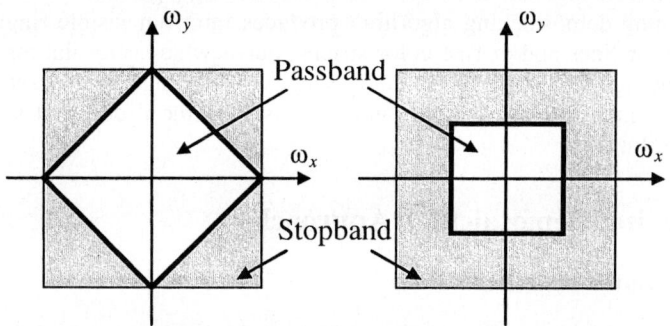

(a) Mosaicked green pixels (b) Mosaicked red and blue pixels

Fig. 1. Fundamental frequency pass-band

$$g_{m,n} \begin{cases} \neq 0 & , \text{ if } m+n \text{ is odd} \\ = 0 & , \text{ if } m+n \text{ is even} \end{cases} \quad (1)$$

$$r_{m,n} \begin{cases} \neq 0 & , \text{ if if } m \text{ and } n \text{ are odd} \\ = 0 & , \text{ if otherwise} \end{cases} \quad (2)$$

$$b_{m,n} \begin{cases} \neq 0 & \text{, if if m and n are even} \\ = 0 & \text{, if otherwise} \end{cases} \quad (3)$$

The original R-, G-, and B- signals to be recovered are represented as the 2D arrays, $q_{m,n}, f_{m,n}, a_{m,n}$, respectively.

$$q_{m,n}, f_{m,n}, a_{m,n} \quad ; (m,n) \in \{0, \cdots, 2N-1\}^2 \quad (4)$$

The linear operators s, ρ are defined as the composite operators of the blur operator due to the optical low-pass filter and the hold process with the 100% pixel aperture. If we apply these operators to the sharpening-demosaicking approach, severe ringing artifacts will occur near color edges. Hence, instead of them, we employ the band-limited versions $\tilde{s}, \tilde{\rho}$ of the operators s, ρ. The operator $\tilde{s}$ is defined by limiting the frequency response of the operator s within the frequency pass-band corresponding to the mosaicking pattern of the G-signals, whereas the operator $\tilde{\rho}$ corresponds to the R- and B- signals.

Recovery Formula for the G-Signal

Information about the original G-signal $f_{m,n}$ is included only in the mosaicked G-signal $g_{m,n}$, and then we define the discrete fidelity energy:

$$\sum_{\substack{m,n=0 \\ m+n: odd}}^{2N-1} \left| \{\tilde{s} * f\}(m,n) - g_{m,n} \right|^2 \quad . \quad (5)$$

We define the $2N \times 2N$ DFT $\hat{g}_{\xi,\eta}$ of the G-signal $g_{m,n}$.

$$\hat{g}_{\xi,\eta} = \sum_{m,n=0}^{2N-1} g_{m,n} \cdot e^{-i2\pi \frac{m \cdot \xi}{2N}} \cdot e^{-i2\pi \frac{n \cdot \eta}{2N}}, \quad (\xi,\eta) \in \left\{ -\frac{2 \cdot N}{2} + 1, \cdots, \frac{2 \cdot N}{2} \right\}^2 \quad (6)$$

In the same manner, the $2N \times 2N$ DFTs $\hat{\tilde{s}}_{\xi,\eta}, \hat{f}_{\xi,\eta}$ of $\tilde{s}_{\xi,\eta}, f_{\xi,\eta}$ are defined. We reformulate the fidelity energy of (5) in the DFT domain as follows:

$$\frac{1}{N^2} \cdot \sum_{\substack{\xi,\eta=-N+1 \\ (-N+1 \leq \xi+\eta \leq N \; \& \; -N+1 \leq \xi-\eta \leq N) \\ or \; (\xi,\eta)=(0,N)}}^{N} \left| \frac{1}{2} \cdot \hat{\tilde{s}}_{\xi,\eta} \cdot \hat{f}_{\xi,\eta} - \hat{g}_{\xi,\eta} \right|^2 \quad . \quad (7)$$

We estimate the partial derivative of the fidelity energy with respect of f in the DFT domain, and we derive the equation.

$$\hat{e}_{(G)\xi,\eta} = 0 \quad , \quad \hat{e}_{(G)\xi,\eta} = \begin{cases} \overline{\hat{\tilde{s}}}_{\xi,\eta} \cdot \left\{ \frac{1}{2} \cdot \hat{\tilde{s}}_{\xi,\eta} \cdot \hat{f}_{\xi,\eta} - \hat{g}_{\xi,\eta} \right\} \\ \quad , if \; (-N+1 \leq \xi+\eta \leq N \; \& \; -N+1 \leq \xi-\eta \leq N) \; or \; (\xi,\eta)=(0,N) \\ 0 \quad , otherwise \end{cases} \quad (8)$$

Recovery Formulas for the R-Signal and the B-Signal

Information about the original R-signal $q_{m,n}$ is included only in the mosaicked R-signal $r_{m,n}$, and then we define the discrete fidelity energy:

$$\sum_{\substack{m,n=0 \\ m,n:\,odd}}^{2N-1} \left|(\tilde{\rho}*q)(m,n) - r_{m,n}\right|^2 . \tag{9}$$

We reformulate the fidelity energy of (9) in the DFT domain, and we derive the equation minimizing the fidelity energy.

$$\frac{1}{2}\cdot\hat{e}_{(R)\xi,\eta} = 0 \quad , \quad \hat{e}_{(R)\xi,\eta} = \begin{cases} \overline{\hat{\tilde{\rho}}}_{\xi,\eta} \cdot \left(\frac{1}{4}\cdot\hat{\tilde{\rho}}_{\xi,\eta}\cdot\hat{q}_{\xi,\eta} - \hat{r}_{\xi,\eta}\right) & , \text{ if } (\xi,\eta) \in \left\{-\frac{N}{2}+1,\cdots,0,\cdots,\frac{N}{2}\right\}^2 \\ 0 & , \text{ otherwise} \end{cases} \tag{10}$$

In the same way as in the case of the original R-signal $q_{m,n}$, we derive the equation for the recovery of the original B-signal $a_{m,n}$.

$$\frac{1}{2}\cdot\hat{e}_{(B)\xi,\eta} = 0 \quad , \quad \hat{e}_{(B)\xi,\eta} = \begin{cases} \overline{\hat{\tilde{\rho}}}_{\xi,\eta} \cdot \left(\frac{1}{4}\cdot\hat{\tilde{\rho}}_{\xi,\eta}\cdot\hat{a}_{\xi,\eta} - \hat{b}_{\xi,\eta}\right) & , \text{ if } (\xi,\eta) \in \left\{-\frac{N}{2}+1,\cdots,0,\cdots,\frac{N}{2}\right\}^2 \\ 0 & , \text{ otherwise} \end{cases} \tag{11}$$

The equations of (8), (10) and (11) are independent of each other, and their solution set is uniquely given. The solutions correspond to the inverse operations of the band-limited blur operators $\tilde{s}, \tilde{\rho}$. This prototypal sharpening-demosaicking approach restores only spatial frequency components of color signals lower than the Nyquist frequency corresponding to the mosaicking pattern of each primary color filter, but it often produces visible ringing artifacts near sharp color edges. Moreover, in the case of the Bayer's RGB color filter array, since the RGB three primary colors occupy different spatial-frequency pass-bands as shown in Fig.1, restored R and B color images will not be sharpened to the same degree as a restored G image, and thus false color artifacts are often visible near sharp color edges. To overcome these difficulties, we introduce the concept of the super-resolution into the prototypal sharpening-demosaicking approach.

3 Super-Resolution Approach

3.1 Total-Variation-Based Super-Resolution for Deblurring

F. Malgouyres and F. Guichard [8] introduced the sub-sampling into the total-variation method [9] for the deblurring, and studied the minimization of the energy functional:

$$\lambda \cdot \int_{\Omega} |\nabla v| \cdot d\Omega + \sum_{m,n=0}^{N-1} \left|(\tilde{s}*v)(m,n) - u_{m,n}\right|^2 \quad , \lambda > 0 . \tag{12}$$

They proved that for a cylindrical function whose DFT is supported by a line, the minimization of the energy functional of (12) admits a solution cylindrical along the same line. The cylindrical function mathematically models the 1D structure of a step edge. The total-variation-based oversampling-deblurring approach of (12) restores frequency components higher than the Nyquist frequency from observed blurry frequency components so that it can enlarge images while preserving image structures defined as the cylindrical functions, and thus it can preserve image edges without producing ringing artifacts.

3.2 Super-Resolution Sharpening-Demosaicking

We introduce the TV-based super-resolution into the sharpening-demosaicking.

Recovery Formula for the G-Signal
We reformulate the energy functional by introducing the total-variation energy into the discrete energy functional of (5), as follows:

$$\lambda \cdot \sum_{m',n'=0}^{2N-1} |\nabla f|_{(m',n')} + \sum_{\substack{m,n=0 \\ m+n:\,odd}}^{2N-1} |\{\tilde{s} * f\}(m,n) - g_{m,n}|^2 \quad , \tag{13}$$

$$|\nabla f|_{(m',n')} = \sqrt{\left(\Delta^x f_{m',n'}\right)^2 + \left(\Delta^y f_{m',n'}\right)^2 + \beta^2} \quad , \quad \Delta^x f_{m',n'} = f_{m'+1,n'} - f_{m',n'}, \quad \Delta^y f_{m',n'} = f_{m',n'+1} - f_{m',n'}.$$

and we derive the iterative algorithm minimizing the energy functional of (13).

$$f_{i,j}^{(n+1)} = f_{i,j}^{(n)} + \varepsilon \cdot \left[\lambda \cdot \left\{ \left(\frac{\Delta^x f_{i,j}^{(n)}}{|\nabla f|_{(i,j)}^{(n)}} - \frac{\Delta^x f_{i-1,j}^{(n)}}{|\nabla f|_{(i-1,j)}^{(n)}} \right) + \left(\frac{\Delta^y f_{i,j}^{(n)}}{|\nabla f|_{(i,j)}^{(n)}} - \frac{\Delta^y f_{i,j-1}^{(n)}}{|\nabla f|_{(i,j-1)}^{(n)}} \right) \right\} - \frac{IDFT_{(2N \times 2N)}\left[\hat{e}_{(G)\xi,\eta}^{(n)}\right]_{(i,j)}}{N^2} \right] \tag{14}$$

Recovery Formulas for the R-Signal and the B-Signal
For the R-signal we reformulate the energy functional by introducing the total-variation energy into the discrete energy functional of (9), and we derive the iterative algorithm.

$$q_{i,j}^{(n+1)} = q_{i,j}^{(n)} + \varepsilon \cdot \left[\lambda \cdot \left\{ \left(\frac{\Delta^x q_{i,j}^{(n)}}{|\nabla q|_{(i,j)}^{(n)}} - \frac{\Delta^x q_{i-1,j}^{(n)}}{|\nabla q|_{(i-1,j)}^{(n)}} \right) + \left(\frac{\Delta^y q_{i,j}^{(n)}}{|\nabla q|_{(i,j)}^{(n)}} - \frac{\Delta^y q_{i,j-1}^{(n)}}{|\nabla q|_{(i,j-1)}^{(n)}} \right) \right\} - \frac{IDFT_{(2N \times 2N)}\left[\hat{e}_{(R)\xi,\eta}^{(n)}\right]_{(i,j)}}{2 \cdot N^2} \right] \tag{15}$$

In the same manner, for the B-signal we derive the iterative algorithm:

$$a_{i,j}^{(n+1)} = a_{i,j}^{(n)} + \varepsilon \cdot \left[\lambda \cdot \left\{ \left(\frac{\Delta^x a_{i,j}^{(n)}}{|\nabla a|_{(i,j)}^{(n)}} - \frac{\Delta^x a_{i-1,j}^{(n)}}{|\nabla a|_{(i-1,j)}^{(n)}} \right) + \left(\frac{\Delta^y a_{i,j}^{(n)}}{|\nabla a|_{(i,j)}^{(n)}} - \frac{\Delta^y a_{i,j-1}^{(n)}}{|\nabla a|_{(i,j-1)}^{(n)}} \right) \right\} - \frac{IDFT_{(2N \times 2N)}\left[\hat{e}_{(B)\xi,\eta}^{(n)}\right]_{(i,j)}}{2 \cdot N^2} \right] \tag{16}$$

Equations (14), (15) and (16) are independent of each other. The G-, R-, B-signals to be recovered are separately updated according to these three equations.

3.3 Spatially Adaptive Control of the TV Image Regularization

The TV-based super-resolution restores spatial frequency components higher than the Nyquist frequency, and sharpens color edges effectively without producing ringing artifacts and false color artifacts. However, as side effects, the TV image regularization influences frequency components lower than the Nyquist frequency, and when we render the weighting parameter λ excessively large, the TV image regularization will tend to smooth out original signal variations excessively in texture image regions, and hence fine textures will be degraded. To remedy the drawback, we introduce a spatially adaptive technique that changes the weighting parameter λ of the TV energy term dependently on the local saliency of color edges around a pixel.

The algorithm of the spatially adaptive control is as follows:

1) Compute the map of edge magnitude by applying the detection filters of directional salient edges to the mosaicked R-, G-, B- images,
2) Diffuse the edge magnitude into neighboring pixels by convolving the edge-magnitude map with the averaging mask whose weighing coefficients are inversely proportional to the distance from the center pixel,
3) Interpolate and magnify the diffused edge-magnitude map to the image size to be recovered,
4) Set the value of the weighting parameter λ of the TV energy term proportional to the diffused edge-magnitude of each pixel.

4 Performance Evaluations

To evaluate the effectiveness of our super-resolution sharpening-demosaicking methods for the Bayer's RGB color filter array, we use artificially generated test RGB-mosaicked natural images, and restore high-resolution RGB color images from them with our super-resolution sharpening-demosaicking methods. For the experiments, we artificially generate test RGB-mosaicked images from original RGB color image data that we get by scanning color films, taken with an analog camera, by using a very high-resolution RGB line sensor. The raw RGB data of the original color images are arranged in an array of horizontally 4096-pixel size by vertically 4096-pixel size, and intensity of each primary color is expressed in 12-bit word length. To produce test RGB-mosaicked color images mimicking color images taken with a single solid-state color image sensor using the RGB color filter array, first we apply the smoothing process mimicking the optical low-pass filtering to the original raw RGB data, and then sub-sample the RGB color images according to the mosaicking pattern. We apply our super-resolution sharpening-demosaicking method to the artificially generated test RGB-mosaicked images.

Fig. 2 compares an enlarged color-edge part of the color image demosaicked with our prototypal sharpening-demosaicking method without the super-resolution technique (SD) [7], with that demosaicked with our super-resolution sharpening-demosaicking method with the spatially adaptive TV image regularization (SD-ATV). SD produces visible ringing artifacts near sharp color edges, whereas SD-ATV reproduces sharper edges than SD, without producing ringing artifacts.

Fig. 3 and Fig.4 compares an enlarged texture part of the color image demosaicked with SD-ATV, with that demosaicked with our super-resolution sharpening-demosaicking method with the non-adaptive TV image regularization (SD-TV). SD-TV smoothes out fine textures, whereas SD-ATV preserves them, because the diffused edge-magnitude map is estimated as almost zero, and thus the TV-based image regularization hardly operates.

Super-resolution Sharpening-Demosaicking   253

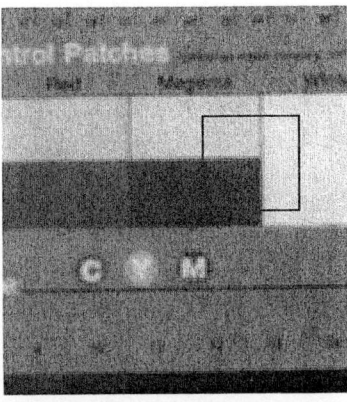
(a) Original image

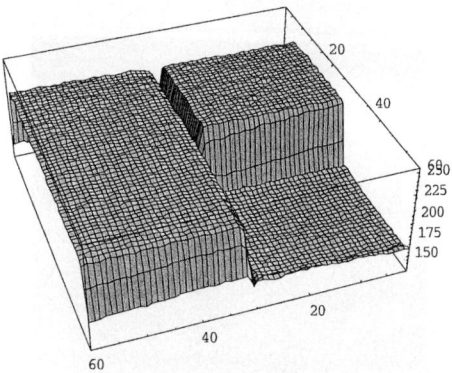
(b) Intensity variation of the original G-image

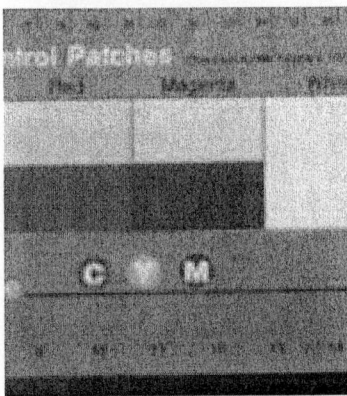
(c) Restored image with SD

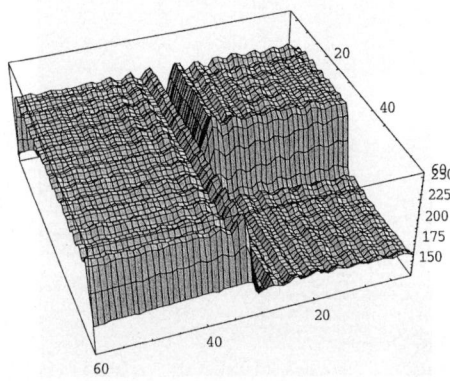
(d) Intensity variation of the restored G-image with SD

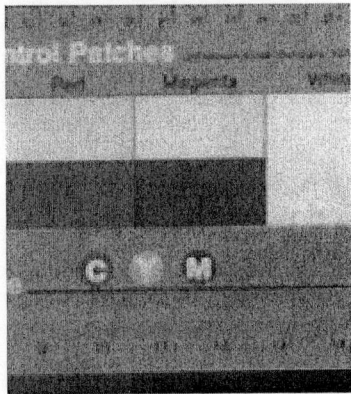
(e) Restored image with SD-ATV

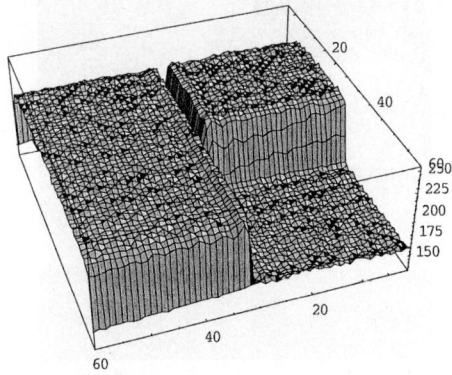
(f) Intensity variation of the restored G-image with SD-ATV

Fig. 2. Example of image restoration with the sharpening-demosaicking methods

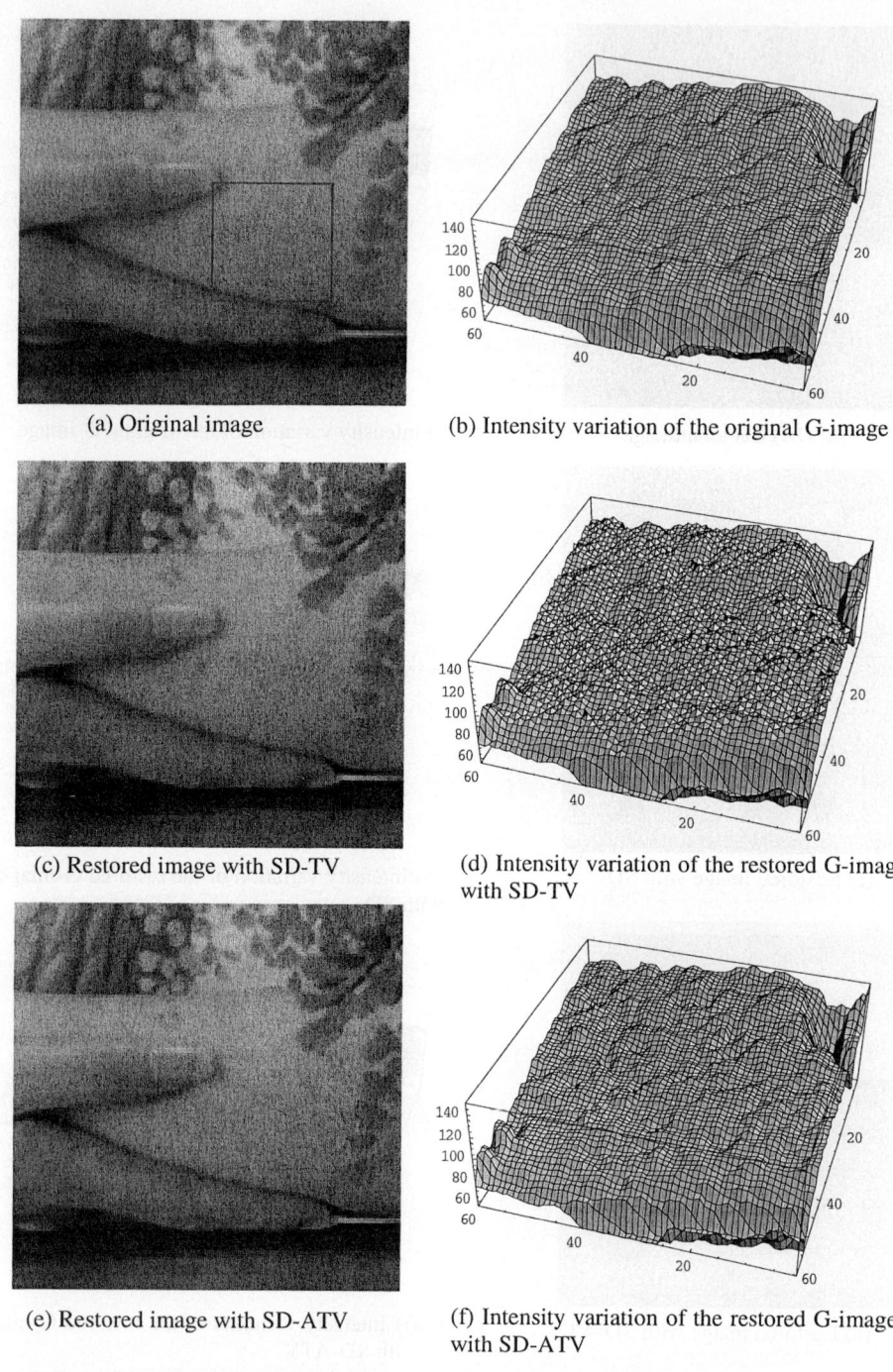

Fig. 3. Example of image restoration with the sharpening-demosaicking methods

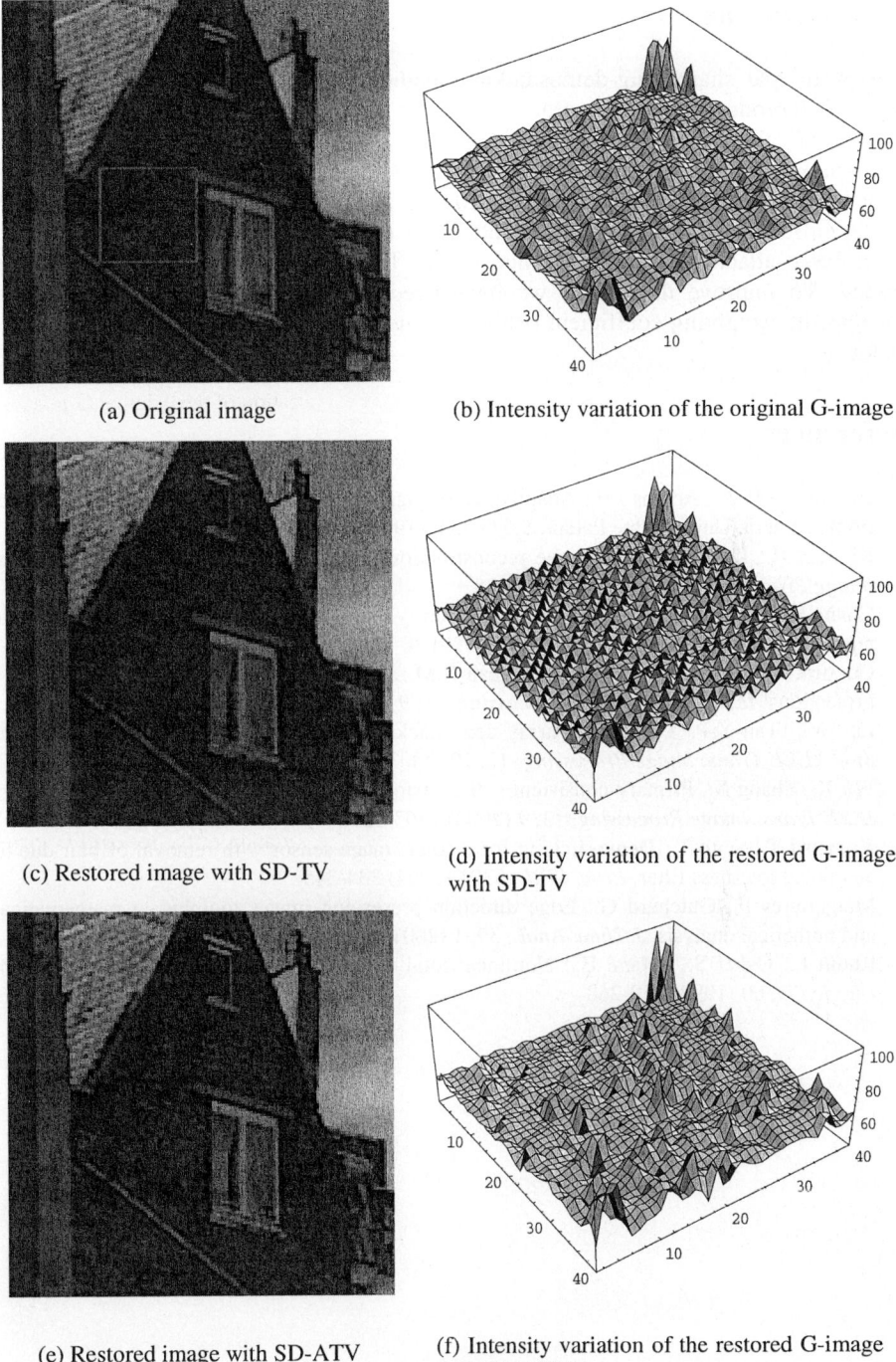

Fig. 4. Example of image restoration with the sharpening-demosaicking methods

5 Conclusions

The prototypal sharpening-demosaicking method for the Bayer's RGB color filter array often produced ringing artifacts near color edges. To suppress those artifacts, we introduced the TV-based super-resolution. The super-resolution sharpening-demosaicking method restores spatial frequency components higher than the Nyquist frequency without producing ringing artifacts. However, the introduction of the TV energy influences frequency components lower than the Nyquist frequency, and if we excessively attach greater importance to the TV energy, fine textures will be degraded. To improve this point, we introduced a spatially adaptive technique that changes the weighting coefficient of the TV energy term dependently on local image features.

References

1. Hamilton J.F. Jr., Adams J.E.: Adaptive color plan interpolation in signal sensor color electronic camera, United State Patent, 5,629,734 (1997)
2. Kimmel R.: Demosaicking: image reconstruction from color CCD samples, *IEEE Trans. Image Processing*, 7, 3 (1999) 1221-1228
3. Chang E., Cheung S., Pan D.Y.: Color filter array recovery using a threshold-based variable number of gradients, *Proc. SPIE*, 3650 (1999) 36-43
4. Gunturk B. K., Altunbasak Y., Mersereau R.M.: Color plan interpolation using alternating projections, *IEEE Trans. Image Processing*, 11, 9 (2002) 997-1013
5. Lu W., Tan Y-P.: Color filter array demosaicking: new method and performance measure, , *IEEE Trans. Image Processing*, 12, 10 (2003) 1194-1210
6. Wu X., Zhang N.: Primary-consistent soft-decision color demosaicking for digital cameras, *IEEE Trans. Image Processing*, 13, 9 (2004) 1263-1274
7. Komatsu T., Saito T.: Demosaicking for a color image sensor with removal of blur due to an optical low-pass filter, *Proc. SPIE*, 5301 (2004) 334-345
8. Malgouyres F., Guichard G.: Edge direction preserving image zooming: a mathematical and numerical analysis, *J. Num. Anal.*, 39, 1 (2001) 1-37
9. Rudin L., Osher S., Fetami E..: Nonlinear total variation based noise removal algorithm, *Physica D*, 60 (1992) 259-268

Gradient Based Image Completion by Solving Poisson Equation

Jianbing Shen, Xiaogang Jin, and Chuan Zhou

State Key Lab of CAD&CG, Zhejiang University,
Hangzhou 310027, P.R. China
{Jianbing Shen, Xiaogang Jin, Chuan Zhou}@cad.zju.edu.cn

Abstract. Image completion is a method to fill the missing portions of an image caused by the removal of one or more foreground or background elements. In this paper a novel image completion algorithm is proposed for removing significant objects from natural images or photographs. The completion is realized in the following three steps. First, a gradient-based model is presented to determine the gradient-patch filling order. This step is critical because a better filling order can improve the continuation of image structures. Second, we implement the gradient-patch update strategy by measuring the exponential distance between the source patch and the target one in gradient domain. In order to find a better patch matching and propagating algorithm, we incorporate the gradient and color information together to determine the target patch. Third, a complete image is achieved by solving the Poisson equation with the updated image gradient map. Some experimental results on real-scene photographs are given to demonstrate both the efficiency and image equality of our novel method.

1 Introduction

The removal of objects or large objects, known as image completion, has become an important task in photo editing or film post-production. Given an input image I with an missing or unknown region, the goal of image completion is to propagate structure and texture information from the known or existing regions $I - \Omega$ to Ω. The removed parts can be filled in by various interactive procedures such as clone brush strokes and compositing processes. However, filling the background hole seamlessly and automatically from existing neighborhood information of damaged images is still a difficult problem. A professional skilled artist usually completes them by meticulous work.

A number of approaches related to image completion have been proposed in computer graphics and computer vision literatures, [4, 5, 6, 9, 16]. Bertalmio [4] used PDE-based method to repair damaged images. The idea is to extend the structures inward arriving at the boundaries of the damaged area. For an image in which only small portions are missing, this approach can achieve highly smoothed results. However, the lack of texture in a large reconstructed area is easily visible. Therefore this approach is ineffective for filling in large holes in the natural images. Levin [2] extended the idea by measuring global image statistics based on the prior image knowledge besides the local color information. Drori et.al. [6] incorporated pyramid image approximation and adaptive image fragments together to achieve impressive results.However, the method is very slow due to the high computational complexity.

Recently, some researchers have considered example-based method as a way to achieve image region completion with objects or large objects removal [3,5,6, 9,16]. One of the first attempts to use example-based synthesis for object removal was by Harrison [8], which filled the pixels in the target region by the level of "texturedness" of the pixel's neighborhood. Although the intuition sounds, strong linear structures were often overruled by nearby noise. Jia [9] presented a technique for filling image regions through explicitly segmenting the unknown area into different homogeneous texture areas using tensor voting method, but their approach requires both an expensive segmentation step and a difficult choice about what constitutes a boundary between two textures. More recently Criminisi et.al. [5] addressed a example-based image inpainting algorithm with region filling, who used the angle between the isophote direction and the normal direction of the local boundary to define the searching order of the patches, so that the structure of the missing region can be filled before filling in the texture. Sun [19] introduced a novel structure propagation approach to image completion. In their system, the user manually specifies important missing structure information by extending a few curves or line segments from the known to the unknown regions. Their approach synthesizes image patches along these user-specified curves in the unknown region using patches selected around the curves in the known region. Structure propagation is formulated as a global optimization problem by enforcing structure and consistency constraints. If only a single curve is specified, structure propagation is solved using Dynamic Programming. When multiple intersecting curves are specified, the Belief Propagation algorithm is adopted to find the optimal patches. After completing structure propagation, the remaining unknown regions are filled using patch-based texture synthesis.

Our gradient domain techniques and Poisson equation solving techniques also relates to those used for high dynamic range compression [7], Poisson image editing [11], image fusion for context enhancement [13], interactive photomontages [1], Poisson image matting [14] and removing photography artifacts [18]. In our approach we propagate the missing image components by selecting the most similar gradient of the target region with that of the source regions, then the missing background components of the damaged image can be restored with the inpainted gradient map by directly solving the Poisson equation.

The rest of the paper is arranged as follows. Section 2 describes the details of our gradient-based completion mechanism in three key stages. Section 3 shows the results and compares with other previous schemes. In Section 4, we conclude our proposed algorithm with a discussion on future directions.

2 Gradient-Based Image Completion Algorithm

In this section, we describe an outline of our image completion algorithm. A digital photograph is firstly used as the input image which containing a manually masked area as the unknown region, then the unknown region is filled in gradient domain by the image information in known area.

We use similar notation as that used in the image completion literature [4, 5, 6, 16]. We denote the unknown region (the region to be filled) by Ω, the known region by Ψ, the contour region by $\partial\Omega$, the source and target gradient patches by Ψ_s, Ψ_t respectively. At each step, a target fragment is firstly completed by adding more details to it from a source fragment consists of gradients, using the gradient-based patch priorities defined in our paper to determine the patch filling order. Secondly, a source gradient patch is selected by measuring the adjusted appearance of the source patch with the target patch, enforcing the searching area in the neighborhood around the previous source patch in the gradient domain. Thirdly, we solve Poisson equation with the updated gradient map to reconstruct a complete image. The experimental results show our algorithm is none-blurring and well structure maintaining.

2.1 Gradient-Based Filling Order

Features describing image content, such as color histogram, gradient, texture, shape and object composition, are usually introduced to extract image salient information. These features are then used to determine the filling order of target patches. Zhang et.al. [16] incorporated the textureness in the neighborhood for determining the filling order, and Criminisi et.al [5] used the angle between the isophote direction and the normal direction of the local boundary to define the searching order of the patches, so that the structure of the missing region can be filled before filling in texture. In this paper we calculate the patch filling order using image gradient feature in a manner similar to that in [5].

The confidence term $C(p)$ is initialized to zero if p is removing or damaged; otherwise it is set to one [5], where p is the pixel under consideration. The second relevant term is called the gradient term $G(p)$, which corresponds to the local shape feature, and its value is based on the magnitude of the gradient information at location p. The gradient term is computed as follows:

$$G(p) = \frac{1}{|A|} \sum_{p_i \in A} \sqrt{Gx^2(p_i) + Gy^2(p_i)} \qquad (1)$$

$$C(p) = \begin{cases} 0, & \forall p \in \Omega \\ 1, & \forall p \in I - \Omega \end{cases} \qquad (2)$$

where A denotes the neighborhood area around pixel p, and $G = [Gx, Gy]$ denotes the gradient field of an image for the horizontal and vertical directions using a simple forward difference.

For a given patch Ψ_s centered at the point p for some $p \in \partial\Omega$, where p is the pixel under consideration, we define its filling order as the following formula:

$$P(p) = C(p) \cdot G(p) \qquad (3)$$

$$C(p) = \frac{\sum_{q \in \Psi_s \cap (I \setminus \Omega)} C(q)}{|\Psi_p|} \qquad (4)$$

The gradient term $G(p)$ may be considered as a measure of the amount of edge and structure information surrounding the pixel p. The purpose for calculating the patch priority value $P(p)$ is to encourage the linear structures to be filled first with the larger values, therefore, this can help to propagate the broken lines into the connected ones.

2.2 Patch Matching and Propagating

After all patch filling priorities on the filling-boundary have been computed, the gradient patch Ψ_T with the highest priority is firstly selected to propagate. Then the target region is filled with extracted data based on the source region Ψ_S. As noted before, under the assumption that the content in the unknown area is similar to the content of the known region for the similarity measurement [16], the traditional inpainting techniques propagate pixel-information via diffusion [4,6], which results in blurry fill-in and line un-continuous, especially of large regions. Criminisi [5] propagated the filling patches by direct sampling of the source region. Similarly, we solve this problem by gradient-patch sampling and gradient-patch copying algorithm. However, we do not use the common Sum of Squared Difference (SSD), which is widely used in image completion to measure the similarity between space patches. The reason is that the SSD does not always suffice to provide the desired completion results as described in [15].

Since a well-suited similarity measurement between gradient patches is the heart of the algorithm that directly influences the final completion result, we use an exponential similarity measure as follows:

$$s(\Psi_S, \Psi_T) = e^{d_c(\Psi_S, \Psi_T) + d_g(\Psi_S, \Psi_T)} \qquad (5)$$

$$d_c(\Psi_S, \Psi_T) = \sum_{(x,y)} ||\Psi_S^c(x,y) - \Psi_T^c(x,y)|| \qquad (6)$$

$$d_g(\Psi_S, \Psi_T) = \sum_{(x,y)} ||\Psi_S^g(x,y) - \Psi_T^g(x,y)|| \qquad (7)$$

$$\Psi_S = argmin_{\Psi_i \in \Phi} \frac{s(\Psi_S, \Psi_T)}{|\Psi_S|} \qquad (8)$$

where Ψ_S^c, Ψ_T^c represent the R, G, B color information of the source patch and the target one, while Ψ_S^g, Ψ_T^g represent the corresponding gradient information. Once a gradient patch to the highest priority location p is copied, we then fill it with data extracted from the known region Ψ. The confidence at all previously damaged pixels in Ψ_S is updated using formula (4).

As described in the above sections, now we have gotten the final updated gradient map $G' = [Gx', Gy']$ of the source image for the following restoration through Poisson equation solver.

2.3 Image Reconstruction by Solving Poisson Equation

Image reconstruction from gradients fields is an approximate invariability problem, and it is a very active research area. In 2D, a modified gradient vector field $G' = [Gx', Gy']$ may not be integrable. Let I' denote the completion image propagated from G', we can use one of the direct methods recently proposed [7] to minimize $|\nabla I' - G|$, so that $G = \nabla^2 I'$. Involving a Laplacian and a divergence operator, I' can be obtained by solving the Poisson differential equation:

$$\nabla^2 I' = div([Gx', Gy']) \qquad (9)$$

Since both the Laplacian ∇^2 and div are linear operators, approximating them using standard finite differences yields a large system of linear equations. We use the full multigrid method [12] to solve the Laplacian equation with Gaussian-Seidel smoothing iterations. This leads to $O(n)$ operations to reach an approximate solution, where n is the number of pixels in the image.

To solve the Poisson equation more efficiently, an alternative is to use a "rapid Poisson solver", which uses a sine transform based on the method [12] to invert the Laplacian operator. However, the complexity with this approach will be $O(n(log(n)))$. The images were zero-padded on both sides, and Dirichlet boundary conditions instead of Neumann boundary conditions were used to avoid the scale/shift ambiguity [18] in the gradient restoration.

3 Experimental Results and Discussions

Our algorithm has been applied to a variety of full color natural photographs with complex background structures. Since visual perceptual completion is the ability of the visual system to fill in missing areas [6], it is commonly accepted that the quality of the results apparently corresponds to the human perception of the appearance in the completed images. Our experimental results visually demonstrate that the proposed algorithm can get satisfactory image completion. Moreover, we compared our results with the ones of earlier work.

Figure 1 demonstrates the advantage of our gradient-based patch compensation to match the target patch. This image is downloaded from the website http://www.cis.rit.edu/fairchild/personal.php. Even the removing region (the foreground person) covers about 39%, our method can still restore the missing background reasonably.

Figures 2, 3 show comparisons of the results obtained by our gradient-based method with the ones obtained by other proposed methods. In both cases, our method performs better than the previous techniques designed for the restoration of small scratches. For the example shown in Figure 3, where larger objects are removed, our approach outperforms earlier work dramatically in terms of perceptual quality. In figures 2, 3, we can find the blur introduced by the diffusion process and the lack of texture in the synthesized area with the previous methods described [4,6]. The images obtained by our approach provide more detailed and coherent results than the other ones.

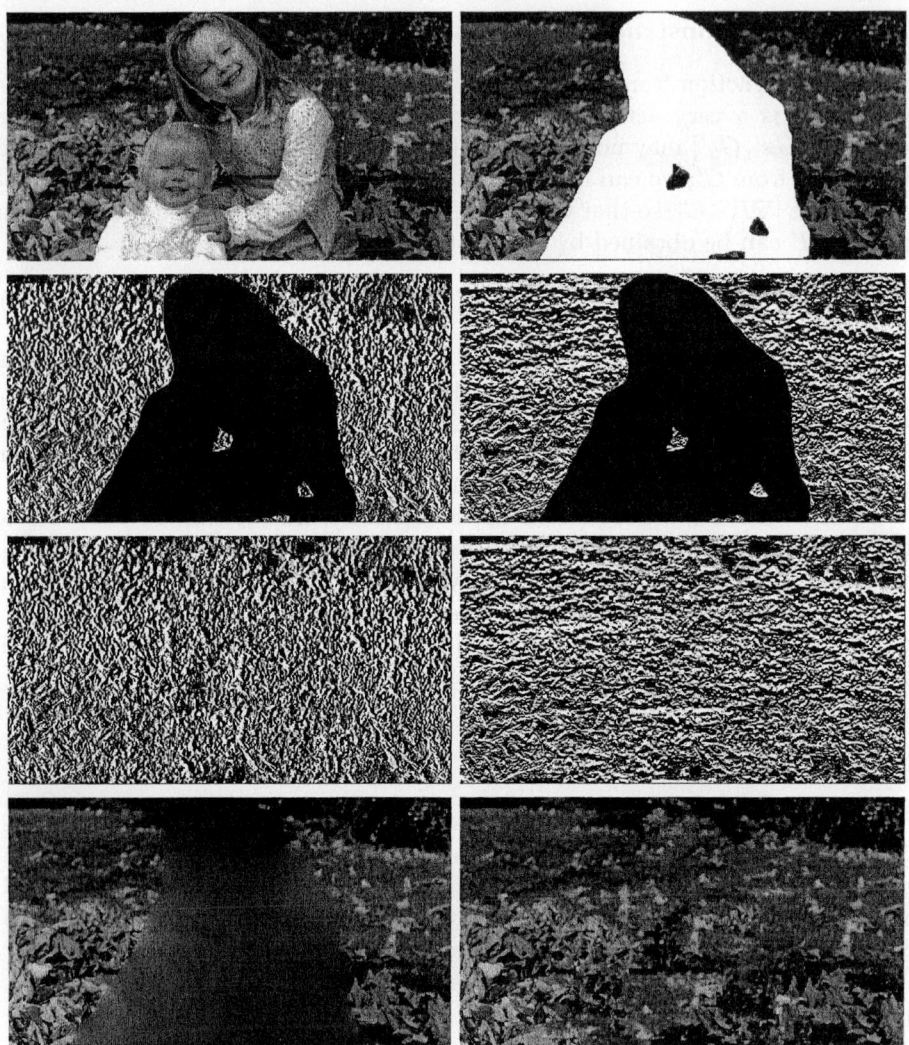

Fig. 1. Algorithm comparisons. Top left: original image. Top right: the figure needs to be removed (in white with red boundary). First middle left: the initial gradient map in horizontal direction. First middle right: the initial gradient one in vertical direction. Second middle left: the gradient map after propagating in horizontal direction. Second middle right: the gradient one after propagating in vertical direction. Bottom left: results obtained by inpainting method [4]. Bottom right: results obtained by our method.

When comparing the performance of a new completion algorithm with the previous ones, the subjective image quality evaluation testing, which is based on many observers that evaluate image quality, is not enough. We need an objective image quality testing based on mathematical calculations. The objective quality

Fig. 2. Algorithm comparisons. Top left: original image. Top right: the microphone needs to be removed. Middle left: results obtained by inpainting method [4,6]. Middle right: results obtained by our method. Bottom left: the enlarged area from the marked region in top-right image. Bottom right: the enlarged area from the marked region in bottom-left image.

evaluation is easier and faster than the subjective one because no observers are needed. In this paper, we utilize the Peak Signal Noise Ratio (PSNR), which is the most widely used objective image quality metrics, to evaluate the complete image results in red, green, blue channels separately. Table 1 shows our new algorithm has better performance in PSNR than previous algorithms.

The performance of our method is dependent on the availability of the similar content in the known area. In case of no available patches in the known area to synthesize the unknown one, our algorithm may not work well. Our algorithm also has limitation when dealing with curved structures in still photographs.

Table 1. PSNR (dB) comparison between different completion algorithms

Channel	Algorithm	Fig.1	Fig.2	Fig.3
Red	Bertalmio [4]	11.0962	32.2705	16.8124
	Drori [6]	11.4835	32.4725	17.1017
	Criminisi [5]	11.9430	32.8189	17.4278
	Our Method	12.5741	33.6307	19.3317
Green	Bertalmio [4]	12.0853	32.9155	16.9019
	Drori [6]	12.4321	33.5248	17.1027
	Criminisi [5]	12.6542	33.8171	17.6515
	Our Method	13.1995	34.4735	19.1372
Blue	Bertalmio [4]	11.1060	33.6374	16.0834
	Drori [6]	11.3595	34.1269	16.3772
	Criminisi [5]	11.6643	34.6080	16.5796
	Our Method	12.0598	35.3863	18.2548
Mask(pixels)		78824	3235	7997

Fig.4 shows the results of our gradient-based algorithm on one of the examples used from [6]. As it can be observed by comparing the result from [6] and our completion result, our algorithm does not introduce the edge blur and the ghost artifact. Our result is similar to or slightly better than Drori's [6].

Some limitations remain in our approach. The gradient-based method works well if the missing structures can be represented by a set of linear structures. Our approach also shares the most common limitation of example-based techniques [4, 5, 6, 9, 19]: if there are not enough samples in the image, it will be impossible to synthesize the desired structure or texture. Our approach has no ability to handle depth ambiguities, where the missing area covers the intersection of two perpendicular regions as shown in Fig.5. In our algorithm, pixel colors are represented in RGB color space, we may achieve the better experimental results in the CIE lab color space because of its property of perceptual uniformity and its more meaningful similarity distances than in RGB color space [21, 5].

Fig. 3. Algorithm comparison. Top left: original image from [4]. Top right: the target region covers 13% of the total image area. Middle left: the result of region filling by traditional image inpainting [4]. Middle right: result from [6]. Bottom left: the result image by example-based completion [5]. Bottom Right: the final image where the bungee jumper has been completely removed and the occluded region reconstructed by our automatic algorithm.

Fig. 4. Algorithm comparison. Top left: A photo of the oil painting "Still Life with Apples", P. Cezanne, c. 1890, The Hermitage, St. Petersburg. Top right: The manually selected target region. Bottom left: results obtained by [6]. Bottom right: results obtained by our gradient method. Notice the ghost artifact disappears since no smoothing is introduced at any stage of our algorithm.

Fig. 5. Our approach does not handle depth ambiguities. Top left: A synthesis image in which the missing area covers the intersection of two perpendicular regions [6]. Top right: a nature image with the same ambiguity. Bottom left: results obtained by [6]. Bottom right: results obtained by our method.

4 Conclusions and Future Work

A novel gradient-based image completion algorithm by solving Poisson equation has been proposed in this paper. Experiments and analysis both demonstrates the feasibility and efficiency of our new proposed algorithm.

Our image completion approach can be divided into three major steps. First, a gradient-based model is presented to determine the gradient-patch filling order. Second, the gradient-patch update strategy is implemented by measuring the exponential distance of the source patch with the target one in gradient domain. In order to find a better patch matching and propagating algorithm, we incorporate the gradient and color information together to determine the target patch. Third, a complete image is achieved by solving the Poisson equation with the updated image gradient map.

Currently, we are intending to extend our approach from still photography completion to video gradient completion and meshs gradient completion [20]. The difficulties in removing objects from video include global motion compensation and maintaining consistency of the unknown area over the whole video sequence [15, 17].

Acknowledgement

This work was supported by 973 Program (No.2002CB312101), National Natural Science Foundation of China (No. 60273054, 60340440422) and Fok Ying Tung Education Foundation (No. 91069).

References

1. Agarwala, A., Dontcheva, M., Agarwala, M., Drucker, S., Colburn, A., Curless, B., Salesin, D., and Cohen, M.: Interactive digital photomontage. In proceedings of ACM SIGGRAPH, ACM Press. (2004) 294-302.
2. Levin, A., Zomet, A., and Weiss, Y.: Learning how to inpaint from global image statistics. ICCV. (2003) 305-361.
3. Bornard, R., Lecan, E., Laborelli, L., and Chenot, J. H.: Missing data correction in still images and image sequences. In ACM Multimedia, France. (2002) 355-361.
4. Bertalmio, M., Sapiro, G., Caselles, V., and Ballester, C.: Image inpainting. In proceedings of ACM SIGGRAPH, ACM Press, (2000) 417-424.
5. Criminisi, A., Perez, P., and Toyama, K.: Object removal by exemplar-based inpainting. IEEE Transactions on Image Processing. (2004) 1200-1212.
6. Drori, I., Cohen-Or, D., and Yeshurun, H.: Fragment-based image completion. In proceedings of ACM SIGGRAPH, ACM Press. (2003) 303-312.
7. Fatal, R., Lischinski, D., and Werman, M.: Gradient domain high dynamic range compression. In proceedings of ACM SIGGRAPH. (2002) 249-256.
8. Harrison, P.: A non-hierarchical procedure for re-synthesis of complex texture. In WSCG, Czech Republic, (2001) 190-197.
9. Jia, J., and Tang, C. K.: Image repairing: Robust image synthesis by adaptive tensor voting. CVPR, Madison, WI. (2003) 643-650.

10. Press, W., Teukolsky, S., and Vetterling, W., and Flannery, B.: Numerical Recipes in C: The Art of Scientific Computing. Cambridge University Press. (1992).
11. Perez, P., Gangnet, M., and Blake, A.: Poisson image editing. In proceedings of ACM SIGGRAPH, ACM Press. (2003) 313-318.
12. Raskar, R., Tan, K., Feris, R., Yu, J., and Turk, M.: Non-photorealistic camera: depth edge detection and stylized rendering using multi-flash imaging. In proceedings of ACM SIGGRAPH, ACM Press. (2004) 679-688.
13. Raskar, R., Ilie, A., and Yu, J.: Image fusion for context enhancement and video surrealism. NPAR. (2004) 85-95.
14. Sun, J., Jia, J., Tang, C.K., and Shum, H.Y.: Poisson matting. In proceedings of ACM SIGGRAPH, ACM Press, (2004) 315-321.
15. Wexler, Y., Shechtman, E., and Irani, M.: Space-Time Video Completion, CVPR, Washington, D.C., USA, (2004) 120-127.
16. Zhang, Y.J., Xiao, J.J., and Shah, M.: Region Completion in a Single Image, EUROGRAPHICS, Grenoble, France, Short Presentations. (2004).
17. Zhang, Y.J., Xiao, J.J., and Shah, M.: Motion Layer Based Object Removal in Videos, WACV. (2005) 516-521.
18. Agrawal, A., Raskar, R., Nayar, S., and Li, Y.: Removing Flash Artifacts using Gradient Analysis. In proceedings of ACM SIGGRAPH, ACM Press. (2005) to appear.
19. Sun, J., Yuan, L., Jia J., and Shum, H.Y.: Image Completion with Structure Propagation. In proceedings of ACM SIGGRAPH, ACM Press. (2005) to appear.
20. Sharf, A., Alexa, M., and Cohen-Or, D.: Context-based surface completion. In Proceedings of ACM SIGGRAPH, ACM Press. (2004) 878-887.
21. Kasson, J.M., Plouffe, W.: An analysis of selected computer interchange color spaces. In Proceedings of ACM SIGGRAPH, ACM Press. (1992) 373-405.

Predictive Directional Rectangular Zonal Search for Digital Multimedia Processor

Soon-Tak Lee[1] and Joong-Hwan Baek[2]

[1] Telechips Inc. KORAD Bldg., 1000-12 Daechi-dong Gangnam-Gu, Seoul, Korea
stlee@telechips.com
[2] School of Electronics, Telecommunication & Computer Engineering,
Hankuk Aviation University, Koyang City, South Korea
jhbaek@mail.hangkong.ac.kr

Abstract. Motion estimation is the biggest part of any video encoding system since it could significantly affect the encoding time and output quality. Until now, several motion estimation algorithms that have the fast motion estimation and a good PSNR are proposed. However these are not considered an embedded system processor using SDRAM as a video frame memory. In this paper, we propose new fast predictive block matching algorithm, named *predictive directional rectangular zonal search*. Comparing with existing algorithms, it has not only similar output quality, but more efficient operating with SDRAM. It makes possible to design a hardware motion estimator into a compact one. A motion estimation hardware block that is based on the proposed algorithm for H.263 and MPEG-4 video encoder, is implemented by $0.13 \mu m$, 1.2 V CMOS technology.

1 Introduction

Ubiquitous environment is expected to realize services which people can obtain various types of information in anytime and anywhere. The number of smart cellular phones including camera/camcoder devices is increasing around the world.[8] These devices are mostly used for visual communication or to record the visual information, but they can also be used as input devices to realize novel user interfaces. Hence, these have to be existed with us anytime and anywhere. But, mobile terminals and hand-held devices often add unique constraints to use - limited user time, low transmission bandwidth, low power, low-resolution display, etc.[7] Therefore, in ubiquitous environment, one of main objective is to minimize the required computing power.

To minimize the battery consumption at these embedded systems, high performance and low power video en/decoder are needed. In case of MPEG-4 or H.263 video encoder implementation for embedded system, there is strong need to consider not only the video compression standard, but also the characteristics of that.

In video encoder, motion estimation can consume approximately from 66% up to 90% of the computational power of the encoder, and it is the most computational intensive part for the video encoding process.[1][2][5]

Usually, embedded system works only at low frequency, narrow memory bandwidth and limited battery power. Even if we use outstanding motion estimation algorithm, a software motion estimator has a huge computational complexity and high computation power is required. Therefore, hardware motion estimator is needed to reduce processor operating frequency and power consumption of processor.

In the motion estimation process, large data are read from reference frame data. Most embedded system use SDRAM as a main system memory. SDRAM is small, priced low and easy to purchase. However, it only shows a good efficiency of reading and writing data, which are located in linear address. To access the data in SDRAM, memory controller must send two kind of address. One is RAS(row address signal) and the other is CAS(column address signal). SDRAM is divided into several blocks. RAS signal selects one of these blocks and CAS catches the real data. When memory controller read the data in same block, it sends RAS signal just one time and changes CAS only. SDRAM shows better read/write performance at continuously located data than at scattered data. For that reason, a motion estimator has to read the reference frame data, which are located in continuous address as much as possible for maximize the SDRAM read efficiency.

In this paper, we suggest the Predictive Directional Rectangular Zonal Search(PDRZS) for low-power video encoding system. This algorithm considers the efficient operate with SDRAM and direction of motion vectors. These are spatially and temporally adjacent macroblocks in a sequence. PDRZS is tested by well-known ten MPEG test video sequences. Comparing to existing well-known motion estimation method - APDZS(advanced predictive diamond zonal search), it shows better efficiency at SDRAM operation as well as an almost same output quality. In addition, it can make a simple and small hardware than APDZS.[3]

PDRZS is implemented by $0.13 \mu m$, 1.2V CMOS technology.

2 Advanced Predictive Diamond Zonal Search (APDZS)

One of very important characteristic of APDZS is the usage of a predictor, which is usually taken as the predictor used for the motion vector coding process.

In case of MPEG-1/2, the predictor takes the motion vector of the previous block that is located in the left, whereas in H.263/MPEG-4 takes the median value of the motion vectors on the adjacent blocks at the top, left and top-right.[6] The motion vectors that have spatially and temporally adjacent macroblocks in a sequence are highly correlated each other.[3][4][6]

There is high correlation between the motion vectors of spatially and temporally adjacent macroblocks in a sequence.[3][4]

APDZS predicts the candidate motion vector, and searches the best motion vector by using diamond search pattern. During the search process, APDZS terminates the search process early by using an adaptive threshold technique. [3][4]

Though APDZS shows a fast and good PSNR value, it is not suitable for video encoder at embedded system, because of following reasons;

The difficulty of hardware implementation as a small and low-power.
The inefficient cooperation with SDRAM.

To implement the diamond search pattern as a hard-wired logic, many decision logics are needed. Decision logic increases the hardware size. The linearity of reference frame data is more decreased in diamond pattern than rectangular pattern. As a result of this, the SDRAM operation efficiency can be decreased.

3 Predictive Directional Rectangular Zonal Search (PDRZS)

In this paper, we propose the PDRZS. It has a good SDRAM operation efficiency and almost same performance comparing to APDZS.

3.1 Motion Vector Distribution

Table 1 is the simulation results using PMVFAST with full search. These are shown by the motion vector characteristic during predictive motion estimation process.[4]

Table 1. Motion Vector Directions of Test Sequences

Video Sequence	Direction of $\overrightarrow{MV}_{candi}$			
	X		Y	
	Direction of $\overrightarrow{MV}_{diff}$			
	x	Y	X	Y
Carphone	651	433	146	133
Coastguard	57	71	16	3
Container	35	19	0	3
Foreman	2721	1206	778	1276
Football	1366	944	660	1078
Garden	255	188	4	1
hall monitor	282	156	59	94
Mobile	45	27	31	23
Salesman	24	9	2	14
table tennis	2470	1668	104	282
Total	7906	4721	1800	2907
Percent	62.612%	37.388%	38.241%	61.759%

During the process of motion estimation,

$S_C = \{\forall \overrightarrow{MV}_{candi}\}$, $\overrightarrow{MV}_{candi}$ is the candidate motion vector of the current block.

$\overrightarrow{MV}_{candi} = (x_{candi}, y_{candi})$

$X = \{\overrightarrow{MV}_{candi} | \overrightarrow{MV}_{candi} \in S_C \land |x_{candi}| \geq |y_{candi}|\}$

$Y = \{\overrightarrow{MV}_{candi} | \overrightarrow{MV}_{candi} \in S_C \land |x_{candi}| < |y_{candi}|\}$

In the simulation, the probabilities of $\mathbf{X}$ and $\mathbf{Y}$

$$P(\mathbf{X}) = \frac{\mathbf{X}}{(\mathbf{X}+\mathbf{Y})} = \frac{12627}{(12627+4707)} = 0.728$$

$$P(\mathbf{Y}) = 1 - P(\mathbf{X}) = 0.272$$

Set $\mathbf{S}_B = \{\forall \overrightarrow{MV}_{best}\}$, $\overrightarrow{MV}_{best}$ is the best motion vector of the current block.

$$\overrightarrow{MV}_{diff} = \overrightarrow{MV}_{best} - \overrightarrow{MV}_{candi} = (x_{diff}, y_{diff})$$

$$\mathbf{X}_X = \{\overrightarrow{MV}_{best} | \overrightarrow{MV}_{best} \in \mathbf{S}_B \wedge |x_{candi}| \geq |y_{candi}| \wedge |x_{diff}| \geq |y_{diff}|\}$$
$$\mathbf{X}_Y = \{\overrightarrow{MV}_{best} | \overrightarrow{MV}_{best} \in \mathbf{S}_B \wedge |x_{candi}| \geq |y_{candi}| \wedge |x_{diff}| < |y_{diff}|\}$$

$$\mathbf{Y}_X = \{\overrightarrow{MV}_{best} | \overrightarrow{MV}_{best} \in \mathbf{S}_B \wedge |x_{candi}| < |y_{candi}| \wedge |x_{diff}| \geq |y_{diff}|\}$$
$$\mathbf{Y}_Y = \{\overrightarrow{MV}_{best} | \overrightarrow{MV}_{best} \in \mathbf{S}_B \wedge |x_{candi}| < |y_{candi}| \wedge |x_{diff}| < |y_{diff}|\}$$

The probabilities of $\mathbf{X}_X, \mathbf{X}_Y, \mathbf{Y}_X$ and $\mathbf{Y}_X$

$$P(\mathbf{X}_X) = \frac{7906}{(7906+4721)} = 0.626$$

$$P(\mathbf{X}_Y) = 1 - P(\mathbf{X}_X) = 0.374$$

$$P(\mathbf{Y}_X) = \frac{1800}{(1800+2907)} = 0.382$$

$$P(\mathbf{Y}_Y) = 1 - P(\mathbf{Y}_X) = 0.618$$

From above simulation, if $\overrightarrow{MV}_{candi}$ is x direction, usually $\overrightarrow{MV}_{diff}$ is x direction. If $\overrightarrow{MV}_{candi}$ is y direction, usually $\overrightarrow{MV}_{diff}$ is y direction. So to speak, effective motion estimation can be operated by selecting the pattern in Figure 1a or Figure 1b depending on the direction of $\overrightarrow{MV}_{candi}$.

3.2 Predictive Directional Rectangular Zonal Search

Here is the algorithm for the proposed PDRZS for estimating the motion vector $\overrightarrow{MV}_{current}$ of the current block.

$\overrightarrow{MV}_{candi}$ is the candidate motion vector of the current block. If the absolute value x of $\overrightarrow{MV}_{candi}$ is bigger than y, the horizontal rectangular search pattern in Figure 1a is selected for searching, and in the opposite case, the vertical rectangular search pattern in Figure 1b is selected.

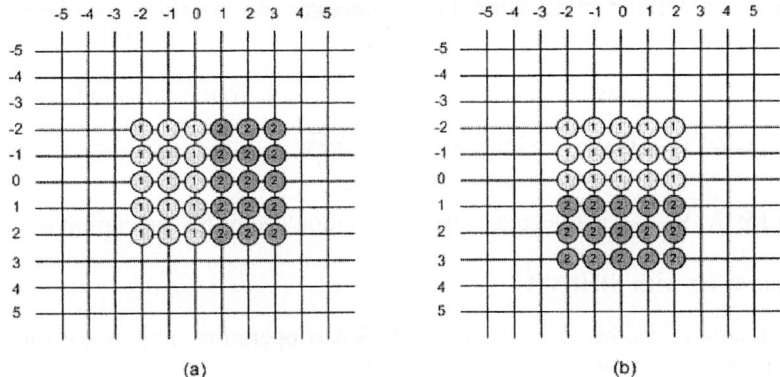

Fig. 1. Search Patterns in PDRZS (a) horizontal rectangular pattern. (b) vertical rectangular pattern.

Step 0: Initialization. Set threshold parameter T.

Step 1: Calculate SAD at motion vector $(0,0)$. If ($SAD \leq T$) then $\overrightarrow{MV}_{current} = (0,0)$ and go to Step 16.

Step 2: Get the $\overrightarrow{MV}_{candi}$. If ($|x \text{ of } \overrightarrow{MV}_{candi}| > 0$) then go to Step 10.

Step 3: Select half of the vertical rectangular search pattern, numbered as one in fig 1b and calculate SADs by using 2-D SAD engine in fig 2.

Step 4: If ($MinSAD \leq T$) then $\overrightarrow{MV}_{current} = \overrightarrow{MV}(MinSAD)$ and go to Step 16.

Step 5: $\overrightarrow{MV}_{current} = \overrightarrow{MV}(MinSAD)$ and bestSAD = MinSAD.

Step 6: Select half of the vertical rectangular search pattern, numbered as two in fig 1b and calculate SADs by using 2-D SAD engine.

Step 7: If ($MinSAD \leq T$) then $\overrightarrow{MV}_{current} = \overrightarrow{MV}(MinSAD)$ and go to Step 16.

Step 8: If (bestSAD > MinSAD) then $\overrightarrow{MV}_{current} = \overrightarrow{MV}(MinSAD)$.

Step 9: Go to Step 16.

Step 10: Select half of the horizontal rectangular search pattern, numbered as one in fig 1a and calculate SADs by using 2-D SAD engine.

Step 11: If ($MinSAD \leq T$) then $\overrightarrow{MV}_{current} = \overrightarrow{MV}(MinSAD)$ and go to 16.

Step 12: $\overrightarrow{MV}_{best} = \overrightarrow{MV}(MinSAD)$ and $bestSAD = MinSAD$.

Step 13: Select half of the horizontal rectangular search pattern, numbered as two in fig 1a and calculate SADs by using 2-D SAD engine.

Step 14: If ($MinSAD \leq T$) then $\overrightarrow{MV}_{current} = \overrightarrow{MV}(MinSAD)$ and go to 16.

Step 15: If ($bestSAD > MinSAD$) then $\overrightarrow{MV}_{current} = \overrightarrow{MV}(MinSAD)$.

Step 16: $\overrightarrow{MV}_{current}$ is selected as the best motion vector for the current block.

3.3 Operating with SDRAM

Diamond pattern has the weakness at the SDRAM operation. That is not suitable for SDRAM burst operation.

Table 2 shows the simulation result of SDRAM operation using APDZS and PDRZS. Simulation was executed on Verilog simulator using memory controller and reference frame buffer in Figure 2 by using APDZS and PDRZS. SDRAM memory controller settings are as below.

Clock(bus frequency) : 100 MHz
CAS latency : 3 cycle
Delay of RAS to CAS cycle : 30ns(nano second)
Delay of Read to Precharge : 30ns
Delay of Refresh to Idle : 30ns
Delay of Precharge to Refresh : 80ns
Refresh cycle : 320ns

Table 2. SDRAM Operation Test Results

Method	Ready cycle (1 frame)	Transfer cycle (1 frame)	Total transfer cycle (1 frame)	Compare Total transfer time	Waiting Period
APDZS	31991	26840	58831	100.000%	54.378%
PDRZS	23977	24585	48562	82.545%	49.374%

Table 2 also shows the simulation result. PDRZS is 17.455% faster at total SDRAM operation than APDZS and 5% better at SDRAM operation efficiency.

4 Hardware Implementation

Based on proposed algorithm-PDRZS, we implemented the motion estimator with about 95K gates and 2048 bytes of on-chip memory using a synthesizable Verilog Hardware Description Language.

4.1 Motion Estimation Block

The core part of this motion estimator is SAD calculator. Block diagram of SAD calculator is shown in Figure 2. Motion estimation is the function that searches a

Predictive Directional Rectangular Zonal Search for Digital Multimedia Processor 275

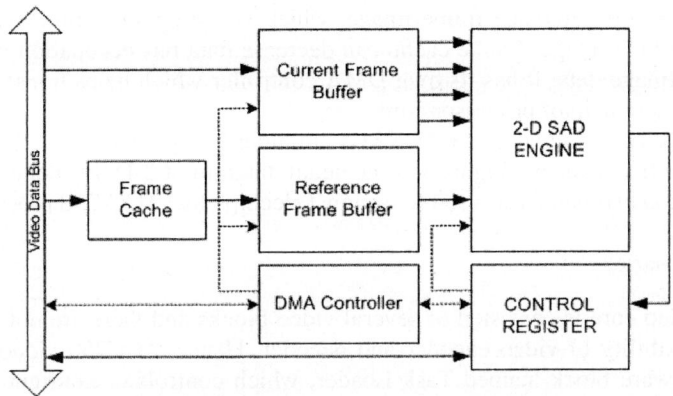

Fig. 2. Block Diagram of SAD Calculator

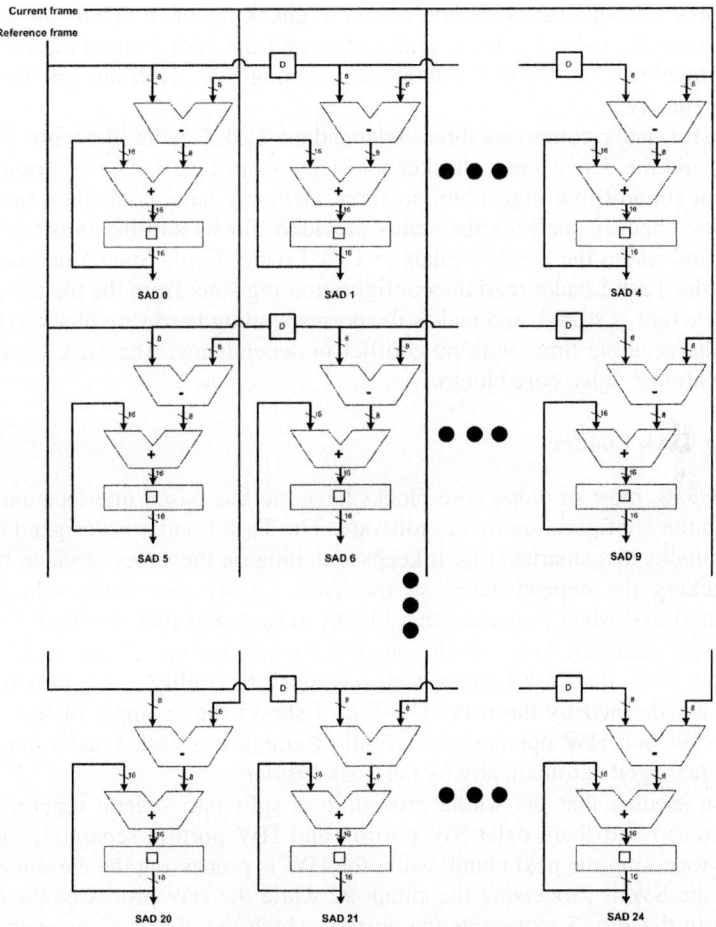

Fig. 3. 2-D SAD Engine

macroblock in the reference frame image, which is analogous with a macroblock in the current frame image. Frame cache can decrease data bus occupation by the reference frame image data. It has its own DMA controller which helps transfer the frame data without any help of processor core.

This block can calculate max 25 SADs simultaneously, which are 20x20 areas in the reference frame image. Figure 3 is the detail diagram of 2-D SAD engine.

This motion estimator was used to design Telechips Inc. TCC-750 processor.

4.2 Task Loader

TCC750 video core is consisted of several video blocks and there are not tightly coupled for flexibility of video encoder and decoder. Hence, TCC750 video core has a special hardware block, named Task Loader, which controls or configures the other video blocks, and manages the dependency between video blocks by means of the predefined data structures including control/depend information.

With Task Loader, the CPUs don't need to check the each video hardware status, and not to start the video hardware at the accurate time after waiting until the dependencies are resolved. Therefore the parallelism among S/W, H/W and another H/W can be obtained easily.

The Task Loader comprises three independent Task Loader elements, the arbitration logic, and the dependency checker for elements in Fig. 4. The arbitration method is based on round-robin algorithm, so three elements have equivalent priority. The Dependency checker analyzes the status of video blocks and the information of the next task, and issues the Ready signals to Task Loader Finite State Machines (FSMs). And then, the Task Loader read the configuration registers from the memory in which the data structure is stored, and makes the corresponding hardware block to start processing at the accurate time, with no conflict in dependency. The Task Loader is able to manage almost video core blocks.

4.3 Using Task Loader

In the TCC750, most of video core blocks have the bus-based interface and need the control and the configuration by the software. The Task Loader is designed to manage the video blocks in a smarter way. It keeps watching on the states of video blocks and keeps checking the dependencies, so the Task Loader determines which block it makes to start and when it makes other blocks to start. For that, the Task Loader utilizes the novel data structure, which contains the information of execution order and dependency. Also, the Task Loader itself has much flexibility to supports the various data structure defined by the user. The Fig. 5 shows the example of the system, in which the SW and HW operate concurrently through the Task Loader, and the HW blocks are managed automatically by the Task Loader.

You can assume that the whole procedure is split into several repetitive chunks (sub-procedure) and there exist SW portion and HW portion separately. The CPUs can keep processing the next chunk while the HW is processing the current chunk. As the Fig 5, the SW is processing the chunk #2 while the HW processes the chunk #1. The shade in the Fig. 5 represents the portion which the chunk #2 is processed. The

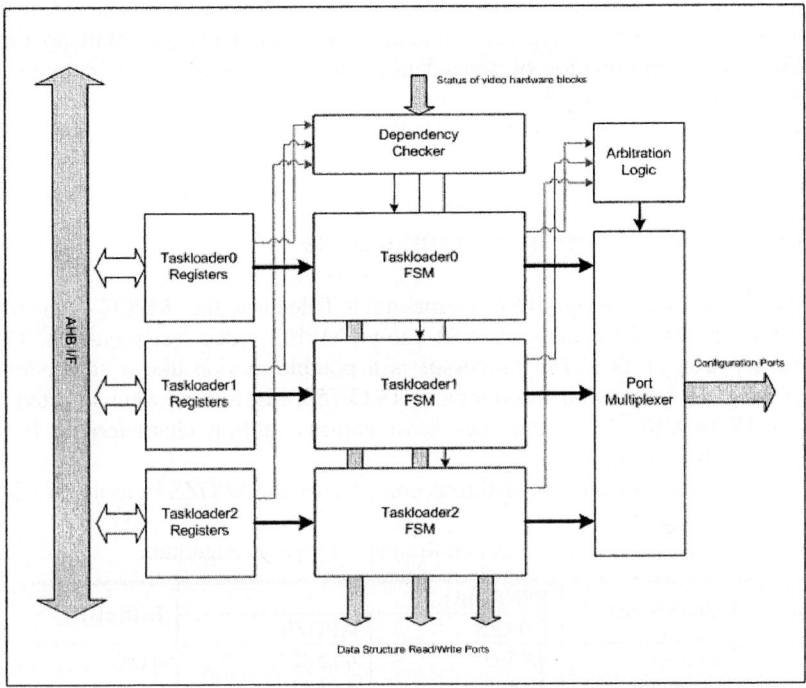

Fig. 4. Task Loader Hardware Architecture

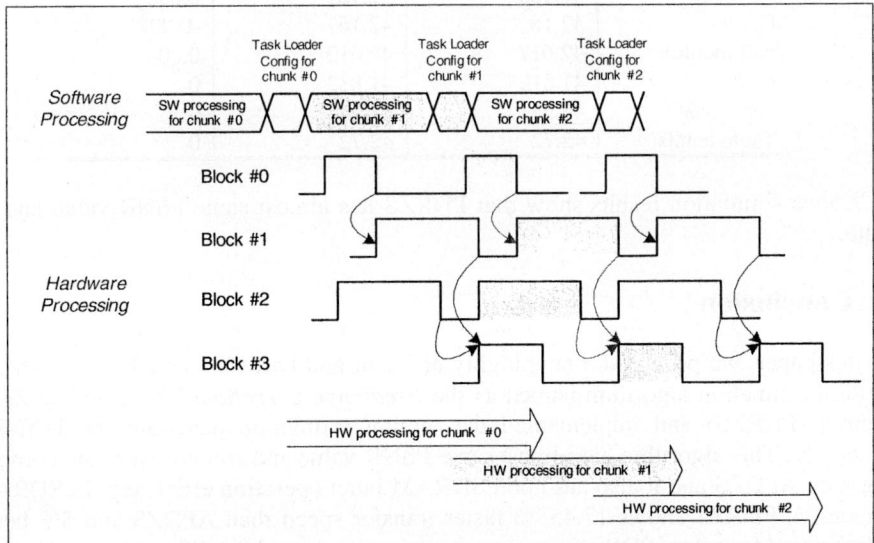

Fig. 5. The parallelism of HW and SW

CPUs need not to check the interrupt or the status of hardware blocks. Moreover, the hardware blocks can also operate concurrently without delayed start-up time. The arrows represent the relation of dependency with two blocks. If one block processing is done, the corresponding block pointed by the arrow is ordered to start by the Task Loader. Because there is no start-up delay, the whole performance of the hardware is improved.

5 Simulation Results and Comparisons

The proposed PDRZS algorithm is embedded Telechips Inc. MPEG-4 encoder software and was tested by using 10 well-known MPEG video test sequence. The main application area of TCC-750 processor is a potable device like a camcoder-phone. Considering the main application area of TCC-750, resolutions were selected ranging from QCIF to CIF. Test sequences have various motion characteristic from low-motion to high-motion.

In Table 3, the proposed algorithm is compared with APDZS in terms of PSNR.

Table 3. Simulation Results of Proposed Algorithm

Video sequence	PSNR(dB)		Diff(dB)
	PDRZS	APDZS	
Carphone	43.595	43.587	0.008
Coastguard	43.647	43.647	0
Container	43.97	43.97	0
Foreman	43.57	43.547	0.023
Football	42.185	42.127	0.058
Garden	42.16	42.167	-0.007
hall monitor	42.617	42.613	0.004
Mobile	41.812	41.812	0
Salesman	43.94	43.94	0
Table tennis	42.72	42.72	0

Above simulation results show that PDRZS has almost same PSNR value and bitrate.

6 Conclusion

In this paper, we proposed a new highly efficient and hardware suitable block-based motion estimation algorithm named as the *Predictive Directional Rectangular Zonal Search* (PDRZS) and implemented the motion estimation hardware for TCC-750 processor. This algorithm has almost same PSNR value and compression rate comparing with APDZS and it also has good SDRAM burst operation efficiency. In SDRAM operation, PDRZS shows 17.455% faster transfer speed than APDZS and 5% better efficiency. Moreover, PDRZS is easy to make a simple and small hardware. Telechips Inc. designed the motion estimation block of TCC-750 multimedia processor using PDRZS by $0.13 \mu m$, 1.2V CMOS technology. TCC-750 processor is especially suitable for portable video en/decoding devices.

References

1. Cavalli, F., Cucchiara, R., Piccardi, M., Prati, A.: Performance analysis of MPEG-4 decoder and encoder. Video/Image Processing and Multimedia Communication 4th EURASIP-IEEE Region 8 International Symposium on VIPromCom, Vol., Iss., 2002 pp. 227-231
2. Stechele, W.: Algorithmic complexity, motion estimation and a VLSI architecture for MPEG-4 core profile video codecs. VLSI Technology, Systems, and Applications, 2001. Proceedings of Technical Papers, 2001 International Symposium on, Vol., Iss., 2001 pp. 172-175
3. Tourapis, A.M., Au, O.C., Liou, M.L.: Highly efficient predictive zonal algorithms for fast block-matching motion estimation. Circuits and Systems for Video Technology, IEEE Transactions on, Vol.12, Iss.10, Oct 2002 pp. 934-947
4. Tourapis, A.M., Au, O.C., Liou, M.L.: Fast block-matching motion estimation using predictive motion vector field adaptive search technique(PMVFAST), ISO/IEC JTC1/SC29/WG11 MPEG2000/M5866, Noordwijkerhout, NL, Mar. 2000.
5. S. Ballista, F. Casalino, C. Lande, MPEG-4: a multimedia standard for the third millennium. 1, IEEE Multimedia, 6(4), 1999, pp. 74-83
6. Pereira F., Ebrahimi T., The MPEG-4 book, Prentice-Hall, 2002
7. Chang, S.F.: Content-Based Video Summarization and Adaptation for Ubiquitous Media Access. Image Analysis and Processing, 2003.Proceedings. 12th International Conference on, Vol., Iss., 17-19 Sept. 2003 pp. 494-496
8. Senda, S.; Nishiyama, K.; Asahi, T.; Yamada, K.: Camera-typing interface for ubiquitous information services. Pervasive Computing and Communications, 2004. PerCom 2004. Proceedings of the Second IEEE Annual Conference on 14-17 March 2004 pp. 366 - 369

Motion Field Refinement and Region-Based Motion Segmentation

Sun-Kyoo Hwang and Whoi-Yul Kim

Division of Electrical and Computer Engineering, Hanyang University,
Haengdang-Dong, Seongdong-Gu, Seoul, Korea
sunkyoo@vision.hanyang.ac.kr, wykim@hanyang.ac.kr

Abstract. In this paper, we propose a method to refine a motion field from image sequences and region-based motion segmentation using the motion information. An initial motion field is generated by a block matching algorithm. We compute the motion profile at each block and define the motion confidence measure from the motion profile. In the refining process, we regulate the motion vectors with low confidence to those with high confidence. In the segmentation stage, each frame of the image sequence is partitioned into regions by a watershed algorithm and a motion vector is assigned to each region. After constructing a region adjacency graph, the graph is segmented by the normalized cuts algorithm. The experiments show that the proposed method provides satisfactory results in motion segmentation from image sequences with or without camera motion.

1 Introduction

Motion segmentation or moving object segmentation is an essential process in analyzing video data. They are base technologies for object-based compression in MPEG-4 [1] and content-based retrieval in MPEG-7 [2]. Therefore, the development of a fast and accurate algorithm for motion segmentation remains an important research problem in video processing.

Various approaches for motion segmentation have been proposed. Tsaig et al. have proposed a Markov Random Field (MRF) based moving object segmentation algorithm [3], [15]. They modeled MRFs on a region adjacency graph and used the motion information to classify regions as foreground or background. By treating the region as an elementary unit for the MRF model, they efficiently reduced the computational complexity. Shi et al. have proposed a motion segmentation algorithm based on a normalized cuts algorithm [4]. A normalized cuts algorithm is a kind of graph partitioning method that overcomes some drawbacks of the conventional minimum cut method. A normalized cut can be obtained by eigen-analysis on a weighted graph. In [4], each pixel is treated as a vertex of the graph and the motion similarity between pixels is assigned on the graph edge as a weight. Smith et al. [5] have developed a Bayesian framework for segmenting a video sequence into ordered motion layers. Their approach focused on the relationship between the edges in consecutive frames.

The estimation of an accurate motion field plays an important role in all of these methods. However, general motion estimation algorithms often generate an inaccurate motion field due to reasons such as noise, aperture, or shadow effects. Therefore, a refining process is required as part of the post-processing of the conventional motion estimation algorithm.

This paper presents a method to refine the initial motion field and to segment moving objects in image sequences by using this refined field. The initial motion field is estimated by a general block matching algorithm and the motion profile of each block is also computed simultaneously. From the motion profile, the confidence of each motion vector is computed and is used to refine the initial motion field. The refined motion field is used to compute a prominent motion vector for each region of the region adjacency graph, which is generated from an image by the watershed algorithm. Final segmentation is obtained by the normalized cuts algorithm. We applied the normalized cuts algorithm on the region adjacency graph (RAG) to speed up the processing time without a loss of accuracy. A block diagram of the proposed method is depicted in Fig. 1.

This paper is organized as follows: Section 2 explains the motion refinement method. In Section 3, we show how to construct a region adjacency graph and segment the graph by using the normalized cuts algorithm. Section 4 shows the experimental results on some video data. Finally, we conclude in section 5.

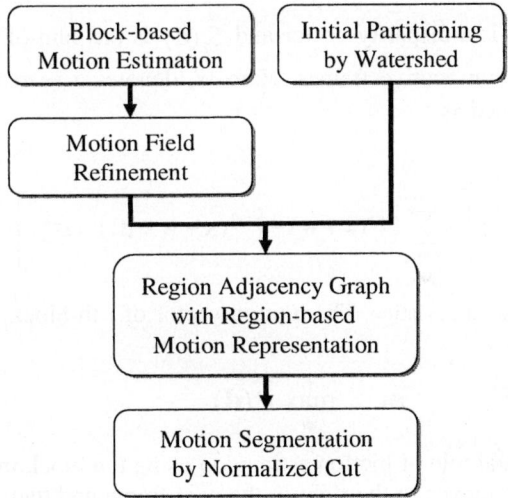

Fig. 1. Block diagram of the proposed method

2 Refined Motion Field Generation

Block matching and optical flow are the most common methods for motion estimation [6]. Especially, the block matching method is widely used due to its lesser hardware complexity. However, the method often fails when a block contains multiple objects with different motions or an aperture problem occurs. In addition noise and shadow have been obstacles to the estimation of an accurate motion vector. Therefore, post-processing to increase the accuracy of motion estimation is required.

2.1 Initial Motion Field and Motion Profile

Various types of block matching methods have been proposed such as the full search, three-step search [6], and diamond search algorithm [7]. Even though the full search method is a rather slow algorithm because the method tests all the candidate blocks exhaustively within the search area, it shows the best performance in accuracy. During the full search process, we can also get useful information, called the motion profile [4].

The motion profile was originally proposed as a measure of the probability distribution of that motion vector at a pixel. Shi et al. used the motion profile in [4] to compute the motion similarity of two image pixels. In this paper, however, we compute the motion profile at each block and use that data in computing the motion confidence. Let $I^t(\mathbf{x})$ denote the image function at time t and at pixel location $\mathbf{x} \in R^2$.

The motion profile of the i-th block can be defined as

$$P_i(\mathbf{d}) = \frac{S_i(\mathbf{d})}{\sum_{W_s} S_i(\mathbf{d})}, \qquad (1)$$

where $\mathbf{d} = (d_x, d_y)$ is a disparity vector and $S_i(\mathbf{d})$ is the sum of the squared difference (SSD) of two consecutive frames. Here W_s denotes a search window where $\mathbf{d}$ exists. $S_i(\mathbf{d})$ is defined as

$$S_i(\mathbf{d}) = \exp\left[-\sum_{\mathbf{w} \in W_b} \left(I^t(\mathbf{x}+\mathbf{w}) - I^{t+1}(\mathbf{x}+\mathbf{w}+\mathbf{d}) \right)^2 / \sigma_{ssd}^2 \right], \qquad (2)$$

where σ_{ssd} is the standard deviation. The motion vector of i-th block, $\mathbf{m}_i = (u_i, v_i)$, is defined as

$$\mathbf{m}_i = \max_{\mathbf{d}} P_i(\mathbf{d}). \qquad (3)$$

Fig. 2 shows an example of motion estimation using the block matching algorithm. The man in Fig. 2(a) moves to the right in the next frame and there is no camera motion. The motion vectors located at the boundary of the man in Fig. 2(b) generally depict the motion correctly. However, the motion vector in the other areas such as the left wall and the man's shirt shows some errors. These motion vectors obtained incorrectly need to be refined in the post process. Fig. 2(c)–(f) show the motion profile of blocks denoted as **A–D** in Fig. 2(a).

2.2 Motion Field Refinement

We think that it is desirable to regulate unreliable motion vectors with reliable ones in the neighborhood. To do this, a confidence measure of the estimated motion should be defined.

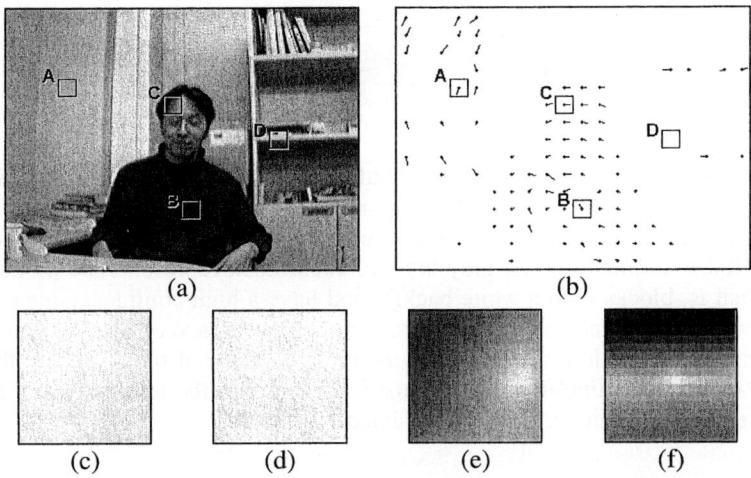

Fig. 2. Motion profile in various locations. (a) is the reference frame. The man in (a) is moving from left to right in front of a static camera. (b) shows the initial motion field acquired by the block matching algorithm. (c) to (f) shows the motion profile of block A to B in (a).

The distribution of the motion profile tells us the level of confidence of the estimated motion. If the motion profile at a block contains a single Gaussian distribution, we think that the estimated motion at the block is reliable as shown in Fig. 2(e) and (f). If the motion profile contains almost uniform distribution, however, the estimated motion vector can be considered ambiguous as illustrated in Figs. 2(c) and (d).

We define the confidence of the motion vector of the i-th block as

$$c_i = \text{var}(P_i) . \tag{4}$$

This is a very simple but reasonable definition of the level of confidence of the motion vector, implying that the motion vector obtained from the motion profile is considered reliable if the value of c_i is high. If the c_i has a low value, it means that the motion vector obtained from the motion profile is uncertain or likely to contain an error. We can suppose that the motion profiles of Fig. 2(c) and (d) have a low value of c_i and those of Fig. 2(e) and (f) have high value of c_i.

The refined motion vector field $\mathbf{m}^r = (u^r, v^r)$ minimizes the energy functional,

$$\varepsilon = \iint \mu \left[(u_x^r)^2 + (u_y^r)^2 + (v_x^r)^2 + (v_y^r)^2 \right] + c_i \left| \mathbf{m}_i^r - \mathbf{m}_i \right| dxdy . \tag{5}$$

This equation is similar to the gradient vector flow (GVF) equation in [8]. When c_i is low, the energy is dominated by the Laplacian of the motion vector, which acts like a smooth filtering. When c_i is large, the energy is minimized by setting $\mathbf{m}_i^r = \mathbf{m}_i$.

By using the calculus of variations [12], equation (5) can be minimized by solving the following Euler-Lagrange equations

$$\begin{cases} \mu\nabla^2 u^r - c_i(u^r - u) = 0 \\ \mu\nabla^2 v^r - c_i(v^r - v) = 0 \end{cases}, \tag{6}$$

where ∇^2 is the Laplacian operator. Equation (6) can be solved numerically by iterative methods. For details, see [8].

Fig. 3 shows the result of the motion field refinement. Figs. 3(a) and 3(b) show two consecutive images in sequence. There is no camera motion involved and only the person is moving from left to right. Fig. 3(c) shows the initial motion field generated by the full search method. The gray-level of each block represents the motion confidence. That is, blocks with a white background have a high confidence measure. Fig. 3(d) shows a refined motion field. To prevent the appearance of a new motion vector in blocks with no motion, we displayed the motion vector of blocks where the initial motion existed. Note that the incorrect motion vectors in the left wall are effectively diminished and those in the shirt are regulated.

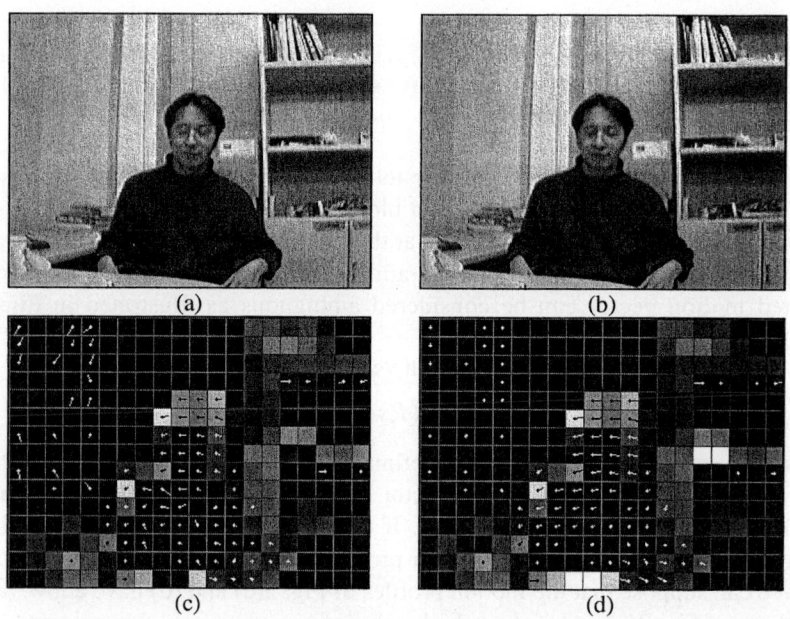

Fig. 3. Initial motion field and refined motion field. (a) and (b) are consecutive images in sequence. (c) shows the initial motion field and the refined motion field is displayed in (d).

3 Region-Based Motion Representations and Segmentation

A region is a set of pixels that have similar features such as gray-level, color, or motion. By treating regions as the elementary unit for image processing, we can reduce the computational complexity without a corresponding loss of accuracy.

3.1 Region Adjacency Graph (RAG)

To partition an image into a set of homogenous regions, we used the watershed algorithm [9], [10]. The watershed algorithm segments an image into uniform regions by interpreting the input image as a topological surface. From the result of the watershed algorithm, we construct a region adjacency graph (RAG) $G = (V, E)$. Fig. 4 shows the detailed process for the construction of RAG with a block diagram.

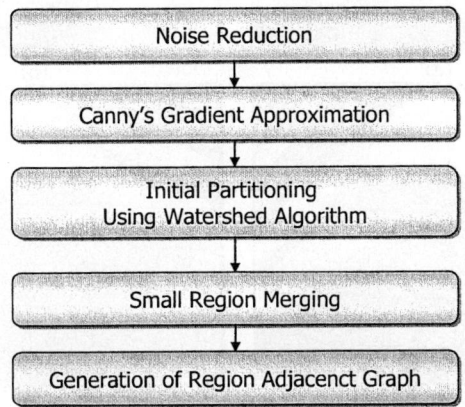

Fig. 4. Block diagram for constructing a region adjacent graph

As the watershed algorithm is very sensitive to noise, it is preferable to use a noise reduction filter in the pre-processing. To reduce noise in this paper, we used an anisotropic diffusion filter [13]. The anisotropic diffusion filter removes noise effectively without destroying the topological structure of an image. To acquire the Canny's gradient approximation of an input image [14], the image is convolved with the first derivative of a Gaussian:

$$G(x) = \frac{-x}{\sqrt{2\pi}\sigma^3} e^{-x^2/2\sigma^2}, \tag{7}$$

where σ is the standard deviation of the Gaussian. After applying the watershed algorithm to $G(x)$, tiny regions are merged into neighborhood regions. This merging step is required to reduce the computational complexity in the graph partitioning. Fig. 5 shows an example of the initial partitioning for the construction of the RAG.

Let $R=\{R_1, R_2, ..., R_n\}$ denote a set of regions obtained by the watershed algorithm. R can be thought as a set of the vertices of the RAG. For region-based motion segmentation, we assign a motion vector to each region. The motion vector of a region can be computed from the refined motion field by a simple averaging operation as follows:

Fig. 5. Initial partitioning of an image. (a) is a selected frame of a video, (b) is the result of the anisotropic diffusion filter, (c) is the result of the watershed algorithm and (d) is the final partitioning with small region merging.

$$\mathbf{m}_{R_i} = \frac{1}{N} \sum_{(x,y) \in R_i} \mathbf{m}^r_{(x,y)} . \tag{8}$$

Note that the block-based motion representation is converted to a region-based one and the image segmentation problem is converted to a graph partitioning problem.

If two regions R_i and R_j are adjacent, it is considered that there is an edge E_{ij}. The weight on the edge of RAG represents the motion dissimilarity of the two regions. The motion dissimilarity between i-th and j-th region is simply defined as

$$d(i, j) = \left| \mathbf{m}_{R_i} - \mathbf{m}_{R_j} \right| . \tag{9}$$

3.2 Graph Partitioning

We used a normalized cuts algorithm to partition the RAG [4], [11]. A normalized cut, proposed by Shi, gives the criterion to partition a graph into perceptually significant groups. A normalized cut can be obtained by a simple eigen-analysis on the modified weight matrix.

Let $G = (V, E)$ be a weighted graph where V is a set of vertices and E is a set of edges. The graph can be separated into two disjoint sets, A, B, $A \cup B = V$, $A \cap B = \emptyset$ by removing edges between the two sets. The total weight on the edges removed is called the *cut*: $cut(A, B) = \sum_{u \in A, v \in B} w(u, v)$. Finding a partition which minimizes the cut separates the graph effectively; however, it has undesirable bias when there is a set with a small number of vertices. To overcome the shortcomings of the conventional cut, a *normalized cut (Ncut)* is proposed:

$$Ncut(A, B) = \frac{cut(A, B)}{assoc(A, V)} + \frac{cut(A, B)}{assoc(B, V)}. \tag{10}$$

where $assoc(A, V) = \sum_{u \in A, t \in V} w(u, t)$ is the total connection from nodes in A to all nodes in the graph and $assoc(B, V)$ is similarly defined. Minimizing the normalized cut partitions the graph without the biased effect.

To partition the graph with the normalized cut, we compute the weight matrix $\mathbf{W}$ with $\mathbf{W}(i, j) = w_{ij}$ and a diagonal matrix $\mathbf{D}$ which has the diagonal element with $\mathbf{d}(i) = \sum_j w_{ij}$. In the normalized cuts framework, the eigen-analysis of the generalized eigenvalue system $(\mathbf{D} - \mathbf{W})\mathbf{y} = \lambda \mathbf{D}\mathbf{y}$ gives the best partitioning. This generalized eigenvalue system can be transformed into a standard eigenvalue system as equation (11). For details, see [11].

$$\mathbf{A}\mathbf{z} = \lambda \mathbf{z}$$
$$\begin{cases} \mathbf{A} = \mathbf{D}^{-1/2}(\mathbf{D} - \mathbf{W})\mathbf{D}^{-1/2} \\ \mathbf{z} = \mathbf{D}^{1/2}\mathbf{y} \end{cases} \tag{11}$$

In our segmentation method, the weight on the graph edge is assigned by the motion similarity of the two adjacent regions:

$$w_{ij} = \begin{cases} \exp(-d(i, j) / \sigma_m^2) & Depth(i, j) < k \\ 0 & \text{Otherwise} \end{cases}, \tag{12}$$

where $d(i, j) = |\mathbf{m}_i - \mathbf{m}_j|$ is the motion difference and $Depth(i, j)$ is the depth of the connectivity from i-th to the j-th vertex.

4 Experimental Results

The proposed segmentation method is applied to two video sequences with or without the camera motion. The experiment was performed with a 1.8GHz Pentium IV PC with 512Mbyte RAM and was implemented with Microsoft visual C++ .NET. The motion similarity is considered for regions where the depth is not greater than 5(k=5).

Fig. 6 shows the segmentation result from a synthesized image sequence. In this image sequence, the background composed with small squares is moved to the lower-left and the foreground object composed with larger squares is moved to the upper-right (Fig. 6(a),(b)). Fig. 6(c) shows the motion vector of each region by a different color. Regions with the same color have the same motion vector. This motion information is used to compute the motion similarity between adjacent regions and the segmentation result by using the normalized cuts algorithm is presented in Fig. 6(d).

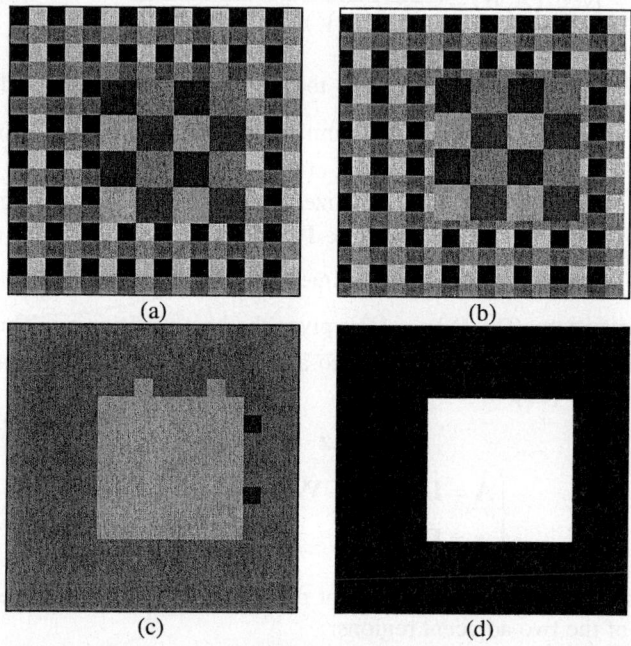

Fig. 6. Initial motion field and refined motion field. (a) and (b) are consecutive images in sequence. (c) shows the initial motion field and the refined motion field is displayed in (d).

Fig. 7 shows the segmentation result of videos without camera motion. In Fig. 7(a), a person is moving from left to right in the front of a static camera. Because the video is generated by a web camera, it contains an excessive amount of noise. Nevertheless, the proposed method separated the person neatly (Fig. 7(b)). Fig. 7(c) is a selected frame of a video which is obtained in the same way and the segmentation result is shown in Fig. 7(d).

Fig. 8 shows the result of the motion segmentation of the foreman video. Because the video contains complex camera motion, the segmented results have an undesirable background patch. However, we think it is satisfactory because it is fully automatic segmentation.

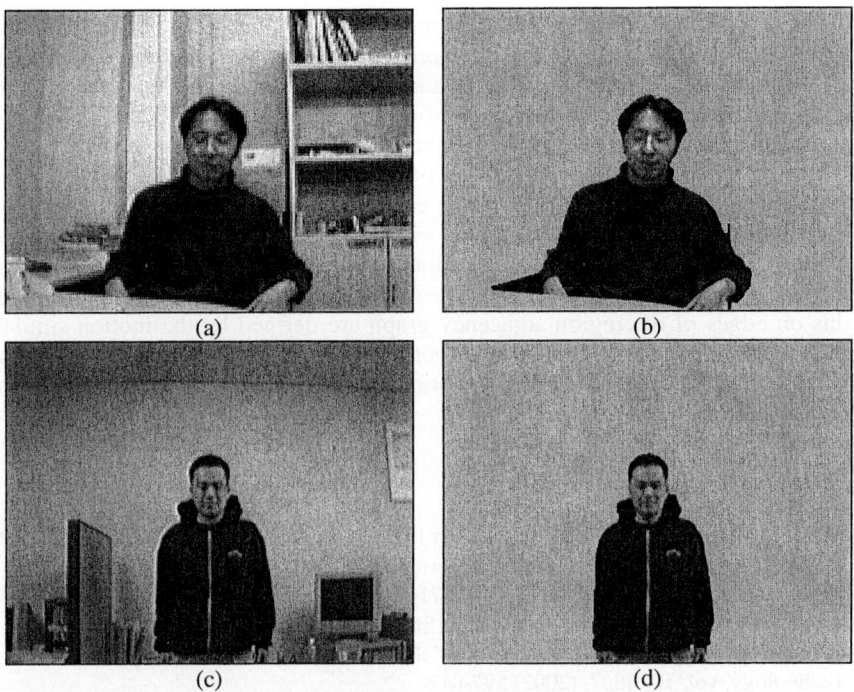

Fig. 7. Segmentation results from a video without camera motion. (a) and (c) are selected frames acquired by web camera. (b) and (d) show the segmentation results.

Fig. 8. Segmentation results from a video with camera motion. (a) is a selected frame from the "foreman" sequence and (b) shows the segmentation result.

5 Conclusion

We proposed a region-based motion segmentation method, where the estimated motion vector is refined with a motion confidence measure. To compute the initial motion field, we used a well-known block matching algorithm. While searching the motion vector of each block, we also computed the motion profile which was originally proposed as a measure of the probability distribution of motion vectors. In this paper, we computed the variance of the motion profile and used that as the motion confidence measure. With the motion confidence measure, unreliable motion vectors are regulated with reliable ones in the neighborhood.

To transform the input image into a set of homogenous regions, we used the watershed algorithm. By treating regions as an elementary unit for further processing, we reduced the computational complexities without a corresponding loss of accuracy. Each frame is converted into a region adjacency graph and the graph is partitioned into perceptually significant groups by means of the normalized cuts algorithm. The weights on edges of the region adjacency graph are defined by the motion similarity which is computed by using the refined motion field. Experiments show that the proposed method gives satisfactory segmentation results for various videos with or without camera motion.

References

1. MPEG-4 Video Verification Model Version 15.0, ISO/IEC JTC1/SC29/WG11 N3093, (1999)
2. Bober, M. "MPEG-7 Visual Shape Descriptors," IEEE Trans. Circuits and Systems for Video Technology, vol. 11, no. 6, (2001) 716-719.
3. Tsaig, Y. and A. Averbuch, "Automatic Segmentation of Moving Objects in Video Sequences: A Region Labeling Approach," IEEE Trans. Circuits and Systems for Video Technology, vol. 12, no. 7, (2002) 597-612.
4. Shi, J. and J. Malik, "Motion segmentation and tracking using normalized cuts," Sixth International Conference on Computer Vision, (1998) 1154-1160.
5. Smith, P., T. Drummond, and R. Cipolla, "Layered motion segmentation and depth ordering by tracking edges," IEEE Trans. Pattern Analysis and Machine Intelligence, vol. 26, no. 4, (2004) 479-494.
6. Tekalp, A. M., Digital video processing, Prentice-Hall, (1995) 72-116.
7. Zhu, S. and K-K. Ma, "A New Diamond Search Algorithm for Fast Block-Matching Motion Estimation," IEEE Trans. Image Processing, vol. 9, no. 2, (2000) 287-290.
8. Xu, C. and J. L. Prince "Snakes, Shapes, and Gradient Vector Flow," IEEE Trans. Image Processing, vol. 7, no. 3, (1998) 359-369.
9. Vincent, L. and P. Soille, "Watersheds in digital spaces: an efficient algorithm based on immersion simulations," IEEE Trans. Pattern Analysis and Machine Intelligence, vol. 13, no. 6, (1991) 583-598.
10. De Smet, P. and D. De Vleeschauwer, "Performance and Scalability of a highly optimized rainfalling watershed algorithm," Proc. Int. Conf. on Image Science, Systems and technology, (1998) 266-273.
11. Shi, J. and J. Malik, "Normalized cuts and image segmentation," IEEE Trans. Pattern Analysis and Machine Intelligence, vol. 22, no. 8, (2000) 888-905.
12. Strang, G., "Introduction to Applied Mathematics," Wellesley-Cambridge Press, (1986).
13. Perona, P. and J. Malik, "Scale Space and Edge Detection Using Anisotropic Diffusion," IEEE Trans. on Pattern Analysis and Machine Intelligence, vol. 12, no. 7, (1990) 629-639.
14. Canny, J., "A computational approach to edge detection," IEEE Trans. Pattern Analysis and Machine Intelligence, vol. 8, (1986) 679–698.
15. Geman, S. and D. Geman, "Stochastic relaxation, gibbs distributions and the Bayesian restoration of images," IEEE Trans. Pattern Analysis and Machine Intelligence, vol. 6, (1984) 721–741.

Motion Adaptive De-interlacing with Horizontal and Vertical Motions Detection

Chung-Chi Lin[1], Ming-Hwa Sheu[1], Huann-Keng Chiang[1], and Chishyan Liaw[2]

[1] Graduate School of Engineering Science and Technology,
National Yunlin University of Science & Technology,
123 University Rd. Section 3, Touliu, Yunlin 640, Taiwan
`cclin@thu.edu.tw`, `{sheumh, chianghk}@yuntech.edu.tw`
[2] Department of Computer Science and Information Engineering, Tunghai University,
181 Taichung-Kung Rd. Section 3, Taichung 407, Taiwan
`liaw@thu.edu.tw`

Abstract. A motion adaptive de-interlacing technique with horizontal and vertical motions detection is proposed and its performances are examined. Object movement happens quite often in film broadcasting and normally they move horizontally, vertically, or diagonally. The movements tend to destabilize the quality of performance such as jagged effect, blurred effect, and artifacts effect, while de-interlacing technique is utilized. In our proposed method, de-interlacing begins with object motion detection, which is to ensure that the interfield information is used precisely. The proposed method also utilizes intrafield de-interlacing by median edge dependent interpolation, Median EDI, while the object movement is not detected. The simulation results show that the proposed algorithm exhibits better performances than other interpolation algorithms.

1 Introduction

The current NTSC system uses the interlaced scan technique to display video sequence. However, the technique creates undesirable visual artifacts and makes the lines flicker, twitter, and crawl as results of the interlaced scan. On the other hand, the technique of interlaced scan is unsuitable for devices like LCD displays, personal computer monitors, and HDTV that require a progressive scan format. Moreover, the new display systems support progressive scan in order to reduce artifacts in display and improve the quality of the picture. Thus, de-interlacing techniques are important to the quality of display.

Currently, the most popular broadcast picture format is 480-line interlacing. In digital broadcast, new picture progressive formats with 480 or 720 lines are used. Therefore, picture format conversion techniques are important for multi-format broadcast with one source. Numerous de-interlacing techniques have been proposed for interlaced to progressive scan conversion [1]-[17], which can be roughly classified into intrafield de-interlacing, interfield de-interlacing, motion adaptive de-interlacing, and motion compensated de-interlacing.

Intrafield de-interlacing [2]-[7] uses a single field to reconstruct one complete frame. The most simple and conventional methods are line doubling and bilinear interpolation in the vertical direction. The technique works fairly well for low frequency images with no degradation. However, it either creates a jagged effect in the oblique edge or generates blurring effects, particularly in the high frequency area. To redress these problems, the edge-based line average, ELA [2], method is widely used. The edge-based line average method extracts edge information and calculates the average between lines as interpolation. This method provides good results when the edge can be correctly estimated. Nevertheless, it has shortcomings when wrong edge information is used, and it is sensitive to small pixel values. Park *et al.* [3] proposed an edge dependent interpolation, EDI, algorithm based on a horizontal edge pattern. The EDI algorithm has a visually good performance in intrafield de-interlacing.

Interfield de-interlacing [2], [8]-[11] generates a full progressive frame by directly merging two consecutive fields. Normally the video quality is better than that of intrafield de-interlacing in static area, but the line-crawling effect occurs in motion area.

Motion adaptive de-interlacing [2], [7]-[9], [12]-[14] has the advantages of both intrafield de-interlacing and interfield de-interlacing. If non-motion is detected, interfield de-interlacing is able to present a pleasing resolution with low computational complexity; otherwise, intrafield de-interlacing is used. Lin *et al.* [13] described a motion adaptive de-interlacing algorithm that consists of ELA-Median directional interpolation with same-parity 4-field horizontal motion detection. The same-parity 4-field horizontal motion detection detects horizontal motion and makes accurate determination about where objects are going to move.

Motion compensated de-interlacing [8]-[10], [14]-[17] is to present a macroblock searching for a most similar block in the two successive even or odd fields and calculates its motion vectors to form a new field. However, this approach is more complex to implement and it is difficult to obtain good results without reliable motion estimation. Jung *et al.* [15] described a de-interlacing method using motion compensated interpolation. In the algorithm, the bi-directional motion is estimated between the same parity fields, i.e., the previous and next field, and the motion vector is refined in the interpolated field.

The motion adaptive de-interlacing techniques are capable of improving the quality of the visual results. However, most of them focus on the horizontal motion detection only; nevertheless, their performances are also affected by vertical motion. The vertical motion tends to destabilize the quality of performance while de-interlacing technique is utilized. It either generates a jagged effect, blurring effect, or artifacts effect. This paper presents a motion adaptive de-interlacing that includes intrafield de-interlacing by median edge dependent interpolation, Median EDI, and interfield de-interlacing with 4-field horizontal motion detection and 4-field vertical motion detection. In section 2, the proposed algorithm is discussed in detail. In section 3, extensive simulation results are presented. Finally, the conclusions are given in section 4.

2 The Proposed Method

In our proposed method, the first stage of de-interlacing is motion detection, which detects horizontal motion and vertical motion as well. If the motion is detected, then the interfield information is used for interpolation according to different directional motions. If the motion is not detected, then intrafield de-interlacing is used for interpolation by Median EDI. The block diagram of our proposed method is illustrated in Fig. 1. In the rest of this section, the scheme of interfield de-interlacing with horizontal and vertical motions detection is discussed in section 2.1, followed by intrafield de-interlacing using median edge dependent interpolation in section 2.2.

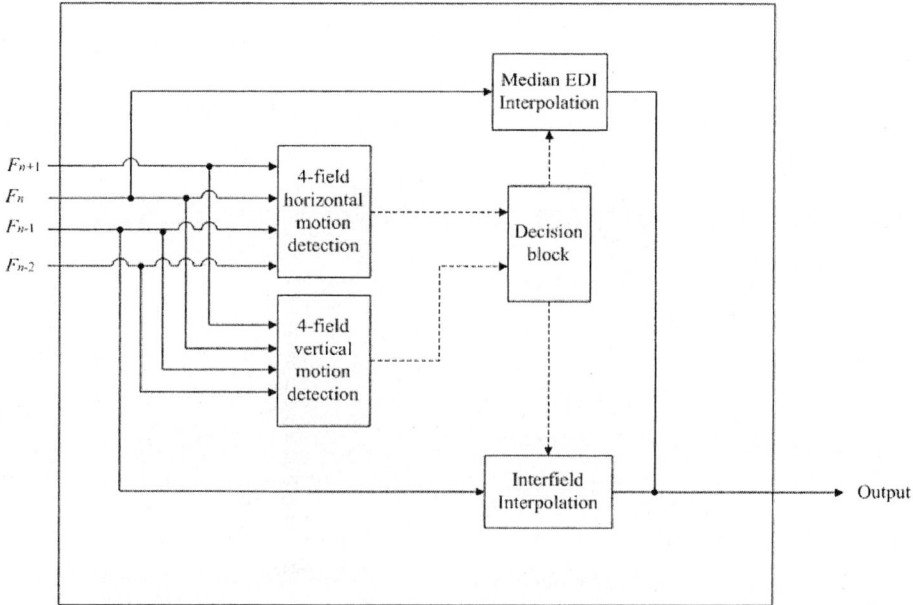

Fig. 1. Block diagram of proposed method (solid-line: data flow; dash-line: control line)

2.1 De-interlacing with Horizontal and Vertical Motions Detection

We now start from horizontal and vertical motions detection of our method. Let $F_{n-2}(i,j)$, $F_{n-1}(i,j)$, $F_n(i,j)$, and $F_{n+1}(i,j)$ denote as the field before previous field, the previous field, current field, and the next field, respectively, where the two dimensional spatial indices (i,j) are $i=1, ..., W$ and $j=1, ..., H$; and W and H are the width and the height of frame, respectively. In motion detection, the absolute difference value of pixels within 2-field [12], field F_{n-1} and F_{n+1}, leads to a wrong decision if the object moves too fast. Consequently, line crawling effect occurs due to the erroneous detection. The 4-field motion detection with extra field difference between F_{n-2} and F_n detects more motion information than 2-field motion detection; thus the line crawling effect can be eliminated.

In 4-field horizontal motion detection [13], five directional temporal interpolations are used to achieve higher resolution than that of interfield interpolation as shown in Fig. 2. The method uses a 1×3 block to find the absolute difference value of block matching between F_{n-1} and F_{n+1} for five directional temporal interpolation. If the minimum difference of block matching is smaller than the threshold T_1, and the pixel difference between F_{n-2} and F_n is also smaller than the threshold T_2, the temporal prediction of horizontal motion will be adopted.

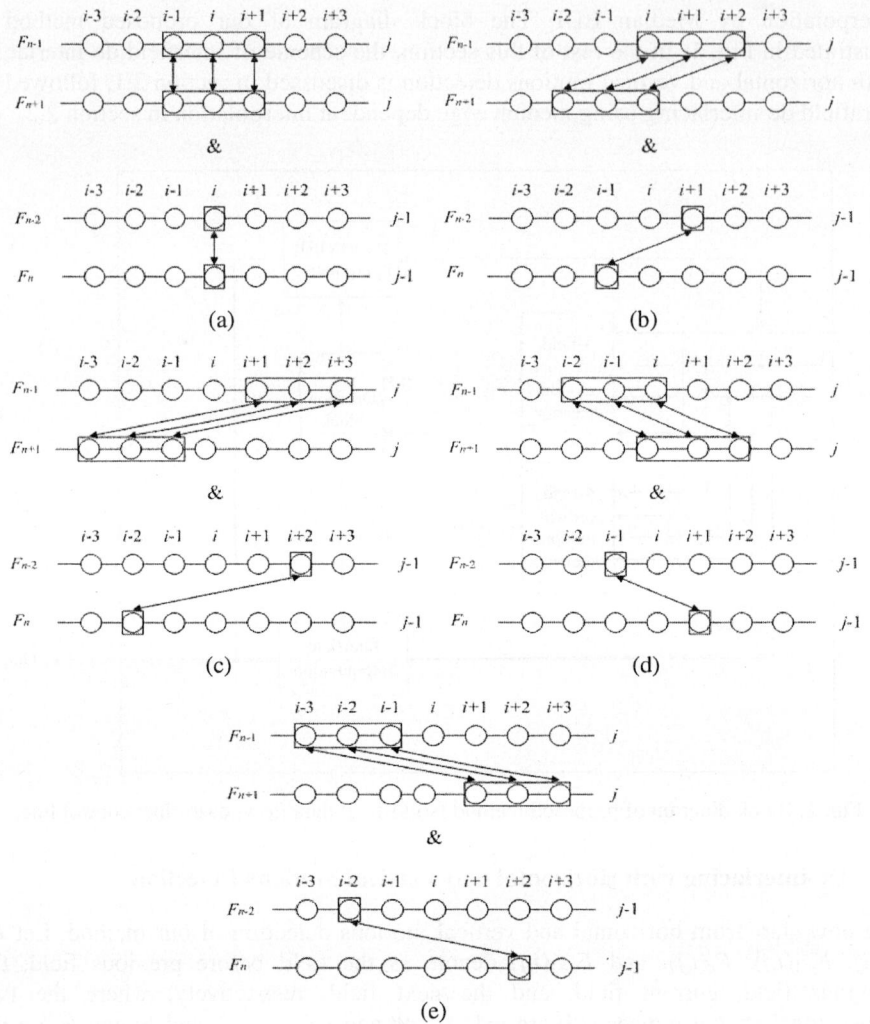

Fig. 2. 4-field horizontal motion detection

Normally, the object moves horizontally, vertically, or diagonally. In 4-field vertical motion detection, the upward and downward directional motions are discussed. We separate vertical motion to be the upward, downward, and diagonal motions that ten directional temporal interpolations are used to achieve higher resolution than that of interfield interpolation. In Fig. 3, five directional temporal interpolations of upward $90°$ motion and upward diagonal $30°$, $45°$, $135°$, and $150°$ motions are used. The method uses a 1×3 block to find the absolute difference value of block matching between F_{n-1} and F_{n+1} for five directional temporal interpolation. If the minimum difference of block matching is smaller than the threshold T_1, and the pixel difference between F_{n-2} and F_n is also smaller than the threshold T_2, the temporal prediction of upward or upward diagonal motions will be adopted. The method for the temporal prediction of downward and downward diagonal motions is processed similar to that of upward motion and upward diagonal motions detection.

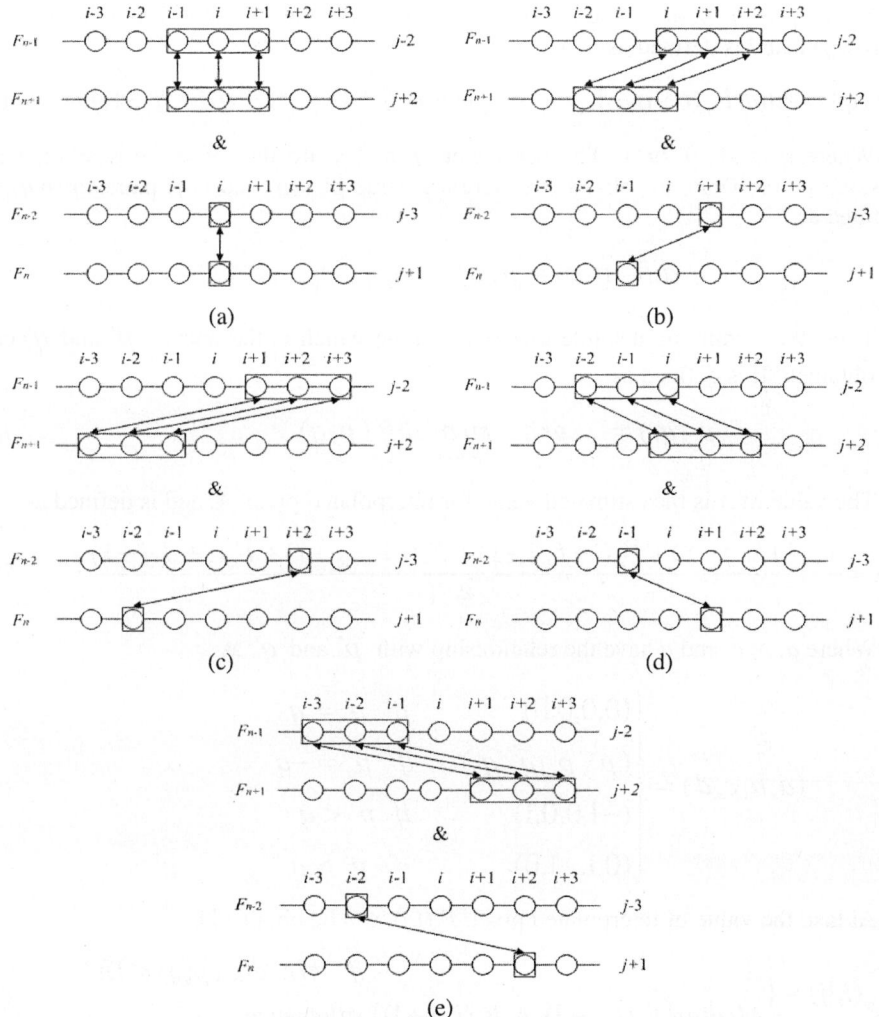

Fig. 3. 4-field upward motion and upward diagonal motions detection

2.2 Intrafield De-interlacing Using Median EDI

Edge dependent interpolation [3] is a technique of intrafield de-interlacing but some artifacts occurs due to erroneous detection in a non-dominant directional edge region. In this section is proposed to the Median EDI that it can eliminate the artifacts by interpolating the missing pixels according to the classification of the edge region.

In current frame, the value of interpolated pixel, $F_n(i,j)$, is decided by Median EDI method that the value of interpolated pixel. Let $u(p)$ be the sum of the values of three consecutive pixels in row $j-1$, and be defined as

$$u(p) = sum(F_n(i+p-1, j-1), F_n(i+p, j-1), F_n(i+p+1, j-1)), \qquad (1)$$

Where p is -1, 0, or 1. The $v(q)$ is the sum of the values of three consecutive pixels in row $j+1$ and is defined as

$$v(q) = sum(F_n(i+q-1, j+1), F_n(i+q, j+1), F_n(i+q+1, j+1)), \qquad (2)$$

Where q is -1, 0, or 1. The parameters p and q are the reference position with missing pixel. Thus, the absolute difference value of $u(p)$ and $v(q)$ pair, $diff(p,q)$, is defined as

$$diff(p,q) = |u(p) - v(q)| \quad , \qquad (3)$$

Thus, the minimum absolute difference value which is the pair of p' and q' can be obtained. It is defined as

$$(p', q') = \arg\min_{-1 \le p,q \le 1} diff(p,q) \quad , \qquad (4)$$

The value of A is the estimated value for interpolated pixel, A, and is defined as

$$A = \frac{F_n(i+a, j-1) + F_n(i+b, j-1) + F_n(i+c, j+1) + F_n(i+d, j+1)}{4}, \qquad (5)$$

Where a, b, c, and d have the relationship with p' and q' as

$$(a,b,c,d) = \begin{cases} (0,0,0,0) & \text{if } p' = q' \\ (p', p', q', q') & \text{if } p' = -q' \\ (-1,0,0,1) & \text{if } p' < q' \\ (0,1,-1,0) & \text{if } p' > q' \end{cases} \qquad (6)$$

At last, the value of interpolated pixel, $F_n(i,j)$, can be obtained by

$$F_n(i,j) = \begin{cases} A & \text{if } \min diff(p,q) < Th \\ Median(F_n(i, j-1), A, F_n(i, j+1)) & \text{otherwise} \end{cases} \qquad (7)$$

Where a threshold parameter Th needs to be set in advance. This method could avoid artifacts while erroneous detected in a non-dominant directional edge region.

3 Simulation Results

The proposed algorithm is coded in C++ and executed on personal computer. To evaluate the performance of de-interlacing with horizontal and vertical motions, three threshold values used in the simulations are set empirically to: $T_1 = 45$, $T_2 = 15$, and $Th = 15$. The test video sequences are illustrated in Table 1. The performances of our proposed algorithm with that of bilinear, ELA [2], EDI [3], and Lin [13] are analyzed. In table 2, the proposed method has better performance than other algorithms. Fig. 4 to Fig. 6 demonstrates that our proposed algorithm for horizontal and vertical motions detection present a more pleasing visual quality. The average PSNR of the results from our method and from different interpolation methods for various sequences are compared in Table 3. And Fig. 7 shows the PSNR performance of the various de-interlacing methods on some video sequences. The results also show that the proposed algorithm has better average PSNR than other algorithms.

Table 1. The test video sequences

Video Sequences	Frame size	Number of frame
Akiyo	176x144	300
Coastguard	176x144	300
Container	176x144	300
Hall Monitor	176x144	325
Mother and Daughter	176x144	300
Weather	360x243	300
Table Tennis	352x288	300
News	176x144	300
Silent	176x144	450

Table 2. PSNR in Fig. 4-6

Name	Bilinear	ELA	EDI	Lin [13]	Proposed
Akiyo	36.25	34.86	36.30	49.61	50.36
Coastguard	27.12	26.66	26.93	29.46	29.73
Container	26.75	26.37	26.55	34.96	35.16
Hall monitor	28.39	27.65	28.27	37.79	38.35
Mother and Daughter	32.75	32.64	32.89	46.20	46.91
Weather	24.10	25.15	25.24	37.62	38.69
Table Tennis	26.39	24.87	26.07	36.58	37.43
News	30.50	27.65	29.94	39.46	41.97
Silent	32.01	31.30	31.97	44.73	45.19

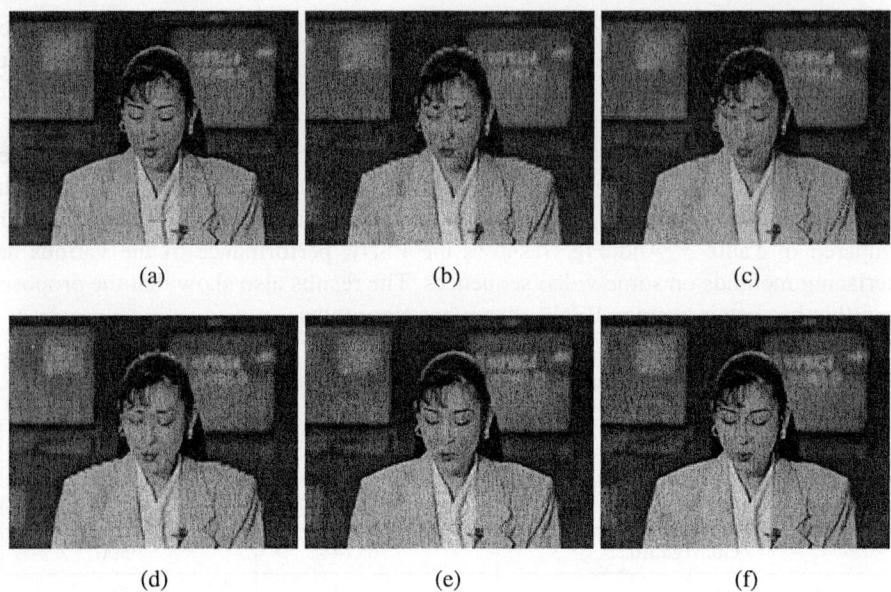

Fig. 4. Akiyo (a) Original (b) Bilinear (c) ELA (d) EDI (e) Lin [13] (f) Proposed

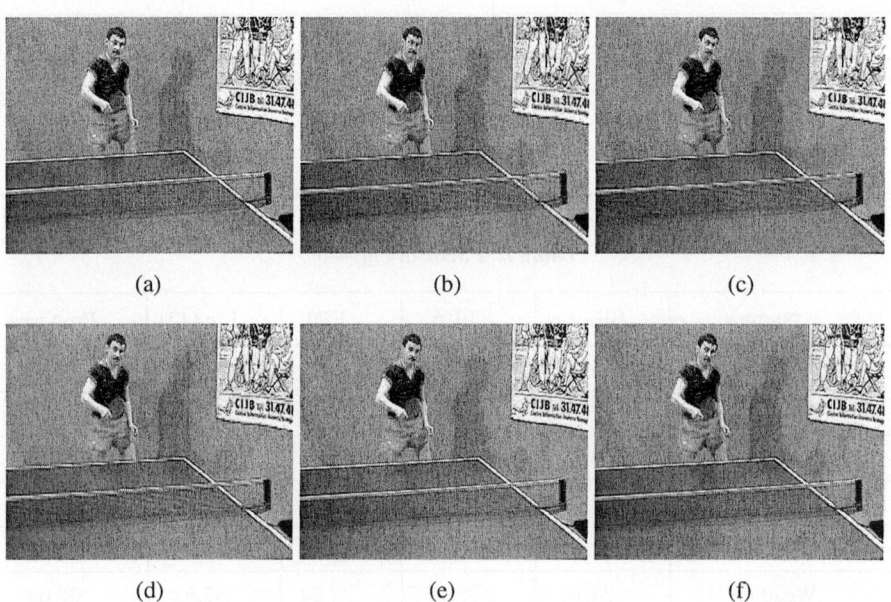

Fig. 5. Table Tennis (a) Original (b) Bilinear (c) ELA (d) EDI (e) Lin [13] (f) Proposed

Fig. 6. News (a) Original (b) Bilinear (c) ELA (d) EDI (e) Lin [13] (f) Proposed

Table 3. Average PSNR of the various de-interlacing methods on some video sequences

Average	Bilinear	ELA	EDI	Lin [13]	Proposed
Akiyo	36.14	35.00	36.22	41.48	42.34
Coastguard	26.57	26.23	26.42	27.06	27.32
Container	26.11	25.81	25.92	33.20	33.48
Hall monitor	27.75	27.06	27.64	34.62	35.23
Mother and Daughter	34.01	33.79	34.13	39.39	39.90
Weather	23.29	24.21	24.21	31.00	31.33
Table Tennis	27.44	26.40	27.26	32.06	32.54
News	30.02	27.55	29.54	35.73	36.46
Silent	32.28	31.58	32.27	36.51	36.92

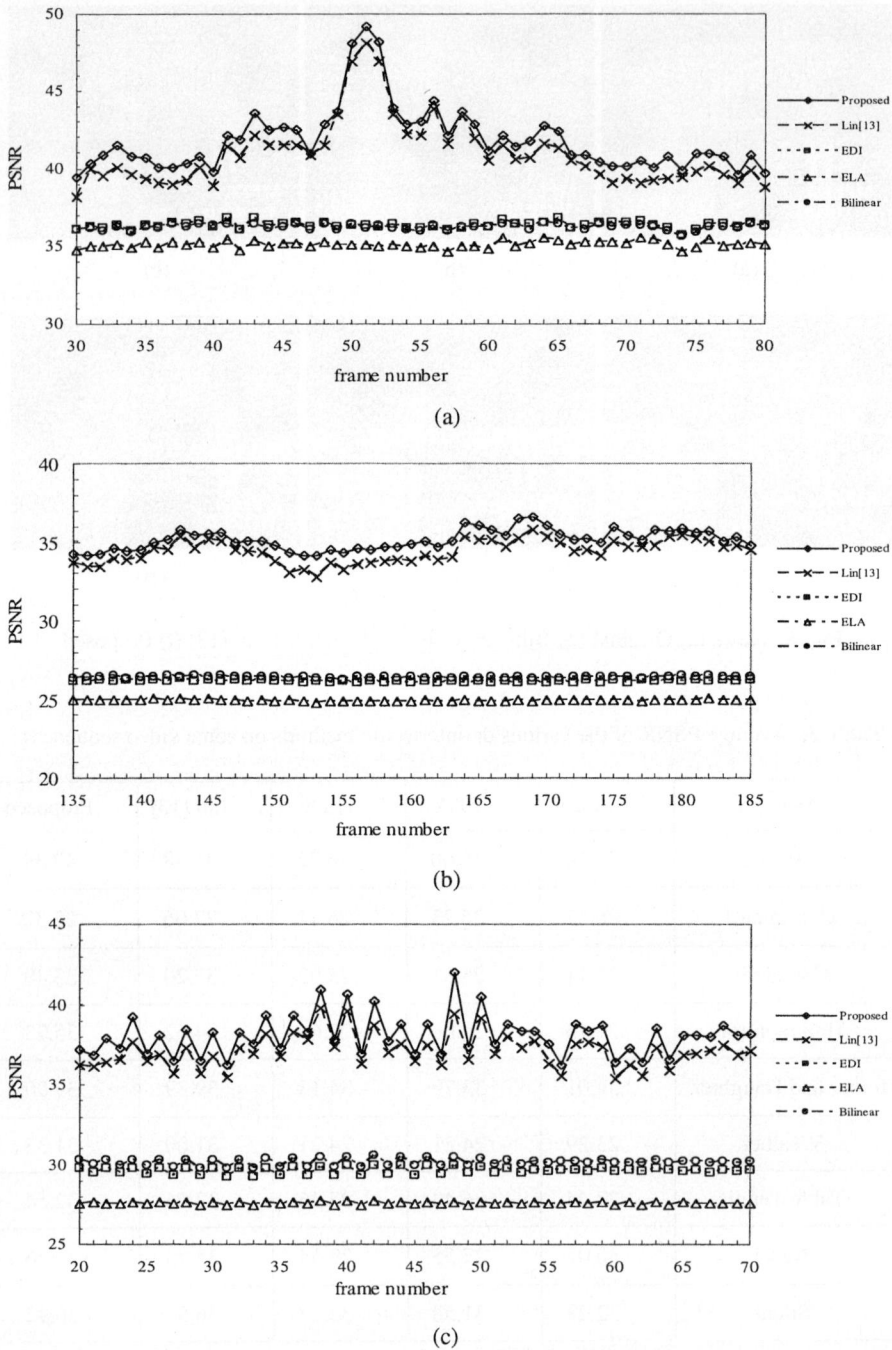

Fig. 7. PSNR performance of the various de-interlacing methods on some video sequences (a)Akiyo (b)Table Tennis (c)News

4 Conclusion

In this paper, we propose a new scheme of horizontal and vertical motions detection algorithm for motion adaptive de-interlacing technique. We propose the horizontal and vertical motions detection scheme, which is executed to ensure that the interfield information can be used more efficient. After the horizontal motion information and vertical motion information are produce. The decision block selects the result for interpolated pixel according to the information of horizontal motion, vertical motion, and Median EDI. The results of our experiments show that the quality of picture can be improved by horizontal and vertical motions detection algorithm. Furthermore, the simulation results also show that our proposed algorithms present a higher quality of video sequences than other interpolation algorithms.

Acknowledgement

This work was partially supported by Chung-Shan Institute Science and Technology of Taiwan with Dr. Ping-Kuo Weng and Mr. Ying-Yih Wu under the Grant BV94G09P.

References

1. G.D. Haan and E.B. Bellers, "Deinterlacing - an overview," *Proceedings of The IEEE*, vol. 86, pp. 1839-1857, Sep. 1998.
2. M. Lee, J. Kim, J. Lee, K. Ryu, and D. Song, "A new algorithm for interlaced to progressive scan conversion based on directional correlations and its IC design," *IEEE Trans. Consumer Electronics*, vol. 40, pp. 119-129, May 1994.
3. M.K. Park, M.G. Kang, K. Nam, and S.G. Oh, "New edge dependent deinterlacing algorithm based on horizontal edge pattern," *IEEE Trans. Consumer Electronics*, vol. 49, pp. 1508-1512, Nov. 2003.
4. Y. Kim, "Deinterlacing algorithm based on sparse wide vector correlations," *SPIE Optical Engineering*, vol. 2727, pp.89-99, 1996.
5. H.S. Oh, Y. Kim, Y.Y. Jung, A.W. Morales, and S.J. Ko, "Spatio-temporal edge based median filtering for deinterlacing," in *Digest of the Int. Conference on Consumer Electronics*, pp. 52-53, June 2000.
6. H. Yoo and J. Jeong, "Direction-oriented interpolation and its application to de-interlacing," *IEEE Trans. Consumer Electronics*, vol. 48, pp. 954-962, Nov. 2003.
7. H.Y. Lee, J.W. Park, T.M. Bae, S.U. Choi, and Y.H. Ha, "Adaptive scan rate up-conversion system based on human visual characteristics," *IEEE Trans. on Consumer Electronics*, vol. 46, pp. 999-1006, Nov. 2000.
8. R. Li, B. Zheng, and M.L. Liou, "Reliable motion detection/compensation for interlaced sequences and its applications to deinterlacing," *IEEE Trans. Circuits and Systems for Video Technology*, vol.10, pp. 23-29, Feb. 2000.
9. J. Kovacevic, R.J. Safranek, and E.M. Yeh, "Deinterlacing by successive approximation," *IEEE Trans. Image Processing*, vol. 6, pp. 339-344, Feb. 1997.
10. D. Han, C. Shin, S. Choi, and J. Park, "A motion adaptive 3-D deinterlacing algorithm based on the brightness profile pattern difference," *IEEE Trans. Consumer Electronics*, vol. 45, pp. 690-697, Aug.1999.

11. C. Sun , "De-interlacing of video images using a shortest path technique," *IEEE Trans. Consumer Electronics*, vol. 47, pp. 225–230, May 2001.
12. S.F. Lin, Y.L. Chang, and L.G. Chen, "Motion adaptive interpolation with morphological operation and 3:2 pulldowned recovery for deinterlacing," *IEEE International Conference on Multimedia and Expo,* Aug. 2002.
13. S.F. Lin, Y.L. Chang, and L.G. Chen, "Motion adaptive interpolation with horizontal motion detection for deinterlacing," *IEEE Trans. Consumer Electronics*, vol. 49, pp. 1256-1265, Nov. 2003.
14. S.G. Lee and D.H. Lee, "A motion-adaptive de-interlacing method using an efficient spatial and temporal interpolation," *IEEE Trans. Consumer Electronics*, vol. 49, pp. 1266-1271, Nov. 2003.
15. Y.Y. Jung, B.T. Choi, Y.J. Park, and S.J. Ko, "An effective de-interlacing technique using motion compensated interpolation," *IEEE Trans. Consumer Electronics*, vol. 46, pp. 460-466, Aug. 2000.
16. O. Kwon, K. Sohn, and C. Lee, "Deinterlacing using directional interpolation and motion compensation," *IEEE Trans. Consumer Electronics*, vol. 49, pp. 198-203, Feb. 2003.
17. K. Sugiyama and H. Nakamura, "A method of de-interlacing with motion compensated interpolation," *IEEE Trans. Consumer Electronics*, vol. 45, pp. 611 – 616, Aug. 1999.

All-in-Focus Image Generation by Merging Multiple Differently Focused Images in Three-Dimensional Frequency Domain

Kazuya Kodama[1], Hiroshi Mo[1], and Akira Kubota[2]

[1] National Institute of Informatics,
Research Organization of Information and Systems,
2-1-2 Hitotsubashi, Chiyoda-ku, Tokyo 101-8430, Japan
{kazuya, mo}@nii.ac.jp
[2] Interdisciplinary Graduate School of Science and Engineering,
Tokyo Institute of Technology,
4259-G2-31 Nagatsuta, Midori-ku, Yokohama 226-8502, Japan
kubota@ip.titech.ac.jp

Abstract. This paper describes a method of image generation based on transformation integrating multiple differently focused images. First, we assume that objects are defocused by a geometrical blurring model. And we combine acquired images on certain imaging planes and spatial frequencies of objects by using a convolution of a three-dimensional blur. Then, we reconstruct an all-in-focus image from the acquired images based on spatial frequency analysis using three-dimensional FFT. Some experiments of image generation utilizing synthesized images and real images are shown and extension of the method integrating multiple differently focused images in three-dimensional frequency domain is discussed.

1 Introduction

In order to generate a certain image by using multiple differently focused images, conventional methods [1-14] usually analyze each acquired image independently and merge them into a desired image. These methods are not easy to extend for merging very many images. In this paper, we propose the method for integrating multiple differently focused images as structured three-dimensional information. Then, it is analyzed in the frequency domain and transformed to desired images directly[15].

A three-dimensional filter derived from our geometrical blurring model combines spatial information of the scenes and integrated acquired images with a space-invariant equation using a convolution. By transforming the equation into the frequency domain, we analyze preserved frequency components of the scenes on integrated acquired images. Then, we design a filter that transforms them to an all-in-focus image without any depth estimation.

Some experiments of an all-in-focus image generation utilizing synthesized images and real images are shown.

2 Geometrical Features of Our Blurring Model

In our method, first, we assume that images are acquired with an ideal geometrical blurring model as Fig.1. We define r_{ij} as a radius of the blur on the image plane P_j produced from objects which are focused on the image plane P_i. The radius r_{ij} can be expressed with the radius of the lens (L) and the distance between the lens plane and the image plane P_i, P_j (v_i, v_j, respectively) as follows:

$$r_{ij} = \frac{|v_i - v_j|}{v_i} L \ . \tag{1}$$

Here, we correct the size of the acquired image to be fit to the image acquired on a certain image plane P_b[11]. Using the distance between the lens plane and the plane P_b (v_b), the corrected radius of the blur $\bar{r}_{ij}$ can be expressed as follows:

$$\bar{r}_{ij} = \frac{v_b}{v_j} r_{ij} = \frac{v_b}{v_j} \frac{|v_i - v_j|}{v_i} L \ . \tag{2}$$

On the other hand, a radius of the blur on the plane P_i produced from objects which are focused on the plane P_j is expressed as follows:

$$\bar{r}_{ji} = \frac{v_b}{v_i} r_{ji} = \frac{v_b}{v_i} \frac{|v_i - v_j|}{v_j} L \ . \tag{3}$$

Therefore, we obtain the following relation:

$$\bar{r}_{ji} = \bar{r}_{ij} \ . \tag{4}$$

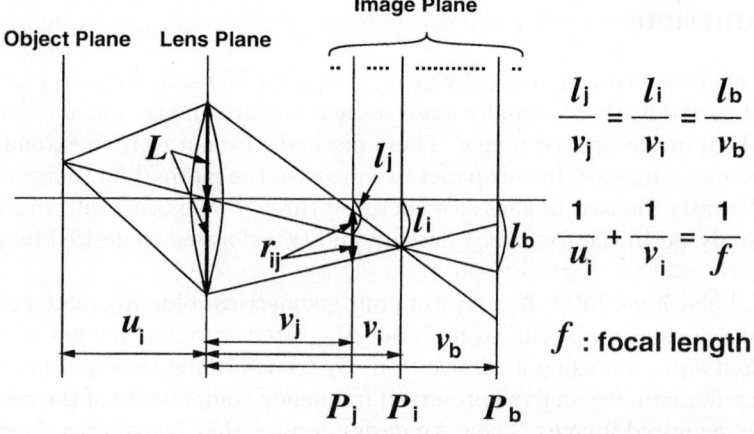

Fig. 1. A geometrical blurring model

In the same way, each radius of the blur produced between three image planes P_i, P_j, P_k (the distance from the lens plane is denoted by $v_i \geq v_j \geq v_k$, respectively) is expressed as follows:

$$\bar{r}_{ik} = \frac{v_b}{v_k} \frac{v_i - v_k}{v_i} L \;, \tag{5}$$

$$\bar{r}_{ij} = \frac{v_b}{v_j} \frac{v_i - v_j}{v_i} L \;, \tag{6}$$

$$\bar{r}_{jk} = \frac{v_b}{v_k} \frac{v_j - v_k}{v_j} L \;. \tag{7}$$

Therefore, we also obtain the following relation:

$$\bar{r}_{ik} = \bar{r}_{ij} + \bar{r}_{jk} \;. \tag{8}$$

Based on the relations above, by setting $v_0 \sim v_{N-1}$ appropriately, we can acquire multiple differently focused images under the condition using a certain $r(\geq 0)$ as follows:

$$\bar{r}_{ij} = |j - i| r \;. \tag{9}$$

3 Scene Analysis Using a Multi-focus Imaging Sequence

We correct the size of the acquired images under the condition described in the previous section and create a multi-focus imaging sequence. Then, we line the sequence up along the orthogonal axis (z–axis) to image planes (x, y) as Fig.2. The acquired image on the image plane P_i is put at $z = i$ after the size correction. This three-dimensional structure which consists of a multi-focus imaging sequence is denoted by $g(x, y, z)$.

And here, let us introduce images which consist of only focused regions of each acquired image. The other regions are set to 0. When the size of these images is corrected and they are lined up in the same way as $g(x, y, z)$, we can define the three-dimensional structure denoted by $f(x, y, z)$, which represents

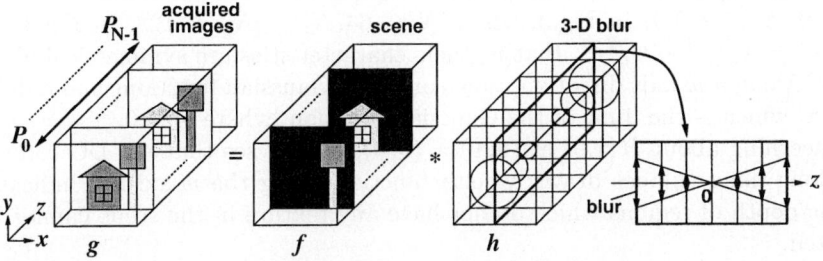

Fig. 2. A three-dimensional blur combines the scene and the acquired images

spatial information of the scene. If the scene is corrected in the manner derived from a perspective imaging, it equals $f(x,y,z)$ except occluded regions.

Under the condition in the previous section, a certain three-dimensional blurring filter $h(x,y,z;r)$ can combine $f(x,y,z)$ and $g(x,y,z)$ by using a convolution as Fig.2. Finally, we obtain the following relation:

$$g(x,y,z) = h(x,y,z;r) * f(x,y,z) \ . \tag{10}$$

In the frequency domain, the convolution is transformed as follows:

$$G(u,v,w) = H(u,v,w;r)F(u,v,w) \ . \tag{11}$$

Therefore, by analyzing characteristics of $H(u,v,w)$, we are able to know how the multi-focus imaging sequence $g(x,y,z)$ preserves spatial frequency components of the scene $f(x,y,z)$.

4 Characteristics of Three-Dimensional Blurs

Let a Gaussian blur with the variance of σ^2 be denoted by $b(x,y;\sigma)$. Here, we replace a geometrical blur, the radius of which is R, with a Gaussian blur of $\sigma = R/\sqrt{2}$ [9]. Then, the three-dimensional blurring function $h(x,y,z;r)$ can be expressed as follows:

$$h(x,y,z;r) = \begin{cases} b(x,y;r|z|/\sqrt{2}) & (rz \neq 0) \\ \delta(x,y) & (rz = 0) \end{cases} . \tag{12}$$

In the frequency domain, $h(x,y,z;r)$ is transformed as follows:

$$H(u,v,w;r) = \begin{cases} Nb(w;r(K_x^2 u^2 + K_y^2 v^2)^{1/2}/\sqrt{2}) & (r(u^2+v^2) \neq 0) \\ N\delta(w) & (r(u^2+v^2) = 0) \end{cases}, \tag{13}$$

where if the corrected size of images is denoted by (N_x, N_y), $K_x = N/N_x$, $K_y = N/N_y$. For simplicity, we rewrite $H(r) = H(u,v,w;r)$ and show characteristics of $H(1.0)$ and $H(0.0)$ in Fig.3, where $N = 64, N_x = N_y = 128$. In Fig.3, we define $s^2 = K_x^2 u^2 + K_y^2 v^2$, that is, their characteristics are symmetrical along ellipses. Along a w-axis direction, they consist of Gaussian functions and a delta function, which is the limit of the Gaussian function, where $\sigma \to 0$.

Concerning about $H(1.0)$ at $(u,v) = (0,0)$, we can see that the DC component along image planes draws a delta function along the w-axis. It indicates that the depth of regions which do not have any texture in the scene cannot be estimated.

$H(0.0)$ denotes the three-dimensional filter corresponding to acquired images with an ideal pin-hole camera. In this case, all of acquired images is the same all-in-focus image and $H(0.0)$ consists of only a delta function along the w-axis.

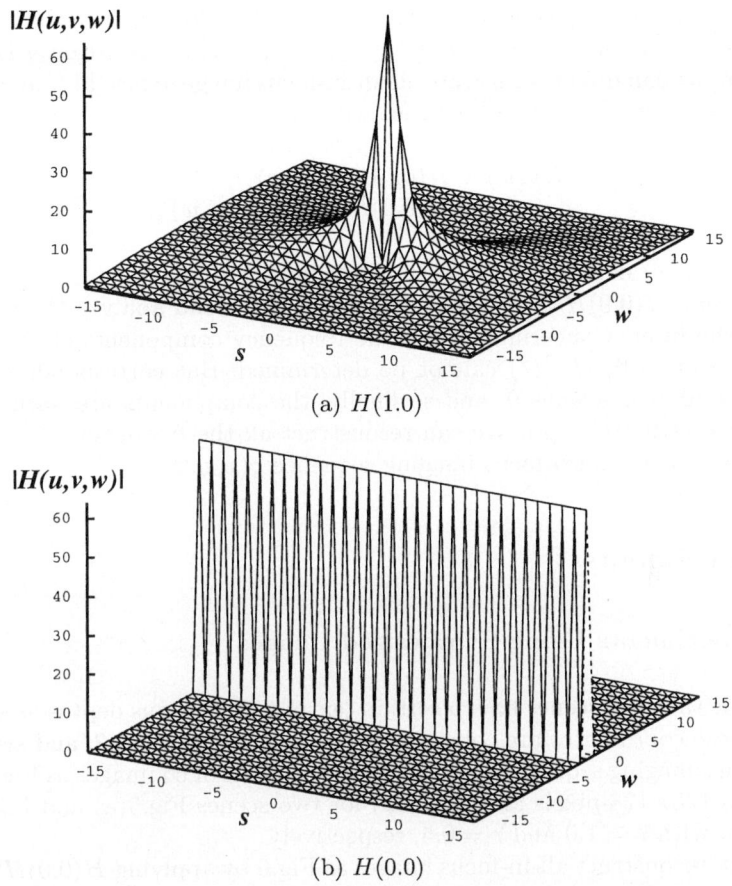

(a) $H(1.0)$

(b) $H(0.0)$

Fig. 3. Characteristics of three-dimensional blurs

It indicates that with this filter we can acquire complete information of the scene texture, but on the other hand, the depth information is completely lost.

For acquiring spatial frequency information of the scene, it is preferable that $|H(r)|$ is, to a certain extent, larger than 0 constantly. When we take a close look at the high frequency component along image planes of $H(1.0)$ in detail, we notice that $|H(1.0)|$ is constantly close to 1, where the distance between (u,v) and $(0,0)$ increases larger. It indicates that the depth information of the regions which have clear textures can be precisely estimated.

5 Image Generation by a Three-Dimensional Filtering

As we described in the previous section, even utilizing multi-focus imaging sequences, the scene $f(x, y, z)$ itself cannot be estimated completely because there are regions where $|H(r)| \simeq 0$ around w-axis except $w = 0$. On the other hand, concerning about the frequency component of $H(r)$ along $w = 0$, that is, (u, v)-plane, $|H(1.0)|$ is smaller than $|H(0.0)|$, but larger than 1 constantly. Therefore, in general, we can directly generate an all-in-focus image $a(x, y, z)$ (any z will do) from the multi-focus imaging sequence without any scene estimation as follows:

$$\begin{aligned} A(u, v, w) &= H(0.0)F(u, v, w) \\ &= H(0.0)H^{-1}(r)G(u, v, w) , \end{aligned} \quad (14)$$

where $A(u, v, w)$ denotes $a(x, y, z)$ in the frequency domain.

We define $H(0.0)H^{-1}(r)$ above as a single filter and analyze the characteristics of the filter. Concerning about the frequency components of $H(r)$ whose power is near to 0, $H^{-1}(r)$ cannot be determined. But corresponding components of $H(0.0)$ is always 0, and so finally, the components are harmless as a single filter $H(0.0)H^{-1}(r)$. We can reconstruct all the frequency component of $a(x, y, z)$ from the multi-focus imaging sequence $g(x, y, z)$.

6 Experiments

6.1 Experiments Using Synthesized Images

We assume that two scenes have a certain texture and various depths as shown in Fig.4, whose coordinates are corrected in the same way as Fig.2, and synthesize multi-focus imaging sequences $g(x, y, z)$ which consist of 64 images as Fig.5. Each image has 128×128 pixels and $g(x, y, z)$ for two scenes Fig.5(a) and Fig.5(b) is structured with $r = 1.0$ and $r = 0.5$, respectively.

We can reconstruct all-in-focus images as Fig.6 by applying $H(0.0)H^{-1}(r)$ to multi-focus imaging sequences. The results show that the desired images which are clearly focused in all regions are reconstructed. It is notable that the re-

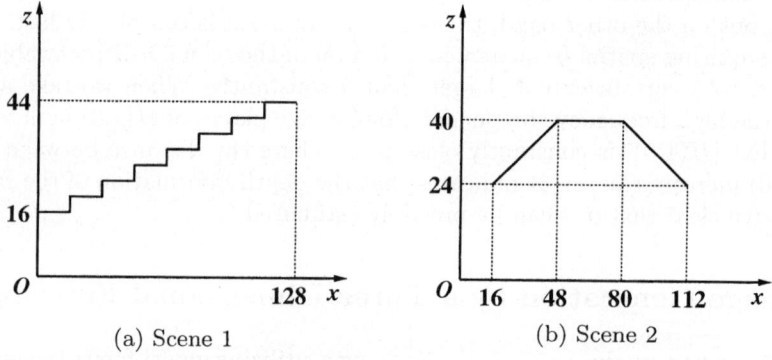

Fig. 4. Assumed depths of the scenes (at arbitrary y)

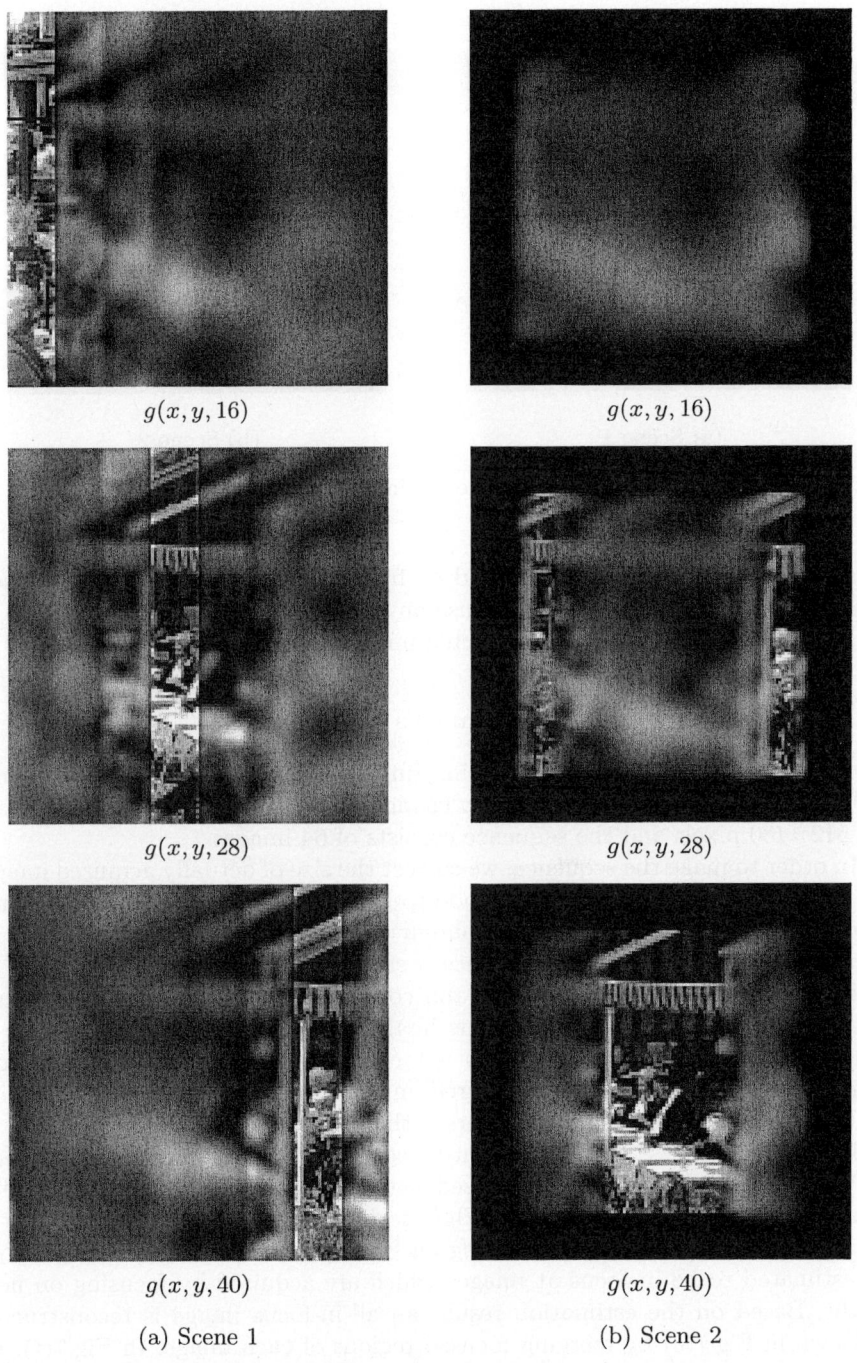

Fig. 5. Synthesized multi-focus imaging sequences $g(x,y,z)$

(a) Scene 1 (b) Scene 2

Fig. 6. Reconstruction of all-in-focus images $a(x,y,0)$

constructed images are not interfered by frequency components of $H(r)$ where $|H(r)| \simeq 0$. In addition, we do not use any window function, but there are no obvious distortions on the reconstructed images.

6.2 Experiments Using Real Images

We experiment using a multi-focus imaging sequence of real images as shown in Fig.7(a)-(c), which are acquired by changing focus consecutively. Each image has 512×480 pixels and the sequence consists of 64 images.

In order to make the sequence, we correct the size of actually acquired images and apply a focus interpolation method to the corrected images to be fit to the condition described in Sect.2 based on our previously proposed method[12]. As a result, we estimate that the sequence is structured with $r = 0.41$.

If we can know camera features and control camera parameters well, such pre-processings to make a multi-focus imaging sequence become very easy. In that case, the focus interpolation is not necessary and r is determined from camera parameters. The size of acquired images also can be corrected according to the camera features and parameters without any estimation.

In Fig.7(d)-(f), we show the reconstruction results of a conventional select-and-merge method[11] and our proposed method. Fig.7(d) is the focus estimation result by the conventional method. White regions are estimated to be in focus at images which are acquired by focusing on far depths. Conversely, black regions are estimated to be in focus at images which are acquired by focusing on near depths. Based on the estimation result, an all-in-focus image is reconstructed as shown in Fig.7(e) by merging focused regions of each image. In Fig.7(f), we show an all-in-focus image reconstructed by our proposed method.

In Fig.8, we show comparison of the upper half of the reconstructed images in detail. The conventional method has visible artifacts derived from the inaccurate

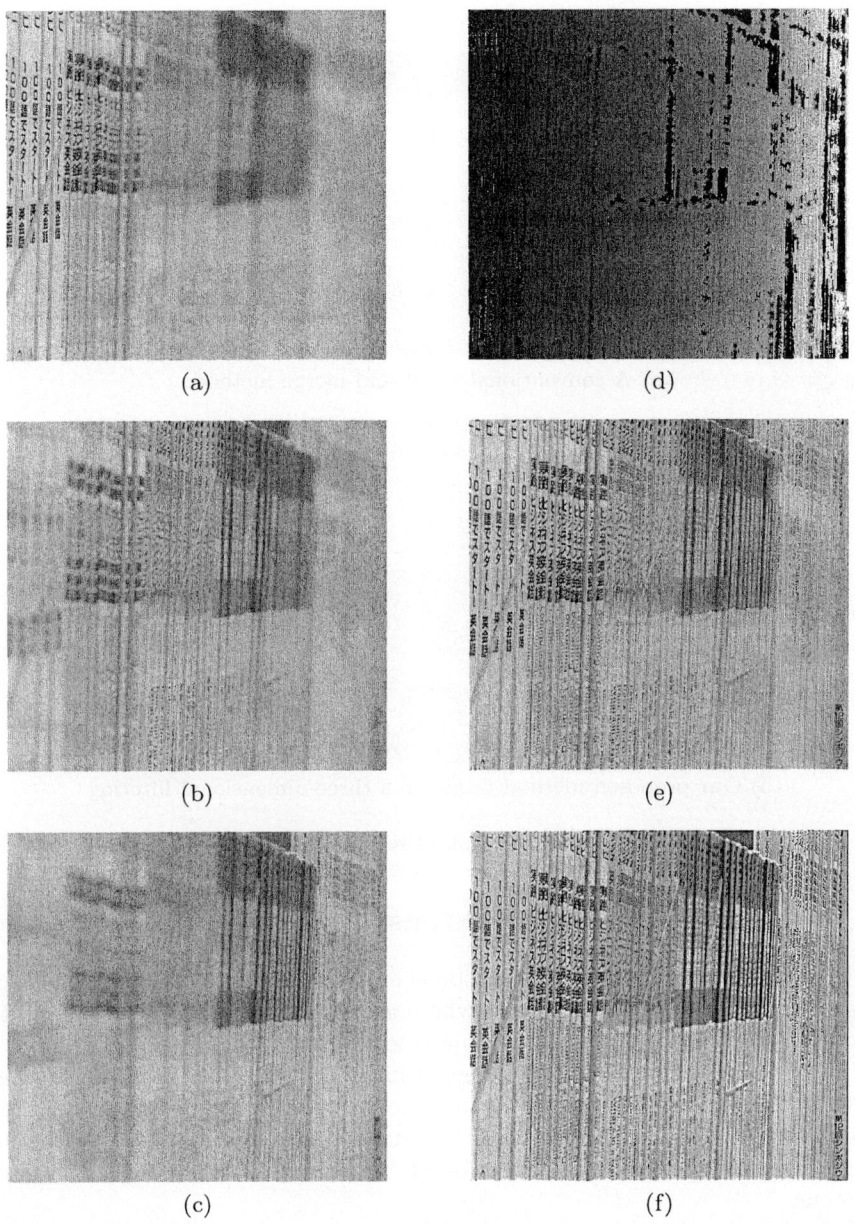

Fig. 7. Reconstruction of an all-in-focus image from real images: (a) $g(x,y,16)$, (b) $g(x,y,28)$, (c) $g(x,y,40)$, (d) the focus estimation result, (e) a conventional select-and-merge method, (f) our proposed method

focus estimation in Fig.7(d). We can see that our proposed method provides the reconstructed image that is more stable.

(a) A conventional select-and-merge method

(b) Our proposed method based on a three-dimensional filtering

Fig. 8. The upper half of reconstructed images

7 Discussion for Future Extension

The experiments in the previous section show that reconstruction of all-in-focus images needs frequency components where $w = 0$ of the scene $f(x, y, z)$, and the components are preserved well on a multi-focus imaging sequence $g(x, y, z)$.

In the same way, any various images which are expressed with only the preserved frequency components on the multi-focus imaging sequences $g(x, y, z)$ can be reconstructed by using our method. It is useful future extension of the method for image generation and reconstruction of some visual information derived from the scene.

For example, the three-dimensional blur corresponding to acquired images with a certain virtual iris as shown in Fig.9, where the center is (s, t) and the radius is r, can be expressed as follows:

$$h(x, y, z; r, s, t) = b(x + sz, y + tz; r|z|/\sqrt{2}) . \qquad (15)$$

In the frequency domain, it is transformed as follows:

$$H(u, v, w; r, s, t) = b(w - (su + tv); r(u^2 + v^2)^{1/2}/\sqrt{2}) . \qquad (16)$$

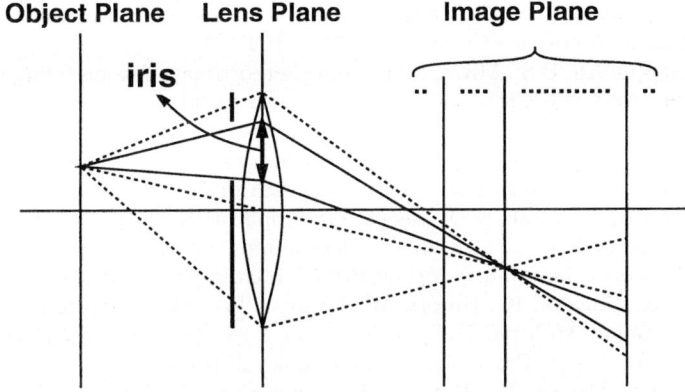

Fig. 9. A generalized blurring model

We can generate various images by using this generalized blurring filter. At $(s,t) = 0$ and $r = 0$, it equals the filter for all-in-focus images with an ideal pin-hole camera discussed in this paper.

8 Conclusion

In this paper, we proposed a novel method of all-in-focus image reconstruction. Based on the spatial frequency analysis of a structured multi-focus imaging sequence using a three-dimensional filter, an all-in-focus image is directly reconstructed from the sequence without any depth estimation.

As a future work, we will extend the method for generating more various images from multi-focus imaging sequences. And we would like to analyze actual blurs of ordinary lenses in comparison with our blurring model for applying this method to real images more robustly.

References

1. Subbarao, M., Wei, T.-C., Surya, G.: Focused Image Recovery from Two Defocused Images Recorded with Different Camera Settings. IEEE Transactions on Image Processing, Vol.4, No.12 (1995) 1613-1627
2. Sezan, M.I., et al.: Survey of Recent Developments in Digital Image Restoration. Optical Engineering, Vol.29, No.4 (1990) 393-404
3. Burt, P.J., Kolczynski, R.J.: Enhanced Image Capture Through Fusion. Proc. 4th ICCV (1993) 173-182
4. Burt, P.J.: A Gradient Pyramid Basis for Pattern-Selective Image Fusion. Proc. SID 1992 (1992) 467-470
5. Toet, A.: Image fusion by a ratio of low-pass pyramid. Pattern Recognition Letters 9, North-Holland (1989) 245-253

6. Pavel, M., Larimer, J., Ahumada, A.: Sensor Fusion for Synthetic Vision. AIAA Computing in Aerospace Conference (1991) 164-173
7. Li, H., Manjunath, B.S., Mitra, S.K.: Multi-Sensor Image Fusion Using the Wavelet Transform. 1994 IEEE International Conference on Image Processing, Vol.I (1994) 51-55
8. Subbarao, M., Gurumoorthy, N.: Depth Recovery from Blurred Edges. Proc. Computer Vision and Pattern Recognition '88 (1988) 498-503
9. Subbarao, M., Agarwal, N.B., Surya, G.: Application of Spatial-Domain Convolution/Deconvolution Transform for Determining Distance from Image Defocus. Computer Vision Laboratory, Stony Brook, Tech.Report 92.01.18 (1992)
10. Kodama, K., Aizawa, K., Hatori, M.: Iterative Reconstruction of an All-Focused Image by Using Multiple Differently Focused Images. 1996 IEEE International Conference on Image Processing, Vol.III (1996) 551-554
11. Kodama, K., Aizawa, K., Hatori, M.: Generation of arbitrarily focused images by using multiple differently focused images. SPIE Journal of Electronic Imaging, Vol.7, No.1 (1998) 138-144
12. Kubota, A., Kodama, K., Aizawa, K.: Registration and blur estimation methods for multiple differently focused images. 1999 IEEE International Conference on Image Processing, Vol. II (1999) 447-451
13. Kubota, A., Aizawa, K.: Inverse filters for reconstruction of arbitrarily focused images from two differently focused images. 2000 IEEE International Conference on Image Processing, Vol.I (2000) 101-104
14. Aizawa, K., Kodama, K., Kubota, A.: Producing Object-Based Special Effects by Fusing Multiple Differently Focused Images. IEEE Transactions on Circuits and Systems for Video Technology, Vol.10, No.2 (2000) 323-330
15. Kodama, K.: Image Generation Based on Transformation Integrating Multiple Differently Focused Images (in Japanese). Proc. the 8th Image Media Processing Symposium, I-4.03 (2003) 73-74

Free-Hand Stroke Based NURBS Surface for Sketching and Deforming 3D Contents

Jung-hoon Kwon, Han-wool Choi, Jeong-in Lee, and Young-Ho Chai

221 Heukseok-dong, Donhjak-ku, Chung-Ang University,
Seoul 156-756, Republic of Korea
{guessyetts, chlnuri, velab-jeongin}@hotmail.com,
yhchai@cau.ac.kr
http://velab.cau.ac.kr

Abstract. This research is to make a series of NURBS surfaces for the virtual 3D conceptual design and the styling process by applying arbitrary free-hand strokes. The surface can be modified in real-time calligraphic stroke based free form deformation. The suggested algorithm is used to create 3D NURBS surfaces for styling object using free-hand strokes with the posture information of the input wand. The algorithm presented in this paper can help product designers in the conceptual engineering stage, even if he or she has no idea about the shape of a target product.

1 Introduction

Design is one of the most important aspects of the overall product development process. It determines not only the visual appearance but also the aesthetic and visual impact of the product in order to give it the 'added value' and 'desirability'. Recently the speed of design development cycles tends to increase in accordance with the change of user requirements. Consequently, companies invest a huge amount of time and manpower in developing the innovative shapes of products and the timesaving design process.

In spite of the risk, the conceptual design and the engineering design have not been integrated because while nearly all phases in the engineering design are computerized nowadays, there is less use of computers in the conceptual design in which intuitive and flexible tools such as pens and paper are mainly used. Moreover the current CAD software used for engineering design does not provide intuitive sketching applications. These interfaces are typically based around 2D views and 2D input, and users must communicate 3D information using 2D input devices such as a mouse, joystick, or tablet. Consequently, this '2D-to-3D' paradigm, in which 3D shape is built up from 2D inputs, unfortunately forces users to comprehend a rigid mathematical structure and model 3D shapes by relying on a large and complex toolset. The toolset is needed to compensate any inevitable loss of profiles, which are needed to create 3-dimensional models.

Such complexity of current CAD systems illustrates the concrete limit in freely expressing ideas characteristic in conceptual design. Therefore, such approach may hinder the efficiency of design process. To overcome this problem, we have found the possibility of a novel design paradigm. The ongoing research and the increased computer performance contribute to the acceleration of the integration of the sketch phase into the rest of the design cycle by applying the computerized format instead of the analogue such as pens and paper, to the sketch manner.

Especially, the use of Virtual Reality (VR) techniques, instead of traditional 2 dimensional devices (monitor, keyboard and mouse), have made possible sketching directly in 3D space in a more intuitive fashion. These demonstrated the unexploited potential of real 3-dimensional design in VR. Virtual Reality offers a better perception of 3-dimensionality, providing direct drawing and positioning via 3D interaction to express the design concepts. Thus, according to our vision, VR can offer the ideal unconstrained interface for free artistic expression and bridge the gap between creative experimentation and precise manufacturing-oriented modeling.

There have been a number of 3-dimensional construction systems built up of the VR techniques in recent years. 3-Draw[1] system and FreeDrawer[2] are sketching systems, which have demonstrated that developing 3D models on the computer by drawing directly in 3-dimensional space is natural and quick. And in Surface Drawing[3], surfaces are created by moving a hand, instrumented with a special glove, through space in a semi-immersive 3D display and interaction environment. The user's hand is acting as a guide for a plane to construct a surface. The HoloSketch[4] supports several types of 3D drawing objects and animation in three-dimensional space.

The user interfaces of these systems keeping the number of low level interactions to a minimum, as well as the command set, support to express the user's thinking in a fast way, while it provides little functionalities to be capable of sophisticated creation to build complex 3D models. For instance, 3-Draw system allows only the placement of lines and HoloSketch works well for models that are made of theses primitives but do not readily extend to the larger class of all surfaces. Surface Drawing is not suitable to express tidied and beautified 3D models by reason of lack of skill to refine the human hand's irregular shake.

We propose a smart sketching system, a 3-dimensional modeling tool for curve drawing and deformation in an immersive VR system. It provides direct control over the creation of a wide range of intricate and sophisticated shapes by moving the wireless wand through space. Each of the systems discussed above has some similarities to our system, but the novel construction method and the calligraphic stroke based deformation procedure make the system functionally quite distinct. In particular construction method for surfaces is achieved through the skinning algorithm including derivatives based on an angle (orientation) of the wand. The deformation is accomplished by means of some calligraphic free-hand strokes that are drawn for the target curve on the final shape. Users are allowed to freely create, modify, and erase surfaces based on the wand's motions. A compact toolset and the construction process by means of gestures allow both beginners and experts to have free access to quick and easy 3D form creation and deformation.

2 The Calligraphic Stroke Based Virtual Surface Construction

Most 3D modeling software requires artists to create shapes using mathematical controls. We observe that many artists have difficulty conceptualizing with these tools.

Therefore, even when presented with sophisticated modeling tools, artists often use pencils to think about models before specifying them with software. This process forces a 3-dimensional task to be conducted in 2 dimensions. Since the object being created is 3-dimensional, this thought process would ideally take place in 3 dimensions.

In this paper we propose a 3-dimensional sketching and modeling interface that support 3D input and output, running on the immersive VR system. This medium allows the users to directly create 3D models by moving a 3D input device through space. At first the points of a free hand calligraphic stroke are interpolated into a NURBS curve. Secondly each profile value of selected curves is set equal. Thirdly a set of curves is converted into a single NURBS surface by the skinning algorithm. Finally a user can modify the shape of a NURBS surface by drawing additional calligraphic strokes.

2.1 Free Hand Calligraphic Strokes for NURBS Curves

By moving the wand through 3-dimensional space, a user draws lines on free-hand drawings, which are automatically interpolated into a suitable NURBS curve. Using the given data, which consists of drawing points, an appropriate parameter value and the knot vector are computed. And then we can interpolate given a set of points with pth-degree non-rational B-spline curve through the $(n+1) \times (n+1)$ coefficient matrix of linear equations, which is set up by evaluating the B-spline basis functions. Here n is the number of control points.

Before curves are converted into a skinned surface, there are several elements we should consider for its order and profile value. Skinning algorithm is a method that uses more than two curves to form surfaces. However, changing the order yields different skinned surfaces even with the use of the same curves. Thus, setting the order of the curves given for skinning is important. A user has to select certain curves, which will be combined to constitute a network of curves, in the appropriate order.

Moreover, another aspect to consider is that the values contained in each curve on the same network, which will describe the shape of the desired surface, must be identical. Through the degree elevation algorithm and the knot refinement algorithm these curves will have the same degree and be defined on the same knot vector. The degrees must be set at the biggest values among those contained in each curve. If the knot vectors of curves are not identical, the new knot vector, which is composed of the maximum multiplicity of all knots, has to be defined. The knot refinement algorithm enables the new knots to be inserted into the established knot with their multiplicities. Consequently, these unified curves apply to the section curves of the skinned surface, and their profiles are carried over in the skinning direction of profiles of the skinned surface.

2.2 The Skinning with Derivatives of Edges

Skinning is one of the most powerful and widely used methods for surface construction: It defines a surface using two or more given section curves. A series of curves functions as a frame of a skinned surface. It can help a user intentionally find the most efficient way to represent the desired shape before beginning the modeling process.

We present the enhanced skinning algorithm differently from the general skinning algorithm. Our skinning algorithm is based on the construction interpolating both points and derivatives determined from the position and the angle of the wand. The resulting skinned surface passes through the given section curves and assumes the given derivatives at the prescribed points by applying the standard B-spline interpolation method. Especially consideration for derivatives gives emphasis on the importance of the motions of the wand. As the wand is moved in an immersive environment as shown in Figure 1, data including the position and the angle of the wand are sent to the tracking computer. The derivatives are determined from the angle between the right and the left maker of the wand.

Fig. 1. Derivatives by the tracked motion of wand

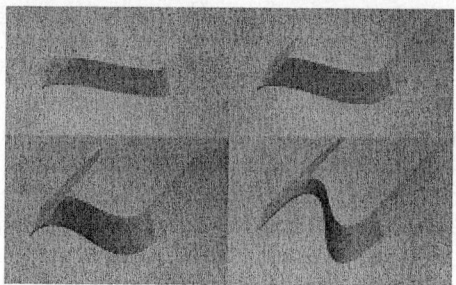

Fig. 2. Various shapes by changing the derivative condition

The reason for using the derivatives is that each derivative gives rise to one additional knot and control point, and, hence to one additional linear equation. There are some advantages of using derivatives for the skinning algorithm. As the derivatives are added to the skinning algorithm, the number of equations increases double, so we can get a double control points. We can get double control points by the skinning algorithm including derivatives because the derivatives formula is used to set up the additional equation. Hence, we can approach to the precise and various shapes of a skinned surface due to the doubled control points. Most of all, the final shape of the skinned surface encompasses the posture information of the wand, which implies the extra meaning besides positioning of the 3D input device. Figure 2 shows the resulting surface through the skinning algorithm with different derivatives. In consideration of these aspects, we improved the modification techniques through manipulating the derivative condition instead of the control point of section curves.

2.3 Object Creation by NURBS Surfaces

When creating an object interactively, we clearly require techniques that enable us to manipulate the shape of the object intuitively. However designing skinned surfaces is often a fastidious process. Mostly the skinned surface is defined, modified, and manipulated with operations on the section curves. A surface shape is difficult to control due to its dependence on the number, shape, and positioning of these curves. Moreover, in commercial computer design tools, designers can obtain more desirable shapes by assiduously manipulating their control points.

This modification method is definitely not suitable if developing the interactive system that supports the 3D input, since exactly selecting spatial positions is hard in these systems. Hence we have implemented the novel modification technique to be fast and easy enough for the user to be able to efficiently work efficiently. In this paper, we propose the method to modify curves and surfaces by drawing more calligraphic strokes.

A user is allowed to control the derivative condition such as the direction and the size. The derivative conditions play an important role in determining the overall shape of the surface[5]. Even though a set of the section curves is still fixed, just changing direction and size of derivatives can cause wide differences of the control point net, and so the accomplished shapes are diversified too.

In an attempt to capture the flavor of the sketching system, we initiated construction of each sample model of a boat. To begin, the user first draw four curves which function as the frames of the boat model. Next, the user can construct the surface that links the two curves, step by step, via the skinning algorithm with derivatives. The hull shape of the boat can be diverse according to the change of derivatives conditions as shown in Figure 3.

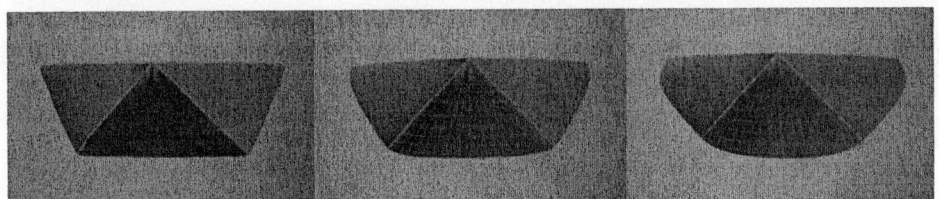

Fig. 3. Diverse hull shape by applying different derivative

A car model is constructed in a similar manner with the boat; first drawing the curves that describes the frame of the car, and then expanding these curves into the skinned surface via the skinning algorithm. Finally, both sides of the car are wrapped with the Coons surfaces. Moreover user can attempt to create the various edge shapes of the model by changing the derivative condition, as illustrated in Figure 4.

Fig. 4. Car model by skinned and Coons surfaces

3 Deformation and Sculpting of NURBS Surface

3.1 NURBS Surfaces Deformation with Calligraphic Stroke

The constructed surface can be deformed by free-hand calligraphic strokes proposed in the last chapter. The input stroke will be a target curve of deformation. The original surface will be updated into a new surface including the target curve by calligraphic stroke deformation. A designer can complete a rough 3D sketch using 3D strokes as if he or she sketches directly on a 2D sketchbook. Calligraphic strokes for deformation can be drawn at any side of surface such as upside and underside, as shown in Figure 5. Sederberg & Parry[6] proposed a method by which solid geometric modeling could be deformed using tensor product Bernstein polynomial and lattices.

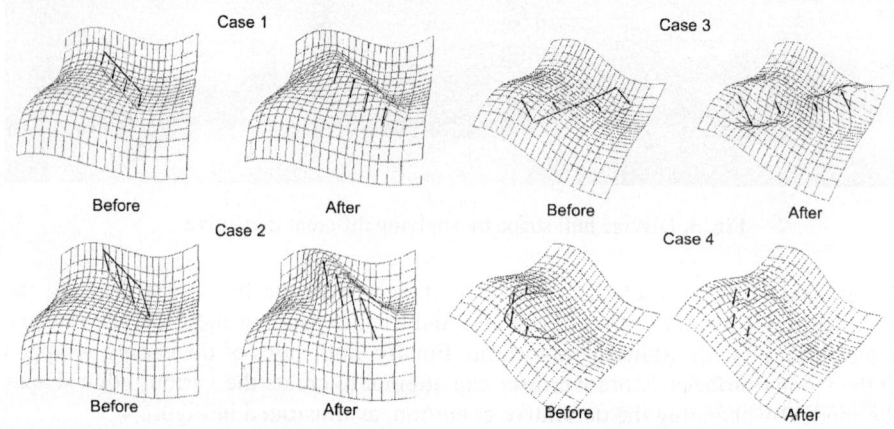

Fig. 5. Sample calligraphic strokes for the target curve

Various deformation methods using lattices were proposed by Coquillart[7], Mac-Cracken and Joy[8]. Hsu, Hughes, and Kaufman[9] found a new way of free-form deformation using pseudo-inversed direct manipulation. Paul Borrel[10] deformed a surface, locally displacing with constraint area. Wesche and Seidel[2] and Schkolne, Pruett and Schröder[3] proposed another deformation method, which use special tool or motion in virtual 3D environments.

But the deformation methods in the previous literature require completely different procedure compared with the modification of 2D sketch in the general design process. Using 3D stroke, however, much of researcher's concern is placed on drawing surface, instead of surface deformation. The deformation method, which is adopting and using the calligraphic stroke as target curve on the final shape make a designer draw and modify a model easily and efficiently by using drawing skill of the general 2D sketch.

A user's stroke in 3D sketching system is to be target curve of surface deformation. And the orientation of wand in 3D stroke defines the direction that determines deformation area in the surface. The sequence of the deformation by calligraphic strokes based on the above equation become as follows:

1. The user drawing calligraphically a stroke with 3D input system. The stroke becomes the target curve on NURBS surface for deformation.
2. We now calculate corresponding projected points on surface using the position and the orientation of stroke. First of all, we consider only one point in the target curve. Surface is translated by using the matrix by which target point is translated into origin of axes of coordinates, and rotated by using the matrix by which target normal is rotated to positive direction of z-axis. Next, we search parametric values of u and v on the surface that become the nearest point to the origin, which is now the same as the target point. The values of u and v become deformation point on the surface. The distance from deformation point to target point (deformation value) becomes diagonal element of surface points, $\Delta q^{k,l}$, matrix. NURBS basis functions are determined with the value of u, v at the calculated deformation points.

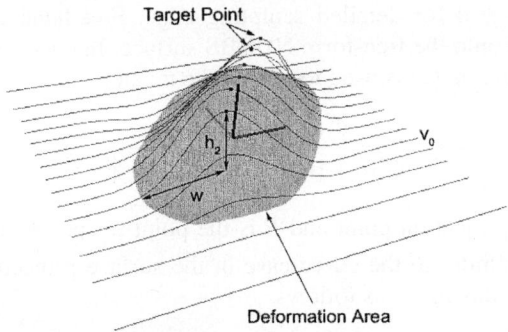

Fig. 6. Two polynomials for the approximation of deformation

3. The rest elements of $\Delta q^{k,l}$ matrix except diagonal element are interpolated by two third order polynomials. We use the polynomial at both sides of the target curve. The rest elements of the matrix are determined by referencing Figure 6. After calculating the displacement in both directions of u, v, and then the values are averaged to fill in the matrix $\Delta q^{k,l}$.
4. The basis functions are calculated and pseudo-inversed to determine the change of the control points of the deformed surface.

When a designer draws an object, he or she expresses the volume and area by drawing its outlines. The deformation by calligraphic strokes is the deformation of NURBS surface using designer's intentional strokes in 3D space such as outline drawings on a 2D sketchbook.

3.2 NURBS Surface Sculpting by Multi-resolution Trimming

NURBS surfaces are widely used in the engineering design since it could create smooth surface using minimal number of data. But its intuitive deformation is quite difficult especially for the detailed modification. Most literatures show a rough deformation so that these techniques may results some distortion or even separation when applied in the sharp deformation. Coquillart[7] applied a lattice to deform a certain area into the special shape. Coons [11] surface can be used for filling in a space for deformation. Wang [12] showed that the separation of surfaces with knot insertion could be used in the detailed trimming with continuous curvature. Virtual sculpting tool [13] [14] is developed using the surface feature constraints, but this deformation requires many control points for conserving the whole deformed shape. Deformation can be implemented by trimming the target surface and the selected area rendering.[15] Similar idea is applied in the sub-division surface with multi-resolution.[16]

In this paper, both the surface trimming and multi-resolution surface are used for the detailed sculpting including sharp edge of free form surface. The calligraphic free-hand strokes are also used for the target sculpting curves. In order to triangulate the surface, the NURBS surface is stored in grid type UV map that can be expanded into the multi-resolution grid for detailed sculpting edge. Free-hand calligraphic curves have to be projected onto the free-form NURBS surface. In curve projection by Newton iteration, the Equation (1) is used to update the u value.

$$u_{i+1} = u_i - \frac{C'(u_i) \cdot (C(u_i) - P)}{C''(u_i) \cdot (C(u_i) - P) + |C'(u_i)|^2} \tag{1}$$

where, $C(u_i)$ is the projection point and P is the point for projection. The conditions for termination are similar to the curve case in the surface projection but are simply extended to both u, v directions as follows.

a. Point coincidence

$$|S(u_i, v_i) - P| \le \varepsilon_1 \tag{2}$$

b. Zero cosine

$$\frac{|S_u(u_i,v_i)\cdot(S(u_i,v_i)-P)|}{|S_u(u_i,v_i)||(S(u_i,v_i)-P)|} \le \varepsilon_2 \quad \frac{|S_v(u_i,v_i)\cdot(S(u_i,v_i)-P)|}{|S_v(u_i,v_i)||(S(u_i,v_i)-P)|} \le \varepsilon_2 \qquad (3)$$

c. The parameter does not change significantly

$$|(u_{i+1}-u_i)S_u(u_i,v)+(v_{i+1}-v_i)S_v(u_i,v_i)| \le \varepsilon_1 \qquad (4)$$

where, ε_1 is a measure of Euclidean distance and ε_2 is a zero cosine measure. Figure 7 shows a sample projection of free-hand calligraphic curve on surface.

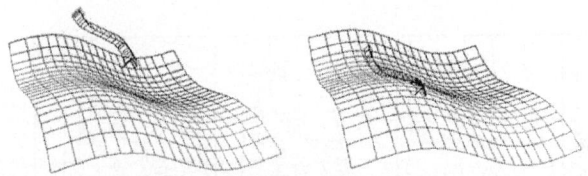

Fig. 7. Projection of calligraphic stroke

Since the surface is stored in the grid type UV map, curve projection is actually the process to find boundary grids as shown in Figure 8. Jordan Curve Theorem is used to determine the exterior, interior and boundaries of all 2 dimensional UV grids.

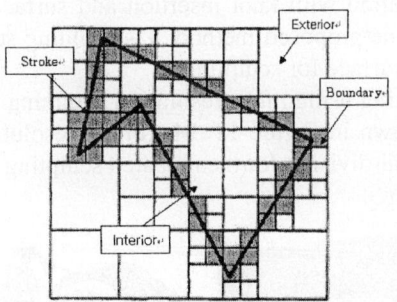

Fig. 8. Projected strokes on 2 dimensional UV map

Sculpting is implemented by two separate surfaces, the original NURBS surface and sculpting curves which have generally constant cross sectional shape. The boundary area is required to be defined by smaller grids, so that the sculpting effect is maximized. The Figure 9 shows the sharp boundary by quad-division interpolation of UV map.

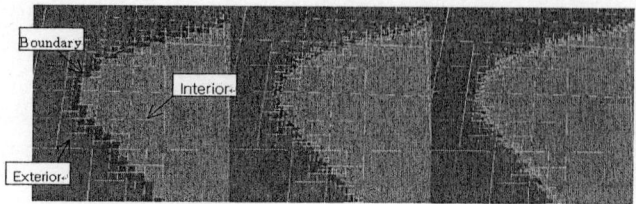

Fig. 9. Boundary grids by quad-division interpolation

This multi-resolution surface can be used for the surface trimming without changing the topology of the target surface. Boundaries and interior grids are simply replaced with the sculpting effect in different levels as shown in Figure 10.

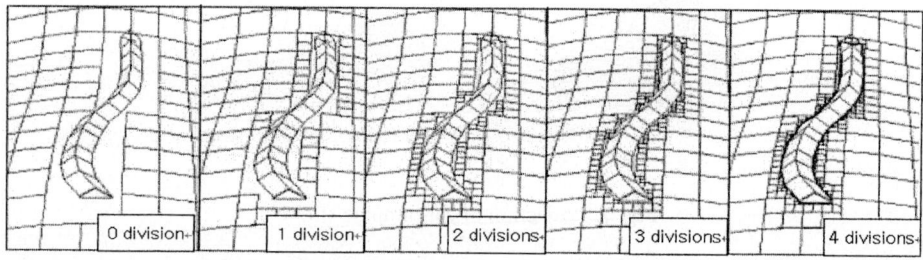

Fig. 10. Projection of calligraphic stroke

To show the effectiveness of the NURBS surface sculpting using multi-resolution trimming, direct deformation with knot insertion and surface trimming with separation are compared with the proposed method. Two folding strokes are applied on the 10 by 10 cubic NURBS surface for sculpting.

NURBS surface sculpting using multi-resolution trimming shows satisfactory result without distortion as shown in Figure 11. Maximum resolution is set for preventing the unwanted precise quad-division for the repeated sculpting curves.

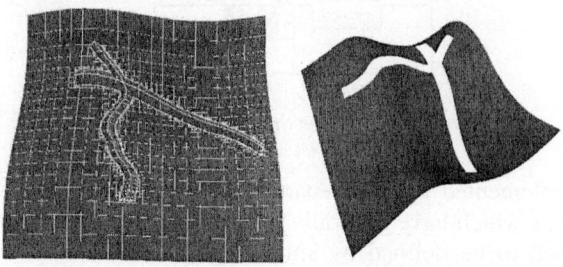

Fig. 11. Sculpting by multi-resolution trimming

4 Conclusion

We describe a smart sketching system, which demonstrates an innovative 3D modeling technique to construct and deform 3-dimensional models. The user directly draws free-hand strokes using a wireless wand as an input device. A set of curves with derivatives is converted into a surface by the skinning algorithm, of which the shape can be interactively modified by additional stokes. We can explain that the significant point of this construction method is the intimate relations between the shape of surfaces and the motions of the wireless wand.

Our smart sketching system is expected to solve the problems of the 2D interfaces, which force users to comprehend a rigid mathematical structure and a complex toolset. Its compact toolset and the effective and sophisticated manipulation is enough to accomplish complex projects, yet accessible for both experts and beginners.

Most of existing surface deformation algorithms makes a user learn how to use the new deformation tool to design model. But surface deformation with calligraphic strokes helps the user approach easily to the intuitive 3D deformation interfaces. The general users don't need to learn new skill or the way of using tool, and are able to design model in 3D virtual space as they draw on a sketchbook. Some detailed sculpting interfaces are required to be implemented to finish the precise styling such as filleting, grooving and making a hole in the surface.

References

1. Sachs, E., Roberts, A., & Stoops, D., 3-Draw: A Tool for Designing 3D Shapes, IEEE computer Graphics & Applications, 11(6) (1991) 18-26.
2. Wesche, G., Seidel, H., FreeDrawer - A Free-Form Sketching System on the Responsive Workbench, In Proceedings of VRST2001, Banff, Alberta, Canada, (2001) 167-174.
3. Schkolne, S., Pruett, M., & Schroder, P., Surface Drawing: Creating Organic 3D Shapes with the Hand and Tangible Tools, In Proceedings of SIGCHI 2001, ACM Press Seattle, WA, USA, (2001) 261-268.
4. Deering, M. F., HoloSketch: A Virtual Reality Sketching/ Animation Tool, ACM Transactions on Computer-Human Interaction, 2(3) (1995) 220-238.
5. Ugail, H., Bloor, M., & Wilson, M., Techniques for Interactive Design Using the PDE Method, ACM Transactions on Graphics, 18(2) (1999) 195-212.
6. Sederberg, T. S., Parry, S. R., Free-Form Deformation of Solid Geometric Models, In Proceedings of SIGGRAPH '86, Computer Graphics, 20(4) (1986) 151-160.
7. Coquillart, S., Extended Free-Form Deformation: A Sculpturing Tool for 3D Geometric Modeling, In Proceedings of SIGGRAPH '90, Computer Graphics, (1990) 187-196.
8. MacCracken, R., Joy, K. I., Free-Form Deformations with Lattices of Arbitrary Topology, In Proceedings of SIGGRAPH '96, Computer Graphics, (1996) 181-188.
9. Hsu, W. M., Hughes, J. F., & Kaufman, H., Direct Manipulation of Free-Form Deformations, In Proceedings of SIGGRAPH '92, Computer Graphics, 26(2) (1992) 177-184.
10. Borrel, P., Simple Constrained Deformation for Geometric Modeling and interactive Design, ACM Transaction on Graphics (TOG), 13(2) (1994) 137-155.
11. Piegl, L., Tiller, W., The NURBS books (2nd ed.). Berlin, Heidelberg, Germany, Springer, (1997).
12. Wang, X., Geometric Trimming and Curvature Continuous Surface Blending for Aircraft Fuselage and Wing Shapes, M.S. Thesis, Mechanical Engineering, Virginia Polytechnic Institute and State University (2001).

13. Zheng, J. M., Chan, K.W., Gibson, I., Surface Feature Constraint Deformation for Freeform Surface and Interactive Design, Proceedings of ACM Symposium on Solid Modeling and Application (1999).
14. Janis, P. Y., Wong, R., Lau, W.H., Ma, L., Virtual 3D Sculpting, Journal of Visualization and Computer Animation, John Wiley & Sons, 11(3) (2000) 155-166.
15. Cheung, K. L, Lau, W. H., Li, W. B., Incremental Rendering of Deformable Trimmed NURBS Surfaces, Proceedings of ACM VRST (2003).
16. Biermanny, H., Martinz, I., Bernardiniz, F., Zoriny, D., Cut-and-Paste Editing of Multiresolution Surfaces, Proceedings of Computer Graphics and Interactive techniques (2002).

Redeeming Valleys and Ridges for Line-Drawing

Kyung Gun Na[1], Moon Ryul Jung[1], Jongwan Lee[2], and Changgeun Song[3]

[1] Dept. of Media Technology, Sogang University, Korea
{gun, moon}@sogang.ac.kr
[2] Dept. of Physics, Hallym University, Korea
[3] Dept. of Information Engineering and Telecommunications,
Hallym University, Korea

Abstract. This paper presents a new method of line drawing based on the hypothesis that artists draw the lines that decompose the object into parts, and the lines that help convey the shapes of the parts. But they draw these lines differently depending on the viewpoint. Contours are the most obvious part-decomposing lines. Valley lines, which typically delimit convex parts, are also part-decomposing lines. As shape-conveying lines, ridge lines on each part are chosen; they are good at conveying the shape of parts in that they are maxima of the principal curvatures on the part surface. So, valley and ridge lines are good candidates in line-drawing. But they have been dismissed because they are view-independent unlike contours. But because of their shape-conveying capability, they have a strong intuitive appeal as candidates for line-drawing. So we propose a way to "redeem" them by making them view-dependent: *Valley and ridge lines are given strengths depending on how the view direction relates to the surface normals to the lines.* On the other hand, when valleys and ridges are extremely strong, for example, when they are sharp edge lines, they are drawn regardless of viewpoint. We have found that the view-dependent valley and ridge lines are quite stable with respect to viewpoint change.

1 Introduction

When painting, artists can use all kinds of techniques to convey the 3D shape of objects effectively. These techniques use the light intensity, color tone, shadow etc. When drawing objects with only lines, artists use their intuition to capture feature lines, which can depict 3D shapes well. So we ask "what lines do artists draw?"

Contours, the lines at which "the surface turns away from the viewer and becomes invisible"[4], are basic [11]; children use them a lot when depicting objects. Contours were used by many NPR (non-photorealistic rendering) line drawing systems [14,6,7,10]. But artists also draw lines other than contours. Various hypotheses have been proposed about what lines they draw. The most obvious choices are the salient geometric features of objects, e.g., creases, ridges, and valleys [14,10,9]. Recently Costa Sousa et al. [2] proposed a line-drawing method that draws individual creases, contours, mesh boundaries, convex edges, and concave edges.

DeCarlo et al. [4] suggested the revolutionary idea of *suggestive contours*. These are lines "seen" from the current viewpoint that become contours when seen from nearby viewpoints. The nearby viewpoints used to define suggestive contours correspond to the *mind's eye* of the artist.

However, the suggestive contour is not sufficiently stable with respect to viewpoint change. That is, the suggestive contours can change abruptly as the viewpoint changes. To solve this instability problem, DeCarlo et al. constrained the set of nearby views by prohibiting them from being close to parallel to the normal vector on the surface. DeCarlo et al. [3] have presented ways to improve temporal coherence in dynamic viewing conditions (but not yet in animation).

In computer vision, there is growing consensus that to recognize some shape human beings decompose the shape into parts. If we think that line drawing is one way to represent how one recognizes a given shape, drawing lines at boundaries among parts is a good strategy. But line drawing techniques developed for NPR have not paid an explicit attention to the observation that lines are for decomposing the object into parts and conveying the shapes of parts. So the meanings of proposed lines were not clear enough. This paper is an attempt to take this important observation into consideration. But then which are parts to recognize?

There are basically two ways to recognize parts. The first method is to define a prior set of basic shapes that are possible parts. Then we need to find these basic shapes in the object. Then the boundary lines are determined from the recognized parts. Or we can define computational rules to detect *boundaries* between parts. The parts are implicitly determined when the boundaries are determined. The latter approach is more general and robust, and more suitable for our purpose.

As a general criteria for finding boundaries between parts, the "minima rule" has been suggested[8]. According to this rule, human vision defines part boundaries along valley lines, that is, at negative minima of the principal curvatures on surfaces[5]. In other words, all negative minima of the principal curvatures form boundaries between parts. There have been some work that use this idea for mesh segmentation [12]. An extreme case of valley lines are concave creases, which are obvious boundaries between parts.

Once parts are defined by valley lines, the shape of each part can be better conveyed by drawing ridge lines on them. For example, the bridge of the nose is a ridge line, and drawing it usually help convey the shape of the nose. A ridge line is the locus of points at which the larger principal curvature (with positive value) assumes a local maximum along the direction of the principal curvature. The part surrounded by valley lines is typically convex. The ridge line on the convex part typically represent the locally highest region of the part relative to the bottom. So drawing ridges helps convey the shape of the part.

In summary, valleys and ridges have clear intuitive meaning which is useful for line drawing. But as they are, valleys and ridges are view independent, so they are not suitable for artistic line drawing. For this reason, DeCarlo et al. [4] dismisses them as lines for line-drawing. But we want to "redeem" valley and ridge lines as lines for line-drawing, and propose a way to make valleys and ridges dependent on viewpoint. When a ridge on a surface is seen from above, its significance as a locally highest region is greatly reduced because this fact is not conveyed by the ridge line. In such cases, it is not worthwhile to draw ridges. We capture this intuition increasing the strength of a ridge as the view direction diverges from the surface normal at the ridge. In contrast, when a valley is seen from above, its significance as the boundary between parts is the strongest. We capture this intuition by reducing the strength of a valley as the view direction diverges from the surface normal at the valley. Ridges or valleys whose strengths are below user-defined thresholds are not drawn. On the other hand, when valleys and ridges are extremely strong, for example, when they are sharp edge lines, they are drawn regardless of viewpoint. The thresholds are determined through the process of trial and error. We present a variety of results, which confirms our expectation. The supplementary video, which displays view-dependent valleys and ridges as the viewpoint changes gradually, is a real time recording.

2 Valley and Ridge Lines

2.1 Principal Curvatures

The principal curvatures of a surface at a given point are the maximum and minimum of the normal curvature of the point. For mesh, the principal curvature at vertex v can be represented by using the normal variation between n_v and n_f, where n_v is the normal vector at the vertex v and n_f is the normal vector to a face f adjacent to vertex v (See Figure 1(a)). The smaller $n_v \cdot n_f$ is, the greater the normal variation between n_v and n_f. If $n_v \cdot n_f$ is the smallest for a particular face f, then the normal variation is maximum between n_v and n_f. The maximum normal variation can be considered an approximation of a principal curvature. If the face f is below the tangent place at vertex v as in Figure 1(a), the maximum normal variation is considered positive. If the face f is above the tangent place at vertex v, the maximum normal variation is considered negative. We represent the magnitude of the maximum normal variation by $1 - min_{f \in faces(v)}(n_v \cdot n_f)$, where $0 < min_{f \in faces(v)}(n_v \cdot n_f) < 1$.

2.2 Ridge and Valley Points

There are several methods for detecting ridge and valley lines[13,15]. Here we describe a simple but effective method of detecting ridges. As shown in Figure 1(b), if a point p on the surface has the maximum (positive) principal curvature greater than those of its neighbor points on the maximum principal curve of the point, that point is called a ridge point. Connecting neighboring ridge points forms a ridge curve, and the tangent vectors on a ridge curve are perpendicular to the maximum principal directions.

To detect a ridge point, we compare the maximum normal variation of a vertex v and those of neighboring points along the principal direction of the vertex. See Figure 2 for the procedure of detecting ridge vertices.

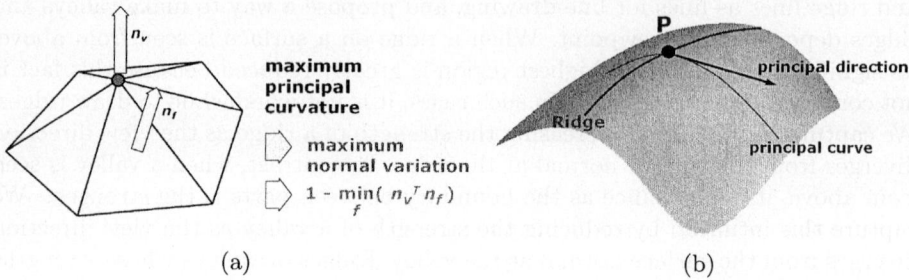

Fig. 1. (a): The maximum normal variation as the principal curvature. (b): If the maximum (positive) principal curvature of p is greater than that of neighboring points on the maximum principal curve passing through p, then p is a ridge point. Connecting nearby ridge points form a ridge.

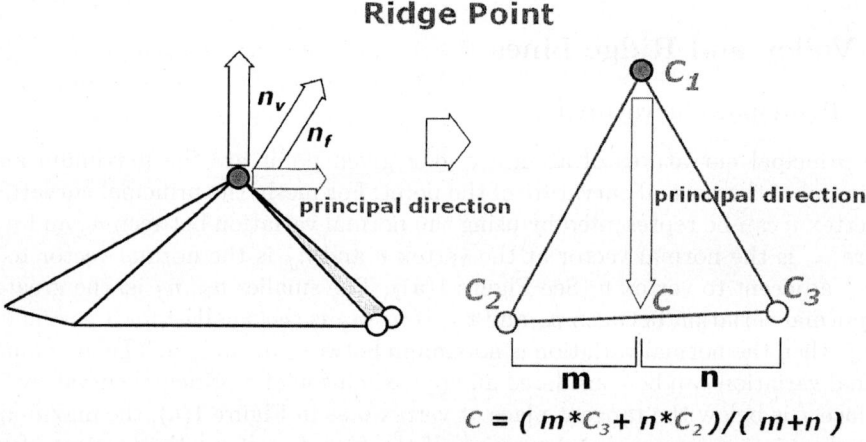

Fig. 2. Left: The principal direction is the projection to the tangent plane of the face normal n_f of the face f, where $n_v \cdot n_f$ is the smallest. Right: Let C1 be the maximum normal variation of the vertex. Let C be the maximum normal variation of the intersection point between (the projection to the face f of) the principal direction and an edge of the face. C is computed using the maximal normal variations C2 and C3 of the edge vertices, respectively, as shown in the figure. If $C1$ is greater than both the maximum normal variation C of the point on the edge (visible in the figure) and that of the point on the edge on the other side (invisible) intersected by the principal direction of the vertex, the vertex is a ridge point. Here we use the 1-ring neighborhood to detect a ridge point.

Valley points are determined in the same way as ridge points. The difference is that the neighbor faces of a valley point are above the tangent plane at the valley point, whereas the neighbor faces of a ridge point are below the tangent plane.

2.3 Detecting Ridge and Valley Lines

A ridge or valley line is formed by connecting ridge or valley points, respectively. Because we apply the same connecting method to ridge and valley points, we describe the method only for ridges. A ridge line is formed in two steps: connecting ridge points to form ridge edges and connecting ridge edges to form ridge lines. We have two rules for forming ridge edges:

1. If there are two ridge vertices on edges of a mesh triangle, the are connected by a straight segment to form a ridge edge.
2. If each edge of a mesh triangle contains a ridge vertex, these vertices are connected to the centroid of the triangle formed by the vertices. It results in three ridge edges.

A ridge line is formed by connecting ridge edges by means of the hysteresis thresholding technique [1]. In general, finding ridge lines in a high-resolution mesh is itself a problem. A multi-resolution search for ridges may give a better result, but in the present context, this is a side issue.

We want to detect sufficiently strong ridges, because drawing too many ridges would look cluttered. One solution to this problem is to detect ridge points by using the 1-ring neighborhood, and let the user set the threshold for sufficiently strong ridge points. Another solution is to use the 2- or 3-ring neighborhood to detect ridge points. Using wider local neighborhoods eliminates weak ridge points. It turns out that the first method gives a better result. But the better result of the threshold method relies on user intervention.

2.4 The View-Dependent Strength of Valleys and Ridges

Given valleys and ridges, whether they are drawn as lines or not and how they are drawn depend on their "view-dependent strengths". We determine the strength of a valley or ridge by how the normal vector to the valley or ridge is related to the view direction. For example, look at Figure 3. When the view direction is close to the surface normal to a ridge line, the ridge line does not help convey the shape of the part, and it is given a weak strength. In contrast, when the view direction is close to the surface normals to a valley line, the valley line greatly helps decompose parts along it.

The strength of a ridge point p is computed as follows:

$$ridge\_strength(p) = (1 - (n_p \cdot v)) \tag{1}$$

Here n_p is the normal to the vertex p and v is the view direction. The strength of a ridge edge e is computed as the arithmetic mean of $ridge\_strength(p1)$ and $ridge\_strength(p2)$ with the same proportionality coefficient for all ridge points. The $p1$ and $p2$ are the end points of a ridge edge. The equation for the strength of a ridge edge implies that the strength is the least when the ridge edge is seen right from above, that is, from the view direction parallel to the normal vector.

But, we put a constraint on the view dependency of ridge and valley lines. It has been observed that artists draw ridges and valleys regardless of viewpoint,

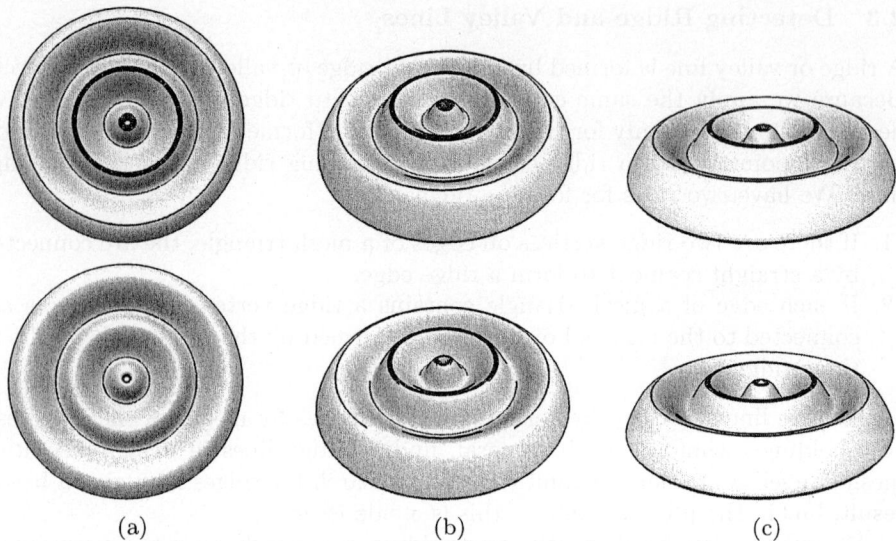

Fig. 3. Top: Ridges and valleys drawn independent of the viewpoint. Bottom: Ridges and valleys drawn dependent on the viewpoint. (a) The view direction is close to the surface normals to the valleys and ridges: (Top) Both the ridges and valleys are drawn strong. (Bottom) Only the valleys are drawn strong. (b) The view direction gets close to the tangent planes to the valleys and ridges: (Top) Both the ridges and valleys are drawn strong. (Bottom) the valleys begin to fade away and the ridges begin to emerge. (c) The view direction is close to the tangent planes to the valleys and ridges: (Top) Both the ridges and valleys are drawn strong. (Bottom) Only the ridges are drawn strong.

when they are extremely strong. To reflect it, the ridge strength equation is modified as follows:

$$ridge\_strength(p) = normalvar(p) + (1 - (n_p \cdot v)) \qquad (2)$$

The $normalvar(p)$ is the maximum normal variation of a ridge point p. It represents the view-independent strength of the ridge point. So, the strength of a ridge edge becomes great if its points have strong maximum normal variations.

The strength of a valley point p is computed as follows:

$$valley\_strength(p) = normalvar(p) + (n_p \cdot v) \qquad (3)$$

The strength of a valley edge e is computed in the same way as ridge edges. The equation for the strength of a valley edge implies that the strength is the greatest when it is seen right from above, that is, from the view direction parallel to the normal vector.

A valley or ridge edge is chosen for drawing if their strength is above a given threshold, which is determined by trial and error.

2.5 The Brightness and Thickness of Lines

For visualization purposes, we determine the brightness of each segment(edge) of ridges or valleys according to the maximum normal variations $normalvar(p1)$ and $normalvar(p2)$. Here, the $p1$ and $p2$ denote the end points of an edge. We have found that visually pleasant results are obtained if the thickness is proportional to the strength of ridge and valley segments.

3 Experiments and Results

We experimented with various models. We drew lines using purely geometric valleys and ridges, and also drew lines based on their view-dependent strengths, as shown in Figures 4, 5, and 6. Table 1 shows the threshold for the view-dependent strengths of ridges and valleys.

Table 1. The thresholds for the view-dependent strengths of ridges and valleys

name	vertex	threshold for ridge strength	threshold for valley strength
man	6,737	0.25	0.50
venus	19,847	0.42	0.45
buddha	38,768	0.70	0.53
athena	7,546	0.88	0.35
turtle	14,276	0.30	0.38
elephant	19,753	0.23	0.30
griffin	33,570	0.40	0.37
greek	4, 742	0.35	0.43

The supplementary video shows the view-dependent valleys and ridges, obtained as the viewpoint changes continuously. The view dependent valleys and ridges convey the shape reasonably well. The video shows that the view dependent valleys and ridges are quite stable with respect to viewpoint change. The viewer would not accept lines appearing or disappearing suddenly as the viewpoint changes gradually. So it is important that lines in line drawing are stable i.e. not too sensitive to viewpoint change.

4 Conclusions

In this paper, we have proposed an NPR line drawing technique. It aims at "redeeming" valley and ridge lines for artistic line drawing, by making them sensitive to viewpoint moderately. The collection of lines to be drawn is predetermined by geometry. But the ability to select which parts to draw from the given collection gives a reasonable illusion that the lines change as the viewpoint changes.

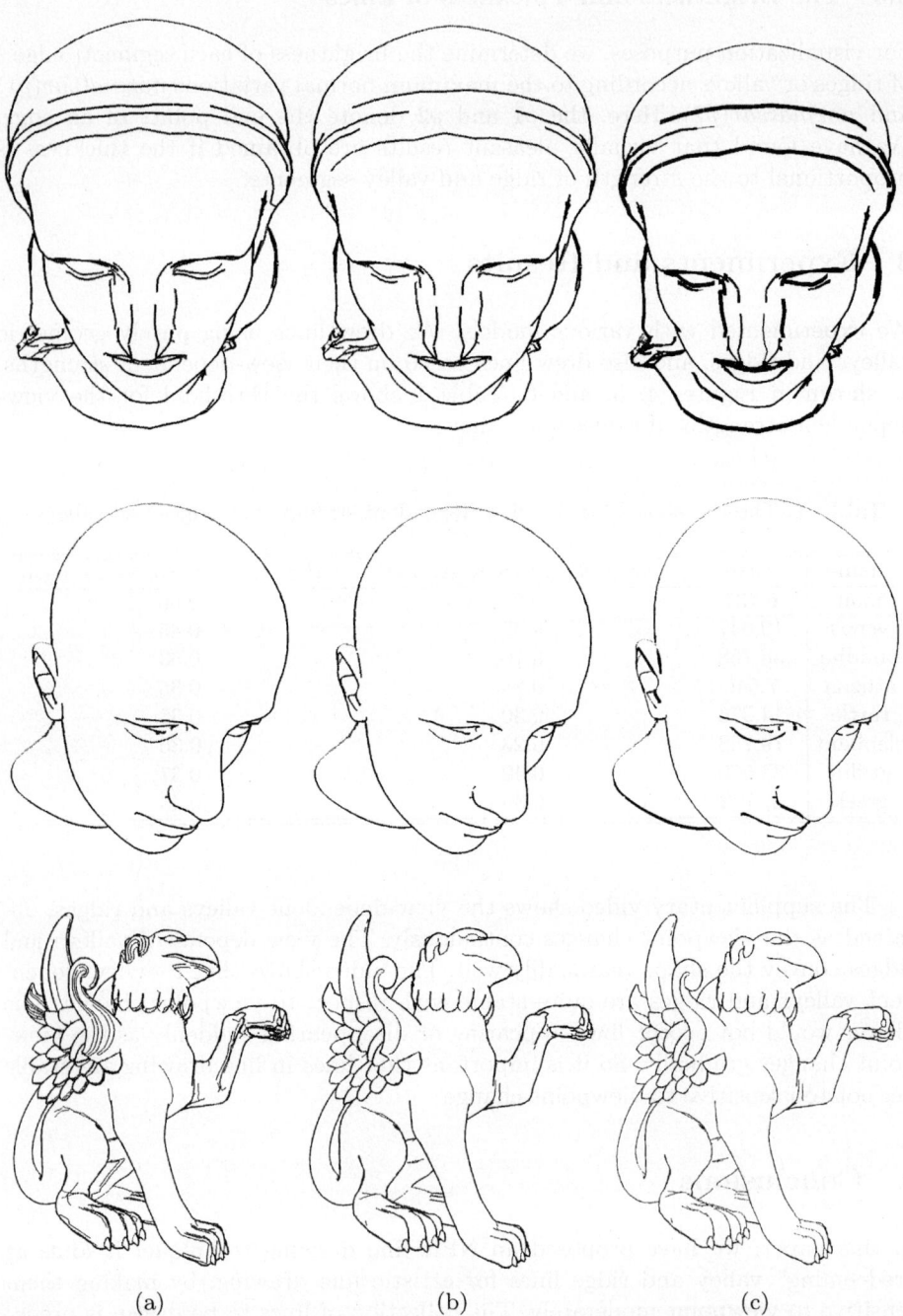

Fig. 4. (a): View independent. (b): view dependent. (c): view dependent: The thickness of lines is proportional to the strength of ridge and valley segments.

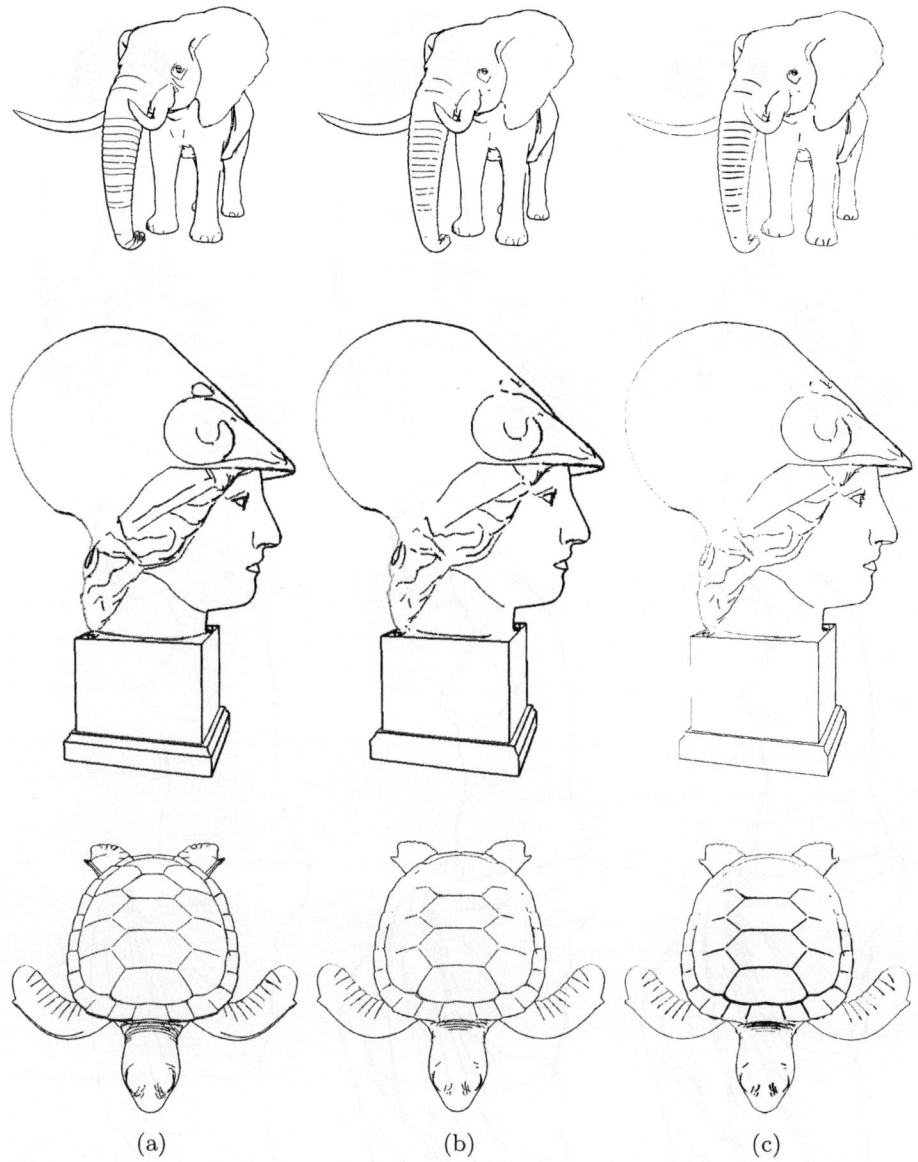

Fig. 5. (a): View independent. (b): view dependent. (c): view dependent: The thickness of lines is proportional to the strength of ridge and valley segments.

When we compare our method with suggestive contours, it turns out that the lines drawn are less affected by viewpoint change. But this disadvantage pays off in that our method is more stable than suggestive contours with respect to viewpoint change.

The strength of valleys and ridges also depends on the magnitude of their curvature. But we did not incorporate it in this study, except that we use the

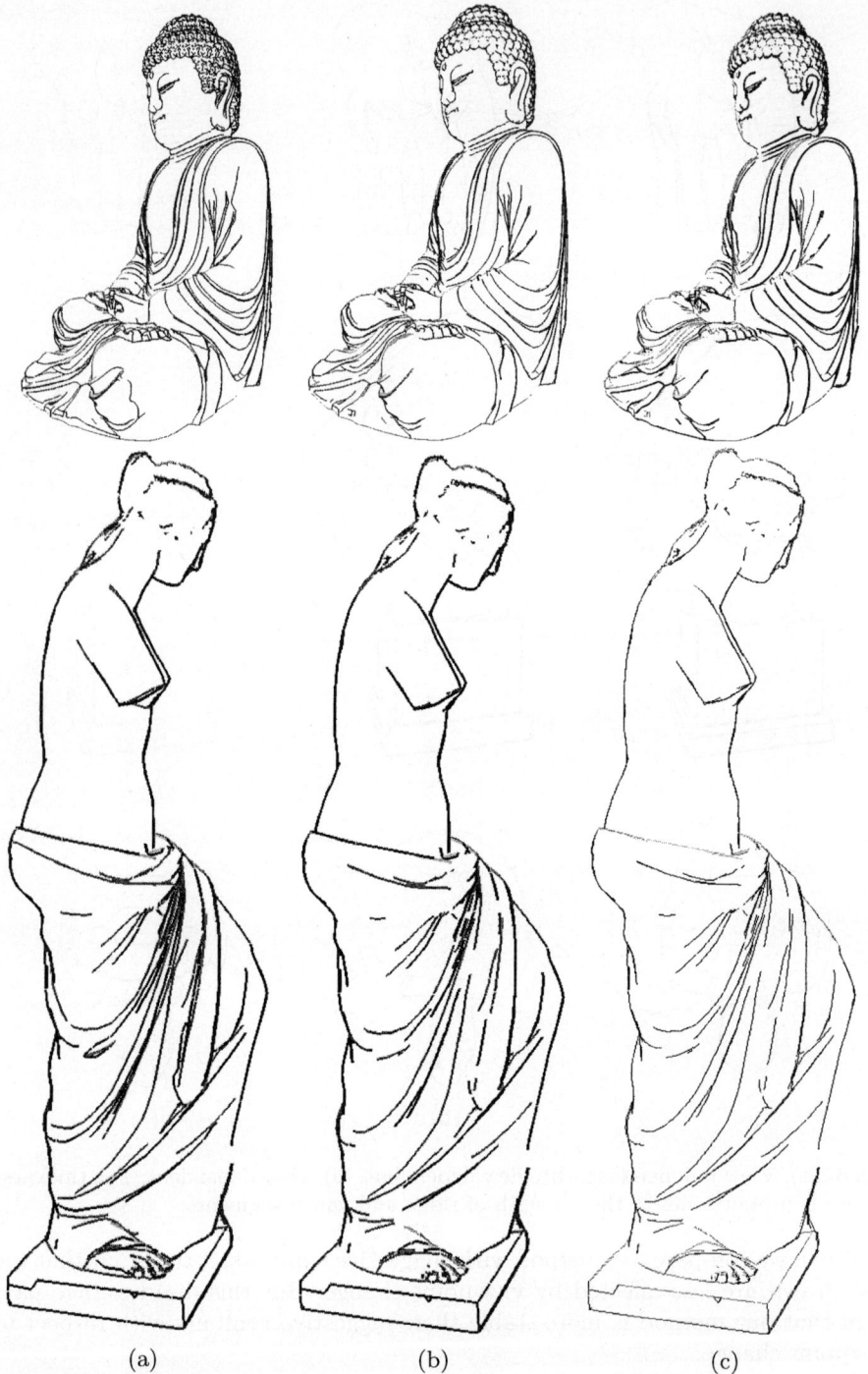

Fig. 6. (a): View independent. (b): view dependent. (c): view dependent: The thickness of lines is proportional to the strength of ridge and valley segments.

curvature to decide whether to draw ridges and valleys regardless of viewpoint. It is because it is extremely uncertain how to combine this factor with the dependency on viewpoint.

Future improvements include extending our system with other algorithms for shape feature analysis (including more accurate curvature estimation methods). It would also be useful to have automatic selection of threshold values for the valley and ridge strength which vary over different regions of the model. This locally adaptive thresholding helps balance the number of lines for different regions.

Acknowledgements

This work was supported by the Korea Science and Engineering Foundation (KOSEF) for three years. There was also additional support of the Regional Innovation System (RIS) of Ministry of Commerce, Industry and Energy, Korea.

References

1. J. Canny. A computational approach to edge detection. *IEEE PAMI*, 8(6):679–698, 1986.
2. M. Costa Sousa and P. Prusinkiewicz. A few good lines: suggestive drawing of 3D models. In *Eurographics 03*, 2003.
3. D. DeCarlo, A. Finkelstein, and S. Rusinkiewicz. Suggestive contours in dynamic scenes. In *NPAR 2004*, pages 848–855, 2004.
4. D. DeCarlo, A. Finkelstein, S. Rusinkiewicz, and A. Santella. Suggestive contours for conveying shape. In *SIGGRAPH 03*, pages 848–855, 2003.
5. A. Girshick, V. Interrante, S. Haker, and T. Lemoine. Line direction matters: an argument for the use of principal directions in 3d line drawings. In *First International Symposium on Non-Photorealistic Rendering*, pages 43–52, 2000.
6. B. Gooch, P. Sloan, A. Gooch, P. Shirley, and R. Riesenfeld. Interactive technical illustration. In *Proc. of the 1999 Symposium on Interactive 3D Graphics*, pages 31–38, 1999.
7. A. Hertzmann and D. Zorin. Illustrating smooth surfaces. In *SIGGRAPH 2000*, pages 517–526, 2000.
8. D. Hoffman and M. Singh. Salience of visual parts. *Cognition*, pages 29–78, 1997.
9. V. Interrante, H. Fuchs, and S. Pizer. Enhancing transparent skin surfaces with ridge and valley lines. *IEEE Visualization*, pages 221–228, 1995.
10. R. Kalnins, L. Markosian, B. Meier, M. Kowalski, J. Lee, P. Davidson, M. Webb, J. Hughes, and A. Finkelstein. Wysiwyg NPR: Drawing strokes directly on 3D models. In *SIGGRAPH 02*, pages 755–762, 2002.
11. J. Koenderink. What does the occluding contour tell us about solid shape? *Perception*, pages 321–330, 1984.
12. Y. Lee, S. Lee, A. Shamir, D. Cohen-Or, and H.-P. Seidel. Mesh scissoring with minima rule and part salience. *Computer Aided Geometric Design*, accepted for publication, Elsevier Science, 2005.
13. A. Lopez, F. Lumbreras, J. Serrat, and J. Villanueva. Evaluation of methods for ridge and valley detection. *IEEE PAMI*, 21(4):327–335, 1999.

14. L. Markosian, M. Kowalski, S. Trychin, L. Bourdev, D. Goldstein, and J. Hughes. Realtime nonphotorealistic rendering. In *SIGGRAPH 97*, pages 415–420, 1997.
15. H. Tanaka, M. Ikeda, and H. Chiaki. Curvature-based face surface recognition using spherical correlation-principal directions for curved object recognition. In *Third IEEE International Conference on Automatic Face and Gesture Recognition*, pages 372–377, 1988.

Interactive Rembrandt Lighting Design

Hongmi Joe, Kyoung Chin Seo, and Sang Wook Lee

Department of Media Technology, Sogang University,
1 Shinsu-dong, Mapo-gu, Seoul, Korea 121-742
{jjoengmi, jiniseo, slee}@sogang.ac.kr

Abstract. The paper presents an efficient way of designing lighting setup for rendering 3D face model. Specifically, we focus on obtaining lighting direction for Rembrandt lighting. A Rembrandt patch is a triangle defined as the bright region surrounded by self and cast shadows on a check area, and we use the self- and cast-shadow curves for computing the direction of main lighting. A user graphically specifies a Rembrandt patch on a 3D model. From the user input, lighting directions are estimated from the cast- and self-shadow geometry on a 3D face model. The final lighting direction is decided among the candidates predicted by the self and cast shadows. The presented method lets a user interactively design and achieve Rembrandt lighting by alleviating repetitive manual search for the light direction by trial and error. Experimental results show the effectiveness of the presented method. It suggests appropriate Rembrandt lighting directions quickly and easily.

1 Introduction

Lighting is an important factor in generating images in both real and graphical environments. Basic function of the lighting is to make objects visible for observers. In addition, lighting has more subjective functions in making films and photographs [1][2][3]. Feelings such as mood, dramatic situations, emotion and tension can be added to a scene by adequate lighting [4][5]. Moreover, in case of a close up shot, designing proper lighting is one of the key issues in conveying detailed emotional expressions of a character. Figure 1 shows photographs taken under four kinds of standard lighting setups used frequently by photographers. Different impressions from the characters can be created by different lighting designs.

Much expertise in lighting is usually required to make professional lighting conditions. Even with much expertise, many trials are normally needed. Whenever the object changes its position/orientation, lighting should change its whole setup every time. For rendering of synthetic images using 3D modeling software like Maya[TM] or 3D Studio Max[TM], the lighting control should be no less stringent [6]. Even if hardware accelerated rendering techniques support fast verification process of rendered results, it takes time to find an accurate lighting condition by trial and error.

Our motivation for the work presented in this paper is to develop a software system that suggests lighting directions for the common users who may not be familiar with lighting design. We focus on the Rembrandt lighting which is frequently used for close up shot of the character's face. We propose an efficient approach to the design of Rembrandt lighting based on simple graphical interaction by a user. A user draws

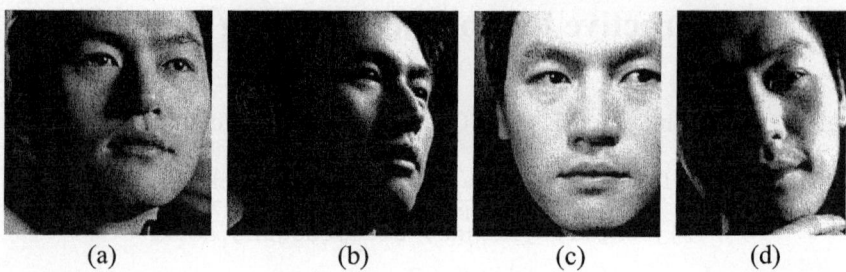

Fig. 1. Lighting for portrait photography : (a) open loop lighting (b) close loop lighting (Rembrandt lighting) (c) butterfly lighting (d) one side lighting

the shadow curves/lines of a Rembrandt patch on a model face and the system automatically computes the light direction. In contrast to the forward rendering process with manually specified lighting conditions, we inversely calculate lighting directions to fit the expected result.

There have been a number of approaches to the estimation of light directions from shading and shadows. However, there have been only a few applications of the basic techniques to the lighting design problem of creating desired effects in computer-generated images. To the best of our knowledge, Rembrandt lighting design has not been specifically investigated before.

Estimation of illumination direction from shading has been investigated under assumption of point light source [7][8]. Sato *et al.* showed an approach to the estimation of multiple point light sources from shadows [9]. Recent research has paid attention to the recovery of multiple illumination directions [10] on a textured surface [11][12]. Our work benefits from the results in [10][11][13] for estimating light direction from shadows. For computer cinematography, several researchers have presented methods for lighting design. Poulin *et al.* proposed a sketch-based input method for highlight and shadows [14]. Pellacini *et al.* showed an interface for placing shadows like a 3D primitive with 3D objects and inversely calculated the lighting conditions [15]. A fast rendering algorithm for interactive design of shadow was presented by Gershbein *et al.* [16]. Interactive lighting design systems have been proposed for theaters [17] and environments [18]. Wang *et al.* present an image-based estimation method with arbitrary geometry for virtual reality [19][20].

The rest of the paper is presented as follows. In section 2, we introduce the Rembrandt lighting and its important features. Section 3 describes the whole process from user input to lighting-direction estimation. Experimental results are shown in Section 4. Finally, we conclude our work and discuss future work.

2 Rembrandt Lighting

The Rembrandt lighting (closed loop lighting) is originated from a painting style created by a Dutch painter, Harmensz van Rijn Rembrandt, in the seventeenth century. In his portraits, he depicted the detailed facial expressions using contrast between shadows and lightings. The lighting used by Rembrandt is adopted by film directors since it is effective for close up shot of actor in movies. Therefore, it became one of the standard lighting for person.

Under the Rembrandt lighting, shadows are connected on a cheek of face as can be seen in Figure 1(c). That is why we call the Rembrandt lighting the closed loop lighting. Lighting designers determine the appropriate lighting conditions by constantly checking this closed loop of shadows.

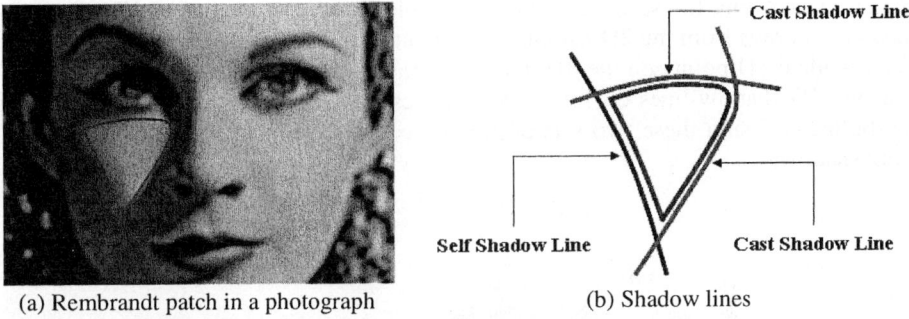

(a) Rembrandt patch in a photograph   (b) Shadow lines

Fig. 2. Rembrandt patch

The triangle shaped bright region surrounded by shadows is called *Rembrandt patch* as shown in Figure 2(a). We seek to estimate a lighting direction inversely by extracting lighting directions from the shadow information. Boundary lines of the Rembrandt patch are composed of three shadow lines. Moreover, the shadow lines are generated by two types of shadows. As presented in Figure 2 (b), one (blue line) is a self shadow line which is formed by surfaces that do not receive direct illumination. The self shadow is also called attached shadow. Another (green line) is a cast shadow line projected by the nose ridge. The other (magenta line) is also a cast shadow line projected by the region of the eye. Whenever the light source changes its position, these three shadow lines are located on different positions.

The "illumination-from-shadow" techniques give us the candidates of illumination directions, and we use these two kinds of shadow information. If users sketch the desired positions of shadows, lighting directions are estimated based on the illumination geometry of the self- and cast- shadows.

3 Proposed Method

Basic idea of our system is to estimate all the possible illumination directions from the desired shadows sketched by a user and decide a final lighting direction for the Rembrandt lighting based on a consensus of the computed directions. Figure 3 describes whole process of our system. Firstly, user sketches two lines on 3D face model (Figure 3(a)). One is a cast-shadow line, the other being a self-shadow line. We apply estimation algorithms to obtain possible illumination directions to fit each shadow line as illustrated in Figure 3(b) and 3(c). Among two groups of possible illumination directions, we decide the final direction that satisfies the illumination constraints given by the cast and self shadows as illustrated in Figure 3(d). With suggested illumination directions, we can visually check the result by forward rendering. To obtain more accurate lighting directions, we can repeat the whole process by modifying the position of the shadow curves a few times.

A user may sketch lines or curves on the 3D face to specify the desired region where the Rembrandt patch will be shown. The user clicks their mouse on the position of lines or curves. We construct 2D spline curves from a set of input points on the screen [21]. Along the spline curves, we sample sufficient number of 2D points and then project rays from the 2D-sampled points into 3D mesh in the direction of camera. We calculate 3D points on the 3D mesh by a ray-triangle intersection algorithm [22]. For two 2D shadow lines on screen coordinates, we obtain corresponding 3D points on the mesh. Using these two sets of 3D vertices, we estimate illumination direction from shadow.

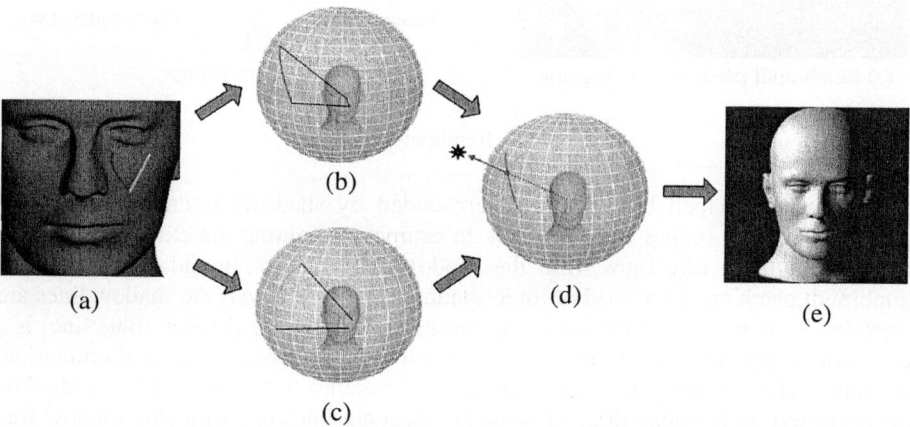

Fig. 3. Diagram of proposed system: (a) sketching shadow lines, (b) illumination from cast shadow, (c) illumination from self shadow, (d) final lighting direction (e) proof rendering

3.1 Illumination Direction from Self Shadow

For vertices corresponding to the self shadow curve, possible illumination directions are calculated. At first, normal vectors of the vertices are mapped onto the Gaussian sphere [23] as depicted in Figure 4(a). We apply the Hough transform to fit the mapped points into circles [24]. Instead of choosing one circle with minimum error value, we collect possible circles within threshold error value. Possible lighting directions are calculated by getting each normal vector of the plane including each circle as shown in Figure 4(b). The possible lighting directions are projected onto the sphere (we call *light direction sphere*) enclosing the face model like Figure 3(b).

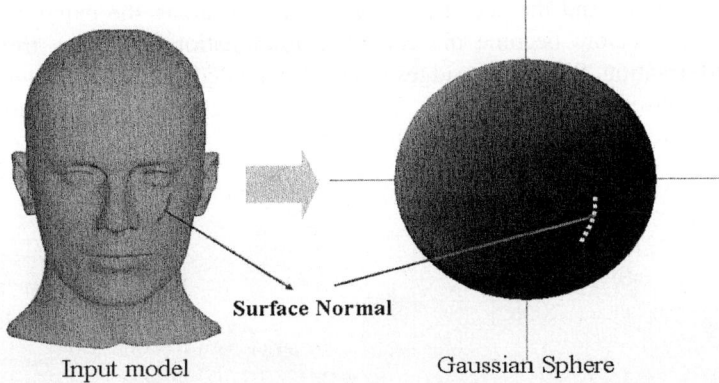

(a) Mapping surface normals of input model to that of Gaussian sphere

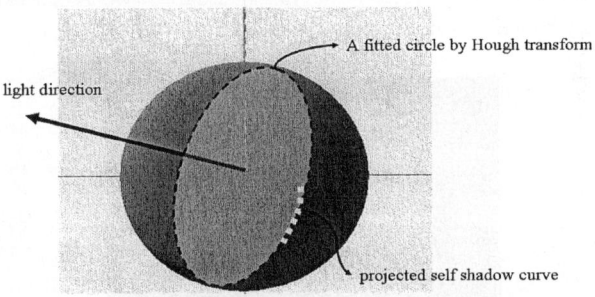

(b) Hough transform on a Gaussian sphere

Fig. 4. Estimating illumination direction from self shadow

3.2 Illumination Direction from Cast Shadow

To estimate light directions from cast shadow curve, we need to know which part of the face model is casting shadows. Since the cast shadow curve of a Rembrandt patch is generated by the nose ridges, we may extract the nose silhouette as viewed from the points on the cast-shadow curve. However, it is time consuming, if not impossible, to determine the nose ridges seen from those shadow boundary points. Therefore, approximate nose ridges are found from a side view of the face model.

As shown in Figure 5(a), we cast rays from the sampled vertices on the shadow curve and then check where each ray intersects with the surface or not. Boundary curve is determined as a nose ridge curve. Figure 5(b) depicts the extracted boundary line. Figure 5(c) shows a result of finding nose ridges. There exists one-to-many correspondence between the extracted boundary curve and the user-specified shadow curve. All the possible direction vectors are computed from the set of 3D points along the shadow curves and the set of 3D points sampled along the extracted boundary curves. These vectors become the candidate illumination directions from the cast shadow information. Since false ridges are often included, we apply a simple filtering algorithm to discard the false ridges. The smoothed lighting directions are projected on the light direction sphere as shown in Figure 3(c).

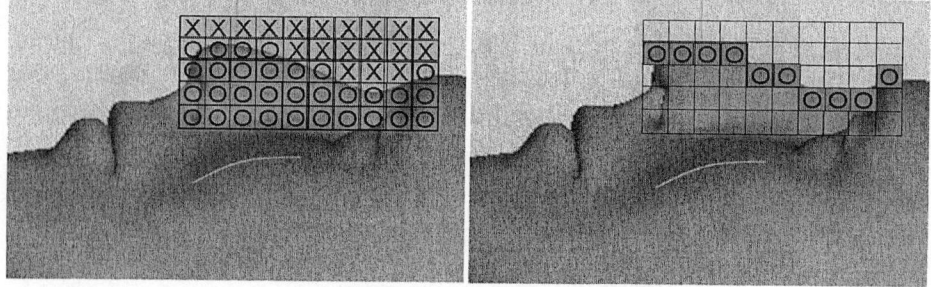

(a) Ray casting from the shadow curve   (b) Boundary curve

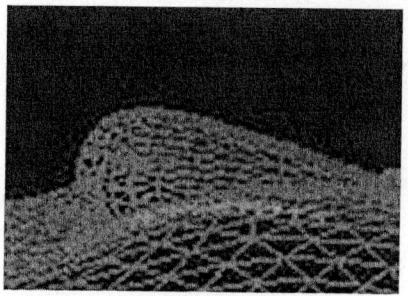

(c) A result of nose ridge line

Fig. 5. Finding nose ridge line

3.3 Determination of Final Lighting Direction

We decide the final direction to fit the two shadow curves using the possible directions for the Rembrandt lighting calculated in section 3.2 and 3.3. Both directions from cast and self shadow are mapped on the light direction sphere. Therefore, we merge them into one light direction sphere and calculate intersection between two groups of directions. In most cases, two lines are intersected as shown in Figure 3(d). Therefore, we decide the final light direction as the intersecting point on the light direction sphere. If the directions are not intersected each other, we simply find one pairs of light directions with minimum distance and decide a middle point between the pairs as the final direction.

4 Experimental Results

We have carried out experiments using 3D face models generated by Maya^{TM}. The model is composed of more than 10,000 triangles. Our algorithm is tested on a PC with P4 2.8GHz CPU and 512 MB RAM. We implement our system with Visual C++ and OpenGL in Windows environment.

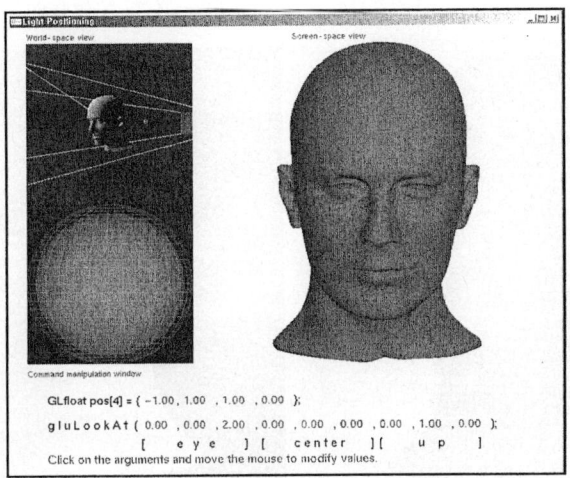

Fig. 6. User interface

Figure 6 shows our interface for supporting interactive design of Rembrandt lighting. Using this interface, we graphically specify the desired shadow curves on the target 3D face model. After drawing the shadow curves on the 3D face model, we can check the estimated lighting directions displayed on both Gaussian sphere and 3D space interactively. Moreover, we check the rendering image by the estimated lighting direction. Whenever users change the position of the shadow curves, all process from calculating lighting directions to rendering images are displayed in our GUI interactively.

Figure 7 explains the effectiveness of our algorithm. From the user input in Figure 7(a), we confirm that the shadows rendered with the estimated illumination direction are closely fitted to the input lines as shown in Figure 7(d). Figure 7(b) is a rendered image using an illumination direction calculated by only cast shadow information. Figure 7(c) presents also a rendered image with an illumination direction calculated by only self shadow information.

We also make experiments with a 3D scanned face model of a real person. As presented in Figure 8, results show a strong possibility to extend our work to real world environment. In addition, we compare working time for designing Rembrandt lighting between without and with our algorithm. Figure 8(b) and 8(c) show an example of rendered results with lighting direction with only manual search and estimation by our algorithm. The result is similar with each other but it takes longer time to search the lighting directions manually. The subjective tests with 10 persons show that people spend from 15 minutes to 1 hour on manually searching the accurate Rembrandt lighting direction. In comparison, it takes less than 2 minutes to search with our algorithm.

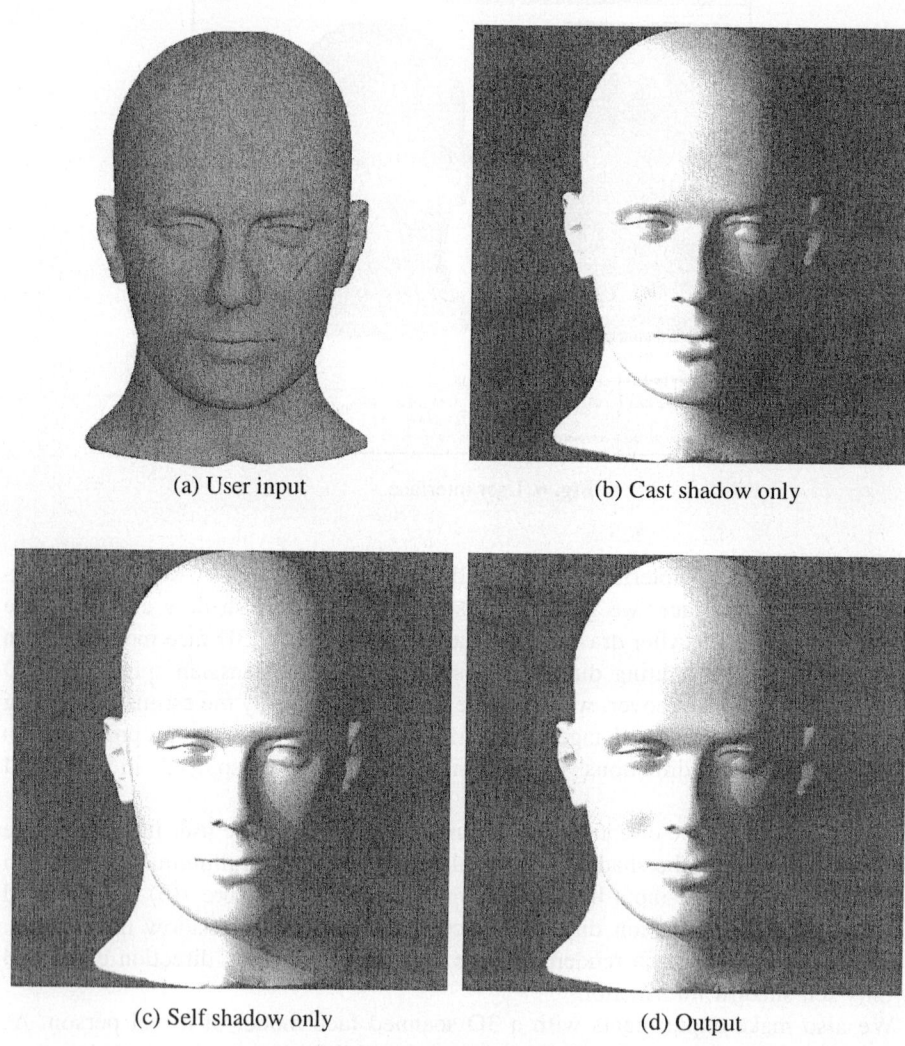

(a) User input (b) Cast shadow only

(c) Self shadow only (d) Output

Fig. 7. Experimental results with a 3D face mesh model

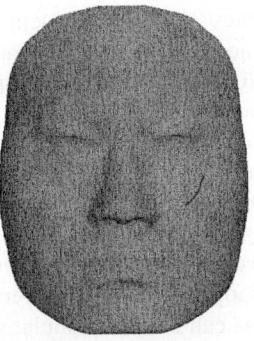

(a) User input

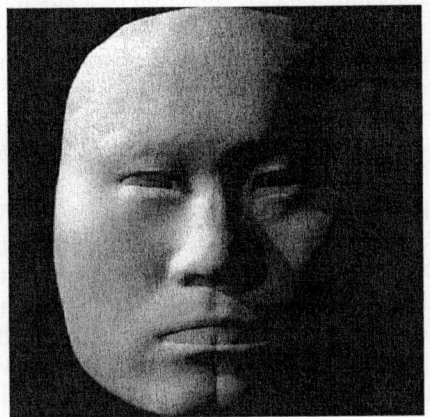

(b) Output by a designer

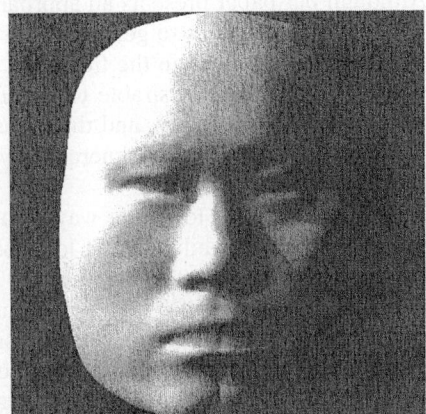

(c) Output by our system

Fig. 8. Experimental results with a 3D scanned face model

5 Conclusion and Future Work

In this paper, we propose an easy way of designing Rembrandt lighting on graphical 3D environment. We present an algorithm that estimates the lighting direction from the specified shadow curves and suggests lighting directions for Rembrandt lighting. Our intuitive interface enables users to design lighting condition interactively. Without much expertise in lighting design, users can design their lighting condition for Rembrandt illumination with the help of our system. Our system facilitates searching for the accurate lighting by avoiding exhaustive trials.

Although we present effectiveness of our method through experiments, we note some limitations in our work. Since the computation of the candidate lighting directions from the cast shadow curves rely on the ridges on a face model, false ridges result in errors. An effective method for collecting valid ridge curves should be developed to improve the accuracy. Another problem is to merge the candidate lighting directions where there is no intersection. Instead of finding a nearest lighting direction among the candidate lighting directions computed from the cast and the self shadow curve, we may obtain better directions for the Rembrandt effect by interpolating the candidate directions. The method for manual specification of Rembrandt patch also leaves room for improvement. Curves as well as vertices can be used to control the position of shadow curve more delicately.

Techniques for designing lighting for other illumination effects than Rembrandt will be a subject of our future work. We intend to extend our system to other standard lighting settings, such as open-loop lighting and butterfly lighting. The lighting directions of standard lighting settings can be also calculated using the shadow curves. For various kinds of lighting settings, we can construct the database of lighting settings and give users more options when they choose the lighting settings.

Although our paper presents an approach for estimating the direction of a key light which mainly contributes to generate the shadows, the directions of fill light and back light should be estimated in the future. In addition to estimating the Rembrandt lighting direction, it will be desirable to calculate the different properties of lighting settings such as size, intensity, and distances of light. For example, soft shadow along the Rembrandt patch can be generated by estimating the size of light as well as the lighting direction..

We also have plans to find a way to utilize the developed method for real-world lighting design. The availability of lost-cost and high-performance range sensors will make it possible to instantly capture the 3D geometry of a performer's face and to guide the lighting design for photography and film. Using the proper photometric and geometric calibration procedure, we can simulate the rendering result using our software and find proper positions of the object and the lights. In the real world, all we have to do will locate the object and the lights on the pre-calculated positions. Instead of estimating the lighting directions based on known 3D geometry information, it will be useful to obtain the lighting direction from images in many applications.

Acknowledgments

This work was supported by the Intelligent Robotics Development Program, one of the 21st Century Frontier R&D Programs funded by the Ministry of Commerce, Industry and Energy of Korea.

References

1. Tracy, K.: The Complete Idiot's Guide to Portrait Photography. Alpha (2002)
2. Millerson, G.: Technique of Lighting for Television and Motion Pictures. Focal Press (1982)
3. Alton, J.: Painting With Light. University of California Press (1995)
4. Lowell, R.: Matters of Light & Depth. Lower Light Management (1999)
5. Zettl, H.: Sight, Sound, Motion: Applied Media Aesthetics. 3rd edn. Wadsworth Publishing (1998)
6. Barzel, R.: Lighting controls for computer cinematography. J. Graph. Tools 2 (1997) 1–20

7. Pentland, A.: Finding the illuminant direction. JOSA 72 (1982) 448–455
8. Yang, Y., Yuille, A.: Sources from shading. In: Proceedings CVPR '91, IEEE Computer Society (1991) 534–539
9. Sato, I., Sato, Y., Ikeuchi, K.: Illumination distribution from shadows. In: Proc. IEEE Conf. Computer Vision and Pattern Recognition (CVPR '99). (1999) 306–312
10. Zhang, Y., Yang, Y.H.: Illuminant direction determination for multiple light sources. In: Computer Vision and Pattern Recognition, 2000. Proceedings. IEEE Conference on. Volume 1. (2000) 269–276
11. Wang, Y., Samaras, D.: Estimation of multiple illuminants from a single image of arbitrary known geometry. In: ECCV '02: Proceedings of the 7th European Conference on Computer Vision-Part III, London, UK, Springer-Verlag (2002) 272–288
12. Li, Y., Lin, S., Lu, H., Shum, H.Y.: Multiple-cue illumination estimation in textured scenes. In: ICCV '03: Proceedings of the Ninth IEEE International Conference on Computer Vision. Volume 2., Washington, DC, USA, IEEE Computer Society (2003) 1366–1373
13. Zhang, Y., Yang, Y.: Multiple illuminant direction detection with application to image synthesis. PAMI 23 (2001) 915–920
14. Poulin, P., Fournier, A.: Lights from highlights and shadows. In: SI3D '92: Proceedings of the 1992 symposium on Interactive 3D graphics, New York, NY, USA, ACM Press (1992) 31–38
15. Pellacini, F., Tole, P., Greenberg, D.P.: A user interface for interactive cinematic shadow design. In: SIGGRAPH '02: Proceedings of the 29th annual conference on Computer graphics and interactive techniques, New York, NY, USA, ACM Press (2002) 563–566
16. Gershbein, R., Hanrahan, P.: A fast relighting engine for interactive cinematic lighting design. In: SIGGRAPH '00: Proceedings of the 27th annual conference on Computer graphics and interactive techniques, New York, NY, USA, ACM Press/Addison-Wesley Publishing Co. (2000) 353–358
17. Dorsey, J.O., Sillion, F.X., Greenberg, D.P.: Design and simulation of opera lighting and projection effects. In: SIGGRAPH '91: Proceedings of the 18th annual conference on Computer graphics and interactive techniques, New York, NY, USA, ACM Press (1991) 41–50
18. Schoeneman, C., Dorsey, J., Smits, B., Arvo, J., Greenburg, D.: Painting with light. In: SIGGRAPH '93: Proceedings of the 20th annual conference on Computer graphics and interactive techniques, New York, NY, USA, ACM Press (1993) 143–146
19. Wang, Y., Samaras, D.: Estimation of multiple directional light sources for synthesis of augmented reality images. Graphical Models 65 (2003) 185–205
20. Wang, Y., Samaras, D.: Multiple directional illuminant estimation from a single image. In: IEEE CPMCV Workshop (in conjunction with ICCV 2003). (2003)
21. Moller, T., Trumbore, B.: Fast, minimum storage ray-triangle intersection. J. Graph. Tools 2 (1997) 21–28
22. Akenine-Moller, T., Haines, E.: Real-Time Rendering. 2nd edn. AK Peters, Ltd. (2002)
23. Horn, B.K.: Extended gaussian images. PIEEE 72 (1984) 1656–1678
24. Duda, R.O., Hart, P.E.: Use of the hough transformation to detect lines and curves in pictures. Commun. ACM 15 (1972) 11–15

Image-Based Generation of Facial Skin Texture with Make-Up

Sang Min Kim, Kyoung Chin Seo, and Sang Wook Lee

Department of Media Technology, Sogang University,
1 Shinsu-dong, Mapo-gu, Seoul, Korea 121-742
{i12cuagain, jiniseo, slee}@sogang.ac.kr

Abstract. This paper presents a new approach to the realistic rendering of facial skin and to the transform of bare-skin colors into make-up ones based on the BTF measurement from 2D photographs. We develop an apparatus to capture skin texture images under various lighting and viewing directions. Instead of physical modeling of human skin layers, our approach is based on the BTF (Bidirectional Texture Function) for skin texture generation and rendering. We present a method to add make-up effects to bare skin using a color transformation between the BTFs of bare skin and skin with make-up. Experimental results demonstrate that the presented method generates realistic skin texture and cosmetic effects.

1 Introduction

In the field of computer graphics and multimedia, realistic rendering of skin has become an important research topic recently. Human skin has spatial variations of its texture and shows complex optical properties. Therefore, it is difficult to render 3D face skin model realistically using simple synthetic skin texture. Moreover, makeup changes the reflectance of the skin as shown in Figure 1. Reflectance properties change due to the addition of cosmetic substance. In this paper, we analyze the makeup effects from photographs and present a method for synthesizing realistic texture with makeup from the photographs taken from the real skin.

Some of the previous research has focused on modeling reflectance characteristics of skin. Translucency of skin has been explained by subsurface scattering [1][2]. While BRDF representation has been dealing with reflectance on the surface, BSSRDF includes reflectance properties caused by scattering beneath the surface. However, this approach is more useful to homogenous materials like marbles. On the other hand, human skin is composed of different materials like melanin, hemoglobin, and collagen. Research based on Dermatology and Optics have analyzed human skin as multi-layered structure and inhomogeneous material [3][4][5] but it concentrate on color characteristics of skin. A rendering technique considering multilayered structure was also investigated by Hanrahan *et al.* [6]. It should provide an effective way of synthesizing skin images if realistic physical parameters are given.

Image-based approach has obtained the reflectance properties from captured photographs of skin. BRDF property of human skin is estimated from photographs captured under varying light directions [7]. In spite of accurate representation of the reflectance

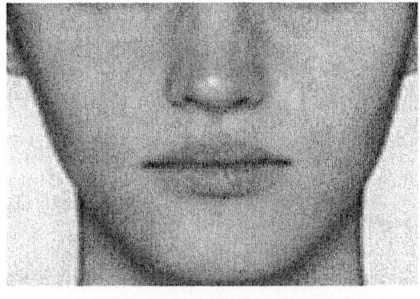
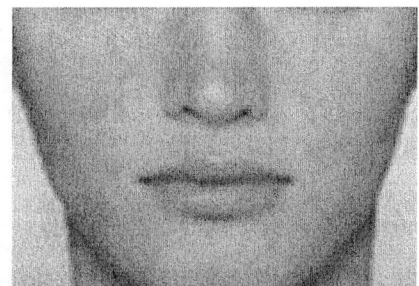

(a) Bare skin (b) Skin with make-up

Fig. 1. Appearance change after makeup

properties, the BRDF model cannot include characteristics of the human skin texture because it is the model for reflectance of one point on the object surface. Instead, BTF model [8] includes spatial variation of materials. The 6-dimensional BTF function includes spatial variation of texture while 4-dimensional BRDF shows reflectance ratio of a point on the surface. Rendering 3D surfaces using sampled BTF data is presented by Tong *et al.* [9]. They propose the synthesis of BTF data by texton-based analysis. Suykens *et al.* approximate BTF database using a factorization method for hardware accelerated rendering [10]. The BTF database is decomposed into small texture maps and synthesized in the graphics hardware. Koudelka *et al.* focus on compression of large dataset of BTF [11]. The BTF images are aligned using a rectified method and represented as a weighted sum of basis images. For the diagnosis purpose of skin diseases, Cula *et al.* presents skin texture modeling based on the BTF [12][13]. After capturing small part of skin images under varying lights and viewing directions, they extract features to recognize specific types of skin diseases.

In this paper, we present a practical rendering method using photographs and adding makeup effects. Our rendering method includes all the effects on the skin such as spatial variation of texture and complex optical properties. We discuss the addition of make-up effects to facial skin data based on the BTF model. After measuring BTF data for bare and make-up skin, we perform color transformation between corresponding data sets. For rendering of 3D model, we generate texture maps using a texture quilting technique.

The rest of this paper is organized as follows. Section 2 describes the reflectance model used in our method. We present whole process from data acquisition to rendering in section 3. Experimental results are shown and discussed in section 4. In section 5, we conclude our work and discuss future work.

2 Reflectance Model: BTF

To represent reflectance information including the spatial variation of human skin texture, we use the BTF (Bidirectional Texture Function). The collection of BTF data is illustrated in Figure 2. Under various lighting directions ω_i and viewpoints ω_o, we capture the reflectance for all points x on local region of texture. The BTF f is denoted by :

$$f(x, \omega_i, \omega_o),\qquad(1)$$

where x is 2D spatial location on the surface and ω_i and ω_o are incident lighting direction and camera viewing direction in the spherical coordinates, respectively. The BTF is a 6-dimensional representation of texture and reflectance. Since the BTF function accounts for complex reflections due to specularity, interreflection, shadow/masking effect by macrostructure in addition to shading, it has been considered as a potentially effective representation for complex surfaces such as skins. In this paper, we construct the BTF database for a small region of human facial skin.

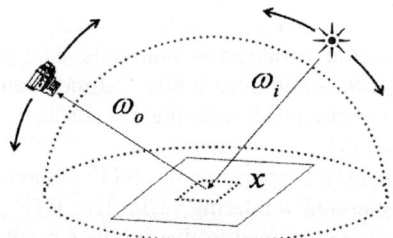

Fig. 2. Bidirectional Texture Function

3 Proposed Method

Basic motivation of our work presented in this paper is to transfer a make-up effect of a face onto another face. The makeup effect is computed from two sets of BTFs: one from a bare skin and another from the same skin with makeup. The overall process is depicted in Figure 3. Firstly, we capture BTF data of bare and makeup skin of the same face under uniformly sampled lighting and viewing directions. Using these pairs of BTF data sets, we observe how much colors are changed by applying makeup, which we call cosmetic factor. We add the makeup effect to new person's bare skin by multiplying its BTF dataset by the cosmetic factor. Among the transferred BTF data set, we collect skin patches corresponding to the surface normals of local surfaces on a 3D model and then use a texture synthesis technique to generate texture image for mapping. The generated texture map includes texture details and reflectance variations under a specific lighting direction, and can be used to render realistic 3D human face.

3.1 Acquiring BTF Datasets

The acquisition of BTF datasets of human skin is done by capturing hundreds of photographs of facial skin with sampled lighting and viewing directions. For the effective use of the BTF, the lighting directions $\omega_i(\phi_i, \theta_i)$ and viewing directions

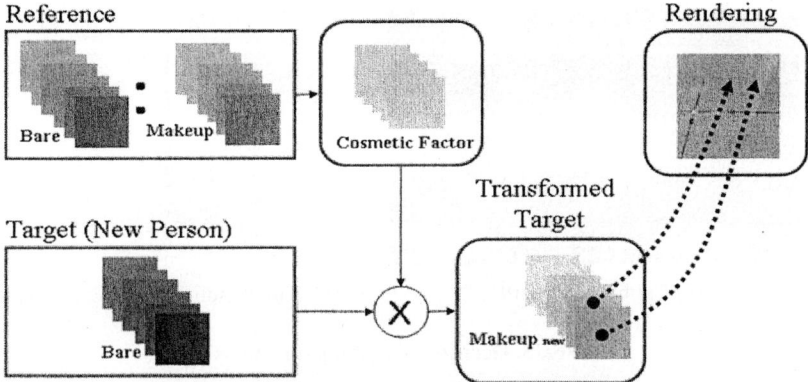

Fig. 3. Diagram of overall process

Fig. 4. Apparatus to control lighting directions

$\omega_o(\phi_o, \theta_o)$ in Equation 1 have to be known accurately. We design an arc-shaped apparatus as shown in Figure 4 to efficiently control lighting directions. BTF images are captured in uniformly sampled intervals in illumination and viewing angles.

For the accurate measurement of lighting and viewing directions, we designed a calibration board as shown in Figure 5(a). Checkerboard patterns are printed and four needles are attached around the square hole for skin viewing. We attach this calibration board to the skin region of interest. Using the printed checker board patterns, conventional calibration method is used for the viewing directions $\omega_o(\phi_o, \theta_o)$. The shadows cast by the four needles give us the clues for the estimation of the lighting directions, $\omega_i(\phi_i, \theta_i)$. As depicted in Figure 5(b), the zenith angle of the incident light direction, θ_i, is estimated using the simple geometric relationship between the shadow length a and the needle length b as follows:

$$\theta_i = 90 - \tan^{-1}(b/a). \tag{2}$$

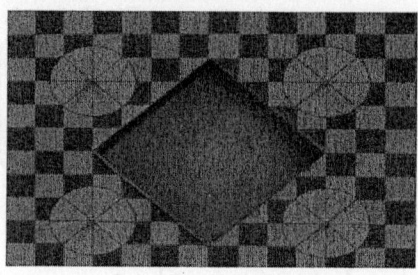 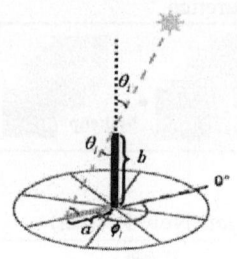

(a) Calibration board (b) Calculation of lighting direction

Fig. 5. Decision of lighting directions

We determine the final zenith angle of the lighting direction by averaging all the directions calculated from the 4 needles. The azimuth angle ϕ_i of the lighting direction is also calculated by averaging the azimuth angles of the shadows cast by 4 needles. We calculate a shadow vector from starting and ending point of the shadow. We get the azimuth angle from the difference between the shadow vector and the reference vector calculated from printed circle. The remaining parameter x, spatial location of skin image, is registered after warping every skin regions into a rectangular one. As a result, we organize image irradiance for each corresponding location, lighting direction, and viewing direction.

3.2 Cosmetic Factor: Transformation Between Two BTF Datasets

When people apply makeup, a new layer composed of cosmetic substances covers the bare skin layer as shown in Figure 6(b). We generate the optical effect of this new layer based on a simplified analysis of reflectance. The radiance from the skin layer structure is formulated as the multiplication of the irradiance $E(x, y, \lambda)$ and an exponential function based on the Lambert-Beer theory [14]. The reflectance equation of the skin with makeup, $L_M(x, y, \lambda)$, at specific a location (x, y) over spectrum is denoted by :

$$L_M(x, y, \lambda) = \exp(C(x, y) + B(x, y))E(x, y, \lambda), \qquad (3)$$

where $B(x, y) = -\rho_b(x, y)\sigma_b(x, y)$ and $C(x, y) = -\rho_c(x, y)\sigma_c(x, y)$. $\rho(x, y)$ is the pigment density of the layer and $\sigma(x, y)$ is the cross section of the layer. The subscripts b and c denote bare skin layer and cosmetic layer, respectively. We assume that the bare skin has one layer structure and that the skin with makeup is represented as two layer structure. The reflectance of the bare skin, $L_B(x, y, \lambda)$, is denoted by:

$$L_B(x, y, \lambda) = \exp(B(x, y))E(x, y, \lambda). \qquad (4)$$

The difference by makeup, which we call the cosmetic factor $\Delta(x, y)$, is obtained by dividing Equation 4 by Equation 3.

$$\Delta(x, y) = \exp(C(x, y)) = \frac{L_M(x, y, \lambda)}{L_B(x, y, \lambda)}. \tag{5}$$

Inversely, we add the cosmetic effect to new BTF skin data of arbitrary person by multiplication of $\Delta(x, y)$ as follows:

$$L'_M(x, y, \lambda) = L'_B(x, y, \lambda)\Delta(x, y), \tag{6}$$

where $L'_B(x, y, \lambda)$ denotes the radiance of BTF dataset of new person's bare skin and $L'_M(x, y, \lambda)$ is a newly generated BTF dataset mixed with cosmetic effects. Eventually, we use $L'_M(x, y, \lambda)$ to render a 3D face model by texture mapping.

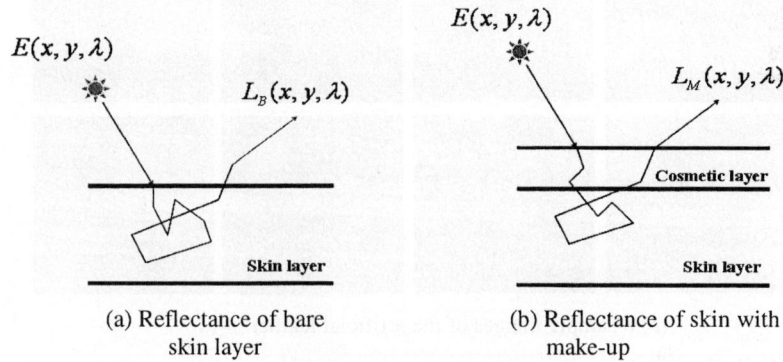

(a) Reflectance of bare skin layer

(b) Reflectance of skin with make-up

Fig. 6. Reflectance of skin layer

3.3 Texture Generation and Rendering on 3D Face Model

We generate a texture map composed of BTF data patches for rendering 3D human face model. Global lighting and viewing conditions are set up in advance. Surface normal of each polygon of the 3D face model and the known global lighting and global viewing direction are used to calculate lighting direction $\omega_i(\phi_i, \theta_i)$ and viewing direction $\omega_o(\phi_o, \theta_o)$. The corresponded texture patches for each polygon of the 3D model, $f(x, \omega_i(\phi_i, \theta_i), \omega_o(\phi_o, \theta_o))$, is drawn from the BTF data set. If the BTF patch with corresponding light direction and viewing direction does not exist in the data set, we select a BTF patch nearest the corresponding directions. Instead of mapping the retrieved patches to the corresponding polygon one by one, we make a texture map by merging all patches into one. To generate a seamless texture map, we utilize an image quilting method [15] instead of directly copying BTF patches on the corresponding location of texture map. We can simply render the 3D model using the synthesized texture map.

4 Experimental Results

Experiments have been carried out for leather datasets and human skin datasets using our proposed method. We use a Sony XC-003 3CCD color video camera connected to Matrox MC-II capture board for the image acquisition. After attaching the calibration board to the skin region of interest, we perform standard camera calibration. Before experimenting with real human skins, we test the BTF-based rendering method using an artificial leather patch. We construct a BTF data set using 1200 captured

(a) 8 sample images of the artificial leather

(b) Rendering result

Fig. 7. Rendering result of a cylinder with artificial leather texture

images. In order to render a cylinder, 100 BTF patches with corresponding lighting and viewing directions are collected among the dataset. As presented in Figure 7(a), the appearance of the artificial leather sample changes under various lighting directions. The selected eight images are captured from a fixed viewing direction and different lighting directions. Figure 7(b) shows a rendering result using the corresponding image samples. It can be seen that our approach produces realistic spatial shading of texture according to the surface orientation change.

Figure 8 shows the experimental results for generating cosmetic effects. We generate three BTF datasets for same person by adding makeup base and powder. Figure 8 (b) and Figure 8 (c) are the captured images after applying make-up base and adding powder to the same skin region, respectively. After calculating the cosmetic factors, we transform the bare skin with the cosmetic factors. Figure 8 (d) and (e) show the synthesized skins with makeup base and additional powder, respectively.

Using the cosmetic factors, we transform the different person's skin as shown in Figure 9. We take photographs of two person's bare skins as shown in Figure 9 (a) and (d) and transform each bare skin to a skin with makeup base and a powdered skin using the cosmetic factors computed from the datasets in Figure 8. Figure 9 (b), (c), (e), and (f) show the synthesized results with the cosmetic factors of a different person.

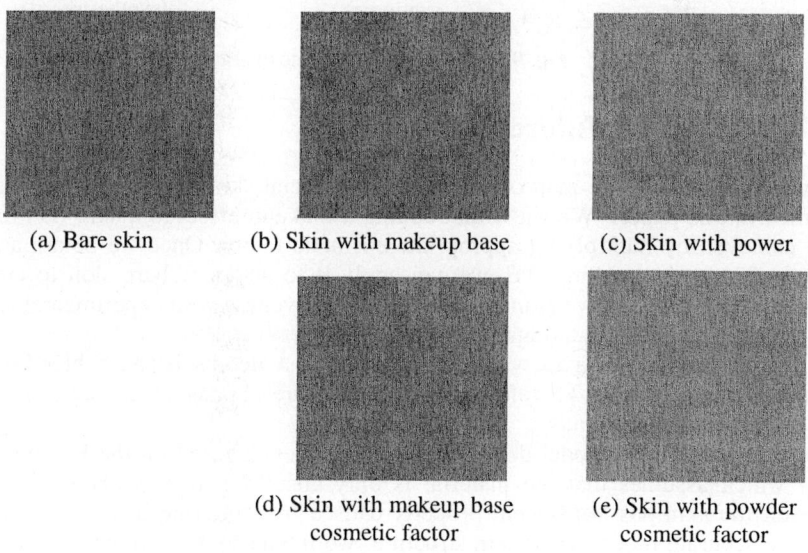

(a) Bare skin (b) Skin with makeup base (c) Skin with power

(d) Skin with makeup base cosmetic factor (e) Skin with powder cosmetic factor

Fig. 8. Simulation result using cosmetic factors

Results using human facial skin are shown in Figure 10. Instead of whole face, we focus on the cheek area which has approximately 900 polygons. Figure 10 (a) and 10 (b) show the rendered results using reference BTF dataset which are captured to calculate the cosmetic factor. Rendering result of bare skin of target person is presented in Figure 10 (c). A face with synthesized makeup is obtained by multiplying the cosmetic factor is shown in Figure 10 (d). The results show that appearance changes due to applying cosmetics are transferred onto new BTF dataset.

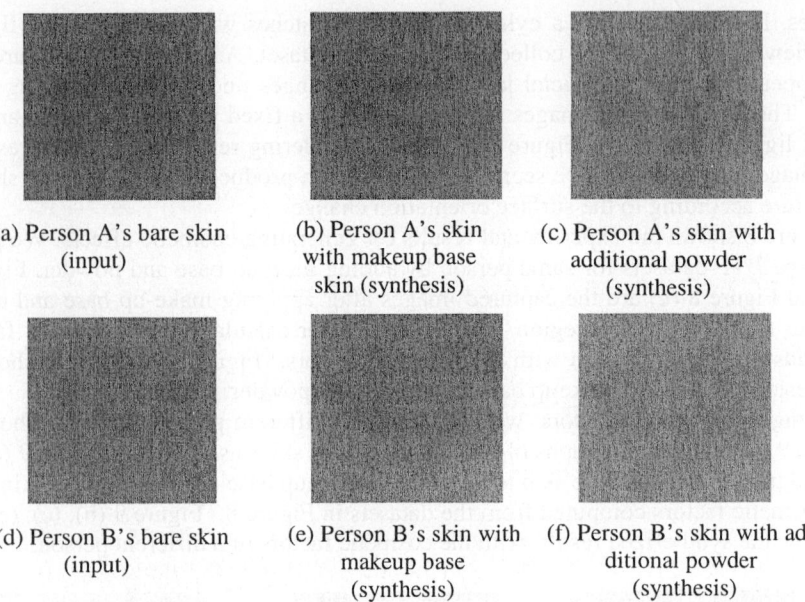

Fig. 9. Synthesis results by cosmetic factors

5 Conclusion and Future Work

The generation of texture map of texture map of facial skin with realistic makeup is presented in this paper. We show that adding a makeup effect to a skin BTF can be easily achieved by multiplying appropriate cosmetic factor. Once we obtain a set of cosmetic factors for a skin BTF, we can apply it to any new bare skin to create a makeup effect, and we have demonstrated the effectiveness with experimental results. Below, we discuss the limitations and future work.

To make the texture map without seam, we lost details because blending and smoothing are included. Therefore, improved texture expansion methods are desirable for preserving the details.

The cosmetic factor model developed in this paper is based on the Lambert-Beer theory which assumes that the material is only absorbing light without scattering. However, the skin has translucent property caused by scattering inside the material. For more accurate modeling of skin structure, we intend to develop new models that account for multi-layered structure and scattering beneath the surface. We plan to investigate various approaches to modeling the reflectance change by makeup including image-based decomposition of pigments based on a scattering model such as the Kubelka-Munk model.

We are currently working to improve the efficiency of our measurement system. The results shown in this paper is limited to one skin region. By developing a system for the automatic control of lighting and viewing directions, we will be able to capture the BTF data more efficiently and obtain more skin samples from various facial regions. This will make the synthesized facial skin more realistic. We are also investigating to develop more accurate camera and light calibration methods. Efficiency in temrs of data storage can be achieved by data compression. It will be useful in many applications to reduce the size of BTF data by compression or to find a new compact representation instead of stacking multiple images.

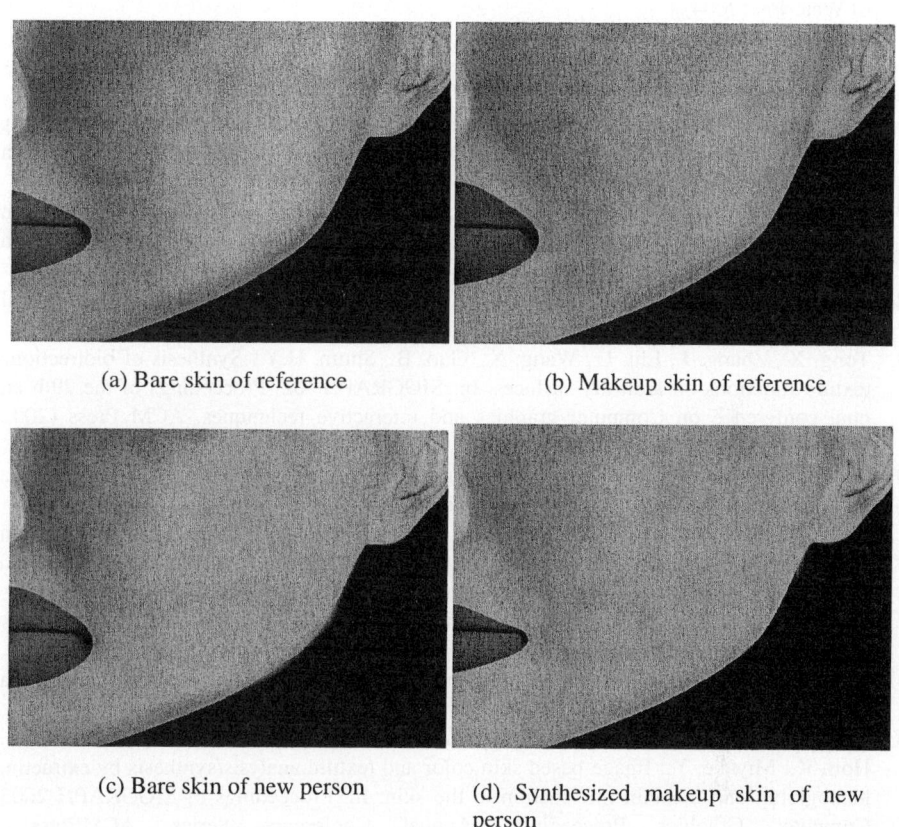

(a) Bare skin of reference
(b) Makeup skin of reference
(c) Bare skin of new person
(d) Synthesized makeup skin of new person

Fig. 10. Rendered results

Acknowledgments

This work was supported by the Intelligent Robotics Development Program, one of the 21st Century Frontier R&D Programs funded by the Ministry of Commerce, Industry and Energy of Korea.

References

1. Jensen, H., Marschner, S., Levoy, M., Hanrahan, P.: A practical model for subsurface light transport. In: Proceedings of SIGGRAPH 2001. (2001) 511–518
2. Jensen, H.W., Buhler, J.: A rapid hierarchical rendering technique for translucent materials. In: SIGGRAPH '02: Proceedings of the 29th annual conference on Computer graphics and interactive techniques, ACM Press (2002) 576–581

3. van Gemert, M., Jacques, S., Sterenborg, H., W.M.Star: Skin optics. IEEE Transactions on Biomedical Engineering 36 (1989) 1146–1154
4. Krishnaswamy, A., Baranoski, G.V.G.: A study on skin optics. Technical Report CS-2004-01, Natural Phenomena Simulation Group, School of Computer Science, University of Waterloo (2004)
5. Angelopoulou, E.: Understanding the color of human skin. In: Proceedings of the SPIE Conference on Human Vision and Electronic Imaging VI. Volume 4299., SPIE Press (2001) 243–251
6. Hanrahan, P., Krueger,W.: Reflection from layered surfaces due to subsurface scattering. In: Proceedings of the 20th annual conference on Computer graphics and interactive techniques, ACM Press (1993) 165–174
7. Marschner, S.R., Westin, S.H., Lafortune, E.P.F., Torrance, K.E., Greenberg, D.P.: Imagebased brdf measurement including human skin. In: Proceedings of 10th EurographicsWorkshop on Rendering. (1999) 139–152
8. Dana, K., van Ginneken, B., Nayar, S., Koenderink, J.: Reflectance and texture of real-world surfaces. ACM Transactions on Graphics 18 (1999) 1–34
9. Tong, X., Zhang, J., Liu, L., Wang, X., Guo, B., Shum, H.Y.: Synthesis of bidirectional texture functions on arbitrary surfaces. In: SIGGRAPH '02: Proceedings of the 29th annual conference on Computer graphics and interactive techniques, ACM Press (2002) 665–672
10. Suykens, F., vom Berge, K., Lagae, A., Dutre, P.: Interactive rendering with bidirectional texture functions. Computer Graphics Forum 22 (2003)
11. Koudelka, M.L., Magda, S., Belhumeur, P.N., Kriegman, D.J.: Acquisition, compression, and synthesis of bidirectional texture functions. In: 3rd International Workshop on Texture Analysis and Synthesis (Texture 2003). (2003) 59–64
12. Cula, O.G., Dana, K.J.: Bidirectional imaging and modeling of skin texture. IEEE Transactions on Biomedical Engineering 51 (2004) 2148–2159
13. Cula, O.G., Dana, K.J., Murphy, F.P., Rao, B.K.: Skin texture modeling. International Journal of Computer Vision 62 (2004) 97–119
14. Tsumura, N., Ojima, N., Sato, K., Shiraishi, M., Shimizu, H., Nabeshima, H., Akazki, S., Hori, K., Miyake, Y.: Image-based skin color and texture analysis/synthesis by extracting hemoglobin and melanin information in the skin. In: Proceedings of SIGGRAPH 2003. Computer Graphics Proceedings, Annual Conference Series, ACMPress / ACMSIGGRAPH (2003) 770–779
15. Efros, A.A., Freeman, W.T.: Image quilting for texture synthesis and transfer. In: Proceedings of SIGGRAPH 2001, ACM Press / ACM SIGGRAPH (2001) 341–346

Responsive Multimedia System for Virtual Storytelling*

Youngho Lee[1], Sejin Oh[1], Youngmin Park[1], Beom-Chan Lee[2], Jeung-Chul Park[3],
Yoo Rhee Oh[4], Seokhee Lee[6], Han Oh[7], Jeha Ryu[2], Kwan H. Lee[3], Hong Kook Kim[4],
Yong-Gu Lee[5], JongWon Kim[6], Yo-Sung Ho[7], and Woontack Woo[1]

[1] GIST U-VR Lab., Gwangju 500-712, S.Korea
{ylee, sejinoh, ypark, wwoo}@gist.ac.kr
[2] Human-Machine-Computer Interface Lab.
{bclee, ryu}@gist.ac.kr
[3] Intelligent Design & Graphics Lab.
{jucpark, lee}@kyebek.gist.ac.kr
[4] Speech, Audio, and Language Communications Lab.
{yroh, hongkook}@gist.ac.kr
[5] Nanoscale Simulation Lab.
lygu@gist.ac.kr
[6] Network Media Lab.
{shlee, jongwon}@netmedia.gist.ac.kr
[7] Visual Communications Lab.
{ohhan, hoyo}@gist.ac.kr

Abstract. In this paper, we propose Responsive Multimedia System (RMS) for a virtual storytelling. It consists of three key components; Multi-modal Tangible User Interface (MTUI), a Unified Context-aware Application Model for Virtual Environments (vr-UCAM), and Virtual Environment Manager (VEManager). MTUI allows users to interact with virtual environments (VE) through human's senses by exploiting tangible, haptic and vision-based interfaces. vr-UCAM decides reactions of VE according to multi-modal input. VEManager generates dynamic VE by applying the reactions and display it through 3D graphics and 3D sounds, etc. To demonstrate an effectiveness of the proposed system, we implemented a virtual storytelling system which unfolds a legend of Unju Temple. We believe the proposed system plays an important role in implementing various entertainment applications.

1 Introduction

With the rapid advancement of hardware and software, entertainment computing industry has been popularized during the last decade. Nowadays, it is common for users to interact with virtual environment (VE) in various kinds of application areas including simulation, training, education, and entertainment. In this regard, many VR systems have been developed in various types to show its effectiveness.

Many researchers have studied about virtual reality system for virtual storytelling. Most virtual storytelling system integrates multimedia presentation, multimodal interfaces. The representative examples are KidsRoom (Bobick et al., 1996), NICE (Roussos, M et al., 1997) and Larsen and Petersen's (1999) storytelling environment

---
* This work was supported in part by CTRC, and in part by MIC through RBRC at GIST.

[1][2][3]. They combined the physical and the virtual world into interactive narrative play space. They also make a child's bedroom or a CAVE-like environment changed as an unusual world for fantasy plays by using images, lighting, sound, and vision-based action recognition. They offers interactive story through reactions to the user's actions. However, their interfaces are not natural to control general VE since they exploits specific devices (3D wand) or vision-based tracking system. Moreover, these systems reduce user's interest because they only show same responses without considering users. Moreover, they make users perceive gaps between real and virtual environments by ignoring changes in the real environments.

We present Responsive Multimedia System (RMS) for virtual storytelling with immersive multimedia contents. It consists of three key components; a multi-modal tangible user interface (MTUI), a Unified Context-aware Application Model for Virtual Environments (vr-UCAM), and virtual environment manager (VEManager). MTUI allows users to interact with virtual environments through human's senses by exploiting tangible, haptic and vision-based interfaces. vr-UCAM decides suitable reactions based on multi-modal input [4][5]. Finally, VEManager generates dynamic VE through 3D graphics and 3D sounds, etc.

The proposed RMS has the following advantages. It allows users to naturally interact with virtual environments through multimodal interfaces, such as tangible, haptic and vision-based interfaces. It also shows adaptive reactions according to the user's input through the multimodal interfaces. Moreover, it provides users with realistic virtual environments by exploiting 3D graphics and 3D sounds. Therefore, it maximizes user's interest through interactive and immersive virtual story telling system.

To demonstrate a usefulness of the proposed system, we designed interactive story about 'Unju Temple'. We described several events on specified locations of the temple and then classified them as applicable points for vr-UCAM. Moreover, it shows narrative stories stimulated not only by human physical senses but also by their experiences, knowledge and emotion without limitations of space and time. We also implemented bi-directional interactive 3D web for enjoying contents through the web site. We expect that RMS can evoke personal experience, knowledge, feeling and senses of participants through the virtual storytelling.

This paper is organized as follows. We describe the conceptual design for proposed system in Section 2. In Section 3 and 4, we explain the detailed explanation of RMS and implementation. Finally, the conclusion and future works are presented in Section 5.

2 Conceptual Design of Responsive Multimedia System

In proposed RMS, we divide Environment into four parts as basic elements for storytelling: user, real surrounding, virtual object and virtual surrounding. We assume that these are basic elements for storytelling. All virtual objects and surroundings are connected with an input and output relationship. In this architecture, the start point of interaction can be user or a virtual object. Once users manipulate a real surrounding, user's gesture is acquired from multi-modal interface then it is delivered to virtual objects or virtual surroundings. Then the virtual object shows suitable responses according to the acquired input. Then the virtual object selects animated actions according to the context acquired [16]. Also these animated actions bring an effect to the virtual surrounding. On the other hand, the virtual surroundings influence environmental condition according to the context. As shown in Fig.1, the proposed RMS is composed of a table-type multi-modal tangible user interface (MTUI), a unified context-aware application model for virtual environments (vr-UCAM), and virtual environment manager (VEManager).

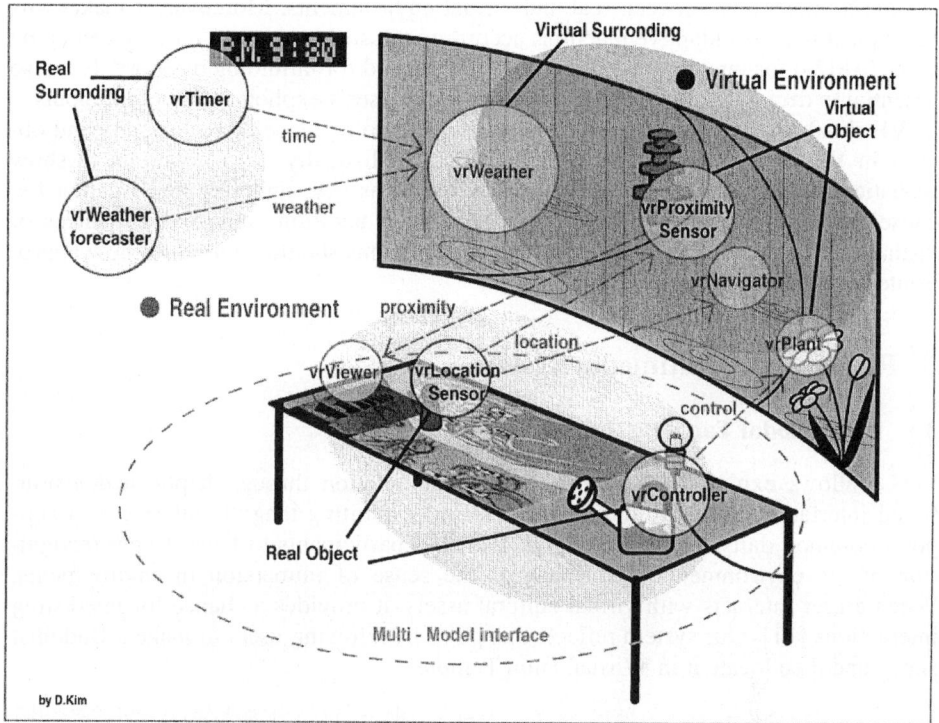

Fig. 1. Conceptual Design of RMS; It supports seamless integration of vrSensor and vrService. Left side is real environment and right side is virtual environment.

To design multi-modal user interface, we consider which modality have to be integrated in RMS. Human perceive the environment in which they live through their senses (e.g. vision, hearing, touch, smell, and taste)[6][7]. Since vision, hearing, and touch are the main factors of human sense, we select these three modalities. On the other hand, human express their own intention with voice, hand/body movement, facial express, and so on. Considering mapping of different human-action modalities to computer-sensing modalities, position/motion and video sensing devices can sense multiple human actions. For instance, facial expression and hand or eye movement can be sensed through the vision sensor. Therefore, we integrate position/motion and video sensing devices in prototype of RMS

We design multi-modal tangible user interface as a form of table since we want to use various types of objects on the table. It has table screen, LCD projector, table glasses, sound devices and one workstation. We include vision-based and haptic interface for the multi-modality in it. So users can manipulate the tangible object and watch information from table screen. Users also sense touch from direct manipulation of tangible object. From the vision-based tracking system, user's gesture and motion are detected by tracking position/motion of tangible object. Clearly, force feedback from haptic device stimulates human's touch sense.

We can improve realism of user's experience by exploiting vr-UCAM2.0 (a Unified Context-aware Application Model for Virtual Environments) [371]. It supports seamless interaction between real and virtual environments. Moreover, it makes virtual object to show adaptive reactions according to user's context. Thus, we can apply vr-UCAM2.0 for integration of the whole system and for unfolding the story. It is also essential to decide pertinent responses suitable for user's explicit and implicit inputs.

VE should provide realistic immersion. It needs to be modeled realistically and objects in VE have to show animated sequences realistically. It is important to show realistic 3D terrain and environment factors such as sky, lightning and weather because users can feel the mood of environment. In addition, animated sequences of virtual objects should be considered. These animations should be used to show appropriate responses to unfold a scenario.

3 Responsive Multimedia System

3.1 Multi-modal Tangible User Interface

MTUI allows exploration and interactive manipulation through haptic and vision-based interfaces. Since we designed MTUI by exploiting tangible interfaces, it supports common daily interaction [8][9]. It assists participants to have deeper recognition of the environments, and enhances the sense of immersion in environments. When a user interacts with virtual cultural assets, it provides a chance for interesting interactions [11]. Our system reflects this point by allowing users to make a Buddhist statue and then locate it in 'Virtual Unju Temple'.

3.1.1 Vision-Based Interface

ARTable is a table-based tangible user interface system which uses a projector and two cameras to display information and to track tangible objects [10]. One of the cameras is placed over the table to capture its surface and augment virtual objects on it. By showing what is happening in the VE within real space, the augmentation helps the user to know how the table and the VE are related. Another camera and the projector are placed under the table. By using half-transparent material, the table could show projection images on the table and the camera could see objects on the table surface. The objects are attached with ARToolKit markers on their bottom so that marker detection is not interfered with users' hand occlusion [13]. And if the objects are needed to be tracked in 3D space, markers are also attached on them.

In RMS, ARTable displays a map with indications of interaction cues through the projector and users manipulate tangible objects to interact with the VE. Although most virtual reality systems are equipped with a 3D joystick for the navigation, it is easy to lose users' current location and direction in VE. Thus we give a location and meaning of it to the user to help user's perception of the VE. Tangible objects are more familiar form than 3D joystick or mechanical devices especially to the novice

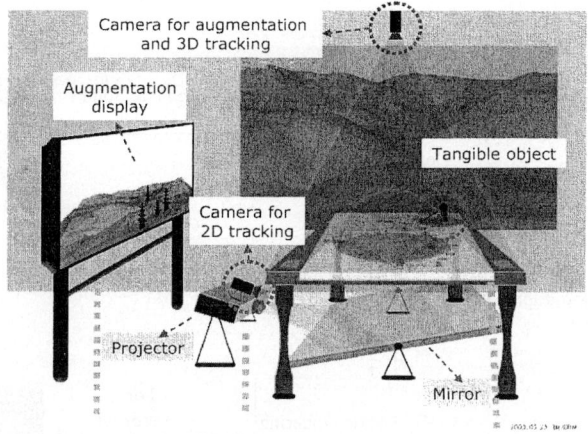

Fig. 2. ARTable and Display

users. Thus they are sensible to manipulate and reflect where the user wants to navigate or what the user want to do.

ARTable is composed of table-type frame, projector, two cameras, table screen, and various types of tangible objects as shown in Fig. 2. Calibration is an off-line process for a transformation between two cameras. After calibration, we can calculate the poses of AR Markers attached on the tangible object. The table and AR display show information to help users' interaction. Tangible objects support various interactions for VEs. And we also display a map of VE on the table screen and we calibrate position of tangible object and the map.

3.1.2 Haptic Interface

A system configuration for haptic interaction is shown in Fig. 3. This system is mainly composed of three parts: database, graphic, and haptic process. The database has rough Buddhist image generated by a modeling tool such as Maya or 3D Max. Each 3D model is represented by geometric vertex, face, color, and texture as obj file format.

The geometric data are used for performing graphic and haptic deformation in each process. Since the graphic and haptic process has their own thread, two processes run at 30Hz and 1 KHz, respectively. In the graphic process, an immersive virtual environment which has a virtual sculpting background is created and a rough Buddhist model is loaded for achieving deformation. Each virtual object is loaded with realistic texture mapping to provide a user with immersive interaction. In order to enhance performance of graphic rendering, each object is optimized by display list and indexed geometry methods which are commonly used for computational optimization of graphic rendering.

In the haptic process, 3 DOF haptic interaction and haptic deformation are performed in 1 KHz rate. 3 DOF haptic interaction is implemented by graphic hardware based haptic rendering algorithm that can deal with any type of object data such as surface-based or volume-based 3D representation as well as primitive models since only the graphic rendering contexts are referred for the collision detection and force

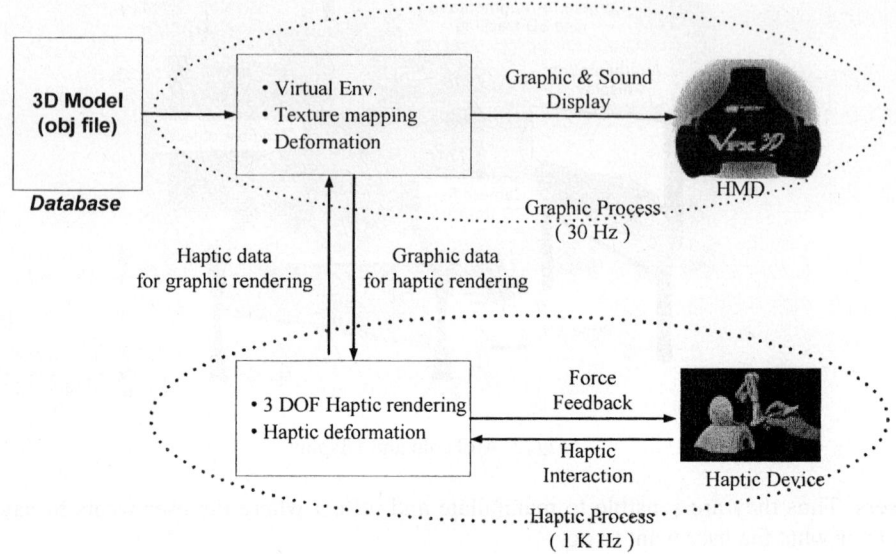

Fig. 3. Haptic Interaction Configuration

generation. In addition, it does not use any pre-computed hierarchy of object data such as bounding boxes or voxmap because the data structure of the on-line the LOMI is small enough to be updated in real-time [12].

After collision detection is performed by graphic hardware based haptic rendering algorithm, then 3 DOF haptic deformation is performed according to 3 DOF force computation between HIP (Haptic Interaction Point) and IHIP (Ideal HIP) [12]. At this time, contact point (IHIP) between haptic interaction point and a surface of 3D model is determined, and then triangles nearby contact point are remeshed. Deformed region are specifically decided by reaction force, and weight factors of moving vertices which determine deformed shape is calculated in the deformed region. Then geometry information of deformation is transferred to graphic process for rendering graphic context. In calculating deformation forces, weight factors of each vertex in deformed region are considered to generate reaction force.

3.1.3 Networked Synchronization for Collaborative Haptic Interaction
We applied server/client architecture. The client sends his or her haptic cursor position to server. The server manages and updates the virtual object states by using the data and sends the update information of virtual objects to all clients. The client architecture supporting the proposed scheme consists of three layers: application, synchronization, and network layer, as shown in Fig. 4. This layered architecture intends to assist the application developer by isolating the synchronization and network issues. Also, it supports easy expansion of a haptic application into a network version with the proposed scheme.

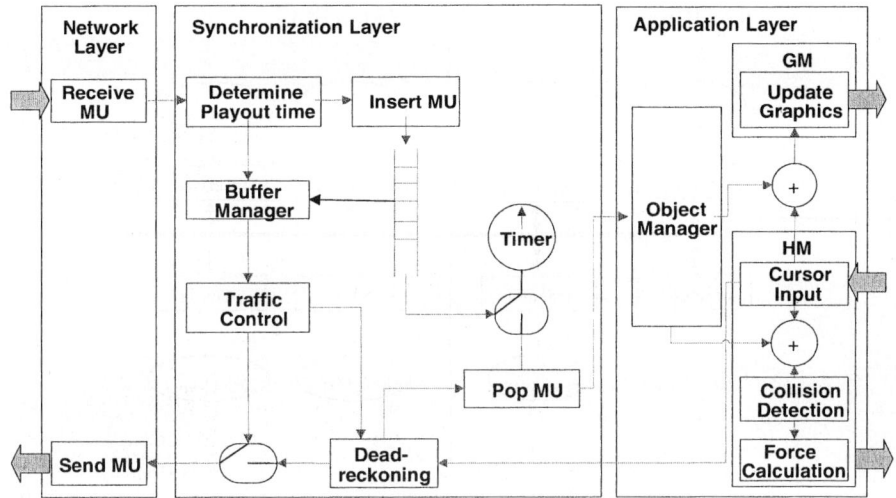

Fig. 4. Architecture for the delay jitter compensation

The synchronization layer relieves the deterioration of haptic interaction quality caused by network delay (jitter) and loss by using the adaptive playout and transmission rate controls. The adaptive playout determination algorithm adaptively controls the playout time according to current network delay distribution to filter out short-term fluctuations and to control appropriate buffering (i.e., waiting) time for smooth haptic interactions. The transmission rate determination algorithm control the transmission rate based on the number of MUs in current buffer. The rate control is achieved by filtering out MUs by exploiting the dead-reckoning scheme.

Finally, the network layer communicates with the other nodes (server or clients) by the MUs. We implement the transmission protocol that refers to the control method of RTP (real-time transport protocol). Additional features such as time stamp and sequence number are expected for the control in consideration of the case to send the state of the VEs. Extra headers to assist the adaptive QoS control of haptic interaction are placed on top of RTP.

3.2 vrSensor and vrService of vr-UCAM

vr-UCAM2.0 (A Unified Context-aware Application Model for Virtual Environments) is a framework for designing reactive virtual environments [12]. It makes virtual objects to show personalized reactions according to user's context. That is, it is aware of user's situation through the user's explicit interactions. Furthermore, it infers user's implicit context (e.g. preference, intention, emotion, etc) from the explicit situation. Finally, it offers adaptive responses according to the context.

The vr-UCAM2.0 consists of vrSensor, vrSCM and vrService. vrSensor generates the context from detected changes. vrSCM supports seamless context sharing between real and virtual environments. vrService decides specific services by analyzing

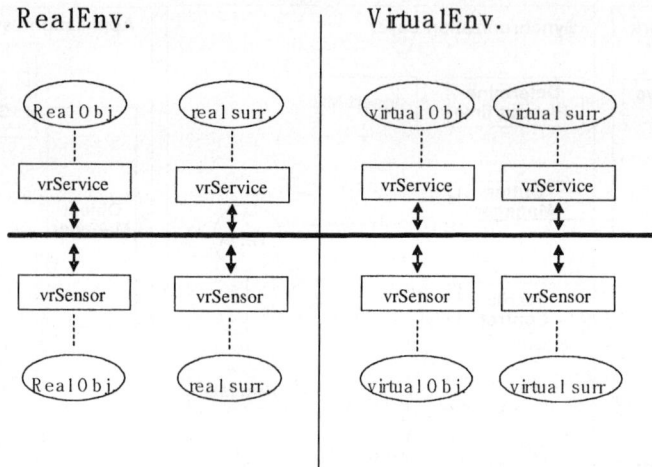

Fig. 5. Circles represent object or surrounding in Environment. Each element is attached to vrSensor or vrService of vr-UCAM. All elements communicate each other over the network.

contexts generated from other vrSensors and vrServices. Thus, it detects user's preliminary context through user's input with tangible objects and haptic interface. Then, it comprehends the user's explicit and implicit contexts, and then it makes virtual environments to show personalized reactions according to extracted contexts. The Fig. 5 exhibits the relationship between four elements which is based on the vr-UCAM2.0.

3.3 Virtual Environment Manager (VEManager)

VEManager is composed of physical engine and environment engine. Physical engine supports interaction between virtual object and virtual surrounding based on collision detection. Environment engine has a role to control virtual surroundings such as weather, temperature, humidity and so on. In this approach, LOD for a massive terrain model and 3D sound generation are important.

3.3.1 Levels of Detail

The RMS contains a number of fine 3-D objects and a massive terrain model. In order to display these models at a specified frame rate, we implement the Level-of-Detail (LOD) technique. The LOD technique is to construct a number of progressively simpler versions of an object and to select one of them for display as a function of range. Three-dimensional objects which locate a great distance from the eyepoint are rendered in less detail, while relatively close objects are represented in great detail. The LOD technique saves rendering time significantly and improves overall display performances. In this system, two types of LOD schemes are used. One is for 3-D objects placed on the terrain, and the other is for the terrain model.

For 3-D objects placed on the terrain, we prepare multiple models of an object with varying levels of detail and associate them with one node called pfLOD provided by OpenGL Performer. A pfLOD node contains an x, y, z location of the center of LOD processing which defines the point used in conjunction with the eyepoint for

LOD range-switching calculations. During the culling phase of frame processing, we compute the distance from the eyepoint to the object and select which LOD model to display.

The LOD scheme for the terrain model is slightly different from the above LOD scheme. The terrain model is so large that the entire terrain cannot fit into a single LOD range. In order to address this problem we use Active Surface Definition (ASD). The ASD is a real-time surface meshing and morphing library and an ASD surface contains several hierarchical LOD meshes. When Performer renders an ASD surface, a pfASD node which defines necessary information such as the structure or the evaluation function selects triangles, not model, from many different LODs and combines them into final surface. This approach enables to render the large terrain model that is too large to select single LOD without requiring a lot of system memory.

3.3.2 3D Sound Generation for RMS

The 3D sound generating system consists of two modules: one module is a converter to generate an appropriate sound format and the other one is an interface with the speaker system. Fig. 6 shows a functional procedure of the 3D sound generating system for RMS. The sound generation system first searches a file from a sound file server whenever RMS requests a sound to the sound generating system. After that, the file format of the sound file is modified into the format that can be dealt with the interface with the sound system that supports 5.1-channel speaker system for RMS to give a realistic sound.

For example, consider a sound file stored in the sound file server with the MPEG-1 stereo format. In this case, the sound generating system applies a technique to convert this stereo sound file into a sound file with a 5.1 channel format. Moreover, the sound generating system can play out the sound with the spatial sound effect if RMS gives the direction and distance between the user's position and an object that generates some sound. That is, the sound generating system can relatively control the volumes of five speakers by using the direction information and adjust the loudness for each speaker according to the distance in VE.

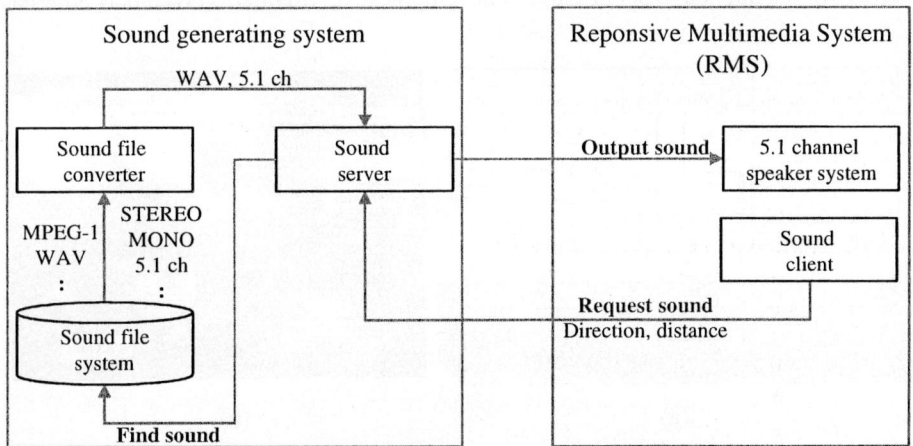

Fig. 6. 3D sound generating system for RMS

3.4 Bi-directional Interactive 3D Web

G3 (GIST 3DWeb) started as an effort to enrich the interactiveness in the virual Unju temple. G3 allows one to revisit the statues and monuments seen in the virtual Unju temple on his/her personal computers. The direction of interactiveness is bi-directional because one not only can see but can apply paintings to these objects. And surprisingly, this personal artistic works can be seen on the next visit to virtual Unju temple. G3 is implemented as an Active-X control and thus can be run as a stand alone MS-Windows application or as an embedded object in a web page (restricted to MS-Explorer). G3 is digitally signed with a certificate from thawte USA (487 East Middlefield Road Mountain View, CA 94043, http://www.thawte.com/) for secure delivery over the Internet.

4 System Integration and Demonstration

We integrated hapic interface, ARTable, 3D Sound system, VRManager, and vr-UCAM into the RMS. Fig. 7 (a) shows structure and information flow of RMS. We built Database and Sound server to save 3D Model and to play 5.1 channel sound. With the haptic interface, we deform 3D model and deliver it into the DB over the network. We display this deformed content in VE and we download it from the 3D web site. We connect ARTable, Haptic interface and VE with sound server. When trigger signal is delivered to the sound server, it selects proper sound file to play through 5.1 channel speaker installed in the room. We designed 3D web server to allow users to interact our contents over the network.

Various equipments were deployed into RMS as shown in Fig. 7 (b). There was three-channel stereoscopic display system. The clustered 3 workstations for cylindrical 3D stereoscopic display, 2 workstations for vision-based and haptic interface, and 1 workstation for sound and database server. In addition to workstation, we installed two cameras, haptic device, and 5.1 channel sound system.

All objects in real and virtual environment were connected with each other using vr-UCAM. We applied vrSenor class to development of vrTimer, vrWeatherForcaster,

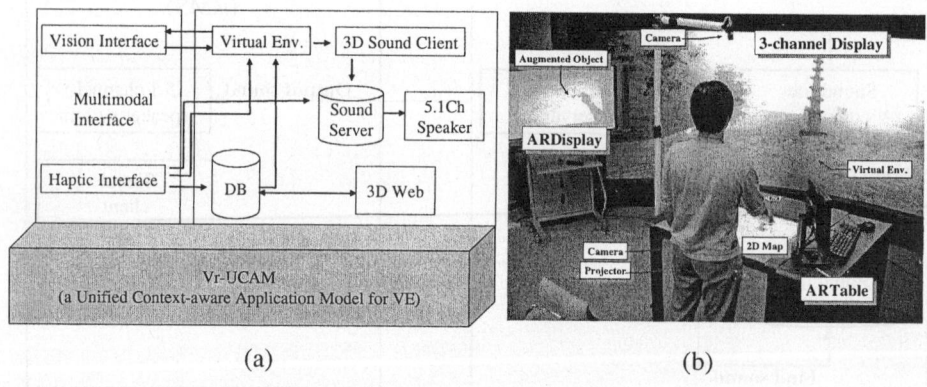

Fig. 7. (a) System Architecture and (b) Demonstration of RMS

vrLocationSensor, vrPot and vrShovel. The role of vrTimer was acquisition of time. vrWeatherForecast detected the changes of weather of real environment. vrLocationSensor found the location of object. vrShovel recognized the user's gesture of purring water and the gesture of transferring of object respectively. We applied vrService class to implement vrWeather, vrPicture, vrNavigator and vrPlant. vrWeather changed the weather and time of VE according to the messages generated by vrSensor. For the navigation, vrNavigatior changed the coordinate of VE according to message from vrLocator. When a user approached specific location, vrPicture showed photos of that location. vrPlant grew up a tree in virtual environment. It used message from vrTime, vrPot, vrWeatherForcaster. Virtual plant grew up by taking water and nourishment which were acquired from multi-modal interface and virtual surrounding.

RMS supported users' natural interactions with VE [15]. Users can easily see how to use the interface and feel comfortable with the interface that looks just like an everyday objects in real world. For example, users can move real object that is connected to vrNavigator in VE. Users can carve stone when users beat stone with a hammer shaped device. If users want to pour water on flower, all they need to do is tilt bottle-shape tangible object.

5 Conclusion and Future Work

In this paper, we proposed Responsive Multimedia System for a new approach to virtual storytelling. We made a multimodal tangible user interface for natural interaction by exploiting vision based and haptic interfaces. VEManager provided intelligent responses by showing dynamic scene and animations. Most important feature of our system is that we combined context-aware application model, called vr-UCAM, with VR System. However, there are several possible enhancements to improve the proposed system. We have plans to find an evaluation scheme of our storytelling. We will also apply the concept of artificial life to generate life-like virtual objects. In the future, RMS will be used for providing personalized virtual story according to user' context.

References

1. Bobick, Aaron & Intille, Stephen et al. (1996) "The KidsRoom: A Perceptually-Based Interactive and Immersive Story Environment,". Technical report, MIT Media Laboratory.
2. Roussos, M., Johnson, A., Leigh, J., Barnes, C., Vasilakis, C., and Moher, T. (1997). "The NICE project: Narrative, Immersive, Constructionist/Collaborative Environments for Learning in Virtual Reality." In *Proceedings of ED-MEDIA/ED-TELECOM 97*, Calgary, Canada, June 1997, pp. 917-922.
3. Larsen, C.B. & Petersen, B.C. (1999)" Interactive Storytelling in a Multimodal Environment." Aalborg University, Institute of Electronic Systems
4. Seokhee Lee, Youngho Lee, Seiie Jang, Woontack Woo, "vr-UCAM : Unified Context-aware Application Module for Virtual Reality," *ICAT*, pp. 495-498, 2004.
5. Sejin.Oh, Youngho Lee, Woontack Woo, "vr-UCAM2.0: A Unified Context-aware Application Model for Virtual Environments," *ubiCNS*, 2005.

6. D.L. Hall, "An Introduction to Multisensor Data Fusion," *Proc. of the IEEE*, pp.6-23, vol.85, no.1, Jan. 1997
7. B. V. Dasarathy, "Sensor fusion potential exploitation: Innovative architectures and illustrative approaches", *Proc. IEEE*, vol.85, pp.24- 38, Jan. 1997
8. H. Ishii, B. Ullmer, "Tangible Bits: Towards Seamless Interfaces between People, Bits and Atoms," *in Proc. of ACM CHI*, pp. 234-241, Mar. 1997
9. Sejin Oh, Woontack Woo, "Manipulating multimedia contents with Tangible Media Control System," *ICEC*, Vol.3166, pp. 57-67, 2004.
10. Y.Park, W.Woo, "Context based AR Interaction Table using Tangible Objects," *ubiCNS*, 2005
11. K. Salisbury, F. Barbagli, and F. Conti, "Haptic Rendering: Introductory Concepts", IEEE *Computer Graphics and Applications*, vol. 24, No. 2, pp. 24-32, 2004.
12. Jong-Phil Kim, Beom-Chan Lee, and Jeha Ryu, "Haptic Rendering with Six Virtual Cameras", *HCI international* 2005. (accepted)
13. ARToolKit (http://www.hitl.washington.edu/research/shared_space/download)
14. Yochen Hiltmann, "Miruk: Die Heiligen Steine Koreas," *Edition Qumran im Campus Verlag*, 1993
15. Youngho Lee, Sejin Oh, Woontack Woo,"A Responsive Multimedia System (RMS): VR Platform for Immersive Multimedia with Stories," *ICVS* 2005 (accepted)
16. Seiie Jang, Woontack Woo, "Unified Context Representing User-Centric Context: Who, Where, When, What, How and Why," *1st International Workshop on Personalized Context Modeling and Management for UbiComp Applications* (accepted)

Communication and Control of a Home Robot Using a Mobile Phone

Kuniya Shinozaki[1], Hajime Sakamoto[2], Takaho Tanaka[3], and Ryohei Nakatsu[1]

[1] Kwansei Gakuin University, School of Science and Technology,
2-1 Gakuen, Sanda 669-1337, Japan
{scbc0052, nakatsu}@ksc.kwansei.ac.jp
http://www.nirvana.ne.jp/updatefile/nakatsu/
[2] Hajime Laboratory
sakamoto@nirvana.ne.jp
[3] The Kansai Electric Power Co. Ltd., Research & Development
tanaka.takaho@a2.kepco.co.jp

Abstract. Research and development of humanoid/animal robots is being actively pursued, and it is expected that in the near future these robots will be introduced into our homes as "home robots." The key function of these robots is their ability to communicate with humans. Since communication via mobile phones is becoming increasingly common among us, it is essential for these robots also to be able to communicate using mobile phones. In this paper we propose the concept of a home robot and describe the essential functions that we consider are essential for the robot. Then, as one of the key functions of the robot, we explain the basic architecture and construction of the communication/control function of the robot, which uses mobile phones as a primary medium.

1 Introduction

In addition to conventional industrial robots, various types of humanoid robots and pet robots are being actively studied and developed [1][[2][3][4][5]. The characteristics of these robots are that they can act as real animals such as cats and dogs or walk like humans. However, these robots are still not at the level of contributing to the material aspect of our lives. What they can do is entertain people by their animal- or human-like behaviors, thereby contributing to the mental aspect of our lives. In that sense, these robots are puppets rather than industrial robots or home electrical appliances. The present generation of robots are, of course, much more expensive than puppets and it is difficult for consumers to purchase them as everyday goods. Why, then, do these robots attract our interest? One answer to this question is that people expect these robots to be something more than mere puppets; they probably expect some degree of communication capability. Children tend to think of their puppets as living things and communicate with them with their imagination. Their communications, however, are limited within the bounds of their imagination. On the other hand, it is expected that robots can communicate with human using speech and gestures, and in that sense, communication with these robots is real.

By possessing the capability of carrying out real communications with humans, these robots could become our partners and members of our society. But how do we expect these robots behave as members of our society? So far it seems that lay people, as well as researchers, seem interested only in the hardware aspect of robots, though sooner or later the above question will become the essential one on which we must focus.

In this paper, as a first step toward answering this question, we propose the concept of a home robot that would be introduced into our homes in the near future. We also propose the communication capabilities these robots should have. Then, as an example of one of these robots, we will describe an animal-type robot that we have researched and developed. Moreover, since we consider that communication between humans and these robots via mobile phone is one of the essential functions that these robots should have, we will describe the architecture and the function of the communication capability possesses by the prototype robot in relation to mobile phones.

2 Concept and Functions of a Home Robot

2.1 Concept

Let us suppose that humanoid/pet robots would be introduced into our homes as "home robots." How should they appear, and what functions should they have? Let us try to answer these questions.

(1) Appearance
In the near future, most home electrical appliances will be connected through a network and have the capability of communicating with humans. There should, however, be a basic difference between these products and home robots. We expect home robots to be like members of our own family rather than simple machines. For that purpose, the robots would need to look like animals or humans.

(2) Communication Capabilities
Regarding their communication capabilities, it is imperative that the robots have far superior capabilities to conventional computers and home electrical appliances. The required communication capabilities are:

Verbal Communication: Since verbal communication forms the basis of our daily lives, it is necessary that home robots should have the same type of capability. It would be best for them to have a verbal communication capability because we would want to communicate with them by voice. On the other hand, is it appropriate for the robots to talk to human using synthesized speech? The answer to this question is that as we want to realize somewhat different types of communication to conventional ones, it would be acceptable for the robots to have that capability.

Nonverbal Communication: In human-to-human communication, nonverbal information such as gestures, facial expressions and emotions involved in speech play a very important role. Therefore, even in communication between home robots and humans, nonverbal communication would have a very significant effect on the relationship. Moreover, the basic reason why a home robot should have the appearance of a human/animal is that it would be easier for us to communicate with it based on nonverbal information. In human-pet communication, we try to guess the emotions/intentions of our pets based on their facial expressions and gestures, which makes such communication more fruitful. Likewise, the nonverbal communication capabilities required for home robots are given below.

Gesture expression capability
Gesture identification capability
Capability of making facial expressions
Capability to identify facial expressions
Capability to identify expression of emotions using voice
Capability to identify emotions involved in speech

These are the functions for which, despite a long research history, satisfactory research results have not yet been obtained. It is therefore worthwhile spending many more research resources on these topics.

2.2 A Prototype of a Home Robot

As an example of the above-mentioned home robots, we are now researching and developing humanoid and pet robots. Because it is difficult to estimate beforehand which type of robot consumers would accept as home robots, it is necessary for robot researchers/developers to develop various types of humanoid/pet robot as well as various types of applications for them. Releasing them into the market, however, might tell us which is best, based on sales and consumer feedback.

The details of our humanoid robot, including its positioning, functions, and capabilities, will be described in a different paper; in this paper, we only describe the pet robot we are researching and developing. Currently, the most popular pet robot is "AIBO" by Sony, which has a dog-like appearance and the capability of expressing various types of dog-like behaviors. Moreover, these behaviors appear themselves depending on the history of interactions between an AIBO and its users. This function could give users the feeling that they can really teach AIBO how to behave and that it could learn based on its interactions with users. On the other hand, the problem with AIBO is that it has the appearance of a dog and all of its behaviors are those of a dog. Although users might easily feel empathy toward the robot because of this, they would expect that AIBO would behave exactly like a dog. However, there is a limit to the number of behaviors AIBO can display, meaning that users would soon lose interest in AIBO and this is what has in fact happened.

Based on the above considerations, we have started researching our own pet robot. The prototype robot we have developed features the following capabilities.

(1) Communications using voice
Utilizing speech recognition and speech synthesis capabilities, the robot can verbally communicate with users.

(2) Processing of image input from robot eyes
Through processing images obtained through the robot's cameras, the robot can identify objects around it and understand its surroundings. It also features the function of sending images to a mobile phone.

(3) Sensing capabilities utilizing various types of sensors

The robot includes has several types of sensors such as touch sensors, distance sensors, and so on. By utilizing them, it can recognize the world surrounding it and carry out appropriate decisions, and by combining this information with the image processing data, we can realize the robot's autonomous capabilities.

Figure 1 shows a diagram of the robot's hardware construction, and Table 1 presents its specifications In addition, Fig. 2 illustrates its appearance. The robot looks like an animal but it cannot be identified as any specific one. Using this characteristic, we want to develop various types of interaction capabilities for the robot and want to create new method of communication between the robot and its users.

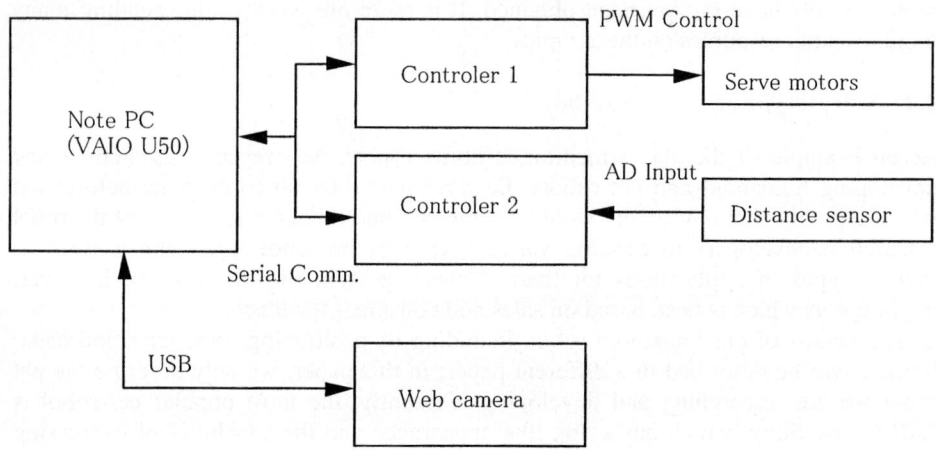

Fig. 1. Hardware construction of the robot

Table 1. Hardware specifications of the prototype robot

Item	Example
Height	366 mm
Width	254 mm
	331 mm
Weight	4.5 Kg
Controller	32-bit micro-processor (for servo motors)
	32-bit microprocessor (for sensors)
	Notebook PC (VAIO U50) (to control the processors and speech/image processing)
Actuator	Servo motor (S5050)
Camera	Web camera
Sensor	Distance sensors × 10, Touch sensors×5
Battery	Nickel hydrogen 7.2 V

Fig. 2. The appearance of the prototype robot

2.3 Autonomous Functions of the Robot

By combining and integrating the above-mentioned basic functions, this robot has the capability of behaving autonomously. From among the various autonomous functions humans possess, we have developed and installed the following functions that we consider a home robot should have.

(1) The function to fulfill its desires
First is a desire-behavior model [6], which is represented by a network. The network consists of "nodes," each of which corresponds to one desire, and "links" among nodes and sensor inputs through which the activation energy is sent. The sensor inputs--including speech and images-- feed energies into the network. Furthermore, activation energies are sent from node to node via the links. If the sum of these energies exceeds a predetermined threshold on one of the nodes, the desire corresponding to it would appear and the corresponding sequence of actions would present themselves.

(2) The function to reach its destination by avoiding obstacles around it
Many of the behaviors to fulfill the apparent desire feature the action of moving from a present position to a destination. In this case if there are some obstacles on the way toward the destination, the robot detects them using its image processing function and moves toward the destination by avoiding those obstacles.

(3) The function to decide the priority between its own desire and the command given

In addition to the above autonomous function, sometimes users issue commands to the robot. Typical commands are speech commands and button inputs activated by a mobile phone and sent to the robot. One important issue for the robot is how to realize a good balance between internal autonomous behavior and external commands. If the priority is placed on the external command, then the robot will become a remote-controlled one. On the other hand, if the priority were placed on the internal autonomous function, then although the interactive behavior of the robot would be interesting, it would become difficult for users to control the robot. Especially in the case of security checks, the lack of a function to obey the outer command could prove fatal. Therefore, to realize an appropriate balance between autonomous behaviors and external commands, we have introduced chaos theory. By adopting a multiple chaos control mechanism [7], we successfully set the balance to an appropriate point between autonomy and command. In addition to this, by employing the chaos control system, it was possible to introduce appropriate fluctuation of robot behaviors. Figure 3 show the construction of the software that realizes the above autonomous function.

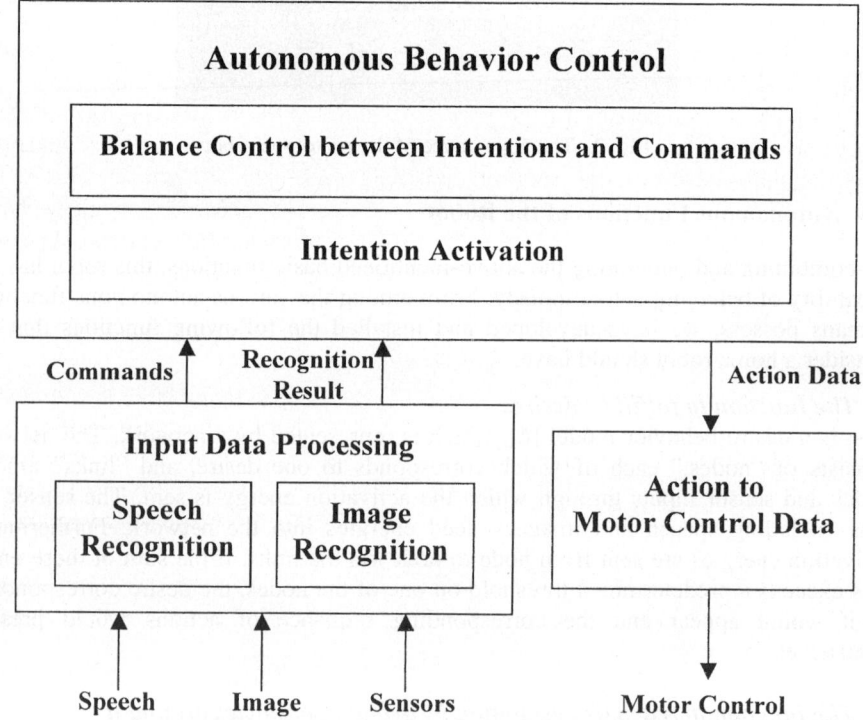

Fig. 3. Software construction of the prototype robot

3 Communications/Control of the Home Robot Using a Mobile Phone

3.1 Concept

If we consider a home robot as a member of our family, it is essential to realize a communication capability between the robot and us. This can be achieved through mobile phones. Some of the cases where we communicate with the robot using mobile phones are as follows.

(1) Communications with the robot
When we are out of our home, frequently we communicate with other family members via mobile phones. Sometimes it is to inform them of important messages, and sometimes it is with requests. It is also common that we want to enjoy ourselves and relax by communicating with other members of our family. This means that the robot should also include this type of communication capability.

(2) Security check
Sometimes we give orders to our family members when we are away from home. These orders might be a request to check the closure of doors/windows, or to turn on/off the air conditioners, and so on. In the case of human communications, since humans have high-level judgment capabilities, it would be enough to give high-level commands. In the case of a robot, however, even if it receives a high-level command to check the security of the next room, it would be very difficult to achieve this function. Therefore, instead of assessing the level security by itself, it would be better for the robot to send images captured by its camera to a mobile phone. The user would then be able to check the security by himself/herself, making it essential for the robot to have the capability of sending images to a mobile phone.

(3) Communication intermediary
It could be convenient to realize communications between a user and other members of the family, utilizing the robot as an intermediary. For example, when there is an aged person who does not understand how to operate a mobile phone, the robot could become an intelligent mobile phone that can mediate communications between the family member and a user. In the case when there is a baby who cannot operate mobile phone, the robot would go near the baby and send its image to a mobile phone or output the voice of the user (mother in most cases) to the baby. In this way, the user can check how the baby is behaving even when he/she is away from home or cannot talk to the baby directly.

3.2 Communication Modes of a Mobile Phone

To fulfill the above functions, we have realized a mobile communication capability between the robot and its users. Basically there are three modes of communication using mobile phones.

(1) Voice communication
Just as with conventional telephone communications, communications using voice is the basis of mobile communications. In this case the telephone network is used to send the information between both sides.

(2) Video communication
Recently, most mobile phones have been equipped with a digital camera, making some form of video communication possible. Now, most of the mobile network operators, including NTT Docomo, are supplying this communication capability to mobile phone users in Japan. The video mode requires a far wider frequency range than does the standard voice telephone network.

(3) Internet communication
In addition to the above communication modes, it is possible to communicate through the Internet. Each mobile communication company supplies its own Internet service; in the case of NTT Docomo, the service is called "'i-mode." The service provider prepares a server, and when a user accesses the server, application programs described by JAVA can be downloaded, allowing the application to run on the user's mobile phone. Using this mode, by pushing one of the mobile phone buttons, the user can send information corresponding to the button to the receiver.

3.3 Construction of the Overall System

System construction
Among the above functions of the mobile phones, we have realized a communication function based on image communications and Internet communications. By adopting this architecture, the below services could be realized.

Employing the image communication capability, the following can be done.

* A user can watch the image sent from the robot camera on a mobile phone display.
* By sending a voice signal from a mobile phone to the robot, the robot can output the voice directly. The robot can also input the voice to a speech recognition function, change it into a command, and carry out that command.
* The voice response of the robot can be sent to the mobile phone.
* By utilizing the above function, a user can communicate with the autonomous robot by voice, give it orders and receiving image sent from it.
* Using the Internet mode:
* By pushing one of the buttons on a mobile phone, the corresponding command can be sent to the robot.
* By downloading the information sent from the robot to the server, the user can obtain desired information.

With these functions, the user can control the robot's actions by pushing appropriate buttons, and obtain information gathered by the autonomous robot. For example, the user could watch snapshots of room images taken by the robot or could view the history of the robot's behaviors.

The system

Figure 4 shows the overall construction of the system, and Fig. 5 provides a top-page view of the robot communications Web page on a mobile phone. Figure 6 illustrates how a user controls and/or communicates with the robot using voice or buttons.

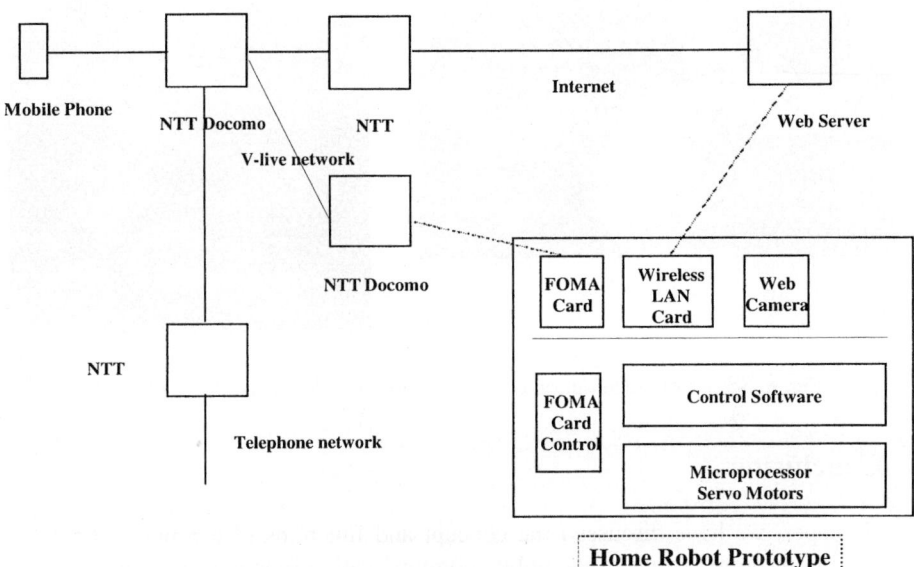

Fig. 4. Construction of the overall system

Fig. 5. Top page view of robot web site

Fig. 6. Scenes of voice/button communication bewteen a user and the robot

4 Conclusion

In this paper, we have discussed the concept and functions of a robot that can live with us in our home, focusing its mobile communication function. First, we proposed the concept of a home robot that could be introduced into our homes in the near future and would help us with various aspects of our lives. Furthermore, we discussed the various functions that this type of robot should have. We then introduced an example of an animal-type home robot that we are developing and discussed the robot's software and hardware. In addition, we indicated that communication capability, especially a mobile phone-based communication capability, is the key for this type of robot to be a success. This was followed by a description of the concept and architecture of the robot's communication function that makes it possible for us to control and to communicate with the robot.

We are now evaluating the various robot functions, including the mobile phone-based communication capability. These results should provide us with a clearer vision as to which functions the home robot should have, and from there we will develop the second prototype of the robot.

References

1. http://www.honda.co.jp/robot/
2. http://www.sony.net/SonyInfo/QRIO/
3. http://www.humanoid.waseda.ac.jp/index.html
4. Nakaoka, S., et al.: Leg Motion Primitives for a Dancing Humanoid Robot. Proc IEEE Int. Conf. Robotics and Automation, IEEE (2004) 610-615

5. Wama T., et. al.: Realization of Tai-chi Motion Using Humanoid Robot - Physical Interactions with Humanoid Robot. Building the Information Society, Kluwer Academic Publishers (2004) 59-64
6. Maes P.,: How to Do the Right Thing. Connection Science, Vol.1, No.3 (1989) 291-323
7. Liu, Y. and Davis, P.: Dual Synchronization of chaos. Physical Review E, 61 (2000) 2176-2179

Real-Time Stereo Using Foreground Segmentation and Hierarchical Disparity Estimation

Hansung Kim, Dong Bo Min, and Kwanghoon Sohn

Dept. of Electrical and Electronics Eng., Yonsei University,
134 Shinchon-dong, Seodaemun-gu, Seoul 120-749, Korea
khsohn@yonsei.ac.kr
http://diml.yonsei.ac.kr

Abstract. We propose a fast disparity estimation algorithm using background registration and object segmentation for stereo sequences from fixed cameras. Dense background disparity information is calculated in an initialization step so that only disparities of moving object regions are updated in the main process. We propose a real-time segmentation technique using background subtraction and inter-frame differences, and a hierarchical disparity estimation using a region-dividing technique and shape-adaptive matching windows. Experimental results show that the proposed algorithm provides accurate disparity vector fields with an average processing speed of 15 frames/sec for 320x240 stereo sequences on a common PC.

1 Introduction

One of the most important problems in 3D image processing is to locate corresponding points in the images, a process referred as disparity estimation. As shown in Fig. 1, stereo imaging involves two separate image views of a single world point w. The objective is to find the corresponding pair I_1 and I_2 in the

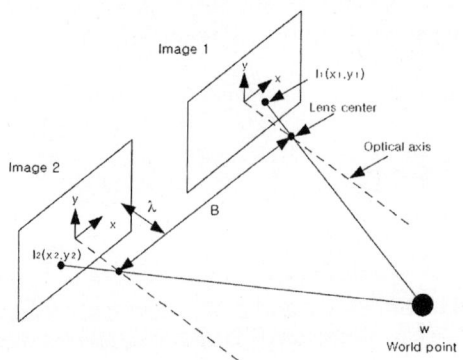

Fig. 1. Stereo geometry

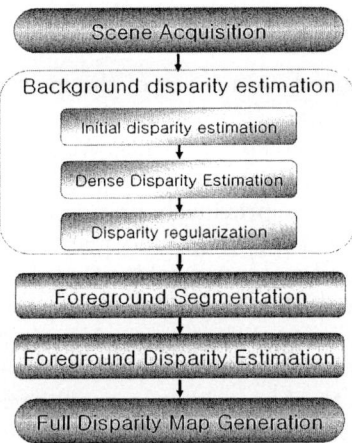

Fig. 2. Block diagram of the proposed algorithm

image pair. If we assume that the cameras are identical and the coordinate systems of both cameras are aligned in parallel, the determination of disparity from I_1 to I_2 becomes finding a function $d(x,y)$ such that:

$$I_2(x,y) = I_1(x + d(x,y), y) \tag{1}$$

A number of studies have been reported on the correspondence problem since the 1970's. D. Scharstein and R. Szeliski recently discussed the taxonomy of existing stereo algorithms [1] and a test bed for the quantitative evaluation of the algorithms [2]. However, most of them have serious limitations on being applied to common applications since they do not work in real-time. Several real-time methods were recently proposed [3][4][5], but they were implemented on DSP for acceleration or show poor quality to be used for wide-ranging applications.

We have previously proposed a two-stage algorithm to find smooth and precise disparity vector fields in a stereo image pair [6]. The algorithm has consisted of a dense disparity estimation and edge-preserving regularization. It results in such a clean disparity map with good discontinuity localization, but the computational cost is so high that it does not work in real-time. In this paper, we propose a fast disparity estimation algorithm using background registration and object segmentation. We assume that a stereo camera set does not move, and there is no moving object for a few seconds in an initialization step for generating background information. Accurate and detailed disparity information for background is estimated in advance, then only disparities of moving foreground regions are calculated and merged into background disparity fields.

Fig. 2 shows a block diagram of the proposed system. As a preprocessing, acquired image sequences are low-pass filtered to reduce noise effect and rectified since we assume that stereo images are captured in parallel stereo cameras in disparity estimation. We use a real-time stereo rectification function provided by Triclops SDK [7].

2 Foreground Segmentation

Real-time foreground segmentation is one of the most important components of the proposed system, since the performance of the segmentation decides the efficiency and quality of the final disparity fields. We propose a foreground segmentation technique using background subtraction and inter-frame differences based on the technique which we have previously proposed [8]. Fig. 3 shows overall segmentation process. At first, the background masks $I_{min}(x,y)$ and $I_{max}(x,y)$ are modeled with minimum and maximum intensities of the first N frames, respectively, because the background information is very sensitive to noise and change of illumination. Then, the frame difference mask $I_{fd}(x,y)$ is calculated by the difference between two consecutive frames. In the third step, an initial foreground mask is constructed from the frame difference and background difference masks by the OR process, that is, if a pixel of current frame satisfies one of Eq. (2), it is determined to be belonged to an initial foreground region. Th_{tol} and Th_{fd} mean threshold values for background and frame difference regions, respectively.

$$I_{cur}(x,y) < I_{min}(x,y) - Th_{tol}$$
$$I_{cur}(x,y) > I_{max}(x,y) + Th_{tol} \qquad (2)$$
$$I_{fd}(x,y) > Th_{fd}$$

However, due to the camera noise and irregular object motion, there exist some noise regions in the initial mask. One of the conventional ways to eliminate the noise regions is using the morphological operations to filter out small regions. Therefore, we refine the initial mask by a closing process and eliminate small regions with a region-growing technique.

Finally, in order to smooth the boundaries of foreground and to eliminate holes inside the regions, we propose a profile extraction technique. This technique is remodeled from Kumar's profile extraction technique [9]. A weighted one pixel thick drape moves from one side to the opposite side. The adjacent pixels of the drape are connected by elastic spring, so it covers object but does

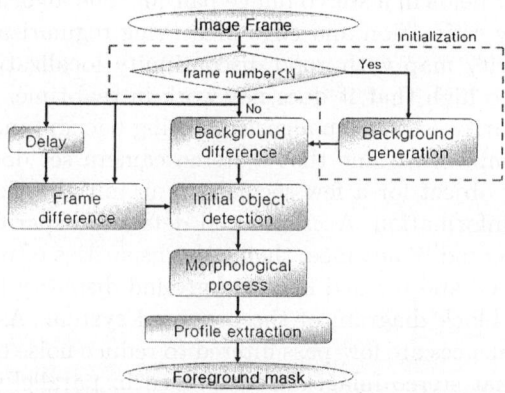

Fig. 3. Real-time segmentation algorithm

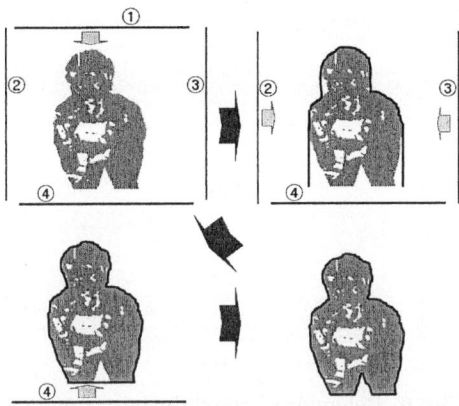

Fig. 4. Profile extraction process

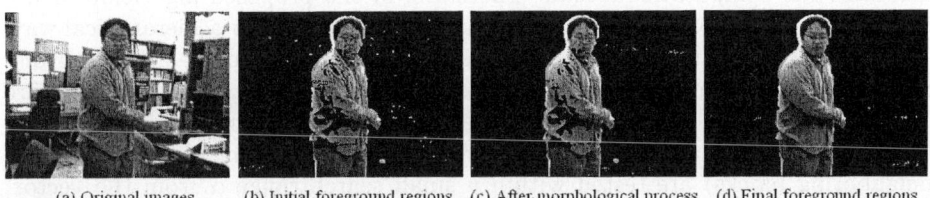

(a) Original images   (b) Initial foreground regions   (c) After morphological process   (d) Final foreground regions

Fig. 5. Segmentation results

not infiltrate into gaps whose widths are smaller than a threshold M. This process is performed from all quarters and the region wrapped by four drapes is decided as a final foreground region. Fig. 4 shows the profile extraction process applied to an initial object.

Segmentation results by the proposed method are shown in Fig. 5. The image is captured in typical office environment without any special lighting equipment. Fig. 5 (b) is the result of initial object detection from Fig. 5 (a). Main object are detected well, but they include noises on background and object boundaries. In Fig. 5 (c), we can see that noises are eliminated and object surfaces are smoothed by a morphological process. However, many holes still exist inside the objects. Fig. 5 (d) is the final segmentation result. After applying the profile extraction technique, good semantic foreground regions are obtained.

3 Disparity Estimation

3.1 Background Disparity Estimation

In windows-based algorithms, the reliability and efficiency depend on the size of a matching window. Large window sizes provide reliable but not detailed results. Moreover, employing a large window for each pixel in dense disparity estimation

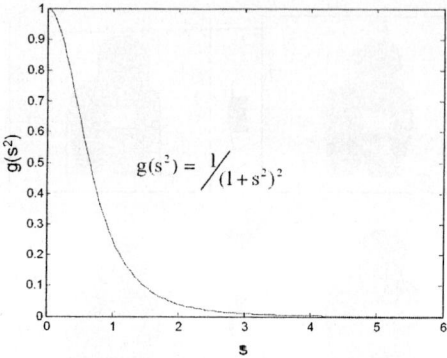

Fig. 6. Behavior of the diffusivity function

increases the computational load. Therefore, in the proposed algorithm, dense disparity information of background is initially estimated in a hierarchical way.

The first step in hierarchical estimation is a BxB block-based initial disparity estimation. In the second step, dense disparity vectors for each pixel are estimated based on the initial block vectors. In order to cover all the probable disparity candidates, 9 initial vectors (1 from the current block and 8 from neighboring blocks) are tested within a small search range α from the vector. In order to improve computational efficiency in disparity estimation, we use a region-dividing technique which we have previously proposed [6]. The technique performs point matching in the order of the possibility of correct matching and divides the region into sub-regions at the true matching point. After the region splits into two sub-regions in matching process, the search ranges of points in each sub-region are restricted to the corresponding sub-region.

However, in the disparity vectors estimated by the above-described method, spatial correlation of the estimated vector fields is not considered. In order to provide more accurate and reliable background disparity fields, we refine the fields by regularizing them by means of the following nonlinear diffusion equation with an additional fidelity term [6].

$$\frac{\partial d}{\partial t} = \lambda \ div \left(g(|\ \nabla I_l(x,y)\ |^2)\nabla d(x,y)\right)$$
$$+ (I_l(x,y) - I_r(x+d,y))\frac{\partial I_r(x+d,y)}{\partial x} \quad (3)$$
$$where \ \ g(s^2) = 1/(1+s^2)^2$$

$g(|\nabla I_l|^2)$ is a diffusivity function which plays the role of discontinuity marker. Fig. 6 shows the behavior of the function $g(|\nabla I_l|^2)$. Therefore, this function reduces smoothing on object boundaries to preserve their discontinuities. In order to solve Eq. (3), we discretize the parabolic system by finite differences, and find the regularized disparity field in recursive manner by updating the field using Eq. (4).

$$\frac{d^{k+1}(x,y) - d^k(x,y)}{\tau} = \lambda \left\{ \frac{\partial}{\partial x} \left(g\left(\left|\frac{\partial I_l(x,y)}{\partial x}\right|^2 \right) \times \frac{\partial d^k(x,y)}{\partial x} \right) \right.$$
$$+ \frac{\partial}{\partial y} \left(g\left(\left|\frac{\partial I_l(x,y)}{\partial y}\right|^2 \right) \times \frac{\partial d^k(x,y)}{\partial y} \right) \right\}$$
$$+ \left(I_l(x,y) - I_r(x+d^k,y) \right) \times \frac{\partial I_r(x+d^k,y)}{\partial x} \quad (4)$$
$$+ \left(d^k(x,y) - d^{k+1}(x,y) \right) \times \left(\frac{\partial I_r(x+d^k,y)}{\partial x} \right)^2$$

3.2 Foreground Disparity Estimation

The most important requirement of foreground disparity estimation is a processing speed because the fields of foreground must be updated in every frame. Hierarchical disparity estimation used in background disparity estimation is applied to the blocks which include foreground regions except a regularization step. Initial search ranges are also restricted by the neighbor background disparities since the foreground objects always exist in front of background region. Eq. (5) shows the search range decision where SR_{Max} and SR_{Min} mean maximum and minimum search range, respectively, and d_{ln} and d_{rn} are left and right neighboring background disparities of the foreground region on the same scanline.

for **L → R** disparity
$$SR_{max} = Min(d_{ln}, d_{rn}) \quad (5)$$
for **R → L** disparity
$$SR_{min} = Max(d_{ln}, d_{rn})$$

As a result, search ranges are restricted by three factors: background disparity, region-dividing technique and hierarchical estimation. Thus, the processing time of foreground estimation is greatly reduced.

In matching process, however, conventional rectangular window yield false result around object boundaries because the result is highly influenced by strong feature. In background disparity estimation, wrong disparities around the regions are corrected by regularization, but it can result in errors in foreground estimation. For example, in the cases of points A and B in Fig. 7, although they belong to different regions, the same disparity vectors are assigned because of the strong edge between them. In order to avoid this type of problem, we propose a new matching window which provides a high degree of reliability around the boundary region by deforming its shape according to the flow of the features. Let Ω denote the contour of the matching window. Starting from a sufficiently small contour Ω_0, the contour expands in the direction of non-increasing $|\nabla I|$ until a maximum size NxN is reached. Fig. 8 shows an example of window generation in the 1D case. The window does not cross strong feature so that the correct sharp boundary of disparity vectors can be obtained, as shown in Fig. 9, where

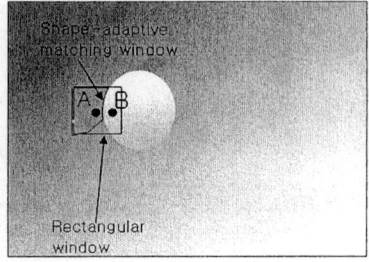

Fig. 7. Rectangular window and the proposed window

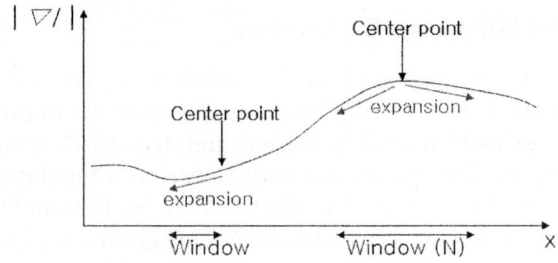

Fig. 8. Window generation in 1D case

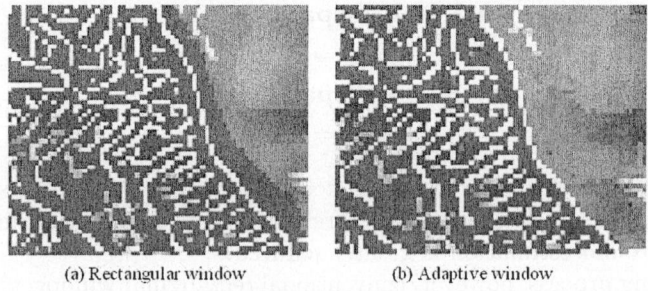

Fig. 9. Matching results using a rectangular window and the proposed window

white lines represent the real edges of the object. However, the adaptive window may decrease the matching power in highly textured regions. Thus, the shape-adaptive window is applied only for pixels in the block, where the maximum difference of disparity to other surrounding blocks is larger than ϵ.

Finally, estimated foreground disparity fields are merged into background disparity fields. We check the reliability of the disparity for the pixels in boundary blocks which include the boundary between background and foreground in order to compensate errors induced by wrong foreground segmentation. Final disparities of the pixels in boundary blocks are determined by the following conditions.

$$\text{if}(|\mathbf{I_r(x,y)} - \mathbf{I_l(x+d_{fore},y)}| < |\mathbf{I_r(x,y)} - \mathbf{I_l(x+d_{back},y)}|)$$
$$d_{final}(x,y) = d_{fore}(x,y) \quad (6)$$
else
$$d_{final}(x,y) = d_{back}(x,y)$$

4 Simulation Results

The proposed algorithm is applied to stereoscopic sequences captured by Digiclops which provides a rectified stereo sequence with a speed of 30 frames/sec [7]. The size of images is 320x240 and we used a PC with a Pentium IV 3.0 GHz CPU and 512 Mbytes memories. The parameters used in the simulation are listed in Table 1.

At first, we compared the performance of the proposed algorithm with other 4 fast algorithms in Table 2. For the objective evaluation, we applied the algorithm to the still images of Fig. 10 provided on Scharstein's homepage with ground truth disparity maps [2], and compared accuracy of the estimated disparity fields. We used two measures of quality. The first is BMP (bad matching percentage) of the estimated disparity map employed by Zitnick and Kanade [10], which is defined as:

Table 1. Parameters used in simulation

Stage	Parameter	Values
Foreground segmentation	Background generation	N = 50
	Background difference	$\text{Th}_{tol} = 10$
	Frame difference	$\text{Th}_{fd} = 5$
Disparity estimation	Block size	B = 8
	Dense disparity range	$\alpha = 2$
	Shape-adaptive window	$\varepsilon = 2$
Disparity regularization	Lagrange multiplier	$\lambda = 2000$
	Time step size	$\tau = 0.0001$
	Number of iteration	T = 150

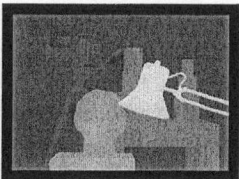

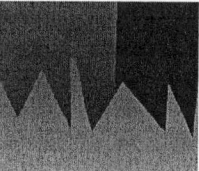

(a) Head and lamp　　　　　　　　　　(b) Sawtooth

Fig. 10. Test images and true disparity fields

Table 2. Comparative performance of algorithms

	Bad Matching Percentage (%)		RMSE (pixel)	
	Head and lamp	Sawtooth	Head and lamp	Sawtooth
Multi-window [11]	4.48	2.18	1.3980	1.2973
Max-Surface [12]	9.25	6.72	1.5294	1.6933
Real-time-DP [4]	4.22	6.11	1.1255	1.7542
MMHM [5]	8.00	3.03	1.6242	1.3069
Hierarchical	5.22	2.46	1.1047	1.3028
Final disparity	4.07	2.25	0.9193	0.9094

$$B = \frac{1}{N} \sum_{x,y} \delta\left(d_e(x,y), d_T(x,y)\right) \tag{7}$$

$$\text{where } \delta(a,b) = \begin{cases} 1, & \text{if } |a-b| > 1 \\ 0, & \text{else} \end{cases}$$

The second is RMSE (Root-Mean-Squared Error) of the estimated map. The RMSE between the estimated map $d_e(x,y)$ and the ground truth map $d_T(x,y)$ can be calculated by:

$$RMSE = \left(\frac{1}{N} \sum_{x,y} (d_e(x,y) - d_T(x,y))^2\right)^{1/2} \tag{8}$$

The proposed algorithm does not deal with a boundary problem, thus a border of 20 pixels was excluded from the evaluation.

In Table 2, the "Hierarchical" row means the results before regularization, that is, we can regard them as a performance of foreground estimation though the effect from the segmentation is not considered. In the BMP evaluation, the results of applying the proposed algorithm are somewhat inferior to several algorithms in the "Head and lamp" images, and it is a good second to the graph cut algorithm in the "Sawtooth." However, the proposed algorithm gives the best results in the RMSE category. Figs. 11 and 12 show the disparity maps of the "Sawtooth" and the "Head and lamp," respectively. In examining the results, the multi-window and the real-time DP algorithms are superior in terms of finding discontinuities, but they have problems in error propagation in the horizontal direction. The max-surface and the MMHM algorithms show a good result with the "Sawtooth," but produces prominent errors in some regions in the case of the "Head and lamp." The proposed algorithm results in reasonably clean maps with good discontinuity localization. However, the algorithm fails to find disparity in a narrow background such as the area between the arms of the lamp.

Table 3 shows the average running time analysis of our algorithm when one person moves in a scene. The system requires about 6-7 seconds for initialization before it works. After that, our algorithm shows an average speed of 15 frames/sec. According to referenced papers, Multi-window shows about 5 frames/sec, Max-Surface 2 frames/sec, Real-time-DP 8 frames/sec without

Table 3. Processing speed (msec)

Stage	Step	Time
Initialization	Background generation	1852
	Background disparity Estimation	5156
Main processing	Capturing and rectification	28.26
	Initial segmentation	9.69
	Morphological process	4.64
	Silhouette extraction	6.45
	Disparity estimation	17.81
	Total	66.85

MMX optimization, and MMHM 5 frames/sec. Considering both processing speed and quality of disparity fields, the proposed algorithm shows the best results.

Fig. 13 is the snapshot of test sequence and estimated background disparity fields. The image sequences are captured in natural condition without any special lighting equipment or any arrangement of objects for extracting good results. We can see that the proposed algorithm results in such a clean map with good discontinuity localization. Fig. 14 show several frames from the resulting sequences; the left one is segmented foregrounds and the right one final disparity fields in each pair. In the final disparity fields, we can easily imagine a 3D structure of the scene.

5 Conclusion

In this paper, we propose a real-time disparity estimation algorithm using background registration and foreground segmentation. Dense background disparity

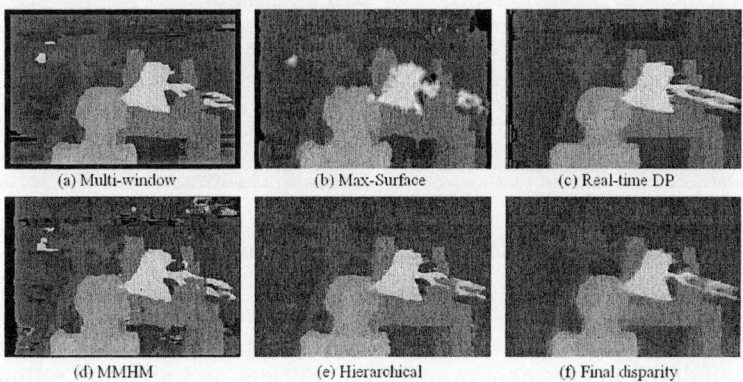

Fig. 11. Disparity fields of "Head and lamp"

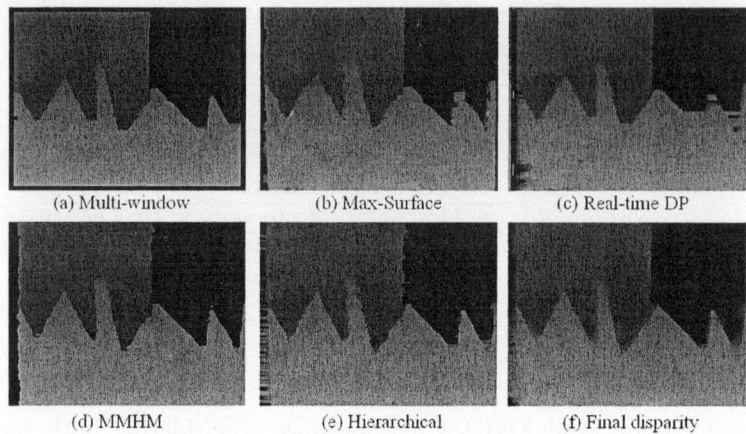

Fig. 12. Disparity fields of "Sawtooth"

Fig. 13. Test sequence and estimated background disparity

Fig. 14. Results of foreground segmentation and final disparity

information is calculated in advance and only disparities of moving object regions are updated in the main process. For efficient and accurate estimation, a real-time segmentation algorithm, hierarchical disparity estimation and shape-adaptive windows are proposed. The performance of the proposed algorithm was evaluated in objective and subjective ways. Computation time mainly depends on the image size, and it was about 15 frames/sec for image pairs having a resolution of 320x240 on a common PC.

As a future work, we have to develop more powerful segmentation algorithm. The performance of the segmentation decides the efficiency and quality of the final disparity fields. Especially, foreground regions classified into background due to wrong segmentation make serious errors in final fields since the fields are not updated. The second perspective of our work will be to improve accuracy of disparity fields at object boundary regions. It is also planned to develop a complete 3D modeling algorithm from multiple stereo cameras. We are currently investigating a depth fields merging algorithm with camera calibration.

Acknowledgements

We would like to thank Dr. D. Scharstein and Dr. R. Szeliski for supplying the ground truth data on their homepage, and Dr. Y. Ohta and Dr. Y. Nakamura for the imagery from the University of Tsukuba. This work was supported by the Ministry of Information and Communication, Korea, under Information Technology Research Center (ITRC) Support Program.

References

1. Scharstein, D., Szeliski, R.: A Taxonomy and Evaluation of Dense Two-frame Stereo Correspondence Algorithms. IJCV, Vol.47, (2002) 7-42
2. http://www.middlebury.edu/stereo
3. Schreer, O., Brandenburg, N., Kauff, P.:Real-time Disparity Analysis for Applications in Immersive Teleconference Scenarios - a Comparative Study. Proc. ICIAP (2001) 346-351
4. Forstmann, S., Ohya, J., Kanou, Y., Schmitt, A., Thuering, S.: Real-time Stereo by Using Dynamic Programming. Proc. CVPR (2004) pp.29
5. Muhlmann, K., Maier, D., Hesser, J., Manner, R.: Calculating Dense Disparity Maps from Color Stereo Images, an Efficient Implementation. IJCV, Vol.47 (2002) 79-88
6. Kim, H., Choe, Y., Sohn, K.: Disparity Estimation Using Region-dividing Technique with Energy-based Regularization. Optical Engineering, Vol.43, No.8 (2004) 1882-1890
7. http://www.ptgrey.com/
8. Kim, H., Kitahara, I., Kogure, K., Hagita, N., Sohn K.: Sat-Cam: "Personal Satellite Virtual Camera". Proc. PCM, Vol.3 (2004) 87-94
9. Kumar, P.,Sengupta, K., Ranganath, S.: Real Time Detection and Recognition of Human Profiles using Inexpensive Desktop Cameras. Proc. ICPR, Vol.1 (2000) 1096-1099
10. Zitnick, L., Kanade, T.: A Cooperative Algorithm for Stereo Matching and Occlusion Detection. IEEE Trans. PAMI, Vol.22, No.7 (2000) 675-684
11. Hirschmuller, H.: Improvements in Real-time Correlation-based Stereo Vision. Proc. CVPR Stereo Workshop (2001) 141-148
12. Sun, C.: Fast Stereo Matching Using Rectangular Subregioning and 3D Maximum-surface Techniques. IJCV, Vol.42, No.1 (2002) 7-42

Multi-view Video Coding Using Illumination Change-Adaptive Motion Estimation and 2-D Direct Mode

Yung-Lyul Lee, Yung-Ki Lee, and Dae-Yeon Kim

Sejong University, Department of Internet Engineering, DMS Lab.,
98 KunJa-Dong, KwangJin-Gu, Seoul, Korea
yllee@sejong.ac.kr

Abstract. A MVC (Multi-view video coding) method, which uses both an illumination change-adaptive ME (Motion estimation)/MC (Motion compensation) and a 2-D (Dimensional) direct mode, is proposed. A new SAD (sum of absolute difference) measure for ME/MC is proposed to compensate Luma pixel value changes for spatio-temporal motion vector prediction. Illumination change-adaptive (ICA) ME/MC uses the new SAD to improve both MV (motion vector) accuracy and bit saving. The proposed 2-D direct mode that can be used in inter-view prediction is an extended version of the temporal direct mode in MPEG-4 AVC. The proposed MVC method obtains approximately 0.8dB PSNR increment compared with the MPEG-4 AVC simulcast coding.

1 Introduction

An adaptive spatio-temporal predictive coding [1] and illumination change-adaptive ME/MC based on the MPEG-4 AVC [2] for MVC are proposed for applications such as the 3DTV and free viewpoint video. A new 2-D inter-view direct mode for the efficient prediction is proposed when the spatio-temporal prediction uses the IBBP structure. The 2-D inter-view direct mode calculates the motion vector of an MB in the current bi-predictive (B) picture when the collocated MB of subsequent P (Predictive) picture refers to an inter-view (spatial prediction) picture, since the current temporal direct mode in the MPEG-4 AVC standard [2] could not be applied to the spatial predictive inter-view picture for MVC. In the proposed illumination change-adaptive (ICA) ME/MC, the pixel values on the current block are subtracted by the average pixel value of the current block and the pixel values on the reference block in the reference frame are subtracted by the average pixel value of the reference block in the reference frame, and then ME/MC is performed by SAD (Sum of Absolute Difference) between the two difference blocks.

The proposed method is compared to the MPEG-4 AVC [2] simulcast coding in terms of objective quality for the various multi-view test video sequences [3]. The proposed method shows better PSNR (peak signal to noise ratio) results than the MPEG-4 AVC [2] simulcast coding.

This paper is consists of the following five sections. In section 2, we introduce the way how the reference picture ordering for MVC is defined. In section 3 and 4, the detailed algorithm of the proposed method is described. Finally, simulation results and conclusions are given in section 5 and 6, respectively.

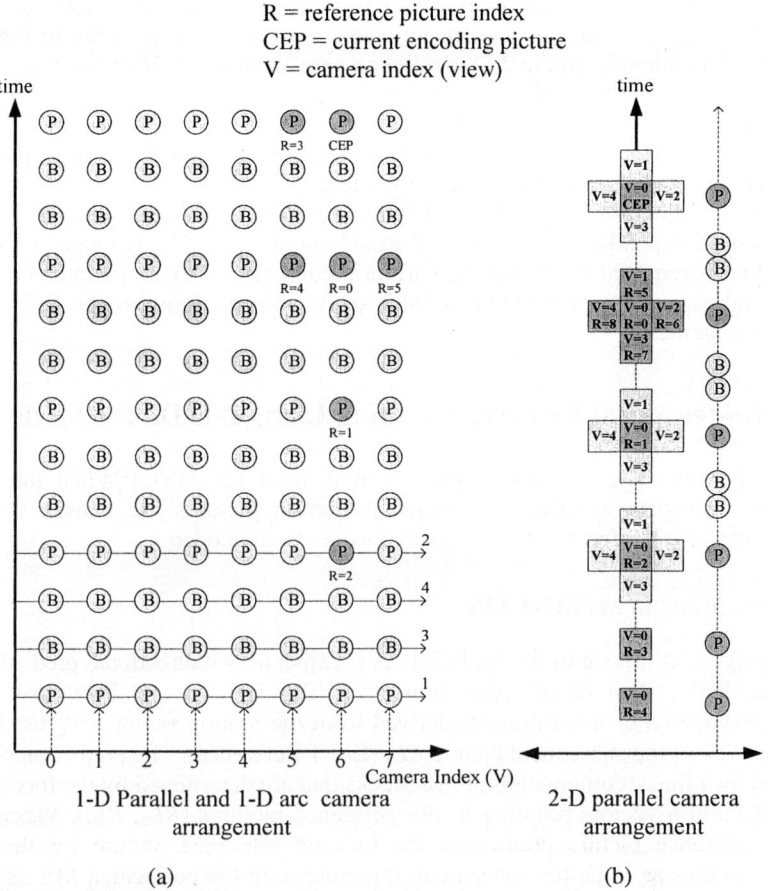

Fig. 1. Reference picture ordering of (a) 1-D parallel and 1-D arc camera arrangements and (b) 2-D parallel camera arrangement

2 Encoding/Decoding Order

In this paper, 1-D parallel, 2-D parallel and 1-D arc data sets [3] for MVC are used as the input data. The reference picture index R, which is used for reference picture indices in the encoder and decoder, for the 1-D parallel and 1-D arc camera arrangement and 2-D parallel camera arrangements are defined as shown in Fig. 1(a) and Fig. 1(b), respectively. The encoding/decoding orders of MVC between inter-view in the 1-D parallel and 1-D arc data sets are shown in Fig. 1(a). The arrow direction 1 means that the encoding/decoding of MVC starts from camera index 0 to camera index 7 in the same time axis. The P (Predictive) pictures in the arrow direction 2 following the arrow direction 1 are encoded by referencing the pictures in the arrow direction 1. The B (Bi-predictive) pictures in the arrow direction 3 following the arrow direction 2 are encoded by referencing the pictures in the arrow directions, 1 and 2. The B (Bi-predictive) pictures in the arrow direction 4 following the arrow direction 3 are encoded in the same way as the B pictures in the arrow direction 3. The pictures in the 2-D parallel camera arrangement that has five cameras can be encode in the similar way to those in the 1-D parallel and arc camera arrangement. The coding structure of IBBPBBP in Fig. 1(a) and (b) is applied to each view. In Fig. 1, R is the reference picture index, CEP means the current picture to encode/decode, and V is the camera (view) index.

For the encoding and decoding, the reference picture index R as shown in Fig. 1(a) and (b) is used depending on the camera arrangement types. The number of reference pictures that is required to encode the current picture are set to six pictures in the 1-D parallel and arc camera arrangements and set to nine pictures in the 2-D parallel camera arrangement.

3 Spatio-temporal Predictive Coding Using 2-D Direct Mode

In this paper, the spatio-temporal prediction is used for MVC. When the spatial prediction coding is applied, the spatial prediction pictures are chosen from the previous inter-view reference P pictures that were already coded.

3.1 Direct Mode in MPEG-4 AVC

The temporal direct mode in the MPEG-4 AVC [2][4] uses bidirectional prediction and allows residual coding of the prediction error. The forward and backward motion vectors (MV_0, MV_1) of this mode are derived from the motion vector MV_C used in the co-located MB of the subsequent picture RL_1 (List 1 Reference). The prediction signal is calculated by a linear combination of two blocks that are determined by the forward and backward motion vectors pointing to two reference pictures (RL_0, RL_1). When using multiple reference picture prediction, the forward reference picture for the direct mode RL_1 is chosen to be the subsequent P picture with the co-located MB as shown in Fig 2. The forward and backward motion vectors for direct mode blocks are calculated as follows:

$$MV_0 = \frac{TD_B}{TD_D} MV_C$$
$$MV_1 = \frac{TD_B - TD_D}{TD_D} MV_C \quad \dotfill \quad (1)$$

where MV_0 is the forward motion vector, MV_1 is the backward motion vector, and MV_C is the motion vector of the co-located block in the subsequent P picture.

3.2 Proposed 2-D (Two Dimensional) Direct Mode

For MVC, the spatio-temporal prediction is usually used for improving coding efficiency. If the motion vector used in the co-located block of the subsequent P picture for the direct mode block of the current B picture points to the inter-view reference picture, a new 2-D direct mode is required, since the temporal direct mode

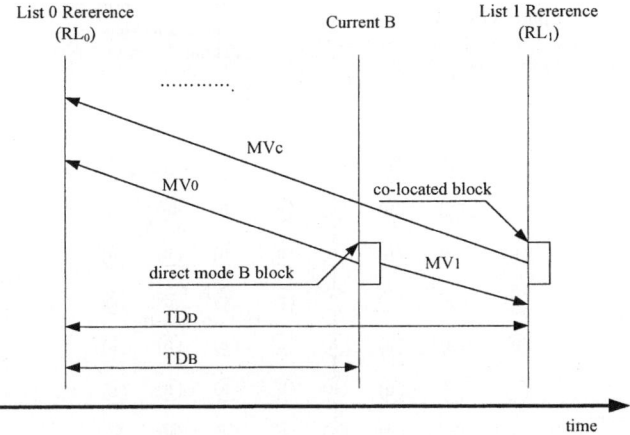

Fig. 2. A direct mode block has the forward and backward motion vectors MV_0 and MV_1 pointing to two reference pictures RL_0 and RL_1 in MPEG-4 AVC

for 2-D video coding does not support the inter-view reference picture as the RL1 picture. Therefore we proposed the 2-D direct mode block for referring to the spatial (inter-view) prediction picture. Fig 2 illustrates 2-D direct mode in which the horizontal-axis i is the cameras index and the vertical-axis is time. In Fig. 3, P(i,t) is the P picture that has the camera index i and time t, and B(i,t-1) is the B picture that has the camera index i and time t-1.

When the current block (16×16 or 8×8 block) of $B(i,t-1)$ picture is coded as the 2-D direct mode, the motion vector of the co-located block of the subsequent $P(i,t)$ points to the block of $P(i-1,t-3)$ picture. In order to make the prediction block of the current block of $B(i,t-1)$ picture, the interpolated block of the two blocks pointed by two motion vectors to $P(i-1,t-3)$ and $P(i,t-3)$ pictures is calculated.

The two forward motion vectors (MV_{F1}, MV_{F2}) of this mode are derived from the motion vector MV_C used in the co-located MB of the subsequent picture $P(i,t)$ and the forward prediction block R_F is calculated by the interpolation of two prediction blocks, R_{F1} and R_{F2}, as follows:

$$MV_{F1} = MV_C \left.\frac{TD_B}{TD_D}\right|_{to\ P(i-1,t-3)}, MV_{F2} = MV_C \left.\frac{TD_B}{TD_D}\right|_{to\ P(i,t-3)}$$
$$R_F = (3R_{F1} + R_{F2} + 2)/4 \qquad\qquad (2)$$

where MV_{F1} and MV_{F2} point to the blocks in $P(i-1,t-3)$ and $P(i,t-3)$ pictures, respectively, and R_{F1} and R_{F2} are the reference blocks pointed by MV_{F1} and MV_{F2}, respectively.

The two backward motion vectors (MV_{B1}, MV_{B2}) of this mode are derived from the motion vector MV_C used in the co-located MB of the subsequent picture $P(i,t)$ and the backward prediction block R_B is calculated by the interpolation of two prediction blocks, R_{B1} and R_{B2}, as follows:

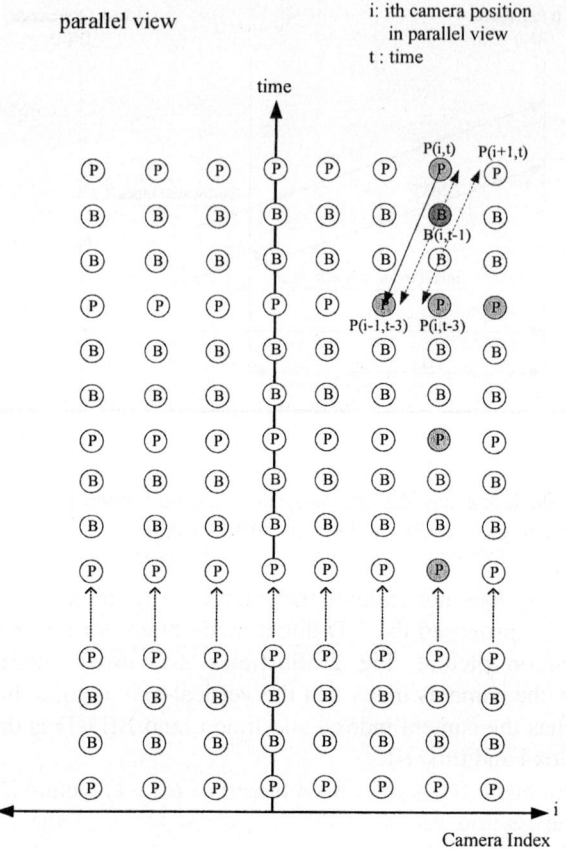

Fig. 3. An example of 2-D direct mode

$$MV_{B1} = MV_C \left. \frac{TD_B - TD_D}{TD_D} \right|_{to\ P(i,t)}, MV_{B2} = MV_C \left. \frac{TD_B - TD_D}{TD_D} \right|_{to\ P(i+1,t)}$$
$$R_B = (3R_{B1} + R_{B2} + 2)/4 \quad \dots\dots\dots\dots\dots\dots\dots\dots\dots\dots\dots (3)$$

where MV_{B1} and MV_{B2} point to the blocks in $P(i,t)$ and $P(i+1,t)$ pictures, respectively, and R_{B1} and R_{B2} are the reference blocks pointed by MV_{B1} and MV_{B2}, respectively.

In the experiments, the existing MPEG-4 AVC [2] reference frames for the prediction are used for temporal prediction except the stored B picture and the 2-D direct mode is used only for the spatial prediction. When using the proposed 2-D direct mode, only the residual data and 2-D 8×8 or 16×16 direct mode are encoded so that the coding efficiency is improved.

In case that the current block (16×16 or 8×8 block) of the $B(i,t-1)$ picture is coded as the 2-D direct mode and the motion vector of the co-located block of the subsequent $P(i,t)$ points to the block of the $P(i-2,t-3)$ picture in Fig 3, the proposed 2-D direct mode is applied in a similar way to eqs. (2) and (3) by changing the weighting factors.

4 Illumination Change-Adaptive (ICA) Motion Estimation and Compensation

In MVC, there are illumination changes in general between the inter-views and same views. Therefore this paper also proposes an MB-based ICA.

Assume that the current frame is denoted by $f(i,j)$ with spatial coordinates (i,j), and the reference frame is $r(i,j)$. The conventional *SAD* calculation for the motion estimation of $S \times T$ blocks, such as 16×16, 16×8, 8×16, 8×8, 8×4, 4×8, and 4×4, is performed as follows:

$$SAD(x, y) = \sum_{i=0}^{S-1}\sum_{j=0}^{T-1} | f(i, j) - r(i+x, j+y) | \quad\quad\quad\quad\quad\quad\quad\quad (4)$$

where *(x, y)* represents a motion vector. In order to compensate the illumination change, *NewSAD* is defined as follows:

$$NewSAD(x, y) = \sum_{i=0}^{U-1}\sum_{j=0}^{V-1} | (f(i, j) - M_{curr}) - (r(i+x, j+y) - M_{ref}) | \quad\quad (5)$$

where M_{curr} and M_{ref} are the average pixel values of the current block and reference block, respectively. In the experiments, U and V are set to 16 or 8. The difference signals of $U \times V$ blocks are coded in integer 4×4 DCT and quantization as in the MPEG-4 AVC [2][5] standard. For the illumination change-adaptive ME/MC, the MB_type is first decided. When the proposed ME/MC is used, the minimum one bit flag to the maximum four flag bits indication for the $S \times T$ block is used with the 8 bits M_{curr} value depending on the flag.

5 Simulation Results

For the experiments, the spatio-temporal reference frames, the MB-based ICA ME/MC and the 2-D direct mode are used in the seven MVC data sets [6]. Although the PSNR values can be slightly degraded, the fast ME [7] method that is called the hexagonal search in the current JM7.6 [8] is used only for the proposed method to speed up the simulation results. The anchor bit-streams coded in the MPEG-4 AVC simulcast mode were used for comparison to the proposed method. All experiments were performed with SIF (320×240) YUV 4:2:0 sequences. Table 1 describes the properties of the various test data sets which form a representative set of the data. These data sets vary in the number of cameras/views N, the arrangement of the cameras, distance between cameras D, as well as properties of the images in terms of image size S and frame rate F. The 10 seconds of each view is used for testing. The MPEG-4 AVC anchors were encoded according to the coding conditions for test data sets in Table 2 with the AVC encoding parameters as specified in the Table 3. For the test, the software used for AVC was JM7.6.

The proposed method also uses the IBBPBBP... structure. Five spatial predicted pictures among ten reference pictures are used in the 2-D parallel data sets as the number of reference pictures, and 3 spatial predicted pictures among 6 reference

Table 1. Properties of the various test data sets

Data Set Name	Image Property	Camera Parameter
Race1, Race2, Flamenco1, Golf2	S: 320x240, F: 30fps	N: 8, D: ~20cm, A: 1-D parallel
Flamenco2, Crowd	S: 320x240, F: 30fps	N: 5, D: ~20cm, A: 2-D parallel
Aquarium	S: 320x240, F: 10fps	N: 16, D: ~2 cm, A: 1-D arc

Table 2. Coding conditions for test data sets

Class	Test Sequences	Bit-rates [kbps/camera]		
A (easy)	Flamenco1, Golf2, Race2, Aquarium	64 kbps	128 kbps	256 kbps
B (difficult)	Race1, Flamenco2, Crowd	128 kbps	256 kbps	512 kbps

Table 3. MPEG-4 AVC parameters

Feature / Tool / Setting	AVC Parameters
Rate control	Yes
RD optimization	Yes
Specific settings	Loop filter, CABAC
Search range	±32 for SIF
# Reference picture	5
I-frame period	1 sec
GOP Structure	IBBP...

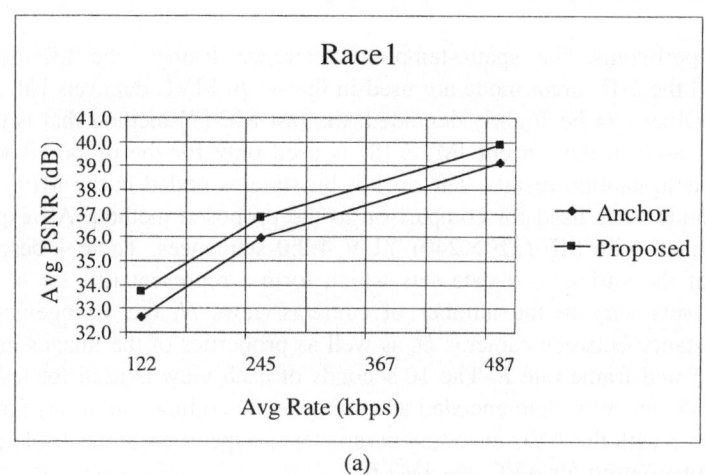

(a)

Fig. 4. Comparison of PSNR between the MPEG-4 AVC simulcast and proposed method: (a) race1: 1-D parallel data set, (b) race2: 1-D parallel data set, (c) flamenco1: 1-D parallel data set, (d) golf2: 1-D parallel data set, (e) flamenco2: 2-D parallel data set, (f) crowd: 2-D parallel data set, and (g) aquarium: 1-D arc data set

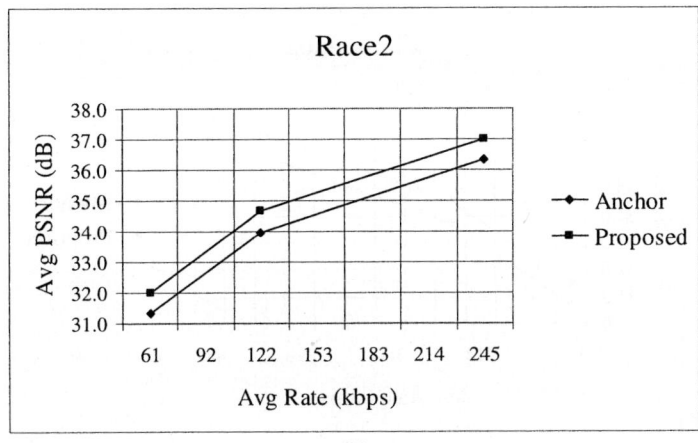

(b)

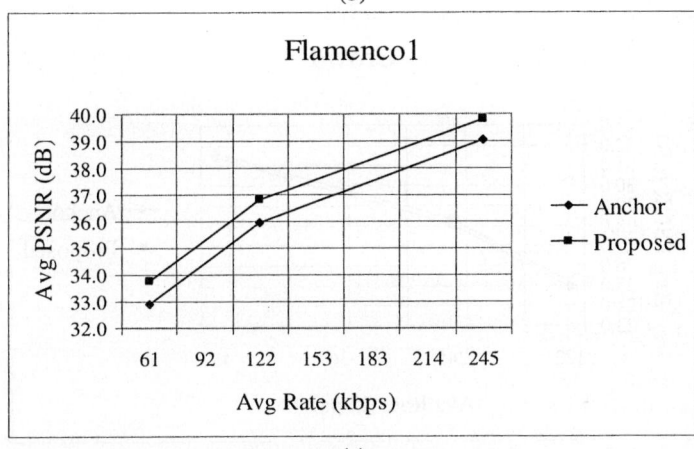

(c)

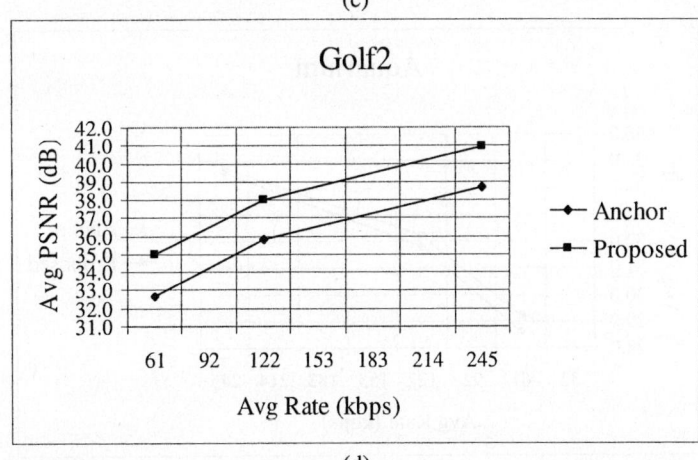

(d)

Fig. 4. (*Continued*)

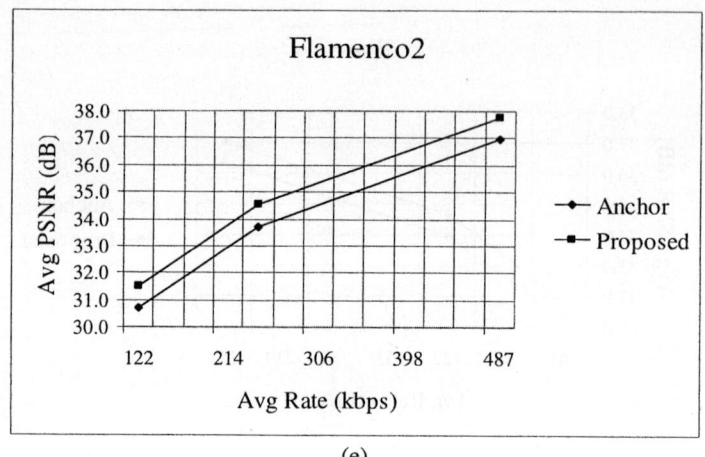

(e)

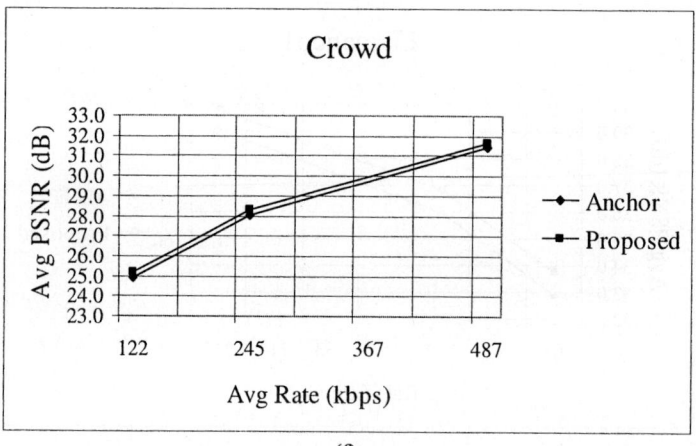

(f)

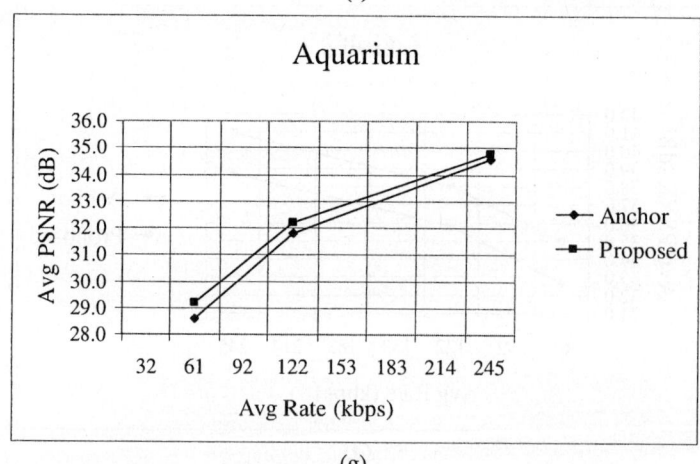

(g)

Fig. 4. (*Continued*)

pictures are used in the 1-D parallel and 1-D arc data sets as the number of reference pictures. The more spatial predicted pictures can be considered but we restricted the number of spatial prediction pictures in the experiments. The proposed 2-D direct mode is applied only for spatial predicted pictures, and the proposed MB-based ICA ME/MC is used for all spatio-temporal reference pictures. Fig. 4shows that rate distortion curves of the "Race1", "Race2", "Flamenco1", "Golf2", "Flamenco2", "Crowd", and "Aquarium" sequences, in which the frame rates are 30Hz except the "Aquarium" sequence with 10 Hz frame rates. The proposed method obtains approximately 0.7dB, 0.9dB, 0.8dB, 2.2dB, 0.8dB, 0.2dB, and 0.4dB PSNR improvement in each test sequence compared with the MPEG-4 AVC simulcast method, as shown in Fig. 4(a) ~ (g).

In Table 4, 5 and 6, we compared the proposed method to the MPEG-4 simulcast AVC anchor in terms of the quantitative bitrates and PSNRs.

Table 4, 5 and 6 show the average PSNR values of all camera views for the given bit rates of the 2-D parallel data set, 1-D arc data set, and 1-D parallel data set, respectively.

Table 4. Average PSNR comparison for the given bitrates (2-D parallel data set)

Flamenco 2			
Anchor		Proposed	
Avg Rate	Avg PSNR	Avg Rate	Avg PSNR
128.4	30.7	128.4	31.5
256.8	33.7	256.7	34.5
513.4	37.0	513.1	37.8
Crowd			
Anchor		Proposed	
Avg Rate	Avg PSNR	Avg Rate	Avg PSNR
128.3	24.9	128.4	25.2
256.4	28.1	256.6	28.3
512.7	31.5	512.8	31.7

Table 5. Average PSNR comparison for the given bitrates (1-D arc data set)

Aquarium			
Anchor		Proposed	
Avg Rate	Avg PSNR	Avg Rate	Avg PSNR
66.4	28.6	66.9	29.2
131.7	31.8	131.3	32.2
256.4	34.5	260.2	34.7

Table 6. Average PSNR comparison for the given bitrates (1-D parallel data set)

Race 1			
Anchor		Proposed	
Avg Rate	Avg PSNR	Avg Rate	Avg PSNR
129.0	32.6	128.8	33.7
257.5	35.9	257.6	36.8
513.6	39.1	514.8	39.9
Race 2			
Anchor		Proposed	
Avg Rate	Avg PSNR	Avg Rate	Avg PSNR
64.3	31.3	64.6	32.0
128.3	34.0	128.8	34.6
256.3	36.3	257.0	37.0
Flamenco 1			
Anchor		Proposed	
Avg Rate	Avg PSNR	Avg Rate	Avg PSNR
64.3	32.9	65.3	33.8
128.5	36.0	129.6	36.8
256.7	39.0	257.4	39.8
Golf 2			
Anchor		Proposed	
Avg Rate	Avg PSNR	Avg Rate	Avg PSNR
64.4	32.7	64.6	35.0
128.3	35.8	128.6	38.0
256.4	38.7	256.7	40.9

6 Conclusion

We proposed a MVC method that improves the PSNR by approximately more than 0.7dB for a given bit rates. Our method is a kind of extended version of MPEG-4 AVC. By using the proposed method that uses both 2-D direct mode and ICA ME/MC, the coding efficiency in MVC can be improved. Therefore, the proposed method can be considered as a MVC tool in the future MVC standard [9]. The simulation is performed on without the intrinsic and extrinsic camera parameters. If the camera parameters are given for the test data sets, we believe that we can improve the coding gain more.

Acknowledgement

This research is partly supported by the Ubiquitous Autonomic Computing and Network Project, the Ministry of Information and Communication (MIC) 21st Century Frontier R&D Program in Korea.

References

1. Yung-Lyul Lee and Woo-Chul Sung, "Multi-view video coding using 2D direct mode," *ISO/IEC JTC1/SC29 WG11* m11266, Palma de Mallorca, Spain, October 2004.
2. T. Wiegand, Final draft international standard for joint video specification H.264, *Joint Video Team (JVT) of ISO/IEC MPEG and ITU-T VCEG*, JVT-G050, March 2003.
3. "Call for Evidence on Multi-View Coding," *ISO/IEC JTC1/SC29/WG11* N6720, October 2004.
4. M. Flierl and B. Girod, "Generalized B pictures and the draft JVT/H.264 video compression standard," *IEEE Trans. Circuits Syst. Video Technol.*, vol. 13, pp. 587–597, July 2003.
5. H. Malvar, A. Hallapuro, M. Karczewicz, and L. Kerofsky, "Low-Complexity transform and quantization in H.264/AVC," *IEEE Trans. Circuits Syst. Video Technol.*, vol. 13, pp. 598–603, July 2003.
6. R. Kawada, "KDDI multiview video sequences for MPEG 3DAV use," *ISO/IEC JTC1/SC29/WG11* m10533, Munich, March 2004.
7. Zhibo Chen, Peng Zhou, Yun He, "Fast Motion estimation for JVT," JVT-G016.doc, *Joint Video Team (JVT) of ISO/IEC MPEG & ITU-T VCEG*, 7th meeting, Pattaya, TH, 5-13 March 2003.
8. http://bs.hhi.de/~suehring/tml/download/old_jm/jm76.zip
9. "Survey of algorithms used for Multi-view Video Coding (MVC)," *ISO/IEC JTC1/SC29/WG11*, N6909, HongKong, China, January 2005.

Fast Ray-Space Interpolation with Depth Discontinuity Preserving for Free Viewpoint Video System

Gangyi Jiang[1,2], Liangzhong Fan[1,2], Mei Yu[1,3], Xien Ye[1], Rangding Wang[1], and Yong-Deak Kim[4]

[1] Faculty of Information Science and Engineering,
Ningbo University, Ningbo 315211, China
[2] Institute of Computer Technology, Graduate School of Chinese Academy of
Sciences, Beijing 100871, China
[3] National Key Laboratory of Machine Perception,
Peking University, Beijing 100871, China
[4] Division of Electronics Engineering, Ajou University, Suwon 442-749, Korea

Abstract. Ray-space representation is the main technology to realize free viewpoint video system with complicated scenes. Ray-space interpolation is one of key problems to be solved. A new fast ray-space interpolation method that can preserve depth discontinuity is proposed in this paper. Discontinuity features of ray-space data are first extracted by using adaptive threshold, then, a cross check operation is carried out between neighboring epipolar lines to refine the extracted feature points. After that, ray directions of feature points are determined, and ray-space interpolation is implemented in the regions segmented by feature points. Experimental results show that the proposed method achieves much higher *PSNR* than the pixel matching based interpolation method and the block matching based interpolation method, and the quality of rendered intermediate viewpoint images is also improved greatly. In addition, the proposed interpolation method requires low computational cost and is suitable for hardware implementation.

1 Introduction

As 2D image communication systems have been widely used, 3D image system enhancing the reality of virtual environment is considered as promising next generation of multi-media system[1]. MPEG has been working on the exploration of 3D audio-visual (3DAV) since December 2001. 3DAV was classified into three main application scenarios, that is, Free Viewpoint Video(FVV), omni-directional video and interactive stereo video[2]. In FVV system, user can freely control the viewpoint position of any dynamic real-world scene in real time. The techniques in FVV systems can be classified into two categories, that is, model-based rendering(MBR) and image-based rendering(IBR) methods. MBR representation is obtained by converting the original multi-view images to a 3D model with texture information. Since the model matching and texture analysis are time-consuming, MBR is not suitable for full real-time applications. IBR, on the other hand, requires only sampled images to generate high-quality novel views. Ray-space representation is a newly developed method of IBR, used to describe 3D information by converting the original multi-view images to "ray" parameters. FVV system based on ray-space representation was demonstrated in M8595[3]. Unlike other IBR methods, the ray-space representation can generate an arbitrary viewpoint image without complicated analysis and rendering process. It has been approved that the ray-space representation is very suited to realize a full real-time FVV without any restriction on scene[4].

One of the key technologies to make the ray-space based FVV system feasible is ray-space interpolation. In the real world situation, it is difficult to set many cameras very closely. However, the ray data captured by the camera setup is too sparse in viewpoint axis to apply the ray-space method[5]. Therefore, it is necessary to generate the absent ray data by some approaches. Ray-space interpolation is a technique that generates the missing ray from two or more views of a scene. The main difficulty of ray-space interpolation is how to find the best correspondence among points in multi-view images. Two types of interpolation methods had been discussed, that is, the pixel matching based interpolation(PMI) and block matching based interpolation(BMI) methods[6]. These methods find the correspondence from neighboring viewpoint image with minimum mean square error (MSE) criterion. The PMI method performs well when the disparity is small, but fails in textureless regions. The BMI method makes better correspondence detection than the PMI method except for depth discontinuous regions.

In this paper, feature points at regions with discontiguous depth is first extracted, then, the correspondences of the feature points are determined with sum of MSE (SMSE) criterion by utilizing the correlation between multiple epipolar lines. The correspondence of feature points determined by the new method is more accurate than the above two conventional methods. The rest of paper is organized as follows. In section 2, a practical camera setup is described to capture multi-view images. The related work of ray-space interpolation is briefly reviewed in section 3. Feature point extraction and refining, multiple epipolar matching interpolation algorithm based on feature points are described in section 4. Experimental results are given in section 5.

2 Ray-Space Representation of Multi-view Images

Ray-space representation is one of IBR techniques[7], which derives from the plenoptic function. It describes the rays in a scene as 4D function $f(x, y, \theta, \phi)$, where (θ, ϕ) denotes the direction of the ray, (x, y) denotes the intersection of the ray and the reference plane, and $f(x, y, \theta, \phi)$ represents the intensity of the specific ray. An important feature in ray-space is that an image with respect to a certain viewpoint is given as a sub-space of ray-space[8].

Fig.1(a) shows a camera setup to capture multi-view images for the ray-space based FVV system, where real cameras labeled 1, 2, 3 and 4 are horizontally arranged with the same interval. Virtual cameras, drawn transparently

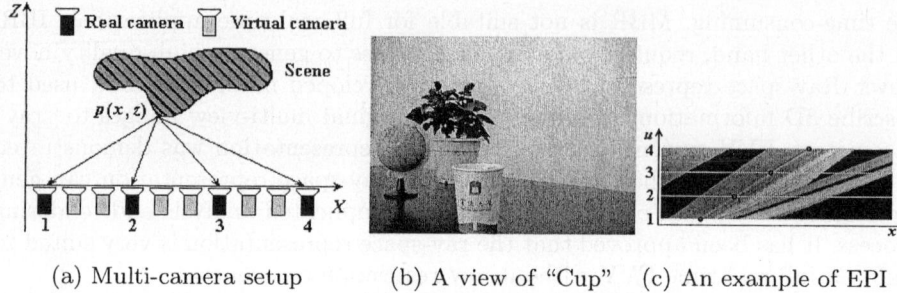

(a) Multi-camera setup   (b) A view of "Cup"   (c) An example of EPI

Fig. 1. Ray-space representation of multi-viewpoint images

in Fig.1(a), are also required to render arbitrary views, these virtual viewpoint images are interpolated from the captured real images. Fig.1(b) is a view of "Cup" scene as an example, and Fig.1(c) shows an example of epipolar plane image (EPI) of a real scene, where four horizontal lines correspond to the same scanlines captured by the real cameras. Here, we call the EPI in Fig.1(c) as a ray-space slice. The point $p(x, z)$ in the scene projected to EPI is represented by the four red points in Fig.1(c), and it is proved that these points in the EPI form a locus of straight line. The slope of the line represents the inverse depth. Based on these properties, we conclude that this matching process requires only one-dimensional searching operation in an EPI.

3 Related Ray-Space Interpolation Methods

Ray-space based FVV system can render novel views easily, but it requires relatively dense sampling of the scene, that is, the use of a large number of cameras. It is not supported in MPEG at all, and would require a new major standardization effort including definition of many new tools. In the real world situation, it is difficult to set many cameras very closely. Thus, the ray-space data obtained is usually too sparse in viewpoint axis to apply the ray-space method. Therefore, it is necessary to generate missing ray data by some approaches[9].

Fig.2(a) shows the PMI method, it simply searches the best pixel pair from two nearest EPI lines for interpolation. When the pixel "a" in EPI line-1 and the pixel to be interpolated are given, the position of the pixel 'b" in EPI line-2 can be determined. The absolute difference value between pixels "a" and "b" in the two EPI lines is considered as their similarity error measure. The procedure is repeated for all possible pixel pairs, and the pixel pair with lowest error is regarded to indicate the direction of the ray. This matching method has good performance in edge region when the searching range is small.

Fig.2(b) shows the BMI method. Given a block "A" in EPI line-1 and the location of pixel to be interpolated, a block "B" in EPI line-2 can be found. Then the MSE can be calculated for block "A" and block "B". The same procedure is done for the next block, which has one pixel shift from block "A". After finding all MSE values in the assigned maximum disparity, the middle pixels of block

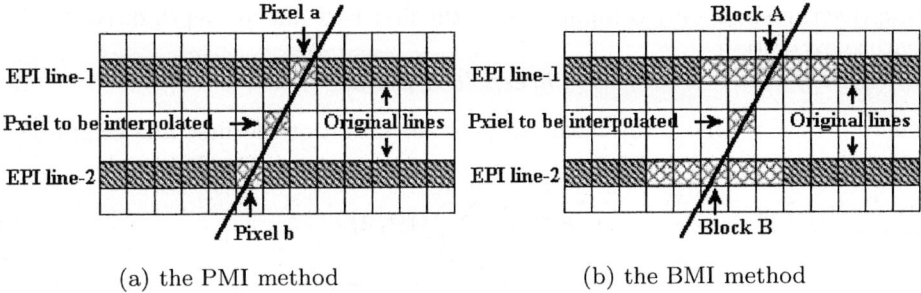

Fig. 2. Conventional interpolation methods

pairs with the minimum MSE value is considered as the best correspondence among all calculated MSE values. This method can detect the correspondence better than the PMI method except for depth discontinuous regions[10].

4 The Proposed Ray-Space Interpolation Method

As mentioned above, correspondence between pixels calculated in the conventional interpolation methods is similar to block based stereo matching. Error matching may occur in background regions or depth discontinuous regions, especially when the searching range is large, and as a result, the arbitrary viewpoint image rendered from ray-space interpolated with these methods usually exists obvious distortion.

In this section, a new fast depth discontinuity preserving interpolation algorithm is described. First, we explain our depth discontinuity feature extraction and feature refining method. Then, multi-epiploar line matching method is used to determine correspondence of feature points. Finally, a region-based interpolation method is presented.

4.1 Depth Discontinuity Feature Extraction

Ambiguity in textureless regions is an important factor resulting in inaccurate correspondence for many matching algorithms. However, it is unreasonable for a scene to be artificially altered by placing a textured background behind the objects of interest in order to make the scene more amenable to the particular matching algorithm. In fact, textureless, nearly fronto-parallel surfaces can be handled quite nicely as long as assumption that intensity variation accompanies depth discontinuities.

Given an EPI $I(x,u)$ with size of $W \times H$, a gradient image $G(x,u)$ is calculated as

$$G(x,u) = |I(x+1,u) - I(x,u)| \tag{1}$$

Due to an EPI is composed of the same scanlines of multi-view images, all lines in an EPI correspond to a scanline of a scene. Considering computational cost, adaptive threshold only computed from the first EPI-line for depth discontinuity feature extraction

$$Threshold = \mu + \sigma \quad (2)$$

where μ and σ denote the mean and the deviation of the first line of gradient image,

$$\mu = \frac{1}{W} \sum_{i=0}^{W-1} G(i, u) \quad (3)$$

$$\sigma = \sqrt{\frac{1}{W} \sum_{i=0}^{W-1} (G(i, u) - \mu)^2} \quad (4)$$

Thus the depth discontinuity feature map $\{f(x, u)\}$ is acquired by

$$f(x, u) = \begin{cases} 1, & \text{if } G(x, u) \geq Threshold \\ 0, & \text{otherwise} \end{cases} \quad (5)$$

As image noise is unavoidable, if it occurs in the EPI, it is usually detected as discontinuity feature point by the above feature extraction method. These errors will be propagated in the next processing step, so that the interpolated arbitrary viewpoint image will be degraded. Therefore a feature refining process is performed to eliminate these noises.

Here, a cross-check operation is applied to the discontinuity feature map in our method. When a pixel $I(x, u)$ is extracted as a discontinuity feature point, pixel $I(x+d, u+1)$ will be determined as its correspondence with the disparity d by MSE criterion. If the feature point $I(x, u)$ is not a noise, a disparity $-d$ is most probably searched for pixel $I(x+d, u+1)$ when EPI line u is as the reference line. So if the absolute values of the two disparities are not equal, $I(x, u)$ is regarded as a noisy point, and will be eliminated from the discontinuity feature map.

4.2 Multiple Epipolar-Based Matching Method

As mentioned in section 3, the PMI and BMI methods just utilize nearby EPI line information to determine the correspondence, and often fail at textureless regions or depth discontinuous regions. In view of an EPI is converted from

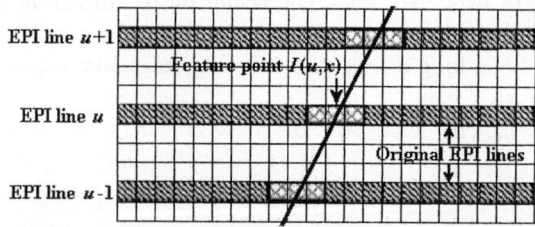

Fig. 3. Multiple epipolar matching method

multi-view images, we take advantage of the information of multiple EPI lines to enhance correctness in correspondence determination.

Fig.3 shows our multiple epipolar matching method. The pixel at position (x, u) in EPI line u denotes a discontinuous feature point. Multiple epipolar information can be incorporated for matching by the following function

$$SMSE(d) = \frac{1}{2M} \sum_{k=-M}^{k=M} \left[\frac{1}{2W+1} \sum_{w=-W}^{w=W} |I(x+w+d_{u+k}, u+k) - I(x+w, u)| \right] \quad (6)$$

where M represents the number of EPI lines nearby EPI line u, W denotes the size of matching window, d_{u+k} denotes the disparity between EPI line $u+k$ and EPI line u. The range of d_{u+k} is constrained from zero to maximum disparity. This above function is called as sum of mean square error(SMSE). The direction of current feature point is selected by

$$d_{best} = \arg\min_{d} \{SMSE(d)\} \quad (7)$$

4.3 Region-Based Interpolation

Fig.4(b) shows the result of discontinuity feature map after feature extraction, feature refining and multiple epipolar line matching processing. The sparse EPI is split into different regions by the extracted feature points, and it is clear that depth discontinuous information of objects is extracted correctly. Fig.5 illustrates the region-based interpolation method. If a, b and c, d represent four neighboring feature points in the original EPI lines, positions of e, f and g, h can be computed from line equation easily, their intensities are linear interpolated from intensities of these feature points, then, the pixels between e and g and the pixels between f and h can be bi-linearly interpolated. Fig.4(c) shows a slice interpolated by the proposed method, the quality of which is acceptable.

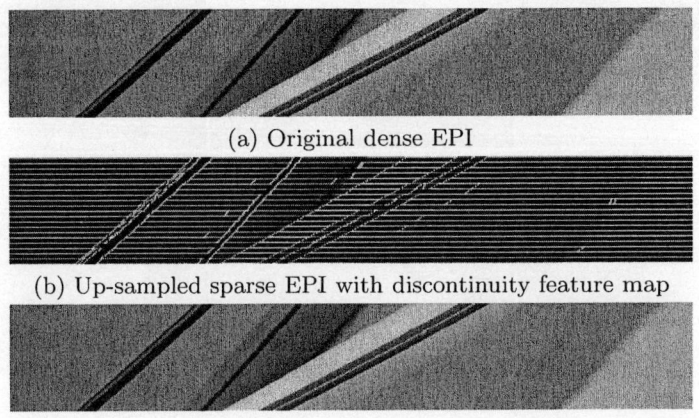

(a) Original dense EPI

(b) Up-sampled sparse EPI with discontinuity feature map

(c) EPI interpolated by the proposed method ($PSNR=32.96$dB)

Fig. 4. Result of 117th EPI interpolation of "Cup" (camera interval=5mm)

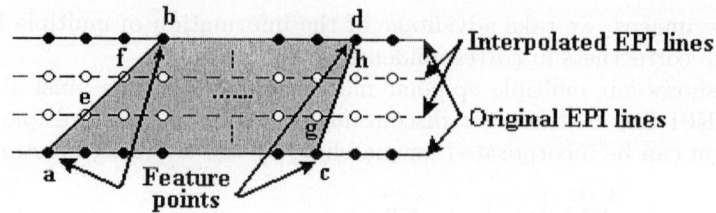

Fig. 5. Region-based interpolation

5 Experimental Results and Analyses

We perform experiments on three test sets of real data called "Xmas", "Cup" and "Toy" on a PC with CPU of PIII 850MHz and RAM of 256M. Fig.6 gives the three test multi-view image sets. "Xmas" is available from Tanimoto Lab, of which 101 viewpoint images are captured synchronously with camera interval of 3mm, the size of the images is 640×480, and the distance between cameras and object is about 30cm. For the "Cup" and "Toy" sets, the camera interval is 1mm, the number and the size of images are the same as "Xmas", but the maximum disparity of the two sets are much larger than that of "Xmas". Firstly, these multi-view images are converted into 480 EPIs with different camera interval, the resolutions of EPI are 480×21, 480×11, 480×6, 480×5, respectively. Different interpolation algorithms are applied to these sparse EPIs to generate the dense ones, and then the interpolated dense EPI is compared with actual dense EPI converted from real images with *PSNR* criterion.

(a) "Xmas"   (b) "Cup"   (c) 'Toy"

Fig. 6. Three test multi-view image sets for ray-space interpolation.(The upper is the most left images, and the lower is the most right images).

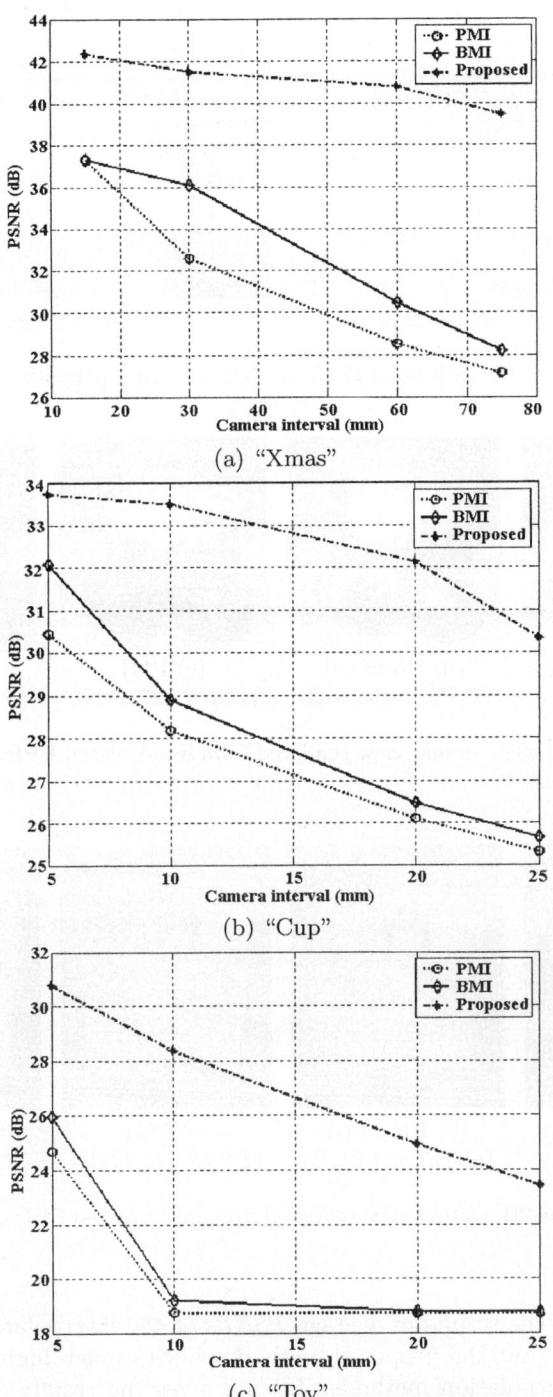

Fig. 7. *PSNR*s of the rendered virtual viewpoint images

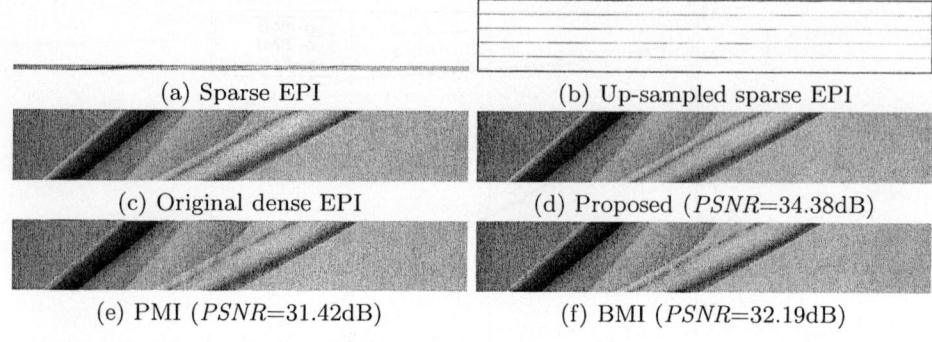

Fig. 8. Results of the interpolated 153th EPI of "Cup" (camera interval=20mm)

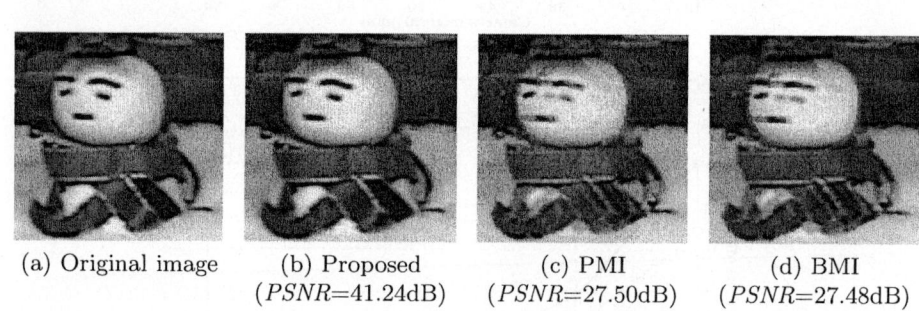

Fig. 9. Part of the 99th virtual view rendered from interpolated EPIs of "Xmas" (camera interval=75mm)

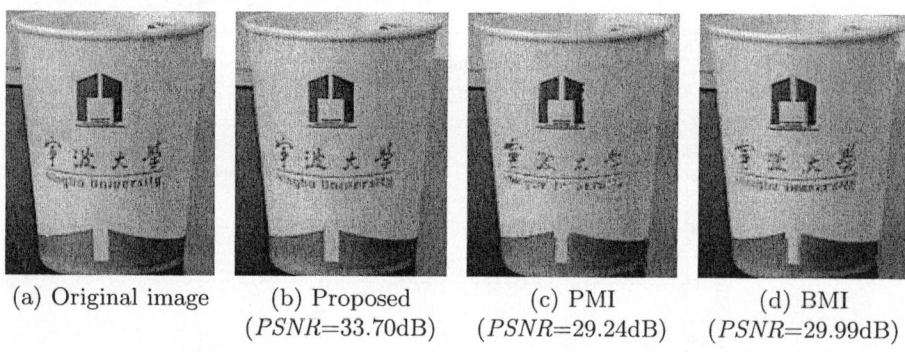

Fig. 10. Part of the 2th virtual view rendered from interpolated EPIs of "Cup" (camera interval=20mm)

Table 1 gives the results of average *PSNR*s of 480 interpolated EPIs respectively, it is clear that the proposed method achieves much higher *PSNR*s than conventional interpolation methods. Table 2 gives the results of average computational *TIME* of interpolating 480 EPIs respectively, the running time of conventional interpolation methods increases as camera interval increases, but

Table 1. Average *PSNR*s of 480 interpolated EPIs unit:dB

Test sets	Camera interval	PMI	BMI	Proposed method
Xmas	15 mm	40.05	39.50	44.07
	30 mm	35.93	37.50	42.83
	60 mm	31.98	33.22	41.55
	75 mm	30.60	31.48	40.51
Cup	5 mm	33.88	34.66	35.62
	10 mm	32.00	32.33	34.95
	20 mm	30.42	30.69	33.80
	25 mm	29.67	29.93	32.31
Toy	5 mm	27.60	28.55	32.08
	10 mm	22.45	23.19	29.64
	20 mm	22.02	22.44	26.74
	25 mm	21.98	22.31	25.68

Table 2. Average computational *TIME* of interpolating 480 EPIs unit:ms

Test sets	Camera interval	PMI	BMI	Proposed method
Xmas	15 mm	22	64	45
	30 mm	41	113	47
	60 mm	87	221	47
	75 mm	94	285	55
Cup	5 mm	41	113	52
	10 mm	78	202	53
	20 mm	149	379	57
	25 mm	190	463	56
Toy	5 mm	243	595	114
	10 mm	636	1772	72
	20 mm	774	2029	56
	25 mm	805	2036	64

the proposed method keeps approximately constant running time under different camera intervals, and the running time is much saved compared with the PMI or BMI methods especially under large camera interval. Fig.7 shows average *PSNR*s of virtual viewpoint images rendered from interpolated EPIs, it is seen that *PSNR*s of the three test sets have been improved greatly by the proposed method compared with the PMI or BMI methods.

Fig.8 gives an example of interpolated EPIs, the proposed method outperforms the conventional methods with more than $2 \sim 3$dB in generating the dense EPI. Fig.9 and Fig.10 show parts of virtual images rendered from EPIs interpolated with the above three interpolation methods. It is obvious that the proposed method is much better than conventional methods in keeping edges

(a) Left view (b) Right view

Fig. 11. Rendered stereo images from ray-space data, interpolated by the proposed method (camera interval=60mm)

and fine textures of objects. The characters and some edges of pattern on the cup are well kept by the proposed method, while they are damaged by the two conventional methods. The experiments of "Xmas" give similar results. After generating dense ray-space data, it is easy to render stereo images by selecting appropriate data. Fig.11 shows a rendered virtual stereo image pair from the interpolated EPIs, of which the camera interval between the left and the right views is 60mm.

6 Conclusions

Ray-space representation has superiority in rendering arbitrary viewpoint images of complicated scene in real-time, and it has been attracting more and more attention. Interpolation is one of the key techniques to make the ray-space based FVV system feasible, and it also determines the cost of application and the quality of rendered image. In this paper, a new fast ray-space interpolation method with depth discontinuity preserving is proposed, which improves visual quality as well as *PSNR*s of rendered virtual viewpoint image greatly, compared with the conventional PMI and BMI methods. In addition, the proposed method requires low computational cost and is suitable for hardware implementation.

The future work will focus on the exposed or occluded objects, which is also a challenge for traditional multi-view image coding as well as stereoscopic image processing.

Acknowledgements. This work was supported by the Natural Science Foundation of China (grant 60472100), the Natural Science Foundation of Zhejiang Province (grant RC01057), the Ningbo Science and Technology Project of China (grant 2003A61001, 2004A610001, 2004A630002), and the Zhejiang Science and Technology Project of China (Grant 2004C31105).

References

1. Takano, T., Naemura, T., Harashima, H.: 3D Space Coding Using Virtual Object Surface. Systems and Computers. **32** (2001) 47–59
2. Smolic, A., Kamata, H.: Report on Status of 3DAV Exploration. ISO/IEC JTC1/SC29/WG11 **N5558** (2003)
3. Smolic, A., Kimata, H.: Report on 3DAV Exploration. ISO/IEC JTC1/SC29/WG11 **N5878** (2003)
4. Bangchang, P.N., Fujii, T., Tannimoto, M.: Experimental System of Free Viewpoint Television. In: Proc. of SPIE, Stereoscopic Displays and Virtual Reality Systems, Australia. **5006** (2003) 554–564
5. Kobayashi, T., Fujii, T., Kimoto, T.: Interpolation of Ray-Space Data by Adaptive Filtering. In: Proc. of SPIE, Electronic Imaging 2000. **3958** (2000) 252–259
6. Tehrani, M.P., Fujii, T., Tanimoto, M.: Offset Block Matching of Multi-View Images for Ray-Space Interpolation. The journal of the Institute of Image information and Television Engineers. **58** (2004) 540–548
7. Kimata, H., Kitahara, M., Kamikura, K.: System Design of Free Viewpoint Video Communication. In: The Fourth International Conference on Computer and Information Technology, Wuhan, China. (2004) 52–59
8. Fan L., Jiang G., Yu M.: Realization of FTV Based on Ray Space Representation. Journal of Computer-Aided Design & Computer Graphics. (to appear)
9. Fujii, T., Tanimoto, M.: Acquisition and display systems of FTV (Free-viewpoint TeleVision). In: Proc. of SPIE, Three Dimensional TV, Video and Display, Japan. **5243** (2003) 96–103
10. Droese, M., Fujii, T., Tanimoto, M.: Ray-Space Interpolation based on Filtering in Disparity Domain. In: Proc. of 3D Image Conference 2004, Tokyo, Japan. (2004)

Haptic Interaction with Depth Video Media

Jongeun Cha[1], Seung-man Kim[2], Ian Oakley[1],
Jeha Ryu[1], and Kwan H. Lee[2]

[1] Human-Machine-Computer Interface Lab., Dept. of Mechatronics,
Gwangju Institute of Science and Technology,
1 Oryong-dong, Buk-gu, Gwangju 500-712, Republic of Korea
{gaecha, ian, ryu}@gist.ac.kr
http://dyconlab.gist.ac.kr
[2] Intelligent Design & Graphics Lab., Dept. of Mechatronics
{sman, lee}@kyebek.gist.ac.kr
http://kyebek9.gist.ac.kr

Abstract. In this paper we propose a touch enabled video player system. A conventional video player only allows viewers to passively experience visual and audio media. In virtual environment, touch or haptic interaction has been shown to convey a powerful illusion of the tangible nature - the reality - of the displayed environments and we feel the same benefits may be conferred to a broadcast, viewing domain. To this end, this paper describes a system that uses a video representation based on depth images to add a haptic component to an audio-visual stream. We generate this stream through the combination of a regular RGB image and a synchronized depth image composed of per-pixel depth-from-camera information. The depth video, a unified stream of the color and depth images, can be synthesized from a computer graphics animation by rendering with commercial packages or captured from a real environment by using a active depth camera such as the Zcam^{TM}. In order to provide a haptic representation of this data, we propose a modified proxy graph algorithm for depth video streams. The modified proxy graph algorithm can (i) detect collisions between a moving virtual proxy and time-varying video scenes, (ii) generates smooth touch sensation by handling the implications of the radically different display update rates required by visual (30Hz) and haptic systems (in the order of 1000Hz), (iii) avoid sudden change of contact forces. A sample experiment shows the effectiveness of the proposed system.

1 Introduction

The rapid development of telecommunication technologies such as enhanced CPU speed and power, low cost memory, and ultra fast communication networks has led to the digital multimedia age, where viewers can enjoy and be immersed in high quality video and audio media. Typically, some interaction such as selecting interactive icons with a wireless keyboard or a remote control is also allowed. That interaction is generally a menu-based dialogue where the viewer selects an option from several ones provided on screen. However, recently viewers' demands for a more realistic and interactive experience with video media are growing and there is interest in exploring the possibilities of an interactive experience with the video media beyond passive watching and listening, i.e. touching and manipulating the video media content directly. Such an interaction style, known as haptic interaction, has the potential to create a truly immersive experience for the viewers by providing a powerful illusion of the tangible nature of the displayed environments.

Traditionally, haptic interaction has been integrated with fully synthesized virtual reality (VR) worlds where several users can share the virtual contents simultaneously. Recently, O'Modhrain and Oakley [1] discussed the potential role that haptic feedback might play in supporting a greater sense of immersion in broadcast content. In addition, they explored two potential program scenarios: the creation of authored haptic effects for children's cartoon and the automatic capture of impact data to be streamed and displayed in the context of a live sport broadcast. However, since the media is based on 2-dimensional information, the possible haptic interaction is limited to 2-dimensions. If the media includes 3-dimensional information, more useful interactions may become possible. For example, it will become possible to touch and explore an object-of-interest such as a peculiar shaped object or the face of a famous actor's face [2]. When an actor is touching his lover on the face in a scene, viewers may want to touch her also to increase immersion in the scene and feel as if they had become the actor.

Typically, in order to represent a 3-dimensional scene, polygonal 3D meshes are used. But, they are not appropriate for 3D video media because of the redundancy of connectivity information, complex level-of-detail, compression, and progressive transmission [3]. To bridge the gap between simple 2D texture mapping and full 3D modeling of a video object, a depth image based representation was proposed [4]. In this system, the 3D video media is a combination of regular video (general RGB image) and synchronized per-pixel depth information (depth image), see Fig. 1. Currently, the European IST project ATTEST [5] has created a novel 3D-TV system by means of a depth image-based representation. They created 3D content by capturing real dynamic environments with an active range camera, and compressed and transmitted them with MPEG codecs. In the 3D-TV system, the viewers could see the 3-dimensional real-world scene stereoscopically.

 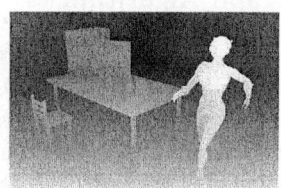 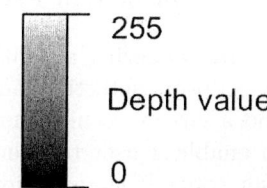

Fig. 1. General RGB image and synchronized per-pixel depth information

In order to provide an interaction force, haptic rendering, the process to display the haptic attributes of surface and material properties of virtual objects in real time via a haptic interface, need to be employed. Haptic rendering, however, requires significantly higher update rates (on the order of 1 kHz) than graphic rendering for smooth and stable force calculation. The main bottleneck of the haptic rendering process is the collision detection between the virtual scene and the current haptic interaction point. While a pre-computed "hierarchical bounding boxes" approach has been employed to achieve fast collision detection in the majority of previous works, e.g. [6, 7, 8, 9], they are not applicable in the case of depth video that requires the construction of a new bounding box for each frame. Also, an extremely large model, such as depth image, slows down the collision detection considerably (697,430 triangles in 720×486 resolution depth image). Walker and Salisbury [10] proposed a proxy graph algorithm for extremely large static topographic maps of over 100 million triangles, which is essentially the same as a single frame depth image. With this technique, they not only reduced the overall number of collision detection operations, but also optimized the collision detection by capitalizing on the special structure of the vertically monotone height field.

In this paper we propose a modified proxy graph algorithm for depth video streams, because the proxy graph algorithm exhibits some problems when applied to depth video streams. First, it fails to detect some collisions between a virtual haptic interaction point and depth video changing its shape frame by frame. Secondly, it produces piecewise-continuous contact forces because of significantly different video and haptic update rates. Finally, it generates sudden large changes in force at scene transitions making the haptic interface unstable.

2 Modified Proxy Graph Algorithm for Depth Video Streams

In order to explain the proposed idea, this section provides a brief review of proxy-based haptic rendering algorithms with detailed summary of the proxy graph algorithm [10]. Then, the problems and solutions involved in applying this algorithm (i.e. the proposed modified proxy graph algorithm) to a stream of depth images are explained in detail.

2.1 Overview of Proxy Graph Algorithm

Haptic rendering algorithms are essentially composed of the coupled processes of collision detection and response between a haptic interaction point (HIP) and a virtual scene. Their objective is to model the forces from this interaction to enable a user to touch, feel and manipulate virtual objects. Typically, the user controls the position of a point in the virtual world, and a force vector is generated based on the distance between this point and what is termed a proxy point which is constrained to remain on the surface of objects in the scene. This can be easily imagined in the case of a user exploring a virtual plane.

Initially, when the user is not in contact with the plane, the proxy and the haptic interaction point are coincident, and no forces are applied. As the user moves onto, and then penetrates the plane, the proxy remains on its surface while the HIP penetrates into the surface, and the user feels forces proportional to the distance between these two points. A typical algorithm renders these forces using a linear spring model.

A key process in a proxy algorithm is the minimisation of the distance between the HIP and the proxy point. As the HIP moves within an object, the proxy must be moved to an appropriate location on its surface in order to provide a realistic force. In the example of the plane mentioned above, this is trivial, but is more complex when considering realistic virtual objects such as polygonal meshes. A typical solution is to generate a list of constraint planes. In each update, this list is initially empty, and the proxy is moved towards the HIP until it is coincident or until collision with a polygon prevents further motion. In the case of collision, the polygon is added to the list of constraints, and a new goal location reflecting this constraint becomes the proxy's optimal destination. It can be shown that in a polygonal mesh, three such iterations will restrict the proxy's motion to a single point, a constrained local minima. Proxy algorithms based on these concepts are commonplace, as they are simple to implement, robust and reliable [9, 12, 13].

However, a weakness of this constraint resolution process is that it restricts the number of polygons a user can traverse in a given update cycle to one. This is essentially due to the fact that constraints are not released when a user moves to an adjacent polygon. Given the 1000 Hz refresh rates required for smooth haptic display, this limitation only becomes evident when considering very large or dense meshes, in which a user can move across multiple triangles in a single millisecond. In these situations, the constraint model yields an undesirable feeling of viscosity, due to the proxy point lagging behind the user's actual position. While this can be remedied by simply modifying the basic algorithm to release constraints when new polygons are encountered, this entails considerable additional processing, and is currently an unrealistic solution. Walker and Salisbury [10] describe the proxy graph algorithm, a alternative constraint resolution method to address this issue. Essentially, they restrict proxy motion to the vertices of the mesh, and choose among vertices simply by selecting the gradient that slopes towards the target most rapidly. Although, this approach can result in erroneous proxy positioning, these errors are usually minor, and allow a large number of polygons to be traversed efficiently within a single update.

Depth images are simply height maps. They consist of an evenly spaced two dimensional array of elevations. A triangle based surface can be derived from them by the simple precedent of adding horizontal and diagonal lines between each element. They are also vertically monotone, with each horizontal point possessing only a single point above or below it. In the context of their proxy graph algorithm, Walker and Salisbury [10] discuss several optimisations to collision detection algorithms that can be used with this type of data structure. Firstly, the HIP path can be projected onto the two-dimensional

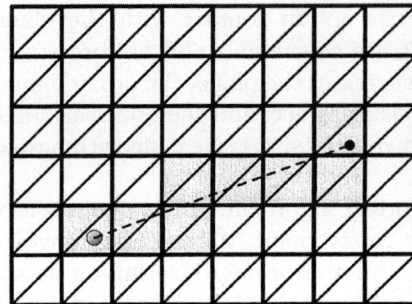

Fig. 2. Local triangulation for collision detection

representation of the height map in order to generate a list of candidate polygons which should be checked for collisions (Fig. 2). Secondly, cells within this candidate list that possesses elevation values below that of the HIP path can simply be discarded. These optimisations, in conjunction with those related to constraint resolution described above, yield an algorithm which executes extremely rapidly when applied to large data-sets.

2.2 Collision Detection Correction with Depth Video Streams

The proxy graph algorithm was developed for haptic interaction with the large static topographic maps. In contrast, the surface triangulated from the depth video is dynamic - it changes its shape frame by frame. Consequently, when the current surface transforms into the next surface, the collision detection fails in some cases and the haptic device can go through the surface as shown in Fig. 3(a, b).

These kinds of problems occur in haptic interaction with a moving rigid-body object, which can pass through the previous proxy. Ruspini [14] corrected this problem by moving the previous proxy position with respect to the movement of the object in the same local frame of the object as shown in Fig. 3(c). However, the same method cannot be applied to the depth video streams because the surface moves regardless of the local coordinates. To remedy this situation, the surface depth is stored by projecting the proxy position on to the surface. When the surface moves upward, the proxy is also moved by that amount, as shown in Fig.4. This ensures that the surface cannot pass through the proxy.

2.3 Local Surface Interpolation

Humans can sense force vibrations well in excess of 300Hz. For smooth and stable force display, generally, a high haptic update rate (>1000Hz) is required. The depth video refresh rate (30Hz) is much slower than the haptic update rate. This performance gap may cause the contact force to be piecewise continuous, that is to say, a viewer will perceive the discrete change of the depth video surface. Ruspini [14] proposed a proxy blending method in haptic interaction with deformable

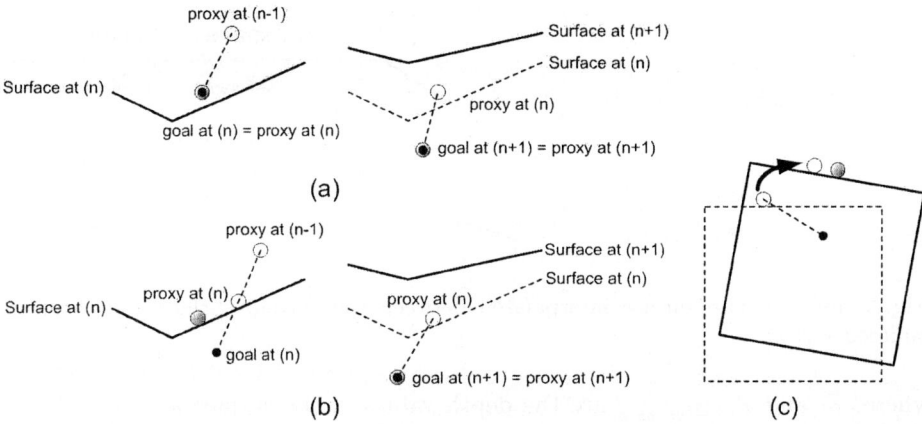

Fig. 3. Illustration of the collision detection failure of the proxy graph algorithm with depth video: The general proxy algorithm checks the collision between the surface and the line segment connecting the current goal and the previous proxy. (a) When the surface goes up with the device position in the vicinity of the surface, the surface can pass through the line segment in frame (n+1). (b) Even though the first collision is detected and the proxy position is determined at frame (n), the algorithm regards proxy is inside of the frame (n+1) when the surface goes up. (c) The previous proxy contacting on the rigid-body surface is moving in the same local coordinate and maintains the same contact point.

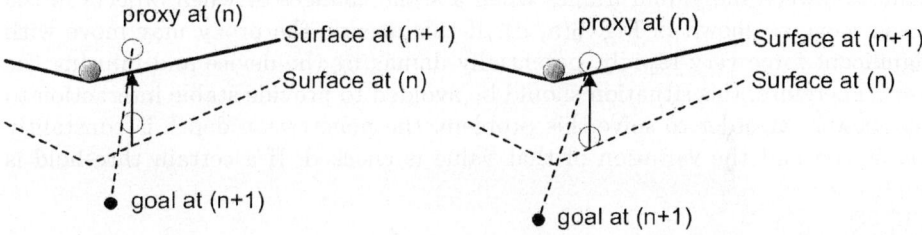

Fig. 4. Correction of the previous proxy position out of or on the surface by the amount of the surface movement

objects, which interpolates an intermediate proxy between the old proxy constrained to the old surface and the current proxy constrained to the current surface. This method requires additional time to calculate two proxy positions during the blending period and resultant force is delayed by about one frame.

In this paper as shown in Fig. 5, we interpolate the local intermediate surface needed to be used in collision detection between the current and the next depth video local surface using Eq.(1), since the next depth image can be obtained at the current time by buffering.

$$Z_{intermediate} = Z_t + \Delta Z_{graphic} \frac{\Delta t_{haptic}}{\Delta t_{graphic}} = Z_t + (Z_{t+\Delta t_{graphic}} - Z_t) \frac{\Delta t_{haptic}}{\Delta t_{graphic}} \quad (1)$$

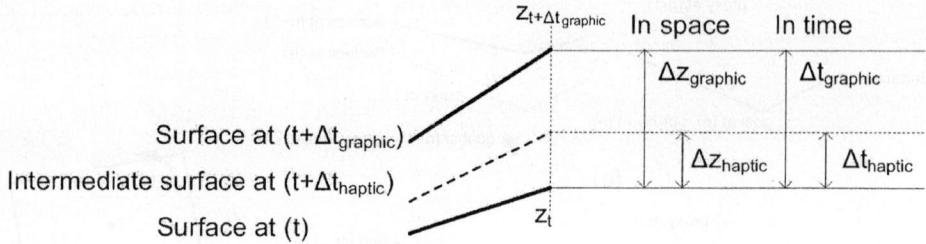

Fig. 5. Intermediate surface interpolated between the current surface and the next buffered surface

where, Z_t and $Z_{t+\Delta t_{graphic}}$ are the depth values of the surface at time (t) and $(t + \Delta t_{graphic})$, respectively, $\Delta t_{graphic}$ is the graphic update time (about 30ms), and Δt_{haptic} is the elapsed time from time (t) to current haptic update time. Δt_{haptic} can be obtained by counting the clocks from (t). Since, our system is running on the MS Windows which is not a real time OS, $\Delta t_{graphic}$ is not an exact constant. However, subjective evaluation by users confirms that this interpolation process is sufficient to give the apparent continuous force.

2.4 Sudden Change of the Proxy Position

During the stream of the depth video, there can be dramatic changes in depth values between individual frames when a scene changes or when objects in the scene move as shown in Fig. 6(a, b). If this occurs, the proxy may move with significant force very rapidly, potentially damaging the device and injuring the user. Therefore, this situation should be avoided to provide stable interaction to the viewer. In order to solve this problem, the penetration depth is constantly monitored and the variation of that value is checked. If a certain threshold is

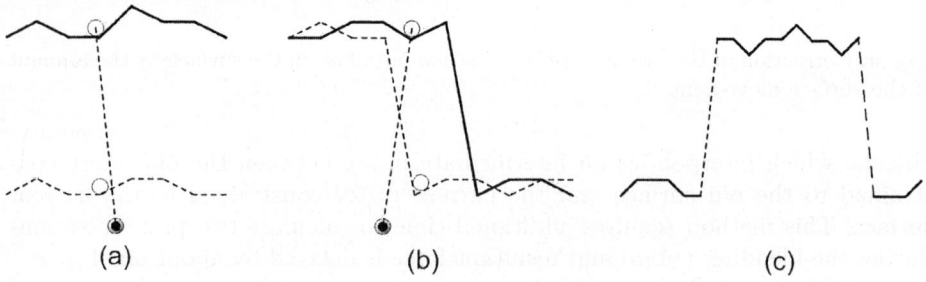

Fig. 6. Sudden change of the proxy position: (a) While the scene changes to another, the previous proxy on the old surface abruptly goes up on the higher new surface. (b) The proxy around the object edge goes up to another higher moving object. (c) The viewer is prevented from touching the object's edge surface that comes from an occlusion.

exceeded, we make the proxy collocated with the device position to make the
force zero for safety. In other words, when the force changes abruptly, the proxy
is allowed to pass through the surface. Consequently, at the moment of scene
change the viewer will not experience a dangerous force increase. Additionally,
the viewer is prevented from touching an object's edge surface (the dotted surface
in Fig. 6(c)) that comes from an occlusion at the camera view.

3   Example and Results

A sample experiment had been performed to verify the effectiveness of the proposed algorithm as shown in Fig. 7. The depth video can be easily synthesized
by rendering a computer graphics animation in off-line rendering packages (e.g.
Discreet 3DS MAX or Alias Maya), where the depth image can be saved by
reading Z-buffer as shown in Fig. 8(a). In recent years, with the technological
advancement of active depth sensors such as the ZCam^{TM} depth camera [11],
depth video can be directly captured in real time as shown in Fig. 8(b). However,
depth video usually contains quantization errors and optical noises, mainly due
to the reflectivity or color variation of the objects being filmed. When the raw
depth map is applied to haptic interactions, the high frequency geometric errors
produce distort feeling such as a jagged texture and a tremor.

To enhance depth map, we applied a median-filtering technique to reduce
noise. Then, we adaptively sampled feature points using 1st-gradient analysis,
since depth variation greatly affects the quality of a reconstructed surface. The
Delaunay triangulation technique situated the feature points in 2D space. Although a 3D surface is reconstructed by projecting a 2D triangular mesh into a
3D space based on the filtered depth value, it still contains local noise that produce jagged surfaces. For that reason we applied Gaussian smoothing to the 3D
mesh to enhance the smoothness of the surface. Finally we rendered the 3D surface with a commercial animation package (Maya) to generate a smooth depth

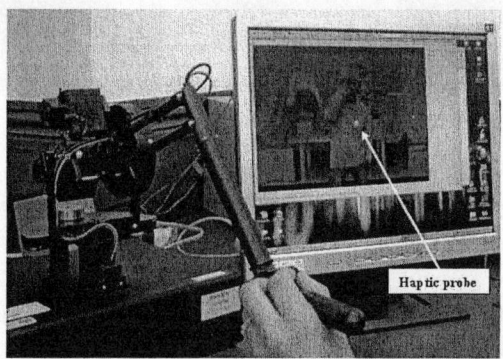

Fig. 7. Haptically enhanced depth video player

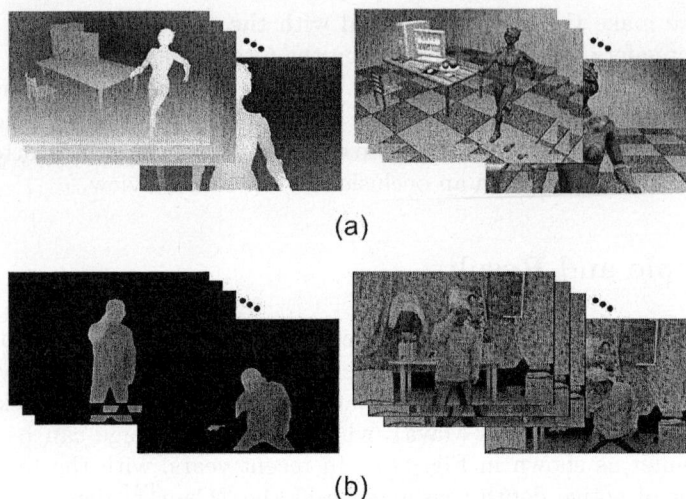

Fig. 8. Depth videos synthesized from computer graphics animation and (b) captured and smoothed from Zcam^{TM}

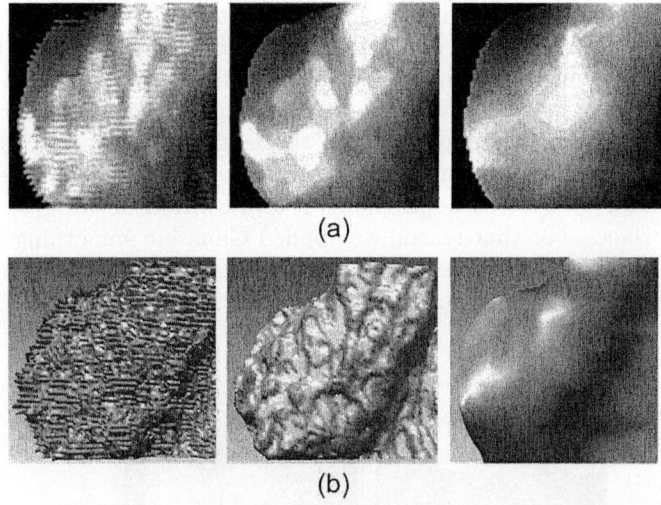

Fig. 9. Depth video enhancement captured from Zcam^{TM}: (a) The raw, median-filtered and Gaussian smoothed depth images. (b) Corresponding mesh models to the depth images

map from a reconstructed 3D surface. Fig. 9 shows the zoomed part of a raw, median-filtered and Gaussian smoothed set of depth images. We experimented with SD (standard definition, 720x486 pixels) depth videos. In order to display these two depth videos with OpenGL, we assigned column index, row index and depth value to x, y and z positions, respectively. Also, each point was set as the color value corresponding to the captured RGB image and then all points are triangulated by adding a diagonal edge. However, for faster graphic rendering, we reduced the resolution to 360x243 pixels. We did not, however, reduce the resolution in the haptic rendering. Moreover, for more immersion in the depth video, viewers wore CrystalEye shutter-glasses which provide a stereoscopic view.

This application was implemented to run on an Intel based PC (Dual 3.0Ghz Pentium IV Xeon, 1GB DDRRAM, nVidia QuadroFX 1300 PCI-Express) under Microsoft Windows XP using PHANToM premium 1.5/6 DOF made by SensAble Technologies. PHANToM haptic interfaces provide high-performance 3D positioning and force feedback plus a 3 degree-of-freedom orientation sensing gimbal. The haptic rendering algorithm was implemented using PHANToM Device Drivers Version 4.0 and HDAPI. The HDAPI is a low-level foundational layer for haptics and provides the functions to acquire 3D positions and set the 3D forces at a near realtime 1Khz servo rate.

Table 1. Haptic computation time during each update

	Without contact	With contact
Average time(milliseconds)	0.017	0.070

Table 1 shows the results of the depth video haptic rendering performance tests. The haptic computation time for each haptic update was measured using a high-resolution timer provided in Windows. The minimum computation time is obtained with the haptic interface away from the surface and the maximum one is measured by moving the haptic interface rapidly across the surface. The proposed modified proxy graph algorithm operates comfortably within the 1kHz update rate.

This example verified that we were able to stably touch and acquire the shape of the scene. Also, we could interact with a moving object and feel the smooth movement. Even if the scene was changed to another and a closer object showed up abruptly, we could penetrate the surface without feeling sudden force increase.

4 Conclusion

The depth video based haptic rendering algorithm was successfully implemented to allow the viewers to directly touch the 3-dimensional scene captured in a depth video. This is an initial stage to provide the viewers with more realistic and interactive experience by touch. At the present time, this algorithm offers the ability to touch a scene in video media and an application scenario is to touch unusual or interesting on-screen objects or an actor's face to acquire the shape or feeling of the skin. We believe that the synergy of the viewers' demand, the producer's creativity, and this kind of technical capability will make touch enabled media rich and abundant.

Acknowledgements

This work was supported by the Ministry of Information and Communication (MIC) through the Realistic Broadcasting IT Research Center (RBRC) at Gwangju Institute of Science and Technology (GIST).

References

[1] O'Modhrain, S., Oakley, I.: Touch TV: Adding Feeling to Broadcast Media, Proc. European Conf. Interactive Television: from Viewers to Actors, Brighton, UK (2003) 41-47
[2] Cha, J., Ryu, J., Kim, S., Eom, S., Ahn, B.: Haptic Interaction in Realistic Multimedia Broadcasting, Proc. 5th Pacific-Rim Conf. Multimedia on Advances in Multimedia Information Processing, Part III, Nov./Dec. (2004) 482-490
[3] Ignatenko, A., Konushin, A.: A Framework for Depth Image-Based Modeling and Rendering, Proc. Graphicon-2003, Sep. (2003) 169-172
[4] Kauff, P., Cooke, E., Fehn, C., Schreer, O.: Advanced Incomplete 3D Representation of Video Objects Using Trilinear Warping for Novel View Synthesis, Proc. PCS'01 (2001) 429-432
[5] Redert, A., Op de Beeck, M., Fehn, C., IJsselsteijn, W., Pollefeys, M., Van Gool, L., Ofek, E., Sexton, I., Surman, P.: ATTEST - Advanced Three-Dimensional Television System Technologies, Proc. 1st Int. Symp. 3D Data Processing, Visualization and Transmission, Padova, Italy (2002) 313-319
[6] Salisbury, K., Brock, D., Massie, T., Swarup, N., Zilles, C.: Haptic rendering: Programming touch interaction with virtual objects, Proc. 1995 ACM Symp. Interactive 3D Graphics (1995) 123-130
[7] Gottschalk, S., Lin, M., Manocha, D.: OBB-Tree: A hierarchical structure for rapid inter-ference detection, Proc. ACM SIGGRAPH 1996 (1996)
[8] Inc. SensAble Technologies: GHOST^{TM}: Software developer's toolkit, Programmer's Guide (1997)
[9] Ruspini, D., Kolarov, K., Khatib, O.: The haptic display of complex graphical environments, Proc. ACM SIGGRAPH 1997 (1997) 345-352
[10] Walker, S., Salisbury, K.: Large Haptic Topographic Maps: MarsView and the Proxy Graph Algorithm, Proc. ACM SIGGRAPH 2003 Symposium on Interactive 3D Graphics (2003) 83-92
[11] http://www.3dvsystems.com/
[12] Zilles, C., Salisbury, K.: A Constraint Based God-Object Method For Haptic Display, Proc. IEE/RSJ Int. Conf. on Intelligent Robots and Systems, Human Robot Interaction, and Cooperative Robots, Vol 3 (1995) 146-151
[13] Ho, C., Basdogan, C., Srinivasan, M.: Efficient point-based rendering techniques for haptic display of virtual objects, Presence: Teleoperators and Virtual Environments, Vol.8, no. 5 (1999) 477-491
[14] Ruspini, D., Khatib, O.: Dynamic Models for Haptic Rendering Systems, Proc. Advances in Robot Kinematics: ARK'98, Strobl/Salzburg, Austria (1998) 523-532

A Framework for Multi-view Video Coding Using Layered Depth Images

Seung-Uk Yoon, Eun-Kyung Lee, Sung-Yeol Kim, and Yo-Sung Ho

Gwangju Institute of Science and Technology (GIST),
1 Oryong-dong, Buk-gu, Gwangju 500-712, Korea
{suyoon, eklee78, sykim75, hoyo}@gist.ac.kr

Abstract. The multi-view video is a collection of multiple videos capturing the same scene at different viewpoints. Since the data size of the multi-view video linearly increases as the number of cameras, it is necessary to compress multi-view video data for efficient storage and transmission. The multi-view video can be coded using the concept of the layered depth image (LDI). In this paper, we describe a procedure to generate LDI from the natural multi-view video and present a framework for multi-view video coding using the concept of LDI.

Keywords: Multi-view video coding, layered depth image, MPEG 3DAV.

1 Introduction

The multi-view video is a collection of multiple videos capturing the same scene at different camera locations. If we acquire multi-view videos from multiple cameras, it is possible to generate video scenes from any viewpoints, which means that users can change their views within the range of captured videos and can feel the visible depth with view interaction. The multi-view video can be used in a variety of applications including free viewpoint video (FVV), free viewpoint TV (FTV), three-dimensional TV (3DTV), surveillance, and home entertainment.

Although the multi-view video has much potential for a variety of applications, one big problem is a huge amount of data. In principle, the multi-view video data are increasing linearly as the number of cameras; therefore, we need to encode the multi-view video data for efficient storage and transmission. Hence, it has been perceived that multi-view video coding (MVC) is a key technology to realize those applications.

ISO/IEC JTC1/SC29/WG11 Moving Picture Experts Group (MPEG) has been recognized the importance of MVC technologies, and an ad hoc group (AHG) on 3-D audio and visual (3DAV) has been established since December 2001. Four main exploration experiments (EE) on 3DAV were performed from 2002 to 2004: EE1 on omni-directional video, EE2 on FTV, EE3 on coding of stereoscopic video using multiple auxiliary components (MAC), and EE4 on depth/disparity coding for 3DTV and intermediate view interpolation. In response to the Call for Comments issued in October 2003, a number of companies have expressed their interests for a standard that enables FTV and 3DTV. After MPEG called interested parties to bring evidences on MVC technologies in October 2004 [1], some evidences were recognized in January 2005 and a Call for Proposals (CfP) on MVC has been issued in July 2005. Then, the responses to the Call will be evaluated in January 2006.

In this paper, we propose a framework for MVC using the concept of the layered depth image (LDI) [2] and we also describe a procedure for generating LDI from the natural multi-view video. While most of the proposed MVC techniques are some extension of predictive video coding algorithms, our framework takes a completely different approach based on the concept of the layered depth image (LDI), which is an efficient image-based rendering (IBR) technique. In addition, we generate LDI frames from the natural multi-view video, which is different from the previous LDI generation methods mainly using 3-D synthetic objects.

The paper is organized as follows. After we review some algorithms for multiple view video coding in Section 2, we explain the concept of LDI in Section 3. In Section 4, we describe details of the LDI generation procedure from the natural multi-view video. Then, we propose a framework for multi-view video coding using LDI in Section 5. After experimental results are presented in Section 6, we draw conclusions in Section 7.

2 Algorithms for Multi-view Video Coding

The major objective of multi-view videos is to provide free views using captured videos from different viewpoints. In order to provide such a functionality, it is essential to compress and encode the huge amount of multi-view video data. Several algorithms have been proposed for multi-view video coding in response to the Call for Evidence of MPEG 3DAV [1]. They include the Group of GOP (Go-GOP) prediction using shared reference picture memory [3], illumination change adaptive motion estimation/motion compensation and two-dimensional (2-D) direct mode [4], inter-camera motion prediction [5], spatio-temporal decomposition or checkerboard decomposition [6], and the predictive coder based on view interpolation [7]. All the proposed methods employ H.264/AVC, which is one of the most efficient video coding algorithms.

The key idea of the proposed multi-view video coding algorithms is to utilize spatial and temporal relationships among captured videos. As we apply motion estimation along the temporal direction in a single video, we can perform disparity estimation among different views in the multi-view video. In other words, they try to exploit the spatio-temporal correlation among adjacent views. Those methods outperform the simulcast coding scheme that encodes each view independently using H.264/AVC.

Unlike those algorithms, our proposed framework is based on the conversion between multi-view videos and LDI frames. It is possible to efficiently encode multi-view videos using the concept of LDI because one of the functionalities of IBR is to provide the view interaction using view generation.

3 Concept of the Layered Depth Image

Image-based rendering (IBR) techniques have been received much attention as an attractive alternative to traditional geometry-based rendering (GBR). While GBR requires elaborate modeling and long processing time, IBR uses 2-D images as primitives to generate an arbitrary view of the 3-D scene. Therefore, IBR requires a proper amount of computational resources and does not bothered by the complexity of 3-D objects in the scene. In addition, it is easier to acquire a photo or a picture than complex 3-D models of the scene.

Among a variety of IBR techniques, the layered depth image (LDI) is one of the most efficient rendering methods for 3-D objects with complex geometries. It represents the current scene using an array of pixels viewed from a single camera position. However, each LDI pixel contains not just color values, but also several other attribute values. It consists of color, depth between the camera and the pixel, and other attributes that support rendering of LDI. Three key characteristics of LDI are: (1) it contains multiple layers at each pixel location, (2) the distribution of pixels in the back layer is sparse, and (3) each pixel has multiple attribute values. Because of these special features, LDI enables us to render arbitrary views of the scene at new camera positions. Moreover, the rendering operation can be performed quickly with the list-priority algorithm proposed by McMillan [8].

When the rays are emanating from a reference viewpoint (an LDI camera), it is possible to store intersecting points between rays and an object. Each intersecting point contains color and depth information.

Figure 1 represents the conceptual diagram of LDI [2]. As shown in Fig. 1, the first intersecting points construct the first layer of LDI, the second ones build up the second layer, and so on. Consequently, each layered depth pixel has different number of depth pixels, which contain color and depth information.

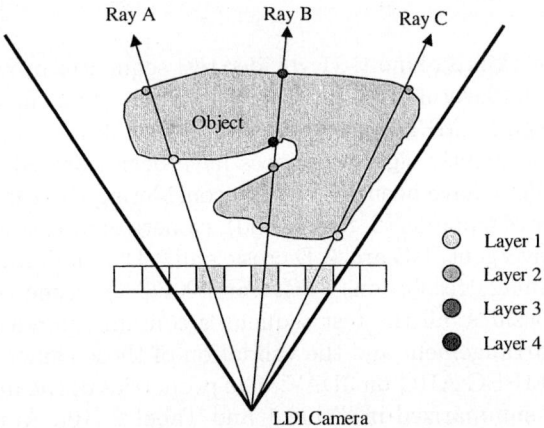

Fig. 1. Concept of the layered depth image

4 Generation of LDI from the Natural Multi-view Video

It is possible to generate LDI by storing intersecting points with color and depth, but this method can only be applied to 3-D computer graphics (CG) models. Since rays cannot go through the real object, we need another approach to generate LDI from natural images.

Figure 2 shows the generation process of LDI using multiple color and depth images [2]. The LDI scene viewed from the camera C_1 is constructed by warping pixels in other camera locations, such as C_2 and C_3.

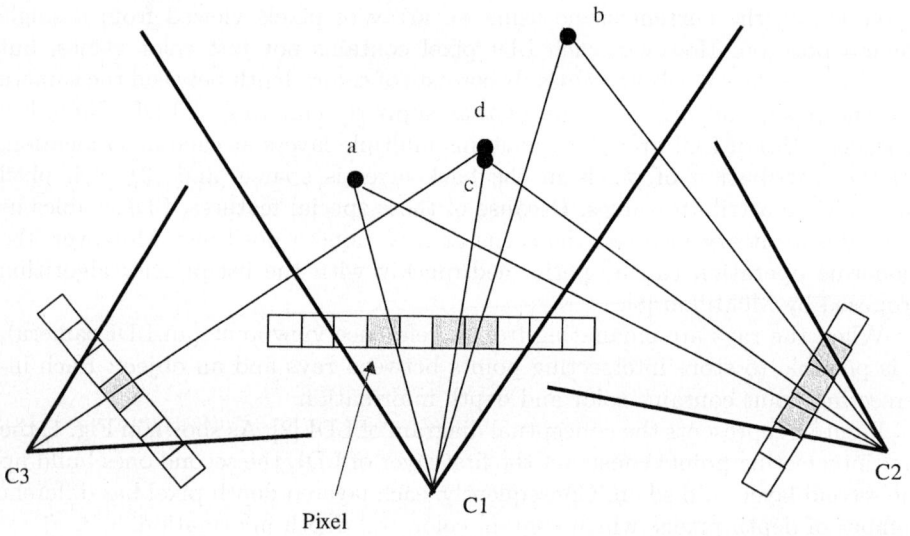

Fig. 2. LDI generation from multiple depth images

There are various kinds of multi-view video test sequences provided by MPEG AHG on 3DAV [1][9]. Several proponents provide about 20 sequences with different properties. Recently, MPEG has been issued the call for proposals (CfP) on MVC [10] and consequently eight sequences have been selected as the test sets for CfP on MVC. They have been selected by considering the variety of features, such as the number of cameras (5, 8, and 100), camera arrangements (1-D parallel, 1-D parallel convergent, 1-D arc, 2-D cross, and 2-D array), frames per second (15, 25, and 30), image resolutions (VGA and XVGA), scene complexity, and camera motions. Besides, all the test sequences contain camera parameters for their own camera arrangement and the validation of those camera parameters is now under way in MPEG AHG on 3DAV. The properties of the multi-view video test sequences are summarized in Table 1 and Tabel 2 [10]. Among them, Microsoft Research (MSR) provided the multi-view video sequence, Breakdancers with camera parameters and depth information [11][12].

Table 1. Properties of MPEG 3DAV test sequences. (A: available, N/A: not available).

Property	KDDI	MERL	HHI	Nagoya Univ.	MSR
Sequences	Flamenco Objects Crowd Golf, Race	Ballroom Exit	Jungle Uli	Rena Akiko Akko&Kayo	Breakdancers Ballet
No. of Cameras	5/8	8	8	100	8
Camera Parameters	A	A	A	A	A
Depth Information	N/A	N/A	N/A	N/A	A

Table 2. Test data sets for CfP on MVC

Data Set	Sequences	Image Property	No. of Cameras	Camera Arrangement
MERL	Ballroom	VGA, 25fps	8	1-D parallel
MERL	Exit	VGA, 25fps	8	1-D parallel
KDDI	Race1	VGA, 30fps	8	1-D parallel
KDDI	Flamenco2	VGA, 30fps	5	2-D parallel (cross)
HHI	Uli	XVGA, 25fps	8	1-D parallel convergent
MSR	Breakdancers	XVGA, 15fps	8	1-D arc
Nagoya Univ.	Rena	VGA, 30fps	100	1-D parallel
Nagoya Univ.	Akko&Kayo	VGA, 30fps	100	2-D array

If we use the test data set without depth information as the natural video input to generate LDI, we need to estimate disparity from those multi-view images. Using the parallel camera arrangement, disparity can be computed by using a stereo matching algorithm and depth values can be obtained from estimated disparity by calculating $z = bf/d$, where z is the depth, b is the baseline, f is the focal length, and d is the disparity. As shown in Fig. 3, we can obtain one depth map per two parallel images captured from adjacent cameras in the case of the 1-D parallel camera configuration. We have estimated disparity and depth values for the KDDI-A test sequences. Since there are eight cameras in the KDDI-A test set [1], seven depth maps are acquired for the first frame using the stereo matching algorithm [13].

There are several problems in generating LDI frames from the test sets without depth information. Although we can easily compute depth images from disparity maps under the parallel camera arrangement, the quality of the computed depth map is not sufficient. Figure 4 presents histogram equalized depth maps acquired from the KDDI-A data set: Flamenco1 and Race2. As shown in Fig. 4, it is difficult to figure out depth positions of objects within the computed depth map. One of the main reasons is related to the image rectification that can correct the misalignment of parallel images [14]. The other reason could be the accuracy of the stereo matching algorithm that we used. We exploited a kind of the real-time disparity estimation technique [13], which focuses on the fast computation rather than the accuracy of estimation. If we use a more stable and accurate method and perform more iterations or refinements, we

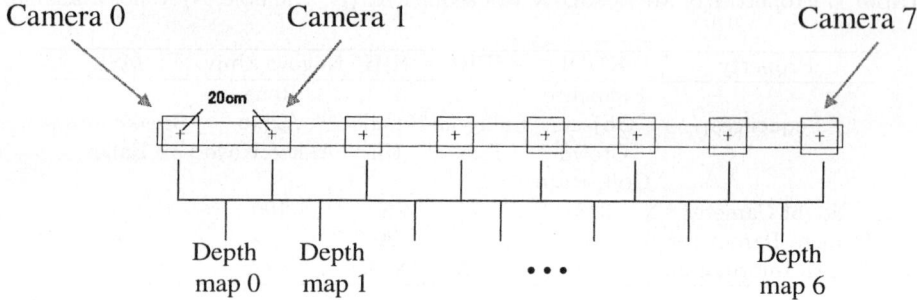

Fig. 3. Depth map extraction for KDDI-A test sequences

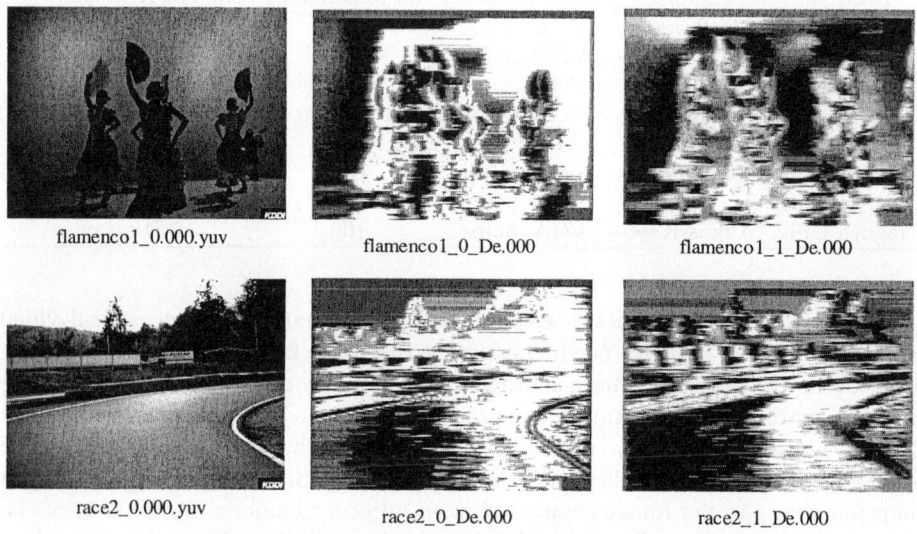

Fig. 4. Estimated depth maps for the KDDI-A data set: Flamenco1 and Race2

can obtain more reliable results. However, it is very time consuming and it requires another preprocessing and postprocessing to get sufficient quality of depth maps.

Because of these reasons, we are now focusing on the test set from MSR. MSR data include a sequence of 100 images captured from eight cameras; the camera arrangement is 1-D arc with about 20cm horizontal spacing. Depth maps computed by stereo matching algorithms are provided for each camera together with the camera parameters: intrinsic parameters, barrel distortion, and rotation matrix [11][12]. The exact depth range is also included. Figure 5 shows some of sample depth images of the MSR data set. As we can observe in Fig. 5, the depth images from MSR are more reliable than the calculated depth maps from the KDDI data set.

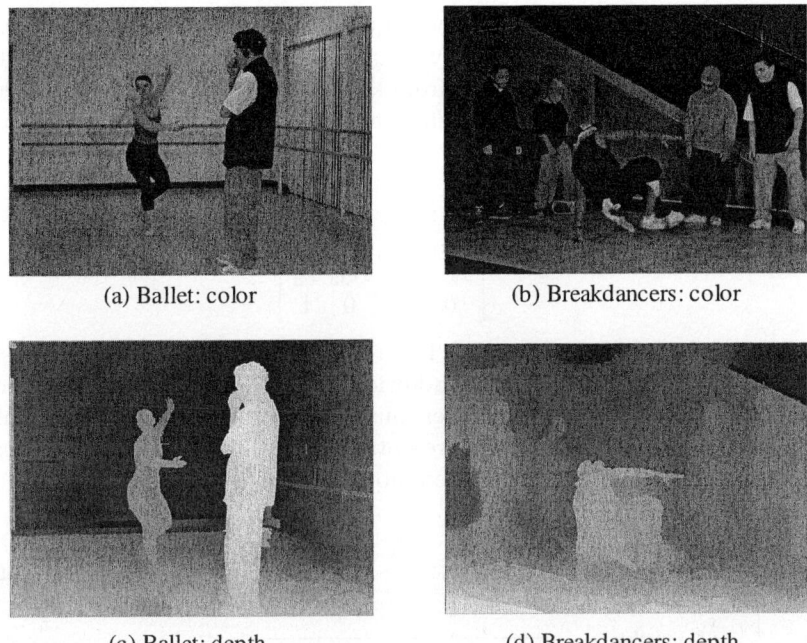

(a) Ballet: color (b) Breakdancers: color
(c) Ballet: depth (d) Breakdancers: depth

Fig. 5. Test images from Microsoft Research: 1024x768

After obtaining depth information from the multi-view video, we perform 3-D warping to generate a single LDI using multiple depth images. We use the following incremental 3-D warping equation [2] because the original McMillan's warping equation [15] is very complex and has many parameters to be computed. If we use the incremental warping equation, we can avoid those problems and reduce the computational complexity for 3-D warping. When $C_1 = V_1 \cdot P_1 \cdot A_1$, $C_2 = V_2 \cdot P_2 \cdot A_2$, the transform matrix $T_{1,2} = C_2 \cdot C_1^{-1}$. C is a camera matrix, V is the viewport matrix, P is the projection matrix, and A is the affine matrix.

$$T_{1,2} \cdot \begin{bmatrix} x_1 \\ y_1 \\ z_1 \\ 1 \end{bmatrix} = \begin{bmatrix} x_2 \cdot w_2 \\ y_2 \cdot w_2 \\ z_2 \cdot w_2 \\ w_2 \end{bmatrix} = T_{1,2} \cdot \begin{bmatrix} x_1 \\ y_1 \\ 0 \\ 1 \end{bmatrix} + z_1 \cdot T_{1,2} \cdot \begin{bmatrix} 0 \\ 0 \\ 1 \\ 0 \end{bmatrix} \quad (1)$$

where (x_1, y_1) is the pixel location in C_1, z_1 is the depth at (x_1, y_1). (x_2, y_2) is the warped pixel location in C_2.

The camera matrix C can be easily calculated for 3-D synthetic scenes. While the viewport matrix is computed from the image resolution, the projection matrix is automatically determined by OpenGL according to the orthogonal/perspective view, and the affine matrix is computed from the rotation and translation matrix. However, it is difficult to estimate these three matrices in the natural video because the meanings of projection and affine matrices are not clearly defined. For this reason, we try to calculate the camera matrix C without estimating each V, P, and A matrix from the natural multi-view video. Because the MSR data set contains a 3x4 affine matrix, the camera matrix C can be computed by

$$C = \begin{bmatrix} R_{11} & R_{12} & R_{13} & T_1 \\ R_{21} & R_{22} & R_{23} & T_2 \\ R_{31} & R_{32} & R_{33} & T_3 \\ 0 & 0 & 0 & 1 \end{bmatrix} \quad (2)$$

where R is a 3x3 rotation matrix and T is a 3x1 translation matrix. We construct the camera matrix C by adding an additional row. This is reasonable because the camera matrix C is a 4x4 homogeneous matrix, consisting of rotational and translational components. Figure 6 presents the overall procedure for generating LDI from the natural multi-view video, not from 3-D synthetic models.

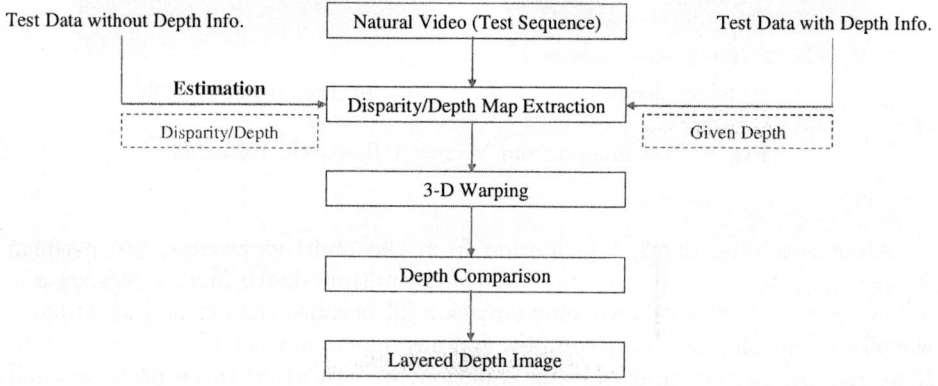

Fig. 6. Generation of LDI from the natural multi-view video

5 Framework for Multi-view Video Coding Using LDI

An important aim of the multi-view video is to provide view-dependant scenes from the pre-captured multiple videos. This goal is similar to the functionality of image-based rendering (IBR) techniques, the novel view generation using 2-D input images. Inspired by this idea, we propose a framework for multi-view video coding using the concept of LDI.

As shown in Fig. 7, the first color and depth frames of the multi-view video are collected and warped to the selected LDI view by Eq. 1. Consequently, eight color and eight depth images construct the first frame of LDI sequence. In this paper, the LDI sequence and LDI frames have the same meaning, which is the collection of LDIs. Once we obtain the LDI frames from the above procedure, the reconstruction of multiple views is a basic functionality of LDI. Since LDI contains all the necessary information to generate an arbitrary view, it can reproduce any viewpoints by using the incremental 3-D warping. In addition, we can apply LDI coding algorithms to compress the generated LDI frames.

We obtain LDI frames from multi-view video test sequences by 3-D warping using the given depth images. Since there is information loss caused by depth comparison and thresholding in generating LDI, the compensation procedure is required before reconstructing the original multi-views. The depth thresholding is closely related the quality of reconstructed views. The reconstruction quality decreases as we increase the threshold value.

In the encoding step, LDI data could be preprocessed [16] and H.264/AVC is applied to those processed data adaptively. One important thing to be considered in the encoding process is to exploit the special characteristics of LDI, which are described in Section 3. Because each layer of LDI contains empty pixels, we should fill or remove those vacant holes before applying H.264/AVC.

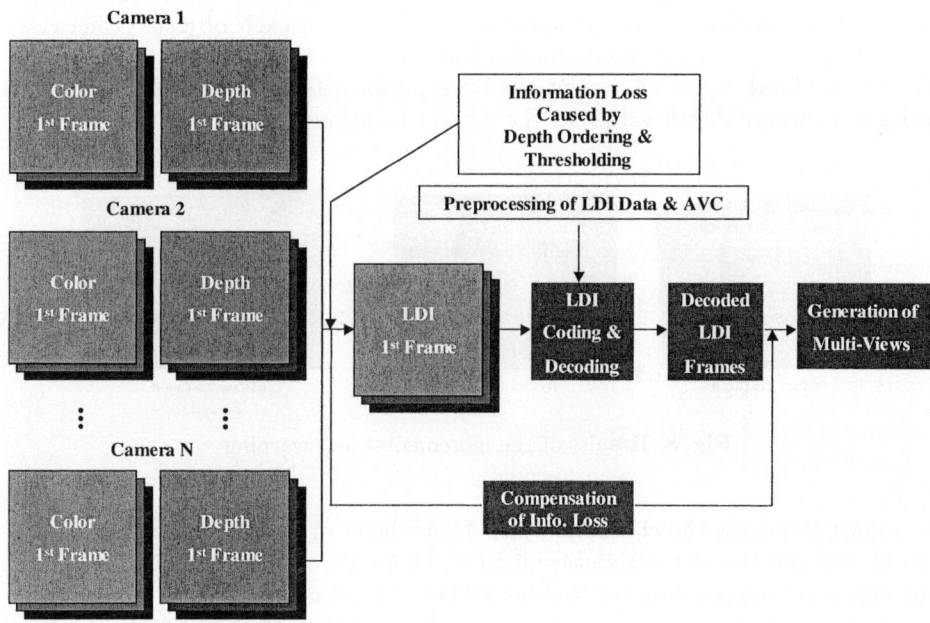

Fig. 7. Framework for multi-view video coding using LDI

6 Experimental Results and Analysis

We have generated LDI frames from Ballet and Breakdancers sequences of the MSR data set by using the incremental 3-D warping. We have used the depth images provided by MSR, not the estimated depth maps. For eight color and depth frames of multi-view videos, we perform the incremental 3-D warping to construct LDI frames. In other words, the first eight color and depth frames of

Ballet and Breakdancers are used to generate the first LDI frame, the second 16 images are used to construct the second LDI frame, and so on.

The main part of generating LDI frames from the natural multi-view video is the incremental 3-D warping. Figure 8 shows the results of 3-D warping using the constructed camera matrix. We can observe that actors are slightly rotating as the camera number changes. In order to identify the warping results clearly, we do not interpolate holes. White pixels in each image represent the holes, which are generated by the 3-D warping. In Fig. 8, camera number 4 is the reference LDI view and the warping has been performed from other camera locations to the reference LDI view. When the warping is carried out from the left cameras (camera 0, 1, 2, and 3) to the reference camera, major holes are created along the right side of the actors. On the other hand, holes are mainly distributed in the left side of the actors as the warping is done from the right cameras (camera 5, 6, and 7) to the LDI view.

When we perform the 3-D warping, it is needed to align warped images carefully before the depth comparison. It is clear that the depth comparison should be accomplished at the same pixel location of each object. Otherwise, warped images are overlapped and the result becomes similar to an afterimage. The block-based image alignment has been performed after the 3-D warping in order to compare depth values at the correct locations.

(a) Cam. 0 to Cam. 4   (b) Cam. 1 to Cam. 4   (c) Cam. 7 to Cam. 4

Fig. 8. Results of the incremental 3-D warping

Figure 9 depicts the characteristics of each layer of the constructed LDI. We can clearly see the characteristics of LDI. There are no holes in the first layer but holes are increased as the number of layers increase.

Table 3 lists the data size between multi-view frames of the test sequence and the generated LDI frame [17]. In Table 3, the sum of frames implies the summation of the data size of eight color and eight depth images. It is clear that the data size is reduced by converting multi-view video to LDI frames even without any encoding process.

There are several issues to be considered in future experiments. First, the relationship between the number of layers and the quality of reconstructed multi-views should be analyzed carefully. Second, shape adaptive transforms, such as a shape-adaptive discrete cosine transform (SA-DCT) and a shape-adaptive discrete wavelet transform (SA-DWT), could be used to encode LDI data because H.264/AVC supports only the 4x4 integer transform. Finally, we will conduct

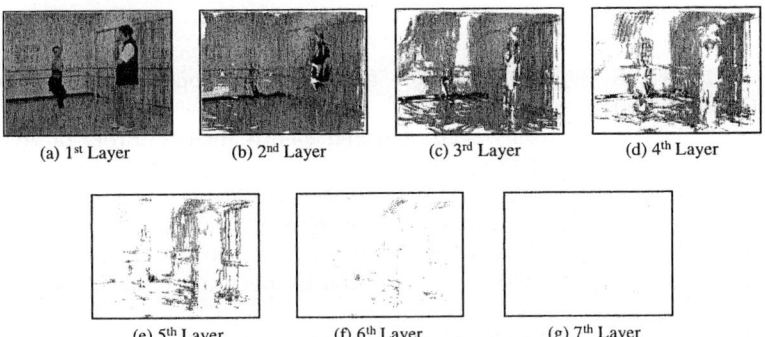

Fig. 9. Pixel distribution in each layer of the constructed LDI

Table 3. Comparison of data size between multi-view frames and LDI frame [kBytes]

Ballet	1st 8 frames	2nd 8 frames
Sum of frames (Color + Depth)	25,165.9	25,165.9
LDI frame	14,078.0	14,061.6
Breakdancers	1st 8 frames	2nd 8 frames
Sum of frames (Color + Depth)	25,165.9	25,165.9
LDI frame	12,726.6	12,689.7

more experiments on the data aggregation and efficient encoding methods using more test sequences with depth information.

7 Conclusions

In this paper, we have described a procedure to generate layered depth images (LDIs) from the natural multi-view video and also proposed a framework for multi-view video coding (MVC) using the concept of LDI. Unlike previous algorithms for MVC, we exploit the concept of image-based rendering techniques. Incremental 3-D warping has been successfully performed using the newly constructed camera matrix. Furthermore, the data size of the original multi-view frames has been reduced by converting them to LDI. From these experimental results, we have observed that our framework is useful for efficient coding of multi-view video data.

Acknowledgements. This work was supported in part by Gwangju Institute of Science and Technology (GIST), in part by the Ministry of Information and Communication (MIC) through the Realistic Broadcasting Research Center (RBRC), and in part by the Ministry of Education (MOE) through the Brain Korea 21 (BK21) project.

References

1. ISO/IEC JTC1/SC29/WG11 N6720: Call for Evidence on Multi-view Video Coding. October (2004)
2. Shade, J., Gotler, S., Szeliski, R.: Layered Depth Images. Proc. of ACM SIGGRAPH, July (1998) 291–298
3. ISO/IEC JTC1/SC29/WG11 m11570: Multi-view Video Coding using Shared Reference Picture Memory and Shared Motion Vector Memory. October (2004)
4. ISO/IEC JTC1/SC29/WG11 m11588: Multi-view Video Coding using Illumination Change-adaptive Motion Estimation/Motion Compensation and 2D Direct Mode. October (2004)
5. ISO/IEC JTC1/SC29/WG11 m11596: Response to Call for Evidence on Multi-view Video Coding. October (2004)
6. ISO/IEC JTC1/SC29/WG11 m11700: Responses received to CfE on Multi-view Video Coding. October (2004)
7. ISO/IEC JTC1/SC29/WG11 m11762: Response to Call for Evidence on Multi-view Video Coding. October (2004)
8. McMillan, L.: A List-Priority Rendering Algorithm for Redisplaying Projected Surfaces. UNC Technical Report TR95-005, University of North Carolina (1995)
9. ISO/IEC JTC1/SC29/WG11 N7094: Preliminary Call for Proposals on Multi-view Video Coding. April (2005)
10. ISO/IEC JTC1/SC29/WG11 N7327: Call for Proposals on Multi-view Video Coding. July (2005)
11. Interactive Visual Media Group at Microsoft Research, http://www.research.microsoft.com/vision/ImageBasedRealities/3DVideoDownload/
12. Zitnick, C.L., Kang, S.B., Uyttendaele, M., Winder, S., and Szeliski, R.: High-quality Video View Interpolation using a Layered Representation. Proc. of ACM SIGGRAPH, August (2004) 600–608
13. A Study on Real-time Extraction of Depth and Disparity Map for Multi-viewpoint Images. ETRI Research Report, November (2002)
14. ISO/IEC JTC1/SC29/WG11 m11292: Multi-view Video Coding using Image Stitching. October (2004)
15. McMillan, L.: An Image-based Approach to Three-Dimensional Computer Graphics. Ph.D. Dissertation, University of North Carolina at Chapel Hill (1997)
16. Yoon, S.U., Kim, S.Y., and Ho, Y.S.: Preprocessing of Depth and Color Information for Layered Depth Image Coding. LNCS 3333, October (2004) 622–629
17. ISO/IEC JTC1/SC29/WG11 m11916: Preliminary Results for Multi-view Video Coding using Layered Depth Image. April (2005)

A Proxy-Based Distributed Approach for Reliable Content Sharing Among UPnP-Enabled Home Networks

HyunRyong Lee and JongWon Kim

Networked Media Lab., Department of Information and Communications,
Gwangju Institute of Science and Technology (GIST),
Gwangju 500-712, Korea
{hrlee, jongwon}@netmedia.gist.ac.kr

Abstract. We propose a proxy-based distributed scheme for reliable streaming services among UPnP(universal plug and play)-enabled home networks. We design a "SHARE" module that extends HG (home gateway) with a UPnP-compatible protocol. By relaying SSDP (simple service discovery protocol) messages used in the UPnP device architecture, the SHARE module provides connectivity that is needed to control other UPnP devices for streaming services among home networks. To provide reliable streaming services in a distributed way, the SHARE module tries to coordinate the distribution of streaming loads among multiple senders by using many-to-one distributed streaming. It also tries to provide reliable streaming services based on the system and network resource status of each sender by leveraging the UPnP QoS services. Based on the UPnP components, the SHARE module provides the transparent content sharing to users. Through design-level verification and partial implementations of the proposed SHARE module, we validate the feasibility of our work.

1 Introduction

As networking technologies penetrate wide varieties of devices for daily usage, home networks are becoming a reality. Homes are also beginning to build in-house home networks and getting connected with high-speed access networks. As of today, lots of innovative and versatile types of home networking appliances are being designed to meet the demands of home consumers. Based on protocols such as UPnP (universal plug and play) [19], HAVi (home audio video interoperability) [20], and Jini [21], the proliferation of next-generation convergence devices will promote the explosive generation of ordinary content by home consumers and the sharing of content among themselves.

With the advent of A/V (audio/video) home network that owns variety and abundant of content, in near future, people will want to make the community based on their interests for content sharing among home networks as people do on current P2P (peer to peer) file sharing community. Thus, we can visualize a new kind of community model by linking home networks together as shown in

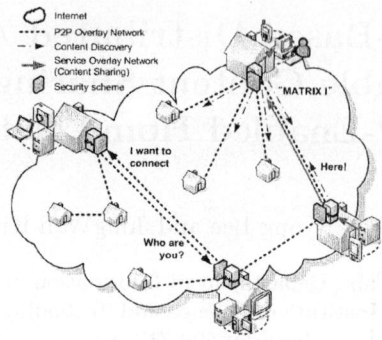

Fig. 1. Illustration for digital home community (DHC)

Fig. 1. In this community model (dubbed as DHC: digital home community), all participating home networks represented by HG (home gateway) are connected by a special kind of P2P overlay networks [1]. We may view the DHC as more formalized home-network-extended construction of current P2P file sharing community. In this regard, the European *ShareIt!* [1] project seems the closest match so far. The *ShareIt!* project develops and demonstrates a system of right-managed content sharing among homes connected by the broadband Internet with a P2P network of set-top boxes with storage. The *ShareIt!* develops discovery and delivery models for content and associated applications. It tries to enable seamless integration of broadcast, broadband, and stored content by developing an end-to-end suite of P2P protocols and by paying particular attention to DRM (digital rights management) issues.

However, existing home networking protocols (especially UPnP) are not ready to support the content sharing service among home networks, since their targets are small local networks like home and office intranet. Thus, based on the UPnP protocol, we propose a proxy-based scheme to provide content sharing service among home networks in a distributed way. Especially, as a method of content sharing service, we focus on a streaming service that is widely used for content transfer and requires QoS support. Since the streaming service in DHC consumes the resources of home networks, the streaming services can affect the quality of other services and may be affected by resource status of home networks. So, the proposed approach should provide a reliable streaming service based on the available resource of home networks while it tries to minimize the quality degradation of other services in home networks. The proposed approach also needs to provide the streaming service to home users in a transparent way. In this paper, to meet above requirements, we propose a module for HG called SHARE that provides the reliable streaming service by utilizing distributed streaming and by checking service availability of each sender based on the UPnP protocol [3, 4, 5]. Based on the UPnP components, the SHARE module

---

[1] In this paper, it is assumed that a hierarchical and secure overlay network could be built to support the DHC.

provides the transparent content sharing. We can summarize the roles and contributions of the proposed SHARE module as follows: 1) **a UPnP protocol extension** to let UPnP devices to discover and control other UPnP devices in remote home networks, 2) **a transparent interface** for content sharing, compatible with the existing UPnP AV architecture [4], and 3) **a distributed streaming scheme** that selects senders based on the system and network resource status and ensures the quality of streaming and other services in the home networks.

The outline of the paper is as follows. In Section 2, we discuss the requirements for the DHC and target of this paper. Detailed discussion on the proposed SHARE module follows immediately. Implementation results are covered in Section 3. Section 4 discusses and compares the SHARE module to related work. We conclude the paper in Section 5. Note that, from now on, we will use home network to refer 'UPnP-enabled home network' for the sake of simplicity.

2 SHARE Module for Reliable Streaming Service in a Distributed Way

Before discussing about the proposed SHARE module, it is worthwhile to introduce the requirements for the DHC and our research target in this paper. To effectively support the concept of DHC, P2P-overlay networks that consist of home networks should be formed as shown in Fig. 1. To achieve this, the HG in each home network should paly a proxy role for internal devices. Thus we need to extend the HG so that it can recognize the required P2P-overlay networking. By reflecting the hierarchical decomposition of home networks, the extended HG should effectively support the discovery and the sharing of devices and content. It also allows the DHC users to effectively manage various devices and content in their home networks. Also, there should be appropriate QoS techniques to provide robust and reliable services, especially for content sharing services. In addition, it needs to address the involved security concerns such as authentication, authorization, confidentiality, and integrity. By integrating solutions for above issues, we can support a lot of services that may be requested by users in the DHC.

Among above issues, in this paper, we only focus on the reliable and transparent content sharing service through streaming among home networks in a distributed approach. To assist the reliable and transparent streaming service in a distributed way, we design the SHARE module as shown in Fig. 2. The SHARE module is divided into three sub-modules: the HomeConnector, the virtual MS (media server), and the MediaDistributor. The HomeConnector manages the connection setup that is needed to control UPnP devices for streaming service among HGs and the MediaDistributor governs necessary communications for distributed streaming and service availability checking. The virtual MS provides the transparent content sharing and segment-based proxy caching. As shown in Fig. 2, the proposed SHARE module is additional component to the UPnP protocol. The SHARE module does not change the UPnP protocol. Instead,

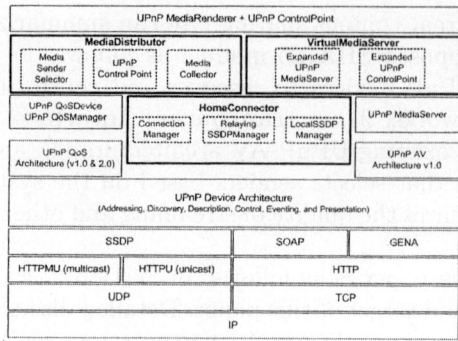

Fig. 2. The SHARE module for HG and its relation with the UPnP protocol. The boxes with solid line are the proposed SHARE module components.

the SHARE module is combined with the UPnP protocol for the reliable and transparent content sharing among home networks.

2.1 HomeConnector for Inter-home Connections

The main role of HomeConnector is to connect multiple home networks as a VPN (virtual private network) does. Basically, connections among home networks are required to control and get information from the UPnP devices in remote home networks. Before discussing the required extensions, let's look into the UPnP protocol itself. In the UPnP network, the UPnP CP (control point) [2] should control the UPnP devices to transmit media content. Basically, each UPnP CP can discover other UPnP devices by sending and by receiving SSDP (simple service discovery protocol) [12] messages. When it receives the SSDP messages, each UPnP CP can proceed with subsequent procedures such as description, control, eventing, and presentation. By accessing the URL contained in *LOCATION* parameter of SSDP messages (shown in Fig. 3), the UPnP CP can get the information for subsequent procedures. Thus if we can exchange the SSDP messages, the UPnP CP can initiate the discovery and control of other UPnP devices in separate UPnP networks. However, it is not trivial to enable the multicast-delivery SSDP messages among home networks.

To solve this problem, we propose the HomeConnector in this paper. It is divided into three components: the connection manager, the local SSDP manager, and the relaying SSDP manager. Fig. 4 shows the components of HomeConnector and its interaction. The connection manager manages the list of home networks that home consumers want to connect. The local SSDP manager captures the SSDP messages from its home network and sends them to the relaying SSDP manager. The relaying SSDP manager then relays them to other counter-part relaying SSDP manager. When the relaying SSDP manager receives the relayed

---

[2] UPnP CP controls the operation of one or more UPnP devices in order to accomplish the desired behaviors.

```
NOTIFY * HTTP/1.1
LOCATION: http://203.237.53.107:64750/
HOST: 239.255.255.250:1900
SERVER: Windows NT/5.0, UPnP/1.0, Intel CLR SDK/1.0
NTS: ssdp:alive
USN: uuid:7c905674-0083-4c3b:service:ConnectionManager:1
CACHE-CONTROL: max-age=1800
NT: urn:schemas-upnp-org:service:ConnectionManager:1
Content-Length: 0
```

Fig. 3. An example of the SSDP message

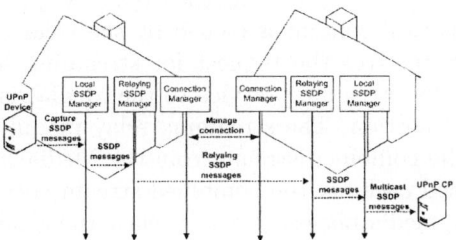

Fig. 4. The Components of HomeConnector and its interaction

SSDP messages from counter-part relaying SSDP manager, it forwards the relayed SSDP messages to the local SSDP manager. The local SSDP manager finally multicasts the relayed messages to its own home network. Like this, the HomeConnector makes the connections and lets the UPnP CP to control other UPnP devices in different home networks.

2.2 Virtual Media Server for Transparent Content Sharing

In this section, we discuss the way to provide transparent content sharing among home networks. We propose additional components that can be combined with the components of UPnP AV architecture for the transparent content sharing.

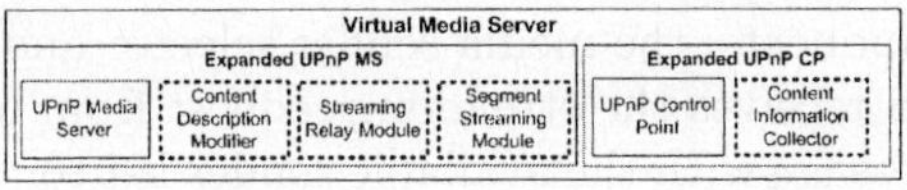

Fig. 5. The components of virtual MS

Although the HomeConnector can make the connections among home networks, it can support nothing more than the connections among home networks. If there is no method that plays a proxy role for users, users will be confused with many discovered devices and content. Thus we propose the sub-module, called the virtual MS, for the transparent content sharing. As shown in Fig. 5, the virtual MS is divided into two components: the expanded UPnP CP and the expanded UPnP MS [3].

---

[3] In the UPnP AV network, the UPnP MS is able to access its content and transmit it to another device via the network using some type of transfer protocol.

Based on the connections that are formed by the HomeConnectors, the expanded UPnP CP discovers the remote UPnP MSs and gets content information from the remote UPnP MSs. To get the content information from the remote UPnP MSs, the expanded UPnP CP uses the Browse() and Search() interfaces that are defined in the UPnP AV content directory service [8]. After gathering of the content information from the remote UPnP MSs, the expanded UPnP CP sends the gathered content information to the expanded UPnP MS. By modifying the collected information of content like the *protocolInfo* parameter that indicates the URL for content retrieving, the expanded UPnP MS lets local users to search the content as if content is owned by the local UPnP MS. When the expanded UPnP MS receives the request for streaming service from users, it forwards the request for streaming service to the MediaDistributor that will be discussed in the next section. The streaming relay module of expanded UPnP MS, then, receives the combined stream from the MediaDistributor. After performing segment-based caching, the combined stream is sent to the UPnP MR (media renderer) i.e., media player. When it relays the combined stream, it does segment-based caching, where contents are divided into group of segments and specific segment group is stored at storage of HG for distributed streaming. To distribute segments of content to different HGs in the DHC such that any segment group is equally likely to appear at any HG, the RanSub [15] can be used. The RanSub is a scalable approach to distributing changing, uniform random subsets of global state to all nodes of an overlay tree.

In the proposed approach, users only need to communicate with the original UPnP components like UPnP MS. They don't need to know internal and external operations of the virtual MS and communicate with additional components of the virtual MS. Note that the virtual MS is discovered by user as one UPnP MS.

2.3 MediaDistributor for Segment-Based Distributed Streaming

As the most important sub-module of SHARE module, the MediaDistributor is assisting the efficient and reliable streaming service in a distributed way. It is divided into two components: the media sender selector and the media collector. When the virtual MS receives the streaming request from users, it forwards the streaming request message with the available sender list to the MediaDistributor as shown in Fig. 6. The available sender list contains the information of HG that has content segment for requested streaming service. Based on this list, the MediaDistributor begins its work. It is designed to facilitate the distributed streaming scheme that receives media streams from multiple senders. With the P2P-style distributed approach, it mitigates the performance bottleneck problem of centralized approach by selectively determining where to get segments. It checks the service availability of every possible sender based on the system and network resource status. This may alleviate the quality degradation of other services of HG and increase the quality of streaming service, since requests for streaming service are sent to selected senders that have enough resource. The minimization of HG's quality degradation is an important and practical issue, because the HG with the SHARE module is the main device that connects between home network and the Internet. It also can be used as a UPnP MS in home network. Thus, to check the service availability of each possible sender is important. In this paper, we only consider the resource status at the point of the receiving of streaming request and do not propose method to adapt streaming to the dynamic resource status. To support more actual streaming, we need to solve the issues that are can be caused by the dynamic resource status. In the proposed approach, the HG resources are reserved and utilized based on the UPnP QoS services [6, 5] for the reliable streaming.

The media sender selector of MediaDistributor determines which node (i.e., HG with SHARE) will stream the target stream content with sufficient resource. The available bandwidth of each path (i.e., from source HG to destination HG) will guide the decision. But the media sender selector uses the system and network resource information simultaneously. Basically, the delay, the one factor of streaming quality, is the sum of following factors: transmission delay, propagation delay, queueing delay, and nodal processing delay. Although the nodal processing delay is not the main factor of delay, it can affect the total delay. Thus, in this paper, we propose the way to consider the network and system resource status at the same time. To estimate the available bandwidth from itself to each sender, the SHARE module can use the TFRC (TCP-friendly rate control) algorithm proposed in [16]. TFRC protocol is designed to provide TCP-friendly traffic, and results in less fluctuation in sending rate than TCP does. To check the resource status of each sender, the media sender selector utilizes the UPnP QoS services. In the UPnP QoS architecture v1.0 [5], the QoSDevice service [7] is defined. The QoSDevice service exposes its static QoS capabilities through the GetQoSDeviceCapabilities interface and its run time QoS state of the device through the GetQosState interface. Especially, the GetQosState interface provides information about its currently active traffic streams. The resource information that is returned by the GetQosState interface may include the utilization of processor to do transfer in the case of the media server and its buffer size in the case of intermediate device. In the UPnP QoS architecture v2.0 [6], the services for monitoring like network monitoring service (called QoSMonitor service) and network rotameter service are being discussed. These services are defined to provide feedback to other QoS elements allowing for intelligent decisions. The QoSMonitor service provides more specific and detailed network status information such as the number of ports, average latency for each link, the ongoing connections, the load of the processor doing the switching, the throughput, etc. For more detailed description for possible resource information, refer to [6]. But this resource information is not fixed. Based on the collected system and network resource information of each possible sender, the media sender selector determines which sender can offer reliable streaming. Fig. 7 shows pseudo code for the routine for sender selection of media sender selector. The current algorithm for the sender selection of the media sender selector is a preliminary version. The proposed algorithm chooses the sender when it determines that the checked sender has sufficient resource for the content streaming. It does not check all possible senders and select senders that have the highest resource availability. Basically, there are multiple issues that are related to the algorithm for media sender selection. It needs to determine the segment size and number of segment groups for effective distributed streaming. It should solve the tradeoff problem between the number of segment groups and system overhead for segment mergence. It also needs to provide load balanced distributed streaming among multiple sender. To solve these problems, we are trying to get the relation between system overhead and streaming quality in real testbed. By simulating the algorithm based on the result from real test, we will enhance the algorithm for media sender selection. With the SetUpTrafficQoS() that is defined in the UPnP QoSDevice service, after media sender determination, the media sender selector allocates certain amount of HG resources for distributed streaming. This pre-allocation of system resources may block problems that can occur because of limited resource.

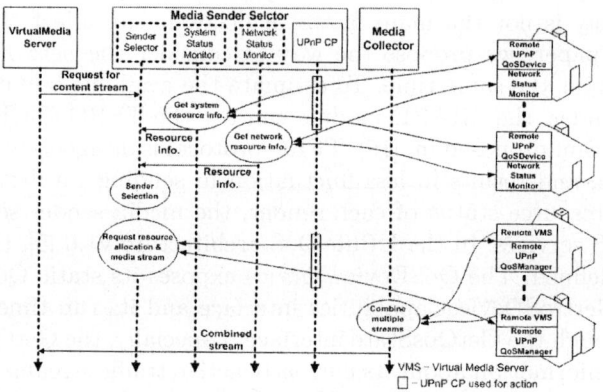

Fig. 6. The procedures for MediaDistributor

Since the MediaDistributor utilizes the distributed streaming, there should be a module to collect and combine multiple segmented streams into one stream. The media collector coordinates the arrival of different media data segments and reconstructs media data in their original and continuous order before feeding them to the UPnP MR. For better streaming service, the media collector should be able to accommodate the dynamic set of peer senders and the end-to-end network congestion.

3 Implementation and Verification

To verify the proposed design, until now, a prototype of HomeConnector component is realized while the MediaDistributor component and the virtual MS are partially prototyped. They are implemented in C over .NET platform by leveraging the open-source version of UPnP AV architecture. The preliminary

```
While(need more segment)
{
    //find the senders that own specific segment
    Sender = Find_Candidate_Sender(Segment_number, Candidate_Sender);

    //find sender that has sufficient resource
    while(no candidate sender)
    {
        //make the connection between receiver and sender
        Make_Connection(Sender);

        //get system and network resource information
        Sender.S_Info = Get_Resource_Information(Sender);

        //check the service availability
        if(Check_Service_Availability(Sender.S_Info)){

            //add selected sender to sender list
            Add_Sender(Sender);

            //request resource allocation to selected sender
            Request_Resource_Allocation(Sender);

        }

        //shift pointer in linked list
        Shift_Sender_Pointer(Sender);
    }

    Segment_number++;
}

Int Check_Service_Availibity(Sender.S_Info){
    if(Sender.S_Info enoughs for streaming) return 1;
    else return 0;
}
```

Fig. 7. Pseudo code for sender selection routine of media sender selector

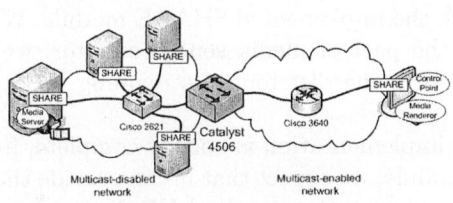

Fig. 8. Testbed to verify the HomeConnector

prototype implementation is verified over a testbed network that mimics the HG-connected digital homes as shown in Fig. 8. First, we apply the HomeConnector component to virtual home networks, where the native IP multicast is supported within its own boundary. To check the connection formed by the HomeConnector between two networks, we use the DeviceSniffer [17] that is UPnP tool made by Intel. The DeviceSniffer monitors all SSDP messages. By using the DeviceSniffer, we verify that the SSDP messages are exchanged between two networks. It is confirmed that, with the implemented module, we can enable the UPnP CP to discover and control other UPnP devices in another network. Moreover, using the established connection, we can receive streaming content from the UPnP MS in another UPnP network.

Next, the media collector and the media sender selector of MediaDistributor are tested. To verify that it can support the transparent distributed streaming service, we use two nodes that own segments of media content. In this implementation, we focus on the verification of the transparent streaming service based on the UPnP AV architecture. Thus, we conclude that two nodes are enough

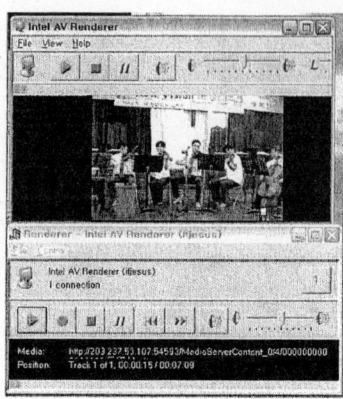

Fig. 9. The image of implementation result

to verify the implementation purpose. The media sender selector requests the segment-based streaming to the counter-part virtual MS. At this stage, we simply assume that there is no resource limitation, since we focus on the verification for the transparent streaming service. After buffering, the media sender selector starts to send combined stream to the UPnP MR. Fig. 9 shows the image of content playback through the implemented SHARE module. With the implemented media collector and the part of media sender selector, we can verify that the SHARE module supports the distributed streaming service and is compatible with the UPnP CP.

Although current implementation is not yet complete, from the partially implemented SHARE module, we expect that it can provide the distributed content streaming and cooperate with the standard UPnP devices. Based on future implementation of the media sender selector, we will enhance the algorithm of media sender selector for sender selection.

4 Related Work

To make the connections among separated UPnP networks, Intel proposes a tool named as DeviceRelay [17]. The DeviceRelay can mirror the UPnP devices onto a different network that also has an running instance of the running DeviceRelay. The DeviceRelay will automatically mirror all UPnP devices from one network on to the other networks. A UPnP CP on the other network can interact with mirrored devices. DeviceRelay should maintain the descriptions of all devices to mirror. With the DeviceRelay, the media can not be transferred. Unlike the DeviceRelay that needs to maintain the descriptions of all devices to mirror, the HomeConnector only needs to maintain a list of home networks to connect. The HomeConnector can make a virtual network that can send and receive media as conventional VPN does, too.

There have been many researches for distributed streaming. In Jeon and Nahrstedt [9], peer clients, which are fully connected together, not only receive multimedia streams from a server, but also send cached streams to peer clients like a proxy server upon its request. Before finishing segmented playback, clients request next segment to another peer. Like this, it can provision small initial delay and low jitter during playing time. However clients depend on only one sender that has limited resource at a specific time. Built on top of Gnutella [18], the GnuStream [11] takes into consideration the underlying P2P network dynamics and heterogeneity. In the GnuStream, the client distributes streaming loads in proportion to the current capability of peer sender. But the GnuStream does not consider system resource status of each sender that can affect the quality of streaming service. Guo et al. [13] presents a novel and efficient design of a scalable and reliable media proxy system supported by P2P networks. They address both scalability and reliability issues of streaming media delivery in a cost-effective way. In their work, each peer should act as a client, a streaming server, and an index server that contain information about peers who owns content. Even though it uses P2P technology for scalability, client depends on only one sender at specific time and it doesn't care about resource status of the sender. Most the proposed P2P streaming approaches assume that all peers can support streaming service without any resource limitation. But every system has limited resource that can affect the streaming quality. Unlike the above approaches, the SHARE module leverages UPnP QoS services and bandwidth estimation algorithm to check the service availability based on system and network resource status. The SHARE module distributes streaming loads onto multiple senders effectively while it tries to minimize the quality degradation of other services in home networks.

5 Conclusion

The proposed proxy-based SHARE module can help us to realize the vision of the DHC. It can support the reliable and transparent content streaming service among home networks based on the UPnP protocol in a distributed way. We need to enhance the decision algorithm of media sender selector for sender selection. Also, the design of interface is required to better support the hierarchical and secure P2P overlay networks for the DHC [10].

Acknowledgements. This research is supported by Korea Research Foundation (KRF-2004-041-D00463).

References

1. J. Walker, O. J. Morris, and B. Marusic, "Share it! - The architecture of a rights-manges network of peer-to-peer set-top boxes," in Proc of EUROCON, 2003.
2. Digital Living Network Alliance, "DLNA home networked device interoperability guidelines," 2004.
3. UPnP forum, "UPnP Device Architecture 1.0," Dec. 2003.
4. J. Ritchie and T. Kuehnel, "UPnP AV Architecture 0.92," May. 2003.

5. D. Hlasny, J. Manbeck, N. Gadiruju, and S. Palm, "UPnP QoS Architecture 0.931," Dec. 2004.
6. M. Hartskamp, R. Chen, and P. Sharma, "UPnP QoS Networking Monitoring Service," Mar. 2005.
7. N. Gadiraju, R. Bopardikar, and S. Palm, "UPnP QoS QoSDevice Service," Aug. 2005.
8. K. Debique, T. Igarashi, S. Kou, J. Moonen, J. Ritchie, G. Schults, and M. Walker, "UPnP AV Content Directory Service," June. 2002.
9. W. Jeon and K. Nahrstedt, "Peer-to-peer Multimedia Streaming and Caching Service," *Proc. of ICME 2002, Vol. 2, 26-29,* , 2002.
10. X. Bai, S. Liu, P. Zhang, and R. Kantola, "ICN: Interest-based clustering network," *Proc. of Fourth International Conference on Peer-to-Peer Computing*, Aug. 2004.
11. X. Jiang, Y. Donh, D. Xu, and B. Ahargava, "Gnustream: A P2P Media Streaming System Protype," *Proc. of IEEE International Conference on Multimedia and Expo*, July. 2003.
12. Y.Y. Goland, T. Cai, P. Leach, Y. Gu, and S. Albright, "Simple Servicee Discovery Protocol/1.0," *Internet Engineering Task Force Internet Draft (draft-cai-ssdp-v1-03.txt)* , Oct. 1999.
13. L. Guo, S. Chen, S. Ren, X. Chen, and S. Jiang, "PROP: a Scalable and Relialbe P2P Assisted Proxy Streaming System," *Proc. of the 24th International Conference on Distributed Computing Systesms*, 2004.
14. Z. Zhang, Y. Wang, H. Du, and D. Su, "Video Staging: A Proxy-Server-Based Approach to End-to-End Video Delivery over Wide-Area-Networks," *ACM transaction on networking, VOL. 8, NO. 4*, Aug. 2000.
15. D. Kostic, A. Rodrigues, J. Albrecht, and A. Vahdat, "Using Random Subsets to Build Scalable Network Services," *Proc. of the USENIX Symposium on Internet Technologies and Systems*, Mar. 2003.
16. S. Floyd, M. Handley, J. Padhye, and J. Widmer, "Equation-based congestion control for unicast applications," *Applications, Technologies, Architectures and Protocls for Computere Communication, pp.43-56*, Oct. 2000.
17. DeviceRelay, *http://www.intel.com/cd/ids/developer/asmo-na/eng/downloads/upnp/tools/index.htm.*
18. Gnutella, *htttp://www.gnutella.com/.*
19. Universal Plug and Play, *http://www.upnp.org/.*
20. Home Audio Video Interoperability, *http://www.havi.org/.*
21. Jini Technology, *http://www.jini.org/.*

Adaptive Distributed Video Coding for Video Applications in Ad-Hoc Networks

Ke Liang[1], Lifeng Sun[2], and Yuzhuo Zhong[2]

[1] School of Software, Tsinghua University,
Beijing 100084, China
liangk03@mails.tsinghua.edu.cn
[2] Department of Computer Science, Tsinghua University,
Beijing 100084, China
{sunlf, zyz}@mail.tsinghua.edu.cn

Abstract. In nowadays distributed video coding systems, side information is generated at the decoder using motion estimation. Therefore, the high computational complexity is swaped from the encoder to the decoder. In order to reduce the computational complexity at the decoder, generating the side information using extrapolation may be a compromise, but it brings a drawback of rate-distortion performance. To compensate this drawback, we proposed an Adaptive Distributed Video Codec (ADVC) based on multilevel coset codes. In our implementation, the temporal similarities among successive frames can be exploited substantially, and the side information is available at the encoder that achieves more accurate correlation. The simulation results show the proposed ADVC has a better rate-distortion performance than non-adaptive distributed video codec (DVC), especially in low-rate scenarios . . . .

1 Introduction

State-of-the-art video coding standards, like H.26x and MPEG, have a heavy encoder due to the predictive or interframe coding. At the same time, they also have a lightweight decoder, which is regarded as a "slave" mode relative to the encoder. As a result, the encoder is almost 5 or 10 times complex than the decoder in the conventional codec. We can see that the conventional coding schemes have been used for many "downlink" systems like broadcasting and video-on-demand systems, in which videos are encoded once but need to be decoded many times. However, we may be interested in the dual scenarios such as compressing video at low-power nodes in ad-hoc networks. We can get a light encoder if the task of motion estimation is not included in the MPEG or H.263 encoder, but the corresponding rate is huge. Fortunately, the distributed video coding (DVC) scheme emerges, which has a simple encoder but a complex decoder with a accredited rate.

The DVC scheme is based on Slepian-Wolf theorem [1] and Wyner-Ziv theorem [2]. To appreciate the two theorems, let X and Y denote two statistically dependent Gaussian random processes, which are encoded by two independent encoders but decoded by a joint decoder. The Slepian-Wolf theorem establishes the achievable rate region for probability of decoding error to zero : $R_X + R_Y \geq H(X,Y)$, $R_X \geq H(X|Y)$, $R_Y \geq H(Y|X)$ [1]. The Wyner-Ziv theorem proves the inequality : $R_{X|Y}^{WZ}(D) - R_{X|Y}(D) \geq 0$ [6]. $R_{X|Y}^{WZ}(D)$ denotes the rate required when the side information are available at the decoder only, $R_{X|Y}(D)$ denotes the rate required when the side information are available at the both sides. The two results suggest that an intraframe encoder - interframe decoder system can achieve similar efficiency of an interframe encoder - decoder system.

In current practical distributed video coding frameworks [3][4][5], the decoders are complex due to the shift of motion estimation from the encoder to the decoder. However, the framework with heavy decoder is not desirable when all the terminals are low-power mobile devices without powerful stations for transcoding. What's more, in practically distributed video codec [6], there is still a performance gap from H.263+ interframe coding ranges from 2 to 3 dB because the temporal statistics are not exploited adequately.

In this paper, we propose an adaptive distributed video coding codec (ADVC) using multilevel coset codes [7]. The proposed codec is a transform-domain codec because the DCT transform enables the encoder to exploit the spatial statistics within a frame, thus achieves better rate-distortion performance. The quantized DCT coefficients of to-be-encoded frames are treated as sources. To reduce the complexity at the decoder, the quantized DCT coefficients of the previous frame are treated as the side information, therefore the side information can be easily generated at both sides of the codec. There are two reasons that bring a drawback of rate-distortion performance, one is the inaccurate side information comparing to the side information generated using motion-compensated interpolation, the other is the error caused by quantization. To compensate this drawback, number of Wyner-Ziv frames [3] in a single slice can increase due to the strong correlation among the successive frames, on the other hand, side information is available at the encoder in aid of achieving more accurate correlation between the to-be-encoded frame and the side information.

The rest of the paper is organized as follows: In section 2, we will review some practical transform-domain distributed video codec currently. In section 3, we will describe the proposed distributed video coding codec. In section 4, we will discuss the simulation details and compare the performance of the pro-posed codec to conventional H.263+ codec. Finally, section 5 conclude the paper.

2 Overview of Related Distributed Video Codec

Results from [3][6] show that the transform-domain Wyner-Ziv video codec can achieve better rate-distortion performance than pixel-domain Wyner-Ziv video codec because the spatial transform can exploit the statistics dependencies within a frame.

Aaron and Girod developed a typical transform-domain Wyner-Ziv video codec using turbo codes [3][6]. In their implementation, video sequences are partitioned into two subsets. One subset of frames, called *key frames*, is encoded using conventional codec. Another subset of frames, called *Wyner-Ziv frames*, is encoded using a Wyner-Ziv encoder. A blockwise DCT is performed at each Wyner-Ziv frame. The transform coefficients are independently quantized and grouped together into coefficients bands, and then be compressed by a Slepian-Wolf turbo coder. In their implementation, the number of Wyner-Ziv frames between two key frames is fixed and cannot be changed in the encoding process.

Puri and Ramchandran develop a similar transform-domain Wyner-Ziv video codec with the acronym PRISM [4]. Like the Aaron and Girod's implementation, a blockwise DCT is followed by uniform scalar quantization. Each block is encoded independently, and only about 20 percents of the coefficients in it are syndrome encoded, the remaining coefficients are conventionally entropy-coded. The encoder also sends CRC of quantized coefficients to aid motion compensation at the decoder. In their implement, there are no key frames if all of one frame's blocks have large noise compare to the previous frame's co-located blocks. Rate-distortion results are similar to the Aaron and Girod's results.

3 Proposed Adaptive Distributed Video Codec

In above two transform-domain distributed video codec, side information is generated at the decoder using motion estimation. In our implement, side information is the quantized DCT coefficients of the previous frame, and source is the quantized DCT coefficients of the to-be-encoded frame.

We also divide the video sequence into key frames and Wyner-Ziv frames as defined in [3]. The to-be-encoded frame is divided into non-overlapping spatial blocks (block size we choose is 8×8) also. A *slice* denotes a video sequence in which the first and the last frame are encoded as key frames(it is similar to GOP in the conventional coding schemes, we use it in the paper to distinguish between DVC and the conventional coding schemes). Frames between the two key frames are all encoded as Wyner-Ziv frames. the slice can be extended due to the high correlation among these video sequences. The Wyner-Ziv frames in a non-extended slice are called *original Wyner-Ziv frames*. The additional Wyner-Ziv frames in an extended slice are called *extended Wyner-Ziv frames*. Number of original Wyner-Ziv frames in the slice is the value of the slice.

In our implement, key frames are encoded by conventional H.263+ intraframe encoder, and Wyner-Ziv frames are encoded by Coset encoder based on multilevel coset codes.

3.1 Multilevel Coset Partition

Let X denotes the source to be encoded, Y denotes the side information. They both are quantized DCT coefficients in two co-located blocks. We partition the source X into cosets of a multilevel code according to side information Y.

Consider an n-level partition for example (as shows in Fig. 1, $X=30, Y=27$). First, the codebook of source is partitioned into two cosets at level-0, one coset is odd numbers, the other coset is even numbers. The index of coset containing odd numbers is 1, and the index of coset that containing even numbers is 0.

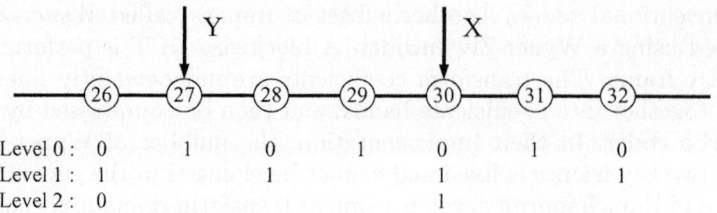

Fig. 1. Coset partition: X is the source, Y is the side information, the number of levels depends on the noise (or distance) between X and Y

Then, as is showed in the above example, X's index of coset at level-0 is 0 (even number), therefore in the next step, the coset which index is 0 will be partitioned again into two subcosets at level-1. The number of levels that should partition the source to depends on the distance (or noise) between the source X and the side information Y.

Let $\triangle = |X - Y|$ denotes the distance (or noise) between the source X and the side information Y. $d = 2^{i+1}$ denotes the distance of each coset at level i. To decode without error, the following inequations should be satisfied:

$$\triangle < \frac{d}{2} \Rightarrow \triangle < 2^i \tag{1}$$

So X will be partitioned $i+1$ times, and $i+1$ indexes will be transmitted to the decoder. Return to the example showed in fig.1, $\triangle = 3$, so $i = 2$, and therefore 3 coset indexes (1 1 0) should be transmitted to the decoder.

Let $U = (U_0, U_1, \ldots, U_n)$ denotes the vector that X is partitioned into an $n+1$ path lattice, $U_i (0 \leq i \leq n)$ denotes the index of coset at level i. We transmit coset indexes U to the decoder, so the encoding rate is [9]:

$$R = I(U;X) - I(U;Y) \tag{2}$$

We use the chain rule of information theory given as [9] and get a similar result as [8]:

$$\begin{aligned} R &= I(U_0, U_1, \ldots, U_n; X) - I(U_0, U_1, \ldots, U_n; Y) \\ &= I(U_0; X) + I(U_1; X|U_0) + \ldots + I(U_n; X|U_0, U_1, \ldots, U_{n-1}) \\ &\quad I(U_0; Y) + I(U_1; Y|U_0) + \ldots + I(U_n; Y|U_0, U_1, \ldots, U_{n-1}) \\ &= (I(U_0; X) - I(U_0; Y)) + (I(U_1; X|U_0) - I(U_1; Y|U_0)) + \ldots \\ &\quad + (I(U_n; X|U_0, U_1, \ldots, U_{n-1}) - I(U_n; Y|U_0, U_1, \ldots, U_{n-1})) \\ &= \sum_{i=0}^{n} R_i \end{aligned} \tag{3}$$

As is showed by (3), the encoding rate R can be partitioned into n components, each component R_i denotes the encoding rate at level i. In [8], syndrome coding is performed with linear error correction codes to compress the coset indexes at each level (or band) to achieve a desired rate.

In our implement, X is not encoded at each level band using separately encoder like [8]. We transmit all the coset indexes of a single X to the decoder. If the to-be-encoded source X is a vector, we partition the encoding rate of $X(R)$ into m components, each component r_i ($0 \leq i \leq m$) denotes the rate of each sample in X.

Let the source $X = (x_0, x_1, \ldots, x_{63})$ (block size is 8×8) denotes a vector of quantized DCT coefficients (after operation of zigzag) of a block, r_i ($0 \leq i \leq 63$) denotes the rate of each sample x_i after zigzag. R_i denotes the rate of X at level i. R denotes the encoding rate of X, so R have two representations (as is showed in fig.2):

$$R = \sum_{i=0}^{n} R_i = \sum_{i=0}^{63} r_i \qquad (4)$$

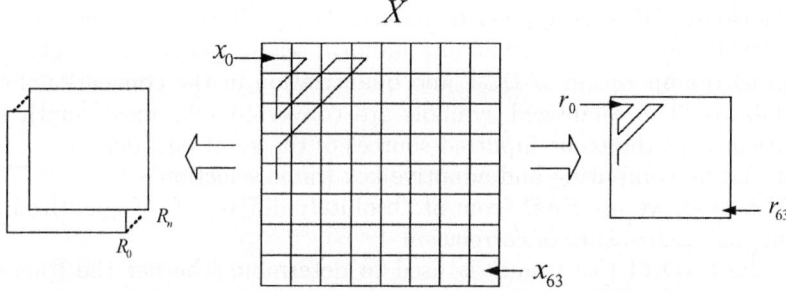

Fig. 2. Two different representations of R

To achieve a desired rate, only coset indexes of low frequency coefficients are transmitted to the decoder because the low frequency DCT coefficients contain most of block's information.

We now describe the framework of the proposed codec: ADVC (Adaptive Distributed Video Codec).

3.2 Framework of ADVC

The proposed framework of ADVC is simple and flexible, in another word, both the encoder and the decoder are lightweight. The main features of the proposed framework are: 1)The to-be-encoded frame and the side information are all quantized DCT coefficients; 2)Side information is available at the encoder; 3)The slice can be extended at the encoder to exploit the strong correlation among the successive frames.

Encoder. The proposed encoder (fig.3) includes two separate encoders, one is a conventional encoder (we use H.263+ encoder here), and another is a Wyner-Ziv encoder based on multilevel coset codes.

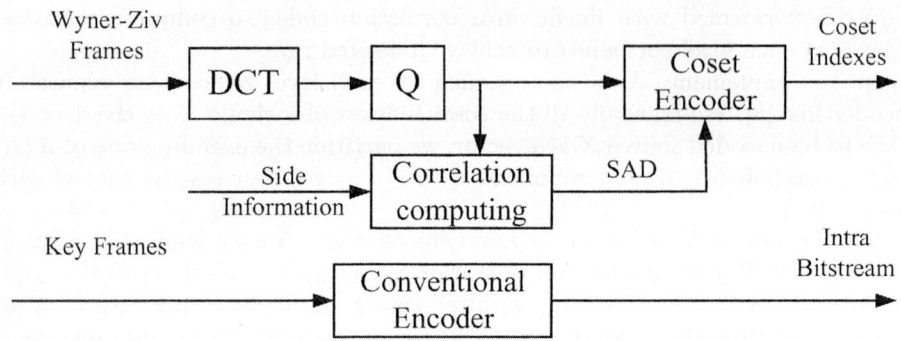

Fig. 3. ADVC encoder, the side information is quantized coefficients of the previous frame

1. Spatial transform and quantization
   A blockwise DCT is applied to reduce the spatial redundancy, after that, the DCT coefficients are sent to a uniform scalar quantization. This step is akin to the operation of DCT and quantization in the conventional coding standards. The quantized symbols are converted into fixed-length binary codewords as the to-be-inputted sources of the coset encoder.
2. Correlation computing and adaptive key frame selection
   In this step, we use SAD (sum of absolutely difference) of quantized coefficients as the measure of correlation.

   The SAD of two frames is used to determine whether the frame after the last original Wyner-Ziv frame in one slice is encoded as an extended Wyner-Ziv frame or be encoded as a *key frame* (the start of a new slice).
   If the frame is encoded as a Wyner-Ziv frame, the SAD of two co-located blocks is used to classify the to-be-encoded block into many classes by which the block is encoded using matched approaches. Two extremely modes are skip mode and intra mode. The block in the to-be-encoded frame is intra-encoded in the intra mode and is not encoded at all in the skip mode. The coset coding mode is between these two extremely modes.

   Comparing to the encoder in [3], it is a additional module which may increase the computational burden. But this process can enhance the compression efficiency, and the additional computational burden is tolerable in practice. Comparing to the same process in [4][8], we can get a more accurate correlation because we use side information here.
3. Coset partition and encoding
   As is mentioned above, we select the quantized DCT coefficients of the previous frame as the side information, on the other hand,The source is the quantized DCT coefficients of the to-be-encoded frame.

   For a to-be-encoded block, the number of the coset indexes that should be transmitted to the decoder is determined by the SAD of quantized DCT coefficients between the block and the co-located block in the previous frame. Then, how to choose the number? We consider this problem that minimize

the lagrangian cost: $J = D + \lambda R$, λ is a nonnegative real number, R is the rate, D is the expected distortion.

Let the vector $X = (x_0, x_1, \ldots, x_{63})$ denotes the source, and the victor $Y = (y_0, y_1, \ldots, y_{63})$ denotes the side information. They are regarded as two Gaussian memoryless sources and both are zigzagged. The estimate of X at the decoder is denoted as $X' = (x'_0, x'_1, \ldots, x'_{63})$. Let Vector $U = (u_0, u_1, \ldots, u_{63})$ denotes the coset indexes that should be transmitted to the decoder. The rate at each sample is $R_i = H(U_i|Y_i)$, and the distortion at each sample is $D = ||x_i - x'_i||^2$. So the langrangian cost function is: $J = \sum_{i=0}^{63}(D_i + \lambda R_i) = \sum_{i=0}^{63} J_i$. For Gaussian source, $D_i = \sigma_i^2 2^{-2R_i}$, σ_i is the variance of x_i. Let $\frac{\partial J_i}{\partial R_i} = 0$, so that $\lambda_i = 2ln2\sigma_i 2^{-2R_i}$. We only transmit the coset indexes of low frequency coefficients (m) to the decoder, so that:

$$J = \sum_{i=0}^{m} 2ln2 \cdot \sigma_i^2 \cdot \frac{R_i}{2^{2R_i}} + \sum_{j=m+1}^{63} \sigma_j^2 \quad (5)$$

To minimize the langrangian cost function, an appropriate m should be selected according to the SAD of the two blocks. In our implement, $m \in \{6, 10, 16, 20\}$. The larger SAD of two blocks, the larger m should be selected.

Decoder. The proposed decoder (fig.4) is similar to the decoder in [3][4], but it is a lightweight decoder. We generate the side information using extrapolation from the previous frames.

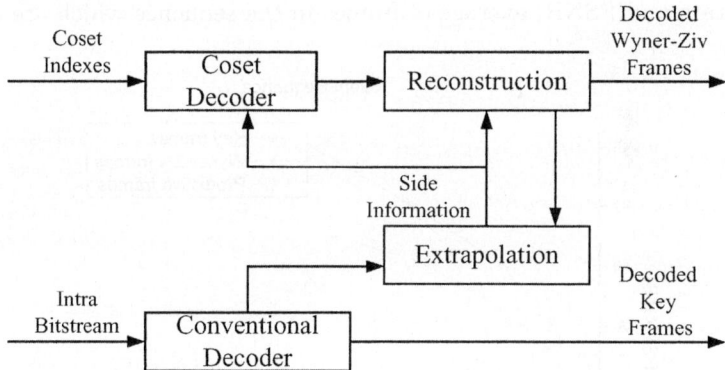

Fig. 4. ADVC decoder, the side information is quantized coefficients of the previous frame, extrapolated by the key frame or Wyner-Ziv frame

In our implement, the quantized coefficients of the previous frame are used directly as the side information. So the IDCT operation is avoided, therefore, the complexity of the proposed decoder is lower than the decoder in [3] and [4].

If the previous frame is a key frame, side information can be easily generated by the inverse VLC module of the conventional decoder. If the previous frame is a Wyner-Ziv frame, side information will be generated by the reconstruction module in the decoder.

Because the source and the side information are all quantized DCT coefficients, and then the coset indexes are lower-part of the source's binary representation, so we can decode without multistage decoding. So the complexity of the proposed decoder is reduced further.

Given the coset indexes of the to-be-decoded frame, the coset decoder decodes the low frequency DCT coefficients of the blocks using the coset indexes without error, the high frequency DCT coefficients of the blocks are the copy of the co-located DCT coefficients of the side information.

This lightweight decoder may brings a drawback of rate-distortion performance because of the inaccurate side information that generated by extrapolation from the previous frame. To compensate this drawback, the encoder should transmit enough coset indexes adaptively based on similarities between the source and the side information.

4 Simulation Results

We choose two QCIF sequence for simulation, silent sequence and foreman sequence. Silent sequence is a low-motion sequence, and foreman sequence is a high-motion sequence. In each sequence, the frame rate is set to 15 Fps. To change the rate, we varied the number of the quantization levels.

We first compare the rate-distortion performance of different frames which are encoded using different encoding approaches (fig.5 and fig.6), The plots show the rate and PSNR, average of frames in the sequence which are encoded

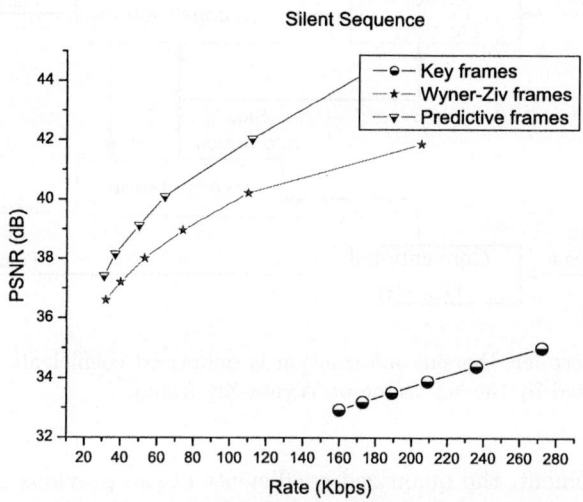

Fig. 5. Rate and PSNR comparison of silent sequence for frames using different encoding approaches. Side information is extrapolated by the previous frame in Wyner-Ziv coding.

using the same approaches: (1) key frames (DCT-based intraframe coding), (2) Wyner-Ziv frames (Wyner-Ziv coding), (3) predictive frames (H.263+ interframe coding).

We then compare the rate-distortion performance of the whole sequence (fig.7 and fig.8), The plots show the rate and PSNR, average of all frames in the sequence: (1) DCT-based intra-frame coding, (2) H.263+ interframe coding with slice=3 (I-P-P-P-I predictive structure), (3) non-adaptive DVC (Distributed

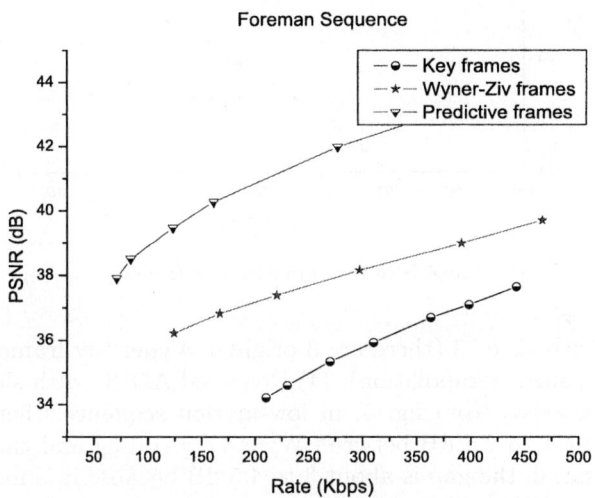

Fig. 6. Rate and PSNR comparison of foreman sequence for frames using different encoding approaches. Side information is extrapolated by the previous frame in Wyner-Ziv coding.

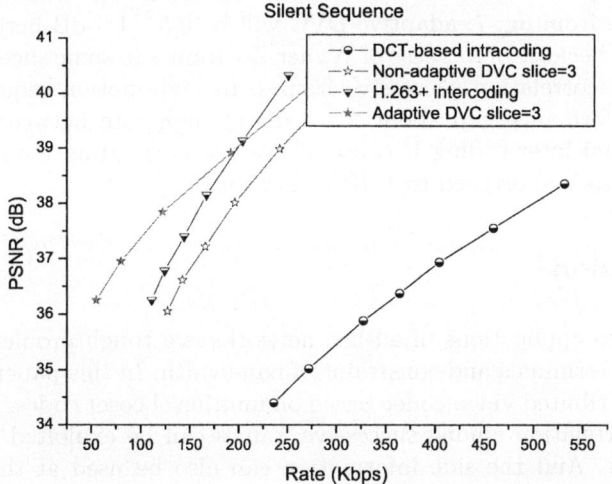

Fig. 7. Rate and PSNR comparison of silent sequence

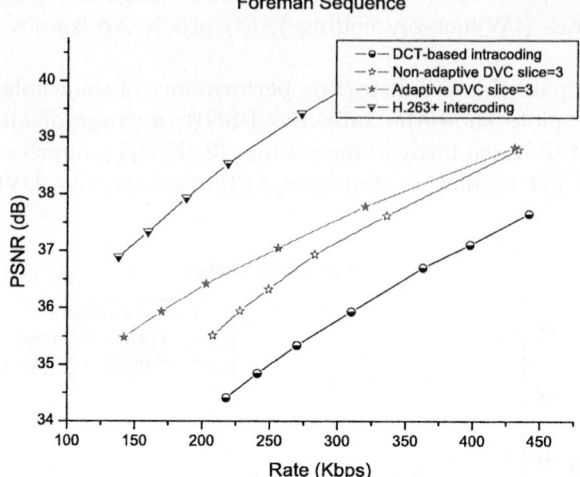

Fig. 8. Rate and PSNR comparison of foreman sequence

Video Codec) with slice=3 (there are 3 original Wyner-Ziv frames in one slice) using previous frame extrapolation), (4) Proposed ADVC with slice=3.

It can be observed from fig. 5, in low-motion sequence, there is a performance gap about 1 to 2.5 dB between Wyner-Ziv coding and the conventional intercoding, in fig. 6. the gap is about 3 to 4.5 dB because it is more difficult to extrapolate an accurate side information in high-motion sequence. This performance gap in foreman sequence (fig. 6) is smaller than Wyner-Ziv coding with motion-compensated extrapolation implemented in [3] (in [3], the gap between H.263+ interframe coding and the Wyner-Ziv codng with MC-E is about 5 dB at low rate) because in our implement, the side information is available at the encoder to compute correlation between the source and the side information.

We can see from fig. 7, adaptive DVC will be 0.5 - 1.5 dB better than non-adaptive DVC because of increase of Wyner-Ziv frames in some slices where there are some high correlation successive frames. In high-motion sequence (fig. 8), there is a performance gap about 2 - 3 dB at high rate between ADVC and the conventional inter-coding because of the low correlation among successive frames. The gap is shortened to 1 dB at low rate.

5 Conclusion

Real-time video applications in ad-hoc networks is a tough problem because of the low-power terminals and constraint of bandwidth. In this paper, we propose a adaptive distributed video codec based on multilevel coset codes. In our implement, high correlation among successive frames can be exploited substantially at the encoder. And the side information can also be used at the encoder to compute more accurate correlation. The proposed ADVC is a lightweight codec, both the encoder and the decoder is simple and flexible. We can see from simulation results that the proposed lightweight ADVC has a good rate-distortion performance at low rate. We can see from the simulation results that the gap performance between the H.263+ interframe coding and the ADVC decreases as the rate decrease, so it is desirable for video applications with mobile devices in ad-hoc networks.

The implemented ADVC is far from complete and will be enriched in future work. The rate-distortion performance of the proposed codec is dependent on the similarity among successive frames. More accurate side information will achieve better rate-distortion performance. Our ongoing work includes generation of better side information and good transcoding strategy for multi-receiver video applications, what's more, the performance of the proposed ADVC in error prone environment should be concerned.

Acknowledgement

This work was supported by National Natural Science Foundation of China under Grant No. 60432030 and No.60273008

References

1. Slepian, D. and Wolf, J.K.: Noiseless coding of correlated information sources. IEEE Transactions on Information Theory. Vol 19, (1973) 471-480
2. Wyner, A. D. and Ziv, J.: The rate-distortion function for source coding with side information at the decoder. IEEE Transactions on Information Theory. Vol 12, (1976) 1-10
3. Aaron, A. Rane, S. Setton, E. Girod, B.: Transform-domain Wyner-Ziv codec for video. Proc. SPIE Visual Communication and Image Processing. San Jose (2004)
4. Puri, R. and Ramchandran, K.: PRISM: A New Robust Video Coding Architecture Based on Distributed Compression Principles. 40th Allerton Conference on Communication, Control and Computing. vol 6, (2002) 379-381
5. Liveris, A. Xiong, Z. and Georghiades, C.: A distributed source coding technique for correlated images using Turbo codes. IEEE Communications Letters, vol 6, (2002) 379-381
6. Girod, B. Aaron, A. Rane, S. and Rebollo-Monedero, D.: Distributed video coding. Proceedings of the IEEE, Special Issue on Video Coding and Delivery, vol 93, (2005) 71-83
7. Wachsmann, U. Fischer, R. and Huber, J.: Multilevel codes: Theoretical Concepts and Pratical Design Rules. IEEE Transactions on Information Theory. Vol 45, (1999) 1361-1391
8. Majumdar, A. Ramchandran, K.: PRISM: an error-resilient video coding paradigm for wireless networks. Proceeding of the First International Conference on Broadband Networks. (2004) 478-485
9. Cover, T. M. and Thomas, J. A.: Elements of Information Theory. New York, Wiley, (1991)

High Speed JPEG Coder Based on Modularized and Pipelined Architecture with Distributed Control

Fahad Ali Mujahid[1], Eun-Gu Jung[1], Dong-Soo Har[1],
Jun-Hee Hong[2], and Hoi-Jeong Lim[3]

[1] Department of Information and Communications,
Gwangju Institute of Science and Technology, Republic of Korea
{fahad, egjung, hardon}@gist.ac.kr
[2] Department of Electrical Engineering, Kyungwon University
hongpa@kyungwon.ac.kr
[3] Department of Orthodontics School of Dentistry,
Dental Science Research Institute Chonnam National University
hjlim@chonnam.ac.kr

Abstract. The design of an efficient reusable IP based Extended JPEG encoder is presented in this paper. This encoder uses user-defined quantization and Huffman tables that can be reconfigured at run-time. It has a modularized and pipelined architecture with distributed control for each block. A simple interface makes integration of the modules in various systems simple and straightforward. The design when targeted on FPGA operated at speed of up to 90MHz and when mapped on $0.25\mu m$ CMOS process the design can operate at speeds over 450MHz, which is faster than any of the similar JPEG encoder designs reported.

1 Introduction

New multimedia and communications products are increasingly based on System-on-Chip (SoC). Applications in the same domain have many algorithmic similarities. These complex algorithms have many similar blocks, but due to lack of design methodology designers do not exploit this fact. Most of the modules made for an application can be easily used in other similar products with little or no change, thus enabling reuse of intellectual property (IP).

Reuse of intellectual property (IP) is a crucial strategy for design teams who need quicker time-to-market. Designers now face cycle times as short as 3 months for the ICs that drive hot items such as cell phones and digital cameras. Designers must also contend with the fact that IC complexity is growing at a rate of 58% per year, but design productivity is increasing at only 21% per year.

Creating IP specifically formatted for the reuse needs of the system designer helps bridge this gap. Reuse provides both IP creators and system designers a method for sharing best practices and strategic blocks. The challenge for system designers, then, is to develop complex designs within the required cycle times. This can be accomplished only with new design methodologies and entirely different concepts for chip design. IP reuse is a critical part of system design methodology.

In the past, work has been done on the development of SoC based multimedia systems [2], but they were unable to fully exploit the potential of this design methodology that emanates from the regular structure of involved algorithms. Although those systems adopted independent blocks for the realization of the encoder, the control was centralized. Due to the globally central control, the adjoining blocks become dependent on the sequence and the timing of signals from controller, which limits the flexibility of the design, and makes it complicated. This also increases the amount of effort required to verify the design after integration.

In this paper, we have proposed a JPEG [1] encoder with distributed control. The control for different data processing units is embodied in the pertinent units. Once the optimized and verified implementation of basic blocks is achieved, they can be used for the construction of larger complex systems by only conforming to the handshake protocols, thereby reducing the system development time.

The remaining part of the paper is organized as follows. Design methodology is presented in section 2. Data-Dominated IP components are discussed in section 3. Use of NoC model for our methodology is discussed in section 4. Design of some main IP components of an image compression system is discussed in section 5. In section 6 we present implementation of JPEG encoder based on our design methodology. Section 7 gives the details of the conformance of the encoder with the ISO requirements. Section 8 discusses the performance of the presented architecture based on the synthesis results and presents comparison of those results with the other JPEG solutions presented in the literature. Finally, Section 9 draws conclusions based on the proposed design methodology and suggestions for future work.

2 Design Approach

Architectures customized to match the computation and the data flows of an application have demonstrated considerable performance improvement compared with general purpose architectures [3]. It is becoming clear that the design of complex signal processing systems on a single chip will be effective only if complex building blocks are used. This can be achieved through the use of structured design methodologies, which employ existing components and systems for the construction of new systems. Studies show that 70% of new designs correspond to existing components that cannot be reused because of a lack of methodologies and tools [4]. To enhance the reusability, cores developed for DSP must employ modular design methodology. In such a design, a complex system is segregated in to hierarchical sub-parts to make it more manageable.

Once the partitioning of a complex system into sub-parts is achieved, reusable IP design approach can be used. Now pre-designed reusable IP cores wrote in different HDLs, from various sources are integrated on a single chip. Studies have shown that use of pre-designed IP functions shortens the overall design cycle by many months, potentially reducing a two year design cycle to six months or less [5]. As an added advantage use of these cores also minimizes the design risk as the solutions are silicon-proven.

A significant factor to the effective and persistent use of IPs is their extent of reusability, i.e., their ability to migrate from one design to another and from one process to another. The design and quality of the IP core also play a significant role. Previous investigations have proven that architectures that seem good for a certain design implementation may not be suitable over broad level due to lack of modularity and parameterization that is need for design reuse. For a particular application, the process of choosing an algorithm mapping is often complex. Factors such as regularity, data interconnects and I/O requirements must also be kept in mind to reach an optimal solution for a broad range of application. To make the IP reusable with minimum effort the code must be highly structured and modular.

3 Data-Dominated IP Components

The target domain of our methodology is that of embedded data-dominated applications. This domain includes real-time cost-sensitive applications which deal with large amounts of complex data types. This occurs especially in real-time multi-dimensional signal processing applications, notably multi-media processing and advanced communication front-ends, which handle indexed array signals. Our methodology directly applies for both these classes, which contain many important applications such as video coding, medical image archival, multi-media terminals, artificial vision, speech and audio coding, xDSL modems, and wireless LAN modems.

In current design practice, internally optimized reused components are put together in a system, with a custom glue and global control logic added around it. This strategy leads to a good solution if the designer is well familiar with all IP blocks and they are designed with enough flexibility to enable the designer to use them in the mode particular to his application. Such a design may give rise to a significant buffer overhead to handle the control signals sequencing and mismatch between the data production and consumption in the different component. For data-dominated applications, this has a severe negative impact on the power, area, and system latency. Reusing components of a much finer granularity is an unsatisfactory solution, since this allows only for a very partial reuse of the design effort.

To avoid both a major performance and cost penalty and the redesign cost, we propose a new system-level IP reuse methodology intended for soft IP components in custom hardware context. It will remedy the identified problems with only a small penalty in terms of design time (compared to the time required for a redesign). But it will also provide added flexibility.

4 Use of NoC Model in Reusable Description

We will use the concept of NoC in design of our reusable IP components for data dominated application. In the proposed methodology we treat each IP block as

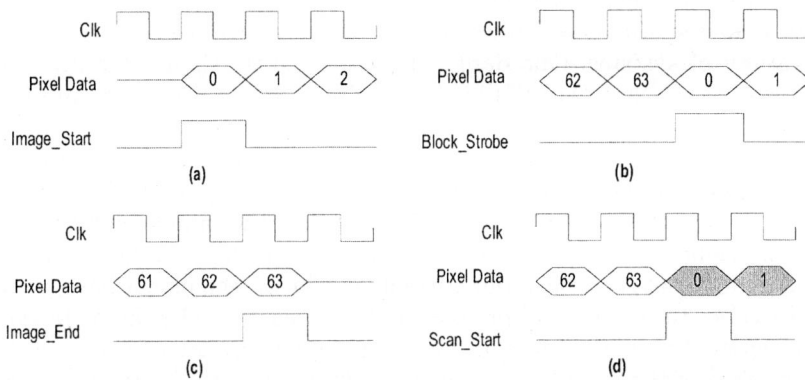

Fig. 1. (a) Image_Start signal; (b) Block_Strobe signal; (c) Image_End signal; (d) Scan_Start signal

a separate processing unit. Each of the blocks will have its own control module and they will communicate with other modules through a fixed protocol. This approach will significantly reduce the reuse time as control for module is already embedded and there is no need to make a central controller.

In general our reuse methodology aims at finding a better trade-off in the exploration pace of design time versus design cost and performance. This translates into two objectives:

- Reusing previous design effort maximum possible extent.
- Losing as little freedom as possible, when reusing parts of designs without change.

In the next section we will explain the steps to develop the IP components for an image processing system, which will be later used for implementation of a JPEG encoder, to show the realization of our objectives.

5 IP Component Design with Distributed Control

In this section step-by-step we will discuss the design process of Soft IP component with distributed control. For explanation we will discuss how we designed components for our image compression system.

5.1 Protocol Signals

The first step in the development of IP components under this methodology is to develop a comprehensive and diverse protocol for communication between the IP modules. The design of the protocol should be done keeping in mind the computational characteristics of data and different algorithms in which it can be used. It should prove the designer maximum flexibility.

For the development of our image compression system, from the computational characteristics of multimedia and image processing algorithms and knowledge of the images, the handshake protocol for the modules can be based on few simple and diverse signals that will enable them to be easily integrated in a variety of systems. Our design uses five one-bit signals for this purpose. These five signals are Data_Valid, Image_Start, Block_Strobe, Scan_Start and Image_End. The counters and the rest of the controls in the IP modules are sequenced by these signals. Scan_Start is not used in case of gray scale images where we have only one image component, and it is only used in case of colored images. The sequence of these signals is related to the sample count in the data and is shown in Figure 1. Data_Valid indicates if the data coming with the clock edge is valid or not. In case of our current system, all the blocks have a throughput of one so this signal is not used and is fixed to active high. Image_Start signal marks the start of data in an image and is asserted for one cycle with the first pixel of the image. Block_Strobe signal marks the start of an 8x8 block and is asserted for one cycle with the first pixel of every 8x8 block. Image_End signal marks the end of the image data and is asserted for one cycle with the last pixel of the image. Scan_Start signal is used where the image has more than one component and each component is red in a separate scan. Scan Start is asserted for one cycle with the first pixel in every scan for different components. With this kind of distributed control logic along with simple handshake protocol the system modifications and enhancements can be performed with least amount of rework.

5.2 DCT/iDCT Module

In the JPEG encoder DCT constitutes the major portion of the processing. We have designed a flexible 2-D DCT unit which supports different modes to handle different block sizes.

The user can also set different levels of pipeline stages to achieve desired clock frequency. For applications that do not require very high throughput the user can also configure the unit to perform 2-D DCT operation using single 1-D module, this will reduce the area of the overall unit to half. The DCT module is implemented using Chen's algorithm [6], e.g., the row-column decomposition 2-D DCT generating two 1-D DCT. This significantly reduces the computational complexity from $O(N^4)$ to $O(N^3)$. DCT module uses a 16x64 dual port transpose memory between the two 1-D DCT modules. DCT module is tested with standard test vectors [7] and works within the tolerance range. Figure 2 shows the design of a 1-D configurable DCT unit.

For quantization a ready-made off the shelf module is used and the quantization tables can be updated at run-time. If the user does not initialize the tables, default tables are used.

5.3 Zig-Zag Scanning

To facilitate entropy coding of the DCT quantized coefficients data is reordered placing low frequency coefficients before high frequency coefficients. Figure 3 shows two of the scan orders.

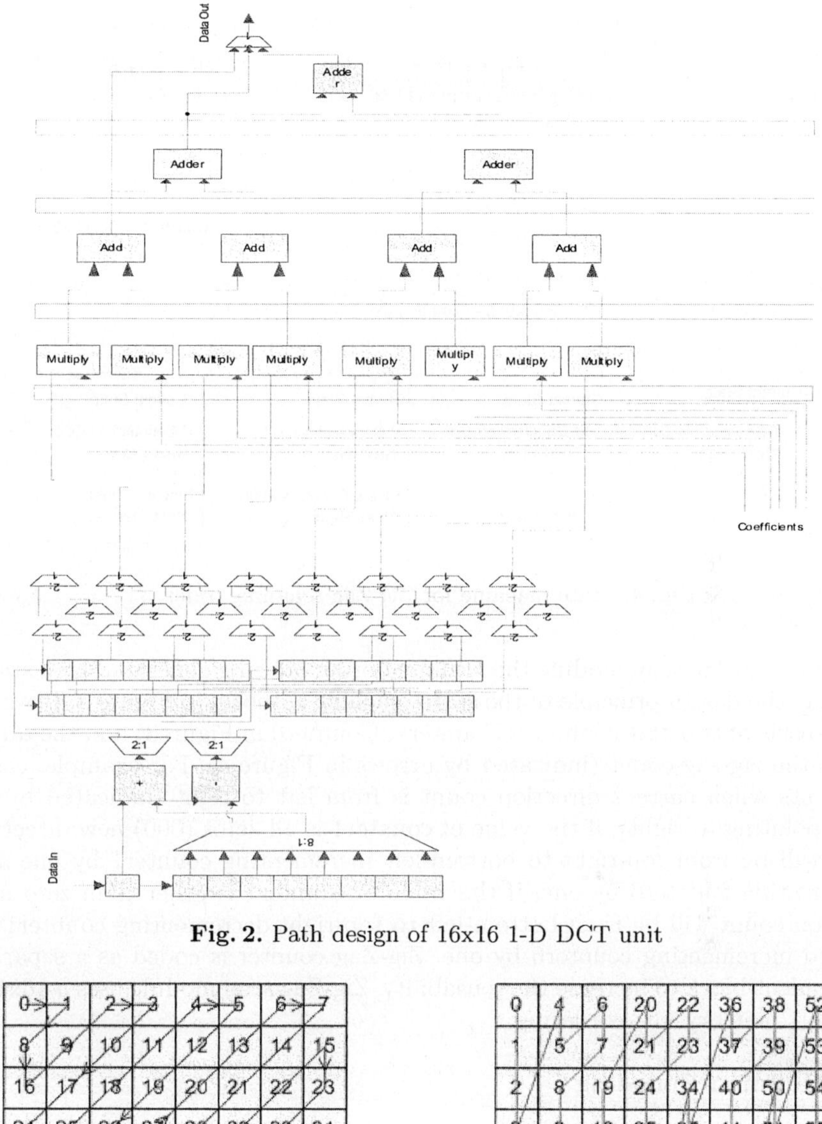

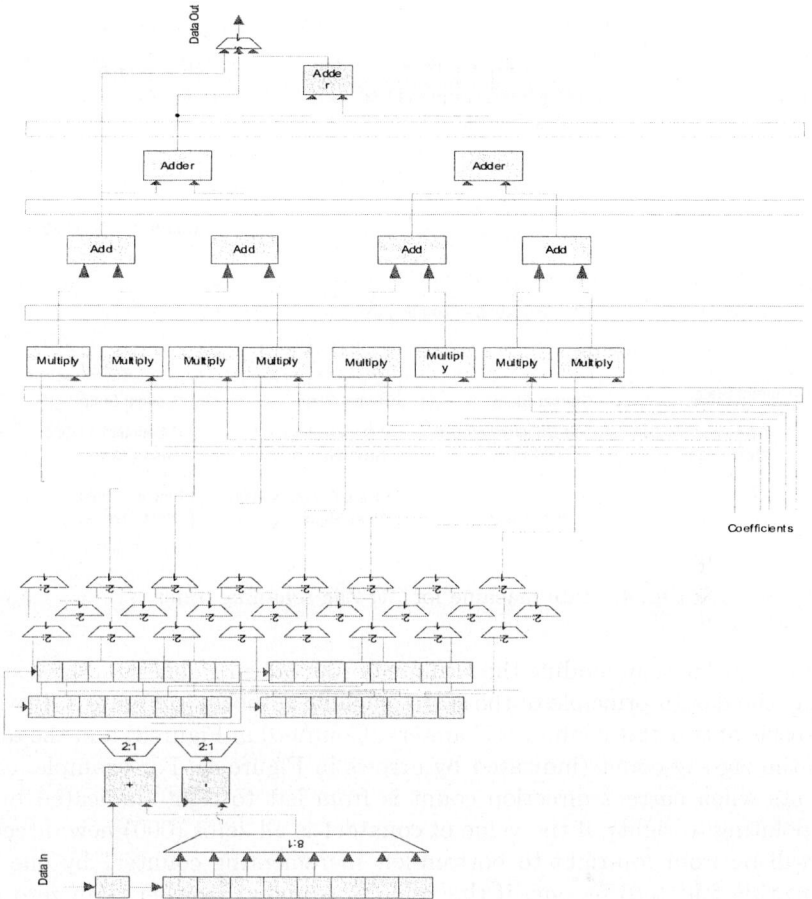

Fig. 2. Path design of 16x16 1-D DCT unit

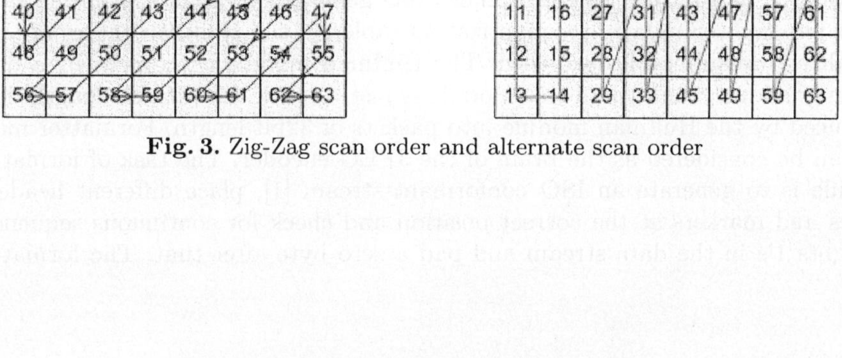

Fig. 3. Zig-Zag scan order and alternate scan order

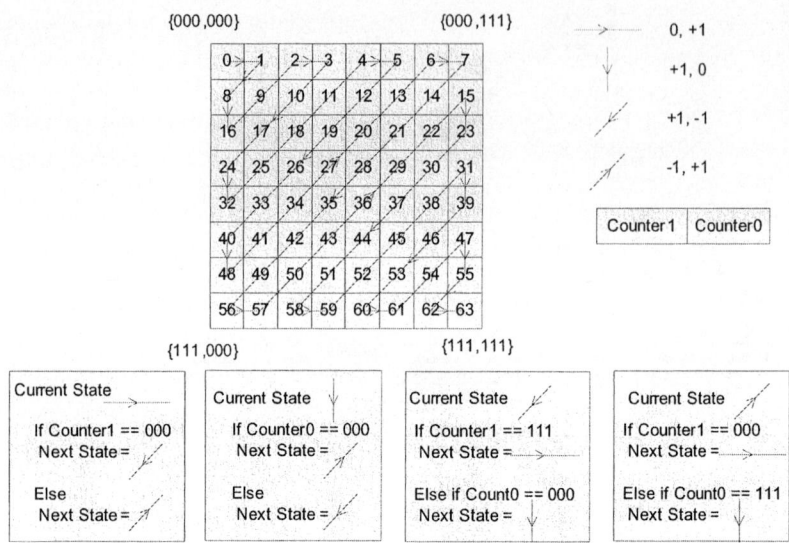

Fig. 4. State machine for Zig-Zag scanning order

In the Zig-Zag scan module the scanning order is being generated by a statemachine, the design principle of the state-machine is shown in Figure 4. It works on the basis of two 3bit counters (Counter1, Counter0 in Figure3) and the direction of the zig-zag count (indicated by arrows in Figure 4). For example, case1 represents when current direction count is from left to right (indicated by an arrow pointing to right), if the value of counter1 is all zeros (000) new direction count will be from top-right to bottom-left incrementing counter1 by one and decrementing counter0 by one, if the value of counter1 is other than zero new direction count will be from bottom-left to top-right decrementing counter1 by one and incrementing counter0 by one. Zig-Zag counter is coded as a separate independent block to increase the reusability. Zig-Zag scan module uses a 16x128 dual port memory for reordering.

5.4 Huffman Encoding

The Huffman encoder and Huffman table generator are coded as separate modules to give the designers the flexibility to use hard wired tables or ones that can be updated at runtime. The Huffman table generator can transform one table entry per cycle. Similarly to quantization tables, if the Huffman tables are not initialized, default tables are used. The Huffman module is followed by a data packing module, the task of this module is just to pack the variable length data produced by the Huffman module into packets of 32bit length. Formatter module can be considered as the brain of the JPEG encoder. The task of formatter module is to generate an ISO conformant stream [1], place different headers, tables and markers at the correct position and check for continuous sequences of eights 1's in the data stream and pad a zero byte after that. The formatter is based on synchronous state machines which can be easily modified through the change of parameters to enable different JPEG options available e.g. mode of operation [1]. Some other options like image size, quantization table select, Huffman table select and bit precision are programmable and can be changed at run-time by changing the register values.

With the proposed reconfigurable design methodology the gate count of the over all system may increase by a small number, but the gains achieved in terms of speed and ease of integration in new systems are significant. To upgrade, or modify the system we can simply take out any module and replace it with some other module without any effect on the adjoining modules i.e., we can replace the Huffman encoder module with an Arithmetic coding module or the DCT module with wavelet transform module easily by just conforming to the handshake protocol. In case of the use of global control such a change would mean restructuring of the whole controller. Thus for reconfigurable architectures distributed control enhances the reusability of the IP modules, making the task development and modification of systems easier.

6 Implementation of JPEG Coder Based on Distributed Control

The JPEG encoder design is a good example of reusable IP based multimedia system core. It is the most commonly used digital image compression algorithm. JPEG, standing for Joint Photographic Experts Group, is a standardized image compression mechanism. It is designed for compressing full-color or gray-scale continuous-tion still images of natural, real-world scenes, like photographs, naturalistic artwork, and similar material. It is lossy, which means that decompressed image is not quite the same as the original image. It is designed to the limitations of human eye, which is a known fact that small color changes are perceived less accurately than small changes in brightness. The degree of lossiness can be varied by adjusting compression parameters.

We built an Extended Baseline JPEG encoder, with sequential encoding. Our system consists of following units.

- Scan converter
- DCT unit (Discrete Cosine Transform)
- Quantization unit
- Zig-Zag Scan unit
- Run-Length coder unit
- Huffman coder unit
- Data Packing module
- FiFo module
- Header generation and Formatter unit

In our implementation DCT, Quantization, Zig-Zag scan, Run-Length coder, and Huffman coder were reusable IP's, built using proposed methodology. While Scan converter, Data Packing, FiFo and Formatter modules were custom built for our system. Figure 5 shows the block diagram of the system.

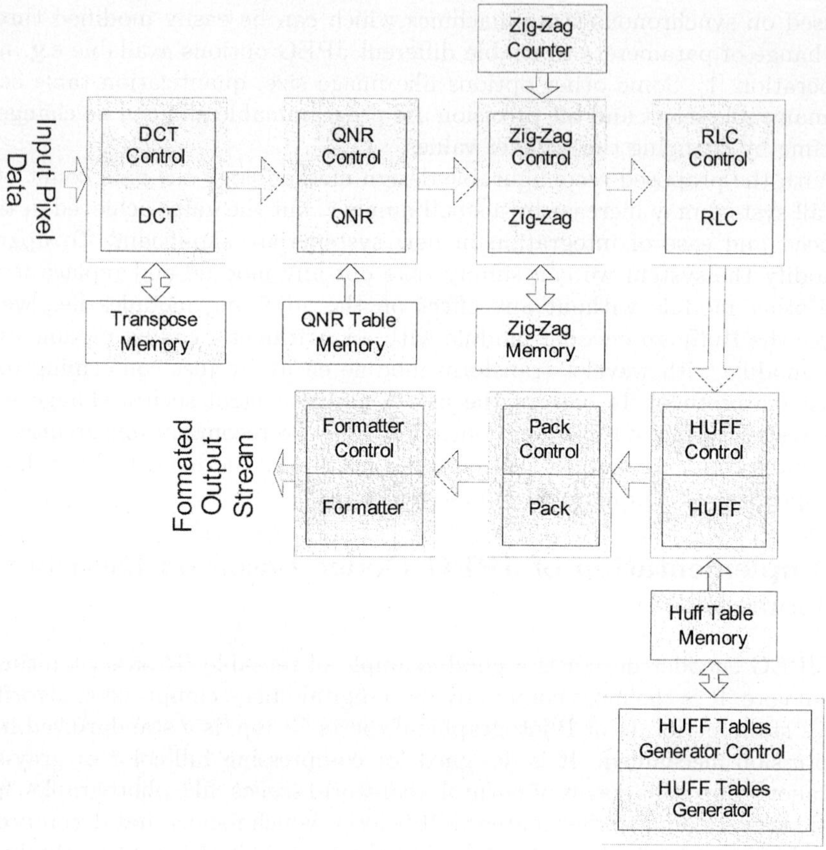

Fig. 5. JPEG encoder block diagram

7 Conformance and Statistical Considerations

All the IP cores are combined to make a JPEG encoder. The output stream of the encoder conforms to the extended baseline standard [1] and can process 8 and 12bit image data. Various images with different sizes are used for functional

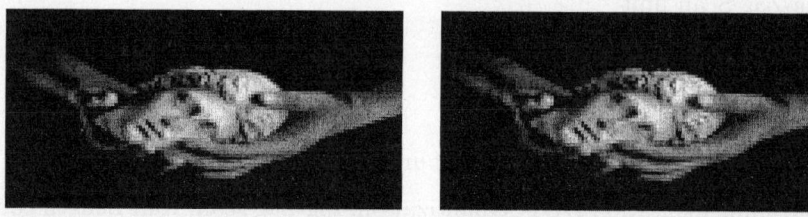

Fig. 6. Orignal hands.bmp (9272 Bytes) along with compressed hands.jpg (1548 Bytes) image produced by the implemented hardware

verification. The compressed bit-streams can be decoded correctly with a variety of image processing software's. Figure 6 illustrates the compressed image generated by the encoder along with the original image. Due to the fixed word length in fixed point arithmetic errors are incurred during DCT and quantization steps. The ISO standard [1] sets stringent limits on the errors caused due to loss of precision. The blocks were tested with random numbers and ISO standard test-vectors [7]. The design meets the Peak Mean Square Error and Overall Mean Square Error specifications. As the encoder has the support for run-time programmable quantization and Huffman tables the user can program these to control the quality of the compressed image.

8 Performance

In terms of performance the core can handle 8bit and 12bit image data with a throughput of one sample per cycle. The core was successfully tested on an FPGA device running at 90MHz, which can easily support the standard NTSC and PAL rates at a good resolution. It might be mentioned here that the system clock was set to 90MHz due to initial set requirements of the project and it can be further increased by changing the parameters and increasing the number of pipeline stages in the design. The modules containing the critical paths in the design were synthesized with anam cell library at $0.25\mu m$ CMOS and all modules successfully synthesized well above 450MHz. Full parameters for CMOS are not present due to non availability of memory compiler. The HDL code is parameterized in a manner to able the user to control the pipeline stages, thus the design can be synthesized at even higher clock speeds based on the requirements.

Table 1. Comparison with recent JPEG IP designs reported in litrature

Author	Technology	Clk Rate (MHz)
Fahad	FPGA	90MHz
	$0.25\mu m$	450MHz
Chung-Jr Lian	$0.6\mu m$	40MHz
J.K.Hunter	FPGA	30MHz
	$0.35\mu m$	100MHz
S. Okada	$0.6\mu m$	18MHz

The complete design, implementation and testing of the encoder was accomplished within a couple of months. Table 1 compares the performance of the proposed encoder with a few of the JPEG designs reported in the literature [8-10].

9 Conclusions

Reusable IP design is a new paradigm that promises shorter time-to-market and superior flexibility. Many multimedia and communication applications that employ algorithms with similar computation characteristics can benefit from this approach. Performance of a reusable IP depends on the extent of design approach. To make an IP reusable the code must be structured and modular. Use of distributed control increases the flexibility and scalability of the architecture by making the code more structured and modular. IP modules design with this approach can also be used more easily in a new bread of systems, based on reconfigurable architectures. JPEG was used as an initial test case for the presented design approach. Undoubtedly the design surpasses other available encoders. Thus based on the proposed JPEG architecture an image compression system can be swiftly built for diverse applications. While the study proved superior performance of the use of distributed control for reusable IP design, future work will involve new IP modules for development of upcoming video compression standards and their mapping in dynamically reconfigurable architectures.

Acknowledgements

This work has been supported in part by the Center for Distributed Sensor Network (CDSN) at GIST, in part by IC Design Education Center (IDEC), in part by the KAIST/GIST IT-21 Initiative in BK21 of Ministry of Education, and in part by the GIST Technology Initiative (GTI).

References

1. ISO/IEC, International Standard DIS 10918-1, Digital Compression and Coding of Continuous-Tone Still Images.
2. Hao-Chieh Chang, Li-Lin Chen, Chung-jr Lian and Liang-Gee Chen, "IP DESIGN OF A RECONFIGURABLE BASELINE JPEG ENCODER", Proceedings of IEEE, AP-ASIC 1999.
3. Kiran Bondalapati and Viktor K. Prasanna, "Reconfigurable Computing Systems", Proceedings of the IEEE, Vol. 90, No. 7, July 2002.
4. Ahmed Amine Jerraya, Hong Ding, Polen Kission and Maher Rahmouni, "Behavioral Synthesis and Component Reuse with VHDL", Kluwer Academic Publishers Nov 1996.
5. Dave Bursky, "Accelerating system design by leveraging intellectual property rating", Microelectronics Design, Vol.2, No.1, Feb 1998.
6. A. Madisetti and A.N. Willson, Jr., "A 100 MHz 2-D 8×8 DCT/IDCT processor for HDTV applications", IEEE Transactions on Circuits and Systems for Video Technology, , Vol: 5 , Issue: 2 , pp: 158-165, April 1995
7. ISO/IEC, International Standard DIS 10918-2, Digital Compression and Coding of Continuous-Tone Still Images: Compliance testing.
8. Chung-Jr Lian, Liang-Gee Chen and Hao-Chieh Chang, "Design and Implementation of JPEG Encoder IP Core", Proceedings of the ASP-DAC 2001.
9. J. K. Hunter, J. V. McCanny and A. Simpson, "JPEG encoder system-on-a-chip demonstrator", Proceedings of Thirty-Third Asilomar Conference on Signals, Systems, and Computers, Vol. 1, pp: 762-766, 24-27 Oct. 1999.
10. S. Okada, Y. Matsuda, T. Watanabe, K. Kondo, "A single chip motion JPEG codec LSI", IEEE Transactions on Consumer Electronics, Vol: 43, Issue: 3, pp: 418-422, Aug. 1997.

Efficient Distribution of Feature Parameters for Speech Recognition in Network Environments

Jae Sam Yoon, Gil Ho Lee, and Hong Kook Kim

Dept. of Information and Communications,
Gwangju Institute of Science and Technology (GIST), Gwangju 500-712, Korea
{jsyoon, ghlee, hongkook}@gist.ac.kr

Abstract. In network or ubiquitous environments, there are difficulties in performing large vocabulary speech recognition by a small device due to its limited power. Therefore, an approach, so-called distributed speech recognition (DSR), that distributes the processing modules of automatic speech recognition into a device and a server has been attractive. Of all processing modules of DSR, quantization of feature parameters plays a main role in terms of the transmission bandwidth and the recognition performance. In this paper, we propose an efficient quantizer of feature parameters by incorporating the correlation between successive analysis frames of speech. The proposed quantizer is based on the predictive multi-stage vector quantization scheme and designed with different bit rates by trading off with the performance of speech recognition. It is shown from speech recognition experiments that the DSR system employing the proposed quantization method can reduce a bit rate by 20% with a comparable recognition performance to the ETSI DSR standard.

1 Introduction

Automatic speech recognition (ASR) systems in wireless communications or IP network environments can be configured depending on the applications of ASR systems, the limitation of computing resource, the existence of a network protocol supporting the ASR system design, etc [1]. Generally, one of the following three scenarios can be considered: embedded approach (or client-based system), bitstream-based approach (or server-based system), and distributed speech recognition (DSR) approach (or client/server-based system) [2]. In the embedded approach, all the recognition processing is executed at the client side and then the recognition result is used for speech-enabled services such as name dialing or a form-filling application. However, if the service requires large vocabulary speech recognition for dictation or call center applications, it is not practical to assign such a heavy computational load to a client device that has low computing power. Contrary to the embedded approach, the sever in the client/server-based approach receives speech signals from the client through networks such as Internet and telephony systems, and then performs the conventional speech recognition. The drawback of this approach is to degrade the performance of speech recognition because speech signals are distorted by speech coding and

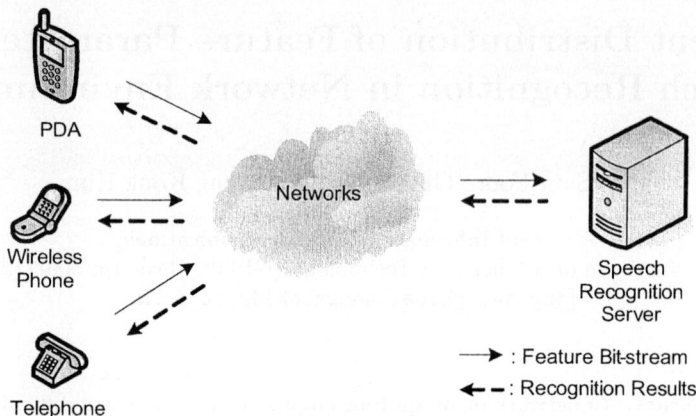

Fig. 1. Configuration of a distributed speech recognition system

channel errors. In order to overcome this problem, the DSR approach has been proposed. Figure 1 shows a typical configuration of DSR, where feature extraction for speech recognition is completed at the client side while speech decoding and understanding are processed at the server side.

The DSR technology has been developed with the growth of Internet and wireless communications technology. Recently, European Telecommunications Standards Institute (ETSI) published a standard DSR front-end [3]. The standard includes the fundamental modules for DSR such as feature extraction, feature compression, bit-stream formatting and decoding, error protection and mitigation. Figure 2 shows the overall structure of the front-end for DSR. The feature extraction module is to obtain salient features that are useful for acoustic modeling at the server. In order to make a DSR system robust to background noise, a speech enhancement algorithm can be applied prior to the feature extraction [4][5]. In the feature compression module, a split vector quantizer (SVQ) is used in the standard. After that, the bit sequence is passed into the bit-stream formatting module and packets are made to be transmitted to a remote server. However, most of the communication channels suffer from bit errors or packet losses, which results in performance degradation of speech recognition. In the DSR standard, cyclic redundancy checksum (CRC) is used as a channel coder in the error protection and mitigation module. At the server, channel errors are corrected by CRC codes from the transmitted bit-stream and feature parameters are decoded. Finally, a speech decoding process is done to recognize what a user located at the client has said.

In this paper, we aim at improving the transmission bandwidth for DSR while maintaining the performance of speech recognition. In other words, we propose an efficient vector quantizer in the feature compression module so that the proposed quantizer can compress feature parameters with a lower bit rate than that used in the standard.

Following this introduction, we review what kinds of processing should be done at the client for the distribution of speech recognition algorithms in

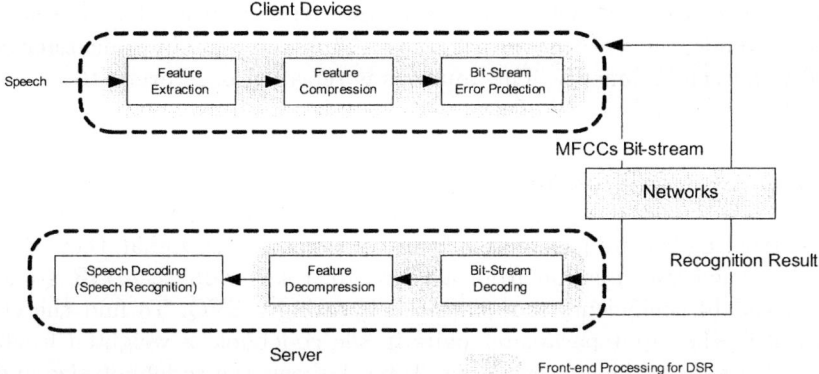

Fig. 2. Distributed structure of the front-end for a DSR system

Section 2. In Section 3, an efficient feature quantization scheme, so-called safety-net predictive VQ (PVQ), is proposed. After that, we evaluate the performance of speech recognition when the proposed quantizer is used for DSR in Section 4. Especially, we compare the performance of speech recognition by varying the bit-rate of safety-net PVQ, and discuss a trade-off between the bit rate and the performance of speech recognition. Finally we summarize our contributions in Section 5.

2 Client Processing in the DSR Standard

In this section, we will describe which processing is performed at the client for DSR. There are feature extraction, feature compression, and framing erasure and error protection processing. For more detailed description, refer to the ETSI standard document [3].

2.1 Feature Extraction

This module is to extract feature parameters for speech recognition. As feature parameters, mel-frequency cepstral coefficients (MFCCs) and a logarithmic energy are widely used. In order to obtain them, speech signals are first sampled by using a A/D converter whose sampling frequency is one of the three sampling frequencies such as 8, 11, and 16 kHz. Next, the feature extraction module applies a notch filter to remove a DC bias from the input speech, and then divides the signal into a segment of 25 msec long. Typically, a logarithmic energy over the speech segment is calculated. Simultaneously, the speech segment is pre-emphasized by using a first-order zero filter. And then, a Hamming window of length 25 msec is applied to the pre-emphasized signal. Next, the magnitude of the windowed signal is calculated by applying a 256-point fast Fourier transform (FFT) for 8 kHz and 11 kHz or a 512-point FFT for 16 kHz. Mel-scaled log spectrum is computed after applying 23 mel-filter banks to the magnitude spectrum. Finally, 13 MFCCs $\{c_0,\cdots,c_{12}\}$ are extracted from the mel-scaled log spectrum. Thus, the feature vector becomes 14 dimensional by concatenating 13 MFCCs and the log energy. This analysis is repeated once every 10 ms, which results in a frame rate of 100 Hz.

2.2 Feature Compression

After extracting feature parameters from the input speech signal, they are compressed for the transmission from a client to a server in the DSR standard. Pairs of the 14 coefficients are quantized by using a SVQ. To find the closest codeword to the input parameter pairs in the codebook, a weighted Euclidian distance is used for the VQ encoding. Table 1 shows the codebook size and the weighting matrix for the feature pairings, where I is a 2×2 identity matrix, $W = \begin{bmatrix} 1446.0 & 0 \\ 0 & 14.7 \end{bmatrix}$ for 8 kHz or 11 kHz sampling rate, and $W = \begin{bmatrix} 1248.9 & 0 \\ 0 & 12.7 \end{bmatrix}$ for 16 kHz sampling rate.

As shown in the table, a feature vector that consists of 13 MFCCs and a log energy denoted by logE is split into 6 subvectors. Each subvector is quantized with a corresponding subvector codebook. The number of bits for each subvector codebook is 6 except for the last one. As a result, 44 bits once every frame are required to quantize feature parameters, which corresponds to a bit rate of 4.4 kbits/s because we extract 100 feature vectors per second.

Table 1. Split vector quantization codebook size for the feature pairings

Pairings	Codebook Size (bits)	Weight
(c_1, c_2)	6	I
(c_3, c_4)	6	I
(c_5, c_6)	6	I
(c_7, c_8)	6	I
(c_9, c_{10})	6	I
(c_{11}, c_{12})	6	I
(c_0, logE)	8	W

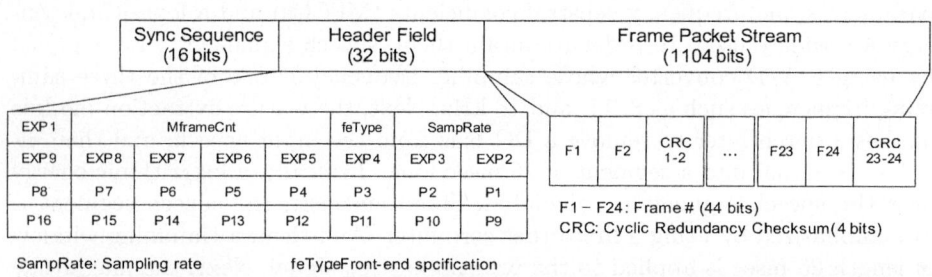

Fig. 3. Multiframe bit-stream format

2.3 Bit-Stream Formatting and Error Protection

In this subsection, we describe how to make a bit-stream to transfer the features with an error protection. Basically, a multiframe format is used for the quantized bits over 24 frames, where the multiframe format includes a synchronization sequence field, a header field, and a frame packet stream field as shown in Fig. 3. The synchronization sequence field of a 16-bit length is placed in the beginning of each multiframe bit-stream. The header field is composed of sampling rate (2 bits), front-end specification (1 bit), multiframe counter (4 bits), undefined 9 bits for future expansion, and cyclic code parity bits (16 bits). The frame packet stream field contains 1104 bits that are from 24 feature vectors and twelve 4-bit CRCs.

2.4 Bit-Stream Decoding and Error Detection

In the server, the transmitted, bit-stream decoded indices from the frame packet stream are used to lookup the estimates of the front-end features. In the DSR standard, errors of the bit-stream transmitted are detected by two methods: CRC and data consistency. If the CRC computed from the transmitted bit-stream does not match the received CRC, it is declared that the frame has bit errors and a processing for the error concealment is performed. On the other hand, the data consistency check is applied if the CRC test is failed. The detail algorithm of the data consistency check is referred to as described in [3].

3 Proposed Vector Quantization

In general, the performance of a speech recognition system is compared by measuring word accuracy or word error rate. In addition to the measurement, the transmission bandwidth should be taken into account for a DSR system, which related to how many users can be serviced with a single speech recognition server. Here, we refer to the bandwidth as the number of bits per frame for feature parameters or a bit-rate in bits/s. As described in the previous section, a feature vector extracted from each frame is compressed with 44 bits/frame. Thus, in this work we propose a quantization scheme with a lower rate than 44 bits/frame, while maintaining word error rate.

The proposed quantization scheme is based on the interframe correlation of MFCCs and a safety-net structure [6]. First of all, we investigated the degree of the correlation of MFCCs in order to verify the use of PVQ. For this end, we measured the interframe correlations from 3,200 frames collected from the utterances spoken by 2 males and 2 females. The correlation, $CR(i, k)$, is defined by $CR(i,k) = (\sum_{n=0}^{N-1-k} c_{i,n} c_{i,n+k})/(\sqrt{\sum_{n=0}^{N-1-k} c_{i,n}^2} \sqrt{\sum_{n=0}^{N-1-k} c_{i,n+k}^2})$, where i is the quefrency index, k is the interval of frames, N is the total number of frames, and $c_{i,n}$ is the ith MFCC of the nth frame. Figure 4 shows interframe correlations of each MFCC according to different number of interests. From this measurement, we found out that each MFCC of a frame was highly correlated with that of the past one frame. Especially, among all the MFCCs, c_0 has the largest correlation which was larger than 0.95. So, we divided MFCCs into two

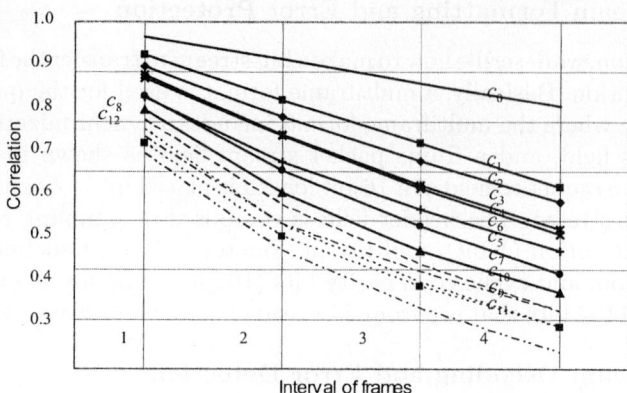

Fig. 4. Interframe correlations of MFCCs

subvectors to increase the prediction performance of PVQ: a 1-dimensional vector, $\mathbf{C}_1 = [c_0]$, and a 12-dimensional vector, $\mathbf{C}_2 = [c_1 \; c_2 \cdots c_{12}]^T$.

Next, we consider how to improve the performance of speech recognition by mitigating the error propagation due to the frame erasure by unreliable communication channels. Thus, we finally propose a safety-net PVQ by combining the PVQ described above with a memoryless VQ to remove the weakness of a PVQ due to the error propagation. For each frame a full search of both the predictive VQ and the memoryless VQ is performed. The best candidate, with respect to a distortion criterion, is encoded and transmitted. In addtion, the safety-net PVQ provides better robustness even when interframe correlation is low. That is, the predictive VQ and the memoryless VQ are performed to focus on highly correlated vectors and lowly correlated vectors, respectively. Figure 5 shows the proposed safety-net PVQ structure [1]. An input MFCC vector of the nth frame is split into 2 subvectors as

$$\mathbf{C}[n] = \begin{bmatrix} \mathbf{C}_1 \\ \hline \mathbf{C}_2 \end{bmatrix} = \begin{bmatrix} c_0 \\ \hline c_1 \\ \vdots \\ c_{12} \end{bmatrix}. \tag{1}$$

Then, each subvector is quantized by its corresponding safety-net PVQ, where a selector determines one of either PVQ or the memoryless VQ depending on the Euclidean distance measure. In PVQ, prediction is based on a past one quantized MFCC vector such as

---

[1] In the standard DSR, logE is quantized with c_0. However, we only quantize c_0 in this work because the DSR system using the proposed VQ is recognized with 13 MFCCs, excluding logE. Thus, to be a fair comparison of bit rate, the proposed quantizer should be compared with 42 bits/frame instead of 44 bits/frame.

$$\mathbf{C}_{ip}[n] = \alpha_i \hat{\mathbf{C}}_i[n-1], \tag{2}$$

where α_i is the prediction coefficient of the past one frame of the ith subvector in (1). Especially, we construct the memoryless VQ and PVQ for $\mathbf{C}_2$ with a multi-stage VQ because the multi-stage VQ is generally known to be efficient in search and training of VQ for high dimensional vectors [7]. Finally, we need to assign the number of bits to five quantization indices (i_1-i_5).

For i_1 and i_2, one bit is assigned to each index because they are used to select the memoryless VQ or PVQ as shown Fig. 5. In order to assign the number of bits to i_3, i_4 and i_5, we divided speech database into two parts. The first one, which consisted of 172,800 American, English and Korean frames, was used for training the safety-net VQ and the rest, which consisted of 48,400 frames, was used for the evaluation of the VQ. Actually, the number of bits for PVQ is closely related to the value of α_i. Therefore, we first select an optimal α_i and then assign the proper number of bits to each index when PVQ works with the selected optimal α_i.

As a criterion of selecting α_i, we used the following Euclidean distance measure.

$$D\left(\mathbf{C}, \hat{\mathbf{C}}\right) = \frac{1}{N} \sum_{n=0}^{N-1} \sqrt{\sum_{i=0}^{K-1} (c_{i,n} - \hat{c}_{i,n})^2}, \tag{3}$$

where K is the number of subvector components, N is the total number of frames, and $c_{i,n}$ and $\hat{c}_{i,n}$ are the ith components of unquantized and quantized subvectors of the nth frame, respectively. K was set to 1 and 12 for $\mathbf{C}_1$ and $\mathbf{C}_2$,

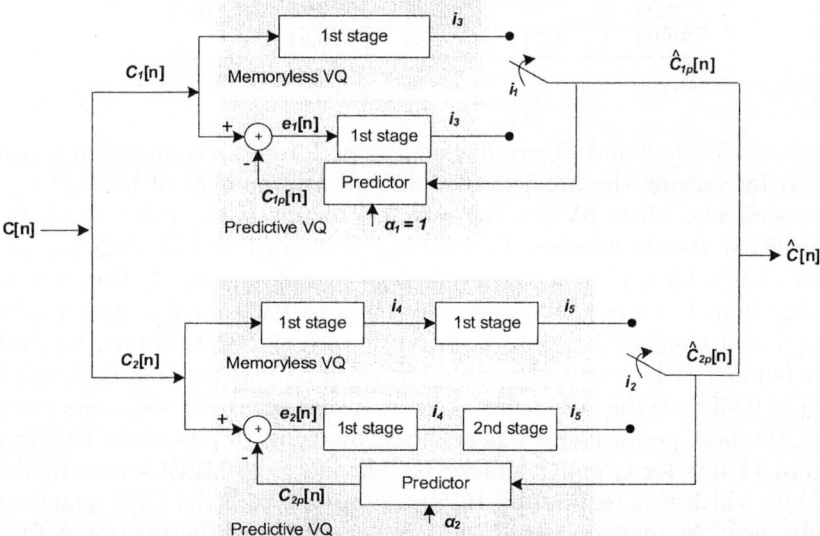

Fig. 5. Safety-net PVQ combining a predictive VQ with a memoryless VQ

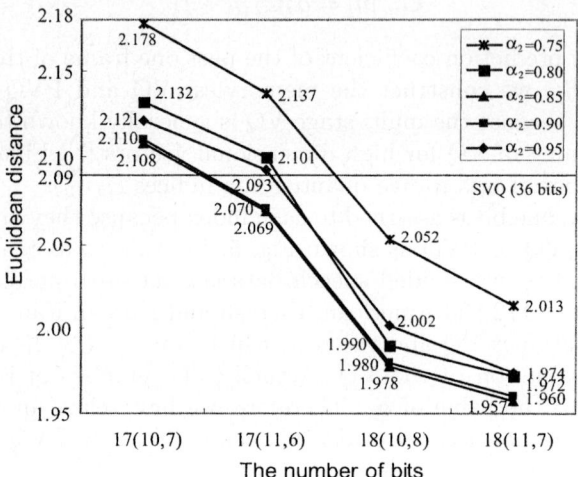

Fig. 6. Performance comparison by varying the prediction coefficient and the number of bits for C_2, where (a,b) in the x-axis represents the number of bits assigned for the first and second stage, respectively

Table 2. Performance comparison by varying the prediction coefficient and the number of bits for C_1

α_1	Safety-net PVQ			SVQ
	4 bits	5 bits	6 bits	8 bits
1	0.72	0.36	0.18	
0.95	1.18	0.71	0.42	0.41
0.90	1.54	0.88	0.51	

respectively. Table 2 and Figure 6 show the performance comparison measured from (3) by varying the prediction coefficient and number of bits for C_1 and C_2, respectively, where SVQ is the scheme of split vector quantization that is used in ETSI standardization. Comparing to the distance of SVQ, the proper number of bits for C_1 should be set to 5 or more when $\alpha_1=1$. However, when α_1 is less than 1, we need to assign more bits to PVQ for C_1. As a result, we set $\alpha_1=1$ and assigned 5 bits to i_3 for a bit rate of 25 bits/frame. Similarly, a proper number of bits for C_2 becomes 18 when α_2 was between 0.75 and 0.95, and $\alpha_2 = 0.85$ gave the best result. Moreover, exhaustive experiments provided us that the best performance was achieved by using 18 bits when 18 bits were split into 11 bits for i_4 and 7 bits for i_5. Therefore, 13 MFCCs were quantized by 25 bits which was reduced by 19 bits compared with the SVQ quantizer. In a similar way, we increased the total number of bits of the safety-net PVQ to 30 bits, 35 bits and 40 bits per frame while $\alpha_1=1$ and $\alpha_2=0.85$. Table 4.1 shows the specific bit allocation of i_3, i_4 and i_5 for the four bit rates.

Table 3. Bit allocation for the proposed safety-net PVQ

Index	Function	Number of bits			
i_1	Prediction selector for C_1	1	1	1	1
i_2	Prediction selector for C_2	1	1	1	1
i_3	VQ index for C_1	5	6	8	11
i_4	First stage VQ index for C_2	11	12	13	14
i_5	Second stage VQ index for C_2	7	10	12	13
	Total	25	30	35	40

4 Speech Recognition Experiments

4.1 Speech Recognition Task

In order to evaluate the performance of the DSR system employing the proposed quantization scheme, we constructed a large vocabulary continuous speech recognition (LVCSR) system. Actually ETSI had developed a database for LVCSR and named it the AURORA 4 database [8].

The database was derived from the Wall Street Journal 5000-word closed-loop task and divided into training and test sets. There were two different sets according to the noise condition for training acoustic models, which were clean-condition training set and multi-condition training set recorded at sampling rates of 8 kHz and 16 kHz. In our experiments, the 8 kHz-multi-condition training set was used. The training set was constructed by adding six different noises (cars, babble, street traffic, train station, restaurants, and airport) to the 7138 utterances recorded by the Sennheiser close talking microphone and several far talking microphones. In the AURORA 4 database, fourteen test sets were defined in order to evaluate the speech recognition performance under the different microphone conditions and noisy environments. Among the fourteen test sets, we selected seven test sets, where each set was composed of 330 utterances recorded by the Sennheiser close talking microphone at a rate of 8 kHz under the clean and the six noisy conditions.

4.2 Speech Recognition System

As mentioned in Section 2.1, 13 MFCCs were used for speech recognition feature parameters. In addition to the energy normalization for c_0, we applied cepstral mean normalization for the remaining 12 MFCCs. Finally, the feature vector becomes 39 dimensional by concatenating delta and delta-delta coefficients to $(c_0, \cdots, c_{12})$.

We used HTK [9] for training and testing. Pruning was applied to speed up training. The lexicon of the word was extracted from the publicly available CMU version 0.6 dictionary [10]. Each pronunciation of the word was placed with both long and short interword silences in the lexicon of the recognition system. Acoustic models of the recognition system were based on the context-dependent, 4-mixture, cross-word triphone models. All combinable triphone models were expanded from the 41 monophone models which included long and short interword silence models, and the mixtures of triphone models were tied by employing the decision tree. The bigram language model for a 5000-word closed vocabulary [11] was used with standard backoff probabilities for smoothing. The language model factor was set to 18 and the word insertion penalty was set to -5 in decoding phase.

4.3 Bandwidth vs Recognition Performance

In order to evaluate the effect of the proposed quantizer on the performance of a DSR system, we compared the performance of the systems such as 1) the baseline system that uses unquantized MFCCs, 2) the standard DSR system recommended by ETSI ,where MFCCs are quantized by SVQ, 3) the DSR systems using MFCCs quantized by the proposed safety-net PVQ operating at four different number of bits/frame from 25 bits/frame to 40 bits/frame with a step of 5 bits/frame. The performance of the DSR systems was measured by the word error rate (WER) averaged over all the test conditions.

Table 4 shows the average WER of each system for seven different test conditions. The baseline system gave the lowest WER because the feature parameters used for the baseline system were not quantized. Compared with the standard DSR system, the performance of the DSR system using the safety-net PVQ was degraded when the number of bits for the quantizer was 25 bits/frame or 30 bits/frame. However, the WER was lowered by increasing the number of bits to 35 bits/frame or 40 bits/frame. From the table, it could be stated that the proposed safety-net PVQ could reduce the number of bits per frame by 9 bits while the performance of the DSR system using the proposed quantizer was comparable to that of the standard DSR system.

Table 4. Word error rate (%) of different ASR configurations on the task of the AURORA 4 database under multi-condition training

ASR System	Baseline	Std. DSR	DSR used safety-net PVQ			
Test Cond. | Bits (bits/frame)	Unquantized	44	25	30	35	40
Clean	18.21	18.92	19.39	19.30	19.04	18.23
Car	20.34	20.81	22.98	22.60	22.06	22.10
Babble	29.63	30.79	30.97	30.23	29.39	29.70
Restaurant	31.70	33.22	33.03	33.18	32.39	32.26
Street	32.51	32.71	34.19	33.64	31.68	32.47
Airport	28.21	28.73	29.93	28.13	28.53	27.72
Train station	32.84	33.79	35.36	33.16	33.53	32.93
Average	27.63	28.42	29.41	28.61	28.09	27.92

5 Conclusion

In this paper, we have proposed an efficient vector quantizer (VQ) to compress feature parameters with less number of bits than the DSR standard. In contrast with split VQ (SVQ) used in the DSR standard, the proposed quantizer was based on a predictive VQ with multiple stages by utilizing the high correlation of MFCCs over the successive analysis frames. In addition, a safety-net structure was combined into the multi-stage predictive VQ to make the quantizer robust to the channel errors. It was shown from the recognition experiments that the DSR system employing the proposed VQ could reduce relatively the number of bits/frame by 20% compared with the standard DSR system.

The DSR system, employing the proposed VQ, has advantages over the standard DSR system. We can provide a voice-enabled service to more users because the DSR system using the proposed VQ can be implemented with a lower bit rate than standard DSR system. Second, instead of increasing the number of users, we can improve the performance of speech recognition under a noisy channel condition by allocating the remaining bits to the channel coder.

Acknowledgment

This research was partially supported by the University Fundamental Research Program of the Ministry of Information and Communication, Republic of Korea and by University IT Research Center Project.

References

1. Viikki, O.: ASR in portable wireless devices. Proc. IEEE Workshop on Automatic Speech Recognition and Understanding, Tranto, Italy (2001) 96-102.
2. Kim, H. K., Cox, R. V. : A bitstream-based front-end for wireless speech recognition on IS-136 communications system. IEEE Speech Audio Process, Vol. 9, No. 5, (2001) 558-568.
3. ETSI ES 201 108 v1.1.3, Speech Processing, Transmission and Quality aspects (STQ); Distributed speech recognition; Front-end feature extraction algorithm; Compression algorithms, ETSI, (2003).
4. Yifang, X., et al.: Roubust recongition of noisy speech using speech enhancement. Proc. IEEE International Conference on Signal Processing, Beijing, China, (2000) 734-737.
5. Zhigang, C., Wentao, Z.: Speech enhancement based on minimum mean-square error short-time spectral estiamtion and its realization. Proc. IEEE International Conference on Intelligent Systems, Vol. 2, (1997) 1794-1797.
6. Zhu, Q., Alwan, A.: An efficient and scalable 2-D DCT-based feature coding scheme for remote speech recognition. Proc. IEEE International Conference on Acoustics, Speech, and Signal Processing, Salt Lake City, UT (2001) 7-11.
7. Juang, B. H., Gray, A. H.: Interframe LSF quantization for noisy channels. Proc. IEEE International Conference on Acoustics, Speech, and Signal Processing, Paris, France (1982) 597-600.
8. Hirsch, G.: Experimental framework for the performance evaluation of speech recogntion front-ends on a large vocabulary task. ETSI STQ Aurora DSR Working Gruop (2002).

9. Young, S., et al.: The HTK Book (for HTK Version 3.2). Microsoft Corporation, Cambridge University Enginnering Department (2002).
10. The CMU Pronouncing Dictionary. http://www.speech.cs.cmu.edu/cgi-bin/cmudict, Speech at Carnegie Mellon University, Carnegie Mellon University, PA, (2001).
11. Paul, D., Necioglu, B.: The Lincoln large-vocabulary stack-decoder HMM CSR. Proc. IEEE International Conference on Acoustics, Speech, and Signal Processing, Minneapolis, MN (1993) 660-663.

Magnitude-Sign Split Quantization for Bandwidth Scalable Wideband Speech Codec

Ji-Hyuk You, Chul-Man Park, Jung-Il Lee, Chang-Beom Ahn,
Seoung-Jun Oh, and Hochong Park

VIA-Multimedia Center, Kwangwoon University,
447-1 Wolgye-Dong, Nowon-Gu, 139-701, Seoul, Korea
hcpark@mail.kw.ac.kr, via-staff@viame.re.kr
http://www.viame.re.kr

Abstract. New quantization method based on magnitude-sign split scheme for bandwidth scalable wideband speech codec is proposed. In the high-band codec, the signal is band-pass filtered and each band is transformed independently into DCT domain. The DCT coefficients are split into magnitude and sign, and each is quantized separately based on its unique characteristics. In addition, the quantized gain parameter in the low-band codec is utilized in the high-band codec for an enhanced performance. The 19.8kbps bandwidth scalable wideband codec consisting of G.729E for low-band and the proposed codec for high-band is developed, and it is confirmed that the proposed codec has better subjective performance than 24kbps G.722.1.

1 Introduction

Voice quality is a decisive factor in high-quality digital speech communications. One strategy for enhancing the voice quality is to expand the bandwidth of transmitted speech, which requires a higher sampling rate and the development of new wideband speech codec [1]. In addition, digital speech communications usually use the packet-based networks whose channel capacity is varying over time, and the transmission of voice packet with fixed length is not suitable for these networks. To solve this inefficiency in the packed-based speech communications, the voice packet is divided into several independent layers and those layers are selectively transmitted depending on the given channel capacity. The codecs which enable the layered packet structure are called *scalable codecs*, and can provide the optimal performance by means of channel-adaptive transmission of layers [2]. The wideband speech codec to be designed, therefore, has to have the scalable structure for maximum enhancement of quality compared with the conventional narrow-band communications.

One of the layer structures is to assign the frequency band to each layer and to control the bandwidth of transmitted signal based on the channel capacity. For example, in two-layered 7kHz wideband codec with one layer corresponding to the low-band and the other to the high-band, the wideband speech communication with 7kHz bandwidth is serviced in a normal condition, and when the channel capacity is reduced, only the low-band layer is transmitted, thereby providing the narrow-band speech communications without the high-band layer.

Many researches on bandwidth scalable wideband speech codecs have been reported [2, 3, 4]. In general, the wideband signal is divided into low-band signal and high-band signal with 4kHz boundary, and the low-band signal is processed by standard narrow-band speech codecs such as G.729 to maintain the compatibility with the current narrow-band communications with 4kHz bandwidth. The high-band signal is usually processed based on a transform coding, and the spectral coefficients are quantized utilizing their characteristics.

In this paper, new quantization scheme for bandwidth scalable wideband speech codec is developed, which consists of split quantization of spectral magnitude and sign, selective quantization of spectral sign with a small number of bits, and the usage of low-band information in high-band codec for better quantization efficiency. The overall codec structure assumes G.729, G.729E and G.723.1 as the low-band codec for compatibility. Finally, the subjective performance of the proposed codec is measured and compared with the standard wideband speech codec.

2 Structure of Proposed Codec

The specification of the proposed bandwidth scalable wideband speech codec is summarized in Table 1. The frame size is designed to be 30msec in order to use G.723.1 as well as G.729 and G.729E as the low-band codec. If G.729 or G.729E is used in the low-band, 3 frames of 10msec are processed as in one basic frame. The look-ahead is 5msec as in G.729.

Overall structure of the proposed codec is depicted in Figure 1. Wideband input speech is first converted into narrow-band speech by low-pass filtering and down-sampling, which is then encoded by the standard narrow-band codec such as G.729, G.729E and G.723.1. The high-band codec extracts high-band information directly from the wideband input and encodes the high-band information using the proposed high-band codec, where the low-band parameters are utilized for better performance.

Table 1. Specification of the proposed speech codec

Sampling Rate		16 kHz
High-Band Bit Rate		8 kbps
Overall Bit Rate	with G.729	16kbps
	with G.729E	19.8kbps
	with G.723.1	13.3/14.4kbps
Frame Size		30 msec
Two Low-Pass Filtering Delay		3 msec
Look-Ahead		5 msec

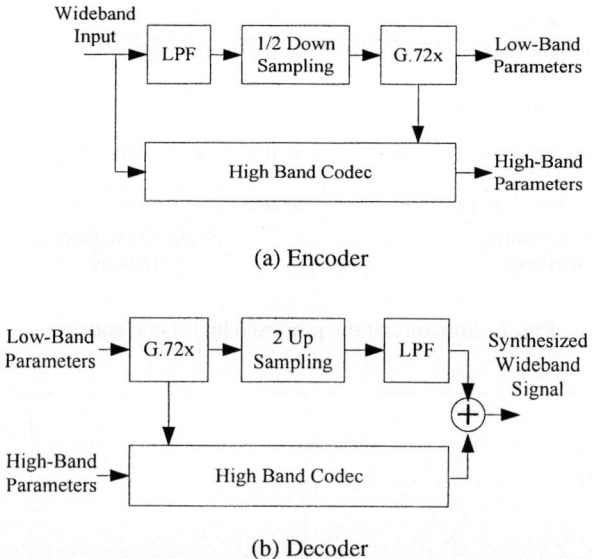

Fig. 1. Overall structure of the proposed bandwidth scalable wideband speech codec. (a) Encoder; (b) Decoder.

3 Proposed High-Band Codec

3.1 Overall Structure

When designing the high-band codec, the constraint of scalable codec needs to be considered; the transmission of high-band packet to decoder is dependent on the time-varying channel capacity, which enforces that the high-band codec be operated independently for each frame and cannot use the inter-frame operations such as frame prediction.

The wideband input is split into spectral bands using auditory filter bank and quantized in the frequency domain as depicted in Figure 2. First, the input is divided into 4 critical bands using Gammatone filter which has an impulse response $g(t)$ [5, 6],

$$g(t) = at^{N-1} e^{-2\pi b B(f_c)} \cos(2\pi f_c t + \phi)$$

where f_c is the center frequency, $B(f_c)$ is the bandwidth, and N, a, b, ϕ are filter parameters. The frequency response of Gammatone filter is depicted in Figure 3. Only four upper bands in Figure 3 are used in the proposed codec, whose center frequency and bandwidth are given in Table 2.

The Gammatone filter is implemented in IIR structure in encoder to reduce the processing delay, and in FIR structure in decoder to eliminate the error propagation. The order of filter is decided such that total filtering delay in both encoder and decoder does not exceed the look-ahead delay of 5msec.

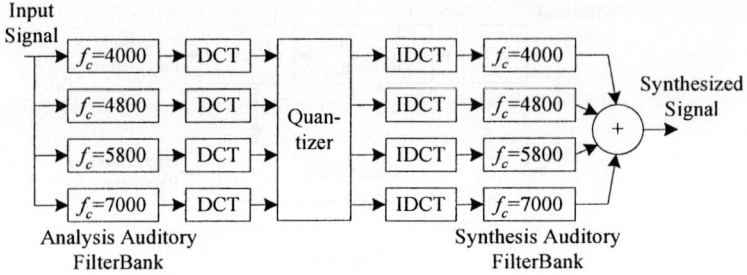

Fig. 2. Structure of the proposed high-band codec

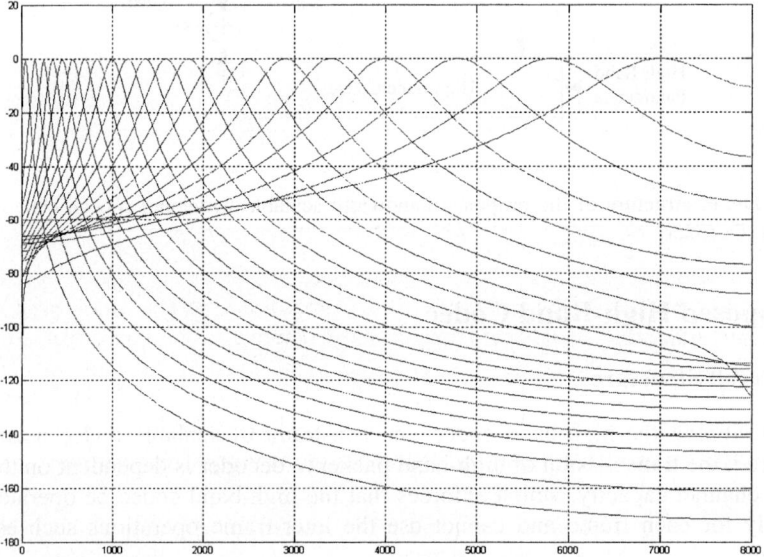

Fig. 3. Frequency response of Gammatone filter

Next, each band-passed signal is transformed into the frequency domain by DCT. In other words, for each 30msec-frame, the 480-sample output of each Gammatone filter is applied to 480-point DCT without down-sampling, resulting in 480 DCT coefficients. Since DCT is applied to the band-passed signal, only those coefficients inside the corresponding band are quantized and transmitted. The index of coefficients for each band is given in Table 3. Windowing is not applied to the signalwhen computing DCT, and the distortion by this effect is eliminated in the synthesis stage by overlapping operation in FIR filtering. Finally, high-performance quantizer for 206 DCT coefficients is designed, which completes the development of new high-band codec.

Table 2. Band center frequency and bandwidth of Gammatone filter

	Center Frequency(Hz)	Bandwidth(Hz)
Band 0	4000	457
Band 1	4800	543
Band 2	5800	651
Band 3	7000	780

Table 3. DCT index of each frequency band(DCT size is 480)

	First Index	Last Index	# of Coeff.
Band 0	220	263	44
Band 1	264	317	54
Band 2	318	383	66
Band 3	384	425	42
Sum			206

3.2 Magnitude and Sign of DCT Coefficient

For an efficient quantization of DCT coefficients, it is necessary to take advantage of its correlation property. Table 4 shows the correlation coefficients of adjacent DCT coefficients and those of adjacent magnitudes, where Korean speech of 10 minutes from NTT database is used. It is evident that there exists no useful correlation between DCT coefficients, while relatively high correlation between DCT coefficient magnitudes exists. This analysis, therefore, leads to an idea of new split quantizer which splits the DCT coefficient into its magnitude and sign, and quantizes each element separately based on its unique characteristics.

Table 4. Correlation between index k and $k+1$ of DCT coefficients and DCT coefficient magnitudes

	DCT coefficient	DCT coeff. magnitude
Band 0	0.0047	0.5901
Band 1	0.0018	0.6162
Band 2	0.0056	0.6492
Band 3	0.0001	0.6469

3.3 Quantization of DCT Coefficient Magnitude

In order to achieve an efficient quantization by utilizing the high correlation of DCT magnitudes, those of each band are transformed again by DCT. DCT coefficients after this stage are called the *second-stage DCT coefficients* and denoted by $dct[n][k]$ for band n. For example, in band 0, 44 DCT coefficient magnitudes are transformed by 44-point DCT, resulting in the 44 second-stage DCT coefficients. The structure of quantizer based on this concept including sign quantization module is depicted in Figure 4.

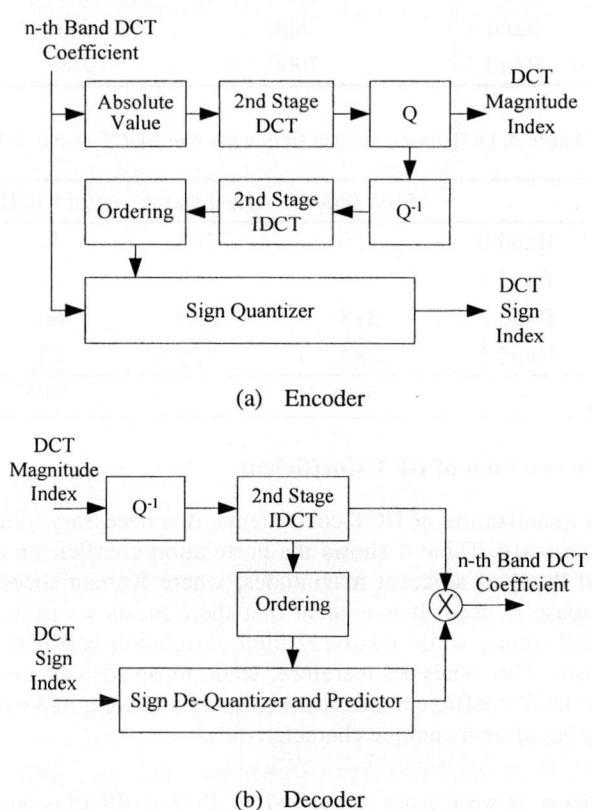

Fig. 4. Structure of DCT coefficients quantizer

Due to the high correlation of DCT magnitudes, the energy of second-stage DCT coefficients will be concentrated in the lower index region; note that the energy was evenly distributed before the second-stage DCT. For example, Figure 5 is the energy of the second-stage DCT coefficients of band 0, which clearly shows that the most of energy is concentrated in the lower index region.

Table 5 shows the experimental results of energy compaction by the second-stage DCT; more than 80% of the energy is concentrated in $dct[n][0] \sim dct[n][10]$, and more than 90% in $dct[n][0] \sim dct[n][30]$ for all bands. In addition to the numerical results, perceptual transparency of the speech, which is reconstructed only with $dct[n][0] \sim dct[n][30]$, is also confirmed by the extensive hearing tests.

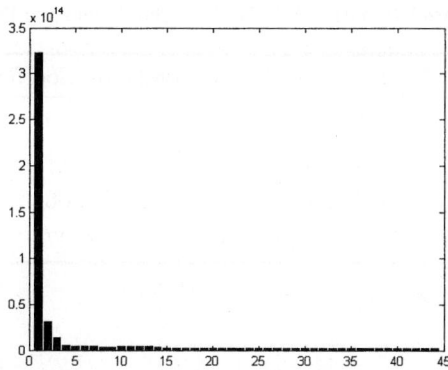

Fig. 5. Energy of the second-stage DCT coefficients in band 0

Table 5. Energy distribution after the second-stage DCT

	2nd DCT Size	$dct[n][0]\sim dct[n][10]$	$dct[n][0]\sim dct[n][20]$	$dct[n][0]\sim dct[n][30]$
Band 0	44	82.23 %	88.58 %	93.83 %
Band 1	54	81.68 %	87.02 %	91.29 %
Band 2	66	82.91 %	87.29 %	90.83 %
Band 3	42	84.96 %	90.56 %	95.32 %

Based on these numerical analyses and subjective tests, new spectral coefficients quantizer is designed which quantizes only $dct[n][0]\sim dct[n][30]$ and removes the rest of the second-stage DCT coefficients. The DC value, $dct[n][0]$, is scalar quantized for each band because its value is very large compared with others, $dct[n][1]\sim dct[n][30]$. Furthermore, DC values are predictive quantized along the bands because of high correlation between adjacent bands. For example, a quantized fixed codebook gain of G.729 or G.723.1 in the low-band has high correlation with DC value of band 0, because the fixed codebook gain represents the overall energy of the low-band signal. Therefore, the DC value of band 0 is predicted from the quantized fixed codebook gain of low-band codec which is always transmitted as the basic layer, and the prediction error is scalar quantized after μ-law companding. Similarly, DC values between bands in the high-band also have high correlation, and DC of one band is predictive scalar quantized from the previous band. The AR-model predictor with order of one is used in all bands. Table 6 shows the correlation coefficient of DC values between bands, which confirms the feasibility of predictive quantizer for DC value. In addition, all bands have very similar values in correlation, which allows a single quantizer for all bands. Finally, Figure 6 shows the distribution of prediction error of band 0, based on which a symmetric quantizer is used.

Table 6. Correlation of G.729 fixed codebook gain and DC of each band

	Correlation Coefficient
CB Gain : DC[0]	0.8239
DC[0] : DC[1]	0.8311
DC[1] : DC[2]	0.8506
DC[2] : DC[3]	0.8327

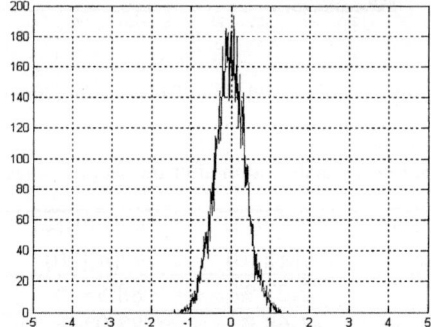

Fig. 6. Distribution of DC prediction error in band 0

The rest of the second-stage DCT coefficients, $dct[n][1] \sim dct[n][30]$, is vector quantized after RMS-normalization. Since the correlation between DC and RMS value within a band is very high as shown in Table 7 and Figure 7, the RMS value is predicted from the quantized DC value of the corresponding band and the error is scalar quantized after companding in a similar way to DC quantizer.

The resulting 30 normalized coefficients are split into 3 subvectors of 10 dimensions and each 10-dimensional subvector is vector quantized with 9 bits each. There exist 4 bands and 3 subvectors for each band, $dct[n][1] \sim dct[n][10]$, $dct[n][11] \sim dct[n][20]$, $dct[n][21] \sim dct[n][30]$, and $4 \times 3 \times 9 = 108$ bits in total are required for quantization. Based on the importance measure of each band, however, the number of bits is reduced without noticeable perceptual degradation as follows. In two most important bands, all 3 subvectors are quantized and transmitted using $6 \times 9 = 54$ bits; in the third important band, only two lower subvectors, $dct[n][1] \sim dct[n][10]$ and $dct[n][11] \sim dct[n][20]$, are quantized and transmitted using $2 \times 9 = 18$ bits, and in the least important band, only one subvector, $dct[n][1] \sim dct[n][10]$, is quantized and transmitted using 9 bits. In this selective quantization, only 9 subvectors are quantized and $9 \times 9 = 81$ bits in total are required. The degree of importance of each band is measured simply by the band energy, and 4 bits are used to transmit the ranking information of band.

Table 7. Correlation between DC and RMS of each band

	Correlation Coefficient
DC[0] : RMS[0]	0.9912
DC[1] : RMS[1]	0.9911
DC[2] : RMS[2]	0.9869
DC[3] : RMS[3]	0.9909

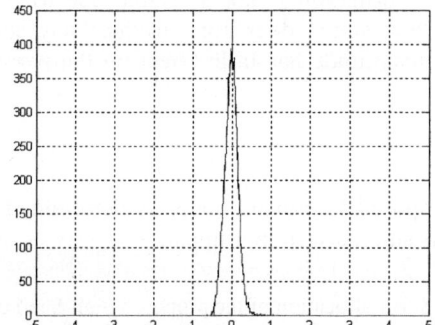

Fig. 7. Distribution of RMS prediction error in band 0

3.4 Quantization of DCT Coefficient Sign

Since the sign of DCT coefficient has almost random distribution, no structured quantization scheme is possible and the sign quantization requires 1 bit per sign, resulting in 206 bits for sign quantization only, which is too large for allowed 240 bits of 8kbps target bits rate. However, inverse DCT can be considered as a linear combination of sinusoidal signals, where the sign of each coefficient corresponds to the binary phase of each frequency component. It is well known that the phase of frequency component has little effect to the perceptual quality of resulting speech. Furthermore, the sign of smaller coefficient has relatively less contribution to the speech reconstruction and can be chosen randomly without any noticeable perceptual degradation, which has been confirmed by the perceptual listening tests after eliminating the signs of small coefficients.

Therefore, new quantization method for sign information is proposed which chooses the signs to be quantized adaptively based on the coefficient magnitude. More specifically, 206 DCT coefficients in 30msec frame are sorted in a descending order of magnitude, and 115 signs corresponding to the coefficients of large magnitude are quantized with 1 bit per sign. The 91 remaining signs are not transmitted and its value is predicted in the decoder. In sign quantization, therefore, no information related to the frequency value is used, and the magnitude of each spectral coefficient is the only decisive factor.

In this way, the sign information can be transmitted to the decoder very efficiently with only 115 bits. Since the decoder has to know the same magnitude ordering as in the encoder for proper operation, the sorting is based on the magnitude of the quantized DCT coefficients which are available before the sign quantization as shown in Figure 4.

To preserve the frame continuity, those signs not transmitted to the decoder are predicted subject to the minimal discontinuity for each frequency component. In other words, the sign of each DCT coefficient is selected such that the last sample of the corresponding frequency component in the previous frame is connected most smoothly to the first sample of that component in the current frame. Since a set of those frequency components whose signs are not transmitted is changed every frame, the prediction error is not accumulated at certain components.

If the previous sign information is not available due to packet loss, all missing signs are randomly chosen, which does not introduce any additional distortion because the sign of small magnitude has little effect on the perceptual quality as mentioned above.

3.5 Bit Allocation

Bit allocation of the proposed high-band codec is determined after various analysis and listening tests, and is summarized in Table 8.

Table 8. Bit allocation of the proposed high-band codec

		Band 0	Band 1	Band 2	Band 3	Sum
DCT Magnitude	DC	6	6	6	6	24
	RMS	4	4	4	4	16
	VQ		9 × 9			81
	Classification		4			4
DCT Sign			115			115
Total Sum						240

4 Performance Analysis

The subjective performance of the proposed bandwidth scalable wideband speech codec was measured by an informal preference test. The low-band is encoded by 11.8kbps G.729E and the high-band is encoded by the proposed 8kbps high-band codec, resulting in a 19.8kbps bandwidth scalable codec. 20 Korean speech sentences in total by 5 male speakers and 5 female speakers are used, and 24kbps G.722.1 wideband codec is used as a reference codec [7]. As in Table 9, the preference test results show that the proposed scalable codec has much better subjective performance than 24kbps G.722.1.

Table 9. Preference test results of the proposed codec

	Proposed	No Preference	G.722.1
Male Speech	70.0%	27.5%	2.5%
Female Speech	55.0%	40.0%	5.0%

5 Conclusions

In this paper, new bandwidth scalable wideband speech codec with a magnitude-sign split quantization was developed. The low-band signal is encoded with the standard codec for compatibility. The high-band signal is band-passed and each band is transformed into DCT domain and quantized by magnitude-sign split scheme. Then, the magnitudes are transformed again by DCT to achieve an efficient quantization. The sign is quantization based on the ordering information, and only a subset of signs is transmitted. The subjective performance of the proposed 19.8kbps scalable codec was confirmed to be better than that of 24kbps G.722.1 wideband codec.

The proposed codec is yet to be optimized in performance. More intelligent band-ranking decision and bit allocation, a better selection scheme for the coefficient magnitude subvector and the coefficient signs based on the psychoacoustic model are under research to improve the performance.

Acknowledgment

This work was supported by Research Grant of Kwangwoon University in 2005.

References

1. 3GPP TS 26.190: AMR wideband speech codec; Transcoding functions (2001)
2. Koishida, K., Cuperman, V., Gersho, A.: A 16-kbit/s bandwidth scalable audio coder band on the G.729 standard, IEEE ICASSP (2002) 1149–1152
3. McCree, A.: A 14kbps wideband speech coder with a parametric highband model, IEEE ICASSP (2000) 1153–1156
4. Kim, K. T., Jung, S. K., Park, Y. C., Youn, D. H.: A new bandwidth scalable wideband speech/audio coder, IEEE ICASSP (2002) 657–660
5. Ambikairajah, E., Epps, J., Lin, L.: Wideband speech and audio coding using Gammatone filter bank, IEEE ICASSP (2001) 773–776
6. Kubin, G., Kleijn, W. B.: On speech coding in a perceptual domain, IEEE ICASSP (1999) 205–208
7. ITU G.722.1: Coding at 24 and 32 kbit/s for hands-free operation in systems with low frame loss (1999)

Self-timed Interconnect with Layered Interface Based on Distributed and Modularized Control for Multimedia SoCs

Eun-Gu Jung[1], Eon-Pyo Hong[1], Kyoung-Son Jhang[2], Jeong-A Lee[3], and Dong-Soo Har[1]

[1] Department of Information and Communications,
Gwangju Institute of Science and Technology, Republic of Korea
{egjung, ephong77, hardon}@gist.ac.kr
[2] Department of Computer Engineering, College of Engineering,
Chungnam National University, Republic of Korea
sun@cnu.ac.kr
[3] Department of Computer Engineering,
Chosun University, Republic of Korea
jalee@chosun.ac.kr

Abstract. In this paper, a high performance asynchronous on-chip bus designed in a Globally Asynchronous Locally Synchronous (GALS) style is proposed. The asynchronous on-chip bus is capable of handling multiple outstanding transactions and in-order completion to achieve a high performance, which is implemented with distributed and modularized control unit in a layered interface. The architecture of asynchronous on-chip bus is discussed and implemented for simulations. Simulation results show that throughput of the proposed asynchronous on-chip bus with multiple outstanding transactions and in-order transaction completion is increased by 31.3%, while power consumption overhead is only 6.76%, as compared to an asynchronous on-chip bus with a single outstanding transaction.

1 Introduction

Asynchronous On-Chip Buses (OCBs) [1,2,3] have been proposed for a low power Global Asynchronous Interconnection(GAI) in Globally Asynchronous Locally Synchronous (GALS) style. Similarly to synchronous OCBs [3,4] widely used for System-on-a Chip(SoC) design, the asynchronous OCBs take small silicon area and have low latency. In a synchronous OCB, new features such as multiple outstanding transactions and in-order transaction completion have been introduced in [4] to meet the high performance requirement of SoCs.

A high performance asynchronous OCB with multiple outstanding transactions and in-order transaction completion is proposed here. These features are embodied efficiently through a layered architecture with distributed and modularized control units, as a master interface and a slave interface of an asynchronous OCB are implemented. To the best knowledge of authors, an asynchronous OCB with these new features has not appeared in the literature until now.

This paper is organized as follows. Section 2 contains basic concepts and Sect. 3 presents the proposed layered architecture. In Sect. 4, the implementation of an asynchronous OCB with distributed and modularized control units for the layered architecture are explained in details. Furthermore, Sect. 5 shows simulation environments and results. Finally, Sect. 6 gives conclusions.

2 Backgrounds

A single outstanding transaction is supported by most OCBs, where each master interface issues only one command prior to the arrival of the corresponding response [3]. When an OCB supports multiple outstanding transactions, each master interface can generate another command before the response for previous one arrives, bringing higher performance [4].

When a master interface issues several commands, the corresponding responses may arrive out of order. If each master IP supports out-of-order transaction completion, the order of a sequence of responses does not cause problems, since master IPs dispose responses in order. However, if each master IP supports only in-order transaction completion, each master interface must rearrange a sequence of responses with a reorder buffer (ROB) [4].

3 Architecture of Asynchronous OCB

The increasing design complexity in implementing a high performance asynchronous OCB makes it difficult to design a centralized control unit. The design may suffer from increased area cost, long synthesis time, and degraded performance due to poor optimization [2,5]. As a solution, a layered architecture has been considered in [6]. However, it is not suitable to apply the layered architecture directly to the implementation of communication protocols for an asynchronous OCB, because the design environment of SoC differs from that of off-chip network. Hence, a layered architecture customized for an asynchronous OCB is proposed here. The asynchronous OCB for Master IP and Slave IP in Fig. 1 is a simplified model of the layered architecture with distributed and modularized control units. The asynchronous OCBs have a master interface and a slave interface for communications. Each interface consists of three layers:physical layer, data link layer, and transport layer. The physical layer is concerned with data encoding, filtering, and bus driving. The data link layer is involved with flow control and access control. The transport layer is associated with flow control for read/write transactions, bust transactions, split transactions, multiple outstanding transactions, and in-order transaction completion. Since the proposed asynchronous OCB employs a single physical addressing, network layer is not needed.

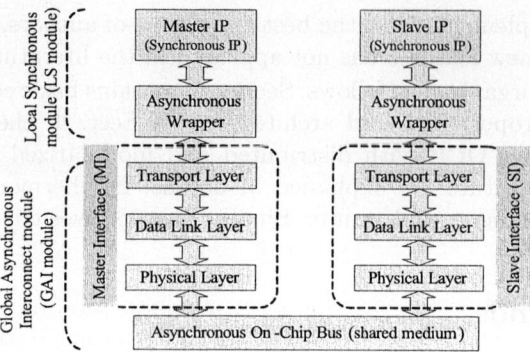

Fig. 1. GALS system with an asynchronous OCB based on the layered architecture

4 Implementation

4.1 Asynchronous Handshake Protocol for Asynchronous OCB

In general, two-phase signaling incurs lower performance, as compared to four-phase signaling, when combined with common data encoding scheme. However, an asynchronous handshake protocol with two-phase signaling might have higher performance in case of data transfer under an OCB environment, because data transfer time through long wire dominates encoding and decoding time of an asynchronous handshake protocol. Figure 2 shows simulation results (at 0.25um CMOS process) of two asynchronous handshake protocols with different wire lengths, where both handshake protocols use a 1-of-4 data encoding scheme for Delay Insensitive (DI) communication. The asynchronous handshake protocol with two-phase signaling takes less time for data transfer when wire length is larger than 1mm, as plotted in Fig. 2(a). Also, this protocol consumes less power with wire lengths greater than 4mm (see Fig. 2(b)). Hence, two-phase signaling and DI data encoding are used for an asynchronous OCB, while four-phase signaling and bundled data encoding in [1] are applied to design of a controller of each interface.

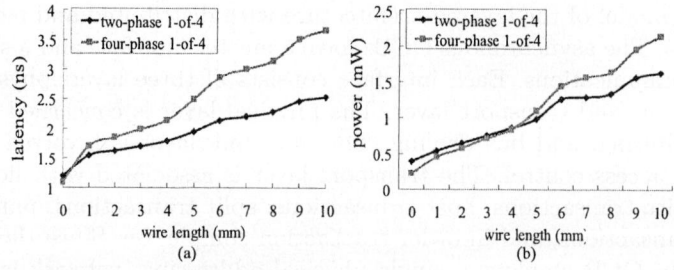

Fig. 2. Simulation results according to wire length: (a)latency; (b)power consumption

4.2 Proposed Asynchronous OCB

Figure 3 shows the proposed layered interfaces of asynchronous OCB with multiple outstanding transactions and in-order transaction completion (MI-OCB) features. The layered interfaces for Master IP and Slave IP are designed with distributed and modularized control units corresponding to partitioned functionality of each layer. Each interface consists of three layers. Each sub-block in each layer is a control circuit generated from a Signal Transition Graph (STG) by petrify synthesis tool [7].

A master interface and a slave interface are divided into two parts by a horizontal dashed line. The upper part of the master interface transfers information of a master IP to the slave interface, and the lower part gets information of a slave IP from the slave interface and transfer it to the master IP. For the slave interface, the upper part gets information of the master IP from the master interface, and the lower part transfers information of the slave IP to the master interface.

The behavior of both interfaces is as follows. The master IP activates the master interface, as illustrated in Fig. 3(a), to transfer information of the master IP to the slave. To create a token, the controller AHPC-T1 of transport layer uses *issue_rin* and *issue_ain* signals related to multiple outstanding transactions. The

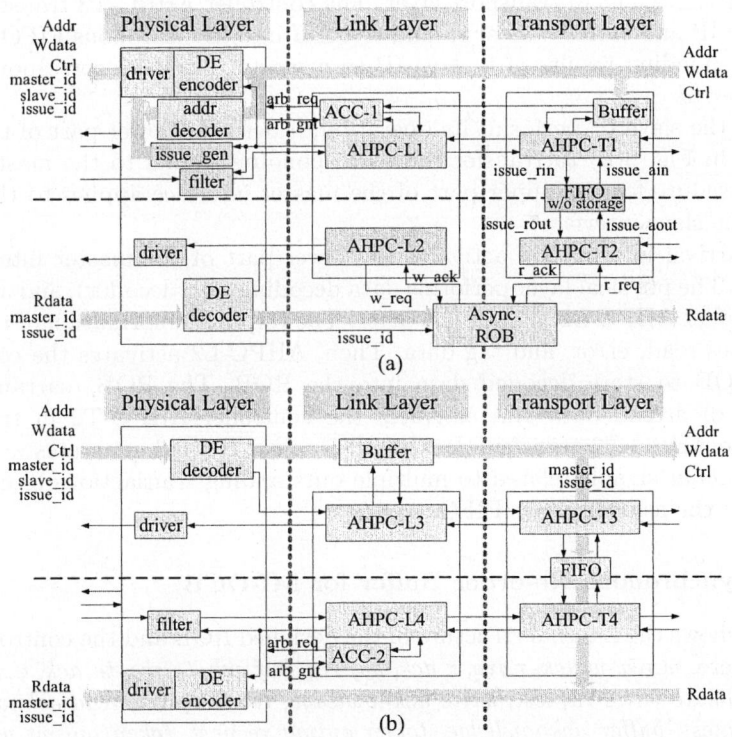

Fig. 3. Layered interface for MI-OCB: (a)master interface; (b)slave interface

token is generated and inserted into asynchronous FIFO without data storage, when the master interface is activated and the asynchronous FIFO has an empty slot. The asynchronous FIFO controls the number of issues by means of tokens stored. The token in the asynchronous FIFO is consumed by an arrival response from the slave interface and then the asynchronous FIFO can accommodate a new token. Hence, the scheme for multiple outstanding transactions is enabled by the token mechanism. The data link layer uses *arb_req* and *arb_gnt* signals to obtain the permit to access the command channel and then activates the physical layer. The physical layer transfers information of a master IP to a slave IP through command channel. The physical layer performs data encoding (DE encoder), address decoding (addr decoder) to select a slave IP, filtering (filter), and bus driving (driver). Also, the issue_gen sub-block of the physical layer generates one tag data item per issue. The tag data items are used for rearranging a sequence of arrival responses.

The transferred information from the master interface activates the slave interface as shown in Fig. 3(b). The physical layer performs data decoding, followed by the activation of the controller AHPC-L3 in data link layer. The information consists of address, write, control, and tag data. The tag data contain identifiers *master_id*, *issue_id*, *slave_id* of the source (master), the issue, the sink (slave), respectively. The AHPC-L3 stores decoded data into a buffer and activates the controller AHPC-T3 of transport layer. The controller AHPC-T3 transfers data to a slave IP and stores *master_id* and *issue_id* into asynchronous FIFO to send the corresponding results of a slave IP to a master interface corresponding to the *master_id*.

After the slave IP performs its operation, it activates lower part of the slave interface in Fig. 3(b) to transfer the corresponding results to the master. The same procedure for the upper part of the master interface applies to the lower part of the slave interface.

The arrival information activates the lower part of the master interface in Fig. 3(a). The physical layer performs data decoding (DE decoder), and activates the controller AHPC-L2 in data link layer. The response information of the slave IP includes read, error, and tag data. Then, AHPC-L2 activates the controller of the ROB to store decoded data into the ROB. The ROB rearranges the sequence of arrival data and activates the controller AHPC-T2 in transport layer. The AHPC-T2 transfers data to the master IP, and generates *issue_rout* and *issue_aout* signals related to multiple outstanding transactions to consume a token in the asynchronous FIFO.

4.3 Asynchronous Re-order Buffer for MI-OCB

Figure 4 shows the internal structure of the designed ROB and the controllers involved. Here, *w_req*, *w_ack*, *r_req*, *r_ack*, *buf_req*, *buf_ack*, *to_req*, *to_ack*, *ti_req*, and *ti_ack* indicate *write request*, *write acknowledge*, *read request*, *read acknowledge*, *buffer request*, *buffer acknowledge*, *token output request*, *token output acknowledge*, *token input request*, and *token input acknowledge*, respectively. In the initial state, ROB starter in Fig. 4 generates a token and supplies it to the first cell

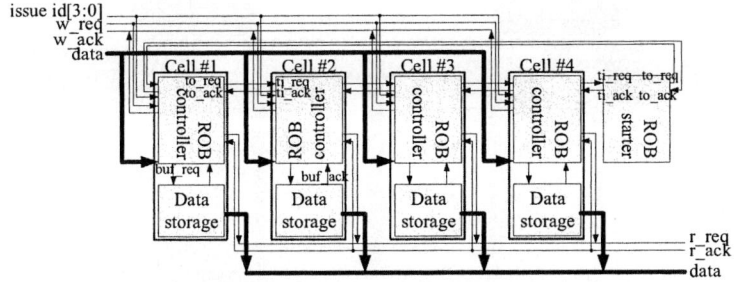

Fig. 4. Internal structure of proposed asynchronous ROB

(Cell #1), permitting the first cell to transfer a stored response to a master IP. When a new response from a slave arrives, the proposed asynchronous ROB stores it into an appropriate cell according to the *issue_id* item. The sequence of the stored responses may be out of order. When the cell with a stored response gets the token, it transfers the response to a master IP and hands the token over to the next neighbored cell. Followed by three token passing from the first cell (Cell #1), the ROB starter transfers a token from the last cell (Cell #4) to the first cell. If a neighbored cell receiving the token does not have a response, the neighbored cell holds the token until a response from a slave arrives. Hence, the proposed asynchronous ROB always outputs the stored responses in order.

5 Simulations

5.1 Simulation Environment

Two asynchronous OCBs were implemented with 0.25um CMOS process at the transistor level. For comparisons, the asynchronous OCB with a single outstanding transaction (SI-OCB) was considered with a few modifications of the proposed MI-OCB. The FIFO without storage and the issue_gen block were eliminated for the the master interface of SI-OCB. Also, AHPC-T1 and AHPC-L2 were redesigned. The FIFO of transport layer was replaced with a single buffer for the slave interface of SI-OCB. Also, a single buffer instead of the proposed asynchronous reorder buffer was used.

The implemented OCBs consist of 32-bit address bus, 32-bit write data bus, 32-bit read data bus, 16-bit control bus, and 2-bit error bus. In Fig. 5, MI is a master interface and SI means a slave interface. A master is composed of a synchronous IP (Sync. IP), an asynchronous wrapper (Async. wrapper), and a master interface (MI). A slave consists of a synchronous IP, an asynchronous wrapper, and a slave interface (SI). The simulation environment consists of two parts: (1) an implemented part and (2) a virtual part. The implemented part corresponds to the implemented buses and consists of four master interfaces, eight slave interfaces, two arbiters for a command and a response channels, and so on. The virtual part is constructed by using ADFMI of NanoSim from Synopsys and consists of twelve synchronous IPs for master and slave interfaces.

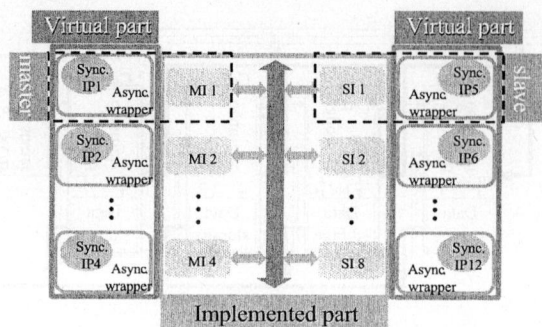

Fig. 5. Simulation environment

Table 1. Simulation parameters of the first case: distribution of bus transactions

	master1	master2	master3	master4
m_case1	1	0	0	0
m_case2	1/2	1/2	0	0
m_case3	1/3	1/3	1/3	0
m_case4	1/4	1/4	1/4	1/4

It is assumed that each synchronous IP is implemented by a synchronous design technique and has an Asynchronous wrapper module to communicate with proposed asynchronous OCBs.

Before measuring performance and power consumption, workloads should be determined, since workloads affect simulation results. However, it is difficult to find appropriate workloads of real applications because real workloads can be obtained when all applications with real input data are modeled exactly. Instead, workloads for simulations are obtained by synthetic workload generation with the following parameters:

- The clock frequency of a synchronous IP.
- The ratio of non-bus transfer time to total transfer time per synchronous IP, where total transfer time consists of non-bus transfer time and bus transfer time.
- The distribution of bus transactions, which indicates how many portion of total bus transactions each master is responsible for.
- The distribution of accessed slaves by each synchronous IP.

These parameters determine the delay of components in the virtual part. In the virtual part, it is assumed that delay of all Asynchronous wrapper modules is always zero to focus on the proposed asynchronous OCB.

Through the synthetic workload generation, various possible situations can be investigated. Two cases where the proposed bus architecture can be utilized well are determined. The first case is that all synchronous IPs have the same clock frequency. Parameters of the first case are as follows:

Table 2. Simulation parameters of the first case: distribution of accessed slaves by each synchronous IP (synchronous IP)

	master1	master2	master3	master4
s_case1	slave 1	slave 3	slave 5	slave 7
s_case2	slave 1,2	slave 3,4	slave 5,6	slave 7,8
s_case3	slave 1,2,3,4	slave 3,4,5,6	slave 5,6,7,8	slave 7,8,1,2
s_case4	slave 1~8	slave 1~8	slave 1~8	slave 1~8

Table 3. Simulation parameters of the second case: clock frequencies and distribution of bus transactions of master IPs

Master	Sync. IP1	Sync. IP2	Sync. IP3	Sync. IP4
Distribution of bus transactions	65%	20%	5%	10%
Clock Frequency (MHz)	300	133	33	33

- The clock frequency of all synchronous IPs are set to an infinite clock frequency, 300MHz, 200MHz, or 100MHz.
- The ratio of non-bus transfer time to total transfer time per synchronous IP is 0. In other words, all transfers of each synchronous IP are always bus transfers.
- For the distribution of bus transactions, four cases are made as shown in Table 1. The master1 is enabled for m_case1, and the master1 and master2 are enabled for m_case2, and so on.
- Table 2 shows the distribution of accessed slaves by each synchronous IP, which consists of four cases. In s_case1, each master communicates with a single dedicated slave. Each master communicates with two, four, and eight dedicated slaves with the same probability for s_case2, s_case3, and s_case4, respectively.
- The total number of bus transactions is 2400.

For the second case, Table 3 and Table 4 show some parameters such as various clock frequencies of all synchronous IPs and distribution of bus transactions of master IPs. It is the more realistic model of a System-on-a-Chip consisting of CPU, DSP, RAM/ROM on-chip memory, and peripheral devices. The synchronous master IP1 (synchronous IP1) has the largest bus transactions, as does CPU dealing with most workloads using high clock frequency. The synchronous slave IP5 (synchronous IP5) can be assumed as an on-chip ROM, and other IPs act as other modules of a System-on-a-Chip. The other parameters of the second case are as follows:

- The ratio of non-bus transfer time to total transfer time per synchronous IP is 0.
- The distribution of accessed slaves by each synchronous IP is s_case4 in Table 2. In other words, each master communicates with all slaves with the same probability.
- The total number of bus transactions is 4800.

Table 4. Simulation parameters of the second case: clock frequencies of slave IPs

Slave	Sync. IP5	Sync. IP6	Sync. IP7	Sync. IP8	Sync. IP9	Sync. IP10	Sync. IP11	Sync. IP12
Clock Frequency MHz)	200	133	133	33	33	33	33	66

5.2 Simulation Results

Figure 6 shows simulation results of the first case. Here, throughput is defined by

$$throughput = N_{trans} \times N_{bit}/T \qquad (1)$$

where N_{trans} is the total number of bus transactions, T indicates the completion time of data transmission, and N_{bit} means the data bit width. Fig. 6(a) shows throughput of MI-OCB when distribution of accessed slaves is s_case1 and a clock frequency of a synchronous IP is varied from 100MHz to infinite. The infinite clock frequency means that response delay of a synchronous IP is zero nanosecond, namely, any synchronous IP with an infinite clock frequency gives a response without any delay. For four clock frequencies, throughput is increased proportionally to the number of enabled masters, which is a profound property of an asynchronous OCB. However, if a few masters use up most bus bandwidth, the throughput increase becomes saturated and the increase of enabled masters has little effect. For example, when all synchronous IPs have the infinite clock frequency, throughput is increased slightly in cases of three and four enabled masters (m_case3, m_case4) because two enabled masters (m_case2) use most of bus bandwidth, as illustrated in Fig. 6(a). This trend can be seen in other distribution of accessed slaves such as s_case2, s_case3, and s_case4. The saturation point is determined by simulation environment parameters such as bus latency, ratio of master clock to slave clock, average burst size, and so on.

Simulation results of Fig. 6(b) show throughput of MI-OCB when the clock frequency of all synchronous IPs is 100MHz and distribution of accessed slaves by each synchronous IP is s_case1, s_case2, s_case3, or s_case4. Among four cases of distribution of accessed slaves, s_case4 has the lowest throughput, since s_case4 has the highest probability of selecting the same slave simultaneously by more than two masters. This high probability of conflict results in the loss of performance. The cases of s_case1 and s_case2 have the highest throughput because all masters communicate with exclusively dedicated slaves (see Table 2).

Figure 6(c) shows normalized throughput of MI-OCB when the distribution of bus transactions is m_case1 and a clock frequency of a synchronous IP is varied from 100MHz to infinite. The normalized throughput is set on the basis of throughput of s_case1 when the frequency of all synchronous IPs is 100MHz. Compared with s_case1 of each clock frequency, the throughput of each frequency at s_case4 is the highest due to multiple outstanding transactions. The improvement of throughput is 5%, 9%, 12%, or, 25%, when the frequency of all synchronous IPs is 100MHz, 200MHz, 300MHz, or infinite, respectively.

Figure 6(d) shows energy consumption per bus transaction of MI-OCB at the first case. Symbols 'min', 'avg', 'max' indicate minimum, average, maxi-

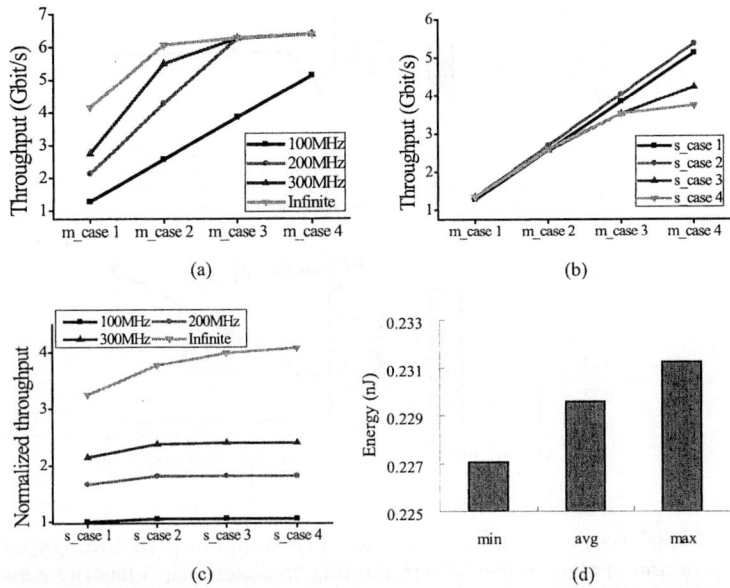

Fig. 6. Simulation results of the first case: (a)throughput of MI-OCB when distribution of accessed slaves is s_case1 and a clock frequency of a synchronous IP is varied from 100MHz to infinite; (b)throughput of MI-OCB when the clock frequency of all synchronous IPs has 100MHz and distribution of accessed slaves by each synchronous IP is s_case1, s_case2, s_case3, or s_case4; (c)normalized throughput of MI-OCB when the distribution of bus transactions is m_case1 and a clock frequency of a synchronous IP is varied from 100MHz to infinite; (d)energy consumption per data transaction of MI-OCB

mum energy consumption for all possible cases which are made by simulation parameters. Sixty four cases are generated by four cases of distribution of bus transactions, four cases of distribution of accessed slaves, and four cases of clock frequency of a synchronous IP. Regardless of sixty four cases, MI-OCB consumes very similar energy because the number of bus transactions is identical.

Figure 7 shows simulation results of the second case. Compared with SI-OCB, throughput of MI-OCB increases by 31.3% due to executing multiple outstanding transactions (see Fig. 7(a)). The plot in Fig. 7(b) shows the effect of the number of outstanding transactions on throughput of MI-OCB, where the throughput corresponding to the number of outstanding transactions equal to one indicates the throughput of SI-OCB. When the number of outstanding transactions is larger than four, the throughput is saturated.

Figure 7(c) shows energy consumption of two asynchronous OCBs. Compared with SI-OCB, MI-OCB consumes the energy increased by 6.76%. However, the increase of energy consumption is insignificant when considering the throughput improvement. Figure 7(d) shows the effect of the number of outstanding transactions on energy consumption per bus transaction for MI-OCB, where the energy

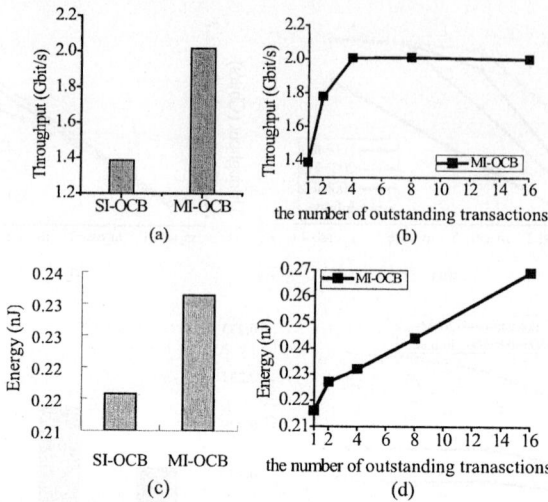

Fig. 7. Simulation results of the second case: (a)throughput; (b)throughput for MI-OCB, as a function of the number of outstanding transactions; (c)energy consumption per bus transaction; (d)energy consumption per bus transaction of MI-OCB, as a function of outstanding transactions

consumption corresponding to the number of outstanding transactions equal to one indicates the energy consumption of SI-OCB. As the number of outstanding transactions increases, power consumption increases since hardware complexity of the proposed asynchronous ROB increases.

6 Conclusions

The proposed asynchronous OCB efficiently accommodate multiple outstanding transactions and in-order transaction completion. A bus interface can be easily extended from asynchronous OCB with a single outstanding transaction (SI-OCB) to asynchronous OCB with multiple outstanding transactions and in-order transaction completion (MI-OCB), due to distributed and modularized control units and partitioned functionality in each layer. Simulation results of performance and power consumption of the implemented asynchronous OCBs reveal that MI-OCB has higher throughput than SI-OCB, while power consumption overhead of MI-OCB is very small. Compared with SI-OCB, throughput of MI-OCB increases by 31.3%. Power consumption overhead of MI-OCB is only 6.76%.

Acknowledgements

This work has been supported in part by the Center for Distributed Sensor Network (CDSN) at GIST, in part by IC Design Education Center (IDEC), in part by the KAIST/GIST IT-21 Initiative in BK21 of Ministry of Education, and in part by the GIST Technology Initiative (GTI).

References

1. Bainbridge, W.J.: Asynchronous System-on-Chip Interconnect. PhD thesis, Univ. of Manchester, UK (2000)
2. Jung, E.G., Choi, B.S., Lee, D.I.: High performance asynchronous bus for SoC. In: Proceedings of IEEE International Symposium on Circuits and Systems. Volume 5., Bangkok, Thailand (2003) 505–508
3. Salminen, E., Lahtinen, V., Kuusilinna, K., Hamalainen, T.: Overview of bus-based system-on-chip interconnections. In: Proceedings of IEEE International Symposium on Circuits and Systems. Volume 2., Phoenix-Scottsdale, AZ (2002) 372–275
4. ARM: AMBA AXI Protocol Specification. (2003)
5. Kim, E., Lee, J.G., Lee, D.I.: Automatic process-oriented control control generation for asynchronous high-level synthesis. In: Proceedings of IEEE International Symposium on Asynchronous Circuits and Systems, Eilat, Israel (2000) 104–105
6. Zimmermann, H.: OSI reference model–the ISO model of architecture for open systems interconnection. IEEE Transactions on Communications **28** (1980) 425–432
7. Cortadella, J., Kishinevsky, M., Kondratyev, A., Lavagno, L., Yakovlev, A.: Petrify: A tool for manipulating concurrent specifications and synthesis of asynchronous controllers. IEICE Transactions on Information and Systems **E-80D** (1997) 315–325

Enhanced Downhill Simplex Search for Fast Video Motion Estimation

Hwai-Chung Fei, Chun-Jen Chen, and Shang-Hong Lai

Department of Computer Science, National Tsing Hua University,
Hsinchu 300, Taiwan, R.O.C
lai@cs.nthu.edu.tw

Abstract. Block-based motion estimation can be regarded as a function minimization problem in a finite two-dimensional space. Therefore, fast block-based motion estimation can be achieved by using an efficient function minimization algorithm instead of using a predefined search pattern, such as the diamond search. The downhill simplex search algorithm is an efficient derivative-free function minimization algorithm. In this paper, we propose several enhanced schemes to improve the efficiency of applying the downhill simplex search algorithm to motion estimation. The proposed enhanced schemes include a new initialization process, a special rounding method, and an early-stop error function evaluation procedure. Experimental results on several benchmarking videos show superior performance of the proposed algorithm over some existing fast block matching methods.

1 Introduction

Due to the strong demand of storing and transmitting an enormous amount of video data, video compression has been a very important and practical problem in recent years. Motion estimation (ME) is an indispensable part in video compression. ME has been popularly utilized to reduce the temporal information redundancy. Block matching algorithms (BMA) are required for ME in many video standards, such as MPEG-1 [1], MPEG-2 [2], MPEG-4 [3], H.263 [4], and H.264 [5]. In BMA, frames are divided into non-overlapping macroblocks, and we need to find a motion vector (MC) in a pre-defined search range for each macroblock. The simplest BMA is the full search (FS) algorithm. This algorithm exhaustively searches over all possible locations in the search range and picks the most suitable block as the MV, so that it finds the optimal solution within the search range. However, FS has a fatal drawback, i.e. the extremely high computational complexity. Therefore, it is not practical to use FS in video compression, especially in real-time applications. To reduce the computational complexity of FS, many fast BMAs, such as three step search [6], new three step search [7], four step search (FSS) [8], and diamond search (DS) [9] are proposed. Fast BMAs strategically check possible candidates in the search range to decrease the number of search points. Most video encoders apply fast BMAs for motion estimation since they can significantly reduce the search time without noticeable video quality degradation. The most important criterion for a fast BMA is to find an accurate MV with as few search points as possible.

In this paper, we propose a fast BMA that uses a derivative-free function minimization algorithm, i.e. the downhill simplex search algorithm, to find MVs between adjacent image frames. The rest of this paper is organized as follow. Section 2 introduces the basic procedures of downhill simplex search. In Section 3, we present our enhanced downhill simplex search algorithm that contains a new initialization process, a special rounding technique, and an early-stop error function evaluation scheme. Section 4 gives experimental results on some real videos and comparison of the proposed algorithm with some previous BMAs. Finally, we conclude this paper in Section 5.

2 Downhill Simplex Search

Downhill simplex search [10] is a derivative-free multidimensional function minimization method. In the downhill simplex search, a collection of n + 1 points in n-dimensional space is called a simplex. In the iterative simplex update process, the point with the highest function value is iteratively replaced by a new point with a smaller function value until the stopping criterion is satisfied. Our goal is to find MVs in 2-D space, so the three points of the simplex form a triangle. Besides, sum of squared errors (SSE) is applied as the function value in this case.

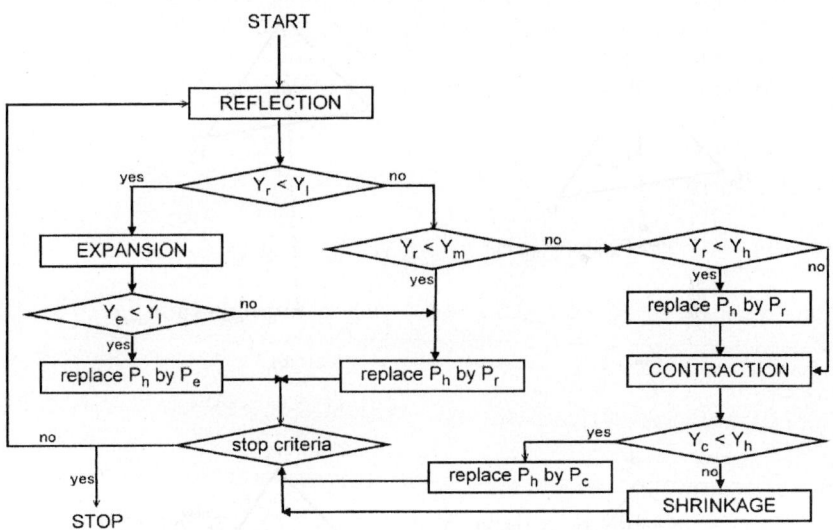

Fig. 1. Flow chart of the downhill simplex search

Downhill simplex search can be roughly divided into two portions. In the first portion, we need to initialize the simplex. It is important since we have better chance to find the correct solution very quickly when the actual solution is near the initial simplex or inside the simplex. After the initial simplex is determined, the simplex is updated iteratively until the stopping criterion is satisfied. Finally, the point with the lowest function value in the simplex is the final solution.

Fig. 1 shows the flow chart of the iterative simplex update procedure. This iterative procedure consists of four main components; namely, reflection, expansion, contraction, and shrinkage. In the reflection step, we define a reflection point P_r as

$$P_r = P_{ave} + \alpha(P_{ave} - P_h) \qquad (1)$$

where α is a positive constant and P_{ave} is the average of all points of the simplex. In the expansion step, we define a expansion point P_e as

$$P_e = P_{ave} + \gamma(P_r - P_{ave}) \qquad (2)$$

where γ is a constant greater than or equal to one. In the contraction step, we define a contraction point P_c as

$$P_c = P_{ave} + \beta(P_h - P_{ave}) \qquad (3)$$

where β is a constant between zero and one. After these points are determined, their SSE values are calculated to see which point can be used to replace the point with the highest value in the simplex. In the shrinkage action, all points except the point with the lowest function value are moved toward this lowest point. Fig. 2 depicts the geometrical interpretation of these operations.

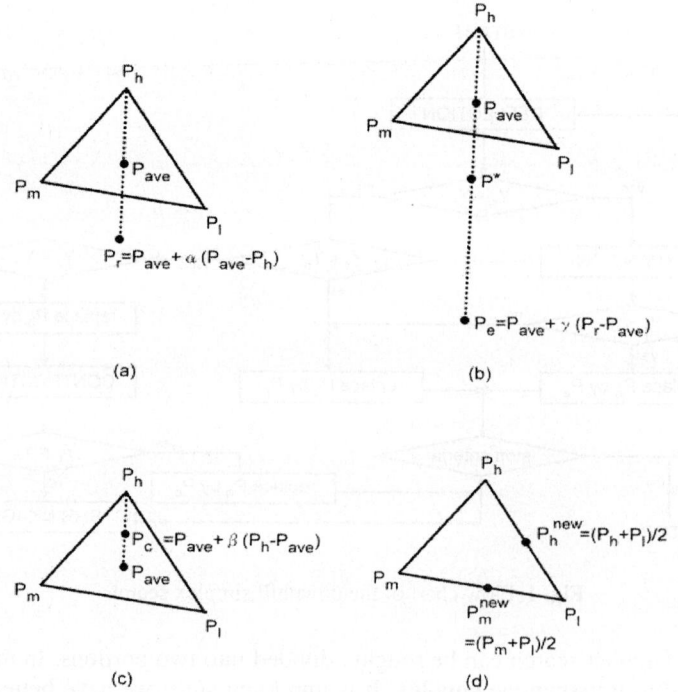

Fig. 2. The four components in the downhill simplex iteration: (a) reflection, (B) expansion, (c) contraction, and (d) shrinkage

Another essential element in the downhill simplex process is when to stop the iteration. In other words, a stopping criterion must be carefully designed. The stopping criterion here is when two of the three points in the simplex are rounded to the same point.

3 Motion Estimation with Enhanced Downhill Simplex Search

In this work, we propose an enhanced downhill simplex search as the BMA to determine the motion vectors for video coding. Throughout the iterative simplex update process, one of the key factors that determine the search performance is the selection of a good initial simplex. A simple initialization method for downhill simplex search is to find three points around the center of the current block. This method works well for blocks with small motion vectors. However, the performance decreases when the motion vectors are large. In this work, we propose to select an appropriate initial simplex from some motion prediction results.

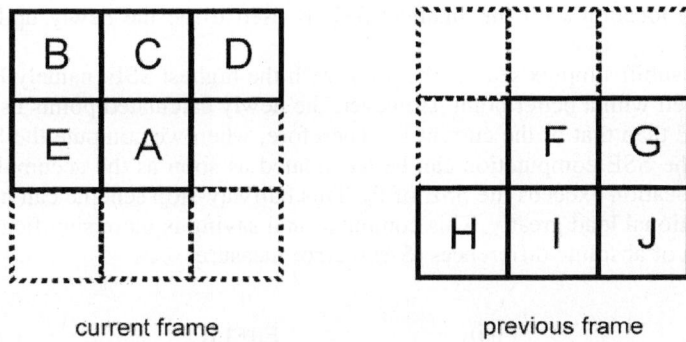

Fig. 3. The blocks used in the motion vector prediction for the initial simplex selection

As the video coding standards predict motion vectors in motion vector encoding processes, we can predict the current motion vector from the estimated motion vectors available in the neighboring blocks at the current or previous frame. As shown in Fig. 3, the MVs of the neighboring blocks at the current and previous frames are utilized. We average the motion vectors of block B, C, D, and E to obtain a candidate, called MV_{c1}, and average the motion vectors of block G, H, I, and J to obtain another candidate, called MV_{c2}. Besides, the motion vector of block F and the original point (0,0) are chosen as candidates MV_{c3} and MV_{c4}, respectively. There are two possible ways to determine an appropriate initial simplex from the four candidates. One is to choose the candidate with the smallest SSE as the starting center and then find three neighboring points for an initial simplex. The other is to choose three points from the four candidates directly to form an initial simplex. The former can provide a more localized simplex, and the latter has the advantage of better computational efficiency. Because we focus on the computational efficiency, the latter is adopted in our experiments.

In addition, the stopping criterion used in the proposed downhill simplex search algorithm is very intuitive. If two of the three points, P_h, P_m, and P_l, lie on the same point, the simplex has degenerated, then the iteration should stop, i.e., the iteration terminates when

$$P_h = P_m \quad \text{or} \quad P_h = P_l \quad \text{or} \quad P_m = P_l \tag{4}$$

Furthermore, the halfway stop skill can be applied in the downhill simplex search. When accumulating SSE of a certain point, if the currently accumulated SSE is larger than that of the target value, we abort the accumulation. Note that this skill is only used in the iteration portion because the initial points may be substituted and no target SSE are set for them.

Finally, we develop a new location rounding scheme in the enhanced downhill simplex search algorithm. The simplest rounding method is to round the search location to the nearest integer position, but this may degrade the accuracy. As shown in Fig. 4, (x,y) is a point with fractional position, and (i,j), (i+1,j), (i,j+1), and (i+1,j+1) are four integer position points nearest to (x,y). The function F represents the SSE function value at that point. The purpose of BMA is to find the block that is most similar to the current block. The computation of SSE at the fractional point requires interpolation, which is quite computational costly but may not improve too much. Instead of using interpolation, we calculate F(i,j), F(i+1,j), F(i,j+1), and F(i+1,j+1), and then the location with the smallest SSE is used to be the newly updated point (x,y).

In the downhill simplex search, the point with the highest SSE, namely P_h, is iteratively replaced with a better point. However, the newly calculated points usually have a higher SSE than that of the current P_h. Therefore, when we compute the SSE of the new point, the SSE computation can be terminated as soon as the accumulative SSE of the new location exceeds the SSE of P_h. This halfway-stop scheme can help reduce the computational load greatly. This computational saving is more significant for SSE than the sum of absolute differences (SAD) error measure.

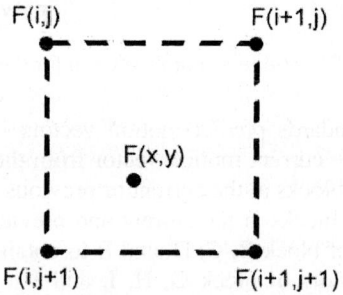

Fig. 4. A new rounding scheme: (x,y) is the position of a new candidate selected from the four nearest grid points from their SSE function values

4 Experimental Results

We compare five BMAs, including full search (FS), four step search (FSS), diamond search (DS), simplex minimization search (SMS) [11], and our proposed downhill simplex search (DSS), through experiments on four benchmarking video sequences (foreman, coastguard, news, and container). When accumulating SSE of a block, every pixel requires three operations, including two additions and one multiplication.

Thus, if all the pixels in the block are counted when calculating SSE at a certain point, it needs 3 x 256 = 768 operations. The foreman sequence is a popular video because it contains different motion directions and large motions near the end of the video. The coastguard sequence contains fast movement through the whole sequence. The news sequence almost remains static in most areas except the small area around the human face. The container sequence contains slow and uniform motions. The formats of these sequences are listed in Table 1 and the results are listed in Tables 2-5. The foreman sequence and coastguard sequence have larger MVs, so our proposed method significantly outperforms the other methods. As shown in Fig. 5 and Fig. 6, our proposed method apparently has higher PSNR than other fast BMAs. When the MVs are large, most fast BMAs, such as DS and FSS, normally require more computational cost for motion estimation. It is evident from the experiments that the numbers of search points required in the proposed method for different types of video sequences are quite stable. The news sequence and container sequence have smaller MVs, almost near zero, so the PSNR differences between the proposed algorithm and other fast BMAs are insignificant, as shown in Fig. 7 and Fig. 8. However, our proposed method can find solutions with much less computational cost than those of other fast BMAs, as shown in Table 4 and Table 5. In fact, our proposed method is much faster than the other BMAs for all of our experiments. This is mainly due to that the initial simplex is carefully selected and the early-stop scheme further boosts the search speed. On the other hand, the accuracy of our proposed method is higher than other fast BMAs in video sequences with large motion (foreman and coastguard sequences) and is similar to other fast BMAs for video sequences with small motion (news and container sequences). Figures 9-12 show the total numbers of operations required in these motion estimation methods for some periods of frames in these test sequences. The average number of operations required in the proposed method is consistently the least among all these BMAs and the computation required in our algorithm does not frustrate significantly even when the MVs during some short periods of a video sequence are quite large.

Table 1. The four test video sequences used in our experiments

Sequence Name	Resolution	Frames
Foreman	176 x 144	320
Coastguard	176 x 144	97
News	176 x 144	200
Container	176 x 144	180

Table 2. Test results of the Foreman sequence

BMA	PSNR (dB)	# of operations (x10^5)
FS	32.17	618.324
FSS	31.73	17.212
DS	31.77	16.114
SMS	31.31	11.175
DSS	31.86	6.309

Table 3. Test results of the coastguard sequence

BMA	PSNR (dB)	# of operations (x10^5)
FS	33.25	618.324
FSS	33.13	15.228
DS	33.17	12.903
SMS	32.53	10.651
DSS	33.24	5.928

Table 4. Test results of the news sequence

BMA	PSNR (dB)	# of operations (x10^5)
FS	37.63	618.324
FSS	37.61	12.678
DS	37.61	9.755
SMS	37.54	10.656
DSS	37.57	5.334

Table 5. Test results of the container sequence

BMA	PSNR (dB)	# of operations (x10^5)
FS	42.17	618.324
FSS	42.17	12.319
DS	42.16	9.309
SMS	42.13	10.543
DSS	42.12	5.589

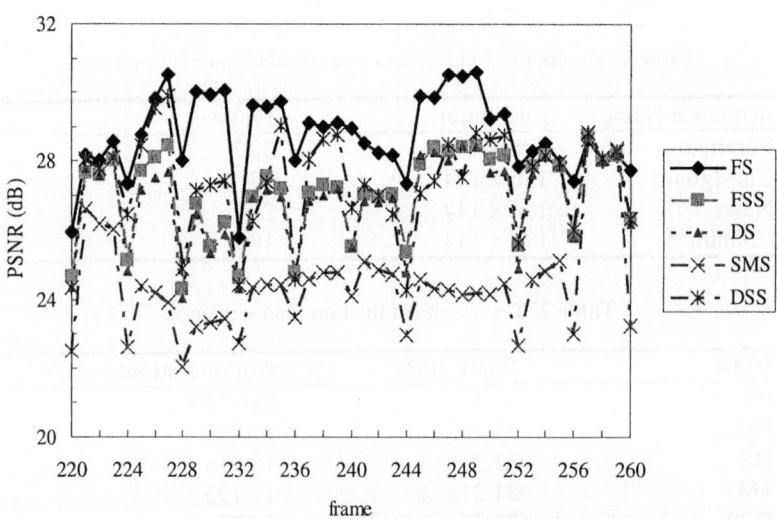

Fig. 5. Result of foreman sequence from frame 220 frame 260

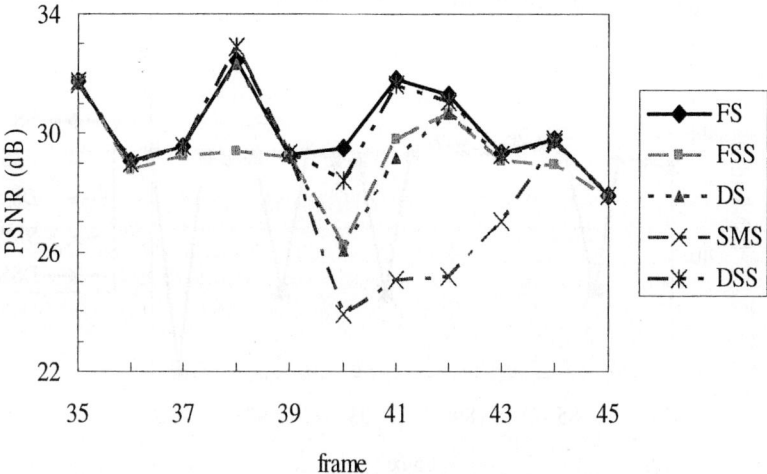

Fig. 6. Result of coastguard sequence from frame 35 to frame 45

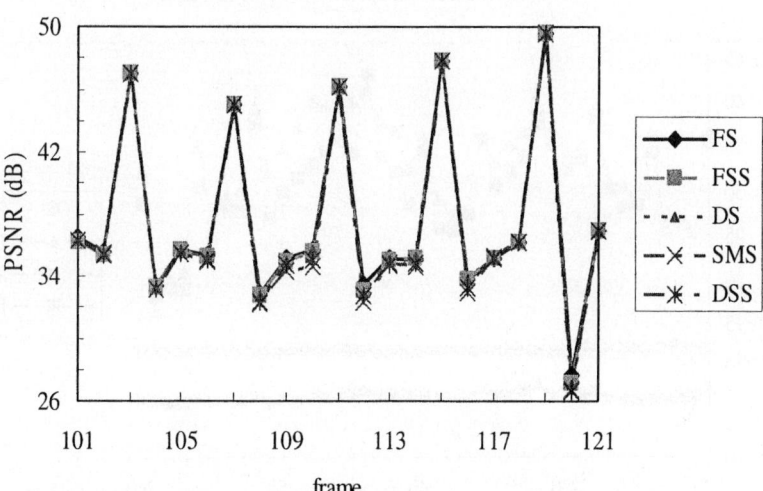

Fig. 7. Result of news sequence from frame 101 to frame 121

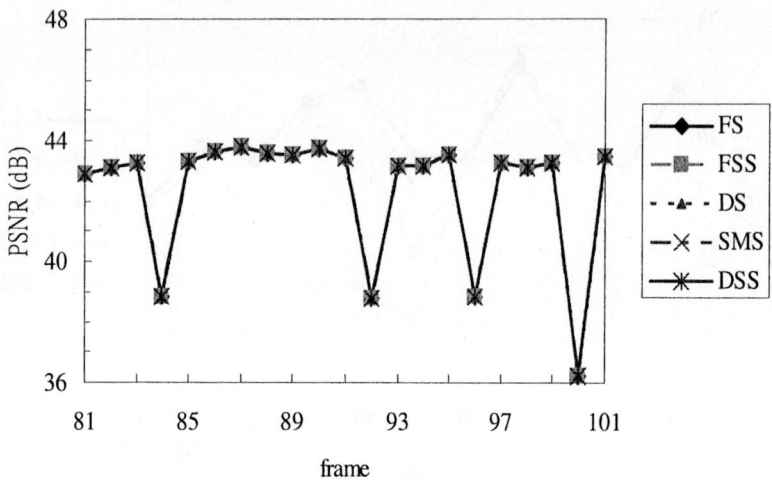

Fig. 8. Result of container sequence from frame 81 to frame 101

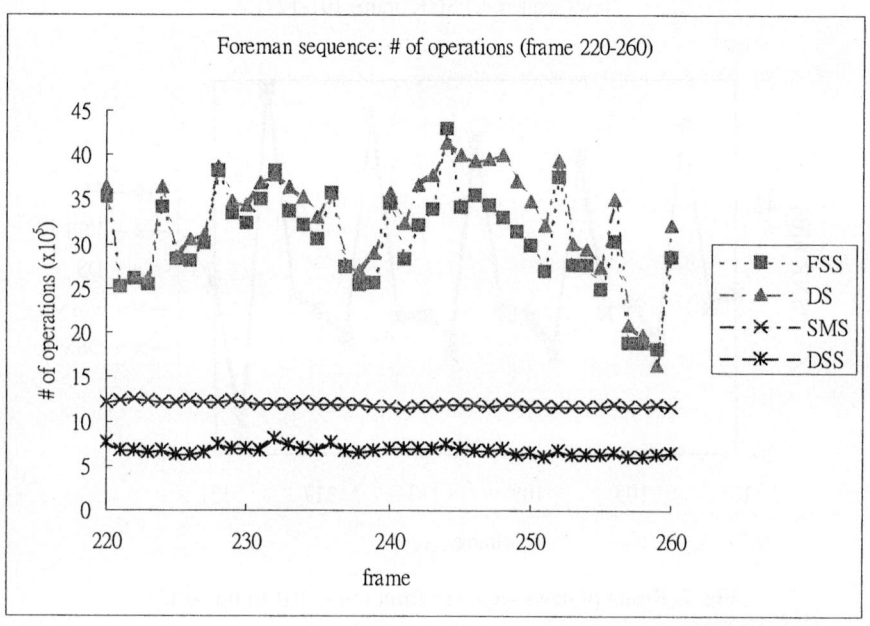

Fig. 9. The number of operations required for the Foreman sequence during frames 220-260

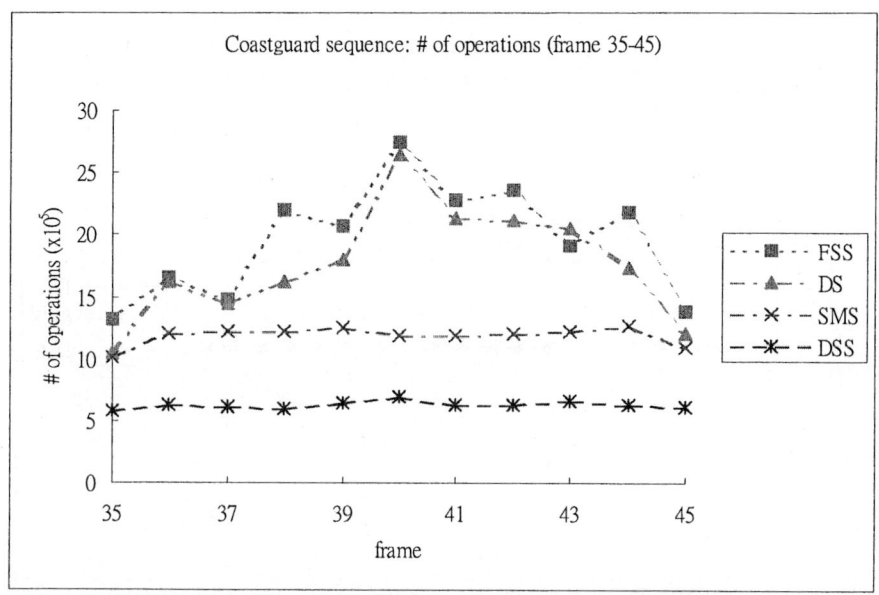

Fig. 10. The number of operations required for the coastguard sequence during frames 35-45

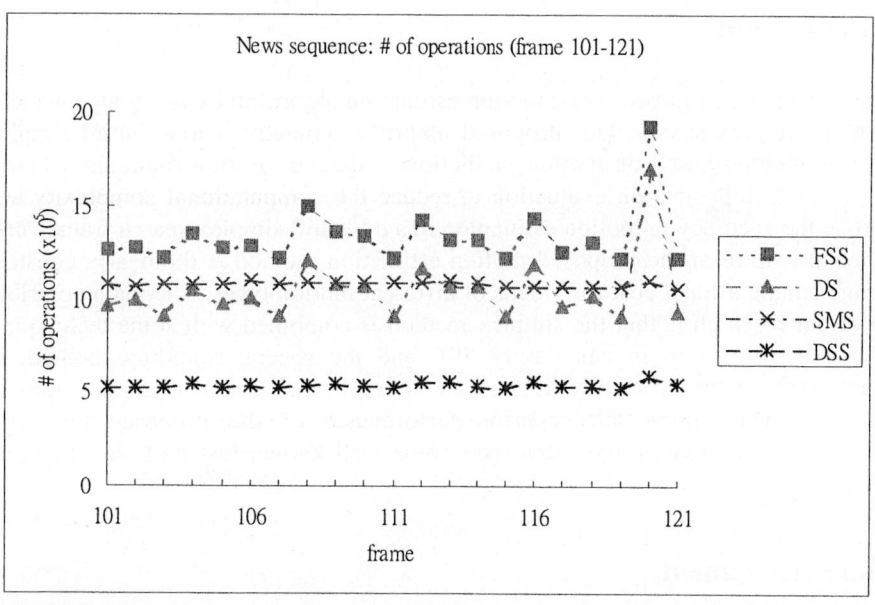

Fig. 11. The number of operations required for the news sequence during frames 101-121

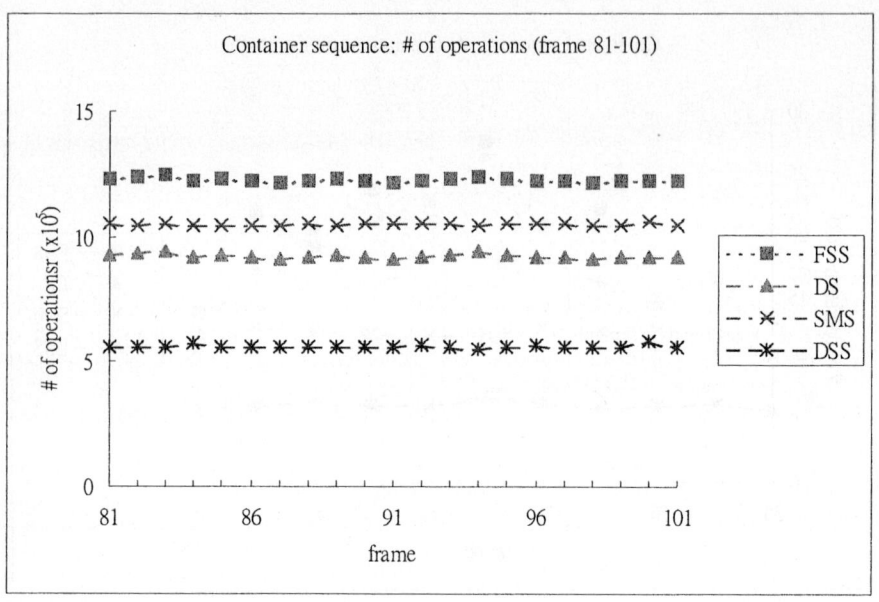

Fig. 12. The number of operations required for the container sequence during frames 81-101

5 Conclusion

In this paper, we proposed a fast motion estimation algorithm by using an enhanced downhill simplex search. Our proposed algorithm contains a new initial simplex selection method based on motion prediction, a special location rounding scheme, and an early-stop function evaluation to reduce the computational complexity and improve the accuracy in motion estimation in a downhill simplex search framework. A special feature of the proposed motion estimation method is the nearly constant average computational cost for videos of different motion types. The main contribution of our research is that the simplex method is combined with some techniques, such as halfway stop in calculating SSE and the special rounding method, to further improve the efficiency. Experimental results on several different types of video sequences show the superior performance of the proposed enhanced downhill simplex search algorithm over some well-known fast motion estimation methods.

Acknowledgement

This work was supported by MOEA research project under grant no. 94-EC-17-A-01-S1-034.

References

1. ISO/IEC 11172, Information technology - coding of moving pictures and associated audio for digital storage media at up to 1.5 Mbit/s. (1993)
2. ISO/IEC 13818, Information technology - Generic coding of moving pictures and associated audio information, Part 2: Video. (1995)
3. ISO/IEC 14496-2. Information technology - coding of audio-visual objects - Part 2: Visual. (1998)
4. ITU-T Recommendation H.263. Video coding for low bit rate communication, Version 2. (1998)
5. ISO/IEC 14496-10 and ITU-T Recommendation H.264. Advanced Video Coding. (2003)
6. Koga, T., Iinuma, K., Hirano, A., Iijima, Y., Ishiguro, T.: Motion compensated interframe coding for video conferencing. Proc. Nat. Telecommun. Conf., New Orleans, LA, Nov. 29-Dec. 3 (1981) G5.3.1-G5.3.5
7. Li, R., Zeng, B., Liou, M.L.: A new three-step search algorithm for block motion estimation. IEEE Trans. Circuits Syst. Video Technol., Vol. 4. Aug, (1994) 438-442
8. Po, L.M., Ma, W.C.: A novel four-step search algorithm for fast block motion estimation. IEEE Trans. Circuits Syst. Video Tech., Vol. 6, June, (1996) 313-317
9. Zhu, S., Ma, K.-K.: A new diamond search algorithm for fast block-matching motion estimation. IEEE Trans. Image Processing, Vol. 9, Feb, (2000) 287-290
10. Nelder, J.A., Mead, R.: A simplex method for function minimization. The Comput. J., Vol. 7, (1965) 308-313
11. Al-Mualla, M.E., Canagarajah, C.N., Bull, D.R.: Video coding for Mobile communications Efficiency, Complexity, and Resilience. Elsevier Science. (2002)

Camera Motion Detection in Video Sequences Using Motion Cooccurrences

Hyun-Ho Jeon, Andrea Basso, and Peter F. Driessen

Department of Electrical and Computer Engineering,
University of Victoria, Victoria, BC V8W 3P6, Canada
{hjeon, abasso, peter}@ece.uvic.ca

Abstract. In this paper, we propose a camera motion detection method that can identify pan, tilt and zoom in a video sequence. The proposed method exploits motion features based on the motion cooccurrence matrix, which is able to provide dominant motion characteristics between two images such as the size of the homogeneous motion area and the direction of motion. We show that motion cooccurrence matrices are quite different for different types of motion and can be used to effectively identify simple camera motion such as pan, tilt and zoom in video sequences. Our method does not rely on the parametric motion model and can be used to qualitatively detect camera motion. Performance of the proposed method is evaluated by experiments for a set of test sequence.

1 Introduction

The estimation of camera motion is important for video coding, indexing and retrieval purposes. In video coding, global motion is estimated to compensate for camera motion to get more precise local motion estimation. The segmentation of the video sequence to be indexed into elementary shots and their characterization on the basis of their motion characteristics such as static shot, panning and zooming is a key element of video indexing and retrieval systems.

Many approaches have been developed to estimate camera motion of video sequences for the purpose of video coding and motion-based video indexing. The traditional camera model based approach [1],[2] represents the motion between two consecutive frames by the global motion model, and the global motion parameters are estimated by robust estimation algorithms. The camera operation can be derived by analyzing the estimated model parameters. Another approach estimates camera motion by analyzing the dominant motion in the image [3],[4]. Angle histograms extracted from the motion vector field or optical flow field are also widely used, but they do not provide information about the spatial distribution of motion in the image.

In this paper, we propose a method of camera motion estimation that can identify pan, tilt and zoom in a video sequence. To identify dominant motion types due to camera operations, we exploit motion features in the frame such as the size of the homogeneous motion area and the direction of motion. We consider the motion cooccurrence matrix, which can express how pairs of motion directions are spatially distributed in the image. We build the motion cooccurrence matrix for each frame using the optical flow field. Cooccurrence matrices have been used for the detection of spatial invariance of intensity patterns in an image [5]. The cooccurrence matrix with a distance d is a 2-dimensional $N \times N$ matrix, where N is the number of quantization levels for the pixel value [5]. The entry *(i,j)* of the matrix specifies the frequency of the neighboring pixels with value j at a distance d from a pixel of value i in the image. The basic idea of the cooccurrence matrix was extended into motion description [6]. It was used to classify uniform motions and unstructured real-world motions. The Cooccurrence matrix was transferred to the temporal domain and used for motion-based video indexing [7]. In section 2, we will describe our proposed method for the camera motion detection. In section 3, experimental results are presented. Section 4 presents our conclusion.

2 Proposed Method

Our proposed method for pan, tilt and zoom detection in video sequences consists of three steps. In the first step, for each frame of the input sequence, we compute the motion cooccurrence matrix. Since each camera motion is characterized by a certain pattern in the motion cooccurrence matrix, we calculate the statistical features of the cooccurrence matrix for each frame in the second step. The statistical features are examined to identify the camera motion type.

2.1 Motion Cooccurrence Matrix

For each frame of an input video sequence, we compute an optical flow field [8]. As we do not need a dense motion field, we calculate optical flow for uniformly sampled image points. Then we compute the magnitude and angle of each optical flow vector. The magnitude and the angle of a flow vector at an image point are given by

$$\rho = \sqrt{v_x^2 + v_y^2}, \quad \theta = \arctan\left(\frac{v_y}{v_x}\right) \qquad (1)$$

where (v_x, v_y) is a flow vector.

Given a flow field, the computation of the motion cooccurrence matrix requires a quantization of the flow vector angle. In the experiments, the angle is quantized into 12 levels with 30-degree interval.

For an $N \times M$ flow field, the cooccurrence matrix entry $C(i,j)$ is defined as

$$C(i,j) = \sharp\{(r,s) | \theta(r) = i, \theta(s) = j, d(r,s) = 1\} \qquad (2)$$

where r and s represent spatial positions of the neighboring flow vectors in the image, $d(r,s)$ represents the spatial distance between two positions r and s, and $\theta(r)$ and $\theta(s)$ are quantized angles of two flow vectors at positions r and s. The operator '$\sharp$' counts the number of flow vector pairs having angles i and j. From Eq. 2, we can see that the homogeneous flow vector field of an image contributes to peaks along the diagonal direction in the matrix.

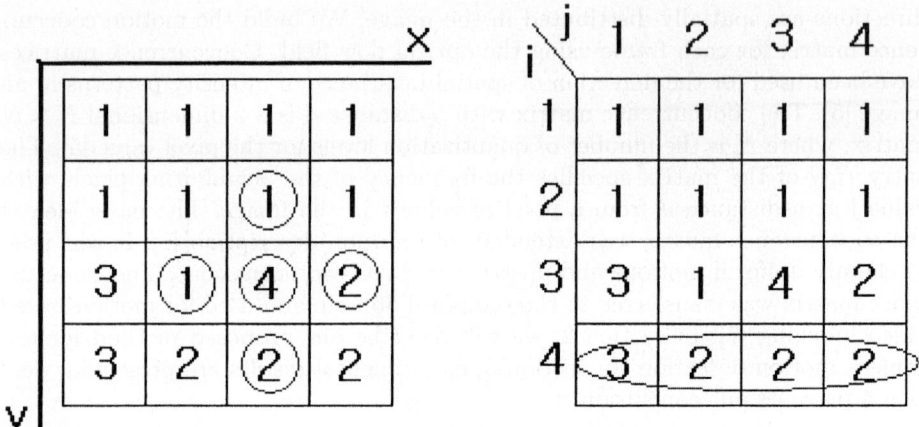

Fig. 1. Construction of a motion cooccurrence matrix

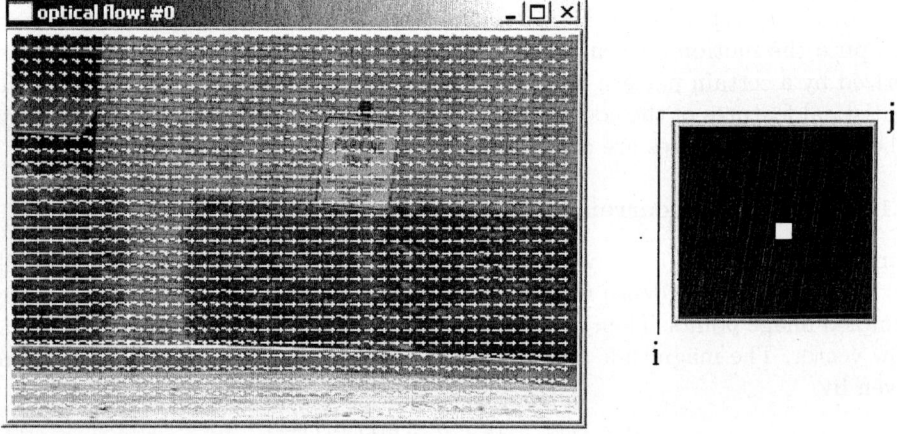

Fig. 2. An example of the motion cooccurrence matrix for the camera panning image overlapped with the optical flow field

Fig. 1 shows construction of a motion cooccurrence matrix. Assume that 4×4 flow field is given. Let each number in Fig. 1(a) represent the quantized angle of a flow vector. For instance, consider the point surrounded by a solid blue circle. The quantized angle of this point, $\theta(r)$ is 4. We consider four neighboring points with $d(r, s) = 1$. These points are marked by red circles. By counting the number of neighboring points for each angle, we get $C(4, 1) = C(4, 2) = 2, C(4, 3) = C(4, 4) = 0$. Corresponding entries of $C(i, j)$ are marked by a blue circle in Fig. 1(b). To obtain a cooccurrence matrix, the number of frequencies over the entire image is accumulated in the corresponding entry.

Fig. 2 shows some examples of motion cooccurrence matrices. In (a) and (b), frames from camera pan-right and zoom-in shots are overlapped with optical

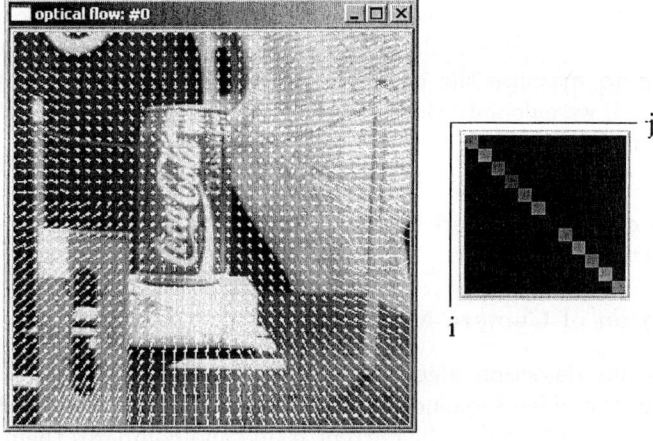

Fig. 3. An example of the motion cooccurrence matrix for the camera zooming image overlapped with the optical flow field

flow fields. (c) and (d) show the computed motion cooccurrence matrices for each camera motion. In pan-right, most of the flow vectors point to the left and a single peak at $180°$ is present in the cooccurrence matrix. In zoom-in, flow vectors are distributed over all the directions. This gives a line of peaks along the diagonal direction.

2.2 Statistical Feature Extraction

To identify camera motion types from the distinctive patterns in cooccurrence matrices, we compute statistical features of the cooccurrence matrices.

One of the most distinctive characteristics due to camera movement is a global distribution of motion over the entire image area. We define Mot_Act by computing the average occurrence of the matrix in each frame. The Mot_Act is close to 1 if there is a high degree of motion due to camera movement or an abrupt scene change.

$$Mot\_Act = \frac{\sum_{i,j} C(i,j)}{Total\ number\ of\ flow\ vector\ pairs} \quad (3)$$

For each flow vector, four neighbors are considered. Therefore, the total number of flow vector pairs is $4 \times N \times M$. Since a panning or a tilting operation typically induces a specific direction of motion in the optical flow field, the percentage of the dominant direction of motion, Dir and corresponding angle index, Max_Angle are defined in Eq. 4 and Eq. 5. During panning or tilting, Dir is close to 1.

$$Dir = \frac{max_{All\ C(i,j)}\{C(i,j)\}}{Total\ number\ of\ flow\ vector\ pairs} \quad (4)$$

$$Max\_Angle = i^*, \text{where } i^* \text{ is the angle index of the maximum } C(i,j) \quad (5)$$

A narrow strip along the diagonal direction in the motion cooccurrence matrix is a distinctive feature of the motion flow field under camera zooming. We define *Spread* to measure the degree of spread of a diagonal strip. For each non-zero $C(i,j)$, we calculate the distance from the diagonal line, $dt(i,j)$. Then *Spread* is defined as

$$Spread = Mean\_dt \times Var\_dt \qquad (6)$$

where $Mean\_dt$ and Var_dt are the mean and variance of the distance measurements, respectively.

2.3 Detection of Camera Motions

The basis of our detection algorithm is to set a pan, tilt or zoom mark for every frame in the video sequence where camera motion is present. It computes Mot_Act, Dir and $Spread$ for the current frame and compares them with corresponding threshold values. Further analysis of these parameters will allow us to mark the current frame as belonging to a specified motion type. During panning or tilting, one dominant motion direction is observable in the current frame's optical flow field. Therefore, both Mot_Act and Dir should be close to the highest value, 1. In real panning or tilting shots, these two parameters are lower than 1 due to noisy vectors and object motion. During zooming, flow vectors are distributed over all directions. So the percentage of the dominant motion direction is much lower than 1. Detailed steps are described in Table 1 and Table 2.

Table 1. Algorithm 1 for pan tilt detection

1:	reset det_boundary
2:	for i=0 to N-1
3:	if $Mot\_Act(i) > T1$ and $Dir(i) > T1$
4:	update det_boundary
5:	else
6:	postprocess(det_boundary)
7:	store(det_boundary)
8:	reset(det_boundary)
9:	end
10:	end

Assuming that the total length of the video sequence is N, algorithm 1 identifies potential pan/tilt shots by counting frames with high Mot_Act and Dir values. For the detected candidate, post-processing is applied to check the duration of the detected motion. We only consider camera motions that last longer than 10 frames. Directions of pan/tilt are also determined at the post-processing module from the angle of the highest bin in the cooccurrence matrix.

Zoom detection is similar to pan/tilt detection. Since motion vector directions are distributed over all directions, Dir is not large any more. Note that the dissolve operation also gives low Dir values because the randomness of the flow

Table 2. Algorithm 2 for zoom detection

```
 1:  reset det_boundary
 2:  for i=0 to N-1
 3:    if Mot_Act(i) > T1 and Dir(i) < T2 and Spread(i) < T3
 4:      update det_boundary
 5:    else
 6:      postprocess(det_boundary)
 7:      store(det_boundary)
 8:      reset(det_boundary)
 9:    end
10:  end
```

vector directions increases due to incorrect motion estimation during the dissolve period. This randomness of the flow directions can be characterized by high *Spread* in dissolve images. The third condition in line 3 is added to avoid false detection due to dissolves. Direction of a zoom (i.e., zoom-in or zoom-out) is determined at the post-processing module. To identify the direction of a camera zoom, we calculate the divergence of a flow vector defined as

$$div = \frac{dv_x}{dx} + \frac{dv_y}{dy} \qquad (7)$$

In each frame, we calculate the divergence of all the flow vectors and average them to get the mean divergence of a frame. Zoom-in or zoom-out can be identified by the positive or negative value of the mean divergence.

2.4 Threshold Selection

In our detection method, we need to set three threshold values, T1, T2 and T3. Since T1 and T2 are introduced to detect the presence of a global motion in images, we fix constant values for them assuming that a global motion is dominant during camera movement. Since T1 is related to the percentage of image areas having non-zero motions, we set $T1 = 0.6$ in the experiments. T2 is related to the number of quantized angular directions. Since we divide the $[0°, 360°]$ into 12 intervals, the percentage of motion vectors in each direction should be 8.3 % in ideal zooming images. We set $T2 = 0.2$ to give tolerance for noise and object motion. In order to automatically obtain an optimal threshold T3, we use the entropy threshold method [9]. This method is known to be efficient for two-class data classification problems. We assume *Spread* of the whole sequence can be split into two distributions, one for the frames belonging to the normal shot and the other for the dissolve shot. Then, the entropy threshold method finds the optimal threshold by searching through all possible threshold values, which optimizes the criterion function. Let the values of *Spread* be in the range $[0, M]$ and uniformly quantized by L bins. Then, let n_i represent the number of frames whose *Spread* values fall within the $i-$th bin, $i \in [0, L-1]$. Two probability distributions are derived from the distribution of *Spread* of an input sequence. Given a threshold t, the probability distribution of *Spread* for the normal frames is defined as

$$\frac{p_0}{P_t}, \frac{p_1}{P_t}, \frac{p_2}{P_t}, \ldots, \frac{p_t}{P_t}, \text{ where } p_i = \frac{n_i}{\sum_{k=0}^{L-1} n_k} \quad P_t = \sum_{i=0}^{t} p_i \quad (8)$$

Similarly, the probability distribution of *Spread* for the potential dissolve frames is defined as

$$\frac{p_{t+1}}{1-P_t}, \frac{p_{t+2}}{1-P_t}, \frac{p_{t+3}}{1-P_t}, \ldots, \frac{p_{L-1}}{1-P_t}, \quad (9)$$

Then, the entropies of the two classes are defined as

$$H_b(t) = -\sum_{i=0}^{t} \frac{p_i}{P_t} \ln \frac{p_i}{P_t} \quad (10)$$

$$H_w(t) = -\sum_{i=t+1}^{L-1} \frac{p_i}{1-P_t} \ln \frac{p_i}{1-P_t} \quad (11)$$

The optimal threshold, t^*, is defined as the central value of the $t^* - th$ bin where t^* has to satisfy the following criterion [9]

$$t^* = argmax_t\{H_b(t) + H_w(t)\} \quad (12)$$

3 Experimental Results

We evaluate the proposed method using test video sequences. The test set consists of 9 video clips from the Internet and documentary videos. The video frames are in 352 × 240 YUV 4:2:0 format and the frame rate is 29.97 frames/sec. Table 3 shows the test set used in our experiments. The number of frames, the boundaries of camera motion and the motion categories of each sequence are summarized in the table. The locations of these boundaries are hand labeled to obtain a ground truth.

The effectiveness of the proposed camera motion detector is evaluated from two frequently used parameters: *Recall* and *Precision*. These two metrics are defined as follows:

$$Rec = \frac{Number\ of\ correctly\ detected\ camera\ motion\ frames}{Number\ of\ overall\ frames\ of\ motion} \times 100$$

$$Prec = \frac{Number\ of\ correctly\ detected\ camera\ motion\ frames}{Number\ of\ frames\ of\ all\ detected\ motion} \times 100 \quad (13)$$

For an input video sequence, we obtain an optical flow field and a motion cooccurrence matrix for each frame. Then, statistical features are extracted as described in Sec. 2. Next, we apply the detection method to identify the pan/tilt/zoom shot boundaries of the input sequence. Fig. 4 shows plots of Mot_Act, Dir and Max_Angle of the test sequence (Hidden Fury #1) over time.

Table 3. Test video sequences

Sequence	Length (frame)	Contents
Senses and sensibility	510	157-339: pan+a moving object
	440	106-309: pan+a moving object
	400	54-220: pan+a moving object
Hidden fury	320	11-294: tilt-up
	240	21-215: pan-left
Wrestling with uncertainty	190	9-18: dissolve + zoom-out
		19-167: zoom-out
		168-179: dissolve
	550	30-139: zoom-out
		140-160: dissolve + zoom-out
		161-539: zoom-out
	290	0-29: dissolve
		30-249: zoom-out
		250-280: dissolve
	320	12-281: zoom-out + a moving object
	410	11-33: dissolve
		34-383: pan-right
		384-405: dissolve
Incredible monuments of Rome	541	27-75: dissolve + zoom-out
		76-271: zoom-out
		300-335: dissolve + zoom-in
		336-465: zoom-in

This sequence contains a 284-frame tilt-up from frames 12 to 295. In the upper plot, Mot_Act and Dir are shown by the solid blue and dotted green lines, respectively. A manually segmented boundary for the camera tilting is marked by the solid black lines. Detected boundaries are marked by dash-dot red lines. The direction of a tilt can be determined from Max_Angle as shown in the lower plot. Since the camera is tilting up in this sequence, most of the flow vectors have $270°$ direction, which corresponds to the quantized direction 9.

Fig. 5 illustrates the plot of Mot_Act, Dir and Max_Angle for the panning sequence. This sequence contains a 195-frame pan-left from frames 21 to 215. 162 frames are correctly detected and 33 frames are missed in this sequence. Decrease of Dir from frame 194 to 215 corresponds to the section of the shot where a man moves independently from the camera movement. Since the camera is panning to the left, most of the flow vectors have $0°$ directions.

If a shot contains camera zoom, Mot_Act will be very large whereas Dir will be small. This is illustrated in Fig. 6, which shows Mot_Act, Dir and $Spread$ over time. The sequence contains two zoom-out shots, one from frames 30 to 139, and the other from frames 161 to 539. Two zoom-out shots are connected by a dissolve. Since the first 110-frame zoom-out shot contains multiple motions that consist of zoom-out, tilt-up and a large moving object, our assumption of a single dominant motion is not valid for this case. To distinguish dissolves from

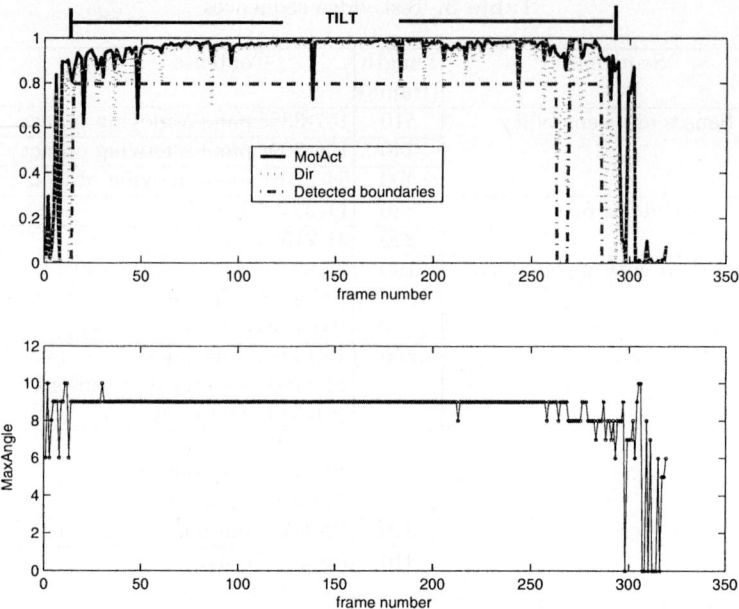

Fig. 4. Plot of *Mot_Act*, *Dir* and *Max_Angle* in the tilt sequence (Hidden Fury ♯1)

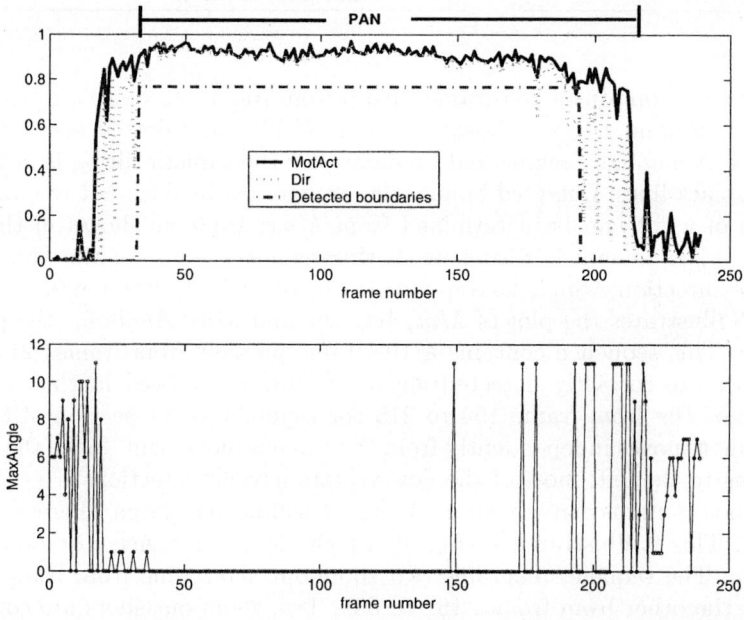

Fig. 5. Plot of *Mot_Act*, *Dir* and *Max_Angle* in the pan sequence (Hidden Fury ♯2)

zooms, we identify frames with high *Spread* values. Threshold T3 is automatically determined by the entropy threshold method as described in Sec. 2. The solid black line in the plot of *Spread* shows the derived threshold level of this sequence. The detected dissolve boundary is marked by the dash-dot red line in this plot. Detected dissolves are excluded from the detected zoom boundaries. Fig. 6 illustrates an example of the zooming sequence mixed with the dissolve. Due to the use of the *Spread* feature, dissolve between frame 140 and frame 160 can be distinguished from zooms and our method can avoid false positive detections of zoom.

The overall performance of the proposed detector for the test video set is estimated by calculating the total number of camera motion frames in the test set, the total number of correctly detected frames, the total number of falsely detected frames and the total number of missed frames. For the test set, *Recall* = 82.2% and *Precision* = 97.0 % values are obtained. If a camera zoom is combined

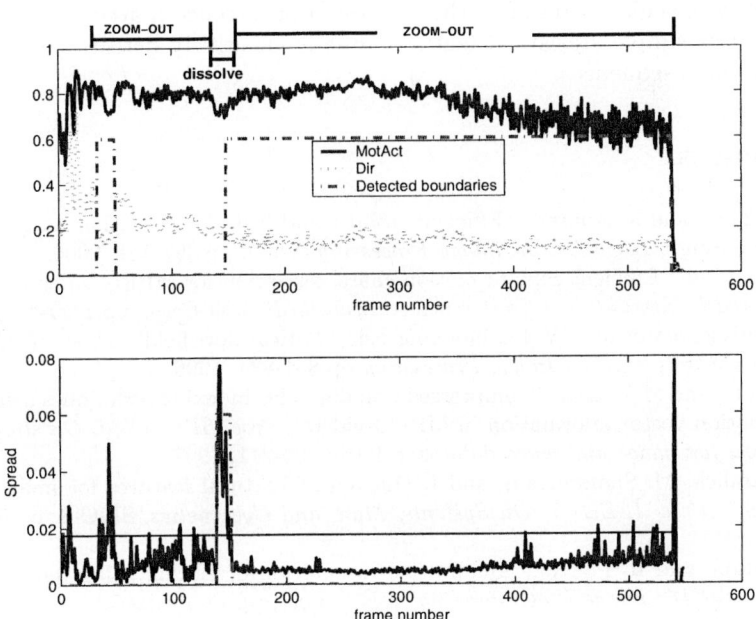

Fig. 6. Plot of *Mot_Act*, *Dir* and *Spread* in the zoom sequence (Wrestling with Uncertainty ♯3)

Table 4. Performance of the proposed camera motion detection method

Motion type	Correct	Missed	False	Recall	Precision
Pan/tilt	1200	179	14	87.0%	98.8%
Zoom	1128	324	58	77.6%	95.1%
Total	2328	503	72	82.2%	97.0%

with pan or tilt, many frames are missed because distribution of motion in the image cannot be characterized by our assumption of uniformity in all directions. Our dissolve detection based on the Spread parameter misses frames at the beginning and the end of dissolves and these missed dissolve frames are often falsely detected as zooms.

4 Conclusion

We propose a camera motion detection method that can identify pan, tilt and zoom in video sequences. Our method exploits global motion features extracted from the motion cooccurrence matrices. Since the motion cooccurrence matrix of motion vector directions between two images provides a compact representation of spatially homogeneous motion areas in the image, it allows us to detect simple camera motions in video sequences. The proposed method does not rely on the parametric motion model that typically requires high computational complexity. To identify specific patterns in the motion cooccurrence matrix, the proposed method uses simple statistical features, but it effectively detects pan, tilt and zoom in video sequences.

References

1. F. Dufaux, and J. Konrad, "Efficient, robust and fast global motion estimation for video coding", *IEEE Tr. on Image Processing*, Vol.9, pp.497-501, 2000.
2. J. Kim et al, "Efficient camera motion characterization for MPEG video indexing", *Proc. IEEE International Conference on Multimedia and Expo.*, pp.1171-1174, 2000.
3. V. Ardizzoneet et al., "Video indexing using optical flow field", *Proc. IEEE International Conference on Image Processing*, pp.831-834, 1996.
4. E. Kobla, and M. Cascia, "Compressed domain video indexing techniques using DCT and motion vector information in MPEG video", *Proc. SPIE Conf. On storage and retrieval for image and video databases V*, pp.200-211, 1997.
5. R. Haralick, M. Shanmugam, and I. Dinstein, "Textural features for image classification", *Proc. IEEE Tr. On Systems, Man, and Cybernetics*, SMC-3, pp.610-621, 1973.
6. R. Nelson, and R. Polana, "Qualitative recognition of motion using temporal texture", *CVGIP: Image Understanding*, vol.56, no.1, pp.78-89, 1992.
7. P. Bouthemy and R. Fablet, "Motion characterization from temporal cooccurrences of local motion-based measures for video indexing", *Proc. IEEE International Conference on Pattern Recognition*, Vol.1, pp.905-908, 1998.
8. B. Lucas, and T. Kanade, "An iterative image registration technique with an application to stereo vision", *Proc. DARPA IU Workshop*, pp.121-130, 1981.
9. J. Kapur, P. Sahoo and A. Wong, "A new method for gray-level picture thresholding using the entropy of the histogram", *Computer Vision Graphics Image Processing*, pp.273-185, 1981.

A Hybrid Motion Compensated 3-D Video Coding System for Blocking Artifacts Reduction

Cho-Chun Cheng[1], Wen-Liang Hwang[1], Zuowei Shen[2], and Tao Xia[3]

[1] Institute of Information Science, Academia Sinica, Taipei, Taiwan
[2] Department of Mathematics, National University of Singapore, Singapore
[3] Center for Wavelet, Approximation and Information Processing (CWAIP), National University of Singapore, Singapore

Abstract. We compare, both objectively and subjectively, the performance of various advanced motion compensation methods, including overlapped block motion compensation (OBMC) and control grid interpolation (CGI), in a 3-D wavelet based coding system. Our results indicate that an OBMC sequence usually has a higher PSNR than those of the other methods, while a CGI sequence usually has the least number of blocking artifacts. We combine these two methods in a hybrid system in order to achieve better visual quality and maintain satisfactory coding efficiency simultaneously. The objective and subjective results indicate that the proposed hybrid method removes more than 50% of blocking artifacts of an OBMC sequence, while simultaneously maintaining a high PSNR performance.

1 Introduction

Recent advances in motion-compensated temporal filtering (MCTF), which are based on discrete wavelet transform (DWT), make it possible to implement highly efficient video codecs in a 3-D structure with spatial, temporal, and SNR scalability [2],[10],[13],[16]. As implemented in most 3-D video coding systems, the block matching algorithm (BMA) is still the predominant method for reducing temporal redundancies due to its relatively low computational complexity. However, it is widely recognized that the discontinuous motion field generated by BMA may cause block-wise varying coefficient statistics and result in unpleasant blocking artifacts that degrade the visual quality of a video [1]. Previous research has suggested that many advanced motion compensation techniques, such as CGI or OBMC, can effectively improve the visual quality of a decompressed video [8],[9],[15]. Attempts to reduce blocking artifacts in 3-D video coding systems have also been reported. The systems in [3],[12] use a filter to smooth the areas where neighboring motion vectors are inconsistent. The early coding results of 3-D subband coding using CGI and OBMC are reported in [11] and [17], respectively.

In this work, the temporal filtering schemes based on advanced motion compensation techniques are described first, including CGI and OBMC. From the preliminary coding results, we observe that even though CGI and OBMC can reduce blocking artifacts in various applications, both methods generate distinct side effects during the de-blocking process. For CGI, although the decompressed sequences are free of blocking artifacts, undesirable blurred edges are often perceived due to the stronger smoothing effect resulting from a completely smooth motion field. In contrast, poor de-blocking results often appear in those areas with high motion activities after applying OBMC. In view of these problems, we develop a novel motion compensation model (OBCG) that can integrate the advantages of CGI and OBMC to achieve better visual quality, and maintain satisfactory coding efficiency simultaneously. Moreover, because OBCG creates inter-dependency relations between neighboring motion vectors (MVs), an iterative motion refinement algorithm based on dynamic programming is proposed for estimating the dependent motion field.

This paper is organized as follows. In Section 2, the frameworks of temporal filtering based on CGI and OBMC are introduced. In Section 3, a novel motion compensation model is presented, and our proposed iterative motion refinement algorithm is formulated. The simulation results are reported and compared with those of conventional methods objectively and subjectively in Section 4. Finally, in Section 5, we present our conclusions.

2 Temporal Filtering Frameworks of OBMC and CGI

In motion compensated 3-D subband coding schemes, temporal filtering is performed along the motion trajectory between video frames. For simplicity, the following discussion assumes that the temporal filter is the Haar wavelet, which is the most popular temporal filter and is used in the majority of 3-D wavelet coding systems.

2.1 Temporal Analysis Filtering

Under a conventional MCTF framework, motion compensation is implemented between a pair of successive frames $\mathbf{F} = (f_1, f_2)$. The highpass subband frame H corresponds to the temporal location of frame f_1, while the lowpass subband has the same temporal position as f_2. During motion compensation, f_1 is partitioned into a group of non-overlapped square blocks, $\mathbf{P} = (P_{0,0}, \cdots, P_{N_1-1,N_2-1})$. Each block then finds its corresponding block with the least distortion measurement in f_2 during the motion estimation operation. Let $f_1(s)$ and $f_2(s)$ denote the pixel intensity at spatial index $s = (x, y)$ of frames f_1 and f_2 respectively. Also, let $\hat{f}_1(s)$ and v^{MC} respectively denote the predicted pixel intensity at s and the corresponding motion vector (MV) obtained by using the MC motion compensation technique. For the Haar wavelet, the temporal filtering scheme is given by

$$H(s) = \frac{1}{\sqrt{2}}[f_1(s) - \hat{f}_1^{MC}(s)], \quad s \in P_{i,j} \qquad (1)$$

$$L(s) = \sqrt{2} f_2(s) + H(s + v^{MC}), \quad s \in P_{i,j} \qquad (2)$$

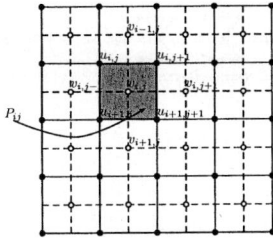

Fig. 1. Configuration of CGI and OBMC. The black nodes on the vertices of each block represent the control points in CGI. The white node in the center of each block represents the MV of each block in OBMC.

The *MC* in Equations 1 and 2 represents the motion compensation technique adopted in temporal filtering. Although CGI and OBMC both try to eliminate unexpected discontinuities in motion-compensated frames, they adopt different concepts. CGI produces a smooth motion field in order to preserve continuity and connectivity in the predicted frame. As shown in Fig. 1, the vertices of each block are chosen as control points, with each point assigned to an MV in the set $\mathbf{U} = (\mathbf{u}_{0,0}, \cdots, \mathbf{u}_{N_1,N_2})$. Let $\mathbf{u}_{i+p,j+q}$ be the p,qth neighboring MV associated with $P_{i,j}$. For each interior pixel in $P_{i,j}$, CGI computes an individual MV by interpolating its neighboring control points. $w_{p,q}(\mathbf{s})$ denotes the scalar interpolation coefficient, and depends on the desired contribution of the p,qth control point to $\mathbf{s}$. Therefore, the temporal filtering scheme of CGI can be formulated by replacing $\hat{f}_1^{MC}(\mathbf{s})$ and $\mathbf{v}^{MC}$ in Equations 1 and 2 with $\hat{f}_1^{CGI}(\mathbf{s})$ and $\mathbf{v}^{CGI}$ respectively, which are given as

$$\hat{f}_1^{CGI}(\mathbf{s}) = f_2(\mathbf{s} - \mathbf{v}^{CGI}) \qquad (3)$$

$$\mathbf{v}^{CGI} = \sum_{p=0}^{1} \sum_{q=0}^{1} w_{p,q}(\mathbf{s}) \mathbf{u}_{i+p,j+q}, \qquad (4)$$

where

$$\sum_{p=0}^{1} \sum_{q=0}^{1} w_{p,q}(\mathbf{s}) = 1, \quad and \quad \mathbf{s} \in P_{i,j}. \qquad (5)$$

On the other hand, OBMC reduces the abrupt changes of pixel intensities between neighboring blocks by using a weighted sum at block boundaries. As shown in Fig. 1, instead of assigning four MVs to every vertex in the CGI scheme, OBMC assigns a single MV to each block, and the MV set is denoted as $\mathbf{V} = (\mathbf{v}_{0,0}, \cdots, \mathbf{v}_{N_1-1,N_2-1})$. Let $\alpha_{p,q}(\mathbf{s})$ denote the weighting factor for the p,qth neighboring MV at $\mathbf{s}$. Then, the temporal filtering scheme of OBMC can be formulated by replacing $\hat{f}_1^{MC}(\mathbf{s})$ and $\mathbf{v}^{MC}$ in Equations 1 and 2 with $\hat{f}_1^{OBMC}(\mathbf{s})$ and $\mathbf{v}^{OBMC}$ respectively, which are given as

$$\hat{f}_1^{OBMC}(s) = \sum_{p=-1}^{1}\sum_{q=-1}^{1} \alpha_{p,q}(s) f_2(s - v_{i+p,j+q}) \qquad (6)$$

$$v^{OBMC} = v_{i,j}, \qquad (7)$$

where

$$\sum_{p=-1}^{1}\sum_{q=-1}^{1} \alpha_{p,q}(s) = 1, \quad |p|+|q| < 2, \quad and \quad s \in P_{i,j}. \qquad (8)$$

2.2 Temporal Synthesis Filtering

Based on the temporal analysis filtering process addressed in the previous section, the temporal synthesis filtering process is straightforward. Let L' and H' denote the temporal subbands received at the decoder side, and f'_1 and f'_2 denote the reconstructed frames of f_1 and f_2 respectively. The general form of connected and multiple connected pixel reconstruction equations can then be formulated as

$$f'_1(s) = \sqrt{2} H'(s) + \hat{f}'^{MC}_1(s), \qquad (9)$$

$$f'_2(s) = \frac{1}{\sqrt{2}}[L'(s) - H'(s + v^{MC})]. \qquad (10)$$

The temporal synthesis filtering scheme of CGI can be formulated by replacing v^{MC} (in Equation 10) with v^{CGI} in Equation 4, and $\hat{f}'^{MC}_1(s)$ (in Equation 9) with $\hat{f}'^{CGI}_1(s)$, which is given as

$$\hat{f}'^{CGI}_1(s) = f'_2(s - v^{CGI}). \qquad (11)$$

In the case of OBMC, v^{MC} can be replaced with v^{OBMC} in Equation 7, and $\hat{f}'^{OBMC}_1(s)$ is given as

$$\hat{f}'^{OBMC}_1(s) = \sum_{p=-1}^{1}\sum_{q=-1}^{1} \alpha_{p,q}(s) f'_2(s - v_{i+p,j+q}). \qquad (12)$$

In the proposed synthesize method, both OBMC and CGI can be decoded in the same framework (by Equations 9 and 10) but with different modules (CGI in Equations 4 and 11, and OBMC in Equations 7 and 12). With this approach, we can alter the video codec with suitable motion compensation schemes in accordance with computational costs, rate constraints, or different requirements of visual quality.

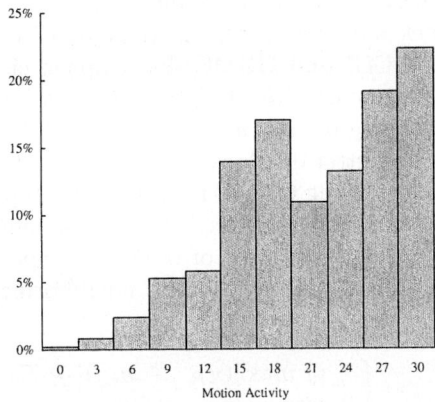

Fig. 2. The average percentage of blocks with blocking artifacts versus motion activity in the *Dancer* and *Foreman* OBMC sequences

3 A Novel Motion Compensation Model

In this work, we develop a novel motion compensation model that integrates the advantages of CGI and OBMC to achieve better visual quality and maintain satisfactory coding efficiency simultaneously. The major operation involved in the de-blocking process is smoothing. The inclusion of OBMC in the H.263 standard demonstrates the effectiveness of the simple smoothing technique in removing blocking artifacts [4]. Even so, some blocking artifacts still exist on sequences after OBMC has been applied. Our observations show that most of the blocking artifacts of OBMC appear along the block boundary of adjacent blocks with highly inconsistent motion vectors. In Fig. 2, the plot shows the average percentage of blocks with blocking artifacts versus the motion activity of various OBMC sequences. The motion activity is measured by calculating the maximum absolute difference between the motion vector of a block and the motion vectors of its neighboring blocks. We can see from the plot that even after OBMC motion compensation is applied, blocking artifacts are still very likely to occur in areas where motion activity is high.

In contrast, CGI, which is regarded as a stronger smoothing operation, provides a completely smooth motion field that includes those areas around and within a block. However, the strong smoothing effect provided by CGI often over-blurs the decompressed video signal and sometimes makes the edge information indistinguishable.

Inspired by the approach that uses a simple filtering mechanism with two different modes to remove blocking artifacts after motion compensation [7], we propose a simple selection mechanism to combine the advantages of the higher PSNR of OBMC and fewer blocking artifacts of CGI. The hybrid method is motivated by our previous experiment results of evaluating OBMC and CGI performances subjectively and objectively on a 3-D wavelet coding system. We decide whether the block should be compensated by OBMC or by CGI. To select a proper mode between CGI and OBMC, local image characteristics must be examined. When the motion activities between neighboring blocks are relatively high, the stronger smoothing operation provided by CGI inside a block, as well as at its boundaries, has a better de-blocking effect. In contrast, when the motion activities are relatively low, using OBMC to smooth a few pixels around a block's boundary is enough to achieve the desired de-blocking effect and retain a high PSNR performance without losing most of the edge properties. In our proposed coding scheme, the motion activities between neighboring areas are examined by using the following measurement:

$$\phi_{P_{i,j}}(\mathbf{v}_{P_{i,j}}) = \begin{cases} 1, if \max |(\mathbf{v}_{P_{i,j}} - v_{i,j})| \geq Threshold \\ 0, otherwise, \end{cases} \tag{13}$$

where

$$\mathbf{v}_{P_{i,j}} = \{v_{i+p,j+q}| -1 \leq p \leq 1; -1 \leq q \leq 1; p,q \in Z\}.$$

$\mathbf{v}_{P_{i,j}}$ represents the set of neighboring MVs associated with $P_{i,j}$. If the difference between the target block's MV ($v_{i,j}$) and any of its neighboring block's MV ($v_{i+p,j+q}$) is larger than a certain threshold, $\phi_{P_{i,j}}$ is set to 1, and CGI is adopted in the target block. Otherwise, $\phi_{P_{i,j}}$ is set to 0 and OBMC is adopted in the target block.

OBCG utilizes most of the settings of OBMC. However, additional motion compensation choices are added to the original OBMC framework. The major feature of our proposed motion compensation model is that it allows each block to be compensated by either CGI or OBMC in accordance with the surrounding motion activities. Therefore, the dependent motion estimation optimization problem of OBCG can be formulated as

$$\min J_{OBCG}(\mathbf{V})$$
$$= \min_{\mathbf{V}} \{ \sum_{i=0}^{N_1-1} \sum_{j=0}^{N_2-1} D_{OBCG}(P_{i,j}, \mathbf{v}_{P_{i,j}})$$
$$+ D_{CGI}(P_{i,j}, \mathbf{v}_{P_{i,j}}) \cdot \phi_{P_{i,j}}]\}, \tag{14}$$

where

$$D_{CGI}(P_{i,j}, \mathbf{v}_{P_{i,j}}) = \frac{1}{N_p} \sum_{s \in P_{i,j}} |f_1(s) - \hat{f}_1^{CGI}(s)| \tag{15}$$

$$D_{OBMC}(P_{i,j}, \mathbf{v}_{P_{i,j}}) = \frac{1}{N_p} \sum_{s \in P_{i,j}} |f_1(s) - \hat{f}_1^{OBMC}(s)|. \tag{16}$$

$D_{CGI}(P_{i,j}, \mathbf{v}_{P_{i,j}})$ and $D_{OBMC}(P_{i,j}, \mathbf{v}_{P_{i,j}})$ denote the prediction error of block $P_{i,j}$ using CGI and OBMC respectively, and N_p represents the number of pixels in $P_{i,j}$. It is worth noting that the motion field of the proposed model can not be solved by optimizing each block's prediction error independently, because each adjacent block pair shares more than one MV. Optimizing each block's prediction error independently leads to considerable performance degradation. Therefore, an iterative motion refinement scheme based on dynamic programming is proposed to solve the dependent optimization problem. First, the original 2-D dependent motion estimation optimization problem of OBCG is decomposed into a series of 1-D problems; then, the iterative motion refinement algorithm of OBCG is performed as follows:

Step 0. Initialize the MV set **V** of each block using BMA, and split **V** into two subsets {**vo**, **ve**}, where **vo** and **ve** denote the MV subset of odd rows and even rows respectively. Moreover, for each $i \in \{i = 1 + 2x | 0 \leq x < \frac{N_1 - 1}{2}, x \in Z\}$, let $\mathbf{vo}_i$ denote the MV subset of the ith odd row, and for each $i \in \{i = 2x | 0 \leq x \leq \frac{N_1 - 1}{2}, x \in Z\}$, let $\mathbf{ve}_i$ denote the MV subset of the ith even row.

Step 1. Set optimization cycle $k = 0$ to $\mathbf{vo}^k = \{\mathbf{vo}_1^k, \mathbf{vo}_3^k, \cdots\}$ and $\mathbf{ve}^k = \{\mathbf{ve}_0^k, \mathbf{ve}_2^k, \cdots\}$ for the initial condition.

Step 2. Use **V** to calculate ϕ, which classifies the motion compensation technique adopted by each block.

Step 3. Odd row processing:
- Fix $\mathbf{ve}^k$ to provide the neighboring condition for odd row optimization, and apply Equation 17, shown below, for each ith row.

$$\mathbf{vo}_i^{k+1} = \arg \min_{\mathbf{vo}_i^{k+1}} (\sum_{j=0}^{N_2 - 1} D_{OBCG}(A_{i,j}, \mathbf{v}_{A_{i,j}})) \quad (17)$$

$$for \ i \in \{i = 1, 3, \cdots\}. \quad (18)$$

- Update $\mathbf{V} = \{\mathbf{vo}^{k+1}, \mathbf{ve}^k\}$, and increase $k = k + 1$.

Step 4. Even row processing:
- Fix $\mathbf{vo}^k$, and apply even row optimization to find $\mathbf{ve}^{k+1}$ by replacing the vo with ve in Equation 17, for $i \in \{i = 0, 2, \cdots\}$.
- Update $\mathbf{V} = \{\mathbf{vo}^k, \mathbf{ve}^{k+1}\}$, and increase $k = k + 1$.

Step 5. Iterate **Steps 2-4** until J_{OBCG} converges to a minimum.

When calculating Equation 17 for the possible paths in the trellis, instead of calculating the prediction error of each non-overlapped $P_{i,j}$, different corresponding areas $A_{i,j}$ should be considered. The corresponding areas are only those overlapped regions affected while refining consecutive MVs. $\mathbf{v}_{A_{i,j}}$ represents the set of neighboring MVs needed to compensate for $A_{i,j}$. Note that the same classification ϕ is adopted at the decoder side, so our proposed dual mode selection model can be perfectly reconstructed without sending any additional overhead.

4 Performance Evaluation

In this section, we perform comparative studies of alternative 3-D subband coding schemes in terms of both objective and subjective evaluations. The video

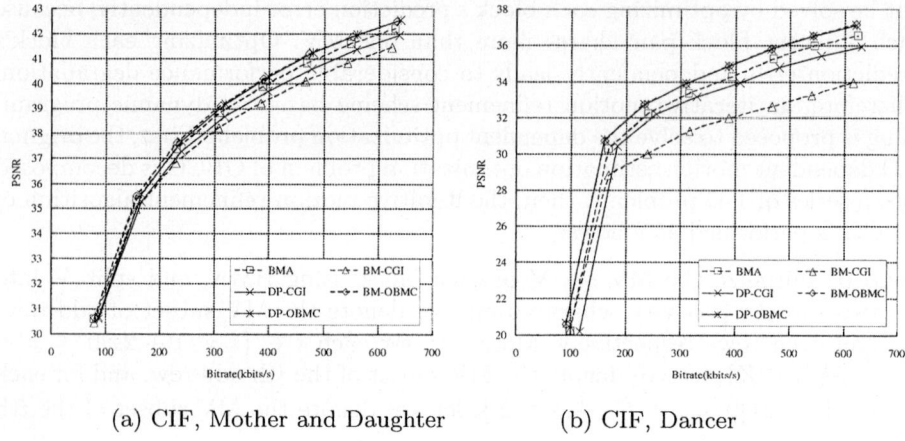

(a) CIF, Mother and Daughter (b) CIF, Dancer

Fig. 3. The PSNR performance of BMA, BM-CGI, DP-CGI, BM-OBMC, and DP-OBMC at various bit rates

sequences used in our experiments are Y-luminance signals of QCIF ($176 \times 144 \times 30 fps$) and CIF ($352 \times 288 \times 30 fps$) formats. Conventional motion compensation based on BMA is implemented using full-search with integer pel accuracy, and a $[-16, 15]$ search range is set for both the horizontal and vertical dimensions. With regard to the proposed motion compensation schemes based on OBCG, the initial motion field for each block is estimated by a full-search BMA. The motion field is then updated using the iterative motion refinement scheme proposed in this work. The bilinear transform is adopted to compute the scalar interpolation coefficients w of CGI, and the 24×24 weighting window proposed in [14] is chosen as the α for our OBMC. First, all of the video signals are applied with three levels of temporal filtering using the Haar filter, and a 3-level spatial DWT with the $9 - 7$ filter is then applied. Finally, the 3-D SPIHT (Set Partitioning in Hierarchical Trees) [6] algorithm is used to encode the wavelet coefficients of each subband to generate a scalable bitstream.

Because both CGI and OBMC create inter-dependency relations between neighboring MVs, the proposed iterative motion refinement algorithm is adopted to improve the coding efficiency. As shown in Fig. 3, the improvement achieved by using the proposed iterative motion refinement scheme based on dynamic programming for CGI (DP-CGI) is significant. The scheme can usually achieve a 0.4 - 1.9 dB gain over the result of CGI, which uses the motion field obtained by BMA(BM-CGI). For OBMC, both BM-OBMC and DP-OBMC achieve considerable performance improvements over the conventional coding scheme based on BMA. The coding gain is about 0.3 - 0.7 dB, on average. The PSNR performance of OBCG for different video sequences at various bit rates is shown in Fig. 4. Because DP-CGI and DP-OBMC represent two special cases of OBCG, the PSNR performance of OBCG usually lies between these two methods. However, OBCG still maintains a 0.3 - 0.4 dB gain over the conventional coding scheme based on BMA.

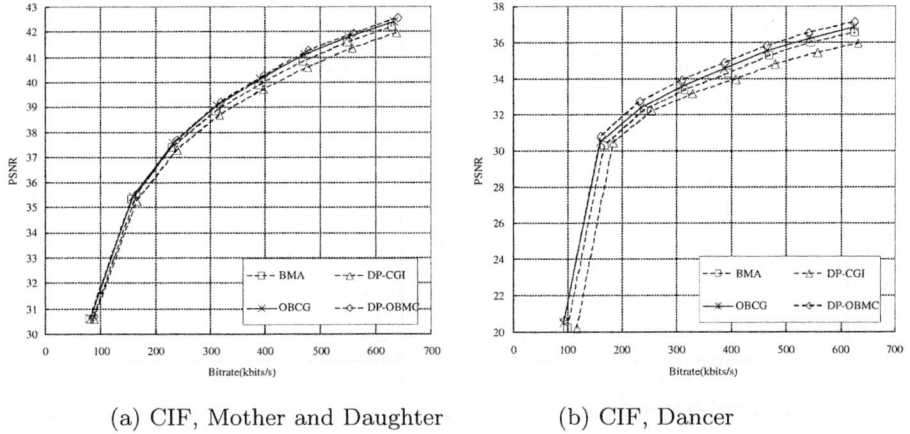

(a) CIF, Mother and Daughter (b) CIF, Dancer

Fig. 4. The PSNR performance of BMA, DP-CGI, DP-OBMC, and OBCG at various bit rates

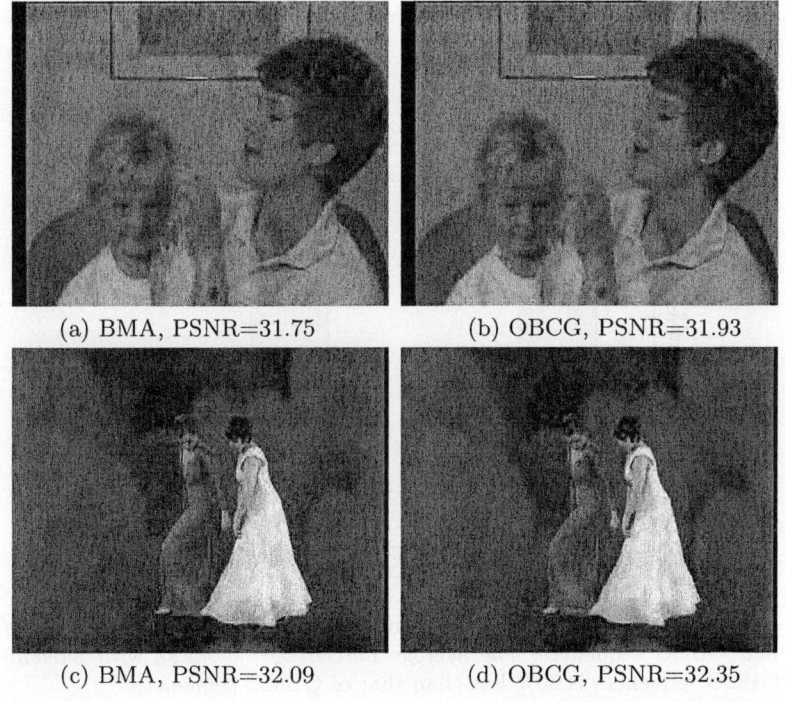

(a) BMA, PSNR=31.75 (b) OBCG, PSNR=31.93

(c) BMA, PSNR=32.09 (d) OBCG, PSNR=32.35

Fig. 5. Perceptual quality: (a),(b) frame 76 of CIF Mother and Daughter at 95 kbits/sec; and (c),(d) frame 50 of CIF Dancer at 200 kbits/sec

For subjective evaluation, the decompressed frames in Fig. 5 show the visual quality of different schemes. It is clear that our proposed 3-D video coding scheme

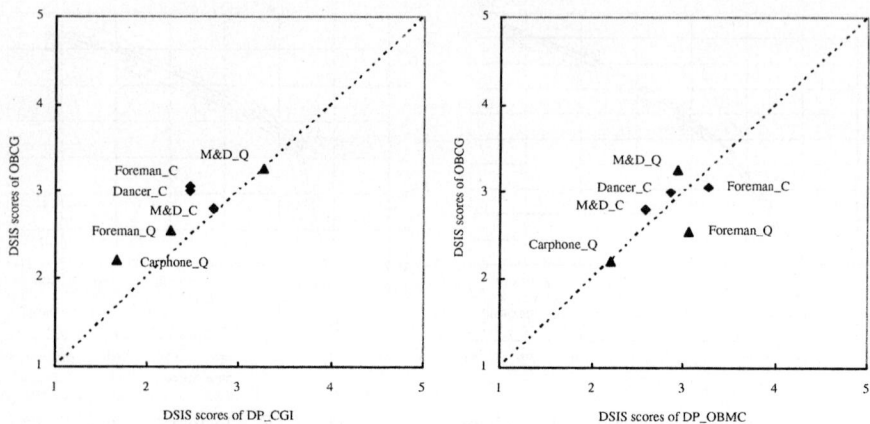

Fig. 6. Perceptual comparison of 3-D video coding systems using DP-CGI, DP-OBMC, and OBCG for various video sequences at low bit rates. (Q: QCIF, and C: CIF).

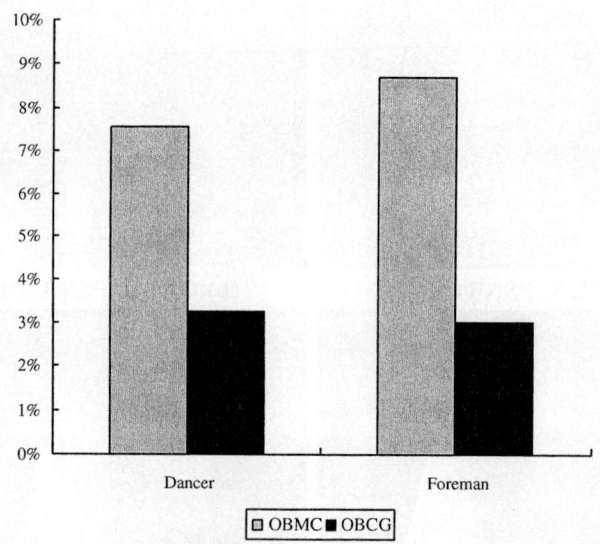

Fig. 7. Comparison of the average percentage of blocks with blocking artifacts of OBMC and OBCG sequences. The average percentage of blocks with blocking artifacts of OBCG sequences is 50% less than that of OBMC sequences.

adapts to various frame features successfully, and removes noticeable blocking artifacts without degrading details. To compare it with conventional de-blocking techniques, more sophisticated subjective tests were conducted. The first subjective tests were conducted according to the requirements of [5], and the DSIS

(Double Stimulus Impairment Scale) was evaluated. While evaluating DSIS, the testers were required to vote using a five-grade impairment scale from 5 (imperceptible) to 1 (very annoying) after being presented with the test materials. The comparative results are shown in Fig. 6. We observe that better subjective performances of OBCG are consistently maintained through different types of video sequences. Although the coding results of DP-CGI and DP-OBMC show the performance bounds of our proposed model in terms of PSNR, the results of subjective evaluation show that the perceptual quality of our proposed model is not necessarily between them. The perceptual quality of most video sequences compressed by OBCG can also outperform both DP-CGI and DP-OBMC. We also demonstrate the results of another subjective test by asking our testers to identify, frame-by-frame, the blocks that contain the blocking artifacts in video sequences encoded by different methods. From the results shown in Fig. 7, we conclude that OBCG reduces more than 50% of the blocking artifacts that appear in OBMC sequences.

5 Conclusions

An iterative motion refinement algorithm is proposed for estimating the dependent motion field and improving the coding efficiency of OBCG. The optimal motion vectors are obtained by applying a sequence of 1-D dynamic programming algorithms. Motivated by the preliminary objective and subjective results, we propose a hybrid OBMC/CGI system, which combines the high PSNR of OBMC sequences and the low blocking artifacts of CGI sequences. The system uses the motion vector of a block to determine by which method a block should be encoded. Experiment results show that our proposed model adapts to various frame features successfully, and leads to improved PSNR and better perceptual quality over the BMA model. Compared to conventional de-blocking techniques, although DP-CGI and DP-OBMC have shown the performance bounds of our proposed model in terms of PSNR, the results of subjective evaluation show that the perceptual quality of our proposed model can outperform them in most cases. In the future, finding a good blocking artifact measurement and including it into our coding system to evaluate the proposed hybrid system will be the focus of our work.

References

1. M.C. Chen and A.N. Willson, Jr.: Motion-vector optimization of control grid interpolation and overlapped block motion compensation using iterated dynamic programming. *IEEE Trans. on Image Processing*, vol. 9, no. 7, pp. 1145-1157, July 2000.
2. S.-J. Choi and J.W. Woods: Motion-compensated 3-D subband coding of video. *IEEE Trans. on Image Processing*, vol. 8, no. 2, pp. 155-167, February 1999.
3. K. Hanke, T. Rusert, and J.-R. Ohm: Motion-compensated 3D video coding using smooth transitions. *Proc. SPIE Visual Communications Image Processing*, vol. 5022, pp. 933-940, 2003.

4. ITU-T: ITU-T Recommendation H.263: Video coding for low bitrate communication. *The International Telecommunication Union*, 1996.
5. ITU-R: ITU-R Recommendation BT.500-11: Methodology for the subjective assessment of the quality of television pictures. *The International Telecommunication Union*, 2002.
6. B.-J. Kim, Z. Xiong, and W.A. Pearlman: Low bit-rate scalable video coding with 3-D set partitioning in hierarchical trees. *IEEE Trans. on Circuits and Systems for Video Technology*, vol. 10, no. 8, pp. 1374-1387, December 2000.
7. S.D. Kim, J. Yi, H.M. Kim, and J.B. Ra: A deblocking filter with two separate modes in block-based video coding. *IEEE Transactions on Circuits and Systems for Video Technology*, vol. 9, no. 1, pp. 156-160, February 1999.
8. Y. Nakaya and H. Harashima: Motion compensation based on spatial transformation. *IEEE Transactions on Circuits and Systems for Video Technology*, vol. 6, no. 3, pp. 243-250, June 1994.
9. M.T. Orchard and G.J. Sullivan: Overlapped block motion compensation: an estimation-theoretic approach. *IEEE Trans. on Image Processing*, vol. 3, no. 5, pp. 693-699, September 1994.
10. J.-R. Ohm: Three-dimensional subband coding with motion compensation. *IEEE Trans. on Image Processing*, vol. 4, no. 3, pp. 339-367, 1994.
11. J.-R. Ohm: Motion-compensated 3-D subband coding with multiresolution representation of motion parameters. *Proc. IEEE Int. Conf. Image Processing*, vol. 3, pp. 250-254, 1994.
12. T. Rusert, K. Hanke, and J.-R. Ohm: Transition filtering and optimized quantization in interframe wavelet video coding. *Proc. SPIE Visual Communications Image Processing*, vol. 5150, pp. 682-694, 2003.
13. A. Secker and D. Taubman: Highly scalable video compression using a lifting-based 3D wavelet transform with deformable mesh motion compensation. *Proc. IEEE Int. Conf. Image Processing*, pp. 1029-1032, 2001.
14. K. Shen and E.J. Delp: Wavelet based rate scalable video compression. *IEEE Trans. on Circuits and Systems for VideoTechnology*, vol. 9, no. 1, pp. 109-122, February 1999.
15. G.J. Sullivan and R.L. Baker: Motion compensation for video compression using control grid interpolation. *Proc. IEEE Int. Conf. Acoustics, Speech, Signal Processing*, vol. 4, pp. 2713-2716, 1991.
16. J.W. Woods and P. Chen: Improved MC-EZBC with quarter-pixel motion vectors. *ISO/IEC JTC1/SC29/WG11*, MPEG doc., M8366, Fairfax, May 2002.
17. Y. Wu, R.A. Cohen, and J.W. Woods: An overlapped block motion estimation for MC-EZBC. *ISO/IEC JTC1/SC29/WG11*, MPEG doc., M10158, Brisbane, October 2003.

Fast Panoramic Image Generation Method Using Morphological Corner Detection

Jungho Lee, Woongho Lee, Ikhwan Cho, and Dongseok Jeong

Hitech Center 916ho Inha University, 253 Yonghyun-dong Namgu,
402751 Incheon, South Korea
{julian, ltlee, teddydino}@inhaian.net
dsjeong@inha.ac.kr
http://multimedia.inha.ac.kr/index.html

Abstract. We present a method of building a panoramic image from adjacent images. The panoramic image is constructed using several images taken by adjacent cameras or parsed from a video, and used for photogrammetry or many computer graphic applications. The perspective transformation, which is estimated from the appropriate corresponding pairs of images, can be used to construct the panoramic image without unwarranted distortion. We used the corner points for the corresponding features, and morphological structures were utilized for fast and robust corner detection. We used the criterion of the corner strength, which guarantees the robust detection of the corner in most situations. For the transformation, 8 parameters were estimated from perspective equations, and bilinear color blending was used to construct a seamless panoramic video. The experiments showed that the proposed method yields fast results with good quality under various conditions.

1 Introduction

The automatic construction of high-resolution image mosaics is an active area of research in the fields of photogrammetry, computer vision, image processing and computer graphics. Image mosaics can be used for many different applications. The most traditional application is the construction of large aerial and satellite photographs from collections of images [1]. More recent applications include scene stabilization, change detection, video compression and video indexing uses mosaic image to increase the field of view and resolution of the camera [2], [3], [4], [5].

A number of techniques have been developed for the stitching process. A simple and hardware-intensive way is to use a lens with a very large field of view such as a fish-eye lens, while another way is to record a cylindrical panoramic image on a long film strip [6]. The image mosaic or stitching methods are widely used for panoramic image generation in computer graphics, because they are relatively independent of the hardware and induce less distortion. These methods use image processing techniques such as template matching, edge detection, or perspective transformation [7], [9], [12]. Most of these methods use corresponding points in partially conjoined images to accomplish perspective transformation [7], [8], [12], [13]. Template matching with simulated annealing [14] and the high-curvature detection of contours [7] are commonly used methods, but these algorithms require a large number of calculations. The number of calculations or processing speed are very important factors when image mosaics are adopted for change detection or background extraction for video compression.

In this paper, we propose an efficient and fast image mosaicing method, which uses morphological corner detection for corresponding point matching. The results obtained with the proposed method show that it provides a fast processing speed and nearly distortionless images.

First, we describe the overall method of image mosaicing in section 2. The detail algorithms used in the proposed method are presented in sections 3 and 4. Finally, we discuss the experimental results and future works in section 5.

2 Procedure of Image Mosaicing

Panoramic images are generated by applying the mosaic process to several con-joined images, which were acquired at the same time and location from adjacent cam-eras or a panning camera. Our mosaic method of generating panoramic images can be classified into four stages. First, the overlap lengths between the conjoined images, which limit the boundary of the processing region, are measured. The images obtained from multiple adjacent cameras or a continuously panning camera have overlapped regions. If the overlap lengths are known, the processing time required to find the corresponding pairs is drastically decreased. Second, four corresponding points are decided between two adjacent identical scenes. These points can be obtained through a corner point detection and simple pattern matching process. Third, the perspective transformation parameters are calculated from the coordinates of the four corresponding pairs. Because the relative directions or locations of the cameras are unknown and a wide angle optical lens has distortions in its boundaries, the panoramic image cannot be made with a simple cut and paste method. Therefore we have to apply a perspective transformation to one side of two adjacent images. We used the 8-parameter model for the perspective transformation [7], [8], [12], [13]. The parameters of this model can be obtained by mathematical approximation from the coordinate relations of the four corresponding pairs. Finally, we apply bilinear color blending, which eliminates the ghost effect of the panorama image on the transformed image.

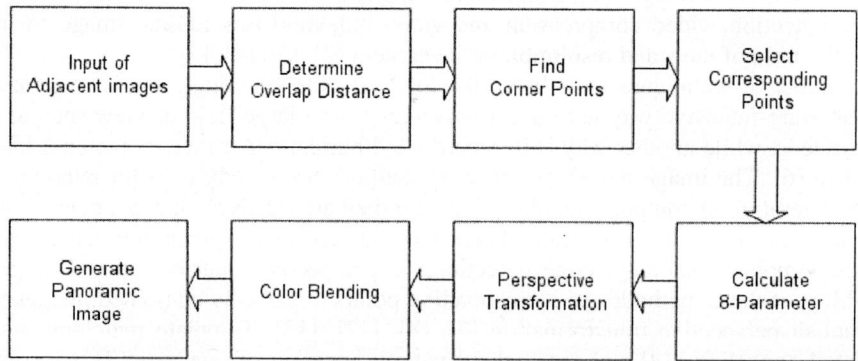

Fig. 1. The block diagram of mosaic process

All computer vision based operations are based on grey images, except for the color blending step, which eliminates the ghosts from the resultant image. A block diagram of the proposed mosaic method is shown in Fig. 1.

3 Find Corresponding Pairs

This section describes the second stage which includes the calculation of the overlap distance of the adjacent images, the corner detection of the overlapped images and the pattern matching of the corner points which are found. If the overlap distance is known, the processing time can be reduced, by restricting the processing area. Pattern matching allows two corner points of adjacent images to be selected as matched points. To minimize the distortion of the perspective transform, the four corresponding pairs have to form a nearly perfect rectangle, and it is more effective when the four corresponding points are distant from each other.

3.1 Calculate Overlapping Distance

Before finding the corresponding pairs, we can determine the overlapping distance between the adjacent images. If we have this information, we can reduce the scope of the region which contains the corresponding points. This has the advantage of decreasing the processing time, as well as reducing the number of mismatched pairs.

We used the simple MSE (mean square error) described below to find the overlapping distances. If we calculate the MSEs while increasing the overlapping region from the lower boundary to the upper boundary of overlap, which is determined by the installation of the camera, the exact overlapping distance has the minimum MSE (1). In equation (1), the overlap is the candidate distance, and u(m,n) is the gray level of the pixel situated at the coordinates (m,n) of the input image.

$$\sigma_{MSE}^2 = \frac{1}{OverlapArea} \sum_{n=0}^{height} \sum_{m=0}^{Overlap} |u(m,n) - u'(Overlap - m, n)|^2 \quad (1)$$

We utilize an image pyramid to reduce the complexity of the arithmetic operation, which is induced by the use of the MSE [10]. Each image is down-sampled with a ratio of half and quarter and, in this way, the overlap distance is gradually estimated from the quarter level image to the original level image.

3.2 Corner Detection

Some features such as edges, census transformed points, high-curvatures or corner points are employed to find corresponding pairs. We utilize the corner points to determine the corresponding pairs. Usually, corner points are not affected by the difference in contrast between images or deformable transformations. The distributions of the corner points of the same scene are very similar. Most of them have a companion on the other side of the image with almost the same location.

There are many methods of detecting corner points, but we need a method with low computational complexity. Robert Laganiere proposed the use of morphology to find the corner points [11]. In his method, the corner strength is calculated with morphological masks, such as those shown in Fig. 2.

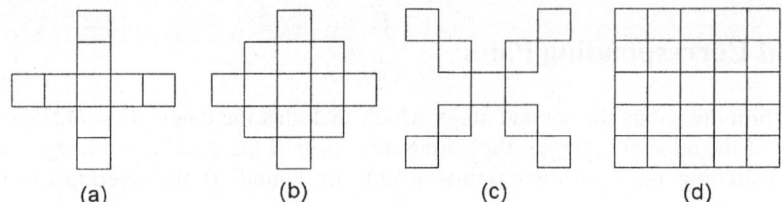

Fig. 2. Morphological masks (a) Cross, (b) Diamond, (c) X, (d) Square

The strength of the corner can be represented by the difference between the asymmetric morphological closings. The asymmetric closing(c) is the dilation (δ) of an image using a given structuring element, followed by its erosion (ε) using another structuring element. This is described in (2).

$$I^c_{cross, diamond} = \left(I^\delta_{cross}\right)^\varepsilon_{diamond} \qquad (2)$$

The corner strength is obtained using a relation such as that described in (3). This is accomplished by comparing two images, which are acquired from two different operators. Basically, the value of C(x, y) corresponds to the difference in brightness between the corners and their background.

$$C_{cross, X}(I) = \left| I^c_{cross, diamond} - I^c_{X, square} \right| \qquad (3)$$

However, Laganiere's method determines the corner point simply through the use of threshold values of the corner strength based on some fixed value. This can induce the over detection or insufficient appearance of corner points. Therefore, a criterion is needed which guarantees robust corner detection in general situations. We propose a criterion method of determining the corner strength, which finds local peaks in a corner strength map. This method operates automatically without any predefined parameters.

An example of a corner strength map is presented in Fig. 3 with 3D rendering. Some hills are observed in this map, and these are the possible corner points. The proposed method considers the top of a hill to be a corner point, and an algorithm, which finds the local maxima, is applied to the corner strength map. We used two memory maps, one of which denotes the appearance of the peaks and the other represents their height, in order to decrease the computational cost.

On the other hand, any tiny peaks caused by noise should be excluded from the detection of the corners. Therefore, these tiny peaks were removed by thresholding before the identification of the peak points. Fig. 4 shows the result of the corner detection method using a static threshold and that of the proposed method. The proposed method is able to locate the corner points with a consistent level of accuracy under any conditions.

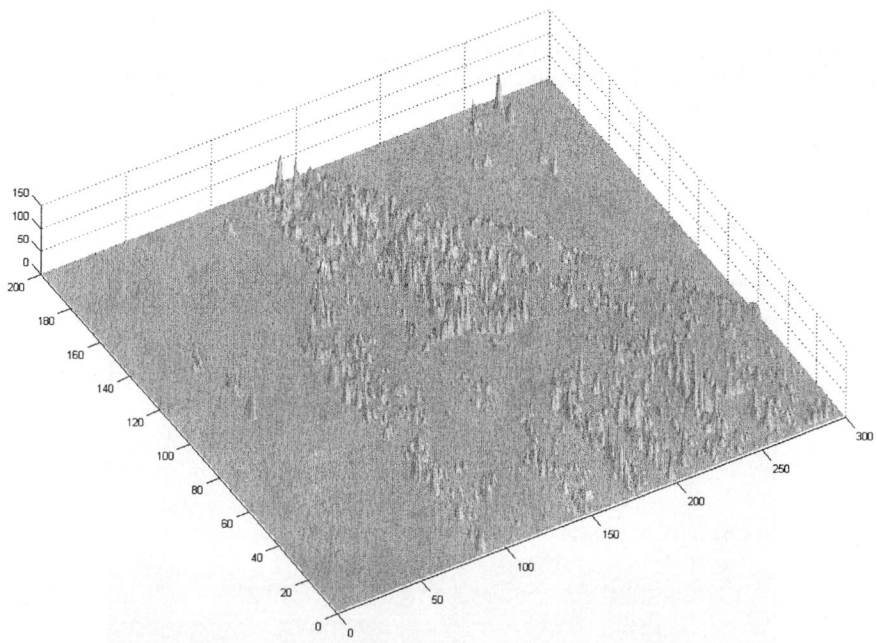

Fig. 3. The corner strength map of an image after eliminating any tiny peaks. Some hills are observed in this map, and these are the possible corner points.

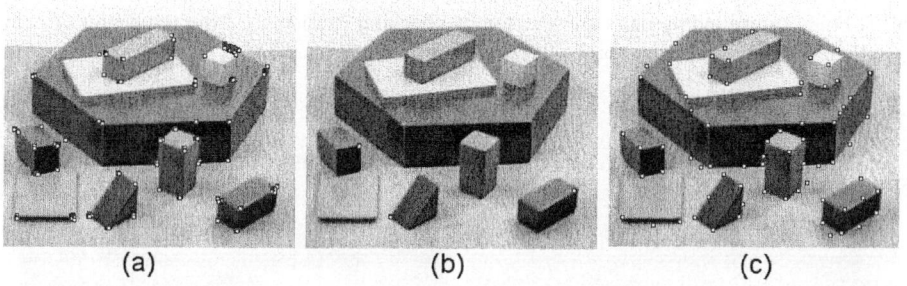

Fig. 4. Detected corners of blox image (a) Laganiere's method with threshold=20, (b) Laganiere's method with threshold=40, (c) proposed method

3.3 Pattern Matching

To estimate the 8-parameters used for perspective transformation, we need four pairs of matched points in the adjacent images. As stated above, corner detection simply find corners without any correspondences between two images. As a result, associating the corners of the adjacent images remains to be done.

Template matching is performed here, in order to determine which corners in the left and right images are exactly matched. At first, one template that is related to the corner point in the left image is chosen, and it is compared to the other templates of the right image. The information pertaining to the relative location within the image and the MSEs between the templates is employed to determine the matched pairs. A corner point that has a minimum MSE value and a suitable location is selected to form the corresponding pair. However, some pairs have large MSE values, because some isolated corner points do not have corresponding pairs. These pairs could be removed simply by applying a suitable threshold value. In this paper, a 60*60 template that includes the corner point in the center is used.

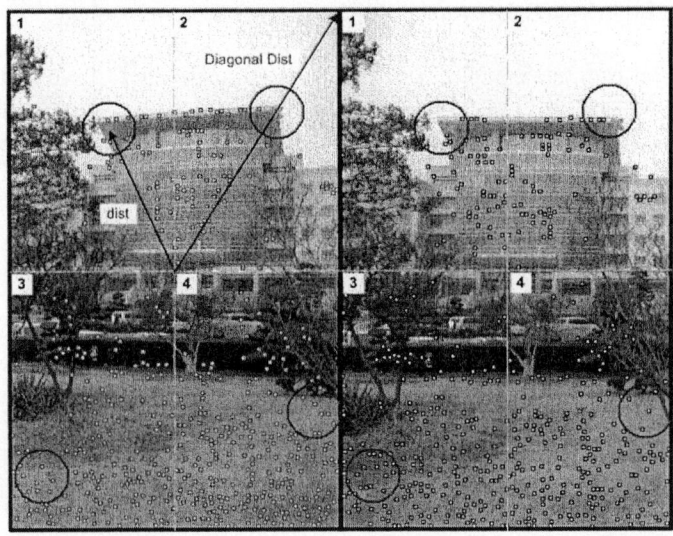

Fig. 5. Four corresponding pairs are selected by checking its distance from the center of overlapped image. The most distant pair will be selected in every quadrant.

Fig. 6. Four corresponding pairs (a) Left image (b) Right image

After template matching, there are many matched points between the two overlapped regions. Therefore, it is necessary to decide which point is the most suitable for perspective transformation. In our experiments, the distortion of the transformed image was reduced at the tetragon which connects the four corresponding points had a large area. Fig. 5 explains the decision of corresponding points and Fig. 6 shows the four matched pairs of images obtained from adjacent cameras. The red cross-marks represent the corresponding points.

4 Perspective Transformation and Color Blending

Perspective transformation maps one arbitrary 2D quadrilateral into another. Generally, the 8-parameter model is used to transform panoramic images [7], [8], [12]. We can represent such a transform as X'=Hx, where X' is the vector of the resultant image $(x', y', 1)$, x is the vector of the earlier image $(x, y, 1)$, and H is a transform matrix. We can write this transform in more detail as equation (4)

$$\begin{bmatrix} x'W \\ y'W \\ W \end{bmatrix} = \begin{bmatrix} h_0 & h_1 & h_2 \\ h_3 & h_4 & h_5 \\ h_6 & h_7 & h_8 \end{bmatrix} \begin{bmatrix} x \\ y \\ 1 \end{bmatrix} \qquad (4)$$

Generally $h_8 = 1$ and $W = h_6 x + h_7 y + 1$.
Then we can derive the projection result as (5) and (6)

$$x' = \frac{h_0 x + h_1 y + h_2}{h_6 x + h_7 y + 1} \qquad (5)$$

$$y' = \frac{h_3 x + h_4 y + h_5}{h_6 x + h_7 y + 1} \qquad (6)$$

To find proper parameters, we iteratively update the transform matrix H using iterative equation (7)

$$H_n = H_{n-1}(I + D_n) \qquad (7)$$

Where

$$D = \begin{bmatrix} d_0 & d_1 & d_2 \\ d_3 & d_4 & d_5 \\ d_6 & d_7 & d_8 \end{bmatrix}$$

Resampling image I_1 with the new transformation, X'=H(I+D)x, is the same as warping the resampled image by means of the expression X''=(I+D)x, i.e. the new projection equation can be written in the form of equations (8) and (9).

$$x'' = \frac{(1+d_0)x + (1+d_1)y + d_2}{d_6 x + d_7 y + (1+d_8)} \qquad (8)$$

$$y'' = \frac{d_3 x + (1+d_4)y + d_5}{d_6 x + d_7 y + (1+d_8)} \qquad (9)$$

We wish to minimize the squared error metric (10).

$$E(d) = \sum_n \left[I_1(x_n'') - I_0(x_i) \right]^2 \qquad (10)$$

If four corresponding pairs (*X1*, *Y1*) (*x1*, *y1*), (*X2*, *Y2*) (*x2*, *y2*), (*X3*, *Y3*) (*x3*, *y3*), and (*X4*, *Y4*) (*x4*, *y4*) are given, we can estimate the 8-parameters ($h_0, h_1, h_2, h_3, h_4, h_5, h_6, h_7$) required to minimize equation (10) [7], [8]. These equations can be solved iteratively with the matrix form [13].

If we know the parameters, we can deform one image, in such a way as to allow the two adjacent images to be merged. In general, when we stitch two adjacent images together, some unwanted discontinuities of intensity or color will exist in their common areas. Therefore, a method of adjusting the two images is needed, in order for them to have similar intensities. In this paper, the bilinear blending technique is used to construct a seamless panorama according to the distance [12]. After adjusting the two images, the intensities of the common area will blend together.

5 Experimental Results and Conclusions

In this paper, we presented a novel method of building a panoramic image. To validate his method, raw images were taken with two CCD cameras installed on a tripod mount at an angle of 15 degrees and the resolution was 704*480. We constructed panoramic images for approximately 200 pairs of scenes taken from several locations. In each case, the panoramic image was successfully and seamlessly constructed with good quality.

The average processing time of these 200 pairs of images was about 0.78 seconds per pair, when the algorithm was implemented in the Microsoft Visual C++ 6.0 language and executed on an Intel Pentium 4 CPU operating at 2.6GHz. The results of the proposed method as compared to those of template matching with the SA (simulated annealing) method are presented in Table 1.

The processing time was measured from image loading to panoramic image generation, and the SAD (sum of absolute difference) was calculated before the ghost image elimination process with color blending. The results in this table show that the proposed method is superior to the SA method in terms of the processing time and quality. The processing time was decreased by about 44% and the SAD was also slightly decreased. However, the proposed method exhibits a large variation of processing time, because each pair of scenes has a different number of corners and the time required for the template matching process is proportional to the number of corners. Fig. 7, Fig. 8 and Fig. 9 shows the resultant images which were constructed by the proposed method.

Table 1. Experimental results obtained with the proposed method compared to those obtained with the Template Matching with Simulated Annealing method. Experiments were conducted for 200 pairs of images. The processing time was measured in milliseconds in the same environment.

		Proposed	TM with SA
Processing Time (ms)	Average	783.5	1407.25
	Standard Deviation	339.99	31.58
	Minimum	359	1312
	Maximum	1906	1781
SAD	Average	40.45	44.86
	Standard Deviation	2.00	2.38
	Minimum	26.26	33.21
	Maximum	58.12	60.65

Fig. 7. Result of horizontally captured images obtained by panning the camera. Experimental result of two distant image mosaic.

We propose a fast and reliable image mosaicing method, the core of which is a robust procedure for finding correspondences between two adjacent images. The proposed method is automatic, relatively fast and robust to many conditions, such as differences in contrast between the cameras or variations in the relative position of the camera. The corners identified using this method are sufficiently good to find correspondences between pairs of adjacent scenes. However, the number of corners that are found should have uniformity for the consistency, and this will be the subject of a future work.

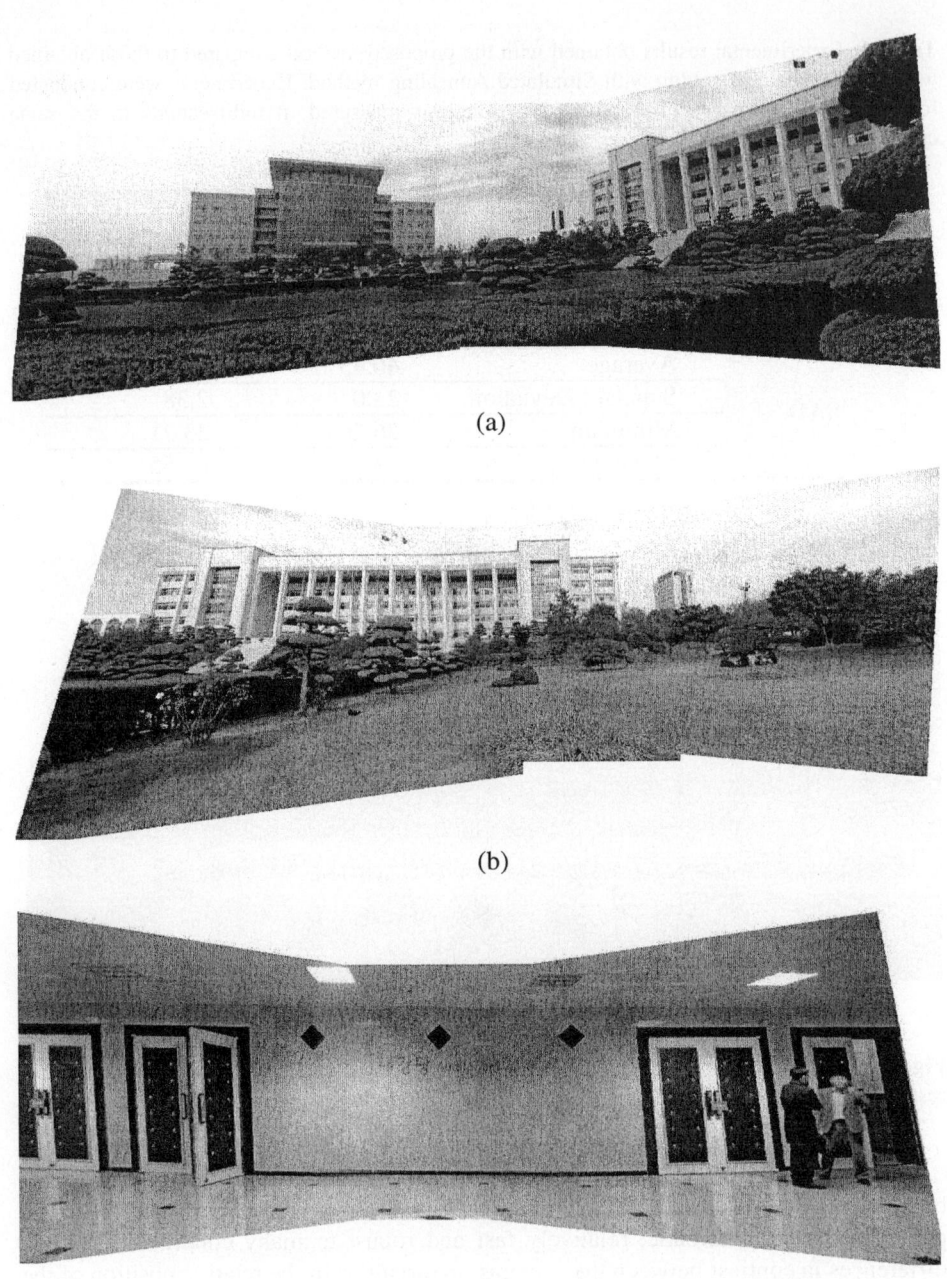

Fig. 8. Results of horizontally captured images obtained by panning the camera. Experimental results of three (a) Distant images (b) Medium distance images (c) Close images.

Fig. 9. Result of vertically captured images obtained by panning and tilting the camera. Experimental result of three medium distance vertical images.

Acknowledgements

This work was supported by INHA UNIVERSITY Research Grant.

References

1. Kenney, C.S., Manjunath B.S.: A condition number for point matching with application to registration and postregistration error estimation. IEEE Transaction on Pattern Analysis and Machine Intelligence (PAMI), Vol. 25. (2003) 1437 - 1454
2. M. Hansen, P. Anandan, K. Dana, G. van der Val, P. Burt: Real-time scene stabilization and mosaic construction. IEEE Workshop on Application of Computer Vision (1994) 54-62
3. M.Irani, S.Hsu, P.Anandan: Video compression using mosaic representations. Signal Processing: Image Communication, Vol.7. (1995) 529-552
4. H.S.Sawhney, S.Ayer: Compact representation of videos through dominant multiple motion estimation. IEEE Transaction on Pattern Analysis and Machine Intelligence (PAMI), Vol. 18 (1996) 814-830
5. S.Mann, R.W.Picard: Virtual bellows: Constructing high quality images from video. International Conference on Image Processing, Vol. I. (1994) 363-367
6. J.Meehan: Panoramic Photography. Watson-Guptill (1990)
7. Hui Chen, Wenping Wang, Ralph Martin: Building Panoramas from Photographs Taken with an Uncalibrated Hand-held Camera. Proceedings of Vision, Modeling and Visualization 2000(VMV00). (2000) 221-230

8. Smolic A., Wiegand T.: High-resolution video mosaicing. Image Processing Proceedings International Conference on, Vol. 3. (2001) 872 – 875
9. Chiou-Ting Hsu, Tzu-Hung Cheng, Beuker, R.A., Jyh-Kuen Horng: Feature-based video mosaic. Image Processing Proceedings International Conference on, Vol. 2. (2000) 887 – 890
10. Whichello A.P., Hong Yan: Document image mosaicing. Pattern Recognition Proceedings Fourteenth International Conference on, Vol. 2. (1998) 1081-1083
11. Laganiere R.: Morphological corner detection. Computer Vision Sixth International Conference on. (1998) 280-285
12. Jun-Wei Hsieh: Fast stitching algorithm for moving object detection and mosaic construction. Image and Vision Computing, Vol. 22, Issue 4, (2004) 291-306
13. H.Y. Shum, R. Szeliske: Construction of Panoramic Image Mosaics with Global and Local Alignment. Panoramic Vision. Springer-Verlag New York (2001) 227-268
14. Dong-Keun Kim, Byung-Tae Jang, Chi-Jung Hwang: A planar perspective image matching using point correspondences and rectangle-to-quadrilateral mapping. Image Analysis and Interpretation 2002 Proceedings, (2002) 87-91

Generation of 3D Building Model Using 3D Line Detection Scheme Based on Line Fitting of Elevation Data

Dong-Min Woo[1], Seung-Soo Han[1], Young-Kee Jung[2], and Kyu-Won Lee[3]

[1] Information Engineering Department, Myongji University,
Gyeonggido, Korea 449-728
{dmwoo, shan}@mju.ac.kr
[2] Computer Engineering Department, Honam University,
Gwangju, Korea 506-090
ykjung@honam.ac.kr
[3] Computer Engineering Department, Daejun University,
Daejun, Korea 300-716
kwlee@dju.ac.kr

Abstract. This paper presents a new 3D line segment extraction method, which can be used in generating 3D rooftop model. The core of our method is that 3D line segment is extracted by using line fitting of elevation data on 2D line coordinates of ortho-image. In order to use elevation in line fitting, the elevation itself should be reliable. To measure the reliability of elevation, in this paper, we employ the concept of self-consistency. We test the effectiveness of the proposed method with a quantitative accuracy analysis using synthetic images generated from Avenches data set of Ascona aerial images. Experimental results indicate that our method generates 3D line segments almost 10 times more accurate than raw elevations obtained by area-based method. Also, our proposed method shows much improved accuracy over the cooperative hybrid stereo method. Using a simple 3D line grouping scheme, 3D line segments are shown to generate a precise 3D building model effectively.

1 Introduction

3D building model of urban area can be regarded as one of the most useful multimedia data. It has been basically applied to environmental monitoring and surveillance. Recently, it can be used in new applications such as virtual city touring and simulation of urban development. An efficient technique to generate 3D site model of broad urban area is stereo processing of aerial or satellite images. There has been a significant body of research in stereo matching technique, which is broadly divided into area-based method [1-4] and feature-based method [5-7].

Area-based method is especially useful in the generation of 3D natural terrain model, since it can generate dense elevation map for each grid in the area. The current state of area-base method has been advanced to achieve a very precise terrain model in terms of the use of multi-resolution scheme [2], NCC(Normalized Cross-Correlation), NSSR(Narrow Search Sub-pixel Registration)[1], etc. However, this method is not very successful in 3D line extraction for the building model generation, since it generates smoothed elevation around the boundaries or edges of buildings by the nature of correlation or SSD(Sum of Squared Difference) necessarily incorporated in the area-based stereo matching. Feature-based method might be basically effective in the site model generation, since the matching process is based on the features such as 2D line segment, corner point, edge, zero-crossing, etc. Those features can be core elements constructing building rooftops. One of major difficulties in 3D line extraction process by the feature-based stereo matching of complex urban images is a increasing number of possible 2D line matching combination, which may lead to the high possibility of false line matching, as well as significant computational cost.

In this context, there has been a necessity for a research on how to incorporate area-based method with feature-based method. Hybrid stereo matching is based on the incorporation of area-based method with feature-based method. The way of this incorporation has been studied mainly as the combination of area-based and feature-based methods [8-9], and the generation of more improved urban model was reported. By this combinational method, however, perspective distortion [4] cannot be avoided, since correlation window or SSD window needs to be used in the stereo matching process. Also, these combinational hybrid methods assume that features should be similarly extracted in both images, which can be hardly achieved in the real situation. The recent introduction of cooperative hybrid stereo method [10] is based on the idea that the feature matching is directed by the reliable disparity evaluated by area-based method. Since this scheme significantly reduced the number of possible matched 2D line pairs, reliable 3D lines of building could be extracted to generate 3D building model.

To extract more accurate 3D line segments of buildings, in this paper, we suggest a new scheme using both DEM (Digital Elevation Map) and ortho-image obtained by area-based stereo. The core of our scheme is that 3D line segment is constructed by using line fitting of elevation data on 2D line extracted from ortho-image. Since we use only reliable elevation based on self-consistency [11], we can construct precise 3D line segments which can be key elements to build 3D model.

2 3D Line Extraction

2.1 2D Line Detection

Our 3D line extraction scheme begins with the 2D line detection from ortho-image, shown in Fig. 1, so that we can locate orthographical coordinates of 3D line. To detect 2D lines from ortho-image, edge detection is carried out first and then 2D lines are formed from edges. We employed Canny edge detector, since it is optimal according to the criteria where edge is defined and comes up with thin edges. To obtain 2D line segment, we use Boldt algorithm [13] based on token grouping. The method extracts a basic line element, token, in terms of the properties of line, and constructs 2D line using grouping process. It is efficient in detecting 2D lines of large structure appeared in urban image.

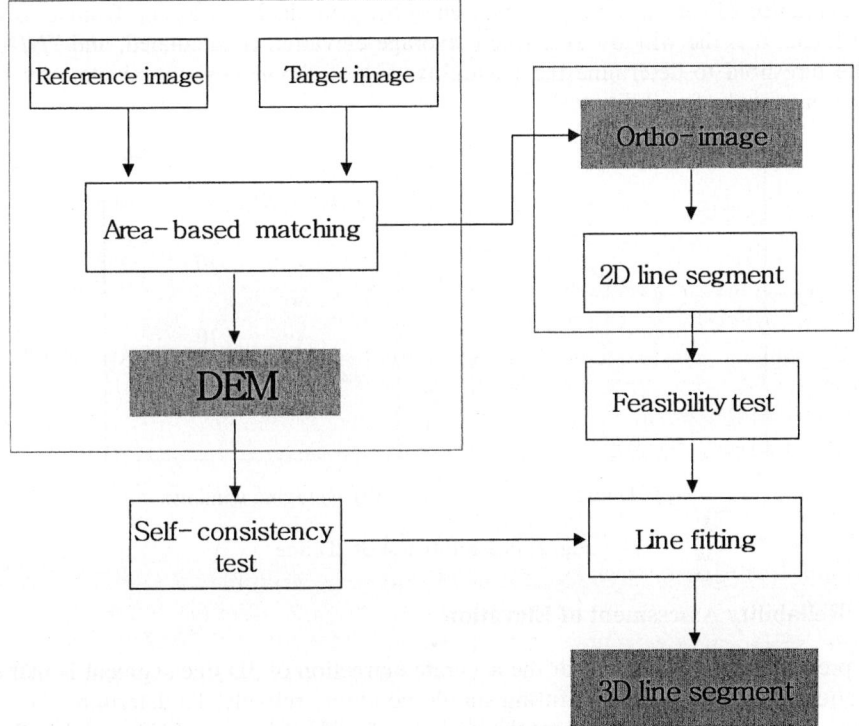

Fig. 1. 3D line extraction process

2.2 Feasibility Test of 2D Line

2D line segments detected from ortho-image might be caused by planar patterns or shadows, as well as boundaries of building rooftop. To remove 2D line segments irrelevant to building rooftop, we carry out feasibility test for all 2D lines detected from ortho-image by testing whether 2D line can be feasible to be constructed into 3D line. We utilize the fact that 3D line should exist along the depth or elevation discontinuities.

The feasibility test begins with the calculation of average elevation of upper, bottom, left and right area of a coordinate on 2D line segment. The criteria for the feasibility test are the difference between upper and bottom average elevations and the difference between left and right average elevations. Equation (1) shows the condition for the feasibility test in terms of the feasibility criteria.

$$\left| (\tfrac{1}{n}) \sum_{i=-n}^{i=-1} dem\,(i,j) - (\tfrac{1}{n}) \sum_{i=1}^{i=n} dem\,(i,j) \right| + \\ \left| (\tfrac{1}{n}) \sum_{j=-n}^{j=-1} dem\,(i,j) - (\tfrac{1}{n}) \sum_{j=1}^{j=n} dem\,(i,j) \right| < THD_{fitness} \qquad (1)$$

In equation (1), *dem(i,j)* is the elevation of the grid displaced by (i,j) from a 2D line coordinate, n is the window size where average elevation is calculated, and $THD_{fitness}$ is the threshold to determine the feasibility. Fig. 2 shows how to calculate average elevations for the feasibility test.

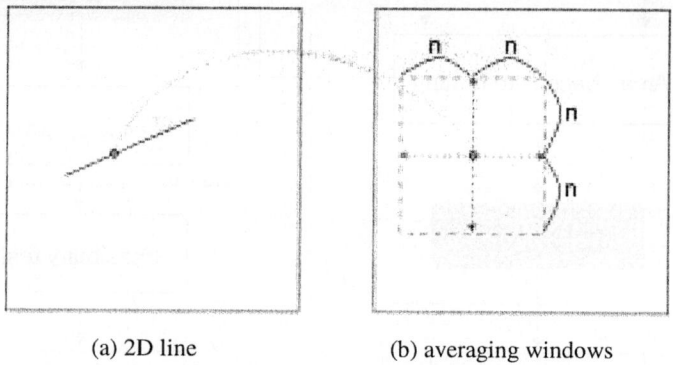

(a) 2D line   (b) averaging windows

Fig. 2. Feasibility test of 2D line

2.3 Reliability Assessment of Elevation

The preliminary requirement for the accurate extraction of 3D line segment is that the elevation data used in 3D line fitting should be highly reliable. To determine the reliability of elevation data, we adopt the concept of self-consistency [11], which reflects our expectation that reversing the target and reference images will lead to similar result when the image matching algorithm find correct correspondence and come up with reliable elevation. Therefore, the difference of the elevations provides a measure of consistency and reliability, and equation (2) indicates the condition for the reliable elevation data.

$$\left| Z_{ab}(i,j) - Z_{ba}(i,j) \right| < THD_{Height} \tag{2}$$

where Zab(i,j) and Zba(i,j) are two elevation data obtained by reversing the reference and target images, a and b. Also, THDHeight is the threshold to determine the degree of self-consistency. The elevation data determined as reliable by equation (2) can be used in 3D line fitting. Since we have two elevation for each (i,j), the average value of two elevations are actually participated in line fitting such as

$$\left(Z_{ab}(i,j) + Z_{ba}(i,j) \right) / 2 \tag{3}$$

2.4 3D Line Fitting

3D line segments are extracted by line fitting of reliable elevation data, as shown in Fig. 3. In order to minimize the error of the estimated 3D line as small as possible, in this paper, we adopt a line fitting in a sense of LSE(least squared error). In this paper, we define the fitted 3D line as the intersection of two plane equations, $ax + by = 1$ and $cy + dz = 1$.

To evaluate the coefficients, a, b, c and d, we substitute n 3D coordinates (x_1,y_1,z_1), (x_2,y_2,z_2), ... , (x_n,y_n,z_n) of reliable elevations for two plane equations, such that

$$
\begin{aligned}
ax_1 + by_1 &= 1 & cy_1 + dz_1 &= 1 \\
ax_2 + by_2 &= 1 & cy_2 + dz_2 &= 1 \\
&\vdots & &\vdots \\
ax_n + by_n &= 1 & cy_n + dz_n &= 1
\end{aligned}
\qquad (4)
$$

Since we have far more than 2 coordinates for each line segment, equation (4) is over-determined. The LSE estimation of the coefficients in equation (4) can be computed by well-known pseudo inverse as in equation (5).

$$
\begin{array}{ll}
A \cdot X1 = B & C \cdot X2 = B \\
A^T A \cdot X1 = A^T B & C^T C \cdot X2 = C^T B \\
X1 = (A^T A)^{-1} A^T B & X2 = (C^T C)^{-1} C^T B
\end{array}
\qquad (5)
$$

$$
A = \begin{bmatrix} x_1 & y_1 \\ x_2 & y_2 \\ \vdots & \\ x_n & y_n \end{bmatrix} \quad
C = \begin{bmatrix} y_1 & z_1 \\ y_2 & z_2 \\ \vdots & \\ y_n & z_n \end{bmatrix} \quad
X1 = \begin{bmatrix} a \\ b \end{bmatrix} \quad
X2 = \begin{bmatrix} c \\ d \end{bmatrix} \quad
B = \begin{bmatrix} 1 \\ 1 \\ \vdots \\ 1 \end{bmatrix}
$$

After determining the coefficients of the 3D line equation, we obtain the 3D line segment by finding 3D starting and end points, which can be the orthographically nearest positions on 3D line from two starting and end points of 2D line segments.

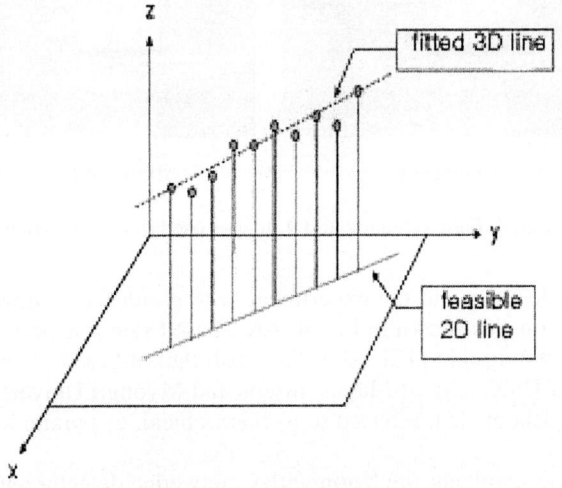

Fig. 3. 3D line fitting

3 Experimental Results

The experimental environment is set up, based on Ascona aerial images of Avenches area. Since Avenches data include 3D models of terrain and buildings, these data can be efficiently utilized for the analysis and the accuracy assessment of the suggested scheme.

To provide a detailed accuracy analysis, in this experiment, we use ortho-image and 3D model of Avenches area as a pseudo ground truth. A photo realistic ray-tracing program is used to synthesize images of the surface from arbitrary viewpoint. Fig. 4 shows 4 synthetic images generated from altitude of 1000m.

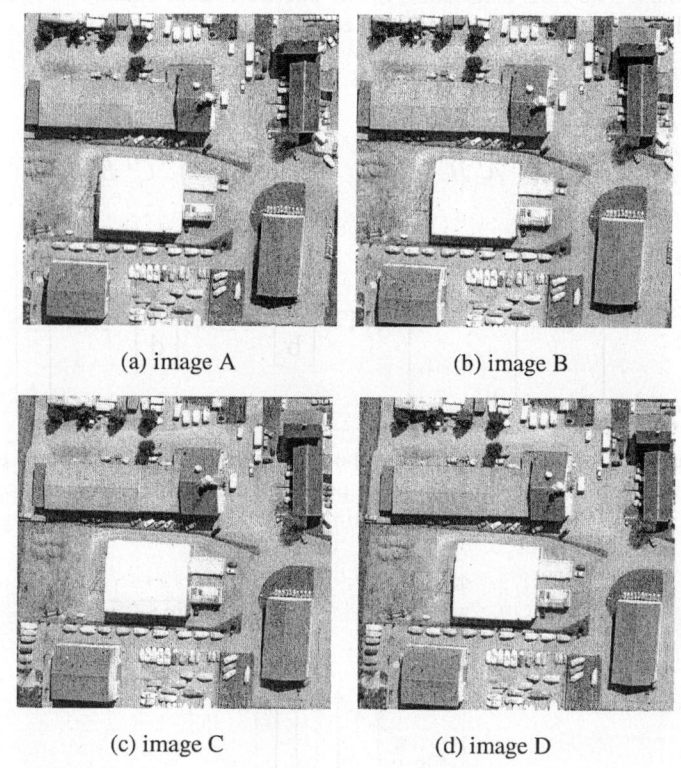

(a) image A   (b) image B

(c) image C   (d) image D

Fig. 4. Four synthetic aerial images used in the experiment

The first step to carry out the experiment is to reconstruct DEM and ortho-image from overlapped images shown in Fig. 4. Area-based stereo is performed on synthetic images with Terrest system [12], which is a correlation-based 3D reconstruction system developed at University of Massachusetts and Myongji University. We employed multi-resolution scheme [2], referred to as hierarchical, or pyramid processing, to our Terrest system.

To find 3D line segments, we begin with Canny edge detector and Boldt line finder to find 2D line segments in ortho-image. To get the feasible 2D line segments, the feasibility test is carried out for filtering of all the 2D line segments detected. The threshold for the feasibility test is set to 1m. Fig. 5 (a) and (b) show ortho-image and the filtered feasible 2D line segments, based on the area-based reconstruction result from image A and image B of Fig. 4. As in Fig. 4, it is noticed that some 2D line segments caused by shadow and small planar patterns are effectively filtered out by our feasibility test.

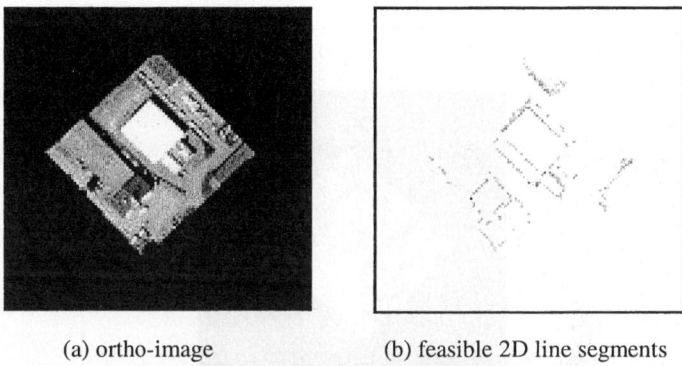

(a) ortho-image (b) feasible 2D line segments

Fig. 5. 2D line segment detection

In our 3D line fitting, only reliable elevations should be used in the estimation of 3D line. To measure the reliability, we calculate the difference of DEMAB and DEMBA. Fig. 6 (a) shows DEMAB and (b) shows DEMBA. Fig. 7 represents this difference in gray scale image, where the light part shows a high consistency or reliability in elevation. In this experiment, we set the threshold to be 1m, which means the elevation difference within 1m can be determined as reliable. The reliable points on 2D line segments are also displayed.

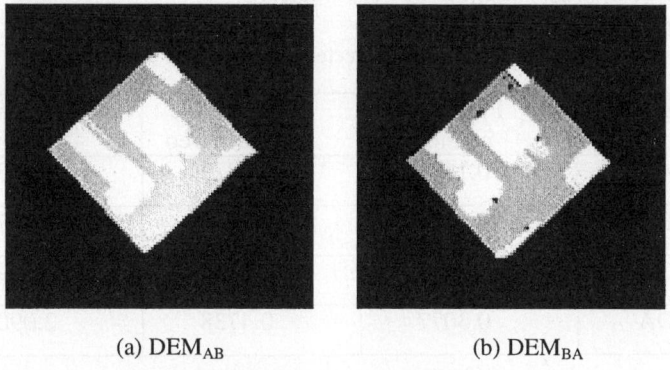

(a) DEM_{AB} (b) DEM_{BA}

Fig. 6. DEM reconstructed from image A and B

3D line fitting experiments using LSE were carried out for 4 image pairs, AB, BC, CD and DA. Table 1 shows the comparison between the extracted 3D line segments and the ground truth line segments supplied by Avenches data set. To represent the quantitative accuracy of 3D line segments extracted by our suggested scheme, we obtain the error by calculating the average distance between the extracted 3D line segments and the ground truth line segments as in equation (6).

$$\frac{\sum \frac{e_{1i}+e_{2i}}{2} \times d_i}{\sum d_i} \tag{6}$$

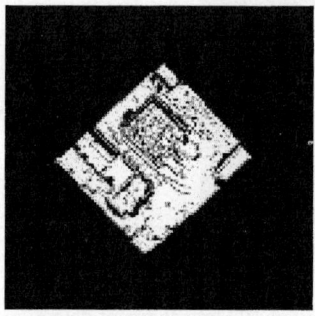

Fig. 7. Reliability evaluation of elevation using self-consistency

In equation (6), e_{1i} is the distance from the starting point of line segment i to the ground truth 3D line, while e_{2i} is the distance from the end point of line segment i to the ground truth 3D line and d_i is the length of line segment i. Error analysis show that 3D lines from image pair BC are most accurate with the average error of 0.16m and that 3D lines from image pair DA have a little more errors relatively with the average error of 0.30m. Since average errors are shown consistently regardless of image pair, the suggested method is thought to be very stable.

Table 1. Average errors of detected line segments (unit: meter)

Image pair	Proposed method	Cooperative hybrid stereo	Area-based stereo
AB	0.1681	0.8827	2.1534
BC	0.1624	0.4664	2.1670
CD	0.2383	0.6138	2.1290
DA	0.3077	0.4738	2.0904

To verify the effectiveness of the suggested method, we need to show the accuracy comparison with other methods. Thus we compare our result with elevation obtained by area-based stereo and cooperative hybrid stereo method. On the boundaries of the buildings, i.e. lines of 3D model, raw elevations have average errors of 2.0m – 2.2m,

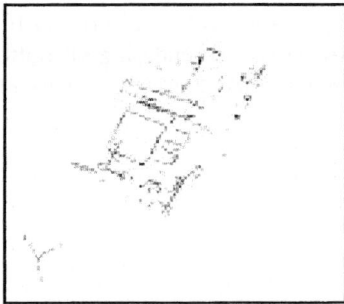

Fig. 8. Fused 3D line segments

which are 10 times more than our errors. Furthermore, our method shows much improved accuracy over cooperative hybrid stereo method.

To show the applicability of our suggested method to the site model, we try an experimental 3D model generation by using a fundamental 3D grouping scheme. Prior to the grouping, 3D line segments extracted from image pairs AB, BC, CD, DA are fused so that we can get 3D line segment information as much as possible for the grouping. In this process we perform a grouping of similar 3D line segments. Similarity of 3D line segments are calculated by the average distance. The grouped 3D lines are evaluated as a single 3D line in terms of LSE (Least Squared Error) estimation. Fig. 8 represents the rendering of fused 3D line segments.

The used 3D grouping scheme assumes that the rooftop consists of rectangular elements. Under this very limited assumption, we carry out 3D grouping by junction extraction and rooftop generation, based on properties of building and hypothesis generation. The grouping begins with the detection of junctions from 3D lines. Fig. 9 (a) shows junctions detected from 3D lines. Among these junctions, we find L-corner and T-corner which can be constructing elements for the building. L-corners and T-corners build the hypothesis of the rooftop as shown in Fig. 9 (b), since the rooftop element is assumed to be rectangular. Each hypothesis is verified by the properties of rooftop we define, and the building rooftop is generated as in Fig. 9 (c).

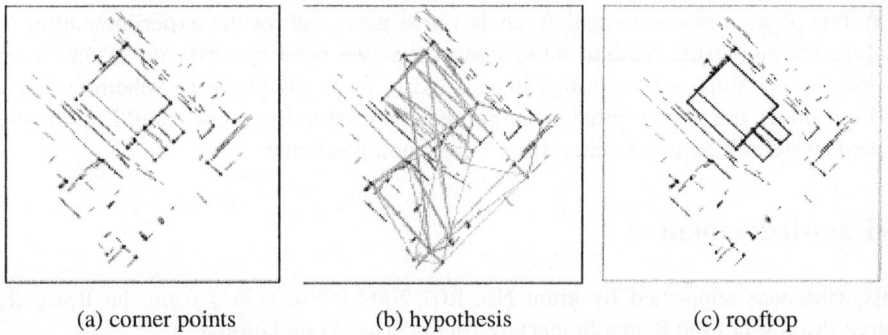

(a) corner points   (b) hypothesis   (c) rooftop

Fig. 9. 3D grouping to obtain the rooftop model

The generated rooftop is transformed to AUTOCAD file format so that we can realize its 3D structure. Fig. 10 shows 3D rendering of rooftop from AUTOCAD format and we find that the suggested hybrid stereo can be very effectively applied to the 3D modeling of urban area.

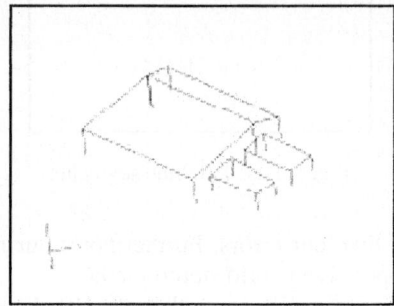

Fig. 10. 3D view of detected rooftop model

4 Conclusions

In this paper we suggested a new 3D line segment detection method using DEM and ortho-image which can be obtained by conventional area-based stereo method. Experimental results show that the suggested method comes up with 3D line segments almost 10 times more accurate than raw elevations obtained by area-based method. This accuracy can be achieved, due to line fitting of only reliable elevations in a least squared error sense. With this accuracy, we believe that the suggested method can be efficiently utilized in the area of 3D site modeling from urban imagery. To show the applicability of our suggested method to the generation of 3D model of urban area, we perform the experiment on the generation of 3D rooftop model using a fundamental 3D grouping scheme. Since the generated 3D rooftop model reflects the shape of actual building, it is verified that our suggested method can be very effectively utilized in 3D model generation.

In this paper, only one small Avenches area was used for the experimentation. To analyze the suggested method more intensively, we need to carry out extensive experiments including various urban images. Also, basic 3D grouping scheme was carried out under the very limited assumption. The continuing work should be directed toward a research on more generalized 3D grouping scheme.

Acknowledgement

This work was supported by grant No. R01-2002-000-00336-0 from the Basic Research Program of the Korea Science & Engineering Foundation.

References

1. Panton, D. J.: A Flexible Approach to Digital Stereo Mapping. Photogrammetric Engineering and Remote Sensing, Vol. 44 (1978) 1499-1512
2. Hannah, M.: A System for Digital Stereo Image Matching. Photogrammetric Engineering and Remote Sensing, Vol. 55 (1989) 1765-1770
3. Hung, Y., Chen, C., Hung, K., Chen, Y., Fuh, C.: Multipass Hierarchical Stereo Matching for Generation of Digital Terrain Models from Aerial Images. Machine Vision and Applications, Vol. 10 (1998) 280-291
4. Mostafavi, H.: Image Correlation with Geometric Distortion Part II: Effects on Local Accuracy. IEEE Trans. Aerospace and Electronic, Vol. 14 (1978) 494-500
5. Grimson, W.: Computational Experiments with Feature Based Stereo Algorithm. IEEE Trans. Pattern Analysis and Machine Intelligence, Vol. 7 (1985) 17-34
6. Marr, D., Poggio, T.: A Computational Theory of Human Stereo Vision. Proc. Royal Society of London Vol. 204 of B (1979) 301-328
7. De Vleeschauwer, D.: An Intensity-based, Coarse-to-fine Approach to Reliably Measure Binocular Disparity. CVGIP: Image Understanding, Vol. 57 (1993) 204-218
8. Kanade, T., Okutomi, M.: A Stereo Matching Algorithm with an Adaptive Window: Theory and Experiment. IEEE Trans. Pattern Analysis and Machine Intelligence, Vol. 16 (1994) 920-932
9. Han, K., Bae, T., Ha, Y.: Hybrid Stereo Matching with a New Relaxation Scheme of Preserving Disparity Discontinuity. Pattern Recognition, Vol. 33 (2000) 767-785
10. Woo, D., Schulz, H., Jung, Y., Lee, K.: Generation of 3D Urban Model Using Cooperative Hybrid Stereo Matching. Lecture Notes in Computer Science, Vol. 3331 (2004) 222-229
11. Leclerc, Y., Luong, Q., Fua, P.: Self-consistency: A Novel Approach to Characterizing the Accuracy and Reliability of Point Correspondence Algorithms. DARPA Image Understanding Workshop (1998)
12. Schultz, H., Woo, D., Riseman, E., Stolle, F.: Error Detection and DEM Fusion Using Self-consistency. IEEE Int. Conf. on Computer Vision, Vol. 2 (1999) 1174-1181
13. Boldt, M., Weiss R., Riseman, E.: Token-based Extraction of Straight Lines. IEEE Trans. Systems Man Cybernetics, Vol. 19 (1989) 1581-1594

Segmentation of the Liver Using the Deformable Contour Method on CT Images

Seong-Jae Lim[1], Yong-Yeon Jeong[2], and Yo-Sung Ho[1]

[1] Gwangju Institute of Science and Technology (GIST),
1 Oryong-dong, Buk-gu, Gwangju 500-712, Korea
{sjlim, hoyo}@gist.ac.kr
[2] Chonnam National University Medical School,
8 Hack-dong, Dong-gu, Gwangju 501-757, Korea

Abstract. Automatic liver segmentation from abdominal computed tomography (CT) images is one of the most important steps for computer-aided diagnosis (CAD) for liver CT. However, the liver must be separated manually or semi-automatically since surface features of the liver and partial-volume effects make automatic discrimination from other adjacent organs or tissues very difficult. In this paper, we present an unsupervised liver segmentation algorithm with three steps. In the preprocessing, we simplify the input CT image by estimating the liver position using a prior knowledge about the location of the liver and by performing multi-level threshold on the estimated liver position. The proposed scheme utilizes the multiscale morphological filter recursively with region-labeling and clustering to detect the search range for deformable contouring. Most of the liver contours are positioned within the search range. In order to perform an accurate segmentation, we produce the gradient-label map, which represents the gradient magnitude in the search range. The proposed algorithm performed deformable contouring on the gradient-label map by using regular patterns of the liver boundary. Experimental results are comparable to those of manual tracing by radiological doctors and shown to be efficient.

Keywords: Liver segmentation, Morphological filtering, Deformable contouring, Computer-Aided Diagnosis(CAD).

1 Introduction

Liver cancer is one of the most common internal malignancies worldwide. The hepatocellular carcinoma is common in Asia and metastasis is common in the West. Computed tomography (CT) has been identified as accurate noninvasive imaging modalities in the diagnosis of the liver cancer. Designing and developing computer-assisted image processing techniques to help doctors improve their diagnosis has received considerable interests over the past years [1]. CT images are interpreted by radiologists. However, image interpretation by human beings is often limited due to the non-systematic search patterns of themselves, the presence of structural noise in the image, and the presentation of complex disease states requiring the integration of a vast amount of image data and clinical information.

Recently, the computer-aided diagnosis (CAD), defined as a diagnosis introduced by a radiologist who uses the output from a computerized analysis of medical images as a "second opinion" in detecting lesions, assessing extent of disease, and making diagnostic decisions, is being used to improve the interpretation components of medical imaging [2],[3]. Considerable and serious efforts have been made toward the development of CAD systems in diagnostic radiology.

However, CAD research for liver against mammogram and chest radiographs is to be insufficient because the liver segmentation that plays an important role for CAD is difficult. This is mainly due to the following two facts. The first one is the proximity of the liver and other organs or muscles having similar intensity values. It makes resolution difficult by observation of intensity discontinuity alone because of the partial-volume effects (PVE), i.e., the mixing of different tissue types in a single voxel. PVE causes edge blurring between different tissue types and reduces the accuracy and reliability of measurements taken on the image. The second one is the shape variation across patients even on the same patient [4].

For image segmentation, there are various approaches, such as feature thresholding, contour-based methods, region-based methods, clustering, and template matching [5]. Each of these approaches has its advantages and disadvantages in terms of applicability, suitability, performance, and computational cost. Particularly, any approaches cannot guarantee desirable results on liver segmentation without considering characteristics of the abdominal CT image.

In this paper, we propose an automatic liver segmentation algorithm in abdominal CT images, which is a combination of region-based and contour-based approaches. Our algorithm exploits multiscale morphological filtering and the deformable contour method using labeling-based search algorithm to address these problems. In order to increase the robustness of the method, we use an estimated liver position (ELP), which is composed of control points and fitted into the patient map. ELP enables us to find robust patient contour and is used to perform proper liver segmentation [6].

2 Segmentation of the Liver

Mainly, the liver is approximated to muscle and gastrointestinal tract. Since adjacent organs have similar intensity values as the liver, a direct liver-extraction approach may extract undesirable boundaries resulting from its adjacent organs as fault positive/negative errors [1]. In order to cope with the problem, we present a new segmentation scheme, consisting of three stages: image simplification as preprocessing, search range detection using multiscale morphological filtering, and contour-based segmentation using the labeling-based search algorithm.

2.1 Image Simplification

For image simplification, we consider a prior knowledge of the liver on the abdominal CT image, such as shape, location, and intensity value.

Estimated Liver Position (ELP). For histogram considering only pixels within the patient contour, we introduce the ELP. In order to find the ELP, we use prior knowledge, such as a general location, shape and attenuation of the liver. An abdominal CT image typically consists of six components: background/air, liver, soft tissue, bone/vessel, kidney, and gastrointestinal tract. The liver is generally located in the left side of abdominal CT images and existed within the ribs [2]. We use the fact that the liver is positioned within the ribs. Since the attenuation of the ribs is almost white gray-level like the bone, we can easily detect the ribs. Figure 1 shows the estimation result of the liver position.

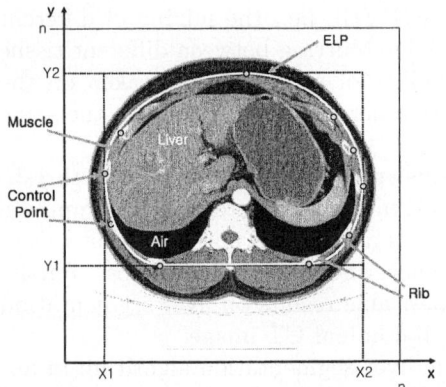 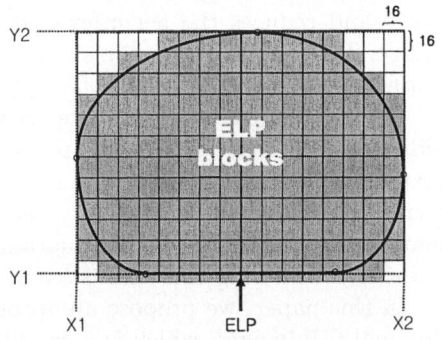

Fig. 1. Estimation of Liver Position   **Fig. 2.** ELP Blocks

In Fig. 1, the four patient extensions $(X1, X2, Y1, Y2)$ in the x and y direction are calculated by finding control points. Those control points are determined by the outmost point of each rib. Finally, the ELP becomes the spline curve connecting all of the control points, as shown Fig. 1. The liver is always located with in the ELP. For more accurate and simple processing, we make the ELP blocks, which are 16x16 blocks including the ELP, as shown in Fig. 2.

Histogram Analysis. We analyzed the intensity distribution of about 20 number of CT samples that are manually segmented liver and adjacent muscle, as shown in Fig. 3. In addition, we interpret Hounsfield numbers correspond to the liver and muscle into the gray level. Finally, we found that the intensity distribution of the liver is similar to the Gaussian distribution. In Fig. 3, however, attenuation of the liver and muscle is overlapped on some places. Hence, we estimate a threshold δ from the overlapped location to divide two objects. Assuming a Gaussian distribution with mean μ and standard deviation σ, the probability $P\{x; |x - \mu| \leq 2\sigma\} \simeq 95\%$, we can propose to set δ equal to 2σ [7].

Since the distribution function is similar to the normal distributed Gaussian function, as shown in Fig. 3, we estimate the mean μ_l for the liver and μ_m for the muscle by finding peaks in the intensity distribution of the ELP. We then obtain the standard deviation σ_l for the liver and σ_m for the muscle by fitting the gaussian density function on the intensity distribution function. Finally, we decide the threshold value δ_l for the liver and δ_m for the muscle. Thus, the ELP is classified into three classes by using the threshold value: liver class($\mu_m + \delta_m < C \leq \mu_l + \delta_l$), chaos class($\mu_l - \delta_l < C \leq \mu_m + \delta_m$), and non-liver class(others), where C is the class. Multilevel thresholding based on the analysis of the intensity distribution makes many other organs or tissues disappear in ELP blocks and identifies the liver and adjacent region as clear or blurred liver region.

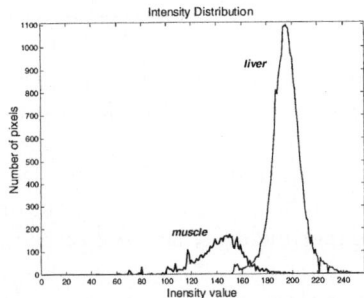

Fig. 3. Histogram of Several CT Samples

2.2 Search Range Detection

We find the first and second search region by performing multiscale morphological operations on the threshold image of the image simplification for the precise liver boundary.

Multiscale Morphological Filtering. Preprocessing classifies each pixel into the clustered liver class and the scattered non-liver class. Accordingly, we perform mathematical morphology filtering to reduce the scattered class and detect the liver object. This set theoretic, shape oriented approach treats the image as a set and the kernel of operation as another set, commonly known as structuring element. Different standard morphological operations, namely erosion, dilation, opening, and closing, are basically set theoretic operations between these two sets. The shape and the size of the structuring element play an important role in detecting or extracting features of the given shape and size from the image [5].

In constructing a morphological filter, we use erosion and dilation with a flat structuring element as follows [8], [9],

$$(f \ominus B_n)(x,y) = min\{f(x+l, y+m)|(l,m) \in B_n\} \quad (1)$$

$$(f \oplus B_n)(x,y) = max\{f(x-l, y-m)|(l,m) \in B_n\}. \quad (2)$$

Though the structuring element B takes care of the shape of the features during processing the image, it cannot equally treat the objects of the same shape but of the different size. Thus, for processing objects based on their shape as well as size, we incorporate a second attribute to the structuring element: its scale or composition. The types of morphological operations are termed as multiscale morphology [10]. Multiscale filtering are defined by

$$(f \ominus kB_n)(x,y) = \{(((f \ominus \underbrace{B_n) \ominus B_n) \cdots \ominus B_n}_{k \text{ times}})(x,y)\} \quad (3)$$

$$(f \oplus kB_n)(x,y) = \{(((f \oplus \underbrace{B_n) \oplus B_n) \cdots \oplus B_n}_{k \text{ times}})(x,y)\} \quad (4)$$

where k is an integer representing the scale factor of the structuring element B and n is the size of B. Multiscale filtering is performed by using the composition of the kth order morphological erosion and dilation operations with the multisize structuring elements of the 5x5 and 3x3 flat size. The size of structuring elements is decided by analyzing the number of remained regions or pixels of the threshold image, and the k value is experimentally set to 4 or 5.

First Search Range Detection. For the detection of the first search region, firstly, we find the initial liver region by performing multiscale opening. In multiscale opening, the erosion operation of k times, as its first step, eliminates bright features that do not fit within the structuring element and unconnected and scattered features in the threshold image. Then, it dilates iteratively same times to the erosion operation to restore the contours of components that have not been completely removed by the first step [2].

In the second stage, multiscale filtering using the fixed order of filtering composition causes dispersed pixels of tissues. It is due to the various shape or size of the liver by patients. In order to solve this problem, we perform on the 4-connected region-labeling algorithm based on the breadth-first search approach [11]. After the performance of the region-labeling algorithm, the largest labeled region is marked out for the coarse liver region.

The labeled liver region still has noise, such as adjoining muscles. Thus, we classify the labeled image into three classes by using the modified K-means algorithm. The adjacent tissues or muscles to the liver mainly have a higher or lower intensity value than that of the liver. Therefore, we use three centroids for the modified K-means algorithm that the middle centroid corresponding to the mean value of the liver is just computed again and the others are fixed to the max and min intensity value in the labeled liver region. This processing divides the region into the adjacent noise which will be reduced and the initial liver region.

The first search region is constructed by performing the different order's composition between erosion and dilation operations of the mathematical morphological opening on the clustered initial liver region by

$$(f \circ iB_n)(x,y) = ((f \ominus iB_n) \oplus (i+j)B_n)(x,y) \quad (5)$$

where i is the scale factor of the structuring element and j is a parameter which decides the size of search range. Generally, i is set to 2 and j is 4 or 5.

Second Search Range Detection. In the clustering, instead of reducing the adjacent noise, any liver region can be reduced. In order to address this problem, reverse filtering of the first morphological filtering is performed on the region of the original image corresponding to the previous labeled region. Multiscale morphological closing recovers some regions of the liver which are damaged or reduced in the previous morphological opening. The second search region is constructed based on the result of the morphological closing, region-labeling, and modified K-means clustering similar to the previous processing.

Multiscale morphological closing is defined, respectively, by

$$(f \bullet iB_n)(x,y) = ((f \oplus iB_n) \ominus (i+j)B_n)(x,y) \quad (6)$$

The final search range is determined by excluding the second search region from the first search region. Since most of the liver boundaries are located in this search range, precise automatic liver segmentation is possible by using the deformable contour algorithm within this range. Furthermore, the initial liver boundary which will be a guidepost for the search algorithm constructed by extension of the second search region to the original liver size.

2.3 Contour-Based Liver Segmentation

The initial liver boundary acquired by morphological filtering is a coarse liver contour. Therefore, we present the labeling-based search algorithm that deforms the initial liver boundary within the search range to find clear and final liver contour. For the search algorithm, we make a gradient-label map.

Gradient-Label Map. Since the slice thickness of our CT data set is 5mm, PVE is occurred at the boundary of the adjacent object. Because occurrences of PVE yield a gradual intensity fall across the boundaries of objects, a labeling-based search algorithm with an intensity partition that is sufficiently fine results in labeled images whose isolabel contours form conspicuous patterns. Because isolabel-contour patterns resemble isoelevation contours on topographical maps, we refer to the labeled images as isolabel-contour maps. If we observe an area within an isolabel-contour map that extends from one object's center to its boundary within the search range, we see a distinct pattern. Where the intensity gradient is monotonic in the raw image, the pattern of labels in the isolabel-contour map is monotonic as well. We observe dense contour patterns in the areas of abrupt intensity gradients and widespread contour patterns in the areas of gradual intensity gradients [4]. In order to make a gradient-label map, we enhance the isolabel-contour map by using the gradient magnitude into the weighing factor.

The spatial gradient of the search range image is approximated by using of a morphological gradient operator, expressed by

$$G(f) = \{(f \oplus B_n)(x,y) - (f \ominus B_n)(x,y)\} \quad (7)$$

The gradient image usually indicating borders between neighbor regions within search range is weighted by being reversed and normalized.

Labeling-Based Search Algorithm. We can describe the entire patterns of liver contours by classifying into three patterns in a gradient-label map as a relationship of the intensity distribution.

- Pattern 1: The liver is adjacent to the air region which has low intensity value.
- Pattern 2: The liver is touched to the ribs or the kidney which has high intensity value.
- Pattern 3: The liver is adjoined to the stomach, the intensity value within the liver boundary is distributed through the low gray-level.

The deformable contouring is started from the lowest located pixel of the initial liver contour toward the clockwise direction on the gradient-label map. Fig. 4 shows the eight directions which the current pixel can proceed. Liver boundary is smooth since the liver is the human organ. Therefore, the directions that the current pixel can proceed are three directions indicated by the small arrows in Fig. 4. Among the three directions, the center direction is determined by the initial liver contour obtained in the second stage. If the current pixel is located on the initial liver contour, then the next direction is determined by the initial liver contour. Otherwise, the next direction is the same as the previous direction. The other two possible directions are on either side of the center direction, as shown in Fig. 4. All of three directions are the candidate pixels.

Arrows indicate pixels considered for cost function within 9x9 window.

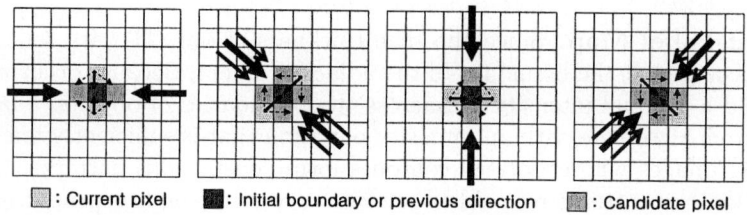

Fig. 4. Search Map

For the optimal path from each pixel, we formulate the local cost function at each candidate pixel. We can get a correct liver contour by finding optimal path which is the minimal cost value. The local cost function combining three features is defined as,

$$l(p,q) = w_D \cdot f_D(p,q) + w_B \cdot f_B(q) + w_I \cdot f_I(q) \tag{8}$$

where each w is the weight of the corresponding feature function. The p and q are two neighboring pixels in the gradient-label map, and $l(p,q)$ represents the local cost on the directed link from p to q and the two pixel value components, f_B and f_I, are "initial boundary" and "intensity distribution" cost functions. [12].

The f_D is a function of gradient direction which adds smoothness constraint to the boundary by associating a relatively high cost for sharp changes in boundary direction. The gradient direction feature cost is

$$f_D(p,q) = \frac{2}{3\pi}\{acos[d_p(p,q)] + acos[d_q(p,q)]\} \tag{9}$$

where $D'(p)$ is the unit vector perpendicular to the gradient direction at a point p. In addition, $d_p(p,q) = D'(p) \cdot L(p,q)$ and $d_q(p,q) = L(p,q) \cdot D'(q)$ are vector dot products and $L(p,q)$ is the normalized bidirectional link or the unit edge vector between pixels p and q and simply computes the direction of the link between p and q so that the difference between p and the direction of the link is minimized [12].

One of the two pixel components, $f_B(q)$ is the function estimating the state of the candidate pixel about the initial boundary. The state is inside or outside position in the gradient-label map. For the pixel component of the intensity distribution, we formulate the cost function, $f_I(q)$, by following the search map, as shown in Fig. 4. Functions $f_B(q)$ and $f_I(q)$ are

$$f_B(q) = \frac{1}{255}\{I(q) \cdot s\} \quad and \quad f_I(q) = \frac{1}{255}\{I(q) \cdot P(n)\} \tag{10}$$

where $I(q)$ is the pixel value at q and s is the weight of the state. If pixel is "inside" and "outside", s is 0.4. Otherwise, s is 0.2. $P(n)$ indicates a kind of the pattern as mentioned above. Each pattern is decided by searching neighboring pixels of each candidate pixel on bidirectional large arrows within the 9x9 window, as shown in Fig. 4. If the current pixel goes to the perpendicular direction, then the neighboring eight pixels of the candidate pixel that correspond to the initial boundary or previous direction are examined whether those are on the above pattern. The neighboring pixels within 9x9 window of the other candidate pixels are also examined. $P(n)$ value is experimentally determined but if the candidate pixel satisfies the pattern, $P(n)$ can generally take a value from 0.2 to 0.4. Otherwise, $P(n)$ is set to 1.

3 Experimental Results and Analysis

We experimented several samples with various shapes and irregular texture of 10 patients. All of the samples are contrast-enhanced abdominal CT images of venous phase.

Fig. 5 shows the results of each process of the proposed algorithm. Fig. 5(a) shows the original CT image. Fig. 5(b) depicts the multilevel threshold image on ELP blocks. We simplified the CT image using multilevel thresholding, which is decided by considering the feature of the gaussian distribution. It is due to the intensity distribution of the liver which is similar to the gaussian distribution. We can see that many other organs and tissues are eliminated in the threshold image.

However, unconnected or small tissues are remained. In order to reduce these objects and preserve the liver region, we perform recursively multiscale morphological filtering with region-labeling and clustering, as shown in Fig. 5(c) and Fig. 5(d). The appropriate composition of the order of morphological operations with region-labeling and clustering makes the suitable search range for the liver contour as depicted in Fig. 5(c) and Fig. 5(d). Final search range is formed by subtracting the second search region from the first search region, as shown in Fig. 5(e). In addition, for deformable contouring, we construct the initial liver boundary by extension of the second search region to original liver size, as shown in Fig. 5(f).

Lastly, deformable contouring based on the labeling-based search algorithm finds the final liver contour in the search range. For deformable contouring we make the gradient-label map weighted by gradient magnitude on search range, as shown in Fig. 5(g). Final liver contour is determined by computing the minimum cost function considering the gradient direction, the intensity distribution and the pattern features of the liver, as shown in Fig. 5(h) and Fig. 6.

The results of the proposed algorithm were evaluated by comparing to results of manual tracing by radiologist. The exclusive-or method is used for the comparable measure. Table 1 shows the comparison of automatic and manual segmentation of the liver. The correctness average is about 96.8% and the error is about 3.2%. Fig. 5(h) and Fig. 6 show results of segmentation on the five patients. In addition to this, Table 1 presents results of the comparison of the area and error rate on the various locations in the abdominal CT of a patient.

Table 1. Comparison of automatic vs. manual segmentation of the liver (mm^2)

Sample	Auto.	Manual	Error(%)	Sample	Auto.	Manual	Error(%)
1	4493.17	4600.03	0.02320	9	9721.03	10085.35	0.03612
2	9492.12	9302.13	-0.02042	10	8225.13	7961.23	-0.03315
3	14498.81	14254.97	-0.01711	11	7510.97	6074.00	-0.02366
4	12832.21	12576.27	-0.02035	12	6321.27	6699.13	0.05640
5	12341.24	12688.73	0.02739	13	5006.03	5133.93	0.02491
6	13381.12	13017.53	-0.02793	14	4524.13	4675.53	0.03238
7	11194.59	11584.49	0.03366	15	3407.97	3536.56	0.03636
8	10320.27	10655.81	0.03149	16	3007.97	3056.56	0.01590

4 Conclusions

In this paper, we have proposed a new algorithm for automatic liver segmentation using a prior knowledge and the deformable contour method based on morphological filtering. We used the prior knowledge about the location of the liver in CT image and introduced the estimated liver position (ELP). Histogram analysis within the ELP is used to decide the adequate threshold value for multilevel thresholding that reduced computational complexity. In addition, multiscale morphological filtering using region-labeling and clustering detects the search

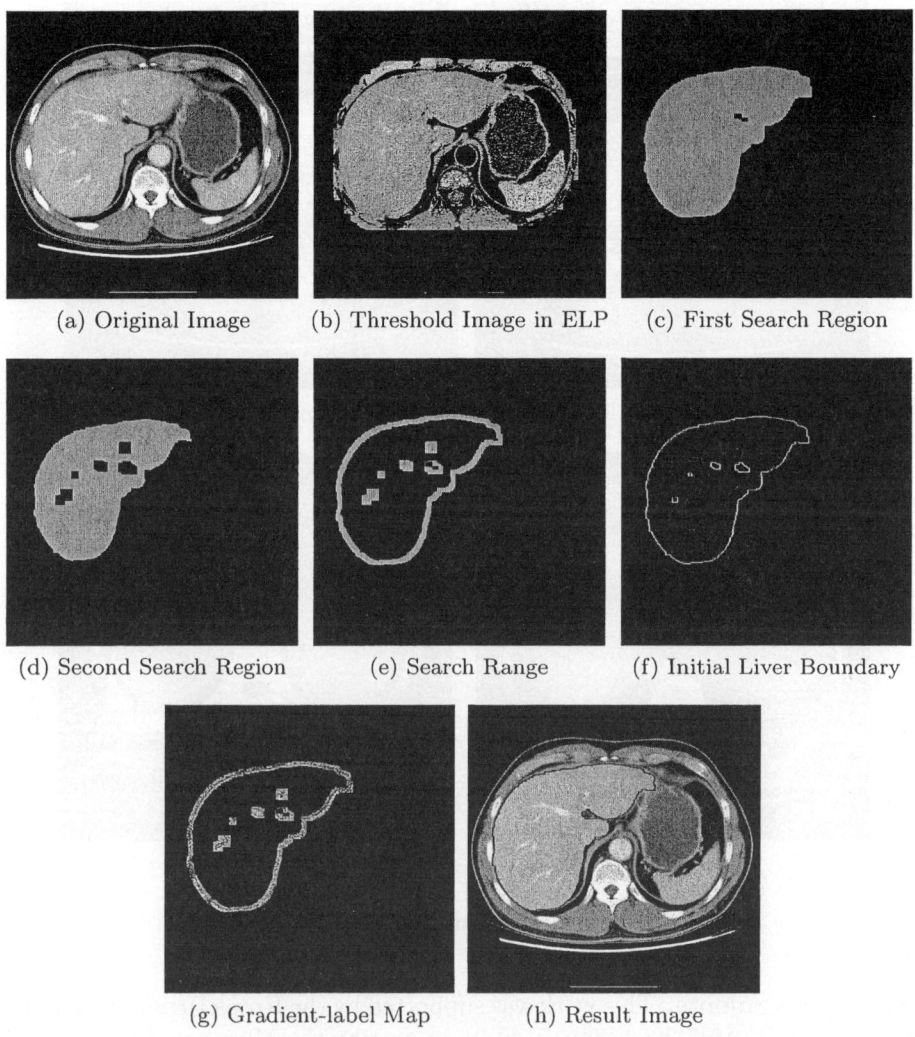

Fig. 5. Experimental Results of Patient 1

range and the initial liver boundary for the deformable contouring. The final contour is found by using the labeling-based search algorithm on the gradient-label map. The search algorithm considering partial-volume effect (PVE) computes the minimum cost function composed of the gradient magnitude, the gradient direction and the pattern of the intensity distribution. The final results are compared to manually segmented image by the radiologist, and we could know that the false positive/negative results were effectively suppressed. This algorithm is the effective automatic segmentation algorithm of the liver in CT images for the first step of the computer-aided diagnosis (CAD) and computer-aided surgery (CAS) systems. It will assist radiologists by improving their diagnosis.

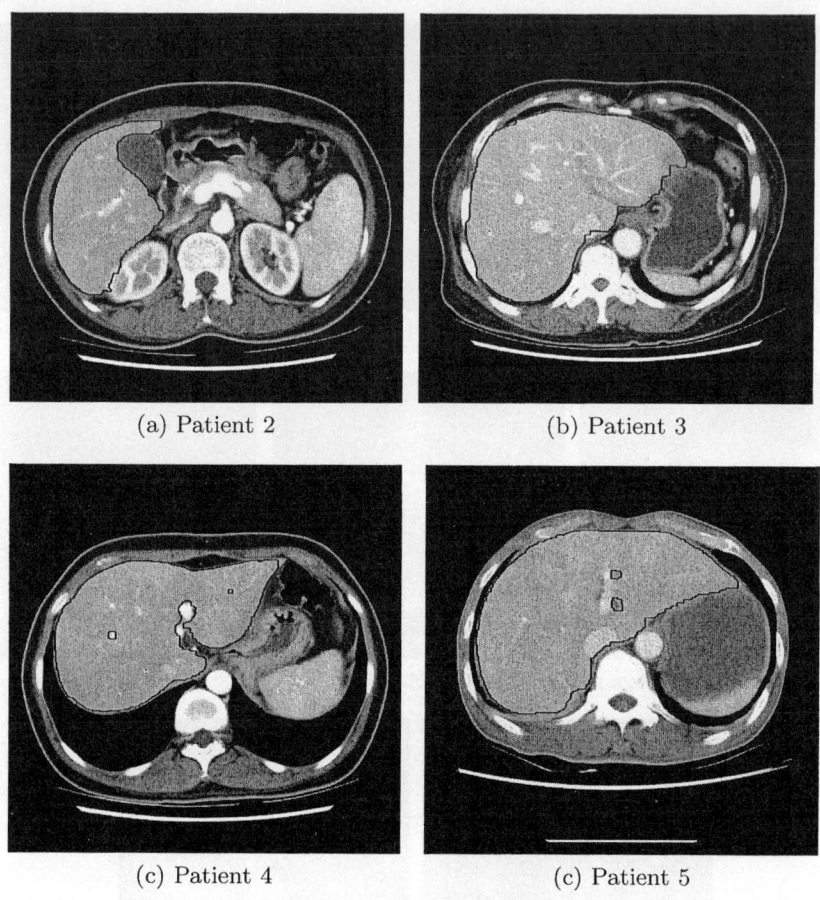

(a) Patient 2   (b) Patient 3

(c) Patient 4   (c) Patient 5

Fig. 6. Experimental Results

Acknowledgements. This work was supported by the Korea Research Foundation Grant (No. M07-2004-000-10140-0), in part by the Ministry of Information and Communication (MIC) through the Realistic Broadcasting Research Center (RBRC) at Gwangju Institute of Science and Technology (GIST), and in part by the Ministry of Education (MOE) through the Brain Korea 21 (BK21) project.

References

1. Chen, E.L., Chung, P.C., Chen, C.L., Tasi, H.M., Chang, C.I.: An Automatic Diagnosis System for CT Liver Image Classification. IEEE Transaction on Biomedical Engineering, Vol. 45, No. 6 (1998) 783-794
2. Lim, S.J., Jeong, Y.Y., Lee, C.W., Ho, Y.S.: Automatic Segmentation of the Liver in CT Images Using the Watershed Algorithm Based on Morphological Filtering. Proceeding of the SPIE, Vol. 5370 (2004) 1658-1666

3. Giger, M.L., Karssemeijer, N., Armato, S.G. III.: Guest Editorial : Computer-Aided Diagnosis in Medical Imaging, IEEE Transaction on Medical Imaging, Vol. 20, No. 12 (2001) 1205-1208
4. Shiffman, S., Rubin, G.D., Napel, S.: Medical Image Segmentation Using Analysis of Isolable-Contour Maps, IEEE Transaction on Medical Imaging, Vol. 19, No.11 (2000) 1064-1074
5. Mukhopadhyay, S., Chanda, B.: Multiscale Morphological Segmentation of Gray-Scale Images, IEEE Transaction on Image Processing, Vol. 12, No. 5 (2003) 533-549
6. Bilger, K., Kupferschlager, J., Muller-Schauenburg, W., Nusslin, F., Bares, R.: Threshold Calculation for Segmented Attenuation Correction in PET with Histogram Fitting, IEEE Transaction on Nuclear Science, Vol. 48, No. 1 (2001) 43-50
7. Kuo, C.H., Tewfik, A.H.: Multiscale Sigma Filter and Active Contour for Image Segmentation, Proceeding of the ICIP (1999) 353-357
8. Gonzalez, R.C., Woods, R.E.: Digital Image Processing, Prentice Hall (2002)
9. Kim, M.C., Choi, J.G., Kim, D.H., Lee, H., Lee, M.H., Ahn, C.T., Ho, Y.S.: A VOP Generation Tool: Automatic Segmentation of Moving Objects in Image Sequences Based on Spatio-Temporal Information, IEEE Transaction on Circuits and Systems for Video Technology, Vol. 9, No. 8 (1999) 1216-1226
10. Maragos, P.: Pattern Spectrum and Multiscale Shape Representation, IEEE Transaction on Pattern Analysis and Machine Intelligence, Vol. 11 (1989) 701-716
11. Gose, E., Johnsonbaugh, R., Jost, S.: Pattern Recognition and Image Analysis, Prentice Hall (1996)
12. Mortensen, E.N., Brrett, W.A.: Interactive Segmentation with Intelligent Scissors, Graphical Models and Image Processing, Vol. 60 (1998)

Radial Projection: A Feature Extraction Method for Topographical Shapes

Yong-Il Kwon[1], Ho-Hyun Park[2,*], Jixue Liu[3], and Mario A. Nascimento[4]

[1] School of Electrical and Electronics Engineering, Chung-Ang University, Korea
kyi0605@hanmail.net
[2] School of Electrical and Electronics Engineering,
Chung-Ang University, Korea
hohyun@cau.ac.kr
[3] School of Computer and Information Science, University of South Australia
jixue.liu@unisa.edu.au
[4] Department of Computing Science, University of Alberta, Canada
mn@cs.ualberta.ca

Abstract. Topographical images such as aerial and satellite images are usually similar with respect to colors and textures but not in shapes. Thus shape features of the images and the methods of extracting them become critical for effective image retrieval from topographical image databases. In this paper, we propose a shape feature extraction method as well as a similarity function for topographical image retrieval. The method extracts a set of attributes which can model the presence of holes and disconnected regions in images and is tolerant to pre-processing, more specifically segmentation, errors. Experiments suggest that retrieval using attributes extracted using the proposed method performs better than using the Curvature Scale Space (CSS) which is a well known method in the area of shape feature extraction.

1 Introduction

Image retrieval is the process to find images from an image database that match the properties of a given image called a query image. Image retrieval can be done using annotations or actual content. Annotation-based image retrieval requires text annotations to be done manually in advance for each database image, and uses those when a query is processed. This is clearly not practical for any non-trivial image database. On the other hand in content-based image retrieval (CBIR), features such as color, texture and shape are extracted automatically from the actual images, and used for finding images that are similar to a query image [1]. This paper focuses on the CBIR problem. The methods of CBIR depend largely on the types of images such as color-rich (e.g., product catalogs, scenery and flower images), texture-rich (e.g., brick fences, wheat in a farm, ocean waves, and cloth images) and shape-rich images (e.g., trademarks, buildings, traffic sign images). This means that a method that works effectively and

---

* Corresponding author.

efficiently with one type of images may not work well with other types of images. One such type of images that existing methods do not work well with is topographical images, which are the focus of this paper.

When compared to other types of images, topographical images, in particular aerial and satellite images, have the following properties which make their retrieval more challenging. Firstly, because they are usually similar in colors and textures, these features are not very discriminant, i.e., do not help distinguishing those types of images. This makes shape an important feature within topographical image retrieval. Secondly, topographical images are often complex requiring more sophisticated feature extraction than simple shape images. Finally topographical images may have low resolutions and some uncontrollable features, such as reflected lights, which may adversely affect image pre-processing, namely segmentation. All these properties of topographical images need to be addressed by feature extraction methods in order to facilitate their retrieval.

We assume that the original images, e.g., from satellite services, are initially segmented in order to separate background (e.g., sea and clouds) from objects of interest (e.g., islands). (The particulars of the segmentation technique do not matter as far as our proposed technique is concerned.) Once the segmentation process is done the image is transformed into a binary image where 0 and 1 (respectively black and white in the forthcoming figures) represent background and region pixels respectively [7]. Often the whole image is not interesting for retrieval purposes, but rather the objects in it. For instance, if the image contains an archipelago, it may be useful to store the individual islands separately. For that we assume that images go through a "separation" process where the individual objects are stored as images by themselves. (The process through which this is achieved is also orthogonal to our proposal.) Thus at the final of this pre-processing stage one has a database of images, each containing one single object, and we assume such a setting in our work. As an example Figure 1(a) illustrates the image after being segmented into background and foreground and Figure 1(b) shows the individual images which are stored in the database for future retrieval.

A shape can be of one of two types: simple or complex. A simple shape means that it can have only one single region and the region can be described by a polygon without holes. A complex shape means that it can have multiple regions that can be disconnected, e.g., a set of islets forming an archipelago, or can have holes, e.g., lakes inside a portion of land, and can have nested regions as well. Allowing a single object to have disconnected regions is important because minor errors in the segmentation can disconnect regions which are in reality connected. However, at query time, this type of segmentation errors should ideally not affect the final retrieval result.

Existing CBIR systems retrieve images using color, texture, and/or simple shape features [1,6,8]. When these systems are used for topographical image retrieval, it is likely that the retrieval accuracy will not be ideal. Therefore new methods are needed to perform CBIR of topographical images.

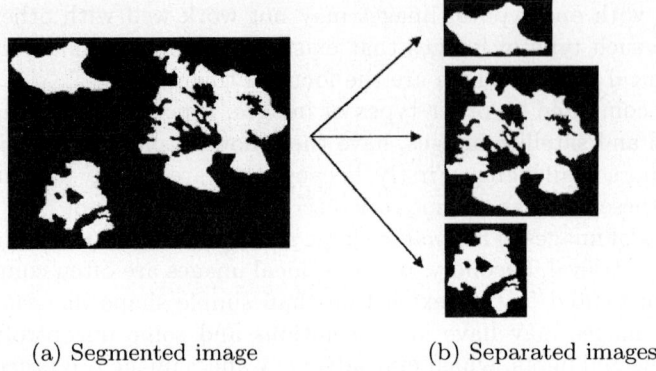

(a) Segmented image   (b) Separated images

Fig. 1. A segmented image and its separated objects

Our main contribution in this paper is the proposal of a shape extraction method called *Radial Projection* (RP) for capturing shape features of topographical images. Given an object, which may have holes and disconnected regions, the method produces a set of attribute vectors to represent the object. Unlike other approaches RP allows the user to define how fine-grained or coarse the object's representation will be. This allows one to carefully trade-off retrieval efficiency, effectiveness and storage space.

The rest of this paper is organized as follows. In Section 2, we briefly review other methods for extracting shape features. In Section 3, we propose our RP technique, describing the feature extraction process in detail and discussing its advantages. In Section 4, we define the distance function to be used in tandem with RP and show how to use it to compare two images efficiently. In Section 5, we show preliminary experimental results and Section 6 concludes the paper.

2 Related Work

Shape feature extraction of images can be divided into region-based methods and contour-based methods [3]. Region-based methods use the pixel distribution of both the boundary and inner pixels of regions while contour-based methods use the pixel distribution of boundary pixels only. The method we proposed in this paper falls in the former category.

As mentioned earlier we consider a binary image of size $S_X \times S_Y$ where each pixel $p(x,y)$ has a value given by a function $f(x,y)$ defined as follows:

$$f(x,y) = \begin{cases} 1 \text{ if } p(x,y) \text{ belongs to a region} \\ 0 \text{ otherwise} \end{cases}$$

One technique used for region-based methods is the Cartesian Projection which can be defined as:

$$p_X(x) = \sum_{y=1}^{S_Y} f(x,y), x = 1, ..., S_X$$

$$p_Y(y) = \sum_{x=1}^{S_X} f(x,y), x = 1, ..., S_Y$$

that is, the list $\langle p_X(x) \rangle$ (respectively $\langle p_Y(y) \rangle$) counts the numbers of region pixels along the Y-axis (respectively X-axis), for each pixel in the X-axis (respectively Y-axis) [7]. Figure 2 shows an example of the Cartesian projection method on the Cartesian coordinates. Each rectangle represents a pixel of the region in a 6×6 (pixels) image. The projected value, i.e., the number of region pixels, is shown along the direction of the projections at the left side for y and at the bottom for x. Once those sets are obtained, two images can be compared using any vector-based distance, e.g., the Euclidean distance.

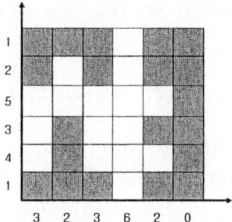

Fig. 2. An example of projection on the Cartesian coordinates

Clearly the Cartesian Projection depend on the orientation of the image. In other words, it is not rotation invariant. As well, it does not take into account the existence of holes and disconnected regions in an object.

A contour-based feature extraction method called *Curvature Scale Space* (CSS) has been proposed in [4,5]. The CSS is reportedly a successful method in the CBIR domain [3]. It has also been extended and advanced by the growth of MPEG [3]. The concept of CSS is that convex and concave segments of a contour are considered as features [5]. Those segments are divided by the inflection points on the contour which have zero curvature. The curvature is the change rate of tangents along the contour. The detail steps of CSS for a region in an image are as follows [3]:

(1) The contour of an object is extracted;
(2) The contour is smoothed by a low pass filter, and the filter gradually removes concave segments;
(3) On each filtering the curvature of the new contour is recalculated and the positions of inflection points are recorded;
(4) Steps (2) and (3) are iterated until all concave segments are removed;
(5) Finally the positions of inflection points on each filtering and the total number of filterings are regarded as feature values.

Like the Cartesian Projection method the CSS is also applicable only to the retrieval of simple shaped objects, i.e., it is not well suited for a complex object which has disconnected regions and holes. Our proposal, presented next, aims exactly at overcoming such limitations.

3 Radial Projection

The basic idea behind our method is to have a user-defined discrete representation of the image using *rays* originating at the object's center of gravity, hence the name *Radial Projection* (RP), which sample the image's content. For each of such rays a set of attributes are computed and the whole set of attributes is used to describe the object's shape.

The first task is to obtain the "origin" of the image space. We assume it to be the centroid of the image and discuss how to obtain it shortly. Next a set of equally spaced rays starting at the object's centroid and ending at the object's boundary is obtained. Assuming the angular space between rays to be θ, i.e., there are $k = 360/\theta$ rays (denoted as $R_1, R_2, ..., R_k$), a ray $R_i, (i = 1, 2, ..., k)$ can be formally defined as:

$$R_i = \langle P_1^i, P_2^i, ... P_{n_i}^i \rangle$$

where each $P_j^i, j = 1, ..., n_i$ is an image pixel $p(x, y)(x \in 1, 2, ...S_X, y \in 1, 2, ...S_X)$ and which holds the following properties:

- P_1^i is the object's centroid;
- $P_{n_i}^i$ is the farthest region pixel along direction $(i-1)\theta$; and
- $d(P_1^i, P_{j+1}^i) > d(P_1^i, P_j^i), \forall j = 1, 2, ...n_i - 1$.

In effect, the properties construct a well-ordered list of pixel originating from the object's centroid to its farthest boundary along the segment of line with slope $(i-1)\theta$. Then for each such ray R_i three attributes are obtained:

(1) Region Pixel Frequency (RPF), i.e., the number of region pixels it contains.
(2) Region Alternation Frequency (RAF), i.e., the number of times the pixels alternate between region and background.
(3) Ray Length (RL), i.e., the length of the ray.

There are several advantages to using these attributes in contrast to previous approaches. The main one is that RAF allows one to capture the notion of holes. As well, since this set of attributes is obtained for each ray and there are $360/\theta$ rays modeling the object, θ being a user-defined parameter, one can make the representation as fine or as coarse as desired. The tradeoff in the latter case is the storage space for the extracted attributes and computational time when comparing two different shapes. Next we show how to obtain the object's centroid and how to compute the three aforementioned attributes.

In order to find the centroid of the region(s) of an object, we compute the total number of region pixels in the corresponding binary image.

$$XY_{sum} = \sum_{x=1}^{S_X} \sum_{y=1}^{S_Y} f(x, y)$$

Then we sum x and y coordinate values of the region pixels respectively.

$$X_{sum} = \sum_{x=1}^{S_X} \sum_{y=1}^{S_Y} f(x, y) \times x$$
$$Y_{sum} = \sum_{x=1}^{S_X} \sum_{y=1}^{S_Y} f(x, y) \times y$$

Finally the centroid of gravity is computed as:

$$(x_c, y_c) = \left(\frac{X_{sum}}{XY_{sum}}, \frac{Y_{sum}}{XY_{sum}} \right)$$

Once the centroid is obtained, the user-defined parameter θ is used to determine the number of k equally spaced rays used to model the object at hand. For the sake of presentation assume the following rewriting of function $f(.,.)$ defined earlier:

$$F(P_i^k) = \begin{cases} 1 \text{ if pixel } P_i^k \text{ belongs to a region} \\ 0 \text{ otherwise} \end{cases}$$

For each such ray R_k the three attributes mentioned above are obtained as follows.

- $RPF_k = \sum_{P_i^k \in R_k} F(P_i^k)$. (This counts how many region pixels are there in a given ray.)
- $RAF_k = \sum_{P_i \in R_k} |F(P_i^k) - F(P_{i+1}^k)|$. (This counts the number of alternations between region and background the rays covers.)
- $RL_k = d(P_1^k, P_{n_k}^k)$. (This is the length of the ray.)

Figure 3 is an example which shows implementation of Radial Projection for topographical images. The left part shows enlargement of a ray which is the elliptic portion of the right part. Each rectangle represents a pixel of the ray and the right-most pixel is the centroid of the object. Starting from the centroid pixel, we project along the arrow, and then we find nine white pixels which are region pixels. Thus the RPF is 9. During the projection process, there are changes of colors between the 3-rd black pixel and the 4-th white pixel as well as between 9-th and 10-th, and between 15-th and 16-th. Therefore, the RAF is 3. Finally we can find the 18-th pixel is the farthest region pixel from the centroid. So the RL is 17.

The features extracted are invariant to translation. This is because if the region is moved to another position, the centroid is also moved, and the values obtained are the same. However, it is not rotation invariant, which is an important requirement. In order to address this we note, for a given object, the maximum value for one chosen attribute, in this work we have used the RL

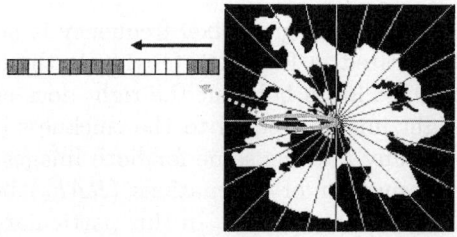

Fig. 3. An example of feature extraction using RP

attribute. The idea is to shift the metadata for the objects with respect to a reference ray, so that the reference ray becomes the first element of the attribute vectors for all objects in a consistent manner, and to make the features rotation invariant. Note that this type of shifting cannot be done when using the Cartesian Projection method discussed earlier. We discuss how to use this shifting criteria within RP further in Section 4. In order to make the metadata also invariant to scaling we divide each attribute value by the average value of the that attribute over all rays. The use of the average value as a normalization factor instead of the maximum is due to the fact that possible noise in the segmentation process may introduce errors which can affect such maximum value, whereas the average value is a more robust statistic.

In summary, for a given shape and a given angular discretization value θ, a set of three attribute values (RPF, RAF and RL) are stored for each of the $360/\theta$ rays R_k. In order to facilitate the comparison of two different shapes we assume that the metadata information for the rays is stored in order starting with the index k which yielded the reference ray and continuing with the rays following that one in a counter-clock wise way. (We present a set of objects and their respective metadata in the next section.)

We now compare our approach with two existing methods to illustrate the advantages of our approach. Recall that the Cartesian Projection [7] uses only the pixel frequency as a feature value. In contrast, our approach is much more granular, using not only the region pixel frequency but also the ray length and the number of region alternations. The ray length can be used to obtain boundary information of an object, and the number of alternations identifies holes and disconnected regions in the object.

Fig. 4. Two images have the same region pixel frequency

A case where using only the region pixel frequency is not enough to distinguish two images is illustrated in Figure 4. Obviously the two images are very different, i.e., the left image has a hole but the right does not. Since the radius of the region in the right image is equal to the thickness of the "ring" in the left image the RPF_k for any k is the same for both images. To distinguish the two images, we use the number of alternations (RAF_k) between regions and background and the length of each ray k. In this particular case the number of alternations is 1 in the left image but 0 in the right image (regardless of the direction used to extract the features).

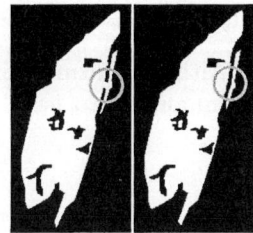

Fig. 5. An example of segmentation error

Figure 5 shows a situation where a segmentation error occurred: a connection between two regions in the right figure is missing (in the area highlighted by the gray circle). The connection which is present in the left image yields a high degree of convexity which is absent in the right image. While this makes CSS produce different metadata for both images the difference in the metadata produced by RP is very small reflecting the user's perception.

4 Distance Function

In this section, we present a method of comparing images on the attribute values calculated from the last section. We can compare a query shape and a shape which is stored in database by computing the distance between features extracted from the two shapes.

Let us consider two shapes I and Q which after the pre-processing and feature extraction detailed above can be represented as the following lists:

$$I = \langle (RPF_1^I, ...RPF_k^I), (RAF_1^I, ..., RAF_k^I), (RL_1^I, ..., RL_k^I) \rangle$$
$$Q = \langle (RPF_1^Q, ..., RPF_k^Q), (RAF_1^Q, ..., RAF_k^Q), (RL_1^Q, ..., RL_k^Q) \rangle$$

where RPF_j^I, RAF_j^I and RL_j^I are the attribute values obtained for ray R_j. Moreover, due to the reference ray mentioned in the previous section we have $RL_1^I \geq RL_j^I, \forall j$. (Similarly for image Q.) Note that it is possible to exist ties for the choice of the reference angle, for now we assume those are broken arbitrarily.

For each attribute type, a similarity measure can be computed using the Euclidean distance:

$$D_{RPF}(I,Q) = \sqrt{\sum_{j=1}^{k}(RPF_j^I - RPF_j^Q)^2}$$
$$D_{RAF}(I,Q) = \sqrt{\sum_{j=1}^{k}(RAF_j^I - RAF_j^Q)^2}$$
$$D_{RL}(I,Q) = \sqrt{\sum_{j=1}^{k}(RL_j^I - RL_j^Q)^2}$$

It is possible that for some applications some of these attributes are more meaningful than others. In order to accommodate that we define a weight for each of those component distances, resulting in the following distance formulation:

$$D(I,Q) = w_{RPF} \times D_{RPF}(I,Q) + w_{RAF} \times D_{RAF}(I,Q) + w_{RL} \times D_{RL}(I,Q)$$

where $w_{RPF}+w_{RAF}+w_{RL} = 1$. Although future work is needed to automatically fine tune such parameters it is important to have the model allowing for it in case the users wish to use it.

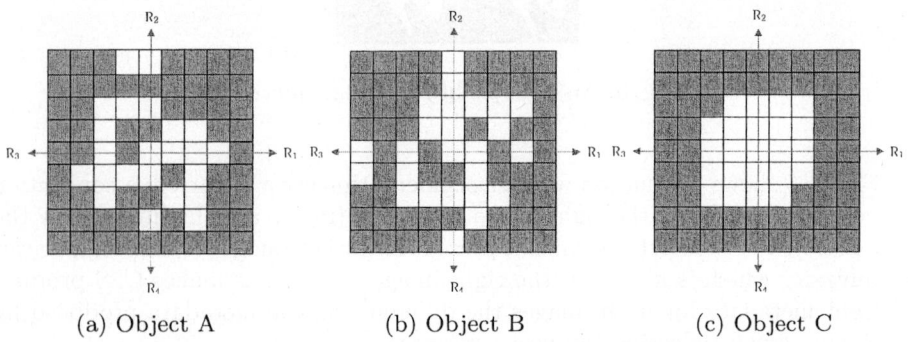

Fig. 6. An example of radial projection and distance function

We illustrate the computation of the similarity distance using the three shapes in Figures 6(a), (b) and (c). To simplify the illustration we use $\theta = 90$ degrees. It is easy to see that object B is a slightly different version of object A when rotated 90 degrees counter-clockwise. On the other hand object C is quite different from A. That is, the similarity function should be such that $D(A,B) < D(A,C)$.

Using the definitions presented in the previous section and the notation above, the set of metadata for objects A, B and C are respectively:

$$A = \langle(3,2,3,4),(4,2,2,0),(4,2,3,3)\rangle$$
$$B = \langle(3,3,3,5),(4,4,2,0),(4,4,3,4)\rangle$$
$$C = \langle(3,3,3,3),(0,0,0,0),(2,2,2,2)\rangle$$

Taking as example object A, note that this already reflects the fact that the attributes have been ordered by $R_2^A, R_3^A, R_4^A, R_1^A$ as RL_2^A has the largest value for the RL attribute. In the case of object B, R_2^A, R_3^A or R_4^A can be the reference ray but we chose R_3^B and for C any of rays could serve as the reference. Using the formulas just presented and all weights equal to 1/3, one obtains $D(A,B) = 1.88$ and $D(A,C) = 2.92$ which agree to our visual perception.

Now let us analyse the complexity of the proposed RP technique. We assume that the segmentation and object separation process is done off-line since they are orthogonal to the retrieval process.

The feature extraction is done for each of the k rays. The number of pixels comprised in a ray can be upper-bounded by $M = \max_{i=1,\ldots,k} |R_i|$. Since these set of pixels have to be, at most, inspected three times (one for each attribute), the time complexity to extract the shape features is $O(k \times M)$, i.e., linear on k since M is a constant.

The distance computation has also linear complexity on the number of rays k since the Euclidean distance is computed a constant number of times, one for each attribute type for feature vectors of length k.

Since both feature extraction and similarity computation can be done in linear time and, as argued earlier, the features extracted are rotation, translation and scale invariant we consider our technique to be a good candidate when compared to the other approaches, such as the Cartesian Projection and CSS. Even though these also have good asymptotical performance, they cannot capture important features of complex shapes. Next we present some preliminary experiments that further suggest the superiority of RP when compared to CSS.

5 Experimental Results

In order to assess our proposed technique we show here some preliminary results, which, despite the small database used, are very encouraging. For the following set of results the weights w_{RPF}, w_{RAF}, w_{RL} were empirically determined to be 0.27, 0.27 and 0.46 respectively.

As discussed in Section 3, RP can extract features from an image regardless of rotation/scale/translation of an image. Figure 7 shows the result of experiments which confirm such robustness.

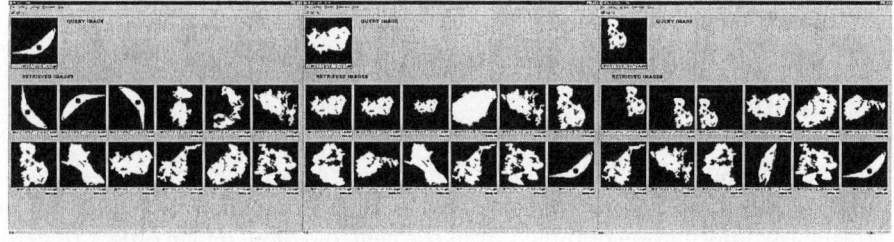

Fig. 7. Experiments for rotation/scale/translation invariance

In the first experiment of Figure 7 we can see that the images which have the identical region but different rotations with the query image are highly ranked. This shows that the images similar to the query image are retrieved without regard to rotation of images. Through the second and third experiments, we can also see that the images which have the same shaped region but different scale and translation are determined as similar images with the query image.

We do not compare RP to the Cartesian Projection technique because the latter is a specialized version of our proposal. That is, if one sets $w_{RPF} = 1$ and $w_{RAF} = w_{RL} = 0$ and projects only on X and Y axes directions then RP is reduced to the Cartesian Projection. Since our proposal uses a superset of the semantically meaningful attributes used by the Cartesian Projection, it ought to be more effective. Next we compare RP with CSS because CSS has been argued to be one of the most powerful shape feature extraction/retrieval methods.

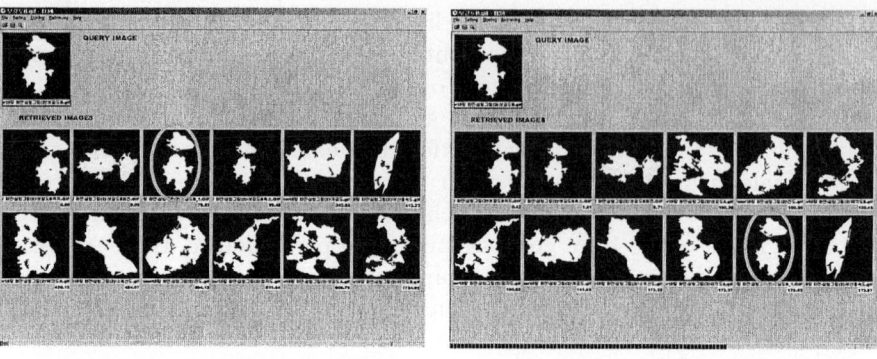

(a) image retrieval using RP   (b) image retrieval using CSS

Fig. 8. Experimental results of topographical image retrieval using RP and CSS

Figure 8 shows the result of a query (displayed in the top left corner of the images) ranked in row major order. We can see that RP ranks all similar shapes at the very top. It is important to note that the third best ranked shape has in reality two regions due to segmentation error. On the other hand, CSS is unable to handle such type of errors and ranks that same shape very lowly. This confirms that RP is robust with respect to segmentation errors which occur frequently in topographical images and can retrieve the desired images effectively.

6 Conclusion

In this paper, we introduced a shape feature extraction method, called *Radial Projection*, suitable for topographical images. It abstract the shape information by storing ray information obtained from the centroid of an image object towards the outer boundary in the polar coordinates. For each ray, the following features are extracted: (1) the region pixel frequency, (2) the region alternation frequency, and (3) the length of the ray, i.e., the distance from the centroid to the farthest pixel of the region. We have shown that these features are more comprehensive than others used in previous works, in the sense that it accounts for region holes and disconnections. As well, we showed how a simple reference angle can simplify the distance computation, resulting in a linear time similarity measure.

The Radial Projection has the following advantages which we have verified through experiments: (1) it can retrieve the images similar to a query image regardless of rotation, scale and translation, and (2) it is robust to segmentation errors and can also extract shape features from the images which have holes and disconnected regions.

We are currently carrying experiments using much larger databases in order to confirm our preliminary results presented in this paper. Future work should be done in the following directions: automatic tuning of the attribute weights used in the similarity computation, using, for instance, relevance feedback; investigating the effect of the chosen reference ray; and finally, the use of an indexing structure in order to speedup query processing.

Acknowledgement

This research was supported by the international joint research grant of the foreign professor invitation program of IITA (Institute of Information Technology Assessment), Korea. Mario A. Nascimento has also been supported by NSERC, Canada.

References

1. Gudivada, V.N., Raghavan, V.V., "Content-based Image Retrieval System", IEEE Computer, Vol. 28, pp. 18-22, September 1995.
2. Kpalma, K., Ronsin, J., "A multi-scale curve smoothing for generalised pattern recognition(MSGPR)", Proceedings of Seventh International Symposium on Signal Processing and Its Applications, Vol. 2, pp. 427-430, July 2003.
3. Manjunath, B.S., Philippe S. and Thomas S., Introduction to MPEG-7 Multimedia Content Description Interface, John Wiley and Sons Publishers, June 2002.
4. Mokhtarian, F., Mackworth, A.K., "A Theory of Multiscale, Curvature-Based Shape Representation for Planae Curves", IEEE Transactions on Pattern Analysis and Machine Intelligence, Vol. 14, pp.789-805, August 1992.
5. Mokhtarian, F., and Bober, M., The Curvature Scale Space Representation: Theory, Applications, and MPEG-7 Standardization, Kluwer Academic Publishers, 2002.
6. Smith, J.R., Shih-Fu, C., "VisualSEEK : a fully automated content-based image query system", Proceedings of the fourth ACM international conference on Multimedia, pp. 87-98, 1997.
7. Milan, S., Vaclav, H. and Roger B., Image Processing, Analysis and Machine Vision, PWS Publishers, 1999.
8. Vasconcelos, N., Kunt, M., "Content-based retrieval from image databases: current solutions and future directions", Proceedings of International Conference on Image Processing, Vol. 3, pp. 48-53, October 2001.

A Robust Text Segmentation Approach in Complex Background Based on Multiple Constraints

Libo Fu[1,2], Weiqiang Wang[1,2], and Yaowen Zhan[1,2]

[1] Institute of Computing Technology,
Chinese Academy of Sciences, Beijing, China 100080
[2] Graduate School of Chinese Academy of Sciences, Beijing, China 100039
{lbfu, wqwang, ywzhan}@jdl.ac.cn

Abstract. In this paper we propose a robust text segmentation method in complex background. The proposed method first utilizes the K-means algorithm to decompose a detected text block into different binary image layers. Then an effective post-processing is followed to eliminate background residues in each layer. In this step we develop a group of robust constraints to characterize general text regions based on color, edge and stroke thickness. We also propose the components relation constraint (CRC) designed specifically for Chinese characters. Finally the text image layer is identified based on the periodical and symmetrical layout of text lines. The experimental results show that our method can effectively eliminate a wide range of background residues, and has a better performance than the K-means method, as well as a high speed.

1 Introduction

Text embedded in images or video frames usually includes plentiful semantic information and thus provides an important clue for the index and retrieval of the contents of images and videos. In the past ten years many research works have been done on text detection, localization in images and videos [1,2,3,4,5], and text tracking in videos [6,7]. However, the issue of text extraction or text segmentation has not been studied extensively [8], especially for text embedded in complex background. Generally an OCR engine is employed to convert pixel text in images into plain text, but it is only able to recognize well-segmented binary images. For text in images or video frames, especially in complex background, a segmentation process aiming at removing background and improving text quality is always needed before text is fed into an OCR engine. However, it is still a challenging task to segment text out completely and accurately from complex background, i.e., there are no broken strokes, no conglutinated strokes and no background residues. A robust text segmentation approach is very significant, since it can prevent the performance of an OCR engine from degrading greatly.

Many algorithms have been proposed to address the issue of text segmentation. Among these algorithms, the threshold-based methods [2,9,10] were first developed to segment text in documents or images with simple background. The related thresholds are generally chosen based on intensity contrast between text and background. These approaches will fail for text embedded in complex background [11]. Otsu in [12] presents a general adaptive threshold method through minimizing the intra-class variance. Although this technique can be applied in text segmentation in complex background, some undesirable background residues are possibly left due to their similarity with text color. This will reduce the recognition rate of an OCR engine greatly.

Some authors have also considered the spatial information of text in their segmentation algorithms. Gao et al. [13] utilize the Gaussian mixtures to model text regions and background. In their method, each Gaussian represents the regions with the same color property. An adaptive searching algorithm based on the constraint of text layout relation is developed to discriminate text and background regions. Chen et al. [4] also use the GMM but the model parameters are estimated based on MRF. A post-processing procedure including the connected component analysis and the grayscale consistency constraint is used to eliminate the components with illegal size or a different gray level value from text. They report their approach yields similar results as the K-means algorithm [12] does, but the latter has a lower computation cost. Ye et al. [14] employ the "edge couple" characteristic of text to sample text pixels, and then a GMM is trained online to model the distribution of the hue and intensity values of text pixels. They employ the spatial connectivity information and the connected components analysis to further refine the segmentation results. Today many preprocessing techniques are also suggested to improve image quality before segmentation, including sub-pixel interpolation [7,15], multi-frame integration for videos [6,7] and character stroke enhancement [15].

In this paper, we propose a robust approach to text segmentation in complex background. The K-means algorithm is first adopted to cluster a detected rectangle text block into K binary image layers, and then an effective post-processing procedure is applied to obtain more complete and accurate segmentation results. Compared with previous works, we present more robust constraints to characterize general text regions based on color, edge and stroke thickness, which can effectively eliminate a wide range of background residues to refine the segmentation results furthest. We also propose the components relation constraint (CRC) which is designed specifically for Chinese characters.

The rest of the paper is organized as follows: we present the details of the proposed text segmentation algorithm in Section 2; the experimental results are reported in Section 3; Section 4 concludes our work.

2 Description of Our Algorithm

We first detect text in images or video frames using the text detection algorithm presented in [5]. After that, each localized text block is rescaled to a proper size using sub-pixel linear interpolation [15]. This rescaling will not only help to improve the text resolution if the height of text blocks is less than 20 pixels, but also make some constraints proposed by us not sensitive to scale. In our experiments, only those characters whose height and width are in the range from 24 to 32 pixels are considered. After scaled, each text block will have the new height of about 40 pixels if it is horizontal, and the width of about 40 pixels or so for vertical. Fig.1 gives two examples of text blocks detected from the frames of TV news and both have extremely complex background.

(a) (b)

Fig. 1. Examples of text blocks with complex background

2.1 Preliminary Segmentation Using K-Means Clustering

For each rescaled text block, the K-means algorithm [12] is applied to cluster pixels into K binary image layers based on their YCbCr color vectors. As for the number of clusters K, our experiments show that choosing K= 3 or K= 4 can be adapted to almost all cases. The explanation can be as follows: (1) text aligning compactly in a well-localized text block generally has uniform color and occupies a considerable large area, thus there are generally no more than four humps in the smoothed gray level histogram of the text block; (2) for text blocks with simple background, the number of humps is usually 2, but even if we vary K from 2 to 3, the integrity of character strokes after clustering is seldom influenced, since the color of text is more homogeneous than the color of background; (3) sometimes only one large hump appears, and this occurs when text has similar color with its surrounding background, a larger K is needed in this case. In our experiments, K= 3 or K= 4 is decided adaptively based on the smoothed gray level histogram of text blocks. A reference line which represents c times the average of all bins of the histogram is set in the histogram to find out the number of isolated humps above it (Fig.2), and c is chosen as 0.8 here. We choose K= 3 when two or three humps appear in the histogram and K= 4 in other cases. After clustering, three or four binary image layers are generated and we assume that text is contained in one of them (i.e. text image layer). Fig.3 gives an example and Fig.3 (a)(b)(c) correspond respectively the three binary image layers generated for the text block in Fig.1 (a). Since it is often difficult to decide immediately which layer is the text image layer, we will let all layers follow the same post-processing procedure presented below.

2.2 Post-processing Based on Multiple Constraints

For each image layer obtained, the connected component analysis is performed to get a set of connected components and those whose height or width are less than two pixels will be removed. Then a group of constraints are applied to further

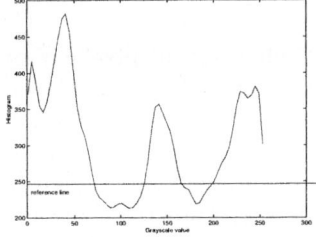 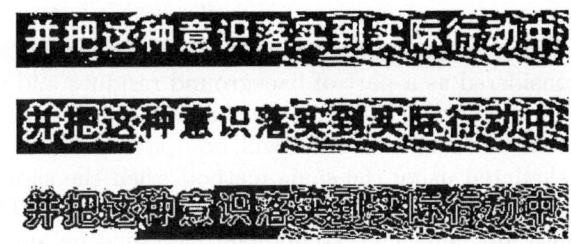

Fig. 2. The smoothed gray level histogram and its reference line for the text block in Fig.1 (a)

Fig. 3. Three binary image layers generated by K-means algorithm (K=3) for the text block in Fig. 1 (a). The image layer (a) is the text image layer.

eliminating the remaining background residues to refine the preliminary segmentation results. These constraints include the color constraint (CC), the edge magnitude constraint (EMC) and the thickness constraint (TC). For Chinese characters, the components relation constraint (CRC) can be additionally applied.

To be concise, we list some notations frequently used here. L denotes the current image layer and C denotes the current connected component; m_L and σ_L denote the mean and the standard deviation of the original YCbCr color value c of the white pixels in L, and $\sigma_L = (E|c-m_L|^2)^{1/2}$, similarly we have m_C and σ_C for C; H_i and W_i are the height and the width of the bounding box of the connected component C_i, $i = 1, 2, \cdots$; H_{max} and W_{max} denote the maximal height and the maximal width permitted for a character, and both are set as 32 pixels in our experiments.

Color Constraint (CC). We assume if a connected component is only made up of text pixels, its pixels should have homogeneous color. However, the low contrast between text and background tends to result in a text connected component polluted by background residues (e.g. conglutinated strokes or connection with background regions (Fig.6 (a))). This kind of residues can not be removed through simple morphological operations such as "H-break", "open" [14,16]. We employ the following cues to identify this kind of connected components: (1) the color distribution of its pixels has a large σ_C and no large number of pixels fall in a certain neighborhood of m_C or (2) the height or the width of its bounding box exceeds H_{max} or W_{max}.

In order to obtain an estimation of the color value of text pixels, we use the operation $\delta(L) = L - L \circ e$ defined in [16] to get a map from the current image layer, where "$\circ$" is the morphological operation "open" and e is a structure element whose size is slightly larger than the scale of character strokes (e.g. 4-5 pixels in our experiments). The components left in the map will have the scale approximating to that of character strokes; we use the mean of the original color values of the pixels in these components as the estimation and mark it as c_T.

For a connected component identified as being polluted by background residues possibly, if a pixel and more than two of its 8-neighbouring pixels satisfy the following condition

$$|c - c_T| > \varepsilon_1 \sigma_C .\qquad(1)$$

where c denotes the color value of the pixel and ε_1 is a coefficient, the pixel will be considered as a part of background residues and removed from the image layer. When all connected components have been processed by the above procedure, their standard deviation will be updated and a new estimation for c_T will be calculated using the same method, then the same procedure will start again to check and process each connected component. This iterative process continues until any connected component identified by our clues as being polluted has no pixels satisfying the condition (1).

For the text pixels either lost in the preliminary segmentation or removed by the above process due to variation of their color from the text color, some morphological operations can be employed to recover them. We use the operation "bridge" to fill the gaps with the width of one pixel and the operation "fill" to fill the holes with the size of one pixel. For the text pixels on the boundary of character strokes (except the corner pixels), the operation "majority" can be used to smooth the contour, i.e. a pixel is set as white if five or more pixels in its 8-neighbourhood are white, otherwise, the pixel is set as black.

Further we assume that all the connected components corresponding to text have homogeneous color. For each connected component, we use m_C as an estimation of the color values of all the pixels in it. If the m_C of a connected component is farthest away from the average color value of the pixels in all other connected components, it will be removed, if the following condition holds

$$\max_k |m_{C_k} - \frac{\sum_{i \neq k} m_{C_i}|C_i|}{\sum_{i \neq k}|C_i|}| > \varepsilon_2 \sigma_L .\qquad(2)$$

where ε_2 is a coefficient. Then σ_L is updated and this iterative process continues when the condition (2) holds.

Edge Magnitude Constraint (EMC). Intuitively the boundaries of those connected components corresponding to text should go with strong edges. Contrarily, for some of those connected components in the same image layer but corresponding to background, their boundaries will not go with strong edges, if the contrast between the two sides of their boundary is low before clustering. So EMC is specifically used to identify and remove such connected components. First an edge magnitude map is calculated. Then for each pixel s on the boundary of the current connected component, we locate the pixel r with the maximal edge magnitude along the normal direction of the pixel s among 1-3 pixels outward and 1 pixel inward. Let r_+ and r_- denote the two neighboring pixels of r on the normal. Among these three pixels, the pixel t that has the maximal color difference from m_C is further determined, i.e.

$$t = \arg\max_{p \in \{r, r_+, r_-\}} |c_p - m_C| .\qquad(3)$$

Let S denote all the pixels obtained through the equation (3) for the pixels on the boundary of the current connected component. If a large percent of the pixels in S have a color value close to m_C, i.e. $|\{p||c_p - m_C| < \varepsilon_3 \sigma_C, p \in S\}| > \varepsilon_4 |S|$, where ε_3 and ε_4 are coefficients, the connected component will be removed, since this condition indicates that the contrast between the connected component and the regions surrounding is too low, which mean it cannot be a part of text.

Thickness Constraint (TC). Character strokes should have proper size, so a connected component will be removed, if its height or width exceeds the thresholds H_{max} and W_{max}. More strictly, character strokes also should have proper thickness. Considering this fact, we project each remaining connected component horizontally and vertically respectively, and obtain the Maximal Continuous Thickness (MCT) for each horizontal scan line and each vertical scan line, as shown in Fig.4. A threshold η is used to locate the large MCT values. For a connected component, if the number of the large MCT values exceeds a threshold m or the length that the consecutive large MCT values last (i.e. the 1-run length) exceeds a threshold n in the horizontal or vertical direction, which means the connected component looks like a large "solid block", it can not be a character stroke and should be removed. In our experiment, $\eta = 10$, $m = 24$ and $n = 6$, which can accept the printed fonts that have larger stroke thickness such as the bold.

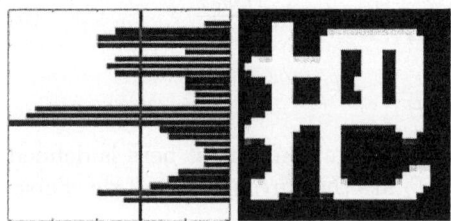

Fig. 4. Maximal Continuous Thickness (MCT) in horizontal direction

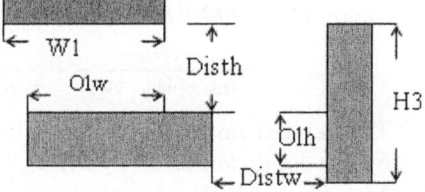

Fig. 5. Definition of spatial relation between sub-components

All the above constraints are applicable for both western language text and Chinese text. Since the characters in the latter generally have regular size and the structure of sub-components, the components relation constraint (CRC) is designed to refine the segmentation of Chinese characters.

Components Relation Constraint (CRC). Almost all Chinese characters have similar width and height under the same font and size, and most of them have the structure of sub-components. Intuitively the sub-components of a Chinese character obey some spatial relation. Thus, a group of rules can be designed to check the spatial relation between these sub-components. Based on the rules, those connected components that satisfy the constraint will be combined to form a new component, and most of the components that correspond to background residues can be excluded from the true characters, if they fail to satisfy the constraint. Finally, a component analysis step can be followed to identify and eliminate these background residues.

To present the rules, we define the following notions: H_{new} and W_{new} denote the height and the width of the new bounding box if two components are combined; k_1-k_6 are the constants determined empirically; H_i and W_i are the height and the width of the bounding box of the connected component i; other notations are illustrated in Fig.5. The rules are as follows:

1. After two components are combined, the new bounding box are not supposed to exceed the maximal dimension, i.e.

$$W_{new} \leq W_{max} \wedge H_{new} \leq H_{max} . \tag{4}$$

2. For two components, if one is completely contained in the bounding box of the other, i.e. $W_{new} = max(W_1, W_2) \wedge H_{new} = max(H_1, H_2)$, they will be combined. Otherwise, they will be checked using the following two rules.

3. For two large components, the length of overlapped part of their horizontal or vertical projection should be large enough and the distance between them should be within a proper range to guarantee the compactness, i.e.

$$\begin{aligned}&\frac{Ol_w}{max(W_1,W_2)} > k_1 \wedge \frac{Dist_h}{min(W_1,W_2)} < k_2 \frac{H_{max}}{W_{max}} \vee \\ &\frac{Ol_h}{max(H_1,H_2)} > k_1 \wedge \frac{Dist_w}{min(H_1,H_2)} < k_2 \frac{W_{max}}{H_{max}} \vee \\ &\frac{Ol_w}{max(W_1,W_2)} + \frac{Ol_h}{max(H_1,H_2)} > k_3 .\end{aligned} \tag{5}$$

The related notions are shown in Fig.5. A large component here is defined by the condition $W \geq T_1 \vee H \geq T_2$, T_1, T_2 are the thresholds, and we choose $T_1 = T_2 = 4$ in our experiment.

4. For a large component and a small component, the similar constraint about the overlapped length and distance is defined below,

$$\begin{aligned}&\frac{Ol_w}{min(W_1,W_2)} > k_4 \wedge \frac{Dist_h}{min(W_1,W_2)} < k_5 \frac{H_{max}}{W_{max}} \vee \\ &\frac{Ol_h}{min(H_1,H_2)} > k_4 \wedge \frac{Dist_w}{min(H_1,H_2)} < k_5 \frac{W_{max}}{H_{max}} \vee \\ &\frac{Ol_w}{min(W_1,W_2)} + \frac{Ol_h}{min(H_1,H_2)} > k_6 .\end{aligned} \tag{6}$$

All the components in the same image layer are first ordered according to their areas. The calculation of check and combination starts from the components with the largest area, since a large component is more reliable than a smaller one on locating a character. For a component, if more than one component around it satisfy the condition for combination, the component, which keeps the most compactness with it, is chosen, i.e.

$$i^* = \arg\min_{i} \{max(\frac{|cx_i - cx|}{W_{new}}, \frac{|cy_i - cy|}{H_{new}})\} . \tag{7}$$

where (cx, cy) is its geometric center, and (cx_i, cy_i) is the geometric center of the component checked. Two combined components are viewed as a new component, and the process continues until no components can be combined.

After above processing, all the components are further checked through their size, aspect ratio and filling ratio of their bounding boxes. If the height or width is too small, or the aspect ratio or filling ratio is not in the predefined range, the component will be removed. Here, special rules are designed for the Chinese character "one". Any component with similar structure will be checked through its spatial relation with other components in the image layer and decided whether it is really a character. The results in each step for the text block in Fig.1 (b) are shown in Fig.6.

Fig. 6. (a) The initial text image layer of Fig.1 (b). (b) Result after applying CC. (c) Result after applying EMC. (d) Result after applying TC. (e) Result after applying CRC. (f) Final result.

After all the above steps come to the end, most background residues will have been removed, except those very similar with character strokes. Some of the left background residues may fall in the bounding boxes of true characters, CC can be used again within the bounding box to identify them. However, they cannot be eliminated when they have very similar color with text.

2.3 Selection of the Text Image Layer

After the elimination of background residues from each image layer, we will identify the text image layer from the K image layers and use it as the input to an OCR engine. The text image layer generally exhibits a periodical and symmetrical layout, while a great many connected components in the background image layers are removed by the post-processing step. Thus, they can be easily distinguished through many methods, such as projection profile [3], spatial variance [1] or frequency domain methods.

We employ the X-axis projection profile in our system (Fig.7). The profile is first smoothed and then binarized. A half of the average value of the profile

Fig. 7. Result after residue elimination for each layer in Fig.3 and corresponding projection profile after smoothing and thresholding

is used as the binarization threshold. We use the following cues to identify the text image layer: (1) the binarized profile of the text image layer has the largest number of 1-run lengths; (2) the 1-run lengths occur regularly and the spacings between them are small, which make these spacings have a small mean and a small standard deviation.

3 Experimental Results

In our experiments, 394 text blocks from video frames at a resolution of 720*576 and 157 text blocks from video frames at a resolution of 352*288 are used as test datasets. Two datasets contain 3446 Chinese characters and 2096 Chinese characters respectively. All the text blocks have complex background and those in the latter set are degraded by us using a Gaussian blur function with a radius of 2 pixels. To evaluate the performance of our algorithm, character extraction rate (CER), character recognition rate (CRR) and extra error recognition rate (ERR) are calculated on each dataset. Here CER, CRR and ERR are defined as:

$$CER = \frac{N_x}{N}, \ CRR = \frac{N_c}{N}, \ ERR = \frac{N_e}{N_r}. \tag{8}$$

where N_x is the number of characters completely extracted without losing strokes or being connected with background residues, N_c is the number of characters correctly recognized by OCR, N_e is the number of background residues that are wrongly recognized as characters by OCR, N_r is the total number of characters outputted by the OCR engine, and N is the true total number of characters.

We compare our algorithm with K-means algorithm to show how much gain can be obtained from the proposed constraints. The experiments are carried out on a PC with CPU Pentium IV 1.4G and 512 M memories, and the text recognition is implemented by the commercial software HWOCR 5.0. The following parameters are used for the coefficients and the constants in our algorithm during the experiments: $\varepsilon_1 = 1.75$ and $\varepsilon_2 = 1.6$ in CC, $\varepsilon_3 = 2.5$ and $\varepsilon_4 = 0.3$ in EMC, they are all determined experimentally; In CRC, k_1-k_2 are respectively set as 0.6, 0.9, 0.5, 0.8, 1 and 0.8 based on the spatial relation between sub-components

Table 1. Performance comparison on the first dataset

	CER	CRR	ERR	Speed(Chars/s)
Our algorithm	96.5%	93.9%	1.2%	145
K-means	97.8%	68.4%	4.1%	376

Table 2. Performance comparison on the second dataset

	CER	CRR	ERR	Speed(Chars/s)
Our algorithm	94.1%	74.2%	0.7%	139
K-means	88.5%	69.8%	5.3%	438

of printed Chinese characters, they are not sensitive to scales and fonts. The experimental results on the two datasets are summarized in Table 1 and Table 2 respectively. The speed in the tables refers to the speed of text segmentation, without including OCR time.

We can see from the experimental results that CRR are improved greatly from 68.4% to 93.9% for the first dataset but just by 4.4% for the second dataset. The explanation is that background residues usually appear isolated in the first dataset while connected with text regions due to blur in the second. In the first dataset, the employment of all proposed constraints has removed almost all the isolated residues, but the CC may break or discard character stokes, which results in the slight decrease of CER. In the second dataset, the CER increases due to the further segmentation by the CC on those connected components where text is connected with background residues. However, a small increase of 4.4% in CRR shows that the CC is inadequate to give an accurate further segmentation for those seriously conglutinated strokes. The fall of ERR in both datasets also proves the effectiveness of the proposed residue elimination method.

Although the time cost of our algorithm is as 2.5-3 times as that of the direct K-means, it can still meet the real-time demand. Since all the image layers independently follow the same procedure in our algorithm, when computed parallelly, the time cost can be reduced to as 1.5-2 times as that of K-means. The first dataset has 8.74 characters per block and the second is 13.34, so K-means has a lower speed on the first dataset. Our algorithm has a relatively lower speed on the second dataset, because the CC is executed more frequently and the computational complexity of the CC and the CRC are nonlinear.

4 Conclusion

In this paper, we propose a text segmentation algorithm in complex background based on clustering and post-processing. A group of robust constraints are designed which can effectively eliminate a wide range of background residues, and thus have overcome some drawbacks of the existing text segmentation methods when applied in complex background. Moreover, these constraints are independent from each other and from the initial segmentation algorithm, thus they can be applied optionally on demand. The experiments show that our algorithm works well in extremely complex background and is competent for lightly blurred text. Our algorithm also has a parallel computational architecture and can meet real-time demand.

Acknowledgements

This work has been supported by the National Hi-Tech R&D Program (the 863 Program) under contract No.2003AA142140.

References

1. Zhong, Y., Karu, K., Jain, A.K.: Locating text in complex color images. Pattern Recognition, 28(10), pp.1523-1535, October, 1995.
2. Wu, V., Manmatha, R., Riseman, E.: Finding text in images. Proceedings of ACM International Conference on Digital Libraries, Philadelphia, pp.1-10, 1997.
3. Jain, A.K., Yu, B.: Automatic text location in images and video frames. Pattern Recognition, 31(12), pp.2055-2076, 1998.
4. Chen, D., Odobez, J.-M., Bourlard, H.: Text detection and recognition in images and video frames. Pattern Recognition, 3(37), pp.595-608, 2004.
5. Ye, Q., Gao, W., Wang, W., Zeng, W.: A robust text detection algorithm in images and video frames. 4th IEEE Pacific-Rim Conference on Multimedia, Singapore, 2003.
6. Li, H., Doermann, D., Kia, O.: Automatic text detection and tracking in digital video. IEEE Trans. on Image Processing, 9(1), pp.147-156, 2000.
7. Lienhart, R., Wernicke, A.: Localizing and segmenting text in images and videos. IEEE Trans. on Circuits and Systems for Video Technology, 12(4), April, 2002.
8. Jung, K., Kim, K.I., Jain, A.K.: Text information extraction in images and video: a survey. Pattern Recognition, 37(5), pp. 977-997, May, 2004.
9. Trier, O.D., Jain, A.K.: Goal-directed evaluation of binarization methods. IEEE Trans. on Pattern Recognition and Machine Intelligence. 17(12), December, 1995.
10. Tsai, C.M., Lee, H.J.: Binarization of color document images via luminance and saturation color features. IEEE Transactions on Image Processing, 11(4), 2002.
11. Lienhart, R.: Video OCR: a survey and practitioner's guide. In Video Mining, Kluwer Academic Publisher, pp. 155-184, October, 2003.
12. Otsu, N.: A threshold selection method from gray-level histograms. IEEE Trans. on System, Man and Cybernetics, 9(1), pp.62-66, 1979.
13. Gao, J., Yang, J.: An adaptive algorithm for text detection from natural scenes. Computer Vision and Pattern Recognition, Vol.2, December, 2001.

14. Ye, Q., Gao, W., Huang, Q.: Automatic text segmentation from complex background. IEEE International Conference on Image Processing, Singapore, October, 2004.
15. Sato, T., Kanade, T., Hughes, E., Smith, M.: Video OCR for digital news archives. IEEE Workshop on Content-based Access of Image and Video Databases, Bombay, India, pp.52-60, January, 1998.
16. Tang, X., Gao, X., Liu, J., Zhang, H.: A spatial-temporal approach for video caption detection and recognition. IEEE Trans. on Neural Networks, 13(4), July, 2002.

Specularity-Free Projection on Nonplanar Surface

Hanhoon Park, Moon-Hyun Lee, Sang-Jun Kim, and Jong-Il Park

Division of Electrical and Computer Engineering,
Hanyang University, Seoul, Korea
{hanuni, vivendi, markjun}@mr.hanyang.ac.kr
jipark@hanyang.ac.kr

Abstract. In projection display systems, specular reflection may distract users and obscure the projected useful information. This paper demonstrates that the specular reflection can be avoided by redundantly illuminating the display surface using multiple overlapping projectors and cameras. Our initial system using two projectors and a single camera is presented. The system automatically estimates where specular reflection occurs and which projector generates the specular reflection. Then, the system blanks the light of the projector falling on the specular region while boosting the other projector's light so that the additional light is projected onto the surface consistently. Through experiments, it is shown that the system eliminates specular reflection successfully while maintaining a good image quality.

1 Introduction

Projectors can display images with very high spatial resolution and dynamic range. Moreover, the projectors are getting cheaper and their size is getting smaller. These advances led the projectors to become ubiquitous. Recently, projection display technology has gained significant attention and has been employed for a variety of applications including the construction of seamless high resolution display [1], immersive 3-D virtual environment generation [2], and synthesis of interesting visual effects or useful information on 3-D objects [3,4]. These systems typically exploit camera-projector synergy in two ways: (1) by casting light into the environment to observe the resulting change in scene appearance; (2) by modifying the projected images in response to camera input. For instance, the projection-based augmented reality system can be calibrated by projecting a known test-pattern from projectors and observing the patterns using cameras. Then, the calibrated system projects appropriately pre-warped graphic image so that the projected image appears fitted on the projection surface.

In general, projection display systems use a single projector and thus may have losses; shadow or occluder light distracts users in front projection displays; specular reflection obscures useful information in projection-based augmented reality. The shadow and occluder light could be eliminated and suppressed based on multiple overlapping projectors and cameras, respectively [5]. However, to the best of our knowledge, no solution has been provided for specular reflection. This paper provides a computational framework for solving the specular reflection problem.

The solution for eliminating specular reflection is to redundantly illuminate the projection surface using multiple overlapping projectors. In this paper, our initial system using two projectors and a camera is presented. However, the method can be easily applied to the case of M projectors and N cameras. The system automatically estimates where specular reflection occurs and what projector generates the specular reflection. Then, the system blanks the light of one projector falling on the region while boosting the other projector's light. To do this, the geometric relationship between the projectors and the projection surface should be known, which is estimated by applying a calibration method to the image captured by a camera[1]. The system can successfully eliminate specular reflection while maintaining a good image quality.

The rest of this paper is organized as follows. In Section 2, the details of the proposed method for avoiding specular reflection are explained. Some experimental results are given in Section 3 and conclusion is drawn in Section 4.

2 Method

In this section, the main idea of specularity-free projection system is given first and the detailed methods follow in order.

2.1 Concept

Fig. 1 shows the concept of our system for eliminating specular reflection using multiple overlapping projectors. Notice that:

i. Assuming the projectors are calibrated and the geometry of projection surface is known, projection from two projectors can be exactly overlapped by prewarping the projection images and thus users feel as if there is only a single projection (see Fig. 2);
ii. Two projectors which are separated at a distance would hardly produce specular reflection at the same time at the same point of the projection surface.

Therefore, it would be possible to make users free from specular reflection by blocking the projection from one projector which produces the specular reflection. For instance, at P_1 in Fig. 1, the projection by PROJECTOR 2 is blocked and the user sees the boosted projection by PROJECTOR 1 that does not have specular reflection. On the contrary, at P_2 in Fig. 1, the projection by PROJECTOR 1 is blocked and the user sees the boosted projection by PROJECTOR 2 that does not have specular reflection.

---

[1] Homography can be exploited when the projection surface is planar as in [10]. However, it cannot be applied to the cases that the projection surface is nonplanar.

2.2 Calibration and 3-D Reconstruction

We use a modified version of the well-known Zhang's calibration method [6] for calibrating projectors and cameras. For robust calibration, coplanar 3-D points and their corresponding 2-D points are required [7]. In Zhang's calibration method, the points on a real planar pattern correspond to 3-D points and their projected (or imaged) points correspond to 2-D points. On the contrary, the projected points correspond to 3-D points and the points on a source pattern of a projector correspond to 2-D points in our method. The coordinates of the projected points are computed from the image captured by a camera as follows (see Fig. 3). It is assumed that the real distance between the four corner points of the white plane are known. The coordinates of the grid points are computed using the relative distance between the grid points and the four corner points in the camera image.

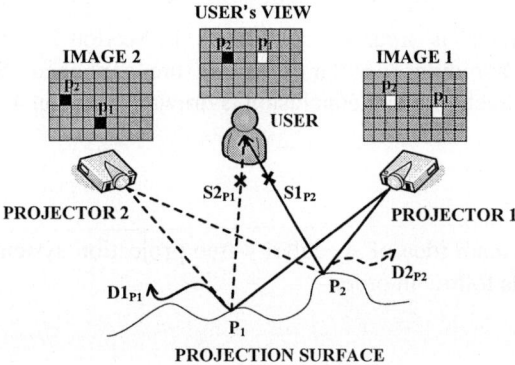

Fig. 1. Concept of eliminating specular reflection using multiple projectors. The user is led to see only the diffuse reflection from each projector.

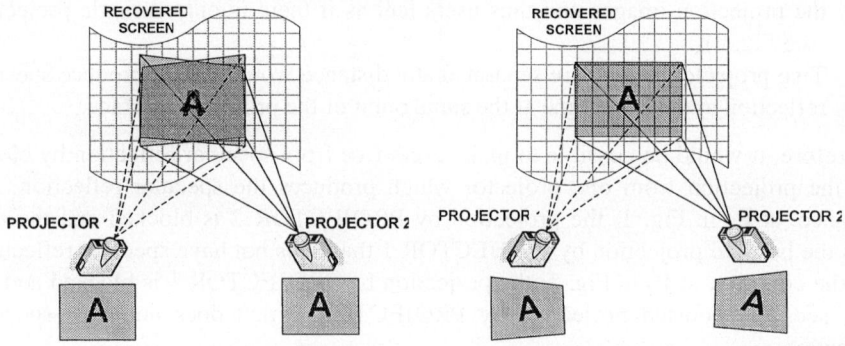

Fig. 2. Geometric registration. Left image: without geometric registration, right image: with geometric registration which is achieved by prewarping the images before projecting them. The details are explained in Section 2.2 and 2.3.

$$\begin{pmatrix} x \\ y \\ 1 \end{pmatrix} = P_1 \begin{pmatrix} X \\ Y \\ 0 \\ 1 \end{pmatrix} = H_{o-p} \begin{pmatrix} X \\ Y \\ 1 \end{pmatrix} = H_{o-p} H_{c-o} \begin{pmatrix} u \\ v \\ 1 \end{pmatrix} \qquad (1)$$

where

P_1 : projection matrix of PROJECTOR1

H_{o-p} : homography that takes object coordiantes to projector coordinates

H_{c-o} : homography that takes camera coordinates to object coordinates

Given the corresponding 3-D and 2-D points, the optimization algorithm [6] of Zhang's method is used as it is. After calibrating projectors and cameras using the proposed calibration method, the geometry of projection surface is recovered using a linear triangulation method [7]. Let **P** and $\mathbf{P_c}$ be the projection matrix of projector and camera, respectively. The relationship between the homogeneous coordinates of projection surface $\tilde{M}(X,Y,0,1)$, projector homogeneous coordinates $\tilde{m}(x,y,1)$, and camera homogeneous coordinates $\tilde{c}(u,v,1)$ is represented as

$$\tilde{m} = P\tilde{M} , \; \tilde{c} = P_c\tilde{M} .$$

The homogeneous scale factor is eliminated by a cross product as

$$\tilde{m} \times (P\tilde{M}) = 0, \; \tilde{c} \times (P_c\tilde{M}) = 0 .$$

An equation of the form $A\tilde{M} = 0$ can then be composed, with

$$A = \begin{bmatrix} xp^{3T} - p^{1T} \\ yp^{3T} - p^{2T} \\ up_c^{3T} - p_c^{1T} \\ vp_c^{3T} - p_c^{2T} \end{bmatrix}$$

where p^{iT} and p_c^{iT} are the rows of P and P_c respectively. This is a redundant set of equations, since the solution is determined only up to scale. A has a 1-dimensional null-space which provides a solution for $\tilde{M}$ and can be computed using Singular Value Decomposition (SVD) [7].

The projection surface is polygonally represented using the recovered points on surface [9] because the surface is piece-wise planar.

2.3 Geometric Registration

Let u_i, v_i (i=1,2) be the x-, y-coordinates of two projected images. Geometric registration indicates that projection from two projectors is exactly overlapped ($u_1 = u_2$, $v_1 = v_2$) without distortion and thus users feel as if there is only a single projection.

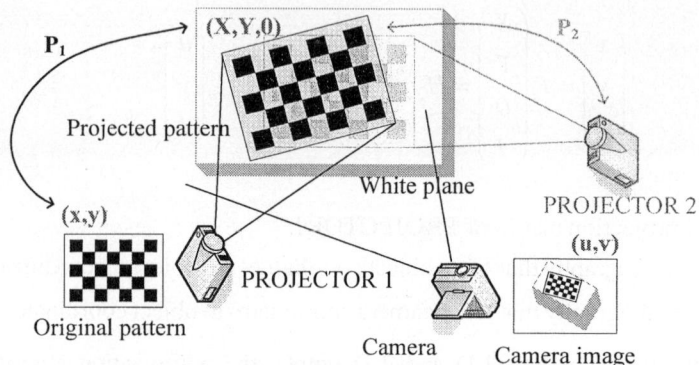

Fig. 3. Modified Zhang's calibration [8]. The projected points (X,Y,0) correspond to 3-D points and the points (x,y) on a source pattern of a projector correspond to 2-D points. The coordinates of the projected points are computed from the image coordinates (u,v) captured by the camera. All the relationship is defined as homography.

Without geometric registration, two projected images are distorted and not exactly overlapped ($u_1 \neq u_2$, $v_1 \neq v_2$) because their coordinates are transformed by different projection matrix (homography) in Eq. (2).

$$\begin{pmatrix} u_i \\ v_i \\ 1 \end{pmatrix} = H_{p_i-c} \begin{pmatrix} x \\ y \\ 1 \end{pmatrix}, \quad i=1,2 \qquad (2)$$

where

H_{p_i-c} : homography that takes i - th projector coordiantes to camera coordinates.

If the projection images are prewarped as follows:

$$\begin{pmatrix} x_i' \\ y_i' \\ 1 \end{pmatrix} = H_{p_i-c}^{-1} \begin{pmatrix} x \\ y \\ 1 \end{pmatrix}, \quad i=1,2 \cdot \qquad (3)$$

Then, the coordinates of two projected images in the camera coordinate system becomes same as each other as follows.

$$\begin{pmatrix} u_i' \\ v_i' \\ 1 \end{pmatrix} = H_{p_i-c} \begin{pmatrix} x_i' \\ y_i' \\ 1 \end{pmatrix} = H_{p_i-c} H_{p_i-c}^{-1} \begin{pmatrix} x \\ y \\ 1 \end{pmatrix} = \begin{pmatrix} x \\ y \\ 1 \end{pmatrix}. \qquad (4)$$

Eq. (2) is available only when the projection surface is planar. However, 3D projection surface is polygonally reconstructed in the previous section and thus Eq. (2) can be used to define the relationship between projectors and camera coordinates regarding each polygon.

2.4 Detection of Specularity

The projector which generates specular reflection is easily estimated using surface normal as in Eq. (5) and (6). As shown in Fig. 4, the angle θ between $-\vec{n}$ and $(\vec{p}_i + \vec{u})$ is small at the specular region.

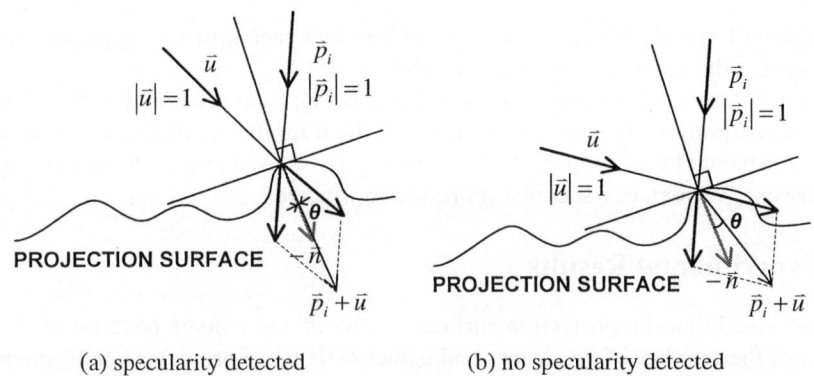

(a) specularity detected   (b) no specularity detected

Fig. 4. Detection of specularity. θ represents the angle between two vectors. When θ is less than a certain constant (ε), specularity is detected. $\vec{n}$ represents the unit surface normal. $\vec{p}_i$ represents the unit directional vector of i-th projector. $\vec{u}$ represents the unit directional vector of user's viewpoint.

$$\theta_i = \cos^{-1}\left(\frac{-\vec{n} \cdot (\vec{p}_i + \vec{u})}{|\vec{p}_i + \vec{u}|}\right), \quad 0° \leq \theta_i \leq 90°, \; i = 1,2 \tag{5}$$

where $\vec{n}$: surface normal, $|\vec{n}| = 1$

$\vec{p}_i$: directional vector of i-th projector, $|\vec{p}_i| = 1$

$\vec{u}$: directional vector of user's viewpoint, $|\vec{u}| = 1$

The projector regarding a minimum θ generates specular reflection.

$$k = \arg \min_i \{\theta_i\}, \quad i = 1,2. \tag{6}$$

The process is performed patch-wise because the surface is assumed to be piecewise planar and thus the surface is reconstructed polygonally in Section 2.2 (the points within a patch have the same surface normal).

At a point of surface, both projectors may not generate specular reflection when both θ_1 and θ_2 are larger than a constant (ε). In this case, the projection by two projectors is weighted-summed as follows.

$$I = wI_{p_1} + (1-w)I_{p_2} \qquad (7)$$

where

$$w = \frac{\sin(\theta_1)}{\sin(\theta_1)+\sin(\theta_2)}, \quad \frac{\sin(\varepsilon)}{\sin(\varepsilon)+1} \leq w \leq \frac{1}{1+\sin(\varepsilon)}.$$

The value of w is determined by the possibility that each projector generates specular reflection at the point of surface as follows.

On the contrary, both projectors may generate specular reflection at the same time at the same point of the projection surface, which rarely occurs because two projectors are separated at a distance. In this case, Eq. (6) is used as it is. It indicates that the weaker one between two specular reflection is projected.

3 Experimental Results

It is assumed that the projection surface is smooth and convex because of the limitation of the number of projectors and cameras. If more projectors and cameras are used, this limitation can be alleviated. Two projectors (SONY VPL-CX6 and PLUS V-1080[2]) and one camera (PointGrey Dragonfly) were used in our experiments.

A convex surface was polygonally reconstructed (5×7 quadrilaterals). In experiments, a grid pattern (5×7 quadrilaterals) was projected on the surface to reconstruct the surface. Only the corner points of the grid pattern were estimated by applying the linear triangulation to the projector image and camera image. To evaluate the accuracy of the reconstruction method, a synthetic image was projected onto a convex surface using two projectors with geometric registration which is explained in Section 2.3. As shown in Fig. 5, one can feel as if there is only a single projection.

To estimate where the specular reflection occurs, Eq. (6) was used. The resulting values (θ) were represented by the images (see Fig. 6). After comparing between the values of the corresponding points, the light of the projector associated with the higher value was blocked. In case of both projectors does not generate specular reflection (aforementioned in Section 2.4), two lights were weighted-summed.

---

[2] The different projectors can be used in our method because the method is geometry-based one. Radiometric compensation methods can be used to enhance the quality of projection image.

A real image using two projectors with geometric registration was projected onto a planar and convex surface. In both cases, the specular reflection was successfully eliminated (see Fig. 7 and Fig. 8). To show where the specular reflection is generated by two projectors, the image of each projector was also projected independently. The patch including specular reflection was not projected. In case of a convex surface, the results w.r.t. two different user's viewpoints were given to show how the projection changes according to user's viewpoint. All the results are convincing. In case of a nonplanar surface, the final projection was partially affected by both projectors. In case of a planar surface, the final projection was almost determined by one of projectors because the surface normal is almost same at the whole surface.

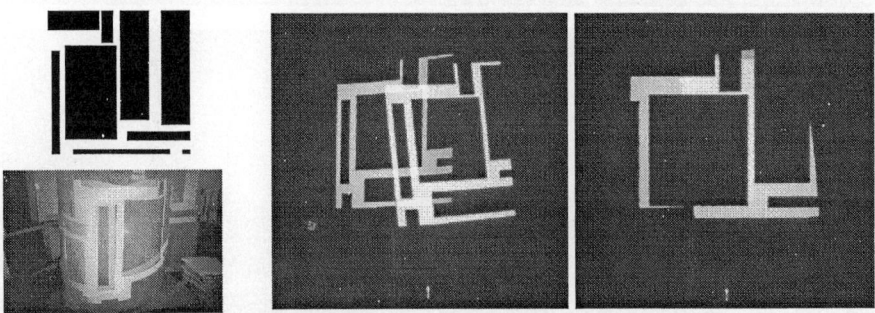

Fig. 5. Results of geometric registration. Left-top image: original image, left-bottom image: projection surface, middle image: without geometric registration, right image: with geometric registration.

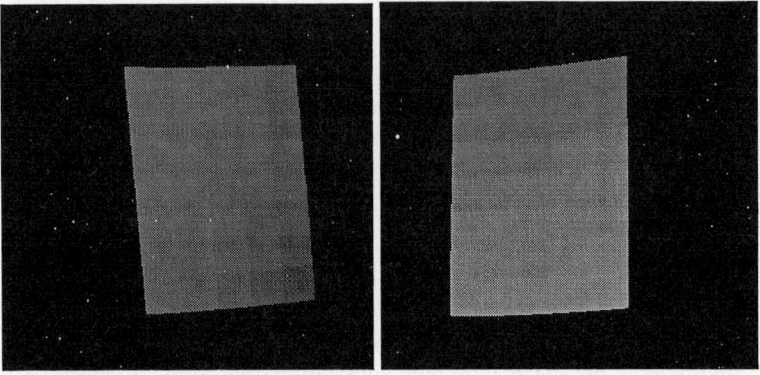

Fig. 6. An example of visualization of the degree of specularity generated by two projectors. The brighter pixels have a higher probability of specular reflection. For instance, left projector generates the specular reflection in the left-top side of a surface. The surface looks blocky because the surface is polygonally reconstructed.

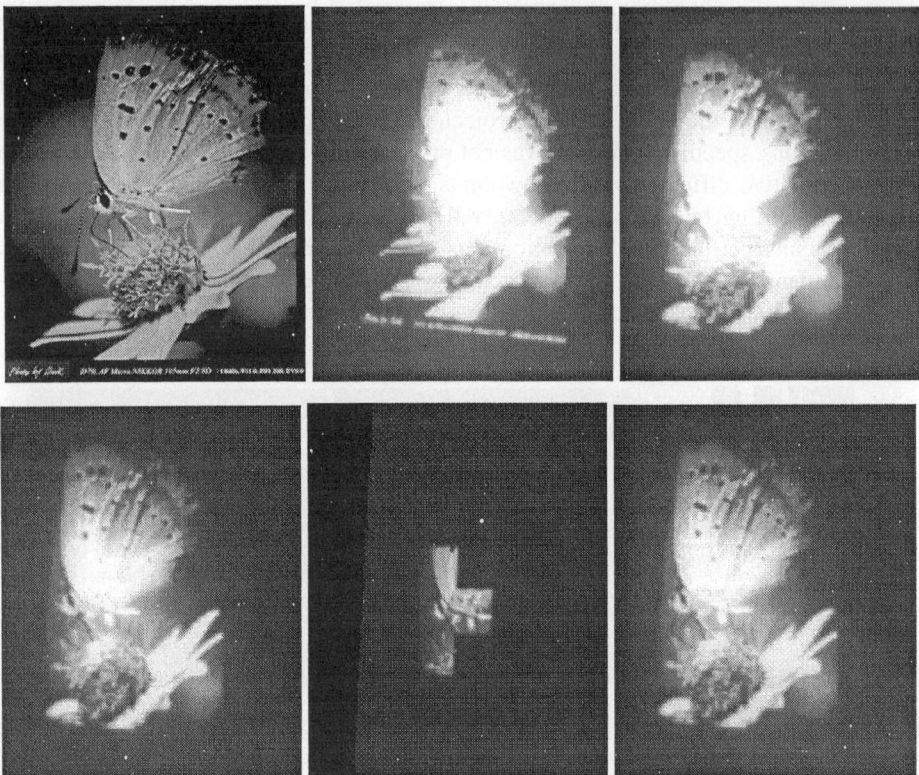

Fig. 7. Elimination of specular reflection on a planar surface. The projection surface is divided by small patches and each planar patch is independently processed. However, the final projection is almost determined by the right projector because the surface normal is almost same at the whole surface. Left-top image: original image, middle-top image: merged image without geometric registration and specular elimination, right-top image: merged image with only geometric registration (the image texture looms because of specluar reflection), left-bottom image: merged image with geometric registration and specular elimination, middle-bottom image: contribution of the left projector, right-bottom image: contribution of the right projector.

4 Conclusion

In this paper, it was confirmed that specularity-free projection was achieved using a multi-projector-camera system that redundantly illuminates the projection surface. The method would be useful for any application that uses reflective surfaces as screen, e.g. watery or bloody surface in the medical field.

Currently, we are trying to employ radiometric compensation methods for enhancing the quality of projection image. The practical issues associated with eliminating specular reflection from a complicated projection surface using multiple projectors and multiple cameras should be further explored and are currently under extensive investigation.

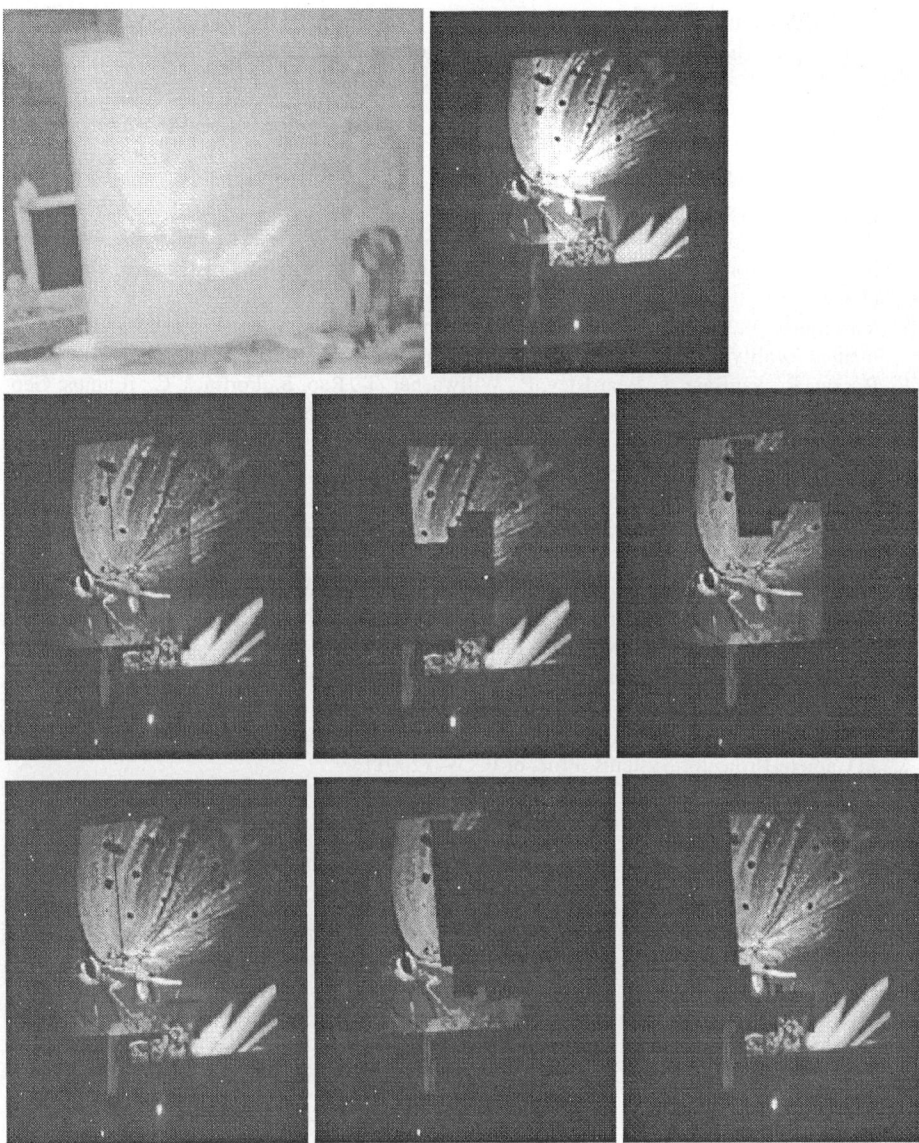

Fig. 8. Elimination of specular reflection on a convex surface. The convex surface can be considered to be piecewise planar. Each planar patch is independently processed. Left-top image: convex projection surface, right-top image: merged image with only geometric registration (the image texture looms because of specluar reflection), left-middle image: merged image with geometric registration and specular elimination when the user's viewpoint was located at the middle of two projectors, middle-middle image: no-specular projection of the left projector, right-middle image: no-specular projection of the right projector, left-bottom image: merged image with geometric registration and specular elimination when the user's view-point was shifted to the left projector, middle-bottom image: contribution of the left projector, right-bottom image: contribution of the right projector.

Acknowledgement. This study was supported by a grant(02-PJ3-PG6-EV04-0003) of Ministry of Health and Welfare, Republic of Korea.

References

1. Surati, R.: Scalable Self-Calibrating Display Technology for Seamless Large-Scale Displays. PhD thesis, MIT (1999)
2. Raskar, R., Brown, M., Yang, R., Chen, W., Welch, G., Towles, H., Seales, B., Fuchs, H.: Multi-Projector Displays Using Camera-Based Registration. Proc. of IEEE Visualization. (1999)
3. Yasumuro, Y., Imura, M., Manabe, Y., Oshiro, O., Chihara, K.: Projection-based Augmented Reality with Automated Shape Scanning. Proc. of Electronic Imaging. (2005)
4. Raskar, R., vanBaar, J., Beardsley, P., Willwacher, T., Rao, S., Forlines, C.: iLamps: Geometrically Aware and Self-Configuring Projectors. Proc. of SIGGRAPH, Vol. 22. (2003) 809-818
5. Cham, T.-J., Rehg, J.M., Sukthankar, R., Sukthankar, G.: Shadow Elimination and Occluder Light Suppression for Multi-Projector Displays. Proc. of CVPR. (2003)
6. Zhang. Z.: Flexible camera calibration by viewing a plane from unknown orientations. Proc. of ICCV. (1999) 666-673
7. Hartely, R., Zisserman, A.: Multiple View Geometry. Cambridge University Press (2003)
8. Kang, G.-C.: Direct-Projected Augmented Reality for Intelligent Surgery. MS thesis, Hanyang University, Korea (2005) (In Korean)
9. Kazhdan, M.: Shape Representations and Algorithms for 3D Model Retrieval. PhD thesis, Princeton University (2004)
10. Sukthankar, R., Stockton, R., Mullin, M.: Smarter Presentations: Exploiting Homography in Camera-Projector Systems. Proc. of ICCV. (2001)

Salient Feature Selection for
Visual Concept Learning*

Feng Xu[2], Lei Zhang[1], Yu-Jin Zhang[2], and Wei-Ying Ma[1]

[1] Microsoft Research Asia, 100080, Beijing, P.R. China
{leizhang, wyma}@microsoft.com
[2] Department of Electronic Engineering, Tsinghua University,
100084, Beijing, P.R. China
f-xu02@mails.tsinghua.edu.cn
zhang-yj@mail.tsinghua.edu.cn

Abstract. Image classification could be treated as an effective solution to enable keyword-based semantic image retrieval. In this paper, we propose a novel image classification framework by learning semantic concepts of image categories. To choose representative features for an image category and meanwhile reduce noisy features, a three-step salient feature selection strategy is proposed. In the feature selection stage, salient patches are first detected and clustered. Then the region of dominance and salient entropy measures are calculated to reduce non-common salient patches for the category. Based on the selected visual keywords, SVM and keyword frequency model categorization method are applied to classification, respectively. The experimental results on Corel image database demonstrate that the proposed salient feature selection approach is very effective in image classification and visual concept learning.

1 Introduction

It is challenging to search images based on their content from a large-scale image database and web pages due to the semantic gap between low level features and high level semantic concepts. An alternative solution is to search images by text keywords, which makes the automated or semi-automated image categorization and annotation increasingly important. A successful annotation and categorization will significantly enhance the performance of content-based image retrieval systems by filtering out images from irrelevant classes during matching.

Many good results have been reported in two class image classification tasks, such as city vs. landscape [1], indoor vs. outdoor [2]. Recently, many promising approaches for general object recognition were proposed and demonstrated to be promising to solve multiple class image classification tasks. Fergus *et al* proposed constellation model, which is learned in a Bayesian manner, to recognize six classes of objects [3]. The model could be learned from unlabeled and unsegmented cluttered scenes in a scale invariant manner, and is capable of recognizing

---

* This work was performed when the author Feng Xu was visiting Microsoft Research Asia.

six object classes. This classification scheme was further improved by Li et al to classify more categories with less training samples [4]. A good application of this scheme is filtering Google images [5]. Taking into account shape, appearance, occlusion and relative scale, the constellation model well describes an object in multiple semantic aspects with low-level features, and demonstrates promising potentials in image understanding. However, its computational cost is too expensive in both learning and recognition, and it is difficult to extend the algorithm to large-scale image databases. Csurka et al proposed bags of key-points of objects as features. Based on that, the visual vocabulary is constructed by k-means clustering algorithm. Both Naive Bayes and SVM classifiers are applied to categorization [6]. After training, labels are propagated to 116 categories. But the discriminative binary classifier is inefficient and classification results are affected by noisy points significantly. Another method for image classification based on discovered knowledge from annotated images using WordNet was proposed in [7]. The novelty of this work is the automated class discovery and the classifier combination using the extracted knowledge.

As another way to support keywords based image retrieval, image annotation has been an active research topic in recent years. Many automatic image annotation techniques have been proposed in the literatures. The limitation of pages does not allow us to survey all these works. Instead we try to emphasize some of these works that are most relevant to our proposed work. A typical annotation method is implemented based on classification in [8], in which multi-level annotation was proposed. Images are first segmented, and then salient object are detected by region classification. In this method, semantics perfectly correspond to salient objects. However, the salient object detection depends on syntax classification tree and is difficult to be scaled up. "Video Google" [9] applies text retrieval method to efficiently index video frames. To speed up the retrieval, local salient features are detected and represented by SIFT descriptors, and then SIFT descriptors are quantized into visual keywords. Thus the video retrieval problem is converted to the document-term text retrieval problem and inverted file is utilized to obtain dramatically efficient retrieval performance. However, no correspondence between low-level feature and semantics is constructed. Therefore it is appropriate only for similar frames in one movie. Generally, generative model performs successfully in image annotation due to its scalability. A representative work is reported in [10, 11], in which *correspondence latent Dirichlet allocation* model is proposed. By LDA model, latent correspondence between image regions and keywords is achieved. However, this type of model mainly focuses on the probabilities of correspondences between image regions and text, ignoring feature analysis for images, which may lead to weak semantic concepts.

On the other hand, it is useful to have access to high-level information about objects contained in images to manage image collections. To achieve this goal, high-level information must be learned and modeled from low-level features. A significant number of models have been proposed to model objects from low-level features. As low-level features are usually noisy and uninformative, feature selection is of great importance and needs to be conducted before modeling object.

Nuno et al [12] exploited recent connections between theoretic feature selection and minimum Bayesian error solutions to derive feature selection algorithms that are optimal in a discriminant feature sense without compromising scalability. However, they did not provide feature selection from image content, in which semantic feature is not included. In fact, there are few feature selection methods proposed, especially for image classification and concept learning.

Recent progresses in object recognition and image annotation have shown that local salient features are more informative in describing image content than global features [3, 6, 8, 9]. In image classification, features are required to be common and representative within the same class and discriminative for different classes. In object semantic learning, the model should emphasize the object in an image category. Therefore it is essential to select the common salient features and meanwhile reduce noisy features contributed by only a few images. Here, noisy features are defined as the salient points at non-common parts of all the images in the same category. However, to the best of our knowledge, there is no related works explicitly eliminating noises. Thus a robust salient feature selection strategy based on image category is crucial and worthy of investigation. Based on the selected features, the visual keyword dictionary can be constructed and the frequencies of visual keywords can be utilized for categorization.

In this paper, we propose a novel image classification algorithm. First, a three step salient feature selection (FS) strategy is explicitly conducted. For every image category, the salient patches are detected and quantized by k-means clustering algorithm. Then a visual keyword dictionary is constructed. Thereafter, the region of dominance [13] is calculated for every visual keyword to select most representative salient features, and the salient entropy is used to evaluate the distribution of the salient patches and choose the most common visual keywords. That is, the salient patches are selected by the number of salient patches in one cluster, the region of dominance, and the salient entropy. Based on the selected patches, the frequencies of visual keywords are counted and used for categorization. And the SVM classifier, as the widely used discriminative classification model, is also applied.

The rest of the paper is organized as follow: Section 2 presents the salient feature selection strategy; Section 3 presents the classification methods, including visual keyword frequency model and SVM; Section 4 shows the experimental results to evaluate the performance of the proposed techniques; Section 5 gives conclusions.

2 Salient Feature Selection Strategy

Most traditional classification methods use global low level features. Recently, many general object recognition approaches prefer local salient features. In these approaches, all the local salient features are integrated together, and used to train the classifier [3, 6]. However, noisy salient features appearing on background severely deteriorate the classification accuracy as these salient features are usually contributed by only a few images in an image category and thus are not common for this category. To model an image category, it is essential to conduct salient feature selection to choose the most representative salient features before image categorization, because such features are capable of expressing an object away from different backgrounds. In this section, we describe the proposed salient feature selection strategy in detail. Three steps are included: salient patch detection, visual keywords construction and representative visual keywords selection.

2.1 Salient Patch Detection

In the first step, salient patches are detected by the local salient feature detector proposed by Kadir and Brady [14]. Other detectors are also possible for this task, such as SIFT proposed in [15]. This detector aims at finding regions that are salient over both location and scale. For each point on an input image, a number of intensity histograms are calculated in circular regions of different radiuses (scales). The entropy of each histogram is then calculated and the local maximum is selected as a candidate region. The regions with the highest saliencies over the image provide the features for visual keywords construction. In practice, this method provides stable identification of features over a variety of sizes and copes well with intra-class variability.

Once the salient regions are identified, they are cropped from the image and rescaled to the size of a small pixel patch. Because a high dimensional Gaussian is difficult to manage, principal component analysis (PCA) is performed on the patches from all images. Then each patch is represented by a vector of the coordinates within the first 15 principal components, which is the category feature for classification.

2.2 Visual Keyword Construction

The 15-dimensional salient features are then quantized to construct the visual keyword collection.

The vector quantization is performed on the extracted feature vectors of all the images within one category. The vector quantization is conducted here by k-means clustering. Clusters correspond to the 'visual keywords' for the category. Cluster histogram of the salient patches shows the distribution of the salient patches, in which each bin is a visual keyword. Those visual keywords with large number of salient patches or over a predetermined threshold are considered as the most important features and selected to describe the category, while the visual keywords with small number of salient patches are considered as noises from different backgrounds. Fig. 1 illustrates an example of cluster histogram. The shadowed bins denote the selected clusters.

2.3 Representative Visual Keywords Selection

Those visual keywords with large number of salient patches are not always the most informative. Some non-discriminative and non-representative visual keywords may be contributed by a few images, which should be excluded. Through

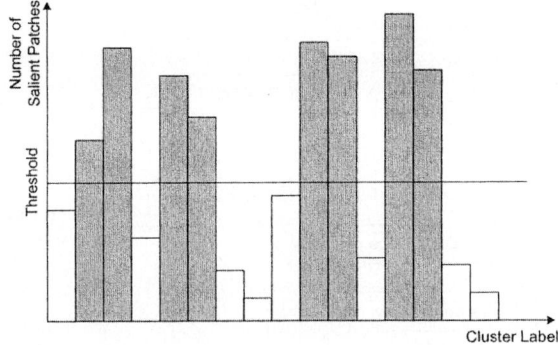

Fig. 1. Visual keywords are denoted as clustered bins. The higher bins (*shadowed bins*) are selected and the lower bins (*white bins*) are discarded.

the most similar noise and the most non-common noise exclusion, the representative visual keywords are selected.

The nearest clusters are considered as the most similar noises, which can be excluded by the region of dominance (ROD) [13]. ROD is defined as the maximal distance between the current bin and the detected local maximums whose number of salient patches is greater than that in the current bin in the 15-dimensional feature space. The larger the distance is, the more dominant the cluster is. If the maximal distance between the current cluster and the selected clusters is smaller than the threshold, the current cluster is regarded as similar to one of the detected local maximums and will not be preserved as visual keyword.

The most non-common noises can be excluded by the salient entropy. The salient entropy is defined as below:

$$H(n) = -\sum_{m=1}^{M} p_m(n) \log\bigl(p_m(n)\bigr) \qquad (1)$$

where n denotes the index of the cluster, m denotes the index of images and M denotes the total number of images in one category. $p_m(n)$ is the ratio between the number of salient patches in the n-th cluster of the m-th image and the total number of the salient patch of this cluster in all the images. Salient entropy reflects the distribution of a certain salient patch cluster in each image within the same category. The more uniform the distribution is, the more common the selected feature is. So the visual keywords with larger entropies are preserved. According to the entropy measure, those visual keywords appearing in only a few images are excluded, despite of the large number of salient patches in the histogram.

This three-step salient feature selection strategy can be modeled as a feature filter shown in Fig. 2.

Through this feature filter, the most important and common features are reserved while noisy patches on background are removed as many as possible.

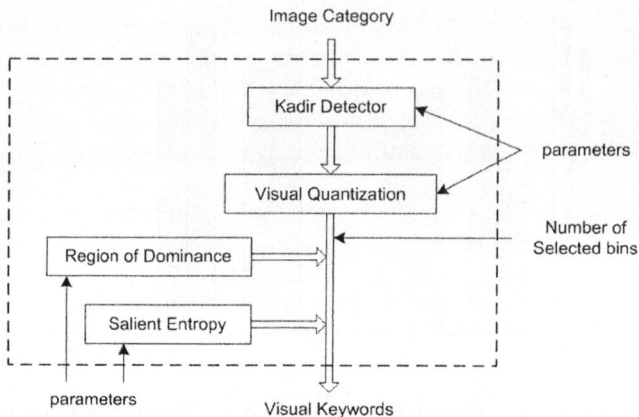

Fig. 2. Feature Filter includes detection, quantization, region of dominance and salient entropy. The selected features can be tuned by some parameters outside of the filter box.

Fig. 3. Image examples from *Ship* and *Firework* categories illustrate salient patches in Corel Collection. In the two categories, the upper row shows all the salient patches and the lower row shows the selected salient patches respectively.

Then for each reserved patch, low level features can be extracted to further model the object.

Some images from Corel image database are shown in Fig. 3 to demonstrate the salient feature selection results. The upper and lower two rows are examples from ship and firework categories respectively. In each category, the first row shows the salient patches without noise reduction while the second row shows the salient patches after feature filtering. For illustration, here, five visual keywords are constructed and different colors represent different visual keywords. After feature filtering, three common visual keywords for ship category, two common visual keywords for firework category are preserved respectively. The same color in the upper and lower rows denotes the same preserved visual keywords. From these examples, it can be found that the preserved salient patches correspond to a certain semantic visual keywords. For example, in the ship category the patches marked in yellow denote the hull, especially where the windows are located.

3 Visual Categorization

Once the feature descriptors have been selected, the problem of generic visual categorization is reduced to that of multi-class supervised learning. During training, labeled images are used to train multiple classifiers for distinguishing different categories. Here two types of classifiers are applied, support vector machine (SVM) and visual keyword frequency model.

3.1 Categorization by SVM

As SVM is a well-known classifier to produce state-of-the-art results in high-dimensional problems, we apply SVM classifier to the image classification.

SVM classifier aims at finding a hyperplane which separates two-class data with maximal margin [16]. The margin is defined as the distance of the closest training point to the separating hyperplane. For given observations x, and the corresponding labels y which take values ± 1, SVM will find a classification function:

$$f(x) = sign(w^T x + b) \qquad (2)$$

where w and b are the parameters of the classifying plane.

In the visual categorization task, x is the selected feature vector, in which the representative salient patches from each visual keyword in an image are concatenated according to the visual keyword cluster label order. Each representative salient patch is achieved by averaging all the salient patches in the same visual keyword cluster, and the averaged intensity information is used to form the feature vector. In fact, the similarity measure is the combination of the similar salient patches in the classification. If the salient patches in each visual keywords between two images are correspondingly similar, these two images are considered to be similar. The elements of the concatenated feature vector with the visual semantics are used to measure the similarity between two images. If a certain visual keyword does not appear in an image, the corresponding element in the feature vector is set to zero. Thus, the concatenated feature vector well represents the object concept. In order to apply SVM to multi-class problems we take the one-against-all approach. That is, given an m-class problem, we train m SVM classifiers. Each classifier distinguishes images in one category from all the other m-1 categories. Given a query image, we assign it to the class with the largest SVM output.

3.2 Categorization by Visual Keyword Frequency Model

Assume we have a set of labeled images $I = \{I_i\}$ and a visual keyword vocabulary $V = \{v_t\}$ of representative salient patches (i.e. cluster centers). Each feature vector of the salient patch (15-dimensional vector) extracted from an image is labeled with the visual keywords to which it lies closest in feature space. Then we count the number $N(t, i)$, the times of visual keyword v_t occurs in image I_i. To categorize a new image, we apply the Bayesian rule and take the largest posteriori score as the prediction.

$$P(C_j|I_i) \propto P(C_j)P(I_i|C_j) = P(C_j)\prod_{t=1}^{|V|} P(v_t|C_j) \tag{3}$$

where C_j is the class label, $|V|$ denotes the total number of the visual keywords in all the category. And the class-conditional probability of visual keyword is estimated as below:

$$P(v_t|C_j) = \frac{\sum_{\{I_i \in C_j\}} N(t,i)}{\sum_{s=1}^{|V|}\sum_{\{I_i \in C_j\}} N(s,i)} \tag{4}$$

In the simplest case, the class probability is the uniform distribution, i.e. $P(C_j) = \frac{1}{J}$, J denotes the total number of the image categories. And in this case, the class-conditional probability can be regarded as the visual keyword frequency. For a new image, all the salient patches are labeled as its closest visual keywords. Then if most of these visual keywords belong to one category, this image can be classified into this category. Such a simple classifier is usually used in text classification and applied to video retrieval by some literature [9].

4 Experimental Results and Discussions

The experiments are conducted on Corel image database. The Corel image database includes 50 categories with labels corresponding to object semantic concepts. Each image category consists of 100 images.

We present results from two experiments. First, we investigate the performance of the SVM classifier by classification accuracy. Then, we explore the performance of the keyword frequency model classifier on the same problem. The benchmark metric for classification evaluation is *classification precision* α, defined as:

$$\alpha = \frac{\phi}{\phi + \varepsilon} \tag{5}$$

where ϕ is the number of true positive samples that are correctly classified to their corresponding semantic category, ε is the number of true negative samples that are irrelevant to the corresponding semantic category and are classified incorrectly.

In SVM classification, each category is classified by linear binary classifier. Using kernel SVM will possibly improve the performance, but here our main purpose is comparing the performance between with salient feature selection and without salient feature selection, in which linear SVM performs well. The features with feature selection and without feature selection are used respectively. For SVM classifier with salient feature selection, the salient patches are arranged as the cluster labels. For SVM classifier without salient feature selection, the salient patches are also detected. Because the numbers of salient patches in different images are different, the image is partitioned into grids and the average salient patch in each grid is arranged.

We also investigate the impact of the ratio between the number of training images and the number of test images. First, 80 images randomly chosen from each image category are used to train SVM classifier and the other 20 are used to test the classifier. Second, 60 images are used for training and 40 are used for testing. The average precisions of these four experiments are shown in Table 1.

Table 1. The average classification precision by SVM. The ratios of image numbers in training set and test set are 4:1 and 3:2 respectively.

Training : Test	4:1	3:2
Without FS	0.6369	0.5167
With FS	0.75	0.6167

From this table, it can be found that the average classification precision is significantly improved by the salient feature selection strategy. Since the most important and common features are selected by the proposed salient feature selection strategy, the features employed in classification can distinguish different image categories more effectively. On the other hand, as the performance of SVM classifier is determined by the training set, higher classification precision can be achieved by using more training set.

In visual keyword frequency model classifier, randomly chosen 80 images are used to train the classifier and the other 20 are used to test for each category. The classification precision for each category and the average precision are shown in Table 2.

From Table 2 and Fig. 4, it can be concluded that this classification method is effective for large-scale image database. Visual keywords are constructed by k-means clustering algorithm and selected by means of salient entropy and region of dominance. Therefore images can be represented by some visual keywords. The combination of salient patches is much stronger in describing object than that of pixels. Each visual keyword corresponds to a certain semantic concept.

For some image categories, the classification precisions are quite high, such as Building, Bus, Firework, Road Sign, Space and Stamp categories. In these categories, the concept is more concrete so that the selected visual keywords can represent the objects more precisely. However, there are also some image

Table 2. The classification precisions of 50 image categories and the average precision by visual keyword frequency. In each image category, 80 images are used for training and test is implemented on the other 20 images.

Class Name	Balloon	Beach	Bird	Bobsled	Bonsai
Precision	0.20	0.60	0	0.80	0.20
Class Name	Building	Bus	Butterfly	Car	Cat
Precision	0.85	1.00	0.50	0.40	0.60
Class Name	Cougar	Dessert	Dog	Eagle	Elephant
Precision	0.05	0.20	0.10	0.50	0.50
Class Name	Firework	Fitness	Flag	Foliage	Fox
Precision	0.95	0.60	0.65	0.60	0.05
Class Name	Goat	Horse	Indoor	Jewelry	Lion
Precision	0.05	0.50	0.80	0.50	0.10
Class Name	Model	Mountain	Mushroom	Owl	Penguin
Precision	0.75	0.70	0.80	0.30	0.70
Class Name	Plane	Porpoise	Reptile	Rhinoceros	Road Sign
Precision	0.40	0.65	0.30	0.40	0.90
Class Name	Royal Guard	Ship	Ski	Space	Stamp
Precision	0.65	0.60	0.80	0.90	0.90
Class Name	Subsea	Sunset	Surfing	Tiger	Train
Precision	0.40	0.50	0.40	0.50	0.70
Class Name	Vallum	Vegetable	Waterfall	Wave	Wolf
Precision	0.60	0.30	0.60	0.90	0.40
Average classification precision			52.7%		

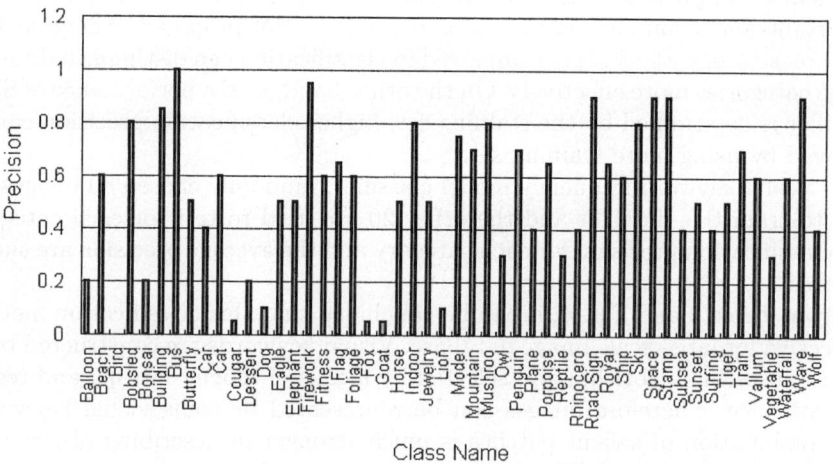

Fig. 4. The classification precisions of 50 image categories. The height of each column denotes the magnitude of each image category and the precision magnitudes among categories are independent.

categories not appropriate to be modeled by this classification method, such as Bird category. The possible reason is that the image content is too diversity to be extracted the salient objects. It may be better to model the concept with both local and global features.

Although the visual keyword frequency model classification method is similar to that reported in [6], the results cannot be directly compared with each other due to the different image database. However, only seven image categories are used in the experiment in [6] while fifty image categories are used in our experiment. Some precisions in Table 2 suggest that our approach will give as good results as that in [6]. On the other hand, our approach is more appropriate to be extended to larger scale image databases with more specific object semantic concept, which is more promising in image search and indexing, especially on the web.

5 Conclusions and Future Work

We have presented a novel framework to classify images based on semantic category concept. The salient feature selection strategy is effective in generating visual keywords to describe image categories. Through salient feature selection, objects are emphasized while non-common noise features are reduced. In image classification, the visual keyword frequency model and SVM are both applied. The experimental results on Corel image database demonstrate that the proposed salient feature selection and image classification algorithm are effective and efficient.

However, there are also some limitations in our algorithm. First, the discriminative features between image categories are not well leveraged. The discriminative information can potentially improve the classification performance. Second, classification algorithm with more object semantic concept can be applied, instead of the numerical vector measure. We will continue investigating these problems in the future.

Acknowledgement

The authors Feng Xu and Yu-Jin Zhang are partially supported by NSFC Project 60172025.

References

1. Aditya Vailaya, Anil Jain, Hong Jiang Zhang, On Image Classification: City vs. Landscape, Pattern Recognition, 31 (12), 1921-1935, 1998.
2. M. Szummer, R. Picard, Indoor-outdoor image classification, IEEE International Workshop on Content-based Access of Image and Video Databases, 42-51, 1998.
3. R, Fergus, P. Perona, A Zisserman, Object Class Recognition by Unsupervised Scale-Invariant Learning, *Proceedings of the IEEE Computer Society Conference on Computer Vision and Pattern Recognition*, II/264-II/271, 2003.

4. Li Fei-Fei, Rob Fergus, Pietro Perona, A Bayesian Approach to Unsupervised One-Shot Learning of Object Categories, *Proceedings of the IEEE International Conference on Computer Vision*, 1134-1141, 2003.
5. R. Fergus, P. Perona, A. Zisserman, A Visual Category Filter for Google Images, *Proceedings of the 8th European Conference on Computer Vision*, 242-256, 2004.
6. Gabriella Csurka, Christopher R. Dance, Lixin Fan, Jutta Willamowski, Cedric Bray, Visual Categorization with Bags of Keypoints, *The 8th European Conference on Computer Vision - ECCV*, 11-14, 2004.
7. Ana B. Benitez, Shih-Fu Chang, Image Classification using Multimedia Knowledge Networks, *IEEE International Conference on Image Processing*, 613-616, 2003.
8. Jianping Fan, Yuli Gao, Hangzai Luo. Multi-Level Annotation of Natural Scene Using Dominant Image Components and Semantic Concepts. MM'04. 540-547.
9. Josef Sivic, Andrew Zisserman. Video Google: A Text Retrieval Approach to Object Matching in Videos. *Proceedings of the Ninth IEEE International Conference on Computer Vision* (ICCV 2003).
10. D.M. Blei, M.I.Jordan. Modeling Annotated Data. SIGIR 2003, 127-134.
11. D.M. Blei, A.Y. Ng, M.I. Jordan. Latent Dirichlet Allocation. Journal of Machine Learning Research, 3: 993-1022, 2003.
12. Nuno Vasconcelos, Manuela Vasconcelos. Scalable Discriminant Feature Selection for Image Retrieval and Recognition. CVPR 2004.
13. Yanxi Liu, Robert T. Collins. A Computational Model for Repeated Pattern Perception using Frieze and Wallpaper Groups. CVPR 2000.
14. T. Kadir, M. Brady. Scale, saliency and image description. IJCV, 45(2): 83-105, 2001.
15. David G. Lowe. Object Recognition from Local Scale-Invariant Features. *Proc. of the International Conference on Computer Vision*.1999.
16. V. Vapnik. Statistical Learning Theory. Wiley, 1998.

Contourlet Image Coding Based on Adjusted SPIHT

Haohao Song, Songyu Yu, Li Song, and Hongkai Xiong

Institute of Image Communication and Information Processing,
Shanghai Jiao Tong University, SHANGHAI 200030, P.R. China
{songhaohao, syyu, xionghongkai}@sjtu.edu.cn
songli@qantsoft.com

Abstract. Contourlet is a new image representation method, which can efficiently represent contours and textures in images. In this paper, we analyze the distribution of significant contourlet coefficients in different subbands and propose a contourlet image coding algorithm by constructing a virtual low frequency subband and adjusting coding method of SPIHT (Set Partitioning in Hierarchical Trees) algorithm according to the structure of contourlet coefficients. The proposed coding algorithm can provide an embedded bit stream, which is very desirable in heterogeneous networks. Our experiments demonstrate that the proposed coding algorithm can achieve better or competitive compression performance when compared with traditional wavelet transform with SPIHT and wavelet-based contourlet transform with SPIHT, which both are embedded image coding algorithms based on two non-redundant transforms. At the same time, benefiting from genuine contourlet adopted in the proposed coding algorithm, more contours and textures in the coded images are preserved to ensure superior subjective quality.

1 Introduction

Efficient representation of visual information lies at the heart of image compression. For 1-D piecewise smooth signals, wavelets have been served as a right representation tool. In addition, fast transform and convenient tree structures (e.g. zerotree and spatial-orientation tree) provide the key factors for the success of wavelets in image compression. EZW [1], SPIHT [2], and EBCOT used in JPEG2000 [3] are famous embedded wavelet image coding algorithms.

However, two-dimensional signals are smooth away from discontinuities across smooth curves. Such signals resemble natural images where discontinuities are generated by edges – referred to points in the image with sharp contrast in the intensity, whereas edges are often gathered along smooth contours that are created by typically smooth boundaries of physical objects. The commonly used separable wavelets in 2-D obtained by a tensor-product of 1-D wavelets are only good at capturing the discontinuities at edge points, but do not see the smoothness along contours. Thus, more powerful schemes are needed in higher dimensions [4] [5].

In recent years, many efficient representations are proposed for two-dimensional signals such as images. Ridgelet [6] by Candès and Donoho achieves high efficient representation of linear singularities in images. Ridgelet transform is done by viewing ridgelet analysis as a form of wavelet analysis in the Radon domain. Many attempts have been made to use ridgelet for image compression [7] [8].

However, in images, edges are typically curved rather than straight. Ridgelet cannot represent curves efficiently. Curvelet [9] by Candès and Donoho can be suited for objects which are smooth away from discontinuities across smooth curves. Later, the authors proposed the second-generation curvelet [10].

Additionally, bandelet [11] by Pennec and Mallat, wedgelet [12] by Donoho and beamlet [13] by Donoho and Huo all can represent contours of objects in images efficiently.

Contourlet [4] [5] is presented by Do and Vetterli as a new image representation method. Although Contourlet transform (CT) is a overcomplete transform with a redundancy factor 4/3 that would increase the rate for a given distortion, it can efficiently represent image containing contours and textures [14]. Recently, some approaches have been attempted to use CT for image compression.

A low bit-rate image coding using CT was proposed in [15]. It uses a scalar quantizer with a zero bin that is twice as large as the other bins to code contourlet coefficients. Recently, a coding technique based on a mixed CT and wavelet transform (WT) was presented [16]. The transform is optimized through an iterative projection process in the transform domain in order to minimize the quantization error in the image domain. Both algorithms cannot produce embedded bit stream.

In [17], a wavelet-based contourlet transform (WBCT) is proposed, which is a non-redundant transform. Authors used WBCT in conjunction with SPIHT to propose an embedded image coding algorithm. Experimental results show that the coding algorithm is competitive to WT with SPIHT, especially for a category of images that have a significant amount of textures and oscillatory patterns and therefore are not "wavelet-friendly" images. But due to the frequency scrambling resulting from the downsampling of the high frequency (HF) subbands in wavelet, WBCT non-linear approximation results might result in larger distortion than contourlet results in some image regions such as contours and textures. It means that CT might be more efficient in representing contours and textures than WBCT. At the same time, the computing complexity of the coding algorithm in [17] will increase fast due to the repositioning algorithm when moving forward along the scales.

Because wavelet incurs frequency scrambling and genuine CT is more efficient in representing contours and textures, we propose a new contourlet image coding algorithm based on adjusted SPIHT. It combines genuine CT with SPIHT efficiently by (1) adopting adaptive subband coding order scheme, (2) constructing a virtual low frequency (LF) subband and (3) adjusting coding structure of SPIHT properly. The proposed coding algorithm can produce embedded bit stream. Experimental results show that compared with traditional WT with SPIHT and WBCT with SPIHT, the proposed coding algorithm has better or comparative objective quality of reconstructed images with lower computational complexity. Meanwhile, more contours and textures are preserved in the proposed coding algorithm and the visual effect is better than those mentioned above.

The rest of the paper is organized as follows. Section 2 will present contourlet transform for image. In Section 3, SPIHT algorithm is introduced briefly. Contourlet image coding algorithm based on adjusted SPIHT is addressed in Section 4. Section 5 contains experimental results. Section 6 concludes the paper and discusses possible future work.

2 Contourlet Transform

Contourlet was proposed by Do and Vetterli at 2001. It is a double filter bank structure for obtaining sparse expansions for typical images with smooth contours. In this double filter bank, the Laplacian pyramid (LP) is first used to capture the point discontinuities, then followed by a directional filter bank (DFB) to link point discontinuities into linear structures. The overall result is an image expansion using basic elements like contour segments, and thus is named contourlet [5].

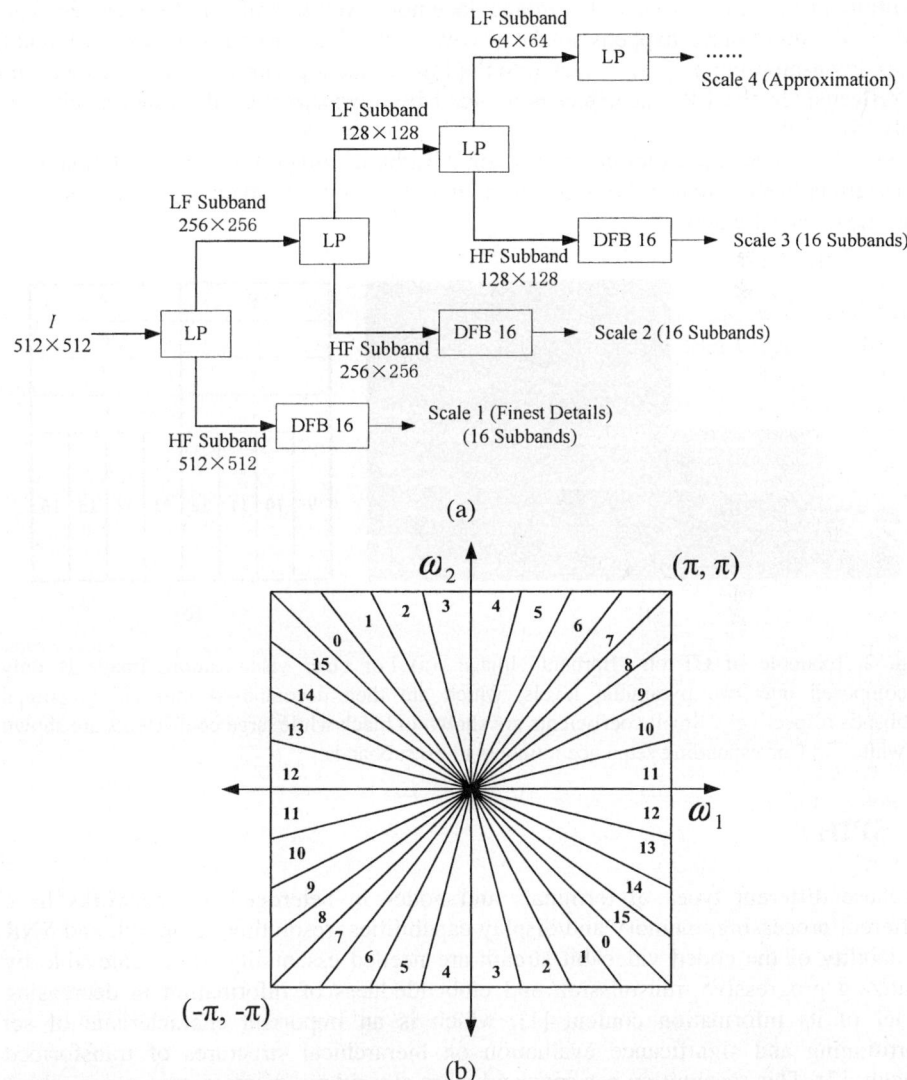

Fig. 1. CT for a 512 ×512 image. (a) Transform flowchart. (b) Frequency partitioning with 16 real wedge-shaped frequency bands.

Fig. 1 shows CT for a 512 ×512 image. HF subband images from the LP are fed into a DFB so that directional information can be captured. The scheme can be iterated on LF subband image. CT decomposes images into directional subbands at multiple scales.

CT has several distinguishing properties as follows: (1) seamless translation to the discrete world; (2) 2-D frequency partition on centric squares; (3) fast filter bank algorithms and convenient tree structures; (4) compactly supported contourlet frames; (5) flexible refinements for the spatial resolution and the angular resolution.

In contrast to the critically sampled wavelet scheme, the LP has the distinguishing feature that each pyramid level generates only one bandpass image (even for multidimensional cases), and this image does not have "scrambled" frequencies. This frequency scrambling happens in the wavelet filter bank when a highpass channel, after downsampling, is folded back into the low frequency band, and thus its spectrum is reflected. In the LP, this effect is avoided by downsampling the lowpass channel only [5].

Fig. 2 shows the example of CT on "Barbara" image. We noticed that only contourlets which match both location and direction of image contours produce significant coefficients.

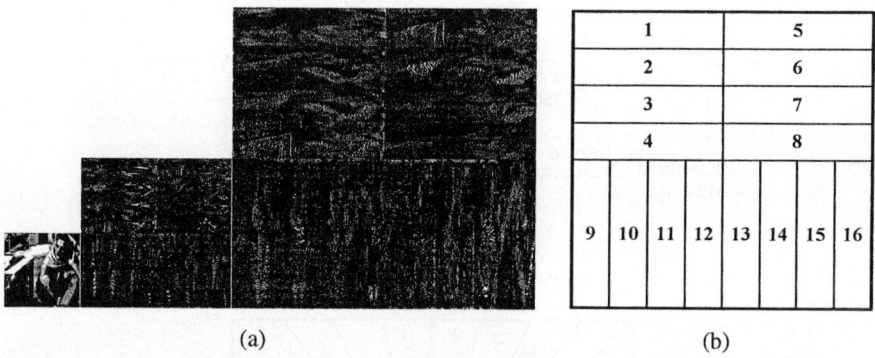

Fig. 2. Example of CT on "Barbara" image. (a) For clear visualization, image is only decomposed into two pyramidal levels, which are then decomposed into 16 directional subbands respectively. Small coefficients are shown in black while large coefficients are shown in white. (b) Corresponding sequence numbers of 16 subbands.

3 SPIHT

Because different types of terminals and nodes in heterogeneous networks have different processing, memory and display capabilities, resolution, temporal, and SNR scalability of the coded video bit stream are needed essentially. It is achievable by realizing progressive transmission and embeddedness of information in decreasing order of its information content [1], which is an important characteristic of set partitioning and significance evaluation on hierarchical structures of transformed images [2]. This recognition has spawned more algorithms in image processing which include EZW, SPIHT, and EBCOT. It is noticeable that these three algorithms are all constructed on the basis of WT.

SPIHT was proposed by Said and Pearlman at 1996. It utilizes three basic concepts: (1) searching for sets in spatial-orientation trees in a WT; (2) partitioning the WT coefficients in these trees into sets defined by the level of the highest significant bit in a bit-plane representation of their magnitudes; and (3) coding and transmitting bits associated with the highest remaining bit planes first.

The following sets of coordinates are used in SPIHT:

$O(i, j)$: set of coordinates of all offspring of node (i, j).
$D(i, j)$: set of coordinates of all descendants of node (i, j).
$L(i, j) = D(i, j) - O(i, j)$.

In the practical implementation, SPIHT defines three ordered lists to store the significance information: list of insignificant sets (LIS), list of insignificant pixels (LIP), and list of significant pixels (LSP). In all lists each entry is identified by a coordinate (i, j), which in LIP and LSP represents individual pixels, and in LIS represents either set $D(i, j)$ or $L(i, j)$. To differentiate between them, the algorithm defined that a LIS entry is of type A if it represents $D(i, j)$, and of type B if it represents $L(i, j)$.

SPIHT is extremely fast in execution. It has better compression performance than EZW and comparable compression performance with EBCOT but with lower computing complexity. It is the reason why SPIHT is adopted in this paper.

4 Contourlet Image Coding Based on Adjusted SPIHT

Advanced modern image coding algorithm should satisfy three main properties as follow: (1) producing embedded bit stream, the reception of code bits can be truncated at any point and the image can still be decompressed and reconstructed to adapt different types of terminals and nodes in heterogeneous networks; (2) owning high compression performance and making reconstructed image have good objective quality; (3) preserving contours and textures of objects in the coded images and satisfying human perceptual property as much as possible.

A contourlet image coding algorithm based on adjusted SPIHT is proposed in this paper. By adopting an adaptive subband coding order scheme, our proposed coding algorithm can scan and code significant coefficients as much as possible when bit stream is truncated at any point in order to satisfy the demand of embedded coding algorithm. Compression performance can be improved further by constructing virtual LF subband and registering the relation of father to children (RFC) between LF image and HF images. As genuine CT is adopted, frequency scrambling does not happen and more contours and textures can be preserved in our proposed coding algorithm. Benefiting from the above measures, the proposed coding algorithm can satisfy three main properties of advanced modern image coding algorithm well.

4.1 Analysis of Distribution of Significant Contourlet Coefficients in Different Subbands

Embedded coding algorithm demands that the coefficients with larger magnitude should be transmitted first because they contain a larger content of information. Based on the analysis of distribution of significant contourlet coefficients in different subbands, we propose an adaptive subband coding order scheme that can satisfy the demand of embedded coding.

Table 1 shows distribution of significant contourlet coefficients of 4 standard test images (8 bit/pixel (bpp), 512×512) at different thresholds. 4-scale LP and 16 directional decomposition at each scale is performed on each HF image.

Table 1. Distribution of significant contourlet coefficients of 4 standard test images at different thresholds. There, threshold 1=128, threshold 2=64, threshold 3=32. 16 subbands are sorted by the number of significant coefficients above corresponding threshold in subbands in descending order. 01-16 are the sequence numbers of 16 subbands as illustrated in Fig. 2 (b).

Image	Threshold 1	Threshold 2	Threshold 3
Barbara	06/04/05/02/13/01/03/12/09/10/07/16/11/14/15/08	06/04/05/02//03/01/13/07/16/09/10/12/11/15/14/08	06/04/05/03/02/07/01/16/13/09/10/12/15/11/14/08
Goldhill	13/04/05/12/11/14/16/03/06/15/02/10/09/07/01/08	13/04/12/05/11/14/16/03/10/15/06/02/09/07/01/08	13/04/12/05/11/14/16/15/03/10/06/02/01/07/09/08
Mandrill	13/12/14/16/04/11/03/06/15/09/05/02/10/01/07/08	13/12/14/11/16/15/04/10/03/06/09/02/05/01/07/08	13/12/14/16/11/15/04/10/03/06/09/02/05/01/07/08
Fingerprint	13/12/14/16/11/15/10/09/04/07/01/05/02/03/06/08	13/12/14/11/15/16/04/10/09/01/07/05/02/03/06/08	13/12/14/11/15/16/04/10/09/05/03/06/02/07/01/08

By analyzing Table 1, we found that although distribution of significant contourlet coefficients varies with images, the orderliness of distribution at different thresholds is kept for every image. In general, if a subband has more significant coefficients at higher threshold, it will have more significant coefficients too at lower threshold in all probability. Based on the analysis above, we propose an adaptive subband coding order scheme that can scan and code significant coefficients as much as possible when bit stream is truncated at any point in order to satisfy the demand of embedded coding.

Our proposed coding algorithm is initialized orderly according to subband significance. Subband significance is defined as the number of significant coefficients in the subband. The more a subband contains significant coefficients, the more significant the subband is. This ensures that significant coefficients can be scanned and coded as much as possible. By testing many images, we found that the order of subband significance basically does not change when threshold descends at 32 (i.e. when bit-plane descends at 5). Therefore, the order of subband significance is initialized as its order at threshold = 32.

In order to decode correctly, the initialization order of subbands need to be coded. As there are only 16 subbands in each scale in the proposed coding algorithm, if the order of first 15 subbands has been decided, the sixteenth subband must have been decided too. This means that only the sequence numbers of first 15 subbands need be coded in-order. Relative to being able to coding more significant coefficients and all output bits, the bits used to code the sequence numbers are negligible.

4.2 Construction of Virtual LF Subband

In the proposed coding algorithm, image is decomposed by LP firstly. Subsequently, each scale HF image is decomposed by DFB. The number of directional decomposition at each scale HF image is same ($N=16$) as illustrated in Fig. 2 (a). In contourlet HF image, the size of ith scale is 4 times as that of $(i+1)$th, and they are all decomposed into 16 subbands. It is easy and clear to find RFC among HF images i.e. tree structure like zerotree in EZW and spatial-orientation tree in SPIHT.

However, there is not apparent direction in approximation image i.e. LF image, especially when the size of LF image is very small in CT. LF image is not performed directional decomposition further. So we can not construct tree structure between LF image and HF images directly.

It is well known that the more zero coefficients an algorithm can cluster together, the higher compression ratio it can achieve. As for tree structure, the higher tree is, the easily above condition is achieved. Therefore, we want to construct RFC between LF image and HF image, which can make tree structure higher in contourlet coefficients.

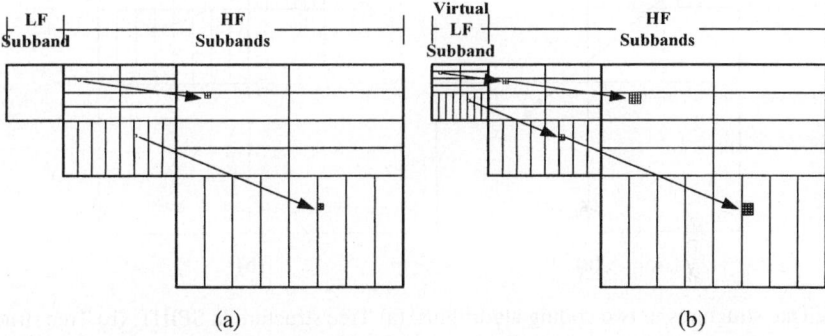

Fig. 3. The comparison of tree structures. (a) Tree structure in contourlet coefficients without virtual LF subband. (b) Tree structure in contourlet coefficients after constructing virtual LF subband.

In our proposed coding algorithm, a virtual LF subband is constructed. It has the same size and contains the same pixels as the original LF image, but is partitioned imaginarily. Unlike HF images, virtual LF subband is partitioned spatially into 16 subbands but not performed directional decomposition. It makes the construction of RFC between LF image and HF images easy. Fig. 3 shows the comparison of tree structures between in contourlet coefficients without virtual LF subband and in contourlet coefficients after constructing virtual LF subband. It is obvious that when image is decomposed by LP into the same scales, tree structure in contourlet coefficients after constructing virtual LF subband is higher than that in contourlet coefficients without virtual LF subband (i.e. the height of tree structure in contourlet coefficients is added by 1). Therefore, the construction of virtual LF subband can achieve better compression performance.

4.3 Adjusted SPIHT for Contourlet

Because SPIHT was proposed based on WT, its definition of some concepts, initialization content and coding structure is not suitable for CT. In order to make the most of SPIHT to code contourlet coefficients, it must be adjusted properly.

Unlike wavelet decomposition, where each scale image except the highest scale only contains 3 subbands LH, HL and HH, each scale image in contourlet decomposition contains more subbands. In our proposed coding algorithm, 16 subbands are contained in each HF image. In SPIHT, spatial-orientation trees are constructed as shown in Fig. 4 (a). In order to adopt SPIHT to code contourlet coefficients, we organize scales and subbands into a new format.

In the proposed coding algorithm, each scale image including virtual LF image is regarded as a whole firstly and is set in the same direction. Because virtual LF image is decomposed into 16 directions too, tree structure can be constructed easily from virtual LF image to the highest frequency image as shown in Fig. 4 (b).

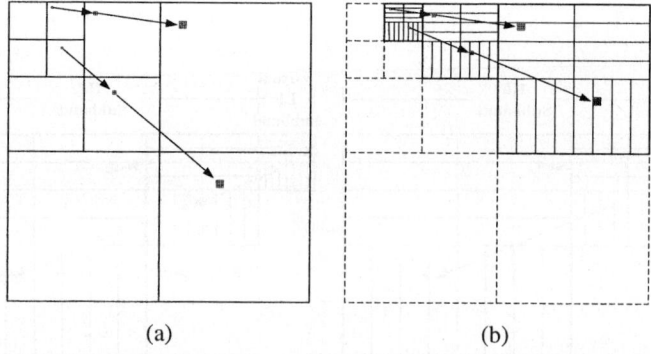

(a) (b)

Fig. 4. Tree structures in two coding algorithms. (a) Tree structure in SPIHT. (b) Tree structure in the proposed coding algorithm. There, virtual LF image has been decomposed into 16 subbands and is constructed RFC with HF images.

In initialization, all coefficients belonging to the highest scale are added to LSP and only those with descendants are also attached to the LIS as type A entries in SPIHT. However, in our proposed coding algorithm, genuine LF coefficients are added to LSP and each subband of virtual LF image is added orderly to LIS according to subband significance as type A entries. By proper adjusting in initialization, the proposed coding algorithm can easily make use of SPIHT to code contourlet coefficients.

Furthermore, because the highest bit-plane of coefficients in LF image is higher than that of coefficients in HF images with a great probability, we output two quantization-steps (QP) $n1$ and $n2$. QP $n1$ is the value of the highest bit-plane of coefficients in LF image, and QP $n2$ is the value of the highest bit-plane of coefficients in all HF images. In the proposed coding algorithm, LIS list will be checked only when *n1* decreases to the value of *n2*. Thus, many bits can be saved for signing spatial-orientation zerotrees in higher bit-planes and compression performance is improved further. In practical coding, only *n1* and the difference between *n1* and *n2* are output.

In order to illuminate our adjustment in the process of initialization, the proposed initialization for contourlet coefficients in SPIHT is presented in its entirety below.

Initialization:

1) output QP *n1* and the difference between QP *n1* and QP *n2*.
2) add coordinates *(i, j)* ∈ genuine LF subband to LIP.
3) add each subband of virtual LF image constructed in 4.2 orderly to LIS according to the subband code order (subband significance) determined in 4.1 as type A entries.

By determining subband code order, constructing virtual LF subband and adjusting the initialization of SPIHT, our proposed algorithm can scan and code contourlet coefficients efficiently.

5 Experimental Results

In order to validate the high efficiency of the proposed image coding algorithm, extensive experiments have been carried out on 4 standard test images (8 bit/pixel (bpp), 512×512) at bit-rates of 0.15 bpp and 0.25 bpp. We presented 4-scale decomposition and used the 9/7 biorthogonal filters [18] for WT and the filters from Phoong *et al.* [19] for LP and the directional decomposition for each scale with *N*=16 separately. The output bit stream isn't further compressed with an arithmetic coder.

Table 2. Comparison of coding results on three coding algorithms (average PSNR in dB)

Image	Bit-Rate (bpp)	The proposed coding algorithm (dB)	Traditional WT with SPIHT(dB)	WBCT with SPIHT(dB)
Barbara	0.15	23.42	23.59	21.41
	0.25	26.15	26.46	24.73
Goldhill	0.15	26.74	25.77	25.22
	0.25	27.70	27.30	27.04
Mandrill	0.15	20.59	19.16	19.05
	0.25	21.71	20.39	19.88
Fingerprint	0.15	23.59	22.35	21.81
	0.25	26.02	26.44	25.06

Table 2 shows that average PSNR results with the proposed coding algorithm are 1.4 dB higher than original WT with SIPHT at best, and are 0.7-2.0 dB higher than WBCT with SPIHT in [17] respectively, which are both embedded image coding algorithm. Fig. 5 and Fig. 6 present the visual quality comparison of the proposed coding algorithm with original WT with SIPHT and WBCT with SPIHT, respectively. It is clear that the better subjective quality can be acquired by the proposed coding algorithm as genuine contourlet is adopted and more contours and textures are preserved. At the same time, the proposed coding algorithm has lower computing complexity than the coding algorithm in [17] as repositioning algorithm is discarded.

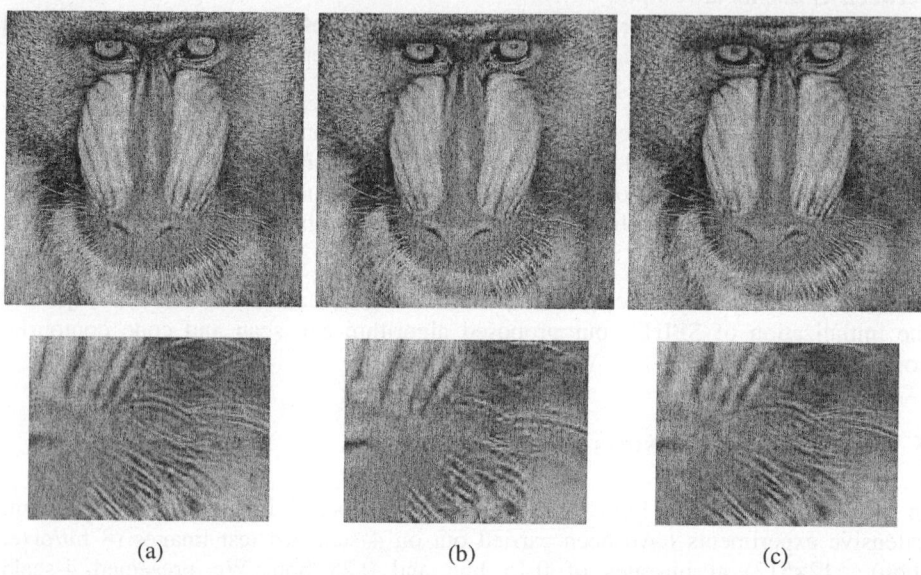

Fig. 5. The coding results of "Mandrill" image at 0.25 bpp. (a) The proposed coding algorithm. (b) WT with SPIHT. (c) WBCT with SPIHT.

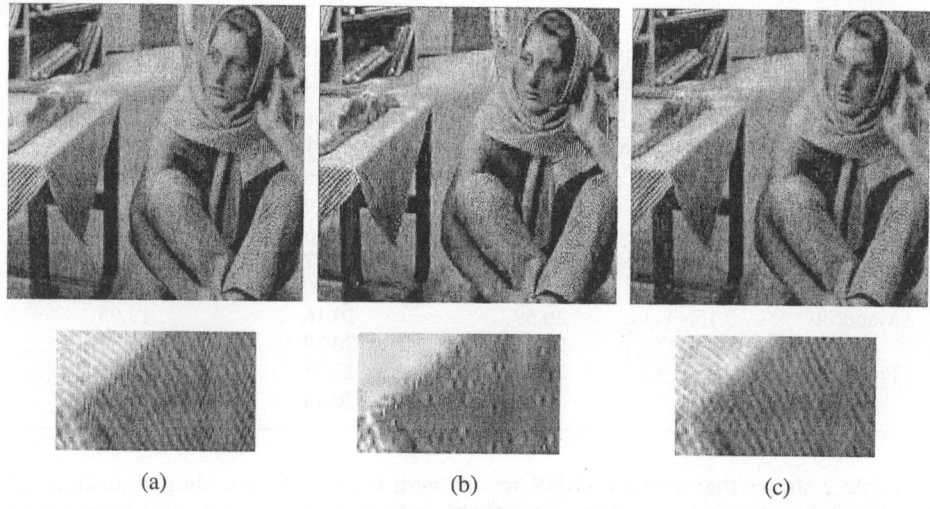

Fig. 6. The coding results of "Barbara" image at 0.25 bpp. (a) The proposed coding algorithm. (b) WT with SPIHT. (c) WBCT with SPIHT.

6 Conclusion

This paper analyzed distribution of significant contourlet coefficients in different subbands and proposed a contourlet image coding algorithm based on adjusted SPIHT by adopting adaptive subband coding order scheme, constructing a virtual LF subband and adjusting coding structure of SPIHT properly. Experimental results show that the proposed coding algorithm has better or competitive compression performance than traditional WT with SPIHT and WBCT with SPIHT. At the same time, because genuine contourlet is adopted, the visual effect of the proposed coding algorithm is superior to them by preserving more contours and textures in the coded images.

In future work, we will investigate the correlation of contourlet coefficients in different directional subbands and different scales. CT for motion compensated image, expanding CT to 3-D and corresponding application for 3-D object image coding will be studied.

Acknowledgement

The authors acknowledge the financial support of RFDP No.20040248047 and Shanghai NSF No.04ZR14082.

References

1. Shapiro, J.M.: Embedded Image Coding Using Zerotrees of Wavelet Coefficient. IEEE Trans. on Signal Processing **41** (1993) 3445-3462
2. Said, A., Pearlman, W.A.: A New, Fast and Efficient Image Codec Based on Set Partitioning in Hierarchical Trees. IEEE Trans. Circuits Syst. Video Technol **6** (1996) 243-250
3. Taubman, D.: High Performance Scalable Image Compression with EBCOT. IEEE Trans. on Image Processing **9** (2000) 1158-1170
4. Do, M.N., Vetterli, M.: Contourlets: A Directional Multiresolution Image Representation. In: The IEEE International Conference on Image Processing (ICIP'2002), Rochester. Vol. 1. (2002) 357-360
5. Do, M.N., Vetterli, M.: The Contourlet Transform: An Efficient Directional Multiresolution Image Representation. Submitted to IEEE Trans. on Image Processing
6. Candès, E.J., Donoho, D.L.: Ridgelets: a Key to Higher-Dimensional Intermittency? Phil. Trans. R. Soc. Lond. A. (1999) 2495-2509
7. Do, M.N., Vetterli, M.: Orthonormal Finite Ridgelet Transform for Image Compression. In: The IEEE International Conference on Image Processing (ICIP'2000), Vancouver, Canada. Vol. 2 (2000) 367-370
8. Granai, L.: Radon and Ridgelet Transform Applied to Motion Compensated Images. EPFL, No 02.10 (2002)
9. Candès, E.J., Donoho, D.L.: Curvelets – a surprisingly effective nonadaptive representation for objects with edges. In: Cohen, A., Rabut, C., Schumaker, L.L. (eds.): Curve and Surface Fitting. Vanderbilt University Press, Saint-Malo (1999)
10. Candès, E.J., Donoho, D.L.: New Tight Frames of Curvelets and Optimal Representations of Objects with Smooth Singularities. Department of Statistics, Stanford University, Tech. Rep. (2002)

11. Pennec, E.L., Mallat, S.: Sparse geometric image representation with bandelets. IEEE Trans. on Image Processing **14** (2005) 423-438
12. Donoho, D.L.: Wedgelets: nearly-minimax estimation of edges. Ann. Statist. **27** (1999) 859–897
13. Donoho, D.L., Huo X.: Beamlets and multiscale image analysis. Multiscale and Multiresolution Methods. Springer Lecture Notes in Computational Science and Engineering. Vol. 20 (2001) 149-196
14. Do, M.N.: Directional multiresolution image representations. Ph.D.thesis, EPFL, Lausanne, Switzerland (2001)
15. Eslami, R., Radha, H.: On low bit-rate coding using the contourlet transform. In: Proc. of Asilomar Conference on Signals, Systems, and Computers, Pacific Grove, USA. (2003) 1524-1528
16. Chappelier, V., Guillemot, C., Marinkovic, S.: Image Coding With Iterated Contourlet and Wavelet Transforms. In: The IEEE International Conference on Image Processing (ICIP '2004). Vol. 5 (2004) 3157 – 3160
17. Eslami, R., Radha, H.: Wavelet-based contourlet coding using an SPIHT-like algorithm. In: Proc. of Conference on Information Sciences and Systems, Princeton. (2004) 784-788
18. Antonini, M., Barlaud, M., Mathieu, P., Daubechies, I.: Image coding using wavelet transformation. IEEE Trans. Image Processing **1** (1992) 205-220
19. Phoong, S.M., Kim, C.W., Vaidyanathan, P.P., Ansari, R.: A new class of two-channel biorthogonal filter banks and wavelet bases. IEEE trans. on Signal Processing **43** (1995) 649-665

Using Bitstream Structure Descriptions for the Exploitation of Multi-layered Temporal Scalability in H.264/AVC's Base Specification

Wesley De Neve[1], Davy Van Deursen[1], Davy De Schrijver[1], Koen De Wolf[1], and Rik Van de Walle[2]

[1] Ghent University - IBBT, Multimedia Lab, Sint-Pietersnieuwstraat 41, B-9000 Ghent, Belgium
Wesley.DeNeve@UGent.be
http://multimedialab.elis.ugent.be

[2] Ghent University - IBBT - IMEC, Multimedia Lab, Sint-Pietersnieuwstraat 41, B-9000 Ghent, Belgium

Abstract. In this paper, attention is paid to the automatic generation of XML-based descriptions containing information about the high-level structure of binary multimedia resources. These structural metadata can then be transformed in order to reflect a desired adaptation of a multimedia resource, and can subsequently be used to create a tailored version of the resource in question. Based on this concept, two technologies are presented: MPEG-21 BSDL and a modified version of XFlavor being able to create BSDL compatible output. Their usage is elaborated in more detail with respect to the valid exploitation of multi-layered temporal scalability in H.264/MPEG-4 AVC's base specification, and in particular with a focus on a combined usage of the sub-sequence coding technique and Supplemental Enhancement Information (SEI) messages. Some performance measurements in terms of file sizes and computational times are presented as well.

1 Introduction

Scalable video coding is a major point of interest in the community of digital video coding. The technology in question is supposed to pave the way for the deployment of several new multimedia architectures. The latter should make it possible to tackle the tremendous diversity in terminals and networks as used in the present-day and future multimedia ecosystem. It is important to be aware of the fact that an efficient solution for this heterogeneity does not only imply the usage of scalable video coding, but also requires the usage of a complementary adaptation decision taking engine and a complementary content adaptation system [1]. Hence, a question that arises is how to optimally customize a scalable bitstream according to a given set of constraints (e.g., device and network characteristics, user preferences, natural environment). A solution for the content adaptation problem, based on the description of the high-level structure of compressed bitstreams in the eXtensible Markup Language (XML), is elaborated in more detail in this paper.

The outline of the paper is as follows: after having given an overview of the temporal scalability features in H.264/AVC's base specification in Section 2, a short description of two bitstream structure description languages is provided in Section 3, as well as a discussion on how they can be used to customize (scalable) bitstreams. Section 4 discusses some performance results as obtained in the context of H.264/AVC while Section 5 concludes this paper.

2 Temporal Scalability in H.264/MPEG-4 AVC

2.1 Context

ITU-T H.264 / MPEG-4 (Part 10) Advanced Video Coding (commonly abbreviated as H.264/AVC) is a new and standardized specification for digital video coding, characterized by a design that targets efficiency, robustness, and usability. Because of its support for a wide range of bit rates, H.264/AVC can even be considered as a universal standard for digital video coding. It is expected that H.264/AVC will have a powerful impact on both consumer and professional video applications in the years to come, especially when taking into account the tools that were added to the standard in the course of 2004 and that are known as the Fidelity Range Extensions (FRExt) [2]. Hence, there is a good chance that H.264/AVC will be used in very diverse usage environments, thus making it relevant to gain an insight into the tools this standard makes available with respect to bitstream customization.

In the first version of the H.264/AVC specification, as approved in the spring of 2003, there are only tools available for enabling multiple representations of the same content and for enabling multi-layered temporal scalability. The latter can be defined as the ability to remove some coded pictures from a bitstream while still obtaining a decodable remaining sequence of pictures (frame dropping or stream thinning). The most important tools in this context are switching or synchronization slices and Supplemental Enhancement Information messages (SEI messages) for signaling the appearance of sub-sequences and sub-sequence layers. Switching slices make it possible to switch between alternate representations of the same video content (simulstore), to recover from data losses or errors, and to apply trick modes such as fast-forward and fast-reverse. Switching slices will not be discussed in further detail in this paper.

The sub-sequence coding technique will be explained in more detail in the next section, as well as some closely related concepts, such as pyramid encoding and explicit Group Of Pictures structures (GOP structures). To conclude this section, it is worth noting that work is currently going on in order to address the need for more advanced scalability tools in H.264/AVC (e.g., to allow spatial, and fine and coarse grain quality scalability). This activity, again conducted by the Joint Video Team (JVT), is known as Scalable Video Coding (SVC) and will most probably result in a second amendment to the H.264/AVC standard.

2.2 Sub-sequences: Background and Signaling

Before providing more details pertaining to the sub-sequence coding technique, it is interesting to have a closer look at some design features of H.264/AVC, especially when taking into account the fact that temporal scalability is often realized in its predecessors by the disposal of bidirectionally predicted pictures.

First, in H.264/AVC there is no such thing as an I picture, a P picture, or a B picture since the recommendation only defines I slices, P slices, and B slices. In addition, it is allowed to construct a coded picture that consists of a mixture of different types of slices. Second, B slices can be used as a reference for the reconstruction of other slices, a concept known as generalized B slices. Hence, it should be clear that for exploiting temporal scalability in H.264/AVC or for enabling fast forward operations, a subtle approach is needed in order to obtain a bitstream that is valid in terms of its syntax and semantics (e.g., correct reference picture management).

The recommended way for achieving temporal scalability in H.264/AVC is to make use of the sub-sequence coding technique. The latter was introduced by Hannuksela as the enhanced concept of a GOP [4]. A sub-sequence represents a number of inter-dependent pictures that can be disposed without affecting the decoding of any other sub-sequence in the same sub-sequence layer or any sub-sequence in any lower sub-sequence layer. It is hereby possible to assign coded pictures in a bitstream to sub-sequences and sub-sequence layers in multiple ways, provided that the structure fulfills the requirements for dependencies between sub-sequences. Typically, each picture will belong to exactly one sub-sequence, and each sub-sequence will belong to exactly one sub-sequence layer in any sub-sequence structure. In short, a sub-sequence layer contains a subset of the coded pictures in a sequence while a sub-sequence is a set of coded pictures within a sub-sequence layer. An example will be provided in Subsection 4.2.

In order to signal the appearance of sub-sequences, sub-sequence layers, and their dependencies, it is possible to insert SEI messages in the compressed video data. SEI messages, introduced for the first time in H.263+, can assist in processes related to decoding, display or other purposes. However, SEI messages are not required for constructing the luma or chroma samples by the decoding process. Three types of SEI messages are defined for sub-sequences. The sub-sequence information SEI message maps a coded picture to a certain sub-sequence and sub-sequence layer. The sub-sequence layer characteristics SEI message and the sub-sequence characteristics SEI message provide statistical information on the indicated sub-sequence layer and sub-sequence respectively (e.g., the number of sub-sequence layers, the average frame and bit rate). Furthermore, the dependencies between sub-sequences are indicated in the sub-sequence characteristics SEI message. Hence, bitstream extraction tools and decoders can use this metadata to scale down a bitstream in the temporal domain or to implement a feature such as a fast-forward mode, without having to delve deeply into the syntax of a compressed bitstream. It is interesting to know that similar adaptation hints are currently standardized in the context of the activities with respect to H.264/AVC SVC.

In practice, sub-sequences will most probably be created by relying on pyramid encoding or an explicit GOP structure. Pyramid encoding organizes the coded pictures of a bitstream in several layers of data dependencies, hereby making use of the following rule of thumb: the layers are ordered hierarchically based on their dependency on each other such that any picture in a layer shall not be predicted from any picture on any higher layer. When making use of this technique, the pictures in the enhancement layers are typically (hierarchically) B slice coded pictures [3]. The latter constraint is weakened when making use of an explicit GOP structure. Such a structure not only makes it possible to specify explicitly the type of slice to use but also makes it possible to specify the layer that will contain the slice. For instance, the explicit GOP structure coding technique allows to add an I slice coded picture to an enhancement layer.

2.3 Syntax Considerations: A View from the Trenches

Several syntax elements can be important when exploiting temporal scalability in the base version of H.264/AVC, such as the nal_ref_idc, frame_num, gaps_in_frame_num_value_allowed_flag, fixed_frame_rate_flag, and slice_type syntax elements, as well as the syntax elements in the sub-sequence related SEI messages. For instance, the sub-sequence information SEI message shall not be present unless gaps_in_frame_num_value_allowed_flag, as available in the Sequence Parameter Set (SPS) referenced by the picture associated with the sub-sequence SEI message, is equal to one. The latter is necessary in order to allow the intentional disposal of slices that are used for the reconstruction for other slices, a scenario that is likely to occur when dealing with multi-layered temporal scalability. Otherwise, the decoder might invoke error concealment procedures due to the fact that the syntax element frame_num is a way to achieve picture loss robustness: a gap in its value indicates a missing reference slice.

The fact that frame_num is primarily a loss robustness feature, is reflected in the way that the behavior of frame_num depends on whether the picture is a reference picture or not (i.e., on the value of nal_ref_idc): frame_num acts as a counter that increments each time a reference picture is decoded. As such, it is possible for a decoder to detect that some picture(s) are missing and to conceal the problem without losing track of what is going on. Since the proper decoding of a non-reference picture is not necessary for the proper decoding of other pictures that arrive later, frame_num was designed so that a missing non-reference picture would not cause frame_num to indicate the presence of a problem when a non-reference picture is missing[1]. Note that the value of frame_num is reset to zero whenever a new coded video sequence begins.

The syntax element sub_seq_frame_num, as available in a sub-sequence information SEI message, is a variant of the syntax element frame_num. The behavior is the same: it acts as a counter that is only incremented when the associated picture is used as a reference. However, the difference lies in the fact that sub_seq_frame_num belongs to one sub-sequence and not to a coded video

---

[1] A better name for frame_num would probably have been ref_pic_num.

sequence. Hence, the value of `sub_seq_frame_num` is reset to zero whenever a new sub-sequence begins. As such, it is still possible for a decoder to detect the loss of a reference slice when gaps are allowed in the value of `frame_num`. Further, it is also interesting to know that the first syntax element of a sub-sequence information SEI message (i.e., `sub_seq_layer_num`) represents the number of a sub-sequence layer, while the second syntax element (i.e., `sub_seq_id`) identifies a sub-sequence within a particular sub-sequence layer.

With respect to the semantics of the `slice_type` syntax element, it is relevant to be aware of the fact that a value in the range 5–9 specifies, in addition to the coding type of the current slice, that all other slices of the current coded picture shall have the same type.

3 Bitstream Structure Description Languages

3.1 Context

In order to be able to deliver scalable video in a heterogeneous environment, it is important to be aware of the need of complementary logic that makes it possible to exploit the scalability properties of the parent bitstream. This bitstream extraction process typically involves the removal of certain data blocks and the modification of the value of certain syntax elements.

One way to realize the scenario as just mentioned, is to rely on automatically generated XML-based descriptions that contain information about the high-level structure of scalable bitstreams. These structural metadata can subsequently be transformed (an operation in the semantic domain) in order to reflect a desired adaptation of a scalable bitstream, and can then be used to automatically create an adapted version of the bitstream in question (an operation in the compressed domain). In other words, the Bitstream Structure Descriptions (BSDs[2]) can be used as an intermediate format to customize scalable bitstreams (without requiring a recode of the compressed video data). As such, the BSDs act as an abstraction of the compressed bitstream since their high-level nature only requires a limited knowledge about the bitstream structure: one no longer has to reason about the bitstream in terms of motion vectors or transform coefficients, but one can think in terms of layers and packets. Moreover, the XML-based formalism also allows the usage of many already existing tools for manipulating XML documents, as well as a straightforward integration with other metadata standards such as MPEG-7.

The structural metadata also enable other applications. For instance, one can think of correcting wrong coded syntax elements without the need of a recode or recompilation of the media data: e.g., correcting aspect ratio information, correcting four-character codes in file containers (FourCCs), ... Such operations are sometimes called header hacks. Further possible applications with regard to BSDs are multiplexing and demultiplexing, automatic video summarization, scene selection, and bitstream syntax validation.

---

[2] In MPEG-21 terminology, a BSD stands for Bitstream Syntax Description.

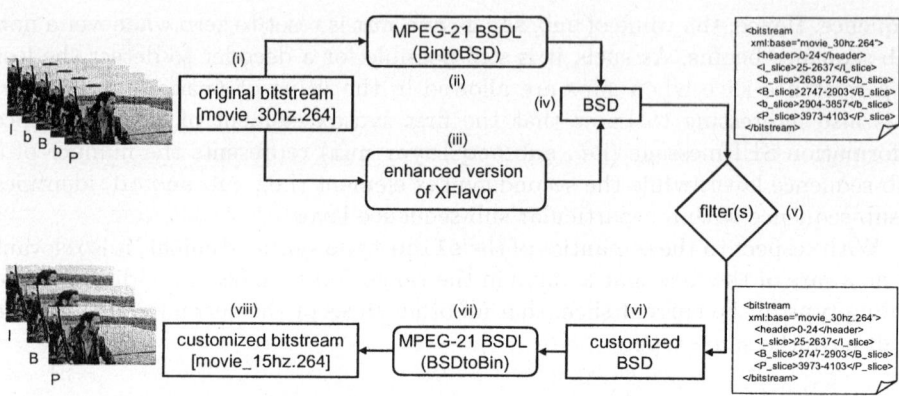

Fig. 1. High-level representation of the joint MPEG-21 BSDL/XFlavor approach

```
<xsd:element name="seq_parameter_set_rbsp">                          class Seq_parameter_set_rbsp {
  <xsd:complexType>
    <xsd:sequence>
      <xsd:element name="profile_idc" type="xsd:unsignedByte"/>          bit(8) profile_idc;
      <xsd:element name="constraint_set0_flag" type="bt:b1"/>            bit(1) constraint_set0_flag;
      <xsd:element name="constraint_set1_flag" type="bt:b1"/>            bit(1) constraint_set1_flag;
      <xsd:element name="constraint_set2_flag" type="bt:b1"/>            bit(1) constraint_set2_flag;
      <xsd:element name="reserved_zero_5bits" type="bt:b5"               bit(5) reserved_zero_5bits = 0;
                   fixed="0"/>
      <xsd:element name="level_idc" type="xsd:unsignedByte"/>            bit(8) level_idc;
      <xsd:element name="seq_parameter_set_id"
                   type="jvt:UnsignedExpGolomb"/>                        ue seq_parameter_set_id;
      <xsd:element name="log2_max_frame_num_minus4"
                   type="jvt:UnsignedExpGolomb"/>                        ue log2_max_frame_num_minus4;
      <xsd:element name="pic_order_cnt_type"
                   type="jvt:UnsignedExpGolomb"/>                        ue pic_order_cnt_type;
      <xsd:element name="if_pic_order_cnt_type_eq_0" minOccurs="0"       if ( pic_order_cnt_type.value == 0 )
                   bs2:if="./jvt:pic_order_cnt_type = 0">
        <xsd:complexType>
          <xsd:sequence>
            <xsd:element name="log2_max_pic_order_cnt_lsb_minus4"
                         type="jvt:UnsignedExpGolomb"/>                  ue log2_max_pic_order_cnt_lsb_minus4;
          </xsd:sequence>
        </xsd:complexType>
      </xsd:element>
      <!-- ... -->                                                       /* ... */
    </xsd:sequence>
  </xsd:complexType>
</xsd:element>                                                       }
```

Fig. 2. Partial description of the SPS syntax in BSDL (left) and XFlavor (right)

In the following sections, a short overview is given of two languages that provide solutions for discovering the structure of a multimedia resource in order to generate its XML description and for the generation of an adapted multimedia resource using a transformed description. To be more specific, more details will be provided with respect to MPEG-21 BSDL (MPEG-21 Bitstream Syntax Description Language) and a modified version of Flavor/XFlavor (Formal Language for Audio-Visual Object Representation) that is able to output BSDL compatible descriptions. A profound comparison between the languages as just mentioned will be provided in a forthcoming paper, as well as a discussion of the merits of the enhanced version of XFlavor. Figure 1 shows a high-level overview of our harmonized MPEG-21 BSDL/XFlavor approach. The different steps in the operational flow are as follows: (i) the parent H.264/AVC bitstream; (ii) a BSD is created by making use of MPEG-21 BSDL; (iii) a BSD is created by making use of the enhanced version of XFlavor; (iv) MPEG-21 BSDL and the modified version of XFlavor allow to create an equivalent BSD (but not necessarily an identical one); (v) filter(s) for customizing a BSD in order to meet the constraints of a certain usage environment; (vi) the customized BSD; (vii) MPEG-21 BSDL allows to create an adapted bitstream, guided by the customized BSD (bitstream extraction); (viii) the tailored child H.264/AVC bitstream. A partial description of H.264/AVC's Sequence Parameter Set (SPS) datastructure in MPEG-21 BSDL and XFlavor is illustrated by Figure 2. Such descriptions are used by the MPEG-21 BSDL and enhanced XFlavor tool chain in order to automatically create a BSD for an arbitrary H.264/AVC bitstream. Note that MPEG-21 BSDL is built on top of W3C XML Schema (the metadata community's point of view) while XFlavor is built on top of the principles of object oriented languages such as C++ and Java (the developers community's point of view).

3.2 The MPEG-21 Bitstream Syntax Description Language

MPEG-21 BSDL is a language that enables the (partial) description of the syntax of (scalable) bitstreams. The technology, built on top of W3C XML Schema, was created by Philips Research, France [6]. The primary motivation behind its development is to assist in customizing scalable bitstreams. In order to avoid a large overhead and unnecessary computations, the language in question will most often only be used for the description of the high-level structure of a bitstream. BSDL falls under the umbrella of the Bitstream Syntax Description tool of the MPEG-21 Multimedia Framework, just like the gBS Schema language [8]. The MPEG-21 standard attempts to realize the ideal of easily exchanging any type of information without technical barriers.

The generic character of the BSDL technology lies in the format independent nature of the logic responsible for the creation of the BSDs and for the generation of the adapted bitstreams. To be more specific, it is not necessary to update the different pieces of software involved in order to support a new (scalable) video coding format since all information necessary for discovering the structure of the bitstream is available in the BSDL description of (a part of) the syntax of the coding format. As such, BSDL allows to construct a universal adaptation engine.

With respect to the first version of H.264/AVC, a generic BSDL schema was developed that allows to describe its Annex B syntax up to and including the slice header datastructure (independent of the profile@level combination used) [9].

3.3 The Formal Language for Audio-Visual Object Representation

Flavor, developed by Columbia University, was initially designed as a declarative language with a C++-like syntax to describe the bitstream syntax on a bit-per-bit basis. Its aim is to simplify and speed up the development of software that processes audiovisual bitstreams by automatically generating the required

C++ and Java code to parse the data, hence allowing the developer to concentrate on the processing part of the software. Flavor was enhanced to support XML features (XFlavor), resulting in the development of tools for generating an XML description of the bitstream syntax and for regenerating an adapted bitstream [7]. As discussed in [8], there are, however, some fundamental differences to BSDL, stemming mainly from the original focus of the two technologies. For instance, in XFlavor, the complete bitstream data are actually embedded in the BSD, resulting in potentially huge descriptions, while BSDL uses a specific datatype to point to a data range in the original bitstream when it is too verbose to be included in the description. This is why, unlike XFlavor, BSDL is rather a description language than a representation language, and can describe a bitstream at a high syntactical level instead of at a low-level, bit-per-bit basis.

Recently, we developed an extension to XFlavor that allows to create BSDL compatible BSDs when taking into account certain restrictions. As such, an XFlavor-alike description was developed for the first version of the H.264/AVC standard, allowing to discover its Annex B syntax up to and including the slice header datastructure. However, the XFlavor-alike description only allows to process H.264/AVC bitstreams that contain one Sequence Parameter Set (SPS) and one Picture Parameter Set (PPS).

4 Simulations

4.1 Context

In this section, experimental performance measurements are presented in terms of file sizes and computational times. Two use cases are targeted: a download-and-play scenario and a simulstore-based streaming scenario. In both scenarios, the goal is to make use of an H.264/AVC bitstream that has provisions for the exploitation of multi-layered temporal scalability in order to target three different usage environments: a desktop computer able to process video data at 30 Hz, a portable entertainment device able to process video data at 15 Hz, and a cell phone able to process video data at 7.5 Hz. The bitstreams in question (Foreman; CIF resolution; 300 pictures; 30 Hz) are compressed by making use of the pyramid encoding technique and are compliant with H.264/AVC's Main Profile. With respect to the streaming scenario, three slices per picture are used for improved error robustness while the download-and-play scenario only uses one slice per picture. It is also important to know that both scenarios are relying on I slice coded pictures, P slice coded pictures, and B slice coded pictures (i.e., all slices in the same picture share a common value for the slice_type syntax element). The resulting bitstreams contain one SPS and one PPS.

To demonstrate the usefulness of the proposed techniques, simulations were carried out for bitstreams having the following GOP structure: $I_0 p_2 P_1 p_2 P_0$, $I_0 b_2 B_1 b_2 P_0$, $I_0 p_3 P_2 p_3 P_1 p_3 P_2 p_3 P_0$, and $I_0 b_3 B_2 b_3 B_1 b_3 B_2 b_3 P_0$. The $I_0 b_2 B_1 b_2 P_0$ coding pattern is shown in Figure 3. Every picture (frame) contains three slices. Each slice is tagged with its type and the value of frame_num. Each sub-sequence information SEI message is tagged with the value of the sub_seq_frame_num

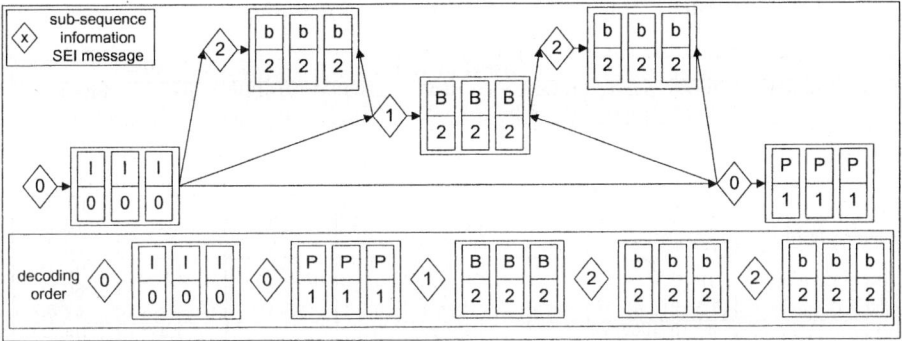

Fig. 3. The $I_0b_2B_1b_2P_0$ coding pattern for the streaming scenario

syntax element, making it possible to identify a sub-sequence layer. It is clear that the $I_0b_2B_1b_2P_0$ coding pattern contains three different sub-sequences and that each sub-sequence is part of a different sub-sequence layer. Hereby, 'P' and 'p' denote a P slice coded reference picture and P slice coded non-reference picture, respectively. As such, the settings used are in line with the ones as applied in the complementary paper by Tian et al. [5]. The first two GOP structures offer three-level temporal scalability while the last two GOP structures offer four temporal resolutions. The value of the quantization parameter for the base layer is equal to 28 and is increased by two for every additional layer.

The simulations were done on a PC having an AMD Athlon4 1600+ CPU and 512 MB of RAM at its disposal. The operating system used was Windows Server 2003, running the Java 2 Runtime Environment (SE version 1.4.2_07). SAXON 6.5.2 was used in order to apply Extensible Stylesheet Language Transformations (XSLTs) to BSDs. The H.264/AVC bitstreams were created by relying on the JM 9.4 reference software. Half of them were manually annotated with SEI metadata by relying on the BSDL approach. Version 1.1.3 of the MPEG-21 BSDL reference software was used. In order to make a fair comparison with the extended version of XFlavor, the generic BSDL schema was simplified such that it is only possible to describe bitstreams that contain one SPS and PPS.

4.2 Simulation Results

This section covers a selection of the performance results that were obtained. Due to place constraints, only the results for the most challenging scenario are shown, i.e., the streaming scenario. From Table 1, it is clear that the obtained values for the different metrics are almost all independent from the GOP structure used. The latter only has a clear impact on the amount of data dropped: obviously, the bit rate reduction is higher when exploiting temporal scalability in case of a GOP structure that embeds P slice coded pictures. This is for instance relevant in case one has to pay for the amount of data transfered.

Table 1. Simulation results for the streaming scenario

	coding pattern	fps (Hz)	MPEG-21 BSDL					XFlavor+	
			parse time (s)	transform time (s)	BSD (KB)	cBSD (KB)	BSDtoBin (s)	parse time (s)	bitstream size (%)
no SEI	IpPpP	30	3696.2	-	1895.1	18.5	-	1.2	100.0
		15	-	2.3	1571.5	10.6	5.4	-	76.9
		7.5	-	2.2	924.9	6.2	3.9	-	53.5
	IpPpPpPpP	30	3722.1	-	1975.3	19.2	-	1.1	100.0
		15	-	2.5	1571.5	10.8	5.5	-	78.1
		7.5	-	2.4	791.4	6.4	3.8	-	56.9
	IbBbP	30	3975.4	-	1998.0	17.7	-	1.2	100.0
		15	-	2.4	1713.6	10.4	5.3	-	86.2
		7.5	-	2.3	924.1	6.2	3.9	-	67.5
	IbBbBbBbP	30	4066.6	-	1964.8	17.2	-	1.3	100.0
		15	-	2.5	1655.4	10.6	5.2	-	87.4
		7.5	-	2.4	864.0	6.4	3.8	-	70.1
SEI	IpPpP	30	300.9	-	793.9	12.0	-	0.7	100.0
		15	-	1.8	561.6	7.4	3.1	-	76.8
		7.5	-	1.7	287.1	4.5	2.4	-	53.4
	IpPpPpPpP	30	300.2	-	793.7	11.6	-	0.7	100.0
		15	-	1.8	561.6	7.3	3.0	-	78.0
		7.5	-	1.7	287.1	4.6	2.3	-	56.8
	IbBbP	30	301.0	-	793.7	11.8	-	0.6	100.0
		15	-	1.8	561.6	7.3	2.9	-	85.9
		7.5	-	1.8	287.1	4.5	2.3	-	67.3
	IbBbBbBbP	30	300.4	-	793.5	11.4	-	0.6	100.0
		15	-	1.7	561.5	7.3	2.7	-	87.1
		7.5	-	1.7	287.0	4.5	2.1	-	69.7

With respect to the bitstreams that do not carry SEI, the following observations can be made. The amount of time, as needed by the parser that is available in the MPEG-21 BSDL reference software package, is unacceptably high in order to create a BSD (3865s on the average). This can be explained by the fact that a lot of XPath expressions have to be executed for resolving the necessary dependencies in order to correctly guide the parsing process. Those XPath expressions are needed for retrieving information about the structure of the bitstream as discovered so far. Due to the fact that H.264/AVC's syntax is described with a rather fine granularity (the resulting BSDs contain info up to and including the slice header syntax structure), the parser is forced to delve deeply into the structure of an H.264/AVC bitstream. It is supposed by the authors that this fundamental problem cannot be solved without relying on some non-normative extensions to MPEG-21 BSDL. From that point of view, it is interesting to notice that an equivalent BSD can be created by our modified version of XFlavor in hardly more than one second. XFlavor has much faster access to the information already gathered thanks to its object oriented nature: only simple indexing operations are needed. Note that the BSDs, as created by our extended version of XFlavor, also produce a certain overhead when comparing them with the BSDs as produced by the BSDL software: the average size of a full BSD is 2594.1 KB in case of XFlavor and 1958.3 KB in case of BSDL (not shown in Table 1).

Table 1 also makes clear that the resulting BSDs can be compressed very efficiently. Compression factors of up to 182 are possible when using common compression software (WinRAR). Adapting a BSD can be done very efficient as well. The latter only takes a few seconds. The syntax elements frame_num and `nal_ref_idc` are used to guide the adaptation process in the case of bitstreams that do not carry SEI. For bitstreams containing sub-sequence information SEI messages, the sub-sequence layer identification information (stored in the syntax element `sub_seq_layer_num`) and the value of `nal_unit_type` are used to guide the adaptation process. Customized bitstreams can also be created very fast when making use of the MPEG-21 BSDtoBin tool, especially due to the fact that this process does not require the evaluation of expensive XPath-expressions. The only things that have to be taken care off, are the appropriate binarization of certain values by performing look-ups in the BSDL schema and the selection of the appropriate data packets from the parent bitstream by performing look-ups in the BSD. Both types of BSDs can be used in order to create a customized bitstream since BSDL-based and XFlavor-based BSDs are completely equivalent.

When relying on SEI messages, there is no need to delve deeply into the syntax for gathering the necessary information in order to be able to exploit temporal scalability. This can immediately be derived from the cost needed for generating a BSD: the amount of time has dropped significantly in case of the MPEG-21 BSDL parser (from 3865s on the average to 300s on the average) because of the fact that very few XPath expressions have to be evaluated. The uncompressed BSDs are also two to three times smaller, resulting in a positive impact with respect to the time needed for adapting such a lightweight BSD and for customizing the corresponding bitstream. Hence, the sub-sequence information SEI messages make it straightforward to exploit multi-layered temporal scalability by relying on BSDs.

It is also important to note that BSDL is more fitted for dropping sub-sequence layers (static content adaptation) in pre-coded bitstreams, while the disposal of individual sub-sequences is more of interest to streaming servers for achieving short-term, immediate, and accurate bit rate adjustment (dynamic content adaptation). One can also see that the presence of the sub-sequence information SEI messages hardly has an impact on the size of the compressed bitstreams, while those content adaptation hints are well suited for enabling fast and intelligent bitstream customization[3].

5 Conclusions

In this paper, two languages were discussed that provide solutions for discovering the structure of a scalable bitstream in order to generate its XML description and for the generation of an adapted bitstream using the transformed description. Their (combined) usage was developed in more detail with respect to the valid exploitation of multi-layered temporal scalability in H.264/AVC's base specification. Special attention was paid to the usage of the sub-sequence coding technique, enabling the easy and efficient identification of disposable chains of pictures when processing pre-coded bitstreams. Some performance measurements in terms of file sizes and computational times were presented as well, illustrating the feasibility of the presented concepts. Our results show that the

---

[3] As such, there is a correspondence with gBS Schema's marker concept.

sub-sequence related SEI messages have a positive impact on the efficiency of the bitstream customization process, especially due to the fact that those content adaptation hints assist in abstracting the coding format to be manipulated. As such, the BSDs, together with the sub-sequence coding technique and the sub-sequence related SEI messages, offer an elegant and practical solution for the exploitation of multi-layered temporal scalability in H.264/AVC's base version.

Acknowledgements

The authors would like to thank Gary Sullivan and Miska Hannuksela for providing information about the sub-sequence coding technique and the vision behind the `frame_num` syntax element.

The research activities that have been described in this paper were funded by Ghent University, the Interdisciplinary Institute for Broadband Technology (IBBT), the Institute for the Promotion of Innovation by Science and Technology in Flanders (IWT), the Fund for Scientific Research-Flanders (FWO-Flanders), the Belgian Federal Science Policy Office (BFSPO), and the European Union.

References

1. Lerouge, S., Lambert, P., Van de Walle, R.: Multi-criteria Optimization for Scalable Bitstreams. Proceedings of the 8th International Workshop on Visual Content Processing and Representation, p. 122-130, Springer, (Madrid), September 2003
2. Sullivan, G., Topiwala, P., Luthra, A.: The H.264/AVC Advanced Video Coding Standard: Overview and Introduction to the Fidelity Range Extensions. Applications of Digital Image Processing XXVII **5558** (2004) 454–474
3. Schwarz, H., Marpe, D., Wiegand, T.: Hierarchical B pictures. Doc. JVT-P014, Poznan, Jul. 2005
4. Hannuksela, M.: Enhanced Concept of a GOP. Doc. JVT-B042, Geneva, Jan. 2002
5. Tian, D., Hannuksela, M., Gabbouj, M.: Sub-sequence Video Coding for Improved Temporal Scalability. Proc. ISCAS 2005, Kobe, Japan, May 23-26, 2005
6. Amielh, M., Devillers, S.: Bitstream Syntax Description Language: Application of XML-Schema to Multimedia Content Adaptation. In WWW2002: The Eleventh International World Wide Web Conference, (Honolulu, Hawaii), May 2002.
7. Hong, D., Eleftheriadis, A.: XFlavor: Bridging Bits and Objects in Media Representation. Proceedings, IEEE Int'l Conference on Multimedia and Expo (ICME), Lausanne, Switzerland, August 2002
8. Panis, G., Hutter, A., Heuer, J., Hellwagner, H., Kosch, H., Timmerer, T., Devillers, S., Amielh, M.: Bitstream Syntax Description: A Tool for Multimedia Resource Adaptation within MPEG-21. Signal Processing: Image Communication **18** (2003) 721-747
9. De Neve, W., Lerouge, S., Lambert, P., Van de Walle, R.: A Performance Evaluation of MPEG-21 BSDL in the Context of H.264/AVC. Applications of Digital Image Processing XXVII **5558** (2004) 555–566

Efficient Control for the Distortion Incurred by Dropping DCT Coefficients in Compressed Domain

Jin-Soo Kim[1] and Jae-Gon Kim[2]

[1] Division of Information Communication and Computer Engineering,
Hanbat National University, San 16-1, Dukmyoung-dong, Yuseong-ku, Taejon 305-719, Korea
jskim67@hanbat.ac.kr
[2] Broadcasting Media Group, Electronics and Telecommunications Research Institute, 161,
Gajeong-dong, Yuseong-ku, Taejon 305-350, Korea
jgkim@etri.re.kr

Abstract. The primary goal of this paper is to facilitate the rate-distortion control in compressed domain, without introducing a full decoding and re-encoding system in pixel domain. For this aim, the error propagation behavior over several frame-sequences due to DCT coefficients-drop is investigated on the basis of statistical and empirical properties. Then, such properties are used to develop a simple estimation model for the CD distortion accounting for the characteristics of the underlying coded-frame. Experimental results show that the proposed model allows us to effectively control rate-distortions into coded-frames over different kinds of video sequences.

1 Introduction

Recently, transcoding based on dropping some parts of bitstream in compressed domain is considered mainly due to the low computational complexity and simple implementation issues [1], [2]. This paper deals with a FD (frame-dropping) – CD (coefficient-dropping) scheme that provides the trade-offs between spatial and temporal qualities as well as extending the range of rate reduction. By combining frame-dropping and DCT coefficient-dropping, it is possible to simply adapt the bit rate of a pre-coded video to dynamic available bandwidth, especially in streaming applications. However, the FD-CD transcoder is subject to drift due to the loss of high-frequency information [2], [3], [4]. As time goes on, this error progressively increases, resulting in the reconstructed frames becoming severely degraded. Therefore, in the FD-CD scheme, it is necessary to reduce or minimize the visual quality fluctuations due to these drift errors in compressed domain [5].

Some conventional works in FD-CD transcoder has focused on the optimal selections of the amount of dropped coefficients within a frame. But, drift is also accumulated and often results in significant visual quality degradation. In [2], each coded DCT coefficient is treated as intra-coded one and its propagated/accumulated errors are ignored [3], [4]. In this paper, we analyze the drift error characteristics incurred by the CD and we propose an effective estimation model that, adaptively, describes well the characteristics of propagation errors. Furthermore, based on this model, how to allocate distortions into coded frames in compressed domain is developed.

2 The Statistical Properties and Estimation Model of CD Errors

2.1 The Statistical Properties of CD Errors

In this paper, it is assumed that only a contiguous string of DCT coefficients at the end of each block is dropped [2], [3]. Let $y_j = \{y_{j,i}\}_{i=1,\ldots,M}$ denote the frame j having M blocks, where $y_{j,i}$ is the decoded block i of frame j. Based on this notation, let $\hat{y}_{j-1}$ and $\hat{y}_j$ represent the decoded frames $j-1$ and j, respectively, degraded by CD operation. Then, decoded blocks with and without CD can be expressed as follows:

$$y_{j,i} = C_{j,i}(y_{j-1}) + e_{j,i}$$
$$\hat{y}_{j,i} = C_{j,i}(\hat{y}_{j-1}) + \hat{e}_{j,i} \quad . \tag{1}$$

where $C_{j,i}(y_{j-1})$ is the motion compensated (MC) component with reference to frame $j-1$ and $e_{j,i}$ is the decoded prediction error. Thus, the MSE (Mean Square Error) distortion of block i of frame j, $D_{j,i}(k_i)$, when coefficients of which the scan order is greater than k_i are dropped (that is, k_i is a new breakpoint of the block i), is given by

$$\begin{aligned} D_{j,i}(k_i) &= \frac{1}{N}\|y_{j,i} - \hat{y}_{j,i}\|^2 = \frac{1}{N}\|C_{j,i}(y_{j-1}) - C_{j,i}(\hat{y}_{j-1}) + e_{j,i} - \hat{e}_{j,i}\|^2 \\ &= \frac{1}{N}\sum_{k=0}^{N-1}\{A_{j,i}(k) + E_{j,i}(k) - \hat{E}_{j,i}(k)\}^2 \\ &= \frac{1}{N}\sum_{k=0}^{N-1}A^2_{j,i}(k) + \frac{2}{N}\sum_{k=k_i}^{N-1}A_{j,i}(k)E_{j,i}(k) + \frac{1}{N}\sum_{k=k_i}^{N-1}E^2_{j,i}(k) \end{aligned} \tag{2}$$

where N is the block size and $A_{j,i}(k) = DCT\{C_{j,i}(y_{j-1,i}) - C_{j,i}(\hat{y}_{j-1,i})\}$, $E_{j,i}(k) = DCT_k(e_{j,i})$, $\hat{E}_{j,i}(k) = DCT_k(\hat{e}_{j,i})$, $k = 0,\cdots,N-1$. Accordingly, it is noted that the CD distortion involves not only the propagated errors and the current error, but the correlated error as well.

Property 1. The MSE in the j-th frame can be approximated to $D_j = \frac{1}{M}\sum_{i=1}^{M}D_{j,i}(k_i)$

$\cong \frac{1}{NM}\sum_{i=1}^{M}\left\{\sum_{k=0}^{N-1}A^2_{j,i}(k) + \sum_{k=k_i}^{N-1}E^2_{j,i}(k)\right\}$. That is, the correlated error is negligible and thus, the distortion of the j-th frame is determined by the sum of the current error and the propagated errors.

Proof) The proof is straightforward based on the fact that $A_{j,i}(k)$ and $E_{j,i}(k)$ are statistically independent and their expected values are zero for $NM \gg 1$ [6]. □

Property 2. When CD is applied to multiple coded-frames, together, the overall distortion of each frame can be expressed by the sum of the current error and the propagated errors from the CD operations of previous frames.

Proof) The proof is similar to that of Property 1. □

2.2 CD Control and Simulation Results for CD Errors

There may be many CD control algorithms [2], [3], [4]. In order to keep a uniform quality within each kept frames and to result in more comfortable spatial quality, in this paper, we assume that the defined CD operations have to evenly distribute the dropped coefficients in the spatial range. Accordingly, we consider only *Lagrangian Optimization CD* (LOCD), which tries to find an optimal truncation point for each block within an optimization window of one frame [2], [3]. This is accomplished by using *Lagrangian* search to minimize the distortion caused by the CD. For the j-th frame with bit budget B_{keep}^j, the problem is to find a new breakpoints set $\bar{k} = (k_1, k_2, ..., k_M)$. The problem is formulated as follows:

$$\underset{\bar{k}=(k_1,k_2,...,k_M)}{\text{minimize}} \sum_{i=1}^{M} \sum_{k=k_i+1}^{N-1} z_{i,k}^2 \text{ such that } \sum_{i=1}^{M} \sum_{k=1}^{k_i} b_{coeff}^{i,k} \leq B_{keep}^j. \quad (3)$$

where $z_{i,k}$ and $b_{coeff}^{i,k}$ is the dequantized-DCT coefficient and the amount of coded bits for the k-th symbol in the i-th block, respectively.

Fig.1 compares each component of the CD distortion. In this experiment, "Foreman" sequence coded 1.5Mbps in CIF is transcoded to 800kbps by CD with uniform rate reduction among frames and FD of all B-frames dropping [3]. This result makes sure that the correlated term can be ignored while the current CD error and the propagated errors are dominant. So, Property 1 is very useful.

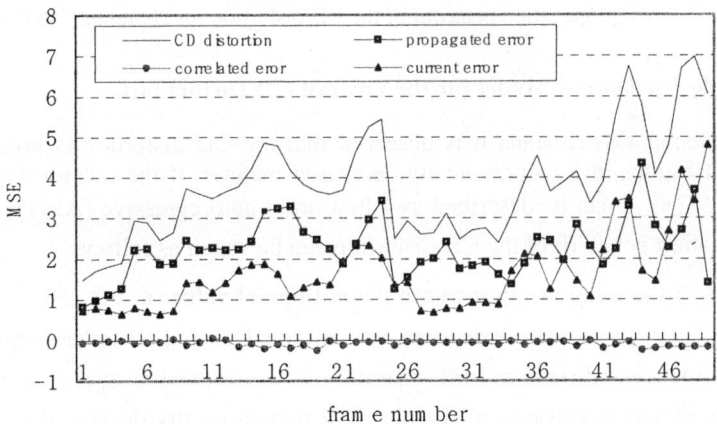

Fig. 1. Each component of the CD distortion for "Foreman" sequence

Additionally, Fig.2 shows the simulation results that CD is applied to each frame individually to investigate the error propagation behavior. In Fig.2, "X_15%" indicates the result of 15% rate-reduction of the X-frame, only while keeping other coded-frames not transcoded. It is noted that the sum of the propagated errors from the past frames and the current error ("sum_15%") is well approximated to the result of CD applied to all frames together ("all_15%"). Therefore, the estimation of CD distortion becomes feasible due to the modeling of error propagation of each frame, independently. Accordingly, as stated in Property 2, when CD is applied to multiple frames simultaneously, each CD distortion can be approximated by the sum of the current error and the propagated errors from the CD operations of all previous frames.

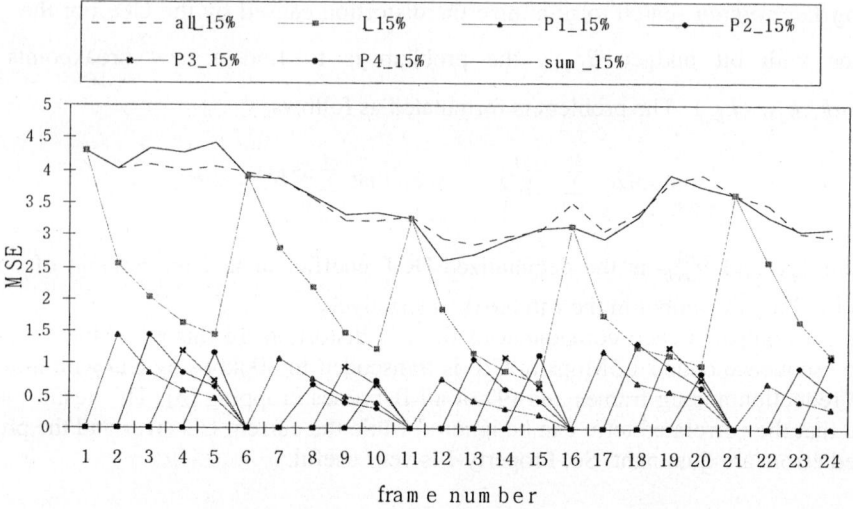

Fig. 2. Error propagation behavior of the CD distortion for "Foreman" sequence

2.3 Simple Estimation Model for the Overall CD Distortions

From the above experiments, it is observed that the CD distortion is propagated to subsequent frames in a monotonically decreased manner. If the relationship between $y_{j,i}$ and $C_{j,i}(y_{j-1})$ can be described as a first-order autoregressive [AR(1)] sequence, the propagation behavior of the CD distortion can be stated as follows:

Property 3. If the relationship between the m-th pixel value of $y_{j,i}$ and the m-th MC value of $C_{j,i}(y_{j-1})$ in scan order can be described as a first-order autoregressive [AR(1)] sequence and random MSE distortion $\delta_j(0)$ is added to $C_{j,i}(y_{j-1})$, the distortion is propagated to subsequent samples in a monotonically decreased manner, i.e., $\delta_j(p) = \zeta \delta_j(p-1)$, for $\zeta \leq 1$, $p \geq 1$.

Proof) An AR(1) process x_{j+1} is defined as $x_{j+1} = \lambda x_j + \varepsilon_{j+1}$, $0 \leq \lambda \leq 1$, $j \geq 0$. Let $\hat{x}_j$ denote the degraded signal incurred by adding random distortion to x_j [7]. For a given MSE distortion $\delta_j(0) = E[(x_j - \hat{x}_j)^2]$,

$$\delta_j(1) = E[(x_{j+1} - \hat{x}_{j+1})^2] = \lambda^2 E[(x_j - \hat{x}_j)^2] = \lambda^2 \delta_j(0)$$

is obtained. According to this relationship, $\delta_j(0) \geq \delta_j(1)$ is found. The extension of this proof gives $\delta_j(0) \geq \delta_j(1) \geq \cdots \geq \delta_j(p-1)$ for $p \geq 1$. □

According to Property 1 and 2, an overall distortion of the j-th frame is simply approximated as follows:

$$D_j = D^j(0) + \sum_{p \geq 1} D^{j-p}(p). \tag{4}$$

where the first term is the distortion caused by CD applied to the j-th frame and the second term is the propagated distortions from the CD operations of previous frames. From the Property 3, a model describing propagation behavior of each CD distortion is proposed in a recursive and adaptive manner as follows:

$$D^{j-p}(q) = \rho_{j-p+q} D^{j-p}(q-1), \quad p \geq q \geq 1. \tag{5}$$

where $D^{j-p}(0)$ means the distortion caused by CD applied to the $(j-p)$-th frame. The propagation behavior in (5) is shown in Fig.3. The model parameter ρ_{j-p+q} is dependent on the coded-frame $(j-p+q)$ and is introduced to represent how much the previous distortion $D^{j-p}(q-1)$ contributes to the current one $D^{j-p}(q)$ in a monotonically decreased manner as follows:

$$\rho_{j-p+q} = \alpha_{j-p+q} \{1 + \beta_{j-p+q}\} \cdot \gamma_{j-p+q}, \quad |\rho_{j-p+q}| \leq 1. \tag{6}$$

Here α_{j-p+q} expresses the power portion compensated from the $(j-p+q-1)$-th frame in the overall power of all inter-coded blocks $\forall i \in S$ in the $(j-p+q)$-th frame, β_{j-p+q} and γ_{j-p+q} are introduced to reflect the portion of the not-coded block and the portion of inter-coded blocks at the $(j-p+q)$-th frame, respectively. α_{j-p+q} is given

$$\alpha_{j-p+q} = \sum_{i \in S} P^{inter}_{j-p+q,i} \bigg/ \sum_{i \in S} P_{j-p+q,i}. \tag{7}$$

where $P^{inter}_{j-p+q,i}$ and $P_{j-p+q,i}$, which denote the propagated power and the total power of the inter-coded block i, respectively, can be simply estimated in the DCT domain. Based on our empirical investigation, to take into account different decaying slopes of the propagation error, $\beta_{j-p+q} = (M^{not}_{j-p+q}/M)^{0.5}$ is obtained, where M^{not}_{j-p+q} is the number of not-coded block in inter-coded macroblocks of frame $(j-p+q)$, and $\gamma_{j-p+q} = (M^{not}_{j-p+q} + M^{mc}_{j-p+q})/M$, where M^{mc}_{j-p+q} is the number of MC-coded blocks in frame $(j-p+q)$.

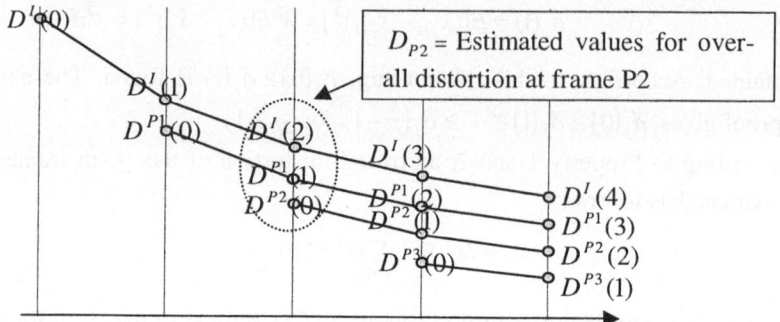

Fig. 3. Adaptive modeling of CD distortions within one GOP

2.4 Simulation Results for Simple Estimation Model

The effectiveness of the CD distortion estimation using the proposed model is tested for two quite different sequences, i.e. "Akiyo" and "Stefan" sequences. The "Akiyo" and "Stefan" sequences in CIF format are coded at 1.2 Mb/s and 1.5 Mb/s with GOP (size = 15, sub-GOP size = 3), respectively. Then, uniform ratio of bits per frame is truncated. Fig.4 and Fig.5 show the experimental results. In Fig.4, for instance, "X_25%CD_model" indicates the trajectory of the estimated distortion caused by the 25% CD of the X-frame, based on (5), and "Sum_models" denotes the sum of all the individual models as defined in (4). "All_25%CD" is the plot of the practically measured distortion at the 25% CD of all coded frames for "Akiyo". These experimental results show that the estimated distortion model well approximates the measured distortion. Particularly, it is noted that, in the case that the activity of moving objects is very low like "Akiyo" sequence, the decaying slope of CD errors is not steep. This

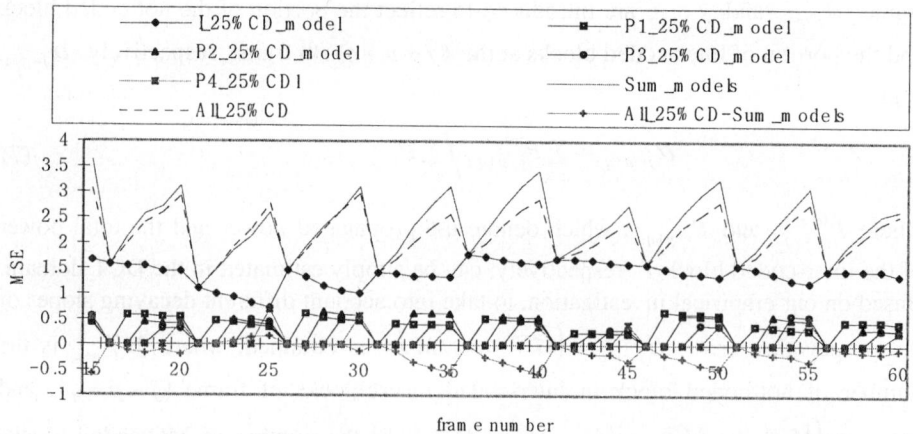

Fig. 4. The results of the estimation of the CD distortion for "Akiyo" sequence

result is mainly due to the fact that "Akiyo" sequence has larger percentage of not-coded blocks in inter-coded macroblocks and so the CD errors of I-frame are critical. On the other hand, since "Stefan" sequence has larger percentage of intra-coded blocks and so intra-refresh effects are working, the slope of CD errors is steeply decaying.

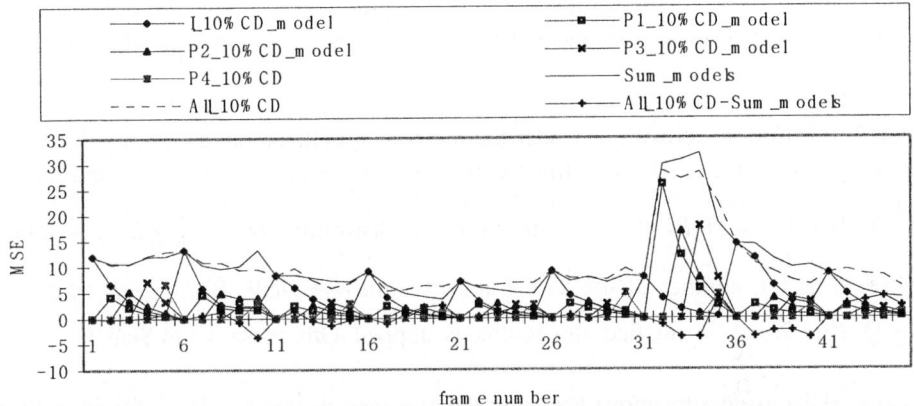

Fig. 5. The results of the estimation of the CD distortion for "Stefan" sequence

3 Rate-Distortion Control Using Proposed Estimation Model

3.1 A GOP-Based Rate-Distortion Control Algorithm for a Pre-coded Video

The challenge of handling (3) in FD-CD transcoder is how to allocate a given bit budget into the kept frames in compressed domain. Some conventional works on the rate-distortion control in FD-CD transcoder has focused on the uniform rate-based CD (URCD) [2], [3], [4]. URCD operates simply as follows: based on the target bit rate, a uniform ratio of bits is dropped from each frame. Then, the optimal selections of dropped coefficients within a frame are achieved by uniformly distributing into each DCT block, based on (3). In [3], Wang has used a new CD rate-allocation scheme to obtain better visual quality. The scheme allocates the larger number of coefficients to be dropped into several frames having strong decoding dependency in the temporal direction

In this paper, the distortion estimation model is applied to develop a content-adaptive rate-distortion control algorithm. That is, the main goal of rate-control scheme is to allocate a given bit-budget into coded-frames within one GOP, while keeping overall distortions per frame to be as constant as possible. For this aim, let's represent an index of the ordered picture coding type within single GOP, i.e. $s \in \{I, P1, P2, \cdots, \}$. Then, let us suppose a coded frame with the picture coding type s undergoes transcoding from $r(s)$ into $r'_i(s)$ [$r(s) > r'_i(s)$ with iteration index i]. By using these notations, (3) is modified to develop the GOP-based rate-distortion control as follows:

Step 1. (Uniform ratio of bit reduction) Let us denote R and $R' (< R)$ as the amount of original bit counts over one GOP (after only FD is applied) and the amount of target bit counts over one GOP (after both FD-CD are applied), respectively. As presented in [3], a uniform ratio of bits, denoted as $\eta = \dfrac{R'}{R} = \dfrac{r'(s)}{r(s)}$, is calculated for one GOP window. Then, based on the (3), a coded frame with the picture coding type s undergoes the CD operation under the rate constraint $r'_0(s) = \eta \cdot r(s)$ where index 0 means initial bit allocation.

Step 2. (Distortion estimation) Under the previous bit allocation, an overall distortion of the coded frame s, D_s, is estimated by using (4). Based on the estimated distortions, D_s for $s \in \{I, P1, P2, \cdots, \}$, the averaged distortion, $D_{avg} = \dfrac{1}{S} \sum_s D_s$, is found where S is the number of the kept frames within one GOP. If $|D_{avg} - D_s| \leq \varepsilon_d$ for $s \in \{I, P1, P2, \cdots, \}$ is satisfied, this routine is stopped. Otherwise, go to Step 3.

Step 3. (Distortion allocation) By using the averaged distortion, D_{avg}, found in Step 2, a newly allocated bit count with the i-th iteration, $r'_i(s)$ for $s \in \{I, P1, P2, \cdots, \}$, is re-allocated such that $|D_{avg} - D_s| \leq \varepsilon_d$ can be satisfied, based on (3).

Step 4. (Rate check) For the newly re-allocated rates, $r'_i(s)$, $s \in \{I, P1, P2, \cdots, \}$ found in Step 3, if the condition $\left| \sum_s r'_i(s) - R' \right| \leq \varepsilon_r$ is satisfied, this routine is stopped. Otherwise, go to Step 5.

Step 5. (Rate re-allocation) A newly allocated bit counts with the $(i+1)$-th iteration is re-allocated as $r'_{i+1}(s) = r'_i(s) + \dfrac{R' - \sum_s r'_i(s)}{\sum_s r(s)} r(s)$ and undergoes the CD operation under the rate constraint $r'_{i+1}(s)$. And then, go to Step 2.

3.2 Simulation Results for the Proposed Rate-Distortion Control Algorithm

As conducted in the previous experiments, all B-frames are dropped and then, the allowable bit-budget is allocated to the kept frames by three algorithms, i.e. URCD [2], Wang's allocation [3], and the proposed algorithm. First, "Akiyo" sequence coded at 1.2Mb/s is transcoded to 500kb/s. Fig.6 shows the simulation results where "Before_CD" represents the amount of bits per frame before dropping coefficients. Since all P-frames of "Akiyo" sequence consist of inter-coded blocks, the propagation errors bring the severe blurring of successively predicted frames. "Wang' allocation" distributes more bits into I-frame, P1-frame, $\cdots$, in decreasing manner. But, it is noted that decoded quality fluctuations is very severe, while the averaged distortion is lowest at some frames. Also, URCD suffers from severe smoothing and the CD distortions are also accumulated.

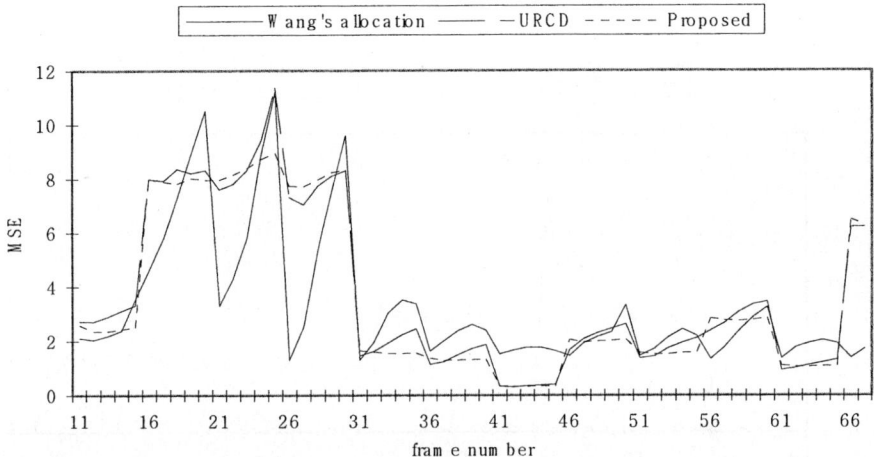

(a) MSE per frame

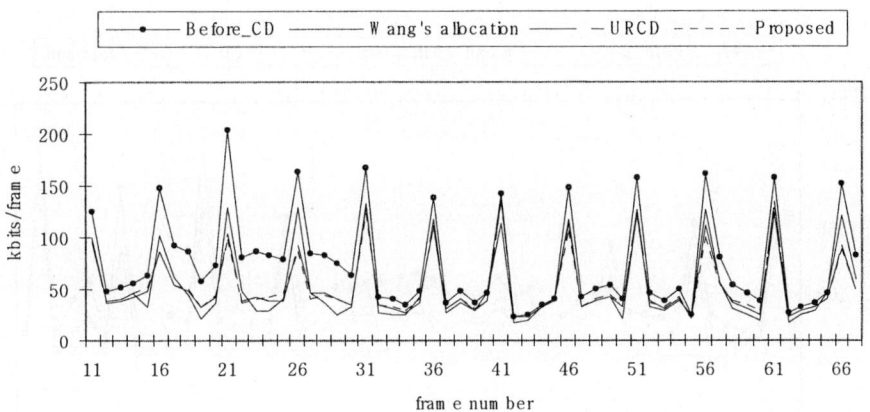

(b) kbits per frame

Fig. 6. The simulation results of rate-distortion control for "Akiyo" sequence

In Fig.7, "Foreman" sequence coded at 1.5Mb/s is reduced to 800kb/s. Compared with "Akiyo" sequence, "Foreman" sequence has smaller number of inter-coded blocks and so the predictive frames do contribute to a smaller drift error. Accordingly, "Wang's allocation" is not effective to this kind of coded sequence. In contrast with this scheme, since URCD treatseach coded frame as intra-coded one, it is found that to drop a uniform ratio of bits per frame has an effect on the allocation of nearly uniform distortion per frame. But, URCD does not fail to adaptively control the drift errors. From the above simulations, it is evident that the proposed scheme is very effective, even if the algorithm is designed for the duration of one GOP window.

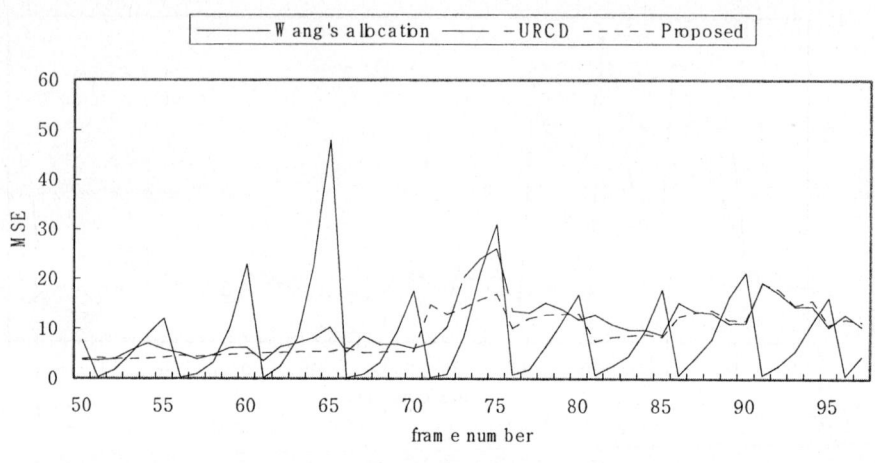

(a) MSE per frame

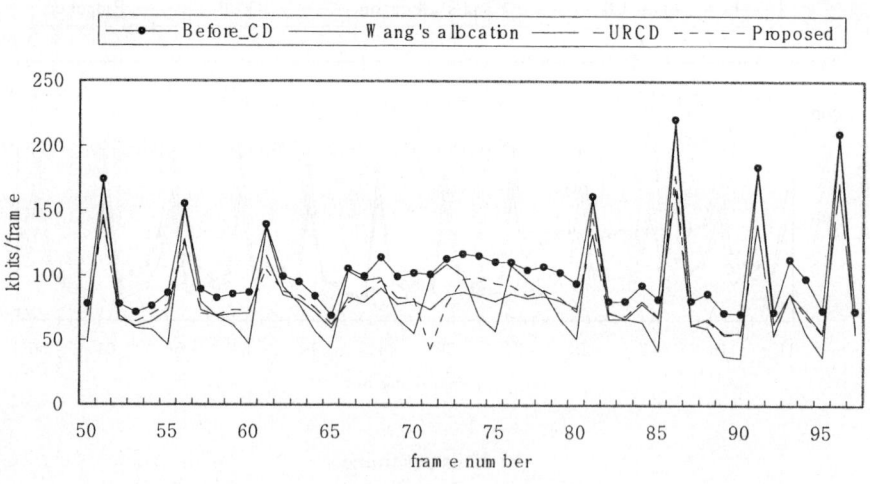

(b) kbits per frame

Fig. 7. The simulation results of rate-distortion control for "Foreman" sequence

4 Conclusions

In this paper, we have focused on the transcoding based on dropping some parts of bitstream in compressed domain. Under the assumption of evenly distributing the dropped coefficients in the spatial range, a novel estimation model describing propagation of the CD distortion is proposed. To develop the estimation model, essential statistical properties of the CD distortion are investigated along with empirical observations. Several experiments with different compressed sequences have shown the effectiveness of the estimation model. That is, the proposed model enables us to efficiently estimate the distortion depending on the amount of coefficient dropping in compressed domain. Furthermore, without introducing a full decoding and re-encoding system in pixel domain, it is shown that the proposed model can be easily extended to find how to allocate nearly uniform distortions among frames and how to control an effective rate-distortion control in compressed domain. Additionally, it is expected that, by exploiting additional coded-information such as motion vectors, quantization parameters for each coded frame, much better performance can be achieved.

As further works, it is necessary to analyze the error characteristics by dropping coefficients on a variety of compressed frames or video sequences (for example, B-frames, with scene changes, etc.). Additionally, we are trying to apply the proposed distortion model to find a universal FD-CD transcoding algorithm.

References

1. Vetro, A.(ed.): Video Transcoding Architectures and Techniques: An Overview. IEEE Signal Processing Mag(2003). Vol.20, 18-29
2. Eleftheriadis, A.: Dynamic Rate Shaping of Compressed Digital Video, Ph.D. dissertation, Dept. Elec. Eng., Columbia University(1995)
3. Wang, Y., Kim, J.G., Chang, S.F.: Content-based Utility Function Prediction for Real-time MPEG-4 Video Transcoding. ICIP'03, Vol.1, 189-192.
4. Kim, J.G., Wang, Y., Chang, S.F.: Content-Adaptive Utility-based Video Adaptation. ICME-2003, Baltimore Maryland(2003)
5. Kim. J.G.(ed.): An Optimal Framework of Video Adaptation and Its Application to Rate Adaptation Transcoding. ETRI Journal(2005), Vol.27, No. 4, pp.341-354
6. Eude, T.(ed.): On the Distribution of the DCT Coefficients. Proc. of ICASSP-94(1994), Vol.5, 365-368
7. Batra, P., and Eleftheriadis, A.: Analysis of Optimal Dynamic Rate Shaping of Markov-1 Sources. Proc. of ICIP-2003, Barcelona, Spain(2003)

Kalman Filter Based Error Resilience for H.264 Motion Vector Recovery

Ki-Hong Ko and Seong-Whan Kim

Department of Computer Science, Univ. of Seoul, Jeon-Nong-Dong, Seoul, Korea
Tel: +82-2-2210-5316, fax: +82-2-2210-5275
jedigo@venus.uos.ac.kr, swkim7@uos.ac.kr

Abstract. We propose an error concealment technique to recover lost motion vectors at the H.264 decoder side. To recover the lost motion vectors, there are two simple techniques: (1) no prediction, where the lost motion vectors are set to zeros, and (2) the prediction using the average or median of spatially adjacent blocks' motion vectors [1]. In this paper, we propose a Kalman filter based scheme for motion vector recovery, and experimented with two test image sequences: Mobile&Calendar and Susie. The experimental results show that our Kalman filter based motion vector recovery scheme improves at average 2 dB PSNR over conventional H.264 decoding with no error recovery. We also improve our scheme using Hilbert curve scan order for Kalman input, and we get 0.512 – 1.652 dB PSNR improvements with better subjective quality over line-by-line scan order.

1 Introduction

Video transmission over bandwidth limited wired/wireless channels usually requires highly compressed bit stream, and they are more fragile to transmission errors than less compressed video streams. There are many researches to guarantee video quality over transmission errors, and we can classify them into two main categories: (1) forward error concealment (or error resilience coding), which improves robustness of encoded bit stream against the transmission errors; (2) decoder error concealments, which recovers or estimates lost information [2, 3]. In this paper, we propose a Kalman filter based motion vector recovery technique for H.264 video error concealment. Kalman filter is a recursive procedure, in which the process and measurement noise are assumed to be independent and normally distributed [4, 5, 6]. Because motion vectors are usually highly correlated with the adjacent blocks' motion vectors, we can improve the Kalman filter based motion vector recovery using Hilbert curve based sequencing for adjacent motion vector in
put for Kalman prediction.

This paper is organized as follows. We review the H.264 motion vector prediction scheme and Kalman filter in section 2. In section 3, we propose a Kalman filter based motion vector recovery scheme, and improve the scheme using Hilbert curve scan order for maximizing the correlation between motion vectors in the Kalman prediction input. In section 4, we presented the experimental results, and conclude in section 5.

2 Related Works

In this section, we will review the motion vector estimation scheme for H.264 video coding standards, and the basic theory of Kalman filter for better estimation.

2.1 Motion Vector Prediction in H.264

H.264 video coding scheme still uses motion vector estimation like other previous video coding schemes: MPEG-1, MPEG-2, and MPEG-4. Moreover, it uses motion vector prediction to exploit the inter-blocks' motion vector correlation, and sends the difference MVD (motion vector difference: MV(E) – MVP(E)) between the estimated motion vector (MV(E)) and predicted motion vector (MVP(E)). In H.264 standard, we can use variable block size motion estimation: 16x16, 8x16, 16x8, 8x8, 4x8, 8x4,

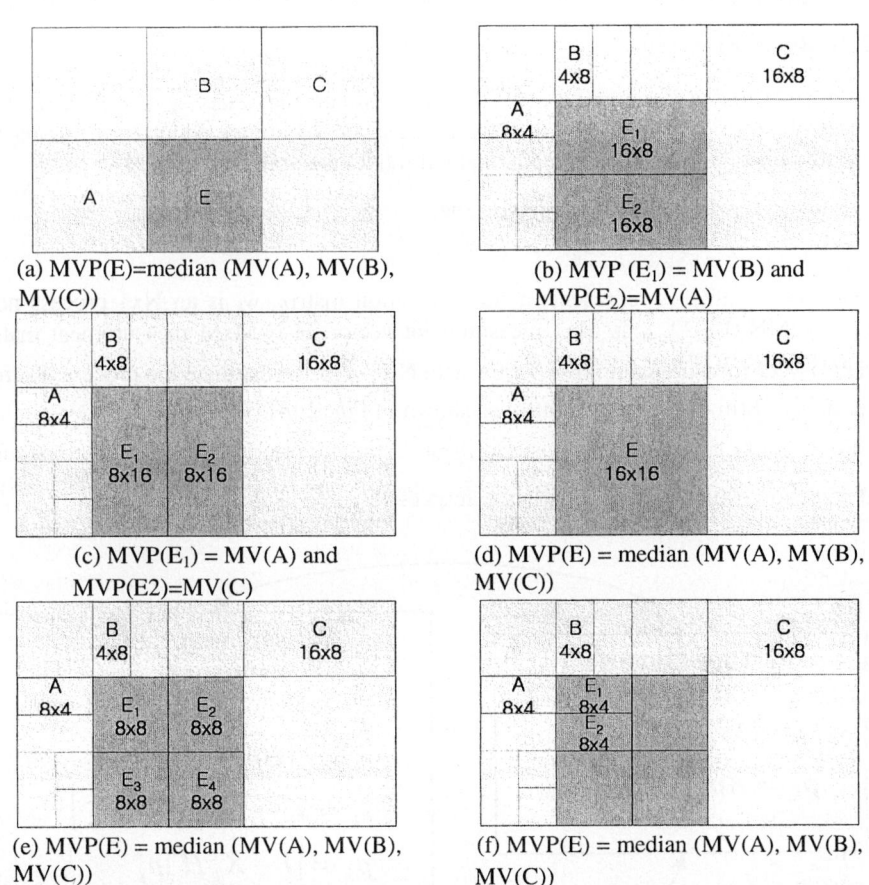

Fig. 1. H.264 motion vector prediction [8]: MV (motion vector estimation), MVP (motion vector prediction)

or 4x4 block based. As shown in Fig. 1, we can predict the motion vector MVP(E) of the current block E from the three neighboring blocks: A, B, and C. Depending on the size of neighboring blocks, we can use different prediction scheme [7, 8]. Fig. 1(a) shows that the size of all neighboring blocks is same. Fig. 1(b) shows that E has two 16x8 partitions E_1 and E_2. Fig. 1(c) shows that E has two 8x16 partitions E_1 and E_2. Fig. 1(d) shows that the sizes of E's neighbor blocks are different. Fig. 1(e) shows that E has four 8x8 partitions E1, E2, E3, and E4 and the sizes of E's neighbor blocks are different. Fig. 1(f) shows that E has two 8x4 partitions E_1 and E_2. Two special cases are (1) if we do not have B and C, we use A's motion vector for MVP(E); (2) if the current block's mode is SKIPPED, we compute median(MV(A), MV(B), MV(C)) for MVP(E).

At encoder side, H.264 computes the motion vector MV using motion vector estimation and the motion vector prediction MVP(E) using the guideline as shown in Fig. 1. From MV and MVP(E), we compute MVD, which is the difference between MV and MVP(E), and send only the MVD.

2.2 Kalman Filtering

A Kalman filter is a recursive procedure to estimate the states s_k of a discrete-time controlled process governed by the linear stochastic difference equation, from a set of measured observations t_k. The mathematical model is expressed as in (1).

$$s_k = As_{k-1} + w_{k-1}$$
$$t_k = Hs_k + r_k \qquad (1)$$

The NxN matrix A represents a state transition matrix, w_k is an Nx1 process noise vector with N(0, σ_w^2), t_k is Mx1 measurement vector, H is MxM measurement matrix, and r_k is Mx1 measurement noise vector with N(0, σ_r^2). To estimate the process, Kalman filter uses a form of feedback control as shown in Fig. 2 [4]. We define $\hat{s}_k^-$, $\hat{s}_k$, p_k^- and p_k as the priori state estimate, posteriori state estimate, priori estimate error covariance, and posteriori estimate error covariance, respectively. K is the Kalman gain.

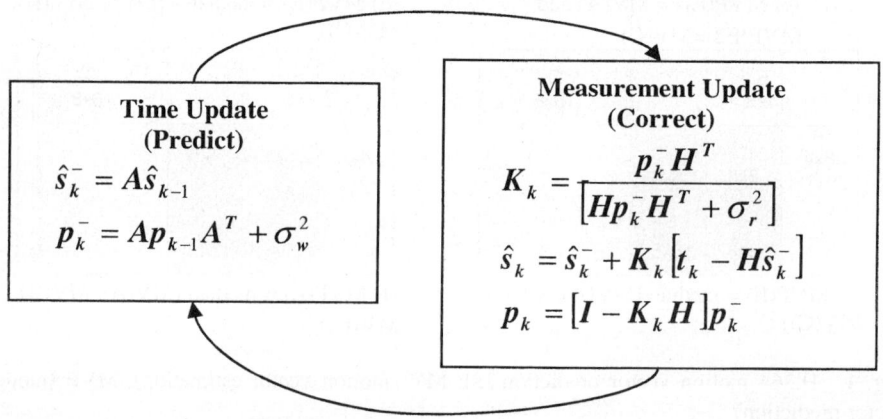

Fig. 2. Kalman filter cycle [4]

Kalman filter is very powerful, and even when the precise nature of the modeled system is unknown, we can predict the system once it has the properties that the measurement noise varies with N(0, σ^2). In H.264 video coding scheme, we use the difference between computed motion vector and predicted motion vector for each image blocks. We can assume that the motion vector difference varies with N(0, σ^2), and Kalman filter can be successful for estimate the motion vector difference.

3 Motion Vector Recovery Using Kalman Filter

From NAL (network abstraction layer) packets, we can normally get MVD and residual textures. Fig. 3 shows the modified H.264 decoder with Kalman filter based motion vector recovery for MVD loss.

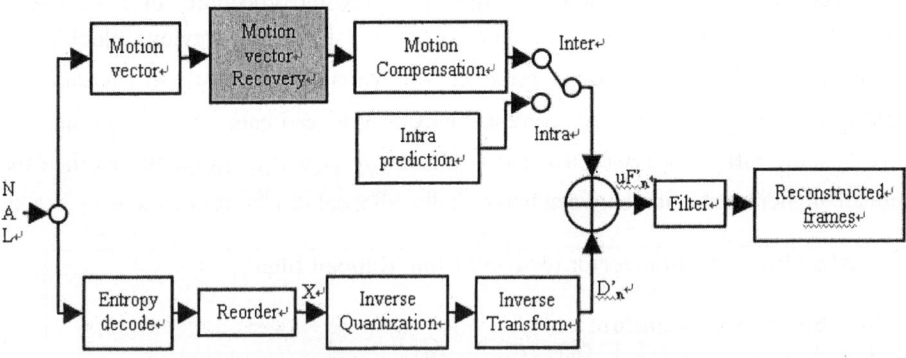

Fig. 3. Kalman filter based motion vector recovery

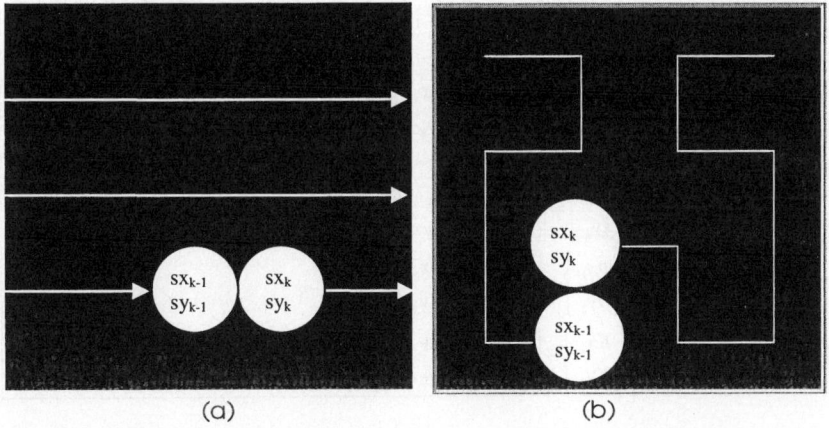

Fig. 4. Kalman prediction input sequencing design using (a) line-by-line scan order and (b) Hilbert curve scan order

We used line-by-line scanning pattern (Fig. 4(a)) for [$sx_0, sx_1, ..., sx_{k-1}, sx_k...$] sequencing. However, we can use a different scanning as shown in Fig. 4(b), to maximize the inter-correlation between MV estimates. If we don't get MVD because of the error occurrence, we predict MV to recover the lost MV.

In our Kalman prediction model, we define the state s = [sx, sy] as the MV estimate, and we can establish a state model as in (2). Likewise, we define the measurement t = [tx, ty] as in (3). We used MVP(E) for the measurement input [tx, ty].

$$sx_k = a_1 sx_{k-1} + wx_{k-1} \qquad sy_k = b_1 sy_{k-1} + wy_{k-1} \qquad (2)$$
$$wx_{k-1} \sim N(0, \sigma_w^2) \qquad wy_{k-1} \sim N(0, \sigma_w^2)$$
$$\sigma_w^2 = E[(wx)^2] = E[(wy)^2]$$

$$tx_k = sx_k + rx_k \qquad ty_k = sy_k + ry_k \qquad (3)$$
$$rx_k \sim N(0, \sigma_r^2) \qquad ry_k \sim N(0, \sigma_r^2)$$
$$\sigma_r^2 = E[(rx_k)^2] = E[(ry_k)^2]$$

To recover lost motion vectors, we use the following procedure. In Time Update step, we compute a priori MV estimate [$\hat{sx}_k^-, \hat{sy}_k^-$] from the previous block's MV estimate [$\hat{sx}_{k-1}, \hat{sy}_{k-1}$], and also a priori error covariance as in (4). In Measurement Update step, we compute the current block's MV estimate [$\hat{sx}_k, \hat{sy}_k$] and the corresponding error covariance using (5). We set $\sigma_w^2 = 0.75$, $\sigma_r^2 = 0.25$. We assume that there are higher correlation between horizontally adjacent blocks, and set $a_1 = b_1 = 0.98$.

Algorithm: Motion vector recovery using Kalman filter

Step 0: **Initialization:**
$$\begin{bmatrix} sx_0 \\ sy_0 \end{bmatrix} = \begin{bmatrix} 0 \\ 0 \end{bmatrix}, \quad \begin{bmatrix} px_0 \\ py_0 \end{bmatrix} = \begin{bmatrix} 0 \\ 0 \end{bmatrix}$$

Step 1: **Time Update:**
$$\begin{bmatrix} \hat{sx}_k^- \\ \hat{sy}_k^- \end{bmatrix} = \begin{bmatrix} a_1 & 0 \\ 0 & b_1 \end{bmatrix} \begin{bmatrix} \hat{sx}_{k-1} \\ \hat{sy}_{k-1} \end{bmatrix} \qquad (4)$$

$$\begin{bmatrix} px_k^- \\ py_k^- \end{bmatrix} = \begin{bmatrix} a_1 & 0 \\ 0 & b_1 \end{bmatrix} \begin{bmatrix} px_x \\ py_{k-1} \end{bmatrix} \begin{bmatrix} a_1 & 0 \\ 0 & b_1 \end{bmatrix}^T + \sigma_w^2$$

Step 2: **Measurement Update:**
$$\begin{bmatrix} \hat{sx}_k \\ \hat{sy}_k \end{bmatrix} = \begin{bmatrix} \hat{sx}_x^- \\ \hat{sy}_k^- \end{bmatrix} + \begin{bmatrix} Kx_k \cdot (tx_k - \hat{sx}_k^-) \\ Ky_k \cdot (ty_k - \hat{sy}_k^-) \end{bmatrix} \qquad (5)$$

$$\begin{bmatrix} px_k \\ py_k \end{bmatrix} = \begin{bmatrix} (1 - Kx_k \cdot px_x^-) \\ (1 - Ky_y \cdot py_y^-) \end{bmatrix}$$

$$\begin{bmatrix} Kx_k \\ Ky_k \end{bmatrix} = \begin{bmatrix} px_k^- / (px_k^- + \sigma_r^2) \\ py_k^- / (py_k^- + \sigma_r^2) \end{bmatrix}$$

---

4 Experimental Results

We evaluated our motion vector recovery schemes with the standard test sequences: Mobile&Calendar and Susie. We compared H.264 motion vector prediction with

(a) Mobile&Calendar: 56th frame.　　　　(b) Susie: 117th frame.

Fig. 5. Lost motion vector error profile for Mobile&Calendar and Susie

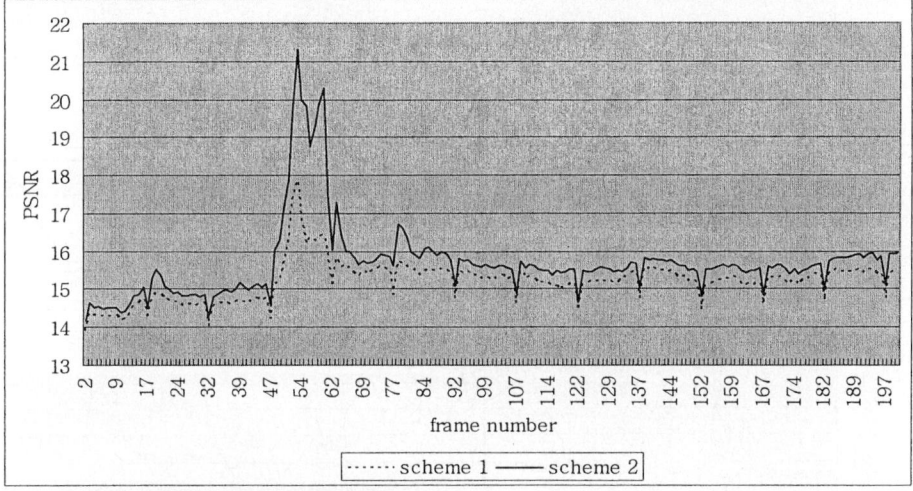

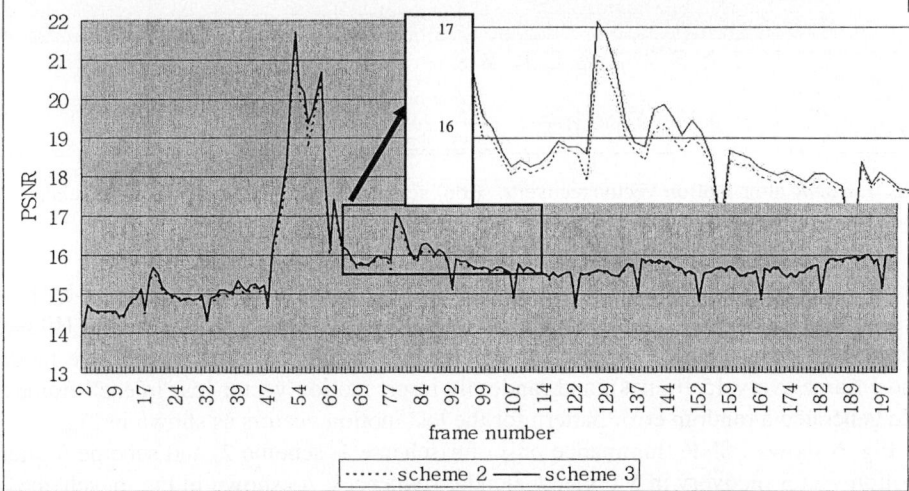

Fig. 6. PSNR after motion vector recovery: (top) scheme 1 and scheme 2, (bottom) scheme 2 and scheme 3 for Mobile&Calendar sequence with average error rate=9.9%

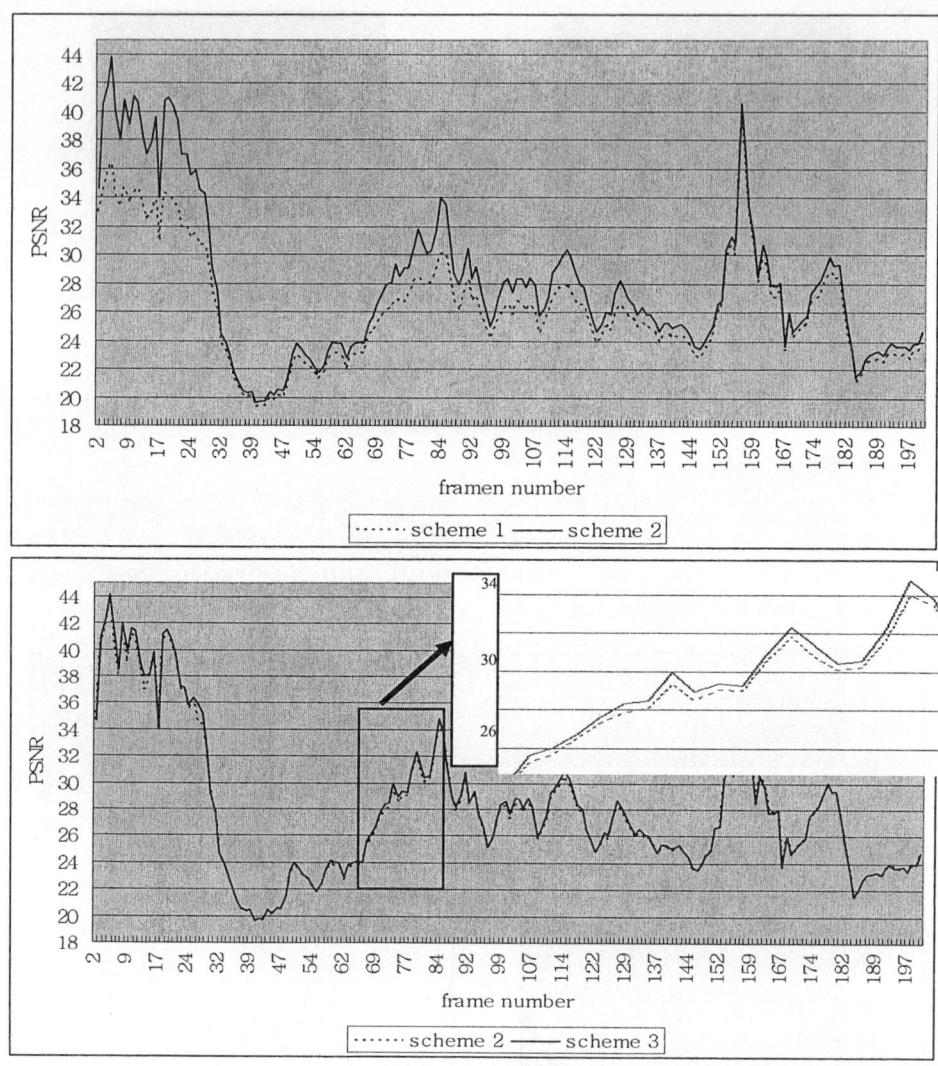

Fig. 7. PSNR after motion vector recovery: (top) scheme 1 and scheme 2, (bottom) scheme 2 and scheme 3 for Susie sequence with average error rate = 8.93%

MVD loss (scheme 1), Kalman filter based motion vector prediction with line-by-line scan input (scheme 2), and Kalman filter based motion vector prediction with Hilbert curve scan input (scheme 3). We used H.264 video compression (no B frame mode and I frame every 15 frames), and randomly insert motion vector loss in each frames. We generated a random error pattern for the lost motion vectors as shown in Fig. 5.

Fig. 6 shows PSNR (luminance only) for scheme 1, scheme 2, and scheme 3 after motion vector recovery in Mobile&Calendar sequences. As shown in Fig. 6, scheme 2 is better than scheme 1 with 0.179 dB – 3.894 dB improvements, and scheme 3 shows 0.002 dB – 0.594 dB improvements over scheme 2.

Fig. 8. Subjective comparison for Mobile&Calendar: (a) No error, (b) scheme 1: PSNR=16.377 dB, (c) scheme 2: PSNR=18.772 dB, (d) scheme 3: PSNR=19.365 dB

Fig. 7 shows PSNR (luminance only) for scheme 1, scheme 2, and scheme 3 after motion vector recovery in Susie sequences. As shown in Fig. 7, scheme 2 is better than scheme 1 with 0.292 dB – 7.403 dB improvements, and scheme 3 shows -0.446 dB – 1.652 dB improvements over scheme 2.

Fig. 8 and Fig. 9 compare the image quality for scheme 1, scheme 2, and scheme 3 in Mobile&Calendar and Susie sequences. As shown in Fig. 8 and Fig. 9, scheme 2 and scheme 3 are better than scheme 1 in subjective quality, and scheme 3 is usually better than scheme 2. However, scheme 2 is better than or equal to scheme 3 when there is much motion. In that case, we cannot get the advantages of Hilbert curve to maximize the local inter-correlation between adjacent blocks' motion vectors.

For detailed subjective quality, we enlarged the image regions. Fig. 10(b) shows the region, in which scheme 2 is better than scheme 3 (calendar details in (b) are

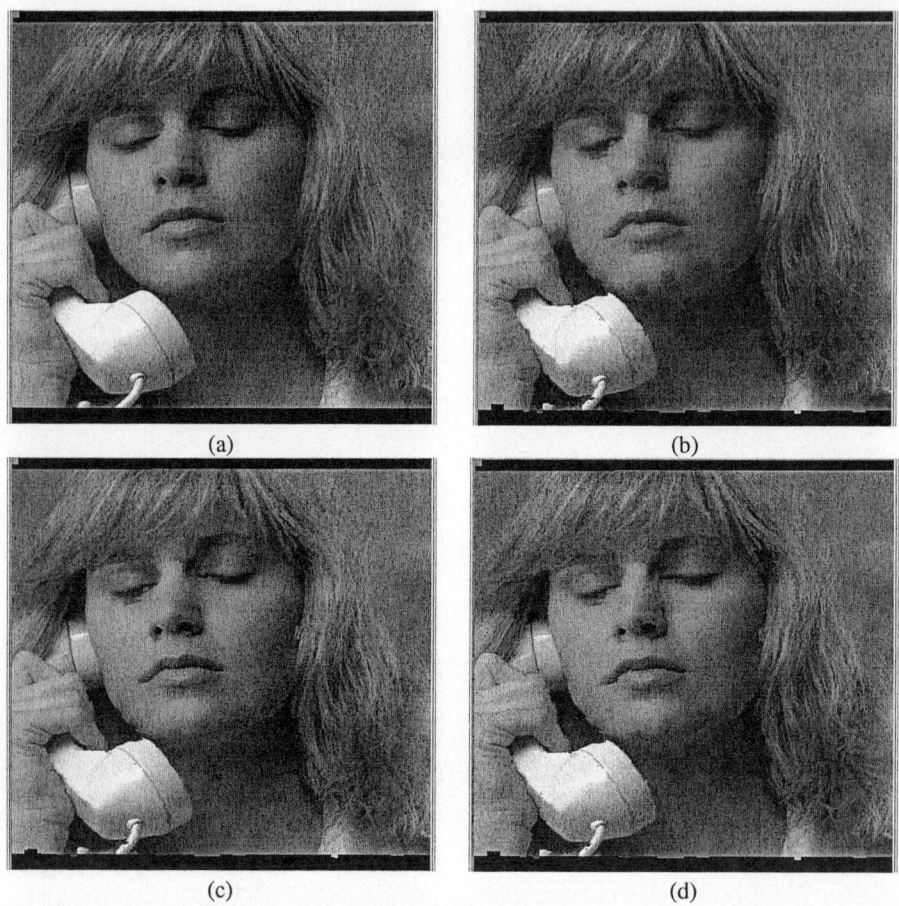

Fig. 9. Subjective comparison for Susie: (a) No error, (b) scheme 1: PSNR=26.497 dB, (c) scheme 2: PSNR=27.976 dB, (d) scheme 3: PSNR=28.357 dB

better than (c)). In this case, the area of calendar's number in Fig. 10(b) are better than in Fig. 10(c), because the real motion of calendar in Mobile&Calendar moves from left to right. Therefore it makes scheme 2 outperforms scheme 3. Fig. 10(e) shows the region, in which scheme 2 is better than scheme 3 (face details in (e) are better than (f)). In this case, the area of Susie's noise and eye in Fig. 10(e) are better than in Fig. 10(f), because the real motion of Susie's face moves from left to right. Therefore it makes scheme 2 outperforms scheme 3.

Fig. 11(c) shows the region, in which scheme 3 is better than scheme 2 (edge details along the ball is missing in scheme 2). In this case, the motions of ball and train move from right to left, which is inverse direction to usual line-by-line scan order. Fig. 11(f) shows that the edge details are preserved in the scheme 3 case because the motion of phone moves from down to up.

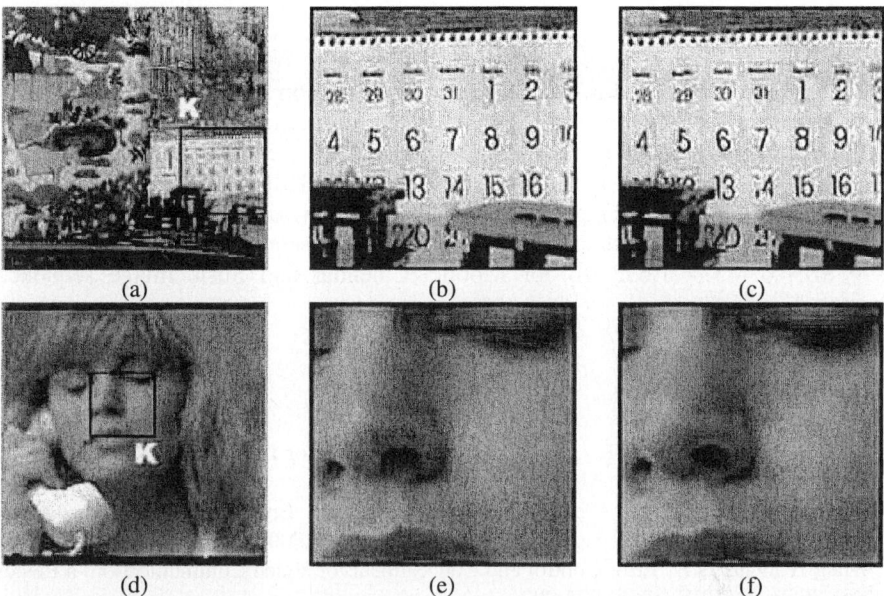

Fig. 10. Regions where scheme 2 is better than scheme 3. (a, d) show the regions, (b, e) show the result from scheme 2, (c, f) show the result from scheme 3

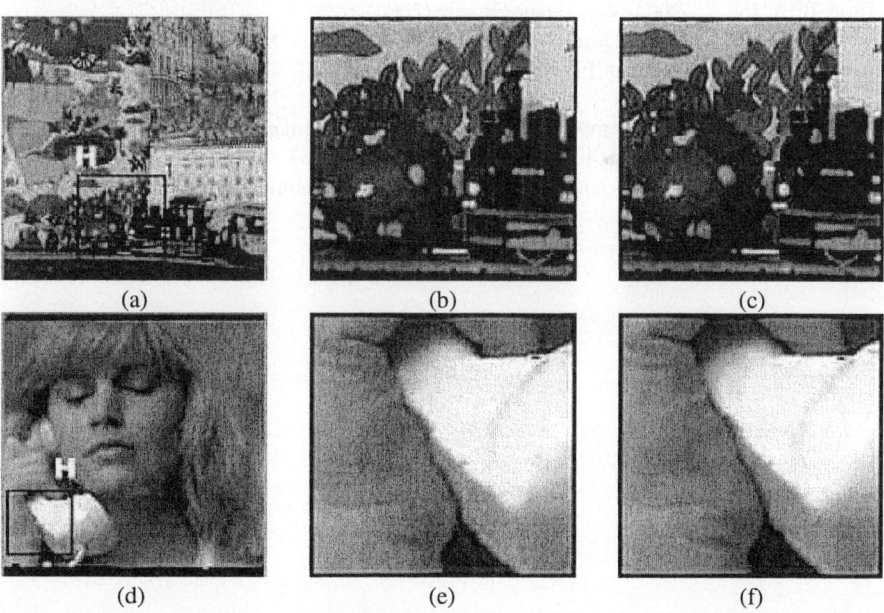

Fig. 11. Regions where scheme 3 is better than scheme 2: (a, d) the regions, (b, e) show scheme 2 enlarged, (c, f) shows scheme 3 enlarged

5 Conclusions

In this paper, we proposed a Kalman filter based motion vector recovery technique. From our definition of Kalman model for the motion vector recovery, we used H.264 motion vector prediction for our measurement input. To exploit the inter-correlation between adjacent blocks' motion vectors, we used Hilbert curve scan order for Kalman filter input sequencing. We showed that motion vector recovery using Hilbert curve scan order is better than line-by-line scan input sequencing more than 0.179 − 3.894 dB, -0.445 − 1.652 dB for Mobile&Calendar and Susie image sequences, respectively.

References

1. Lam, W.M., Reibman, A.R., Liu, B.: Recovery of Lost or Erroneously Received Motion Vectors, Proc. ICASSP'93, Minneapolis, MN 417-420
2. Wang, Y., Wenger, S., Wen, J., Katsaggelos, A.K.: Error Resilient Video Coding Techniques, Vol. 17. IEEE Signal Processing Magazine (2000) 61-82
3. Wang, Y., Zhu, Q.F.: Error Control and Concealment for Video Communication: a Review, Vol. 86. Proc. IEEE (1998) 974-997
4. Welch, G., Bishop, G.: An Introduction to The Kalman Filters, available in http://www.cs.unc.edu/~welch/kalman/index.html
5. Gao, Z.W., Lie, W.N.: Video Error Concealment by using Kalman-Filtering Technique, Proc. IEEE ISCAS-2004, Vancouver Canada (2004)
6. Kuo, C.M., Hsieh, C.H., Jou, Y.D., Lin, H.C., Lu, P.C.: Motion Estimation for Video Compression using Kalman Filtering, Vol. 42. No. 2. IEEE Trans. on Broadcasting (1996) 110-116
7. Aign, S. and Fazel, K.: Temporal & spatial error concealment techniques for hierarchical MPEG-2 video codec, Proc. Globecom'95(1995) 1778-1783
8. Richardson, I.E.G.: H.264 and MPEG-4 Video Compression, John Wiley & Sons (2003) 170-176

High Efficient Context-Based Variable Length Coding with Parallel Orientation

Qiang Wang[1], Debin Zhao[1,2], Wen Gao[1,2], and Siwei Ma[2]

[1] Department of Computer Science and Technology, Harbin Institute of Technology,
Harbin 150001, China
{qwang, dbzhao}@jdl.ac.cn
[2] Institute of Computing Technology, Chinese Academy of Science,
Beijing 100080, China
{wgao, swma}@jdl.ac.cn

Abstract. Entropy coding is one of the most important techniques in video codec. Two main criteria to assess an entropy coder are coding efficiency and friendly realization characteristic. In the recent development of the H.264/AVC standard, a sophisticated entropy coder, named Context-based Adaptive Variable Length Coding (CAVLC), has been invented, which supplies higher coding efficiency than other VLC-based entropy coders in previous video coding standards. But due to its algorithm's inherit traits CAVLC must be executed in a sequential manner, which results in relative low throughput rate. In this paper, a new well-designed context-based VLC entropy coder for transform coefficients is presented. It exploits coefficient block's inner context information to obtain high coding efficiency, and at the same time context models for successive coding elements are designed to be dependent-free so that the coder is more apt to be parallel. Experimental results show that the proposed entropy coder can exhibit the same coding efficiency as CAVLC. Therefore, a new high performance entropy coder with characteristics of parallel orientation and high coding efficiency is supplied.

1 Introduction

Block-based hybrid video coding framework has been widely employed in video coding standards including the newest H.264/AVC specification [1]. Its key techniques are prediction, transform & quantization, and entropy coding, which serve as eliminating inter-frame, intra-frame and statistical redundancy, respectively. More concretely for entropy coding part, the way it is implemented is to perform a uniquely decodable mapping operation from source symbol to binary codeword and at the same time aim to use minimal bit rate to fulfill this task. There are two major entropy coding methods, commonly referred as variable length coding (VLC) and arithmetic coding. Arithmetic coding makes use of joint probability of multiple symbols to obtain higher coding efficiency, but its fatal disadvantage is high implementation complexity. So VLC-based entropy coder is popular with its reasonable complexity and acceptable efficiency, and has been widely realized in market products.

For VLC coding of quantized transform coefficients in a video coder, a common technique, Zig-Zag scan, is used to translate two-dimensional transform coefficient block into data pairs of zero coefficients' run-length (*Run*) and nonzero coefficient (*Level*) [2]. Mpeg-2, H.263 and Mpeg-4 all adopt this technique. And their VLC tables are therefore designed to try to match the length of VLC codeword to the entropy of (*Run, Level*) pair to gain high coding efficiency (In H.263 and Mpeg-4 (*Run, Level, Last*) is used, *Last* indicating whether current coefficient is the last nonzero one in a block). But they ignore a kind of important context information exiting in coefficient block, that is, the coefficients at block's left-up corner usually have larger magnitude than those at right-down corner and similarly zero coefficients more frequently occur at right-down corner. To get further coding efficiency, CAVLC exploits this kind of context information and is well designed to bring coding efficiency improvement about 0.1~1.0dB at different bit-rate [3] [4].

Strength of CAVLC is its high coding efficiency, but its weakness is it is very difficult to be parallel implemented. This comes from its method of utilizing context information in a tightly dependency way so that a following element's encoding / decoding process can not be started until the encoding / decoding cycle of preceding element is completed. So the processing speed of encoding and decoding module for CAVLC will be a bottleneck for further throughput rate, which will be more serious especially at the decoder side when other following modules are fast enough. This paper focuses on this problem, trying to endow a VLC-based entropy coder with parallel traits while keeping the same high coding efficiency as CAVLC. By developing a new mechanism of utilizing context information, this problem is resolved. For *Run* coding context models are appearance order based and for *Level* coding position-based context models are used. Based on such context models, context-adaptive dependencies between successive coding elements are eliminated. We will see the proposed coder is very efficient, possessing the traits of both parallel orientation and high coding efficiency.

The paper is organized as follows. Section 2 describes CAVLC algorithm in H.264/AVC and analyzes its disability for parallel realization. Section 3 gives the proposed VLC entropy coder including how to build context models and its feasibility for parallel implementation. Section 4 gives coding efficiency comparison among popular VLC entropy coders. And at last the paper is concluded in section 5.

2 CAVLC in H.264/AVC

2.1 Algorithm Description of CAVLC

The major features of CAVLC include: 1) *Level* and *Run* are coded separately, 2) *Level* and *Run* are coded in reverse Zig-Zag scan order with multiple tables adaptive switching, 3) other coding elements able to be context-based encoded such as the number of total nonzero coefficients (substituting for the traditional EOB, End Of Block). In detail there are following coding elements in CAVLC: (1) *TotalCoeff:* number of nonzero coefficients in a 4x4 block, (2) *T1s:* number of successive coefficients with magnitude equal to 1 from the end of *Level* sequence (maximum is limited to 3), (3) *Level:* a nonzero coefficient, (4) *TotalZeros:* number of total zero coefficients before the last nonzero coefficient, (5) *Run_before:* number of successive zero coefficients before a nonzero coefficient.

Further more, an example is given in Figure 1 to exemplify these coding elements' meaning. Additionally it also demonstrates a 4x4 coefficient block is expressed into the form of *Run_before* and *Level* sequence with Zig-Zag scan technique. Corresponding to Figure 1, execution flowchart of CAVLC is shown in Figure 2.

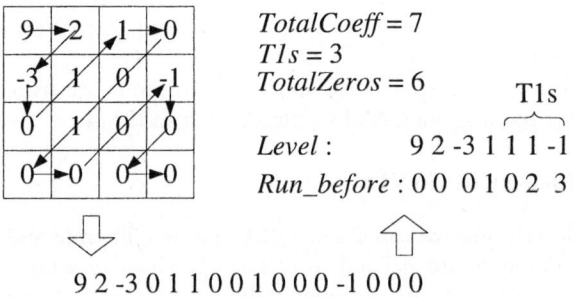

Fig. 1. An example of coding elements in CAVLC

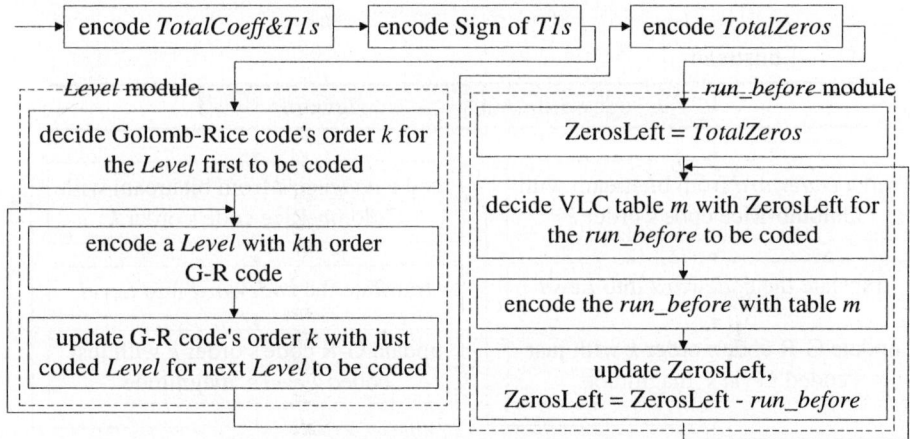

Fig. 2. Block diagram of CAVLC algorithm

From Figure 2 we can see CAVLC adopts coding order as firstly *TotalCoeff&T1s*, then *T1s* coefficients' sign information, *Level*, *TotalZeros* and at last *Run_before*. Most of these elements are context-based encoded. *TotalCoeff* and *T1s* are jointly coded by a specific VLC table selected among multiple tables based on the neighboring blocks' *TotalCoeff* information. *TotalCoeff* is a good context indicator which can reflect motion and texture properties of local areas with less dependency on quantization step size and particular video sequence. More importantly it also serves as helpful context information for coding the following elements. *Level* is encoded with Golomb-Rice (G-R) [5] codes and in reverse Zig-Zag scan order to exploit the increasing tendency of nonzero coefficients' magnitude. In this process the order of

G-R codes is dynamically updated according to previous coded *Level*'s magnitude, which can improve probability matching's precision so for higher coding efficiency. *TotalZeros* are coded based on *TotalCoeff*. For example, in a 4x4 block the maximum value of *TotalZeros* is 10 if *TotalCoeff* equal to 6. So that for a particular *TotalCoeff* CAVLC has a specific VLC table to encode *TotalZeros*. *Run_before* is coded based on the context of number of zero coefficients left to be coded (ZerosLeft) and also in reverse Zig-Zag scan order. After a *Run_before* is coded, ZerosLeft is reduced which corresponds to the possible value range that following *Run_before* can be equal to is shrunk. So CAVLC has different VLC tables for different ZerosLeft instances. For more detailed description about CAVLC, please refer to [3] [4].

2.2 Parsing Bottleneck of CAVLC

From the above description we can see CAVLC has an elaborate and thorough design for what coding elements are needed to efficiently signal a whole block of coefficients. These coding elements are designed with consideration of their ability of being context-based encoded and ability of bringing effective context information to efficiently assist following coding elements' coding. So CAVLC is like a small tightly self-dependant system and is able to deeply exploit inner-block correlation.

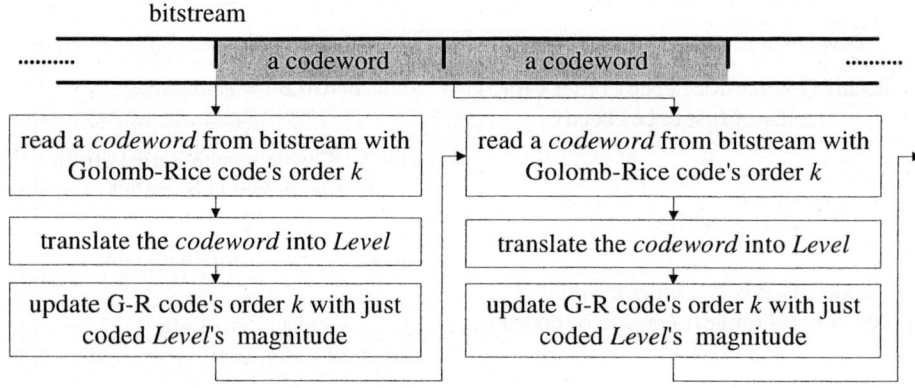

Fig. 3. The sequential parsing manner when *Level* is decoded

But the close dependency between successive coding elements also results in bad influence on realization. The resulted problem is the difficulty of CAVLC's parallel implementation. This problem will be more serious at decoder side when other modules, such as transform and quantization, motion compensation and so on, are fast enough to wait the output of VLC decoding for beginning their process. We call this as parsing bottleneck. Its reason lies in the sequential parsing manner inherent in CAVLC's serial dependency between context models, which determines only after all procedures of decoding the preceding coding elements are finished can the following elements start to decode. Figure 3 shows a bitstream containing *Level* information must be sequential parsed due to G-R code's order k for next *Level* can be decided only when the preceding *Level*'s magnitude is got. The similar instance also exits in decoding *Run_before*. So it is expected that bitstream can be parallel interpreted to improve CAVLC parsing throughput rate.

3 Context-Based VLC with Parallel Orientation

Context information in coefficient block exists there constantly, but a different utilizing method will make the VLC coder behave in different ways. So the task of new coder design currently is to find a new mechanism of utilizing context information to obtain high coding efficiency and at the same time avoid inability of parallel implementation. This section will first propose a new approach of exploiting context information and then based on corresponding context models a new context-based VLC entropy coder for transform coefficients is built. Analysis about its parallel realization is also given.

3.1 A New Way of Exploiting Context Information

It is a well-known observation that as DCT subband frequency increases, the magnitude of nonzero coefficient gets smaller and the run-length of successive zero coefficients becomes longer, which also has been pointed out in [6]. From upper description, we can see CAVLC in H.264/AVC exploits this kind of context. When encoding *Level*, it regards a *Level* increase (here "increase" is defined as in reverse Zig-Zag scan order a *Level* occurs with bigger magnitude than all ever *Level*s) as a context indicator. That is to say, a *Level* increase will bring coder into a new state in which the probability distribution of *Level*s to be encoded is different with the former and a new set of VLC codewords (or another k^{th} order G-R codes) should be applied to fulfill encoding. So CAVLC exploits context information when coding level by defining some threshold values for *Level*'s magnitude to identify the new context appearance. Similarly, CAVLC employs ZerosLeft to identify new context cases for *Run_before* coding.

Another way of exploiting context information or identifying different coding states for *Level*'s context-based adaptive coding is to utilize *Level*'s position information (here 'position' is numbered in Zig-Zag scan order. For example in Figure 1 the position of *Level* '-3' is 2). This is a straightforward idea. [7] has used it to improve the performance of JPEG entropy coder. Due to the characteristic of energy compact of DCT transform or unequal quantization, the positions adjacent to up-left corner of coefficient block usually contain larger magnitude coefficients. So it is reasonable to use position information as context indicator, but it is not enough. When blocks contain different number of nonzero coefficients, the *Level*s even in the same position will have different statistical probability distribution. Table 1 and Table2 list the probability distribution of *Level*'s magnitude at conditions of different coefficient position and different nonzero coefficient number. It can be seen that the statistical characteristics of same coefficient positions show big difference when *TotalCoeff* is different. The data in Table 1 results from Mobile&Calender test sequence in CIF format and Table 2 comes from Foreman test sequence in QCIF format. Similar data can also been obtained in other sequences. So it is necessary to view the same position in cases of different nonzero coefficient number as separate instances, and jointly use position and nonzero coefficients' number to identify different context states.

Table 1. Probability distribution of *Level*'s magnitude at conditions of different position and different nonzero coefficient number in Mobile&Calendar CIF sequence

Abs(*Level*)	*TotalCoeff* = 4			*TotalCoeff* = 10		
	Position = 0	4	11	0	4	11
1	0.796	0.864	0.908	0.509	0.445	0.581
2	0.149	0.120	0.083	0.248	0.278	0.261
3	0.034	0.014	0.007	0.104	0.137	0.098
4	0.011	0.002	0.001	0.050	0.064	0.035
5	0.004	0.000	0.000	0.026	0.030	0.013
…	…	…	…	…	…	…

Table 2. Probability distribution of *Level*'s magnitude at conditions of different position and different nonzero coefficient number in Foreman QCIF sequence

Abs(*Level*)	*TotalCoeff* = 4			*TotalCoeff* = 10		
	Position = 0	4	11	0	4	11
1	0.585	0.867	0.968	0.353	0.430	0.654
2	0.207	0.115	0.028	0.162	0.229	0.264
3	0.093	0.013	0.002	0.097	0.123	0.049
4	0.048	0.003	0.000	0.088	0.115	0.021
5	0.023	0.000	0.000	0.075	0.035	0.007
…	…	…	…	…	…	…

For coding *Run_before*s, a simple method of exploiting context information is to use their appearance order. A later appearing *Run_before* is more adjacent to block's right-down corner so that will be more apt to be larger value. Therefore different appearance order will correspond to different context states. Its validation can be derived from the data shown in Table 1. Similarly, different number of *Run_before*s (the same as the number of nonzero coefficients) can be viewed as different cases to get more accuracy of context exploiting.

In summary, position and appearance order can be used as context indicators for *Level* and *Run_before*'s context-based adaptive coding, respectively. And using the number of nonzero coefficients can further improve context-exploiting accuracy.

3.2 Context-Based VLC with Parallel Orientation

Based on the upper context-exploiting method, a new context-based VLC entropy coder for transform coefficients can be built. Furthermore, if we carefully select and organize the needed coding elements, the new coder can be granted to the trait of parallel orientation.

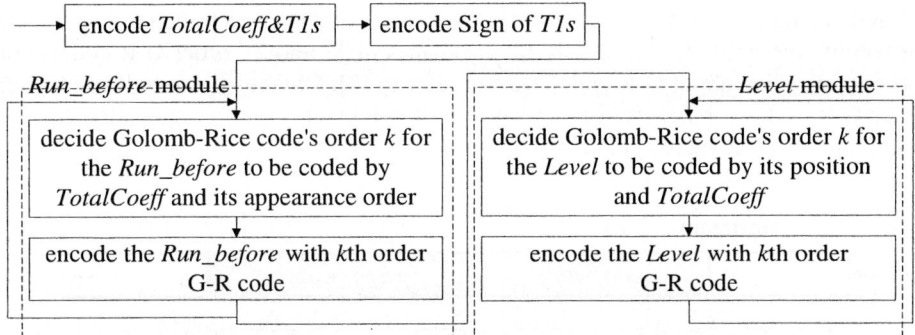

Fig. 4. Block diagram of the proposed context-based VLC coder

To achieve *Level*'s position information when *Level* is coded, *Run_before* should be arranged ahead of *Level* to encode (it is obvious that with *Run_before*s and Zig-zag scan order we can recover each *Level*'s position in coefficient block even in decoder side). And to assist context modeling for *Level* and *Run_before* it is needed to know the number of nonzero coefficients in advance. So *TotalCoeff* is an essential element. Meanwhile it is a more efficient method to express the end of block with respect to EOB. Therefore, the technique of *TotalCoeff&T1s* in H.264/AVC can be borrowed. Considering these factors, the algorithm of the proposed entropy coder is depicted in Figure 4.

Table 3. 1st and 2nd Order Golomb-Rice Codes

Codenumber (N)	Codeword			
	k = 1		k = 2	
	prefix	suffix	prefix	suffix
0	1	0	1	00
1	1	1	1	01
2	01	0	1	10
3	01	1	1	11
4	001	0	01	00
5	001	1	01	01
6	0001	0	01	10
7	0001	1	01	11
...	...	...	...	...

In the proposed coder, G-R codes are adopted for encoding *Level* and *Run_before*, although it is well known that given a source symbol set Huffman codes are optimal VLC codes. The reason for adopting G-R codes is it is not affordable to store a Huffman table for each context cases. G-R codes have regular codeword structure and can be real-time constructed without involving high computation complexity. So it is only needed to simply store G-R code's order k for each context cases to better match their probability distribution. Table 3 shows the shapes of 1st and 2nd order G-R codes. For more information about G-R codes we can refer to [3]. Obviously, we will use higher order G-R codes for *Level*s adjacent to up-left corner of a block, especially the one containing more nonzero coefficients.

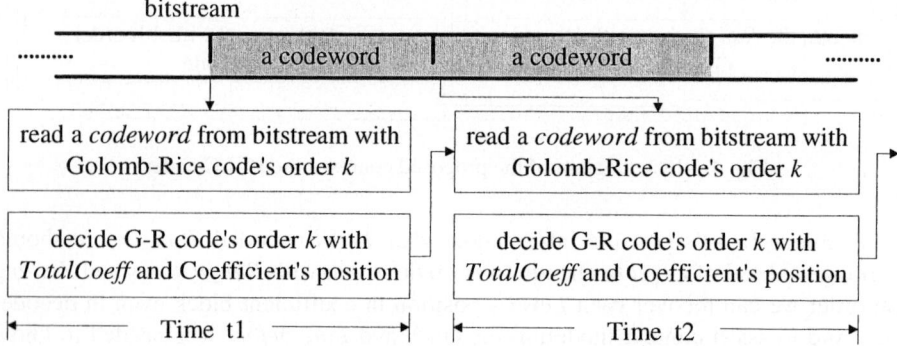

Fig. 5. The parallel parsing manner when *Level* is decoded

The proposed coder possesses the characteristic of parallel implementation. Figure 5 shows a bit-stream containing *Level* information can be parallel or pipeline parsed. From the figure we can see the prerequisite information of order k for reading a G-R codeword from bit-stream can be obtained concurrently with preceding *Level* parsed. This comes from the already decoded *Run_before*s have told each *Level*'s position information, so G-R code's order k. Elimination of tightly context dependency between successive coding elements make it possible to parallel implementation, which is an absorbing feature for realization optimization at most platforms like PC, DSP, ASIC so that the processing time is reduced. Similarly, *Run_before*s also could be parallel encoded and decoded due to context models based on appearance order.

4 Experimental Results

Coding efficiency comparison between the proposed VLC, CAVLC of H.264 and UVLC [8] is carried on. UVLC is a simple entropy coding scheme in infant time of H.264/AVC, which encode transform coefficients like the classical method in MPEG-2 but with Exponential-Golomb codes. The experiment is done at JM76 reference platform developed by JVT. And test conditions are 5 reference frames, 1/4-pixel motion vector resolution, +/-32 pixel motion search range, IPPPP mode and RDO on, which complies with the configuration of H.264 baseline profile. The test sequences include Foreman, Silent, News, Container in QCIF format and Mobile&Calendar,

Paris, Tempete in CIF format. Figure 6 shows the R-D performance of the three entropy coding schemes at most upper sequences. It can be seen the proposed VLC exhibits the same performance as CAVLC and has better performance of 0.1~0.5dB relative to UVLC in different bit-rate. Similar coding results also can be obtained in other two test sequences.

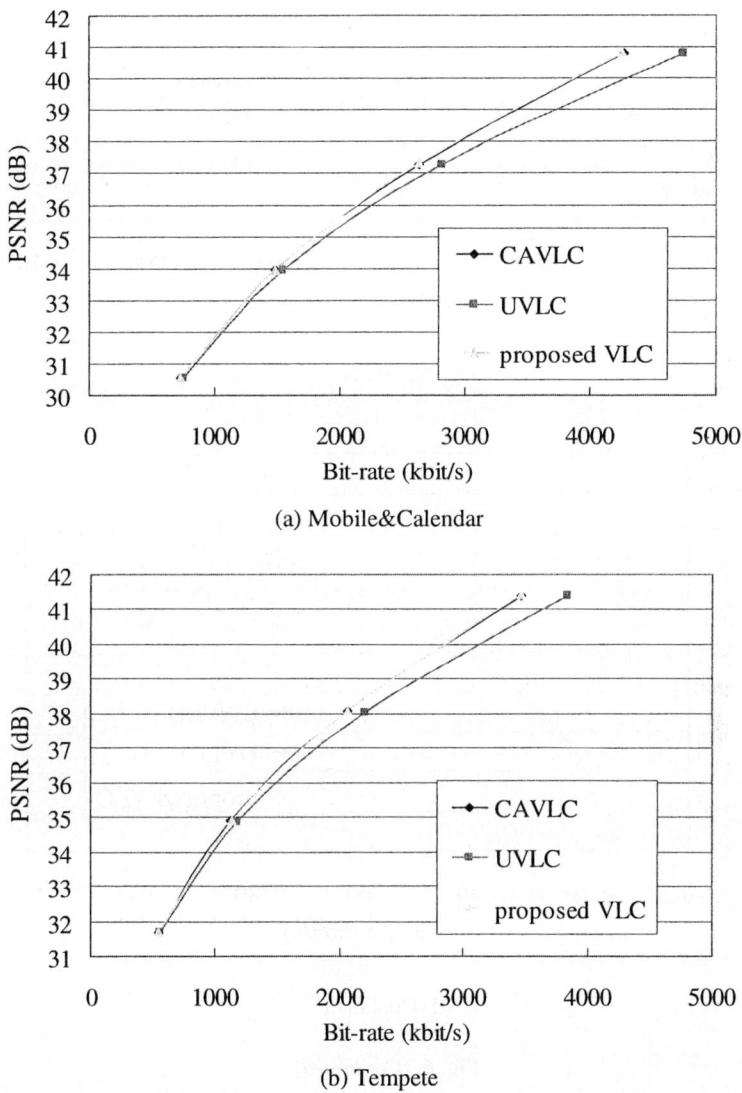

Fig. 6. Rate-Distortion performance comparison among CAVLC, UVLC and the proposed VLC on typical test sequences. (a) Mobile&Calendar sequence, (b) Tempete sequence, (c) Paris sequence, (d) Container sequence, (e) Foreman sequence.

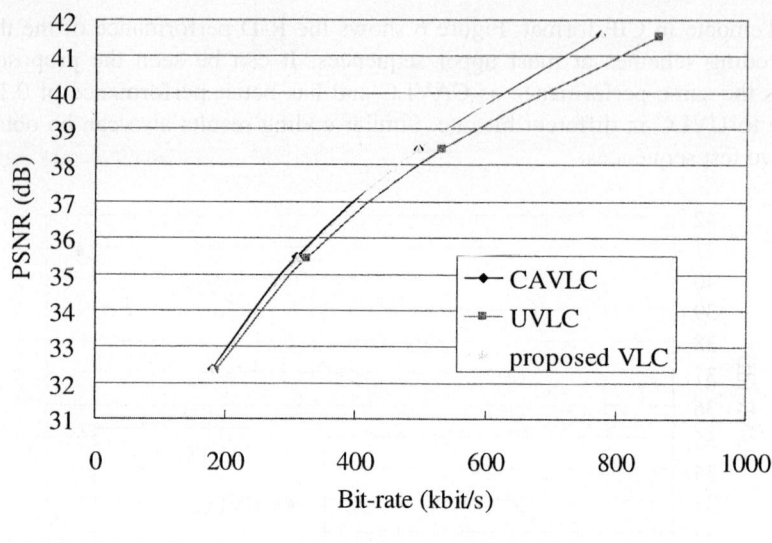

(c) Paris

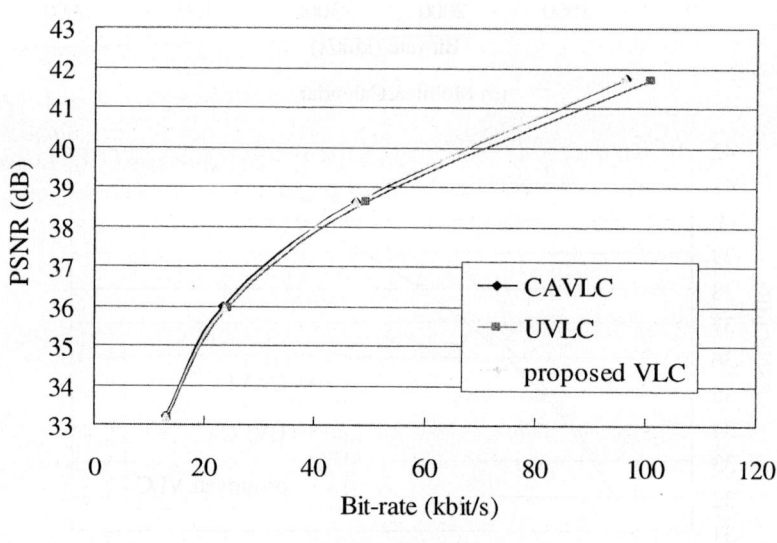

(d) Container

Fig. 6. (*Continued*)

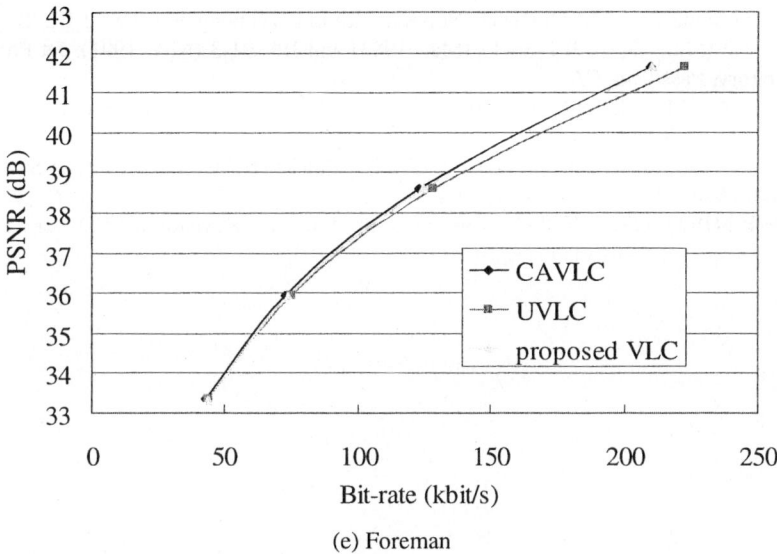

(e) Foreman

Fig. 6. (*Continued*)

5 Conclusions

This paper presents a new context-based VLC entropy coder for transform coefficients. It accomplishes high coding efficiency among VLC family, which comes from effective context models. More importantly, it also holds the characteristic of parallel implementation so that is very suitable for software- and hardware-based realization. This valuable feature is attributed to independency of context models between successive coding elements.

Acknowledgements

This work was supported in part by the National Science Foundation of China (60333020), by the National Hi-Tech Research and Development Program (863) of China (2004AA119010) and by the Beijing Science Foundation (4041003).

References

1. ISO/IEC MPEG, ITU-T VCEG: Text of ISO/IEC 14496 10 Advanced Video Cding 3rd Edition. N6540. Redmond, WA, USA (July 2004)
2. Reader, R.: History of MPEG Video Compression. JVT-EO66. Geneva (Oct. 2002)
3. Bjontegaard, G., Lillevold, K.: Context-Adaptive VLC (CVLC) Coding of Coefficients. JVT-C028. Seattle, WA, USA (May 2002)
4. Au, J.: Complexity Reduction of CAVLC. JVT-D034. Klagenfurt, Austria (July 2002)

5. Rice, R.: Some Practical Universal Noiseless Coding Techniques – Part I-III. Tech. Rep. JPL-79-22 (Mar. 1979), JPL-83-17 (Mar. 1983) and JPL-91-3 (Nov. 1991). Jet Propulsion Laboratory, Pasadena, CA
6. Lakhani, G.: Modified JPEG Huffman Coding. IEEE Trans. Image Processing, Vol. 12 (Feb. 2003), 159-169
7. Lakhani, G.: Optimal Huffman Coding of DCT Blocks. IEEE Trans. Circuits Syst. Video Technol., Vol. 14 (April 2004), 522-527
8. ISO/ICE MPEG, ITU-T VCEG: Working Draft Number 2 Revision 8 (WD-2 rev 8). JVT-B118r8. Geneva, Switzerland (April 2002)

Texture Coordinate Compression for 3-D Mesh Models Using Texture Image Rearrangement

Sung-Yeol Kim, Young-Suk Yoon, Seung-Man Kim,
Kwan-Heng Lee, and Yo-Sung Ho

Gwangju Institute of Science and Technology (GIST),
1 Oryong-dong, Buk-gu, Gwangju 500-712, Korea
{sykim75, ysyoon, sman, leee, hoyo}@gist.ac.kr

Abstract. Previous works related to texture coordinate coding of the three-dimensional(3-D) mesh models employed the same predictor as the geometry coder. However, discontinuities in the texture coordinates cause unreasonable prediction. Especially, discontinuities become more serious for the 3-D mesh model with a non-atlas texture image. In this paper, we propose a new coding scheme to remove discontinuities in the texture coordinates by reallocating texture segments according to a coding order. Experiment results show that the proposed coding scheme outperforms the MPEG-4 3DMC standard in terms of compression efficiency. The proposed scheme not only overcome the discontinuity problem by regenerating a texture image, but also improve coding efficiency of texture coordinate compression.

Keywords: 3-D mesh coding, texture coordinate compression, texture image rearrangement.

1 Introduction

As high-speed networks and the Internet are widely used, various multimedia services with three-dimensional(3-D) audio-visual data have been proposed, such as a realistic broadcasting, immersive 3-D games, and 3-D education tools. These multimedia applications require not only high quality visual services, but also user-friendly interactions.

The 3-D mesh model, which represents 3-D objects by geometry, connectivity, and photometry information, is popular as one of the standard representations of 3-D objects. The geometry information describes 3-D coordinates of vertices, and the connectivity information describes the topology with the incidence relations among vertices, edges and faces. The photometry information includes surface normal vectors, colors, and texture coordinates, which are the attributes of vertices needed to render the 3-D mesh model.

Various processing techniques for the 3-D mesh model have been proposed. The mesh deformation method[1] changes the 3-D mesh model into arbitrary shapes, and the mesh refinement method[2] makes 3-D surfaces more smoothly using subdivision algorithms. In addition, the mesh simplification method[3,4] is widely used to support the level-of-detail(LOD) in the 3-D scene and to transmit the 3-D mesh model data progressively. The 3-D mesh compression method[5] is one of the important techniques in the 3-D mesh processing. In general, the representation of 3-D mesh models requires a tremendous amount of data. In order to store the 3-D mesh data compactly and transmit them efficiently, we need to develop efficient coding schemes for the 3-D mesh model. Figure 1 lists the major approaches for 3-D mesh compression.

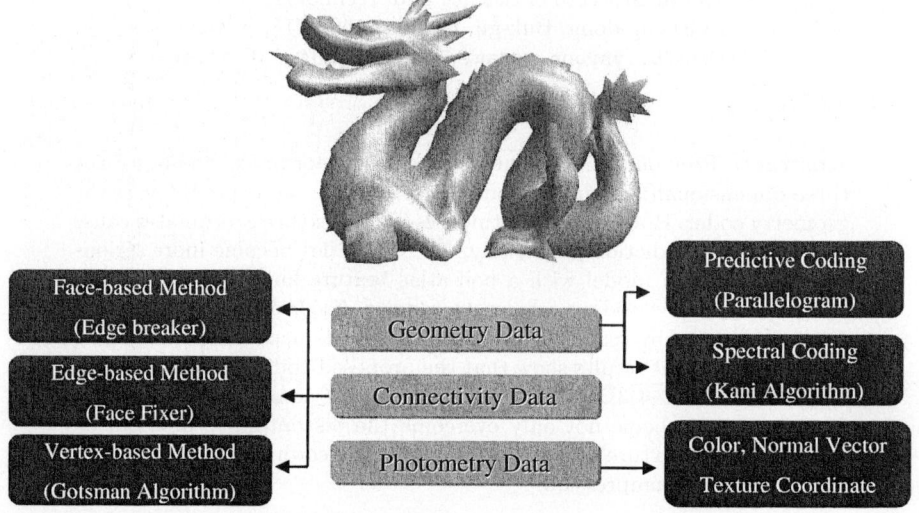

Fig. 1. Approaches for 3-D mesh compression

Previous 3-D mesh coding schemes have focused on compressing geometry and connectivity information. However, we should note that photometry information contribute around 60% to the entire 3-D model data. Especially, when we acquire a 3-D model data from a 3-D data acquisition device, such as a 3-D scanner, we usually employ a texture mapping technique with texture coordinates and texture images instead of colors. The texture mapping makes the acquired models more realistic. Moreover, since the texture coordinate data are corresponding to around 40% of the photometry data, it is necessary for us to develop an efficient texture coordinate coding technique. In this paper, we focus on compressing the texture coordinates.

This paper is organized as follows. Section 2 explains previous works, and Section 3 describes the proposed texture coordinate coding method. After we provide experimental results in Section 4, we conclude in Section 5.

2   Texture Coordinate Coding Algorithms

Texture mapping techniques are widely used to increase the realism of 3-D mesh models. Texture images and texture coordinates are needed to render a 3-D mesh model using a texture mapping technique. The 2-D texture images are mapped into every polygon of a 3-D mesh model according to its texture coordinates.

There are two types of texture images: atlas and non-atlas texture images. Atlas texture images, which assemble the segmented charts into a single texture image, are sometimes convenient to match with 3-D mesh models. Non-atlas texture images are the set of little squares, that are parameterized into a single texture. Figure 2 compares the atlas and non-atlas texture images.

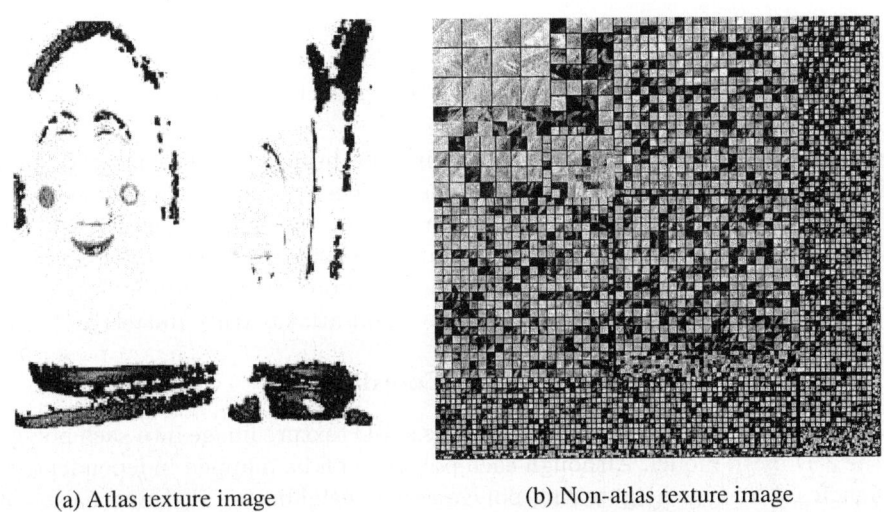

(a) Atlas texture image (b) Non-atlas texture image

Fig. 2. Atlas texture image vs. non-atlas texture image

In general, texture images are commonly coded by the JPEG standard, as still-frame images. According to the quantization design, coding efficiency and quality for texture images will be determined. In this paper, we will not consider the coding for texture images, but the coding for the texture coordinate data. In order to compress texture coordinates, previous works usually exploited the same predictor that was used to code the geometry data. Although there were some efforts to code the texture coordinates by different schemes, they did not increase coding efficiency significantly.

Deering[6] and Taubin et al.[7] traversed all the vertices according to the connectivity information, and coded texture coordinates using a linear predictor. Similarly, Touma and Gotsman[8] encoded the topology information by traversing the vertices, and texture coordinates were coded by predicting them along the traversal order using a parallelogram predictor as shown in Fig. 3. The predicted errors of the texture coordinates were entropy-coded. Isenburg[9] introduced discontinuity problem between the texture images and the texture coordinates during texture coordinate coding, and they proposed a texture coordinate coding scheme with a selective linear predictor.

Although previous texture coordinate algorithms yielded good performance on the 3-D mesh models with atlas texture images, they had problems

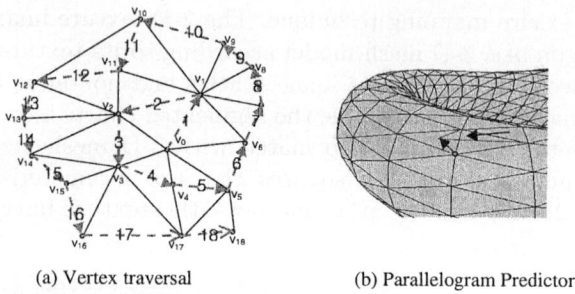

(a) Vertex traversal (b) Parallelogram Predictor

Fig. 3. Vertex traversal and predictive coder

for 3-D models with non-atlas texture images because of discontinuity problem. For realistic multimedia applications, we need to obtain 3-D mesh models from 3-D data acquisition devices to increase the realism. In general, when we obtain 3-D mesh models from a 3-D data acquisition device, most 3-D mesh models include non-atlas texture images. Therefore, we should develop a good coding scheme for texture coordinates with non-atlas texture images.

2.1 Discontinuity in the Texture Coordinates

Texture mapping is a procedure that maps a 2-D texture image into each polygon of the 3-D mesh model. Although each polygon can be mapped independently, it is beneficial to map neighboring polygons into neighboring texture images. We call the process for obtaining suitable texture coordinates as texture parametrization. The texture coordinates are generated through the texture parametrization between vertex coordinates and texture images. The 3-D mesh models with non-atlas texture images cause the texture parametrization to be broken.

When we code the texture coordinates with non-atlas texture images along a vertex traversal order, the coded texture coordinates will be sorted out in an unreasonable order, called as discontinuity in texture coordinates. The predicted

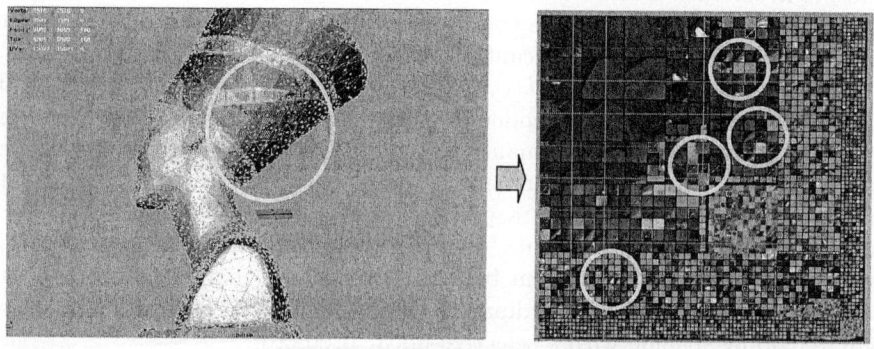

Fig. 4. Discontinuity in texture coordinates

errors of texture coordinates will be increased when we compress the texture coordinates by a predictive coding scheme owing to the discontinuities. As a result, discontinuities in the texture coordinates deteriorate coding efficiency drastically. Figure 4 shows discontinuities in the texture coordinates.

3 Texture Coordinate Coding with Texture Image Rearrangement

In this paper, we propose a new predictive coding scheme for texture coordinate compression using a texture image rearrangement. The main contribution of our proposed scheme is that we remove the discontinuity in the texture coordinates before employing a predictive coder to compress texture coordinates. The proposed scheme can be divided into four parts: analysis of the mesh model, analysis of the texture coordinate, rearrangement of the texture image, and predictive coding of the texture coordinate, as shown in Fig. 5.

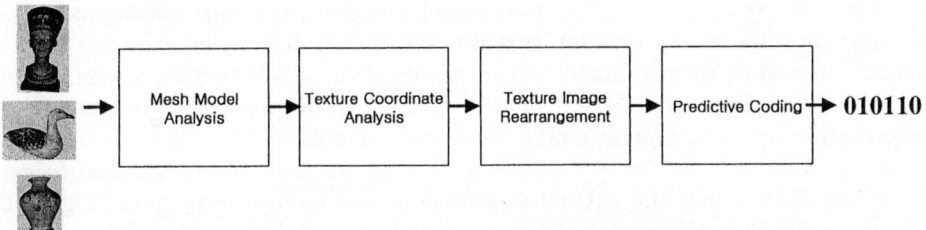

Fig. 5. Overall flow for texture coordinate compression

3.1 Analysis of the Mesh Model

Analysis of the mesh model is a process to extract a texture image and texture coordinates from the 3-D mesh model. The input data format of 3-D mesh models are usually the virtual reality modelling language(VRML)[10]. In order to analyze the 3-D mesh model, we need to obtain a texture image and texture coordinates through a VRML analyzer. From a part of the VRML file to represent the Nefertiti model, we can notice that the Nefertiti model includes a texture image and texture coordinates.

```
texture ImageTexture {
    url "nefert5_T5k1.bmp"
}

texCoord TextureCoordinate { point [
0.333008 1.13184, 0.333008 1.11621, 0.348633 1.13184,
0.192383 1.19434, 0.192383 1.20996, 0.176758 1.19434,
0.750977 1.53027,
```

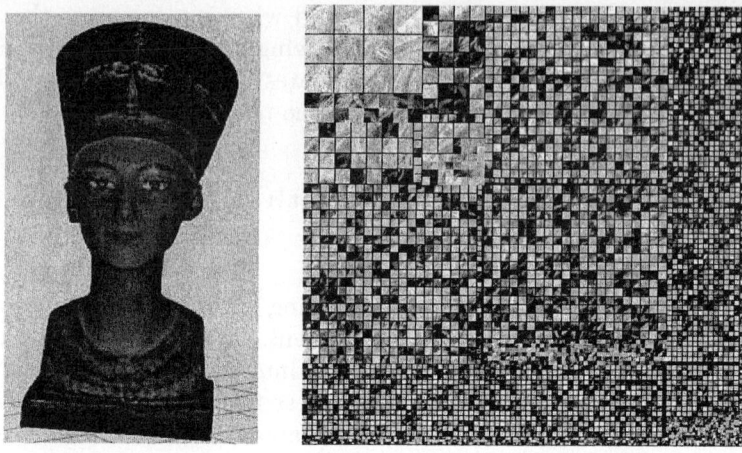

Fig. 6. Example of 3-D mesh model and its texture image

The texture image of the Nefertiti model is $nefer5_t5k1.bmp$, which has 14993 texture coordinates. In general, texture coordinates have x coordinates and y coordinates since they indicate texture positions in a 2-D texture image. With the VRML analyzer, we also extract the geometry information, the connectivity information and other photometry data, such as colors and normal vectors. In order to compress the texture coordinate data, we traverse all vertices to get a coding order using the extracted geometry and connectivity data. Figure 6 describes the Nefertiti model and its texture image.

3.2 Analysis of the Texture Coordinate

In general, texture coordinates are normalized with values between 0 and 1. In order to analyze the texture coordinate, we need to obtain exact texture positions in the texture image from normalized texture coordinates. Texture positions are obtained by multiplying the width and the height of the texture image to texture coordinates as described by Eq.1 and Eq.2.

$$x_{pos} = TextureWidth \times x_{norm} \qquad (1)$$

$$y_{pos} = TextureHeight \times y_{norm} \qquad (2)$$

After obtaining texture positions, we put the texture image and the corresponding texture positions into a memory. We may have an unpredictable problem in extraction of texture positions since the axis of the texture image can be inverse. Therefore, we should make sure that the axis of the texture image should not be inverse.

During the analysis of the texture coordinate, we search for the discontinuous points between a texture image and texture coordinates. In order to obtain the discontinuous points, we first define a searching order. In this paper, we use a vertex traversal algorithm[11,12] supported by 3-D mesh coding(3DMC) in MPEG-4 standards[13] to obtain a searching order. Before searching for discontinuous points, we should define a threshold to determine whether a texture coordinate is discontinuous or not. When distances between a texture coordinate and neighboring texture coordinates are larger than the threshold value, we regard the texture coordinate as a discontinuous point. Finally, discontinuous points are stored in a memory using a data structure.

3.3 Rearrangement of the Texture Image

By the rearrangement of the texture image, we reallocate the texture segments continuously with the discontinuity information. Texture segments are rearranged by the zig-zag order along a coding order. Before rearranging texture segments, we allocate a image buffer so as to store a regenerated texture image.

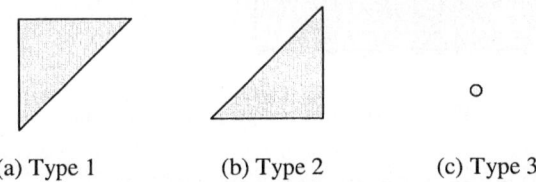

(a) Type 1   (b) Type 2   (c) Type 3

Fig. 7. Types of texture segments

In rearrangement of the texture image, we extract the texture segments corresponding to a triangle face from the texture image. After checking the data structure including the discontinuous information, we allocate texture segments into the image buffer continuously. There are three types of texture segments in non-atlas texture images as shown in Fig. 7. One has a triangle shape with lower direction. Another is a triangle shape with upper direction. The other is a point, which indicates that three texture coordinates are all the same. In order to generate a rearranged texture image, we first classify the type of texture segments. Then, we allocate texture segments into a image buffer by moving the buffer position.

The texture coordinates of a texture segment are changed according to the resolution of a regenerated texture image. In order to use the discontinuous points in a predictive coder, we indicate a flag for each discontinuous points. The flags are used for deceasing the residual errors in the predictive coder. Figure 8 shows an example of texture image rearrangement.

After rearrangement of texture image, we regenerate the texture coordinates corresponding to the reallocated texture image. As soon as we reallocate the texture segments, we calculate the texture coordinates. Finally, we normalize the texture coordinate data by dividing them with the width and height of the regenerated texture image using Eq. 3 and Eq. 4.

$$x_{norm} = x_{pos} \div NewTexutureWidth \qquad (3)$$

$$y_{norm} = y_{pos} \div NewTexutureHeight \qquad (4)$$

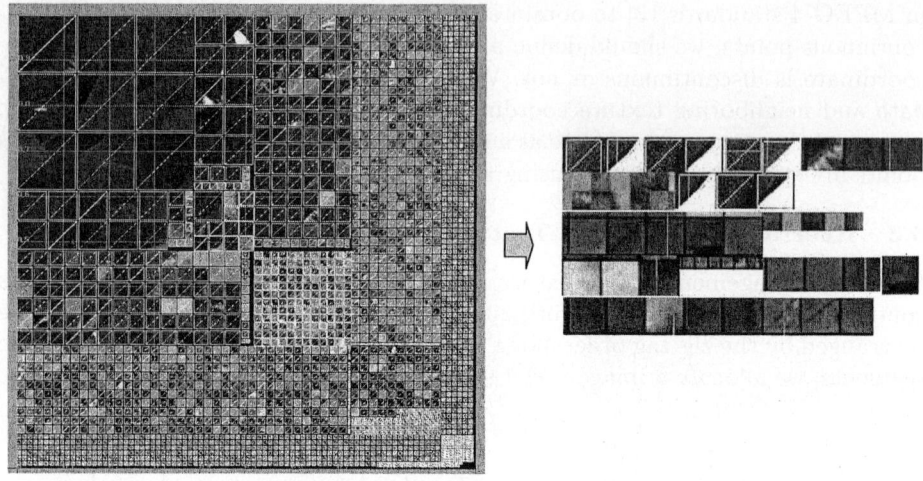

Fig. 8. Texture image rearrangement

3.4 Predictive Coding of the Texture Coordinate

For the predictive coding of texture coordinates, we obtain residual errors using MPEG-4 3DMC. The texture coordinates are coded through the parallelogram predictor along a vertex traversal order. Figure 9 shows the parallelogram predictor. In order to predict a vertex (tx_4, ty_4), we obtain a referred vertex $(tx_4, ty_4)'$ from Eq. 5.

$$(tx_4, ty_4)' = (tx_1, ty_1) + (tx_2, ty_2) - (tx_3, ty_3) \quad (5)$$

From Eq. 6, we can obtain the residual error (ex_4, ey_4). Finally, the residual errors (ex_4, ey_4) are coded through a variable length coder.

$$(ex_4, ey_4) = (tx_4, ty_4) - (tx_3, ty_3) \quad (6)$$

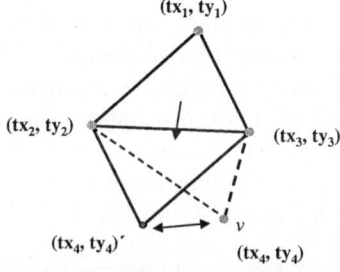

Fig. 9. Predictive coder

4 Experimental Results and Analysis

We have evaluated the proposed algorithm with the Coin model and the Nefertiti model. The Coin model consists of 1468 vertices, 2932 faces and a texture image with 512 x 512 resolutions. The Nefertiti model has 2501 vertices, 4998 faces and a texture image with 515 x 512 resolutions. The Coin model has 8796 texture coordinates and The Nefertiti model has 14993 texture coordinates. Figure 10 shows the tested models and their texture images.

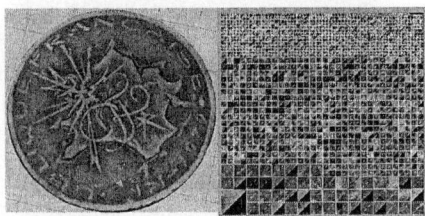

Fig. 10. Tested models and texture images

In order to compress the texture images, we used the JPEG with the quantization table suggested in the standard. Whereas, we used the 3DMC reference software implemented by the MPEG-4 standard for compressing the texture coordinate data. We experimented our proposed scheme for the tested models with a Pentium-4 personal computer including 512 MB memory and a Window operation system.

Table 1. Texture coordinates comparison between 3DMC and the proposed scheme

	3DMC		proposed scheme	
	variance of residuals	predictive coding	variance of residuals	predictive coding
Coin	25.44	168.4 KB	13.22	106.3 KB
Nefertiti	27.64	287.5 KB	14.27	184.3 KB

Table 2. Texture image comparison between 3DMC and the proposed scheme

	3DMC		proposed scheme	
	texture size	JPEG coding	texture size	JPEG coding
Coin	512x512	79 KB	512x612	91 KB
Nefertiti	512x512	96 KB	512x680	112 KB

Table 1 and Table 2 show the comparison results between the MPEG-4 3DMC standard and the proposed scheme. As we can see in Table 1, the proposed scheme had better performance than 3DMC in the texture coordinate coding, since the variances for residuals of texture coordinates along a coding order reduced after rearrangement of texture images. As a result, we could increase

Fig. 11. Rearranged texture images

coding efficiency for texture coordinate compression by a predictive coder, and we could solve the discontinuity problem of texture coordinates for the 3-D mesh models with a non-atlas texture image.

On the other hand, the size of the rearranged texture image was larger than the size of the original texture image, because the texture image was obtained by the zig-zag allocation scheme and included holes sometimes. Rearrangement of the texture image caused the coded data for the texture images to be increased, as shown in Table 2. However, the overall coding efficiency increased by about 30% on average, since the texture coordinates had more information than a texture image. Figure 11 shows the rearranged texture images for tested models. The left image is a rearranged texture image of the Coin model and the right image is for the Nefertiti model.

5 Conclusions

In this paper, we proposed a new algorithm for 3-D mesh texture coordinate coding using a texture image rearrangement. Previous 3-D mesh compression schemes focused on the geometry and connectivity data. However, we can note that photometry information contribute substantial amount in the 3-D model data. Especially, we should have an interest to the texture coordinate coding.

Previous works related to the texture coordinate coding did not consider discontinuities in the texture coordinates. In case of the 3-D mesh model with a non-atlas texture image, discontinuities are more serious. In this paper, we regenerated the texture image according to the texture coordinate coding order so as to remove the discontinuities in a non-atlas texture image. In order to compress the texture coordinate data, we extract the texture images and texture coordinate data from the 3-D mesh models. Then, we reallocate the texture images by the zig-zag order. Finally, we employ a predictive coder so as to compress the residual data along a vertex traversal order.

The proposed prediction coding scheme outperformed the MPEG-4 3DMC since we reduced the residual errors and eliminated the discontinuous points in texture coordinates. The proposed scheme not only overcame the discontinuity problem by regenerating a texture image, but also improved coding efficiency of texture coordinate compression. The proposed scheme can be used for the various multimedia applications needed 3-D mesh model transmission such as 3-D games and 3-D broadcasting systems.

Acknowledgements. This work was supported in part by Gwangju Institute of Science and Technology (GIST), in part by the Ministry of Information and Communication (MIC) through the Realistic Broadcasting Research Center (RBRC), and in part by the Ministry of Education (MOE) through the Brain Korea 21 (BK21) project.

References

1. Desbrun, M., Meyer, M., Alliez, P.: Intrinsic Parameterizations of Surface Meshes. Proceedings of EUROGRAPHICS (2002) 209-218
2. Derose, T., Kass, M., Truong, T.: Subdivision Surfaces in Character Animation. Proceedings of SIGGRAPH (1998) 85-94
3. Hoppe, H.: Progressive Meshes. Proceedings of SIGGRAPH (1996) 99-108
4. Garland, M., Heckbert, P.S.: Surface Simplification Using Quadric Error Metrics. Proceedings of SIGGRAPH (1997) 209-216
5. Rossignac, J.: Geometric Simplification and Compression. Course Notes 25 of SIGGRAPH (1997)
6. Deering, M.: Geometry Compression. Proceedings of SIGGRAPH (1995) 13-20
7. Taubin, G., Rossignac, J.: Geometric Compression through Topological Surgery. ACM Transactions on Graphics (1998) Vol. 17 84-115
8. Touma, C., Gotsman, C.: Triangle Mesh Compression. Proceedings of Graphics Interface (1998) 26-34
9. Isenburg, M., Sneoink, J.: Compressing Texture Coordinates with Selective Linear Prediction. Proceedings of Graphics Interface (2003) 126-131
10. Hartman, J., Wernecke, J.: The VRML 2.0 Handbook. Addison-Welsey Publishing Company (1996)
11. Yan, Z., Kumar, S., Li, J., Kuo, C-C.J.: Robust Coding of 3D Graphics Models using Mesh Segmentation and Data Partitioning. Proceedings of IEEE International Conference on Image Processing (1999) 25-28
12. Kim, S.Y., Ahn J.H., Ho, Y.S.: View-dependent Transmission of Three-dimensional Mesh Models Using Hicrarchical Partitioning. Proceeding on Visual Commnications and Image Processing (2003) 1928-1938
13. Taubin, G., Horn, W., Lazarus, F.: The VRML Compressed Binary Format. ISO/IEC JTC1/SC29WG11 M3062(1998)

Classification of Audio Signals Using Gradient-Based Fuzzy c-Means Algorithm with Divergence Measure

Dong-Chul Park[1], Duc-Hoai Nguyen[1], Seung-Hwa Beack[1], and Sancho Park[2]

[1] Dept. of Information Engineering, Myong Ji University, Korea
{parkd, dnguyen, signal}@mju.ac.kr
[2] Davan Tech Co., Seongnam, Korea
sancho@davan.co.kr

Abstract. Multimedia databases usually store thousands of audio files such as music, speech and other sounds. One of the challenges in modern multimedia system is to classify and retrieve certain kinds of audio from the database. This paper proposes a novel classification algorithm for a content-based audio retrieval. The algorithm, called Gradient-Based Fuzzy c-Means Algorithm with Divergence Measure (GBFCM(DM)), is a neural network-based algorithm which utilizes the Divergence Measure to exploit the statistical nature of the audio data to improve the classification accuracy. Experiment results confirm that the proposed algorithm outperforms 3.025%-5.05% in accuracy in comparison with conventional algorithms such as the k-Means or the Self-Organizing Map.

1 Introduction

Audio data processing is an integral part of many modern multimedia applications. Multimedia databases usually store thousands of audio recordings. These files may be music, speech, or other sounds. The rapid increase in the amount of audio data demands for a computerized method which allows efficient and automated content-based classification and retrieval of audio data. However, the audio is usually treated as an opaque collection of bytes with only the most primitive fields attached: name, file format, sampling rate and so on. This causes the difficulties to the users in searching and retrieving the desired data.

Basically, content-based classification and retrieval of the audio sound can be considered as a pattern recognition problem with two basic issues: feature selection and classification using selected features. Many methods have been proposed to solve this problem. One of the pioneering methods was introduced by the Muscle Fish group [1]. In this technique, acoustical features such as loudness, pitch, brightness, bandwidth, and the harmony are extracted from the audio signals. The mean and covariance computed from the training set of these multi-dimensional features are used to form the feature space. At the same time, Saunders proposed a method that employs a simple threshold of the average zero-crossing rate and energy features to discriminate speech and music signals [2]. As an alternative method, Foote [3] proposed a method that uses Mel-scaled Frequency Cepstral Coefficients (MFCCs) to construct a tree learning vector quantizer. Using the same data set, Li et. al. [4] introduced a new feature extraction scheme using discrete wavelet transform (DWT). Lu et. al. [5] proposed the use of support vector machines (SVM) for audio segmentation and classification. However, in the previous approaches, the acoustic features do not directly attempt to model music signals. Therefore, Tzanetakis et. al. [6] proposed music-oriented features such as rhythmic and pitch contents. This approach gives a very significant insight into the nature of music signals and was utilized in several subsequent works [7,8]. However, one of the shortcomings in the Tzanetakis's research, as well as all the researches mentioned above, is that they didn't exploit thoroughly the statistic information (mean and variance) of audio signals. In those researches, the mean and variance data are put into the feature vectors without any discrimination and then passed through the classifier. In fact, most of the classifiers used in audio classification were designed for general data and did not pay enough attention to the statistical characteristics of the audio data.

In this paper, we propose a novel classification model which can better exploit the statistical nature of audio signals by employing the Gradient-Based Fuzzy c-Means Algorithm with Divergence Measure (GBFCM(DM)). While the GBFCM algorithm has been proven to give high accuracy of clustering [10], the divergence measure was also proven to give better modelling of statistic data like audio signal. Therefore, this combination implies an improvement for audio classification in a term of accuracy.

The content of this paper is organized as follows. Section 2 covers the feature extraction. Section 3 introduces the Gradient-Based Fuzzy c-Means Algorithm with Divergence Measure. Experiments and results are shown in Section 4. Finally, Section 5 concludes this paper.

2 Feature Extraction

Feature extraction is the process of computing a compact numerical representation that can be used to characterize a data pattern. In this paper, we cover the classification of music, speech, and natural sounds. Moreover, the classification of music signals into several genres is also included in the research scope. Fig. 1 and Fig. 2 show samples of audio signals used for experiments in this paper. For this goal, we consider the acoustic feature set proposed by Tzanetakis et. al [6] as the most suitable feature extraction method. Furthermore, we also add the variance information for all the features suggested in [6]. By doing so, our feature set covers 42 features including 20 timbral, 12 rhythmic and 10 pitch features.

1. *Timbral texture features:*

    These features are based on short time Fourier transform (STFT) and are calculated for every short-time frame of sound. The feature vector for describing timbral texture consists of the following features: means and variances of

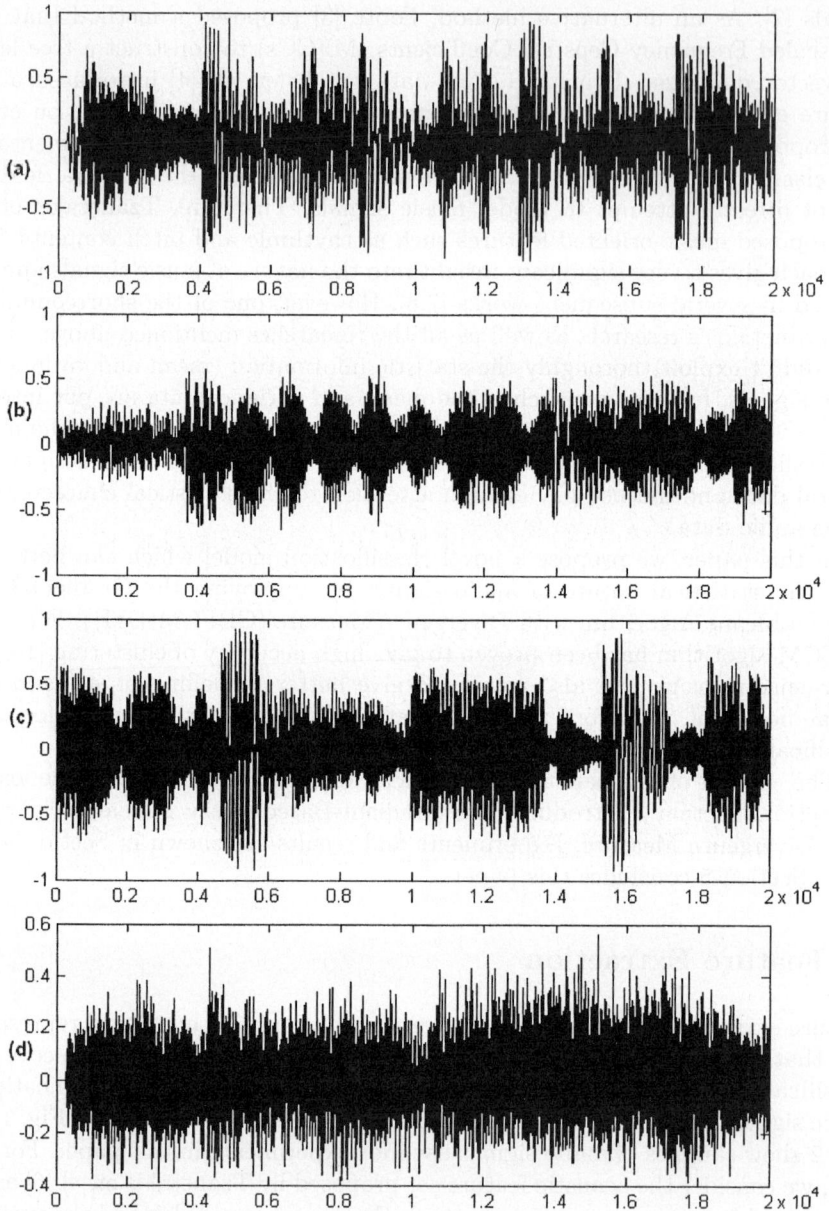

Fig. 1. Sample music excerpts represented in voltage amplitude: (a) Hiphop (b) Folk (c) Pop (d) Rock

spectral centroid, rolloff, flux, zerocrossings over texture window, low energy, and mean and variances of the first five MFCC coefficients over the texture window. This results in a 20-dimensional feature vector.

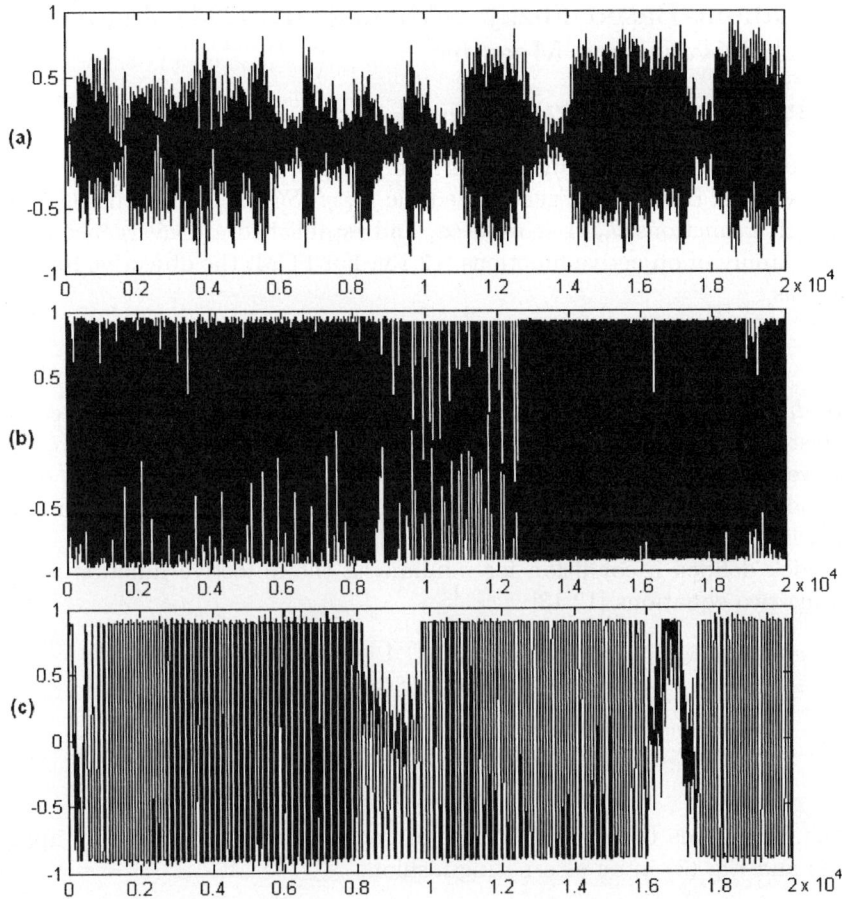

Fig. 2. Sample signal excerpts represented in voltage amplitude: (a) Jazz (b)Country (c) Speech

2. *Rhythmic content features:*

   To represent the rhythmic content, we use the mean and variance of each of the following 6 features: relative amplitude of the first and the second peaks (2 features), ratio of the second and the first peaks(1), period of the first and the second peaks (2), overall sum of the beat histogram. These features are based on detecting the most salient periodicity of the signal by using Discrete Wavelet Transform technique.

3. *Pitch content features:*

   The pitch content features are based on multiple pitch detection techniques [11]. As a total, we use the means and variances of 5 features to represent the pitch content.

3 Gradient-Based Fuzzy c-Means(GBFCM) Algorithm with Divergence Measure

3.1 Fuzzy c-Means(FCM) Algorithm

The objective of clustering algorithms is to group of similar objects and separate dissimilar ones. Bezdek first generalized the *fuzzy ISODATA* by defining a family of objective functions $J_m, 1 < m < \infty$, and established a convergence theorem for that family of objective functions [12,13]. For FCM, the objective function is defined as :

$$J_m(U, v) = \sum_{k=1}^{n}\sum_{i=1}^{c}(\mu_{ki})^m (d_i(x_k))^2 \qquad (1)$$

where $d_i(x_k)$ denotes the distance from the input data x_k to v_i, the center of the cluster i, μ_{ki} is the membership value of the data x_k to the cluster i, and m is the weighting exponent, $m \in 1, \cdots, \infty$, while n and c are the number of input data and clusters, respectively. Note that the distance measure used in FCM is the Euclidean distance.

Bezdek defined a condition for minimizing the objective function with the following two equations [12,13]:

$$\mu_{ki} = \frac{1}{\sum_{j=1}^{c}(\frac{d_i(x_k)}{d_j(x_k)})^{\frac{2}{m-1}}} \qquad (2)$$

$$v_i = \frac{\sum_{k=1}^{n}(\mu_{ki})^m x_k}{\sum_{k=1}^{n}(\mu_{ki})^m} \qquad (3)$$

The FCM finds the optimal values of group centers iteratively by applying Eq. (2) and Eq. (3) in an alternating fashion.

3.2 Gradient-Based Fuzzy c-Means(GBFCM) Algorithm

One attempt to improve the FCM algorithm was made by minimizing the objective function using one input data at a time instead of the entire input data. That is, the FCM in Eq. (2) and Eq. (3) uses all data to update the center value of the cluster, but the GBFCM that is used in this paper was developed to update the center value of the cluster with a given individual data sequentially [10,14]. Given one datum x_k and c clusters with centers at $v_j, (j = 1, 2, \cdots, c)$, the objective function to be minimized is:

$$J_k = \mu_{k1}^2(v_1 - x_k)^2 + \mu_{k2}^2(v_2 - x_k)^2 + \cdots + \mu_{kc}^2(v_c - x_k)^2 \qquad (4)$$

with the following constraint:

$$\mu_{k1} + \mu_{k2} + \cdots + \mu_{kc} = 1 \qquad (5)$$

The basic procedure of the gradient descent method is that starting from an initial center vector, $v_i(0)$, the gradient ΔJ_k of the current objective function can be computed. The next value of v_i is obtained by moving to the direction of the negative gradient along the error surface such that:

$$v_i(n+1) = v_i(n) - \eta \frac{\partial J_k}{\partial v_i(n)}$$

where n is the iteration index and

$$\frac{\partial J_k}{\partial v_i(n)} = 2\mu_{ki}^2(v_i(n) - x_k)$$

Equivalently,

$$v_i(n+1) = v_i(n) - 2\eta\mu_{ki}^2(v_i(n) - x_k) \qquad (6)$$

where η is a learning constant.

A necessary condition for optimal positions of the centers for the groups can be found by the following:

$$\frac{\partial J_k}{\partial \mu} = 0 \qquad (7)$$

After applying the condition of Eq. (7), the membership grades can be found as:

$$\mu_{ki} = \frac{1}{\sum_{j=1}^{c}(\frac{d_i(x_k)}{d_j(x_k)})^2} \qquad (8)$$

Both the FCM and GBFCM have an objective function that related the distance between each center and data with a membership grade reflecting the degree of their similarities with respect to other centers. On the other hand, they differ in the way they try to minimize it:

- As can be seen from Eq. (2) and Eq. (3), all the data should be present in the objective function in the FCM and the gradients are set to zero in order to obtain the equations necessary for minimization [15].
- As can be seen from Eq. (6) and Eq. (8), however, only one datum is present for updating the centers and corresponding membership values at a time in the GBFCM.

More detailed explanation about the GBFCM can be found in [10,14].

3.3 GBFCM with Divergence Measure

In distribution clustering, selecting a proper distance measure between two data vectors is very important since the performance of the algorithm largely depends on the choice of the distance measure[13]. After evaluating various distance measures, the Divergence distance (*Kullback-Leibler Divergence*) between two Gaussian Probability Density Functions(GPDFs), $x = (x_i^\mu, x_i^{\sigma^2})$ and $v = (v_i^\mu, v_i^{\sigma^2})$, $i = 1, \cdots, d$, is chosen as the distance measure in our algorithm[13,16]:

$$D(\boldsymbol{x}, \boldsymbol{v}) = \sum_{i=1}^{d} (\frac{x_i^{\sigma^2} + (x_i^{\mu} - v_i^{\mu})^2}{v_i^{\sigma^2}} + \frac{v_i^{\sigma^2} + (x_i^{\mu} - v_i^{\mu})^2}{x_i^{\sigma^2}} - 2)$$

$$= \sum_{i=1}^{d} (\frac{(x_i^{\sigma^2} - v_i^{\sigma^2})^2}{x_i^{\sigma^2} v_i^{\sigma^2}} + \frac{(x_i^{\mu} - v_i^{\mu})^2}{x_i^{\sigma^2}} + \frac{(x_i^{\mu} - v_i^{\mu})^2}{v_i^{\sigma^2}}) \qquad (9)$$

where x_i^{μ} and $x_i^{\sigma^2}$ denote μ and σ^2 values of the ith component of $\boldsymbol{x}$, respectively, while v_i^{μ} and $v_i^{\sigma^2}$ denote μ and σ^2 values of the ith component of $\boldsymbol{v}$, respectively.

The GBFCM to be used in this paper is based on the FCM algorithm. However, instead of calculating the center parameters of the clusters after applying all the data vectors in FCM, the GBFCM updates their center parameters at every presentation of data vectors. By doing so, the GBFCM can converge faster than the FCM [10,14]. To deal with probabilistic data such as the GPDF, the proposed GBFCM(DM) updates the center parameters, mean and variance, according to the distance measure shown in Eq. (9). That is, the membership grade for each data vector $\boldsymbol{x}$ to the cluster i is calculated by the following:

$$\mu_i(\boldsymbol{x}) = \frac{1}{\sum_{j=1}^{c} (\frac{D(\boldsymbol{x}, \boldsymbol{v}_i)}{D(\boldsymbol{x}, \boldsymbol{v}_j)})^2} \qquad (10)$$

After finding the proper membership grade from an input data vector $\boldsymbol{x}$ to each cluster i, the GBFCM-DM updates the mean and variance of each center as follows:

$$\boldsymbol{v}_i^{\mu}(n+1) = \boldsymbol{v}_i^{\mu}(n) - \eta \mu_i^2(\boldsymbol{x})(\boldsymbol{v}_i^{\mu}(n) - \boldsymbol{x}^{\mu}) \qquad (11)$$

$$\boldsymbol{v}_i^{\sigma^2}(n+1) = \frac{\sum_{k=1}^{N_i}(\boldsymbol{x}_{k,i}^{\sigma^2}(n) + (\boldsymbol{x}_{k,i}^{\mu}(n) - \boldsymbol{v}_i^{\mu}(n))^2)}{N_i} \qquad (12)$$

where
- $\boldsymbol{v}_i^{\mu}(n)$ or $\boldsymbol{v}_i^{\sigma^2}(n)$: the mean or variance of the cluster i at the time of iteration n
- $\boldsymbol{x}_{k,i}^{\mu}(n)$ or $\boldsymbol{x}_{k,i}^{\sigma^2}(n)$: the mean or variance of the kth data in the cluster i at the time of iteration n
- η and N_i : the learning gain and the number of data in the cluster i

Table 1 is a pseudocode of the GBFCM(DM).

4 Experiments and Results

A data set of 2,663 audio signals is used for experiment (379 rock, 341 pop, 337 jazz, 417 hiphop, 369 folk, 320 country, 300 speech, and 200 natural sound). Each signal is a 30s long excerpt, resulting in more than 22 hours of audio data. For

Table 1. The GBFCM Algorithm

```
Algorithm GBFCM(DM)
  Procedure main()
    Read c, ε, m
    [c: initialize cluster, ε: is small value,
    m is a weighting exponent (m ∈ 1,...∞)]
    error := 0
    While (error > ε)
      While (input file is not empty)
        Read one datum x
        [Update GBFCM(DM) center Mean]
```
$$v^\mu(n+1) = v^\mu(n) - \eta\mu^2(v^\mu(n) - x^\mu)$$
```
        [Update GBFCM(DM) membership grade]
```
$$\mu_i(x) = \frac{1}{\sum_{j=1}^{c}(\frac{D(x,v_i)}{D(x,v_j)})^2}$$
```
        e := vμ(n+1) − vμ(n)
      End while
```
$$v_i^{\sigma^2}(n+1) = \frac{\sum_{k=1}^{N_i}(x_{k,i}^{\sigma^2}(n)+(x_{k,i}^\mu(n)-v_i^\mu(n))^2)}{N_i}$$
```
      error := e
    End while
    Output μi, vμ and vσ²
  End main()
End
```

testing, we used 100 excerpts for each genre, the remaining excerpts are used for training. The sets are collected from internet in several formats. After that, the files are converted into 22,050 Hz, 16 bit, mono audio files to be used as input data of feature extraction. During feature extraction, we used the frame size of 23ms (512 samples) and texture window of 1000ms (43 frames). Each excerpt is extracted to get 1 feature vector. The data set and the respective feature vectors are available at http://icrl.mju.ac.kr/audio.html.

For each genre, we model the distribution of its feature vectors by a number of code vectors. Each code vector represents a group with its own mean and covariance matrix. After that, during testing, the genre of each signal is decided using a Bayesian classifier. The classifier decides the genre for each signal by calculating the probability that signal belong to every genre, then chose the genre which gives the highest probability.

$$Genre(x) = \arg\max_i P(x|v_i) \tag{13}$$

$$P(x|v_i) = \sum_{i=1}^{M} c_i \aleph(x, \mu_i, \Sigma_i) \tag{14}$$

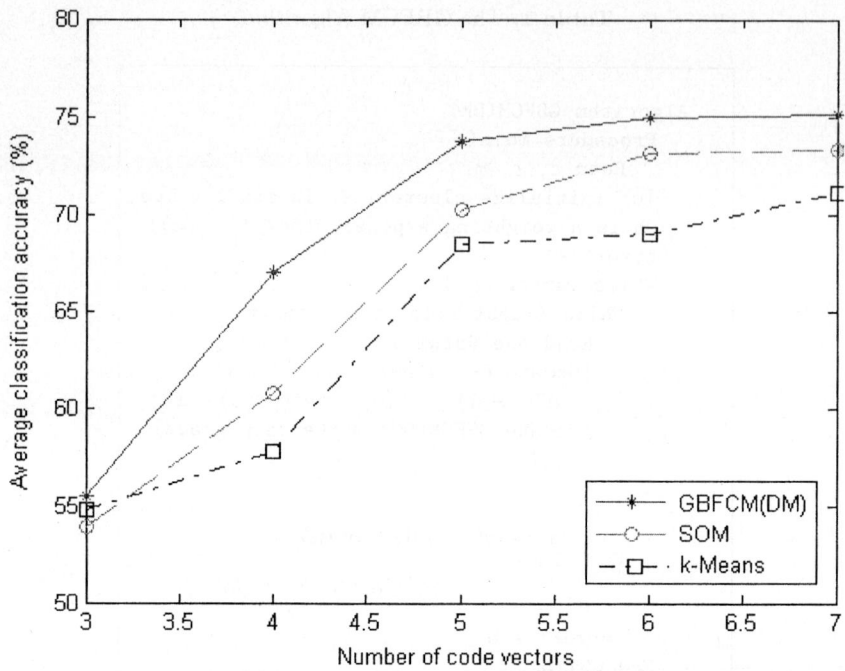

Fig. 3. Classification accuracies for different algorithms

$$\aleph(x, \mu_i, \Sigma_i) = \frac{1}{\sqrt{(2\pi)^d |\Sigma_i|}} e^{-0.5(x-\mu_i)^T \Sigma_i^{-1}(x-\mu_i)} \quad (15)$$

where M is the number of code vectors, c_i is the weight of the code vectors, d is the number of dimensions of the feature vectors (d=42), m_i and Σ_i are the mean and covariance matrix of the $i-th$ group of the genre's distribution, respectively.

The overall classification accuracy of 69.07% is achieved by the GBFCM(DM) using from 3 to 7 code vectors for each genre. Table 2 shows the confusion matrix

Table 2. Confusion matrix of audio genres, using 5 code vectors

	Pop	Rock	Jazz	Hiphop	Folk	Country	Speech	Natutal	Accuracy
Pop	**44**	28	6	5	0	17	0	0	**44%**
Rock	4	**79**	0	0	4	13	0	0	**79%**
Jazz	6	2	**66**	9	11	6	0	0	**66%**
Hiphop	7	0	0	**92**	0	1	0	0	**92%**
Folk	11	7	2	0	**64**	16	1	0	**64%**
Country	25	0	1	11	7	**56**	1	0	**56%**
Speech	0	0	0	3	1	0	**95**	1	**95%**
Nature	0	0	0	0	1	2	0	**97**	**97%**

Table 3. Classification accuracy of different algorithms (unit:%), using 5 code vectors

	Pop	Rock	Jazz	Hiphop	Folk	Country	Speech	Natutal	Average
k-Means	43	71	60	86	57	47	90	94	**68.50**
SOM	41	60	67	91	62	55	91	95	**70.25**
GBFCM	44	79	66	92	64	56	95	94	**73.75**

which describes the detailed classification results for each genre. One significant point can be inferred from the confusion matrix is that pop and country signals are quite likely to be confused. The result also shows that the GBFCM(DM) can discriminate very well speech and non-speech signals, as well as nature and non-nature signals.

To verify the performance of the proposed algorithm, we compare its performance with the performances of some of conventional algorithms such as k-Means and SOM (Self-Organizing Map). The average accuracy of k-Means, SOM, and GBFCM(DM) over all numbers of codebooks are 64.225%, 66.25%, and 69.275%, respectively. Fig. 3 shows the performance in the percentage of correct classification for all three algorithms with several numbers of code vectors in the range from 3 to 7. Specifically, Table 3 shows the performance for each audio genre, using different algorithms with 5 code vectors. Note that the k-Means and SOM algorithm don't use the Divergence Measure, so the input data are 30 dimensional as mentioned in [6]. The results of k-Means algorithm shown in Fig. 3 and Table 3 match with the classification accuracy reported in [6].

From the result shown in Fig. 3 and Table 3, we can infer that the algorithm which uses divergence measure, GBFCM(DM), usually outperforms the k-Means or SOM which use the Euclidean distance measure. The results also show that GBFCM(DM) gives 3.025% - 5.05% better accuracy over the remaining two algorithms.

5 Conclusions

A new approach for modelling and classification of audio signals is proposed in this paper. The paper shows how the mean and variance information of audio signals are modelled using the Gradient-Based Fuzzy c-Means Algorithm with Divergence Measure. To prove the effectiveness of the proposed method, experiments are performed on a database with signals of several genres, including rock, pop, jazz, folk, country, and hip hop musics, speech and natural sounds. Results show that GBFCM(DM) decreases the misclassification rate 3.025%-5.05% over k-Means and SOM.

Acknowledgement

This research was supported by the Korea Research Foundation (Grant # R05-2003-000-10992-0 (2004)). The authors gratefully acknowledge the reviewers for their valuable comments that led to considerable improvements of this paper.

References

1. Wold,E.,Blum,T.,Keislar,D.,Wheaton,J.:Content-based classification, search, and retrieval of audio, IEEE Multimedia, (1996) 27-36.
2. Saunders,J.: Real time discrimination of broadcast speech/music , Proc. Int. Conf. Acoustic, Speech, Signal Processing (ICASSP), (1996) 993-996.
3. Foote,J.:Content-based retrieval of music and audio, Proc. SPIE, Multimedia Storage and Archiving Systems II, (1997) 138-147
4. Li,G.,Khokar,A.: Content-based indexing and retrieval of audio data using wavelets, Proc. Int. Conf. Multimedia Expo II, (2000) 885-888
5. Lu,L.,Li,S.,Zhang,H.: Content-based audio segmentation using support vector machines, in Proc. IEEE Int. Conf. Multimedia and Expo (ICME), Tokyo, Japan, (2001) 749-752
6. Tzanetakis,G.,Cook,P.:Music genre classification of audio signals, IEEE Trans. Speech Audio Process., **10** (2002) 293-302
7. Turnbull,D.,Elkan,C.: Fast Recognition of Musical Genres Using RBF Networks, IEEE Trans. Knowledge and Data Engineering, **17** (2005) 580-584
8. Burred,J.J,Lerch,A.: A hierachical approach to automatic music genre classification, Proc. 6th Int. Conf. Digital Audio Effect, London, UK, (2003)
9. Malheiro,R.,Paiva,R.P.,Mendes,A.J.,Mendes,T., Cardoso,A.: Classification of recorded classical music using neural networks, 4th Int. ICSC Sym. on Engineering of Intelligent Systems , (2004)
10. Park,D.C.,Dagher,I.: Gradient Based Fuzzy c-means (GBFCM) Algorithm, IEEE Int. Conf. on Neural Networks, ICNN-94, **3** (1994) 1626-1631
11. Tolonen,T,Karjalainen,M.: A computationally efficient multipitch analysis model, IEEE Trans. Speech Audio Processing, **8** (2000) 708-716.
12. Bezdek,J.C.: A convergence theorem for the fuzzy ISODATA clustering algorithms. IEEE Trans. Pattern Anal. Mach. Int, **2** (1980) 1-8
13. Bezdek,J.C.: Pattern recognition with fuzzy objective function algorithms, New York : Plenum, (1981)
14. Looney,C.: Pattern Recognition Using Neural Networks, New York, Oxford University press, (1997) 252-254
15. Windham,M.P.: Cluster Validity for the Fuzzy cneans clustering algorithm, IEEE Trans. Pattern Anal. Mach. Int., **4** (1982) 357-363
16. Fukunaga,K.: Introduction to Statistical Pattern Recognition, Academic Press Inc., 2nd edition, (1990)
17. Yang,C.: Music Database Retrieval Based on Spectral Similarity, Stanford Univ Database Group, Stanford, CA, Tech. Rep. 2001-14, (2001)

Variable Bit Quantization for Virtual Source Location Information in Spatial Audio Coding

Sang Bae Chon[1], In Yong Choi[1], Jeongil Seo[2], and Koeng-Mo Sung[1]

[1] Applied Acoustics Laboratory,
School of Electrical Engineering and Computer Science,
Seoul National University,
Shinlim-dong, Kwanak-gu, Seoul, Republic of Korea 151-742
strlen@acoustics.snu.ac.kr
[2] Broadcasting Media Research Group,
Electronics and Telecommunications Research Institute (ETRI),
161 Gajeong-dong, Yuseong-gu, Daejeon, Republic of Korea 305-600

Abstract. In [1,2,3], Binaural Cue Coding (BCC) was introduced for multi-channel spatial rendering for MPEG 4 - SAC (Spatial Audio Coding) to reduce bitrate of multi-channel audio signal. In [4,5], Virtual Source Location Information (VSLI) was introduced to replace Inter-Channel Level Difference, the most determinant parameter in BCC system. Here, Variable Bit Quantization (VBQ) for VSLI is proposed to reduce bitrate at the quantization block in VSLI-based BCC systems removing statistically invalid range.

1 Introduction

The rapid development in electrical engineering has brought about the development of different audio coding technologies with different purposes. Some aim for better quality, while some others target for the lower bitrate. Recently, Binaural Cue Coding (BCC) [1,2,3] was introduced as a basic frame of MPEG 4-SAC (Spatial Audio Coding) technology. By reducing the amount of overlapped information among channels, BCC achieves an efficient compression for multi-channel audio signals. In addition, this compression coding scheme can be applied with other conventional coding technologies independently.

To optimize sound quality and to reduce bitrate, Virtual Source Location Information (VSLI) [4,5] was introduced as an alternative to Inter-Channel Level Difference [1,2], the most determinant parameter among binaural cues [1,2], in the Binaural Cue Coding systems.

In this paper, Variable Bit Quantization (VBQ) is proposed to achieve lower bitrate using the VSLI as a binaural cue in BCC systems. This paper covers historical review on the BCC and the VSLI, and the concept and the efficiency of VBQ.

2 Binaural Cue Coding

Many different audio coding technologies have been developed to achieve lower bitrate. However, most of these audio coders such as AAC [6,7] compress each channel independently. In other words, the redundancy from the overlapped information among channels was not considered to be removed. For this reason, bitrate increases proportionally to the number of channels in multi-channel audio signals in general.

To remove the overlapped information among channels, Binaural Cue Coding (BCC) was introduced to compress multi-channel audio signal into a downmixed signal, either a mono audio signal or two stereo audio signals, with binaural cues to reconstruct original signal at the receiver. The binaural cues are parameters that can describe spatial image of the original signal and they have far lower bitrate compared to the audio signals. Moreover, this BCC can be combined with other different audio coding technologies independently.

2.1 Structure of Binaural Cue Coding System

Fig.1 shows a generic BCC system with five audio input signals. The BCC system has a transmitter and a receiver. The transmitter includes BCC analyzer [1,2] that extracts binaural cues from the original multi-channel audio signals. Equivalently, the receiver includes a BCC synthesizer [1,2] that reconstructs the multi-channel audio signals synthesizing the downmixed audio signal and the extracted binaural cues. As mentioned before, the downmixed audio signal is compressed using an independent audio encoder, AAC in the case of MPEG 4-SAC.

The transmitter transmits AAC-encoded audio of M, the downmixed audio signal of five audio input signals, and binaural cues, Inter-Channel Level Differ-

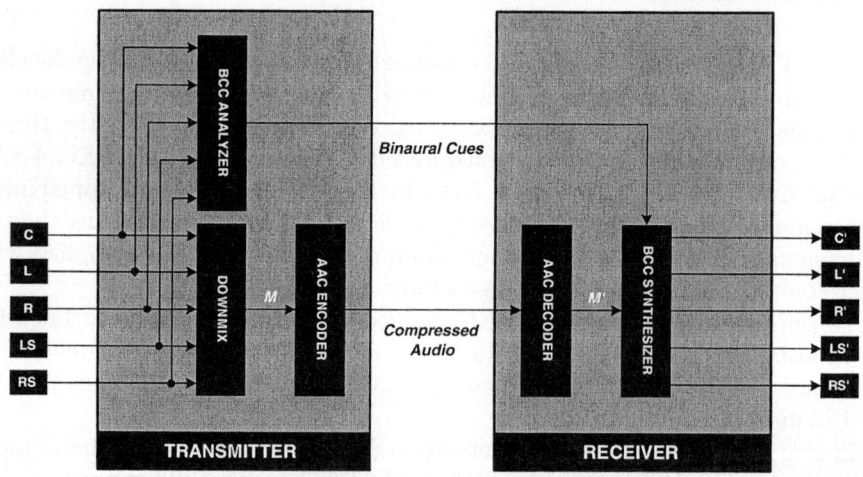

Fig. 1. Generic Binaural Cue Coding System

ence [1,2], Inter-Channel Time Delay [1,2], and Inter-Channel Correlation [1,2], to reconstruct multi-channel audio signals, L', R', C', LS', and RS', at the receiver. When receiver receives transmitted data, AAC decoder reconstructs M'. After that, BCC synthesizer synthesizes five audio signals with the M' and the binaural cues.

2.2 Binaural Cues

Binaural cues are side information that describe the spatial image of multi-channel audio signals. Each binaural cue is extracted based on Equivalent Rectangular Bandwidth (ERB) model [8]. Typical binaural cues are Inter-Channel Level Difference (ICLD), Inter-Channel Time Delay (ICTD), and Inter-Channel Correlation (ICC).

ICLD describes the level difference between one channel and the reference channel, the downmixed audio signal. It plays a very important role in lateralization of the virtually perceived sound source by imitating the shadow effect [13,14,15] for high frequency bands above 1~1.5 kHz.

ICTD describes the time delay between one channel and the reference channel. It plays an important role in lateralization of the virtually perceived sound source by imitating refraction of waves for low frequency bands below 1~1.5 kHz.

ICC describes the correlation between one channel and the reference channel. It plays an important role in determining the width of the rendered source. As the compared channel source gets more similar to the reference channel, ICC converges to 1.

3 Virtual Source Location Information Based BCC

Among typical three binaural cues, the ICLD plays the most important role for the listener to perceive the location of the sound source. However, it seemed more appropriate to consider the location information of the sound source itself than the level difference of the speakers to synthesize spatial image with the knowledge in psychoacoustics. These provided the motive to apply not the ICLD itself, but the virtually panned location information of the sound source to the BCC system considered. For this reason, Virtual Source Location Information applying the Constant Power Panning Law (CPP law) [11,12,13] with ITU-R [14] layout was introduced.

3.1 VSLI Extractor

Fig.2 shows how to extract information at each stage. At stage 1, the center channel audio signal gets divided into LC and RC scaled by $\frac{1}{\sqrt{2}}$ to keep the total power same [4,5]. This stage provides systemic unity to both 5-1-5 system [1,2,3] whose downmixed audio signal is mono and 5-2-5 system [1,2,3] whose downmixed audio signals are stereo. At stage 2, Left Subsequent Vector (LSV)

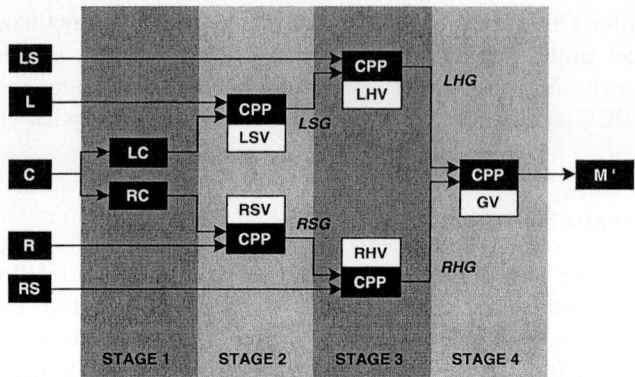

Fig. 2. VSLI Extractor

[4,5] is extracted by Inverse Constant Power Panning (ICPP) from Left (L) signal and Left Center (LC) signal. This process decides the location of virtual source lateralized by L and LC. Right Subsequent Vector (RSV) [4,5] is extracted as LSV at this stage. At stage 3, Left Half-plane Vector (LHV) [4,5] and Right Half-plane Vector (RHV) [4,5] are extracted as in the same way that LSV and RSV were extracted at the previous stage. Finally, Global Vector (GV) [4,5] is extracted at stage 4 from LHV and RHV.

3.2 VSLI Synthesizer

Fig.3 shows how to synthesize audio signal from M', the reconstructed downmixed audio signal, and the VSLIs at the VSLI synthesizer. At stage 1, M' is divided into Left Half-plane Gain (LHG) and Right Half-plane Gain (RHG) according to GV with CPP law. At stage 2, LHG is divided into LS' and Left Subsequent Gain (LSG) and RHG is divided into RS' and Right Subsequent

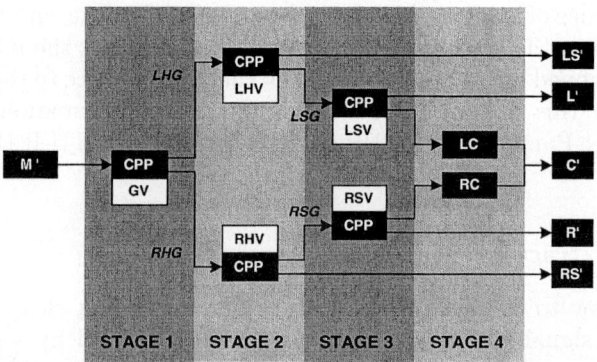

Fig. 3. VSLI Synthesizer

Gain (RSG). Through these four stages, each signal of five channels can be synthesized.

3.3 VSLI-Based BCC vs. ICLD-Based BCC

Accumulative Kullback-Leibler distance measurement [15] was performed as an objective assessment and listening tests as a subjective assessment. These two experiments confirmed that VSLI based BCC is superior to the ICLD based SAC both objectively and subjectively [4,5].

4 Variable Bit Quantization for VSLI

In the field of audio coding technology, quantization method is very important because it determines the average bitrate. Variable Bit Quantization (VBQ), the proposed quantization method, provides lower bitrate compressing up to 15 percent more than a typical quantization method by reducing systemic redundancy of VSLI-based BCC without affecting the sound quality.

4.1 Motive

Fig.4 shows general loudspeaker layout according to ITU-R standard for 5.1 channel audio systems, which VSLI is based on. Here, it is obvious that LSV is localized between L and C/LC, $[-\frac{\pi}{6}\ 0]$, LHV is localized between LS and C/LC, $[-\frac{11\pi}{18}\ 0]$, RSV is between C/RC and R, $[0\ \frac{\pi}{6}]$, and RHV is localized between C/RC and RS, $[0\ \frac{11\pi}{18}]$.

However, it can be noticed that some part of the quantization range of LHV and RHV are wasted. As fig.5 shows, LHV does not lateralize between LSV and

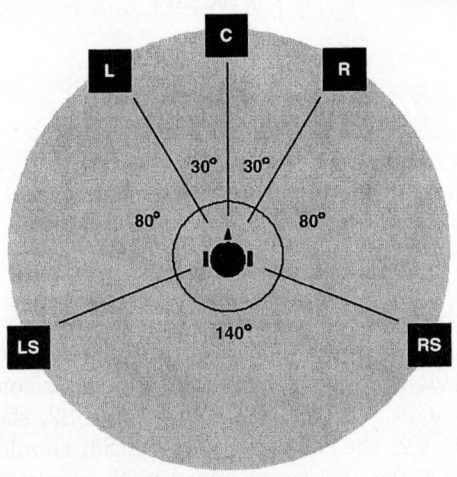

Fig. 4. ITU-R Recommended Layout

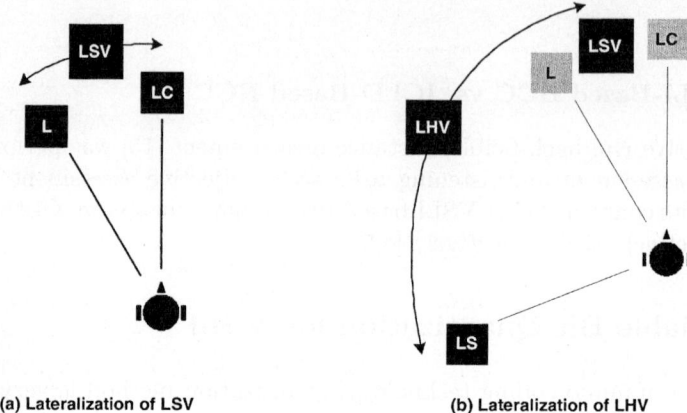

(a) Lateralization of LSV   (b) Lateralization of LHV

Fig. 5. VSLI Extraction

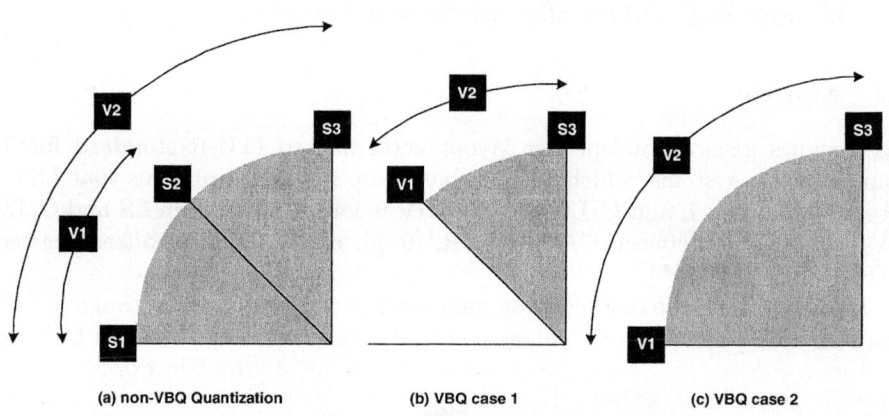

(a) non-VBQ Quantization   (b) VBQ case 1   (c) VBQ case 2

Fig. 6. non-VBQ vs. VBQ

LC once LSV is decided between L and LC. For the same reason, RHV does not lateralize between RC and R. It is possible to reduce bitrate from this point of view. Hence, Variable Bit Quantization (VBQ) is proposed in this paper.

4.2 Variable Bit Quantization

The VBQ is a quantization method for VSLI-based BCC system. VBQ assigns different number of bits to the VSLI at current stage according to the layout and the VSLI at previous stage. Fig.6 shows a comparison between VBQ and non-VBQ with two stages. V1, the VSLI for S1 and S2, should be in the range of [S1 S2] at stage 1. V2, the VSLI for V1 and S3, should be in the range of [V1 S3] at stage 2. However, V2 is quantized in the range of [S1 S3] when non-VBQ quantization is applied. In an extreme case, V1 is around the location of

S2 as shown in Fig.6-(b) shows. In this case, the bit assignment for V2 wastes almost half of the range. On the other hand, the bit assignment by VBQ for V2 does not waste any range because it assigns the number of bits depending on the range of [V1 S3]. The worst case of the VBQ method is when V1 equals S1 as in Fig.6-(c). In this case, VBQ system returns exactly the same result to the non-VBQ system.

As mentioned above, it is able to save the number of bits to code the same information by using VBQ. In addition, it is possible to achieve higher resolution when encoding V2 by using VBQ. For example, since the basic resolution of VSLI is 3 degrees, both the range of $[0\ \frac{\pi}{2}]$ and the range of $[0\ \frac{2\pi}{3}]$ use the same number of bits for quantization, 5 bits. Once the number of bits for quantization is decided to 5 bits, the former has the resolution of $\frac{\pi}{64}$ while the latter has the resolution of $\frac{\pi}{96}$. For this reason, VBQ not only remove systematic redundancy in quantization, but also has higher resolution in VSLI.

At the decoding block, the VSLI synthesizer, assigned number of bits by VBQ for V3 can be calculated from V1 and V2 without any transmitted flag information because V1 and V2 are 5 bits each. When V3 is calculated, the number of bits assigned by VBQ for V4 can be calculated from V3. Hence, it is obvious that it is possible to decode V3 and V4 without transmitting a flag about assigned number of bits for V3 and V4.

4.3 Change in VSLI Extraction for VBQ

Structure. From the previous section, it is confirmed that the VSLI-based BCC system wasted information and that it can be saved by using VBQ. To achieve lower bitrate, the VSLI extraction strategy is changed as Fig.7. Because there are only 4 VSLIs to be expressed, the amount of information to extract is already decreased by 20 percent comparing to the conventional model.

In this VSLI extraction strategy, V3 is expressed as the VSLI of all with an only exception of the center. The reason for this is that the V3 in this case has

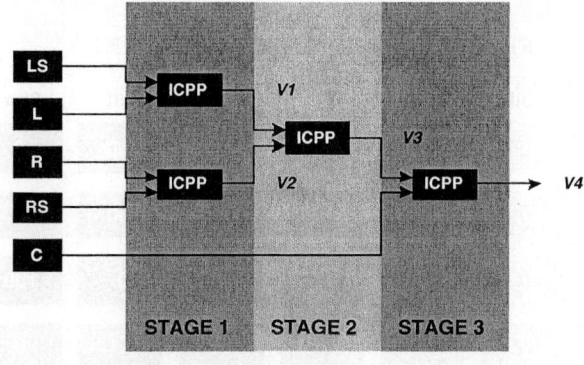

Fig. 7. VSLI Extractor with VBQ

tendency to be positioned close to the center channel statistically. Hence, it is possible to save bits for V4.

Bit Assignment Strategy. The bit are assigned in a way that all of the VLSIs should have a resolution of 3 degree at least. Following this assignment strategy, V1 and V2 are assigned 5 bits with the resolution of 60/32 degree. 0 to 6 bits can be assigned to V3 depending on the result of V1 and V2. In the same way, V4 can be assigned 0 to 6 bits depending on the result of V3. On the other hand, all the VSLIs were assigned 5 bits in non-VBQ system, which is not able to guarantee 3 degree resolution.

4.4 Experiment

The main purpose of VBQ is to reduce bitrate by removing redundancies. To see how much bitrate it reduces, experiments were performed with 5 channel audio signals those were provided by Coding Technology^{TM}, Philips^{TM}, and Dolby^{TM}.

As expected, the result shows that the V4 is now compressed noticeably. The bitrate of V4 was reduced to around 60 percent. When compared with non-VBQ model with 4 stages such as Fig.2, total bitrate was reduced around 25 percent. When compared with non-VBQ model with 3 stages such as Fig.7, total bitrate

	0bit	1bit	2bit	3bit	4bit	5bit	6bit	Avg bit
V1	0	0	0	0	0	100	0	5
V2	0	0	0	0	0	100	0	5
V3	0	0	0	0	0	44	56	5.56
V4	21	16	27	24	10	0.3	0.1	1.87

Fig. 8. Experiment Result - CASTPAN1

	0bit	1bit	2bit	3bit	4bit	5bit	6bit	Avg bit
V1	0	0	0	0	0	100	0	5
V2	0	0	0	0	0	100	0	5
V3	0	0	0	0	0	0	100	6
V4	12	12	24	38	15	0.1	0	2.32

Fig. 9. Experiment Result - CHOSTAKOVITCH

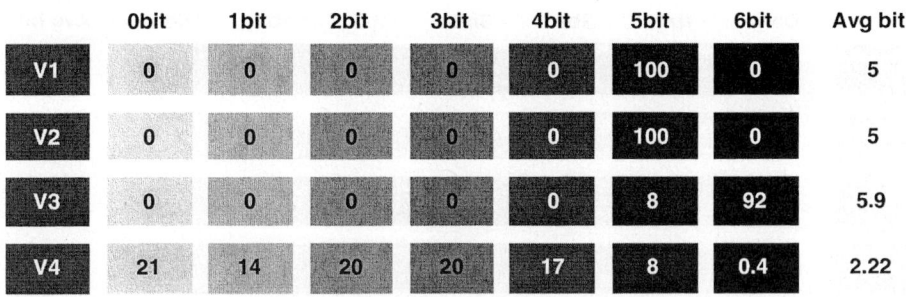

Fig. 10. Experiment Result - POPS

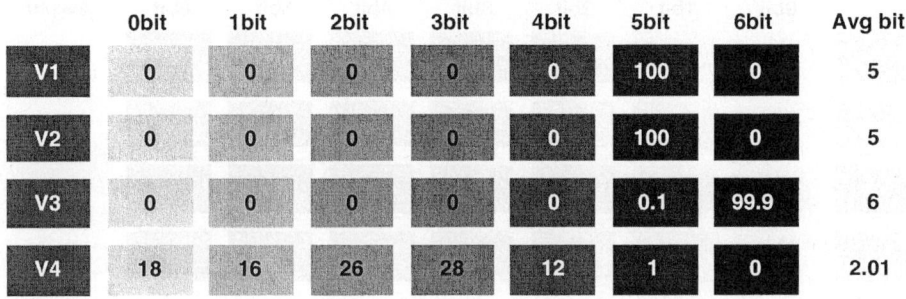

Fig. 11. Experiment Result - POULENC

	0bit	1bit	2bit	3bit	4bit	5bit	6bit	Avg bit
V1	0	0	0	0	0	100	0	5
V2	0	0	0	0	0	100	0	5
V3	0	0	0	0	0	0	100	6
V4	20	17	25	24	13	1	0	1.94

Fig. 12. Experiment Result - JACKSON1

was reduced by about 8 percent even higher resolution of the virtual source is guaranteed. Fig.8~Fig.14 are some of the results from the experiments. .

Each figure shows bit distribution of each sound source. The number in each box is the percentage of the number of bits being used. For example, Fig. 8 shows that 5 bits are assigned to all of V1 and V2, 44 percent of V3, and 0.3 percent of V4 for a sound source, "CASTPAN1".

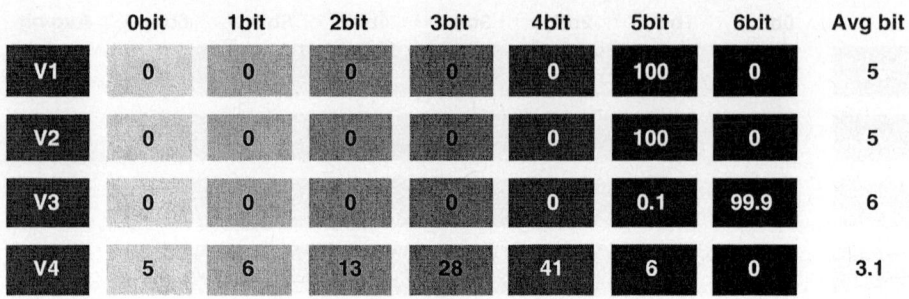

Fig. 13. Experiment Result - INDIE2

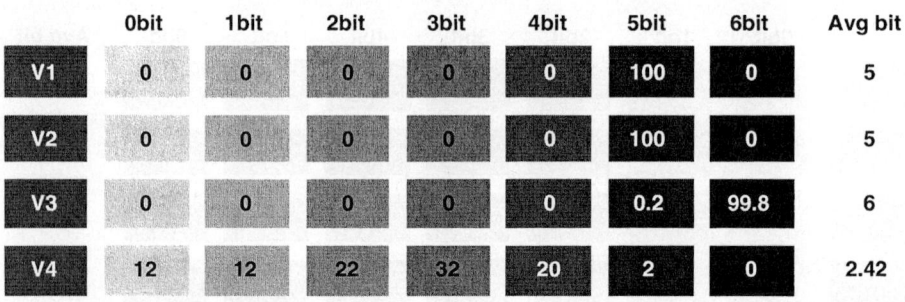

Fig. 14. Experiment Result - INTERVIEW

5 Conclusions

This paper has proposed Variable Bit Quantization for Virtual Source Location Information. The VBQ reduces bitrate by removing statistically meaningless part in the range of quantization. For this reason, the decoded audio signal in the worst case for the VBQ has the same bitrate and the same quality of sound to that of non-variable bit quantized system. Moreover, it is confirmed that VBQ reduced bitrate around 8 percent without deteriorating of sound quality.

References

1. C. Faller and F. Baumgarte, "Binaural cue coding: A novel and efficient representation of spatial audio," in Proc. ICASSP 2002, Orlando, FL, May 2002.
2. F. Baumgarte and C. Faller, "Binaural cue coding - Part I: Psychoacoustic Fundamentals and design principles," IEEE Trans. Speech Audio Processing, vol. 11, pp. 509-519, Nov. 2003.
3. C. Faller and F. Baumgarte, "Binaural cue coding - Part II: Schemes and Application," IEEE Trans. Speech Audio Processing, vol. 11, pp. 520-531, Nov. 2003. S. Haykin, Neural Networks : A Comprehensive Foundation, 2nd Ed., Prentice-Hall, 1999.

4. S. B. Chon, "Binaural Cue Coding for the Multi-Channel Audio with Virtual Source Location Information," M.S. Thesis, Seoul National University, 2005.
5. H. Moon, "Study on multi channel audio compression method with virtual source information," Ph.D. Thesis, Seoul National University, 2005.
6. Generic Coding of Moving Pictures and Associated Audio Information-Part 7: Advanced Audio Coding, ISO/IEC Std. 13 818-7, 1997.
7. M. Bosi, K. Brandenburg, S. R. Quackenbush, L. Fielder, K. Akagiri, H. Fuchs, M. Dietz, J. Herre, G. Davidson, and Y. Oikawa, "ISO/IEC MPEG-2 advanced audio coding," J. Audio Eng. Soc., vol. 45, no. 10, pp 789-814, 1997.
8. B. R. Glasberg and B. C. J. Moore, "Derivation of auditory filter shapes from notched-noise data," Hear. Res., vol. 47, pp. 103-138, 1990.
9. F. L. Wightman and D. J. Kistler, Binaural and Spatial hearing in Real and Virtual Environments. Princeton, NJ: Lawrence Erlbaum, ch. 1, pp. 1-23, 1997.
10. E. A. Macpherson and J. C. Middlebrooks, "Listener weighting of cues for lateral angle: the duplex theory of sound localization revisited," J. Acoust. Soc. Amer., vol. 111, no. 5, pp. 2219-2236, May 2002.
11. James R. West, "Five-Channel Panning Laws: An Analytical and Experimental Comparison," Coral Gables, University of Miami, 1998.
12. Ville Pulkki, "Spatial Sound Generation and Perception by Amplitude Panning Techniques," Helsinki University of Technology Laboratory of Acoustics and Audio Signal Processing, 2001.
13. Ville Pulkki, "Analyzing Virtual Sound Source Attributes Using a Binaural Auditory Model," J. Audio Eng. Soc., Vol.47, No.4, April, 1999.
14. "Multichannel stereophonic sound system with and without accompanying picture," ITU-R 775-1, July, 1994.
15. Y. Stylianou and A. K. Syrdal, "Perceptual and objective detectioin of discontinuities in concatenative speech synthesis," in Proc. International Conference on Acoustics, Speech, and Signal Processing (ICASSP,) vol.2, pp.837-840, May 2001.

The Realtime Method Based on Audio Scenegraph for 3D Sound Rendering

Jeong-Seon Yi, Suk-Jeong Seong, and Yang-Hee Nam

Division of Digital Media, Ewha Womans University,
11-1 Daehyun-dong, Seodaemun-gu, Seoul, South Korea
{vivarena, monica810}@ewhain.net, yanghee@ewha.ac.kr

Abstract. Recent studies have shown that the combination of auditory and visual cues enhances the sense of immersion in virtual reality or interactive entertainment applications. However, realtime 3D audiovisual rendering requires high computational cost. In this paper, to reduce realtime computation, we suggest a novel framework of optimized 3D sound rendering, where we define Audio Scenegraph that contains reduced 3D scene information and the necessary parameters for computing early reflections of sound. During pre-computation phase using our framework, graphic reduction and sound source reduction are accomplished according to the environment containing complex 3D scene, sound sources, and a listener. That is, complex 3D scene is reduced to a set of significant facets for sound rendering, and the resulting scene is represented as Audio Scenegraph we defined. And then, the graph is transmitted to the sound engine which clusters a number of sound sources for reducing realtime calculation of sound propagation. For sound source reduction, it is required to estimate early reflection time to test perceptual culling and to cluster sounds which are reachable to facets of each sub space according to the estimation results. During realtime phase according to the position, direction and index of the space of a listener, sounds inside sub space are played by image method and sounds outside sub space are also played by assigning clustered sounds to buffers. Even if the number of sounds is increased, realtime calculation is very stable because most calculations about sounds can be performed offline. It took very consistent time for 3D sound rendering regardless of complexity of 3D scene including hundreds of sound sources by this method. As a future study, it is required to estimate the perceptual acceptance of grouping algorithm by user test.

1 Introduction

In the field of virtual reality application, it's been crucial that the combination of auditory and visual cues enhance the sense of immersion. But, virtual environments are rapidly becoming very complex, in terms of 3D models and sound sources contained in the 3D scene, but also in terms of complexity of interactivity. For that reason, recent studies have shown that the speed of realtime rendering is improved with the quality of visual, which is concentrated on the field of 3D graphic rendering.

In the field of 3D realtime sound rendering, most studies [7], [8] have not been sufficiently investigated because of a huge amount of computing reverberation effect and realtime calculation according to the position and direction of a moving listener. Therefore, the time-cost of sound rendering for complex 3D environment is getting higher.

To solve this problem, we concentrated on making time-cost of realime computation stable although there are tens of thousands of complex 3D scene of and hundreds of sound sources in virtual environment. In this paper, we suggest the novel approach to reduce the amount of realtime computation for realtime 3D sound rendering using Audio Scenegraph and through clustering sound sources (we limit to consideration of first reflection).

2 Related Works

As discussed previously, because it would be scarcely possible to simulate an application including complex 3D scene and many sounds for realtime sound rendering, the field of realtime 3D sound rendering is relatively young. Basically, calculating sound propagation has been done using various methods: Ray Tracing [1], Image Source [2], [3], and Beam Tracing [4], [5], [6]. Our approach is based on the Image Source method that sound sources are reflected against facets, and calculate early reflection. In fact, although it is necessary to consider seriously the reverberation effect for realistic sound rendering, most studies are concerned with the early reflections because of the huge amount of its computation, and the calculation of reverberation effect is approximated by the values in proportion to reflection time [14].

Recent studies have concentrate upon reducing real-time calculation with maintaining high quality of visual and auditory. In details of graphic reduction for sound rendering, it is necessary to reduce complex 3D scene to facets for efficiently calculating sound propagation. But most methods for scene reduction neglected significant facets like holes or gaps (a human cannot pass, but sound may be propagated easily). Chris [9] solved this problem as optimizing scene information based on geometrical signification of 3D model. But, this is not applied to many realtime 3D sound rendering.

It is necessary to deal with many sound sources for 3D sound rendering. Funkhouser [14] has researched many of 3D sound rendering which achieve realtime computation of propagation paths of static sound as beam tracing. But, because a number of beam tree generated by tracing is proportional to that of sound sources, realtime calculation is higher when sound sources are increased. Unlike this, Nicolas [10] suggested real-time 3D audio rendering method for hundreds of moving sound sources as the method of clustering sounds estimated by perceptual culling according to the position of a listener. This method shows very efficient realtime calculation. However, whenever listener moves, it is required to estimates sound sources by perceptual culling and to clusters the estimated sound sources. Therefore when sound sources are increased, the time-cost for realtime 3D sound rendering is getting higher. And because clustered sounds are played on position of representatives, this is not applied to interactive performance using sounds.

3 Our Approach Using Audio Scenegraph

In this paper, for considering the quality of audiovisual rendering, we separate graphic rendering engine and sound rendering engine, which are connected each other though network. During online, information of a listener like the position and direction is transmitted via network from the graphic rendering engine to the sound rendering engine. (See Fig. 1.).

For graphic reduction during offline phrase, complex 3D scene is divided into subspaces containing significant facets for computation of sound propagation, and the reduced results are represented as Audio Scenegraph we defined, which is transmitted via network to the sound rendering engine. For sound source reduction, it is required to estimate early reflection time to test perceptual culling and to cluster sounds which are reachable to facets of each sub space according to the estimation results. The process of sound source reduction is repeated by the number of sub spaces contained in Audio Scenegraph. During online phrase after pre-computing, sounds are played according to the position and direction of a listener which are transmitted via network whenever a listener moves. In this section, main steps of this approach (they are represented gray boxes in Fig.1) are explained in detail.

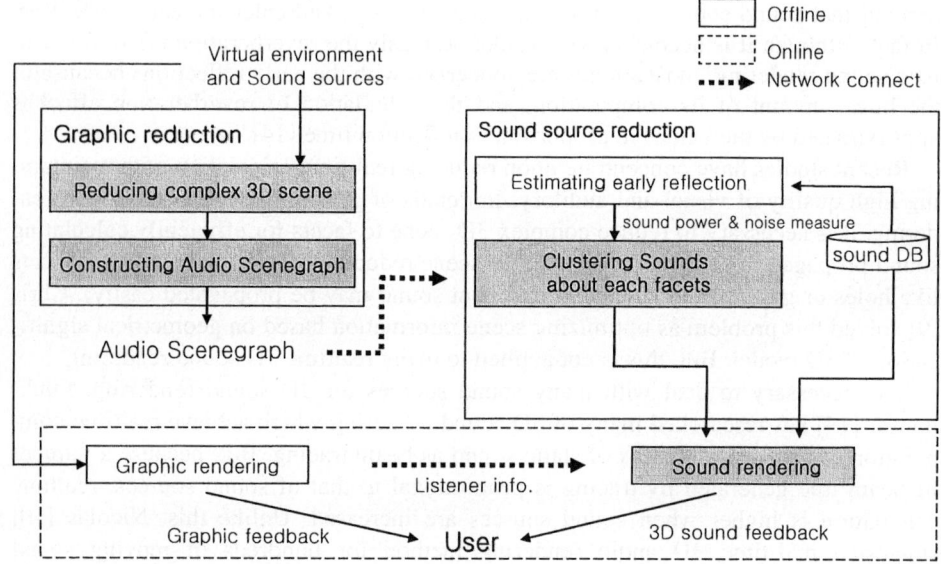

Fig. 1. Real-time 3D Rendering Process. We orderly explain gray boxes in this section.

3.1 Reducing Complex 3D Scene

Even if complex 3D scene is consisted of tens of thousands of polygons, not all of them are important for computing sound propagation. Therefore, we alter polygons into facets as bounding boxes which are necessary for computing sound propagation. Moreover, if there are very small holes or gaps in an occluded sub space, sounds must be going out to other sub spaces. Such a feature should be also considered as virtual facets despite they are not in 3D scene [9]. For example, if the ray of sound propagation is collided with virtual facets, attenuation would not apply to the facets as a zero. It means that it is transmitted without attenuation.

We extend this notion to space partition. When complex 3D scene is divided by a method of space partition (e.g. BSP), all sub spaces are consisted of facets regardless of an interior or an exterior. That is, we regard partitioning results of exterior as virtual facets, and assign the attenuation value of the facet to zero.

3.2 Constructing Audio Scenegraph

In general, a Scenegraph of computer graphics is hierarchically consisted of objects that represent 3D world of application. If it has the purpose for game objects, each node may contain a transformation matrix and, possibly, a renderable object. As the tree is traversed for rendering, transformation matrices are concatenated and objects are rendered with the resulting transform [11].

Audio Scenegraph we propose is similar to the general Scenegraph, but has some differences because of the purpose that the calculation of 3D sound rendering should be quickly computed. Audio Scenegraph has sub space of resulting of space partition, facets contained in sub spaces for applying sound propagation, and sound sources contained in sub spaces. See below pseudo code. (Also see the section 5, Experimental Result. You can confirm Audio Scenegraph used actually). First, complex 3D scene is divided by the method of space partition. Each sub-space has facets embodied by above-mentioned method and position of sound sources contained in the subspace. And each facet has its volume, position, normal, attenuation, and a factor for being noticed if it's a real facet. As we mentioned, we currently consider only early reflections and image source method. If you consider reverberation and diffraction, Audio Scenegraph should be extended.

Pseudo code of Audio Scenegraph

```
sceneRoot: virtual 3D scene tree
numofSpaces: the number of sub spaces
numofObjects: the number of objects in virtual scene
numofSounds: the number of sounds
//space partitioning
numofSpaces = spacePartitioning();
for(int i=0; i<numofSpaces ; i++) {
    obj(i) = NULL; sound(i) = NULL;
    for(int j=0; j<numOfObjects j++) {
        // check whether object are in sub space
        if(isSpaceIn(i, j)) {
            //make a object node
            obj(i) = MakeObjectChild(MakeBoundingBox(j),
                    makeAbsortion(j), calCenterPos(j));
        }
    }
    for(int k=0; k<numofSounds k++) {
        // check a sound space
        if(isSpaceIn(i, k)) {
            //make a sound node
            sound(i)= MakeSoundChild(k, calCenterPos(k));
        }
    }
    sceneRoot.addChild(Obj(i), Sound(i));
}
```

See below example code using Audio Scenegraph. Because each sub space has its facet data, it is convenient to access to each sub space when sound propagation calculates, to apply different attenuation to sub spaces, and to ultimately render sound sources regardless of rendering the graphic view. Our approach sends Audio Scenegraph to sound engine, and then sound engine pre-compute clustering sounds about each facet using this graph. Consequently, it provides rapid computation of sound propagation. Because, 1) we can independently compute 3D realtime sound rendering regardless of graphic scene, 2) we can calculate sound propagation by facets of the graph without checking whether or not the current space is inside, whether or not a sound goes through holes or gaps to other sub spaces.

Example pseudo code using Audio Scenegraph when sounds which are reachable to facets of each sub space are clustered.

```
Root = Audio Scenegraph
while(Root->a number of sub spaces)
   while(Root->sub space->as many as number of facets)
   {   a current facet =
              Root->sub space->facet list[facet index]
       while(Root->a number of sounds)
       {     // estimate sounds inside sub space
           if(! Root->sub space->sound index){
              estimate early reflection
                about a current facet
              if (Early reflection){
                 computing sound propagation
              }
           }
       }
   }
}
```

3.3 Clustering Sounds for Each Facet

First, it is required to estimate early reflection time (20ms up to 80ms). If time of sound propagation is out of the range of early reflection, it is regarded as reverberation and approximated some value (we use reverberation provided to Sound Blaster EAX). And then it is required to test perceptual culling and to cluster sounds which are reachable to facets of each sub space according to the estimation results. The process is repeated by the number of facets of sub spaces contained in Audio Scenegraph. We'll describe detailed in Section 4.

3.4 Realtime 3D Sound Rendering

Consequently, a listener accepts graphic feedback from graphic engine and audio feedback from sound engine. During realtime phase according to the position, direction and index of the space of a listener, sounds inside sub space are played by image method and sounds outside sub space are also played by assigning clustered sounds to buffers. For example, assuming that a listener is in any sub-space consisted of 20 facets and 10 sounds, buffers as 20, the number of facets embodied by above-mentioned sound clustering method are played and sounds inside sub space are played as below 200 by image method and estimating early reflection time. Because we regard the sub space where a listener is currently as the range that listener can receive an interactive response form sounds, sounds inside sub space are played together. Therefore, Even if the number of sounds is increased, realtime calculation is very stable because most calculations about sounds can be performed offline.

4 Clustering Sounds for Each Facet

Whenever listener moves, all sound propagation is re-computed according to the position and direction of a listener. To solve this, one of the efficient methods is used to cluster sounds. But, established methods roughly have two problems. First, whenever sound sources increase, clustering time grows. In this case, it is impossible to avoid increase of realtime calculation. Secondly, if the clustered sounds are just played on the position of representative after clustering sounds, they do not provide instant response when listener touches some sound object. To solve these problems, we suggest that 'pre-clustered sounds for each facet' should be stored in storages of facets. It means that we cluster sounds which are reachable to facets of each sub space during early reflection time and which are culled by perceptual culling method as "Masking effect" [10]. At this time, we use Audio Scenegraph above-defined (you can see example of clustering sounds in section 3.2). Because Audio Scenegraph is consisted of facets for sound propagation, it is easy to access facets collided with sound source.

Fig.2. shows sequence of the progress to cluster sounds for each facet. First, it is required to estimate early reflection time (20ms up to 80ms). If the sound pass early reflection time, it is required to test perceptual culling by using 'perceptual culling theory' by Nicolas [10], Ted [12] as masking effect. And then we cluster sounds which are reachable to facets of each sub space according to the estimation results. That

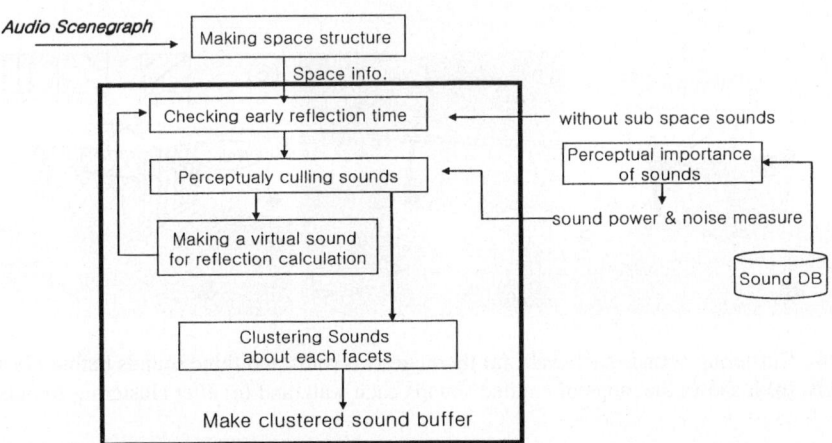

Fig. 2. The method of clustering sounds

is, the sounds which have not been culled are reflected by image sources method against facets of a sub space of them, and the virtual sounds are re-culled by the same estimation. Until sounds are reached to each facet of each sub space, sounds are damped by air absorption, propagation delay and sound absorption of transmitted facets. The results of sounds are added as damped PCM(Pulse Code Modulation) and stored to storage of each facet. See Fig. 3 and Fig. 4. This routine is repeated for all facets.

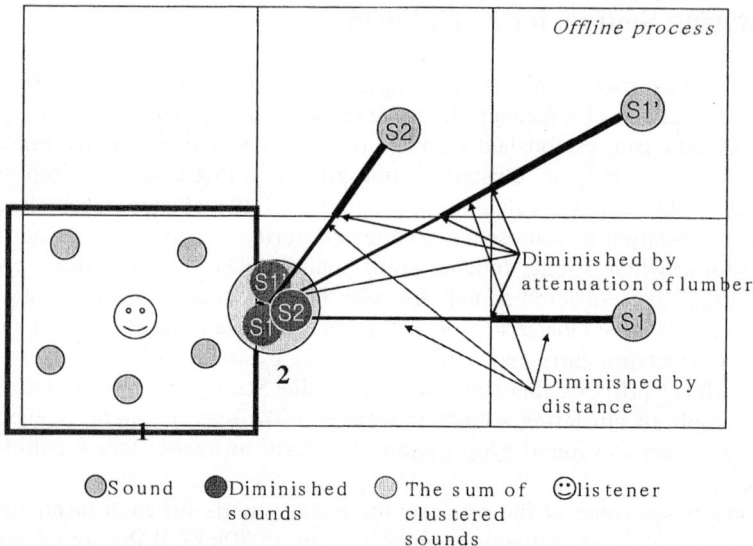

Fig. 3. The overview of clustering sounds. There are three sounds transmitted to facet 2, (S1, S1'(image source), S2). If these sounds are reached to facet 2, their PCM(Pulse Code Modulation)s will be diminished by attenuation of transmitted facets and distance from sounds to facet 2. And then we sum their diminished PCMs and store them to the storage of facet 2.

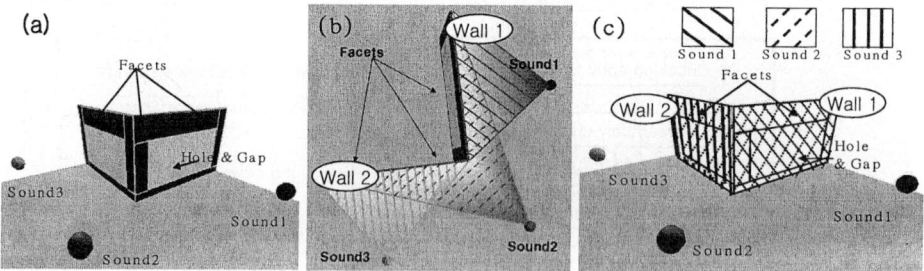

Fig. 4. Clustering sounds each wall: (a) there are two walls and three sounds before clustering sounds, (b) it shows the range of emitted sounds each wall, and (c) after clustering sounds each wall

Sounds stored to storages of facets are just played, which can solve the first problem. Simultaneously, sounds inside current sub space are played, which is able to solve second problem (we regard the space where a listener is currently as the range that listener can receive an interactive response from sounds).

5 Experimental Results

We used two computers connected by a 100Mb/s TCP/IP network, to maximize graphic rendering and sound rendering. See Fig. 5. And for sound rendering we use DirectX 3D Sound as an audio API.

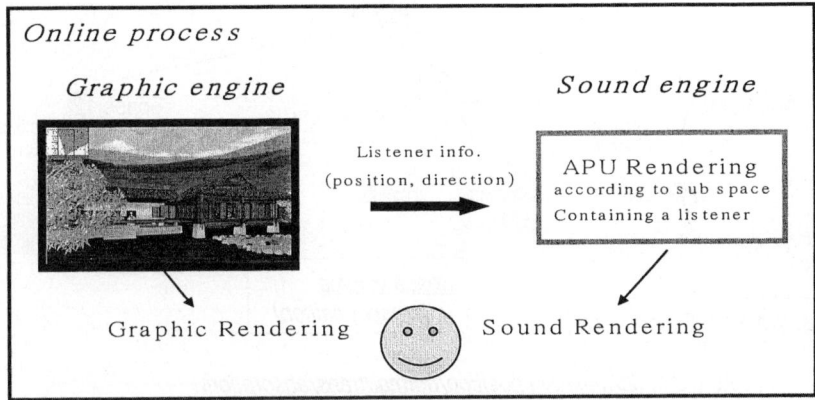

Fig. 5. The system overview. A listener watches a 3D scene from graphic engine and listens to sounds according to his information from sound engine.

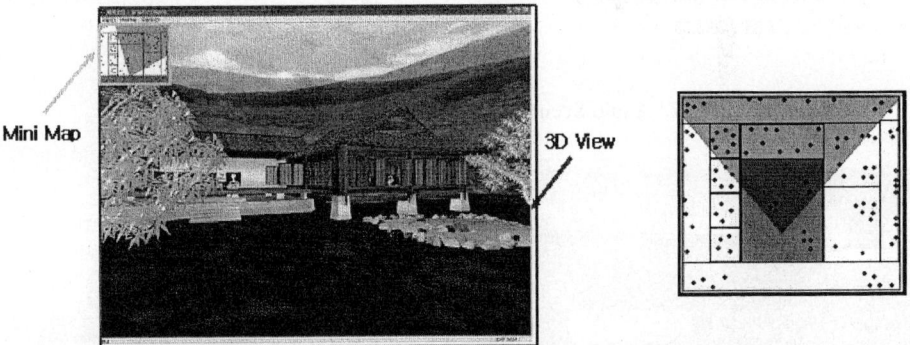

Fig. 6. The interface of graphic engine. Mini Map of the left side of 3D View means violet color shows current space containing moving listener and green color shows the view of a listener at his current position.

For graphic engine, we tested on a 1.7Ghz Intel Pentium 4 CPU, 1Gbyte DRAM, and FireGL 8800 and for sound engine, we tested on a 3.4Ghz Intel Pentium 4 CPU and 2Gbyte SRAM. See Fig. 6. This is our graphic Interface. Listener can navigate with mouse and find his position through Mini map on the left side of screen.

5.1 Results of Graphic Reduction

To test efficiently, we selected traditional Korean house, because it is consisted of a lot of holes and gaps like windows and door. Our complex 3D scene has total 207,720 polygons and is reduced to 414 facets (See Fig. 8).

The resulting scene is represented as Audio Scenegraph we defined (See Fig. 7). Entire scene is consisted of 12 sub spaces and each sub space just has facet index and sound index. The real data of facets and sounds are stored to other storages for efficient sound rendering.

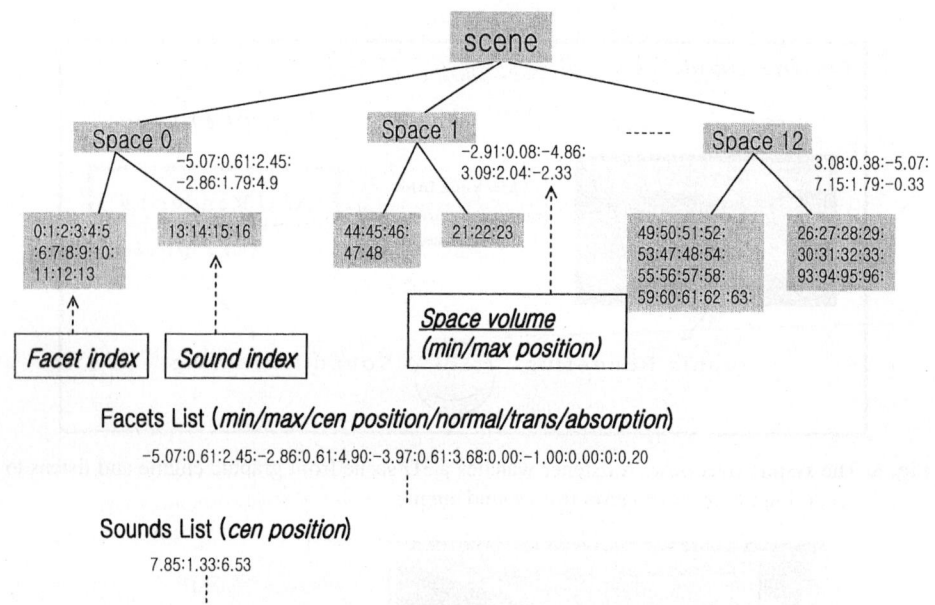

Fig. 7. Audio Scenegraph of our application for testing

Fig. 8. Results of graphic reduction

5.2 Results of Sound Source Reduction

For making proof of stable real-time without regard to a number of sounds, we tested from 100 to 200 with adding 10 sound sources (See Fig. 9 and Table 1). To test robustly, we set the position of a listener at the sub space contains a lot of sounds and facets. That is because played sounds are proportional to facets of sub space. The result shows sable realtime calculation as below 50ms, even if the number of sounds is increased.

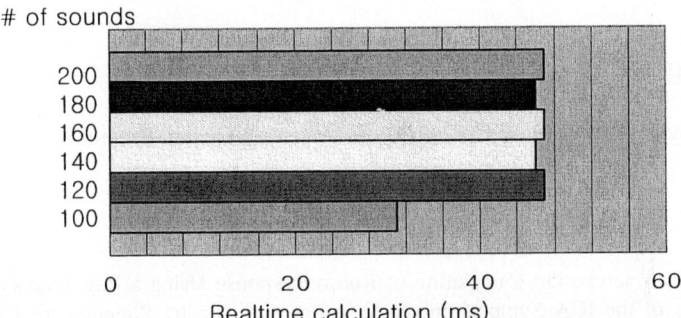

Fig. 9. the chart of realtime calculation: the number of sound sources is increased from 100 to 200

Table 1. Results of realtime calculation

The number of Sounds	Pre-computing time (ms)	Real-time (ms)
100	19,734	31
120	20,218	47
140	28,891	46
160	32,016	47
180	36,172	46
200	38,422	47

Results of Table 1. are tested on sub space which contains 18 facets and 12 sounds. Thus, during online phrase, 18 buffers of storages of facets are played, below 216 sounds by image method of 12 sounds inside sub space are played with sound inside sub space. Because virtual sounds by image method are estimated by early reflection and perceptual culling, played sounds by image method are below 216 (multiply 12 by 18).

6 Conclusions and Future Works

We suggest the method that reduces real-time calculation by using Audio Scenegraph and clustering sounds for each facet. This provides not only reduced real-time calculation, but also improved interactivity for real-time 3D sound rendering. Therefore this approach is useful to the application that sounds should be considered interactively (e.g. games or something for visually impaired people).

However, we have some limitations. 1) This method is suitable for static sound sources. Until now we think dynamic sounds are fewer than static sounds, and dynamic sounds are just played or clustered by Nicolas [10]. Therefore, we will try to extend our approach to dynamic sounds. 2) We did not estimate the reliability of methods through the listener test: perceptual test, interface test, interaction test and so on. Therefore, we will evaluate this method through the listener test.

Acknowledgement

This research was supported by University IT Research Center Project in Korea.

References

1. Vian J., Van Maercke D.: Calculation of Room Response Using a Ray Tracing Method. Proceedings of the ICA Symposium on Acoustics and Theatre Planning for Performing (1986) 74 - 78
2. Allen J., Berkley D., Allen J.: Image Method for efficiently simulating small room acoustics. Journal Acoustical Society of America, Vol. 65. No. 4. (1979) 943-951
3. Borish J.: Extension of the Image Model to arbitrary polyhedra. Journal Acoustical Society of America, Vol. 75. No. 6. (1984) 1827-1836
4. Dadoun N., Kirkpatrick D., Walsh J.: The Geometry of Beam Tracing. Proc. Computational Geometry (1985) 55-71
5. Heckbert P., Hanrahan P.: Beam Tracing Polygonal Objects. ACM SIGGRAPH, Vol. 18. No. 3. (1984) 119-127
6. Tomas F., Nicolas T., Jean-Marc J.: A Beam Tracing Approach to Acoustic Modeling for Interactive Virtual Environments. ACM SIGGRAPH (1998) 21-32
7. Tomas F., Ingrid C., Gary E., Gopal P., Mohan S., Jim W. : Survey of Methods for Modeling Sound Propagation in interactive virtual Environment system. Presence (2003)
8. Topio L., Lauri S. el.3: Creating Interactive Virtual Auditory Environments. IEEE Computer Graphics and Applications (2002)
9. Chris J., Nadia T.: Significant facet Retrieval for real-time 3D Sound Rendering in complex virtual Environments. VRST (2003)
10. Nicolas T., Emmanuel G., George D.: Perceptual audio Rendering of complex virtual Environments. ACM SIGGRAPH (2004)
11. Erich G., Richard H., Ralph J., John V.: Design Patterns: Elements of Reusable Object-Oriented Software. Addison-Wesley (1995)
12. Ted P., Andreas S.: A Review of Algorithms for Perceptual Coding of Digital Audio Signals. Proc. of International Conference on Digital Signal Processing (1997) 179-205
13. James B.: Game Audio Programming. CHARLES RIVER MEDIA Inc. (2002)
14. Tomas F., Patrick M., Ingrid C.: Real-Time Acoustic Modeling for Distributed Virtual Environments. ACM SIGGRAPH (1999)

Dual-Domain Quantization for Transform Coding of Speech and Audio Signals

Jun-Seong Hong, Jong-Hyun Choi, Chang-Beom Ahn, Chae-Bong Sohn,
Seoung-Jun Oh, and Hochong Park

VIA-Multimedia Center, Kwangwoon University,
447-1 Wolgye-Dong, Nowon-Gu, 139-701, Seoul, Korea
hcpark@mail.kw.ac.kr, via-staff@viame.re.kr
http://www.viame.re.kr

Abstract. New quantization method for transform coding of speech and audio signals is proposed. The spectral coefficients obtained by the first transform are split into frequency bands, and those of each band are transformed again on a band basis, resulting in another set of coefficients for each band. Then, the efficiency of Huffman coding in two transform domains is analyzed on a band basis and a domain with better performance is selected for each band as the final quantization domain. In addition, a set of domain selection patterns with frequent occurrence is pre-defined in order to decrease the number of side-information bits for indicating the selected domains. The proposed quantization method based on the dual-domain approach is applied to ITU G.722.1 signal codec and the improvement of quantization performance for various speech and audio signals is verified.

1 Introduction

In transform coding for speech and audio signals, an input signal is transformed to frequency domain and the spectral coefficients are split into several bands for separate processing. Then, the spectral coefficients in each band are quantized based on a human perceptual model, followed by an entropy coding such as variable length Huffman coding if necessary [1]. One of the objectives of transform is to increase the energy compactness of data in transform domain for high coding efficiency using a given Huffman table. In general, however, the coding efficiency of each frequency band varies from band to band because of different statistics of band coefficients, which results in the waste of bits in some bands with high entropy and degraded performance in overall coder. Hence, for the best quantization performance in transform coding, all bands in the transform domain need to have a good data compactness property.

To achieve this goal in the transform coding, multiple Huffman tables are provided and the best one is selected for each band in [2], but many side-information bits and high search complexity are required. Switching between Wavelet transform and Fourier transform depending on the properties of the input signal is proposed in [3]. This method, however, still suffers from the variation of coding efficiency from band to band since the transform method is selected on a frame basis, not on a band basis.

In this paper, a new quantization method of spectral coefficients for transform coding of speech and audio signals is proposed which can provides an enhanced quantization performance by maintaining a high efficiency in Huffman coding for all bands. It computes two sets of coefficients in different domains for each band, and analyzes the domain characteristics with respect to the Huffman coding efficiency. Then, it selects the quantization domain with a better Huffman coding efficiency for each band where the final quantization occurs. In addition, a set of domain selection patterns with frequent occurrence is pre-defined in order to decrease the number of side-information bits which is required to indicate the selected domain of each band. The proposed quantization method is applied to ITU G.722.1 wideband signal codec [4], and the improvement of quantization performance for various speech and audio signals is verified under the structure of G.722.1.

2 Proposed Quantization Method

In order to compare the performance of the proposed quantization method directly with the conventional method employed in the standard codecs, the algorithm development and the performance evaluation of new quantization method assume the structure of a specific standard codec, ITU G.722.1 [4].

2.1 Quantization in G.722.1

The operation of G.722.1 is briefly described. In G.722.1, the input signal is transformed into a frequency domain by MLT (modulated lapped transform), and the transform coefficients are split into bands of 500Hz. The coefficients of each band up to 7kHz are scalar quantized with a given step-size after normalization by a quantized band RMS value. Finally, the quantization indices of each band are coded by Huffman coding. Because the Huffman coding is involved in the quantization, the number of bits required for quantization is determined not only by the quantization step-size but also by the distribution of indices and the Huffman table.

The Huffman table in G.722.1 is designed to assign a small number of bits to zero vectors, which implies that the bands with more zero indices require fewer bits for quantization with the same quantization step-size. In addition, the band with many zero indices further decreases the required number of bits because a sign bit is not necessary for a zero index. Thus, the Huffman coding efficiency can be improved when the band energy is concentrated to a few transform coefficients so that many zero index vectors can result after quantization.

The final step-size of each band is determined among a set of 16 bit allocation patterns after computing the number of bits required by the Huffman coding with each of 16 patterns. Those bit allocation patterns are computed based on the distribution of band energy and the number of available bits, and since the same bit allocation patterns can be determined in the decoder, only four bits are necessary to transmit the bit allocation information.

2.2 Problem Analysis

The problem of quantization method in G.722.1 is first analyzed. Figure 1(a) is a waveform of male voiced speech signal of 20msec which corresponds to 320 samples with 16kHz sampling, and Figure 1(b) is the normalized MLT coefficients following the method in G.722.1, where each vertical grid line represents a 500Hz band with 20 coefficients. Only 14 bands are necessary since bands above 7kHz are discarded in G.722.1. It can be seen that the distribution of MLT coefficients in a band from 2500Hz to 3000Hz (index from 100 to 120 in x-axis) is concentrated to a few points, while that in a band from 3000Hz to 3500Hz (index from 120 to 140) is widely expanded within a band. Therefore, the former band is quantized and Huffman coded very efficiently with the Huffman table in G.722.1, but the latter band is not. This analysis clearly shows the problem of current quantization method and naturally leads to the development of new quantization method which can reduce the variation of index statistics over bands and enable all bands to be coded more efficiently with a given Huffman table by using the coefficients of desired statistics.

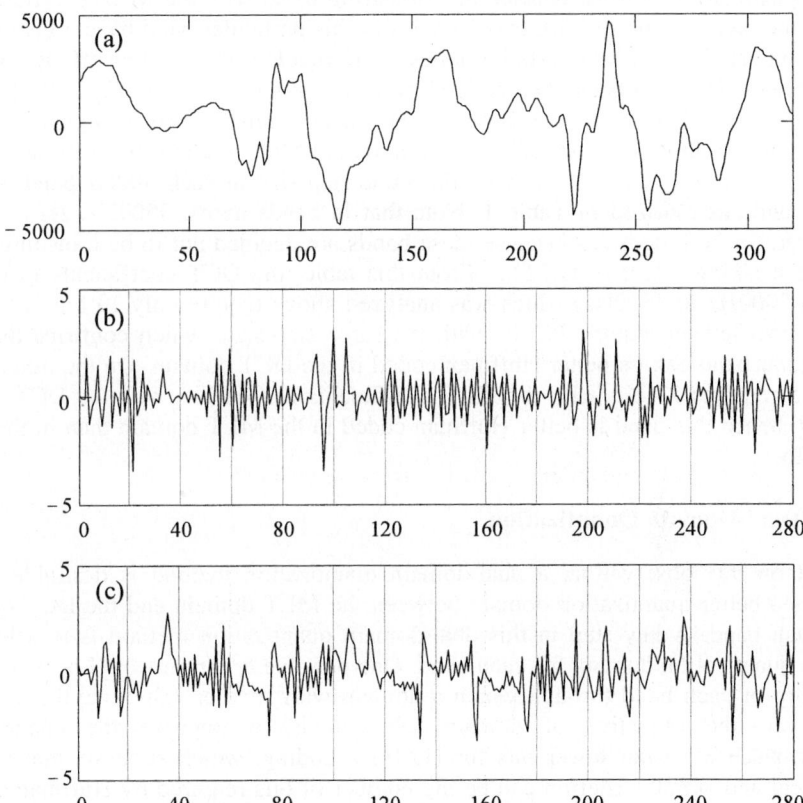

Fig. 1. Male voiced speech. MLT coefficients and DCT coefficients have different statistics and different Huffman coding efficiency for each band. (a) Waveform of 20msec. (b) Normalized MLT coefficients. (c) MLT-DCT coefficients.

As shown in Figure 1(b), not all bands are efficiently coded with a given Huffman table. The statistics of MLT coefficients, however, can be modified by transforming the MLT coefficients by another transform such as DCT, and Figure 1(c) confirms this property. Figure 1(c) shows 20-point DCT coefficients of normalized MLT coefficients in Figure 1(b). In other words, a set of 20 MLT coefficients of each band is considered as a separate 20-sample signal and is applied to 20-point DCT operation, resulting in 20 DCT coefficients for each band. The 20 MLT coefficients are transformed by DCT without windowing or overlapping so that DCT coefficients can be locally invertible in each band.

These DCT coefficients are actually MLT-DCT coefficients, but they are called DCT coefficients in short. Conceptually, the DCT coefficients are time-domain data of band-passed signal because they are generated by DCT operation of band-limited spectral coefficients, while the MLT coefficients are purely frequency domain data. As clearly seen in Figure 1(c), the DCT coefficients in a band from 3000Hz to 3500Hz (index from 120 to 140) have a pulse-like shape with a possibility of many zero quantization indices as desired. Comparing these with the MLT coefficients of the same band in Figure 1(b), two domains in this particular band have a distinct difference in statistics, which further implies a different Huffman coding efficiency.

More evident results can be obtained by an actual computation of quantization and Huffman coding. After quantization and Huffman coding of speech signal in Figure 1(a) by the method given in G.722.1, the number of bits required by Huffman coding of MLT and DCT coefficients with the same step-size in each 500Hz band is computed and summarized in Table 1. Note that in bands above 5500Hz, zero bits are required for both domains because these bands are decided not to be transmitted due to the masking effect in G.722.1. From this table, the DCT coefficients in band 6 (from 3000Hz to 3500Hz) which was analyzed above require only 19 bits, while the MLT coefficients require 29 bits with the same step-size, which confirms that this particular band can be better Huffman coded in the DCT domain. On the other hand, band 5 requires 27 bits with the MLT coefficients and 40 bits with the DCT coefficients; hence this band is better Huffman coded in the MLT domain than in the DCT domain.

2.3 Dual-Domain Quantization

Based on this observation, a dual-domain quantization method is desirable which selects a better quantization domain between the MLT domain and the DCT domain for each band. A key step in this dual-domain quantization method is to select the better quantization domain for each band. One possible criterion would be an entropy measure of each band through which a domain with smaller value may be selected. However, the objective of domain selection is to improve the quantization performance by using fewer bits for Huffman coding, which suggests that a more practical and simple criterion can be the number of bits required by Huffman coding in each domain. In the proposed method, therefore, the MLT and the DCT coefficients for each band are both computed and each coefficient set in each band is Huffman coded independently. Then, the number of bits required by Huffman coding is counted, and finally the domain with fewer bits is selected for each band.

Based on this selection criterion and the results in Table 1, therefore, the signal in Figure 1(a) selects the MLT domain for bands 1, 2, 4, 5, 9, 10, and selects the DCT domain for the rest of bands. As summarized in Table 2, this domain selection strategy achieves the reduction of 34 bits compared with the method in G.722.1 where the MLT coefficients are quantized and Huffman coded in all bands. When all bands are quantized and Huffman coded in DCT domain, 481 bits in total are required.

Table 1. The number of bits for Huffman coding of MLT and DCT coefficients for each band for signal in Figure 1

Frequency Band	0	1	2	3	4	5	6
# of Bits of MLT	89	58	38	68	49	27	29
# of Bits of DCT	88	76	62	62	62	40	19
Frequency Band	7	8	9	10	11	12	13
# of Bits of MLT	24	20	15	20	0	0	0
# of Bits of DCT	16	11	19	26	0	0	0

Table 2. Total number of bits required for quantization and Huffman coding in each domain

Domain	Total # of Bits
MLT in all bands	437
DCT in all bands	481
Selective	403

Note that for each band, the MLT domain and the DCT domain use the same step-size for quantization, resulting in the same quantization performance. The benefit of the dual-domain quantization comes from the difference in Huffman coding performance; hence the proposed method can provide the same quantization performance with a fewer number of bits. On the other hand, if the target bit rate is given, the quantization step-size of can be reduced using the proposed method, and the quantization performance will be enhanced without an increase in the number of bits.

Due to the domain selection in each band, additional fourteen side-information bits, one for each band, are necessary to indicate the selected domain. Therefore, in order for the domain selection strategy to work properly, the effect of bit reduction due to domain selection must be more dominant than the effect of the addition of 14 side-information bits. If the MLT and DCT domains are selected evenly over bands, the effect of bit reduction is maximized; in the worst case, however, if the MLT domain is selected for all bands, there is no bit reduction at all and the additional 14 bits are required, which is often observed in audio signals from experiments.

Figure 2 and Figure 3 show the examples of this potential problem of dual-domain quantization. Figure 2(a) is a 20msec waveform of jazz music, and its MLT coefficients shown in (b) have a desired property for an efficient Huffman coding especially in lower bands. The DCT coefficients shown in (c), however, have poor performance in Huffman coding. In this example, all bands except for band 10 (index from 200 to 220) select the MLT domain, and the dual-domain method requires more bits than the MLT-only method when including the 14 side-information bits.

In contrast to Figure 2, Figure 3(a) which is an onset region of male speech has almost random MLT coefficients with no compaction property as shown in (b). On the other hand, the DCT coefficients in (c) have all pulse-like shapes and good Huffman coding performance. In this example, only band 0 selects MLT domain, and the dual-domain method requires more bits than the DCT-only method.

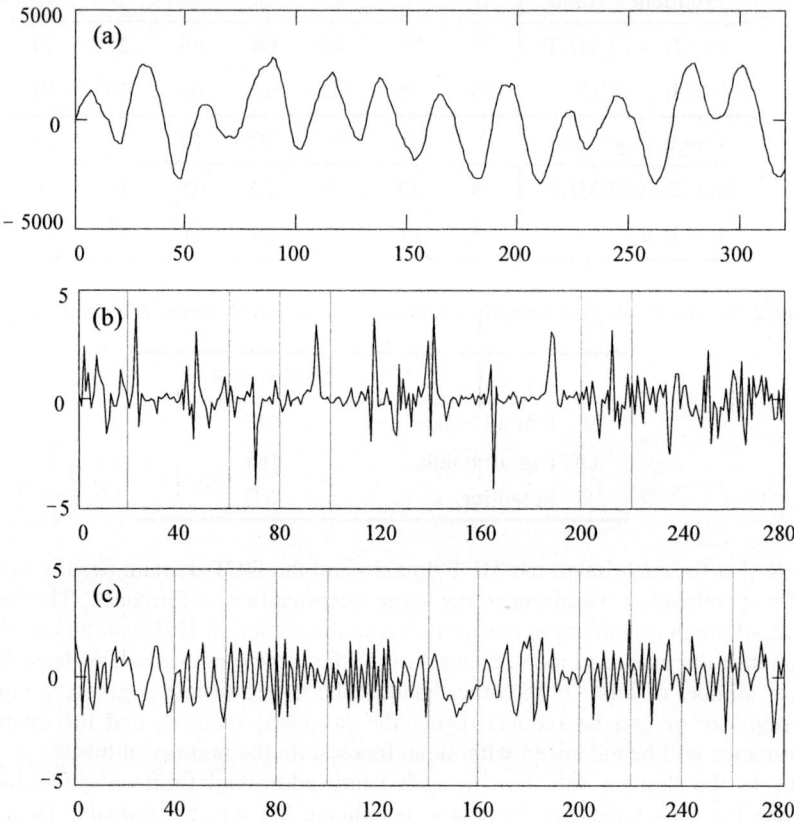

Fig. 2. Jazz music signal. Most of the bands select the MLT domain for better Huffman coding. (a) Waveform of 20msec. (b) Normalized MLT coefficients. (c) MLT-DCT coefficients.

2.4 Selection Modes

To solve the problem of a potential increase in the number of bits by additional side-information bits, a set of domain selection patterns with frequent occurrence is predefined based on extensive statistical analysis of various speech and audio signals. Based on this, the four *selection modes* defined in Table 3 are used as follows. For each frame, the total number of bits for quantization and Huffman coding is counted including the 14 side-information bits for the domain selection as mentioned above, which is the result of mode 0. Next, the total number of bits, when the lower 8 bands select a better domain and the higher 6 bands always use the MLT domain without selection, is counted including 8 side-information bits for the lower bands, which is the result of mode 1. Similarly, the higher 6 bands always use DCT domain and the lower 8 bands select the domain in mode 2, and all bands use MLT domain in mode 3 without any selection process. The number of bits for all 4 modes is then computed, and the one with the least number of bits is selected as the final selection mode. This process can be easily implemented after the MLT and the DCT coefficients of each band are quantized and Huffman coded, and the number of bits is tabulated for each band and domain.

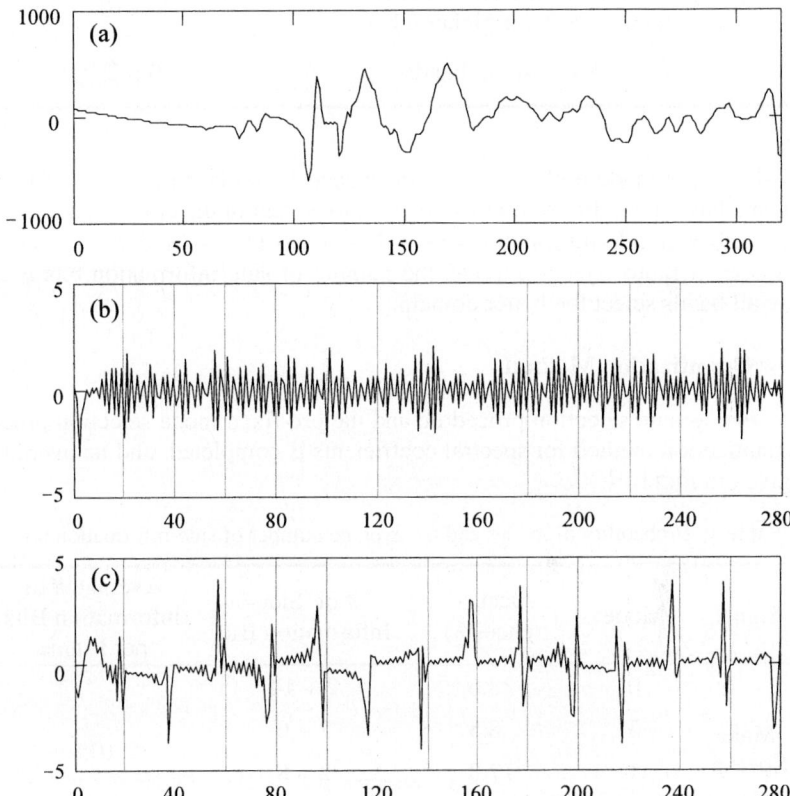

Fig. 3. Onset region of male speech. Most of the bands select the DCT domain for better Huffman coding. (a) Waveform of 20msec. (b) Normalized MLT coefficients. (c) MLT-DCT coefficients.

Using this selection mode, two kinds of side-information bits are required as explained in the last column of Table 3, where the former corresponds to two mode indication bits and the latter to the varying number of domain indication bits. However, the average number of total side-information bits is decreased. For example,

Table 3. Definition of selection modes and the number of side-information bits of each mode

Selection Mode	Description	Total # of Side-Information Bits(Mode + Domain)
0	Selection applied to all bands	2 + 14 = 16
1	Selection applied to lower 8 bands, MLT for higher 6 bands	2 + 8 = 10
2	Selection applied to lower 8 bands, DCT for higher 6 bands	2 + 8 = 10
3	MLT for all bands	2 + 0 = 2

Table 4 shows the mode probabilities of male speech and jazz music of 1000 frames. Two signals have quite different mode distributions, and in the case of jazz music, the average number of side-information bits is 2 + (14×0.314) + (8×0.09) + (8×0.271) = 9.3 bit/frame; without selection mode, the number of side-information bits is always 14 where all bands select the better domain.

2.5 New Quantization Method

Based on the domain selection procedure and the pre-fixed mode selection procedure, a new quantization method for spectral coefficients is completed, and its overall structure is given in Figure 4.

Table 4. Probability of modes and the average number of side-information bits

Signal	Mode	Occurrence(%)	# of Side-Information Bits	Average # of Information Bits per Frame
Male Speech	0	38.6	2 + 14	10.8
	3	8.5	2 + 0	
	1	17.8	2 + 8	
	2	35.1	2 + 8	
Jazz	0	31.4	2 + 14	9.3
	3	32.5	2 + 0	
	1	9.0	2 + 8	
	2	27.1	2 + 8	

The reason that the reduction in the number of Huffman coding bits by the dual-domain method yields the improvement in quantization performance is briefly discussed. In G.722.1, the quantization step-size of each band is determined from a candidate set of 16 step-size patterns over 14 bands by a trial-and-error method based on band energy distribution. In other words, the total number of bits required for Huffman coding of each step-size pattern is counted and the final step-size pattern that comes closest to the number of available bits is selected. Therefore, if the bit reduction in Huffman coding of each band is achieved by the proposed quantization method, the step-size of the corresponding band is automatically decreased in the step-size determination process, which in turn results in the overall enhancement of codec performance.

The computational complexity of the proposed quantization method is increased compared with that of the original method because the proposed one requires the additional operations such as DCT in each band, quantization and Huffman coding for an additional domain. However, the increment is not serious in the aspect of implementation because only 20-point DCT is required and the size of Huffman table is small.

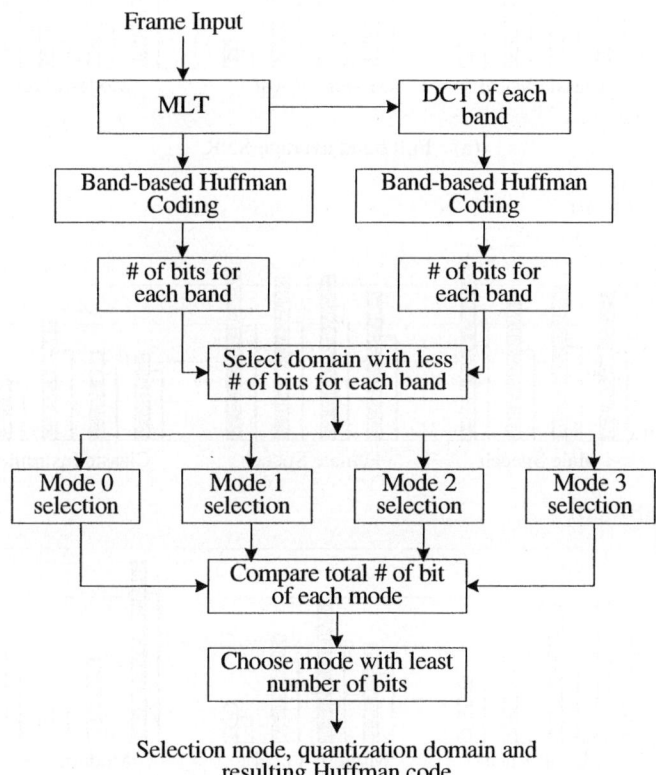

Fig. 4. Overall structure of the proposed dual-domain quantization method

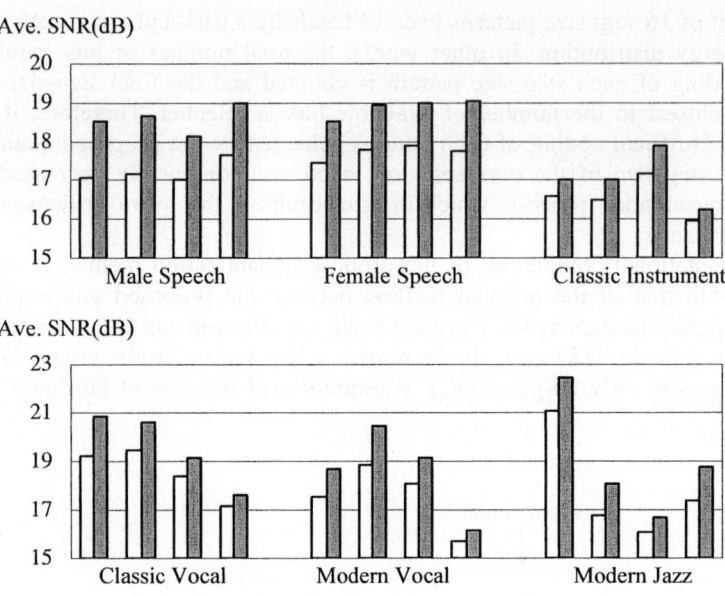

(a) Full band average SNR

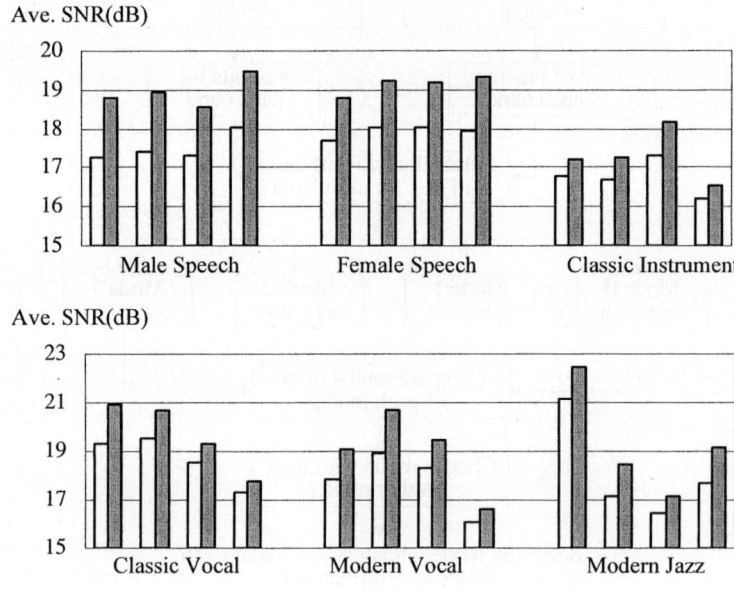

(b) Low band average SNR

Fig. 5. Quantization performance of G.722.1 method (light) and the proposed dual-domain method (dark) in terms of average SNR(dB)

3 Performance Evaluation

The proposed quantization method is applied to G.722.1 codec. Its performance is evaluated in terms of average signal-to-quantization noise ratio (SNR) and compared with that of G.722.1 employing the standard quantization method. In addition, in order to analyze the low-band performance below 4kHz which is perceptually more important than the high-band, the low-band performance up to 4kHz is measured separately from the full-band performance.

The signals used for performance evaluation include male speech, female speech, classic instruments, classic vocal, modern jazz, and modern vocal [5]. Each category contains 4 samples, and thus 24 samples in total are tested in the evaluation.

The evaluation results are shown in Figure 5. In all tested signals and in both full-band and low-band cases, the proposed dual-domain method has higher SNR values than the G.722.1 method with a significant increase. In Figure 5, all cases use the same bit rate of 24kbps for the quantization and Huffman coding. As mentioned before, the proposed method uses a smaller step-size for a given number of bits than G.722.1 by selecting the domain with better Huffman coding performance, and yields the better overall quantization performance with the same bit rate as the G.722.1 method.

4 Conclusions

In this paper, a new quantization method for transform coding of speech and audio signals was proposed. The MLT coefficients in each band are separately transformed again to the DCT domain, resulting in another set of coefficients for each band. The coefficients in two domains have different statistical characteristics in energy distribution and different efficiency in Huffman coding. Then, one domain with better Huffman coding efficiency in a given Huffman table is selected for each band where the final band quantization occurs. To reduce the number of bits for side-information for indicating the selected domain, the pre-defined domain selection patterns with high frequency were defined. The proposed quantization scheme is applied to G.722.1, and it was verified that the proposed method has better quantization performance than the standard method in G.722.1 for various speech and audio samples.

Acknowledgment

This work was supported by the Research Grant from IT-SoC Association in 2005.

References

1. Goyal, V. K.: Theoretical foundations of transform coding, IEEE Signal Processing Magazine (2001)
2. ISO/IEC 11172-3: Information technology-Coding of moving pictures and associated audio for digital storage media at up to about 1.5Mbit/s - Part 3 Audio (1993)
3. Sinha, D., Johnston, J.: Audio compression at low bit rates using a signal adaptive switched filterbank, IEEE ICASSP (1996) 1053-1056
4. ITU Recommendation G.722.1: Coding at 24 and 32 kbit/s for hands-free operation in systems with low frame loss (1999)
5. ITU Recommendation: Subjective qualification test plan for the ITU-T wideband(7kHz) speech coding algorithm around 16kbit/s (1999)

A Multi-channel Audio Compression Method with Virtual Source Location Information

Han-gil Moon[1], Jeong-il Seo[2], Seungkwon Beak[2], and Koeng-Mo Sung[1]

[1] School of Electrical Engineering and Computer Science, Seoul National University,
Shinlim-dong, Kwanak-gu, Seoul, Korea 151-742
fullmoon@acoustics.snu.ac.kr
[2] Broadcasting Media Research Group, ETRI,
Gajeong-dong, Yuseong-gu, Daejeon, Korea 305-700

Abstract. Binaural cue coding (BCC) was introduced as an efficient representation method for MPEG-4 SAC (Spatial Audio Coding). However, in a low bit-rate environment, the spectrum of BCC output signals degrades with respect to the perceptual level. The proposed system in this paper estimates VSLI (virtual source location information) as the side information. The VSLI is the angle representation of spatial images between channels on playback layout. The subjective assessment results show that the proposed method provides better audio quality than the BCC method for encoding multi-channel signals.

1 Introduction

A spatial audio coding technology is emerging in MPEG-4 as a new coding scheme for multi-channel audio signals. Unlike the conventional audio coding scheme, the most noticeable characteristic of the spatial audio coding technology is that the data rates do not increase linearly with the number of audio channels. Therefore, the data rate of SAC system (e.g. BCC) to cover the multi-channels is also much smaller than that of conventional system. In addition, the independent representation of the side information, for reproducing the spatial image in the SAC scheme, helps to control spatial image distortions or modifications separately from the mono/stereo audio coding scheme [1]-[3]. Binaural Cue Coding (BCC) is known to be the most powerful spatial audio coding system. The BCC represents multi-channel signals as down-mixed audio signal and BCC side information. The side information (spatial cue) of BCC contains the spatial localization cues and can be transmitted at a rate of only a few kb/s. The spatial cues defined in the BCC scheme are inter-channel level difference (ICLD), inter-channel time difference (ICTD), and inter-channel correlation (ICC).

A new SAC scheme is proposed with virtual source location information (VSLI) as a new spatial cue in this paper. The VSLI is the angle representation of spatial images between channels on playback layout. The VSLI estimation process is powered by an inverse power panning law. This method is based on Equivalent Rectangular Bandwidth (ERB) [4] partition of frequency band and modification of power panning law [5]-[7]. Coding of inter-channel azimuth angles instead of coding of inter-channel gain offsets has important merit of guaranteeing high inter-channel dynamic range.

The robustness of the proposed VSLI-based SAC system was verified by both objective and subjective preference evaluation. For an objective assessment, the method of Kullback-Leibler distance measure [8] is employed. In case of a subjective assessment, the blind triple-stimulus test [9] was adopted as the subjective preference test to grade the quality difference with respect to the reference (not coded signals) by using the seven grades. The test was performed with the help of GUI MUSHURA test tool [10]. The eleven reference multi-channel contents offered by MPEG audio group [11] were used as the test materials. The results of objective and subjective assessments are presented and analyzed in section IV. Finally, conclusions are drawn in section V.

2 Binaural Cue Coding

2.1 Concept of BCC

The concept of BCC is the separation of the information relevant for the spatial perception of multi-channel audio signals and the basic audio contents. BCC represents multi-channel signals as a mono/stereo audio signal(s) and BCC parameters. The mono/stereo audio signal(s) is just the sum signal derived from all sound sources which are to be part of the spatial image of the multi-channel signals. A basic scheme for coding multi-channel signals with BCC is shown in Fig. 1. In the encoder, a BCC analyzer extracts binaural spatial cues from the multi-channel signals. The multi-channel signals are down-mixed to mono/stereo signal(s) and compressed by AAC encoder. The side information (spatial cue) of BCC contains the spatial localization cues and can be transmitted with a rate of only a few kb/s. The independent representation of the information for reproducing the spatial image in the BCC scheme allows controlling spatial image distortions or modifications separately from the mono audio coding scheme.

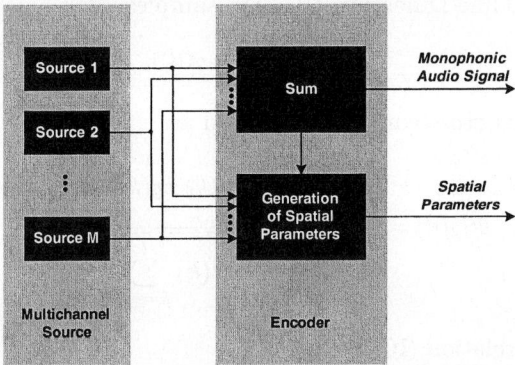

Fig. 1. Generic BCC scheme enhancing a mono audio coder

Since the BCC analysis and synthesis are separated from the mono audio coder, existing mono audio or speech coders can be enhanced for multi-channel coding with BCC.

In general case of **C** playback channels the spatial cues are given for each channel relative to a reference channel. Without loss of generality, channel number **1** is defined as the reference channel. How the spatial cues are defined between the reference channel and each other channel for the partition (subband index) **b** of frame (time index) **k** is shown in Fig. 2. For example, $\{\Delta L_{i,b}, \tau_{i,b}\}$ are the level difference and time difference between channel **1** and channel **i + 1** for the partition **b** of frame **k**.

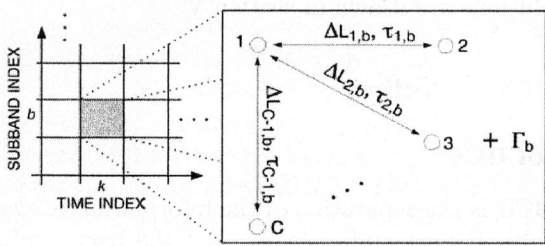

Fig. 2. The spatial cues defined relative to a reference channel for the **b**[th] partition

Commonly used definitions of stationary inter-channel cues for corresponding sub-band signal $x_1(k)$ and $x_2(k)$ of two audio channels with frame **k** are Inter-Channel Level Difference (ICLD) [dB]:

$$\Delta \overline{L} = \lim_{l \to \infty} 10 \log_{10} \left(\frac{\sum_{k=-l}^{l} x_2^2(k)}{\sum_{k=-l}^{l} x_1^2(k)} \right). \tag{1}$$

Inter-Channel Time Difference (ICTD) [samples]:

$$\overline{\tau} = \arg\max_{d} \left| \overline{\Phi}_{12}(d) \right|. \tag{2}$$

with the normalized cross-correlation defined as

$$\overline{\Phi}_{12}(d) = \lim_{l \to \infty} \frac{\sum_{k=-l}^{l} x_1(k) \, x_2(k+d)}{\sqrt{\sum_{k=-l}^{l} x_1^2(k) \sum_{k=-l}^{l} x_2^2(k)}}. \tag{3}$$

Inter-Channel Correlation (ICC):

$$\overline{\Gamma} = \max_{d} \left| \overline{\Phi}_{12}(d) \right|. \tag{4}$$

3 VSLI-Based SAC System

The ICLD describes the amplitude or power difference between the dominant audio channel and the other channels on the assumption that only one dominant audio object exists in one time-frequency partition [12]. However, the inter-channel dynamic range that the ICLD-based SAC (BCC) to cover has to be wide such that the quality of reproduced sound is preserved. Therefore, the quantization requires large number of bits to ensure this sound quality preservation. The conventional BCC uses 15-level uniform quantization for 18dB inter-channel dynamic range. However, 18dB inter-channel dynamic range is not enough to encode wide dynamic range input signal. In this case, the inappropriately quantized maximum level can cause the spectral distortion of original audio signals to occur. The ICLD information is estimated by the ratio between the reference channel band power and the other channel band power. If the reference channel does not contain a specific band signal which is contained in one of the other channels, then the ICLD information between the reference channel and the specific channel is not evaluated. In this case, the specific band information can not be reconstructed at the decoder. The drawbacks of the conventional BCC mentioned above cause the perceptual quality of reconstructed signals to degrade. In this section, VSLI-based newly proposed SAC method is introduced. Basically, VSLI utilizes the angle information of sound image. VSLI encoder estimates angle information of sound image in each band and each frame with multi-channel gain information and VSLI decoder reconstructs each channel gain with the angle information. The per-band and per-frame angle information is called Virtual Source Location Information (VSLI). The sound image localization method called the panning law [6, 7] is extended to the partitions of both frame and band and applied inversely to evaluate the VSLI. The newly propose SAC system with VSLI is structurally similar to the conventional ICLD based BCC system. However, the proposed system uses VSLI as a key parameter instead of ICLD.

3.1 Virtual Source Location Information(VSLI)

The VSLI is azimuth information which represents the geometric spatial information between power vectors of inter-channel frequency bands rather than power ratio such as conventional cue such as the ICLD. In VSLI-based SAC system, all of the source channels are transformed to frequency domain by DFT. Accordingly, the audio input signal in each channel is divided into non-overlapping partitions of time-frequency plane. The cue (VSLI) is extracted under the assumption that the playback layout of multi-channel loudspeakers is fixed as illustrated in Fig. 3.

Inter-channel power vectors form a spatial audio image between adjacent speakers. There are five possible number of the existing spatial sound image denoted as $S1, ..., S5$ in Fig. 3. One spatial image can be represented by one azimuth information. To evaluate the angle information of a spatial image, the power panning law [6, 7] and the notion of time-frequency plane [13] are employed. With the notion of time-frequency plane, the level information of each

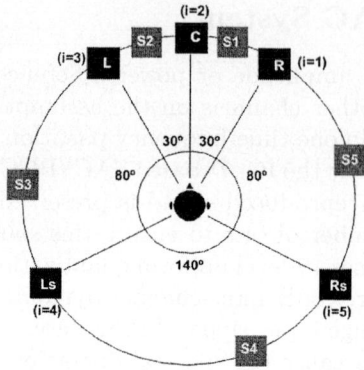

Fig. 3. Playback speaker layout

partition at each time in each channel can be evaluated. For example, the level information $\mathbf{L}_{b,k}^{i}$ of partition $\mathbf{b}$ at time $\mathbf{k}$ in channel $\mathbf{i}$ and $\mathbf{L}_{b,k}^{i+1}$ of partition $\mathbf{b}$ at time $\mathbf{k}$ in channel $\mathbf{i+1}$ are derived from DFT representation of audio input signal as shown in Fig. 4. To estimate the power vector of a spatial sound image between channels, not only the level information, but also the angle between adjacent channels is indispensable. The angle estimation with these two level information $\{\mathbf{L}_{b,k}^{i}, \mathbf{L}_{b,k}^{i+1}\}$ of two adjacent channels is performed with the help of power panning law.

To apply the power panning law inversely, the level information of channel $\mathbf{i}$ and channel $\mathbf{i+1}$ need to be normalized.

$$g_{b,k}^{i} = \frac{L_{b,k}^{i}}{\sqrt{(L_{b,k}^{i})^2 + (L_{b,k}^{i+1})^2}}. \tag{5}$$

$$g_{b,k}^{i+1} = \frac{L_{b,k}^{i+1}}{\sqrt{(L_{b,k}^{i})^2 + (L_{b,k}^{i+1})^2}}. \tag{6}$$

Then, the power panning law is applied inversely to the normalized adjacent channel gains of partition $\mathbf{b}$ at time $\mathbf{k}$, $\{\mathbf{g}_{b,k}^{i}, \mathbf{g}_{b,k}^{i+1}\}$ for position estimation.

$$\theta_{b,k}^{i,i+1} = \cos^{-1}\{g_{b,k}^{i}\}. \tag{7}$$

$$\theta_{b,k}^{i,i+1} = \sin^{-1}\{g_{b,k}^{i+1}\}. \tag{8}$$

Finally, the location information (angle) of virtual source between channel $\mathbf{i}$ and channel $\mathbf{i+1}$ is evaluated (9) with the normalized adjacent channel gains (7) and (8).

$$\theta_{vs} = (\theta_{b,k}^{i,i+1} \times \frac{2}{\pi}) \times (\theta_{i+1} - \theta_i) + \theta_i. \tag{9}$$

The estimated angle value is found to be valid for just one partition $\mathbf{b}$ of one frame $\mathbf{k}$ between channel $\mathbf{i}$ and channel $\mathbf{i+1}$. Therefore, angle values of

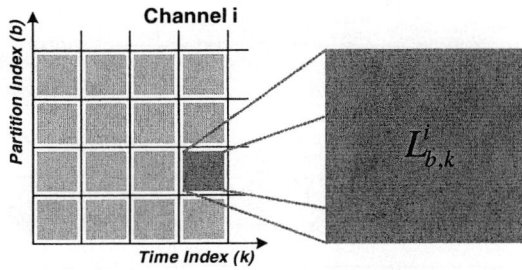

(a) $L_{b,k}^i$ of partition b at time k in channel i

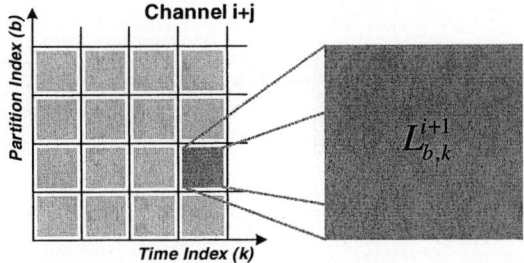

(b) $L_{b,k}^{i+1}$ of partition b at time k in channel i + 1

Fig. 4. Level information $L_{b,k}^i$ and $L_{b,k}^{i+1}$ with time-frequency plane notion

the number of partitioned band are estimated between adjacent channels and transmitted as spatial cues for one frame. The total amount of transmitted information for one frame is **N{partition}**.

The ICLD calculates the power gain directly by using the power ratio between the reference channel and the other channel band power, and then the power gain is applied to the transmitted signal power to reconstruct each channel signal. However, the VSLI obtains the power gain from the angle information indicating the sound source location estimated for the playback loudspeaker layout as in Fig. 3. This characteristic gives VSLI-based SAC system more robust performance that ICLD-based BCC system.

The important advantage of using the VSLI cue is the finite dynamic range of the angle value. Therefore, the angle as a spatial cue can be quantized with a consistent finite maximum level while preserving spatial sound image. The ICLD dynamic range, however, is dependent on the unpredictably varying channel power.

3.2 VSLI-Based SAC System

The schematic diagram of VSLI-based SAC encoder is shown in Fig. 5. The VSLI encoder receives N channels of audio input signal and down-mixed channel(s). It performs a DFT based T/F transform which is used in conventional BCC based SAC encoder. The spectra derived from the T/F transform for each of the

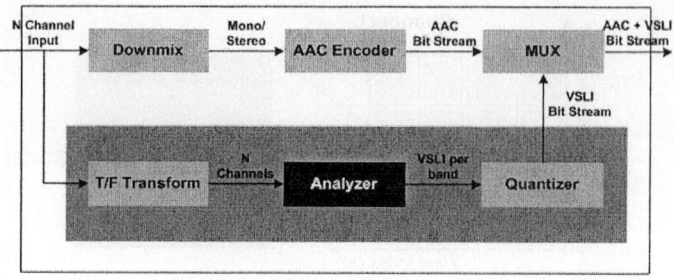

(a) VSLI-based SAC encoder

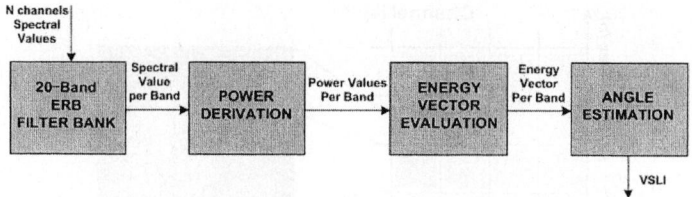

(b) VSLI analyzer

Fig. 5. The schematic diagram of VSLI-based SAC encoder and VSLI analyzer

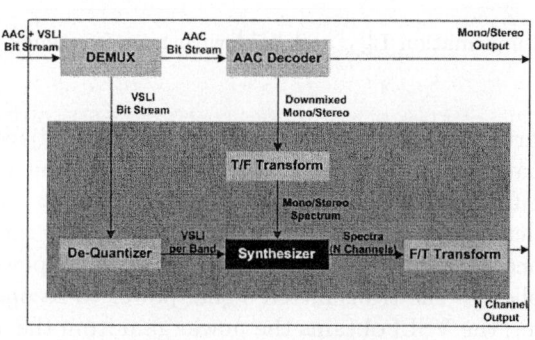

(a) VSLI-based SAC decoder

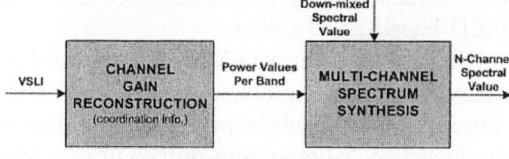

(b) VSLI synthesizer

Fig. 6. The schematic diagram of VSLI-based SAC decoder and VSLI synthesizer

channels are partitioned into 20 ERB partitions approximating the ERB scale. Then, the band energy vectors are derived from the level information of partitioned spectra and the angles of sound images of bands are estimated by means of the energy vectors and the power panning law in VSLI analyzer (as shown in Fig. 5). The down-mixed signal which contains contents is encoded with conventional AAC encoder. Then, the down-mixed signal and the side information (VSLI) are tied up and transmitted.

The schematic diagram of VSLI-based SAC decoder is shown in Fig. 6. The transmitted bit-streams are received by the DEMUX and they are split into the AAC bit-stream and the VSLI bit-stream. The AAC bit-stream is decoded into the mono/stereo audio output for mono/stereo users by conventional AAC decoder. Using the VSLI (the angle information), the VSLI Synthesizer (as shown in Fig. 6) reconstructs N multi-channel gains per band by means of the power panning law. The gains per band (power values per band) are used as key information to recover N multi-channel outputs from the down-mix channel(s). The power values per band and down-mix spectral values are used to estimate the spectra of N channels. Then, the final N channel audio outputs are derived from the N channel spectra after the F/T transform.

4 Experiment

The robustness of the proposed VSLI (information represented by angle) based SAC system can be verified by both objective and perceptual preference measures. Even though the perceptual evaluation is generally accepted as a measuring for the reconstructed audio signal quality, it would be better to provide the objective measure for more generalized reliability. In this chapter, the performance evaluation of VSLI-based SAC system is compared with that of ICLD-based SAC system, both objectively and subjectively. The objective assessment was performed with the help of the method of Kullback-Leibler distance measurement (relative entropy measurement) [8] and the subjective assessment was performed by the ITU-R recommended blind triple-stimulus test [9, 10].

4.1 Objective Assessment

The objective assessment was performed with the help of the method of Kullback-Leibler distance measurement. The Kullback-Leibler distance is a well-known distance measurement tool for measuring perceptual distortion in the field of speech signal processing. It is defined as [8],

$$D_{KL} = \int (P(\omega) - Q(\omega)) \log \frac{P(\omega)}{Q(\omega)} d\omega. \tag{10}$$

This distance was used as the objective measurement in this evaluation. $P(\omega)$ and $Q(\omega)$ denote power spectra of the reference and the decoded signal, respectively. Several D_{KL} were calculated from the reconstructed signals that were decoded by using the ICLD and the VSLI angle with respect to various quantization levels. Eleven reference multi-channel contents from MPEG were used as test materials [11]. Table I shows these materials. In addition to this table, total accumulative D_{KL} of each channel for the eleven contents is shown in table II (e.g. 15-level ICLD means 15-level quantization to each level and 15-level VSLI

Table 1. Test Materials

Index	Material Name	Category
A	BBC Applause	Pathological & Ambience
B	ARL Applause	Pathological & Ambience
C	Chostakovitch	Music (back: direct)
D	Fountain music	Pathological & Ambience
E	Glock	Pathological & Ambience
F	Indie2	Movie sound
G	Jackson1	Music (back: ambience)
H	Pops	Music (back: direct)
I	Poulenc	Music (back: direct)
J	Rock concert	Music (back: ambience)
K	Stomp	Movie sound
L	Total Average	

means 15-level quantization to each angle) From this table, it can be confirmed that VLSI-based results are objectively superior to that of the ICLD-based.

4.2 Subjective Assessment

The blind triple-stimulus test [9] was adopted as a perceptual preference test to grade the quality difference with respect to the reference by using the seven grades (from +3= "A is much better than B" to -3="B is much better than A") comparison scale. The test was performed by using GUI MUSHURA test tool [10].

Eleven reference multi-channel contents offered by MPEG audio group [11] were used as test materials. These materials cover all genres of music from classic music to oriental music as described in table I. The length of all test materials was less than 20 seconds to prevent listeners from becoming worn out and to reduce the total duration of the listening test. Each test material was quantized at various quantization levels as described in table II.

To obtain a fair assessment of the quality of the test materials, the listeners should have experience in listening to sound in a critical way and normal hearing. We referred to the ISO standard 389 as a guideline. Before the assessment, the

Table 2. Accumulative Kullback-Leibler Distance

	15-level ICLD	31-level ICLD	63-level ICLD	15-level VSLI	31-level VSLI
L	230.669381	230.716973	230.662226	229.180312	228.187281
R	233.152649	232.184487	232.012638	227.978998	227.014956
C	197.703029	196.962636	196.762861	207.671739	207.442912
Ls	237.290953	236.492079	236.246915	212.693343	211.083330
Rs	234.877636	234.094557	233.831755	210.179038	207.748244
Total	1134.093648	1130.450732	1129.516395	1087.70343	1081.476723

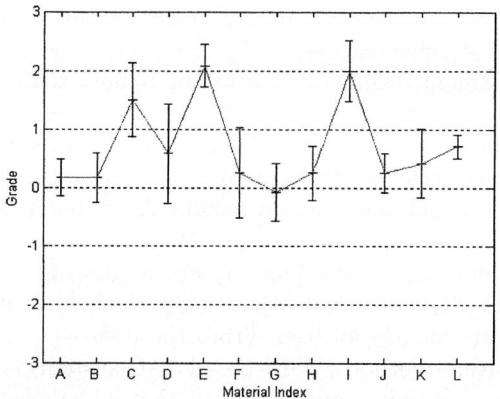

(a) VSLI 15-quantization vs. ICLD 15-quantization

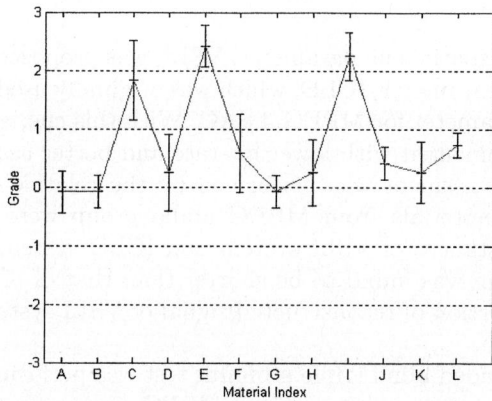

(b) VSLI 31-quantization vs. ICLD 31-quantization

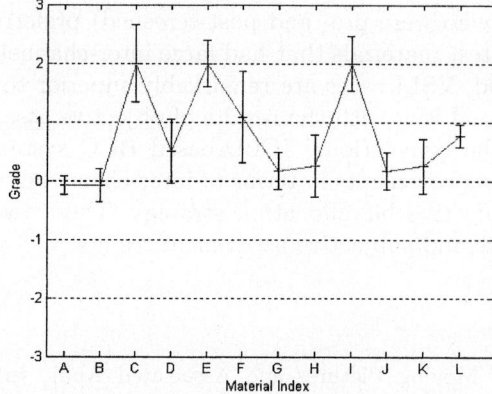

(c) 31-quantization vs. ICLD 63-quantization

Fig. 7. Subjective Assessment Result

listeners were coached to become familiar with all the sound excerpts being tested and their quality level ranges.

Among the assessment results of all listening panels, the results of the listeners who were able to provide consistent repeated responses were selected as data for statistical analysis. Twelve consistent assessment results out of more than 40 assessment results were selected to be used in the analysis.

As shown in Fig. 7, the comparison results show that most VSLI cases are slightly better than ICLD ones. Furthermore, VSLI cases are remarkably superior to ICLD ones for some sequences. The sequences showing superior test results are "Chostakovitch", "Glock", and "Poulenc", which have large inter-channel dynamic ranges or are clearly located. From these results, it is confirmed that the angle representation method (VSLI-based SAC system) is more effective for the sequences having large dynamic ranges or that which clearly localized.

5 Conclusion

In this paper, a new spatial cue parameter, VSLI, was proposed as an alternative to the conventional parameter, ICLD, which was originally used for BCC and was also a candidate parameter for MPEG-4 SAC. With this cue, a VSLI-based SAC system can be implemented with lower bit-rate and better assessment results.

The objective assessment was performed by the relative entropy measurement. Eleven test materials from MPEG audio group were used to measure Kullback-Leibler distances of VSLI system and ICLD system. The overall distance of VSLI system was found to be shorter than that of ICLD system. That is, the spectral distortion of reconstructed signal of VSLI system is smaller than that of ICLD system.

ITU-R recommended blind triple-stimulus test was performed for the subjective assessment. Eleven test materials from MPEG audio group were used for the test as well. Only pre- and post-screened test results were analyzed statistically to improve the confidence level of the assessment. For most of the test materials, the listening panels (who were pre- and post-screened) preferred VSLI case to ICLD case. For some test materials that had large inter-channel dynamic ranges or were clearly located, VSLI cases are remarkably superior to the ICLD ones. These results correspond well with the results of objective assessment.

Compared with the conventional ICLD-based BCC system, the proposed SAC system showed improvements in terms of inter-channel dynamic range and psycho-acoustically effective bit allocation strategy. These two merits can be confirmed by objective and subjective assessment results.

References

1. Generic Coding of Moving Pictures and Associated Audio Information-Part 7: Advanced Audio Coding, ISO/IEC Std. 13 818-7, 1997.
2. M. Bosi, K. Brandenburg, S. R. Quackenbush, L. Fielder, K. Akagiri, H. Fuchs, M. Dietz, J. Herre, G. Davidson, and Y. Oikawa, "ISO/IEC MPEG-2 advanced audio coding," J. Audio Eng. Soc., vol. 45, no. 10, pp 789-814, 1997.

3. D. Shinha, J. D. Johnston, S. Dorward, and S. R. Quackenbush, "The perceptual audio coder (PAC)," in The Digital Signal Processing Handbook, V. Madisetti and D. B. Williams, Eds., chapter 42. CRC Press, IEEE Press, Boca Raton, Florida, 1997.
4. B. R. Glasberg and B. C. J. Moore, "Derivation of auditory filter shapes from notched-noise data," Hear. Res., vol. 47, pp. 103-138, 1990.
5. V. Pulkki, and M. Karjalainen, "Localization of Amplitude-Panned Virtual Sources I: Stereophonic Pannig," J. Audio Eng. Soc., vol. 49, no. 9, pp. 739-752, Sep. 2001.
6. V. Pulkki, "Localization of Amplitude-Panned Virtual Sources II: three-dimensional panning," J. Audio Eng. Soc., vol. 49, no. 9, pp. 753-767, September 2001.
7. West J. R, "Five-channel panning laws: an analytic and experimental comparison", Master's Thesis, Music Engineering, University of Miami, 1998.
8. Y. Stylianou and A. K. Syrdal, "Perceptual and objective detection of discontinuities in concatenative speech synthesis", in Proc. International Conference on Acoustics, Speech, and Signal Processing (ICASSP), vol.2, pp. 837-840, May. 2001.
9. ITU-R Recommendation, "Subjective Assessment of Sound Quality", International Telecommunication Union, BS. 562-3, Geneva, 1990.
10. ITU-R Recommendation, "Method for the Subjective Assessment of Intermediate Sound Quality (MUSHRA)", International Telecommunication Union, BS. 1534-1, Geneva, 2001.
11. ISO/IEC JTC1/SC29/WG11 (MPEG), "Procedures for the Evaluation of Spatial Audio Coding Systems", Document N6691, Redmond, July 2004.
12. C. Faller and F. Baumgarte, "Efficient representation of spatial audio using perceptual parametrization," in IEEE Workshop on Appl. of Sig. Proc. to Audio and Acoust., Oct. 2001.
13. C. Faller and F. Baumgarte, "Binaural cue coding applied to audio compression with flexible rendering," in Proc. AES 113th Conv., Los Angeles, CA, Oct. 2002.

A System for Detecting and Tracking Internet News Event

Zhen Lei[1], Ling-da Wu[1], Ying Zhang[2], and Yu-chi Liu[1]

[1] Center for Multimedia Research, National University of Defense Technology,
Changsha 410073, China
williamjohnmail@126.com, wld@nudt.edu.cn, Yuchiliugfkd66@163.com
[2] Department of Computer and Technology, Tsinghua University, Beijing 100084, China
glwhdxdandan0103@tom.com

Abstract. News event detection is the task of discovering relevant, yet previously unreported real-life events and reporting it to users in human-readable form, while event tracking aims to automatically assign event labels to news stories when they arrive. A new method and system for performing the event detection and tracking task is proposed in this paper. The event detection and tracking method is based on subject extraction and an improved support vector machine (SVM), in which subject concepts can concisely and precisely express the meaning of a longer text. The improved SVM first prunes the negative examples, reserves and deletes a negative sample according to distance and class label, then trains the new set with SVM to obtain a classifier and maps the SVM outputs into probabilities. The experimental results with the real-world data sets indicate the proposed method is feasible and advanced.

1 Introduction

Internet news plays a very important role in the huge Internet information set. According to the latest statistic report of CNNIC, 84.38% of information got from Internet by Chinese users is news. Therefore, research on Internet news is becoming a hotspot in natural language processing (NLP) field. As a new direction of research on NLP, event detection and tracking[1] aims at automatically spotting new, previously unreported events as they happen, and following the progress of the previously spotted events.

The event detection is the problem of identifying stories in several continuous news streams that pertain to new or previously unidentified events. People who need to know the latest news when it happens, such as financial analysts or stock market traders, can use event detection to more quickly identify new events. It consists of discovering previously unidentified events in a chronologically ordered accumulation of stories (retrospective detection), or identifying the onset of new events from live news feeds in real-time (on-line detection). For the purpose of our goal that finds out what happens in the past, the retrospective detection is the right direction to pursue.

A lot of the previous efforts in this field have relied on statistical learning, and have emphasized different kinds of the words somewhat uniformly. We observe that when increasing the weights of subject string the system performance improves and when decreasing them the performance declines. This suggests that it would be beneficial to attribute higher weights on the subject string in order to detect events. Traditional methods of subject extraction from a text mainly depend on the mode of "thesaurus plus match"[2]. Exploiting the special structure of news, we search the full body with title characters to find the repeated word in this paper. These repeated word would express the news subjects very well after simple processing. So we proposed a novel subject extraction-based method to represent the documents. In addition, we also added the time distance to document similarity calculations.

The event tracking is defined to be the task of associating incoming stories with events known to the system. A tracking system's goal is to correctly classify all of the subsequent stories. Automated tracking of events from chronologically ordered document streams is a new challenge for statistical text classification. Existing learning techniques must be adapted or improved in order to effectively handle difficult situations where the number of positive training instances per event is extremely smaller than negative instances and the majority of training documents are unlabelled. K nearest neighbor (KNN), Decision Trees and Rocchio are well-known methods suited to tracking task[3], however SVM is seldom used to tracking task. The main reason, we believe, is that the positive examples are extremely sparse in the training set and SVM is not always fit for learning task of small samples. One solution to this problem is to discount the influence of negative examples by sampling a small portion and ignoring the remaining negative examples. In addition, event detection and tracking requires tracking systems offer a confidence measure, but a standard SVM produces the values that are not probabilities.

In order to overcome the limitation of SVM and use it in our tacking implementation, we present a negative-examples-pruning support vector machine (NEP-SVM). It first prunes the negative samples intermixed in positive class and the densely populated negative examples which are further from positive samples. Then trains the new set with standard SVM to obtain a classifier. Finally we map the SVM outputs into probabilities.

The structure of the paper is as follows. Section 2 and Section 3 detail the proposed event detection and tracking method used in our system respectively. Section 4 presents experimental results. Section 5 gives conclusions.

2 Detection Method Based on Subject Extraction

The goal of an event detection system is to group together stories that discuss the same event and spotting new events as they happen. Fig.1 presents the main idea of a event

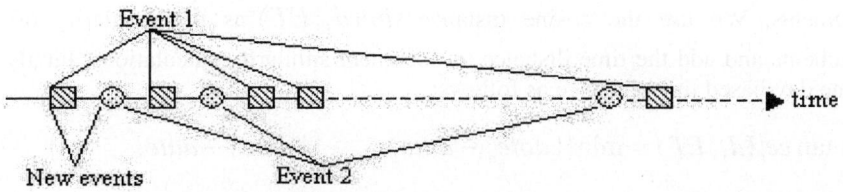

Fig. 1. Event detection task

detection system. A stream of news stories contains stories about different events. Stories on two events are marked in the example, one with squares, and the other one with circles.

2.1 Document Representation

Our approach uses conventional vector space model to represent the documents. Each document is represented by a vector of weighted terms, which can be either words or phrases.

Text subjects, especially subject concepts, precisely and concisely express the main topic and central idea of a whole document. Under this consideration, we give higher weight for subject strings. Normally, concepts in title are related to the news subject and more than 98% of titles can express the news subject clearly[4]. We may obtain important subject strings such as who, what, where by finding the reappearance of some elements appearing in titles and bodies at the same time.

To compare the importance of different subject strings in the news, we need to get the weights of subject strings. Firstly, higher weights should be assigned to longer string. It is because that longer string includes more concrete information than shorter one. Secondly, higher weights should be assigned to high-frequency string. Normally most of news reporters often use some repeated concepts when they wants to explain their important topic. Suppose there are k subject strings $TitSubStr_i$, $i = 1,2,...k$. $TitSubStr_i$'s weight is normalized by the following formula:

$$w(TitSubStr_i)' = 3 * \frac{Len(TitSubStr_i) * Freq(TitSubStr_i)}{\max_{i\ in\ k}\{Len(TitSubStr_i) * Freq(TitSubStr_i)\}} \quad (1)$$

Where $Len(TitSubStr)$ is the length of the subject string $TitSubStr$, $Freq(TitSubStr_i)$ is the frequency of the subject string $TitSubStr$ appearing in the body. For the weight of term in body of document d, we use traditional "ltc" version of the $tf \cdot idf$ scheme[5].

2.2 Similarity Calculation

In our current implementation, a similarity value is calculated while comparing two documents. We use the cosine distance $sim(d_i, ET)$ as the similarity of two documents and add the time distance to document similarity calculations. Firstly, we define day-based time distance as follows:

$$Dis\tan ce_t(d_i, ET) = \min\{|date_d - date_{Event\_B}|, |date_d - date_{Event\_E}|\} \quad (2)$$

Where $date_d$ is the document time, $date_{Event\_B}$ is the beginning time of event ET, $date_{Event\_E}$ is the ending time of event ET.

Given the current document d in the input stream, we impose a time window TW (set to 45 days) of m documents prior to d, and define the modified similarity between d and any event template ET in the time window as follows:

$$sim(d_i, ET)' = \begin{cases} sim(d_i, ET), & if\ Dis\tan ce_t(d_i, ET) = 0 \\ Dis\tan ce_t^{-0.16} * sim(d_i, ET) + 0.15, & if\ Dis\tan ce_t(d_i, ET) \neq 0 \end{cases} \quad (3)$$

If a document's time does not fall into the time window TW, the similarity between that document and the event template is assumed to be 0.

2.3 Event Detection Method

Event detection method used in our system is depicted as follows:

Step 1: Documents are processed sequentially;

Step 2: For each new coming document d_i, prepare a vector space model based on subject extraction of it, including:

- Calculate the $Freq(TitSubStr_{k,d})$ and $Len(TitSubStr_{k,d})$ of subject string;
- Calculate the weight of subject string in title $w(TitSubStr_{k,d})$ and the weight of word in body $w_{i,d}$ respectively;

Step 3: The first document is represented as the first event template ET_1;

Step 4: Each subsequent document is matched against all event templates, and each event template ET_i $(i = 1, 2, \cdots n)$ exists at its processing time;

Step 5: Determine time window $TW = 45$ days, novelty threshold $\theta_{novelty} = 0.56$;

Step 6: If time distance $Dis\tan ce_t(d_i, ET)$ < predetermined time window size

{Calculate the similarities $sim(d_i, ET)'$

If $\arg\max_{ET}\{sim(i, ET)'\} > \theta_{novelty}$

{ d_i is assigned to the most similar event E_{MS};

The representation for template of event E_{MS} is recomputed;}

else

{Perform new event alarm process and label d_i as seed;}

}

else { The similarity between document and event template is not computed;

$sim(d_i, ET)'$ is assumed to be 0;}

3 Tracking Method Based on NEP-SVM

A tracking system's goal is to correctly classify all of the subsequent stories when they arrive. Fig.2 presents the main idea of an event tracking system.

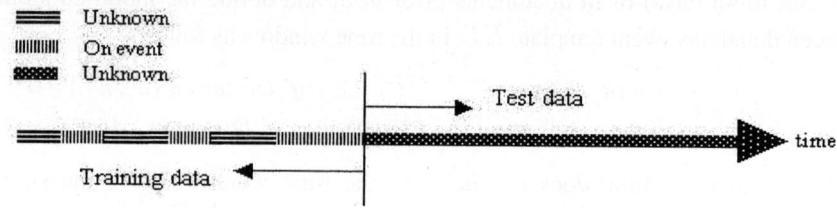

Fig. 2. Event tracking task

3.1 Support Vector Machine

SVM[6] has been shown to work in high dimensional spaces with remarkable performance. It has several merits: (1) Structural risk minimization techniques minimize a risk upper bound on the VC-dimension. (2) SVM can find a unique hyper-plane that maximizes the margin of separation between the classes. (3) The power of SVM lies in using kernel function to transform data from the low dimension space to the high dimension space and construct a linear binary classifier.

3.2 Event Tracking Based on NEP-SVM

Tracking task involves formulating a classifier from a few sample documents that contain discussion of the same topic relevant event. In tracking, the positive examples are extremely sparse in the training set, however the negative examples are densely populated. When training sets with uneven class sizes are used, the classification result based on support vector machine is undesirably biased towards the class with more samples in the training set. That is to say, the larger the sample size, the smaller the classification error, whereas the smaller the sample size, the larger the classification error. In order to compensate for the unfavorable impact caused by this bias, one can discount the influence of negative examples by sampling a small portion in the negative examples or choosing some representative examples from negative examples by clustering algorithm.

We only used a part of negative examples that are close to positive examples and all the positive examples as the training set, because they will be possibly selected as support vectors, whereas it is impossible for the negative examples that are far from the positive examples to be selected as support vectors (see Fig.3). There is no need for SVM to train with them. Therefore, we delete them. In addition, SVM focuses on the samples near the boundary in training time. The samples intermixed in another class (see Fig.3) are usually no good to improve the performance of classifier, instead they may greatly increase the burden of computation and their existence may lead to over-learning and decrease the generalization ability, so a negative example is also deleted if it has different class label from its nearest neighbor.

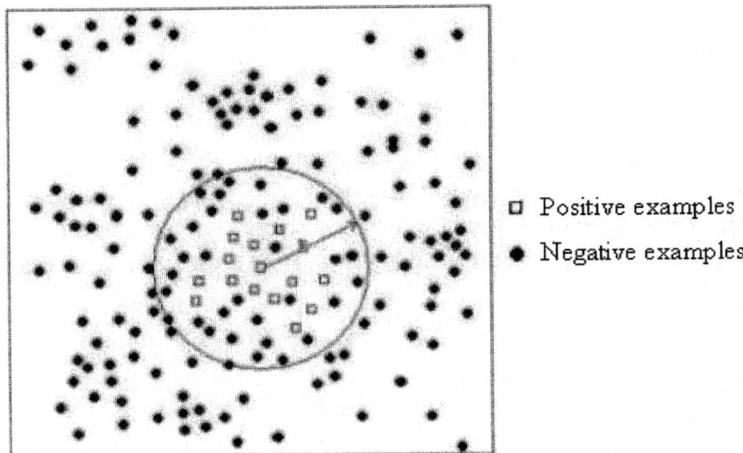

Fig. 3. Choose a part of negative examples and all the positive examples as the training set

With the considerations described above, the NEP-SVM-based event tracking method used in our system is depicted as follows:

Step 1: For each positive sample $ps_i \in \Omega^+$, find the nearest sample Ns_i to each positive sample $ps_i \in \Omega^+$ from all training samples $\{s_j \mid s_j \in \Omega^+ \cup \Omega^-, j=1,2,\cdots,k\}$, $k = N\_p + N\_n$

For $i = 1$ to N_p

$$\{ Ns_i \leftarrow \arg\min_i \sum_{j=1}^{k} Dist(ps_i, s_j); \}$$

Step 2: Decide whether delete Ns_i according to its label

For $i = 1$ to N_p

{If $Ns_i \in \Omega^-$, delete it; $\Omega^- \leftarrow \Omega^- - \{Ns_i\}$; $N\_n \leftarrow N\_n - 1$;}

Step 3: Let $m \leftarrow 1$, $FinalTS \leftarrow \phi$;

Step 4: If $m > N\_p$, go to Step 6;

Step 5: For $j = 1$ to N_n

{ If $Dist(ps_m, ns_j) < R$, $FinalTS \leftarrow FinalTS \cup \{ns_j\}$; $ns_j \in \Omega^-$; }

$m \leftarrow m+1$, go to Step 4;

Step 6: $FinalTS \leftarrow FinalTS \cup \Omega^+$, let $FinalTS$ be the final training sets of SVM;

Step 7: Decision function: $f(e) = \text{sgn}[\sum_{i=1}^{k} y_i \alpha_i (e \cdot e_i) + b]$ is adapted;

Step 8: If $f(e)=1$, then test document $e \in DE$, otherwise $e \notin DE$, DE is defined event;

Standard support vector machines produce an uncalibrated value that is not a probability. But constructing a classifier to produce a posterior probability is very useful, for example, posterior probabilities are required when a classifier is making a small part of an overall decision, and the classification outputs must be combined for the overall decision. In this paper, we adopted a function[7] to map the SVM outputs into probabilities. Instead of estimating the class-conditional densities $p(f \mid y)$, a parametric model is used to fit the posterior $P(y=1 \mid f)$ directly:

$$P(y=1 \mid f) = \frac{1}{1+e^{-f(x)}} \qquad (4)$$

Equation (4) used a logistic link function, and then proposed minimizing a negative log multinomial likelihood plus a term that penalized the norm in an RKHS:

$$-\frac{1}{m}\sum_i (\frac{y_i+1}{2})\log(p_i) + \frac{1-y_i}{2}\log(1-p_i)) + \lambda\|h\|_F^2 \qquad (5)$$

Where $p_i=p(x_i)$. The output $p(x)$ of such a machine will be a posterior probability.

4 Experiment Results

We ran our system on NEM study Corpus[8]. The NEM Study Corpus comprises a set of Internet news stories, which are collected from several influential websites. Each story is represented as a stream of text. It consists of 16560 chronologically ordered news stories. There are 16 events manually identified in this corpus. Each story was assigned a label of "Yes", "No" or "Brief" with respect to each of the 16 events. Except for a small fraction of the articles, each document belongs to exactly one event. We choose 10 events from NEM study corpus to carry out event detection and tracking experiment.

Effectiveness measures of our system were evaluated using the stories related to the 16 selected events. Our experiment is carried out in Pentium 4 2.6Ghz CPU, 512 RAM and Windows 2000 professional system. To evaluate the effectiveness of the event tracking results, six effectiveness measures including Recall, Precision, F1-measure, P_{miss}, P_{false} and $Cost_{norm}$ are used[3].

The effects of using subject extraction (SE) and adding time distance (TD) to document similarity calculations in our event detection method are illustrated in Fig 4.

We observe that introducing time distance increases the performance of the system. Recall, Precision and F1 are higher and P_{miss}, i.e. Miss, is lower than the version without time distance.

Table 1 shows the results of tracking system with using NEP-SVM. The number of positive training examples per event in our system is 4. The macro average method was

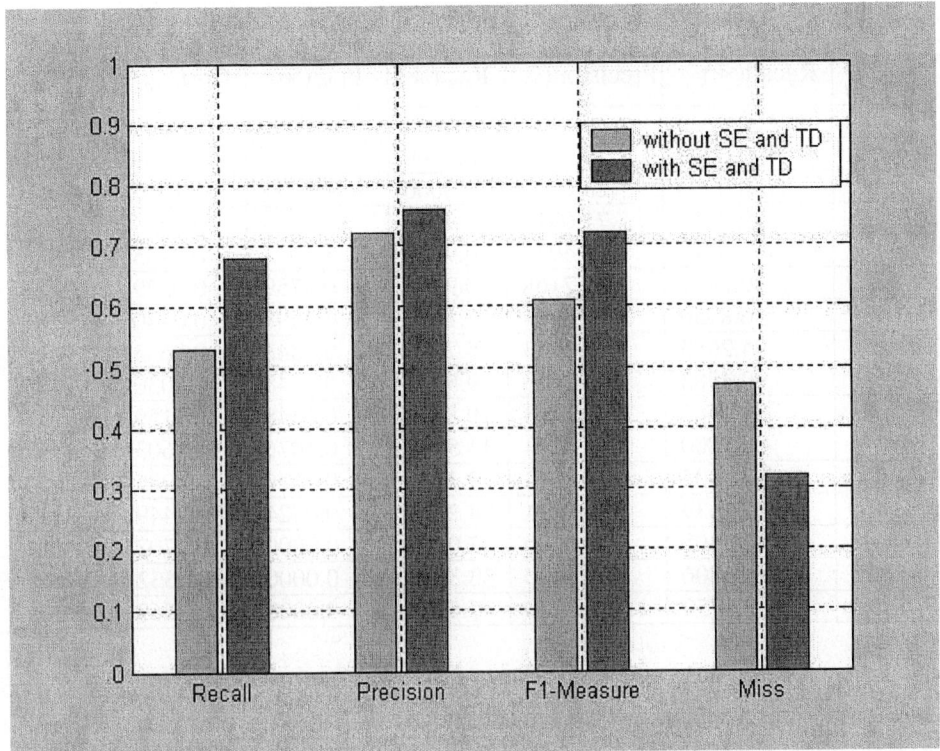

Fig. 4. Comparison of effectiveness measure (Recall, Precision, F1, Miss) between the case of without subject extraction (SE) and time distance (TD) and the case of with SE and TD

adopted to evaluate global performance, which is obtained by computing per-event performance first and averaging them. Table 1 indicates a minimum normalized cost of 0.0329 at a P_{miss} of 0.9583% and a P_{false} of 0.4759%. The optimal tracking threshold is 0.20 in our experiments.

Table 2 shows the results of tracking system with using standard SVM (without probabilistic outputs). Our experiments show that, compared with standard SVM, the performance of NEP-SVM is significantly better than that of standard SVM if appropriate tracking threshold is adopted.

Table 3 and Table 4 show the tracking results on Event 1 and Event5 with using different pruning radius respectively. Experiment results indicate that the performance of tacking system with big pruning radius is not always better than that of tacking system with small pruning radius, for example, the normalized cost of event 1 is 0.0271 when the Pruning Radius R=0.20, but the normalized cost of event 1 is 0.0541 when the Pruning Radius R=0.45. In some cases, using small pruning radius can not only reduce the computational demands of training but also decrease the wrong tracking.

Table 5 shows a result from comparison of four tracking algorithms. As it can be seen from the result, our tracking method based on NEP-SVM with probabilistic outputs showed a better performance than that of Rocchio and Decision Trees,

Table 1. The results of tracking system with using NEP-SVM

$T_{threshold}$	Recall(%)	Precision(%)	P_{miss}(%)	P_{false}(%)	$Cost_{norm}$	F1
0.05	100.0000	10.4918	0.0000	100.0000	4.9000	0.1875
0.08	100.0000	11.2166	0.0000	94.4257	4.6269	0.1984
0.11	100.0000	23.0180	0.0000	43.8711	2.1497	0.3610
0.14	99.0417	71.0919	0.9583	4.5678	0.2334	0.8087
0.17	99.0417	88.4971	0.9583	1.3043	0.0735	0.9284
0.20	99.0417	95.7168	0.9583	0.4759	0.0329	0.9723
0.23	96.8750	97.6901	3.1250	0.2598	0.0440	0.9724
0.26	94.2083	98.3163	5.7917	0.1548	0.0655	0.9610
0.29	90.4583	98.3163	9.5417	0.1548	0.1030	0.9322
0.32	89.1667	98.3163	10.8333	0.1548	0.1159	0.9225
0.35	84.5000	99.4274	15.5000	0.1076	0.1603	0.8973
0.38	80.6805	99.4143	19.3195	0.1076	0.1985	0.8686
0.41	75.7639	99.6774	24.2361	0.0524	0.2449	0.8296
0.44	72.9305	100.0000	27.0695	0.0000	0.2707	0.8117
0.47	66.6806	100.0000	33.3195	0.0000	0.3332	0.7667
0.50	62.3750	100.0000	37.6250	0.0000	0.3763	0.7301

Table 2. The results of tracking system with using standard SVM

Recall	Precision	P_{miss}	P_{false}	$Cost_{norm}$	F1
0.6271	1.0000	0.3729	0.0000	0.3729	0.7329

Table 3. Tracking results of Event 1, $T_{threshold}$=0.29

Pruning Radius	Recall	Precision	P_{miss}	P_{false}	$Cost_{norm}$	F1
R=0.10	1.0000	0.2105	0.0000	0.8287	4.0608	0.3478
R=0.15	1.0000	0.2920	0.0000	0.5359	2.6260	0.4520
R=0.20	1.0000	0.9756	0.0000	0.0055	0.0271	0.9877
R=0.25	1.0000	0.9524	0.0000	0.0111	0.0541	0.9756
R=0.30	1.0000	0.9524	0.0000	0.0111	0.0541	0.9756
R=0.35	1.0000	0.9524	0.0000	0.0111	0.0541	0.9756
R=0.40	0.9750	0.9750	0.0250	0.0055	0.0521	0.9750
R=0.45	0.9750	0.9750	0.0250	0.0055	0.0521	0.9750

the normalized cost of NEP-SVM is reduced by 0.069 and 0.053 respectively, when compared to those of Rocchio and Decision Trees. Though KNN is gaining popularity due to many attractive features and promising performance in the fields of event tracking, the performance of our algorithm is close to that of KNN in minimum normalized cost. As far as F1-Measure and Miss are concerned, NEP-SVM performs better than KNN.

Table 4. Tracking results of Event 5, $T_{threshold}=0.26$

Pruning Radius	Recall	Precision	P_{miss}	P_{false}	$Cost_{norm}$	F1
R=0.10	1.0000	0.8461	0.0000	0.0117	0.0573	0.9167
R=0.15	1.0000	0.9167	0.0000	0.0059	0.0287	0.9565
R=0.20	1.0000	0.7857	0.0000	0.0175	0.0860	0.8800
R=0.25	1.0000	1.0000	0.0000	0.0000	0.0000	1.0000
R=0.30	1.0000	1.0000	0.0000	0.0000	0.0000	1.0000
R=0.35	1.0000	1.0000	0.0000	0.0000	0.0000	1.0000
R=0.40	1.0000	1.0000	0.0000	0.0000	0.0000	1.0000
R=0.45	1.0000	1.0000	0.0000	0.0000	0.0000	1.0000

Table 5. Comparison of different event tracking methods

Method	P_{miss}	P_{false}	$Cost_{norm}$	F1-Measure
Rocchio	8.0788%	0.4306%	0.1019	0.8650
Decision Trees	2.0395%	1.3307%	0.0856	0.9012
KNN	0.9621%	0.4580%	0.0321	0.9568
NEP-SVM	0.9583%	0.4759%	0.0329	0.9723

5 Conclusions

In this paper, we introduced a document representation method that utilizes subject extraction and attributes larger weights for subject strings occurring in both title and body at the same time. We also put forward a new time distance-based similarity measure. Furthermore, we have proposed a NEP-SVM based algorithm to track topic relevant event. The algorithm only used a part of negative examples and all the positive examples as the training set to compensate for the unfavorable impact caused by the populated negative examples. In order to offer a confidence measure the NEP-SVM outputs are mapped into probabilities. With real world data sets, experimental results show the algorithm's effectiveness.

In our future work we plan to concentrate on exploring the suitability of information extraction techniques[9] to event detection and tracking, and their effects on system performance.

References

1. Allan, J., Carbonell, J., Doddington, G., Yamron, J., Yang, Y.: Topic detection and tracking pilot study final report. In Proceedings of the DARPA Broadcast News Transcription and Understanding Workshop, Morgan Kaufmann Publishers, Inc. (1998) 194–218
2. Gao, J.F.: An empirical study of CLIR at MSCN. In Proceedings of the International Workshop ILT&CIP-2001 on Innovative Language Technology and Chinese Information Processing, German Research Center for Artificial Intelligence and Shanghai Jiao Tong University, Shanghai (2001) 55–62
3. Papka, R.: On-line New Event Detection, Clustering, and Tracking. Ph. D. Thesis, University of Massachusetts at Amherst (1999)

4. Chen, G.L., Wang, Y.C.: The research on automatic abstract of Internet information. High Technology Letters (1999) 11(2): 33–36 (in Chinese)
5. Salton, G., Buckley, C.: Term-weighting approach in automatic text retrieval. Information Processing & Management (1988) 24(5): 513–523
6. Kim, K., Jung, K., Park, S., Kim, H.: Support Vector Machines for Texture Classification. IEEE Transactions on Pattern Analysis and Machine Intelligence (2002) 24 (11) 1542–1550
7. Wahba, G.: Support Vector Machines, Reproducing Kernel Hilbert Spaces and The Randomized GACV. Advances in Kernel Methods Support Vector Learning. Massachusetts: MIT Press (1999) 69–88
8. Lei, Z., Wu, L.D., Lei L., Liu Y.C.: A System for Event Detection and Tracking Based on Constructive-Competition Clustering and KNNFL. To appear in the System Engineering Theory and Practice (2006) (in Chinese)
9. Chakrabarti S. Integrating The Document Object Model With Hyperlinks For Enhanced Topic Distillation and Information Extraction. In Proceedings of the 10th ACM-WWW International Conference. Hong Kong: ACM Press. (2001) 211–220

A Video Summarization Method for Basketball Game

Eui-Jin Kim[1], Gwang-Gook Lee[1], Cheolkon Jung[2],
Sang-Kyun Kim[2], Ji-Yeun Kim[2], and Whoi-Yul Kim[1]

[1] Division of Electrical and Computer Engineering, Hanyang University,
Haengdang-dong, Seongdong-gu, Seoul, Korea 133-791
{ejkim, nohoho}@vision.hanyang.ac.kr, wykim@hanyang.ac.kr
[2] Samsung Advanced Institute of Technology,
Giheung-eup, Yongin-si, Gyeonggi-do, Seoul, Korea 449-712
{cheolkon.jung, skkim77, jiyeun.kim}@samsung.com

Abstract. There have been various research efforts on automatic summarization of sports video. However, most previous works were based on event detection and thus cannot reflect the semantic importance of scenes and content of a game. In this paper, a summarization method for basketball video is presented. The proposed method keeps track of score changes of the game by reading the numbers on the score board. Analysis of the score variation yields a video summary that consists of semantically important and interesting scenes such as reversal or pursuit. Experimental results indicate that the proposed method can summarize basketball video with reasonable accuracy.

1 Introduction

With the ever increasing digital video data, needs for new technologies to manage large amount of video data conveniently have also been arising. Automated video summarization is one of the possible solutions to offer a quick review of a video. In the field of an automatic video summarization research, sports videos have been a popular application because of its popularity to users and its simplicity due to repeated patterns.

Most of previous works on sports video summarization were highly dependent on event detection in selecting significant shots. Ekin et al. proposed a general frame work for sports video summarization where a method of shot type classification distinguishing play/break shots was proposed [1]. The ratio of dominant color in a video frame was used as a key feature for this classification. The proposed framework was applied on soccer and basketball video summarization. Also, a method of goal detection in a soccer video was proposed in [2][3]. In this paper, detection of interesting area in a field (i.e., the penalty area) [2] and detection of slow motions were performed [2][3] in addition to the shot type classification proposed in [1]. These events were combined to detect a special sequence, named cinematic template, which includes a goal event. Zhou et al. proposed a method of event detection in a basketball video [4]. In their research, nine major events (such as offense, fast break, dunk, non-game shots) were detected using motion vector, color, and edge information as features. Babaguchi et al. proposed a method which recognizes characters on the overlay, then detects events with a game descriptor that were obtained from the web site [5]. This method can generate summary that reflects the user preference, but the method needs a special games description that require manual operation. Audio features were also utilized in addition to the above mentioned visual features. Referee's whistle [6] or loudness of sound [7] was used to detect special events in the game.

With these event detection methods reasonable summarization is generated for some types of sports, but it may not be suitable for other types of sports. For example, score of a game is very common yet important feature, and the score information can be directly utilized in generating a summary for soccer or baseball game videos. In general, only two or three goals are scored in a soccer game. Also, ten or less is the most common score in baseball games. However, close to a hundred is not an extraordinary score in a basketball game. This is true for other sports like handball or volleyball. In these sorts of games, changes in scoring are more important than the score itself. Some patterns of scoring are very common and even sometimes occur in a repeated pattern like in a see-saw game that is more exciting to the viewer, and provides a clue for a semantic interpretation of the game. Hence, summarization should be performed based on semantically important scenes rather than specific events of these sports.

In this paper, a summarization method for basketball video is presented. The proposed method analyzes the changes in scoring to reflect the semantic importance of shots. Hence, with the proposed method a video summary is generated that consists of semantically important scenes. A number recognition method is utilized to read the score from the scene. Shot type classification is also performed to include play shots only while excluding non-play shots from the video summary. The overview of the proposed method is illustrated in Fig. 1.

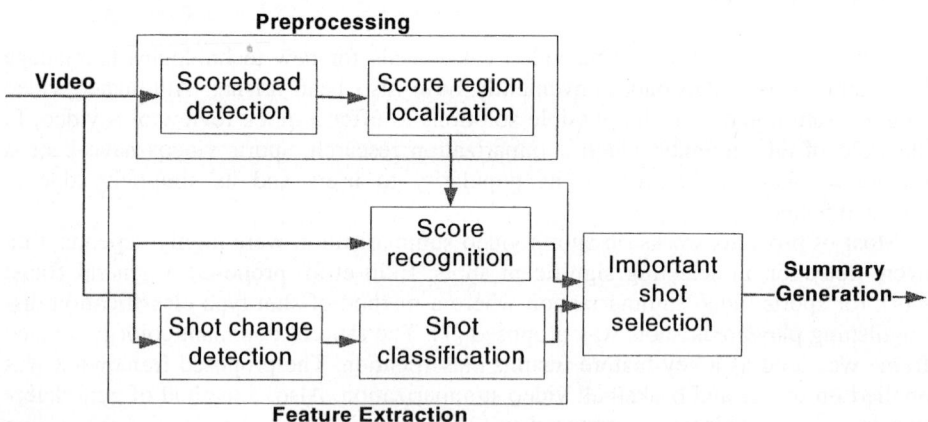

Fig. 1. Block diagram of the proposed system. In the preprocessing process, the location of scoreboard is localized automatically. Then features are extracted through whole video sequence. Type of shots and score of the game are chosen as features for summarization. Finally, the variation of scores is analyzed to decide which part of the video have to be included into the summary video.

Fig. 1 shows the block diagram of the proposed method. First, the input video is segmented into shots by the scene change detection method proposed in [8][9]. Then this step is followed by a feature extraction process. In this process, play shots and non-play shots are classified by the ratio of dominant colors in a shot. To read the score of the game by number recognition method, an initialization process is performed to localize the position of score automatically within the image frame. After the feature extraction step, important shots are chosen by analyzing the variation of recognized scores. Five rules are developed for this shot selection process; 3 point shoot, one-sided lead, see-saw game, pursuit and reversal. These rules can be easily applied to analyze the score in determining semantically important events.

The rest of this paper is organized as follows. In section 2, the preprocessing method is described. In the preprocessing, the location of numbers in the scoreboard is detected. The method of feature extraction is given in section 3. The adopted method for shot classification and score recognition are illustrated in this section. Section 4 describes how the variation of score is analyzed to decide important part of game in generating a summary video. The experimental results on several video sequences of basketball game are given in section 5. Finally section 6 concludes this paper.

2 Preprocessing

To read the score from the video sequence automatically, the score region on the board must be located first. For this localization, candidate regions for scores are obtained first via text localization. Then the score region is determined among these candidate regions using the characteristics of basketball game scores.

2.1 Scoreboard Detection

There were many researches on text localization because of its usefulness for various applications. The text localization also plays an important role in the scoreboard localization, since the scoreboard itself contains other characters. The text area detection method proposed in [10] is used in this paper, which is based on the fact that text regions usually contain many vertical strokes. Equation (1) represents the filter used in this method. In this equation, I represents the input image, x and y are the image coordinates. This filter accumulates the intensity changes along x direction to show high responses with vertical strokes.

$$A(x, y) = \sum_{i=-t}^{t} \frac{\partial I}{\partial x}(x+t, y) \qquad (1)$$

After binarization on the result of filtering described above, text candidate regions are obtained. An automatic thresholding method is used for binarization [11]. However, many false candidate regions are also obtained since the filter just responds to the regions that contain vertical strokes.

As one of such example, Fig. 2 (a) shows an input image of a play shot of the basketball game, and Fig. 2 (b) is the filtered and thresholded output image by Eq. 1. As

 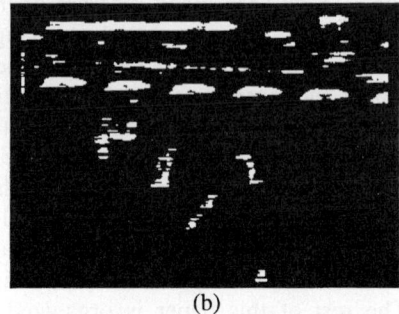

Fig. 2. (a) Shows the original input image and (b) is the filtered output after binarization

shown in Fig. 2 (b), the filtered image contains not only the scoreboard area but also the other textual area from such as advertising signboard or body of players, resulting in false candidates. To eliminate those false candidates, we use an observation that the caption area remains relatively still compared with that of players between image frames. Hence, only the regions which remain static during at least one second are chosen as candidate regions and those are accumulated during the training time. Finally, only the areas of upper 30% within the accumulated regions are considered as the candidate regions for the scoring. With this method, most of the false candidates are eliminated.

2.2 Score Region Localization

Within the candidate regions obtained by the method of previous section, there are many other numbers than the score itself such as the numbers in the clock to show the remaining time or the number of current quarter. To decide only the score regions from those candidate regions, number recognition is performed for each character in the candidate regions and the recognition result is analyzed. The scoring characteristics of a basketball game are utilized in this step: that is, the score is monotonically increased by 1, 2 or 3. On the other hand, the numbers in the clock decreases or increases constantly by one step. In addition, numbers that indicate the current quarter remain still during a quarter. With these simple rules, the score regions are identified and extracted from the candidate regions (Fig. 3).

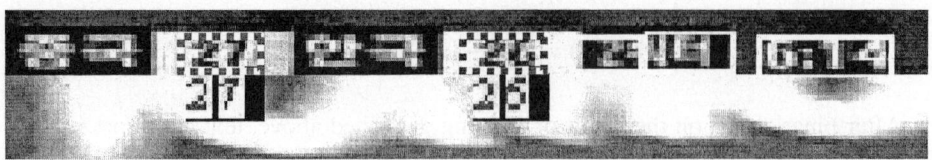

Fig. 3. The result of score region localization: Boxes with dotted line indicate scores of the game for each team. Numbers in white boxes are for time or quarter numbers.

3 Feature Extraction

In this section, the method of feature extraction is described. Two types of features are used in the system: 1) shot type and 2) scoring of the game. For shot types they are first divided into two groups: play shots vs. non-play shots. Non-play shots are of little interest to the viewers and excluded from the resulting video summary. The score of the game is then extracted and analyzed to determine where the important or exciting part of the game is. By applying a set of rules aforementioned to the score changes, semantically important points or parts of the game are then determined. The details of feature extraction process are described in the following section.

3.1 Shot Classification

Play shots of a basketball video provide holistic view of a game to the users and are usually taken by the single main camera located at the center of a stadium. Non-play shots contain audience shots, close-up views or the rest of other shots including videos captured by hand-carry cameras. Some of non-play shots also include scenes when the game is temporally halted by scoring, violation or time-out. Since these non-play shots does not carry any meaning related to the content of a game, they are excluded in the summary. Fig. 4 (a) is an example of play shot which is taken by main camera at a distance to capture the whole game in a frame. Fig. 4 (b) shows an example of non-play shot which captures a player in a close distance.

Fig. 4. Example of a shot classification: (a) play shot, (b) non-play shot, (c) dominant colored pixels in play shot, and (d) dominant colored pixels in non-play shot

To discriminate play/non-play shots, the shot type classification method proposed by Ekin et. al. is adopted in this paper [1]. This approach is based on the fact that long shots (or play shots) contains large number of uniform colored pixels. This ratio of dominant colored pixels and simple thresholds are utilized to classify shots in this method. The dominant color and threshold levels are automatically computed from the initialization process. An example of the use of dominant colored pixel is given in Fig. 4 (c) and (d).

3.2 Score Recognition

To analyze the variation of scores, the scores are recognized at the positions obtained by the preprocessing step. In our system, a neural network was adopted as a classifier for score recognition. A single number region was acquired from the score region and is resized to a size of 16 by 12 to construct an input vector for the classifier.

For the dataset to train the neural network, four types of different Microsoft Windows™ fonts (see, Fig. 5) which resemble the fonts used in usual sports video and their variations added with Gaussian noise were utilized. The trained neural network classifier showed accuracy of 96% from the test performed on 3,000 images captured from three actual basketball videos.

Although our number recognition module yields high accuracy rate, a single false recognition can affect significantly to the summary generation process. For example, if the score of 29:28 were recognized as 29:20 due to false recognition, then summary generation module will be confused with the score and fail to yield a proper one.

For this reason, the recognition results on scores have to be verified before passing it to the summary generation module. A simple consistency check for the scores is applied with two rules to prevent false recognition result. First, the score always increases monotonically and never decreases. Second, the score increases only by one, two, or three at maximum. When a false score that violates these two rules is detected, the system waits for the score from the next shot to replace with.

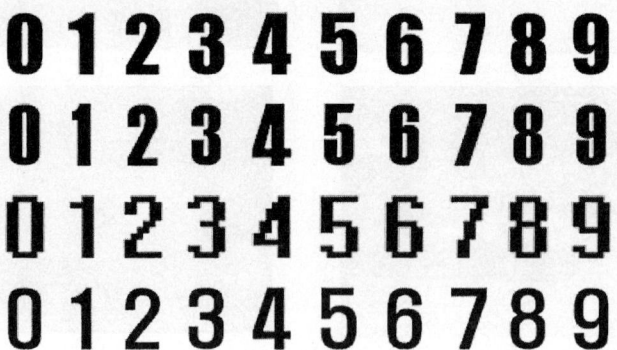

Fig. 5. Four type of fonts which are used in digits training: "Impact", "Haettenschweiler", "MYHead-M" and "system"

4 Summary Generation

In generating a video summary, scenes that are considered important should definitely be included in the summary. In most of previous work, however, event detection techniques were employed to determine whether the scene in question has to be included the summary. For example, goal event detection played a primary role for the summary generation in [2][3]. Also, whole video of a basketball game is divided into nine major events such as offense, fast break, dunk, non-game shot and so on in [4]. However, neither those method based on event detection can reflect the content of a game, nor choose semantically important scene between events.

In our system, the temporal change of scores is analyzed to select semantically important scenes. For this purpose, semantic templates of exciting scenes were defined first as presented in Table 1. In the table, five semantic templates are defined in terms of degree of interest of the game to viewers. These templates are for one-sided game, see-saw game, pursuit, reversal and 3-point shot. One-sided game means that one team overwhelms the other team in a game. For example, one team may scores continuously and this would be exciting to the viewers and also semantically important. See-saw game is opposite to the one-sided game, hence the leading team of the game exchanges hands frequently. Pursuit indicates that the score difference between two teams is getting smaller by scoring of losing team. It is similar to one-sided game since one team gets score constantly hence it induces similar exciting feeling to the viewers. In the reversal, the team that leads the game exchanges hands. The three point shot is also included in the semantic template since it is uncommon and important event in a basketball game. Some of those events may occur almost at the same time or in sequence to yield more exciting moments of the game. For example, pursuit game can be followed by reversal and one-sided game. Also, one-sided game may include successive three point shots which are also more exciting to users.

Table 1. Semantic Templates for Exciting Scenes

Semantic Template	Description
One-sided game	A team leads a game one-sidedly
See-saw game	Lead of the game changes frequently in a short time periods
Pursuit	The score difference of two teams is reduced by the scoring of losing team
Reversal	The winning team exchange hands
3-point shot	Scoring by a three point shot

With these semantic templates, the importance of a video sequence at a given time can be computed as Eq. (2). Here, $I_i(k_t)$ indicates the importance of a video sequence at frame k_t which is obtained by the correlation with the semantic template i.

$$I_{tot}(k_t) = \sum_i w_i I_i(k_t), \text{ when } k_t = \text{score changing frame} \tag{2}$$

The importance of video at a frame k_t by each semantic template is defined as Eq. (3) ~ (7)

$$I_1(k_t) = \mathit{diff}(k_t) - \mathit{min\_diff\_prev}(k_t, T_1) \tag{3}$$

$$I_2(k_t) = \# \text{ change in winning team during a time window around } k_t \tag{4}$$

$$I_3(k_t) = \mathit{max\_diff\_prev}(k_t, T_2) - \mathit{diff}(k_t) \tag{5}$$

$$I_4(k_t) = \begin{cases} \mathit{max\_diff\_next}(k_t, T_3) - \mathit{max\_diff\_prev}(k_t, T_4), \\ \quad \text{if } \mathit{winning}(k_{t-1})! = \mathit{winning}(k_t) \\ 0, \quad \text{otherwise} \end{cases} \tag{6}$$

$$I_5(k_t) = \begin{cases} 1, & \text{if } \mathit{score}(j, k_t) - \mathit{score}(j, k_{t-1}) = 3 \text{ (for } j = 1, 2) \\ 0, & \text{otherwise} \end{cases} \tag{7}$$

In the Eq. (3)~(7), *winning(k)* denotes the index of the leading team in the game at frame *k*. *diff(k)* represent the score difference between wining team and losing team at *k*. *min_diff_next(k, T)* is the minimum score difference during time window *T* next to frame *k*. *max_diff_next(k, T)* is analogous to *min_diff_next(k, T)* but returns the maximum score difference instead of the minimum score differences. Similarly, *min_diff_prev(k, T)* is the minimum score difference during the time window *T* previous to frame *k*. For example, assume that there is 10 points difference at frame 5,000. And the minimum score difference was 2 in the frames from the 4,500 to 5,000. Then *min_diff_prev(5,000, 500)* returns 2 and I_1(5,000) become 8. *score(j, k)* gives that score of team *j* at the time *k*.

Eq. (3) computes the importance of the video sequence at a time by using the semantic template of one-sided game. As shown in the equation, the importance of a scene is decided by the gap between current score difference and the minimum score difference in the past. Hence higher degree of importance is obtained as the leading team runs more score than the losing team. In Eq. (4), the number of changes in the winning team of the game during in a time window is counted to compute the importance of a game reflecting the semantic template of see-saw game. Eq. (5) is the case, after the large score difference between two teams, the losing team is chasing after the other. As the losing team is scoring closer to the winning team, then I_4 become larger. Eq. (6) detects the moment when the reversal occurs. The degree of importance is computed by the summing score differences before and after exchanging hands. The correlation with the semantic template of three point shot is obtained simply by checking the difference between two consecutive scores as shown in Eq. (7).

Using those equations, higher values are obtained when the score change is highly correlated with the defined semantic templates at certain time. Also the degree of importance of scene can be considered even within the same semantic template. For example, a reversal with larger score difference would be more dramatic and gets higher importance since the score difference is included in Eq.(6). Summing the degrees of importance obtained by each semantic template as described in Eq.(2) and the most recent play shot from frame k_t become a candidate shot of the summary. Also the last scoring shot is included in the summary video, since it concludes the game and considered semantically important.

Whether the shot has to be included in a summary is decided by thresholding the degree of importance value obtained by Eq. (2). As the temporal positions of semantically important scenes are determined, the actual shots to compose the summary have to be decided. The play shots prior to the ones above the importance threshold are assembled to generate a video summary. Also, only the last 10 to 20 seconds of the play shot are included in the summary since a time limit of 24 seconds is common in basketball game. This time duration can be changed by user.

To obtain different length of summaries, different thresholds can be used in the scene selection process. Higher threshold value will results in shorter summary video. The shots in the summary obtained with a higher threshold value are all included in the summary that was generated by a lower threshold value. Moreover, the weight w_i in Eq.(2) can be adjusted to reflect the preference of users. For example, one who prefers three point shots can assign more weight in three-point shots to generate a summary containing more three point shots.

The following is a pseudo code to generate video summary within the duration set by a user. The function select_summary_shot in pseudo code takes two arguments; *ShotArray* is an array for the degree of importance of play shots, and *TimeLimit* requested by user. Then the *ShotArray* is sorted in decreasing order for the reasons that will be obvious later. The play shots with highest degree importance will be added to the list in the order of time stamp of each shot until the length of the summary exceed the *TimeLimit*.

Pseudo-code of selecting the summary shot

```
select_summary_shot (ShotArray, TimeLimit)
{
    Duration = 0
    i = 0
    Sort ShotArray with decreasing order of I_tot
    while(TimeLimit> Duration)
    {
        Add ShotArray[i] to summary list
        Duration = Duration + Length of ShotArray[i]
        i++;
    }
}
```

5 Experimental Results

Based on the techniques previously discussed, a prototype system has been developed for summarizing sports video. As input to the system, two full length basketball video (MPEG2, 720x480) of Korean professional basketball league, were used to evaluate the performance of the proposed system. Since our system did not have any advertisement detection module, each quarter of the game was fed separately as input sequence to the system rather than a whole video.

The performance of scene classification is shown in Table 2. Recall and precision indices in Eq. (8) were used as performance measure. In Eq. (8), N_c, N_m and N_f indicate the number of correct detections, missed detections and false detections. The accuracies for detecting play and non-play shots were 85% and 90%, respectively.

$$recall = \frac{N_c}{N_c + N_m} \times 100\%$$
$$precision = \frac{N_c}{N_c + N_f} \times 100\%$$
(8)

Table 2. Experimental results on shot classification

	Precision	Recall
Play shot	89%	82%
Non-play shot	86%	94%

Also it was confirmed that the summary created by the proposed system included important scenes such as one-sided game or reversal. The graph in Fig. 6 shows the variation of the importance value obtained by Eq. (2). At the beginning part of the game, one team was leading the game continuously but with the small difference in scores. There was a reversal, however, at the end of game, and the losing team concluded the game as victory at the end of extended game. Consequently, the higher values occurred at the end of the plot is very stimulating. Finally, to measure the accuracy of the resulting summary, the ratio of important scene in the resulting video was measured and 93% of accuracy was obtained in average. The error was mainly caused by wrong classification of shots.

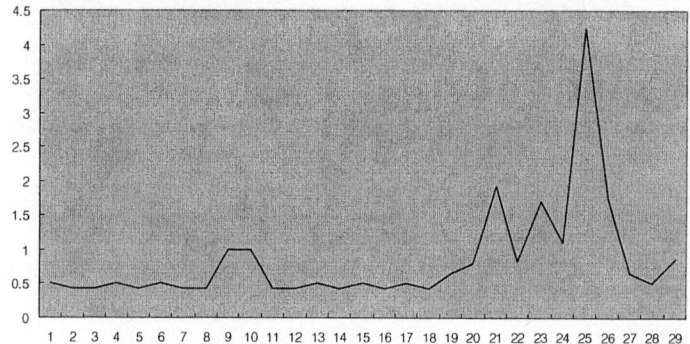

Fig. 6. An example of the variation of the importance value along the time axis

6 Conclusion

In this paper, a novel basketball video summarization algorithm is proposed. Unlike previous works which depend on event detection to create video summary, the proposed algorithm analyzes the patterns of scoring to decide semantically important scenes. Number recognition is employed to obtain scores where the location of scoreboard is detected automatically in the preprocessing step. Also shots of the games are divided into two groups: play and non-play shots by simple shot classification method. Finally, the degree of importance of scenes is computed to generate a summary video in hierarchy using five semantic templates. The resulting summary consists of exciting clips of scoring and is able to capture the flow of the basketball game, like pursuit or see-saw. This algorithm can be applied to other ball games which have similar score events, such as football, volley ball and handball.

References

1. A. Ekin, and A. M. Teklap, : Shot Type Classification by Dominant Color for Sports Video Segmentation and Summarization. International Conference on Acoustics, Speech and Signal Processing, Vol. 3 (2003) 173–176
2. A. Ekin, A. M. Teklap, and R. Mehrotra : Automatic Soccer Video Analysis and Summarization. IEEE Transactions on Image Processing, Vol. 12, No. 7 (2003) 796–807
3. Yao-Quan Yang, Yu-Dong Lu, Wei Chen : A framework for automatic detection of soccer goal event based on cinematic template. Proc. Int. Conf. on Machine Learning and Cybernetics, Vol. 6, 26-29 (2004) 3759 – 3764
4. W. Zhou, A. Vellaikal, and C. J. Kuo : Rule-based Video Classification System for Basketball Video Indexing. ACM Multimedia (2000)
5. Babaguchi N., Kawai Y., Ogura T., Kitahashi T. : Personalized abstraction of broadcasted American football video by highlight selection. Multimedia, IEEE Transactions, Vol. 6, Issue 4 (2004) 575–586
6. Tjondronegoro D.W., Yi-Ping Phoebe Chen, Binh Pham : Classification of self-consumable highlights for soccer video summaries. IEEE International Conference on Multimedia and Expo. Vol. 127-30 (2004) 579–582
7. Leonardi R., Migliorati P., Prandini M. : Semantic indexing of soccer audio-visual sequences: a multimodal approach based on controlled Markov chains. Circuits and Systems for Video Technology, IEEE Transactions, Vol. 14, Issue 5 (2004) 634–643
8. Y. Yusoff, W. Christmas, and J. Kittler : Video Shot Cut Detection Using Adaptive Thresholding. British Machine Vision Conference (2000) 362–372
9. J. Bescos, JM Menendez, G. Cisneros, J. Cabrera, and JM Martinez : A Unified Approach to Gradual Shot Transition Detection. Proc. Int. Conf. on Image Processing, Vol. 3 (2000) 949–952
10. Wolf, C, Jolion, J.-M, Chassaing, F : Text Localization, Enhancement and Binarization in Multimedia Document. 16th International Conference on Pattern Recognition, Vol. 2 (2002) 11–15
11. N. Otsu : A threshold selection method from gray-level histograms. IEEE TRansactions on Systems, Man and Cybernetics, 9 (1979) 62–66,

Improvement of Commercial Boundary Detection Using Audiovisual Features

Jun-Cheng Chen[1], Jen-Hao Yeh[1], Wei-Ta Chu[1], Jin-Hau Kuo[1], and Ja-Ling Wu[1,2]

[1] Department of Computer Science and Information Engineering,
National Taiwan University
[2] Graduate Institute of Networking and Multimedia, National Taiwan University,
No.1, Sec 4, Roosevelt Rd., Taipei, Taiwan 106, ROC
{pullpull, littleco, wtchu, david, wjl}@cmlab.csie.ntu.edu.tw

Abstract. Detection of commercials in TV videos is difficult because the diversity of them puts up a high barrier to construct an appropriate model. In this work, we try to deal with this problem through a top-down approach. We take account of the domain knowledge of commercial production and extract features that describe the characteristics of commercials. According to the clues from speech-music discrimination, video scene detection, and caption detection, a multi-modal commercial detection scheme is proposed. Experimental results show good performance of the proposed scheme on detecting commercials in news and talk show programs.

1 Introduction

The devices of digital video recording have become very common nowadays. Popularity of various devices for capturing and storage boosts the applications of time shifting recording on digital TV and broadcasting videos. Automatic detection and removal of commercials play an important role in digital home applications because commercials are often unwanted information when audiences browse recorded videos.

There are different ways to deal with the commercial detection problems. In the literature, for removing commercial segments in featured films, Lienhart et al. [1] use a combination of video features and commercial recognition scheme to achieve this goal; Duygulu et al. [3] mix audio features and detect video duplicate sequences to remove commercials in TV news programs; Juan et al. [4] use recognition of key frames on shots; Albiol et al. [6] apply template matching on TV station identification logo occurrence; Liu et al. [7] use adaboost with time constraint to detect commercial breaks.

The methods described above work well in conventional TV programs. However, we found that most of the prescribed approaches don't work well due to the advance of video technology. Recently, the traditional black frame insertion and the "always-on" assumption of TV station logo during commercials are not always valid. On the other hand, commercials have some intrinsic characteristics. For example, commercials often have music and have less caption ratio than programs. Hence, from clues of speech-music discrimination, video scene detection, and caption detection, an efficient three-level commercial detection scheme is proposed. It consists of detecting commercial break candidates, boundary refinement, and outlier (i.e. non-commercial parts) removing.

The organization of this paper is as follows. In Section 2, we address the problem and provide an overview of our system. Section 3 delineates how to find commercial-break candidates. Section 4 and Section 5, respectively, describe how to refine the resulting boundaries between commercials and regular TV programs and how to remove outliers. Section 6 presents the experimental results, and finally, Section 7 concludes this paper.

2 Problem Definition and System Overview

2.1 Problem Definition

TV commercial detection has been studied for commercial skipping or other applications for years. Actually, the problem is similar to partition the video data into consistent scenes semantically, which are then classified into programs or commercials.

A commercial break consists of one or more pieces of commercials and there are several commercial breaks in a program video. The problem of commercial detection is to label all possible commercial breaks and find the exact boundaries of them.

2.2 System Overview

The proposed system is illustrated in Fig.1. First of all, the recorded TV programs pass through the shot change detector. The results of shot change detector are used to calculate cuts and strong cuts (will be defined in the next section) per minute, which represent the frequency of shot changes. And then, we use these two features to label candidates of boundaries of commercial breaks. In the boundary refinement stage, the results of speech-music discriminator, video scene detection and caption text detection further characterize commercials and programs. The exact boundaries are

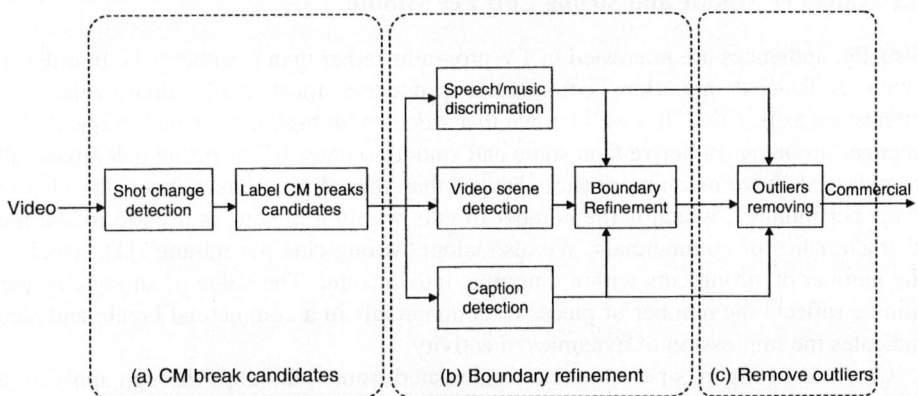

Fig. 1. The block diagram of the proposed commercial detection system

then refined based on the so-obtained characteristics. After boundary refinement, we remove outliers by some observations, such as low average caption ratio and high average music ratio during commercials.

3 Label the Commercial Breaks Candidates

3.1 Cuts and Strong Cuts

A "cut", shot change, shows discontinuity between two individual continuous camera shots. A shot change at frame index t is detected based on the difference of color histograms. In commercial production, directors setup dominant colors according to topics of commercials and make commercials prominent. Different commercials with different topics and styles, therefore, have drastic color difference. To capture this phenomenon, we introduce the feature, "strong cut", to indicate a cut with higher color-histogram difference. The definitions of cut and strong cut are formulated as follows:

$$Type\_of\_Cut(t) = \begin{cases} Strong\ cut, & D(t-1,t+1) > Th_{struct} \\ Cut, & (D(t-1,t+1) < Th_{struct}) \wedge (D(t-1,t+1) > Th_{cut}) \\ No\ shot\ change, & D(t-1,t+1) < Th_{cut} \end{cases} \quad (1)$$

$$\text{and} \quad D(t-1,t+1) = \frac{\sum_{i=1}^{N} |H_{t+1}(i) - H_{t-1}(i)|}{N} \quad (2)$$

Where H_t denotes the YUV color histogram of the t-th frame, N is the total number of bins (e.g., $N=64$). $D(t-1, t+1)$ indicates the average histogram difference between the $(t-1)$-th and the $(t+1)$-th frames. Two thresholds, Th_{struct} and Th_{cut} ($Th_{struct} > Th_{cut}$), are defined to classify shot changes into cut or strong cut.

3.2 Cuts Per Minute and Strong Cuts Per Minute

Usually, audiences are interested in TV programs rather than commercials. In order to catch audiences' attention, commercial producers must make their videos as interesting as possible. It's well known that videos with high motion and frequent shot changes are more attractive than static and smooth scenes. It's also true that almost all commercials have much more shot changes than that of programs. Hence, the idea of "cuts per minute", which is the number of cuts within a minute, is used to model the characteristics of commercials. We also adopt "strong cuts per minute" [1], which is the number of strong cuts within a minute, into account. The value of strong cuts per minute reflects the number of pieces of commercials in a commercial break, and also indicates the impression of dynamics of activity.

Cuts and strong cuts per minute are calculated from video clips through applying a sliding window of length W_s and with T_s overlapping to its neighbors. In our work, W_s is set to 30 second, and T_s is set to 10 seconds. We show examples of strong cuts and cuts per minute in Fig.2. In the figure, we see the typical trend that commercials often have more shot changes than programs and so are strong cuts.

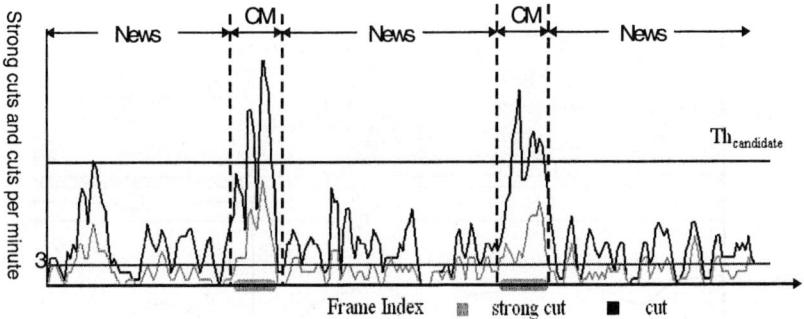

Fig. 2. Examples of strong cuts and cuts per minute

3.3 Mark Commercial Breaks Candidates

We modify the approach proposed in [1] to label commercial-break candidates. As shown in Fig. 2, the segments with large strong cuts and cuts per minute are selected as commercial breaks candidates. First, the segments with strong cuts per minute less than 3 are rejected. Then, the survived segments are further rejected if their cuts per minute do not exceed a threshold $Th_{candidate}$. Generally, the number of commercial breaks is restricted by the law (Enforcement Rules of the Radio and Television Act [11]). For instance, the law regulates that there should be 2 commercial breaks in a 40 minutes long news program. Thus, we can determine $Th_{candidate}$ from this domain knowledge. However, because we don't want to miss any possible cases, a loose threshold is set to allow more false alarms, which will be filtered out by later processes.

4 Boundary Refinement

After previous steps, we just get rough boundaries of commercial breaks. Some program segments may be included in the commercial breaks candidates. To refine the boundaries, we try to capture the characteristics of program-commercial and commercial-commercial changes through the clues of audio, video, and caption texts.

4.1 Audio Features

There are often volume changes between commercials and programs. For example, when commercials start or finish, there is often a very short duration of silence. Moreover, commercials often have background music. So we perform speech-music discrimination proposed in [8], which is constructed on the basis of RMS's (root mean square values) and ZCR's (zero crossing rates) of audio samples. It partitions audio data into segments and classifies each segment as speech or music. In addition to the label of each segment, normalized RMS Matusita distance, the intermediate output of [8], can be used to detect relative significant volume change because it is calculated and normalized with neighbors within a local window. Thus, it's suitable for detecting transitions between commercials and programs.

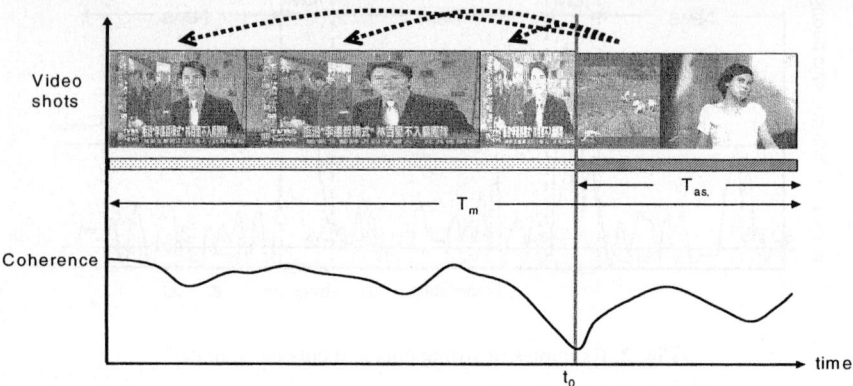

Fig. 3. The computation of video coherence between keyframes. If the shots in T_{as} are quite different to the shots in the rest of the memory, a video scene change is declared to occur at time t_0.

4.2 Video Scene Detection

We assume that the coherence of colors between commercials and programs and between different commercials is low. To discriminate styles of video scenes, we take the scheme of computable video scene with memory model addressed in [2] to simulate the "remembrance" of human. The coherence among shots in the attention span, T_{as}, is computed. Fig.3 illustrates the ideas of video coherence and memory model. We can see that the video scene boundaries are often occurred at the local minimums of the coherence curve. We setup T_{as} as 8 seconds and T_m as 24 seconds for later experiments.

If there is a local minimum in the curve of coherence at time t_0, a "video scene boundary" is declared. The middle frame in a shot is selected as the shot's keyframe in order to avoid the noises generated from special scene transition effects.

4.3 Caption Feature

We take the method developed in [9] to acquire the sizes and the locations of caption texts. In our observations, commercials usually use overlay texts to convey messages to audiences. But these overlay texts often appear only in a short duration at the same location. On the contrary, news or talk show programs often have headlines or captions on the bottom. According to the observation, we focus only on the video texts appeared at the bottom. We define the bottom area as shown in Fig.4 (a), with size frame-width × (0.3 * frame-height). Caption ratio is defined as the number of 8 ×8-pixel blocks that display caption in the bottom area. We use it to indicate the caption characteristics of each segment (c.f. Fig.5). That is,

$cap\_ratio(i)$ = the number of 8×8-pixel blocks that display caption in the bottom area.

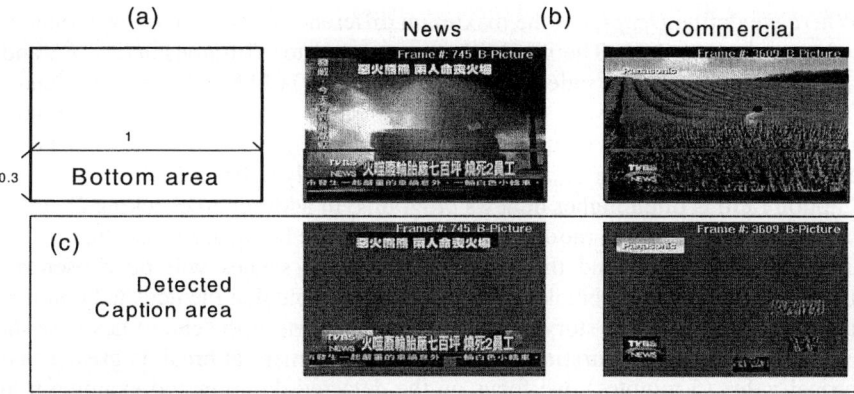

Fig. 4. (a) Definition of bottom area of each frame, (b) keyframes of news and commercials, and (c) the result of caption detection of news and commercial

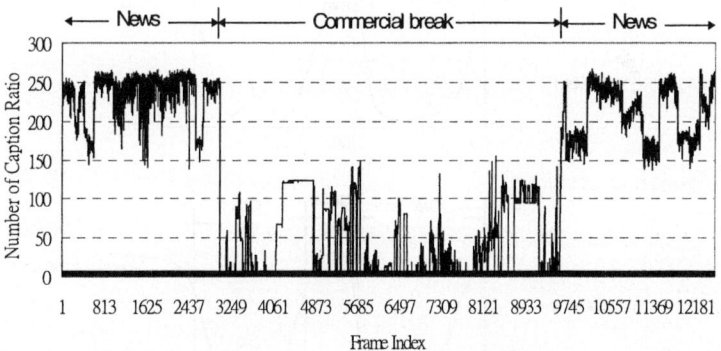

Fig. 5. The caption ratios for each of the frames of an MPEG encoded video (with resolution 320x240). It follows that the caption ratio is lower in commercials than that in news.

4.4 Mark the Exact Boundaries

Transitions of commercials and programs induce scene changes. Large volume changes and caption-ratio changes often occur with scene changes. Thus, we apply our algorithm to commercial-break candidates, and then several video scene boundaries in the suspicious segments are generated. Two types of clues are used to mark the exact boundaries. The first clue is the maximum difference of caption ratio around the video scene boundaries. The second one is volume change. If the j-th video scene boundary satisfies one of the following conditions, we'll retain it. Otherwise, we'll remove it from candidates. That is,

Condition1: $Dcap(j) > Th_{diff\_of\_cap}$ and $\min_{i=L-w,...,L+w} \{cap\_ratio(i)\} < Th_{cap\_ratio}$.

Condition2: $Vc(j) > Th_{vc}$ and $\min_{i=L-w,...,L+w} \{cap\_ratio(i)\} < Th_{cap\_ratio}$.

and $Dcap(j) = \max_{i=L',...,L''} \{cap\_ratio(i)\} - \min_{i=L',...,L''} \{cap\_ratio(i)\}$. (3)

Where we define $Dcap(j)$ as the maximum difference of caption ratios around the j-th video scene boundary. The window size, w, is set to 15 frames and L, L', and L'' are respectively the frame index of j-th, $(j-1)$th, and $(j+1)$th video scene boundaries. $Vc(j)$ is the normalized Matusita distance of RMS values within the duration (3 seconds), where we search volume changes around the j-th video scene boundary. The thresholds $Th_{diff\_of\_cap}$, Th_{cap_ratio}, and Th_{vc} are empirically defined.

Caption ratio is often higher in news programs. In addition to checking $Dcap(j)$, we have to ensure that caption ratio of the j-th video scene boundary is less than Th_{cap_ratio}. Boundaries of the first and the last survived video scenes will be chosen as the boundaries of commercial breaks. However, it's possible that the detected commercial break contains a tiny news story, such as weather reports at the end of news, as shown in Fig. 6(a). Thus, if the duration of the detected commercial break is greater than an empirical value (5 minutes), we focus on the detected duration and examine it again by applying condition 1 and condition 2, as shown in Fig. 6(b).

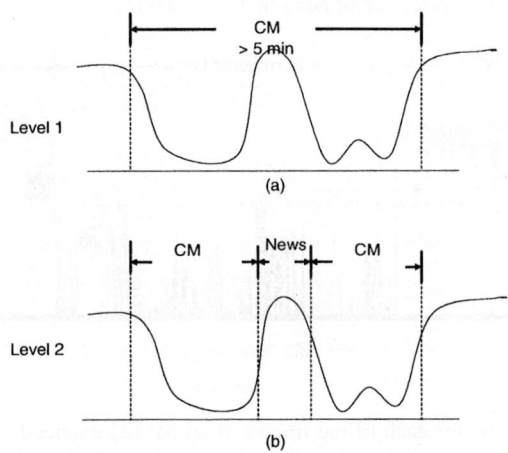

Fig. 6. Illustrations of boundaries refinement

5 Outliers Removing

Some parts of news programs with many shot changes or high motion may be regarded as commercial-boundary candidates at the steps described in Section 3. We observed that commercials often have background music and few long-lasting texts on the bottom. We calculate the average caption ratios and music ratios of segments through results of previous steps. If the average caption ratio of the segment is greater than an empirical threshold or the music ratio of the segment is less than another empirical threshold, this segment will be recognized as some parts of the news program, the so called outliers. These thresholds can be determined by checking the statistical characteristics of different video segments. Fig. 7 shows the histograms of average caption ratio and music ratio. We can see the significant difference between the distributions of two features of commercial breaks and programs, which include talk shows and news programs. We apply outlier removing at the final step because we will get more accurate boundaries of commercial breaks after boundary refinement and this final step is helpful to avoid taking commercial breaks as program segments.

6 Experimental Results

Our experiments are conducted on news and talk show program videos. Our test videos are taken from five different channels in Taiwan. There are 8 news and 2 talk show program videos in our testing dataset and their frame rates are 29.98 frames per second. Their total length is about 7.5 hours. There are 33 different commercial breaks in this dataset. The ground truth consists of the precise timestamps of the commercial breaks for each video sequence.

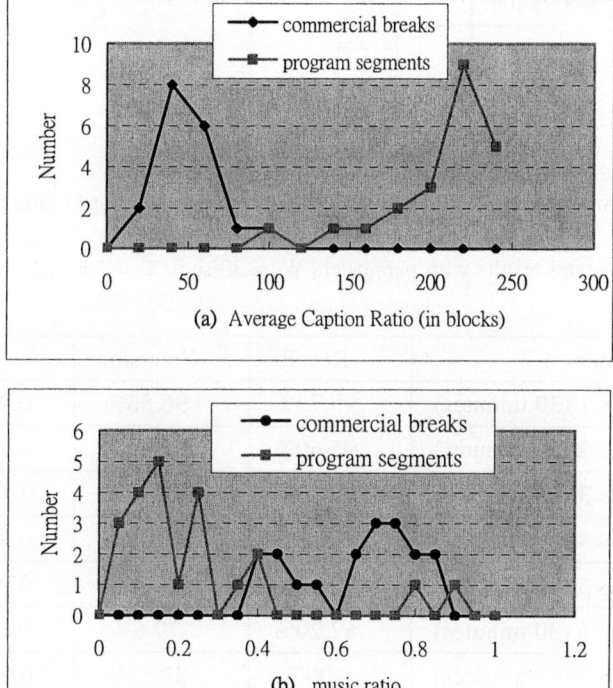

Fig. 7. The histograms of (a) average caption ratio, and (b) the music ratio. Both of them are generated by 18 commercial breaks and 23 program segments from a 5-hour news video.

To estimate the performance of our algorithm, as depicted in Fig. 8, we need to determine the number of frames of commercials correctly identified (true positive: TP), the number of frames of commercials missed (false negative: FN), and the number of frames of programs recognized as commercials (false positive: FP).

We use recall, precision, and F1 metric to show the ability of our algorithm. The definitions of recall, precision, and F1 are shown as follows:

$$\text{Recall} = TP / (TP + FN) \quad (4)$$

$$\text{Precision} = TP / (TP + FP) \quad (5)$$

$$F1 = 2 \times \text{Recall} \times \text{Precision} / (\text{Recall} + \text{Precision}) \quad (6)$$

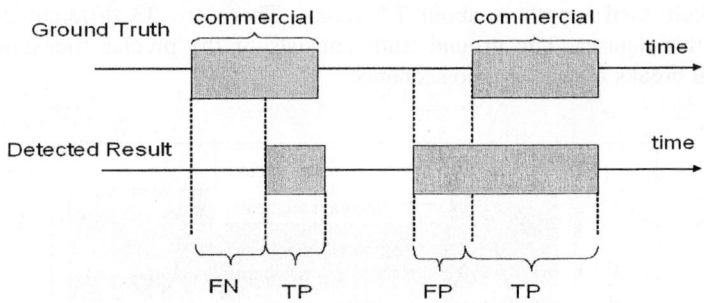

Fig. 8. An example of false negative(FN), true positive(TP), and false positive

Table 1. Experimental results with parameters $W_s = 30(\text{sec})$, $T_s = 10(\text{sec})$, $T_m = 24(\text{sec})$, and $T_{as} = 8(\text{sec})$

Sequences	Recall	Precision	F1
News 1 (30 minutes)	95.70%	96.56%	0.9612807
News 2 (30 minutes)	95.60%	99.90%	0.9770271
News 3 (60 minutes)	76.50%	81.40%	0.788 7397
News 4 (40 minutes)	100%	96.00%	0.9795918
News 5 (40 minutes)	97.66%	98.70%	0.9817724
News 6 (30 minutes)	82.20%	79.6%	0.8084851
News 7 (45 minutes)	100%	82.50%	0.9041096
News 8 (60 minutes)	99.90%	94.60%	0.9717779
Talk show 1 (60 minutes)	99.4%	98.3%	0.9884693
Talk show 2 (60 minutes)	95.2%	97.6%	0.9638506
Average	94.22%	92.52%	0.948485

The recall is the percentage of commercials that our algorithm successfully detects, in terms of duration. The precision is the percentage of actual commercials within what the algorithm detects as commercials. F1 takes recall and precision into consideration at the same time. The corresponding results are listed in Table 1. News 3 and News 6 are taken from the same channel. The results of them have worse performance than others because one of our assumptions, low caption ratio during commercial breaks, is not always valid in these channels. In most cases, our method performs well and averagely achieves 94.22% recall, 92.52% precision and 0.948 F1 metric.

In this work, we further devote our efforts to refine boundaries of commercial breaks. We compare the detection performance of the newly proposed method with our previous work [10], which doesn't integrate audio and caption information. In order to estimate the performance of boundary refinement, average frame difference is calculated as follows:

$$AvgD_j = \frac{1}{N} \sum_{i=1}^{N} fd_i \qquad (7)$$

where fd_i is the frame difference between the i-th detected commercial break and the ground truth, N is the total number of detected commercial breaks in the sequence, and $AvgD_j$ is the average frame difference of the j-th test sequence.

Table 2 shows the average frame difference in 11 sequences. Overall, the proposed method has superior performance and achieves 1641 frame-difference gain in average. Experimental results in Table 2 reveal that our algorithm can determine more precise boundaries.

Table 2. Average frame difference of (a) our proposed algorithm and (b) the algorithm proposed in [10] with parameters $W_s = 30(sec)$, $T_s = 10(sec)$, $T_m = 24(sec)$, and $T_{as} = 8(sec)$

Sequences	Average Frame Difference	
	(a)	(b)
News 1	482	5443
News 2	248	956
News 3	1494	2368
News 4	374	4927
News 5	244	1516
News 6	2035	3465
News 7	1140	563
News 8	504	770
Talk show 1	148	2172
Talk show 2	417	1314
Average	708	2349

7 Conclusion

In this paper, by combining speech-music discrimination, video scene segmentation and caption detection, an effective commercial detection scheme is proposed for news and talk show program videos. From our experiments, the video scene segmentations with caption-change and volume-change detections do help for deciding the exact boundaries of commercial breaks in news videos. Outlier removing based on the average caption ratio and music ratio also performs well. The proposed framework is expected to be applied to other programs with notable caption presentation. However, due to the diversity of the television commercials, of course, the proposed method is not perfect in every situation. More features or model-based approaches should be investigated further in the future.

References

1. Rainer Lienhart, Christoph Kuhmünch and Wolfgang Effelsberg: On the Detection and Recognition of Television Commercials, Proceedings of IEEE International Conference Multimedia Computing and Systems, (1997) 509-516
2. Hari Sundaram and Shih-Fu Chang: Computable Scenes and Structures in Films, IEEE Transactions on Multimedia, Vol. 4, No.4, (2002) 482-491
3. P. Duygulu, M.-Y. Chen, and A. Hauptmann: Comparison and Combination of Two Novel Commercial Detection Methods, Proceedings of IEEE International Conference on Multimedia and Expo, Vol. 2, (2004) 1267 – 1270
4. Juan Maía Sánchez, Xavier Binefa, Jordi Vitrià, and Petia Radeva: Local Color analysis for Scene Break Detection Applied to TV Commercials Recognition, Proceedings of 3rd. International Conference on VISUAL'99, (1999) 237-244
5. B. Satterwhite and O. Marques: Automatic detection of TV commercials, IEEE Potentials, Vol. 23, No. 2, (2004) 9 – 12
6. A. Albiol, M.J. Ch, F.A. Albiol, L. Torres: Detection of TV commercials, Proceedings of IEEE International Conference on Acoustics, Speech, and Signal Processing, vol. 3, (2004) 541-544
7. Tie-Yan Liu, Tao Qin, Hong-Jiang Zhang: Time-constraint boost for TV commercials detection, IEEE International Conference on Image Processing, Vol. 3, (2004) 1617 – 1620
8. C. Panagiotakis and G. Tziritas: A speech/music discriminator based on RMS and Zerocrossings, IEEE Transactions on Multimedia, Vol. 7, No. 1, (2005) 155 – 166
9. Chin-Fu Tsao, Yu-Hao Chen, Jin-Hau Kuo, Chia-Wei Lin, and Ja-Ling Wu: Automatic Video Caption Detection and Extraction in the DCT Compression Domain, accepted by Visual Communications and Image Processing, (2005)
10. Jen-Hao Yeh, Jun-Cheng Chen, Jin-Hau Kuo, and Ja-Ling Wu: TV Commercial Detection in News Program Videos, accepted by IEEE International Symposium on Circuits and Systems, (2005) 4594-4597
11. Enforcement Rules of the Radio and Television Act, article 34, http://www.gio.gov.tw/taiwan-website/1-about_us/6-laws/ra8.htm

Automatic Dissolve Detection Scheme Based on Visual Rhythm Spectrum

Seong Jun Park[1], Kwang-Deok Seo[2], Jae-Gon Kim[3], and Samuel Moon-Ho Song[4]

[1] Mobile Handset R&D Center, LG Electronics Inc., Seoul, Korea
sjpark0420@lge.com
[2] Computer & Telecommunications Engineering Division, Yonsei Univ., Gangwondo, Korea
kdseo@dragon.yonsei.ac.kr
[3] Broadcasting Media Research Group, ETRI, Daejeon, Korea
jgkim@etri.re.kr
[4] School of Mechanical and Aerospace Engineering, Seoul National Univ., Seoul, Korea
smsong@snu.ac.kr

Abstract. The automatic video parser, a necessary tool for the development and maintenance of a video library, must accurately detect video scene changes so that the resulting video clips can be indexed in some fashion and stored in a video database. Abrupt scene changes and wipes are detected fairly well. However, *dissolve* changes have been often missed. In this paper, we propose a robust dissolve detection scheme based on Visual Rhythm Spectrum. The Visual Rhythm Spectrum contains distinctive patterns or visual features for many different types of video effects. The efficiency of the proposed scheme is demonstrated using a number of video clips and some performance comparisons are made with other existing approaches.

1 Introduction

Scene change detection is an important technology for video indexing, browsing and retrieval. Generally, scene changes include both abrupt transitions and gradual transitions, such as wipe and dissolve. The automatic video parsing algorithms usually consist of several parts or sub-algorithms for scene change detection. It must deal with abrupt, as well as gradual scene changes. This collection of shot/scene change scenarios must all be incorporated into the scene detection algorithm. The existing algorithms deal with one or many of these scenarios with different parts of the algorithm dealing with different scenarios. The recent literature on video parsing may be divided into two broad groups. The first of which presents uncompressed domain processing and mainly deals with uncompressed video data and certain features of the video such as object[1], histograms[2], and edges[4]. The second group presents compressed domain processing and considers the DC image [3], [5], [6], [8], [9] and the motion vectors of macroblocks [7]. Many methods have already been proposed for abrupt scene change detection. Whereas, there have been relatively few reported studies on detecting dissolves. Therefore, the robust detection of dissolves is still an open issue and we focus on the detection of *dissolve* changes, where scene changes occur gradually over a longer span of time. The proposed scheme begins by processing the Visual Rhythm reported in [9]. Visual Rhythm is a single image, a sub-sampled version of a full video in which the sampling is performed in a predetermined and in a systematic fashion for a particular scene type. Visual Rhythm Spectrum (VRS) reflects different types of Visual Rhythms of various scene types in the time domain. VRS contains distinctive patterns or visual features for many different types of video effects. The different video effects manifest themselves differently on the VRS. In particular, scene-cuts are presented as perpendicular line and wipes appear as curves that run from the top to the bottom on the VRS. Thus, using the VRS, it becomes possible to automatically detect wipes and scene-cuts simply by determining various lines and curves on the VRS. The dissolves, on the other hand, do not generate any distinguishable lines on the VRS, since during dissolve, every pixel will have characteristics of both outgoing and incoming shots. Thus, *dissolve* changes have been often missed. It is thus more challenging to detect gradual changes like dissolve, as these are often excluded or falsely detected. We found that the dissolving frames do have a visual feature and will show linearly increasing or decreasing luminance and chrominance values. In this paper, we propose a robust dissolve detection scheme exploiting the linear intensity change on the VRS.

2 Visual Rhythm Spectrum

2.1 Visual Rhythm and Pixel Sampling

For the design of an efficient real-time scene change detector, we resort using a portion of the original video. This partial video must retain most, if not all, video edit effects. We claim that our Visual Rhythm, defined below, satisfies this requirement. Let $f_v(x, y, t)$ be the pixel value at location (x, y) and time t of an arbitrary video V. Then, the video V may be represented as:

$$V = \{f_v(x, y, t)\}, \quad x, y, t \in \{0,1,2,\cdots\}. \tag{1}$$

Let $f_T(x, y, t)$ be the representation of a reduced frame of a *spatially reduced video* V_T of the original video V. Each reduced frame, or thumbnails, is a (horizontally and vertically) reduced image of its corresponding frame in the video V. Thus, the spatially reduced video or sequence of thumbnails may be expressed as:

$$V_T = \{f_T(x, y, t)\}, \quad x, y, t \in \{0,1,2,\cdots\}. \tag{2}$$

The relationship between the video V and its spatially reduced video V_T can be represented using their pixel correspondences as follows:

$$f_T(x, y, t) = f_v(rx + k_x, ry + k_y, t), \quad x, y, t \in \{0,1,2,\cdots\}, \quad 0 \le k_x, k_y \le r-1. \tag{3}$$

where k_x and k_y are offsets in pixel units. Using the spatially reduced video, we define the *Visual Rhythm* of the video V as follows:

$$VR = \{f_{VR}(z, t)\} = \{f_T(x(z), y(z), t)\}. \tag{4}$$

where $x(z)$ and $y(z)$ are one-dimensional functions of the independent variable z. Thus, the Visual Rhythm is a two dimensional image consisting of pixels sampled from a three-dimensional data (video). That is, the Visual Rhythm is constructed by sampling a certain group of pixels in each thumbnail and by temporally accumulating the samples along time. Thus, the Visual Rhythm is a two-dimensional abstraction of the entire three-dimensional video content pertaining to a particular scene type.

Depending on the mappings $x(z)$ and $y(z)$, we can obtain various types of Visual Rhythms such as horizontal, vertical, and diagonal Visual Rhythms. According to extensive scrutiny and simulations, we find that the diagonal sampling approach shows the best detection performance. For a constant α, diagonal pixel sampling is achieved by the application of $(x(z), y(z)) = (z, \alpha z)$. Fig. 1 shows two types of gradual scene changes and Fig. 2 shows diagonal sampling strategy for dissolve and wipe. The Visual Rhythm for dissolve results from a repetitive diagonal sampling over many contiguous video frames during the dissolve.

Fig. 1. Gradual shot change types: (a) dissolve (b) wipe

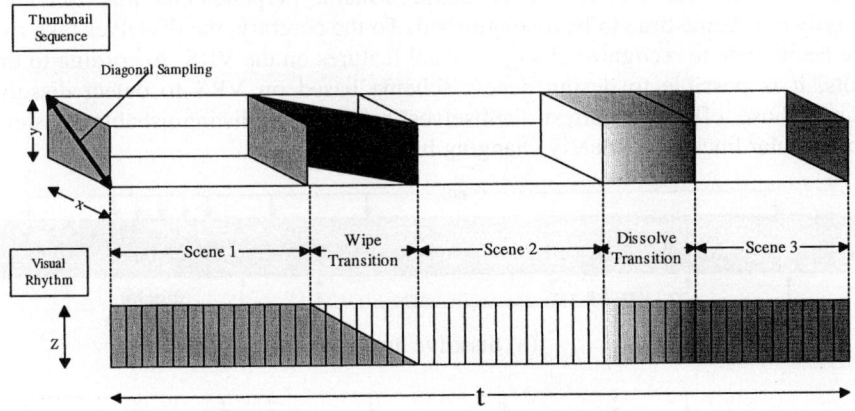

Fig. 2. Visual Rhythm composition from thumbnail sequence

2.2 Characteristics of VRS for Automatic Shot Detection

The Visual Rhythm, an abstraction of a video, is itself a two-dimensional image. It is a depiction of the entire video, which retains visual features of shot changes. In a VRS, pixels along a vertical line are those pixels uniformly sampled along the diagonal of a frame. The vertical lines on a VRS will have similar visual features if the lines are from the same shot. The lines will have different visual features if they belong to different shots. Thus, if there is a shot change, shot boundaries will become apparent on the VRS, as visual features of the vertical lines will change. We will now discuss how different shot changes result in different visual features on VRS.

Fig. 3 shows some typical Visual Rhythm patterns arising from different types of gradual shot changes. Fig. 3(a) shows a typical wipe. Note that this particular wipe appears as an *oblique line* on the VRS. The dissolves, on the other hand, do not generate any distinguishable lines on the VRS, since during dissolve, every pixel will have characteristics of both outgoing (fade-out) and incoming (fade-in) shots. This has been the obstacle for devising an automatic dissolve detection scheme using Visual Rhythm. However, the dissolving frames do have a visual feature and will show linearly increasing or decreasing luminance and chrominance values as indicated in Fig. 3(b).

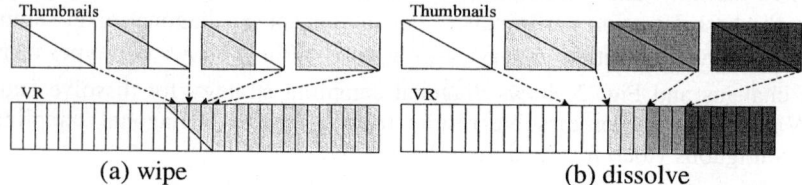

(a) wipe (b) dissolve

Fig. 3. Illustration of Edit Effects on Visual Rhythms

Fig. 4 shows a VRS generated from a real video clip. As explained earlier, and indicated on the figure, edit effects such as cuts and dissolves (including fades) can easily be identified from the VRS. The noticeable difference between the cuts and dissolves is the time duration of the distinguishable perpendicular line. Scene-cuts take only one frame time to be distinguished. To the contrary, the dissolves take much more frame time to recognize changed visual features on the VRS. According to these results, it is possible to design a new scheme based on VRS to detect dissolves, because those effects manifest themselves as visually distinguishable cluster of perpendicular lines with linearly changing luminance values.

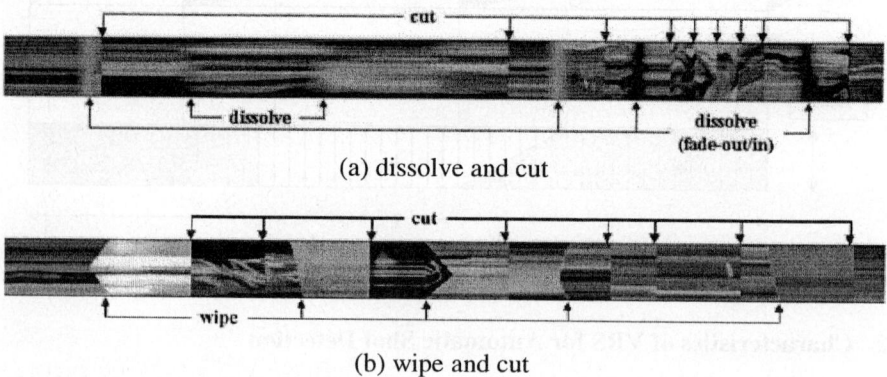

(a) dissolve and cut

(b) wipe and cut

Fig. 4. Visual effects of cut, dissolve, and wipe on the VRS

2.3 Fast Generation of Visual Rhythm

The digital video is usually compressed due to its huge volume. But, because most compression schemes use the discrete cosine transform (DCT) for intra-frame encoding, we can generate the thumbnail sequence only by extracting the DC coefficient in the DCT domain without performing inverse DCT. Since the DC coefficient is actually the average pixel value of the block, the collection of these DC coefficients over the frame can serve as the thumbnail images. Noting this fact, Yeo and Liu [8] introduced the DC image which consists of the DC coefficients of the original frame, and a sequence of DC images called the DC sequence. By accepting the DC image as a thumbnail and the DC sequence as a spatially reduced video, the thumbnail and the original video are related as shown below:

$$f_T(x,y,t) = \frac{1}{8}\sum_{k_x=0}^{7}\sum_{k_y=0}^{7} f_v(8x+k_x, 8y+k_y, t), \quad x,y,t \in \{0,1,2,\cdots\}. \tag{5}$$

As for the P- and B-frames of MPEG, algorithms for determining the DC images have already been developed [5], [11]. Therefore it is possible to generate Visual Rhythms fast for the DCT-based compression schemes, such as Motion JPEG, MPEG, H.261 and H.263 videos.

3 Proposed Dissolve Detection Scheme

The previous discussion indicates that during a dissolve VRS manifests a distinguishable cluster of perpendicular lines with linearly changing luminance values, as shown in Fig. 3(b) and Fig. 4. It means that we should find a linearly changing duration on the VRS in order to detect dissolve, unlike scene-cut and wipe cases where we should find discontinuous perpendicular or oblique lines. The development of a new dissolve detection scheme is based on the following modified chromatic video edit model represented on the VRS for the duration of the dissolve ($0 \le t \le T$):

$$g(z,t) = (1-\frac{t}{T})P(z,t) + \frac{t}{T}Q(z,t), \quad 0 \le t \le T \tag{6}$$

where $P(z,t)$ corresponds to the Visual Rhythm of the outgoing shot $P(z)$ at time t and $Q(z,t)$ the Visual Rhythm of the incoming shot $Q(z)$ at time t. A fade-in is a special case with $P(z,t)=0$ and fade-out $Q(z,t)=0$. Supposing that all the outgoing and incoming frames during dissolve are motionless, $P(z,t)$ could be represented as $P(z)$ and $Q(z,t)$ as $Q(z)$, independent of transition time t. However, for the case of real video containing motion during dissolve, $P(z,t)$ and $Q(z,t)$ should be expressed as:

$$\begin{aligned} P(z,t) &= P(z) + \delta_1(z,t), \quad 0 \le t \le T \\ Q(z,t) &= Q(z) + \delta_2(z,t), \quad 0 \le t \le T \end{aligned} \tag{7}$$

where $\delta_1(z,t)$ represents the displaced Visual Rhythm of $P(z,t)$ from $P(z)$, and $\delta_2(z,t)$ the displaced Visual Rhythm of $Q(z,t)$ from $Q(z)$ on the VRS, respectively. Substituting Eq. (7) into Eq. (6), a *linear dissolve model* could be obtained as follows:

$$\begin{aligned} g(z,t) &= \frac{t}{T}(Q(z)-P(z)) + P(z) + \delta_1(z,t) + \frac{t}{T}(\delta_2(z,t)-\delta_1(z,t)) \\ &= a(z)t + b(z) + v(z,t), \quad 0 \le t \le T \end{aligned} \tag{8}$$

where $b(z) = P(z)$, and $v(z,t) = \delta_1(z,t) + \dfrac{t}{T}(\delta_2(z,t) - \delta_1(z,t))$. According to Eq. (8), the linear dissolve model is composed of three modeling parameters: slope $a(z) = \dfrac{(Q(z) - P(z))}{T}$, intercept $b(z)$, and noise $v(z,t)$ caused by displacement or motion.

In order to find the slope, we apply the linear dissolve model, Eq. (8), for a fixed number of Visual Rhythm data taken from the VRS. The sampling of the data is just like taking $2L+1$ Visual Rhythm strip from the VRS over a sliding window shown in Fig. 5(a). For the calculation of the next slope, we shift the sliding window one frame time to the right and compute the slope again, as shown in Fig. 5(a). If the current frame time is t, then the past L Visual Rhythm data taken between t and $t-L$, and the future L data taken between t and $t+L$ will be applied for the calculation of the slope. The frame time interval between $t-L$ and $t+L$ is called sliding window size of $2L+1$. Since we set the size of the sliding window at $2L+1$, the number of the Visual Rhythm data used for the calculation of the slope at a specific z position at t should be $2L+1$, as shown in Fig. 5(b). We then continue computing the slope for the frame time later than t by shifting the sliding window until the end of the video sequence. Fig. 5(c) shows the estimated slopes for each z position ranging from z_0 to z_M. The dissolve detection becomes the most accurate when the window size is the same as the dissolve duration. The appropriate window size for practical application highly depends on the dissolve duration length. Considering that the common dissolve scene generally takes about 0.3 to 1 second for scene change, the reliable window size for robust detection would be between 10 to 30 for a 30 frame-per-second video sequence. However, longer window size not only takes longer detection time but also shows smoothed slope, resulting in a weak peak, the main obstacle for an easy detection of dissolve. According to this analysis, the most appropriate window size is found to be about 10. For the verification of this analysis, we will touch this issue in the 'Experimental Results' section with real video sequence.

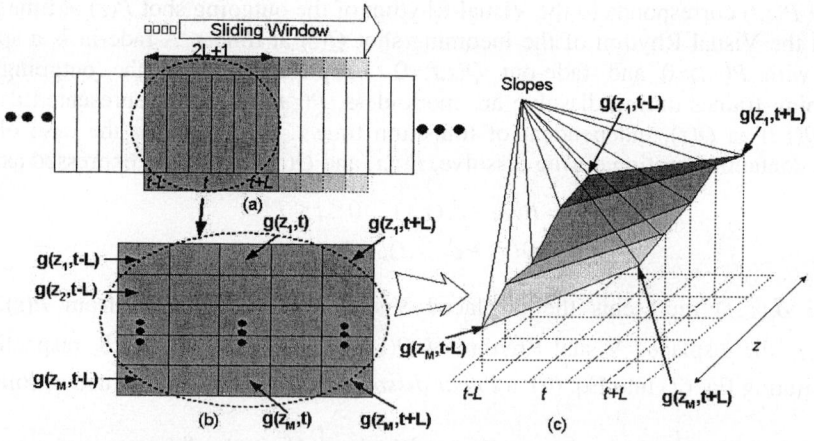

Fig. 5. Slope estimation based on sliding window: (a) shift of sliding window with size of $2L+1$, (b) $2L+1$ data used for the calculation of the slope at each z position at t, (c) estimated slope for each z position at t

According to the above-mentioned sliding window-based approach and Eq. (8), we estimate the slope at position z at frame time t by using $2L+1$ Visual Rhythm data taken from the VRS along time (horizontal direction) as follows:

$$\begin{bmatrix} g(z,t-L) \\ g(z,t-L+1) \\ \vdots \\ g(z,t) \\ g(z,t+1) \\ \vdots \\ g(z,t+L) \end{bmatrix} = \begin{bmatrix} t-L & 1 \\ t-L+1 & 1 \\ \vdots & \vdots \\ \vdots & \vdots \\ \vdots & \vdots \\ \vdots & \vdots \\ t+L & 1 \end{bmatrix} \begin{bmatrix} a(z) \\ b(z) \end{bmatrix} + \begin{bmatrix} v(z,t-L) \\ v(z,t-L+1) \\ \vdots \\ \vdots \\ \vdots \\ \vdots \\ v(z,t+L) \end{bmatrix}. \tag{9}$$

We rewrite Eq. (9) in the generic linear vector model for least squares as follows:

$$\mathbf{g}(z,t) = \mathbf{H}\mathbf{x}(z) + \mathbf{v}(z,t). \tag{10}$$

According to least-squares estimation theory [12], by choosing $\hat{\mathbf{x}}(z)$ such that $\|\mathbf{v}(z,t)\|^2 = \|\mathbf{g}(z,t) - \mathbf{H}\hat{\mathbf{x}}(z)\|^2$ is minimized, we obtained least-squares estimator of $\mathbf{x}(z)$, $\hat{\mathbf{x}}_{LS}(z)$, as

$$\hat{\mathbf{x}}_{LS}(z) = (\mathbf{H}^T\mathbf{H})^{-1}\mathbf{H}^T\mathbf{g}(z,t) \tag{11}$$

where the superscript T denotes the transpose of a matrix. Since we can find $\hat{\mathbf{x}}_{LS}(z)$ from Eq. (11) for all the frame times by shifting the sliding window to the right, $\mathbf{x}(z)$ can be expressed as a 2-dimensional function including time variable such that $\mathbf{x}(z,t) = \begin{bmatrix} a(z,t) \\ b(z,t) \end{bmatrix}$.

For the detection of dissolve, the absolute value $|a(z,t)|$ may be summed vertically (along z) first which may then be used to detect distinguishable peaks in the slope. This is based on the fact that the Visual Rhythms for dissolve do line-up vertically as shown in Fig. 4. Thus, the dissolve changes are detected by first summing $|a(z,t)|$ vertically as follows:

$$s(t) = \sum_{z=1}^{M} |a(z,t)|. \tag{12}$$

And then we determine the peaks in the summed data by using adaptive threshold. Heuristically chosen global threshold is not suitable as the shot content changes from scene to scene. So adaptive thresholds are better than a simple global threshold. Here we use a sliding window method to calculate the thresholds.

The required one dimensional statistics for detecting dissolves are as follows:

$$\mu(t) = \frac{1}{N(B)} \sum_{k \in B} s(t+k). \tag{13}$$

where $\mu(t)$ is the sampled local mean of the slope at t. The set B means the restrained interval, called sliding window. For instance, it may be {-16, -15, ... , -2, -1, 1, 2, ... , 15, 16}, in which case the size $N(B)=32$. The adequate $N(B)$ size needs to be large enough to encompass the whole dissolve duration. Considering that the normal dissolve scene takes about 0.3 to 1 second, the reasonable $N(B)$ size would be between 30 to 40 for a 30 frame-per-second video sequence.

For the detection of dissolves by using $s(t)$ and $\mu(t)$, the following simple adaptive threshold is used:

$$b(t) = \begin{cases} 1, & \text{if } s(t) > \mu(t) \\ 0, & \text{else} \end{cases} \quad (14)$$

Note that $b(t)$ will be set if the value $s(t)$ is above its local mean $\mu(t)$,. The set of frames with $b(t)=1$ will manifest as a visually distinguishable cluster of perpendicular lines on the VRS, which corresponds to a dissolve.

At this point, we may proceed to detect other kinds of visual effects such as scene-cuts and wipes. As shown in Fig. 4, since it is easier to detect scene-cuts and wipes showing much more noticeable effects on the VRS than dissolves, we can first detect them by the previously proposed methods [9] and filter those effects first. As noted in [9], the abrupt changes and wipes can be detected by first summing the derivative image and then by the corresponding adaptive thresholding in [9]. Thereafter, we can finally apply the proposed scheme for detecting dissolves.

4 Experimental Results

To decide appropriate sliding window size $2L+1$ for practical dissolve durations, we first performed experiments on the 'Sunrise' video clip. It contains three dissolve durations as summarized in Table 1 that describes dissolve frame number and length for each dissolve index. Partial display of the video clip sampled from each three dissolve durations is shown in Fig. 6 in order.

Table 1. Three dissolve durations in the 'Sunrise' video clip

Dissolve index	Dissolve frame number	Dissolve length
(a)	19~41	23
(b)	69~82	14
(c)	118~129	12

Fig. 7 describes the dissolve determination process by the proposed scheme. Fig. 7(a) compares the sum of slopes, $s(t)$ in Eq. (12), for the 'Sunrise' video clip by setting the sliding window size $2L+1$ at 5, 11, and 21, respectively. As shown in Fig. 7(a), the most reliable results are obtained when the window size is 11. When the window size is 21, we could detect the first dissolve duration fairly well, however we obtained vague and weak peaks for other two dissolve cases where dissolve durations are much smaller than the window size. On the other hand, for the case of window

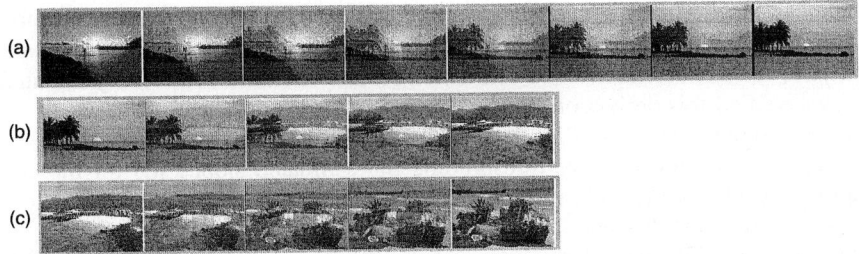

Fig. 6. Dissolve frames sampled from each dissolve index (a), (b) and (c) of 'Sunrise' clip

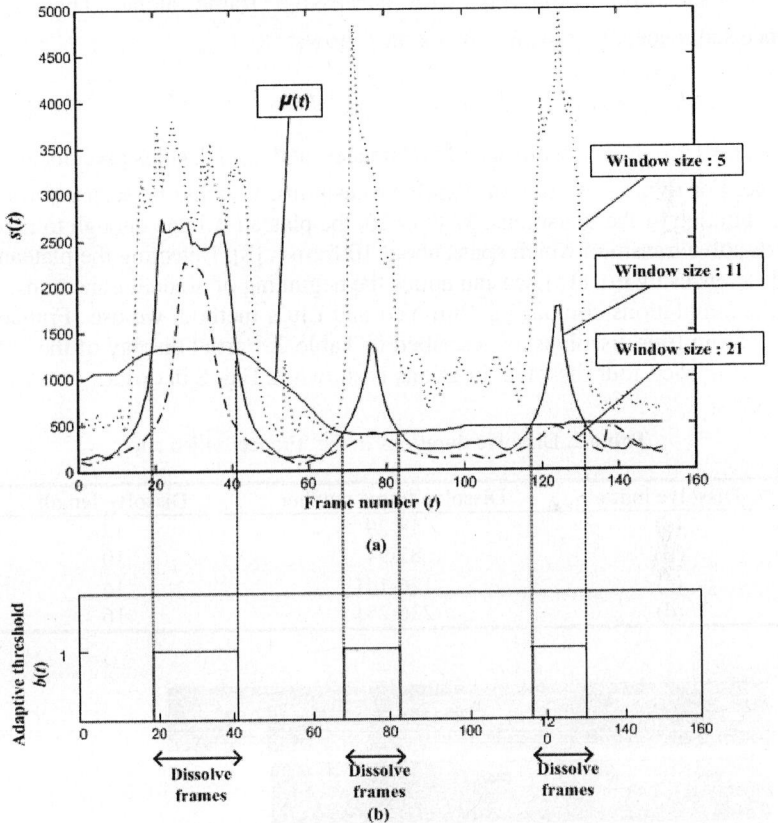

Fig. 7. Dissolve determination by the proposed scheme: (a) estimated slopes for 'Sunrise' video clip using various window sizes of 5, 11, and 21; (b) determined dissolve frames after adaptive thresholding for the case of window size 11

size 5, we could detect all dissolve durations. However, the graph shape is too fluctuating with many local peaks and valleys. Relatively small information quantity used for slope estimation is the cause of this fluctuating graph. The fluctuating result might lead to a false detection. Nevertheless, this does not mean that longer window size is always desirable. Longer window size not only takes longer detection time but also shows smoothed slope, resulting in a weak peak. Therefore, as also mentioned in Section 3, the most reliable slope estimation results could be obtained by taking L=5. And we verified this derivation through extensive simulations with various real video clips containing dissolves. Fig. 7(b) shows the determined dissolve frames after applying Eq. (14) for adaptive thresholding the estimated slopes $s(t)$ for the case of window size 11. As shown in Fig. 7(b), the three dissolve durations are detected well, corresponding to the dissolve frames specified in Table 1.

To show the efficiency of the proposed algorithm, we compare with Yeo and Liu's method [8] which is one of the well-known dissolve detection algorithms. According to [8], they use every frame and compare it to the following kth frame for more robust detection, instead of comparing with successive frame alone. They form the difference sequence $D_t^k, t = 1,2,\cdots N-k$ as follows:

$$D_t^k = d(f_t, f_{t+k}) = |f(x, y, t) - f(x, y, t+k)|. \quad (15)$$

where $f_t, t = 1,2,\cdots N$ is a sequence of DC images, and (x,y) denotes pixel location of the DC image. For robust detection of dissolve transitions, k should be selected to be larger than the duration of the transitions. With k=20, the plateau is large enough to capture the typical dissolve transition which spans about 10 frames [8]. Detecting the plateaus in the frame differences by Eq. (15), we can notice the beginning of gradual transitions.

For the simulations comparing with Yeo and Liu's method, we use 'France' video clip containing four dissolves as described in Table 2. Partial display of the video clip sampled from each four dissolve durations is shown in Fig. 8 in order.

Table 2. Dissolve durations in the 'France' video clip

Dissolve index	Dissolve frame number	Dissolve length
(a)	18-29	12
(b)	82-91	10
(c)	126-141	16
(d)	236-251	16

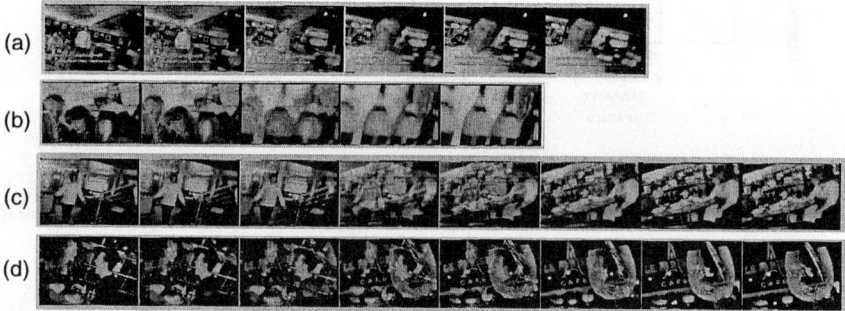

Fig. 8. Dissolve frames sampled from each dissolve index (a), (b), (c) and (d) of 'France' clip

Fig. 9 compares the results for $s(t)$ computed by Eq. (12) and D_t^k by Eq. (15). Note that fixed sliding window size of 11 is used for computing $s(t)$ and frame index $k=32$ to cover the 16 frame duration is employed for evaluating D_t^k. In the case of D_t^k, plateau corresponding to each dissolve duration shows up, thus indicating that a gradual scene transition has taken place. However, the plateaus for the third and fourth dissolves are not so distinctive because of many local peaks and valleys appearing after 150-th frame. Moreover, even some oscillations are observed after 250-th frame, which might result in false dissolve detection. On the contrary, the proposed $s(t)$ clearly discriminates the peaks from local variations with small fluctuation, as can be deduced from the solid line in Fig. 9. Thus, it successfully indicates the four dissolve durations and separates them from local small fluctuations.

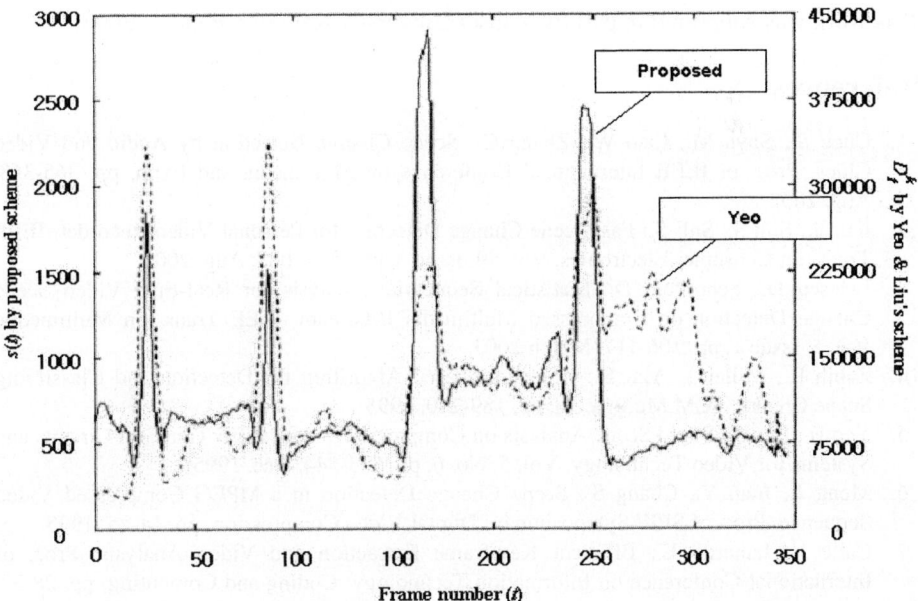

Fig. 9. Results for comparison between the proposed and Yeo's schemes: solid line, left scale— $s(t)$ versus t; dotted line, right scale— D_t^k versus t

5 Conclusion

In this paper, we proposed a new dissolve detection algorithm based on Visual Rhythm Spectrum (VRS) for database construction and systematic arrangement of video contents. VRS contains distinctive patterns or visual features for various types of scene changes. The different video effects manifest themselves differently on the VRS. Especially, the fact that dissolves appear as linear variation on the VRS makes us to devise a new dissolve detection scheme based on the slope estimation.

To find out dissolves, we employed various methods including sliding window-based slope estimation and adaptive thresholding. Although we determined an appropriate window size through extensive simulations on the real video clips, our method can still be improved by employing adaptive sliding window width in the future. We verified the efficiency of the proposed scheme by comparing it with a well-know conventional method.

The proposed algorithm can be applicable not only to raw image but also to various DCT-based digital video standards including Motion JPEG, MPEG-1, MPEG-2, MPEG-4, and H.263.

Once digital videos are indexed by incorporating the proposed dissolve detection scheme, the retrieval and browsing from vast video contents would be much more manageable and convenient.

Acknowledgement

This work was supported in part by Yonsei University Research Fund of 2005.

References

1. Chen S., Shyu M., Liao W., Zhang C.: Scene Change Detection by Audio and Video Clues. Proc. of IEEE International Conference on Multimedia and Expo, pp. 365-368, Aug. 2002.
2. Kim J., Suh S., Sull S.: Fast Scene Change Detection for Personal Video Recorder. IEEE Trans. on Consumer Electronics, Vol. 49, Issue 3, pp.683 – 688, Aug. 2003.
3. Lelescu D., Schonfeld D.: Statistical Sequential Analysis for Real-time Video Scene Change Detection on Compressed Multimedia Bitstream. IEEE Trans. on Multimedia, Vol. 5, Issue 1, pp. 106-117, March 2003.
4. Zabih R., Miller J., Mai K.: A Feature-based Algorithm for Detection and Classifying Scene Breaks. ACM Multimedia, pp. 189-200, 1995.
5. Yeo B., Liu B.: Rapid Scene Analysis on Compressed Video. IEEE Trans. on Circuits and Systems for Video Technology, Vol. 5, No. 6, pp. 533-544, Dec. 1995.
6. Meng J., Juan Y., Chang S.: Scene Change Detection in a MPEG Compressed Video Sequence. Proc. of SPIE Symposium on Digital Video Compression, pp. 14-25, 1995.
7. Calic J., Izuierdo E.: Efficient Key-frame Extraction and Video Analysis. Proc. of International Conference on Information Technology: Coding and Computing, pp. 28-33, April 2002.
8. Yeo B., Liu B.: On the Extraction of DC Sequence from MPEG Compressed Video. Proc. of International Conference on Image Processing, Vol. 2, pp. 260-263, Oct. 1995.
9. Kim H., Park S., Lee J., Song S.: Processing of Partial Video Data for Detection of Wipes. Proc. of SPIE Conference on Storage and Retrieval for Image and Video Databases VII, pp. 280-289, Jan. 1999.
10. Song S., Kwon T., Kim W., Kim H., Rhee B.: On Detection of Gradual Scene Changes for Parsing of Video Data. Proc. of SPIE Storage and Retrieval for Image and Video Database VI, Vol. 3312. pp.404-413, 1998.
11. Song J., Yeo B.: Spatially Reduced Image Extraction from MPEG-2 Video: Fast Algorithms and Applications. Proc. of SPIE Storage and Retrieval for Image and Video Database VI, Vol. 3312, pp. 93-107, 1998.
12. Mendel J.: Lessons in Estimation Theory for Signal Processing, Communications, and Control. Prentice Hall, 1995.

A Study on the Relation Between the Frame Pruning and the Robust Speaker Identification with Multivariate t-Distribution

Younjeong Lee[1], Joohun Lee[2], and Hernsoo Hahn[1]

[1] School of Electronic Engineering, Soongsil University, Dongjak-gu, Seoul, Korea
{youn, hahn}@ssu.ac.kr
[2] Dept. of Internet Broadcasting, Dong-Ah Broadcasting College, Anseong, Korea
vincelee21@naver.com

Abstract. In this paper, we performed the robust speaker identification based on the frame pruning and multivariate t-distribution respectively, and then studied on a theoretical basis for the frame pruning using the other methods. Based on the results from two methods, we showed that the robust algorithms based on the weight of frames become the theoretical basis of the frame pruning method by considering the correspondence between the weight of frame pruning and the conditional expectation of t-distribution. Both methods showed good performance when coping with the outliers occurring in a given time period, while the frame pruning method removing less reliable frames is recommended as one of good methods and, also, the multivariate t-distributions are generally used instead of Gaussian mixture models (GMM) as a robust approach for the speaker identification. In experiments, we found that the robust speaker identification has higher performance than the typical GMM algorithm. Moreover, we showed that the trend of frame likelihood using the frame pruning is similar to one of robust algorithms.

1 Introduction

Ubiquitous computing which is an emerging field from fast conversion of communication and computer technology offers us new environments that can give various services to use small devices while moving. This is supported strongly by the highly developed computer technology and, therefore, ubiquitous computing can be thought of as an idea of invisible computers everywhere. Ubiquitous computing is composed of sensor, communication, process, security, and interface. In these services, an unauthorized speaker can make fraudulent use of the right speaker's ID and his password, even though the systems cannot become aware of it at all. Therefore, security becomes one of major concerns being gradually important to accept those systems. Additionally, the technology preventing false acceptance of another speaker using others' PIN (Personal Identification Number) such as user's ID and password should apply to these services. Speaker identification is more convenient and safer without outflow of personal information because it is no danger of loss or peculation.

In the speaker identification system using speech as speaker's intrinsic information, the parameters of speaker model are obtained from the GMM based on maximum likelihood [1]. However, its performance is degraded by outliers induced by such factors as irregular utterance variations in several sessions, the physical and psychological condition of the speaker, variation of vocal tract, microphones, additive background noise, and speaking styles, etc.[2,3,4]. Even in clean speech, some frames of a speaker's test utterance can be simply more similar to another speaker's model than to the right speaker's one itself[2]. Therefore, the performance of speaker identification is vulnerable to how error data is handled properly. To overcome outliers, there were several robust clustering methods like as fuzzy clustering method[5], noise cluster approach[6], and robust methods (M,R,L estimators)[7,8,9]. Also, we performed the robust adaptation using M-estimator to cope with outliers from several sessions in the previous work[4].

In this paper, to cope with outliers, we applied the frame pruning method and the multivariate t-distribution for robust speaker identification respectively and showed the correspondence between the concepts in the frame pruning and the multivariate t-distribution of robust statistics. The multivariate t-distributions are generally used instead of GMM as a robust approach for the speaker identification [10,11] and the frame pruning algorithm is easily obtained from removing the less reliable log-likelihood of frames[2].

In experiments, the robust speaker identification system showed higher performance than the typical GMM. Also, from the results, we found the similarity between the frames with lower conditional expectation in robust methods and those pruned with less reliable log-likelihood in frame pruning, and then concluded the theoretical basis of the frame pruning method.

The remaining part of this paper is organized as follows. In section 2, we describe the frame pruning method for the speaker identification. The section 3 explains the typical robust algorithms based on the speaker identification. We study on the correlation between the frame pruning and the robust algorithm in section 4. The experimental results are summarized in section 5. Finally, in section 6, we draw conclusions.

2 Frame Pruning for Speaker Identification

Suppose we have T observations $X = \{x_1, \cdots, x_T\}$, $x_t \in R^d$. A d-multivariate normal mixture probability density function is defined by a weighted linear combination of M component densities as

$$p(x_t \mid \lambda) = \sum_{i=1}^{M} \pi_i f_i(x_t) \qquad (1)$$

where the component densities, $f_i(x_t)$ is followed by

$$f_i(x_t) = \frac{1}{(2\pi)^{\frac{d}{2}} |\Sigma_i|^{\frac{1}{2}}} \exp\left\{-\frac{1}{2}\delta(x_t, \mu_i; \Sigma_i)\right\} \qquad (2)$$

$\delta(x_t, \mu; \Sigma)$ is the mahalanobis squared distance between x_t and mean vector μ_i with covariance Σ_i [1].

$$\delta(x_t, \mu; \Sigma) = (x_t - \mu_i)^T |\Sigma_i^{-1}| (x_t - \mu_i) \tag{3}$$

The mixture weights w_i, furthermore satisfy the constraint $\sum_1^M \pi_i = 1$. Collectively, the parameters of speaker's density model are denoted as

$$\lambda = \{\pi_i, \mu_i, \Sigma_i\} \quad i = 1, \cdots, M. \tag{4}$$

Most of speaker identification generally use averaging of the frame scores to compute log-likelihood (L) between speaker model and test utterance with regard to the whole test utterance. If we assumed that all observed vectors are independent observations, the average log-likelihood is obtained from

$$L(\lambda) = \frac{1}{T} \sum_{t=1}^T \log p(x_t|\lambda) = \frac{1}{T} \sum_{t=1}^T \log \left(\sum_{i=1}^M \pi_i f_i(x_t) \right). \tag{5}$$

There are several ways to cope with accumulating the average of total frames like as above eq. (5): normalizing the frame scores[12], replacing the score for a frame with a measure of confidence that the frame was spoken by the target speaker[4]. However, these methods are difficult to be robust when the outliers exist in speech. Even if the case is clean speech, some frames of a speaker test utterance can be simply more similar to another speaker model than to the right speaker model itself[2]. Therefore, to cope with these problems, we apply the frame pruning about the frames with error tendency. Then, the speaker identification becomes more robust.

The frame pruning is the method that the frames with less likelihood are removed after each frame's log-likelihoods are sorted by the value sequentially. Only the remaining frames are use to calculate the average of log-likelihood after the $\alpha\%$ of the lower frames are removed.

$$L'(\lambda) = \frac{1}{T'} \sum_{t=1}^{T'} \log p(x_t'|\lambda) = \frac{1}{T'} \sum_{t=1}^{T'} \log \left(\sum_{i=1}^M \pi_i f_i(x_t') \right), \tag{6}$$

where T' is

$$T' = T * (1 - \frac{\alpha}{100}).$$

3 Robust Mixture Model Based on *t*-Distribution

In this section, we briefly summarized the mixture model based on *t*-distribution as shown [10,11]. The GMM is generally used to model of the multivariate data sets of a wide variety of random phenomenon. However, for a set of data containing a group or groups of observations with longer than normal tails or atypical observations, the use of normal components may inordinately affect the estimation of the mixture model. We deal with a more robust approach by modeling the data by a mixture of t-distribution. Therefore, for such data, the t-distribution is obtained from extending eq. (2) applying the robust M-estimator by Huber and the degree of freedom γ of chi-square random variable [10,11].

We consider ML(Maximum Likelihood) estimation for M-component mixture of t-distributions, given by

$$t(x_t \mid \lambda) = \sum_{i=1}^{M} \pi_i t_i(x_t) \qquad (7)$$

where the component densities are defined by d-multivariate t-distribution of the form

$$t_i(x_t) = \frac{\Gamma\left(\frac{\gamma_i+d}{2}\right) |\Sigma_i|^{-\frac{1}{2}}}{(\pi \gamma_i)^{\frac{d}{2}} \Gamma\left(\frac{\gamma_i}{2}\right) \{1 + \delta(x_t, \mu_i; \Sigma_i)/\gamma_i\}^{\frac{1}{2}(\gamma_i+d)}}, \quad i = 1, \cdots, M, \qquad (8)$$

and $\delta(x_t, \mu; \Sigma)$ is the mahalanobis squared distance. Collectively, the model parameter λ is composed of weight, mean vector, covariance matrix and degree of freedom.

$$\lambda = \{\pi_i, \mu_i, \Sigma_i, \gamma_i\} \quad i = 1, \cdots, M \qquad (9)$$

As we know, if $\gamma_i > 1$, μ_i is the mean of the population, and if $\gamma_i > 2$, $\gamma_i(\gamma_i - 2)^{-1}\Sigma$ is the covariance matrix. The case $\gamma_i \to \infty$ corresponds to a multivariate Gaussian distribution with mean μ_i and covariance matrix Σ_i, and when $\gamma_i = 1$, this becomes multivariate Cauchy distribution. We also notice that multivariate t-distribution can be viewed as a weighted average multivariate Gaussian distribution with the weight Gamma distribution [9,10, 11].

To maximize the probability of t-distribution, we estimate model parameter λ using the ML algorithm. In the EM algorithm, the complete-data is given by following

$$Y_c = \left(Y_0^T, z_1^T, \cdots, z_T^T, u_1, \cdots, u_T\right)^T, \qquad (10)$$

where $Y_0 = \left(x_1^T, \cdots, x_T^T\right)^T$ denotes the observed data set, and $z_1, \cdots, z_T$ has component z_{ti} where z_{ti} are defined by the indicator of component. If x_t belongs to i-th component, $z_{ti} = 1$, otherwise $z_{ti} = 0$. In real data set, there are the incomplete-data, so there needs additive missing data $u_1, \cdots, u_T$, $z_{ti} = 1$ is defined.

To reestimate parameters, the complete log-likelihood function can be defined by

$$\begin{aligned} L(\lambda) &= \sum_{t=1}^{T} \sum_{i=1}^{M} z_{ti} \log t(x_t \mid \lambda) \\ &= \sum_{t=1}^{T} \sum_{i=1}^{M} z_{ti} \{\log(\pi_i) + \log t_i(x_t)\} \end{aligned} \qquad (11)$$

A posterior probability z_{ti} that x_t belongs to i-th component of mixture is obtaind from the EM algorithm.

$$z_{ti} = \frac{\pi_i t_i(x_t)}{\sum_{l=1}^{M} \pi_l t_l(x_t)} \quad (12)$$

The conditional expectation given $z_{ti} = 1$, is followed as

$$u_{ti} = \frac{\gamma_i + d}{\gamma_i + \delta(x_t, \mu_i; \Sigma_i)}. \quad (13)$$

In eq.(13), the degree of freedom γ_i is obtained from the nonlinear Gamma function [10,11]. Using the posterior probability z_{ti}, the parameter for the ML algorithm can be iterlatively estimated by the EM algorithm.

$$\hat{\pi}_i = \frac{1}{T} \sum_{t=1}^{T} z_{ti} \quad (14)$$

$$\hat{\mu}_i = \frac{\sum_{t=1}^{T} z_{ti} u_{ti} x_t}{\sum_{t=1}^{T} z_{ti} u_{ti}} \quad (15)$$

$$\hat{\Sigma}_i = \frac{\sum_{t=1}^{T} z_{ti} u_{ti} (x_t - \mu_i)(x_t - \mu_i)^T}{\sum_{t=1}^{T} z_{ti}} \quad (16)$$

4 The Correlation Between Robust Speaker Identification and Robust Algorithms

Assuming that the maximum log-likelihood in correct recognition is higher than one in the false acceptance, the weight of the frame regarding as outlier is same as zero to neglect the effect of outliers in robust speaker identification. That is, the weight of reliable frame is 1 and the weight of meaningless frame is 0. Its function can take effects as the frame pruning by adjusting the degree of freedom of t-distribution.

Given T sequences of feature vectors $X = \{x_1, \cdots, x_T\}$, $x_t \subseteq R^d$, if outliers exist in X, the process for estimating parameters of GMM is very sensitive in outliers. Therefore, for the reliable estimator, the robust algorithm based on M-estimation method is proposed[3,4,8,9].

$$J = \sum_{t=1}^{T} \rho[\log p(x_t|\lambda)] \qquad (17)$$

In here, $\rho[\cdot]$ is loss function and used to decrease effects of outliers and w_t is weight function, defined as $w_t = \dfrac{\partial \rho[z_t]}{\partial z_t}$, where $z_t = \log p(x_t|\lambda)$.

Applying the weight in the robust algorithm to the frame pruning, the frame pruning algorithm is redefined by

$$L'(\lambda) = \frac{1}{T}\sum_{t=1}^{T}\log p(x_t|\lambda) = \frac{1}{T}\sum_{t=1}^{T} w_t \log p(x_t|\lambda). \qquad (18)$$

After the log-likelihood of each frame is arranged by the size sequentially to calculate w_t, the lowest reliable $\alpha \%$ frames in the ranking frames have $w_t = 0$, otherwise define as $w_t = 1$.

In Cauchy's weight function, w_t is defined by

$$w_t = \left(1 + \frac{r_t^2}{\beta}\right)^{-1}, \qquad (19)$$

where β is scale parameter[3, 4]. Since the data with a large r_t^2 has a small w_t, the influence of outlier can be reduced in eq.(17).

Similarly, as t-distribution is defined from the M-estimator, we can regard the conditional expectation u_{ti} of eq.(13) as the weight of frames.

$$w_t = \frac{1}{M}\sum_{i=1}^{M} u_{ti} = \frac{1}{M}\sum_{i=1}^{M}\left(\frac{\gamma_i + d}{\gamma_i + \delta(x_t, \mu_i; \Sigma_i)}\right) \qquad (20)$$

From above equations, we can know the fact that eq.(20) becomes the form of the robust algorithm. Consequently, the form of eq.(19) is similar to one of eq.(20). As a result, the frame pruning can be regarded as a special case of t-distribution.

Moreover, the tail of t-distribution is longer than one of the normal distribution. If the model is obtained from adjusting properly the degree of freedom of t-distribution, the abnormal data that is considered as outliers in the normal distribution can be included in the robust model. Therefore, the robust algorithm is more effective than the normal distribution for presenting outliers. Also, the removed frame in the frame pruning can be matched to the frame with less Cauchy weight function and less conditional expectation in the robust algorithm.

5 Experimental Results

To show that the frame pruning and the robust algorithm are theoretically related to each other, we performed the robust speaker recognition with them. The speech data consists of two Korean sentences (one is a given sentence, "Yeolryeola-Chamkkae" meaning "open sesame" in Korean, and the other is free one) uttered 15 times each by

100 females and 100 males. Speaker models were trained using 10 utterances of each speaker. The remaining 5 utterances were used for test of the speaker identification. The speech data was sampled at 16 kHz and was parameterized using 12 MFCC and 13 delta cepstrum. The analysis window size was 20ms with 10ms overlap. We used $\alpha = 5\%$ at the frame pruning, and $\beta = 9.0$ at the M-estimator by the Cauchy weight function.

Fig. 1 shows the performance results for the speaker identification with several algorithms for their comparison. The number of mixtures used in these experiments is 5, 8, 11, 14 and 17. Both the frame pruning method and the robust algorithms have higher performance than the GMM for the given sentence as well as the free one. In Fig. 1-(a), the performance of speaker identification is shown as 98.8%, 99.1% 99.5% in the GMM, the frame pruning and t-distribution algorithm, respectively, when the number of mixtures is set to 14. In case of Fig.1-(b), the performance is shown by 99.9%, 99.9%, and 100%, respectively. From the results, the robust methods show superior performance to one using the original GMM algorithm.

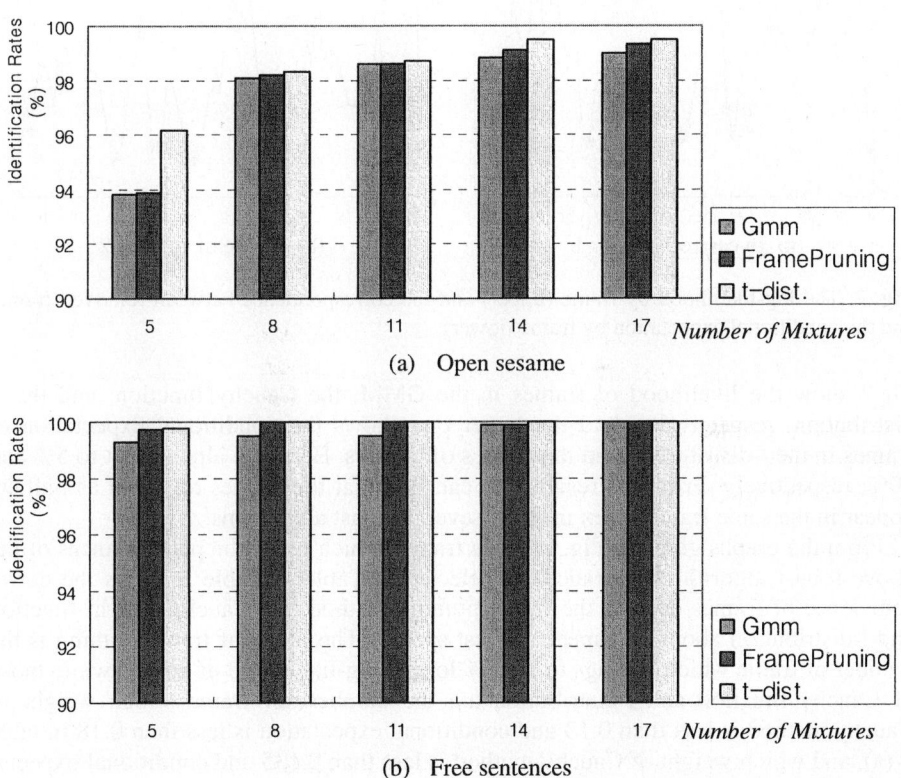

Fig. 1. The performance of speaker identification

To show the relation among several robust algorithms, we performed the following experiments. In Fig. 2, two speakers uttered the same sentence. The upper graphs in

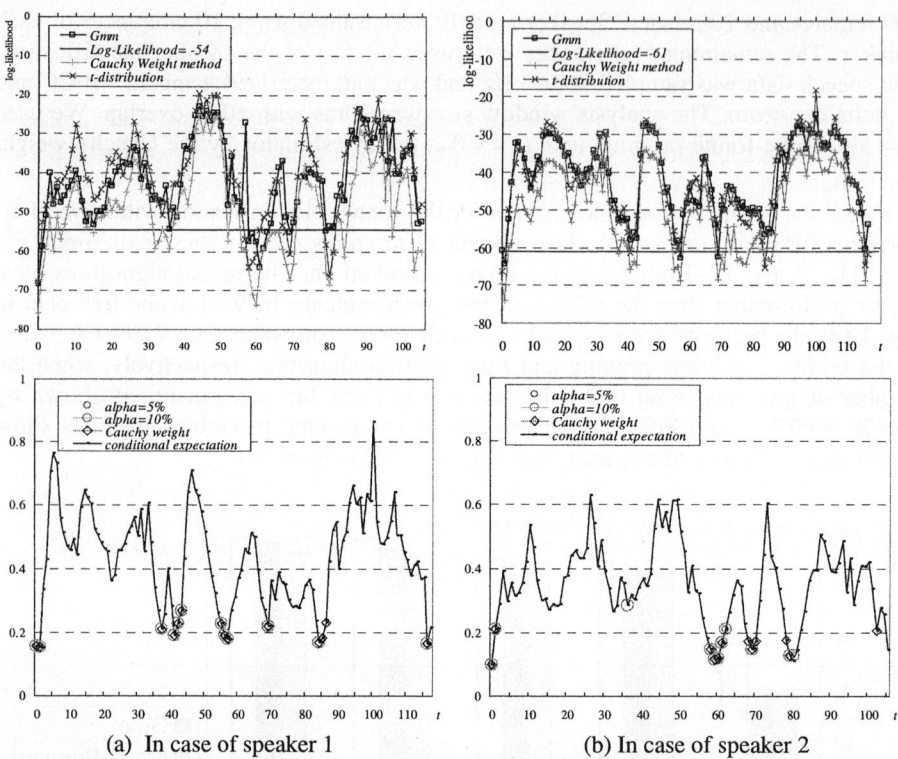

Fig. 2. The log-likelihood by frame (upper) and the correspondence between removed frames and the conditional expectation by frame (lower)

Fig.2 show the likelihood of frames in the GMM, the Cauchy function, and the t-distribution, respectively. And the lower one shows the conditional expectation of frames in the t-distribution and the frames of outliers. Here, the alpha is set to 5% and 10%, respectively. From the results, we can find that the frames regarded as outliers appear in the same frame index in those several robust algorithms.

From the graphs given in Fig. 2, those frames which make the performances of the above robust algorithms degraded are selected in Table 1. Table 1 shows the correspondence of frames each in the frame pruning method, the Cauchy weight function and t-distribution about two speakers' test speech. The index of frame pruning is the number of frame which belongs to the 5% lowest log-likelihood of frames while those of Cauchy function and t-distribution are the numbers of frame which weight of Cauchy method is less than 0.13 and conditional expectation is less than 0.18 in table 1-(a), and which weight of Cauchy method is less than 0.135 and conditional expectation is less than 0.14 in table 1-(b), respectively.

In table 1 and Fig. 1, we can find that the index of the removed frames by the frame pruning method corresponds to those of the frames with low values (low weight or low conditional expectation) in the robust methods. From results, we confirmed that the trend of frames with less log-likelihood using the frame pruning is similar to one in the multivariate t-distribution.

Table 1. The index of frames in the frame pruning and robust algorithms

(a) In case of Speaker 1

Frame Pruning		Cauchy weight function		t-distribution	
Index	$L(\lambda)$ ($\alpha=5\%$)	Index	Weight (≤ 0.130)	Index	u_n (≤ 0.18)
0	-60.876	0	0.127	0	0.158
1	-64.398	1	0.120	1	0.153
57	-62.744	57	0.129	57	0.180
69	-62.576	69	0.129	84	0.169
116	-60.281	116	0.129	116	0.166

(b) In case of Speaker 2

Frame Pruning		Cauchy weight function		t-distribution	
Index	$L(\lambda)$ ($\alpha=5\%$)	Index	Weight (≤ 0.135)	Index	u_n (≤ 0.14)
0	-68.281	0	0.117	0	0.099
1	-58.620	1	0.134	1	0.147
57	-57.278	59	0.125	59	0.118
59	-57.470	60	0.120	60	0.121
60	-64.089	69	0.131	69	0.147
61	-59.160	79	0.129	79	0.128
				80	0.112

6 Conclusions

In this paper, we studied on the relation between the frame pruning and the robust speaker identification with the multivariate t-distribution based on M-estimator. When dealing with outliers, they all show better performance than the convenient methods and actually have same theoretical background. To show their relation, we performed the robust speaker identification by removing less reliable frames in the frame pruning method and the multivariate t-distribution respectively.

In our experiments, the robust speaker identification system shows higher performance than the typical GMM. We can find that the removing of frames with lower weight in the robust algorithm becomes the theoretical basis of the frames pruned in the frame pruning method. As a result, we showed the effectiveness of the speaker identification applying the frame pruning and the multivariate t-distribution and confirmed that the trend of frames with less log-likelihood in the frame pruning is similar to one in the multivariate t-distribution.

Acknowledgement

This work was supported by the Soongsil University Research Fund.

References

1. Reynolds, D.A., Rose, R. :Robust text-independent speaker identification using Gaussian mixture speaker models, IEEE Trans. on SAP, 3(1), (1995) 72-82
2. Bessacier, L. and Bonastre, J.F.: Frame Pruning for speaker recognition, ICASSP98, (1998) 765-768
3. Dav´e, R.N. and Krishnapuram, R.: Robust Clustering Methods: A Unified View, IEEE Trans. On Fuzzy Systems, 5(2), (1997) 270-293
4. Lee, J., Rheem, J. and Lee, K. Y.: Robust Speaker Recognition Against Utterance Variations, LNCS2668, (2003), 624-630
5. Ohashi, Y.: Fuzzy clustering and robust estimation, in 9th Meet. SAS Users Grp. Int., Hollywood Beach, FL, 1984
6. Rajesh, N. D.: Characterization and detection of noise in clustering, Pattern Recognition Letter, 12(11), (1991) 657–664
7. Goodall, C.: M-estimator of location: An outline of the theory, in Understanding Robust and Exploratory Data Analysis, D. C. Hoaglin, F. Mosteller, and J. W. Tukey, Eds. New York: (1983), 339–403.
8. Hampel, F. R., Ponchotti, E. M., Rousseeuw, P. J. and W. A. Stahel: Robust Statistics: The Approach Based on Influence Functions, New York: Wiley, 1986
9. Huber, P. J.: Robust Statistics. New York: Wiley, 1981
10. Peel, D., McLachlan, G.J. : Robust mixture modeling using the t-distribution, Statistics and computing, 10, (2000) 339-348
11. Wang, H., Zhang, Q., Luo, B. and Wei, S. :Robust mixture modeling using multivariate t-distribution with missing information, Pattern Recognition Letters,25, (2004) 701-710
12. Markov, K., Nakagawa, S.: Frame level likelihood normalization for text-independent speaker identification using GMMs, In Proc. ICSLP, (1996) 1764-1767

Auto-summarization of Multimedia Meeting Records Based on Accessing Log

Weisheng He, Yuanchun Shi, and Xin Xiao

Department of Computer Science and Technology, Tsinghua University,
100084 Beijing, China
{hws99, xiaoxin00}@mails.tsinghua.edu.cn,
Shiyc@tsinghua.edu.cn
http://media.cs.tsinghua.edu.cn/~pervasive

Abstract. Computer techniques have been leveraged to record human experiences in many public spaces, e.g. meeting rooms and classrooms. For the large amount of such records produced after long-term use, it is imperative to generate auto summaries of the original content for fast skimming and browsing. In this paper, we present ASBUL, a novel algorithm to produce summaries of multimedia meeting records based on the information about viewers' accessing patterns. This algorithm predicts the interestingness of record segments to the viewers based on the analysis of previous accessing patterns, and produces summaries by picking the segments of the highest predicted interests. We report a user study which compares ASBUL-generated summaries with human-generated summaries and shows that ASBUL algorithm is generally effective in generating personalized summaries to satisfy different viewers without requiring any priori, especially in free-style meetings where information is less structured and viewers' understandings are more diversified.

1 Introduction

With the booming technologies in capture, storage and analysis of multimedia data, human experiences in many public spaces, such as lectures and meetings, are automatically captured as multimedia records[1][2][3][4][5][6]. With such multimedia records growing exponentially, there is an increasing imbalance between the amount of accessible information and the human processing capacity. Thus it is imperative to provide tools for automatic summarization so as to enable viewers to quickly skim over the content.

Our focus is how meeting records, pervasive in our daily life, can be summarized. Meetings are important activities for team communication and coordination, generating a large amount of information which is not formally documented. However, few viewers are willing to sequentially navigate the records since they will have to spend hours on many unimportant, boring and trivial segments before reaching the information they really want. Thus, it will be of great benefits to post-meeting viewers if a summary of the meeting record is available to provide the most relevant information before they decide whether to dig into further details and where to find the interesting information.

Humans are good at summarization. The human summarization process can be divided into two steps: first, we extract low-level features from the record, e.g., what is said or what is done in the meeting, which can be characterized as **events** during the meetings; then, based on these low-level features, we reason what are the interesting parts to be included in summaries. Developments in computer techniques, such as sensing and multimedia analysis, are increasingly enhancing the first step for feature extraction. However, the reasoning step is highly subjective, concerning many implicit and subtle context factors such as viewers' preferences, background, etc., and is therefore too complex for computers to reason without any subjective implications from the viewers themselves.

A valuable source of such subjective implications is the viewers' accessing logs, which is a detailed record of the viewers' operations (rewind, fast-forward, pause, jump, etc.) when they are accessing the meeting records. We have observed that viewers unintentionally embed their understandings to the captured records in their accessing patterns extracted from previous logs, and this knowledge can be leveraged to derive their subjective interests for auto summarization. There have been several research proposed to exploit viewers' logs to summarize multimedia content. One trend[7] is to employ such logs as a minor factor, in combination with other objective features such as slide transition and audio pitch, to generate summaries. Another trend, mainly adopted in video summarization[8][9][10][11], leverages the accessing logs as the major factor for summarization by deriving the viewers' interests to different video segments from their accessing patterns. Other methods, which do not utilize the user logs, require priori knowledge or rules for a specific meeting scenario. For instance, in [12] a meeting ontology is defined to summarize and classify meeting content. However, the priori is usually different between various meetings, thus such method could only be used for specific applications

Meeting record has its unique features. First, a viewer may access several related meeting records and one meeting record may be accessed by more than one viewers. In this sense, the accessing logs are connected both horizontally and vertically, which is largely ignored in previous works. Second, with the aid of computer technologies, meetings can be captured with many indices of explicit semantics. Such indices can act as a bridge between the viewers and computers. On the one hand, viewers can quickly find the information they want by the indices and use them to index into other more detailed multimedia content such as video/audio. On the other hand, computers can infer about viewers' subjective interests from their interaction with the indices. If viewers can be aware of the semantics of such indices, his accessing pattern will be more directed and purposeful, i.e., he will jump to an index and watch its detail only if he feels interested about the semantics related to that index. Thus, a viewer's accessing frequency to a record index reflects his interest in the semantics of that index.

Based on this notion, we present a novel algorithm, ASBUL (**A**uto **S**ummarization **B**ased on **U**ser **L**og), to summarize multimedia meeting records by reasoning viewers' interests from previous logs of accessing the indexing events. Indexing events are low-level, objective events that can be automatically captured by computers and leveraged to mark and index important points in meetings, such as slide transition, user speech, user joining/leaving, etc. The ASBUL algorithm divides the record into segments of similar length, and uses a mathematical model to compute an **interesting value** for each segment by mining the viewers' accessing logs. Segments of the highest interesting value are selected to compose the summary. Compared with other summarization algorithms, ASBUL algorithm has the following two advantages: 1)it can be employed in different situations without requiring any priori knowledge; 2)it analyzes the logs in a personalized manner so that the summaries generated can satisfy viewers with different interests.

The rest of the paper is organized as follows: in section 2 we briefly describe how the accessing logs are collected and stored; then details of ASBUL algorithm is presented in section 3. We report the result of a user study in section 4. Section 5 concludes the paper and outlines our future work.

2 Log Collection

To make the viewers' access to meeting records efficient and meaningful, it is important to automatically capture the necessary indexing events while meetings are recorded. The indexing events to be captured may vary between different meeting scenarios, and two basic criteria for such indexing events are: 1) they cover most of the important information in meetings; 2) they can be automatically detected and captured at a practically acceptable confidence. In our prototype meeting-capture system, the captured indexing events include attendees' speech and their interaction with the electronic whiteboard, e.g. opening documents and making annotations. These events are detected and captured through multiple devices, including microphone array, RF-based location tracking, vision technique and electronic whiteboard. Besides the temporal information (its begin and end time), the metadata of these indexing events also include three semantic dimensions: user, (action) type and keyword, much like the subject, predicate and object in a complete sentence. The user dimension describes the identity of the attendee involved in the event; the type dimension informs the type of action taken in this event, e.g., talking, annotating or changing slide; the keyword contains other important semantic information. e.g., for a talking event it includes the keywords (the keyword set is predefined according to the meeting topic) detected from the speech, and for a document-opening event it includes the title of the document.

To collect viewers' logs, we developed a browser, which visualizes the indexing events as rectangular icons in a timeline, shown in figure1. By clicking on the corresponding icon, viewers can see the metadata of an indexing event. To watch the multimedia content, viewers can play the record in a sequential, VCR-like mode or in a highlight mode. In the highlight mode, viewers can select a single or a group of indexing events either by directly clicking on icons in the timeline or retrieving in the metadata of the indexing events. The multimedia content around the selected events will be played consecutively as user-defined highlights in a pop-up window.

The accessing logs are stored in <Viewer-ID, Event-ID, Access-frequency> triples. The Viewer-ID and Event-ID specify the identity of the viewer and the indexing event, and Access-frequency describes how many times this indexing event has been selected by the viewer to be played in highlight mode. This is because viewers' operations in highlight mode, which we term as a **purposeful access**, are largely based on their own judgment, i.e., a viewer will select an indexing event and watch its details only if he has interest in the semantics of that indexing event. Thus the Access-frequency in the triple can effectively reflect the viewers' interests.

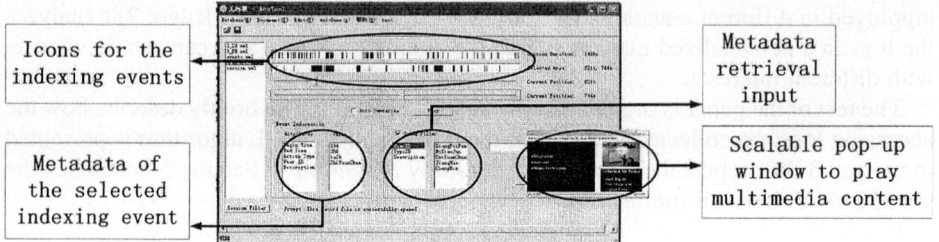

Fig. 1. The browser to access the meeting records

3 ASBUL Algorithm

The ASBUL algorithm can be divided into several parts, and their details will be described in this section.

3.1 Record Segmentation and Interesting Value Computation

The basic idea of ASBUL algorithm is to partition the record into segments and pick those of the highest interesting value into the summary. Thus the first step of ASBUL algorithm is record segmentation. Segment lengths approximate to an empirical value of 15 seconds, and they are not strictly trimmed to 15 seconds so as to avoid segmenting inside an indexing event. (Each indexing event may last for a certain period) Thus the selected indexing events will remain integral in the summary. A segment's interesting value is computed as

$$IV_i = \sum_{e \in E_i} V(e) + f_N \cdot \sum_{e \in E_{i-1}} V(e) + f_N \cdot \sum_{e \in E_{i+1}} V(e) \quad (1)$$

where IV_i is the interesting value of ith segment; $V(e)$ is the interesting value of an individual indexing event e; E_i is the set of indexing events in the ith segment; f_N is a weighing factor to control the influence of one segment on its neighbors. With the introduction of this weighing factor, a segment neighboring very important segments is likely to be picked into the summary even itself does not contain many interesting indexing events. The purpose for this mechanism is to avoid incoherence, a common problem in computer-generated summaries, since the importance of a segment should not only be evaluated by the events it includes, but also by its function to provide context for the more important neighboring segments.

The duration of the summary can be arbitrarily defined by the viewer, the number of segments selected into the summary will equal to the given summary duration. For instance, if the viewer wants a five-minute summary, the ASBUL algorithm will pick up 20 segments which are of the highest interesting value into the summary. (Each segments is about 15 seconds and 20 segments together last for 5 minutes.)

3.2 Interesting Value for Events

As in formula (1), a segment's interesting value is computed by summing up the interesting value of all the indexing events in this segment and its neighbors, thus the essence of ASBUL algorithm is a mathematical model to calculate the interesting value of an individual indexing event based on previous accessing logs.

While evaluating the interestingness of an indexing event to a specific viewer, two types of accessing logs are useful. The first is this viewer's accessing logs to other records in the past, from which his personal interest can be extracted, and we define the evaluation of an indexing event based on this viewer's historical logs as **vertical value**. The second is all viewers' accessing logs to this very indexing event, which can measure the general interestingness of this event as a whole, and we denote this overall metric as **horizontal value**. The interesting value of an indexing event e, $V(e)$, is computed as the sum of its vertical value $VV(e)$ and horizontal value $VH(e)$.

3.2.1 Vertical Value

The purpose of the introduction of vertical value is to ensure the summaries are personalized. Although viewer's interest to an indexing event as a whole can not be directly measured by his accessing logs to other records since no two indexing events are entirely identical, its semantic values, contained in the three dimensions, often reappear in different records. For instance, in meetings between a group of software developers, different modules will be repeatedly discussed and while watching meeting records the interface designer will often stick to the parts when requirements on the interface is discussed or commented; a student reviewing lectures will often directly jump to the addresses given by the instructor if he thinks the most important information in lectures is conveyed by such addresses. Generally if a viewer frequently seeks for the indexing events related to a certain semantic value A, he probably has an enduring interest in A, indicating the chances of his accessing to the indexing events containing A in its metadata are much greater than other events. In this sense, the vertical value of an indexing event can be computed by evaluating the viewer's personal interest to its semantics in three dimensions and then summing them up as follows

$$VV(e) = f_U \cdot I_U(e) + f_T \cdot I_T(e) + f_K \cdot I_K(e) \qquad (2)$$

where e is an indexing event, $I_U(e)$, $I_T(e)$ and $I_K(e)$ are the viewer's interest to the semantic values of its three dimensions (user, type, keyword respectively), and f_U, f_T and f_K are weighing factors.

The computation of $I_U(e)$, $I_T(e)$ and $I_K(e)$ is similar to the Term Frequency-Inverse Document Frequency (TF-IDF) method[13] in text analysis. For example, if the user dimension of an indexing event e is "Jack", $I_U(e)$ is computed as

$$I_U(e) = mean(IU_r("Jack")) = mean(\frac{V_r("Jack")/TV_r}{A_r("Jack")/TA_r}) \qquad (3)$$

where $IU_r("Jack")$ is the viewer's interest to the value "Jack" calculated from his accessing log to a previous meeting record r; $V_r("Jack")$ is his access frequency to all the indexing events in record r whose user dimension is of value "Jack"; TV_r is his access frequency to all indexing events in r; $A_r("Jack")$ is the number of the indexing events in r whose user dimension is of value "Jack"; similarly TA_r is the total number of all indexing events in r. $I_U(e)$ is the arithmetic mean of $IU_r("Jack")$ computed from all records. $I_T(e)$ and $I_K(e)$ are also computed similarly.

3.2.2 Horizontal Value

The horizontal value reflects the general interestingness of an indexing event relative to other indexing events in the record to be summarized. It is computed by analyzing all viewers' accessing logs to this record as

$$WH(e) = \sum_i (SF_i^* \cdot IE(e,i)) / \sum_i SF_i^* \qquad (4)$$

where $IE(e, i)$ is the ith viewer's interest to event e which is directly computed from his accessing logs to e; SF_i is the similarity factor between the current viewer and the ith viewer, measuring the similarity of their interests. Similar to IU_r, $IE(e, i)$ is computed like the TF-IDF method as

$$IE(e,i) = \frac{V(e,i)/TV(i)}{A(e)/TA} = V(e,i) \cdot TA / TV(i) \qquad (5)$$

where $V(e,i)$ is the ith viewer's access frequency to the indexing event e; $TV(i)$ is ith viewer's access frequency to all indexing events. $A(e)$ is the number of e's appearance, which always equals to one, and TA is the total number of all indexing events. Note that the meanings of these four parameters are discussed in the scope of the record to be summarized. (For instance, if the record to be summarized contains five indexing events, then the value o f TA is 5).

Generally viewers who demonstrate similar accessing patterns are likely to share common preferences and similar understandings for what are the interesting segments in the record. Based on this notion, we introduce the similarity factor to the computation of horizontal value. This factor measures the similarity of two viewers' accessing patterns by analyzing previous logs and can in turn inform how much one viewer's accessing patterns can predict another's patterns. The similarity factor is computed as

$$SF_i^* = mean(SF_i(r)) \qquad (6)$$

where $SF_i(r)$ is the similarity factor between the ith and current viewer extracted from their accessing logs to record r; the overall similarity factor, SF_i^*, is the mean of the $SF_i(r)$ calculated from all the records that have been watched by both viewers.

To compute $SF_i(r)$, we adopt a method similar to the calculation of correlation coefficient between two arrays[14]. The access frequency is a reflection of the viewer interest distribution, i.e., the ratio of a viewer's purposeful accesses to a single indexing event divided by the total count of his purposeful accesses to all the events in that record is a quantitative metric to indicate his interest to that indexing event. Thus, if we regard a viewer's access frequencies to the indexing events in one record as an array and compute the correlation coefficient between these arrays, we can have a quantitative metric of the similarity between two viewers' accessing patterns. For expression convenience, we suppose X and Y are the two arrays representing access frequency of the current viewer and the ith viewer to the indexing events in record r, and their similarity factor extracted from r is computed as

$$SF_i(r) = \frac{\sum XY - n\overline{X}\overline{Y}}{\sqrt{(\sum X^2 - n\overline{X}^2)(\sum y^2 - n\overline{Y}^2)}} \quad (7)$$

where $\overline{X}$ is the mean of X and $\overline{Y}$ is the mean of Y. The more the two viewers' accessing patterns resemble each other, the greater $SF_i(r)$ will be, indicating that the ith viewer's understanding, reflected by the value of $IE(e,i)$, will have a greater influence on the prediction of current viewer's interest.

4 User Study

4.1 Methodology

ASBUL algorithm is mainly utilized to generate personalized summaries based on previous accessing logs. Since personalized summarization is largely a subjective issue, the method we employ to evaluate ASBUL algorithm is a user study including two meeting scenarios: a series of presentations on similar topics where the presenter dominates the meeting and our weekly group meeting featured by free discussions between the peers. We select two meeting scenarios because we believe that meetings of different styles will have different features in their summaries. Four meetings for each scenario are captured and used in the user study and their basic information is listed in table 1.

Eight subjects, either meeting attendees or related to the meeting, are recruited in the user study, because generally only those people connected to the meeting will watch the record afterwards. After each meeting is captured, the subjects are encouraged to access the records by the browser introduced in section 2 and their accessing logs are stored in a XML database. Right after each meeting is finished, the corresponding record is made available for access. Finally after all meetings are captured, the subjects are told to summarize the record of the last(fourth) meeting based on their own understanding and interests. The process to manually generate a summary is quite straightforward and easy with a special graphical interface we provide (shown in figure 2). The whole process is quite casual, i.e., the subjects can access the records and generate summaries at their office desks or in their dorms whenever they have time and desire to do so. The length of the summary, either generated by the viewers or by ASBUL algorithm, is about 20% of the original.

A combination of both objective and subjective measures is adopted to evaluate ASBUL-generated summaries. For the objective measure, we compute the percentage

Table 1. Basic information about the captured meetings

Meeting Styles	Avg. length of the original record	Avg. number of indexing events for each record	Avg. duration of each indexing events
Presentation	35:26	73	6.78 (second)
Free Discussion	44:27	89	8.13 (second)

Fig. 2. The graphic tool provided to manually generate summaries. The indexing events are displayed as blue icons in the upper timeline, and the segments already selected into the summary are displayed as green icons in the lower timeline. Subjects can watch the multimedia content in the media player window on the left, and make retrievals in the search pane on the right. Subjects can pick a new segment into the summary in two ways: a) clicking on the buttons beneath the media player window. The starting and stopping position of the segment are determined by the position of the slider-bar when the button is clicked; b) clicking directly on the lower timeline. The starting and stopping position of the segment correspond to the coordinates of the click. By right-clicking on the selected segments (green icons), subject can modify or delete them.

of overlap between subject-generated summaries and ASBUL-generated summaries to quantify the similarity between them. However, since auto summarization deals with strong subjectivity like human understanding and interest, each subject is also asked to complete a questionnaire, in which he can assign a score to several aspects of the ASBUL-generated summary after watching it.

4.2 User Study Results

During this eight-week-long user study, the eight subjects have made 3048 purposeful accesses and based on the logs of these accesses we use the ASBUL algorithm to generate one summary for each subject and each meeting scenario. Thus we have a total of 16 subject-generated summaries and 16 ASBUL-generated summaries. (8 subjects multiplies 2 meeting scenarios for each subject) In this part we will present our analysis to the result of the user study.

First we use the overlap-ratio to measure the difference between summaries generated by the subjects. Totally there are $C(8,2)=28$ values for each scenario and the statistical information is shown in Table2. In this table, we have observed the subjects have displayed very different understandings for what parts in the record are important or interesting, indicating a single-versioned summary, even generated by human expert, can hardly satisfy different viewers simultaneously and it is necessary to generate personalized summaries.

By depicting similarity factors between every two subjects and the overlap-ratio of the summaries they generate into a line chart (shown in figure3), we can see how effective this factor can predict the similarity between viewers' accessing patterns. Since similarity factor is an overall metric and the overlap-ratio here is based on the

Table 2. Overlap-ratio between subject-generated summaries

Meeting Styles	Avg.	Max.	Min.	Standard Deviation
Presentation	35.6%	59.0%	10.3%	17.0%
Free Discussion	38.4%	65.8%	10.9%	17.8%

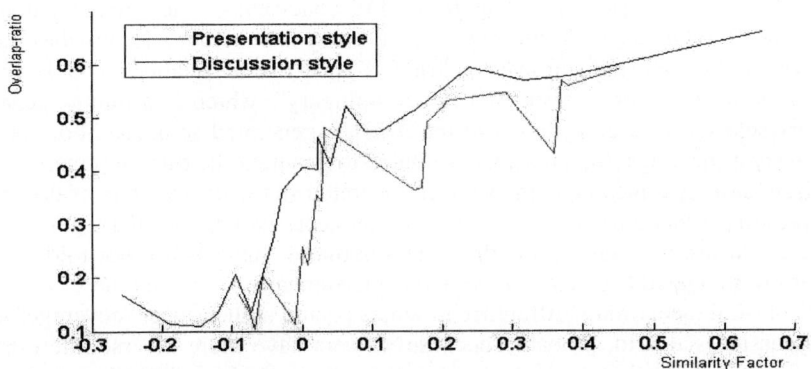

Fig. 3. Relation between similarity factor and overlap-ratio

summaries of a specific record, we do not expect an ideal monotonic relation between them and we can see some local fluctuations in figure3. However, there is a general trend that the overlap-ratio will increase when similarity factor increases, which indicates it is reasonable to use this factor to determine how much one viewer's accessing patterns can contribute to the prediction of another's accessing patterns.

The overlap-ratio between ASBUL-generated summary for a specific subject and the summary manually generated by the subject himself are used as a quantitative metric to measure the quality of auto summarization. Totally there are eight values, one for each subject, and the result is shown in Table3. We can see a considerable overlap-ratio and the average value is significantly greater than the maximum overlap-ratio between the subject-generated summaries (see Table2), suggesting that the ASBUL-generated summary generally covers more interesting points than any of the summaries manually generated by other subjects. Considering the significant variances between viewers' understanding of what are the interesting parts in the record and the cost to manually generate a personalized summary for each viewer, we believe the ASBUL algorithm is an effective alternative.

Table 3. Overlap-ratio between ASBUL-generated summaries and subject-generated summaries. The parameters used in ASBUL algorithm are as follows: f_N=0.4, α=0.5, f_U=0.4, f_T= f_K=0.3.

Meeting Styles	Avg.	Max.	Min.	Standard Deviation
Presentation	67.6%	81.3%	57.0%	11.7%
Free Discussion	71.0%	85.6%	60.5%	8.4%

Table 4. Average score to the aspects listed in the questionnaire. The scores range from 5 to 1, representing "strongly agree", "agree", "no idea", "disagree" and "strongly disagree".

Meeting Styles	Coverage	Conciseness	Continuity	Overall
Presentation	3.25(3.63)	3.75(4.00)	3.25(3.63)	3.50(3.88)
Free Discussion	3.38(2.88)	3.88(3.75)	3.50(3.75)	3.75(3.63)

The aspects listed in the subjective questionnaire include coverage (the summary covers all important points I am interested in), conciseness (the summary does not contain much redundancy), continuity (the summary is coherent and provides reasonable context), overall (the summary provides a good overall quality). The data in the parenthesis are the scores given to a "ruler summary", which is a human-generated summary selected as a comparison to the ASBUL-generated summary. For the presentation style meetings, the presenter is invited to generate the ruler summary; for the free-discussion style meetings, the subject-generated summary which is of the highest overlap-ratio (except the one generated by this subject) with the summary generated by the subject himself is selected as the ruler summary. Subjects are not told how the summary is generated before completing the questionnaire to avoid unnecessary bias.

In Table 4, the maximum difference in scores occurs in the aspect "coverage" of the free-discussion scenario, probably because viewers have more diverse interests in a free-style meeting, making it more difficult for a viewer to find all the key points he is interested in from a summary produced based on the understanding of another viewer. However, the ruler summary has a better coverage for presentation scenario because the knowledge in a presentation scenario is more structured and the presenter certainly has an incomparable understanding for what are the key points. Both summaries are rated fairly well in conciseness, since both human and ASBUL algorithm are not likely to pick segments containing no interesting events or providing no valuable context into the summary. For continuity, although ASBUL-generated summaries still receive poorer scores than ruler summaries, the gaps are not as obvious as in previous work[7]. The overall score has shown that ASBUL algorithm can generate summaries of similar subjective quality to the summaries generated by human.

On the whole, differences in summarizing meeting of the two scenarios are not as significant as we had expected. ASBUL algorithm has more advantage in summarizing free-style meetings largely because in this scenario, the information in meetings is not well structured and results in a more diversified understanding between the viewers, which favors the ASBUL algorithm since it incorporates more personalized factors in the summarization.

5 Conclusion

In this paper, we present an algorithm to summarize multimedia meeting records by using a mathematical model to predict viewers' subjective interests based on their previous logs. The result of a user study shows the algorithm can automatically generate personalized summaries to satisfy different viewers without requiring any priori.

Our future work will continue in two aspects. Firstly, we will put our prototype into long term use and examine if this algorithm will further improve after more data are accumulated and can be learned from. Secondly, in our current implementation most of the parameters, e.g., the vertical weight and horizontal weight, are combined in a linear fashion, we will analyze both theoretically and experimentally if such method is appropriate or there is a better choice.

Acknowledgements

This research is supported by a funding from Lenovo Research Institute. Additionally, we sincerely appreciate those volunteers for their participation and help in our user study.

References

1. Abowd G.D.: Classroom 2000: An experiment with the instrumentation of a living educational environment". IBM Systems J., Vol. 38(4). (1999) 508-530.
2. Heather R.A., Abowd G.D., Geyer W., Fuchs L., Daijavad S., Poltrock S.: Integrating Meeting Capture and Access within a Collaborative Team Environment, Proc. 3rd Int'l Conf. Ubiquitous Computing, 2001, pp. 123-138.
3. Gross R., Bett M., Yu H., Zhu X.J., Pan Y., Yang J., Waibel A..: Towards A Multimodal Meeting Record", IEEE ICME 2000, 2000.
4. S. Mukhopadhyay, B. Smith, "Passive Capture and Structuring of Lectures," Proc. ACM MM'99, 1999, pp. 477-487
5. Baldochi L., Andrade A., Cattelan R., Pimentel M. Architecture and Components for Capture and Access Application. Proc. WebMedia and LA-Web, 2004, pp. 150 – 157
6. Jain, R., Kim, P., Li, Z. Experiential Meeting System. In the Proceedings of ACM SIGMM 2003 Workshop on Experiential Telepresence (ETP03'). 2003, pp. 1-12
7. He L.W., Sanocki E., Gupta A., Grudin J.: Auto-Summarization of Audio-Video Presentations. ACM MM'99 (1999) 489-498
8. Yu B., Ma W.Y., Nahrstedt K., Zhang H.J.: Video Summarization Based on User Log Enhanced Link Analysis. ACM MM'03 (2003) 382-391
9. Babaguchi N., Ohara K., Ogura T.: Effect of Personalization on Retrieval and Summarization of Sports Video. ICICS-PCM 2003 (2003) 940-944.
10. Syeda-Mahmmod T.F., Ponceleon D.: Learning Video Browsing Behavior and its Application in the Generation of Video Previews. ACM MM'01(2001) 119-128.
11. Ma Y.F., Lu L., Zhang H.J., Li M.: An Attention Model for Video Browsing Summarization. ACM MM'02(2002) 533-542.
12. Hakeem, A., Shah M. Onotology and Taxonomy Collaborated Framework for Meeting Classification. Proc. of 17th international conference on Pattern Recognition. (ICPR'04) 2004. pp. 1-5
13. Salton G.: Automatic Text Processing. Addison-Wesley, 1989
14. Whittaker, E. T., Robinson, G.: The Coefficient of Correlation for Frequency Distributions which are not Normal. The Calculus of Observations: A Treatise on Numerical Mathematics, 4th edition. New York: Dover (1967) 334-336.

Towards a High-Level Audio Framework for Video Retrieval Combining Conceptual Descriptions and Fully-Automated Processes

Mbarek Charhad and Mohammed Belkhatir

IMAG-CNRS, BP 53, 38041 Grenoble Cedex 9, France
{charhad, belkhatm}@imag.fr

Abstract. The growing need for 'intelligent' video retrieval systems leads to new architectures combining multiple characterizations of the video content that rely on highly expressive frameworks while providing fully-automated indexing and retrieval processes. As a matter of fact, addressing the problem of combining modalities within expressive frameworks for video indexing and retrieval is of huge importance and the only solution for achieving significant retrieval performance. This paper presents a multi-facetted conceptual framework integrating multiple characterizations of the audio content for automatic video retrieval. It relies on an expressive representation formalism handling high-level audio descriptions of a video document and a full-text query framework in an attempt to operate video indexing and retrieval on audio features beyond state-of-the-art architectures operating on low-level features and keyword-annotation frameworks. Experiments on the multimedia topic search task of the TRECVID 2004 evaluation campaign validate our proposal.

1 Introduction

The size, heterogeneity of content, and the temporal characteristics of video data pose many interesting challenges to the video indexing and retrieval community. Among these challenges is the modeling task for effective content-based indexing and user access capabilities such as querying, retrieval and browsing.

Video data can be modeled based on its visual content (such as color, texture, shape, motion...) [1], [17] audio content [7]. Models such as VideoText [9], VSTROM [2] and VideoGraph [16] whether they use the video annotation (stratification) approach or the keyword-based annotation approach [3], [4] to represent video semantics, fail to model semantic relationships among the concepts expressed in the video. The importance of capturing video semantic associations lies in the fact that it can greatly improve the effectiveness of video querying by providing knowledge-based query processing [13], [4]. This is due to the fact that human beings always have multiple expressions or terms for the same or similar semantics. For example, "sport" and "baseball" do not match syntactically but match conceptually. Furthermore, video semantic associations can be used for flexible, knowledge-based video browsing. Existing visual content-based video browsing approaches are mostly static.

Other techniques for video modeling analyze the semantic content by considering object hierarchies. For example, the model proposed in [1] allows hierarchical abstraction of video expressions representing scenes and events. It provides the possibility to assign multiple interpretations to a given video segment and functionalities for creating video presentations.

However, all tasks involving automated visual characterization at the key-frame level involves heavy computational treatments for low-level extraction while providing very poor recognition results. Indeed, the results of fully-visual manual runs at the TRECVID 2004 evaluation campaign do not go beyond a 0,01 average precision rate [11]. As for now, dealing with fully-automated visual characterization appear to penalize greatly video indexing and retrieval frameworks both as far as the retrieval results are concerned and the computational load involved for low-level feature extraction. As a consequence, text annotations are usually used to describe the video content according to the annotator's expertise and the purpose of this content [9]. However, such descriptions are biased, incomplete and often inaccurate since subjected to the annotator's point-of-view. Also, manual annotation is a costly task which cannot keep pace with the ever-growing size of video collections.

We therefore strongly believe that being able to model aspects related to the audio content is crucial in order to assist a human user in the tasks of querying and browsing. Also, since users are more skilled in defining their information needs using language-based descriptors [14], this modeling task is to consider a symbolic representation of audio features as textual descriptors. Indeed, a user would naturally formulate his desire to being provided with videos where Y is speaking about X with the full-text query " Show me videos where Y is speaking about X.". For this, the traditional keyword-based approaches in state-of-the-art video architectures would appear clearly not satisfactory since they fail to take into account aspects related to conceptual and relational descriptions of the video content. Indeed, we believe that in order to process a query such as "Show videos displaying Bill Clinton speaking" (proposed in the framework of the TRECVID 2004 topic search track), a system is to characterize concepts such as Bill Clinton and relations such as the fact that he is speaking.

In order to process these queries involving non-trivial information needs, we propose in this paper to integrate audio descriptions within a unified full-text framework by considering:

- The specification of a rich video model featuring all characterizations of the audio content. It is based on audio objects, structures abstracting the audio flow related to a video document (they are detailed in section 2).
- The integration of a knowledge representation formalism (conceptual graphs) in order to instantiate the video audio model within a video indexing and retrieval framework and therefore specify indexing, querying and matching processes.
- The specification of fully-automated processes to build and manipulate the conceptual index and query descriptions. Indeed, the strength of our approach relies in the specification of high-level descriptions of the video content while being able to process video corpus of relatively important size.
- The evaluation of our theoretical proposition in the framework of the multimedia topic search track of the TRECVID 2004 evaluation campaign. We will show that it outperforms state-of-the-art systems which do not take into account conceptual and relational characterizations of the video audio content.

In the remainder, we detail in section 2 our conceptual audio framework for video indexing and retrieval. Section 3 deals with the automatic conceptual characterization of audio/speech features and section 4 tackles the index and query conceptual representations. We finally discuss validation experiments conducted on the TRECVID 2004 corpus in section 5.

2 A Bi-facetted Model for Audio Characterization

We propose the outline of an audio model for video indexing and retrieval supported by an expressive knowledge representation formalism. It describes the information related to video shots through audio segment flows and is represented by a bi-facetted structure (fig.1):

- The audio object facet characterizes audio objects (AOs), abstraction of audio elements extracted from the audio flow.
- The audio semantic concept facet provides the semantic description related to each AO. It is based on concepts such as person identity, organization, location… and consists in specifying the speaker identity in each shot as well as the characterization of the audio content being spoken of.

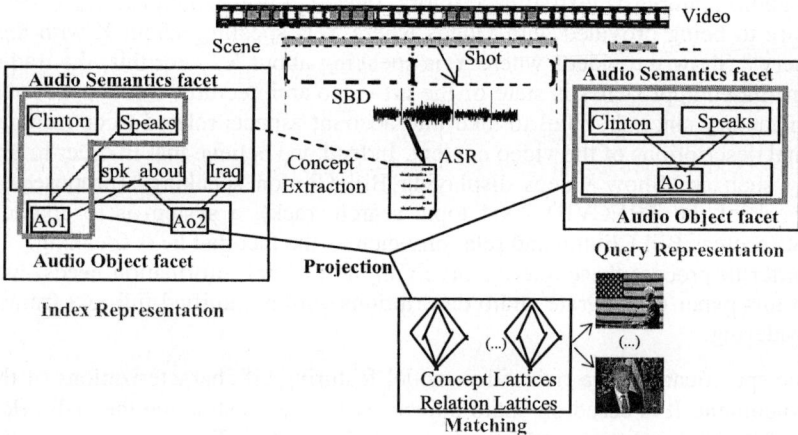

Fig. 1. Video Model and General Description of Indexing, Querying and Matching Processes

In order to instantiate this model as a video retrieval framework, we need a representation formalism capable of representing audio objects as well as the audio semantics they convey. Moreover, this representation formalism should make it easy to visualize the information related to the video shot. It should therefore combine expressivity and a user-friendly representation. As a matter of fact, a graph-based representation and particularly conceptual graphs (CGs) [15] are an efficient solution to characterize the audio content of a video shot. The asset of this knowledge representation formalism is its flexible adaptation to the symbolic approach of multimedia retrieval [14]. It allows indeed to uniformly represent components of our architecture and to develop expressive and efficient index and query frameworks.

Formally, a CG is a finite, bipartite, related and oriented graph. It features 2 types of nodes: the first one between brackets in our CG alphanumerical representation (i.e. as coded in our framework) is tagged by a concept however the second between parentheses is tagged by a conceptual relation. E.g., the CG:[PCM_05] → (Name) → [Conference] → (Location) → [Jeju] is interpreted as: the PCM 2005 conference is held in Jeju.

Concepts and conceptual relations are organized within a lattice structure partially ordered by the IS-A ($\leq$) relation. E.g., Person $\leq$ Man denotes that the concept Man is a specialization of the concept Person, and will therefore appear in the offspring of the latter within the lattice organizing these concepts. Within the scope of the model, CGs are used to represent the audio content of a video shot within index and query stuctures.

The indexing module provides the audio representation of a video shot document in the corpus with respect to the explicited model. It is itself a CG called video shot document audio index graph. In fig. 1, a video shot belonging to the corpus is characterized by a bi-facetted conceptual audio representation.

Also, as far as the retrieval module is concerned, a user full-text query is translated into a video shot conceptual audio representation: the video shot query audio graph corresponding to the bi-facetted audio description. In fig. 1, the query "Find shots of Bill Clinton speaking" is translated into a bi-facetted audio conceptual representation.

The video shot query audio graph is then compared to all audio conceptual representations of video shot documents in the corpus. Lattices organizing audio semantic concepts are processed and a relevance value, estimating the degree of similarity between video shot query and index audio CGs is computed in order to rank all video shot documents relevant to a query.

After presenting our formalism, we now focus on the characterization of the audio content by proposing its conceptual specification and the automatic processes for its generation.

3 Automatic Conceptual Characterization

There are several approaches in the literature for audio segmentation based on speaker change detection. Approaches proposed in [10], [12] assume that the probability of a speaker change is higher around silence regions and use speech-silence detectors to identify the speaker change locations.

Other applications related to audio content characterization through automatic speech recognition (ASR) provide the best segmentation results. The LIMSI system [5] has indeed a 93 % recognition success rate in the TRECVID evaluation task.

ASR consists in analyzing the audio flow for transcribing speech. The output of such process is a structured textual information with temporal descriptions. In our proposition, we use results of speaker-based segmentation and ASR generated in the TRECVID 2004 collection. We aim at analyzing the transcription content for speaker identification in each segment using linguistic patterns. First, we propose to categorize these patterns. Then, we apply them to detect speaker's identities.

We target broadcast news as specific audiovisual content. This kind of documents presents some particularities:

- The number of speakers in this document is limited to three: presenter, reporter and intervening individual.
- The transition between two speakers is often provided except in the case of presenters introducing themselves only at the beginning of news. These expressions may be classified in two groups: those referring to speakers in the next, current or previous segments and those allowing the speakers to identify themselves. These expressions appear just before or after the identity of the person mentioned. All these expressions are called linguistic patterns.

3.1 Speaker Identity Characterization

There are two challenging tasks for video semantic content indexing using audio flow. The first one is specifying who the speaker is in each video segment. As we previously mentioned it, we use linguistic patterns for speaker identity detection. We propose three categories of patterns:

- The first category is for detecting the identity of the speaker who is speaking in the current segment. For example, when the speaker introduces himself: "... this is C.N.N. news I' m [Name]... "
- The second category is for detecting the identity of the speaker who has just spoken in the previous segment.
- The third category is for detecting the identity of the person who will speak (speaker of the following segment).

Table 1 summarizes some of the patterns that we use in our approach gathered by category.

Table 1. List of some linguistic patterns

Previous segment	Current segment	Next segment
thank you...	I'm [name]	tonight with [name]
[name]	[name] CNN	ABC's [name]
thanks... [name]	[name] ABC	[name] reports
[name] reporting	…….	……….
……		

The detection process consists in parsing each segment and identifying passages containing one of these patterns. We then apply a tool for identity recognition. For this, we use a named-entity extraction tool based on two lists of concepts. The first contains a set of first names (~12400) and the second contains common words except family names. We compare neighboring words of each detected pattern with the content of the 2 lists. If neighboring words are for example elements of the first list and not present in the second list, we can estimate that they deal with a person's identity. We then infer the corresponding identity by comparing its localization with respect to a linguistic pattern.

Our approach is summarized in fig. 2 which displays the complete process for automatic speaker identification. We tested our approach on the TRECVID 2004 collection and obtained a success rate of 82 % for automatic speaker's identity recognition.

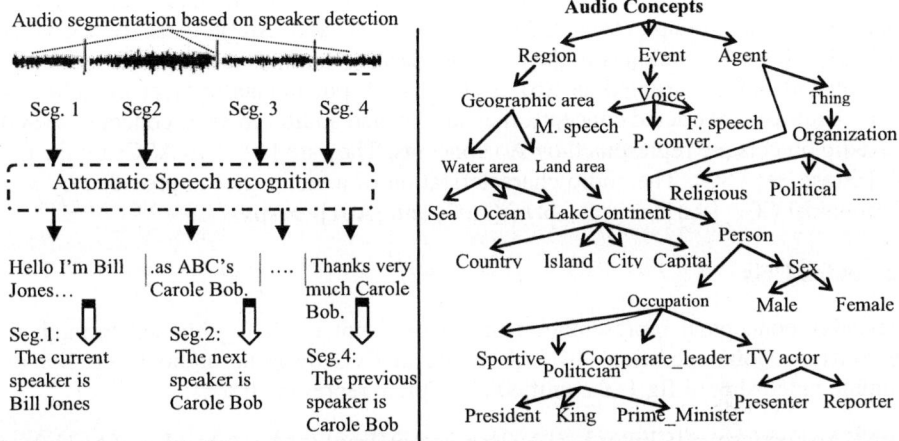

Fig. 2. Identity detection approach: overview   **Fig. 3.** A part of the audio concept lattice

3.2 Conceptual Content Characterization

To extract concepts from audio content, we parse transcriptions files to detect symbolic information by comparing their items to elements in the four concept classes (e.g. person identity, the name of a city, an organization, etc.). We then extract, from each document, the concepts which correspond to each class. This process is based on the projection of each document on the audio concept lattice (partly displayed in fig. 3). We exploit linguistics forms to specify concepts such as the expressions Mr., Mrs. appearing before a person identity or propositions like "in", "at" and "from" before a localization concept (place). Here is the algorithm summarizing the concept extraction process:

Given an audio segment
Extract AOs by projecting the transcription of the audio segment on specific ontologies

- Collect AOs belonging to the concept category person
- Collect AOs belonging to the concept category place
- Collect AOs belonging to the concept category organization
- If AOs belong to the concept category person, specify AOs corresponding to speakers using linguistic patterns.

After presenting the automatic conceptual characterization, we now focus on its conceptual instantiation within a video indexing and retrieval framework. We moreover detail the generation of index and query structures.

4 Conceptual Instantiation Within Index and Query Structures

4.1 CG Representation of the Audio Semantics Facet

Extracted concepts are related through specific audio relations to audio objects (AOs). Considering for example two audio objects (Ao1 and Ao2), these relations are spk(Ao1) where Ao1 belongs to the concept class person translated as Ao1 speaks and spk_abt(Ao1,Ao2) translated as Ao1 is about Ao2. For the audio layer modeling we use all automatic extracted concepts, they are labeled audio semantic concepts (ASC).

Audio objects are represented by Ao concepts. They are linked to ASCs by the CG: [Ao]→(asc)→[ASC]. The audio characterization of a video shot is provided by a set of canonical CGs: [Ao1]→(spk_abt)→[Ao2] and [Ao1] →(spk).

4.2 Index CGs

The index conceptual representation of a video shot is a CG obtained through the combination (**join** operation [14]) of canonical CGs over the audio facet. For our example video shot of fig.1, the unified conceptual representation is:

JOIN[[Ao1]→(asc)→[Clinton] ∩ [Ao2]→(asc)→[Iraq] ∩ [Ao1]→(spk) ∩ [Ao1]→(spk_abt)→[Ao2]]

4.3 Query Module

Our conceptual architecture is based on a unified full-text framework allowing a user to query over the audio layers. This obviously optimizes user interaction since the user is in 'charge' of the query process by making his information needs explicit to the system. The retrieval process using CGs relies on the fact that a query is also expressed under the form of a CG. The representation of a user query in our model is, like index representations, obtained through the combination (join operation) of CGs over all the facets of audio layers. Without going into details, a simple grammar composed of a list of the previously introduced audio concepts, as well as the specified audio relations is automatically translated into an alphanumerical CG structure. For instance, the query string: "Bill Clinton speaking" is translated into the joint unified graph: JOIN[[Ao1]→(asc)→[Clinton] ∩ [Ao1]→(spk)].

The Matching Process. The matching framework is based on an extension of VanRijsbergen's logical model proposed in [18]. We define the relevance of a video shot VS with respect to a query Q as a function of the exhaustivity measure which quantifies to which extent the video shot satisfies the query:

$$\text{Relevance}(VS,Q) = P(VS \rightarrow Q)$$

The exhaustivity function P consists in two operations. It first checks that all elements described within the query graph are also elements of the index graph. For this, we use the CG projection operator to compare video shot query and index graphs. This operator allows to identify within the video shot index graph i all sub-graphs with the same structure as the query graph q, with nodes being possibly restricted, i.e.

they are specializations of q nodes. Πq(i) is the set of all possible projections of query graph q into video shot index graph i. Let us note that several projections of a query graph within an index graph may exist. Then, for each selected video shot, we provide an estimation of its relevance with respect to the query, which corresponds to the quantitative evaluation of their similarity. It is given by the exhaustivity value between query graph q and video shot index graph i:

$$EV(q,i) = MAX\Pi q(i) \; [\Sigma ASCq \text{ concept of } q, ASCi \text{ matching concept of } i \\ IA(ASCi)+Cpt\_Match (ASCq,ASCi)]$$

- The IA function measures the importance of an audio semantic concept and is related to the number of times it is pronounced during the corresponding audio segment.
- The Cpt_Match function is the negative Kullback-Leibler divergence between the probabilities of audio query concepts which are themselves certain (i.e. P(ASCq) equal 1) and the posterior recognition probabilities of audio semantic concepts of graph i.

Let us note that brute-force implementations of the projection operator would result in exponential execution times. Therefore, based on the work in [14], we use an adaptation of the inverted file approach for video retrieval. We specify indeed lookup tables associating audio semantic concepts to the set of image index representations that contain these concepts.

5 Application: TRECVID Topic Search

The CLOVIS[1] prototype implements the theoretical framework exposed in this paper and validation experiments are carried out on the TRECVID 2004 corpus comprising 128 videos segmented in 48817 shots.

AOs are automatically assigned audio semantic concepts as presented in section 5. Finally, all audio alphanumerical representations of CGs linking AOs to audio concepts and relations are automatically generated as presented in sections 3 and 4.

The search task is based on topic retrieval where a topic is defined as a formatted description of an information need text. We therefore design the evaluation task in the context of manual search, where a human expert in the search system interface is able to interpret a topic and propose an optimal query to be processed by the system. Ten multimedia topics and their ground truths developed by NIST for the search task express the need for video concerning people, things, events, locations... and combinations of the former. The topics are designed to reflect many of the various sorts of queries real users propose: requests for video with specific people or people types, specific objects or instances of object types, specific activities or locations or instances of activity or location types.

We compare CLOVIS with the mainstream TRECVID 2004 systems operating manual search on audio features. The National Taiwan University system is based on ASR tokens and high level features (concepts) using WordNet for word-word distances. Approach proposed in this system aligns the ASR word tokens to the corre-

---

[1] Conceptual Layer Organization for Video Indexing and **Search**.

sponding shots by calculating their word-to-word distance with the high-level feature COMF tokens. Without complex algorithms and plenty of computing time, this method does lead to an improvement of the performance of the video information retrieval. The Indiana University system named viewfinder uses only text search based on ASR output. Each query is manually formulated as speech keywords and supported by tf/idf term weighting. Their queries are created by manual construction and selection of visual examples [11].

We propose the top retrieval results for 4 multimedia topics in fig. 4. Average precisions results for each of the 10 topics are provided in fig. 5. The mean average precision over the 10 topics of CLOVIS (0.08019) is approximately 45.54% and 49.05% higher over respectively the mean average precisions of the IU (0.0538), and NTU (0.0551) systems.

The obtained results allow us to state that when performing topic search and therefore dealing with elaborate queries involving conceptual and relational audio characterization and thus require a higher level of abstraction, the use of an "intelligent" and expressive representation formalism (here the CG formalism within our framework) is crucial. As a matter of fact, our framework outperforms state-of-the-art TRECVID 2004 systems by proposing a unified full-text framework optimizing user interaction and allowing to query with precision over audio/speech descriptions.

Fig. 4. Top 4 retrieval results for topics 133, 130, 135 and 136

In the table below, they are proposed with their translation in terms of relevant textual query terms as input to CLOVIS.

Table 2. TRECVID 2004 Topics and CLOVIS transcription

TRECVID topic	CLOVIS transcription
128. US Congressman Henry Hyde's face, whole or part, from any angle	Henry Hyde speaking or being spoken of
129. US Capitol dome	Washington, White House spoken of
130. Hockey rink	Hockey or N.H.L spoken of
133. Saddam Hussein	Saddam Hussein speaking or being spoken of
134. Boris Yeltsin	Boris Yeltsin speaking or being spoken of
135. Sam Donaldson's face. No other people visible with him	Sam Donaldson speaking or being spoken of
136. Person hitting a golf ball	P.G.A. spoken of
137. Benjamin Netanyahu	Benjamin Netanyahu speaking or being spoken of
142. Tennis player	A.T.P. spoken of
143. Bill Clinton speaking	Bill Clinton speaking

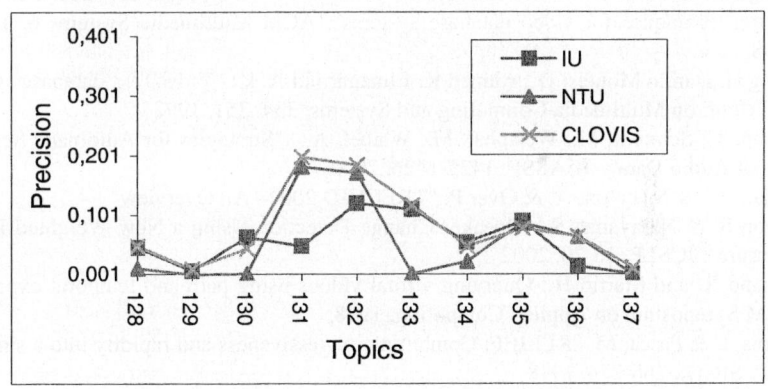

Fig. 5. Average Precision for each of the 10 multimedia TRECVID 2004 topics

6 Conclusion

We proposed the specification of a framework featuring audio characterizations within an integrated architecture to achieve greater retrieval accuracy. We introduced audio objects, abstract structures characterizing the audio content related to a video shot in order to operate video indexing and retrieval operations at a higher abstraction level than state-of-the-art frameworks. We specified the multiple facets, the conceptual representation of index and query structures and finally proposed a unified full-text query framework. Experimental results on the TRECVID 2004 multimedia topic search task allowed us to validate our approach

References

1. Amato G., Mainetto G., Savino P.: "An Approach to a Content-Based Retrieval of Multimedia Data", Multimedia Tools and Applications 7, 9-36, 1998
2. Arslan U., Dönderler M-E, Saykol E, Ulusoy Ö, Güdükbay U: "A Semi-Automatic Semantic Annotation Tool for Video Databases", Workshop on Multimedia Semantics (SOFSEM'02), The Czech Republic, pp. 1-10, 2002
3. Assfalg J., Bertini M., Colombo C.and Del Bimbo A.: "Semantic Annotation of Sports Videos". IEEE MultiMedia 9(2), 52-60, 2002
4. Bertini M, Del Bimbo A., Nunziati W.: "Annotation and Retrieval of Structured Video Documents", in Proc. of Advances in Information Retrieval, ECIR 2003, Pisa, Italy, 14-16, 2003.
5. Gauvain J-L., Lamel L., Adda G.: "The LIMSI Broadcast News transcription system". Speech Communication 37, 89-108, 2002
6. Gong Y., Chua HC, Guo XY: "Image Indexing and Retrieval Based on Color Histograms". Multimedia Tools and App. II, 133-156, 1996
7. Jiang H.,Danilo Montesi D., Ahmed K. Elmagarmid A. k.: "Integrated video and text for content-based access to video databases". Multimedia Tools and Applications, 1999
8. Jiang H.,Abdelsalam Helal A., Ahmed K. Elmagarmid A. k., Joshi A.: "Scene change detection techniques for video database systems". ACM Multimedia Systems 6, 186–195, 1998
9. Jiang H.,Danilo Montesi D., Ahmed K. Elmagarmid A. k.: "VideoText database systems". Int'l Conf. on Multimedia Computing and Systems, 334–351, 1997
10. Kemp, T., Schmidt, M., Westphal, M., Waibel, A.: "Strategies for Automatic Segmentation of Audio Data". ICASSP, 1423-1426, 2000
11. Kraaij, W. & Smeaton, A. & Over P. "TRECVID 2004– An Overview"
12. Kwon S. & Narayanan S.: "Speaker Change Detection Using a New Weighted Distance Measure". ICSLP, 16-20, 2002
13. Lozano R. and Martin H.: Querying virtual videos using path and temporal expressions. ACM Symposium on Applied Computing, 1998.
14. Ounis, I. & Pasca, M. "RELIEF: Combining expressiveness and rapidity into a single system". SIGIR, 266-274, 1998
15. Sowa, J.F. "Conceptual structures: information processing in mind and machine". Addison-Wesley, 1984
16. Tran D. A., Hua K. A., Vu K.: "VideoGraph: A Graphical Object-based Model for Representing and Querying Video Data". ICCM, 383-396, 2000
17. Quénot, G. "TREC-10 Shot Boundary Detection Task: CLIPS System Description and Evaluation". TREC 2001.
18. VanRijsbergen, C.J. "A Non-Classical Logic for Information Retrieval". Comput. J. 29(6), 481-485, 1986

A New Concept of Security Camera Monitoring with Privacy Protection by Masking Moving Objects

Kenichi Yabuta, Hitoshi Kitazawa, and Toshihisa Tanaka

Department of Electrical and Electronic Engineering,
Tokyo University of Agriculture and Technology,
2-24-16 Naka-cho, Koganei-shi, Tokyo 184–8588, Japan
y5645224@gc.tuat.ac.jp, {kitazawa, tanakat}@cc.tuat.ac.jp

Abstract. We present a novel framework for encoding images obtained by a security monitoring camera with protecting the privacy of moving objects in the images. We are motivated by the fact that although security monitoring cameras can deter crimes, they may infringe the privacy of those who and objects which are recorded by the cameras. Moving objects, whose privacy should be protected, in an input image (recorded by a monitoring camera) are encrypted and hidden in a JPEG bitstream. Therefore, a normal JPEG viewer generates a masked image, where the moving objects are unrecognizable or completely invisible. Only a special viewer with a password can reconstruct the original recording. Data hiding is achieved by watermarking and encrypting with the advanced encryption standard (AES). We illustrate a concept of our framework and an algorithm of the encoder and the special viewer. Moreover, we show an implementation example.

Keywords: Privacy protection, security camera, watermarking, JPEG encoding.

1 Introduction

Recently, a large number of security monitoring cameras are set up to deter and investigate crimes. With the increase of these monitoring cameras, how to protect the privacy of recorded objects such as people, cars, and so on is becoming a major problem. Monitoring cameras record not only criminals but also general people, who may not be aware that they are monitored. Moreover, the recorded images can probably be distributed without any permission by these monitored people. Therefore, we should establish a framework for security monitoring which considers the privacy protection.

A simple way to do this is to deteriorate the quality of moving objects. Based on this idea, a non-reversible method which decreases the resolution of objects whose privacy should be protected has been proposed in [1] and [2]. These strategy can make moving objects unrecognizable and still keep the nature of a moving object, that is, we can distinguish whether the moving object is a man, a car, or something else. However, the non-reversible processing loses details of the objects such as human faces, number plates of cars, etc. This implies that the reliability of monitoring cameras for security purpose can be reduced by this deterioration. In other words, if a face image of a criminal, for example, is even slightly destroyed, we may not be able to specify this criminal. In [3], a concept of the reversible method has been proposed. This method can display images with privacies protected or unprotected. However, this system needs a special system when the system reconstructs images as well as it displays images in which the privacy is protected.

In this paper, therefore, we propose a new framework for encoding images recorded by security monitoring cameras. In this framework, an encoder generates a bitstream which gives a "masked" image when a normal JPEG [9] viewer is used for decoding, and a special viewer is needed to reconstruct an input image. In the masked image decoded by a normal viewer, moving objects in an input image are scrambled or erased, so that the privacy of the moving objects can be protected. A special viewer with a password decrypts the moving objects embedded in the bitstream and then reconstructs the input image. Therefore, even if recorded images taken by monitoring cameras are distributed, the objects are unrecognizable, as long as normal JPEG viewers are used.

The rest of this paper is organized as what follows. In Section 2, we clarify requirements which security monitoring cameras satisfy. In Sections 3 and 4, we propose algorithms which implement our new concept. In Section 3, we describe a method of masking and in Section 4, we show how to embed moving objects in a JPEG bitstream by using watermarking [8]. In Section 5, we show experimantal results and discuss about the results. Section 6 concludes our work and mentions open problems.

2   Privacy Protection in an Image Obtained by Security Monitoring

We can classify images into two regions, moving object regions and background regions. Moving object regions are defined as regions including moving objects extracted from the input image by the moving object extraction process [4], [5], [6], [7].

Background regions are defined as regions except the moving object regions. People and cars passing by are extracted as moving objects. If the moving object regions are made invisible or unrecognizable, their privacy can be protected. Moreover, the input image with the moving objects should be reconstructed when it is needed for certain reasons, such as, crime investigation. Although we should preserve the quality of the moving object regions as well as possible, we can reduce the amount of information of the background, because we are more interested in the moving object regions than the background regions. Based on these discussions, we state the requirements of the privacy protection in the fixed monitoring camera system as follows.

1. Masked images should be displayed by normal viewers for compressed images, such as JPEG viewers.
2. Moving objects in masked images should be invisible or unrecognizable.
3. Original input images should be reconstructed by a special viewer with a decodeing password. A decoded images should be reconstructed as close to an input image as possible.
4. An encoder should generate only one JPEG bitstream. A normal and a special viewers can decode a masked and a reconstructed images, respectively only from this bitstream.

3 Masking Method

3.1 Algorithm Overview

Figure 1 shows the flow of a masking method proposed in this paper. We assume that the size of an input image obtained by a monitoring camera is $W \times H$. A JPEG bitstream of a masked image is generated by moving object extraction followed by encoding. The bitstream can be decoded by either a normal or a special JPEG viewer. The former viewer only displays a masked image, where the privacy of moving objects are protected, and the latter viewer reconstructs an input image. In the following, each part is described.

Moving object extraction. For extracting moving objects, we can use the background subtraction methods proposed in [4], [5], [6], or [7], for example. In these methods, a background image is produced by a sequence of input images and moving objects are extracted by taking the difference between an input image and the background image, and then the moving objects are detected. The pixels extracted as a part of the moving object are grouped into connected regions, wich are called moving object regions. The moving object regions are decided whether they need masking process or not, according to the region size which is defined by the number of pixels belonging to that region. Assume that there are K moving object regions in an image. Let $Np(i)(i = 1, 2, \ldots, K)$ be the number of pixels in the ith moving object region. If the ith moving object region satisfies

$$Np(i) \geq Th \quad (i = 1, 2, \ldots, K), \qquad (1)$$

where Th is a threshold, then this region will be masked, and is referred to as a region to be masked. We introduce a binary image which indicates pixels in the masked regions. Let $M_{ij}(i = 1, 2, \ldots, W, j = 1, 2, \ldots, H)$ be a value of the (i, j)th pixel of this binary image. Then, M_{ij} is defined as

$$M_{ij} = \begin{cases} 1 \text{ if the } (i,j)\text{th pixel in the image belongs to region to be masked.} \\ 0 \text{ otherwise.} \end{cases}$$

Encoding. Recall that in the proposed scheme, the privacy of the moving object regions are protected by scrambling/erasing. This step needs three data, that is, an input image, a background image, and a binary image M_{ij} defined above.

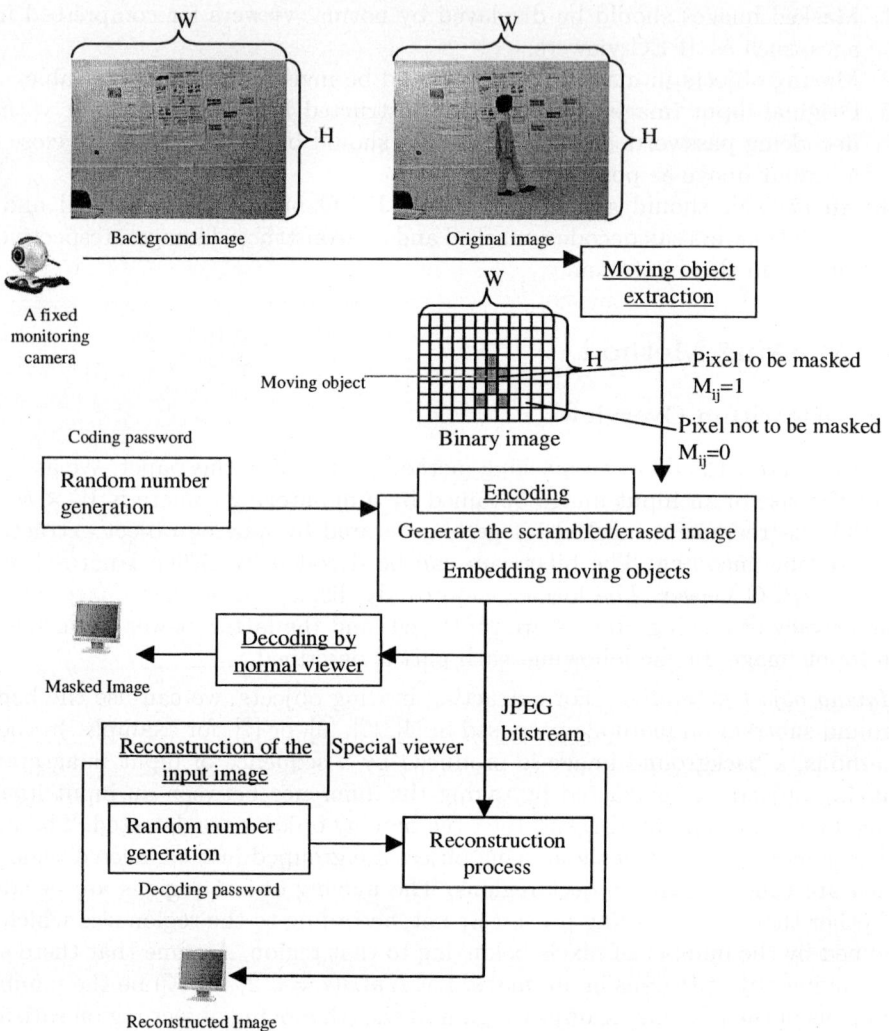

Fig. 1. Flow of Masking process

First, we produce a scrambled/erased image where moving objects are invisible or unrecognizable. Since the special viewer must reconstruct the input image, information of the moving object regions should be embedded in the masked image. This embedded data should be also encrypted for privacy protection. Then, this masked image with embedded data is encoded by a JPEG codec. This part will be more fully explained in Section 4.

Decoding by normal viewers. If we use normal JPEG viewers such as web browsers, they display masked images. Since a masked image is generated such that moving objects are invisible, privacies of these objects are protected.

Reconstruction of the input image. To reconstruct the masked objects, a special viewer with a decoding password is required. The moving objects are decrypted with the password and reconstructed. As a result, a reconstructed image is obtained.

3.2 How to Make Objects Invisible

We propose two schemes for masking that make moving objects invisible. They are listed below.

Scrambling. By the scrambling, the pixels in a moving object region are randomly permutated. As a result, we may not understand what the moving objects are. Although this method can conceal a part of the object, for example a number plate of a car, and a face, some parts of information, such as color, can be recognized.

Erasing. By the erasing, the moving object images are replaced by the corresponding background images. Therefore, the moving objects become invisible. However, in many cases we want to keep a brief shape of an object for some purposes: counting cars and pedestrians, for example. Therefore, in this method we draw peripheral curves of moving objects. This will be illustrated later.

Masked images generated by each method show what is happening, not who is there. We can choose one of the two methods depending on an objective of the system. If a part of information of moving objects, such as color, is desirable to be seen by general users, the scrambling is recommended. If all details of moving objects except the shape should be hidden, we should use the erasing. It should be noted that for reconstruction of an input image including moving objects, information of the moving objects should be embedded in the bitstream generated by the encoder. We will address this problem in the following section.

4 Embedding Moving Objects with Watermarking

This section describes masking methods and how to embed data of moving objects in a masked image by using digital watermarking [8]. Figure 2 shows the simple flow of masking methods with watermarking.

First, moving objects are extracted from an input image. The extracted moving objects are compressed by the JPEG and are encrypted by AES with password. Moving object regions in an input image are hidden by scrambling/erasing. This masked image is transformed by the discrete cosine transform (DCT) and the data of objects that have been encrypted are embedded in DCT coefficients of the masked image. In the following, we describe details of the proposed method.

4.1 Scrambling/Erasing Moving Object Regions

Scrambling. In this method, all pixels in a moving object region are randomly permutated. Assume that there are N pixels in a moving object region. Let

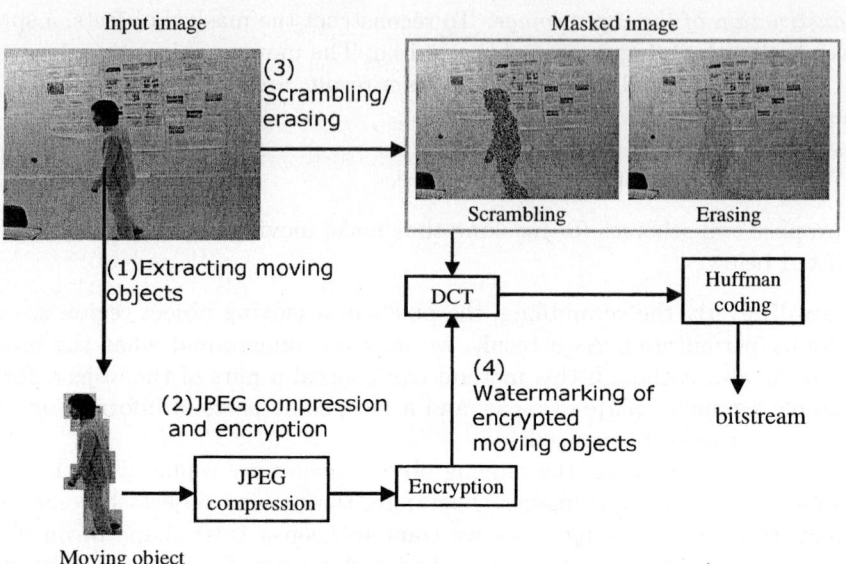

Fig. 2. Flow of masking with watermarking

$R(i)(i = 1, 2, \ldots, N)$ be a generated random number and $P(i)(i = 1, 2, \ldots, N)$ is the ith pixel in this region. Then, the ith replaced pixel is obtained by the permutation defined as

$$\tilde{P}(i) = P(R(i)). \qquad (2)$$

Erasing. In this method, moving objects are made invisible. The pixels in the moving object regions in the input image are replaced by the pixels at the same coordinates in the background image. To illustrate the shape of a moving object, the edge of the moving object is explicitly drawn. We use the binary image (a set of M_{ij}) to specify edges as follows. The pixel of coordinate (i, j) is regarded as a pixel on the edge if $M_{ij} = 1$ and one or over of four pixels in circumference are $M_{ij} = 0$. In other words, when we define N_{ij} as the sum of pixels of the binary image at the upper, the lower, the right, and the left pixels of M_{ij} that is, $N_{ij} = M_{i,j-1} + M_{i,j+1} + M_{i+1,j} + M_{i-1,j}$. If M_{ij} satisfies

$$0 < M_{ij} \times N_{ij} < 4, \qquad (3)$$

then the pixel of coordinate (i, j) is judged as a pixel on the edge.

4.2 Embedding Moving Objects with Watermarking

Encryption of a Moving Object (Fig. 2,(2)). First, an input image is divided into minimum coded units (MCUs). An MCU is a minimum unit of JPEG compression, and the size of an MCU is 8×8. If an MCU includes a moving object region, the MCU is compressed by the JPEG. A bitstream generated by JPEG is stored in an N-byte-length array denoted by $MO[i](i = 1, \ldots, N)$. It

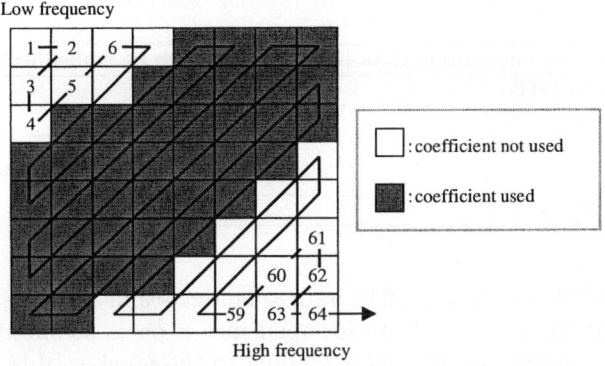

Fig. 3. Position of DCT coefficients for watermarking

should be noted that the bitstream consists of only Huffman codes; therefore, a JPEG header is removed. $MO[i]$ is encrypted by AES [10] and it become $M\tilde{O}[i](i = 1,\ldots,\tilde{N})$ AES is a block encryption method and the block size is 16 bytes, $\tilde{N}$ is a smallest multiple of 16 not less than N.

Watermarking the Encrypted Moving Object (Fig. 2,(4)). We embed $M\tilde{O}[i]$ in the scrambling/erasing image with watermarking. First, we obtain DCT coefficients of the scrambling/erasing image by using a JPEG technique. We use DCT coefficients of middle frequencies for watermarking, because any changes of low coefficients are very noticeable and the changes of high coefficients lead to great changes when the JPEG decoder decodes quantized data. Compared with the low or high frequency DCT coefficients, a small perturbation of a middle frequency DCT coefficient does not visually affect the reconstructed image. Therefore, we propose to embed the moving object data in the middle coefficients indicated in Fig. 3.

Table 1. Grouping of DCT coefficients $QDCTZ\_k(i)$ in each MCU

$1 \leq i \leq 8$	not embedded
$9 \leq i \leq 16$	Position 1
$17 \leq i \leq 24$	Position 2
$25 \leq i \leq 32$	Position 3
$33 \leq i \leq 40$	Position 4
$41 \leq i \leq 48$	Position 5
$49 \leq i \leq 56$	not embedded
$57 \leq i \leq 64$	not embedded

The least signifivcation bits (LSBs) of quantized DCT coefficients are replaced by $M\tilde{O}[i]$ one bit by one bit. For example, if $M\tilde{O}[i]$ = 0x5A = $01011010_{(2)}$ and if the DCT coefficients at the embedding position are $2, 5, 0, 8, 10, 1, 4$, and 3, that DCT coefficients become $2, 5, 0, 9, 11, 0, 5$, and 2.

Table 2. Adaptive embedding position selection by data size

Size of embedding data [bytes]	Position to be embedded
1 to 1800	1
1801 to 3600	1 to 2
3601 to 5400	1 to 3
5401 to 7200	1 to 4
7201 to 9000	1 to 5

Let $QDCTZ\_k(i)(i = 1, 2, \ldots, 64)$ be a quantized and zigzag scanned DCT coefficients. The $QDCTZ\_k(i)$ are grouped into 8 parts as shown in Table 1. The embedding position is decided according to the number of bytes to be embedded. If, the size of input image is 320×240, then the number of MCUs is $(320 \times 240)/16^2 \times 6 = 1800$. The embedding position is dynamically selected by the size of data to be embedded as defined in Table 2.

Remarks on the Use of Watermarking for Embedding the Object Data. The proposed watermarking in masking methods can embed more bits than ordinary watermarking methods do. When watermarking is used in detecting illegal copy or embedding copyright, it should be robust to manipulation of image such as expansion, reduction, and color change. On the other hand, in the proposed masking application, it does not matter in terms of privacy protection if a masked image is attacked and can not be reconstructed. Moreover, the background region in an input image does not include important information. Therefore, the watermarking in this masking application can embed a large size of data, as mentioned in the previous section.

4.3 Decrypting and Reconstruction

First, the encrypted data array $M\tilde{O}[i]$ are extracted from DCT coefficients of the masked image. Then, $M\tilde{O}[i]$ are decrypted by AES. Then, the moving object data is reconstructed with the JPEG decoder. Finally, the reconstructed moving object image is overwritten at the position where there was the moving object in the input image.

5 Experimental Results

Experimental results of masking methods using scrambling/erasing are shown. We apply the proposed methods to a sequence of moving images with 169 frames. In this experiment, the image size acquired from a fixed monitor camera is 320×240 pixels. The frame rate is 5 frames/sec. Figure 4 shows the 131st frame in this sequence whose size is 10.46 KB.

Figures 5(a) and 5(b) show scrambled and reconstructed images, respectively. It can be observed in Fig. 5(a) that pixels in the moving object region are scrambled and the moving object is no longer recognized. However, as seen in

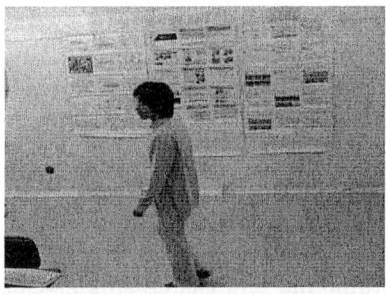

Fig. 4. Input image (the 131st frame)

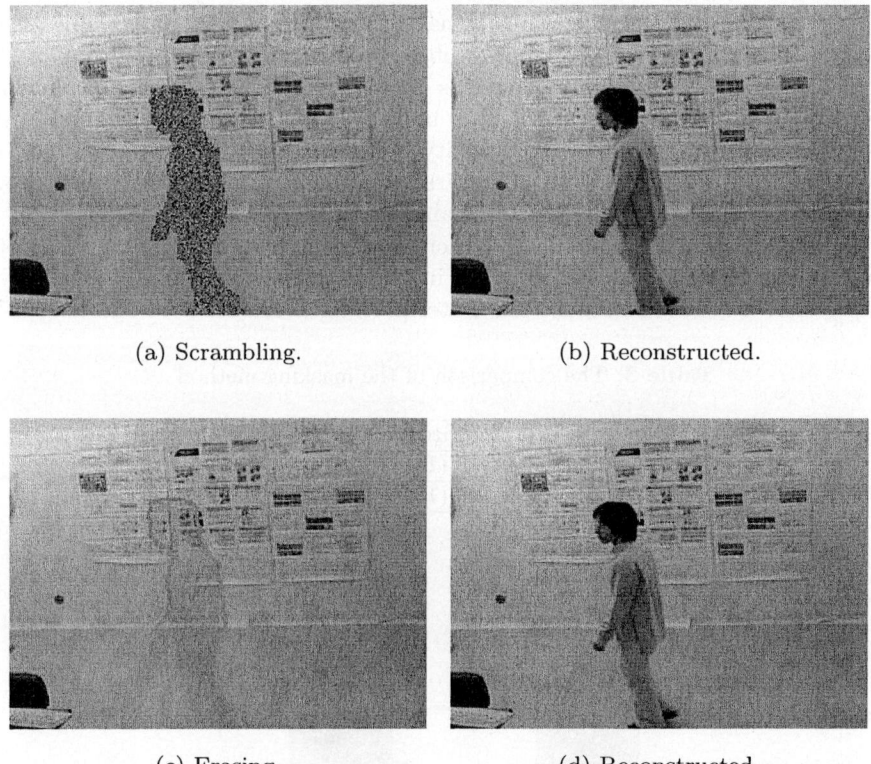

Fig. 5. Masked and reconstructed images generated by two methods

Fig. 5(a) and 5(b), blocking artifacts are visible in the background region due to watermarking. As shown in Fig. 5(b), the moving object region is reconstructed.

In Fig. 5(c), the masked image with an erased object is shown. The moving object is replaced by the background image and it becomes invisible. The reconstructed image is shown in Fig. 5(d). By the erasing, we can hide such information that scrambling can not hide. In the case of scrambling, we can roughly estimate the moving object from the shape and a dominant color, though the face of the moving object can not be recognized.

Table 3 shows comparison of peak signal to noise ratios (PSNRs), the file sizes and the processing times of the scrambleing and the erasing methods. PSNR is defined as

$$PSNR = 10 \times \log_{10} \frac{255^2}{MSE}, \quad (4)$$

where MSE is the mean square error between the original input and reconstructed images. The scrambling and the erasing give similar PSNRs. They are less than 30 dB in the whole images. However, when we compare PSNRs of only the moving object images in the input and reconstructed images, the PSNR of both images are an identical value and it is 46.48 dB. For subjective comparison, the original and reconstructed object images are illustrated in Fig.6. This result shows that the PSNR of the moving object region is higher than that of the whole image. The background image is highly deteriorated by watermarking, however the moving object region gives higher PSNR. This result suggests that each method sacrifices the image quality of the background region to that of the moving object regions, which is desirable because the moving object regions include more important information than its background region.

As seen in Table 3, the file size increases by 92% compared to the input image in the scrambling, and by 63% in the erasing. Efficiency of the JPEG compression is reduced because the watermarking decreases zero run length in

Table 3. The comparison of the masking method

	PSNR [dB]	File Size [KB]	Processing Time [sec]
Scrambling	26.68	20.06 (192%)	46.28
Erasing	26.55	17.06 (163%)	41.88

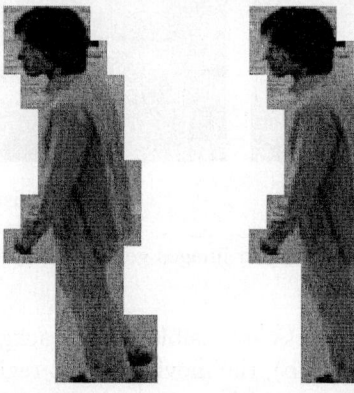

Input image   Reconstructed image

Fig. 6. Images of only the moving object regions.

DCT coefficients. The file size in the scrambling is greater than that of the erasing, because in the scrambling, the adjacent pixels in a moving object region largely differ from each other, which is caused by the interchange of pixels.

The processing time in Table 3is the CPU time required for the encoding process using Pentium4 2.6GHz. It does not include the moving object extraction time.

6 Conclusion

We have presented a novel concept for a security monitoring camera with protecting the privacy of moving objects in recorded images. By using the proposed encoder for security camera recordings, a normal JPEG viewer shows only the masked images, where moving objects are scrambled or erased. Therefore, we need a special viewer with a password to reconstruct an input image. As a result, the privacy of moving objects are strongly protected.

The following problems would be still open. First, we need to decrease the processing time for real-time recording and encoding. Second, experimental results in this paper have shown that the sizes of masked images are grater than those of input images. More efficient compression is necessary. Moreover, flexible selection of DCT coefficients which is used for watermarking would be effective for decreasing the size of output bitstream as well as improving the subjective quality of the reconstructed image.

This research was partially supported by the Ministry of Education, Science, Sports and Culture, Grant-in-Aid for Scientific Research (C), 17560329, 2005.

References

1. I. Kitahara, K. Kogure, and N. Hagita, "Stealth Vision for Protecting Privacy," Proc. of 17th International Conference on Pattern Recognition (ICPR 2004), Vol.4, pp.404-407, (2004)
2. J. Wickramasuriya, M. Alhazzazi, M. Datt, S. Mehrotra and N. Venkatasubramanian " Privacy-Protecting Video Surveillance," SPIE International Symposium on Electronic Imaging (Real-Time Imaging IX), San Jose, CA, Jan. 2005.
3. A. Senior, S. Pankanti, A. Hampapur, L. Brown, Y. Tian and A. Ekin, "Blinkering Surveillance: Enabling Video Privacy through Computer Vision," IBM Technical Paper, RC22886 (W0308-109), August 28, 2003, http://www.research.ibm.com/peoplevision/rc22886.pdf
4. C. Staffer and W. E. L. Grimson, "Adaptive Background Mixture Models for Real-Time Tracking," CVPR99, p. 2246, Fort Colins, CO, June, 1999.
5. A. Lipton, H. Fujiyoshi, and R. S. Patil, " Moving Target Detection and Classification from Real-Time Video," *Proceeding of IEEE WACV98*, November 1998.
6. W. E. L. Grimson, C. Stauffer, R. Romano, and L. Lee, " Using Adaptive Tracking to Classify and Monitor Activities in a Site," IEEE Proc, Computer Vision and Pattern Recognition, pp. 22-31, 1998.
7. R. T. Collins, A. J. Lipton, and T. Kanade, " A System for Video Surveillance and Monitoring," MU-RI-TR-00-12, Robotics Institute, Carnegie Mellon University, May, 2000.

8. S. Katzenbeisser, F. A. P. Petitcolas, F. Petticolas, " Information Hiding Techniques for Steganography and Digital Watermarking," Artech House Publishers, 2002.
9. W. B. Pennebacker, and J. L. Mitchell, " JPEG Still Data Compression Standard," Van Nostrand Reinhold, 1993.
10. Announcing the ADVANCED ENCRYPTION STANDARD (AES), November 26, 2001, http://csrc.nist.gov/publications/fips/fips197/fips-197.pdf

Feature Fusion-Based Multiple People Tracking

Junhaeng Lee, Sangjin Kim, Daehee Kim, Jeongho Shin, and Joonki Paik

Image Processing and Intelligent Systems Laboratory, Department of Image Engineering,
Graduate School of Advanced Imaging Science, Multimedia, and Film,
Chung-Ang University, Seoul, Korea
bi98088@cau.ac.kr

Abstract. This paper presents a feature fusion-based tracking algorithm using optical flow under the non-prior training active feature model (NPT-AFM) framework. The proposed object tracking procedure can be divided into three steps: (i) localization of human objects, (ii) prediction and correction of the object's location by utilizing spatio-temporal information, and (iii) restoration of occlusion using the NPT-AFM[15]. Feature points inside an ellipsoidal shape including objects are estimated instead of its shape boundary, and are updated as an element of the training set for the AFM. Although the proposed algorithm uses the greatly reduced number of feature points, the proposed feature fusion-based multiple people tracking algorithm enables the tracking of occluded people in complicated background.

1 Introduction

Tracking multiple people in video sequences is important for video surveillance and video retrieval, since people are the principle actors in daily activities of interest [1]. The problem of deformable object tracking by analyzing motion and shape in two-dimensional (2D) video is of increasing importance in a wide range of application areas including computer vision, video surveillance, motion analysis and extraction for computer animation, human-computer interface (HCI), and object-based video compression. There have been various research results of object extraction and tracking.

One of the simplest methods is to track difference regions within a pair of consecutive frames [2], and its performance can be improved by using adaptive background generation and subtraction. Based on the assumption of stationary background, Wren *et al.* proposed a real-time blob tracking algorithm, where the blob can be obtained from object's histogram and mean shift approach [3,4].

Shape-based tracking obtains *a priori* shape information of an object-of interest, and projects a trained shape onto the closest shape in a certain image frame. This type of methods include contour-based method [5], active shape model (ASM) [6], state-space sampling, and condensation algorithm [7].

Although the existing shape-based algorithms can commonly deal with partial occlusion, they exhibit several serious problems in the practical application, such as (i) a priori training of the shape of a target object and (ii) iterative modeling procedure for convergence. The first problem hinders the original shape-based method from being applied to tracking objects of unpredictable shapes. The second problem becomes a major bottleneck for real-time implementation. The goal of our work is to develop a general framework to detect and track humans in complex situations, real-time, occlusion, shadow. We assume a stationary camera. (if moving camera, necessary to stabilization.

This paper presents a feature fusion-based multiple objects tracking that matches objects between consecutive frames. The proposed tracking algorithm utilizes feature points for multiple objects tracking, which can track a deformable object by using a greatly reduced number of feature points rather than taking the entire shape. In order to track deformable objects, the proposed algorithm first extracts human objects using motion segmentation, and then masks an ellipsoidal shape to the extracted human object at the head-top position of each human [1]. We then determine if the feature points are inside the ellipsoidal shape. Selected feature points in the following frame are predicted by optical flow. If a feature point is missing or failed in tracking, an additional compensation procedure restores it.

The paper is organized as follows. In section 2 we briefly introduce the framework of the proposed feature fusion-based multiple objects tracking algorithm. Optical flow-based tracking of feature points is presented in section 3, and the restoration of occlusion using NPT-AFM is proposed in section 4. Section 5 summarizes experimental results and section 6 concludes the paper.

2 Framework of the Feature Fusion-Based Tracking

The proposed feature fusion-based tracking algorithm is described in Fig. 1.

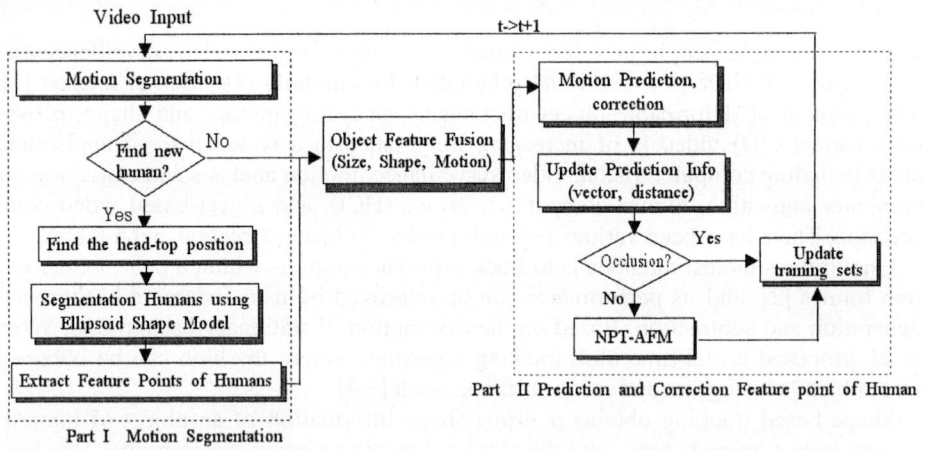

Fig. 1. The proposed feature-based tracking algorithm

Part I represents the motion segmentation block including an initial feature extraction module. The remaining part of the flowchart relates two consecutive frames, named as the tth and the $t+1^{st}$ frames. In Part I, we extract the motion of objects by using a simple optical flow and classify an object motion into four directions such as left, right, upward, and downward. After finding the head-top positions of multiple people, feasible features are extracted by masking an ellipsoidal shape to the extracted human object at the head-top position of each human.

The procedure tracks the shape model that does not include shadow, and predicts the corresponding feature points in the following frame. We keep checking and restoring any missing feature points during the tracking process. If more than 60% of feature points are restored, we decided the set of feature points are not proper for tracking, and redefine a new set of points. We detect occlusion by using motion-based labeling and the NPT-AFM process, which updates training sets at each frame to restore entire shapes from the occluded input.

The advantages of the proposed algorithm can be summarized as: (i) it can track both rigid and deformable objects such as human because a general feature-based tracking algorithm is applied, (ii) it is robust against object's sudden motion because motion direction and feature points are tracked at the same time, (iii) its tracking performance is not degraded even with complicated background because feature points are assigned inside an object rather than near boundary, (iv) ellipsoidal shapes help to find proper feature point and remove shadow, and (v) it contains the NPT-AFM procedure that can restore partial occlusion in real-time.

3 Tracking of Multiple Humans Features Based on Optical Flow

The proposed algorithm tracks a set of feature points based on optical flow. A missing feature point during the tracking is restored by using both temporal and spatial information inside the predicted region. One important contribution of this work is to provide a restoration process for missing feature points, which occurs at almost every frame under realistic, noisy environment.

3.1 Motion-Based Multiple Humans Detection

A person is represented by analyzing the boundary and shape of the foreground blobs. To this end, we should first detect the human region. For the detection of an object region from background, we use Lucas-Kanade optical flow(LKOF). The fundamental condition of optical flow is that intensity of a point on the object does not change during the sufficiently small duration. Let $S_C(x,y,t)$ represent the distribution of intensity in a continuous image, the optical flow condition can be defined as [8][9]

$$\frac{dS_C(x,y,t)}{dt} = 0. \tag{1}$$

By applying the chain rule to (1), we have that

$$\frac{\partial S_C(x,y,t)}{dt}v_x(x,y,t) + \frac{\partial S_C(x,y,t)}{dy}v_y(x,y,t) + \frac{\partial S_C(x,y,t)}{dt} = 0, \tag{2}$$

where $v_x(x,y,t) = dx/dt$, and $v_y(x,y,t) = dy/dt$. From 0, we can evaluate optical flow as

$$\xi_{of}(v(x,y,t)) = <\nabla S_C(x,y,t), v(x,y,t)> + \frac{\partial S_C(x,y,t)}{\partial t} = 0, \quad (3)$$

where $\nabla S_C(x,y,t) = \left[\frac{\partial S_C}{\partial x} \quad \frac{\partial S_C}{\partial y}\right]^T$, and $v(x,y,t) = [v_1(x,y,t) \quad v_2(x,y,t)]^T$. Optical flow that satisfies the constraint given in 0 is prone to noise because the difference approximation between adjacent pixels is used for evaluating derivatives. Error from the optical flow constraint can be measured as

$$E = \sum_{(x,y) \in R} \xi_{of}^2, \quad (4)$$

where R represents a neighboring region, and In minimizing 0. Due to the nature of optical flow, there are many holes, which can are removed by morphological operations. In order to separate a moving object and noise in low-gradient conditions, we used the normalized difference (5), as shown in Figure 2.

$$D_i = \frac{1}{N_i} \sum_{(x,y) \in R_i} |I_t(x,y) - I_{t-1}(x,y)|, \quad (5)$$

where R_i represents the ith segment, and N_i the total number of pixels in R_i.

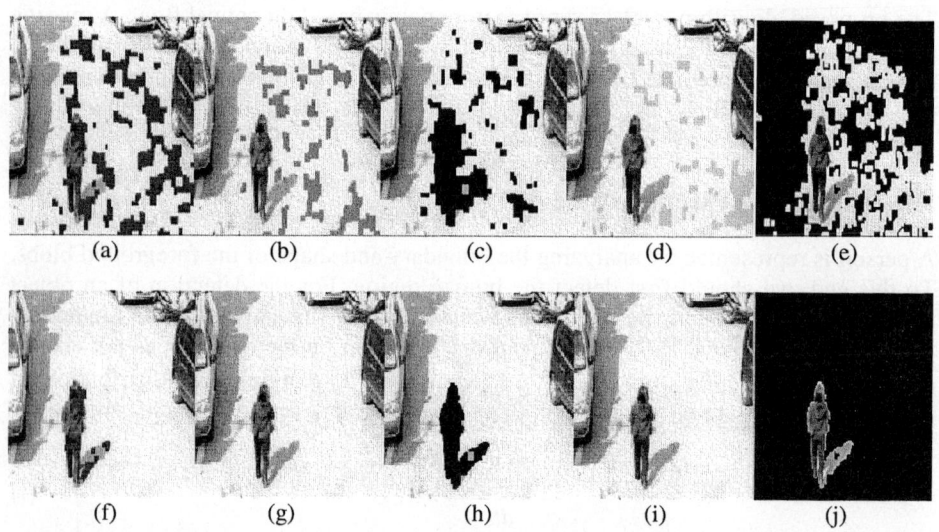

Fig. 2. Results of motion detection in four directions: (a) left to right, (b) right to left, (c) upward motion, (d) downward motion, (e) initial segmentation for the human region, and (f-j) results of noise suppression using the normalized difference given in (1).

3.2 Feature Point Extraction Using Ellipsoidal Shape

After detecting an object from background, we find the head-top position on the foreground boundary. It helps to recognize multiple human locations and potential overlapping. If the head-top position has the highest point in the vertical direction (the direction towards the vertical vanishing point) along the boundary within a range defined by the average size of human head, it can be at candidate of the head as shown in Fig. 3b. If a candidate point does not have sufficient foreground pixels within the model, it is discarded as shown in Fig. 3c [1]. Most of the current shadow removal approaches are based on the assumption that the shadow pixels have the same hue as the background but are of lower intensity [10]. We can extract a set of feasible feature points inside the ellipsoidal shape by using Bouguet tracking algorithm [11].

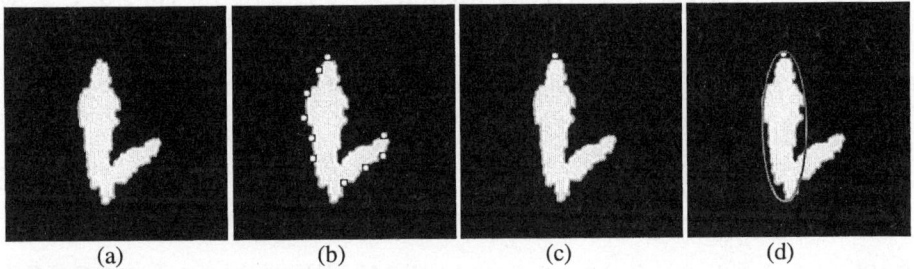

Fig. 3. Ellipsoidal shape-based feature extraction; (a) Result of motion segmentation, (b) candidates of the head-top position, (c) an appropriate head-top candidate, (d) overlapping ellipsoidal shape to the head-top position

Fig. 4. Feasible feature points extraction by overlapping ellipsoidal shape

3.3 Object Matching by Feature Fusion

After extracting a set of feasible feature points, we obtain additional object's information such as size, shape, and motion in the following frame. For robust tracking, an object matching is performed by fusing features between two consecutive frames. In order to avoid cases where one feature fails, tracking system loses an object, or occlusions occur, multiple features are fused. In this subsection, we use the voting algorithm proposed in [2]. The feature fusion algorithm is summarized as follows. Define 1) O_p, an object of the previous image $I(n-1)$; 2) O_c, an object of the current image $I(n)$; 3) s, the variable to count the similarity between O_p and O_c; 4) d, the variable to count the dissimilarity between O_p and O_c, 5) s ++ , an increase of s by one vote; and 6) d ++ , an increase of d by one vote. To compute s and d between O_p and O_c ($t_z < 1$ and $t_s < 1$), three feature fusion function applied as follow [2]:

1. Size fusion: Let

$$r_{ac} = \begin{cases} A_p/A_c : A_p \leq A_c \\ A_c/A_p : A_c \leq A_p \end{cases}, r_{hc} = \begin{cases} H_p/H_c : H_p \leq H_c \\ H_c/H_p : H_c \leq H_p \end{cases}, \text{ and } r_{wc} = \begin{cases} W_p/W_c : W_p \leq W_c \\ W_c/W_p : W_c \leq W_p \end{cases}, \quad (6)$$

where A_c, H_c and W_c are area, height, and width of object O_c. Then

$$\begin{aligned} s++ &: r_{ac} > t_z \lor r_{hc} > t_z \lor r_{wc} > t_z \\ d++ &: r_{ac} \leq t_z \lor r_{hc} \leq t_z \lor r_{wc} \leq t_z, \end{aligned} \quad (7)$$

2. Shape fusion: Let $e_p(e_i)$ be the extent ratio(H_p/W_p) of the shape of $O_p(O_i)$, $d_{ec} = |e_p - e_c|$ then

$$s++: d_{ec} \leq t_s \ , \quad d++: d_{ec} > t_s , \quad (8)$$

3. Motion fusion: Let the previous horizontal and vertical direction of the object be $\delta_p = (\delta_{xp}, \delta_{yp})$ and its current direction be $\delta_c = (\delta_{xc}, \delta_{yc})$. Then

$$\begin{aligned} s++ &: \delta_{xc} = \delta_{xp} \lor \delta_{yc} = \delta_{yp} \\ d++ &: \delta_{xc} \neq \delta_{xp} \lor \delta_{yc} \neq \delta_{yp}, \end{aligned} \quad (9)$$

If vote confidence $\zeta = s/d$ is larger than threshold t_m, object O_p and O_c are similar. Otherwise, the objects are disappeared or occluded.

3.4 Feature Point Prediction and Correction

Sometimes, a tracking algorithm may fail to track a proper feature point in the following frame. A feature point is defined as *untracked* when an error value within small window is over a pre-specified threshold. Especially, a threshold value is determined by the distance between average vectors obtained by spatio-temporal prediction. After the spatio-temporal prediction, re-investigation is performed. Both tracked and untracked feature points are then updated in the list.

In many real-time, video tracking applications, a feature-based tracking algorithm fails due to the following reasons: (i) self or partial occlusions of an object and (ii) feature points on or outside the boundary of the object, which are affected by changing background.

In order to deal with the tracking failure problems, we should correct the erroneously predicted feature points by using the location of the previous feature points and inter-pixel relationship between the predicted points. The proposed algorithm is summarized in Table 1. Spatio-temporal prediction and re-investigation.

Table 2. Spatio-temporal prediction and re-investigation

Step 1	**Temporal prediction**: If the i th feature point at the t th frame is lost in tracking, it is re-predicted as [12] $$\hat{v}_i^{t+1} = v_i^t + \frac{1}{K}\sum_{k=0}^{K-1} m_i^{t-k}, \quad (10)$$ where $m_i^t = v_i^t - v_i^{t-1}$, and K represents the number of frames for computing the average motion vector.
Step 2	**Spatial prediction**: We can correct the erroneous prediction by replacing with the average motion vector of successfully predicted feature points. The temporal and spatial prediction results of step 1 and 2 can be combined to estimate the position of feature points.
Step 3	**Re-investigation of the predicted feature point**: Assign the region including the predicted and corrected feature points temporal and spatial prediction steps. If a feature point is extracted within a certain extent in the following frame, it is updated as a new feature point. If the re-predicted feature points are more than 60% of the entire feature points, feature points estimation repeats.

A temporal prediction is suitable for deformable objects while a spatial prediction is good for non-deformable objects. Both temporal and spatial prediction results can also be combined with proper weights.

4 Restoration of Occlusion Using the NPT-AFM

The most popular approach to tracking 2D deformable objects is to use the object's boundary. ASM-based tracking falls into this category. ASM can analyze and synthesize *a priori* trained shape of an object even if the input is noisy or occluded [13]. On the other hand, *a priori* generation of training sets and iterative convergence prevent the ASM from being used for real-time. We propose a real-time updating method of the training set instead of off-line preprocessing, and also modify the ASM by using only a few feature points instead of the entire landmark points.

4.1 Landmark Point Assignment Using Feature Point

The existing ASM algorithm manually assigns landmark point on the object's boundary to make a training set [13]. A good landmark point has balanced distance between adjacent landmark points and resides on either high-curvature or 'T' junction position. A good feature point, however, has a different requirement from that of a good landmark point. In other words, a feature point is recommended to locate inside the object because a feature point on the boundary of the object easily fails in optical flow or block matching-based tracking [14] due to the effect of changing, complicated background.

A set of n feature points, which is member of the training set, represent the shape of an object as a 2D outline. Instead of using all feature points in a member of the training set, the PCA technique helps to model the shape of the object with fewer parameters. The best set of parameters that represents the optimal location and feature shape of an object can be obtained by matching the shape of models in the training set to the real object in the image. Fig. 5 shows the result of optical flow-based model fitting with 51training shapes. As shown in Fig. 5 (b) and (c), a few mismatches between the feature model and the real object can be found after occlusion.

Fig. 5. Model fitting procedure in the NPT-AFM: (a) optical flow-based feature tracking at the 36th frame, (b) model fitting at the 45th frame, and (c) model fitting at the 52th frame

4.2 Reconstruction of Feature Model and Occlusion Handing

In the AFM algorithm, a feature model obtained from the local feature fitting step does not always match the real object because it has been constructed using a training set of features in the previous frame. A few mismatches between the feature model and the real object can be found in Fig. 6(a). The proposed feature reconstruction algorithm moves an outside feature point toward the average position of all feasible feature points, in other words, inside the object. While moving the outside feature points, we search the best path among three directions toward the average position. If the number of outside feature points is more than 60% of the total feature points, the feature extraction process is repeated. The feature reconstruction process is depicted in Fig. 6.

In addition to reconstructing feature model, occlusion handling is another important function in a realistic tracking algorithm. The proposed NPT-AFM based occlusion handling algorithm first detects occlusion if the labeling region is 1.6 times lager than the original labeling region. The decision is made with additional information such as motion direction and size in the correspondingly labeled object region. If an occlusion is detected, we preserve the previous labeling information to keep multiple object's feature models separately. After handling the occlusion, the feature model should be reconstructed every time. This reconstruction process is performed the size of labeled region is between $0.8L$ and $1.2L$, where L represents the original size of the labeled region.

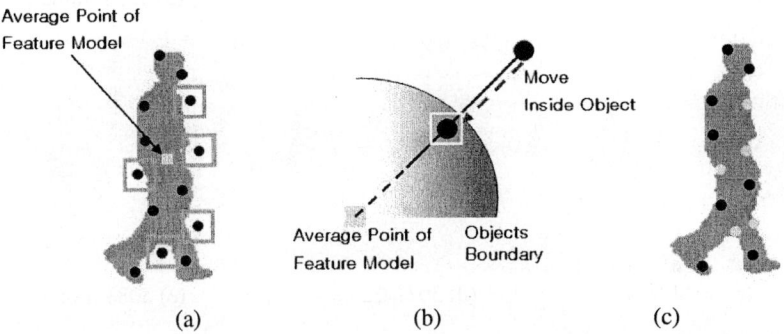

Fig. 6. Reconstruction of the feature model: (a) feature model fitting result, (b) relocation of an outside feature point for feature reconstruction, and (c) result of feature reconstruction

5 Experimental Results

We used 320x240, outdoor video sequences using SONY 3CCD DC-393 color video camera. In order to show the performance of multiple people tracking, We tried to track up to four people by using the proposed algorithm. The result of tracking is shown in Fig. 7 and 8. When people are occluded or after occlusion, we solve the problem using the NPT-AFM algorithm. In Figs. 8(f) and 8(g) a man and a lady are respectively extracted as the initial feature, because predicted and corrected features are over than 60%.

(a) 270 frame   (b) 350 frame   (c) 530 frame

Fig. 7. Results of tracking in sequence with shadow using the proposed algorithm

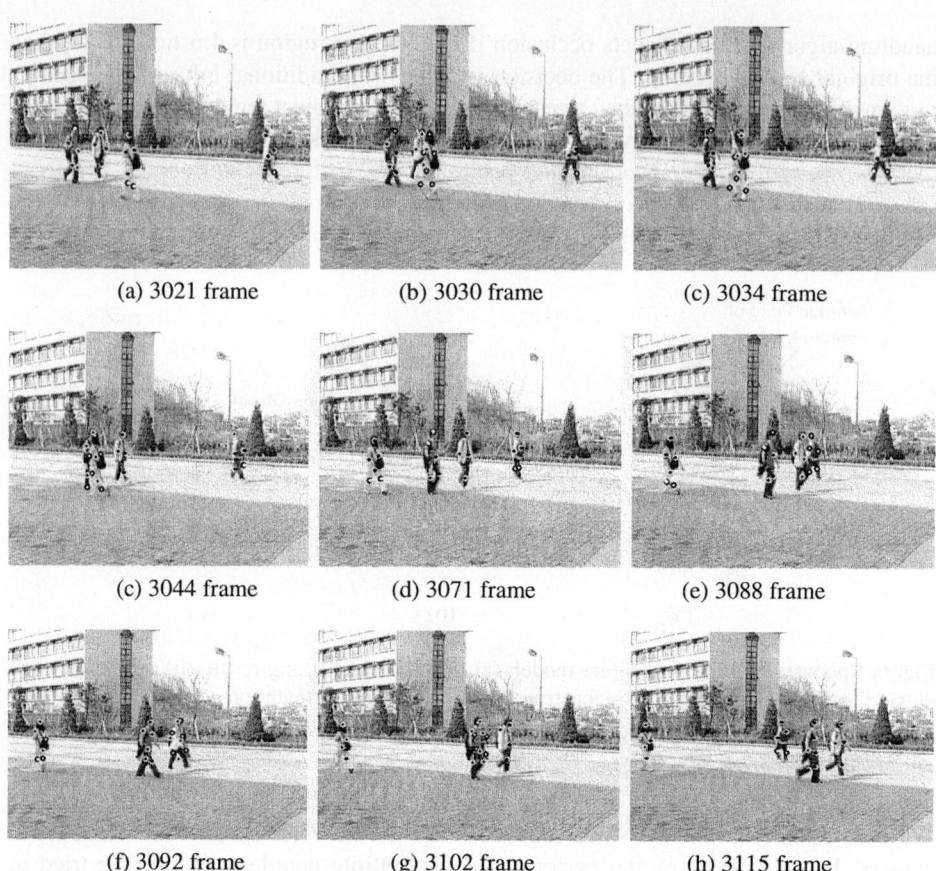

Fig. 8. Results of tracking using the proposed algorithm

6 Conclusions

We presented a novel method for multiple human tracking in video sequences. The proposed tracking algorithm segments people based on motion, extracts a set of feasible feature points inside the ellipsoid shape model for not extract on the shadow, predicts the corresponding feature points in the next frame using optical flow, corrects and reconstructs incorrectly predicted feature points, and finally applies the NPT-AFM algorithm to handle the occlusion problems. NPT-AFM, which is the major contribution of this paper, removes the off-line, preprocessing step for generating a priori training set. The training set used for model fitting can be updated at each frame to make more robust object's shape under occluded situation. Experimental results prove that the proposed algorithm can track multiple people, and is robust with partial occlusion and complicated background with shadows.

Acknowledgment

This work was supported by Korean Ministry of Science and Technology under the National Research Laboratory Project and by Korean Ministry of Information and Communication under the Chung-Ang University HNRC-ITRC program.

References

1. T. Zhao, and R. Nevatia, "Tracking multiple humans in complex situations," IEEE Trans. Pattern Analysis, Machine Intelligence , vol. 26, no. 9, pp. 1208–1221, September 2004.
2. A. Amer, "Voting-based simultaneous tracking of multiple video objects," Proc. SPIE Visual Comm., Image Proc., vol. 5022, pp. 500-5111, January 2003.
3. D. Comaniciu, V. Ramesh, and P. Meer, "Real-time tracking of nonrigid objects using mean shift," Proc. IEEE Int. Conf. Computer Vision, Pattern Recognition, vol. 2, pp. 142-149, June 2000.
4. D. Comaniciu, V. Ramesh, and P. Meer, "Kernel-based object tracking," IEEE Trans. Pattern Analysis, Machine Intelligence, vol. 25, no. 4, pp. 1-14, April 2003.
5. A. Baumberg, Learning Deformable Models for Tracking Human Motion, Ph.D. Dissertation, School of Computer Studies, University of Leeds, UK, October 1995.
6. T. Cootes, C. Taylor, D. Cooper, and J. Graham, "Training models of shape from sets of examples," Proc. British Machine Vision Conf., pp. 9-18, September 1992.
7. M. Isard and A. Blake, "Condensation-conditional density propagation for visual tracking," Int. Journ. Computer Vision, vol. 29, no. 1, pp. 5-28, August 1998.
8. B. Lucas and T. kanade, "An iterative image registration technique with and application to stereo vision," Proc. DARPA Image Understanding Workshop, pp. 121-130, 1981.
9. A. Tekalp, Digital Video Processing, Prentice-Hall Publications, 1995.
10. A. Prati, R. Cucchiara, I. Mikic, and M. Trivedi, "Analysis and detection of shadows in video streams: a comparative evaluation," Proc. IEEE Conf. Computer Vision, Pattern Recognition, vol. 2, pp. 571-576, 2001.
11. J. Bouguet, "Pyramidal implementation of the Lucas Kanade feature tracker description of the algorithms," OpenCV Documentation, Micro-Processor Research Labs, Intel Corporation, 1999.
12. C. Erdem, A. Tekalp, and B. Sankur, "Video object tracking with feedback of performance measures," IEEE Trans. Circuits, Systems for Video Technology, vol. 13, no. 4, pp. 310-324, April 2003.
13. A. Koschan, S. Kang, J. Paik, B. Abidi, and M. Abidi, "Color active shape models for t racking non-rigid objects," Pattern Recognition Letters, vol. 24, no. 11, pp. 1751-1765, July 2003.
14. H. Gharavi, M. Mills, "Block-Matching Motion Estimation Algorithms: New Results," IEEE Trans. Circ. and Syst., PP. 649–651, 1999.
15. S. Kim, J. Kang, J. Shin, S. Lee, J. Paik, S. Kang, B. Abidi, and M. Abidi, "Using a Non-Prior Training Active Feature Model," Pacific-Rim Conf. LNCS, vol. 3333, pp. 69-78, December, 2004.

Extracting the Movement of Lip and Tongue During Articulation

Hanhoon Park[1], Seung-Wook Hong[1], Jong-Il Park[1],
Sung-Kyun Moon[2], and Hyeongseok Ko[3]

[1] Division of Electrical and Computer Engineering, Hanyang University, Seoul, Korea
{hanuni,spacejam}@mr.hanyang.ac.kr, jipark@hanyang.ac.kr
[2] Department of Otolaryngology, Ajou University, Suwon, Korea
smoon@ajou.ac.kr
[3] School of Electrical Engineering, Seoul National University, Seoul, Korea
ko@graphics.snu.ac.kr

Abstract. A method that extracts the 3-D shape and movement of lip and tongue and displays them simultaneously is presented. Lip movement is easily observable and thus extractable using a camera. However, it is difficult to extract the real movement of tongue exactly because the tongue may be occluded by the lip and teeth. In this paper, we use a magnetic resonance imaging (MRI) device to extract the sagittal view of the movement of tongue during articulation. Since the frame rate of the available MRI device is very low (5 fps), we obtain a smooth video sequence (20 fps) by a new contour-based interpolation method. The overall procedure of extracting the movement of lip and tongue is as follows. First, fiducial color markers attached on the lip are detected, and then the data of 3D movement of the lip are computed using a 3D reconstruction technique. Next, to extract the movement of tongue image, we applied a series of simple image processing algorithms to MRI images of tongue and then extracted the contour of tongue interactively. Finally, the data of lip and tongue are synchronized and temporally interpolated. An OpenGL based program is implemented to visualize the data interactively. We performed the experiment using the Korean basic syllables and some of the data are presented. It is confirmed that a lot of experiments using the results support theoretical and empirical observation of linguistics. The acquired data can be used not only as a fundamental database for scientific purpose but also as an educative material for language rehabilitation of the hearing-impaired. Also it can be used for making a high-quality lip-synchronized animation including tongue movement.

1 Introduction

Recently, mechanical cochlea transplant becomes popular and the importance of language rehabilitation program is increasing. However, the language rehabilitation program in progress has been operated with the visit of a curer and thus not effective. The development of language rehabilitation program easily operated at home has been sincerely required. For this purpose, language rehabilitation curers have desired the system that visualizes the exact movement of lip and tongue during pronouncing because it would be helpful for a hearing-impaired person or someone who learns foreign language to learn and practice correct pronunciation. However, there have been few of such a system in the literature.

Lip movement has been a main topic in various fields. In the field of animation, researches on describing lip movement graphically and synchronizing with speech (called *lip synchronization*) have been mainly studied for achieving realistic facial animation [1]. In the field of biometric recognition, researches on recognizing speech from lip movement have been studied (called *lip reading*) [2]. There are several approaches for extracting lip movement. The most popular one is extracting the geometric information of lip contour based on parametric methods. Lip contour can be extracted using prior knowledge such as the color and shape of lip. However, these methods may be sensitive to environmental noise. For accuracy, fiducial markers with a specific color can be attached around mouth [3-6], which are also used in this paper.

Researches on extracting tongue movement are divided into three categories according to the method of acquiring a tongue image: X-ray, ultrasound, and MRI. The most popular method is using X-ray [7]. However, tongue is dimly visible in X-ray image because X-ray penetrates the tongue of low density while teeth and bone is clearly visible in X-ray image because X-ray cannot penetrate the teeth or bone of high density. To improve the image resolution of the part of tongue, barium can be used which is put on tongue. But it has still a problem that tongue is seriously occluded by the bone and teeth. Moreover, X-ray is harmful to the human body. Ultrasound has been mainly used in the research on articulation organ [8]. Ultrasound-based methods are attractive in that it is possible to obtain a video sequence with high frame rate (300 fps) and not harmful to the human body. However, the image resolution is not suitable for analyzing the movement of tongue. The MRI-based method has been actively studied recently and especially 3-D modeling of tongue using the MRI images have gained significant attention [9-12]. Tissue or adipose including lots of water such as tongue is clearly visible in MRI image while bone or teeth is not visible in MRI image. Therefore, tongue is easily detected in the MRI images using a series of simple image processing algorithms. MRI-based method is most suitable for analyzing the movement of tongue and thus used in this paper. Fig. 1 shows the examples of X-ray, ultrasound, and MRI images, which are compared to each other in Table 1.

While the methods associated with extracting the movement of either tongue or lip were relatively investigated, less efforts have been exerted on simultaneous extraction

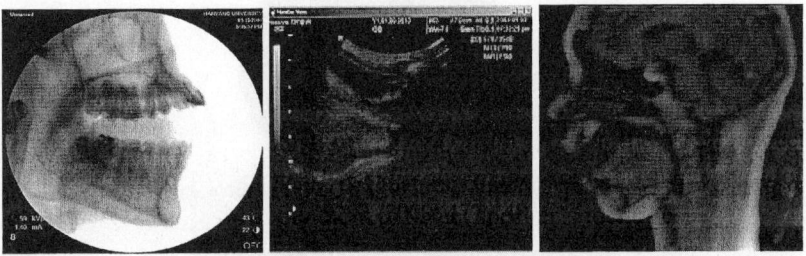

Fig. 1. Examples of X-ray, ultrasound, and MRI images

Table 1. Comparison between X-ray, ultrasound, MRI

	X-ray	Ultrasound	MRI
Image resolution	Fine	Poor	Middle
Capability of acquiring a video sequence	Yes	Yes	Yes
Harmfulness to the human body	Yes	No	No
Frame rate	Middle (10-30 fps)	High (300 fps)	Low (5-10 fps)

of movement of lip and tongue. Therefore, we explore in this paper how to extracts and visualizes the synchronized movement of lip and tongue simultaneously when pronouncing a language. Similar one to our method had been presented and applied to the Swedish [11,12]. In the method, MRI data was use to estimate a 3-D tongue model and electromagnetic articulography (EMA) data was used to estimate the movement of a few points on the tongue. The movement of the whole tongue was estimated from the movement of the points. However, tongue is not modeled and MRI data is directly used to estimate the tongue movement in our method and EMA device is not used.

The rest of this paper is organized as follows. In Section 2, the details of the proposed method for extracting the movement of lip and tongue are explained. Some experimental results are given in Section 3 and conclusion is drawn in Section 4.

2 Method

The movement of lip and tongue is independently extracted using multiple color cameras and MRI device, respectively. Then, the extracted data are merged and synchronized to be visualized simultaneously.

2.1 Modeling of Lip Movement

To compute the 3-D coordinates of lip, the position of lip in the image should be known. To compute the lip position, fiducial color markers with a specific color are attached around mouth (see Fig. 2).

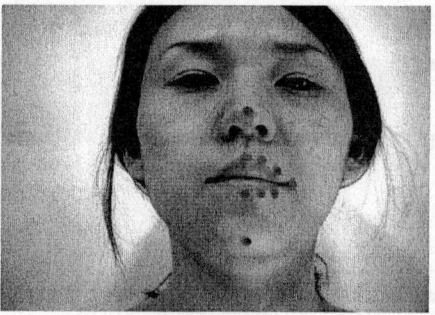

Fig. 2. Fiducial markers attached around mouth. The color of markers is discriminant from that of the face and its material has no specular reflection.

The color of markers is discriminant from that of face and its material has no specular reflection. Then, the markers can be easily detected by transforming the RGB color space into HSV color space and applying a simple cropping and noise-elimination algorithm to the Hue values. The coordinates of markers is computed by fitting the coordinates of the pixels associated with the detected markers to ellipses. For 3-D reconstruction of lip, the position of markers is computed in the images of three calibrated cameras and the 3-D coordinates of markers is computed using a linear triangulation method [13].

2.2 Extraction of Tongue Contour

The movement of tongue is extracted using MRI images. MRI image is clear compared to other radiographic images because tongue is not seriously occluded by the bone and teeth. Moreover, MRI is not harmful to the human body unlike X-ray. However, fast movement of tongue might not be caught because the frame rate of the available MRI device is very low (5 fps). To alleviate the limit, we computed a high-resolution video sequence (20 fps) by temporally-interpolating their intermediate frames of a low-resolution video sequence (5 fps) obtained by the MRI device.

Tongue can be represented as a curve in the image. Thus, the position of tongue in the MRI images is computed using contour detection algorithms. However, tongue may not be discriminant when tongue touches the ceiling or floor of mouth. In this case, the tongue contour is extracted manually. The procedure of detecting tongue contour is as follows.

① Histogram equalization is applied to the tongue image.
② The image is binarized using a cropping algorithm.
③ The noise of image is eliminated using morphology algorithms such as dilation and erosion.
④ Tongue contour is represented using the simple contour representing algorithm, chain code.
⑤ Starting and ending point of tongue contour is specified interactively.

Fig. 3 shows the resulting image of each step.

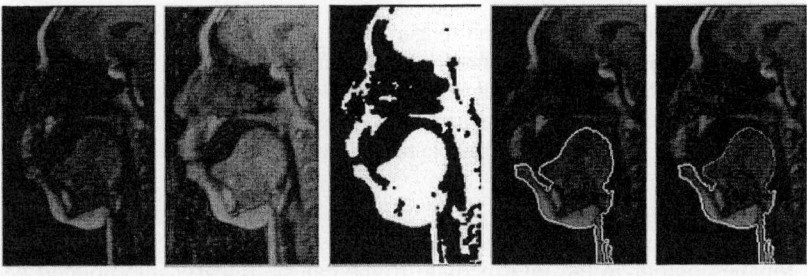

Fig. 3. Process of extracting tongue contour. In the last image, the part of tongue has a different color from the rest of the detected contour.

2.3 Merging of the Movement of Lip and Tongue

The frame rate and length of image sequences of lip (20 fps) and tongue (5 fps) are different because the movement of lip and tongue is independently extracted using three cameras and MRI, respectively (see Fig. 4). Thus, they should be merged and synchronized to be visualized simultaneously. However, it is impossible to define a specific method for synchronization because it is difficult to obtain the lip and tongue images simultaneously and the spending time when pronouncing a language is not uniform. In this paper, the lip and tongue images are synchronized by synthesizing the missing tongue images on the basis of the stretched lip images (see Fig. 5) because the frame rate of lip images is higher than that of tongue images.

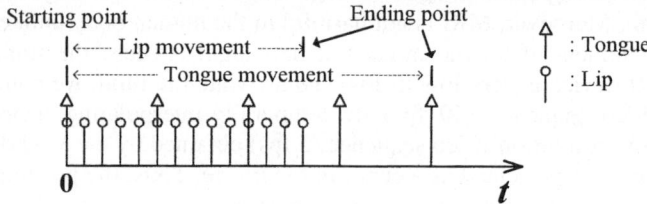

Fig. 4. Lip and tongue movement with different frame rate and length of image sequences

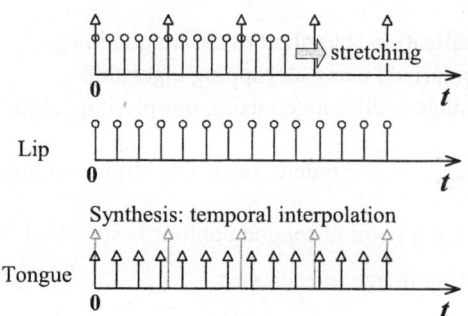

Fig. 5. Synchronization between lip and tongue image sequences. At first, the lip image sequences are stretched in order that the starting and ending points of both image sequences may be consistent with each other because the length of the lip image sequences is shorter than that of the tongue image sequences in our experiments[1]. Next, the tongue image sequences are resampled (synthesized) in order that the sample rate of the tongue image sequences may be same as that of the lip image sequences.

Tongue contour is represented as a curve consisting of adjacent points. The points on the tongue contour in the intermediate frame can be linearly interpolated because

---

[1] The tongue movement cannot be completely caught because the frame rate of MRI image is low. Thus it was intended that the subject pronounced slowly when acquiring the tongue image sequences. Here, it was assumed that the tongue movement was not changed even though the subject pronounces slowly.

the temporal gap between consecutive frames is small. Let $\mathbf{P_1}$ and $\mathbf{P_2}$ be the points on the contours in the consecutive frames. Then, the i-th point P^i on the contour in the intermediate frame is linearly interpolated as follows:

$$P^i = P_1^i * w + P_2^k * (1-w), \quad 0 \leq w \leq 1$$
$$\text{where} \quad k = arg \min_{j=0,1,2,\ldots,N} \text{distance}(P_1^i, P_2^j).$$

This algorithm works even if the number of points on the contours in the consecutive frames is different. However, this can give rise to some troubles in the case that the contour is seriously deformed between consecutive frames as is described in Fig. 6. To resolve the problem, we devise a method in this paper. The upper and lower points on the tongue contour are interpolated independently on the basis of tongue tip which is specified interactively. Fig. 6 illustrates the difference of the naïve linear interpolation and the proposed interpolation method. Fig. 7 shows the examples of applying two methods to real images (w=0.5).

3 Experimental Results and Discussion

The lip movement images were acquired using three IEEE-1394 cameras (Dragon-Fly^{TM} [14]) synchronously at a resolution of 640 by 480 and a frame rate of 20 fps and the images are true-colored. The cameras were positioned in the front, 45 degrees, and 60 degrees of a subject and synchronized in the firm-ware level and the images were saved to BMP files. The images of '녀' are shown in Fig. 8. Nine blue markers were attached on the face of a subject and his/her head was fixed. Seven markers were attached around mouth for tracking the lip movement and two markers were attached on the nose and jaw for matching with the position of mouth in MRI images. The subject is a native speaker of Korean and a 24-year-old woman. Intrinsic and extrinsic parameters of the cameras were calibrated in advance using Zhang's method [15].

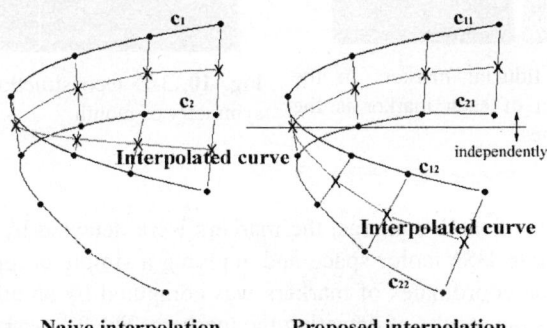

Fig. 6. Difference of the results of using the naïve linear interpolation and the proposed interpolation for synthesizing the intermediate curve. Basically, the points on the interpolated curve are linearly interpolated from each point of curve c_1 and its nearest point on curve c_2. In the proposed method, c_1 and c_2 are split into c_{11}-c_{12} and c_{21}-c_{22}, respectively. The upper points on the interpolated curve are estimated from the points on c_{11} and c_{21}. The lower points on the interpolated curve are estimated from the points on c_{12} and c_{22}.

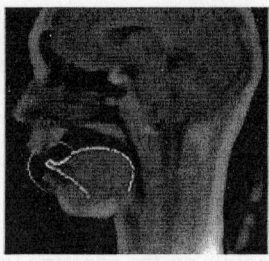 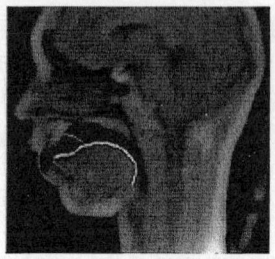

Fig. 7. Interpolated tongue contour using two interpolation methods in Figure 6. Left image: using the naïve linear interpolation. Right image: using the proposed interpolation. In the case of the naïve linear interpolation, the contour was not properly interpolated.

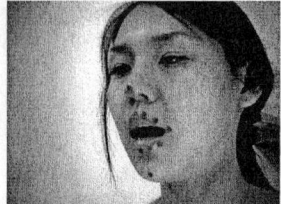 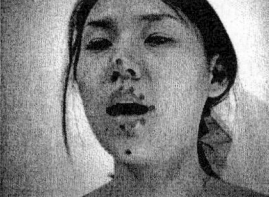 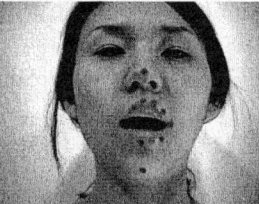

Fig. 8. Acquiring the lip images using three cameras

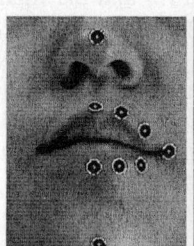 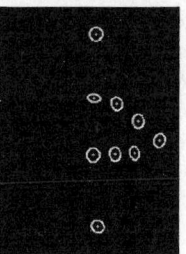

Fig. 9. Detecting fiducial markers in the image. The position of each marker is the center of fitted ellipses.

Fig. 10. 3-D reconstruction of lip using the symmetry of mouth.

From the images of three cameras, the markers were detected by transforming the RGB color space into HSV color space and applying a simple cropping algorithm to the Hue values. The coordinates of markers was computed by an ellipse fitting algorithm. Fig. 9 shows the results of detecting the markers. The 27 markers detected from the images of three cameras were easily corresponded with each other based on the fact that topology of the markers is fixed. The 3-D coordinates of the markers was computed using a linear triangulation method [13]. Since some of mouth region was not visible from some of the cameras, the symmetry of mouth was used for 3-D reconstruction of the whole lip as is shown in Fig. 10.

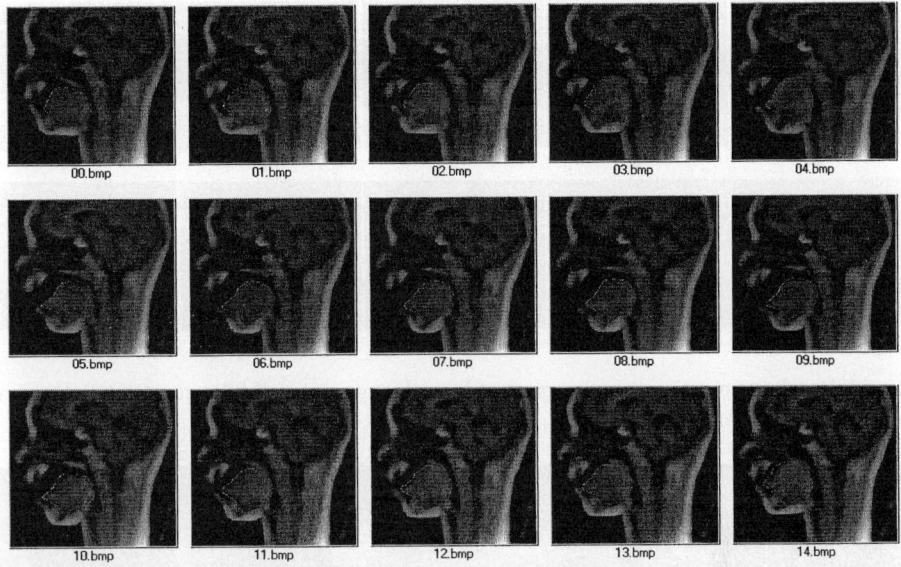

Fig. 11. MRI images of tongue when '가' is pronounced. The detected tongue contour is overlayed.

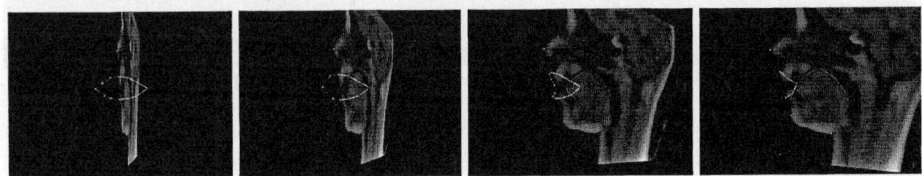

Fig. 12. Movement of lip and tongue visualized from different angles

The sagittal images of tongue were obtained using MRI (MAGNETOM Sonata*, Siemens [16]) at a resolution of 256 by 250 and a frame rate of 5 fps as shown in Fig. 11. The images were saved to DICOM files and converted into BMP files. The tongue contour was extracted from the images using the method explained in Section 2.2.

Spatial arrangement of the movement of lip and tongue was done based on two markers on the nose and jaw. The cues for matching with the lip position could be found from the middle facial features such as nose or jaw because the tongue images were those that captured the lateral section of a head. The relative distance between the center of the upper and lower lip, nose, and jaw were used in the experiment. The lip movement was visualized by 3-D points and lines and the tongue movement was visualized by texture-mapping the MRI images[2] on which the computed tongue contour was drawn using OpenGL. Fig. 12 shows the results of visualizing the movement of lip and tongue from different angles. It may not be easy to capture the movement of

---

[2] The region except tongue in the intermediate MRI image was pixel-wise interpolated in the experiments.

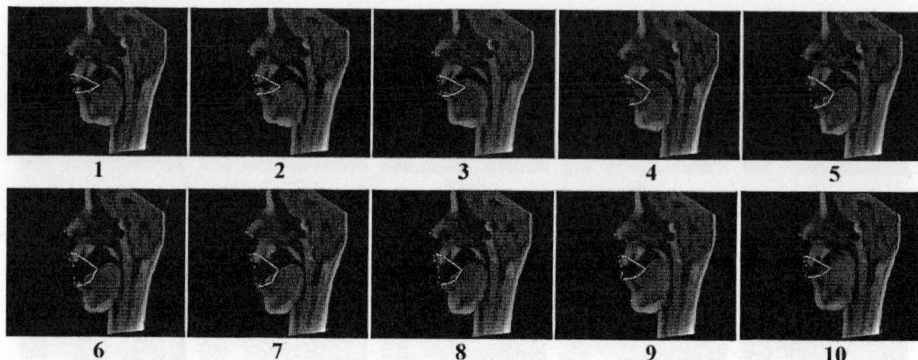

Fig. 13. Results of merging the movement of lip and tongue when '나' is pronounced. A part of the images are presented.

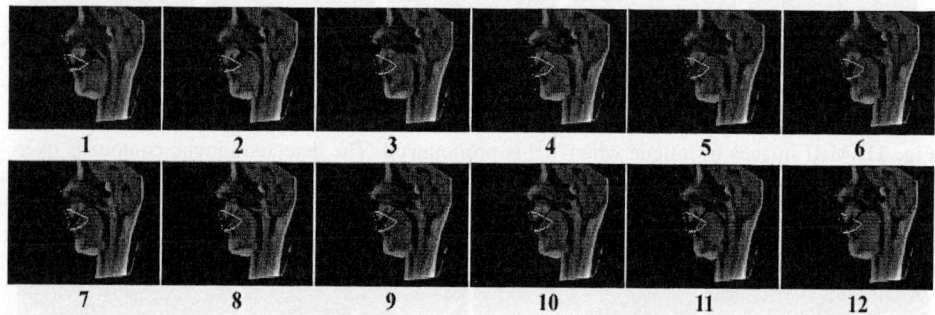

Fig. 14. Results of merging the movement of lip and tongue when '기' is pronounced. A part of the images are presented.

lip and tongue from the rough visualization. It would be improved if the data regarding the movement of lip and tongue is applied to high-quality facial animation.

We performed the experiment on the Korean basic syllables such as '가', '나', '사', '고', '노', '소', '기', '니', '시'. Due to the limited space in this paper, only the results of '나' and '기' are given. Theoretically, '나' consists of 'ㄴ' and 'ㅏ'. 'ㄴ' is pronounced when the tongue tip is touched the back of upper teeth as a nasal and 'ㅏ' when the tongue is positioned in the lower part of mouth [17,18]. In Fig. 13, it is observable that the tongue tip touches the back of upper teeth in the #3 and #4 images and the position of tongue lowers in the #6~#8 images. '기' consists of 'ㄱ' and 'ㅣ'. 'ㄱ' is pronounced when exploding after covering the ceiling of mouth with the back of tongue as a velar plosive and 'ㅣ' when thrusting tongue out and upside while making it widen horizontally [17,18]. In Fig. 14, it is observable that the back of tongue touches the ceiling of mouth in the #4~#6 images and the position of tongue is getting elevated during pronouncing.

4 Conclusion

For achieving effective language rehabilitation, an interactive method which extracts and visualizes the 3-D movement of lip and tongue when pronouncing the Korean language was presented. The results of extraction were demonstrated by visualizing the movement of lip and tongue in different angles using OpenGL. A lot of experiments using the results supported theoretical and empirical observation of linguistics.

More experiments using a word or a sentence should be performed in the future, which will be more useful for the hearing-impaired person or someone who would like to learn Korean language. Also it would be interesting to extend the proposed method to other languages.

Acknowledgement. This work was supported by the Korea Research Foundation Grant (KRF-2003-042-D00167). The authors are grateful to Prof. Jong-Hyo Kim of Seoul National University and Hye-Lim Jeon for their neat help in the experiment.

References

1. Provine, J.A., Bruton, L.T.: Lip Synchronization in 3-D Model Based Coding for Video-Conferencing. Proc. of ISCAS, Vol. 1. (1995) 453-456
2. Chen, T., Rao, R.R: Audio-visual Integration in Multimodal Communication. Proc. of the IEEE, Vol. 86. (1998) 837-852
3. Guenter, B., Grimm, C., Wood, D., Malvar, H., Pighin, F.: Making Faces. Proc. of SIGGRAPH. (1998) 55-66
4. Hager, G.D., Belhumeur, P.N.: Real-time Tracking of Image Region with Changes in Geometry and Illumination. Proc. of CVPR. (1996) 403-410
5. Matsino, K., Lee, C.W., Tsuji, S.: Automatic Recognition of Human Facial Expressions. Proc. of the IEEE. (1995) 352-359
6. Pighin, F., Szeliski, R., Salesin, D.: Resynthesizing Facial Animation through 3D Model-Based Tracking. Proc. of ICCV. (1999) 130-150
7. Laprie, Y., Berger, M.-O.: Extraction of Tongue Contours in X-ray Images with Minimal User Interaction. Proc. of International Conference on Spoken Language Processing, Vol. 1. (1996) 268-271
8. Akgul, Y.S., Kambhamettu, C., Stone, M.: Automatic Extraction and Tracking of the Tongue Contours. IEEE Trans. on Medical Imaging. (1999) 1035-1045
9. Unay, D.: Analysis of Tongue Motion Using Tagged Cine-MRI. Master Thesis, Bogazici University (2001)
10. Stone, M., Davis, E., Nessaiver, M., Gullipalli, R., Levine, W., Lundberg, A.: Modeling Motion of the Internal Tongue from Tagged Cine-MRI Images. Journal of the Acoustical Society of America, Vol. 109, No. 6. (2001) 2974-2982
11. Engwall, O., Beskow, J.: Resynthesis of 3D Tongue Movements from Facial Data. Proc. of Eurospeech. (2003) 2261-2264
12. Engwall, O.: A 3D Tongue Model Based on MRI Data. Proc. of ICSLP. (2000) 901-904
13. Hartley, R., Zisserman, A.: Mutiple View Geometry in Computer Vision. 2nd Ed., Cambridge University Press (2003)
14. Dragonfly Technical Reference Manual, http://www.ptgrey.com
15. Zhang, Z.: A Flexible New Technique for Camera Calibration. IEEE Trans. on Pattern Analysis and Machine Intelligence, Vol. 22, No. 11. (2000) 1330-1334
16. MAGNETOM Sonata*, http://www.healthcare.siemens.com
17. Korean Standard Pronunciation, http://natogi.new21.org/han/pyojun/p202.htm
18. The National Institute of the Korean Language, http://www.korean.go.kr

A Scheme for Ball Detection and Tracking in Broadcast Soccer Video

Dawei Liang[1], Yang Liu[1], Qingming Huang[2], and Wen Gao[1,2]

[1] School of Computer Science and Technology, Harbin Institute of Technology,
Harbin 150001, China
{dwliang, yliu}@jdl.ac.cn
[2] Graduate School of Chinese Academy of Sciences, Beijing 100080, China
{qmhuang, wgao}@jdl.ac.cn

Abstract. In this paper we propose a scheme for ball detection and tracking in broadcast soccer video. There are two alternate procedures in the scheme: ball detection and ball tracking. In ball detection procedure, ball candidates are first extracted from several consecutive frames using color, shape, and size cues. Then a weighted graph is constructed, with each node representing a candidate and each edge linking two candidates in adjacent frames. Finally, Viterbi algorithm is employed to extract the optimal path as ball's locations. In ball tracking procedure, Kalman filter based template matching is utilized to track the ball in subsequent frames. Kalman filter and the template are initialized using detection results. In each tracking step, ball location is verified to update the template and to guide possible ball re-detection. Experimental results demonstrate that the proposed scheme is promising.

1 Introduction

In the past decade, sports video analysis from the standpoint of computer vision has attracted much attention, especially in ball games such as soccer [1-7], American football [8], tennis [9], snooker [10] etc. Through detection and/or tracking of the moving objects (players, ball), several high level analysis can be done, e.g. highlight extraction [2], event detection [10] and tactic analysis [6]. This paper focuses on ball detection and tracking in broadcast soccer video, which is a challenging task.

There are some literatures stating the problem of soccer ball detection and tracking. Chromatic and morphological features are utilized to detect ball in [1]. In [2] the authors use template matching to detect ball in difference image after camera motion compensation at regular intervals, and then ball tracking is carried out between such intervals. In [3] ball's location is initialized manually, after that Kalman filter and template matching are applied to track it. In [4] the authors employ motion information in ball detection and tracking, but in their case the cameras are fixed. A modified version of the directional Circle Hough Transform is used to detect ball in real (not broadcast) image sequences in [5]. In [6], ball candidates are first obtained in each video frame based on playfield detection. Afterwards, Kalman filter is employed to generate candidate trajectories from which ball trajectories are selected and extended. In [7], the authors exploit a coarse-to-fine strategy to identify ball in a single frame after playfield detection, and then CONDENSATION algorithm is used to track the ball.

Although the above-mentioned methods provide certain solutions to the ball detection and tracking issue, the problem is not fully resolved yet. The challenges associated with ball detection and tracking can be attributed to the following factors:

- The ball's attributes (color, shape, size and velocity etc.) change over frames;
- The ball becomes a long blurred strip when it moves fast;
- The ball is sometimes only a little white blob;
- The ball is sometimes occluded by players, merged with lines, or hidden in the auditorium;
- Many other objects are similar in appearance to the ball, such as some regions of the players, some white line segments in the playfield and so on;
- Playfield appearance varies from place to place and from time to time, and cannot be modeled appropriately;
- etc.

Some typical ball samples in broadcast soccer video are shown in Fig.1. These ball samples further testify the challenges of ball detection and tracking in broadcast soccer video.

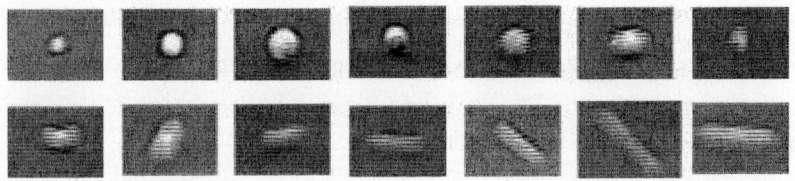

Fig. 1. Some typical ball samples in broadcast soccer video

In this paper, we propose a scheme for ball detection and tracking in broadcast soccer video. It can work well in various playfield conditions. The flowchart is shown in Fig.2. It is composed of two alternate procedures: ball detection and ball tracking. In ball detection procedure, color, shape and size are used to extract ball candidates in each frame. Then a weighted graph is constructed, with each node representing a candidate and each edge linking two candidates in adjacent frames. Finally, Viterbi algorithm is applied to extract the optimal path which is most likely to be ball's path as ball's locations. The method can enhance the robustness of ball detection, since it holds multiple hypotheses of ball's locations. Once the ball is detected, the tracking procedure based on Kalman filter and template matching is started. Kalman filter and the template are initialized using detection results. In each tracking step, ball location is verified to update the template and to guide possible ball re-detection.

The remainder of the paper is organized as follows. In section 2, the method for ball detection is discussed in detail. In section 3, Kalman filter based ball tracking is introduced. Some experimental results are provided in section 4 and the conclusions are presented in the last section.

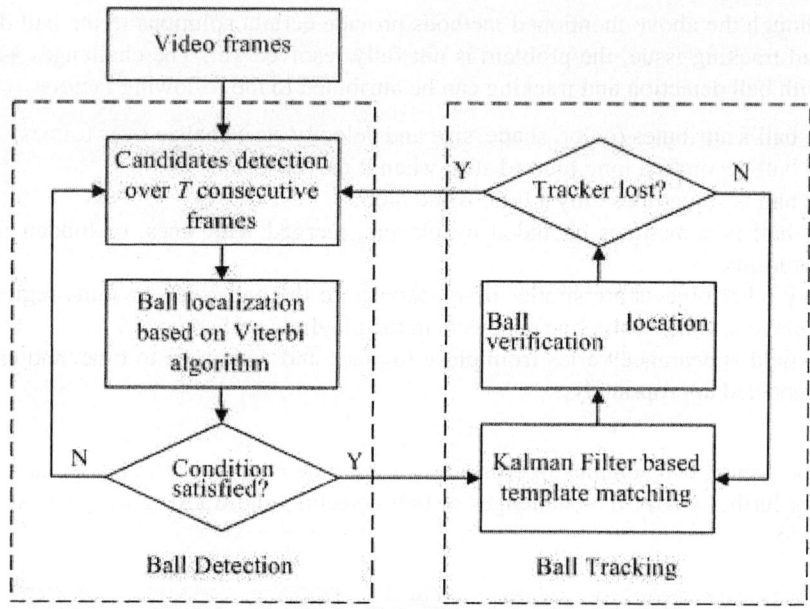

Fig. 2. The flowchart of the proposed scheme

2 Ball Detection

The basic idea of ball detection is to use graph to hold multiple hypotheses of the ball's locations. We extract the optimal path of the graph as the ball's locations rather than identify whether a single object is a ball or not in a single frame, since there are many objects similar to the ball.

2.1 Ball Candidates Detection

Based on the observation that the ball's color is nearly white in long view shots, white pixels are first segmented according to (1) in normalized RGB color space.

$$B(x,y) = \begin{cases} 1 & (r(x,y)-1/3)^2 + (b(x,y)-1/3)^2 \leq a^2 \wedge I(x,y) \geq b \\ 0 & otherwise \end{cases} \quad (1)$$

where B is a binary image and (x, y) is the pixel location, $r(x, y)$ and $b(x, y)$ denote normalized red and blue component, respectively, $I(x, y)$ denotes luminance value. The thresholds are set to $a = 0.05$ and $b = 160$ empirically. Morphological close operation is used to eliminate noises, after that a new region growing algorithm [11] is employed to connect pixels into regions and smooth the boundaries. To obtain ball candidates, several features are used, including the size of the object, the ratio of length and width of the object's minimal bounding rectangle (MBR), the area ratio of the object and its MBR. In order to adapt to various ball appearances, the thresholds are set as loosely as possible to ensure that the true ball region is included in. In our experiment, the threshold of the first feature is set differently as the object appears at different image position, the threshold of the second one is set to 1.5, and the threshold of the third one is set to 0.5.

2.2 Graph Construction

After candidates detection over T consecutive frames, a weighted graph is constructed. Each graph node represents a ball candidate. Since the ball's locations in two adjacent frames are close to each other, only those candidate pairs (between adjacent frames) whose Euclidean distance (in image plane) is smaller than the threshold d_{max} contribute to the graph edge set. According to formula (2) each node is assigned a weight representing how it resembles a ball. Meanwhile each edge is assigned a weight through formula (4) to represent how likely the two nodes correspond to the same object.

$$v_i^t = \begin{cases} 1-\sqrt{c_i^t} & c_i^t \leq 1 \\ 0 & c_i^t > 1 \end{cases} \quad (2)$$

where

$$c_i^t = \frac{1}{M\mu_r^2} \sum_k (\|p_k - \mu\| - \mu_r)^2 \quad (3)$$

$$e_{i,j}^t = (\varpi_s s_{i,j}^t + \varpi_g g_{i,j}^t) / \sqrt{1+(d_{i,j}^t/d_{max})^2} \quad (4)$$

In above formulae, superscript t denotes the relative serial number of frame; subscripts i and j denote the ith candidate in frame t and the jth candidate in frame $t+1$, respectively. In (3), c_i^t is called Circular Variance (CV) [12]. The less CV is, the more the contour resembles a circle. p_k is a contour point, M is the number of contour point, μ is the centroid of the contour, and μ_r is the average distance from contour points to the centroid. In (4) $s_{i,j}^t$ and $g_{i,j}^t$ are the size and the gray level similarity of two candidates respectively with ϖ_s and ϖ_g as the corresponding weights. For simplicity we set $\varpi_s = \varpi_g = 0.5$. $d_{i,j}^t$ is the Euclidean distance (in image plane) of two candidates.

We assume $(\Delta w, \Delta h)$ obeys Gaussian distribution, where Δw is the width difference between MBRs of two candidates, and Δh is the height difference between MBRs of two candidates. Therefore, $s_{i,j}^t$ can be defined as (5), where Σ can be estimated from ball samples. In (6) $g_{i,j}^t$ is the gray level normalized cross correlation of two candidate regions, where vectors $\vec{I}_1$ and $\vec{I}_2$ are obtained through raster scanning of the candidate regions. If the candidate regions are not equal in size, they are adjusted to equal size before scanning.

$$S_{i,j}^t = N(0, \Sigma) \tag{5}$$

$$g_{i,j}^t = \frac{\sum_k \vec{I}_1(k) \cdot \vec{I}_2(k)}{\sqrt{\sum_k \vec{I}_1(k) \cdot \vec{I}_1(k)} \sqrt{\sum_k \vec{I}_2(k) \cdot \vec{I}_2(k)}} \tag{6}$$

2.3 Ball's Path Extraction

Finding the optimal path of a graph is a typical dynamic programming problem. Viterbi algorithm is employed to extract it based on the constructed graph. Note that the graph can be constructed incrementally. Viterbi algorithm is described in Fig.3 similar to that in [13].

---

1. Initialization: $\delta_i^1 = v_i^1$, $\psi_1(i) = 0$, $1 \le i \le N_1$;

2. Recursion: $\delta_j^t = \max\limits_{1 \le i \le N_{t-1},\, d_{i,j}^{t-1} \le d_{\max}} (\delta_i^{t-1} + e_{i,j}^{t-1} + v_j^t)$,

   $\psi_t(j) = \arg\max\limits_{1 \le i \le N_{t-1},\, d_{i,j}^{t-1} \le d_{\max}} (\delta_i^{t-1} + e_{i,j}^{t-1} + v_j^t)$,

   $1 \le j \le N_t$, $2 \le t \le T$;

3. Termination: $q_T = \arg\max\limits_{1 \le i \le N_T}(\delta_i^T)$;

4. Path backtracking: $q_t = \psi_{t+1}(q_{t+1})$, $t = T-1, T-2, \cdots, 1$

Fig. 3. Ball localization based on Viterbi algorithm

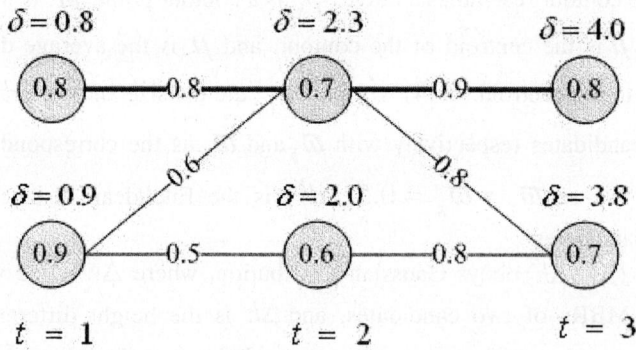

Fig. 4. Illustration of the weighted graph. The optimal path is marked with bold line

Let P_j^t be the optimal path ending at jth candidate in frame t, then the notations in Fig.3 are explained as follows. N_t is the number of candidates in frame t, δ_j^t is the sum of node and edge weights along P_j^t, $\Psi_t(j)$ is the index linking to the candidate in frame $t-1$ on P_j^t, and $\{q_t\}_{t=1,\cdots,T}$ is the optimal path. If the number of candidates on the optimal path is less than T, the observation window is moved forward by one frame and then the ball detection procedure is run again. An illustration of the graph and its optimal path is shown in Fig.4.

3 Ball Tracking

In ball tracking procedure, Kalman filter based template matching (in terms of gray level normalized cross correlation) is exploited. Kalman filter predicts the ball's location in the next frame and filters the tracking result in the current frame. Template matching is used to obtain observation. Kalman filter and the template are initialized using detection results.

Kalman filter addresses the general problem of estimating the state X of a discrete time process that is governed by the linear stochastic difference equation

$$X_{k+1} = AX_k + w_k \tag{7}$$

with a measurement Z that is

$$Z_k = HX_k + v_k \tag{8}$$

The random variables w_k and v_k represent the process and measurement noise respectively. They are assumed to be independent of each other and have normal distribution. In this paper first order dynamics model is employed, i.e.

$$X = \begin{bmatrix} x \\ y \\ \dot{x} \\ \dot{y} \end{bmatrix}, Z = \begin{bmatrix} x \\ y \end{bmatrix}, A = \begin{bmatrix} 1 & 0 & 1 & 0 \\ 0 & 1 & 0 & 1 \\ 0 & 0 & 1 & 0 \\ 0 & 0 & 0 & 1 \end{bmatrix}, H = \begin{bmatrix} 1 & 0 & 0 & 0 \\ 0 & 1 & 0 & 0 \end{bmatrix}, \tag{9}$$

where (x, y) denotes the ball's center, and $(\dot{x}, \dot{y})$ denotes the ball's velocity. Due to lack of space, please refer to [14] for more details about Kalman filter.

A simple but effective method is adopted to make the tracker adaptable to the ball's scale change over frames. A slightly larger block $(x1-\Delta, y1-\Delta, x2+\Delta, y2+\Delta)$ is generated for matched ball region $(x1, y1, x2, y2)$, where $(x1, y1)$ and $(x2, y2)$ are the top-left coordinates and the bottom-right coordinates of the matching region, respectively. The same method in section 2.1 is used to extract object and formula (2) is used to evaluate whether it is a ball. If ball is detected, the template is updated. The number of consecutive missing detections is counted, and if it is larger than a predefined threshold (say 5), the ball detection procedure is run again.

4 Experiments

The proposed scheme is tested on several video clips containing video frames varying from 200 to 1000, with each being MPEG-2 compressed with the resolution of 352×288 at 25 frames per second recorded from TV. Our test video clips are all long

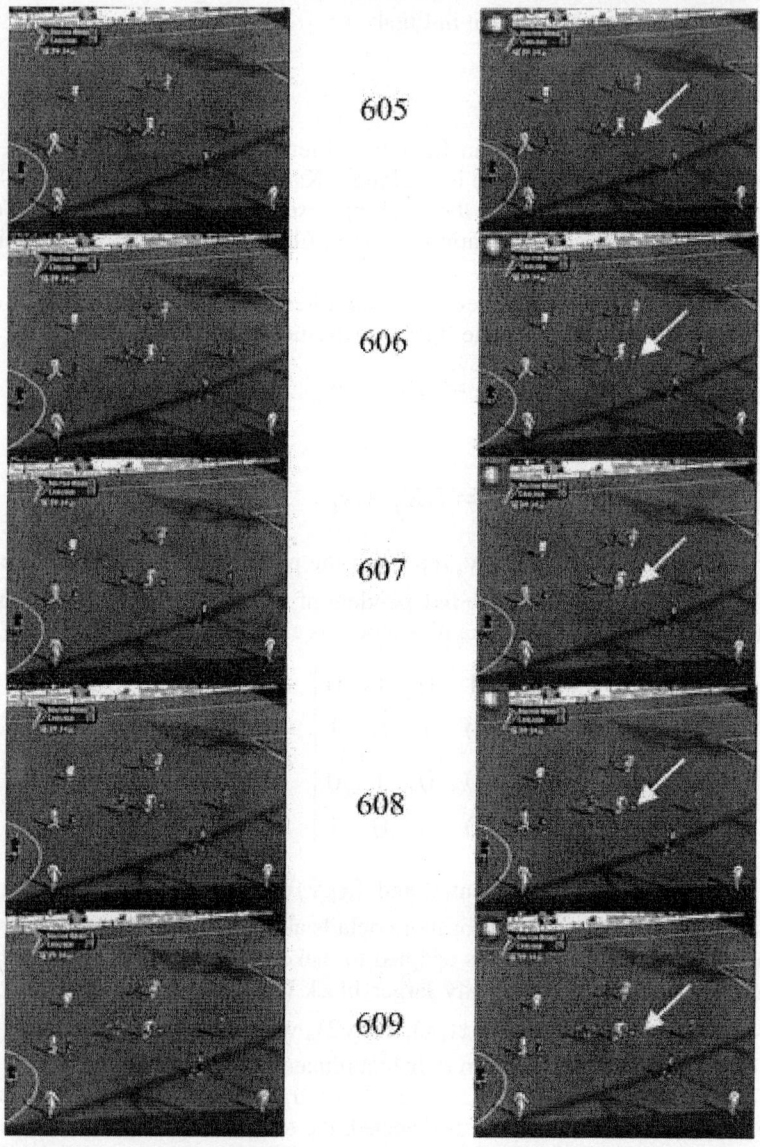

Fig. 5. The ball detection results from frame 605 to 609. In the left column, ball candidates are marked with red rectangle. Extracted ball locations using Viterbi algorithm are shown in the right column with a white arrow indicating the ball's location in each image. The ball is also enlarged and shown on the top left corner of each image to make it seen clearly. The frame number is shown in the middle column.

view shots, since tracking the soccer ball in close-up shots seems to be meaningless for soccer video analysis. In all of the experiments we set $T = 5, d_{max} = 20$.

4.1 Ball Detection

Fig. 5 shows some experimental results of the ball detection procedure. In the left column, ball candidates are marked with red rectangle. In the right column, extracted ball

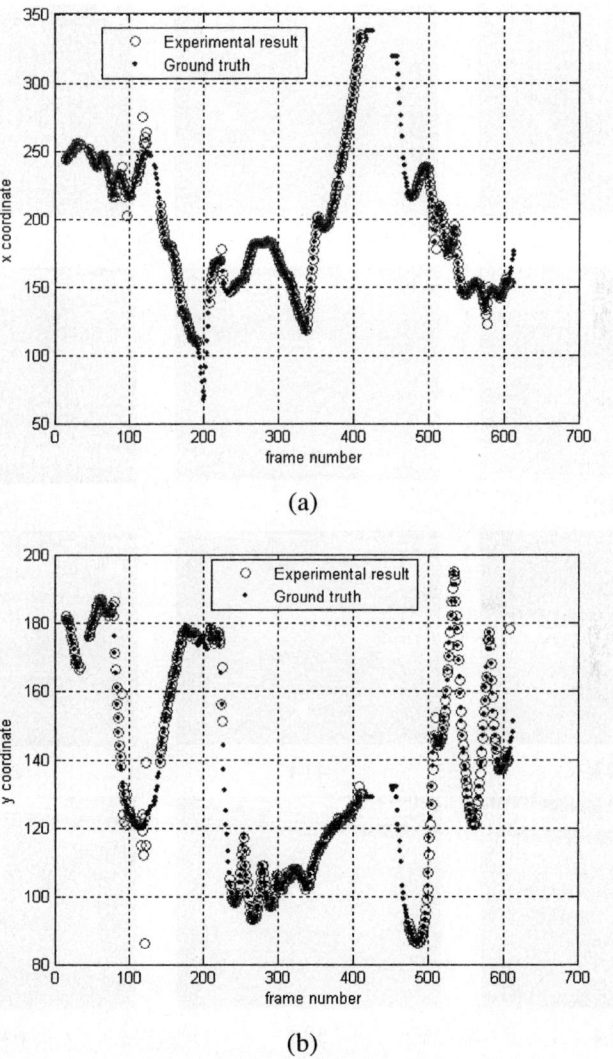

Fig. 6. Ball detection and tracking results on a video sequence with 650 frames. Experimental results are shown in red circle. The ground truths are marked with blue dot. (a) The x-coordinate (in image plane). (b) The y-coordinate (in image plane).

locations based on Viterbi algorithm are also marked with red rectangle with a white arrow indicating the ball's location in each image. The ball is also enlarged and shown on the top left corner of each image to make it seen clearly. Frame number is shown in the middle column. From the results, we can see that the objects that are most likely to be a ball are socks of the player, jersey number, line segments in the playfield and so on. Although so many objects are similar in appearance to the ball, the ball's locations are correctly obtained based on Viterbi algorithm using temporal information.

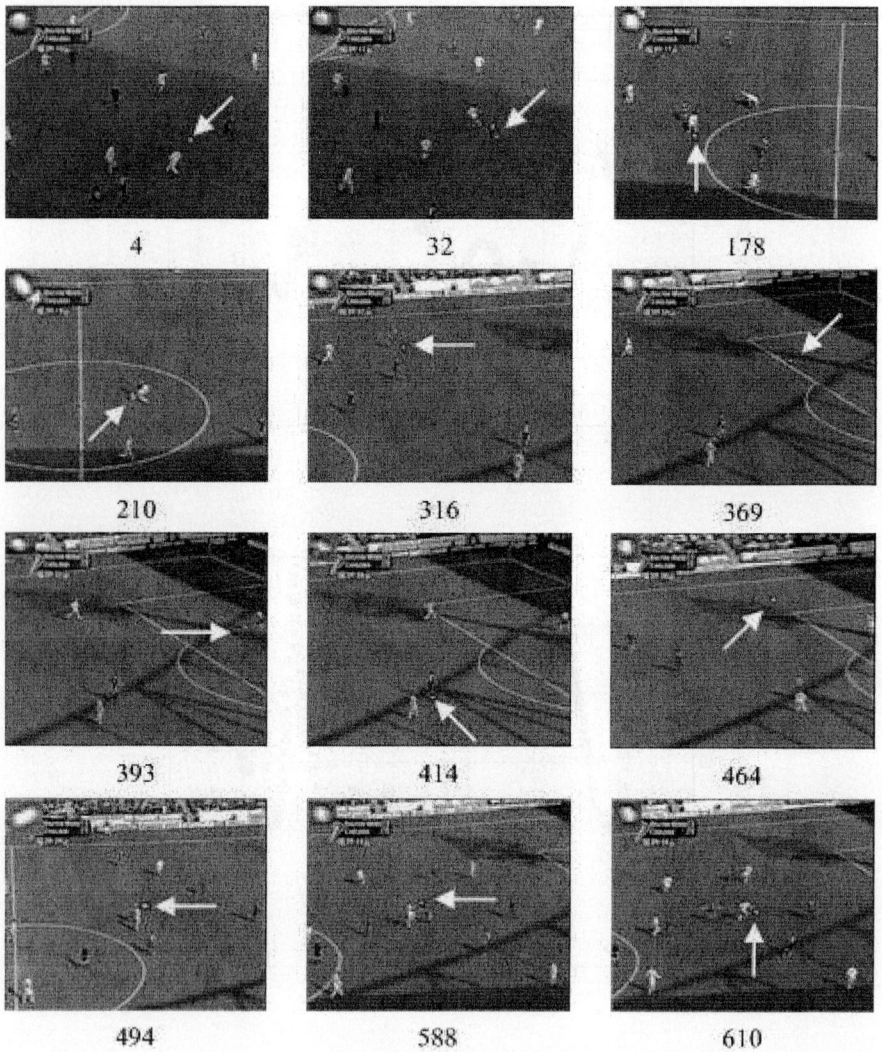

Fig. 7. Some video frames of ball detection and tracking results on a video clip with 650 frames (414 is a false positive)

4.2 Evaluation

Fig. 6 shows ball detection and tracking results on a video clip with 650 frames. The ball's true locations are marked manually on ball's centers. We say a frame contains a ball, if we can find it not depending on the adjacent frames. The experimental result can also be reached at http://www.jdl.ac.cn/user/dwliang/index.htm in video format. Fig. 7 provides some video frames in the process of soccer ball detection and tracking.

To better evaluate the scheme's performance, we did some statistics on two video sequences with each having more than 600 frames. Table 1 provides some statistics of the experimental results. *Precision* and *Recall* rate are used to quantitatively evaluate the experiments. In some clips, such as "sequence1-101-200", the recall rate is very low. This is mainly because that the ball is occluded by players, merged with lines and so on, which makes ball detection and tracking failure. In some clips, such as "sequnce1-401-500", the precision rate is very low. This is mainly because the ball is occluded, and the socks of the player or some line segments are most likely to be the ball. Since the assumption of our scheme is that the ball is nearly circular, our scheme can not deal well with the long blurred case. Nevertheless, from the table, we can observe that the overall precision and recall rate are acceptable.

Table 1. Some statistics of the experiments

Video sequences	Frame number	Ground truth	Experimental results			
		#ball	#detected & tracked	#false positive	Precision (%)	Recall (%)
Sequence1 (bad playfield)	1-100	88	67	2	97.0	73.9
	101-200	92	53	0	100	57.6
	201-300	99	97	10	89.7	87.9
	301-400	97	97	3	96.9	96.9
	401-500	80	62	20	67.7	52.5
	501-600	96	92	5	94.6	90.6
	601-650	48	45	13	71.1	66.7
	total	600	513	53	89.7	76.7
Sequence2 (good playfield)	1-100	92	93	8	91.4	92.4
	101-200	100	99	3	97.0	96
	201-300	94	95	11	88.4	89.4
	301-400	81	71	23	67.6	59.3
	401-500	64	39	3	92.3	56.2
	501-600	82	84	10	88.1	90.2
	601-700	99	99	4	96.0	96.0
	701-719	19	18	3	83.3	78.9
	total	631	598	65	89.1	84.5

5 Conclusions and Future Work

In this paper we propose a scheme for ball detection and tracking in broadcast soccer video. Viterbi algorithm is used to extract the optimal path of a graph as the ball's locations to enhance the robustness of ball detection, and then a Kalman filter based tracker is initialized using the detection results. Since only a small portion of each frame is processed, the tracking procedure runs very fast. A simple but effective method is also employed to verify the ball's locations during tracking and to guide possible ball re-detection. Experimental results show that the scheme can work well even in bad playfield conditions. In future work, we will use the ball's trajectory with other information for high level semantics analysis.

Acknowledgements

This work is partly supported by NEC Research China on "Context-based Multimedia Analysis and Retrieval Program" and "Science 100 Plan" of Chinese Academy of Sciences.

References

1. Gong Y., Sin L. T., Chuan C. H., Zhang H. J., and Sakauchi M.: Automatic Parsing of TV Soccer Programs. In: Proceedings of Second International Conference on Multimedia Computing and Systems (1995) 167-174.
2. Yow D., Yeo B., Yeung M., and Liu B.: Analysis and Presentation of Soccer Highlights from Digital Video. In: Proceedings of Second Asian Conference on Computer Vision (1995) 499-503.
3. Seo Y., Choi S., Kim H., and Hong K.: Where are the ball and players? Soccer Game Analysis with Color-based Tracking and Image Mosaic. In: Proceedings of 9th International Conference on Image Analysis and Processing, vol.2 (1997) 196-203.
4. Ohno Y., Miura J. and Shirai Y.: Tracking Players and Estimation of the 3D Position of a Ball in Soccer Games. In: Proceedings of 15th International Conference on Pattern Recognition, vol.1, (2000) 145-148.
5. D'Orazio T., Ancona N., Cicirelli G., and Nitti M.: A ball detection algorithm for real soccer image sequences. In: Proceedings of International Conference on Pattern Recognition, vol.1 (2002) 210-213.
6. Yu X., Xu C., Leong H. W., Tian Q., Tang Q., and Wan K. W.: Trajectory-Based Ball Detection and Tracking with Applications to Semantic Analysis of Broadcast Soccer Video. In: Proceedings of ACM Conference on Multimedia, (2003) 11-20.
7. Tong X., Lu H., and Liu Q.: An Effective and Fast Soccer Ball Detection and Tracking Method. In: Proceedings of International Conference on Pattern Recognition, vol. 4, (2004) 795-798.
8. Intille S.S., Bobick A.F.: Closed-World Tracking. In: Proceedings of International Conference on Computer Vision (1995) 672-678.
9. Pingali G.S., Opalach A., and Jean Y.: Ball Tracking and Virtual Replays for Innovative Tennis Broadcasts. In: Proceedings of International Conference on Pattern Recognition, Vol. 4, (2000) 152-156.

10. Denman H., Rea N., and Kokaram A.: Content-based analysis for video from snooker broadcasts. Journal of Computer Vision and Image Understanding (CVIU) 92 (2003) 176-195.
11. Ye Q., Gao W., and Zeng W.: Color Image Segmentation using Density-based Clustering. In: Proceedings of International Conference on Acoustics, Speech, and Signal Processing, Vol.3, (2003) 345-348.
12. Peura M. and Iivarinen J.: Efficiency of Simple Shape Descriptors. In: Arcelli C. et. al. (Eds.) Advances in Visual Form Analysis, World Scientific, Singapore (1997) 443-451.
13. Rabiner L.R.: A Tutorial on Hidden Markov Model and Selected Applications in Speech Recognition. In: Proceedings of the IEEE, Vol. 77, No. 2, (1989).
14. Welch G. and Bishop G.: An Introduction to the Kalman Filter. Technical Report TR95-041. Department of Computer Science, University of North Carolina at Chapel Hill. (1995) http://www.cs.unc.edu/~welch/kalman/kalmanIntro.html

A Shape-Based Retrieval Scheme for Leaf Images

Yunyoung Nam[1] and Eenjun Hwang[2],*

[1] Graduate School of Information and Communication,
Ajou University, Suwon, Korea
yynam@korea.com
[2] Department of Electronics and Computer Engineering,
Korea University, Seoul, Korea
Tel.:+82-2-3290-3256
ehwang04@korea.ac.kr

Abstract. Content-based image retrieval (CBIR) usually utilizes image features such as color, shape, and texture. For good retrieval performance, appropriate object features should be selected, well represented and efficiently evaluated for matching. If images have similar color or texture like leaves, shape-based image retrieval could be more effective than retrieval using color or texture. In this paper, we present an effective and robust leaf image retrieval system based on shape feature. For the shape representation, we revised the MPP algorithm in order to reduce the number of points to consider. Moreover, to improve the matching time, we proposed a new dynamic matching algorithm based on the Nearest Neighbor search method. We implemented a prototype system and performed various experiments to show its effectiveness. Its performance is compared with other methods including Centroid Contour Distance (CCD), Fourier Descriptor, Curvature Scale Space Descriptor (CSSD), Moment Invariants, and MPP. Experimental results on one thousand leaf images show that our approach achieves a better performance than other methods.

1 Introduction

Recently, many researchers have proposed and developed methods of content-based image retrieval using image features such as image color, shape, texture, and spatial relationship. In particular, shape-based image retrieval has received efficient and interesting approach. So far, shape recognition methods have been proposed and implemented into face recognition, iris recognition, and fingerprint recognition. Nevertheless, if images contain similar color or texture, shape-based image retrieval method is more effective than other methods using color or texture. For instance, leaves of most plants are green or brown; but the leaf shapes are distinctive and thus can be used for identification.

Like typical content-based image retrieval, shape-based image retrieval consists of three steps. The first step is to detect edge points. Among the existing edge detection methods [1] [2], we use Canny Edge Detection method [3]. The next step is to represent shapes in such a way that it is invariant to translation, rotation, scale, and viewing

---
* Corresponding author.

angle changes. The last step is shape matching that determines how similar shapes are to a given query. The overall retrieval process is illustrated in Fig. 1.

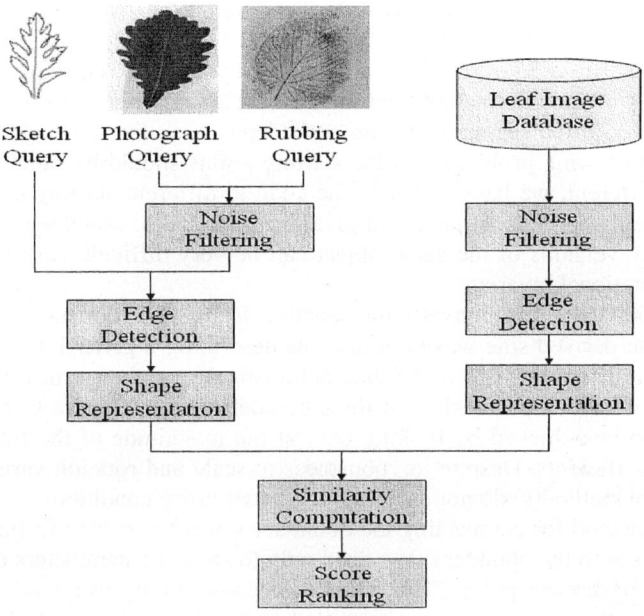

Fig. 1. Overview system

In general, shape representations are classified into two categories: boundary-based and region-based. The former describes a region of interest using its external characteristics [4] (i.e. the pixels along the object boundary) while the latter represents a region of interest using its internal characteristics [1] (i.e. the pixels contained in the region). We choose the external representation since the primary focus is on shape characteristics such as length of boundary, orientation of straight line, joing the extreme points, or number of concaves. For the internal representation, we use a methodology based on the "skeleton" of a shape. In this paper, we use MPP (Minimum Perimeter Polygons) [5-7] for shape representation. MPP is a polygonal approximation method to identify curvature descriptions [8] [9], but it only uses outside boundary of the strip of cells. Nevertheless, it takes long time to retrieve images due to many unnecessary points to consider. In order to solve this problem, we propose a new shape representation method that is based on our improved MPP.

Another important issue of shape-based image retrieval is the effective shape matching method on which the retrieval performance heavily depends. There are several approaches to solving the matching problem. In this paper, we develop a dynamic shape-matching algorithm with the intention to reduce matching time

The rest of this paper is organized as follows. Section 2 describes several shape representation methods. In section 3, we introduce how to segment images and section 4 presents image matching and retrieval. In section 5, some of the experimental results are presented and finally the last section concludes the paper and discusses future work.

2 Shape Representation

Shape-based image retrieval includes edge detection, shape representation and shape matching. In this section, we briefly describe some of the shape representation methods: chain codes [10], Fourier transform [11], and MPP.

Chain codes are used to represent a boundary by a connected sequence of straight-line segments of specified length and direction. This representation is based on 4- or 8- connectivity of the segments. Chain code depends on the starting point, but chain codes have following problems: (i) the starting points should be same. If the starting points are different, we have to rotate the code to different starting points. (ii) Even minor difference in the contour could give different codes. Matching chain codes for slightly noisy versions of the same object can be very difficult. (iii) The representation is not rotational invariant

The Fourier transform converts the function from space domain to frequency domain with the derived sine wave coefficients describing a given 1-D function. While the transform achieves scale invariance automatically, a change in rotation angle of the shape results in a phase shift of the sine coefficients. Therefore, rotation invariance can also be achieved by looking only at the magnitude of the frequency of the frequency coefficients. Despite its robustness to scale and rotation variance, the Fourier transform method(s) do not perform well under noisy conditions.

Another method for compacting the boundary information is to fit line segments or other primitives to the boundary. We need only to store the parameters of these primitives instead of discrete points. This is useful because it reduces the effects of discrete pixelization of the contour.

A boundary can be approximated with arbitrary accuracy by a polygon. In case of a closed curve, the approximation is exact when the number of segments in the polygon is equal to the number of points in the boundary, so that each pair of adjacent points defines a segment in the polygon. MPP is a method for defining curvatures when a change of the slope occurs with the control points approximately uniformly spaced along the curvatures. However, since MPP may include unnecessary points, there is a possibility of low performance for shape matching. In this paper, we improve the MPP algorithm for more effective representation.

Algorithm 1. MPP algorithm

```
1. Obtain the cellular complex.
2. Obtain the region internal to the cellular com-
   plex.
3. Use function boundaries to obtain the boundary of
   the region in step 2 as a 4-connected, clockwise
   sequence of coordinates.
4. Obtain the Freeman chain code of this 4-contected
   sequence using function fchcode.
5. Obtain the convex (black dots) and concave (white
   dots) vertices from the chain code.
6. Form an initial polygon using black dots as ver-
   tices, and delete from further analysis any white
   dots that are outside this polygon.
```

7. Form a polygon with the remaining black and white dots as vertices.
8. Delete all black dots that are concave vertices.
9. Repeat steps 7 and 8 until all changes cease, at which time all vertices with angles of 180° are deleted. The remaining dots are the vertices of the MPP

Fig. 2 shows examples of executing MPP algorithm for two leaf images. (a) and (e) are original images, (b) and (f), (c) and (g), (d) and (h) are results respectively when cell size is 2, 3, 5.

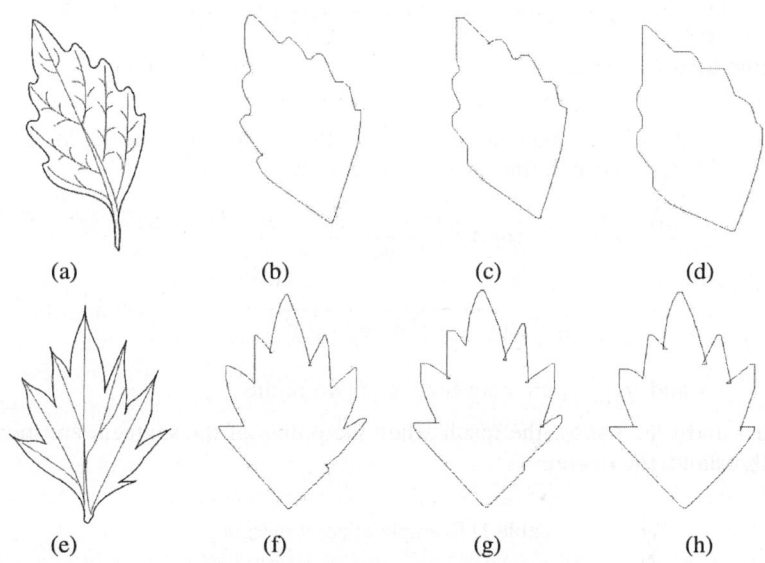

Fig. 2. Image segmentation using MPP

3 Image Segmentation

Image segmentation decomposes an image into regions that correspond to objects. It is an essential preliminary step in most automatic pattern recognition and image analysis process. As mentioned in section 2, shape feature depends on a good image segmentation that results in segmented objects. In this paper, we segment images using boundaries between regions based on discontinuities in gray levels.

MPP algorithm produces convex points and concave points depending on the angle between two points. Therefore, when an image contains plenty of straight lines along the boundary, segmentation may include useless points. To condense these points, we have merged points along boundary if the angle exceeds some threshold as shown in Algorithm 2.

Algorithm 2. Point merging

```
Input:     point : (X, Y) coordinates;
           N : the number of points;
           threshold : specific angle value;

function find_sequence(point, N, threshold){
    for (i=0; i<N; i++){
        a=get_distance(point[i-1], point[i+1]);
        b=get_distance(point[i], point[i-1]);
        c=get_distance(point[i], point[i+1]);
        angle=acos((b^2+c^2-a^2)/(2*b*c));
        if(angle < threshold)
            add_point(result, point[i]);
    }
    return result;
}
```

In this algorithm, a, b, and c are the sides of the triangle. Let the angle opposite the side c be A. Then, we can define cosine A as follows:

$$\cos A = \frac{b^2 + c^2 - a^2}{2bc} \qquad (1)$$

$$a = \sqrt{(x_j - x_i)^2 + (y_j - y_i)^2} \qquad (2)$$

where (x_i, x_j) and (y_i, y_j) are coordinates of two points.

Table 1 and Fig. 3 show the result when the points of the segment are merged using the threshold 160 degree.

Table 1. Example of point merging

Point i	X_i	Y_i	angle(°)	action
0	51	16	108	
1	55	16	108	
2	60	31	176	merging
3	65	51	180	merging
4	70	71	166	merging
5	70	85	135	
6	65	90	135	
7	41	90	135	
8	36	85	135	
9	36	71	166	merging
10	41	51	180	merging

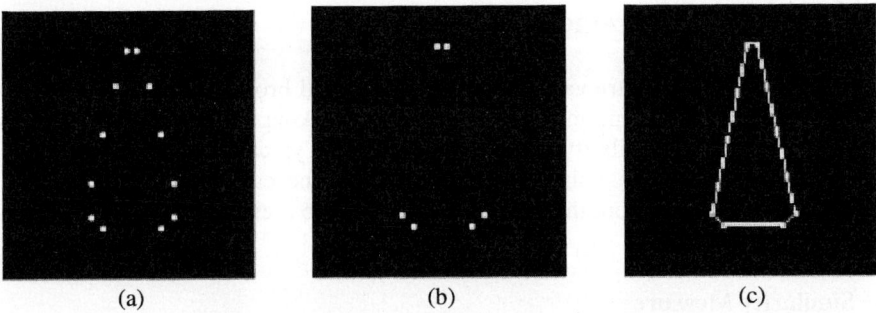

Fig. 3. Image segmentation using point merging

For the invariance, we adjust angles with respect to the longest distance between two points, and then detect left, right, top, bottom points for scale invariance as shown in Algorithm 3. Fig. 4 shows the steps to adjust the original image.

Algorithm 3. Adjustment algorithm

```
Input: crt_1, crt_2 : two points of criterion

function rotating_point (point, N, crt_1, crt_2){
  cos=(crt_2[X]-crt_1[X])/get_distance(crt_1, crt_2);
  sin =sqrt(1- cos^2);
  for (i=0; i<N; i++){
      point[i][X]= cos*(point[i][X]-crt_1[X])+sin*
         (crt_1[Y]- point[i][Y])-crt_1[X];
      point[i][Y]= sin*(point[i][X]-crt_1[X])-cos*
         (crt_1[Y]-point[i][Y])- crt_1[X];
      if(crt_1[Y]<=point[i][Y])
          add_point(result,point[i])
  }
  return result;
}
```

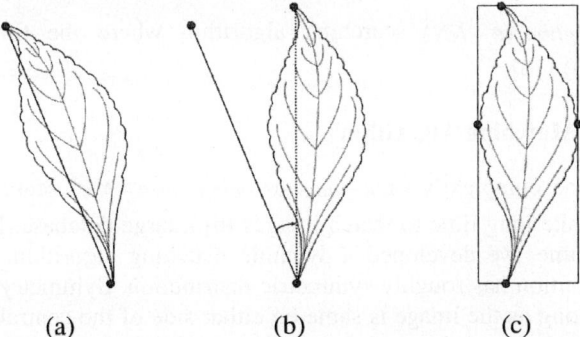

Fig. 4. Image Adjustment based on viewing angle and scale. (a) Original image, (b) Rotational adjustment, and (c) 4-edge points detection for scale invariance.

4 Similarity Measurement and Matching

The final step of image retrieval is image matching and browsing. In this section, we present an efficient dynamic matching method for ranking all database objects in an approximate order of similarity to the query object. Typically, a similarity query is defined as finding the most similar data objects. In the case of image databases, a similarity query is to find out the most similar images to a given image with respect to the features.

4.1 Similarity Measure

After extracting points of interest from images, we perform shape matching to measure the similarity between images. Generally, similarity between two objects is measured by simply evaluating the Euclidean distance [12] between each object's points. Accordingly, the distance between two images can be calculated by the following equation.

$$D(U,V) = \sqrt{\sum_{i=1}^{k}(u_i - v_i)^2} \qquad (3)$$

where U and V are the query and database image, respectively, and u_i and v_i are their i_{th} features, respectively, and k is dimension of the feature space.

According to the Euclidean distance, we can also evaluate similarity between query and database image using the following equation.

$$S(U,V) = \frac{1}{|u|}\sum_{i=1}^{|u|}\min(D_i(u,v)) \qquad (4)$$

where $|u|$ is the number of points of interest extracted from the query image_and $\min(D_i(u,v))$ is the minimum distance between u_i and v_i.

If we use the brute-force algorithm, the time complexity T is $O(|u\|v|) = O(n^2)$ to search the shortest path between u_i and v_i. For the linear time complexity, we use $\varepsilon-nearest\ neighbor(\varepsilon-NN)$ searching algorithm where the time complexity is O(Dpolylog(N)) [13].

4.2 Dynamic Matching Algorithm

Though the time complexity of $\varepsilon-nearest\ neighbor(\varepsilon-NN)$ searching algorithm is linear, it may take long time to match images for a large database. In order to reduce the matching time, we developed a dynamic matching algorithm. The general leaf shape of distribution has roughly symmetric distribution. Symmetry can occur in any orientation as long as the image is same on either side of the central axis. The axis of symmetry is vertical and this makes a good model for symmetry in visual information._Using this property, the matching scope on the shape can be reduced by 1/2×1/2=1/4 times with respect to full matching. Moreover, the matching process may stop when the accumulated similarity value is beyond the threshold.

Even the improved MPP algorithm can produce many points of interest for complicated images. To solve this problem, we created a function called *SMP* based on the sampling methodology. Let $|u|$ and $|v|$ be the number of points of interest extracted from the query image and database image, respectively. If $|u|$ is less than $|v|$, the number of interest points can be reduced by $|v|/|u|$ when we use $SMP(v)$ function. Algorithm 4 below describes the dynamic matching algorithm.

Algorithm 4. Dynamic matching algorithm

```
function dynamic_matching(input_image, db_image, N,
threshold){
   input_point=condensing_point(input_image);
   db_point=condensing_point(db_image);
   if(sizeof(input_point) < sizeof(db_point))
      SMP(db_point);
   for (i=0; i<N/2; i++){
      NN_point=NN_search(input_point[i], db_point);
      Sim = S(input_point[i], NN_point, N/2);
      if(Sim > threshold) {
         Sim = -1;
         break;
      }
   } return result;
}
```

5 Experiments

We have implemented a prototype shape-based leaf image retrieval system as part of a nationwide project that aims to develop an information bank for all domestic aquaplants in Korea. In the experiments, we used PCs with Dual 2.8 GHz Xeon Processors and 1GB of RAM and Microsoft SQL Server 2000 as underlying DBMS.

In order to show the effectiveness of our proposed algorithm, we compare it with other methods including Centroid Contour Distance (CCD), Fourier Descriptor, Curvature Scale Space Descriptor (CSSD), Moment Invariants, and MPP. In addition, we considered a hybrid-search scheme that uses not only leaf shape, but also leaf arrangement for better improvement. Fig. 5 shows a variety of leaf arrangements. We can classify them into alternate (a), opposite (b), and verticillate (c). While the alternate arrangement has one leaf per node, the opposite arrangement has two leaves per node and the verticillate has three or more per node.

The leaf arrangement of user-sketched image is identified by leaf base and the number of leaves per node. The leaf base indicates the shape of the leaf base where it attaches to the stem.

In order to evaluate its performance, we collected 1032 leaf images from "*The Korea Plant Picture Book*" [14]. The representation must be invariant to viewing angle change. For this reason, we adjust the viewing angle using Algorithm 2.

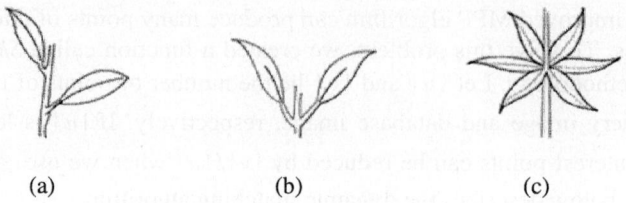

Fig. 5. Leaf arrangement. (a) Alternate, (b) Opposite, and (c) Verticillate

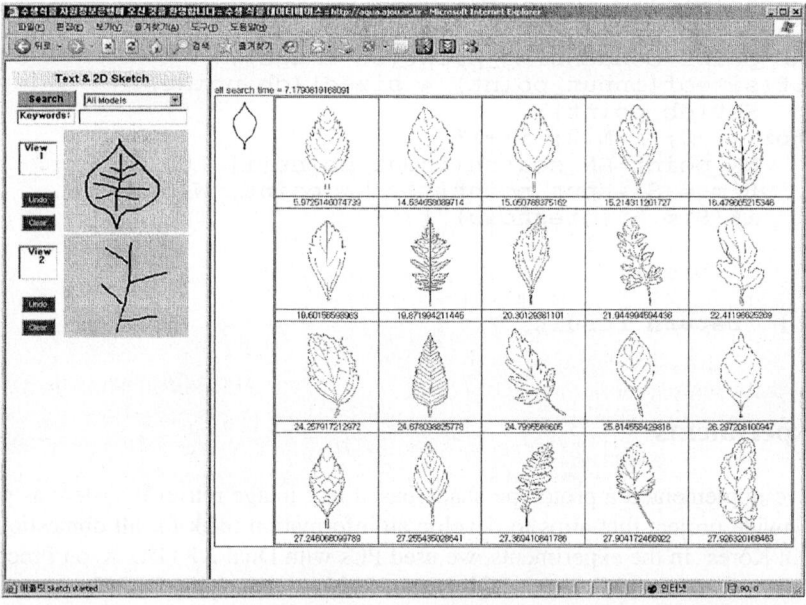

Fig. 6. User Interface

Fig. 6 shows the user interface on the web with sample sketch and its result. Fig. 7 shows the recalls and precisions of the revised MPP, MPP, Fourier Descriptor, CSSD, CCD, and Moment Invariants. Precision is the fraction of retrieved images that is relevant to a query. In contrast, recall measures the fraction of the relevant images that have been retrieved. Recall is a non-decreasing function of rank, while precision can be regarded as a function of recall rather than rank. In general, the curve closest to the top of the chart indicates the best performance.

In this figure, our proposed algorithm achieves approximately 25% better precision and recall than MPP. In addition, precision and recall of the proposed algorithm are 2.11 times better than that of Fourier Descriptor.

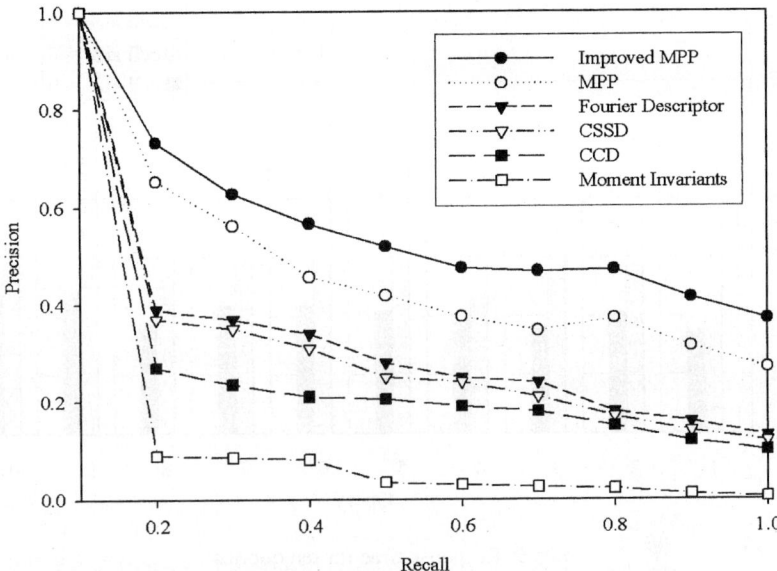

Fig. 7. Precision and recall

Fig. 8 shows ten query images and Fig. 9 shows the response time for ten queries. Table 2 illustrates the average response time of the NN-search and the Dynamic matching with different cell sizes. From the table, we can observe that regardless of matching method used, the response time is decreased as the cell size is increased. Overall, our proposed method achieved approximately 2.2 times faster response time than the NN-search.

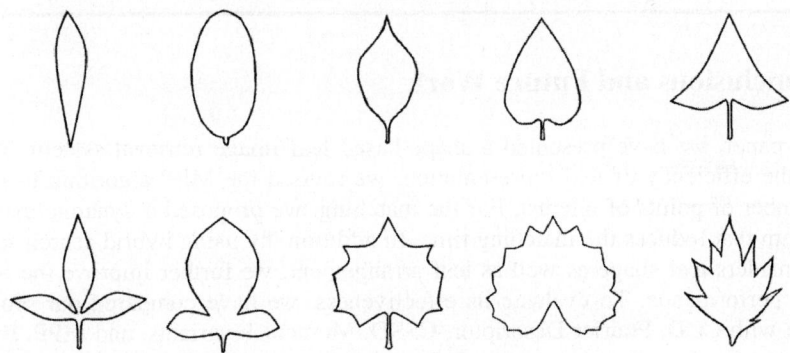

Fig. 8. Ten query images

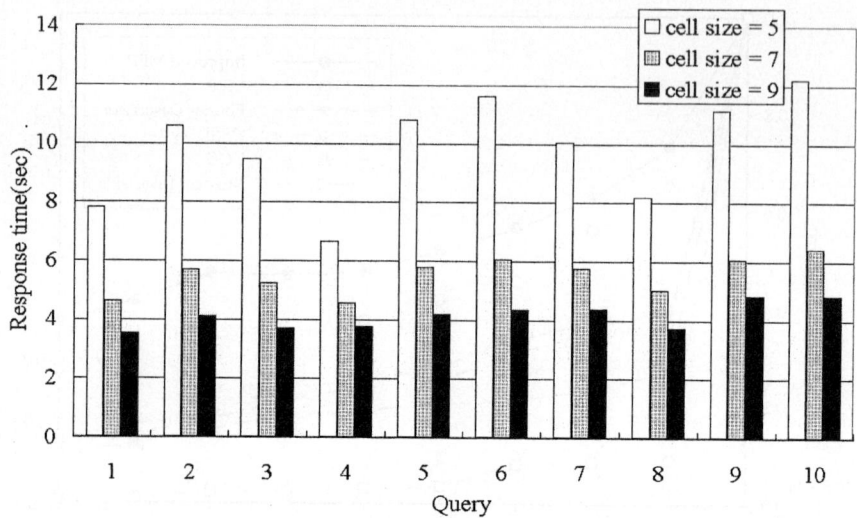

Fig. 9. Response time for ten queries

Table 2. Average retrieval response time in seconds

Cell size	Response Time		A / B
	NN-search (A)	Dynamic matching (B)	
5	29.57	13.57	2.18
7	16.58	7.26	2.28
9	12.45	5.80	2.15

6 Conclusions and Future Work

In this paper, we have presented a shape-based leaf image retrieval system. To improve the efficiency of leaf representation, we revised the MPP algorithm to reduce the number of points of interest. For the matching, we proposed a dynamic matching algorithm that reduces the matching time. In addition, by using hybrid-search scheme that considers leaf shape as well as leaf arrangement, we further improve the overall system performance. To evaluate its effectiveness, we have compared our proposed scheme with CCD, Fourier Descriptor, CSSD, Moment Invariants, and MPP. Experimental results show that the proposed algorithm is more efficient than other methods. In the future, we will improve an efficient shape representation algorithm that uses not only a contour but also a leaf vein.

Acknowledgments

This research was supported by the MIC (Ministry of Information and Communication), Korea, under the ITRC support program supervised by the IITA and a grant (no. BDM0100211) to JRL from the Strategic National R&D Program through the Genetic Resources and Information Network Center funded by the Korean Ministry of Science and Technology.

References

1. Gonzalez, Rafel C., Woods, Richard C.: Digital Image Processing. Addison-Wesley. (1992)
2. Lin, H. J., Kao, Y. T.: A prompt contour detection method. the Distributed Multimedia Systems (2001)
3. Michael Heath, et al.: A Robust Visual Method for Assessing the Relative Performance of Edge Detection Algorithms. IEEE Transactions on Pattern Analysis and Machine Intelligence, Vol.19. No.12. (1997) 1338-1359,.
4. Sundar, H., Silver, D., Gagvani, N., Dickinson, S.: Skeleton based shape matching and retrieval. Shape Modeling International. (2003) 130
5. Kurozumi Y., Davis W.A.: Polygonal approximation by the minimax method. Computer Vision, Graphics and Image Processing. (1982) 248-264
6. Sklansky, Chazin et al.: Minimum perimeter polygons of digitized silhouetts. (1972)
7. Sklansky J.: Finding the Convex Hull of a Simple Polygon. Pattern Recognition Letters, Vol.1 No.2. (1982) 79-84
8. Nishida, H.: Structural feature indexing for retrieval of partially visible shapes. Pattern Recognition, Vol.35. No.1. (2002) 55-67
9. Loncaeic, S.: A survey of shape analysis techniques. Pattern Recognition, Vol.31. No.8. (1998) 983-1001
10. Freeman, H., Saghri, J.: Comparative Analysis of Line Drawing Modelling Schemes. Computer Graphics and Image Processing, Vol. 12. (1980)
11. Chang, C., Wenyin, L. and Zhang, H.: Image Retrieval Based on Region Shape Similarity. Electronic Imaging Storage and Retrieval for Image and Video Databases (2001)
12. Veltkamp, R.: Shape matching: similarity measures and algorithms. Technical Report UU-CS-2001-03, Netherlands (2001)
13. Indyk, P., Motwani, R.: Approximate nearest neighbors: towards removing the curse of dimensionality. The 30 annual ACM symposium on Theory of computing, (1998) 604-613
14. Lee, C.B.: The Korea Plant Picture Book. ISBN-8971871954, Hang-moon-sa, (1982).
15. Petrakis, E., Diplaros, A. and Milios, E.: Matching and Retrieval of Distorted and Occluded Shapes Using Dynamic Programming. IEEE Transactions on Pattern Analysis and Machine Intelligence, Vol.24. No.11. (2002) 1501-1516
16. Choi, W., Lam K. and Siu, W.: An adaptive active contour model for highly irregular boundaries. Pattern Recognition, Vol.34. (2001) 323-331
17. Alt, H., Behrends, B. and Blomer, J.: Approximate matching of polygonal shapes. Ann. Math. Artif. Intell. Vol.13. (1995) 251-266
18. Wang, Z., Chi, Z., Feng, D., Wang, Q.: Leaf Image Retrieval with Shape Features. Lecture Notes in Computer Science, Vol.1929. (2000) 477 - 487
19. Mokhtarian, F., and S. Abbasi.: Matching Shapes with Self-Intersections: Application to Leaf Classification. IEEE Transactions on Image Processing, Vol.13. No.5. (2004) 653-661
20. The MathWorks - MATLAB and Simulink for Technical Computing http://www.mathworks.com

Lung Detection by Using Geodesic Active Contour Model Based on Characteristics of Lung Parenchyma Region

Chul-Ho Won[1], Seung-Ik Lee[1], Dong-Hun Kim[2], and Jin-Ho Cho[2]

Dept. of Control and Instrumentation Engineering, Kyungil University, Gyeongsan, Korea
School of Electronic Engineering and Computer Science,
Kyungpook National University, Korea
chulho@kiu.ac.kr

Abstract. In this paper, the curve stopping function based on the CT number of lung parenchyma from CT lung images is proposed to detect lung region in replacement of conventional edge indication function in geodesic active contour model. We showed that the proposed method was able to detect lung region more effectively than conventional method by applying three kinds of measurement numerically. And, we verified the effectiveness of our method visually by observing the detection procedure on actual CT images. Because lung parenchyma region could be precisely detected from actual EBCT lung images, we were sure that the proposed method could aid to early diagnosis of lung disease and local abnormality of lung function.

Keywords: Lung disease, CT images, geodesic active contour, early diagnosis.

1 Introduction

Today, respiratory diseases are increased by environment elements (eg. air pollution, smoking, etc) and customs. The symptom of lung's faculty is broken out earlier than morphological symptom in diffuse lung disease which the kinds are chronic obstructive pulmonary disease, interstitial lung disease, pulmonary edema, etc[1-2]. Chronic obstructive pulmonary disease breaks out airway obstruction and slows down airflow without symptoms of a lung disease and a heart trouble. This disease breaks out chronic bronchitis which annexes a cough and sputum, abnormal increase of pulmonary alveoli of terminal bronchiole, destroy of partition wall of pulmonary alveoli, decease of elastic recoil pressure, and aerobic respiratory obstruction. These lung diseases cause the change of real CT density in lung tissue. Therefore researches for classification between normal group and lung disease group using CT mean value in lung parenchyma area and quantitative histogram analysis about frequency distribution of CT density are gone recently[3]. For investigation of early detection of lungs alienation, passage chase, drugstuffs effect examination, etc exact detection of lung parenchyma area in lung image using quantitative measurement of lung parenchyma density and density distribution curve is very important.

Lungs contour detection method is used much by active contour model that consider form of interest area and identifying marks of reflex at the same time to detect serial lungs contour. active contour model can find boundary of object that want when do to minimize energy harmonizing internal energy and outside energy as there is balance and early basis model proposed by Kass [4] et al. But, because restriction condition that energy numerical expression should be differentiable and initialization problem affect this method, Amini *et.al*[5] proposed the method using dynamic programming, and greedy algorithm by Williams at al[6] was proposed. Although dynamic algorithm has high computational complexity and time complexity fairly, this is stable and Greedy algorithm has advantages of speed, flexibility and simplicity but has the problem of local solution because it doesn't take advantage of information of previous performance. Existing active contour models have problem that do not extract contour properly because contour can no longer progress inside concave surface area by internal energy when contour came to concavity region, and there is shortcoming that can detect only single object.

Lately, geodesic active contour model is introduced as snake model's geometrical alternative model by Caselles *et.al*[7-8], and is used much for object division by advantage that magic bullet of concave surface problem and detection of multiplex object are possible.

To converge a curve into contour of object, this paper proposes curve stopping function that is based on CT coefficient of area of lung parenchyma instead of used existing edge indication function. The proposed method was compared numerically using various measures and this method can detect better area of lung parenchyma than existing methods and detecting procedure of the area of lung parenchyma was visually verified in lung images.

From detecting the area of lung parenchyma exactly from real EBCT lung image using proposed method, several parameters are obtained by analysis of density distribution curve, and diffuse lung disease and improper functioning of local lung can be diagnosed at early stage.

2 Method

2.1 Geodesic Active Contour Model

Geodesic active contour model was introduced as snake model's geometrical alternative model by V. Caselles *et.al* [7] and derived from geometrical function of following equation (1).

$$S[C] = \int_0^{L(C)} g(C)ds \qquad (1)$$

where curve $C(s) = \{x(s), y(s)\}$ becomes parameter by Euclidian arc length s, and g as edge indication function in image Is spoken brake function because of the role that brakes progress of the curve for border detection of object. A value of this function is small value in edge area and big value in flat area. equation (1) like equation (2) is expressed by Euler Lagrange equation.

$$\frac{dC}{dt} = (g(C)k - <\nabla g, N>)N \qquad (2)$$

where N is normal, and kN is curvature vector.

To consider topological change of curve that progress, level set method that Osher and Sethian[9-10] proposed is used. Geodesic active contour model that expresses curve C using $C = \{(x, y): \phi(x, y) = 0\}$ with $\phi(x, y): \mathbb{R}^2 \to \mathbb{R}$ t is become equation (3) as level set equation's form.

$$\frac{d\phi}{dt} = div\left(g(x, y)\frac{\nabla \phi}{|\nabla \phi|}\right)|\nabla \phi| \tag{3}$$

And, equation (4) is become by including the weighted area minimization term that transforms edge indication function, and acts role that secure the fixed progress speed of curve.

$$\frac{d\phi}{dt} = \left(\alpha g(x, y) + div\left(g(x, y)\frac{\nabla \phi}{|\nabla \phi|}\right)\right)|\nabla \phi| \tag{4}$$

Curve C that express the border of object is derived from level set function and is updated as equation (5).

$$\phi_{t+1} = \phi_t + \left(\alpha g(x, y) + div\left(g(x, y)\frac{\nabla \phi}{|\nabla \phi|}\right)\right)|\nabla \phi| \bullet \nabla t \tag{5}$$

where the updated value of ϕ_{t+1} first is depended on $\alpha g(x, y)$ and, when cost of edge indication function is small indeed, that is, in position on border of object and background the value of ϕ_t decreases and change of curve is restrained. ϕ_{t+1} is affected by $div\left(g(x, y)\frac{\nabla \phi}{|\nabla \phi|}\right)$, which is depended upon cost of edge indication function. Under the small change of ϕ_{t+1}'s cost and deceased curve's progress in the border of object, the object is detected. Therefore, ingredient progress of curve is controlled and the contour of object is detected by edge element, which is appeared in the border of object.

2.2 Edge Indication Function

Edge indication function detects the contour of object and if the value of edge is big in the border of object, this function has small cost and the progress of curve is controlled. In equation (6), $|\nabla I(x, y)|$ is edge operation by the first differential operator, and if $|\nabla I(x, y)|$ is Increased in edge area that indicates the boundary of object, the cost of $g(x, y)$ is decreased and the progress of curve is controlled.[7-8][11]

$$g(x,y) = g(|\nabla I|) = \frac{1}{1+|\nabla I(x,y)|^P} \quad (6)$$

$$|\nabla I(x,y)| = |G_x(x,y)| + |G_y(x,y)| \quad (7)$$

where p is any constant, and equation (7) of edge operation is calculated by gradient operation of x, y in equation (8), (9).

$$G_x(x,y) = I(x-1, y-1) + I(x, y-1) + I(x+1, y-1) \\ - I(x-1, y+1) - I(x, y+1) - I(x+1, y+1) \quad (8)$$

$$G_y(x,y) = I(x-1, y-1) + I(x-1, y) + I(x-1, y+1) \\ - I(x+1, y-1) - I(x+1, y) - I(x+1, y+1) \quad (9)$$

Figure 1 shows detected border line by edge indication function of reference image. The color of the area of lung parenchyma is black and the color of muscle and tissue part is gray in reference image, and the area of lung parenchyma is displayed with gentle change of intensity in organization of the left side lungs top portion. According to repeat achievement, curve converges into the boundary of the area of lung parenchyma, but as see in figure 1 (b), curve is permeated into the interior of the area of lung parenchyma before division of right and left lungs area is completed. The area of imprecise change from muscular tissue into lung parenchyma partial volume effect by partial volume effect in real lungs CT image makes difficult to detect the area of lung parenchyma by edge indication function.

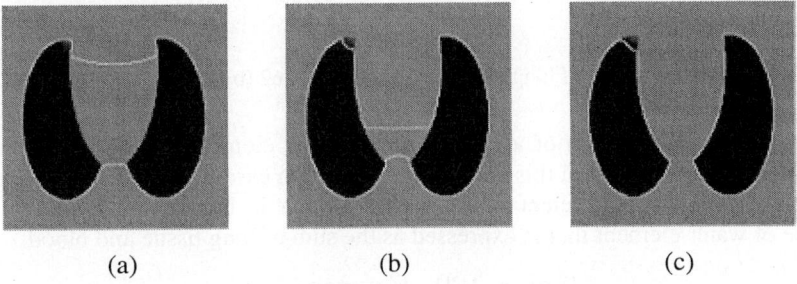

(a)   (b)   (c)

Fig. 1. The contour of detection process by direction function in reference image (a) first process (b) middle process (c) final process

3 Proposed Curve Function

3.1 Characteristic of Lung Parenchyma Area in CT Image

The coefficient of CT or Hounsfield becomes "0" in pure water, and becomes "-1024" in pure air. That of bone becomes about "+1024" in CT image. CT breast image of figure 2 shows muscle and skeleton brightly, and shows relatively darkly lung parenchyma area that has much air. Figure 2 also shows the coefficient of CT of each area of bronchus has near the value of CT coefficient of purity air,"- 1024", because each part of bronchus is empty space actually.

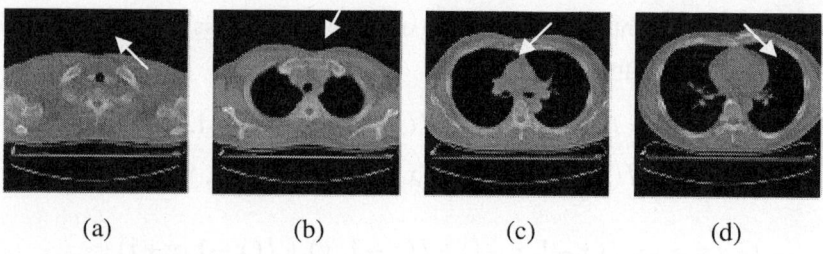

Fig. 2. CT coefficient of bronchus area (a) -963 (b) -965 (c) -965 (d) -988

Lung parenchyma area consists of pulmonary alveoli, and micro vessels are distributed in surroundings of pulmonary alveoli. Therefore, the main component of lung parenchyma is air, but CT coefficient of lung parenchyma is bigger value than "-1024" because lung parenchyma includes pulmonary alveoli and vein.

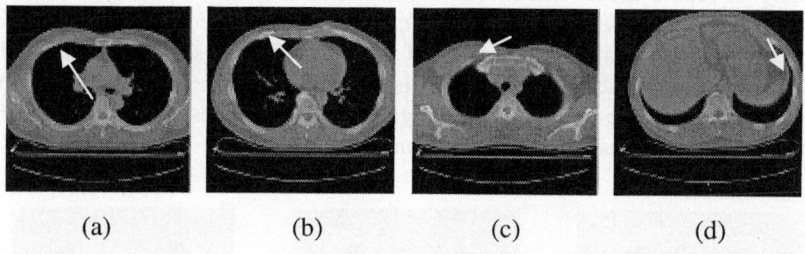

Fig. 3. CT coefficient of lung parenchyma area (a) -862 (b) -853 (c) -868 (d) -850

In equation (1), the sum of air element and water element is 100%, and element that extract water element in this sum is air element. In case of air, CT coefficient is "-1024", but real CT coefficient of lung parenchyma is bigger value than "-1024" because of water element that is expressed as the sum of lung tissue and blood.

$$\%air = 100 - \%water \qquad (10)$$

Figure 4 shows CT coefficients of lung parenchyma in each 200 type of CT lung image about lungs' upper part, middle part and lower part. Table 1 shows average value of CT coefficient of lung parenchyma in each area. Difference of average value of CT coefficient was not big in upper part, middle part and lower part, and the average value of whole lung parenchyma means the value including air, pulmonary alveoli, lung tissue, etc. this value is "- 849.86" as reference value to detect lung parenchyma area.

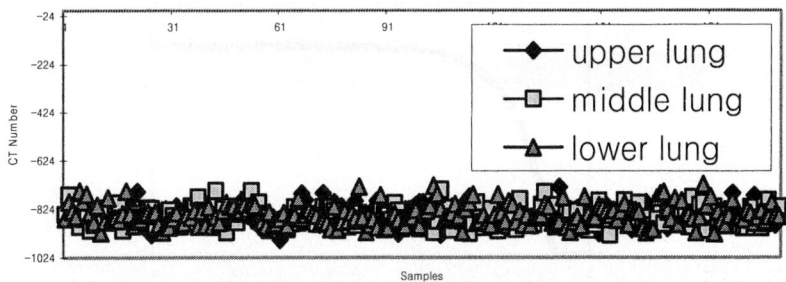

Fig. 4. CT coefficient of lung parenchyma area

Table 1. The average CT coefficient of lung parenchyme area in each part of lung

	Upper lung	Middle lung	Lower lung	Total
Mean	-849.39	-853.405	-846.77	-849.86
S. D.	38.05	36.59	42.179	39.01

3.2 Curve Stopping Function

Because existent edge indication function that detects the boundary of object and background is difficult to detection of lung parenchyma area, new curve progress function is proposed. Curve stopping function is proposed to calculate the average value of CT coefficient, and form of this function is equation (11), and Figure 6 shows this function is exponential function.

$$g(x, y) = 1 - e^{-(\mu(x,y) - \mu_{total})/\tau}, \mu(x, y) \geq \mu_{total} \quad (11)$$

$$\mu(x, y) = \frac{1}{N}\sum_{i=-1}^{1}\sum_{j=-1}^{1} I(x+i, y+i) \quad (12)$$

Where $\mu(x, y)$ is average intensity value of current pixel, and μ_{total}, the average CT coefficient of whole lungs, is "- 849.86", and is time constant of exponential function, and this is factor to control the degree of convergence of curve. In Figure 5, μ_{total} is (-859.86+1024)/2048 = 0.08.

If $\mu(x, y)$ is bigger than μ_{total}, $g(x, y)$ let the progress of curve be rapid. If $\mu(x, y)$ is near to μ_{total} or $g(x, y)$ is small value, has small value the progress of curve is decreased, and consequently curve does not invade into the interior of lung parenchyma.

$$If\ (\mu(x, y) \leq \mu_{total})\ then\ g(x, y) \approx 0, \phi_{t+1} \approx \phi_t \quad (13)$$

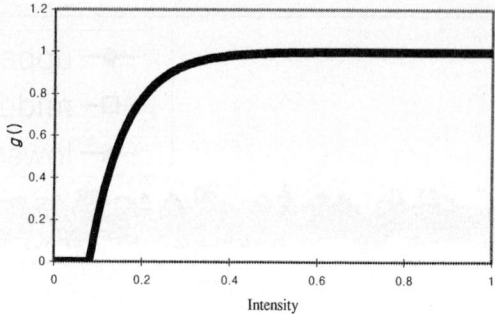

Fig. 5. Edge indication function

Figure 6(a) shows lung parenchyma area which has low value of CT coefficient, and also shows that muscle and tissue which are right and left of lung parenchyma area have big value of CT coefficient. Figure 6(b) shows $g(x, y)$ by change of intensity, and the more curve is approach lung parenchyma area, the more the value of $g(x, y)$ is decreased. the value of $g(x, y)$ is smallest value in lung parenchyma area. Therefore, if CT coefficient is similar to CT coefficient of lung parenchyma, the progress of curve is restrained, and curve is converged to lung parenchyma area, and contour of lung parenchyma is detected finally.

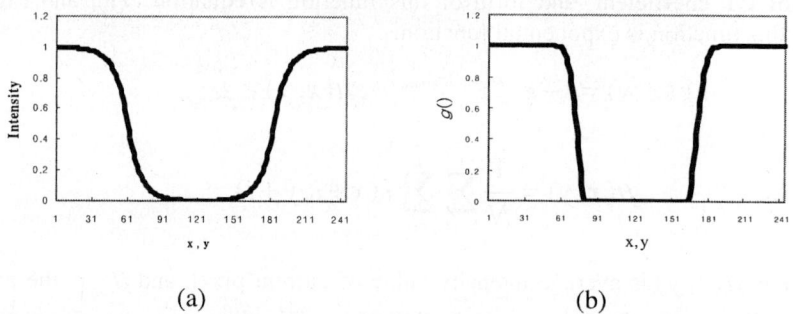

Fig. 6. (a) Curve of intensity in image (b) curve of intensity by edge indication function

4 Experimental Results

To verify effectiveness of contour detection method that uses proposed function, the proposed method was compared with existent methods. Root mean square E_{RMS}, mean absolute error E_{MAE}, and ratio of area R_{AREA} were used to verify this method. Effectiveness of proposed active contour model was verified numerically using three measures comparing points of reference contour with points of detected contour. Distance error root mean square E_{RMS} is equation (14).

$$E_{RMS} = \sqrt{\frac{1}{N}\left\{\sum_{i=0}^{N-1}(r(i)-c(i))^2\right\}} \qquad (14)$$

where N is number of points of relative contour and $r(i)$ and $c(i)$ is point of reference contour and relative contour, respectively. Average mean absolute error E_{MAE} is same with equation (15).

$$E_{MAE} = \frac{1}{N}\left\{\sum_{i=0}^{N-1}|(r(i)-c(i))|\right\} \qquad (15)$$

The cost of this equation is average difference between the coordinate value of reference contour's point $r(i)$ and coordinate value of relative contour's point $c(i)$. Figure 8 shows experimental result for verifying effectiveness of proposed method in reference image. Figure 7(a) shows the difficulty of multiplex object division in existing active contour model, and figure 7(b) shows that contour by edge indication function invades into the interior of lung parenchyma in the top of the left lung and figure 7(c) shows that the contour of lung parenchyma is detected effectively by using curve stopping function.

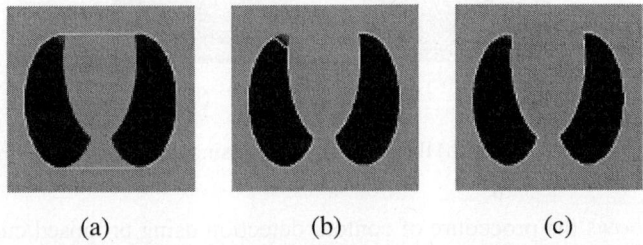

(a)　　　　　　　　(b)　　　　　　　　(c)

Fig. 7. The result of detecting Interest area from reference image (a) active contour model (b) edge indication function (c) geodesic active contour model using curve stopping function

Table 2 shows the detecting results of contour lung parenchyma by existing method and proposed method. E_{RMS}, E_{MAE} mean errors between reference contour and relative contour, and as these errors are small, this detection becomes more correct and as R_{AREA} is near to 1, detection also becomes more correct. We know that proposed model by curve stopping function has small error value than active contour model and edge indication function in E_{RMS} and E_{MAE}, R_{AREA} and becomes also near to 1.

From the initial curve of image 8(a), as procedure of contour detection processes, detected area of left lung parenchyma has more missing area, after 4100th repeat, left and right lung parenchyma area is separated from upper airway, but proper detection of left lung parenchyma area is not achieve[Figure 8 (b)]. Existent edge indication function makes irregular curve of right and left lung parenchyma, and the value of edge operation is decreased in boundary between lung parenchyma area and muscular tissue, and the value of edge indication function is increased. Consequently, existing edge indication function does not achieve faculty that restrains progress of curve in boundary.

Table 2. The measure's result of detecting contour by three methods

	Active contour	Edge indication function	Proposed function
E_{RMS}	11.69	1.24	0.43
E_{MAE}	6.63	0.68	0.18
R_{AREA}	1.65	0.94	0.99

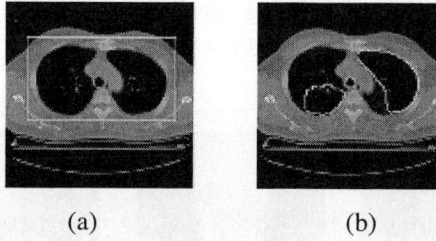

(a)   (b)

Fig. 8. (a) Initial contour (b) the result image by using edge indication function

Figure 10 shows the procedure of contour detection using proposed curve stopping function from initial contour of Figure 9(a). According as repetition is gone, curve is gone by lung parenchyma area from initial contour. In 1900th repeat, the contour of lung parenchyma area and bronchus is detected effectively, and Figure 9(b) shows the image that laps original image over detected contour.

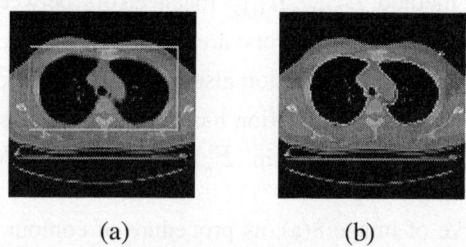

(a)   (b)

Fig. 9. (a) Initial contour (b) the result image by using proposed function

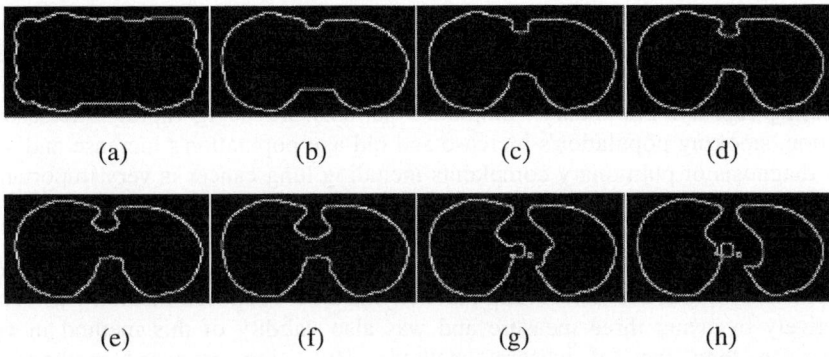

Fig. 10. The procedure of contour detection using proposed curve stopping function (a) 100 times (b) 300times (c) 500times (d) 700times (e) 900times (f) 1100times (g) 1300times (h) 1500times

Proposed contour detection method using curve stopping function is superior than existing methods in numerical comparison of Table 2 and visual comparison of Figure 8 and Figure 9. Figure 11 shows three dimension images are reconstructed by using lung parenchyma areas of 44 slices. Lung parenchyma area is detected by using proposed method. and 44 slices which size is 512 × 512 pixels are acquired from EBCT (electron beam Computer Tomography) equipment of Imatron Inc. 44 CT lung images in various angle show from upper airway to left and right lung parenchyma areas.

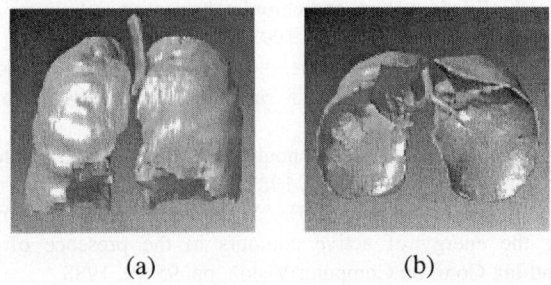

Fig. 11. Three dimension images of (a) front (b) bottom view

5 Conclusions

According to National Health Center data in 2002, the occurrence rate is order of rounds of stomach cancer (20.2%) lung cancer (11.9%) liver cancer (11.3%) large intestine cancer (11.2%) breast cancer(7.4%) thyroid cancer (4.9%) cervical cancer (4.0%) and so on and cancer mortality is order of lung cancer (20.2%) stomach cancer (18.7%) liver cancer (17.7%) large intestine cancer (8.1%) pancreas cancer (4.6%) esophageal cancer (2.4%) and so on. Standpoint to observe here is that the occurrence rate of several cancers related with sanitary conditions ,that is, stomach cancer, liver cancer, cervical cancer etc Is being decreased and the occurrence rate of several cancers involved with dietary life and environmental pollution (industrialization), that is, lung cancer, large intestine cancer, breast cancer, thyroid cancer ,etc. rapidly are being increased. Also, it is true that the mortality by lung cancer, large intestine cancer, cervical cancer and thyroid cancer that can be detected relatively easy early is decreasing rapidly. Pulmonary complaints patients are being rapidly increased by pollution, smoking population's increase and old age population's increase and so on. Early diagnosis of pulmonary complaints including lung cancer is very important for reducing mortality connected with lungs, and exact quantification for statistical data of lung parenchyma area from lung image by CT appliance is essential.

This paper proposed new curve stopping function that use intensity character of lung parenchyma area to detect lung parenchyma area. Proposed method was verified objectively by using three measure and was also validity of this method in visual comparison than that of existent methods. By using proposed method, lung parenchyma area is efficiently detected and by making breast CT image into third dimension image, diagnosis parameters of changes of intensity, volume, etc in lung parenchyma area can be made. This method is expected to be used usefully in early detection of pulmonary complaints, progress level and healing process trace.

Acknowledgement. This work was supported by grant No. R01-2005000101400 from the Basic Research Program of the Korea Science & Engineering Foundation.

References

1. W.L. Foster, E.I. Gimenez, and M.A. Roubidous, "The emphysema: radiologic-pathologic correlations," Radio Graphics. vol. 13, pp. 311-328, 1993.
2. J.C. Hogg,"Bronchiolitis in asthma and chronic obstructive pulmonary diseases," Clinics in Chest Medicine, vol. 14, pp. 733-740, 1993.
3. T. Beinert. J. Behr, and F. Mehnert, "Spirometrically controlled quantitative CT for assessing diffuse parenchymal lung disease," J Comput. Assist. Tomogr., vol. 19. pp. 924-931, 1995.
4. M. Kass, A. Witkin, and D. Terzopoulos,"Snakes: Active contour models," Int. j. Computer Vision, vol. 1, pp. 321-331, 1987.
5. A.A. Amini, S. Tehrani, and T.E. Weymouth,"Using dynamic programming for minimizing the energy of active contours in the presence of hard constraints," In Proc. Second Int. Conf. on Computer Vision, pp. 95-99, 1988.
6. D.J. Williams and M. Shah,"A fast algorithm for active contours and curvature estimation," Computer Vision, Graphic, and Image Processing: Image Understanding, vol. 55, no. 1, pp. 14-26, 1992.
7. V. Caselles, R. Kimmel, and G. Sapiro, "Geodesic active contours," International Journal of Computer Vision, Vol. 22, 61-79, 1997.
8. R. Goldenberg, R. Kimmel, E. Rivlin, and M. Rudzsky, "Fast Geodesic Active Contours," IEEE Transactions on Image Processing, vol. 10, no. 10, pp. 1467-1475, Oct. 2001.
9. S. Osher and J.A. Sethian, "Fronts propagating with curvature dependent speed: Algorithms based on Hamilton-Jacobi formulations," J. Comput. Phys.,vol. 79, 12-49, 1988.
10. J.A. Sethian, "Level Set Methods," Cambridge University Press, 1996.
11. M. Yano, "Boundary Detection with Geodesic Active Contours," Proc. of Distribute Multimedia Systems '99 Aizu-Wakamatsu, July 1999.

Improved Automatic Liver Segmentation of a Contrast Enhanced CT Image

Kyung-Sik Seo and Jong-An Park

Dept. of Information & Communications Engineering,
Chosun University, Gwangju, Korea
nmsu2@hanmail.net

Abstract. This paper presents an improved automatic liver segmentation method using a left partial histogram threshold (LPHT) algorithm. The LPHT algorithm removes other neighboring abdominal organs regardless of pixel variation of contrast enhanced computed tomography (CE-CT) images. After histogram transformation, adaptive multi-modal threshold is used to find the range of gray-level values of the liver structure. The LPHT algorithm is performed to removing other neighboring organs. Then, binary morphological filtering is processed to remove unnecessary objects and smooth the boundary. 48 CE-CT slices of twelve patients were selected to test the proposed automatic liver segmentation. As evaluation methods, normalized average area and area error rate were used. The results of experiments show similar performance between the proposed algorithm and the manual method by a medical doctor.

1 Introduction

Liver cancer is included in fifth main cancers such as lung, breast, colorectal and stomach in the world. It is more serious in eastern and southeastern Asia areas including western and central Africa [1]. The average incidence of liver cancer in this area is 20 per 100,000 and liver cancer is the third highest cause of death from cancer [1]. In Korea, the incidence of a liver cancer is quite high at 19% for male and 7% for female [2]. New cases of liver cancer in the Seoul area have an approximate rate per year as 34.1 for male and 11.5 for female per 100,000 people [2]. In the US, although liver cancer is not included as one of the four major cancers, roughly 20,000 new cases are diagnosed every year. Liver cancer makes up 1.5% of all cancer cases, and once contracted the five-year survival rates are very low, usually less than 10%. The incidence of liver cancer in Black and Hispanic populations is roughly twice that in Caucasians and the incidence of cancer in Vietnamese men is 41.8 per 100,000 people [3]. Prevention is by far the best way to reduce liver cancer as with other cancers. Besides prevention, the early detection and treatment of liver cancer is critical. If the liver is analyzed for early detection, treatment and curing may be easy and human life can be prolonged.

In order to segregate hepatic tumors, the first significant process is to extract the liver structure from other abdominal organs. Liver segmentation using CT images has been dynamically performed because CT is a very conventional and non-invasive technique. Lee extracted the liver using Co-occurrence matrix from CT as the automatic method [4]. Bae et al. used priori information about liver morphology and image processing techniques such as gray-level threshold, Gaussian smoothing, mathematical morphology techniques, and B-splines [5]. Gao et al. developed automatic liver segmentation using a global histogram, morphologic operations, and the parametrically deformable contour model [6]. Tsai proposed an alternative segmentation method using an artificial neural network to classify each pixel into three categories [7]. Also, Husain et al. used neural networks for feature based recognition of liver region [8]. Park et al. built a probabilistic atlas of the brain and extended abdominal segmentation including the liver, kidneys, and spinal cord [9]. Saitoh et al. performed automatic segmentation of liver region based on extracted blood vessels [10]. Seo et al. proposed fully automatic liver segmentation based on the spine [11].

Generally, in order to improve diagnosis efficiency of the liver, the CT image is obtained by contrast media. Hepatic contrast enhancement is dependent on the dose of contrast agent, which is propagated by the blood stream, and increases the attenuation value difference between normal liver parenchyma and tumors. This processing is known as contrast stretching of increasing the dynamic range of the gray levels when low-contrast images come from poor illumination [15]. In spite of this advantage of contrast media, pixel values of contrast enhanced CT (CE - CT) images acquired from the dose of contrast agent are randomly changed. It is hard to segment the liver structure. Also, the middle liver part has a problem to segregate the liver structure because of similar gray-level values of a pancreas in the abdomen. In this paper, an improved automatic liver segmentation method using a left partial histogram threshold (LPHT) algorithm is proposed for overcoming pixel variation of CE-CT images and removing the pancreas which is contact with liver.

In the following section, liver segmentation is performed regardless of randomness of CE-CT images using histogram transformation (HT), adaptive multi-modal threshold (AMT), LPHT, and binary morphological (BM) filtering. Also, we demonstrate experiments and their analysis. Finally, the conclusion will be given in the last section.

2 Improved Liver Segmentation

In this section, improved automatic liver segmentation of a CE-CT image is presented as shown in a block diagram of Fig. 1. Histogram transformation (HT) such as convolution and scaling is described to reduce histogram noise. The adaptive multi-modal threshold (AMT) method based on a piecewise linear interpolation is performed to find the range of gray-level values of the liver structure. Also, the left partial histogram threshold algorithm is proposed to remove neighboring other organs such as pancreas, spleen. Then, binary morphological (BM) filtering is processed for removing of small unnecessary objects and smoothing of the boundary using dilation and erosion.

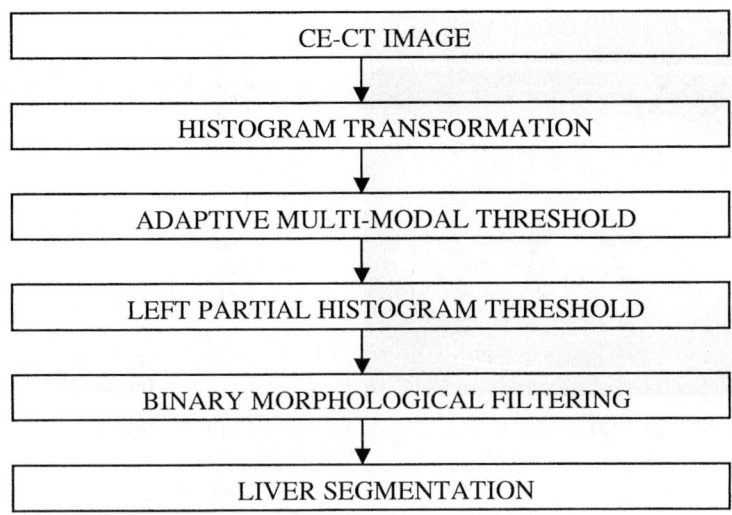

Fig. 1. Block diagram of improved liver segmentation

2.1 Histogram Transformation

In spite of the disadvantage of the pixel variation caused by the contrast enhancement, the CE-CT image gives an advantage of pixel enhancement. Pixel enhancement using a contrast medium comes from increasing the attenuation value of tissue difference between liver and other organs. Pixel variation provides a multi-modal histogram and creates easier segmentation of the histogram.

The histogram in pixel-based segmentation can be used simply to provide statistical information like mean, median, standard deviation, and energy. The histogram is a one-dimensional statistical transformation obtained by counting total pixel numbers for each gray level. Let $I: Z^2 \rightarrow Z$ be a gray-level CT image and (m,n) be a pixel location. Then, $I(m,n) \in Z$. The histogram, $h(k): Z \rightarrow Z$, is defined as [12]

$$h(k) = \{(m,n) \mid I(m,n) = k\} \qquad (1)$$

where k is a gray-level value.

The histogram has small noise to hinder multi-modal threshold. To reduce small noise, histogram transform such as convolution and scaling is proposed. A convolution method as one dimensional low pass filtering is used to smooth the histogram, even though the histogram's horizontal axis is extended and a vertical axis is very increased [13]. Then, the extended horizontal axis is scaled to gray-level values. Fig. 2 shows an example of histogram transformation. Fig. 2(a) is the CE-CT sample image. Fig. 2(b) is the histogram of the sample CE-CT image and Fig. 2(c) is the transformed histogram.

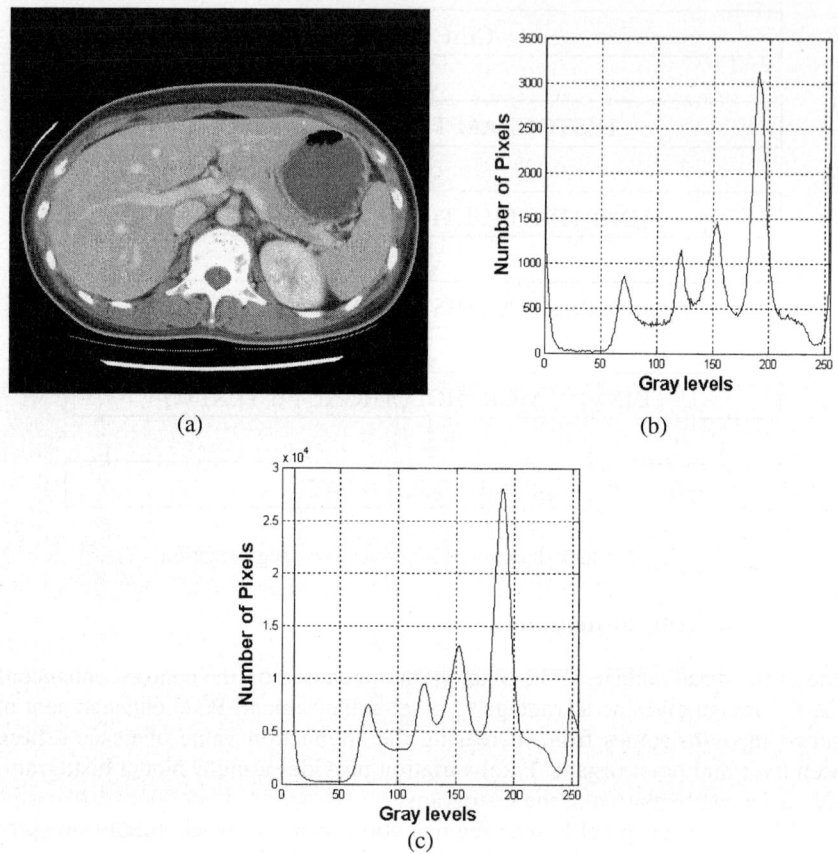

Fig. 2. Histogram transformation: (a) CE-CT image, (b) histogram of the CE-CT image, (c) transformed histogram

2.2 Adaptive Multi-modal Threshold (AMT)

For solving given pixel variation of a CE-CT image, an AMT method is used. The AMT method is processed regardless of histogram variation derived from the contrast enhancement. First of all, after removing the background, bones and extremely enhanced organs such as vessels, we find a global peak in the multi-modal histogram. The left and right valleys are calculated using a piecewise linear interpolation (PLI) method. The PLI method [14] calculates the slope as the line segmentation and its formula is given as

$$f_k = \frac{h_s(k+\gamma) - h_s(k)}{(k+\gamma) - k} \quad (2)$$

where γ is an integer.

Each valley may be founded at the turning point from a negative value to a positive value because each point represents the slope. Left and right valleys become one range of an object. Then, the extracted range is removed from the transformed histogram and this process is repeated until several ranges are found. The important range in this research is the range including gray-level values of the liver. The liver range is located experimentally in the right side of the histogram because of pixel enhancement of CE-CT images. The $ROI : Z^2 \to Z^2$ of the liver is defined as

$$ROI_{liver} = \{(m,n) \mid T_{liver\_l} \leq I(m,n) \leq T_{liver\_u}\}. \quad (3)$$

Fig. 3 shows the AMT method. Fig. 3(a) is the ROI after processing the AMT method and 3(b) is the ROI after removing small objects.

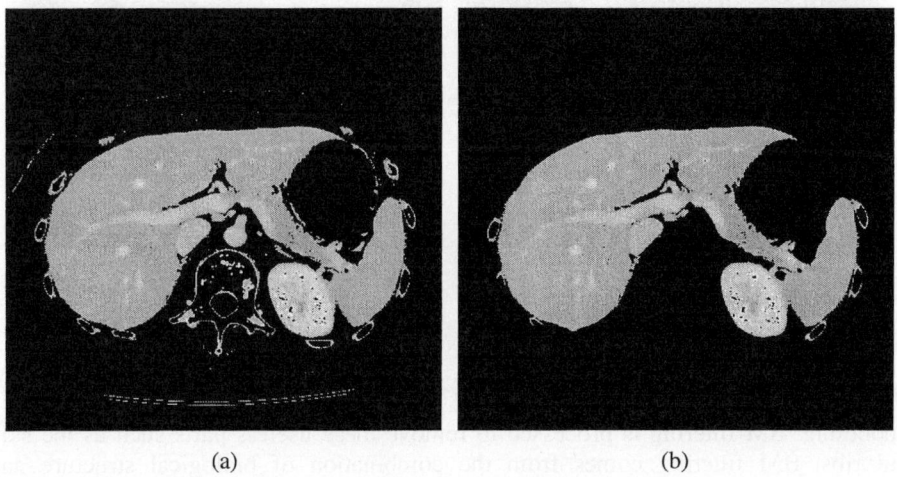

(a) (b)

Fig. 3. Adaptive multi-modal threshold: (a) ROI after AMT, (b) ROI after removing small objects

2.3 Left Partial Histogram Threshold

Left Partial histogram threshold (LPHT) is presented to remove the neighboring pancreas, spleen, and left kidney from the ROI. Let $I_{ROI} : Z^2 \to Z$ be the gray-level ROI. Then, $I_{ROI}(m,n) \in Z$. Let $h_{ROI}(k_1, k_2) : Z \to Z$ be the histogram of I_{ROI} with the range, $[k_1, k_2]$. Let I_{LHTT} be the LPHT image. Then the LPHT algorithm is proposed:

- Find k_{max} where k_{max} is the gray-level value when $h_{ROI}(k)$ is the maximum value.
- Calculate the left partial histogram interval $k_{LI} = (k_{max} - k_1)$.
- Find the left partial histogram threshold value $k_{LHTT} = (k_{max} - k_{LI} / \gamma)$ where γ is the integer value greater than 0.
- Create the LPHT image $I_{LHTT} = \{(m,n) \mid k_1 \leq I_{ROI}(m,n) \leq k_{LHTT}\}$.

Fig. 4 shows an example of the LPHT algorithm. Fig. 4(a) is the LPHT image and 4(b) is the difference image I_{diff} between I_{ROI} and I_{LHTT}.

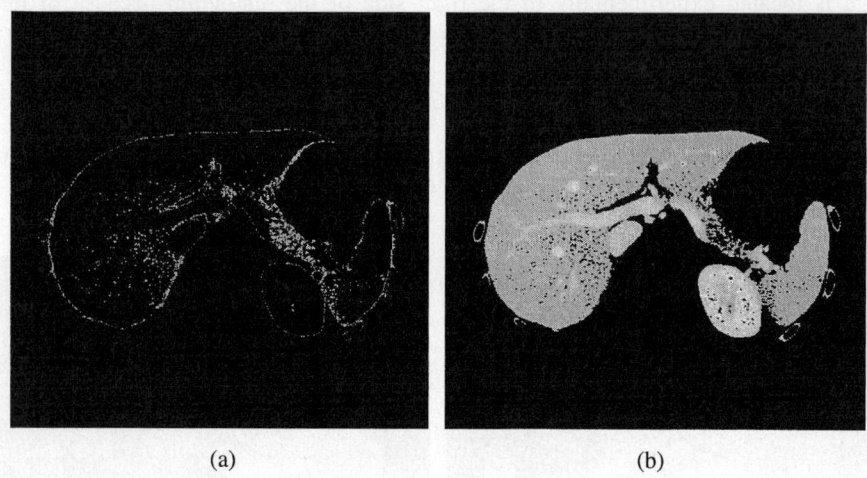

(a) (b)

Fig. 4. Left partial histogram threshold: (a) LPHT image, (b) difference image

2.4 Binary Morphological Filtering

The selected B_{liver} has BM filtering to help better segmentation and boundary smoothing. BM filtering is processed to remove these useless parts such as the skin and ribs. BM filtering comes from the combination of biological structure and mathematical set theories [15, 16]. The shape of a binary object is enhanced and transformed by various binary masks called structure elements. As this transformation is performed in Cartesian coordinates (x,y), spatial performance has a geometric relationship called connectivity [17]. BM filtering is used to combine B_{liver} with a structure element, SE, through various morphological operations. As the SE is the spatial mask, the 8-connected SE is used in this research. Let $SE_2 \subset Z^2$ be a 2 by 2 matrix that consists of 1 and $SE_3 \subset Z^2$ be a 3 by 3 matrix that consists of 1.

There are three main types of BM filtering which are dilation, erosion, and opening [13, 18]. Let $D: Z^2 \to Z^2$ be dilation and $D^i(B): Z^2 \to Z^2$ be iterative dilation (ID) to extend a region. Let $E: Z^2 \to Z^2$ be erosion and $E^i(B): Z^2 \to Z^2$ be iterative erosion (IE) to reduce a region. Let $OP: Z^2 \to Z^2$ be opening and $OP^i(B): Z^2 \to Z^2$ be iterative opening (IO) to smooth thin protrusions. Each filtering is defined as

$$D = \{B \oplus SE\} \qquad (4)$$

$$D^i(B) = \{...((B \oplus SE) \oplus SE)...) \oplus SE\} \quad (5)$$

$$E = \{B \ominus SE\} \quad (6)$$

$$E^i(B) = \{...((B \ominus SE) \ominus SE)...) \ominus SE\} \quad (7)$$

$$OP = \{B \circ SE\} = \{(B \ominus SE) \oplus SE\} \quad (8)$$

$$OP^i(B) = \{...((B \circ SE) \circ SE)...) \circ SE\} \quad (9)$$

where B is a binary input image and i is a iteration number.

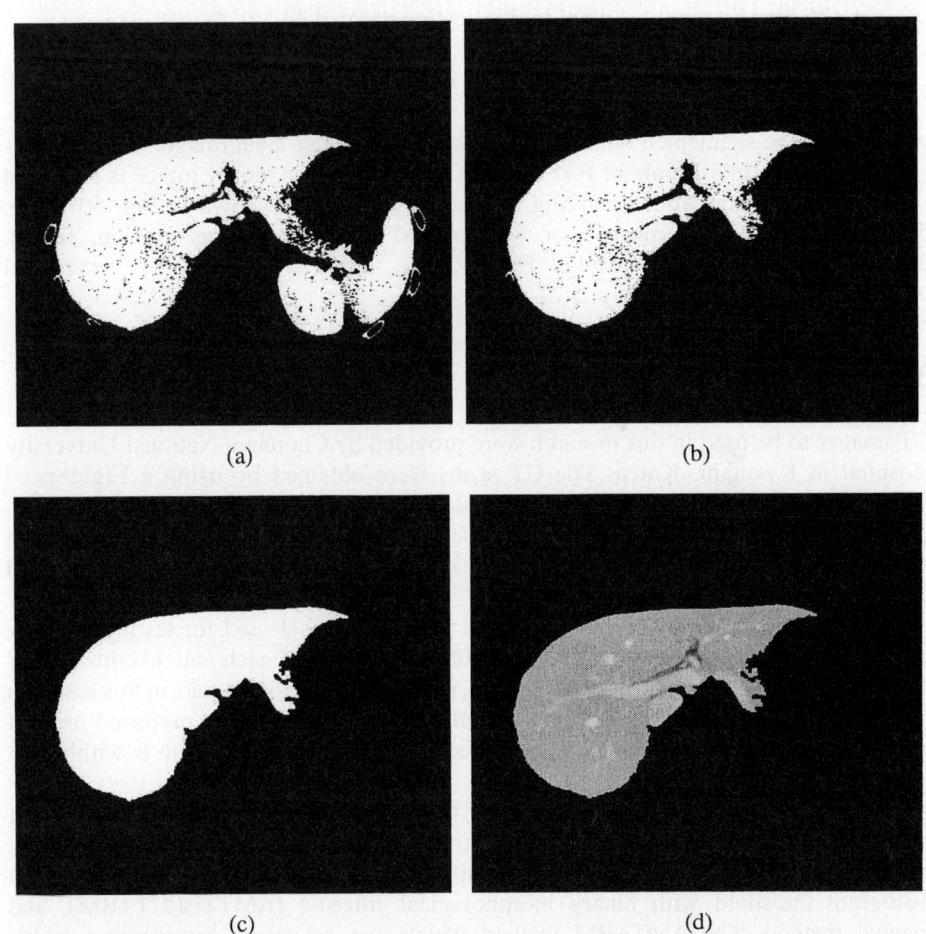

Fig. 5. BM filtering: (a) binary image B, (b) B after removing unnecessary objects, (c) image after various BM filtering, (d) gray-level liver

The combination of each filtering has a specific order because the combination order affects region reduction and expansion. Let $D^1(B) = D$, $E^1(B) = E$, $OP^1(B) = OP$, $D^i(B) = D^i$, $E^i(B) = E^i$, and $OP^i(B) = OP^i$.

Let $CO(B): Z^2 \rightarrow Z^2$ be an ordered combination function of BM filtering. $CO(B)$ used in this research is $\{OP, E, D\}$. In order to smooth the boundary, OP^{10} by SE_3 is first used. Then E^2 by SE_2 is performed to reduce the region and small regions such as the skin and ribs are removed. Also, D^2 by SE_2 is processed to reconstruct the reduction region.

The binary image obtained by BM filtering is transformed to the gray-level image. Let $I_{liver} \subset Z^2$ be a gray-level image. Assuming that B and I have the same size, I_{liver} is obtained by pixel-by-pixel multiplication defined as

$$I_{liver} = \{(m,n) \mid B(m,n) \otimes I(m,n)\} \tag{10}$$

where B is the segmented binary image and I is the gray-level image.

Fig. 5 shows an example of BM filtering processing. The binary image is shown in Fig. 5(a). The image after removing unnecessary objects is shown in Fig. 5(b). Fig. 5(c) show the binary image after various BM filtering such as erosion, filling, dilation, opening, and closing. Finally, the liver is created by gray-level transformation as shown in Fig. 5(d).

3 Experiments and Analysis

CT images to be used in this research were provided by Chonnam National University Hospital in Kwangju, Korea. The CT scans were obtained by using a LightSpeed Qx/i, which was produced by GE Medical Systems. Scanning was performed with intravenous contrast enhancement. Also, the scanning parameters used a tube current of 230 mAs and 120 kVp, a 30 cm field of view, 5 mm collimation and a table speed of 15 mm/sec (pitch factor, 1:3).

Twelve patients including one abnormal patient were selected for testing the new proposed method to segregate a liver structure. CT images of each patient consisted of 4 slices which were hard to segregate. Also, one radiologist took a part in this research in order to segregate the liver structure by the manual method. The proposed method was performed fully automatically and processing time per each patient is within two minutes.

In order to evaluate performance of the proposed algorithm, three different methods were compared such as adaptive multi-modal threshold with binary morphological filtering (AMT+BM), adaptive multi-modal threshold, left partial histogram threshold with binary morphological filtering (AMT+LPHT+BM), and manual method. The AMT+BM method which was processed by adaptive multi-modal threshold and binary morphological filtering was called to the automatic segmented method 1 (ASM 1). As the newly proposed method, the AMT+LPHT+BM method processed by AMT, LPHT, and BM was called to the automatic segmented method 2 (ASM 2). Also, the manual segmented method (MSM) drawn by a radiologist was used for a criterion.

Table 1 shows the normalized average area (NAA) segmented by each method. That is, the segmented liver area of each patient were averaged and normalized by the image size. From the results of this comparison, the ASM 2 including the PHT algorithm has almost same area as the MSM than the ASM 1. Also, as the average NAA of ASM 1, 2, and MSM is 0.1869, 0.1529, and 0.1579 respectively. The NAA difference between ASM 2 and MSM is very small but ASM 1 is relatively larger than MSM.

Table 1. Comparison of normalized average area of ASM 1, ASM 2, and MSM

	ASM 1	ASM 2	MSM
Patient 01	0.1499	0.1198	0.1292
Patient 02	0.2285	0.1773	0.1791
Patient 03	0.1704	0.1557	0.1588
Patient 04	0.2457	0.1922	0.2020
Patient 05	0.1344	0.1216	0.1304
Patient 06	0.2836	0.2090	0.2122
Patient 07	0.2066	0.1856	0.1897
Patient 08	0.1545	0.1482	0.1547
Patient 09	0.1361	0.1142	0.1226
Patient 10	0.1310	0.1080	0.1150
Patient 11	0.1893	0.1453	0.1484
Patient 12	0.2125	0.1580	0.1523

As another comparison method, average error rate (AER) is used. The average AER is defined as

$$AER = \frac{a_{UR} - a_{IR}}{a_{MSR}} \times 100\% \qquad (11)$$

where a_{UR} is the pixel area of UR, a_{IR} is the pixel area of IR, and a_{MSR} is the pixel area of the manual segmented region. Fig. 6 shows the comparison of average AER per each patient based on the MSM between the ASM 1 and ASM 2. The former is 4 ~40% and the latter is 5~13%. In case of the average of all patients, the former is 22.6783 % and the latter is 8.2823 %. From the results of experiments, the proposed method has similar performance as the MSM.

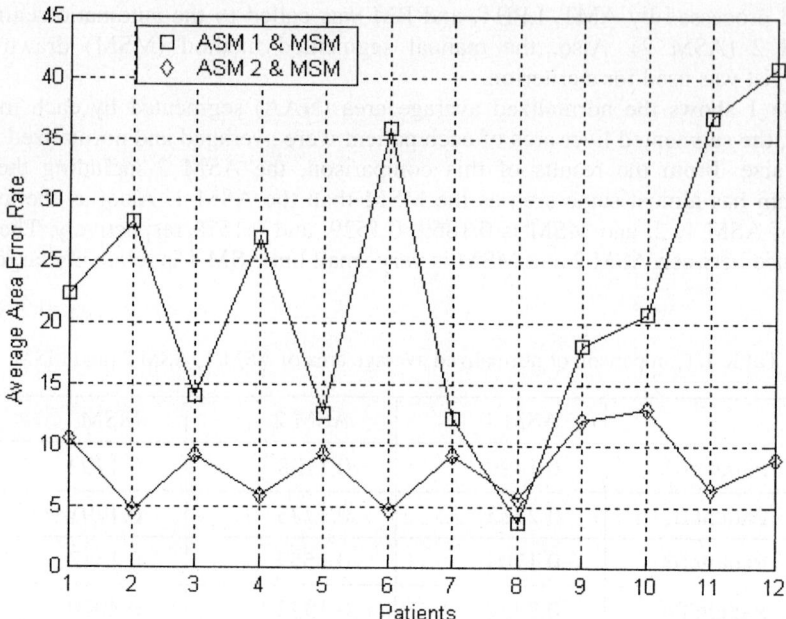

Fig. 6. Comparison of average AER per each patient based on the MSM between the ASM 1 and ASM 2

4 Conclusions

In this paper, we proposed an automatic liver segmentation method using a left partial histogram threshold (LPHT) algorithm. Histogram transformation such as convolution and scaling was used. Next, adaptive multimodal threshold (AMT) was performed to find the range of gray-level values of the liver region. We used proposed LPHT algorithm to overcome pixel variation of CE-CT image and remove the pancreas which is contacted with liver. After LPHT algorithm, the binary morphological (BM) filtering was processed for removing of unnecessary small objects and smoothing of the boundary.

48 CE-CT slices of the middle liver part from twelve patients were selected to evaluate the proposed segmentation method. As the average of normalized average area of the automatic segmentation method 2 using the LPHT and manual segmentation method are 0.1529 and 0.1579 respectively. There are very small difference between ASM 2 and MSM. Also, the average area error rate between the ASM 2 and MSM is 8.2823 %. From the results of experiments, the proposed method has similar performance as the MSM.

Acknowledgements. This study was supported by technological innovation development funds from Small and Medium Business Administration, Korea, 2005.

References

1. Parkin, D. M.: Global cancer statistics in the year 2000. Lancet Oncology, Vol. 2. (2001) 533-54
2. Lee, H.: Liver cancer. The Korean Society of Gastroenterology, Seoul Korea (2001)
3. Miller, B. A., Colonel, L. N., Bernstein, L., et al.: Racial/Ethnic patterns of cancer I the United States 1988-1992. NIH Pub., No. 96-4104. Bethesda MD (1996)
4. Lee, S.: Extraction of the liver from computed tomography using co-occurrence matrix. J. Biomed. Eng. Res., Vol. 22. No. 1. (2001) 9-17
5. Bae, K. T., Giger, M. L., Chen, C. T., Kahn, Jr. C. E.: Automatic segmentation of liver structure in CT images. Med. Phys.,Vol. 20. (1993) 71-78
6. Gao, L., Heath, D. G., Kuszyk, B. S., Fishman, E. K.: Automatic liver segmentation technique for three-dimensional visualization of CT data. Radiology, Vol. 201. (1996) 359-364
7. Tsai, D.: Automatic segmentation of liver structure in CT images using a neural network. IEICE Trans. Fundamentals, Vol. E77-A. No. 11. (1994) 1892-1895
8. Husain, S. A., Shigeru, E.: Use of neural networks for feature based recognition of liver region on CT images. Neural Networks for Sig. Proc.-Proceedings of the IEEE Work., Vol.2. (2000) 831-840
9. Park, H., Bland, P. H., Meyer, C. R.: Construction of an abdominal probabilistic atlas and its application in segmentation. IEEE Trans. Med. Imag., Vol. 22. No. 4. (2003) 483-492
10. Saitoh, T., Tamura, Y., Kaneko, T.: Automatic segmentation of liver region based on extracted blood vessels. System and Computers in Japan, Vol. 35. No. 5. (2004) 1-10
11. Seo, K., Ludeman, L. C., Park S., Park, J.: Efficient liver segmentation based on the spine. LNCS, Vol. 3261. (2004) 400-409
12. Shapiro, L. G., Stockman, G. C.: Computer vision. Prentice-Hall, Upper Saddle River NJ (2001)
13. Pitas, I.: Digital Image Processing Algorithms and Applications. Wiley & Sons Inc., New York NY (2000)
14. Schilling, R. J., Harris, S. L.: Applied Numerical Methods for Engineers. Brooks/Cole Publishing Com., Pacific Grove CA (2000)
15. Gonzalez, R. C., Woods, R. E.: Digital Image Processing. 2nd. Prentice-Hall Inc., Upper Saddle River NJ (2002)
16. Parker, J. R.: Algorithms for image processing and computer vision. Wiley Computer Publishing, New York (1997)
17. Pratt, W. K. : Digital image processing. Wiley-Interscience Publication, New York (2001)
18. Jahne, B.: Digital Image Processing. 5th. Springer-Verlag, Berlin Heidelberg (2002)

Automated Detection of Tumors in Mammograms Using Two Segments for Classification

Mahmoud R. Hejazi and Yo-Sung Ho

Gwangju Institute of Science and Technology (GIST),
1 Oryong-dong, Buk-gu, Gwangju 500-712, South Korea
{m_hejazi, hoyo}@gist.ac.kr

Abstract. A spread pattern of a tumor in medical images is an important factor for classification of the tumor. The spread pattern is generally not considered when we use only one segment for classification. In order to include the spread pattern for tumor analysis, we propose an approach for classification of tumors in mammograms using two segments for a mass. The proposed approach is performed in two stages. In the first stage, the system separates segments of the image that may correspond to tumors using a combination of morphological operations and a region growing technique. In the second stage, segmented regions are classified as normal, benign, or malignant tissues based on different measurements. The measurements pertain to shape, intensity variation around the mass, as well as the spread pattern. Experimental results with mammogram images of the MIAS database show reasonable improvements in correct detection of possible tumors, compared to other approaches.

Keywords: Tumor classification, spread pattern, segmentation, mammogram.

1 Introduction

Classification of objects in digital images is an important task in many applications; especially, in medicine where prevention and early diagnosis are very important. An example of such a task is the checkup done for detecting the breast cancer, which is one of the most common cancers among women and its incidence is rising in recent years. Although the primary prevention is not completely possible since the cause of this disease is not clearly understood, its treatment can be very effective if the breast cancer is detected in its early stages. Among different routine tests, mammography is one of the most common and effective methods for early detection of the breast cancer.

Because mammogram reading is a difficult and ambiguous task, many researchers try to propose automated systems to do this task efficiently. In general, research activities can be divided into two categories. In the first category, they focus on the enhancement and prompt of suspicious regions to draw the attention of physicians to those regions for detecting possible tumors. The objective of activities in the second category is to fully automate mammogram analysis.

Despite of some outstanding works for automation of mammogram analysis, there is still a long way to have a completely reliable automated system for mammogram reading. One of the problems in automated detection of masses in mammograms is the choice of the scale. Masses vary largely in size, ranging from a few millimeters to a few centimeters. Only a few researchers on this area address the issue of scale; however, they validated their proposed methods only on a very small dataset.

Brzakovics proposed a fuzzy pyramid linking method for detection of possible tumors in mammogram images and he classified detected regions to benign and malignant for circular and stellar lesions in a hierarchical fashion [1]. Brzakovic and Neskovic then applied the fuzzy pyramid linking algorithm on a number of different scales to detect abnormal structures over a range of sizes [2]. Ng and Bischof detect the central mass of lesions using a basic template-matching scheme, which was also applied to a number of scales [3]. A circular Hough transform was used by Groshong and Kegelmeyer to detect circumscribed masses by searching for circular blobs. Their algorithm was tuned to provide similar signals for small and large tumors [4].

Mudigonda et al. focused on the development of gradient-based features and texture measures based on gray-level co-occurrence matrices for the classification of mammographic masses [5]. Petroudi et al. proposed a scheme which uses texture models to capture the mammographic appearance within the breast area. They model parenchymal density patterns as a statistical distribution of clustered, rotationally invariant filter responses in a low dimensional space [6]. However, the performance of their approach is restricted by the training set and quality of mammogram images. A neural classification scheme using fractal analysis and spatial moment distributions was proposed by V. Öktem and I. Jouny for detecting malignant tumors [7]. Although they had a low false positive detection, correct detection rate is not reasonable yet.

In this paper, we propose a new approach for automated detection of tumors (of different kinds and scales) in mammograms based on some prognostic factors: mass size, mass shape, intensity variation around mass boundaries, and spread of primary shape [8]. Different from previous works that use only one segment for classification, we extract two segments (inner and outer) for a mass, which helps us to define a spread pattern for a possible tumor if necessary. Classification is then performed using these two segments. Experimental results show that such consideration improves the correct detection of possible tumors and identification of their diagnostic stage.

The paper is organized as follows. Section 2 explains the proposed approach in detail: detection of possible tumors is described in Section 2.1, and feature extraction and tumor classification are detailed in Sections 2.2 and 2.3, respectively. In Section 3, we discuss experimental results and compare them with results of other approaches. Finally in section 4, we conclude our work and address issues for future works.

2 Automatic Detection of Tumors

Although we mainly concentrate on the recognition of three general masses: (1) normal round masses, (2) benign round masses, and (3) malignant round masses, we can also determine the type of non-circular lesions, e.g. star shape and architectural, which are suspicious to be a tumor. In order to classify these types of masses, we use different features, such as size, shape, intensity, and the spread pattern of the primary shape, e.g. ring of dehydration for malignant tumors.

To obtain the abovementioned features in the image, we first separate possible tumors in mammograms by a new segmentation method into two different segments, i.e. inner and outer. This process is done by a combination of morphological operations with a region growing method. Such separation makes the proposed framework distinct from the previous works that are based on one segment.

In the second stage, the detected masses are classified in a hierarchical fashion. In the first level, their sizes are checked. If they are bigger than a maximum threshold value or less than a minimum threshold value, we consider them as non-tumor. Possible tumors then proceeds to the next level of hierarchy, where we use two different classifiers which discriminate a mass based on its shape and edge intensity variations. Such classifications are done for both inner and outer segments of the mass. For both classifiers in this level of hierarchy, we use Multi-Layer Perceptron (MLP) network [9]. Finally, in the last level of classification, the final decision for a mass is made by a rule-based classifier.

2.1 Identification of Possible Tumors

The objective of the first processing stage is to identify possible tumors in mammograms. Generally, identification of possible tumors is a very difficult task due to the rich variations of gray level intensities in mammograms. Here, this process is based on the morphological techniques [10] [11] followed by an intensity growing algorithm, which finally generates two segments for a mass.

Precisely speaking, the segmentation task is accomplished by four steps: (i) cleanup the mammogram from non-informative regions, (ii) marking foreground objects using morphological operations, (iii) determining possible segmented regions by finding the locations of the regional maxima in the marked foreground objects, and (iv) extending segmented regions by connecting components of pixels based on the intensity differences during iterations. Figure 1 shows a typical mammogram and the output of each step. Now, let's examine each step in detail.

Usually, there are some areas in a mammogram image which are not under attention for classification and may increase the processing time. The first step, which is optional, considered for removing these regions. Such a cleanup is done by selecting the breast, or any part of it, as the region of interest.

In the second step, we apply a number of morphological operations for marking the foreground in the image (Fig. 1(b)). These operations are erosion, reconstruction, and dilation, defined by

$$\text{Erosion: } E(I, Se) = I \Theta (-Se) \tag{1}$$

$$\text{Reconstruction: } R_E = \bigcup_{k=0}^{K} [E(I, Se) \oplus I] \tag{2}$$

$$\text{Dilation: } D(I, Se) = I \Theta Se \tag{3}$$

$$\text{Reconstruction: } R_D = \bigcup_{k=0}^{K} [D(I, Se) \oplus E(I, Se)] \tag{4}$$

where I is the original image (after clean up) and S_e is the morphological structural element, which is a disk with radius 20 pixels in this work. Operators $\oplus$ and $\ominus$ are Minkowski addition and subtraction, respectively, which are defined by

$$A \oplus B = \bigcup_{\beta \in B} (A + \beta) \tag{5}$$

$$A \ominus B = \bigcap_{\beta \in B} (A + \beta) \tag{6}$$

In the third step, we find the regional maximal of the reconstructed image from the previous step using a connectivity array of 8-connected neighborhoods (Fig. 1(c)). A regional maximal is a connected set of constant intensity from which it is impossible to reach a point with lower intensity without first ascending, that is, a connected component of pixels with the same intensity value, t, surrounded by pixels whose values are greater than t.

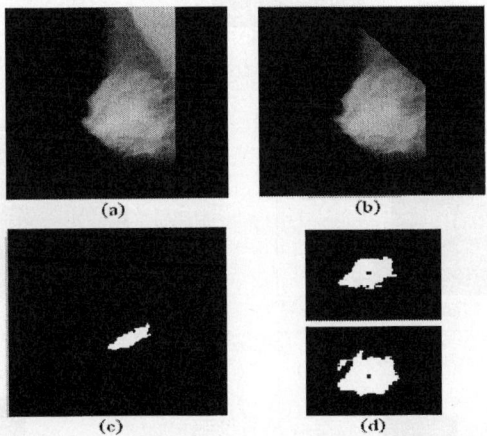

Fig. 1. Different segmentation steps. (a) Original Image. (b) Image after marking foreground. (c) Regional maximal. (d) Inner and outer segments.

Finally, in the last step that is performed iteratively, we extend the regional maximal by allowing more intensity differences for pixels in the primary regional maximal to extract the inner and outer segments. The result of this step is shown in Fig. 1(d). The extension is controlled by the intensity histogram of the primary region, and we continue to extend the region with more intensity values if the weighted average of the intensity histogram changes only in a limited range without significant replacement in the histogram spectrum. Here, we defined two threshold values to control the process; one for the inner segment (T_i) and the other one for the outer segment (T_o) and $T_o > T_i$. However, there are some situations, where inner and outer segments are exactly or almost the same, as in most normal tissues.

In order to clarify the situation, let's examine the process of the regional maximal extension for the mass shown in Fig. 1. The primary intensity histogram for the regional maximal is illustrated in Fig. 2(a). In the first iteration, the extended region has a histogram shown in Fig. 2(b) and the variation is still less than T_i; however, in next iteration, the extended region has a histogram with a variation bigger than T_i, so the inner segment is the one extracted in the previous step. A similar process is done to find the outer segment, but this time with threshold T_o. In this example, the last acceptable extension is related to the histogram in Fig. 2(d). As we can observe in Fig. 2(e), the extension in this step is completely changed the histogram of the primary regional maximal, which is not acceptable.

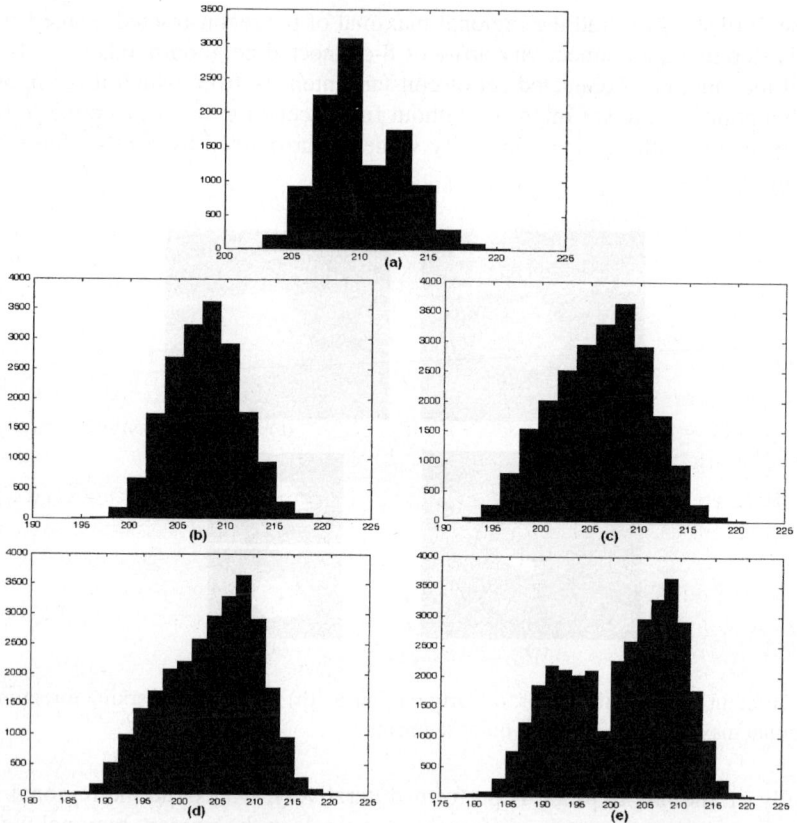

Fig. 2. Extension of the regional maximal in iteration for extracting inner and outer segments. (a) Histogram of the primary regional maximal. (b) Histogram of the extended region after the first iteration (related to the inner segment). (c) Histogram of the extended region after the second iteration. (d) Histogram of the extended region after the third iteration (related to the outer segment). (e) Histogram of the extended region after the fourth iteration (not acceptable).

2.2 Feature Extraction

Having completed the segmentation, and before starting the classification process, we should extract the corresponding features. There are different features used in the classification stage, where each of them is related to one characteristic of the tumor lesions. These features are as follows:

Area. Area is the total number of pixels enclosed in the segmented region. Here, areas are measured for inner and outer segments, separately.

Shape. Shape feature is the signature of the boundary of a mass, obtained by calculating the Euclidian distance between the center and boundary pixels of the extracted region. Later, we will explain how we extract boundaries and calculate the center for a segment. This feature is useful for discriminating circular masses from noncircular ones, which calculated by

$$D_i = \sqrt{((x_i - x_c)^2 + (y_i - y_c)^2)} \qquad (7)$$

where x_i and y_i are the coordinates of the ith edge point, and x_c and y_c are the coordinates of the center of the segmented region. Again, we compute two signatures, one for the inner segment and the other for the outer segment, however, the center of the inner segment is considered as the center point for both segments.

Edge Distance Variation. Edge distance variation is the local intensity changes around the boundary pixels of the extracted region, which is calculated by

$$I_i = abs(I(x_i, y_i) - m_i) \qquad (8)$$

where $I(x_i, y_i)$ is the intensity value of the ith edge point, and m_i is its local mean. Similarly to the previous features, we extract this feature for both segments. Usually, tumors are classified by well-defined edges.

Spread Pattern. Usually, the stage of a breast cancer is based on its size and degree of spread. A typical example of a spread pattern for infiltrating ductal carcinoma [12] is illustrated in Fig. 3. In the progressive stages of a cancer, it may even spread to other parts of the breast or even other parts of the body via lymphatic vessels; however, in this work, we just consider the spread pattern for the situation where the spread is in the original site of the primary mass.

Considering the example of Fig. 3, we can easily observe that a spread pattern may be defined for this kind of tumor if two segments are extracted for the tumor based on the intensity variations around the boundary of its original site. Using this fact, we define a spread pattern as the difference between shapes (signatures) of inner and outer segments. However, this feature is not used for classification in the first and second steps of classification hierarchies. Instead, we compare the inner and outer segments in the rule-based classifier, where, for example, more similar segments can show less possibility for malignancy.

Now, let's examine how we extract edges of the segmented regions and calculate their center. For detecting edges, we apply both the Prewitt and Sobel filters to the segmented inner and outer regions, separately, and then take the union of the results.

$$Edge_s = H_{pr}(S) \cap H_{so}(S) \qquad (9)$$

where $Edge_s$ is the final detected edge for the segment S, and H_{pr} and H_{so} are the results of edge detection for the segment S using the Prewitt and Sobel filters, respectively. Figure 4 shows the result of edge detection for the inner and outer segments of Fig. 1(d).

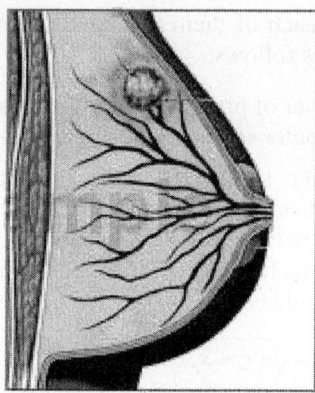

Fig. 3. A typical spread pattern for Infiltrating Ductal Carcinoma [13].

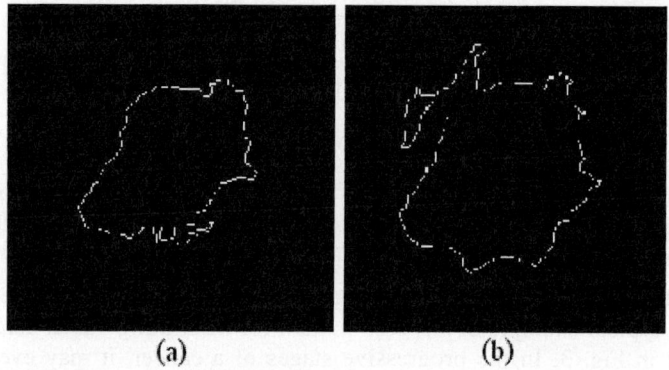

Fig. 4. Boundaries of extracted regions in Fig. 1(d). (a) Edges of inner segment (b) Edges of outer segment.

The second point is related to finding the center of a segment. As mentioned before, we only find the center point for the inner segment, and all measurements for inner as well as outer segments are performed based on this center.

Although there are some useful algorithms which locate the center of a round object, most of them are so complicated [14] [15]. Instead, we use a simple and efficient way for calculating the center that is not necessarily round.

In this method, the mean values of x and y coordinates of edge points are initially considered as coordinates of the center point. We then adjust the coordinates in iteration to find the best position for the center. This adjustment is based on the distribution of edge points around the center. Experiments show that this method is quite successful in locating the center.

2.3 Classification of Extracted Regions

As mentioned before, we perform classification in a hierarchical fashion. Figure 5 shows different levels of classification hierarchy, developed in this work.

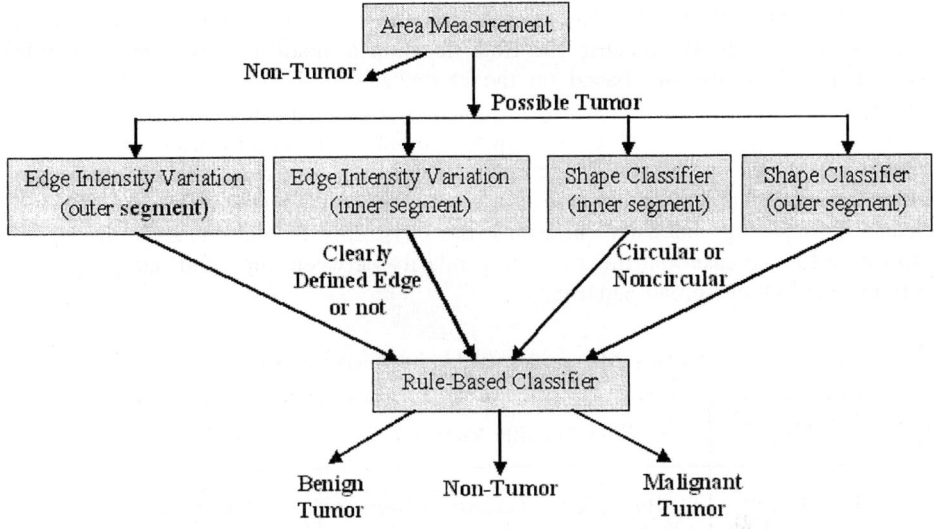

Fig. 5. Levels of hierarchy in the classification stage.

Area Classifier. The area classifier separates the masses to non-tumor and possible tumor based on their sizes, i.e. the area feature. Through experimentation, the minimum and maximum levels are set to be 0.001 and 0.1 of the image resolution, respectively. The segmented area is not a tumor then, if:

$$Area_{out} < Area_{min} \tag{10}$$

$$Area_{in} > Area_{max} \tag{11}$$

where $Area_{in}$ and $Area_{out}$ are the size of inner and outer segments, respectively.

Shape Classifier. For this classifier, we use an MLP network with one hidden layer with 50 neurons, 100 neurons in the input layer, and one output neuron which discriminates between circular and noncircular segments. The input is the shape (signature) feature vector. The classifier has been trained using the backpropagation algorithm for a noise free circle, a number of elliptical shapes with different minor and major access and orientation, as well as some of the real circular and noncircular masses from 80 different mammograms, which are totally around 100 training feature vectors.

Edge Intensity Variation Classifier. For this classifier, similar to the shape classifier, we use another MLP network with one hidden layer with 50 neurons, 100 neurons in the input layer, and one output neuron which discriminates the masses with clearly defined edges (possible tumor cases) from those ones with not clearly defined edges. The input vector is the edge intensity variation feature vector. The classifier has been trained using the backpropagation algorithm for 80 different mammograms.

Rule-Based Classifier. This classifier is somehow the most important one in the classification hierarchy, because the final decision is made in this level. The rules used in this classifier are based on the characteristics of tumors, such as clearly defined edges for the tumor case, determined by experts in this field [8], as well as through experimentation. Table 1 summarizes a list of the major rules. In Table 1, the rules related to the spread pattern are excluded. Based on the rules, the system decides which category the mass belongs to. For example, if both segments are circular with clearly defined edge intensity variations, the possibility of malignancy is increased, especially for the case that there is less similarity between inner and outer segments with respect to their spread pattern.

Table 1. Major rules used in rule-based classifier

Shape	Edge Intensity Variation	Final Decision
Both segments circular	Both segments clearly defined Only one segment clearly defined Neither segments clearly defined	Malignant Benign Non-Tumor
Only one segment circular	Both segments clearly defined Only inner segment clearly defined Only outer segment clearly defined Neither clearly defined	Malignant Possible Benign Possible Malignant Non-Tumor
Neither segments circular	Inner segment clearly defined Only outer segment clearly defined Neither clearly defined	Possible Tumor Undecided Possible Non-Tumor

3 Experimental Results

The processed images, with sizes of 1024 x 1024, have been selected from the Mammographic Image Analysis Society (MIAS) database, which is very well-known in this area, and usually used by researchers to evaluate their algorithms. The dataset consists of a variety of normal mammograms as well as mammograms with different types of abnormalities, such as circumscribed masses, calcification, speculated masses, and so on, with different characteristics and severity of abnormalities [16].

For training, we used 80 mammograms from various categories with different complexity, from highly textured to those that appear hazy. With these data, we trained shape and intensity variation classifiers, and also obtained threshold values for area measurement and some of the rules for the rules-based classifier.

The evaluation was carried out on 60 mammograms including 12 training mammograms and 48 other mammograms (different from the training data). These data contain specific types of tumors including 15 round-shape non-tumors, 15 round-shape benign tumors, and 5 round-shape malignant tumors. The remaining 25 contains noncircular masses (15 tumor and 10 non-tumor cases).

In the segmentation stage, the system was successful in isolating possible tumors. In this stage, while tumors identified in about 88.5% (31/35) of the cases for the complete sample set that consists of circular and noncircular masses, identification was almost precise for the circular tumors (95% (19/20)).

In the classification stage, and in the second level of hierarchy, the mean square error (MSE) for the shape classifier was almost zero. However, there was 3% misclassification for the edge intensity variation classifier, which is caused by imperfect segmentation of noncircular masses.

The overall accuracy of the proposed system for different categories are summarized in Table 2, where the accuracy is defined by the percentage of correct detections and different categories are non-tumor, benign tumor, and malignant tumor for round-shape masses, individually, and all other noncircular cases, together.

Table 2. Percentage of correct detection for different categories

	Using Two Segments	Using Inner Segment Only	Using Outer Segment Only
Normal (circular mass)	86.7% (13/15)	73.3% (11/15)	73.3% (11/15)
Benign (circular lesion)	93.3% (14/15)	80% (12/15)	60% (9/15)
Malignant (circular lesion)	80% (4/5)	60% (3/5)	20% (1/5)
Noncircular (correct detection)	68.0% (17/25)	56% (14/25)	40% (10/25)

From Table 2, we note that the best result is for round-shape benign lesions that have well-defined edges and are segmented almost precisely in the first stage. For non circular cases, the most false detections occurred for calcifications which are usually very small spots in mammograms, and speculated masses which are not identified quite well in the segmentation stage.

In order to show the improvement of the tumor classification in the proposed method, we have included the results of the experiment for the cases where only one segment is used for classification in Table 2. As indicated, the results of classification using two segments show a considerable improvement in the accuracy, compared to the results of classification when we use only of the inner or outer segment for classification.

Besides, a comparison between the proposed approach and some of the previous works shows that the detection accuracy for different types of tumors with different shapes is increased in our proposed system. The results of this comparison have been summarized in Table 3. Although the accuracy of the proposed system is quite reasonable, it is expected to improve even more if we do a more precise segmentation of

Table 3. Comparison of total accuracy in some different approaches

Proposed Approach	AMA [1] (*)	GCM-Based Mass ROI [5]	GCM-Based Mass Margins [5]	Fractal Analysis/ Spatial Moments [7] (**)
82.9% (29/35)	85% (17/20)	74.4% (29/39)	82.1% (32/39)	70% (21/30)

(*) evaluated only for round and star-like tumors
(**) evaluated only for malignant tumors

noncircular masses as well as enough considerations for calcifications and speculated masses.

In Table 3, while the Automated Mammogram Analysis (AMA) approach has been evaluated only for round and star shape tumors, and fractal analysis/spatial moments method consider just malignant tumors, the other approaches have be evaluated for all kinds of masses with different sizes, shapes, and complexities.

4 Conclusion

In this paper, we have presented a novel approach for detection and classification of masses in mammograms. In this work, we extract two segments, inner and outer, for a mass in a mammogram in order to define a spread pattern for tumor lesions. A spread pattern of the tumor in the medical images, in addition to other parameters of the mass, such as size and shape, is an important factor for the classification. Using these two segments, we try to detect tumors in the classification stage which is done in a hierarchical fashion. Experimental results show that tumor detection in this approach outperforms other methods using only one segment for classification. The correct detection rate of the system is expected to be improved further if we perform more precise segmentation for noncircular masses.

Acknowledgments. This work was supported in part by Gwangju Institute of Science and Technology (GIST), in part by the Ministry of Information and Communication (MIC) through the Realistic Broadcasting Research Center (RBRC), in part by the Ministry of Education (MOE) through the Brain Korea 21 (BK21) project, and in part by Institute of Information Technology Assessment (IITA).

References

1. Brzakovic, D., Luo, X.M., Brzakovic, P., An Approach to Automated Detection of Tumors in Mammograms, IEEE Trans. on Medical Imaging, Vol. 9, No. 3 (1990) 232-241
2. Brzakovic, D., Neskovic, M., Mammogram Screening Using Multiresolution-Based Image Segmentation. In: Bowyer, K.W., Astley, S.M. (eds.): State of the Art in Digital Mammographic Image Analysis. World Scientific, Vol. 9 (1994) 103-127
3. Ng, S.L., Bischof, W.F., Automated Detection and Classification of Breast Tumors, Computers and Biomedical Research, Vol. 25 (1992) 218-237

4. Groshong, B.R., Kegelmeyer, W.P., Evaluation of a Hough Transform Method for Circumscribed Lesion Detection. In: Doi, K., Giger, M.L., Nishikawa, R.M., Schmidt, R.A., (eds.): Digital Mammography. Elsevier (1996) 361-366
5. Mudigonda, N.R., Rangayyan, R.M., Desautels, J.E.L., Gradient and Texture Analysis for Classification of Mammographic Masses, IEEE Trans. on Medical Imaging, Vol.19 (2000)
6. Petroudi, S., Kadir, T., Brad, M., Automatic Classification of Mammographic Parenchymal Patterns: A Statistical Approach, In Proc. of the 25th Annual Int. Conf. of the IEEE EMBS Cancun, Mexico (2003)
7. Öktem, V. Jouny, I., Automatic Detection of Malignant Tumors in Mammograms, In Proc. of the 26th Annual Int. Conf. of the IEEE EMBS, USA (2004)
8. Stack, J.P., Redmond, O.M., Codd, M.B., Dervan, P.A., Ennis, J.T., Breast Disease: Tissue Characterization with Gd-DTPA Enhancement Profiles, Radiology, Vol. 174 (1990) 491-494
9. Hu, Y.H., Hwang, J.N., Handbook of Neural Network Signal Processing, CRC Press (2002)
10. Dougherty, E., Lotufo, R., Hands on Morphological Image Processing, SPIE Press (2003)
11. Soille, P., Morphological Image Analysis: Principles and Applications, 2nd edition, Springer-Verlag, Heidelberg (2003)
12. Kopans, D.B., Breast Imaging, 2nd ed., Lippincott Williams & Wilkins, Philadelphia (1998)
13. Nucleus Catalog, http://catalog.nucleusinc.com
14. Aguado, A.S., Montiel, M.E., Nixon. M.S., Using Directional Information for Parameter Space Decomposition in Ellipse Detection, Pattern Recognition, Vol. 29, No.3 (1996) 369-381
15. Ho, C., Chen, L., A Fast Ellipse/Circle Detector Using Geometric Symmetry, Pattern Recognition, Vol. 28, No. 1 (1995) 117-124
16. Suckling, J., Parker, J., Dance, D.R., Astley, S., Hutt, I., Boggis, C.R.M., Ricketts, I., Stamatakis, E., Cerneaz, N., Kok, S.L., Taylor, P., Betal, D., Savage, J., The Mammographic Image Analysis Society Digital Mammogram Database. In: Gale, A.G., Astley, S.M., Dance, D.R., Cairns, A.Y. (eds.): Digital Mammography. Elsevier (1994) 375–378

Registration of Brain MR Images Using Feature Information of Structural Elements

Jeong-Sook Chae[1] and Hyung-Jea Cho[2]

[1] u-Logistics Research Team, Postal Technology Research Center,
Electronics and Telecommunications Research Institute (ETRI), Republic of Korea
chaejs@etri.re.kr
[2] Computer Vision & Multimedia Lab, Department of Computer Engineering,
Dongguk University, Republic of Korea
chohj@dgu.edu

Abstract. In this paper, we propose a new registration algorithm, which can provide more exact criteria for deciphering brain diseases. At the first stage, our algorithm divides the areas of the brain structures to extract their features. After calculating contour and area information, the grouping step is performed. At the next stage, the brain structures are precisely classified with respect to the shape of cerebrospinal fluid and the volume of brain structures. These features are finally integrated into a knowledge base to build up a new standard atlas for normal brain MR images. Using this standard atlas, we perform the registration process after extracting the brain structures from the MR image to be compared. Finally, we analyze the registration results of the normal and abnormal MR images, and showed that the exactness of our algorithm is relatively superior to the previous methods.

1 Introduction

In the field of medical image processing, MR (magnetic resonance) images are now widely used and constantly widen its application areas, due to its superior spatial resolution. Especially for encephalopathy, there are active research efforts on the automatic diagnosis systems, medical treatment planning systems, surgical operation support systems, etc. through focusing on the registration of brain MR images [1][2][3][4][7]. With the development of modern medical imaging technology, a variety of advances have been made in the many areas of the studies for diagnosis of disease and treatment scheduling using acquisition and analysis of medical images. Most commonly used medical imaging technologies include CT(Computed Tomography), MRI (Magnetic Resonance Images), PET (Positron Emission Tomography), and SPECT (Single-Photon Computed Tomography), among which MRI has been more widely used due to its strengths in providing anatomical and pathological information of the body in terms of diagnostics, on the basis of spatial resolution[1]. In addition, the development of recent medical system makes it possible to conduct comprehensive studies on operation aid and medical treatment scheduling system to automatically diagnose and identify diseases, through medical imaging. In particular, cerebral diseases require different methods of diagnosis and scope of treatment, depending on their types and points of attack of diseases, so it is most important to diagnose diseases and set treatment scheduling as correctly and early as possible. To that end, much active research has been performed on registration of normal models with their abnormal counterparts, which can be used as a foundation for more precise diagnosis of disease. This study suggests a new registration algorithm to provide a correct standard for diagnosis of disease. As a preprocessing stage for registration, segmentation of individual regions of brain components and feather extraction of characteristics are performed, followed by analyzing information on contour and size from those selected characteristics. From such information, grouping is done as a first stage of registration and sub categorization of cerebrospinal fluid by shape and size of those brain regions, using information on characteristics of brain components [10]. Based on the knowledge of images of normal people, registration is performed after segmenting regions of components in abnormal image to compare. Finally, we check and analyze comparative results of registration of the image models of normal people and abnormal images, verify accuracy, and conclude this thesis. In this study, we describe related studies in chapter 2, Feather extractions of characteristics of brain components in chapter 3, registration methods in chapter 4, results of experiment and analysis in chapter 5, conclusion and suggestions for further studies in chapter 6.

2 Related Studies

With the rapid development of medical imaging apparatus, in connection with diagnosis, operation, and scheduling of treatment of diseases, a comprehensive study should be done about medical image processing. To set up such a diagnosis system, diagnosis of disease should be done first of all, which is possible by comparative study between normal model images and abnormal ones through medical image processing. Recently, as a technique for comparison between such medical images, registration has been widely studied. The Registration, which has been a major focus of studies in the area of medical image procession, consists of intra-subject registration, inter-subject registration, and image to physical space registration. Characteristics of these algorithms are described below [2][3][4][5][6][7]. The registration, which has been a major focus of studies in the area of medical image procession, consists of intra-subject registration and inter-subject registration. At first techniques are categorized as intra-subject registration of which images are produced out of the same subject and provide different perspectives on the same structure. Moshfegi suggested a technique based on iterative deformation, which needs series of measuring process and is highly sensitive to initial registration error [2]. Second techniques inter-subject registration, refers to cross registration of different subjects. Problems here are related with standard model (atlas) registration of individual images to compare size and appearance among image groups. In general, The atlas itself is created through averaging of image sets, which has undergone registration as different units, mapping on the basis of shared space such as Talairach[3]. Nevertheless, such standard model is not easy to generate in Korea, because of its rarity and high cost as well as poor environment. In this paper, we have resolved this problem by directly creating models for normal people. This study suggests a new standard model through this process, as well as a new method of inter-subject registration, which makes this type of standard model registration available

3 Feather Extractions of the Brain Structural Elements

Chapter 3 explains how to conduct feather extraction of characteristics of brain components, as a previous stage of registration using brain MRI of normal people as input.

3.1 Preprocessing Stage

Because of conditions during photographing, capacity of MRI system, diversity of measurement, and skills of photographer, brain MRI is hard to produce the identical quality for all the images. Therefore, it is impossible to obtain satisfactory results for all the images with the same algorithm, so we need a preprocessing stage to resolve this problem. As a preprocessing stage to conduct extraction of characteristics through region segmentation by elements of the brain MRI, first of all, shading should be emphasized using contrast. Second, after smoothly filtering boundaries among images using median filtering, dithering should be done so that pixel of images can contrast identically with surrounding pixel in shading.

3.2 Stage of Feature Extraction

Feature extraction of the brain structural elements should be done for the head, brain, cerebrospinal fluid, and eyes. Fig. 1 shows the stage of characteristics extraction. Stages of extraction of characteristics information through segmentation of these regions from brain MRI are in the following [2].

For the head region, the head and its background are separated with histogram analysis. Because partial damage is caused to the brain region inside the head with similar background in this process, head region should be extracted by restoring the original image through mask operation with the original image, using restoration algorithm. The brain region is considered in relation with the head region gone through extraction in the previous stage. Extraction of the brain region is possible by performing segmentation of skull layer with high value of shading between the outer scalp and internal area surrounding the brain region to be segmented. Feather extraction of cerebrospinal fluid is carried out by making use of high value of shading of cerebrospinal fluid with the increase of the contrast to maximum after applying reversal to the extracted brain region. The region of eyes can be extracted by measuring density, considering the upper 1/5 area and left-right symmetry. For these characteristic structural elements of the brain, MBR, region, color information and contour should be produced. The information on such characteristics is to be used at the next stage of grouping. Fig. 1 shows the resulting image of segmentation of the brain structural elements with contour of normal people.

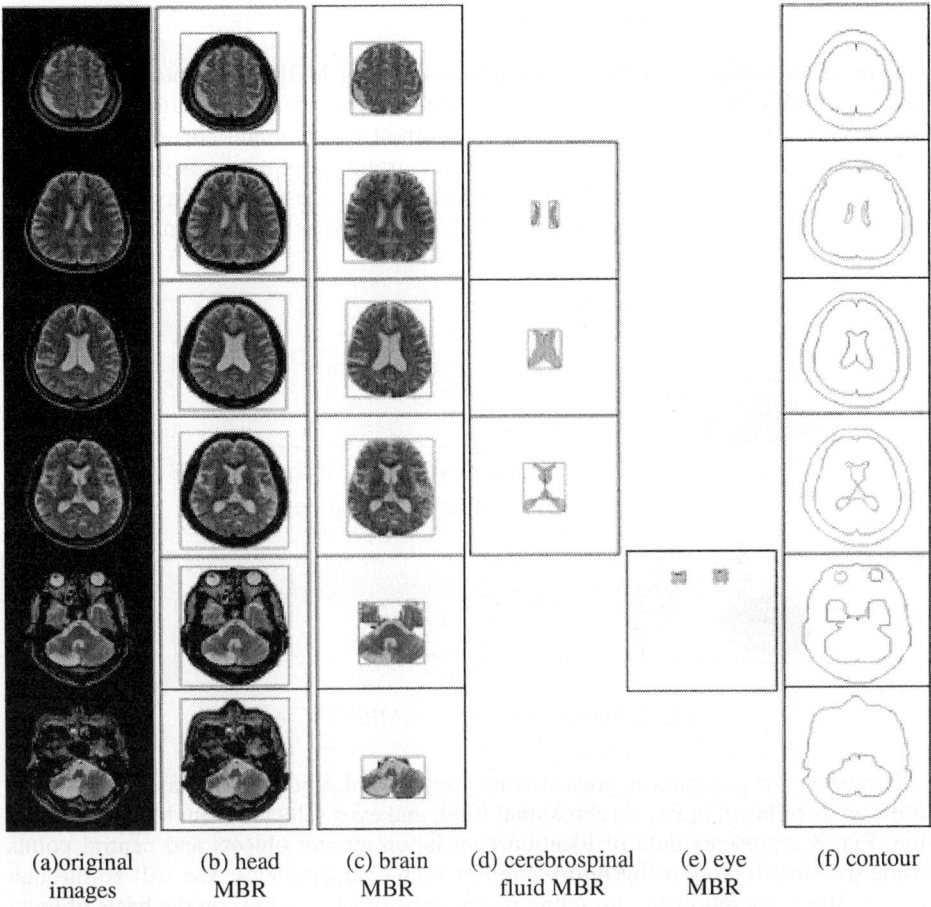

(a) original images　(b) head MBR　(c) brain MBR　(d) cerebrospinal fluid MBR　(e) eye MBR　(f) contour

Fig. 1. Extraction of the brain structures from the normal MR images

4 Registration Algorithms

In chapter 4, registration algorithm is introduced in which automatic grouping of n groups of slide series is done for the feather extraction information, followed by further categorization by shapes of cerebrospinal fluid and size of the brain region. At the first stage of registration, keeping in mind the relationship of location and inclusion among individual objects on the basis of the selected brain components, automatic grouping of n groups of MRI series (20~40 sheets) frame is done for a person. Next, sub categorization is done for each group using detailed information on characteristics. Establishing knowledge base of normal people on the basis of each category of characteristics, registration of models of normal people with abnormal images is done to detect location of slide. For more accurate registration, it is useful to conduct grouping such images by characteristics.

4.1 Method of Brain MRI Grouping

For the relationship of position among objects, using MBR and contour feather extraction of brain MRI components resulted from feather extraction stage of characteristics; grouping is made according to their current position and correlation. Neuroimaging series of a person undergoes automatic grouping of n groups through characteristics of components selected, and sometimes every one may not have the identical number of groups, because imaging is different by types or conditions of diseases. Fig. 2 is a concept map of grouping of brain MRI.

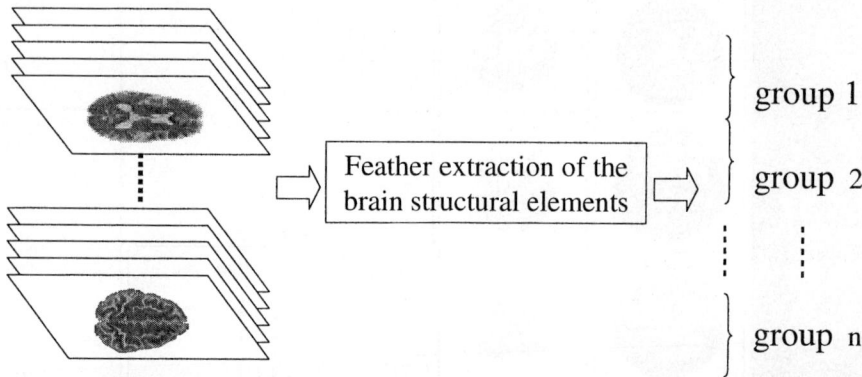

Fig. 2. Automatic grouping of MRI slide series

Parameter for grouping is presented by contour and objects inside as well as MBR of the areas of head, brain, cerebrospinal fluid, and eyes selected from MRI segmentation. Fig. 3 represents data of location correlation among objects and central points inside the head region, using information of such characteristics. We will go through the conditions for automatic grouping of n groups of MRI series, on the basis of location relationship among characteristics information in the next chapter [3].

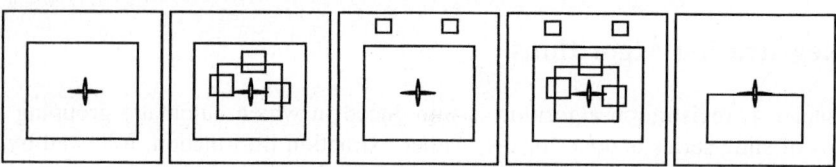

Fig. 3. Relationship of location among objects

4.2 Relationship of Location and Inclusion Among Objects

Relationship of location and inclusion among objects is based on MBR, contour, and area ratio of the brain MRI components as a parameter. MBR of each component of the brain selected as minimum rectangle surrounding the interested area should be produced, followed by defining correlation according to the relationship of location and inclusion among objects with five conditions for grouping. Fig. 4 refers to the overall composition of grouping algorithm.

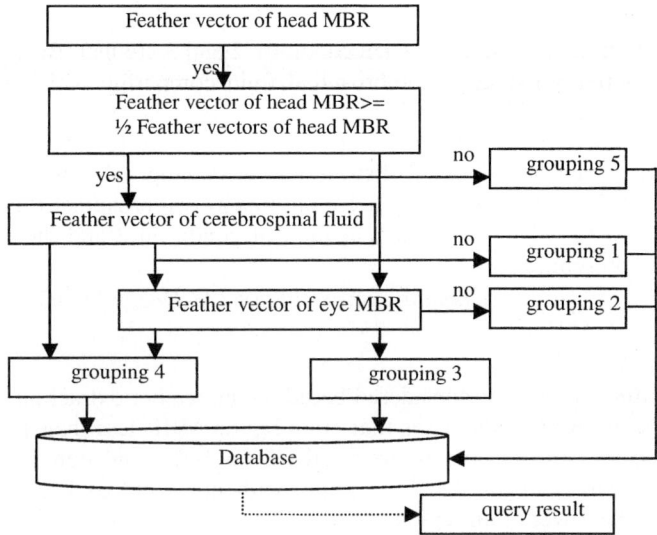

Fig. 4. Flow chart of position and inclusion relationship among objects

1) Condition 1
As a first condition, results from region feather extraction of the head and brain are considered. When MBR and contour are present in the head, there are MBR and contour of the brain area inside this area where MBR height of the brain region is more than 50% of that of the head MBR. A numerical formula is as follows.

$$ccondition1; \frac{H_{brain}}{H_{head}} \geq 0.5 \qquad (1)$$

2) Condition 2
If condition 1 is met, now move to the second condition. In other words, it includes the cases where multiple MBR and contour more than one are in the internal space accounting for 1/3 of the brain region. Experiments show that abnormal people have even 5 to 9 sheets of frame with cerebrospinal fluid extended due to hypertropic condition, while normal people have limited 5 to 6 sheets of frame with cerebrospinal fluid.

$$ccondition2; h_{csf} \leq \frac{1}{3} H_{brain} \qquad (2)$$

3) Condition 3
The third condition is considered only when condition 1 is met as well. Here for categorization you can use existing knowledge that all human beings have eyes in the upper side of the head. Considering upper 1/5 area of the head MBR height as potential space, it includes the cases where MBR and contour are present in this domain, and most domain of the frame containing the eye area is applicable.

$$condition3; h_{eye} \subseteq upper \frac{1}{5} H_{head} \qquad (3)$$

4) Condition 4

The fourth condition is considered when condition 2 and 3 are met. Because abnormal people have relatively extended cerebrospinal fluid comparing with normal people, sometimes their eye region not found in normal people is present in cerebrospinal fluid in frame. Moreover, when tumors or other diseases are found in the frame with the eye region, which has a similar distribution of shading value with cerebrospinal fluid, misrecognition may happen, by selecting this as cerebrospinal fluid. Therefore, it includes the cases where cerebrospinal fluid of condition 2 and the eye region of condition 3 are present.

$$condition4; ccondition2 AND ccondition3 \qquad (4)$$

5) Condition 5

The last and fifth condition is considered based on the feather extraction results of the head and brain. It refers to the cases that brain region MBR less than 1/2 of the head region MBR height in the area where head region MBR and contour are present. Namely, as shown in Fig. 4.9 below, frame with nose and ears is located in the smaller area of the lower brain region.

$$condition5 : \frac{H_{brain}}{H_{head}} \leq 0.5 \qquad (5)$$

4.3 Condition for Sub-classification of Cerebrospinal Fluid

There are four categories of cerebrospinal fluid by shape, under the following conditions.

1) Classification 1

Classification 1 is classified on the basis of information on left-right symmetry of the two cerebrospinal fluids existed left and right. Refer to Fig. 5 for details.

Fig. 5. Classification1 of cerebrospinal fluid

DLb : width of 1/2 area to the left from the central point of the brain region
DRb : width of 1/2 area to the right from the central point of the brain region

$$Di(brain) = \frac{DRb - |DLb - DRb|}{DRb} \qquad (6)$$

From this formulation, we can see that if $D_{i(brain)} = 1$, the brain region is in left-right symmetry. Here, similarity of cerebrospinal fluid can be measured as well. It is possible to calculate similarity of cerebrospinal fluid in the brain region MBR, dividing the brain region into left and right, and first of all, similarity of left cerebrospinal fluid is produced as follows;

$$DistL\ (DLb, dlc) = 1 - \frac{|DLb - dlc|}{|DLb| + |dlc|} \tag{7}$$

DistL, DistR : value of (Li - norm)
DLb, DRb : width of left/right half of the brain region
dlc, drc : distance between left/right/ cerebrospinal fluid and the central point of the brain region

In this formulation, DistL refers to the left half of the brain and similarity distance of cerebrospinal fluid. DistR resulted from this formulation is similarity distance between cerebrospinal fluid and the left half of the brain. When DistL and DistR produced by the formulation are similar with each other, they are further categorized as symmetry. Error of similarity here is set at 0.2, an average of overall image.

$$Classification1(similarity): \frac{|DistL - DistR|}{\max[DistL, DistR]} \leq 0.2 \tag{8}$$

2) Classification 2&3
Classification 2 is classified on the basis of information on density distribution of the central region inside cerebrospinal fluid, when there is only one region of cerebrospinal fluid, as a larger region. First, measure the 1/4 region of the central portion in the cerebrospinal fluid MBR, and then classify as condition 2 if always more than 90%, with condition 3 if less than 90%. Refer to Fig. 6 for details.

Fig. 6. Classification 2&3 of cerebrospinal fluid

D_C = width of cerebrospinal fluid
ni = latitudinal width of the 1/4 region of cerebrospinal fluid
mi = longitudinal width of the 1/4 region of cerebrospinal fluid

Internal area of cerebrospinal fluid is in accordance with the following formulation.

$$A = \sum_{i=0}^{n}\sum_{j=0}^{m} f(i, j) \tag{9}$$

Depending on the following condition of area ratios, they are classified as category 2 or 3.

$$Classification2: 90.0\% \geq A \langle 90.0\% classification3 \tag{10}$$

3) Classification 4

The fourth category of cerebrospinal fluid is classified on the basis of information on one or more small cerebrospinal fluids, which are in left-right symmetry, when there is one cerebrospinal fluid MBR, which does not meet the conditions for category 2 and 3. Refer to Fig. 7 for the condition 4.

Fig. 7. Classification4 of cerebrospinal fluid

Lsc = width between smaller cerebrospinal fluid MBR located at the left 1/2 region to the left from the central point of cerebrospinal fluid region and the central point.

Rsc = width between smaller cerebrospinal fluid MBR located at the right 1/2 region to the left from the central point of cerebrospinal fluid region and the central point They are considered symmetric when they have similar value, and allowable error of similarity is 0.2.

$$Classification 4 : \frac{|Lsc - Rsc|}{\max\{Lsc, Rsc\}} \leq 0.2 \tag{11}$$

4.4 Region Growing

Which extends region by clustering and integrating of input images into the same region when the region currently under processing and neighboring regions sharing characteristics, eventually leads to segmentation of the whole region of an image by extending little by little in such manner. In this study, to restore damaged segmented cerebrospinal fluid throughout multiple preprocessing stages, region growing has been performed. Following Fig. 8 shows damaged cerebrospinal fluid before region growing and referring to restoration resulted from region growing.

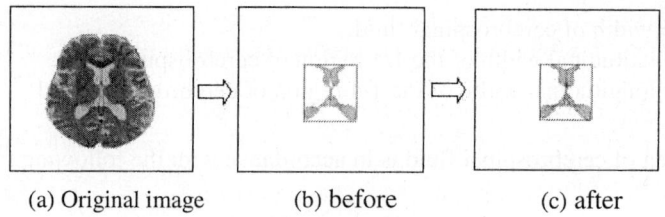

(a) Original image   (b) before   (c) after

Fig. 8. The result of region growing [14]

4.5 A Standard Model Generation and Registration of Abnormal MR Images

For feather extraction of standard models to establish knowledge base of imaging models of normal people, you should select images showing well anatomical characteristics from the 10 MR slide series of normal people, examining with the unaided eyes. Establishing knowledge base of standard models consists largely of two stages. Above all, once selecting models of normal people, you should make standard models by performing feather extraction information on characteristics of the brain components described in chapter 3 for the overall slide series and establishing knowledge base system. After applying the identical algorithm to images of abnormal people in connection with information on characteristics of those standard models, you should determine location of images, by comparing knowledge base DB of standard models of normal people. Data to be used for knowledge base include MBR of each brain structural elements, contour, pixel information, density information, grouping results, MBR of cerebrospinal fluid, and categorization results. By comparing such standard models and abnormal images, you should carry out registration. Refer to Fig. 9 for the details.

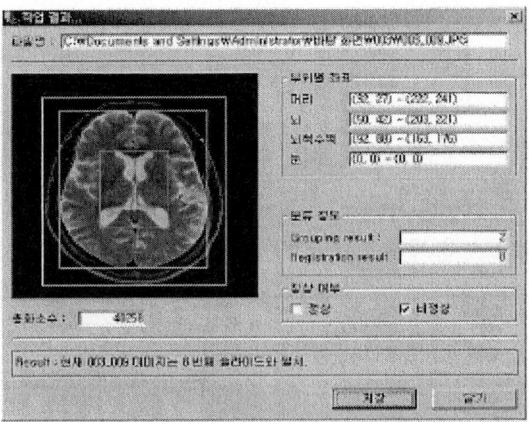

Fig. 9. The result of registration

5 Results

Results and recognitions of registration to standard models of normal people are described in the following. Refer to table 1. for comparison results between recognition ratios of segmented brain components and improved recognition in relation with images of abnormal people. As shown in the recognition ratio, segmentation of head region leads to favorable 100% recognition of the used images. Error of application range of run-length algorithms applied when feather extraction of the eye region is mistaken has an impact on the brain region feather extraction misrecognition as well. According to the analysis of misrecognition of cerebrospinal fluid region, feather extraction of cerebrospinal fluid region has been done 100%, while that of non-cerebrospinal fluid region showing 68 misrecognitions of the total 600 samples. This is because similar objects in cerebrospinal fluid region and location, size, and shading value, which were selected in non-cerebrospinal fluid images, have been recognized as cerebrospinal fluid region. This problem should be resolved later through post processing stage. For the eye region, gray matter area with similar density distribution with eyes in the potential eye region has been recognized as eye region for the most part, although extraction of the eye region has been done correctly for all kinds of images containing eyes. A table 2 shows you the cognition result that performed a grouping about 800 abnormal images about. A registration result of an abnormal image about a standard model is presented to a table 3.

Table 1. The result of feather extractions and accuracy

feather extr.	before preprocessing		after preprocessing	
	false/600 T2	accuracy(%)	false/600 T2	accuracy(%)
head	0/600	100.0%	0/600	100.0%
brain	50/600	91.7%	30/600	95.0%
cereb. fluid	68/600	88.7%	42/600	93.0%
eye	35/600	94.2%	35/600	94.2%

Table 2. Accuracy of grouping algorithm

grouping		original image				
		1	2	3	4	5
	1	95.2%	1.02%	0.00%	0.00%	0.00%
the	2	2.8%	92.7%	3.00%	0.00%	0.00%
result	3	0.00%	5.01%	97.0%	7.02%	0.00%
	4	0.00%	0.00%	0.00%	92.8%	0.00%
	5	0.00%	0.00%	0.00%	0.00%	100.0%

Table 3. Accuracy of a registration algorithm of abnormal MR images

standard model	1	2	3	4	5	6	7	8	9
1	80.8%	0.5%	0.0%	0.0%	0.0%	0.0%	1.1%	5.9%	0.0%
2	0.0%	92.3%	2.0%	1.3%	8.1%	0.0%	0.0%	0.0%	0.0%
3	12.6%	7.2%	88.2%	9.2%	4.7%	2.3%	0.0%	0.0%	0.0%
4	0.0%	0.0%	8.5%	87.8%	0.7%	0.0%	0.0%	0.0%	0.0%
5	0.5%	0.0%	0.0%	0.0%	86.5%	8.1%	0.0%	0.0%	0.0%
6	6.1%	0.0%	1.3%	1.7%	0.0%	89.6%	1.7%	0.0%	0.0%
7	0.0%	0.0%	0.0%	0.0%	0.0%	0.0%	84.3%	0.0%	0.0%
8	0.0%	0.0%	0.0%	0.0%	0.0%	0.0%	12.9%	94.1%	0.0%
9	0.0%	0.0%	0.0%	0.0%	0.0%	0.0%	0.0%	0.0%	100.%

6 Conclusions

This study suggested a method of registration after creating standard models on the basis of the information established by segmenting brain components and feather extraction characteristics of such components. The algorithm suggested here are comprised of series of stages including segmentation and feather extraction of characteristics of brain component region, grouping, sub categorization of brain components, model establishment of images of normal people, and registration of abnormal images. Under this method, it is easy to measure, using their anatomical characteristics as they are. Furthermore, when feather extraction of the brain region was difficult due to quality of images, we used dithering algorithms with surrounding images, and restoration through region growing was used to deal with damaged cerebrospinal fluid region. If error of region segmentation is further improved, this method will be used more effectively as a preprocessing stage of disease diagnosis system. Because it is difficult to obtain standard models (atlas of standard) of existing images, we make it possible to perform diagnosis of disease for abnormal images, by directly creating standard models and conducting registration with images of abnormal people. By conducting grouping after feather extraction brain region characteristics using the algorithm suggested in this study, it is possible to perform registration for all kinds of frames including specific location images reported by previous studies. The algorithm suggested in this study is applied to only one type of image, or MR T2, so it is needed to study how to conduct precise feather extraction and diagnosis of disease through registration with other images. Also, it is necessary to study how to extend this algorithm to other images than those applied in this study.

References

1. G. Subsol, et al., "First steps towards automatic building of anatomical atlases," INRIA (Institut de recherche publique en informatique), TR 2216, 1994.
2. R. Bajcsy and S. Kovacic, "Multiresolution elastic matching", Graphical Models and Image Processing, vol. 46, pp. 1−21, 1989.
3. M. Moshfegi, "Elastic matching of multimodality medical images," Graphical Models and Image Processing, vol. 53, no. 3, pp. 272−282, 1991.
4. C. Davatzikos, et al., "Brain image registration based on curve mapping", Proc. of the IEEE Workshop on Biomed. Image Analysis, pp. 245−254, 1994.
5. C. Davatzikos, et al., "Image registration based on boundary mapping", IEEE Medical Imaging, vol. 15, no. 1, pp. 112−115, 1996.
6. C. Davatzikos, "Nonlinear registration of brain images using deformable models" Proc. of the IEEE Workshop on Math.Methods in Biomedical Image Analysis, San Francisco, 1996.
7. F. S. Cohen, Y. Zhengwei, H. Zhaohui,"Automatic matching of homologous histological sections" IEEE Transactions on Biomedical Engineering, vol.45, no5, pp. 642−649, 1998.
8. D. Collins, P. Neelin, "Automatic 3D inter-subject registration of MR volumetric data in standardized Talairach space",Journal of Computer Assisted Tomography, vol.18 no.2, 1994.
9. F. L. Bookstein, "Principal warps : Thinplate splines and the decomposition of deformations",IEEE Trans. Pattern Anal. Machine Intell, vol. 11, no. 6, pp. 567−585, 1989.
10. C. A. Pelizzari, G. T. Y. Chen, D. R. Spelbring, R. R. Weichselbaum, and C, T. Chen. "Accurate Three-dimensional registration of CT, PET and/or MR images of the brain"Journal of Computer Assisted Tomography, vol. 13, no. 1, pp. 20−26, 1989.
11. R. H. Taylor, S. Lavallee, G. C. Burdea, and R. Mosges In computer integrated surgery, pp. 77−97, MIT Press, Cambridge, MA. 1995.
12. Crane, Randy, "A Simplified Approach to Image Processing," Prentice Hall, 1996.
13. D. H. Ballard and C. M. Brown, "Computer Vision," Prentice Hall, 1982.

Cyber Surgery: Parameterized Mesh for Multi-modal Surgery Simulation

Qiang Liu and Edmond C. Prakash

School of Computer Engineering,
Nanyang Technological University, Singapore 639798
liuqiang@pmail.ntu.edu.sg
asprakash@ntu.edu.sg

Abstract. We present a parameterized representation of virtual organs for surgery simulation purpose. Random 3D input mesh are parameterized and resampled into a regular 2D parameterized model. With this parameterized representation, a high resolution 3D organ mesh can be reconstructed and deformed interactively with a simple and fast free-form deformation method. The amount of deformation and force feed-back can be calculated rapidly. Therefore, haptic rendering can be achieved. In addition, the parameterized mesh can be used to handle collision detection and the contact between multi-objects in an efficient way. With the parameterized mesh, realistic visual and haptic rendering can be provided for interactive surgery simulation.

1 Introduction

Laparoscopic surgery is a popular surgery technique whose benefits are less pain, faster recovery, and shorter hospitalization time. The drawback of this technique is that it is more difficult than traditional surgery procedure, and the surgeons need to learn and adapt themselves to this new type of surgery. To master laparoscopic surgery, massive training and practice is required. With virtual reality technology, surgery simulator can provide cheap and intensive training without the need of cadavers or animals.

One important issue of surgery simulation is to model the virtual human organs in a realistic way, not only visually, but also haptically. Visually, the virtual organs should have adequate number of polygons so that the surfaces can be rendered smoothly. Textures are applied to add colors and details. Some deformation methods should be applied to allow interaction between the user and the virtual organ.

To add haptical realism, a haptic device, such as Phantom developed by SensAble Technologies, can be used to control the movement of the virtual surgery tool. The feedback forces should be calculated and updated in a high frequency (1kHZ at least for Phantom). Therefore, the deformation methods must be fast enough to keep the update rate.

In this paper, we introduce a parameterized representation of the virtual organs for the purpose of surgery simulation. The parameterized mesh has the feature of compact and implicit data representation. This feature is utilized to handle collision detection and the contact between multiple objects in an efficient way. A simple free-form deformation method is introduced. Bound with the parameterized mesh, it provides not only realistic visual deformation, but also fast feedback force update.

The remainder of this paper is structured as follows. Section 2 reviews the related work on parameterized meshes and their application, the deformation methods, and other issues about surgery simulation. In Section 3, we explain the process of parameterizing and resampling arbitrary surfaces into regular parameterized meshes with high resolution. Section 4 and 5 propose the application of parameterized mesh in surgery simulation, and discuss the issues of collision detection (Section 4.1), deformation (Section 4.2), haptic feedback (Section 4.3), and contact between objects (Section 5). In Section 6 we describe our experiment of surgery simulation, and the results are presented. Finally, Section 7 draws the conclusion.

2 Related Work

Some type of surfaces, such as parametric surfaces and PDE surfaces, have natural parameterization. PDE surfaces are defined as solutions of partial differential equations (PDEs). Du and Qin [4] presented an integrated approach that can incorporate PDE surfaces into the powerful physics-based modeling framework.

Unlike parametric surfaces or PDE surfaces, polygon meshes lack a natural parameterization. Grimm [6] used manifolds for representing parameterization. Manifolds have the ability to handle arbitrary topology and represent smooth surfaces. Grimm presented specific manifolds for several genus types, including sphere, plane, n-holed torus, and cylinder. He also introduced an algorithm for establishing a bijective function between an input mesh and the manifold of the appropriate genus. For most applications, the parameter space is preferably on a 2D plane instead of a 3D genus. Lee et al. [9] introduced a piecewise linear parameterization of 3D surface that guarantees one-to-one mapping without foldovers. This technique requires solving a simple, sparse linear system with coefficients based on the geometry of the mesh. The non-negative coefficients are calculated with local straightest geodesics. The resulted parameterization guarantees visual smoothness of isoparametric lines and preserves the conformal structure of the input mesh.

The parameterization of surface meshes provides a solution to various problems in computer graphics, such as texture mapping, remeshing, and geometry images. In texture mapping, the parameters are used to specify the coordinates of the 2D texture image for the corresponding vertices. Alliez et al. [1] introduced a flexible and efficient technique for interactive remeshing of irregular geometry, with the help of parameterization. Gu et al. [7] proposed to take advantage of parameterization and remesh an arbitrary surface onto a completely regular structure called *Geometry Image*, which captures geometry as a simple 2D array of quantized points. Surface information like normals and colors are stored in similar 2D arrays. The connectivity between sample vertices is implicit and therefore the data is more compact. In this paper, we utilize parameterized meshes, which are the same idea as geometry images, to represent virtual organs for the application of surgery simulation.

There exist a number of approaches to model the deformation of the organ, including free form deformation (FFD), mass-spring models, and finite element methods (FEM). A thorough survey of these models can be found in [5]. Although simple, free form deformation (FFD) is a powerful tool that offers great flexibility to to manipulate three dimensional objects, and it is still widely used in computer graphics and animation. For example, Schein and Elber [11] employed FFD to properly place deformable objects in arbitrary terrain. The movement of soft objects can be simulated realistically. De et al. [2][3] introduced a meshless technique, called the method of finite spheres, for real time deformation of soft tissues. When the virtual surgery tool touches the organ model, a collection of sphere nodes are sprinkled around the tool tip, both on the surface of the organ model as well as inside. Because the computationally expensive process of defining the relative location of the nodes and the tool tip, and the process of computing the stiffness matrix are offline, the runtime deformation can be performed in real time.

Hirota et al. [8] introduced a novel penalty method to simulate mechanical contact between elastic objects based on the concept of material depth. The penalty method is used for finite-element simulation. This method results in a reliable and smooth simulation. However, it is not practical for interactive simulation due to the computational cost. Onoue and Nishita [10] proposed a deformation algorithm for ground surfaces composed of granular material such as sand. In this algorithm, objects and granular material on them are represented by a layered data structure called the Height Spans (HS) Map. This method can simulate the contact between solid objects and the granular material in a realistic way so that the volume of the granular material is conserved. The idea of conservation of volume is also adopted in this paper for the simulation of the contact between the organ and other object.

3 Parameterization and Resampling

A parameterized mesh is a regular 2D array of quantized points in the 3D space of the following form.

$$V_{ij} = (x_{ij}, y_{ij}, z_{ij}), 0 \leq i \leq m, 0 \leq j \leq n$$

where i and j are the surface parameters, m and n are the dimensions of the parameterized mesh, and x_{ij}, y_{ij}, z_{ij} are the x, y, z coordinates of the points, respectively.

The virtual organ meshes available are usually arbitrary with low resolution. To be used for surgery simulation, they are first parameterized, then resampled into regular point arrays with high resolution.

3.1 Parameterization

Surface parameterization is the process to map each individual surface patch to an isomorphic triangulation on a 2D plan. An arbitrary mesh is cut along a network of edge paths, and the resulting single chart is parameterized onto a unit square, so that there is a one-to-one correspondence between each vertex V on the original mesh and one point on the parameter space $P = (u, v)$, with $0 \leq u \leq 1$ and $0 \leq v \leq 1$.

There are many solutions readily available for the process parameterization, including the one advocated by Lee et al. [9]. For the sake of easy implementation, we chose to conduct the parameterization of the 3D virtual organ meshes manually with Discreet 3DS Max 6. Figure 1 shows the parameterization of a stomach mesh.

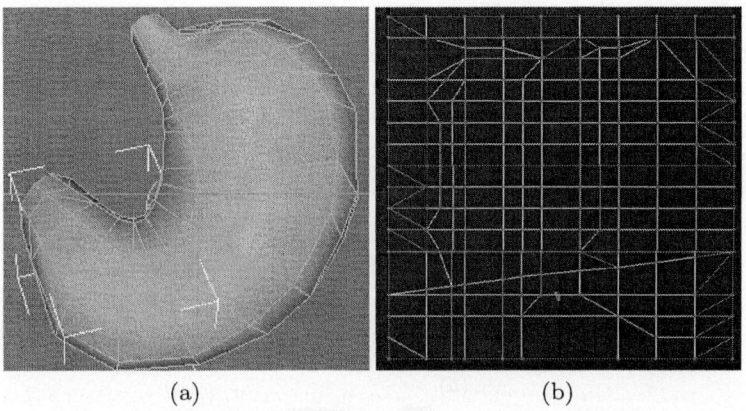

(a)   (b)

Fig. 1. The parameterization of a virtual stomach mesh model. (a) The original 3D stomach model. (b) The UV map of the mesh after manual arrangement.

3.2 Resampling

After parameterization, the model is resampled in $m \times n$ points which are evenly distributed in the parameter space.

Each sampling point is indexed as $P_{ij} = (u_i, v_j)$, in which $1 \leq i \leq m$, $1 \leq j \leq n$, and $0 \leq u_i \leq 1$, $0 \leq v_j \leq 1$. For each sampling point, we check which triangle it lies in. If a sampling point P_{ij} lies in a triangle $V'_1 V'_2 V'_3$, which correspond to triangle $V_1 V_2 V_3$ on the 3D mesh, we calculate the barycentric coordinates (w_1, w_2, w_3) of P_{ij} as

$$w_1 = \frac{u_i(v_2 - v_3) + v_j(u_3 - u_2) + u_2 v_3 - u_3 v_2}{A}$$

$$w_2 = \frac{u_i(v_3 - v_1) + v_j(u_1 - u_3) + u_3 v_1 - u_1 v_3}{A}$$

$$w_3 = \frac{u_i(v_1 - v_2) + v_j(u_2 - u_1) + u_1 v_2 - u_2 v_1}{A}$$

in which A is the area of triangle $V'_1 V'_2 V'_3$ and

$$A = u_1 v_2 + u_2 v_3 + u_3 v_1 - u_1 v_3 - u_2 v_1 - u_3 v_2$$

The barycentric coordinates are used to interpolate the coordinate of a 3D point V_{ij}, which is the corresponding vertex of P_{ij} on the 3D mesh,

$$V_{ij} = w_1 V_1 + w_2 V_2 + w_3 V_3$$

Similarly, the normal of V_{ij} can be calculated via interpolation.

3.3 Reconstruction

After sampling at each point, we get a $m \times n$ point array. Each point corresponds to a vertex on the 3D space, with coordinates and normal information. With this point array, the 3D mesh of the virtual organ can be reconstructed, by connecting the neighboring vertices, as shown in Figure 2. The connectivity of vertices is implicit, and requires no additional storage space.

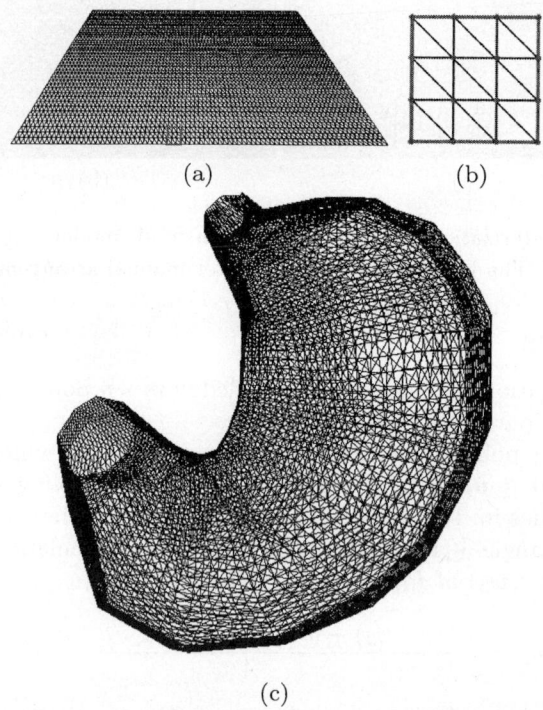

Fig. 2. Reconstruction of the 3D mesh. (a) The 2D point array with neighboring points connected. (b) An up close look of the connection of the points. (c) The reconstructed 3D stomach model mesh.

4 Tool-Organ Interaction

In this section, we present the approaches to simulate the interaction between the surgery tool and the organ. We took advantage of the parameterized mesh and proposed a fast collision detection technique, and a FFD method to simulate the deformation of the organ. With parameterized meshes, the deformations and the feedback forces can be calculated quickly to provide fast update rate.

4.1 Collision Detection

We implement one surgery tool, which is the grasper instrument. The user can control the tool interactively to touch, poke, and grasp the virtual organ. Like most surgery simulators, we assume that only the tool tip touches the organ, and only the collision between the tool tip and the organ is checked. Since the organ mesh is resampled at high density, we can assume that the collision happens only at the vertices of the organ mesh. This reduces the computation to a point-point collision detection.

Before the simulation, the distance between the tool tip and each vertex is calculated. The vertex nearest to the tool tip is the one with shortest distance. During simulation, the nearest vertex V_n is constantly traced and updated. After each time step, we check the neighborhood of the vertex V_n^{t-1}, which is the nearest vertex in the previous time step. The distance between the tool tip and each vertex in the neighborhood is calculated and compared. The new nearest vertex V_n^t is thus updated. The vector from V_n^t to the tool tip is noted as N_t, and the normal of V_n^t is N_n. If $N_t \cdot N_n < 0$, a collision is detected. The vector for V_n^t to the tool tip is the displacement of the vertex V_n^t. This displacement value is transferred to the parameter space to calculate the displacements of the neighboring vertices. The virtual organ is thus deformed.

Since the movement of the tool in one time step is limited, only vertices in a small area need to be checked. The collision detection only involves a small number of point distances calculation and one dot product calculation. Therefore the collision detection is fast and efficient.

4.2 Parametric Deformation of Organ

We designed a fast and easy free form deformation method which is based on the parameterized representation of the organ model. Although the scheme is simple, realistic deformation can be achieved.

Deformation is calculated based on 2D parameter space. When one vertex C is touched by the surgery tool and moved, the amount of displacement $d_c = [d_{xc}\ d_{yc}\ d_{zc}]$ of this vertex is transferred to the corresponding point $P_{i_c j_c}$ on the 2D parameter space. A Gaussian distribution function is evaluated at each surrounding point, and the displacements of these points are calculated with this distribution function as

$$d(P_{ij}) = d_c e^{-\frac{(i-i_c)^2 + (j-j_c)^2}{\sigma}}$$

In the equation above, σ is the standard deviation of the distribution, and it is a parameter that reflects the material property of the organ. The amount of displacement of a vertex V undergoes depends on the distance between it's corresponding vertex V' on the parameter space and $P_{i_c j_c}$. The further V' is from $P_{i_c j_c}$, the less displacement V undergoes.

The 3D coordinates of the corresponding vertex on the mesh are updated based on the calculated displacement of each point. The shape of the 3D organ model is changed accordingly, and hence deformed, as shown in Figure 3. The amount of displacement d_c of the vertex in contact with the tool is restricted to a limit d_{max}. The length of the displacement $\|d_c\|$ is constrained to make sure that $\|d_c\| \leq d_{max}$, so that unrealistic deformation does not happen.

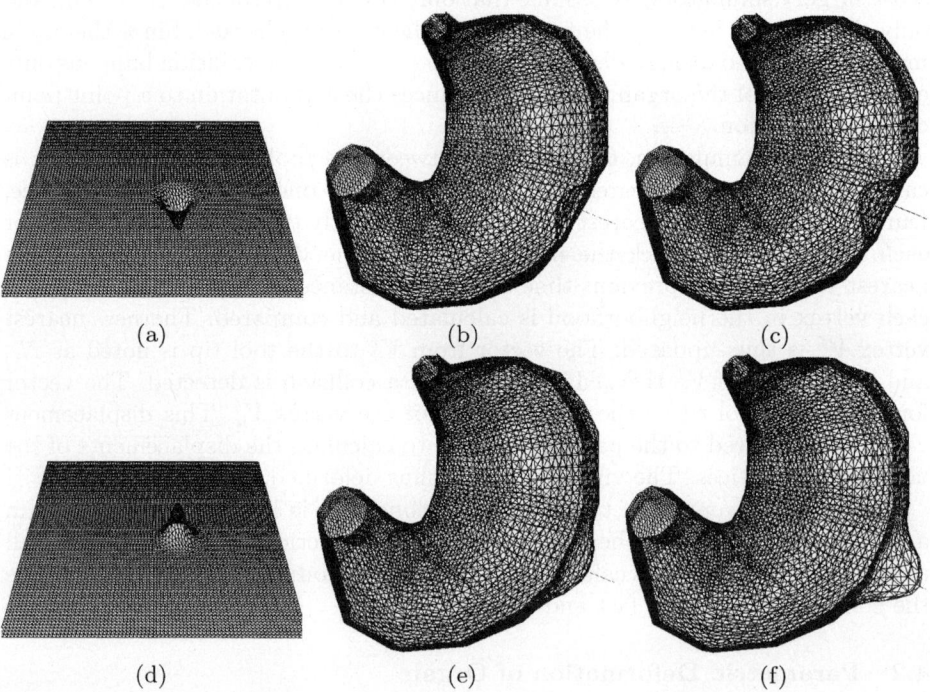

Fig. 3. The deformation of the stomach model with free form deformation: (a) (d) the deformation calculated on the 2D plane; (b), (c), (e), and (f) the deformation mapped onto 3D mesh.

Since the distances between points are evaluated on a discrete 2D mesh, the Gaussian distribution value for each point can be pre-calculated and stored in a look-up table. Moreover, the Gaussian distribution function has the shape of a "bell-shaped" hump. Therefore, before the simulation we can evaluate the Gaussian distribution values at a local area only, and store the values in a look-up table. During the simulation, we only need to check the pre-computed look-up table. Little calculation is needed, and the deformation is very fast.

4.3 Parametric Haptic Force Feedback

We can calculate the feedback force $F = [f_x \ f_y \ f_z]$ directly based on the displacement $d_c = [d_{xc} \ d_{yc} \ d_{zc}]$ of the vertex in contact with the tool tip:

$$f_x = -\Big(\frac{d_{xc}}{|d_{max}|}\Big)^3 f_{max}, f_y = -\Big(\frac{d_{yc}}{|d_{max}|}\Big)^3 f_{max}, f_z = -\Big(\frac{d_{zc}}{|d_{max}|}\Big)^3 f_{max}$$

in which f_{max} is a positive scalar value that indicates the maximum feed back force in one direction. As we can see, it requires little calculation. Therefore, fast update rate can be guaranteed for the haptic device.

5 Contact Between Objects

We proposed a method to handle the contact between the virtual organ and a plane which can deform the organ in a natural way and preserve the volume of the organ approximately. This method can be extended to handle the contact between the virtual organ and another object of any shape. The other object can either be rigid, such as some kind of surgery tool, or be deformable, such as another organ.

The process of our proposed method is show in Figure 4. First, the collision between the organ and the plane is detected. The vertices that penetrate the plane are projected to the plane. The areas around these vertices are then deformed so as to conserve the volume of the organ.

At each time step, the following computations are performed.

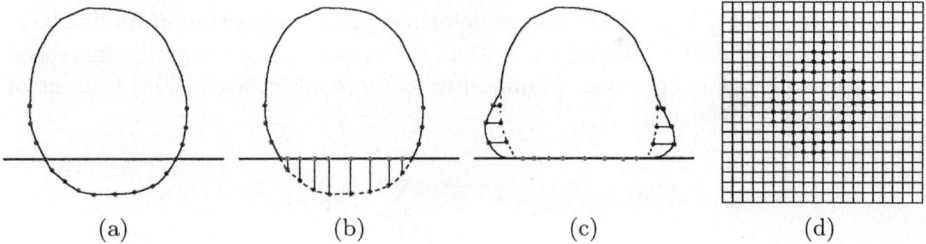

(a)   (b)   (c)   (d)

Fig. 4. The process of the contact between a deformable organ and a plane. (a) The collision between the organ and the plane. (b) The vertices that penetrate the plane (in red color) is projected to the plane. (c) The vertices (in blue color) around the contact area is deformed. (d) The corresponding points in the parameter space.

5.1 Collision Detection

The collision between the plane and the bounding box of the virtual organ is checked first. If collision detected, we further check whether the organ collides with the plane. We just need to check every vertex P_{ij} to see if it is on the other side of the plane. The corresponding points (i, j) of these points on the parameter space are in a set Φ, i.e. $(i, j) \in \Phi$.

5.2 Calculate the Displacements

The vertices that penetrate the plane is displaced by simply projecting onto the plane. The amount of displacement d_{ij} is calculated for each vertex P_{ij}. There are two limits for amount of displacements allowed. One is the maximum amount of displacement allowed for a single vertex d_{Smax}, and the other one is the maximum amount of displacement allowed for the total sum of the displacements of all the vertices that are in contact with the plane d_{Tmax}. If $|d_{ij}| > d_{Smax}$ for $(i,j) \in \Phi$, or $\sum_{(i,j)\in\Phi} |d_{i,j}| > d_{Tmax}$, the positions of all the vertices are set back to the state in the previous time step. The virtual organ is rendered, and we move on to the next time step.

If $|d_{ij}| \leq d_{Smax}$ for $(i,j) \in \Phi$, and $\sum_{(i,j)\in\Phi} |d_{ij}| \leq d_{Tmax}$, the following steps are performed.

5.3 Deformation

After the contact vertices are displaced, the vertices that are around them are deformed, so as to preserve the volume of the organ. The region of the deformation Ψ is decided by the sum of the displacements of the contact vertices $D = \sum_{(i,j)\in\Phi} |d_{ij}|$. The higher the value of D, the larger is the region.

In the parameter space, we check each point (i,j) and find it's nearest contact vertex and their distance s_{ij}. If the value of s_{ij} is higher than a threshold R, the vertex P_{ij} corresponding to (i,j) is in the region of deformation, i.e. $(i,j) \in \Psi$. R is defined as a function of D. The higher the value of D is, the higher is the value of R. In practice, we can pre-define a set of discrete threshold values R_k and its corresponding D_k, where $k = 1, 2, ..., p$.

If the vertex P_{ij} is in the region of deformation, the direction of its displacement d_{ij} is in its normal direction, so that the volume of the organ is increased to compensate the decrease of volume due to the contact area. The amount of displacement is defined as

$$|d_{ij}|_{(i,j)\in\Psi} = e^{-\frac{s_{ij}^2}{\sigma_k}} \sum_{(i',j')\in\Phi} |d_{i'j'}|$$

where σ_k is the standard deviation of Gaussian distribution that corresponds to the threshold value R_k.

Similar to the case where the organ is deformed by the tool, the Gaussian distribution value for each discrete value of s_{ij} can be pre-calculated and stored. During simulation, the distribution values are looked up in the pre-calculated data so as to increase the speed of simulation.

6 Experiments and Results

We implemented the interaction between the tool and organ. We parameterized and resampled two organ models, one stomach model and one liver model, with

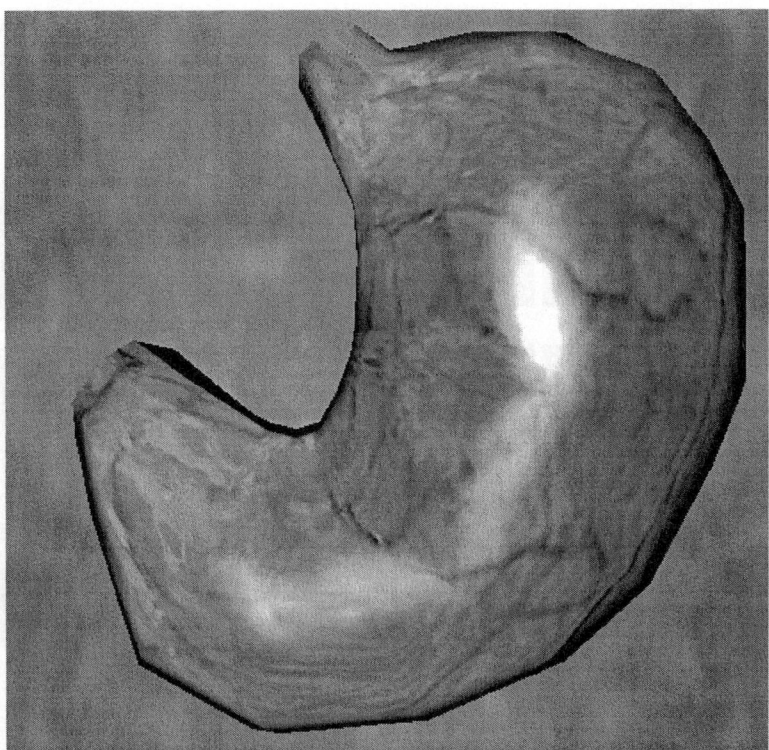

Fig. 5. The stomach model with texture map and bump map. The bump map enhances the appearance of the veins on the surface.

relatively low resolution. Each is resampled by a 81 × 81 point array. Both resampled meshes can be simulated in real time with user interaction. Texture and bump map are used to add realism to the model. The textures of the organs are generated from the snapshots of real laparoscopic surgery. The bump maps are generated with Adobe PhotoShop Normal Map and DDS Authoring Plug-ins developed by nVIDIA. Figure 5 shows a snapshot of the stomach model with texture and bump map.

Mouse input to the system controls the movement of the virtual tool. Figure 6 shows a few snapshots of the surgery simulation with the interaction between the grasper tool and the two organ models. The contact between the virtual stomach and a plane is shown in Figure 7. The experiments on haptic interaction is still in progress.

7 Conclusion and Future Work

We introduced a parameterized representation of 3D organ meshes for the simulation of laparoscopic surgery. Random input virtual organ meshes are parameterized and resampled into regular high resolution models. The high resolution

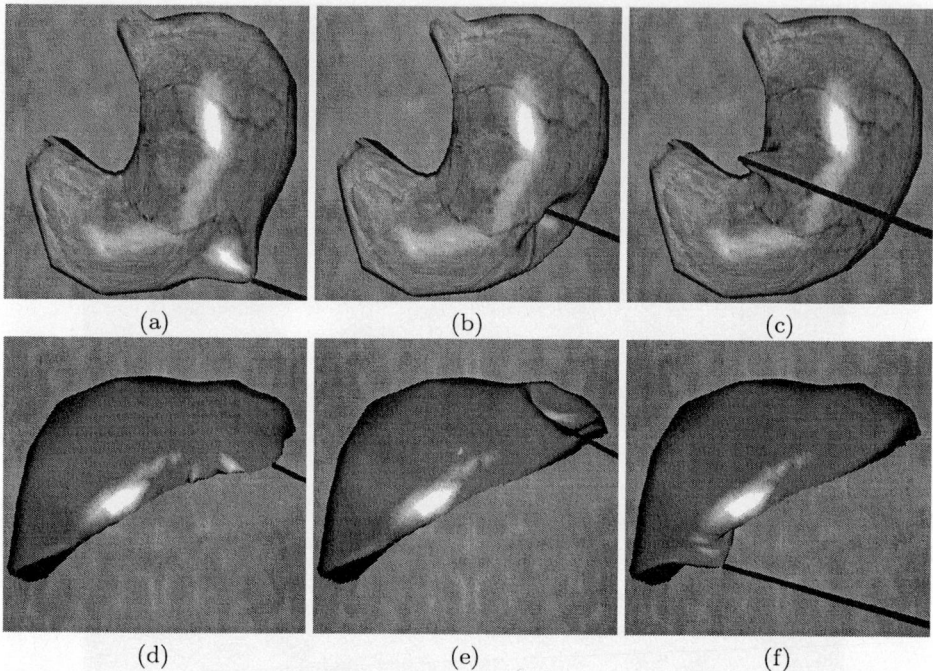

Fig. 6. The deformation of the stomach model with free form deformation. (a)(b)(c) Simulation with the stomach model. (d)(e)(f) Simulation with the liver model.

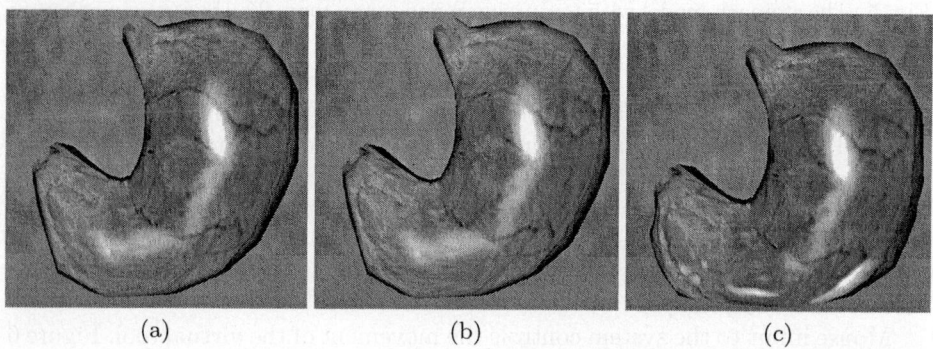

Fig. 7. The process of the stomach model in contact with a plane. The stomach model deforms when it comes in contact with the plane.

models increase the visual quality of the virtual organ. The parameterized mesh is helpful for the simulation in a few aspects. First, it is useful for collision detection. Secondly, we introduced a free-form deformation approach for the parameterized mesh to simulate the interaction between the tool and the organ to achieve an update rate fast enough to provide haptic feedback. Lastly, we also proposed a procedure to handle the contact between the organ and another object.

One limitation of current methods is that the parameterization process is conducted manually. The complexity of the input mesh is limited. In addition, the parameterization quality in terms of least area distortion can not be guaranteed. In future work, we plan to adopt some automatic process, such as the one proposed by Lee et al. [9], for parameterization.

Another direction of future work is to improve the deformation with more sophisticated deformation method, such as mass-spring model and finite element method (FEM). The deformation can be calculated similarly in the 2D parameter space, then transferred back to the 3D mesh. Since the vertices are regularly spaced in the parameter space, no additional remeshing is required for mass-spring model or FEM. More realistic deformation can be produced with these physically based deformation methods. In future work, the contact between multiple deformable organs would be simulated.

References

1. Alliez, P., Meyer, M., and Desbrun, M.: Interactive geometry remeshing. ACM SIGGRAPH (2002) 173–182.
2. De, S., Kim, J., and Srinivasan, M. A.: A meshless numerical technique for physically based real time medical simulations. Medicine Meets Virtual Reality (2001) 113–118
3. De, S., Manivannan, M., Kim, J., Srinivasan, M. A., and Rattner, D.: Multimodal simulation of laparoscopic Heller myotomy using a meshless technique. Medicine Meets Virtual Reality 02/10 (2002) 127–132
4. Du, H., and Qin, H.: Dynamic PDE-based surface design using geometric and physical constraints. Graphic Models **67**(1) (2005) 43–71
5. Gibson S. F., and Mirtich, B.: A Survey of Deformable Modeling in Computer Graphics. Technical Report TR-97-19, Mitsubishi Electric Research Laboratories, Ambridge, MA, USA, 1997
6. Grimm, C. M.: Parameterization using manifolds. International Journal of Shape Modeling **10**(1) (2004) 51–81
7. Gu, X., Gortler, S. J., and Hoppe, H.: Gometry images. ACM SIGGRAPH (2002) 355–361
8. Hirota, G., Fisher, S., and State, A.: An improved finite-element contact model for anatomical simulations. The Visual Computer **19**(5) (2003) 291–309
9. Lee, H., Tong, Y., and Desbrun, M.: Geodesics-based one-to-one parameterization of 3D triangle meshes. IEEE Multimedia **12**(1) (2005) 27–33
10. Onoue, K., and Nishita, T.: An interactive deformation system for granular material. Computer Graphics forum **24**(1) (2005) 51-60
11. Schein, S., and Elber, G.: Placement of deformable objects. Computer Graphics Forum **23**(4) (2004) 727–739

Image Retrieval Based on Co-occurrence Matrix Using Block Classification Characteristics

Tae-Su Kim, Seung-Jin Kim, and Kuhn-Il Lee

School of Electrical Engineering and Computer Science,
Kyungpook National University, 1370, Sankyug-Dong,
Buk-Gu, Daegu 702-701, Korea
{kts1101, starksjin}@ee.knu.ac.kr
kilee@knu.ac.kr

Abstract. A new method of content-based image retrieval is presented that uses the color co-occurrence matrix that is adaptive to the classification characteristics of the image blocks. In the proposed method, the color feature vectors are extracted according to the characteristics of the block classification after dividing the image into blocks with a fixed size. The divided blocks are then classified as either luminance or color blocks depending on the average saturation of the block in the HSI (hue, saturation, and intensity) domain. Thereafter, the color feature vectors are extracted by calculating the co-occurrence matrix of a block average intensity for the luminance blocks and the co-occurrence matrix of a block average hue and saturation for the color blocks. In addition, block directional pattern feature vectors are extracted by calculating histograms after directional gradient classification of the intensity. Experimental results show that the proposed method can outperform conventional methods as regards a precision and a feature vector dimension.

1 Introduction

Recent years have seen a rapid increase in the volume of digital media, such as images, audio, and video, along with the users that store and transmit such information. In particular, efficient searching and retrieval methods for digital images have been investigated due to the spread of digital cameras and growth of the Internet. Image retrieval can essentially be divided into text-based image retrieval systems and content-based image retrieval systems, where the former represents an image using text, such as keywords or sentences. Yet, with this type of system, the same image can be differently annotated because the image contents are represented according to the subjective perception of the classifier, plus manual annotation causes difficulties in the case of a vast database. Meanwhile, content-based image retrieval (CBIR) systems extract feature vectors from visual information on an image, such as color, texture, and shape. This type of system is more objective than text-based image retrieval, as the feature vectors are extracted using automatic annotation without the subjective perception of a classifier. Consequently, many CBIR methods have already been proposed as efficient retrieval methods [1-13].

Swain et al.[1] proposed a CBIR method using a color histogram, which is robust to rotation and a change of image size, as it extracts the global color distribution. However, in the case of a vast database, different images can have a similar color histogram volume as no spatial correlation is included. As such, Huang et al. [2] proposed a CBIR method using a color correlogram, which is a table indexed by color pairs that combines a color histogram and the spatial correlation, making it superior to the method using only a histogram, as it considers the spatial correlation. However, this method requires many computations and large vector dimensions. Therefore, various methods that use a block color co-occurrence matrix (BCCM) have recently been proposed, where the probability of color co-occurrence within blocks is calculated. Specifically, Qiu et al. [3] proposed a CBIR method that derives two content description features, one is a BCCM and the other a block pattern histogram (BPH). However, the BCCM always extracts two representative colors, regardless of the block characteristics, plus it requires many training images and additional storage space for a codebook. As such, Nezamabadi-pour et al. [4] proposed a BCCM that is adaptive to block characteristics, where the blocks are classified into two classes, one is the uniform blocks and the other is the non-uniform blocks. In this method, a uni-color histogram is used to represent the uniform blocks, while a BCCM with two representative colors represents the non-uniform blocks.

These methods that use a BCCM and a color correlogram yield a good performance but require a large quantized RGB color level sized $Q_{RGB} \times Q_{RGB}$ as feature vector dimensions, while a general histogram method sized Q_{RGB}. Accordingly, this paper proposes a new CBIR method using a color and pattern histogram that is adaptive to the block classification characteristics. The proposed method divides an image into blocks, then classifies the blocks as either luminance or color blocks. Thereafter, as a color feature, a block intensity co-occurrence matrix is calculated for the luminance blocks, while a block hue and saturation co-occurrence matrix is calculated for the color blocks. In addition, as a pattern feature, block directional pattern feature vectors are extracted by calculating histograms after performing directional gradient classification of the intensity. Simulation results show that the proposed method is superior to conventional methods with respect to a precision and a vector dimension.

2 Proposed Retrieval Method

A block diagram of the overall CBIR system is shown in Fig. 1. When the user selects a query image, the feature vectors are automatically extracted and the retrieved images shown in a descending order of similarity. A block diagram of the proposed color feature vector extraction process within the overall retrieval system is shown in Fig. 2. and pattern feature vector extraction process shown in Fig. 3. In the proposed method, color features are extracted adaptively according to the block characteristics. First, the image is transformed into the HSI (hue, saturation, and intensity) domain and divided into blocks. Thereafter, the blocks are classified into luminance blocks and color blocks according to the saturation

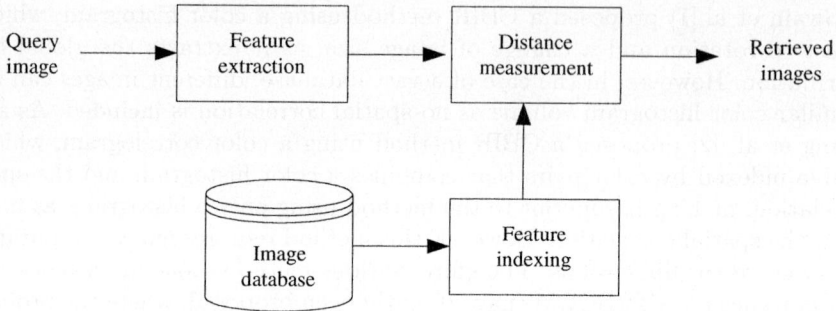

Fig. 1. Block diagram of overall content-based image retrieval system

T_S of each block. The block intensity co-occurrence matrix is then calculated for the blocks with an average saturation smaller than T_S, while the block hue and saturation co-occurrence matrix is calculated for the blocks with an average saturation larger than T_S. In addition to the color features, as a pattern feature, a pattern histogram is calculated by performing directional gradient classification.

2.1 Color Feature Vector Extraction

To extract the color feature vectors, the RGB color space is transformed into HSI color space, where H represents the hue, S indicates the saturation, and I represents the intensity. Specifically, the hue is defined as an angle in the range between 0 and 360 degree, the saturation is the purity of the color and is measured as a radial distance between 0 and 1 from the central axis with intensity, and the intensity is the central vertical axis that represents the average RGB, as shown in Fig. 3 [14]. To extract the color feature vectors that are adaptive to block classification characteristics, the blocks are classified as either luminance blocks or color blocks according to the block average saturation. That is, the block average saturation $\mathbf{S_B}$ and block average intensity $\mathbf{I_B}$ are calculated for the divided blocks $\mathbf{B}$ and the block classification is then performed. The block classification, where $b(k,l)$ represents the bitmap at the $(k,l)th$ block, is performed as

$$b(k,l) = \begin{cases} 0 & if \quad \mathbf{S_B} \geq T_S \\ 1 & otherwise \end{cases} \quad (1)$$

where 0 and 1 represent a color and luminance block, respectively. For the classified blocks, all pixels are then classified as either brighter or darker pixels than each block average luminance $\mathbf{I_B}$. That is, the brightness classification $m(i,j)$ within blocks that represent the bitmap is performed as

$$m(i,j) = \begin{cases} 0 & if \quad I(i,j) \geq \mathbf{I_B} \\ 1 & otherwise \end{cases} \quad (2)$$

For a luminance block that satisfies $b(k,l) = 1$, two representative intensities that represent the average intensity of brighter or darker pixels than the block average

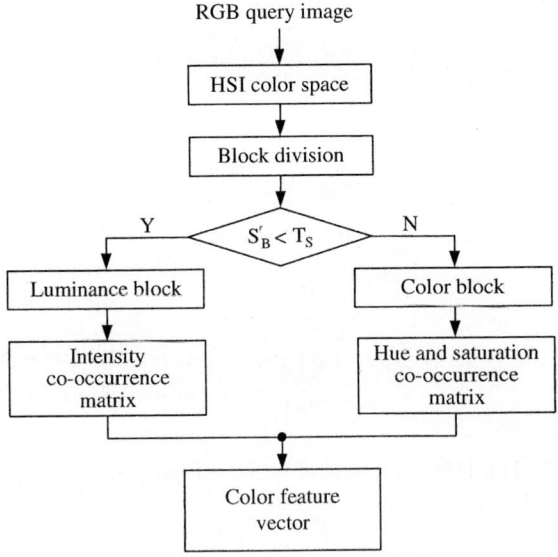

Fig. 2. Block diagram of color feature vector extraction

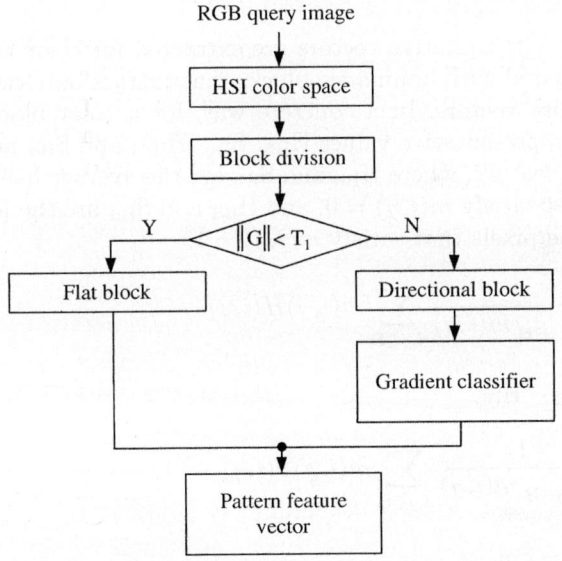

Fig. 3. Block diagram of pattern feature vector extraction

intensity are calculated because these blocks have little color information. That is, I_{Bb} and I_{Bd} where represent the average intensity for the pixels that satisfy $m(i,j) = 0$ and $m(i,j) = 1$ are calculated as follows.

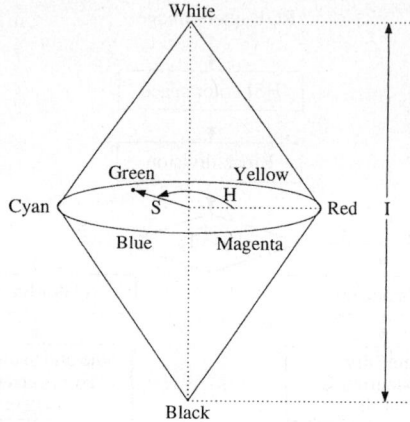

Fig. 4. The HSI color model based on circular color planes

$$I_{Bb} = \frac{1}{\sum_{i,j \in \mathbf{B}} m(i,j)} \sum_{i,j \in \mathbf{B}} m(i,j) I(i,j) \tag{3}$$

$$I_{Bd} = 2I_B - I_{Bb} \tag{4}$$

Meanwhile, four representative vectors are extracted for color blocks with high saturation, compared with luminance blocks that extract only two intensity vectors as the feature vectors. In a concrete way, for a color block that satisfies $b(k,l) = 0$, four representative values H_{Bb}, S_{Bb}, H_{Bd}, and S_{Bd} are calculated to extract the color feature, where H_{Bb} and S_{Bb} are the average hue and saturation for the pixels that satisfy $m(i,j) = 0$, and H_{Bd} and S_{Bd} are the average hue and saturation for the pixels that satisfy $m(i,j) = 1$.

$$H_{Bb} = \frac{1}{\sum_{i,j \in \mathbf{B}} m(i,j)} \sum_{i,j \in \mathbf{B}} m(i,j) H(i,j) \tag{5}$$

$$H_{Bd} = 2H_B - H_{Bb} \tag{6}$$

$$S_{Bb} = \frac{1}{\sum_{i,j \in \mathbf{B}} m(i,j)} \sum_{i,j \in \mathbf{B}} m(i,j) S(i,j) \tag{7}$$

$$S_{Bd} = 2S_B - S_{Bb} \tag{8}$$

After calculating representative values for all blocks, histograms that represent the probability of co-occurrence are calculated for the luminance blocks and color blocks, respectively, as follows.

$$Histo^I(h) = Pr((I_{Bb}, I_{Bd}) \in QI_h) \tag{9}$$

$$Histo^{HS}(h1, h2) = Pr((H_{Bb} \in QH_{h1}, S_{Bb} \in QH_{h1}) \mid (H_{Bd} \in QH_{h1}, S_{Bd} \in QH_{h1})) \tag{10}$$

where QH, QS, and QI represent the quantized hue, saturation, and intensity, h represents the luminance histogram bin, and $h1$ and $h2$ denote the hue and saturation histogram bins, respectively.

2.2 Pattern Feature Vector Extraction

In addition to color the feature vectors, the directional intensity gradient for each block is classified into six classes to extract the pattern feature vectors. Pattern class $\mathbf{C_p}$ is defined as $\mathbf{C_p} = \{C^L, C^{CH}, C^{CV}, C^{D1}, C^{D2}, C^{CR}\}$ where C^L is a no directional flat block, C^{CH} is a horizontal directional block, C^{CV} is a vertical directional block, C^{D1} is a 45 degree directional block, C^{D2} is a 135 degree directional block, and C^{CR} is a no directional complex random block. The directional pattern classification is performed by calculating the directional gradient $\mathbf{G}$ that satisfies $\mathbf{G} = \{G_H, G_V, G_{D1}, G_{D2}\}$. As one example of the four directional gradients, the vertical directional gradient in block location is calculated as follows:

$$G_V(k,l) = \sum_{i=0}^{m-1} \sum_{j=0}^{n/2-1} I_{k,l}(km+i, ln+j) - \sum_{i=0}^{m-1} \sum_{j=n/2}^{n-1} I_{k,l}(km+i, ln+j) \tag{11}$$

After calculating the four directional gradients, the blocks that satisfy $\|\mathbf{G}\| < TH_1$ are classified as C^L, while for the blocks that satisfy $\|\mathbf{G}\| \geq TH_1$, the directional pattern is determined based on the direction with the maximum value among the four directional gradients. For example, the vertical directional change pattern C^{CV} is defined as $C^{CV} = \{\mathbf{B} \mid G_V = MAX(G_H, G_V, G_{D1}, G_{D2})\}$. Thereafter, the pattern histogram $Histo^P$ is extracted by counting six patterns of each block for the overall image.

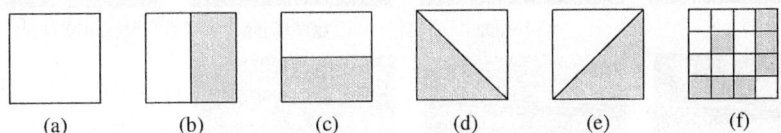

Fig. 5. Directional pattern with (a) non-directional flat block, (b) horizontal direction block, (c) vertical direction block, (d) 45 degree direction block, (e) 135 degree direction block, and (f) non-directional complex random block for pattern feature vector extraction

3 Experimental Results

Experiments were conducted to evaluate the performance of the proposed method. The database included one thousand JPEG-encoded color test images

Fig. 6. (a) Query image and retrieved images from (b) 29.jpg of rank 1 to (k) 571.jpg of rank 10 ranked in a descending order of similarity using Huang's method

Fig. 7. (a) Query image and retrieved images from (b) 3.jpg of rank 1 to (k) 77.jpg of rank 10 ranked in a descending order of similarity using Nezamabadi-pour's method

[4], [6] sized 384×256 or 256×384 and consisting of ten classes, as shown in Table 1. The threshold T_S for experiments was fixed as 0.2 [12] and TH_1 was decided as 13 [4], [7]. As an objective measurement for the evaluation, a pre-

Image Retrieval Based on Co-occurrence Matrix   953

Fig. 8. (a) Query image and retrieved images from (b) 77.jpg of rank 1 to (k) 64.jpg of rank 10 ranked in a descending order of similarity using proposed method

Table 1. Image category for experiment

Class number	Class name
1	Africa people and villages
2	Beach
3	Buildings
4	Buses
5	Dinosurs
6	Elephants
7	Flowers
8	Horses
9	Mountains and glaciers
10	Food

cision and a vector dimension required for extracting the feature vectors were used. A precision calculates the number of images included in the same class as the query image among the retrieved images, represented as

$$P_k = \frac{A_k}{A_k + B_k} \tag{12}$$

where A_k and B_k are the number of images included and not included in the same class as the query image respectively. The rank k had ten interval ranges

Table 2. Precision of retrieved images under equal feature vector dimensions

Rank	Precision %		
	Huang's method [2]	Nezamabadi-pour's method [4]	Proposed method
10	67.43	67.63	71.07
20	62.10	62.15	67.02
30	58.38	58.20	63.74
40	55.46	54.95	60.94
50	53.09	52.10	58.53
60	51.10	49.51	56.34
70	49.37	47.29	54.33
80	47.77	45.29	52.41
90	46.20	43.38	50.51
100	44.64	41.61	48.35

Table 3. Precision of retrieved images according to block size under equal conditionTable 2. Precision of retrieved images under equal feature vector dimensions.

Rank	Precision %	
	4 by 4 block size	8 by 8 block size
10	69.13	68.98
20	64.56	64.61
30	61.55	61.52
40	58.81	59.09
50	56.60	56.83
60	54.44	54.61
70	52.61	52.75
80	50.87	50.98
90	49.31	49.35
100	47.55	47.68

from ten to one hundred, and the distance measure $D(p,q)$ between the query image and the images in the database was

$$D(p,q) = \lambda_1((Histo_p^I - Histo_q^I) + (Histo_p^{HS} - Histo_q^{HS})) \\ + \lambda_2(Histo_p^P - Histo_q^P) \qquad (13)$$

Table 4. Size of color feature vector dimensions required for equal precision

Rank	Precision %	Color feature vector dimension		
		Huang's method [2]	Nezamabadi-pour's method [4]	Proposed method
10	72	4096	1944	640

where λ_1 and λ_2 represent the color and pattern weighting factors, respectively, that satisfy $\lambda_1 + \lambda_2 = 1$. The experiments produced a $\pm 2\%$ change of precision when changing λ_1 between 0.3 and 0.7. Thus, $\lambda_1 = \lambda_2 = 0.5$ was determined as the equal weighting factor.

The query image and retrieved images ranked in a descending order of similarity using conventional methods and the proposed method are shown in Fig. 3, Fig. 4, and Fig. 5. Table 2 shows a precision comparison between the proposed method and conventional methods based on just the color feature vectors, where the comparison was performed by adjusting the quantization level to equal vector dimensions. The proposed method exhibited a higher precision of 3.64 ~ 5.48% than [2] and 3.44 ~ 7.13% than [4], as shown in Table 2. The block size that is used for feature vector extraction is shown in Table 3. A change for the block size has little effect on a precision as shown in Table 3. Also, the vector dimensions required for equal precision are shown in Table 4. Because the change of quantization levels affects on the retrieval performance, the levels were experimentally decided by considering vector dimensions and a precision. The decided quantized levels of the hue, saturation, and intensity are 6, 4, and 8, respectively. Specifically, when the precision was 72% and rank $k = 10$, the required vector dimensions for [2], [4], and the proposed method were 4096, 1944, and 640 respectively. Finally, from the additional six pattern feature vectors, the use of color and pattern feature vectors produced a 1.70 ~ 2.58% higher precision than when using just the color feature vector.

4 Conclusions

A new method of content-based image retrieval was presented that uses a color and pattern histogram that is adaptive to the classification characteristics of the image blocks. First, an image is divided into blocks to exploit the local characteristics, then the blocks are classified as luminance or color blocks according to their saturation. Thereafter, a color histogram is calculated based on the probability of the co-occurrence of a block average intensity among the luminance blocks and the probability of the co-occurrence of a block average hue and saturation among the color blocks. Also, directional pattern classification is performed in six directions to extract the pattern feature. The proposed method exploits a smaller vector dimension than other methods because it extracts the feature vectors that is adaptive to block classification characteristics. Simulation results also confirm that the proposed method can outperform conventional methods as regards the precision.

References

1. Michael J. Swain and Dana H. Ballard: Color indexing. Int. J. Comput. Vis., Vol. 7, No. 1, (1991) 11-32
2. J. Huang, S. R. Kumar, M. Mitra, Wei-Jing Zhu, and R. Zabih: Image indexing using color correlegram. Proc. CVPR97, (1997) 762-768
3. Guoping Qiu: Color image indexing using BTC. IEEE Trans. Image Processing, Vol. 12, No. 1, (2003) 93-101
4. H. Nezamabadi-pour and E. Kabir: Image retrieval using histograms of uni-color and bi-color blocks and directional changes in intensity gradient. Pattern Recogn. Lett., Vol. 25, No. 14, (2004) 1547-1557
5. Yong Rui, Thomas S. Huang, and Shiu-Fu Chang: Image retrieval: Current techniques, promising directions, and open issues. J. Vis. Commun. Image Represent., Vol. 10, No. 1, (1999) 39-62
6. J. Z. Wang, Jia Li, and Gio Wiederhold: SIMPLIcity: semantics-integrated matching for picture libraries. IEEE Trans. Pattern Anal. Machine Intell., Vol. 23, No. 9, (2001) 947-963
7. D. Chen and A. C. Bovik: Visual pattern image coding. IEEE Trans. Commun., Vol. 38, No. 12, (1990) 2137-2146
8. A. Mojsilovic, H. Hu, and E. Soljanin: Extraction of perceptually important colors and similarity measurement for image matching, retrieval, and analysis. IEEE Trans. Image Processing, Vol. 11, No. 11, (2002) 1238-1248
9. Thomas Sikora: The MPEG-7 visual standard for content description-an overview. IEEE Trans. Circuits Syst. Video Technol., Vol. 11, No. 6, (2001) 696-702
10. M. Mirmehdi and R. Perissamy: Perceptual image indexing and retrieval. J. Vis. Commun. Image Represent., Vol. 13, No. 4, (2002) 460-475
11. Y. A Aslandogan and C. T. Yu: Techniques and systems for image and video retrieval. IEEE Trans. Knowl. Data Eng., Vol. 11, No. 1, (1999) 56-63
12. S. Sural, G. Quin, and S. Pramanik: Segmentation and histogram generation using HSV color space for image retrieval. Proc. of ICIP, Vol. 2, No. 2, (2002) 589-592
13. D. K. Park, Y. S. Jeon, C. S. Won, S. J. Park, and S. J. Yoo: A composite histogram for image retrieval. Proc. of ICME, Vol. 1, (2000) 355-358
14. R. C. Gonzalez and R. E. Woods: Digital Image Processing, Prentice Hall, (2002) 295-302

Automatic Generation of the Initial Query Set for CBIR on the Mobile Web

Deok Hwan Kim[1], Chan Young Kim[1], and Yoon Ho Cho[2,*]

[1] School of Computing & information, Dongyang Technical College,
62-160 Kochuk, Kuro, Seoul 152-714, Korea
{dhkim, cykim}@dongyang.ac.kr
[2] School of e-Business, Kookmin University,
861-1 Jungnung, Sungbuk, Seoul 136-702, Korea
www4u@kookmin.ac.kr

Abstract. Despite the rapid growth of wallpaper image downloading service in the mobile contents market, users experience high levels of frustration in searching for desired images, due to the absence of intelligent searching aid. Although Content Based Image Retrieval is the most widely used technique for image retrieval in the PC-based system, its application in the mobile Web environment poses one major problem of not being able to satisfy its initial query requirement because of the limitations in user interfaces of the mobile application software. We propose a new approach, so called a *CF-fronted CBIR*, where Collaborative Filtering (CF) technique automatically generates a list of candidate images that can be used as an initial query in Content Based Image Retrieval (CBIR) by utilizing relevance information captured during Relevance Feedback. The results of the experiment using a PC-based prototype system verified that the proposed approach not only successfully satisfies the initial query requirement of CBIR in the mobile Web environment but also outperforms the current search process.

Keywords: Mobile Content, Collaborative Filtering, Content Based Image Retrieval, Mobile Web, Relevance Feedback.

1 Introduction

With rapid advancement of mobile Web technologies, increasing selection of contents has become available on the mobile Web. Among the many different kinds of mobile contents, wallpaper image for cellular phones, which is used to express the phone owner's emotion, currently ranks at the top of the list of usage [1] and it is expected to stay on top for some time.

Although the wallpaper image downloading market grows rapidly as more developed technologies evolve, users experience high levels of frustration in searching for the specific wallpaper images, due to the inefficient sequential search as shown in Fig. 1. Currently, when users log onto the wallpaper image download

---

* Corresponding author.

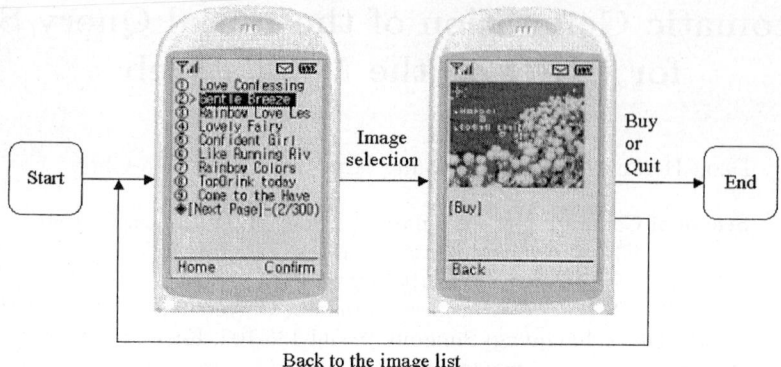

Fig. 1. Current user interface for wallpaper image downloading service

site using a cellular phone, they are presented with the annotation list of images, either a best-seller list or a list generated in some other methods. Users page through the annotation list and take wild guesses to select an entry to check out its visual content hoping that the image will be what he or she wants. If the user likes the image, he or she may make a purchase. Otherwise, the user repeats the same steps until the user either has stumbled over the right one or decides to give up. Using the current method, without any intelligent search aid, the expected number of images the user views before he or she hits the desired image (i.e. target image) far exceeds the acceptable level. To make search processes more acceptable, we need a personalized searching aid that intelligently suggests only the wallpaper images that match the individual user's preference to help users find their target images more efficiently.

Currently, the most widely used technique for image retrieval is Content-Based Image Retrieval (CBIR) [4] [9] that approaches toward the desired images from a large image database step by step starting from an initial query image using their visual features such as color, texture and shape. With the provided query image, CBIR retrieves similar images to the given query and presents the retrieved images to a user. Most of the time, user's target image is not included in the first-round images retrieved by CBIR. To further explore the image database, CBIR employs the relevance feedback (RF) that is an iterative learning mechanism of user's requirement. In CBIR-RF, user interactively provides judgment on the presented images as to whether, and to what degree, they are relevant or irrelevant to her/his request. Then it learns about user's request from the fed back relevance information and applies the newly learned user's preference in the next round of retrieval process [2] [9]. The learning is accomplished in the form of refinements of the query and similarity measure [5] [6] [10].

Despite many successful applications of CBIR in the image search domain in the PC-based Web environment, application of CBIR in the mobile Web environment poses one major problem. Typical CBIR, which operates in a query-by-example (QBE) fashion, assumes that user can provide an initial query image in reasonably good quality using the sophisticated software such as the picture drawing tools. This type of software usually requires rich user interfaces that are not available from the mobile Web environment due to the limited characteristics of mobile peripherals (e.g. cellular phones) such as smaller sized screen, fewer input keys, and less sophisticated browsers. Hence, in order for CBIR to be a feasible alternative in the mobile Web environment, initial query image needs to be provided to CBIR somehow differently rather than by a user.

As a solution to the problem, we propose a *CF-fronted CBIR* approach. The approach uses the Collaborative Filtering technique that is one of the most successful personalized recommendation techniques [7] [8] at the front, and CBIR with RF at the back end. CF is a technique that identifies users whose tastes are similar to those of a target user (i.e. neighbors) and recommends items those neighbors have liked in the past. In our approach, CF is applied to automatically generate the initial query set (IQS) for CBIR through a process of identifying neighbors using relevance information on images fed back from CBIR and providing a list of images that the neighbors, users with similar preferences with the target user, had preferred. Then the target user may select any one of the images in IQS and use it as the starting query image for the subsequent CBIR session. Hence, the CF-fronted CBIR approach resolves the initial query problem of CBIR with a list of images that he would likely prefer, thereby reducing users' search efforts in finding desired wallpaper images on the mobile Web.

We describe the details of CF-fronted CBIR approach and the Initial Query Set Generation Algorithm in Section 2, 3 and 4, respectively. In section 5, we describe the experiment we have conducted to verify the performance of the new approach using the PC-based prototype system and its results. We make a conclusion in Section 6.

2   CF-Fronted CBIR Approach

We propose a new CF-fronted CBIR approach to support a user in finding a desired wallpaper image in the mobile Web environment. This approach consists of two procedures - CF and CBIR-RF procedures. Fig. 2 shows the image search process in the proposed approach.

CF procedure creates the user profile using relevance information and automatically generates an IQS that reflects the target user's preference. When the IQS is presented as shown in (a) of Fig. 2, a user skims through the IQS to see if there are any images of interest. Then, the user selects an entry to view the image, as shown in (b) of Fig. 2. After viewing, the user may decide whether to use the image as a query for CBIR-based search of similar images or to go back to the IQS.

When user decides to use the viewed image as an initial query for further search in CBIR-RF, the image is passed to the CBIR-RF procedure. Then the CBIR-RF procedure, for all images in the database, calculates their distances from the query and generates a list of k most similar images as query results. This procedure then presents the retrieved k images to the user one by one, as shown

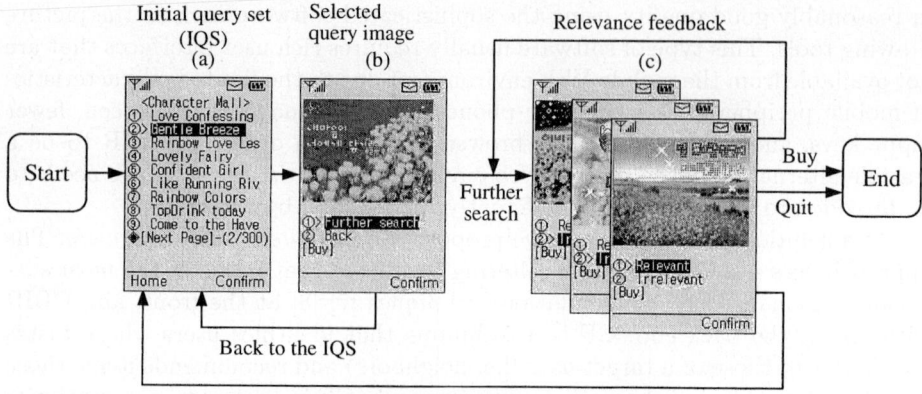

Fig. 2. CF-fronted CBIR process

in (c) of Fig. 2, and interactively elicits the user's relevance judgment on the presented images. Fig. 2 illustrates the case of $k = 3$, where the user is required to feed back the relevance on three retrieved images. For each of k images, the user must declare whether the presented image is relevant or irrelevant to his/her desired image. At any point in this presentation session, the user can also decide to buy an image or quit.

After all of k relevance judgment are made, CBIR-RF procedure updates the relevance information database (RID) with all the fed back relevance judgment, for later use in the CF procedure when the user revisits the mobile Web site. If all of k images are marked as irrelevant (i.e., the user has not found any images relevant to the desired one), the user goes back to IQS and restarts the brand new CBIR-RF search session from the image newly selected. Otherwise, CBIR-RF procedure learns about the user's currently desired image using the relevant set (i.e. a set of images marked as relevant by target user), and applies this information to refine the query and update the similarity measure. It then uses the refined query and similarity measure in the next iteration of retrieval. These iterations continue until the user finds the desired image or quits the image search session.

Fig. 3 shows the CF and CBIR-RF procedures and how those two procedures cooperate to make the CF-fronted CBIR process.

Note that it is beyond the scope of this paper to describe the details of the CBIR-RF procedure since our CF-fronted CBIR approach can be coupled with any CBIR-RF method.

3 Initial Query Set Generation Algorithm

In this section, we propose an algorithm used for generating IQS, from which the mobile user would select an initial query image for CBIR. We devised the

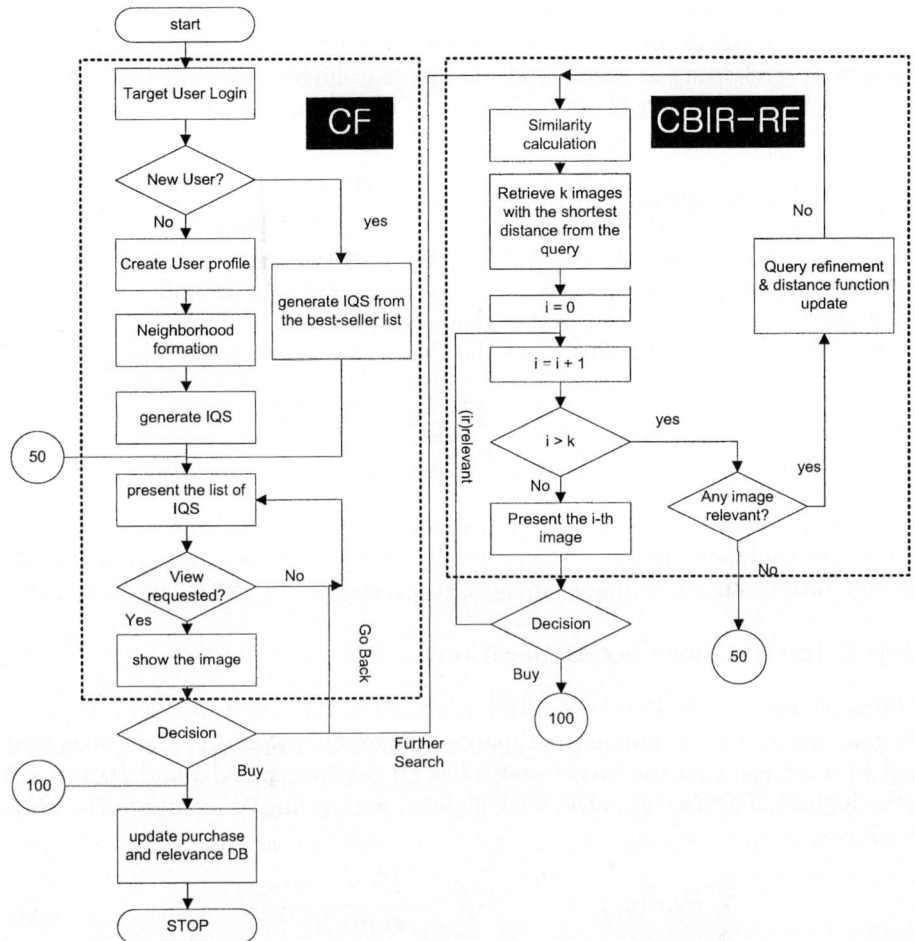

Fig. 3. Internal logic of CF-fronted CBIR process

algorithm using the collaborative filtering that is the most successful technique in the recommendation arena. The CF-based initial query set generation algorithm for a target user u takes three steps.

Step 1: User Profile Creation

CF-based IQS generation depends totally on a user profile, which is a working copy of the relevance information database (RID) that contains information on users' interests in specific images. The information on RID is constantly replaced with newly obtained relevance information fed back from users during CBIR to dynamically reflect the user's most recent preference.

We define the user profile as a matrix of preference ratings $P = (p_{ij})$ where $i = 1$ to M, $j = 1$ to N, where M and N are the total number of users and the total number of wallpaper images, respectively. Because the degree of relevance of an image to the desired image can be expressed in either binary weights (e.g. relevant or irrelevant) or multi-level weights (e.g. highly relevant, relevant, neutral, irrelevant, highly irrelevant), the cells of the rating matrix could have many different values.

Step 2: User Neighborhood Formation

We use $sim(a, b)$ to denote the similarity between two users a and b. We determine the neighborhood, $H = \{h_1, \ldots, h_m\}$ such that $u \notin H$ and $sim(u, h_1)$ is the highest, $sim(u, h_2)$ is the next highest, and so on.

We calculate the similarity using the Pearson-r correlation [8] as follows:

$$sim(a,b) = corr_{ab} = \frac{\sum_{j=1}^{N}(p_{aj} - \bar{p}_a)(p_{bj} - \bar{p}_b)}{\sqrt{\sum_{j=1}^{N}(p_{aj} - \bar{p}_a)^2 \sum_{j=1}^{N}(p_{bj} - \bar{p}_b)^2}} \quad (1)$$

where N is a total number of wallpaper images, p_{aj} and p_{bj} are user a and b's ratings on wallpaper image j, respectively, and $\bar{p}_a$ and $\bar{p}_b$ are user a and b's average ratings on all wallpaper images, respectively.

Step 3: Initial Query Set Generation

$PLS(u, j)$ denotes the *Purchase Likeliness Score* of the target user u for image j. We generate an IQS including n wallpaper images, $Q = \{q_1, q_2, \ldots, q_n\}$ such that $r_j \notin \{$ the images that the target user u has already purchased $\}$ and $PLS(u, r_1)$ is the highest, $PLS(u, r_2)$ is the next highest, and so on. We compute the PLS as follows:

$$PLS(u,j) = \frac{\sum_{i \in H}(p_{ij} - \bar{p}_i) \times sim(u,i)}{\sum_{i \in H} sim(u,i)} \quad (2)$$

Note that, for a new user without any profile information, this algorithm uses the best-seller image list as an IQS.

4 Illustrative Example of IQS Generation

In this section, we demonstrate how initial query set is generated using the algorithm in Section 3.

Let's suppose that Table 1 is a user profile where each of whose elements indicates the preference of the corresponding user on the corresponding image. The profile includes the ratings of 15 users on 10 images. In this example, we use the four possible values of each element: 0, +1, -1, and 2 for unseen, preferred, unpreferred and purchased images, respectively.

Let's think about the case that the system needs to make recommendations to the user U_{15} (i.e. U_{15} is a target user). Using the ratings, recommendations are generated as following steps. First, correlation (i.e. similarity) between the

Table 1. User profile

Ratings		I_1	I_2	I_3	I_4	I_5	I_6	I_7	I_8	I_9	I_{10}
U S E R	U_1	2	0	0	2	0	1	0	0	2	2
	U_2	0	1	0	0	0	0	0	2	0	1
	U_3	2	2	0	-1	1	1	0	0	0	0
	U_4	-1	0	1	0	-1	0	-1	0	-1	0
	U_5	-1	0	0	0	0	0	0	0	-1	0
	U_6	2	0	0	0	0	-1	-1	0	0	0
	U_7	0	0	0	0	-1	2	2	0	0	2
	U_8	-1	0	0	0	-1	0	-1	-1	0	0
	U_9	0	2	2	0	0	0	2	0	0	1
	U_{10}	2	0	0	2	1	0	0	0	0	0
	U_{11}	2	2	0	0	0	0	-1	1	0	0
	U_{12}	0	0	0	0	0	0	0	0	-1	0
	U_{13}	0	0	1	0	2	0	2	0	0	0
	U_{14}	0	2	0	-1	0	0	2	-1	2	-1
	U_{15}	1	0	2	-1	0	0	2	0	0	0

Table 2. Correlation with the Target User

U_1	U_2	U_3	U_4	U_5	U_6	U_7	U_8	U_9	U_{10}	U_{11}	U_{12}	U_{13}	U_{14}
-0.42	-0.26	0.12	0.03	-0.05	0.00	0.21	-0.31	0.63	-0.27	-0.19	0.15	0.54	0.35

target user U_{15} and others are calculated and the result is shown in Table 2. Next, the neighbors, which is a group of customers with high correlations with the target user, are identified. In case of the neighborhood size of five, the users with the top five similarity values, U_7, U_9, U_{12}, U_{13}, and U_{14}, are selected as neighbors. Table 3 shows the neighbors.

The images that can be recommended to U_{15}, who is a target user, are the images that she did not purchase yet. Hence, only a part of the whole profile that is left after excluding the column of the already purchased images by the target user and non-neighbor users (i.e. shaded part of the original profile) is used.

Purchase likelihood score (PLS), which is the weighted average of ratings of the item using the similarity of the each neighbor as weights are shown in Table 4. Recommendations are to be made on the order of highest PLS. The order of the items on the IQS would be I_2 followed by I_5, I_{10}, I_9, I_6, I_1, I_4, and I_8. Any of these images on the IQS may be used as the initial query for CBIR.

Table 3. Neighbors

	I_1	I_2	I_4	I_5	I_6	I_8	I_9	I_{10}	Similarity to U_{15}
U_7	0	0	0	-1	2	0	0	2	0.213
U_9	0	2	0	0	0	0	0	1	0.63
U_{12}	0	0	0	0	0	0	-1	0	0.145
U_{13}	0	0	0	2	0	0	0	0	0.541
U_{14}	0	2	-1	0	0	-1	2	-1	0.349
sum									1.879

Table 4. Initial Query Set

	I_1	I_2	I_4	I_5	I_6	I_8	I_9	I_{10}
PLS	0	1.042	-0.19	0.463	0.227	-0.19	0.294	0.376
order	(6)	(1)	(7)	(2)	(5)	(8)	(4)	(3)

5 Experiment and Results

For the purpose of the performance evaluation of the proposed approach, we developed a Web-based application system running on a PC with exactly the same user interfaces as the cellular phone-based system. Using the system, we carried out the experiments with the intent of answering two major questions:

1. How much performance improvement does the new approach deliver compared to the currently used best-seller-based approach?
2. How does the effectiveness of CF affect the overall performance of the proposed approach?

For the experiments, we used the 230 wallpaper images that Korea Telecom Freetel (KTF), a leading Korean CDMA(code division multiple access) carrier, offered at the time of our experiment. To characterize wallpaper images, we used three color moments based on HSV (hue, saturation, value), a well known visual feature. The mean, standard deviation and skewness of HSV values of all pixels were calculated to represent wallpaper images as vectors in a nine dimensional feature space. In our experiment, we used the less heterogeneous image database that consists of a small number of images that belong to a small number of categories (for example, love, friendship, the bizarre, etc.). For this reason, we used only the color moment for image characterization although it is known that the performance of CBIR improves as more visual features are used.

200 mobile Web customers, who had previously purchased wallpaper images from KTF, participated in the experiment. First, all the participants were asked

to go through all the images and mark the images they had purchased in the past. The collected purchase information is stored as an initial user profile. Then participant starts a search session by selecting a target image to search for from randomly ordered wallpaper images that she has not purchased. For the system's functionality to allow participants to navigate freely for a target image for experiment, we chose the Web interface of the PC over that of the mobile phone. The selected image becomes the target image of the search session.

With the same target image, participant performed two search sessions per period, one using the best-seller-based system and the other using the CF-fronted CBIR (with k=5) system. Participants continued the search session until the target image is shown either because it is selected by the user from IQS / best-seller-based list or because it is returned by CBIR. This experiment was repeated for five periods to see how performance of the system changes by periods where different amounts of ratings are available. Since the quality of recommendations of CF is known to vary by the size of the neighborhood [7], we selected the neighborhood size of 30 after an additional experiment of a single period yielding the best performance.

For the evaluation of the proposed approach, we devised the *views-per-success* (*vps*) metric, which is the number of images a user views before he or she hits the desired image. Basically, *vps* measures the user's effort for a successful search. We used *vps* to compare our proposed approach to the best-seller-based search. Table 5 summarizes our experiment results.

Table 5. Comparison of average performance

	Performance (*vps*)						*vps* reduction
	Period1	Period2	Period3	Period4	Period5	Average	over 5 periods
CF-fronted CBIR [V]	23.01	22.32	19.96	18.57	17.24	20.22	25%
Best-seller-based search [B]	43.98	42.64	41.12	41.89	40.66	42.06	8%
Performance gain*	48%	48%	51%	56%	58%	52%	

* Performance gain of proposed approach over best-seller-based method = $(B - V)/B$

As Table 5 shows, the average *vps* of CF-fronted CBIR approach is about 52% lower than that best-seller-based search, at a significance level of 1%, (i.e. the proposed approach produced performance gains of 52%). Table 5 also shows that the rates of improvement in *vps* over the five periods (i.e. the system's learning speed) is 25% for CF-fronted CBIR approach, 8% for the best-seller-based search. These results indicate that CF-fronted CBIR approach offers not only the lowest *vps* but also the faster performance improvement over 5 periods. Since more rating information becomes available in the user profile, as periods progress, the neighborhood formation becomes more accurate, thereby improving the quality of IQS.

Table 6 summarizes CF's effects over five periods. The results in Table 2 show that better performance of CF help decrease *vps* in three ways. First, the images on the IQS are used more often as an initial query for CBIR-RF because

Table 6. CF's effects over five periods

CF's Effect	Period				
	1st	2nd	3rd	4th	5th
(a) Rate of the images on the first page of IQS becoming an initial query of CBIR	0.33	0.33	0.36	0.36	0.39
(b) Iterations of CBIR-RF per success	4.23	4.08	3.79	3.78	3.66
(c) The rate of the target image being found off the first page of IQS	0.18	0.20	0.24	0.25	0.28

the upper part of IQS contains more relevant images. As Table 6 (a) shows, the average rate of the images on the first page of IQS (that is, top-9 images) becoming an initial query of CBIR-RF increases by period from 0.33 in Period 1 to 0.39 in Period 5. Second, the number of iterations of CBIR-RF per success decreases because the first image used in CBIR-RF is closer to the target image in the feature space. As Table 6 (b) shows, the average number of iterations of CBIR-RF per success decreases from 4.23 in Period 1 to 3.66 in Period 5. Third, the *vps* consumed in CBIR-RF decreases because the likelihood increases that the target image is in the upper part of IQS. As Table 6 (c) shows, the rate of the target image being on the first page of IQS increases from 0.18 in Period 1 to 0.28 in Period 5.

From the experiment result, we can conclude that CF-fronted CBIR is a viable solution to the problems currently encountered in wallpaper image downloading on the mobile Web, and that it can be expected to reduce the search effort. CF-fronted CBIR approach offers the following benefits to both consumers and suppliers of mobile contents: (1) Users can purchase contents with much less search effort and much lower connection time to the mobile Web, because they can much more easily find desired mobile contents. (2) Mobile content providers can improve the profitability of their businesses because lower user frustration in finding desired contents increases revenue through an improved purchase conversion rate (i.e. the number of search sessions that end with purchase divided by the total number of search sessions).

6 Conclusion and Future Research

We proposed a new approach, the CF-fronted CBIR, to address the real problems encountered in wallpaper image downloading services in the mobile Web environment. The approach combines two techniques from different research domains - CF from recommender system and CBIR-RF from image retrieval domains. The new approach resolved the initial query requirement of CBIR by automatically generating initial queries based on previously accumulated relevance information data. We also conducted an experiment using the PC-based prototype system to prove that the approach is a viable alternative and verified that the new approach outperforms the currently used best-seller-based search method.

CF is a recommendation technique based on users' ratings of the past on items. Each rating is supposed to carry the information on corresponding user's preference on the corresponding item. The information content of a single rating in regards to suggesting a particular user's preference on items at the current moment is expected to vary depending on how long ago when the rating was made. However, in CF, these ratings are all treated equally regardless of the time lag between rating and recommendation. Temporal decay factor can be used to discount the information content of ratings over time. The exploration of proper information discounting mechanism for collaborative filtering can be a good area of future research.

As varieties in multimedia contents on the mobile Web increase, the same type of search problems would prevail as they do in case of wallpaper images. With the rapid growth of the mobile Web service, the mobile Web-based recommender system for other types of multimedia contents, such as music on demand (MOD) or video on demand (VOD), will continue to be an area of research interest in the future. To meet the demands for more intelligent search aids from the market, CF-fronted CBIR can be used as a good starting point.

Our approach is applicable to these types of content as long as you can represent the content as a vector in the feature space, as in the case of wallpaper images. However, users can easily provide relevance feedback on wallpaper images after a short viewing; this might not be true for music or videos. So, successful application of our approach to these types of content will require research on the proper interfaces for relevance feedback. We believe that the research on proper interfaces for different types of multimedia content will be a good topic of further research.

Acknowledgements

This work was supported by the new faculty research program 2004 of Kookmin University in Korea.

References

1. Korea internet White Paper 2003.
2. R. Brunelli, O. Mich, "Image Retrieval by Examples," IEEE Transactions on Multimedia, **2**(3) 2000, pp. 164-171.
3. Y.H. Cho, J.K. Kim: Application of Web Usage Mining and Product Taxonomy to Collaborative Recommendations in E-Commerce. Expert Systems with Applications. **26**(2) 2004, pp. 233-246.
4. M. Flickner H. Sawhney, W. Niblack et al. Query by image and video content: The QBIC system. IEEE Computer Magazine, **28**(9) 1995, pp. 23-32.
5. D.H. Kim, C.W. Chung, K. Barnard, "Relevance feedback using adaptive clustering for image similarity retrieval," Journal of Systems and Software, **78**(1) 2005, pp. 9-23.
6. K. Porkaew, K. Chakrabarti, and S. Mehrotra, "Query Refinement for Multimedia Similarity Retrieval in MARS," Proc. 7th ACM Multimedia Conference, November 1999, pp. 235-238.

7. B. Sarwar et al., "Analysis of Recommendation Algorithms for E-Commerce," Proc. ACM E-Commerce Conference, 2000, pp. 158-167.
8. U. Shardanand and P. Maes, "Social Information Filtering: Algorithms for Automating "Word of Mouth". Proc. Conference on Human factors in Computing Systems, 1995, pp. 210-217.
9. X.S. Zhou, T.S. Huang, "Relevance feedback for image retrieval: a comprehensive review," ACM Multimedia Systems Journal, **8** (6) 2003, pp. 536-544. 2.
10. L. Wu et al., "FALCON: Feedback Adaptive Loop for Content-Based Retrieval," Proc. 26th VLDB Conference, 2000, pp. 297-306.

Classification of MPEG Video Content Using Divergence Measure with Data Covariance

Dong-Chul Park[1], Chung-Nguyen Tran[1], and Yunsik Lee[2]

[1] ICRL, Dept. of Information Engineering, Myong Ji University, Korea
{parkd, cntran}@mju.ac.kr
[2] SoC Research Center, Korea Electronics Tech. Inst., Seongnam, Korea
leeys@keti.re.kr

Abstract. This paper describes how the covariance information in MPEG video data can be incorporated into a distance measure and applies the resulting divergence measure to video content classification problems. The divergence measure is adopted into two different clustering algorithms, the Centroid Neural Network (CNN) and the Gradient Based Fuzzy c-Means (GBFCM) for MPEG video data classification problems, movie or sports. Experiments on 16 MPEG video traces show that the divergence measure with covariance information can decrease the False Alarm Rate (FAR) in classification as much as 46.6% on average.

1 Introduction

Many multimedia applications can benefit from retrieval of the video data based on their content such as video on demand, video database, video teleconferencing, etc. Recently, the research on MPEG video content classification has attracted great attention [1,2,3,4,5,6]. When compressed, however, the content classification of the video data may become very complicated. Most of these studies try to exploit the spatial knowledge of the video sequence after decompressing the data. Therefore, classification of compressed video data without going through the decompressing procedure is still an open problem.

Dawood and Ghanbari [1] proposed a linguistic label to model MPEG video traffic and classify it based on the texture and motion complexity. Patel and Sethi [2] proposed a method to analyze the compressed video data directly by using a decision-tree classifier. Their method consists of comparing intensity and row and column histograms of successive I frames of MPEG video using the χ-square test. In the view of data, this approach basically considers the MPEG video data as deterministic time-series data. However, according to Rose's thorough analysis on MPEG data [7], it would be more realistic to consider the MPEG video data as Gaussian Probability Density Function (GPDF) data. The probabilistic nature of the MPEG video data was also accepted by Liang and Mendel [3]. They proposed a classification method involving 2 steps. In the first step, hereafter called the modelling step, they use the Fuzzy C-Means algorithm to model the probabilistic distribution of the log-value of the frame size. In the next step, called the classification step, several classifiers such as the Beyesian classifier and fuzzy classifiers are employed to decide the genre, "movie" or "sport", which a video sequence belongs to. Liang and Mendel, however, utilize the FCM with only mean values of the GPDF data while leaving out the covariance information of the GPDF data. This paper proposes utilizing the entire information, mean and covariance information of the GPDFs in MPEG video data. In addition, several studies confirm that the divergence distance is more suitable for modelling the GPDF data when compared with other distance measures. Therefore, in this paper, we also propose to employ the divergence measure (DM) in modelling MPEG video sequences. These ideas are then applied into the Centroid Neural Network(CNN) and Gradient-based Fuzzy C-Means (GBFCM) as two alternative solutions for modelling the distribution of the log-value of MPEG data.

Section 2 describes the Gradient-based Fuzzy C-Means algorithm. Section 3 introduces the Centroid Neural Network. In Section 4, experiments on MPEG-1 and MPEG-4 video data are examined in order to compare the performance of the GBFCM and the CNN in the case of using both the divergence measure and the Euclidean distance measure. Section 5 concludes this paper.

2 Gradient-Based Fuzzy C-Means Algorithm Using the Divergence Measure (GBFCM(DM))

2.1 Fuzzy C-Means Algorithm

The objective of clustering algorithms is to group similar objects and separate dissimilar ones. Bezdek first generalized the *fuzzy ISODATA* by defining a family of objective functions $J_m, 1 < m < \infty$, and established a convergence theorem for that family of objective functions [8,9]. For FCM, the objective function is defined as :

$$J_m(U, v) = \sum_{k=1}^{n} \sum_{i=1}^{c} (\mu_{ki})^m (d_i(x_k))^2 \tag{1}$$

where $d_i(x_k)$ denotes the distance from the input data x_k to v_i, the center of the cluster i, μ_{ki} is the membership value of the data x_k to the cluster i, and m is the weighting exponent, $m \in 1, \cdots, \infty$, while n and c are the number of input data and clusters, respectively. Note that the distance measure used in the FCM is the Euclidean distance.

Bezdek defined a condition for minimizing the objective function with the following two equations:

$$\mu_{ki} = \frac{1}{\sum_{j=1}^{c} (\frac{d_i(x_k)}{d_j(x_k)})^{\frac{2}{m-1}}} \tag{2}$$

$$v_i = \frac{\sum_{k=1}^{n} (\mu_{ki})^m x_k}{\sum_{k=1}^{n} (\mu_{ki})^m} \tag{3}$$

The FCM finds the optimal values of group centers iteratively by applying Eq. (2) and Eq. (3) in an alternating fashion.

2.2 The Gradient Based Fuzzy C-Means Algorithm Using the Divergence Measure (GBFCM(DM))

The GBFCM was first introduced in [10]. The algorithm attempts to improve the FCM algorithm by minimizing the objective function using one input data at a time instead of the entire input data. That is, the FCM in Eq. (2) and Eq. (3) uses all data to update the center value of the cluster, but the GBFCM that is used in this paper was developed to update the center value of the cluster with given individual data sequentially [10,11]. Given one data x_i and c clusters with centers at $v_j, (j = 1, 2, \cdots, c)$, the objective function to be minimized is:

$$J_i = \mu_{1i}^2(v_1 - x_i)^2 + \mu_{2i}^2(v_2 - x_i)^2 + \cdots + \mu_{ci}^2(v_c - x_i)^2 \quad (4)$$

with the following constraint:

$$\mu_{1i} + \mu_{2i} + \cdots + \mu_{ci} = 1 \quad (5)$$

The group centers are updated as follows:

$$v_{k+1} = v_k - 2\eta\mu_{ki}^2(v_k - x_i) \quad (6)$$

where η is a learning constant and the membership grades are defined as:

$$\mu_{ki} = \frac{1}{\sum_{j=1}^{c}(\frac{d_i(x_k)}{d_j(x_k)})^2} \quad (7)$$

After evaluating various distance measures, the Divergence distance (*Kullback-Leibler Divergence*) between two GPDFs, $x = (x_i^\mu, x_i^{\sigma^2})$ and $v = (v_i^\mu, v_i^{\sigma^2})$, $i = 1, \cdots, d$, is chosen as the distance measure in our algorithm [12,13]:

$$D(x, v) = \sum_{i=1}^{d}(\frac{x_i^{\sigma^2} + (x_i^\mu - v_i^\mu)^2}{v_i^{\sigma^2}} + \frac{v_i^{\sigma^2} + (x_i^\mu - v_i^\mu)^2}{x_i^{\sigma^2}} - 2)$$

$$= \sum_{i=1}^{d}(\frac{(x_i^{\sigma^2} - v_i^{\sigma^2})^2}{x_i^{\sigma^2} v_i^{\sigma^2}} + \frac{(x_i^\mu - v_i^\mu)^2}{x_i^{\sigma^2}} + \frac{(x_i^\mu - v_i^\mu)^2}{v_i^{\sigma^2}}) \quad (8)$$

where x_i^μ and $x_i^{\sigma^2}$ denote μ and σ^2 values of the ith component of x, respectively, while v_i^μ and $v_i^{\sigma^2}$ denote μ and σ^2 values of the ith component of v, respectively.

One epoch of training the GBFCM(DM) consists of two parts: the first is about membership value and weight updates for μ and the second is about weight updates for σ^2. With this scenario, the diagonal covariance for each group is calculated by the following equation:

$$\mathbf{w}_j^{\sigma^2}(m+1) = \frac{\sum_{k=1}^{N_j}[\mathbf{x}_{k,j}^{\sigma^2}(m) + (\mathbf{x}_{k,j}^\mu(m) - \mathbf{w}_j^\mu(m))^2]}{N_j}, \quad j = 1, 2, \cdots, C \quad (9)$$

Table 1. The GBFCM Algorithm

```
Algorithm GBFCM(DM)
  Procedure main()
    Read c, ε, m
    [c: initialize cluster, ε: is small value,
    m is a weighting exponent (m ∈ 1,...∞)]
    error := 0
    While (error > ε)
      While (input file is not empty)
        Read one datum x
        [Update GBFCM(DM) center Mean]
```
$$v^\mu(n+1) = v^\mu(n) - \eta\mu^2(v^\mu(n) - x^\mu)$$
```
        [Update GBFCM(DM) membership grade]
```
$$\mu_i(x) = \frac{1}{\sum_{j=1}^{c}(\frac{D(x,v_i)}{D(x,v_j)})^2}$$
```
        e := v^μ(n+1) - v^μ(n)
      End while
```
$$v_i^{\sigma^2}(n+1) = \frac{\sum_{k=1}^{N_i}(x_{k,i}^{\sigma^2}(n)+(x_{k,i}^\mu(n)-v_i^\mu(n))^2)}{N_i}$$
```
      error := e
    End while
    Output μ_i, v^μ and v^{σ²}
  End main()
End
```

- C,m : the number of clusters and the time index of the epoch.
- $\mathbf{x}_{k,j}^\mu(m)$ or $\mathbf{x}_{k,j}^{\sigma^2}(m)$: the mean or diagonal covariance of the kth data in the in the cluster j at the time of epoch m.
- $\mathbf{w}_j^\mu(m)$ or $\mathbf{w}_j^{\sigma^2}(m)$: the mean or diagonal covariance of the cluster j at the time of epoch m.

Table 1 is a pseudocode of the GBFCM(DM).

3 Centroid Neural Network Using the Divergence Measure (CNN(DM))

3.1 CNN Algorithm

The CNN is an unsupervised competitive learning algorithm based on the classical k-means clustering algorithm. It finds the centroids of clusters at each presentation of the data vector. The CNN first introduces definitions of the winner neuron and the loser neuron. When a data $\mathbf{x}_i$ is given to the network at the epoch (k), the winner neuron at the epoch (k) is the neuron with the minimum distance to $\mathbf{x}_i$. The loser neuron at the epoch (k) to $\mathbf{x}_i$ is the neuron that was the winner of $\mathbf{x}_i$ at the epoch (k-1) but is not the winner of $\mathbf{x}_i$ at the epoch (k). The CNN updates their weights only when the status of the output neuron for the presenting data has changed when compared to the status from the previous epoch.

When an input vector $\mathbf{x}$ is presented to the network at epoch n, the weight update equations for winner neuron j and loser neuron i in CNN can be summarized as follows:

$$\mathbf{w}_j(n+1) = \mathbf{w}_j(n) + \frac{1}{N_j+1}[\mathbf{x}(n) - \mathbf{w}_j(n)] \quad (10)$$

$$\mathbf{w}_i(n+1) = \mathbf{w}_i(n) - \frac{1}{N_i-1}[\mathbf{x}(n) - \mathbf{w}_i(n)] \quad (11)$$

where $\mathbf{w}_j(n)$ and $\mathbf{w}_i(n)$ represent the weight vectors of the winner neuron and the loser neuron at the iteration n, respectively.

CNN has several advantages over conventional algorithms such as SOM or k-means algorithm when used for clustering and unsupervised competitive learning. The CNN requires neither a predetermined schedule for learning gain nor the total number of iterations for clustering. It always converges to sub-optimal solutions while conventional algorithms such as SOM may give unstable results depending on the initial learning gain and the total number of iterations. More detailed description on CNN can be found in [14,15]

Note that the CNN was designed for deterministic data because the distance measure used in CNN is the Euclidean distance.

3.2 Centroid Neural Network Using the Divergence Measure

Though CNN has been applied successfully to deterministic data, it was not designed to work with probabilistic data such as GPDF data. When CNN is applied directly to probabilistic data such as GPDF data, the covariance information should be ignored. In order to deal with the probabilistic data such as GPDF, the winner, g_{w_j}, for the CNN should be determined according to the divergence distance instead of the Euclidean distance. That is,

$$g_{w_j} = \arg\min_w D(g_x, g_w)$$

where $\mathbf{x}$ and $\mathbf{w}$ denote the data vector and the weight vector, respectively.

The concept of winner and loser in CNN can be adopted without any change except for application of the divergence measure for the distance calculation. In this case, however GPDFs have two parameters to consider: mean, μ, and diagonal covariance, Σ. The weight update for mean is the same as the CNN weight update shown in Eq. (10) and Eq. (11). Like CNN, the μ (mean) of the winner neuron moves toward the μ of input data vectors while the μ of the loser neuron moves away from the μ of input data vectors. One epoch of training CNN(DM) consists of two parts: the first concerns the weight updates for μ and the second concerns the weight updates for Σ. Weights updates for Σ are performed once at the end of each epoch while weights for μ are updated at every iteration. That is, after presentation of all the data vectors for weight updates for μ at each epoch, weight updates for μ are suspended until weight updates for Σ are performed with the grouping information of data vectors obtained for μ during the epoch. With this scenario, the diagonal covariance for each group is calculated by the following equation:

$$\sum_{w_j}(n+1) = \frac{\sum_{k=1}^{N_j}[\sum_{x_k j}(n) + (\mu_{x_k j}(n) - \mu_{w_j}(n))]}{N_j}, \qquad j=1,2,...,C$$

where $\sum_{k=1}^{N_j}$ is just a notation for the summation operation while $\sum_{w_j}(n+1)$ and $\sum_{x_k j}(n)$ are notations for covariances. More detailed information on the notations used in the above equation is as follows:

- C, n : the number of clusters and the time index of epoch n.
- $\mu_{x_k j}(n)$ or $\sum_{x_k j}(n)$: the mean or diagonal covariance of the kth data in the in the cluster j at the time of epoch n.
- $\mu_{w_j}(n)$ or $\sum_{w_j}(n)$: the mean or diagonal covariance of the cluster j at the time of epoch n.

Note that the diagonal covariance of each data vector is replaced by the group diagonal covariance value according to the group decided by the mean value of the data vector during the weight update process. The diagonal covariances of all the data vector in a group remain unchanged during the same epoch of the training procedure.

4 Experiments and Results

For experiments, we evaluate the performance of the proposed algorithms on two data sets. The first data set consists of 10 MPEG video traces obtained from http://www3.informatik.uni-wuerzburd.de/MPEG. These are MPEG-1 video traces that are provided by the Institute of Computer Science III, University of Wuerzburg, Wuerzburg, Germany. The total number of GoPs in each data trace is 3333 with 12 frames in each GoP. Each GoP can be represented by the sequence *IBBPBBPBBPBB*. More details about these traces are available at that website. Table 1 shows the titles of the 10 MPEG-1 video streams used in our experiments. Fig. 1 shows an example of MPEG-1 data with I-, P-, and B-frame from the video data *"Two 1993 soccer World Cup matches"* of Table 1.

The second data set consists of 6 MPEG-4 video traces that are obtained from the public website http://www-tkn.ee.tuberlin.de/reseach/trace/trace.html. Table 2 shows the titles of the 6 MPEG-4 video traces in the second data set. These video traces are provided by the Telecommunication Networks Group of the Technical University of Berlin, Berlin, Germany. The total number of GoPs in each data trace is 7500 with 12 frames in each GOP.

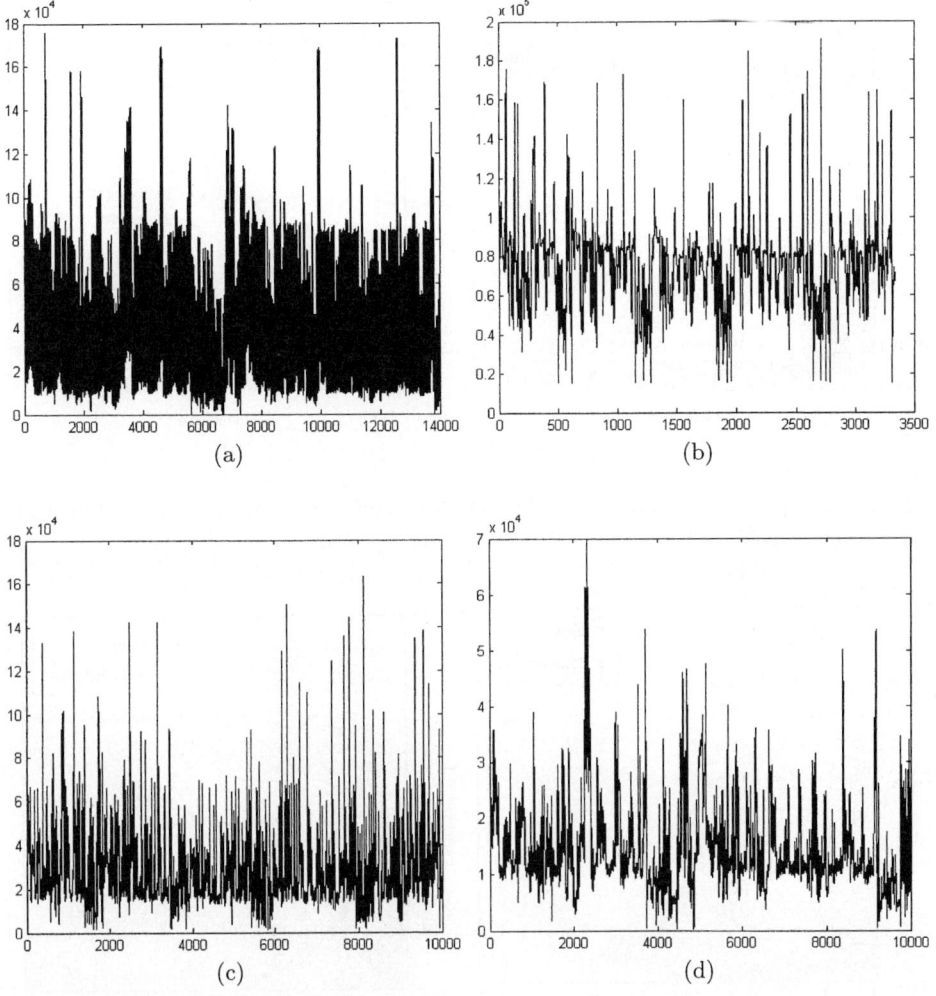

Fig. 1. Example of MPEG data: (a) whole data (b) I-frame (c) P-frame (d) B-frame

Table 2. MPEG-1 Video used for experiments

MOVIE	SPORTS
"Jurassic Park"	"ATP Tennis Final"
"The Silence of the Lambs"	"Formula 1 Race: GP Hockenheim 1994"
"Star Wars"	"Super Bowl Final 1995: SanDiego-San Francisco"
"Terminator 2"	"Two 1993 Soccer World Cup Matches"
"A 1994 Movie Preview"	"Two 1993 Soccer World Cup Matches"

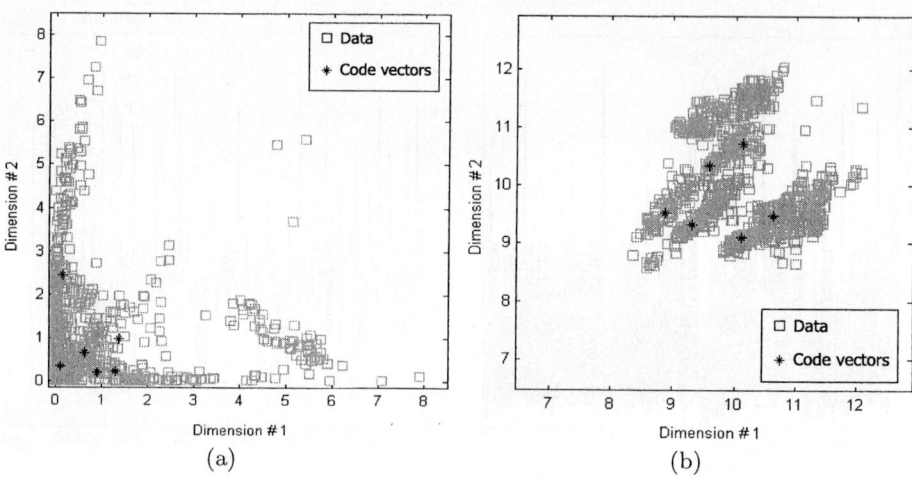

Fig. 2. Example of distribution of MPEG-1 GoPs and their code vectors for Dimension #1 and Dimension #2, presented in mean values: (a)Movie clips (b)Sport clips

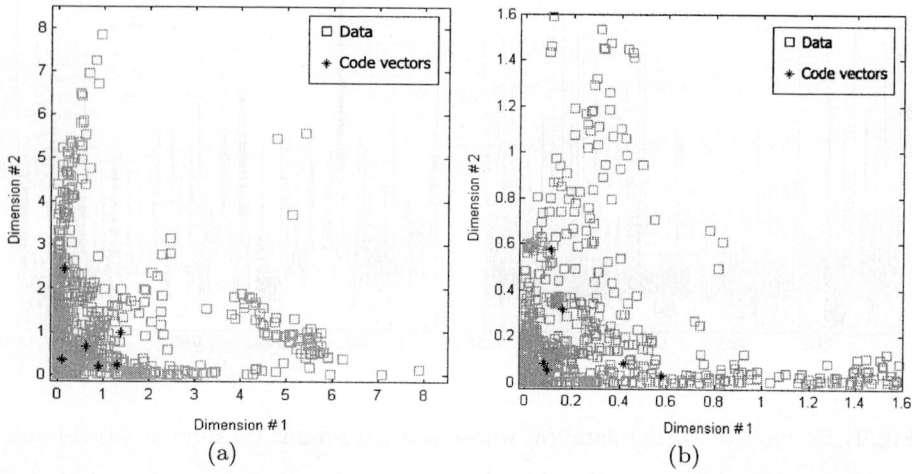

Fig. 3. Example of distribution of MPEG-1 GoPs and their code vectors for Dimension #1 and Dimension #2, presented in covariance values: (a)Movie clips (b)Sport clips

Table 3. MPEG-4 Video used for experiments

MOVIE	SPORTS
"Jurassic Park I"	"Formula 1"
"Silence Of The Lambs"	"Soccer"
"Star Wars IV"	"Alpin Ski"

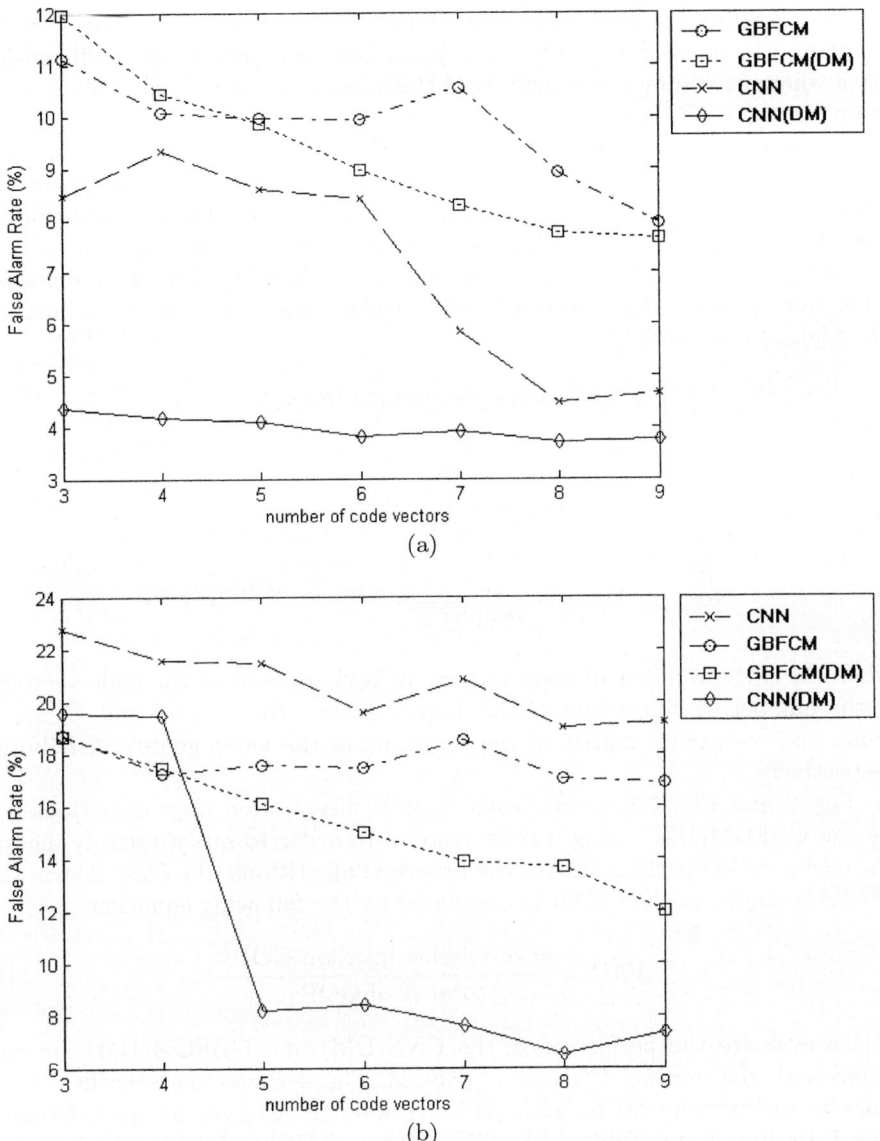

Fig. 4. Experiment results in FAR for different algorithms: (a) Using MPEG-1 data (b) Using MPEG-4 data

For experiments on each data set, we use the first 50% GoPs of each movie for training and the remaining 50% GoPs for testing. We performed the experiments both on the MPEG-1 video traces and MPEG-4 video traces. In each case, the number of clusters in each class of movie and sports was increased from 3 to 9 to find out the sufficient number of cluster that gives the best accuracy.

For applying the divergence measurement, the mean and variance of each of 12 frames in the GoPs are obtained. Each GoP is expressed as 12-dimensional data where each dimension consists of the mean and the variance values of each frame in the GoP. In the training step, the GoPs of each video genre, "movie" and "sport", are clustered into a predetermined number of groups. The mean and covariance of each group are calculated. Base on these mean and covariance values, in the testing step, we calculate the probability that a GoP belongs to "movie" or "sport" using a Bayesian classifier. The classifier decides the video genre for each video trace by calculating the probability that trace belongs to each video genre, then choose the video genre, "movie" or "sport", which gives the highest probability.

$$Genre(x) = \arg\max_i P(x|v_i)$$

$$P(x|v_i) = \sum_{i=1}^{M} c_i \aleph(x, \mu_i, \Sigma_i)$$

$$\aleph(x, \mu_i, \Sigma_i) = \frac{1}{\sqrt{(2\pi)^d |\Sigma_i|}} e^{-0.5(x_i - m_i)^T \Sigma_i^{-1} (x_i - m_i)}$$

where M is the number of code vectors, c_i is the weight of the code vectors, d is the number of dimensions of the feature vectors (d=12), m_i and Σ_i are the mean and covariance matrix of the ith group of the video genre's distribution, respectively.

Fig. 2 and Fig. 3 illustrate some typical distribution approximations done by the GBFCM(DM) using 6 code vectors. In order to quantitatively measure the classification performance of the proposed algorithms, the False Alarm Rate (FAR) is employed. The FAR is calculated by the following equation:

$$FAR = \frac{\text{\# of misclassification GOPs}}{\text{total \# of GOPs}} \quad (12)$$

To evaluate the performance, the CNN(DM) and GBFCM(DM) are compared with the original CNN and GBFCM. Fig. 4 shows the classification results for the experiments on both MPEG-1 and MPEG-4 video traces. As can be seen from Fig. 4 and Table 4, the CNN(DM) and GBFCM(DM) always outperform the CNN and GBFCM, respectively. The reason why the CNN(DM) and GBFCM(DM) always give better result is that the CNN(DM) and GBFCM(DM) utilize the variance information of the frame data while their counterparts do not. This result shows that the divergence measure and covariance information play a very important role in the modelling and classification of MPEG data streams. The results also show that the FARs of MPEG-4 are not as good as MPEG-1's case even though the proposed methods give improvements. This implies that there are room for further research on MPEG-4 data classification.

Table 4. Average FAR(%) for different algorithms

	GBFCM	GBFCM(DM)	CNN	CNN(DM)
MPEG-1	9.78	9.27	7.09	3.97
MPEG-4	17.62	15.23	20.61	11.00

5 Conclusions

A new approach for modelling the probabilistic distribution of log-valued of frame size is introduced in this paper. This paper shows how the divergence measure and covariance information of MPEG video sequences are modelled. The probability information in MPEG video sequences has been incorporated into 2 different clustering algorithms, the GBFCM and CNN, for investigating the effectiveness of the divergence measure and covariance information in MPEG video sequence classification problems in this paper. Experiments and results show that incorporating the divergence measure and covariance information with the clustering algorithm decreases the false alarm rate in classification as much as 46.6% on average.

Acknowledgement. This research was supported by the Korea Research Foundation (Grant # R05-2003-000-10992-0 (2004)).

References

1. Dawood,A.M.,Ghanbari,M.: MPEG video modeling based on scene description. IEEE Int. Conf. Image Processing, Chicago, IL., **2** (1998) 351-355.
2. Patel,N.,Sethi,I.K.: Video shot detection and characterization for video databases, Pattern Recog., **30** (1977) 583-592
3. Liang,Q.,Mendel,J.M.: MPEG VBR Video Traffic Modeling and Classification Using Fuzzy Technique, IEEE Trans. Fuzzy Systems, **9** (2001) 183-193
4. Dimitrova,N.,Golshani,F.: Motion recovery for video content classification. ACM Trans. Inform. Sust., **13** (1995) 408-439
5. Manzoni,P.,Cremonesi,P.,Serazzi,G.: Workload models of VBR video traffic and their use in resource allocation policies. IEEE Trans. Networking, **7** (1999) 387-397
6. Krunz,M.,Sass,R.,Hughes,H.: Statistical characteristics and multiplexing of MPEG streams, in Proc. IEEE Int. Conf. Comput. Commun., INFOCOM'95, Boston, MA, **2** (1995) 445-462
7. Rose,O.: Satistical properties of MPEG video traffic and their impact on traffic modeling in ATM systems, Univ. Wurzburg,Inst. Comput. Sci., Rep., 101 (1995)
8. Bezdek,J.C.: A convergence theorem for the fuzzy ISODATA clustering algorithms, IEEE Trans. Pattern Anal. Mach. Int., **2** (1980) 1-8
9. Bezdek,J.C.: Pattern recognition with fuzzy objective function algorithms. New York : Plenum, (1981)
10. Park,D.C,Dagher,I.: Gradient Based Fuzzy c-means (GBFCM) Algorithm, IEEE Int. Conf. on Neural Networks, ICNN-94, **3** (1994) 1626-1631

11. Looney,C.: Pattern Recognition Using Neural Networks, New York, Oxford University press, (1997) 252-254
12. Bezdek,J.C.: Pattern recognition with fuzzy objective function algorithms. New York : Plenum, (1981)
13. Fukunaga,K.: Introduction to Statistical Pattern Recognition, Academic Press, Inc, 2nd edition, (1990)
14. Park,D.C.: Centroid Neural Network for Unsupervised Competitive Learning, IEEE Tr. on Neural Networks, **11** (2000) 520-528.
15. Park,D.C,Woo,Y.J.: Weighted centroid neural network for edge reserving image compression, IEEE Tr. on Neural Networks, **12** (2001) 1134-1146

Image Retrieval Using Spatial Color and Edge Detection

Chin-Chen Chang[1,2], Yung-Chen Chou[2], and Wen-Chuan Wu[2]

[1] Department of Information Engineering and Computer Science,
Feng Chia University, Taichung, Taiwan 40724, R.O.C.
ccc@cs.ccu.edu.tw
[2] Department of Computer Science and Information Engineering,
National Chung Cheng University, Chiayi, Taiwan 621, R.O.C.
{jackjow, wenn}@cs.ccu.edu.tw

Abstract. To improve the effectiveness and efficiency of CBIR systems, in this paper, we present a novel IR scheme with multiple features, the spatial color and edge percentage features, derived by way of moment-preserving edge detection. Put the above two features together, we come by an effective and efficient IR system. Experimental results show that the proposed method outperforms other similar methods in terms of accuracy and retrieval efficiency.

1 Introduction

Content-based image retrieval (CBIR for short) automatically extracts image features from a query image and then compares these features with those in the images from the database so that similar images to the query one can be picked out [1]. Because of the automatic extraction, the system can retrieve images quickly and efficiently. Image features used by most CBIR methods can be divided roughly into four categories: color layout [2],[3], texture [4], shape [5], and spatial region [6]. The color layout is the most frequently used feature because the human eye is sensitive to color, and that is why the well-known color histogram scheme [3] uses the color feature. Texture and shape features are used mostly to determine edge directions or distribution of images. The edges define the contour of the whole image. Therefore, the edge distribution is an important feature as well. In 1985, Tsai proposed the MP edge detection scheme [7]. The scheme has been used in the field of similar image retrieval as in [8] for example. In 2003, Cheng [8] proposed a CBIR system based on MP edge detection. Nevertheless, the scheme suffers from such shortcomings as being computation-demanding and too much time consumption. In this paper, we intend to improve the shortcomings of Cheng's scheme and utilize multiple features to enhance the retrieval results. First of all, we partition an RGB image into several sub-images, and then, for each sub-image, we extract the color layout and edge percentage features, where the edge percentage feature is acquired through the utilization of the MP edge detection technique. The above features in all the sub-images will be used to represent the original image so as to help find similar images. The remainder of this paper is organized as follows. In Section 2, we will introduce the way we partition digital images and the moment-preserving edge detection method. Then, in Section 3, we will present our proposed method in detail. Also, the experimental results will be shown in Section 4 in order to examine the performance of the proposed scheme. Finally, the conclusions will be in the last section.

2 Related Works

To begin with, let's check out how we can partition images in the first sub-section. Then, in the second, we shall offer a brief review of the image retrieval method [8] based on the moment-preserving edge detection technique.

2.1 Image Partitioning

The color information of an image is important to human vision [2]. In 1991, Swain and Ballard proposed the histogram method [3] based on image color feature. The method statistically calculates the frequencies of color values in the entire image to form a histogram distribution. However, here exists a problem that two dissimilar images may have the same histogram distribution. On the other hand, only generating the mean RGB value of the whole image without revealing individual local features is a poor way to retrieve an image as well. In order to overcome such problem, we will partition an image into several sub-images. These sub-images will be independently processed and can be seen as local representations of the original image. After the partitioning process, we can do feature extraction to each sub-image and obtain the significant features in individual sub-images. Fig. 1 shows the difference between two images before (see Figs. 1(a) and 1(b)) and after (see Figs. 1(c) and 1(d)) image partitioning. As can be seen, the two images in Figs. 1(a) and 1(b) are dissimilar, but if the mean value of the color of the image is used to make the judgment, then we may come to the obvious mistake that the two images are similar. In order to better tell the differences between these images, the images in Figs. 1(a) and 1(b) are partitioned into 2×2 sub-images as shown in Figs. 1(c) and 1(d), respectively. It is certain that the differences between corresponding sub-images can be much more clearly contrasted, leading to an exacter, more accurate comparison result.

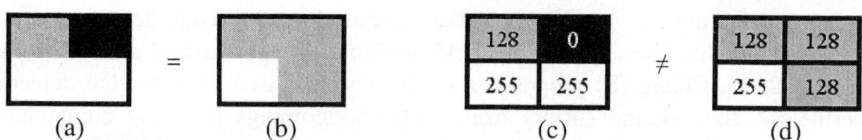

Fig. 1. Example of how image partitioning (2×2 in this case) helps

2.2 Moment-Preserving Edge Detection and Related Retrieval System

In 1985, Tsai [7] presented an edge detection method based on the moment-preserving principle, MP for short. Because the method can be applied only to gray-level images, Yang and Tsai [9] later proposed an advanced MP edge detection method for color images. Both of these methods can effectively detect edge blocks and determine the edge direction and location in a block. The main idea of MP is similar to the concept of momentum conservation in the field of dynamics. The values in a circle, as shown in Fig. 2, are used as the energy magnitude to computes the corresponding values of two intensity levels by using the principle of momentum conservation. We can decide whether an edge exists in the block according to the two intensity levels. Then the location and direction of the edge can be determined.

In 2003, Cheng [8] proposed a novel method for edge detection. Fig. 2 shows a skeleton diagram of Cheng's MP edge detection scheme, where the block size is 4×4, O is the origin of the circle c, and the coordinate $(\bar{x}, \bar{y})$ is the center of gravity of moment. Suppose that there is an edge E in circle c and that the circle is partitioned into two parts, where p_1 and p_2 are the proportions of the square measures of the two parts. In this case, we know that the notation θ is the angle value of the edge direction. Obviously, the distance between $(\bar{x}, \bar{y})$ and the origin can be used to indicate whether the block is an edge block or not. Thus, we can answer this question by using the inequality $\alpha m_0 < \sqrt{m_x^2 + m_y^2}$. Here, m_0 offered by Equation $m_0 = \iint f(x,y)dydx$ is the mean value of circle c; m_x and m_y denote the x-mass moment and y-mass moment respectively, which are derived from Equations $m_x = \iint xf(x,y)dydx$ and $m_y = \iint yf(x,y)dydx$, respectively; and the notation a can be determined experimentally. Note that $f(x,y)$ is the pixel value of coordinate (x,y) in circle c. Cheng claims that the moment values m_0, m_x, and m_y above can be obtained by using three masks (see in [8]). For more details on determining the edge direction, please refer to Cheng's scheme [8].

Then, Cheng uses the edge detection results to develop two image retrieval systems [8]: the visual pattern histogram method and the visual pattern MSE method. Suppose that the block after edge detection proves to contain an edge. The block will be transformed into a visual pattern. For example, Fig. 2(b) shows the visual pattern of the image in Fig. 2(a). There are a total of 45 visual patterns used in Cheng's experiments. The visual pattern histogram method statistically figures out the frequencies of the visual patterns in the whole image to form a histogram with 45 bins. Therefore, we can compute the similarity of two images by comparing the two histograms. As for the visual pattern MSE method, the difference of the parameters h_1 and h_2 in the same visual pattern occurring on two images is computed and accumulated, where h_1 and h_2 are the gray-level values of the parts p_1 and p_2, respectively. When the

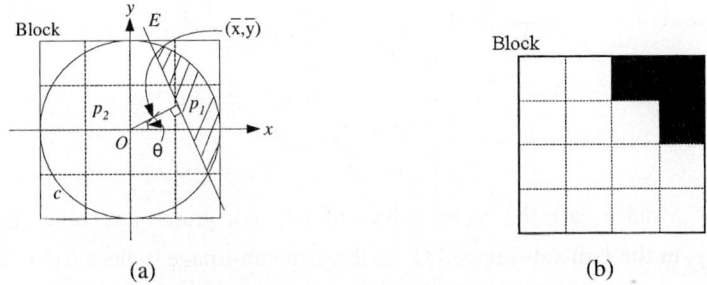

Fig. 2. The diagram for an 4×4 edge detection

accumulated difference is larger, it means that these two images are more dissimilar to each other. Some drawbacks, however, occur in Cheng's two retrieval systems. The visual pattern histogram is a global feature, and global feature representation, as mentioned above, is apt to lead to inaccurate retrieval results. In addition, the visual pattern MSE method requires too much computation cost and is too time-consuming. Besides, the computation of the distance between two images is biased. The distance is the accumulation of differences for the same pattern. However, two images with many identical patterns may have a great distance; that is to say, when most edge directions are similar, two images may still be judged as dissimilar. At the other extreme, two images with few identical patterns may be only a small distance away. According to the above observations, we believe that there are flaws in the visual pattern MSE method.

3 The Proposed Method

In this section, we shall present our image retrieval scheme with multiple features, namely the MFIR scheme. Because the calculation in Cheng's scheme [8] is complicated, the searching process for similar images is time-consuming and inefficient. In our new scheme, we intend to enhance the search efficiency and utilize multiple features—color layout and edge distribution—to improve retrieval accuracy.

3.1 The Feature Extraction Procedure

The goal of the feature extraction procedure is to figure out the color layout and the edge percentage of each sub-image in the image. First, the proposed scheme starts with the partitioning of the entire RGB color image. Then the color layout and the edge percentage features are obtained as follows. Suppose the image is partitioned into 3×3 sub-images. In other words, the image now has 9 sub-images. Then, the color layout feature can be extracted from each sub-image. Because the color space of the image is an RGB color model, we compute the mean values of each sub-image from the three planes, that is, the red (R), green (G), and blue (B) components. The equations are as follows:

$$\overline{r_k} = \frac{1}{w \times h} \sum_{i \in SI_k} \sum_{j \in SI_k} r(i, j) \cdot \qquad (1)$$

$$\overline{g_k} = \frac{1}{w \times h} \sum_{i \in SI_k} \sum_{j \in SI_k} g(i, j) \cdot \qquad (2)$$

$$\overline{b_k} = \frac{1}{w \times h} \sum_{i \in SI_k} \sum_{j \in SI_k} b(i, j) \cdot \qquad (3)$$

Here, $\overline{r_k}$, $\overline{g_k}$, and $\overline{b_k}$ are the mean values of the red, green, and blue components, respectively, in the k-th sub-image; SI_k is the k-th sub-image, where $k = 1, 2, ..., n \times m$ when the size of the image partitioning is $n \times m$; and w and h are the width and height of each sub-image, respectively. In this case, $r(i,j)$, $g(i,j)$, and $b(i,j)$ are the pixel values of the red, green, and blue components of the coordinate (i,j), respectively. The edge percentage feature can be obtained as follows. We make use of the moment-preserving principle, which was introduced in the previous section, to determine whether a block in a sub-image is an edge block. For each sub-image of the entire image, the edge block percentages are computed by using the following equation:

$$Percent_{edge} = \frac{\text{number of edge blocks}}{\text{total number of blocks in a sub-image}}. \qquad (4)$$

In order to improve the recognition ability so as to help with retrieval, the edge distributions of different planes must be taken into account. Hence, the three edge maps of the original RGB color image should be obtained after the practice pf the moment-preserving edge detection method. The three edge maps, shown in Figs. 3(e), 3(f), and 3(g), are drawn from the R, G, and B planes, respectively. Please note that the edge distributions of the three edge maps are different from each other. Fig. 3 illustrates the edge distributions of the red, green, and blue planes on an RGB color image, where Fig. 3(a) is the original image, and Figs. 3(b), 3(c), and 3(d) show the gray level values for the red, green, and blue planes, respectively. After the use of the moment-preserving edge detection method, we get the three edge maps shown in Figs. 3(e), 3(f), and 3(g), respectively. As can be seen, the edge distributions of these edge maps are different from each other because the gray level distributions on different planes are distinct. Then, we can respectively compute the percentages of the edge blocks of each sub-image from the three edge maps by using Equation 4 so as to form as many as 3×n×m edge percentage features, where the size of the image partitioning is n×m.

(a) Girl.jpg (Original) (b) The R plane (c) The G plane (d) The B plane

(e) Edge map of (b) (f) Edge map of (c) (g) Edge map of (d)

Fig. 3. The edge distributions of the R, G, and B planes

Finally, an image can be represented by a feature sequence, such as: $F(I) = \{f_i' \mid i = 1, 2, ..., 2 \times (3 \times n \times m)\}$. Here, $F(I)$ indicates the feature sequence of image I and f_i' indicates the i-th feature of image I. Please note that the first half (i = 1, 2, ..., (3×n×m)) of the feature sequence represents the color layout feature, and the second half (i = (3×n×m)+1, (3×n×m)+2, ..., 2×(3×n×m)) represents the edge percentage feature.

3.2 The Similar Image Matching Procedure

The goal of the similar image matching procedure is to determine whether two given images are similar in the query phase and then to eventually retrieve from the database those images that are similar to the query image. To determine image similarity, the procedure uses the two image features acquired from the feature extraction procedure described above. Our proposed method in the query phase is divided into two stages in order to improve image retrieval performance and save run time. In the first stage, the color layout feature is used. This is because the human eye is sensitive to color, and most images whose color distributions are dissimilar to that of the query image will be filtered out. This practice of filtering out dissimilar color distributions greatly reduces the number of images to be compared in the next stage, and that in turn cuts down the computation overhead. In the second stage, the edge percentage feature is employed to improve retrieval accuracy, where the improvement comes from the preservation of most significant information about the image texture.

$$Dist(Q, I) = \sqrt{\sum_j (f_j^Q - f_j^I)^2} \, . \tag{5}$$

Furthermore, we utilize the metric measurement defined above to compare the resemblance of the two given images, that is, the query image (Q) and the target image (I). Here in this place, $Dist(Q,I)$ represents the degree of difference of similarity and

---

Algorithm: Similar Image Matching
Input: A query image Q
Output: Similar images
Step 1: Run Feature Extraction Algorithm for Q,
Step 2: For I = 1 to N (# of images in database)
  Compute $Sim_c(Q, I)$ by using Equation 6 for the color layout feature,
Step 3: Sort $Sim_c(Q, I)$ in decreasing order of rank,
Step 4: Select the first k% ranked images,
Step 5: For I = 1 to ($N \times k$%)
  Compute $Sim_e(Q, I)$ by using Equation 6 for edge percentage feature,
Step 6: Sort $Sim_e(Q, I)$ in decreasing order of rank,
Step 7: Return the first t ranked similar images to user.

Fig. 4. The algorithm of the similar image matching procedure

f_j^Q and f_j^I indicate the j-th feature of the images Q and I, respectively. Moreover, the similarity degree between Q and I is defined as follows:

$$Sim(Q,I) = \frac{1}{Dist(Q,I)}.\qquad(6)$$

Sim(Q,I) represents the similarity between Q and I. The two images are extremely similar to each other when they have a large value of *Sim()*. On the other hand, a small value of *Sim()* means that the two images are dissimilar. Fig. 4 summarizes the steps of the similar image matching procedure. In Step 4, $k\%$ is determined experimentally, and the notation t in Step 7 stands for the number of images retrieved for the user.

4 Experimental Results

In order to measure and evaluate the retrieval performance of our proposed method, some experiments were conducted. In these experiments, a large database consisting of 1,000 color images in the JPEG format was used. The images in the database were borrowed from the ftp site ftp://db.stanford.edu/pub/wangz/image.vary.jpg.tar. In the database, the size of each image was not restricted. The images were graded manually into 10 classes, including classes of bus, eagle, elephant, flower, portrayal, and so on. Each class was composed of 100 relevant color images. An 1.6 GHz Intel Pentium-IV CPU with 256M RAM was used, and the coding was done in the JAVA language. First, we use the above-mentioned database to evaluate the category retrieval ability of our image retrieval scheme. When an image that belongs to class A is the query image, we expect that those images form the same class A will be show up in the front part of the ranking list. In other words, the higher the rank is, the more similar the target image should be to the query image. In our experiments, we picked out a total of 15 query images for testing.

As Section 3.2 mentioned, the query procedure, that is, the similar image matching algorithm, first executes the feature extraction algorithm for the query image. The feature extraction algorithm is roughly divided into two parts—extraction of the color layout feature and extraction of the edge percentage feature. The two features are extracted from the sub-images acquired when the original image is partitioned. We will probe into the problems associated with image partitioning and edge detection below. First, the original image is partitioned into a number of sub-images. However, the problem is to determine what the ideal number of sub-images is. The purpose of the experiment we shall describe below was to decide upon a satisfactory number of sub-images. In Fig. 5, the various numbers of sub-images resulting from image partitioning are shown. The notation IPn indicates that the original image is partitioned into $n \times n$ sub-images. And the precision is defined to be the proportion of the retrieved similar images belonging to the same class as the query image to those t return images. That is to say, it implies that the retrieval system performs well and can retrieve more similar and relevant images when the precision value is large for a given t. When the value of t increases, the number of relevant images from the retrieved images may or may not increase proportionally. As a result, from the precision formula

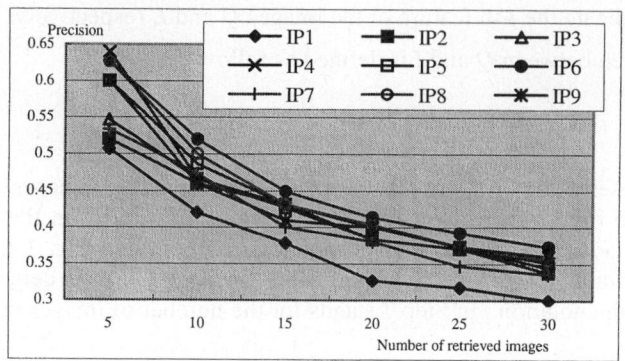

Fig. 5. The image partitioning results with different numbers of sub-images

Equation 7, the curve of the precision to the number of retrieved images t is asymptotically declined.

As can be seen in Fig. 5, the best result occurs when the image is partitioned into 6×6 sub-images. That is to say, in our experiment, 6×6 partitioning resulted in optimal precision rates for the numbers of retrieved images when the 15 query images were used. Furthermore, we have also found that 1×1 partitioning, that is the whole original, non-partitioning image, has the worst results in terms of retrieved precision. When 30 returned images were required by the user, 1×1 partitioning resulted in only about 9 (=0.3×30) retrieved images relevant to the query image.

There is another problem with the edge detection procedure. When edge detection using the moment-preserving principle was carried out, the most important step was to determine the parameter α. Fig. 6 shows how to decide upon a satisfactory α value. In Fig. 6(a), the image is the original image 'Girl.jpg'. The G plane of the original image in the RGB color model is shown in Fig. 6(b). The images shown in Figs. 6(c), 6(d), and 6(e) are the edge maps of Fig. 6(b) with different α values. As can be seen, Fig. 6(c) shows that the image with $\alpha=0.01$ has more edge blocks than the image with $\alpha=0.02$ shown in Fig. 6(e). Generally speaking, some smooth blocks might be

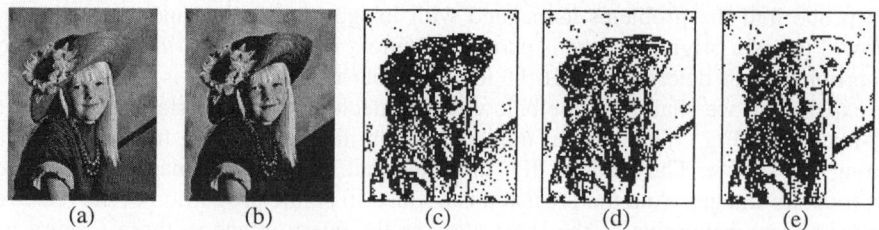

Fig. 6. The binary edge maps of 'Girl.jpg' with different α values: (a) Original image 'Girl.jpg'; (b) The G plane of the original image; (c) Edge map of (b) ($\alpha = 0.01$); (d) Edge map of (b) ($\alpha = 0.015$); (e) Edge map of (b) ($\alpha = 0.02$)

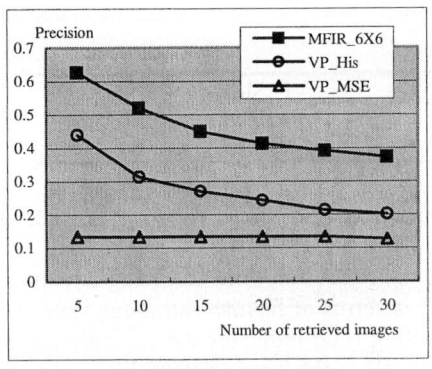 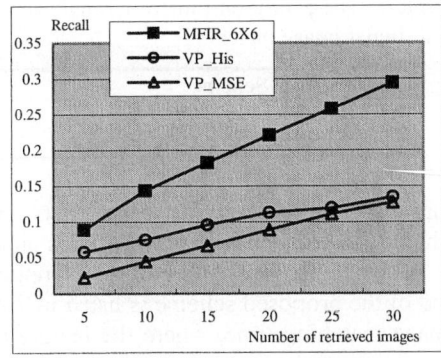

(a) Precision comparison (b) Recall comparison

Fig. 7. The comparison between the proposed scheme and Cheng's scheme

mistakenly treated as edge blocks when too many edge features are extracted. On the contrary, however, if the standard we put on the edge determination is too high, we run the risk of missing significant outlines. For this reason, we suggest that $\alpha=0.015$ is a satisfactory value for extracting a suitable number of edge blocks.

In order to measure retrieval performance, we adopted the precision and recall factors [4]. The precision factor measures how well a search system weeds out what is not wanted. The recall factor measures how well it finds what is wanted. The precision factor (*pre*) and the recall factor are defined, respectively, as follows:

$$pre(Q) = \begin{cases} r/t & \text{if } R \geq t \\ r/R & \text{if } R < t \end{cases}. \tag{7}$$

$$recall(Q) = r/R. \tag{8}$$

Here *pre(Q)* and *recall(Q)* denote the precision degree and the recall value for the query image Q, respectively; r is the number of relevant images from the retrieved images; R is the total number of images relevant to the query Q in the database; and t is the number of retrieved (responsive) images that is given by the user.

Fig. 7 shows the precision and recall performances of the retrieval method using both the proposed features, where the parameter k used in the first stage of the similar image matching algorithm was set to 25 ($k\% = 25\%$), and the features proposed by Cheng [8]. As for the abbreviations in Fig. 7, MFIR_6×6, VP_His, and VP_MSE represent our proposed method with 6×6 image partitioning, Cheng's visual pattern histogram feature, and Cheng's visual pattern MSE feature, respectively. From Fig. 7(a), we learn that the precision of the proposed scheme is better than Cheng's two features when we have the same number of retrieved images (*t*). In other words, when the number of return images is fixed, the proposed scheme can do better similarity comparison and give better retrieval results. Fig. 7(b) shows the abilities of different schemes to retrieve similar images to one query image compare. When the number of return images (*t*) is large, it is more likely to retrieve more similar images, and the recall value would be larger as well. As can be seen in Fig. 7(b), with same number of retrieved images, the proposed scheme does better than the two other features. In

Table 1. The execution time of Cheng's and proposed schemes in terms of feature extraction and similar image matching

Scheme	VP_His	VP_MSE	MFIR_6×6
Feature extracting time (second)	0.7199	0.7199	0.268
Matching time (second)	27.106	358.27	1.56

summary, by the above two contrasts, our proposed scheme is superior to both of Cheng's features in terms of precision and recall.

As for the comparison on time complexity, the execution time of Cheng's features and of the proposed scheme is listed in Table 1 in terms of feature extracting time and image matching time, where the feature extracting time indicates the execution time spent on extracting the features of each image itself in the image database and storing the features in the feature database, and the image matching time is the execution time spent on searching for the similar images to the query image. From Table 1, we observe that the feature extracting time the two of Cheng's features need and the feature extraction time the proposed scheme consumes is about the same. However, there is some significant difference as far as the image matching time is concerned. It is obvious that the matching time the proposed scheme uses, $k\%=25\%$, is the least of all. Since VP_His needs to compare each one of the 45 visual patterns and find out which one the 4×4 block belongs to, plus it also needs to calculate the frequency of each visual pattern, it consumes much time comparing the patterns. In addition, besides comparing the patterns, VP_MSE also needs to determine where the same patterns are in two images before it deals with the difference between the parameters h_1 and h_2 in the same visual pattern. For this reason, the image matching time VP_MSE uses is quite long. By contrast, the proposed scheme consumes little time because the image partitioning, color layout feature calculation, and edge percentage feature derivation are simpler than those of Cheng's features. As can be seen, the proposed scheme gives efficient similar image retrieval results at the cost of little execution time.

In addition, in the similar image matching procedure, $k\%$ is determined experimentally. The figure $k\%$ is used to control the number of similar images to be operated on in the second stage, which is in charge of edge percentage feature comparison. It is clear that any adjustment of $k\%$ will influence the computation time. When $k\%$ is large, it means that the number of similar images there are to compare is large, and in turn that leads to much image matching time. Table 2 shows that $k\%$ affects the retrieval performance in addition to the execution time. For the same return image t, the recall and precision value would increase when $k\%$ gradually increases from 0%. That is because the number of similar images to compare in the second stage increases, which gives a rise to the probability of finding out more similar images. However, when $k\%$ exceeds a certain threshold, the recall and precision of the retrieval system would decrease. This phenomenon reflects the fact that too many similar images to compare interfere the image matching decision. From Table 2, we observe quite clearly that the retrieval system performs well in terms of recall and precision, and the query execution time is scarcely there when $k\%=25\%$. Therefore, we suggest that the $k\%$ be set to 25%. By the way, when $k\%=100\%$, it means that the two features of each image in the database are used in image matching and querying. In this case, the computation time will go straight up the hill, and the retrieval performance is the worst it can be. To conclude, Table 2 proves that the two-stage arrangement ($k\%=25\%$) can effectively filter out most dissimilar images and help retrieve similar images efficiently.

Table 2. The influence of k on the recall value, precision value, and execution time

$k\%$	$t=5$		$t=10$		$t=20$		$t=30$		Time
	Recall	Precision	Recall	Precision	Recall	Precision	Recall	Precision	(second)
0%	0.078	0.560	0.131	0.487	0.229	0.437	0.282	0.376	1.53
25%	0.089	0.627	0.144	0.520	0.221	0.413	0.294	0.373	1.61
50%	0.089	0.627	0.141	0.507	0.218	0.407	0.288	0.362	1.90
75%	0.083	0.587	0.132	0.480	0.198	0.373	0.251	0.324	2.46
100%	0.079	0.560	0.121	0.447	0.182	0.350	0.242	0.316	3.18

5 Conclusions

In this paper, we have proposed an image retrieval scheme that uses multiple image features as well as the moment-preserving edge detection method in order to improve the effectiveness and efficiency. The proposed method not only uses the color layout feature but also takes the edge distribution feature into account. Since the human eye is sensitive to color, the color layout feature is helpful to similar image search. Moreover, for CBIR systems, the edge distribution feature provides important information. Because two features are important, we integrate them together to enhance our image retrieval performance. Experimental results indicate that our proposed method outperforms Cheng's in terms of retrieval accuracy. In addition, because of the use of the two-stage similar image matching in our method, the number of comparisons is greatly decreased. As a result, the total search time is significantly shortened, and the performance is also dramatically improved. In the future, we shall focus on the research and development of video matching. Video data are basically series and series of continuous shots of images, and the neighboring images possess roughly the same color layout and edge distribution. Probably we can search for similar fragments of video data from different shots.

References

1. Flickner, M., Sawhney, H., Niblack, W., Ashley, J., Huang, Q., Dom, B., Gorkani, M., Hafner, J., Lee, D., Steele, D., Yanker, P.: Query by Image and Video Content: The QBIC System. Computer 28 (1995) 23–32
2. Chan, Y.K., Chen, C.Y.: Image Retrieval System Based on Color-Complexity and Color-Spatial Features. Journal of Systems and Software 71 (2004) 65–70
3. Swain, M.J., Ballard, D.H.: Color Indexing. International Journal of Computer Vision 7 (1991) 11–32
4. Chun, Y.D., Seo, S.Y., Kim, N.C.: Image Retrieval Using BDIP and BVLC Moments. IEEE Transactions on Circuits and Systems for Video Technology 13 (2003) 951–957
5. Ma, W.Y., Manjunath, B.S.: Netra: a Toolbox for Navigating Large Image Databases. Proceedings of IEEE International Conference on Image Processing, Vol. 1. Washington DC (1997) 568–571

6. Jing, F., Li, M., Zhang, H.J., Zhang, B.: An Efficient and Effective Region-Based Image Retrieval Framework. IEEE Transactions on Image Processing 13 (2004) 699–709
7. Tsai, W.H.: Moment Preserving Thresholding: a New Approach. Computer Vision, Graphics, and Image Processing 29 (1985) 377–393
8. Cheng, S.C.: Content-Based Image Retrieval Using Moment-Preserving Edge Detection. Image and Vision Computing 21 (2003) 809–826
9. Yang, C.K., Tsai, W.H.: Reduction of Color Dimensionality by Moment-Preserving Thresholding and Its Application for Edge Detection in Color Images. Pattern Recognition Letters 17 (1996) 481–490

$$dis(obj_1, obj_2) = \begin{cases} \|obj_1 - obj_2\| & \text{if } (obj_1, obj_2 \notin \varnothing) \\ \infty & \text{otherwise} \end{cases} \quad (1)$$

For example, if both $image_1$ and $image_2$ are not empty, $dis(image_1, image_2)$ is the Euclidean distance between the two images in low feature space and if there are no images in MMD_1, $dis(image_1, image_2) = \infty$. $mindis$ of two MMDs is defined as minimal value of image, text and audio distances, and $maxdis$ is the maximal value of them. Note that when $dis(object_1, object_2)$ is infinite, it denotes that either $object_1$ or $object_2$ is empty but not the real distance between them. Hence, distance that is infinite should be excluded when calculating $maxdis$.

Here are two heuristic rules that are quite helpful for us to estimate MMD distance.

(1) When judging similarities of two MMDs, if people find two media objects in different MMDs quite similar, they tend to regard the two MMDs as relevant items.

(2) People may be confident about their judgments when all component media objects are similar (or dissimilar) and be confused when some objects are quite similar in two documents whereas others are quite dissimilar.

With an eye to above heuristic rules, we define Unconfidence Factor (UCF) as:

$$UCF = \alpha + \ln(\beta \times margin + 1) . \quad (2)$$

where α and β are smoothing parameters and margin is defined as:

$$margin = maxdis - mindis . \quad (3)$$

If one of the two MMDs contains only one media object of modality M, then UCF is given as:

$$UCF = \frac{1}{\exp(P + \gamma)} . \quad (4)$$

where P is the mean precision of top 20 returned examples in low feature space when query example is of modality M and γ is the smoothing parameter.

The distance between MMDs is given as :

$$MMDdis = \lambda \times mindis + UCF . \quad (5)$$

Where λ is the smoothing parameter.

3 MMD Semantic Space Construction

Manifold learning [4], [15], [16] has received a lot of research attention recently and it has been proved that manifold structure is more powerful than Euclidean structure for data representation in many areas. In this section, we assume that MMD lies on a manifold, and learn the MMD manifold to build the MMD semantic space.

3.1 Semi-semantic Graph Construction and Refinement

To build MMDSS, we first construct a graph $G(V)$ in which MMDs are vertices and the relationships among MMDs are edges. We name $G(V)$ semi-semantic graph for two reasons. First, the weights of edges in SSG are not calculated by Euclidean distances directly, but by means of synthesized distances. Second, there are some text objects in MMDs, which always carry abundant semantic information themselves.

Let Ω denote MMD set in database. We build SSG via the following two steps.

Step 1. local geometrical structure modeling. For each $MMD_i \in \Omega$, there is a corresponding vertex $V_i \in G(V)$ and for any two vertices $V_i, V_j \in G(V)$, we put an edge between them with the weight of W_{ij} which is defined as follows:

$$W_{ij} = \begin{cases} MMDdis(MMD_i, MMD_j), & if\ (MMDdis(MMD_i, MMD_j)) < \varepsilon; \\ \infty & otherwise; \end{cases} \quad (6)$$

where $MMDdis(MMD_i, MMD_j)$ is the distance between MMD_i and MMD_j and ε is a factor that reflects the view of locality.

Step 2. global geometrical structure modeling. We define the length of a path as the sum of the weights along the path. To model the global geometrical structure, we reconstruct the graph by finding the shortest paths in the graph for all pairs of vertices, and then replace the weights W_{ij} by the length of shortest paths between V_i and V_j.

Because the number of MMDs is not large enough, it is difficult to recover the MMD manifold accurately. However, as [4] indicates, we can make use of feedback provided by user to learn a semantic space that is locally isometric to the MMD manifold. A simple but obvious truth is that the latent distances among positive examples and query examples are small and the latent distances among negative examples and positive examples are large. To refine the SSG, we should lengthen the edges among negative examples and positive examples and shorten them among positive examples. As a result, all the edges between the negative and positive examples and those between the negative examples and query examples should multiply a proper factor that is greater than one, and similarly, all the edges between positive examples and query example as well as the edges between any two positive examples should multiply a factor that is smaller than one.

3.2 Multimedia Semantic Space Construction

In this section, we adopt Multidimensional Scaling [17] to build MMD semantics space (MMDSS). We define the distance matrix D as:

$$d_{ij} = \begin{cases} \gamma & if\ (W_{ij} = \infty); \\ W_{ij} & otherwise; \end{cases} \quad (7)$$

where γ is a suitable constant that is big enough. Suppose each MMD M_k is represented by a p dimension vector $x_k = (\mathsf{x}_{k1}, \ldots, \mathsf{x}_{kp})^\mathsf{T}$ in MMDSS. The general b_{ij} term of B is given by:

$$b_{ij} = \sum_{k=1}^{p} x_{ik} x_{jk} = x_i^T x_j\ . \quad (8)$$

Let matrix $A = (a_{ij}) = -\frac{1}{2} d_{ij}^{\ 2}$, and $B = HAH$, where H is the centering matrix, and then we rewrite B as $B = \Gamma \Lambda \Gamma^T$, where $\Lambda = diag(\lambda_1, \ldots \lambda_p)$, the diagonal matrix of the eigenvalues of B, and $\Gamma = (\gamma_1, \ldots \gamma_p)$, the matrix of corresponding eigenvectors. The coordinates matrix X of MMDs in MMDSS is given by:

$$X = \Gamma \Lambda^{\frac{1}{2}}\ . \quad (9)$$

4 Cross-Index and Retrieval in MMDSS

Once MMDSS is built, all MMDs in database are indexed by their coordinates in MMDSS and all the component media objects can be indexed by the coordinates of the MMD which they reside in. If an MMD contains certain media object, we call it the host MMD of the given media object.

4.1 Query Example in Dataset

To query MMD in MMDSS, users can either submit an MMD or a media object. If the query example is an MMD existing in database, the question is very simple. The MMDs that are the k nearest neighbours of the query example in MMDSS will be returned as results. If the query example is a media object that belongs to a certain existing MMD in database, then k MMDs that are closest to the host MMD of the query example are presented to the user. The cross-media retrieval, e.g. query images by audios, is as follows:

(1). Find the host MMD HM of the query example;
(2). Find the k nearest neighbors $N_1, \ldots N_k$ of HM ;
(3). Return all media objects of target modality that belong to $N_1, \ldots N_k$.

For example, if user queries audios by an image I, we first find the host MMD HM of I, and then get the k nearest neighbors $N_1,...N_k$ of HM. After that, l audios $A_1,...A_l$ that reside in $N_1,...N_k$ are returned as results. Because only some of MMDs contain audio objects, l is usually smaller than k.

4.2 Query Example Out of Dataset

If the query example is a new MMD or media object that is not in database, we must introduce it to MMDSS. Because MMDSS is a semantic space and there exists a semantic gulf between low features and high lever semantics, it is very hard to find a mapping function that maps the new items to MMDSS accurately only by low features. However, we can make use of feedback to map the new items into the MMDSS.

Let Ω denote the MMD set in database. If the new item NI is an MMD, we introduce it into the MMDSS by the following two steps.

Step 1. For each $M_i \in \Omega$, calculate the distance $MMDdis_i$ between NI and M_i and present user the k nearest MMDs of NI. User judges the results and marks three to five positive examples.

Step 2. Let P denote the positive example set. For each $p_i \in P$, calculate the distance $MMDdis_i$ between NI and P_i. Let $v = \sum_{i=1}^{n} MMDdis_i$ where n is the number of positive examples. The coordinates of NI are given by:

$$Coord_{ni} = \sum_{P} W_i P_i . \qquad (10)$$

where P_i are coordinates of the ith positive example and W_i is the weight which is defined as :

$$W_i = (v - MMDdis_i)/[(n-1) \times v] . \qquad (11)$$

If the query example is not an MMD but a new media object that is not in database, e.g. an image that is not in any existing MMDs, the mapping approaches are as follows.

Step 1. Find the k nearest media objects of the same modality $Obj_1,...Obj_k$ in database according to low features distances and then find the corresponding host MMDs $MD_1,...MD_k \in \Omega$ which $Obj_1,...Obj_k$ reside in.

Step 2. If the user is querying MMDs, return $MD_1,...MD_k$ as results and then the question is the same as before. If the user is querying images (audios), present user the images (audios) that belong to $MD_1,...MD_k$. Then user judges the results. Let P denote the positive example set. For each $p_i \in P$, find the host MMD MMD_i which

p_i resides in. Let X_i denote the coordinates of MMD_i, the coordinates of the new media object are given by:

$$Coord = \sum_{i=1}^{k} X_i / k .\qquad(12)$$

5 Experiments and Comparisons

To evaluate the effectiveness of our approaches, we experimented with 954 Multimedia Documents consisting of 954 images, 330 audios and 710 texts. The 954 MMDs are divided into 9 semantic categories and spited into two subsets. The first subset contains 900 MMDs and each semantic category contains 100 MMDs. The second subset contains 54 MMDs and each semantic category contains 6 MMDs. The first subset is used to train the MMDSS and the second one is used to test the approaches that introduce new items to MMDSS. We also collect another 30 images and 30 audios as new media objects to test the performance of mapping new media objects into MMDSS.

We define coverage as:

$$coverage = \frac{the\ number\ of\ correctly\ returned\ objects}{the\ number\ of\ relevant\ objects\ in\ database} .\qquad(13)$$

In our experiments, after the SSG is created, only two rounds of feedback are performed in each semantic category before constructing MMDSS. At each iteration of feedback in our experiments, we only require the users provide four positive and four negative examples.

5.1 Query Example in Dataset

In this section, we mainly evaluate the MMD retrieval performances when the query example is in dataset. Figure 1 shows the retrieval performance in MMDSS with different dimensionalities. Users query MMDs by submitting a query example of MMD that is already in MMDSS. If the returned result and the query example are in the same semantic category, it is regarded as a correct result. As figure 1 shows, when top 30 results are returned, about 29 results are correct and the number of correctly returned MMDs reaches 56 when 60 MMDs are returned in the 19-dimension MMDSS. It also can be seen that the retrieval performance highly depends on the dimensionalities of MMDSS, and in our dataset, MMDSS with the dimensionalities between 19 and 21 works best. In our experiments, the mean retrieval precision of top 30 results is over 90% in the 19-dimension MMDSS. When the coverage reaches to 92%, the mean precision is still over 40% in both 19-dimension and 21-dimension MMDSS. Clearly, the retrieval performance of our proposed method is very encouraging.

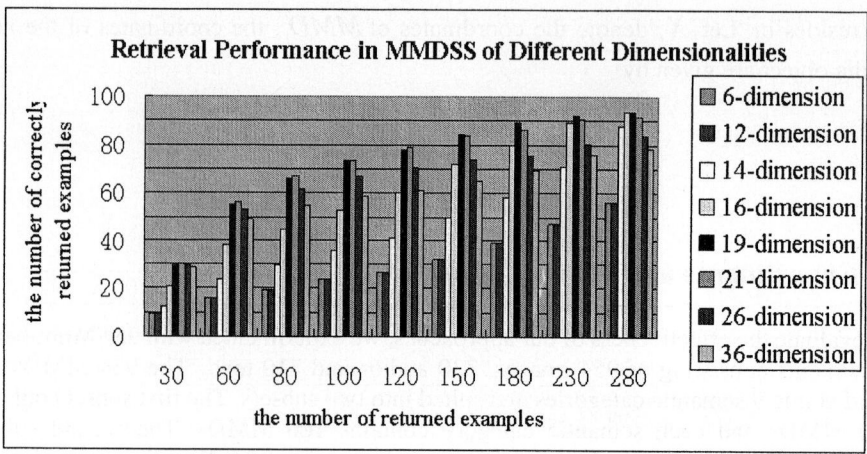

Fig. 1. Retrieval MMDs in MMDSS with different dimensionalities

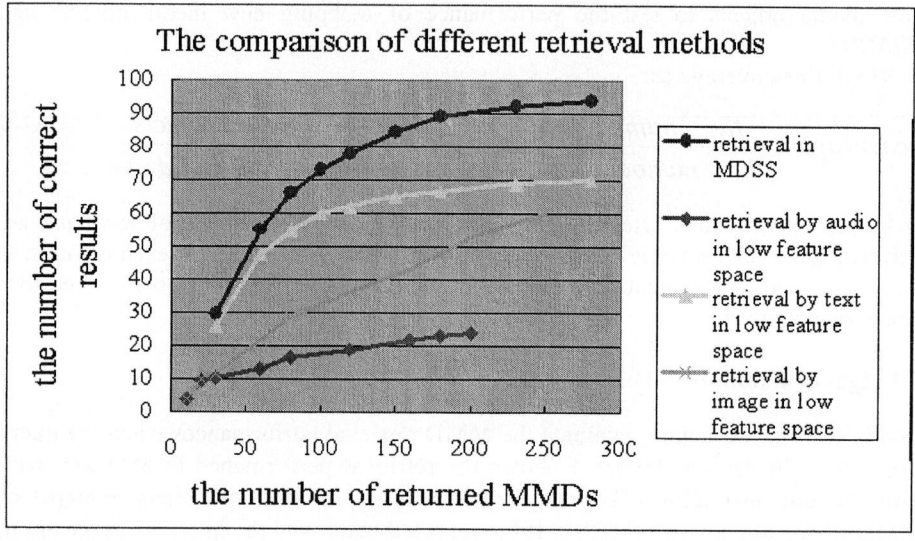

Fig. 2. The comparison of different retrieval methods

Because our method takes all kinds of media objects into consideration, the retrieval performance is higher than the approaches which use only one type of media objects. As can be seen from figure 2, the retrieval performance in MMDSS is much higher than those in low feature space. If top 30 objects are returned, there are over 28.9 correct results on average when retrieving in MMDSS whereas there are 25.6 correct results when retrieving by text in low features space, and the numbers reduce to 12.2 and 10.5 when retrieving by image and audio respectively. The numbers of correct results increase to 55.8, 46.9, 21.8 and 13.2 respectively when 60 results are returned. And since there are about 74 MMDs that contain texts and 35 MMDs that contain audios in each semantic category, the coverage upper limit of querying by text and audio in

Table 1. The mean image retrieval precision and coverage comparison

Query images in low feature space		Query images in MMDSS	
Precision	Coverage	Precision	Coverage
0.5	0.1	0.97	0.29
0.4	0.12	0.92	0.56
0.36	0.29	0.82	0.66
0.30	0.37	0.73	0.72
0.27	0.43	0.65	0.78
0.26	0.53	0.41	0.92

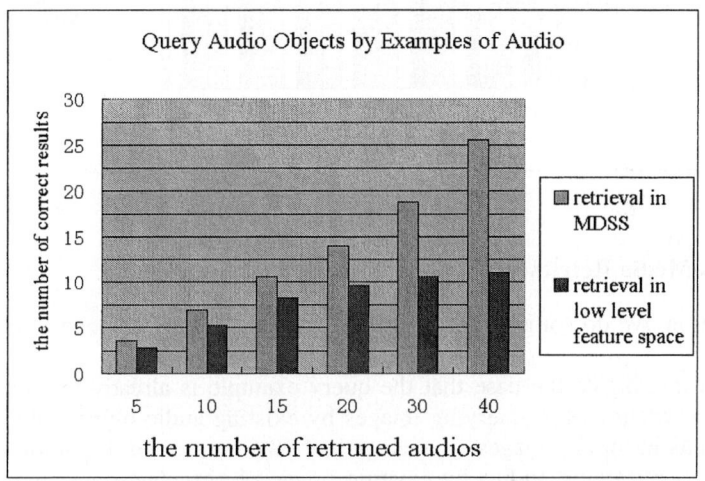

Fig. 3. Query audio objects by examples of audio

low-level feature space are 74% and 35%. However, the coverage in MMDSS reaches 93% when return 280 MMDs. Clearly, our proposed approach is much better than any other methods and we can conclude that MMDSS accurately reflects the semantics of MMDs.

Table 1 shows the results of querying images by the image existing in database and figure 3 shows the experiment results of retrieving audio objects by examples of existing audio objects. As can be seen, the precision of retrieval in MMDSS is much higher than the precision of retrieval in low feature space.

5.2 Query MMDs Outside the Database

If the query MMD is not in the dataset, we call it new MMD or new point because we must introduce it into MMDSS with the help of feedback. As can be seen from figure 4, when top 20 MMDs are returned, there are about 18 correct results after feedback and when top 30 MMDs are returned, there are 25.6 examples are correct. As a result, we can conclude that the new MMD can be accurately introduced into MMDSS.

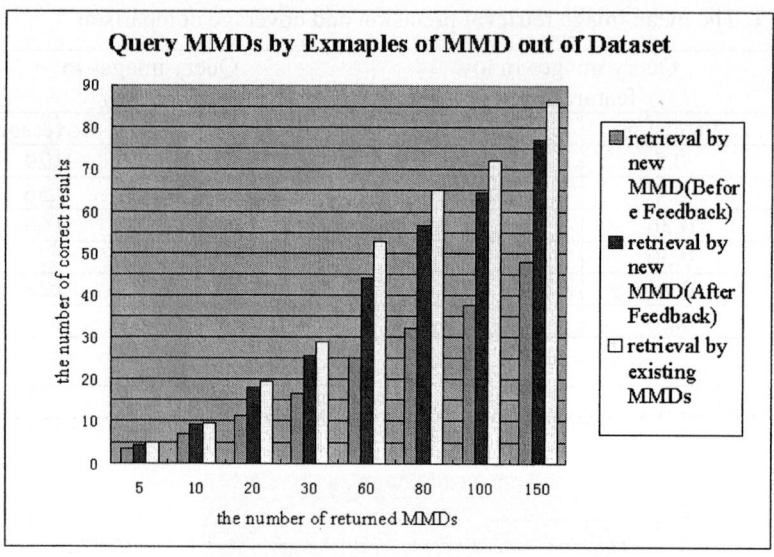

Fig. 4. Query MMD out of dataset

5.3 Cross-Media Retrieval

In this section, we do some experiments to evaluate the performance of cross-media retrieval.

We first investigate the case that the query example is already in dataset. In our experiments, when user is querying images by existing audio objects, there are 19.6 correct results in top 30 images on average and 28.6 correct results in top 60 returns. When user is retrieving audios by existing image objects, there are about 7 correct results in top 10 audios and about 15 correct results in top 30 on average. Table 2 shows the mean cross-media retrieval precision and recall. Clearly, the proposed methods in this paper for cross-media retrieval gain a remarkable performance.

If the query example is not in dataset, we call it new media object or new point as before. In this case, we must map the new objects into MMDSS and then perform cross-media retrieval in MMDSS. It can be seen from figure 5 and figure 6 that the

Table 2. The mean cross-media retrieval precision and recall

Retrieval image by audio		Retrieval audio by image	
Precision	Recall	Precision	Recall
0.82	0.16	0.81	0.10
0.65	0.20	0.69	0.19
0.47	0.29	0.50	0.42
0.45	0.36	0.48	0.45
0.40	0.40	0.43	0.49
0.29	0.81	0.42	0.53

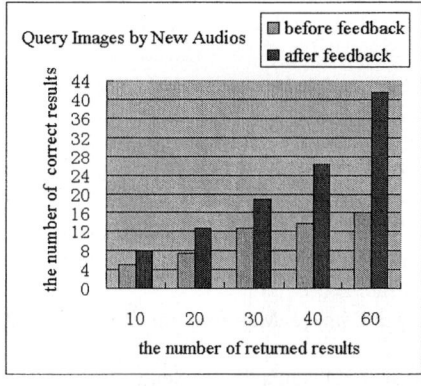 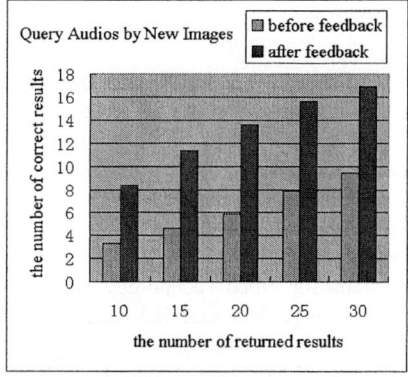

Fig. 5. Query images by new audios   **Fig. 6.** Query audios by new images

overall cross-media retrieval performance of new point is pretty good. When retrieving images by an example of new audio, there are less than 20 correct results in top 60returns before feedback and the number will reach over 40 after the object is introduced into MMDSS. The performance of retrieving audios by new images is quite similar to that of retrieving images by new adios. Clearly, after the new query example being mapped into MMDSS, the retrieval precision is remarkable.

6 Conclusion and Future Work

In this paper, we gave the definition of MMD distance and have proposed a manifold learning method to understand MMD semantics for cross-media retrieval. We have built an MMDSS to index and retrieve MMDs as well as the media objects which reside in them. We also have introduced approaches to introduce the new items that are out of dataset into MMDSS. Comparing with traditional retrieval methods, experiment shows that the MMDSS can accurately understand the MMD semantics and the performance of cross-retrieval in MMDSS is encouraging.

The future work can be focused on the following topics: (1) Exploit more effective methods to discover MMD manifold accurately. (2) Find an accurate way to introduce new items into MMDSS without feedback. (3) Seek for an exact MMD distance estimation algorithm.

Acknowledgement

We would like to thank Hanhuai Shan and Yizi Wu for offering us image and text media objects for experiments. This research is supported by National Natural Science Foundation of China (No. 60272031) and the China-US Million Book Digital Library Project (see http://www.cadal.net).

References

1. H.J. Zhang, D. Zhong. Schema for visual feature based image retrieval [A]. In: Proceedings of Storage and Retrieval for Image and Video Database, USA, 1995. 36-46
2. J. Z. Wang, G. Wiederhold, O. Firschein, and S. X. Wei,"Content-based image indexing and searching using Daubechies' wavelets," International Journal on Digital Libaries, vol. 1, pp. 311-328, 1997.
3. E. Chang, K. Goh, G. Sychay, and G. Wu, "CBSA: Content-Based Soft Annotation for Multimodal Image Retrieval Using Bayes Point Machine". IEEE Trans on Circuits and Systems for Video Technology, vol. 13, No. 1, Jan. 2003.
4. X. He, W.Y Ma, and H.J. Zhang, "Learning an Image Manifold for Retrieval" ACM Multimedia Conference, New York, 2004.
5. Namunu C Maddage, Changsheng Xu., Mohan S Kankanhalli, Xi Shao, "Content-based Music Structure Analysis with Applications to Music Semantics Understanding", ACM Multimedia Conference, New York, 2004.
6. Guodong Guo; Li, S.Z., "Content-based audio classification and retrieval by support vector machines" IEEE Transactions on Neural Networks, Volume 14, Issue 1, Jan. 2003 Page(s): 209 – 215
7. E. Wold, T. Blum, D. Keislar, and J. Wheaton, "Content-based classification,search and retrieval of audio," IEEE Multimedia Mag., vol. 3, pp. 27–36, July 1996.
8. Smoliar, S.W.; HongJiang Zhang;" Content based video indexing and retrieval", Multimedia, IEEE,Volume 1, Issue 2, Summer 1994 Page(s):62 - 72
9. Jianping Fan; Elmagarmid, A.K.; Xingquan Zhu; Aref, W.G.; Lide Wu, "ClassView: hierarchical video shot classification, indexing, and accessing", Multimedia, IEEE Transactions on, Volume 6, Issue 1, Feb. 2004 Page(s):70 – 86.
10. M.Y. Wu, C.Y. Chiu, S.P. Chao,S.N. Y, and H.C. Lin,"Content-Based Retrieval for Human Motion Data",16th IPPR Conference on Computer Vision, Graphics and Image Processing (CVGIP 2003)
11. Meinard M¨uller, Tido R¨oder, Michael Clausen, "Efficient Content-Based Retrieval of Motion Capture Data," Proceedings of ACM SIGGRAPH 2005.
12. Wang, Z. Liu, J. Huang, Multimedia content analysis using audio and visual information [J], IEEE Signal Processing Magazine, 2000, 17(6): 12-36
13. K. Beyer, J. Goldstein, R. Ramakrishnan, and U. Shaft. "When is nearest neighbor" meaningful? International Conference on Database Theory, 1999, 217–235.
14. J. Yang, Y. T. Zhuang, Q. Li. "Search for multi-modality data in digital libraries", Proceedings of 2nd IEEE Pacific-rim Conference on Multimedia, pp.482-489, Beijing, China, 2001
15. H.S. Seung and D. Lee, "The manifold ways of perception", Science, vol 290, 22 December 2000.
16. J.B. Tenenbaum, V.D. Silva, and J.C. Langford, "A global geometric framework for nonlinear dimensionality reduction", Science, Vol 290, 22 December 2000.
17. Kruskal, J. B., and Wish. M. (1977). Multidimensional Scaling. Sage Publications. Beverly Hills. CA.
18. Yueting Zhuang, Congmiao Wu, Fei Wu, Xiang Liu, "Improving Web-based Learning: Automatic Annotation of Multimedia Semantics and Cross-Media Indexing", ICWL 2004, August, Beijing

Multimedia Retrieval from a Large Number of Sources in a Ubiquitous Environment

Gamhewage C. de Silva, T. Yamasaki, and K. Aizawa

Department of Frontier Informatics, University of Tokyo, 707, 5-1-5 Kashiwanoha, Kashiwa-shi, Chiba 277-8561, Japan

Abstract. A system for multimedia retrieval and summarization in a ubiquitous environment is presented. Hierarchical clustering of data from pressure-based floor sensors is followed by video handover to retrieve video sequences showing the movement of each person in the environment. Audio handover is implemented to dub these sequences. Several methods for extracting key frames from the video sequences were implemented and evaluated by experiments. An adaptive spatio-temporal sampling algorithm based on the rate of footsteps yielded the best performance. The measured accuracy of key frame extraction within a difference of 3 seconds is approximately 80%. The system consists of a graphical user interface that can be used to retrieve video summaries interactively using simple queries.

1 Introduction

Multimedia retrieval for ubiquitous environments is an important task with several applications such as taking care of the elderly [1], study of human behavior [2], and aiding recollection of things that were forgotten [3]. With the advancement of image acquisition and storage technologies, there has been a rapid growth of research in this area. The *Ubiquitous Sensor Room* [4], *Aware Home* [1], and *CHIL* [5] are examples of some of the recent and ongoing projects.

However, this task is more challenging compared to summarizing previously edited broadcast media. Ubiquitous environments generate a large amount of video data that increases with time. The content is less structured compared to a single video from a specific category [6][7]. Multiple cameras and microphones are used most of the time, making source selection an additional issue. Because of increased complexity, it is desirable to utilize context and supplementary data from other sensors for more accurate retrieval [8][9].

This research is based on *Ubiquitous Home* [10], a two-room house equipped with a large number of stationary cameras and microphones (Figure 1). Pressure-based sensors mounted on the floor are activated as people move inside the house. Video data are acquired at 5 frames per second. The total amount of data acquired during a single day is approximately 500 Giga Bytes.

Personalized video retrieval and summarization for this environment can be extremely tedious if performed manually. For example, if we want to see what Mr. Smith did in ubiquitous home during his visit in the morning of the 3rd of

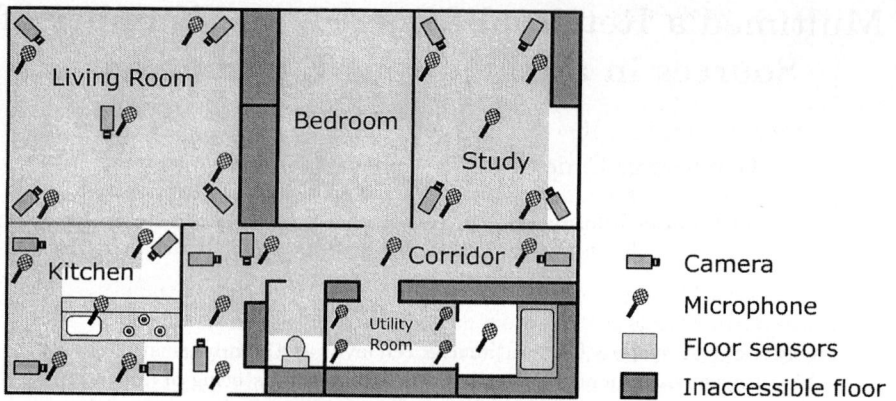

Fig. 1. Ubiquitous home layout and positioning of sensors

September 2005, it is necessary to watch the video from the camera showing the entrance to the house from early morning until the frames showing Mr. Smith entering the house are detected. Thereafter, it is necessary to pause and switch between several cameras to track him as he moves within the house, for the entire duration of his stay.

We intend to create a system where video for the above scenario can be retrieved and summarized as follows: first we enter the date and the time interval. This retrieves a set of key frames showing people who had been inside the house during this time interval. For the people who entered or left the house during this time interval, the key frames showing them entering or leaving the house will be displayed with relevant timestamps. For those who remained inside, a key frame at the start of the time interval is displayed. By browsing only the key frames showing the persons entering the house, we can find the key frame showing Mr. Smith. By clicking on the frame, we can see a video clip or a set of key frames, showing what he did. The cameras and microphones are selected automatically as he moves, so that he can be seen and heard throughout the stay.

We propose to implement the above system by analyzing the floor sensor data to detect the movement of each person in the house. Unlike a video camera or a microphone that covers a limited range, floor sensors cover almost the entire house and provide data in a compact format. This makes it possible to process them faster with relatively low processing power. The results are used for extracting only the relevant portions of audio and video data corresponding to each person's stay. We implement a number of methods for key frame extraction and conduct an evaluation experiment to choose the best method/s.

The structure of the paper is as follows: Section 2 describes the algorithms used in this paper; Section 3 describes our experiment for evaluation of key frame extraction; Section 4 presents the results of this experiment; Section 5 concludes the paper with some suggestions for further study.

2 System Description

2.1 Footstep Segmentation

A 3-stage Agglomerative Hierarchical Clustering (AHC) algorithm, described in our previous work [11], is used to segment sensor activations into footstep sequences of different persons. In the first stage, sensor activations caused by a single footstep are combined based on connectedness and overlap of durations. The second stage forms path segments by clustering the footsteps based on the physiological constraints of walking such as the range of distances between steps, the overlap of durations in two footsteps, and constraints on direction changes. We obtained statistics from several data sets corresponding to walking persons and used the statistics to identify a range of values for each constraint. The third stage compensates for the fragmentation of individual paths due to the absence of sensors in some areas, long steps etc. Context data such as the locations of the doors and furniture, and information about places where floor sensors are not installed, are used for clustering. This algorithm performs well in the presence of noise and activation delays, and despite the absence of floor sensors in some areas of the house. The performance of the algorithm was evaluated using a large data set, and the results were reported in [12].

2.2 Video Handover

The segmented paths are analyzed to create video clips so that the corresponding person is kept in the view as he moves within the house. With several cameras having overlapping views, it is necessary to select cameras in a way that a "good" video sequence can be constructed. There can be different, sometimes conflicting requirements according to the application. For applications related to surveillance and person recognition, it may be desirable to obtain a frontal view of the person in most of the sequence. For personal experience retrieval, a smaller number of transitions between cameras and a good view of the surroundings may be preferred.

We used *position-based handover* [12], an algorithm developed in our previous work, for camera selection. This technique is based on a camera view model that has been created manually. For each camera, the direction of the camera axis and the visibility of a human standing at the location of each floor sensor are recorded as model parameters. In this algorithm, the main objective is to create a video sequence that has the minimum possible number of shots. If the person can be seen from the previous camera (if any), then that camera is selected. Otherwise the viewable regions of the floor for the cameras are examined in a predetermined order and the first match is selected.

2.3 Audio Handover

Audio acquisition capability is a relatively new addition to the ubiquitous home; therefore the work on audio retrieval is still in initial stages. Our intention in this work is to 'dub' the video sequences created by video handover. Although there are a large number of microphones, it is not necessary to use all of them since a microphone can cover a larger range compared to a camera. Furthermore, frequent transitions of microphones can be an annoyance to the listeners.

We implement a simple algorithm for *audio handover*. Each camera is associated with one microphone for audio retrieval. For a camera in a room, audio is retrieved from the microphone that is located in the center of that room. For a camera in the corridor, the microphone closest to the center of the region seen by the camera is selected. This algorithm attempts to minimize transitions between microphones while maintaining a reasonable sound level.

2.4 Key Frame Extraction

We intend to extract key frames from each sequence created by video handover. The extracted set of key frames can provide a summary of the video and serve as an index for browsing the video. The objective of key frame extraction is to create a complete and compact summary of a video sequence [13]. We intend to achieve this objective by minimizing the number of redundant key frames while ensuring that important frames are not missed.

Table 1 summarizes the algorithms we designed for key frame extraction. In all entries, T is a constant time interval. A simple approach to summarize the video is *temporal sampling*, i.e. sampling key frames periodically. Another approach is *spatial sampling*, where key frames are sampled according to the movement of the person in the environment. In case of this work, we implement

Table 1. Algorithms for key frame extraction

Sampling algorithm	Condition for sampling key frame
Spatial	At every camera change
Temporal	Once every T seconds
spatio-temporal	Sample a key frame – at every camera change – If T seconds elapsed with no camera change after the previous key frame
Adaptive spatio-temporal	Sample a key frame – at every camera change – if t seconds elapsed without a camera change where: $t = T(1 - n/20)$ if $1 \leq n \leq 10$ $t = T/2$ if $n > 10$ (n = number of footsteps since last key frame)

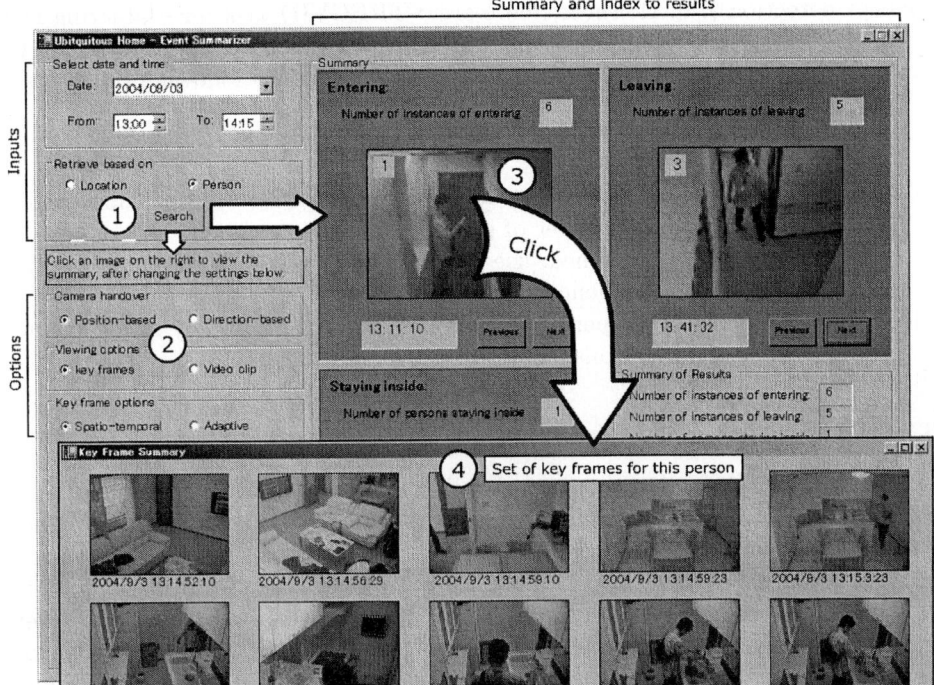

Fig. 2. User interaction with system

spatial sampling by extracting a key frame whenever the camera that is used to show the person is changed. A key frame summary created in this method can help tracing the path the person took. *Spatio-temporal sampling* attempts to combine them to achieve better performance. However, it is evident that we should acquire more key frames when there is more activity and vice versa. Since the rate of footsteps is an indicator of some types of activity, we hypothesize that it is possible to obtain a better set of key frames using an algorithm that is adaptive to the same. *Adaptive spatio-temporal sampling* is based on this hypothesis.

The results are stored in a database, to be retrieved by entering interactive queries through a graphical user interface. The user can retrieve summaries with interactions similar to the scenario described in Section 1. Figure 2 demonstrates interaction with the system for retrieval of key frames to summarize the behavior of a single person.

3 Evaluation Experiment

3.1 Objectives

Evaluation of video retrieval is a relatively new research topic. The TRECVID benchmarks, created in 2001, have evolved to include complex tasks such as concept detection [14]. However, there is no TRECVID task for evaluating key frame extraction at the time of writing [15]. We designed an experiment to evaluate the algorithms for key frame extraction, with the following objectives:

1. Evaluation of the algorithms to select the best algorithm and the correct value for the parameter T
2. Investigate the possibility of extracting an average set of key frames based on those selected by a number of persons
3. If such a set can be obtained, use it for defining accuracy measures for the extracted key frame sequences
4. Obtain feedback on the performance of the algorithms for key frame extraction and identify directions for improvement.

3.2 Description of Experimnent

The experiment consists of a repeated task, referred to as the *key frame extraction task*, performed by multiple test subjects. This is based on a video sequence created by video handover, hereafter referred to as a *sequence*. The task consists of three sections, as described in the following paragraphs.

In the first section, the test subject browses the sequence, and selects key frames to summarize the sequence based on his/her own choice. There is no limit in terms of either the time consumed for selection or the number of frames selected. This section of the experiment is performed first, in order to ensure that seeing the key frames extracted by the system does not influence the subjects when they choose key frames on their own.

In the second section, the subject evaluates sets of key frames (hereafter referred to as *frame sets*) corresponding to the same sequence, created automatically by the system using different algorithms. A total of seven frame sets are presented for each sequence; one created by spatial sampling, two each for the other algorithms with $T = 15$ s and 30 s. The subject ranks each frame set against 3 criteria by answering the questionnaire below.

1. Number of key frames as compared to the duration of the sequence
   (a) too few
   (b) fine
   (c) too many
2. Percentage of redundant key frames
   (a) none
   (b) less than 25%
   (c) 25% to 50%
   (d) more than 50%
3. Number of important frames missed
   (a) none
   (b) 1 to 5
   (c) 6 to 10
   (d) more than 10

In the third section, the subject compares different frame sets and selects the frame set that summarizes the sequence best. For the selected frame set, they answer the following questions:

1. Why do you find it better than other sequences?
2. In what ways can it be improved?

Eight voluntary subjects took part in the experiment. The subjects were regular computer users, but not involved in any work related to video summarization. Each subject completed four repetitions of the key frame extraction task on four different sequences. The subjects were allowed to watch the sequences as many times as they desired. Each subject took 65 to 120 minutes to complete the experiment. This time included short breaks between repetitions, which the subjects were allowed to take if they needed.

4 Results

4.1 Average Key Frame Selection

Figure 3 presents a histogram of key frames selected by the subjects, $f(n)$, for a portion of one sequence. It is evident that key frames selected by different subjects form small clusters corresponding to actions and events they wished to include in their summaries.

The following algorithm was used to form an average key frame set for each sequence. First, we examine $f(n)$ from $n = 0$ and identify non-overlapping windows of 10 frames, within which 50% or more of the subjects selected a key frame. From each window W, an average key frame is extracted using the following equation:

$$k = \left\lceil \frac{\sum_{n \in W} n f(n)}{\sum_{n \in W} n} \right\rceil$$

The average key frames for the frames corresponding to Figure 3 are indicated by black markers on the same graph.

Table 2 compares the average number of key frames the users selected and the number of key frames in the average key frame sets. The numbers are nearly

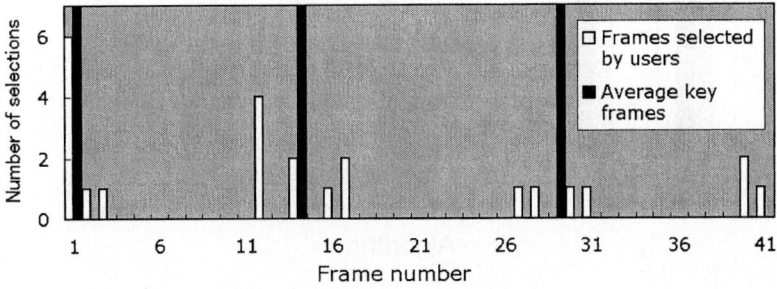

Fig. 3. Average key frames

equal, suggesting that there is strong agreement on the actions and events to be selected as key frames, among different subjects. Therefore, we suggest that it is possible to use these key frame sets in place of ground truth for evaluation of the algorithms for key frame extraction. Furthermore, we propose that the algorithms can be improved by modifying them to retrieve key frame sequences that are closer to the average key frame sets.

Table 2. Comparison of the number of key frames

Sequence Number	1	2	3	4
Average value of the number of key frames selected by subjects	6.5	8	13	32.8
Number of key frames in the average key frame set	6	6	11	30

4.2 Evaluation of Frame Sets

The number of redundant frames or that of missing frames cannot be considered alone to select the best method, since these two measures are somewhat analogous to the *precision* and *recall* measures of information retrieval. Therefore, the best category of responses for each criterion was compared to find out which algorithm has the best overall performance (Figure 4). Adaptive spatio-temporal sampling methods acquired 62% of the total votes, indicating that the algorithm performs much better than the others in key frame extraction. The sum of responses for the three categories is higher when $T = 15$ s, suggesting that 15 s is a

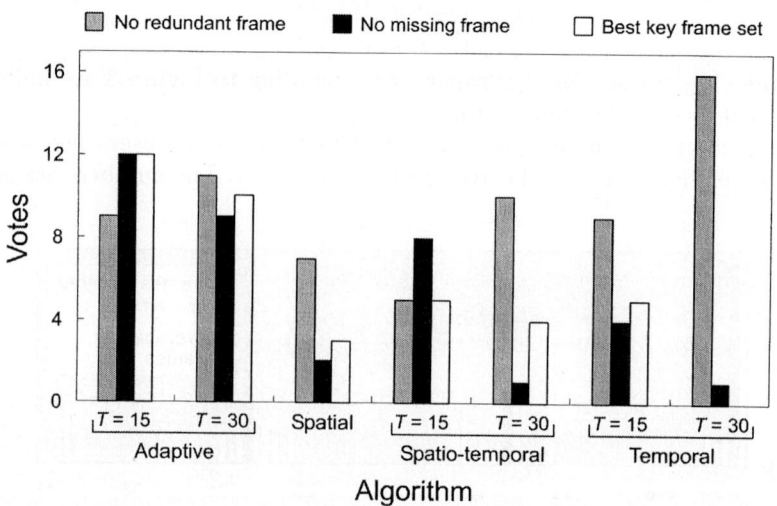

Fig. 4. Comparison of algorithms for key frame extraction

more suitable value for the parameter T. Therefore we select this algorithm and the value of T as the most suitable for key frame extraction in this environment.

4.3 Descriptive Feedback

The subjects used the descriptive questions to express their views about the key frame sets they voted for. The three most common answers for the question "Why do you find it a better summary than other sequences?" are listed below (number of occurrences of each response is indicated in parentheses):

- Minimum number of key frames missed (11)
- Minimum number of redundant frames (6)
- Right number of key frames (5)

The three most common answers to the second question "In what ways can it be improved?" were:

- Add key frames to show interaction with other persons and objects (4)
- Remove redundant key frames (2)
- Try to get a full view of the person in a key frame (2)

4.4 Comparison with Average Key Frames

Figures 5 (a) and 5 (b) show the average key frames and the frame set created by the selected method respectively, for a short sequence. Figure 5 (c) shows the path of the person in the sequence, with locations of the person when the key frames were sampled. There is a high degree of similarity between the two frame sets, as shown by the key frames, locations and timestamps. The algorithm failed to capture the key frame corresponding to the girl picking a camera from the stool, which the test subjects desired to include in their summaries. It extracted two redundant frames as she was within the same view for a longer time.

To evaluate the performance of key frame extraction quantitatively, we define the rank performance, R_n of the algorithm as

$$R_n = \frac{K_n}{N} \times 100\%$$

where K_n is the number of occasions a key frame is present within n frames from that of the average key frame set and N is the number of frames in the average key frame set. Figure 6 plots the cumulative performances against n. The results show that it is possible to extract key frames within a difference of 3 s, with an upper bound of around 80%, using only floor sensor data with this method.

It is evident that the performance is slightly lower for smaller values of n in sequence 3. The person shown in this sequence moves slower and stops for some time in a number of places. As a result, the frames selected by different subjects can be a bit further from those extracted by the algorithm, even when they show the same event or action.

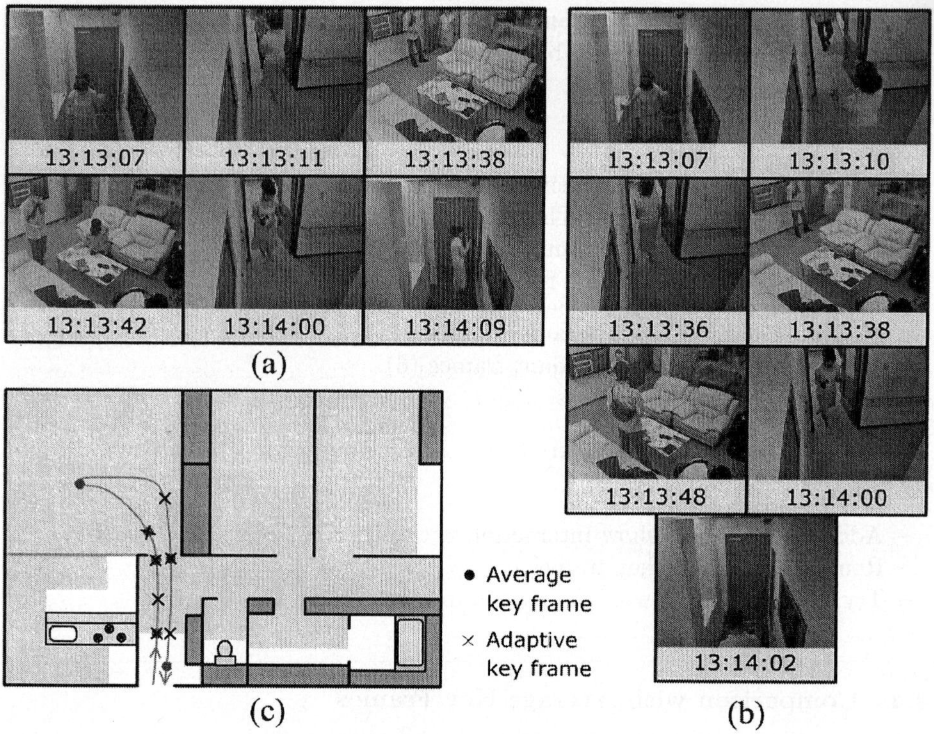

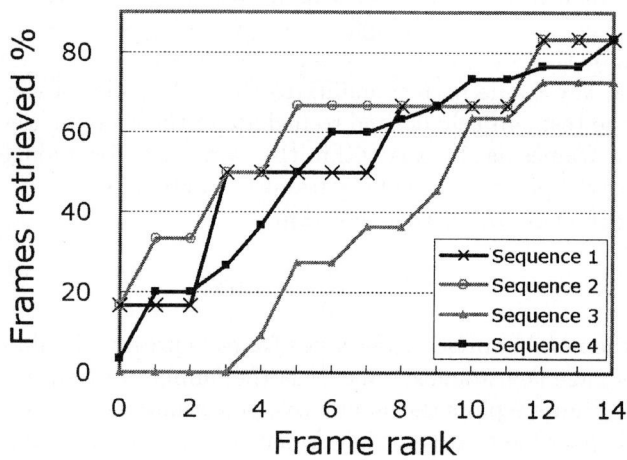

Fig. 5. Comparison of key frame sets

Fig. 6. Cumulative performance of key frame extraction

5 Conclusion

We have implemented personalized video summarization for a ubiquitous environment, by analyzing signals from pressure based floor sensors. Video and audio handover were used to select cameras and microphones for synthesis of continuous video for a given person. A number of algorithms for extracting key frames from the video data were implemented. An experiment was designed and conducted for evaluating the performance of these algorithms. An algorithm that is adaptive to the rate of the footsteps of the person was found to extract key frame sequences that are the best in terms of the number of redundant and missing key frames. Quantitative evaluation based on average sets of key frames showed that about 80% of the most desired key frames can be retrieved using the current algorithms that analyze only the footsteps of a person.

6 Future Work

Future work will focus on extracting key frames to show interaction among persons and between a person and an object. This will increase the completeness of the summaries created by key frame extraction.

Presently video and key frame retrieval is based on date, time and location. This can be enhanced by incorporating retrieval based on different actions. Novel techniques for visualization of results can facilitate more efficient browsing and retrieval. This is important as retrieval is based on interactive querying.

Video handover is currently based on a camera view model that has been created manually. The model has to be updated everytime cameras are adjusted, although minor adjustments do not affect it. Automation of view model acquisition will add more flexibility to video retrieval and remove this tedious task.

At the current state of the work, audio is retrieved using a simple algorithm merely for the purpose of video dubbing. Design and evaluation of better algorithms for audio handover is an interesting future direction. The possibility of using the audio data as a supplementary input for video retrieval is now under investigation.

Acknowledgments

We thank Dr. Hirotada Ueda and Dr.Tatsuya Yamazaki of NICT Keihanna Human Info-communications Laboratory, for experiments in the ubiquitous home. This work is partially supported by CREST of JST, Japan.

References

1. G. A. Abowd, I. Bobick, I. Essa, E. Mynatt, and W. Rogers: The Aware Home: Developing Technologies for Successful Aging, In proceedings of American Association of Artificial Intelligence (AAAI) Conference 2002, Alberta, Canada, July 2002. (2002)

2. T. Mori, H. Noguchi, A. Takada, T. Sato: Sensing Room: Distributed Sensor Environment for Measurement of Human Daily Behavior, Proceedings of INSS2004, pp.40-43, 6 (2004).
3. A. Jaimes, K. Omura, T. Nagamine, and K. Hirata: Memory Cues for Meeting Video Retrieval, Proceedings of CARPE 2004, USA. (2004)
4. Department of Sensory Media - Ubiquitous Sensor Room: http://www.mis.atr.jp/~megumu/IM_Web/MisIM-E.html#usr, ATR Media Information Science Laboratories, Kyoto, Japan. (2002)
5. CHIL - Computers in the Human Interaction Loop: http://chil.server.de/servlet/is/101/, Interactive System Labs, Universitat Karlsruhe (TH), Germany. (2004)
6. J. R. Wang, N. Prameswaran, X. Yu, C. Xu, Qi Tian: Archiving Tennis Video Clips Based on Tactics Information, Proceedings of the 5th Pacific Rim Conference on Multimedia, Part 2 314–321 (1996)
7. Y. Rui, A. Gupta, A. Acero: Automatically Extracting Highlights for TV Baseball Programs, Proceedings of ACM Multimedia 2000, Los Angeles USA. Pp. 105–115 (2000)
8. M. Davis, S. King, N. Good: From Context to Content: Leveraging Context to Infer Media Metadata, Proceedings of ACM Multimedia 2004. Pp. 188-195 (2004)
9. Y. Sawahata and K. Aizawa: Wearable Imaging System for Summarizing Personal Experiences, Proceedings of the 2003 International Conference on Multimedia and Expo, Baltimore, MD. (2003) I-45–I-48
10. T. Yamazaki: Ubiquitous Home: Real-life Testbed for Home Context-Aware Service, Proceedings of Tridentcom2005, pp.54-59, February 23, 2005.
11. Gamhewage C. de Silva, T. Ishikawa, T. Yamasaki, Kiyoharu Aizawa: Video Retrieval in a Ubiquitous Environment with Floor Sensors, In proceedings of IEICE National Conference, March 2005, Japan.
12. Gamhewage C. de Silva, T. Ishikawa, T. Yamasaki, K. Aizawa: Person Tracking and Multi-camera Video Retrieval Using Floor Sensors in a Ubiquitous Environment, In proceedings of CIVR 2005, Singapore. (2005)
13. Song, X., Fan, G.: Joint Key-Frame Extraction and Object-Based Video Segmentation, Motion05 (II: 126-131).
14. M. R. Naphade, J. R. Smith: On the Detection of Semantic Concepts at TRECVID, Proceedings of ACM Multimedia 2004. Pp. 660-667 (2004)
15. TRECVID 2005 Guidelines, http://www-nlpir.nist.gov/projects/tv2005/tv2005.html, National Institute of Standards and Technology, USA. (2005)

Author Index

Abdel-Baki, Nashwa II-141
Ahn, Chang-Beom I-489, I-731
Ahn, Sang-Ho II-337
Ahn, Sangjoon II-48
Aizawa, Kiyoharu I-1005, II-584
Ano, Shigehiro II-429
Ariki, Yasuo II-923
Ashourian, Mohsen II-258, II-349
Avilés, Marcos I-61

Bae, MyungJin II-700
Baek, Joong-Hwan I-269
Baek, SeongHo II-688
Bahn, Hyokyung II-1
Basso, Andrea I-524
Beack, Seung-Hwa I-698
Beak, Seungkwon I-742
Belkhatir, Mohammed I-820
Byeon, Okhwan II-441
Byun, Ju Wan II-1072

Cha, Jongeun I-420, II-176
Cernea, Dan I-84
Chae, Jeong-Sook I-922
Chai, Young-Ho I-315
Chang, Chin-Chen I-981
Chang, Chung-Yuan Knight II-394
Chang, Eun-Young I-73
Chang, I-Cheng I-37
Chang, Pao-Chi II-747
Charhad, Mbarek I-820
Chen, Chun-Jen I-512
Chen, Jun-Cheng I-776
Chen, Tsuhan II-665
Chen, Yiqiang II-1027
Cheng, Cho-Chun I-535
Chiang, Huann-Keng I-291
Cho, Choong-Ho II-224
Cho, Googchun II-981
Cho, Hyung-Jea I-922
Cho, Ikhwan I-547
Cho, Jin-Ho I-888
Cho, Yoon Ho I-957
Choi, Byeong Ho II-514

Choi, Han-wool I-315
Choi, In Yong I-709
Choi, Jin Soo I-234
Choi, Jong-Hyun I-731
Choi, JongUk II-153
Choi, Sang Won II-711
Choi, Seong Jong II-981
Chon, Sang Bae I-709
Choudhry, Umar Iqbal II-818
Chou, Yung-Chen I-981
Chu, Wei-Ta I-776
Chu, Xiaowen II-246
Chun, Seong Soo I-168
Chung, Ki-Dong II-382
Cornelis, Jan I-84

Deklerck, Rudi I-84
de Silva, Gamhewage C. I-1005
Driessen, Peter F. I-524

Fan, Liangzhong I-408
Fang, Zhijun II-405
Fei, Hwai-Chung I-512
Fu, Libo I-594
Fu, Rong II-1027

Gao, Wen I-675, I-864, II-550,
  II-595, II-830, II-946, II-1027
García, Narciso I-61
Gong, Min-Sik II-94
Großmann, Hans Peter II-141

Hahn, Hernsoo I-799
Han, Seung Jo II-489
Han, Seung-Soo I-559
Han, Sunyoung II-48
Har, Dong-Soo I-466, I-500, II-538
Hasegawa, Teruyuki II-429
Hasegawa, Toru II-429
Hayase, Kazuya II-584
He, Wei II-83
He, Weisheng I-809
Hejazi, Mahmoud R. I-910
Hendry II-735

Author Index

Ho, Yo-Sung   I-179, I-361, I-431, I-570, I-687, I-910, II-164, II-176, II-258, II-477, II-514, II-617, II-794
Hong, Eon-Pyo   I-500
Hong, Hyun-Ki   II-772, II-782
Hong, Jin Woo   I-212, I-234
Hong, Jun-Hee   I-466
Hong, Jun-Seong   I-731
Hong, Min-Cheol   II-561
Hong, Seung-Wook   I-854
Hong, Tae Chul   II-200
Hoshino, Haruo   II-429
Hsiao, Fu-Jen   II-665
Hsieh, Ming-I   II-394, II-1015
Hu, Bo   II-830
Huang, Chung-Ling   I-37
Huang, Qian   II-550
Huang, Qingming   I-864, II-830
Huang, Shyh-Fang   II-747
Hur, Namho   I-73
Hwang, Eenjun   I-876
Hwang, Gooyoun   II-465
Hwang, Sun-Kyoo   I-280
Hwang, Wen-Liang   I-535
Hwang, Yong-Ho   II-772

Im, ChaSeop   II-688
Itoh, Kazuo   II-1039

Jang, Euee S.   I-73
Jang, Seok   II-782
Jeon, Hyun-Ho   I-524
Jeon, In-Su   I-144
Jeong, Dongseok   I-547
Jeong, Yong-Yeon   I-570
Jhang, Kyoung-Son   I-500
Ji, Kyunghee   I-191
Jiang, Gangyi   I-408
Jin, Xiaogang   I-257, II-270
Jo, Jinyong   II-441
Joe, Hongmi   I-339
Jun, Kyungkoo   I-25
Jung, Cheolkon   I-765
Jung, Chulho   II-36
Jung, Eun-Gu   I-466, I-500, II-538
Jung, Inbum   II-12
Jung, Kyeong Hoon   II-641
Jung, Moon Ryul   I-327
Jung, Young-Kee   I-559

Kamikura, Kazuto   I-96
Kamimura, Kazuhiro   II-429
Kang, Dong Wook   II-641
Kang, Jung Won   I-191, II-129
Kang, Min-Chang   II-538
Kang, Sanggil   I-202
Kawamori, Masahito   I-224
Kawazoe, Katsuhiko   I-224
Kim, Chan Young   I-957
Kim, Daehee   I-843
Kim, Dae-Yeon   I-396
Kim, Daiyong   I-73
Kim, Deok Hwan   I-957
Kim, Dong Hoon   I-25
Kim, Dong-Hun   I-888
Kim, Dongkook   II-12
Kim, Doohan   II-59
Kim, Eui-Jin   I-765, II-129
Kim, Haelyong   II-235
Kim, Hansung   I-384
Kim, Heesun   II-912
Kim, Hong Kook   I-361, I-477
Kim, Hye-Soo   II-71
Kim, Hyon-Gook   II-676
Kim, Hyunjue   II-117
Kim, Jae-Gon   I-202, I-653, I-787, II-129
Kim, Jae-Won   II-71
Kim, Jin-Soo   I-653
Kim, Ji-Yeon   II-877
Kim, Ji-Yeun   I-765
Kim, JongKuk   II-700
Kim, JongSu   II-688
Kim, JongWeon   II-153
Kim, JongWon   I-361, I-443, II-465, II-501, II-818
Kim, Jun-Yup   II-477
Kim, Ki-Doo   II-641
Kim, Kwanghoon   II-235
Kim, Kyungdeok   II-900
Kim, Kyung-Ho   II-561
Kim, Mi-Ae   II-371
Kim, Munchurl   I-202, II-735, II-806
Kim, Munjo   I-202
Kim, Rinchul   II-981
Kim, Sangjin   I-843
Kim, Sang-Jun   I-606
Kim, Sang-Kyun   I-765, II-877
Kim, Sang Min   I-350
Kim, Sangwook   II-900
Kim, Sehwan   II-176, II-759

Kim, Se-Jin II-224
Kim, Seong-Whan I-664, II-360, II-676
Kim, Seung-Hwan I-179, II-477
Kim, Seung-Jin I-946, II-337
Kim, Seungjoo II-117
Kim, Seung-Man I-420, I-687, II-176
Kim, Sung-Min II-382, II-1072
Kim, Sung-Yeol I-431, I-687, II-164, II-176, II-794
Kim, Taeseok II-1, II-59
Kim, Tae-Su I-946, II-337
Kim, Tae-Wan II-514
Kim, TaeYong II-688
Kim, Whoi-Yul I-280, I-765, II-129
Kim, Wonjung I-120
Kim, Yong-Deak I-408
Kim, Yong Ho I-234
Kim, Yong Tae II-641
Kim, Yoon II-12, II-489
Kim, Young Yong II-200
Kitahara, Masaki I-96
Kitazawa, Hitoshi I-831
Ko, Hyeongseok I-854
Ko, Ki-Hong I-664
Ko, Sung-Jea II-71
Kodama, Kazuya I-303
Koh, Kern II-1, II-59
Komatsu, Takashi I-246
Kong, Hyung-Yun II-187, II-212
Kong, Xiang-Wei II-301
Kon'ya, Yuko I-224
Korekuni, Hitoshi II-889
Kubota, Akira I-303
Kuo, Jin-Hau I-776
Kuwano, Hidetaka I-224
Kwak, Jaiseung II-441
Kwon, Hyoungmoon II-711
Kwon, Jung-hoon I-315
Kwon, Jun-Sik II-772
Kwon, Kee-Koo I-144
Kwon, Ki-Ryong II-337
Kwon, Yong-Il I-582

Lai, Hsu-Te II-1015
Lai, Shang-Hong I-512
Lee, Beom-Chan I-361
Lee, Cheol-Hoon II-94
Lee, Choong-hoon II-312
Lee, Dai-Boong II-105
Lee, Eun-Kyung I-431

Lee, Eunseok II-36
Lee, Gil Ho I-477
Lee, Gun-Woo II-606
Lee, Gwang-Gook I-765, II-129
Lee, Hae-Yeoun II-312
Lee, Haeyoung I-108
Lee, Han-Kyu I-212
Lee, HeeKyung I-212
Lee, Heung-Kyu II-312
Lee, Hyong-Woo II-224
Lee, HyunRyong I-443
Lee, Jeong-A I-500
Lee, Jeong-in I-315
Lee, Joahyoung II-12
Lee, Jongwan I-327
Lee, Joohun I-799
Lee, Joong Yong II-291
Lee, Jui-Yu II-526
Lee, Jumi II-711
Lee, Jungho I-547
Lee, Jung-Il I-489
Lee, Junhaeng I-843
Lee, Kuhn-Il I-946, II-337, II-606
Lee, Kwan-Heng I-361, I-420, I-687, II-176, II-958
Lee, Kyu-Won I-559
Lee, Moon-Hyun I-606
Lee, Sanghee II-36
Lee, Sang-Rak I-25
Lee, Sang Wook I-339, I-350, II-993
Lee, Seokhee I-361
Lee, Seung-Ik I-888
Lee, Seung-Jun II-641
Lee, Soo In I-73
Lee, Soon-Tak I-269
Lee, Sunyoung I-73
Lee, Tae-Hoon II-382
Lee, Won-Hyung II-371
Lee, Wonwoo II-1004
Lee, Woongho I-547
Lee, Yong-Gu I-361
Lee, Yonghee II-981
Lee, Youngho I-361
Lee, Younjeong I-799
Lee, Yung-Ki I-396
Lee, Yung-Lyul I-396
Lee, Yunsik I-969
Lei, Zhen I-754
Li, Houqiang II-854
Lian, Shiguo II-281

Liang, Dawei   I-864
Liang, Ke   I-455
Liaw, Chishyan   I-291
Lim, Chan   II-688
Lim, Dong-Sun   I-144
Lim, Hoi-Jeong   I-466
Lim, Hyesook   I-120
Lim, Seong-Jae   I-570
Lin, Chuang   II-246
Lin, Chung-Chi   I-291
Liu, Jixue   I-582
Liu, Junfa   II-1027
Liu, Qiang   I-934
Liu, Wen-Feng   II-301
Liu, Yang   I-864
Liu, Yazhou   II-946
Liu, Yonghe   II-572
Liu, Yu-chi   I-754
Liu, Zhengkai   II-854
Liu, Zhongxuan   II-281
Lu, Yan   II-629

Ma, Huadong   II-572
Ma, Siwei   I-675
Ma, Wei-Ying   I-617
Markova, Aneta   I-84
Min, Byeongwook   I-73
Min, Dong Bo   I-384
Min, Geyong   II-246
Min, Kyoung Won   II-514
Mo, Hiroshi   I-303
Moallem, Peyman   II-258
Mohebbi, Keyvan   II-349
Moon, Han-gil   I-742
Moon, Nammee   I-191
Moon, Sung-Kyun   I-854
Moon, Young Shik   II-291, II-865
Morán, Francisco   I-61
Mujahid, Fahad Ali   I-466
Munteanu, Adrian   I-84

Na, Kyung Gun   I-327
Nakatsu, Ryohei   I-373, II-1039
Nam, Hyeong-Min   II-71
Nam, Jeho   II-312
Nam, Junghyun   II-117
Nam, Mi Young   II-935
Nam, Yang-Hee   I-720, II-970
Nam, Yunyoung   I-876
Nascimento, Mario A.   I-582

Neve, Wesley De   I-641
Nguyen, Duc-Hoai   I-698
Niimi, Michiharu   II-889
Noda, Hideki   II-889
Noh, Sung-Ryul   I-13

Oakley, Ian   I-420, II-176
Oh, Crystal S.   II-970
Oh, Han   I-361
Oh, Ha Ryoung   II-94
Oh, Hyung Rai   II-24
Oh, Kwan-Jung   II-617
Oh, Ryong   II-224
Oh, Sejin   I-361
Oh, Seoung-Jun   I-489, I-731
Oh, Yoo Rhee   I-361
Ohkubo, Toshiya   II-923

Paik, Joonki   I-843
Pan, Yunhe   I-993
Pan, Zhigeng   II-325
Pang, Yanwei   II-854
Park, Chul-Man   I-489
Park, Dong-Chul   I-698, I-969
Park, Eunyong   II-48
Park, Hanhoon   I-606, I-854
Park, Hochong   I-489, I-731
Park, Ho-Hyun   I-582
Park, Hyun   II-865
Park, Hyuncheol   II-235
Park, Hyunje   II-48
Park, Jeong-Sik   II-453
Park, Jeung-Chul   I-361
Park, Jong-An   I-899, II-489
Park, Jong-Il   I-606, I-854
Park, Jong-Seung   I-13, I-25
Park, Joung Wook   II-958
Park, Ki Tae   II-291
Park, Minsik   I-234
Park, Sancho   I-698
Park, Sang-Hyun   II-453, II-489
Park, Seong Jun   I-787
Park, Si-Yong   II-382
Park, Sujin   I-108
Park, Youngmin   I-361
Prakash, Edmond C.   I-934
Preda, Marius   I-49
Prêteux, Françoise   I-49
Pyun, Jae-Young   II-453, II-489

Qiu, Feng   II-246
Quan, Shan Guo   II-200

Ren, Zhen   II-281
Rhee, Phill Kyu   II-935
Rim, Kee Wook   II-291, II-865
Ro, Yong Man   II-877
Ryu, Byunghan   II-417
Ryu, Jeha   I-361, I-420, II-176
Ryu, Seungwan   II-417

Saito, Takahiro   I-246
Sakamoto, Hajime   I-373
Salomie, Ioan Alexandru   I-84
Schelkens, Peter   I-84
Schrijver, Davy De   I-641
Seo, Dongmahn   II-12
Seo, Hyunhwa   II-417
Seo, Jeong-il   I-709, I-742
Seo, Kwang-Deok   I-787
Seo, Kyong Sok   II-877
Seo, Kyoung Chin   I-339, I-350, II-993
Seo, Kyung-Sik   I-899
Seo, Yang Suk   II-877
Seong, Suk-Jeong   I-720
Seong, Yeong Rak   II-94
Servillat, Florent   II-1039
Sha, Jichang   II-83
Shahab, Qonita M.   II-806
Shen, Jianbing   I-257, II-270
Shen, Zuowei   I-535
Sheu, Ming-Hwa   I-291
Shi, Jiaoying   II-1060
Shi, Yuanchun   I-809
Shimizu, Shinya   I-96
Shin, DongHwan   II-153
Shin, Giroo   II-993
Shin, Jeongho   I-843
Shin, Jitae   II-465
Shin, Sangchul   II-48
Shin, Yoan   II-561
Shin, Yong H.   II-59
Shinozaki, Kuniya   I-373
Sim, Dong-Gyu   I-1
Sohn, Chae-Bong   I-731
Sohn, Kwanghoon   I-384
Song, Changgeun   I-327
Song, Haohao   I-629
Song, Hwangjun   II-24, II-105
Song, Iickho   II-711

Song, Li   I-629
Song, Samuel Moon-Ho   I-787
Song, Zuman   II-653
Suh, Jeong-Jun   II-200
Suk, Jung-Youp   II-606
Sull, Sanghoon   I-168
Sun, Huifang   II-550
Sun, Lifeng   I-455
Sun, Shusen   II-325
Sun, Xiaoming   II-1049
Sun, Xiao   II-83
Sung, Hyun-Sung   II-360
Sung, Koeng-Mo   I-709, I-742
Sung, Mee Young   I-13, I-25

Takao, Nobuteru   II-889
Takiguchi, Tetsuya   II-923
Tanaka, Takaho   I-373
Tanaka, Toshihisa   I-831
Tang, Chih-Wei   I-132
Tao, Dan   II-572
Tao, Jun   II-83
Tao, Pin   II-1049
Tran, Chung-Nguyen   I-969
Tran, Son   I-49
Tung, Yi-Shin   II-841

Van Deursen, Davy   I-641
Van de Walle, Rik   I-641
Van Khuong, Ho   II-187, II-212

Wan, Zheng   II-405
Wang, Hui   II-83, II-653
Wang, Qiang   I-675
Wang, Rangding   I-408
Wang, Weiqiang   I-594
Wang, Wen-Hao   II-665
Wang, Yunli   II-653
Wang, Zhengyou   II-405
Wang, Zhiquan   II-281
Weng, Chung-Yi   II-841
Wolf, Koen De   I-641
Won, Chee Sun   II-1072
Won, Chul-Ho   I-888
Won, Dongho   II-117
Won, Youjip   II-59
Woo, Dong-Min   I-559
Woo, Woontack   I-361, II-176, II-759, II-1004

Wu, Eric Hsiao-Kuang   II-394, II-747, II-1015
Wu, Fei   I-993
Wu, Feng   I-156, II-629
Wu, Ja-Ling   I-776, II-841
Wu, Ling-da   I-754
Wu, Shiqian   II-405
Wu, Wen-Chuan   I-981
Wu, Xiao-feng   II-1039

Xia, Tao   I-535
Xiao, Xin   I-809
Xiong, Hongkai   I-156, I-629
Xu, Feng   I-617
Xu, Jizheng   I-156

Yabuta, Kenichi   I-831
Yamada, Tomokazu   I-224
Yamasaki, Toshihiko   I-1005, II-584
Yang, Seungji   II-877
Yang, Seung-Jun   I-212
Yang, Tian-Lin   I-37
Yang, Ya-Ting   II-841
Yang, Yi   I-993
Yao, Hongxun   II-946
Ye, Xien   I-408
Yeh, Jen-Hao   I-776
Yi, Dong-Hoon   II-501
Yi, Jeong-Seon   I-720
Yim, Changhoon   I-120
Yin, Baocai   II-629
Yin, Hao   II-246
Yoo, Jae Doug   II-958
Yoo, Jo Hyung   II-935
Yoo, Kee-Young   II-723
Yoo, Kil-Sang   II-371
Yoo, Youngil   II-641

Yoon, Eun-Jun   II-723
Yoon, Ja-Cheon   I-168
Yoon, Jae Sam   I-477
Yoon, Seok   II-711
Yoon, Seung-Uk   I-431, II-164, II-176
Yoon, Young-Suk   I-687, II-794
Yoshiyuki, Yashima   I-96
You, Ji-Hyuk   I-489
You, Shingchern D.   II-526
You, Xin-Gang   II-301
Yu, Jiarong   II-1060
Yu, Mei   I-408
Yu, Nenghai   II-854
Yu, Songyu   I-629
Yun, Jae-Woong   II-71

Zeng, Weiming   II-405
Zhan, Yaowen   I-594
Zhang, Daxing   II-325
Zhang, Dongdong   I-156
Zhang, Lei   I-617
Zhang, Mingmin   II-325
Zhang, Nan   II-629
Zhang, Peng   II-830
Zhang, Rong   II-854
Zhang, Wenjun   I-156
Zhang, Xin   II-653
Zhang, Ying   I-754
Zhang, Yu-Jin   I-617
Zhao, Debin   I-675, II-550, II-946
Zheng, Qing-Fang   II-595
Zhong, Yuzhuo   I-455
Zhou, Chuan   I-257, II-270
Zhou, Renqin   II-1027
Zhou, Yongxia   II-1060
Zhuang, Yueting   I-993

Lecture Notes in Computer Science

For information about Vols. 1–3688

please contact your bookseller or Springer

Vol. 3806: M. Kitsuregawa, E.J. Neuhold, A.H. H. Ngu, J.-Y. Chung, Q.Z. Sheng (Eds.), Web Information Systems – WISE 2005. XXI, 771 pages. 2005.

Vol. 3791: A. Adi, S. Stoutenburg, S. Tabet (Eds.), Rules and Rule Markup Languages for the Semantic Web. X, 225 pages. 2005.

Vol. 3789: A. Gelbukh, Á. de Albornoz, H. Terashima-Marín (Eds.), MICAI 2005: Advances in Artificial Intelligence. XXVI, 1198 pages. 2005. (Subseries LNAI).

Vol. 3785: K.-K. Lau, R. Banach (Eds.), Formal Methods and Software Engineering. XIV, 496 pages. 2005.

Vol. 3784: J. Tao, T. Tan, R.W. Picard (Eds.), Affective Computing and Intelligent Interaction. XIX, 1008 pages. 2005.

Vol. 3781: S.Z. Li, Z. Sun, T. Tan, S. Pankanti, G. Chollet, D. Zhang (Eds.), Advances in Biometric Person Authentication. XI, 250 pages. 2005.

Vol. 3780: K. Yi (Ed.), Programming Languages and Systems. XI, 435 pages. 2005.

Vol. 3779: H. Jin, D. Reed, W. Jiang (Eds.), Network and Parallel Computing. XV, 513 pages. 2005.

Vol. 3777: O.B. Lupanov, O.M. Kasim-Zade, A.V. Chaskin, K. Steinhöfel (Eds.), Stochastic Algorithms: Foundations and Applications. VIII, 239 pages. 2005.

Vol. 3775: J. Schönwälder, J. Serrat (Eds.), Ambient Networks. XIII, 281 pages. 2005.

Vol. 3772: M. Consens, G. Navarro (Eds.), String Processing and Information Retrieval. XIV, 406 pages. 2005.

Vol. 3770: J. Akoka, S.W. Liddle, I.-Y. Song, M. Bertolotto, I. Comyn-Wattiau, W.-J. van den Heuvel, M. Kolp, J.C. Trujillo, C. Kop, H.C. Mayr (Eds.), Perspectives in Conceptual Modeling. XXII, 476 pages. 2005.

Vol. 3768: Y.-S. Ho, H.J. Kim (Eds.), Advances in Mulitmedia Information Processing - PCM 2005, Part II. XXVIII, 1088 pages. 2005.

Vol. 3767: Y.-S. Ho, H.J. Kim (Eds.), Advances in Mulitmedia Information Processing - PCM 2005, Part I. XXVIII, 1022 pages. 2005.

Vol. 3766: N. Sebe, M.S. Lew, T.S. Huang (Eds.), Computer Vision in Human-Computer Interaction. X, 231 pages. 2005.

Vol. 3765: Y. Liu, T. Jiang, C. Zhang (Eds.), Computer Vision for Biomedical Image Applications. X, 563 pages. 2005.

Vol. 3764: S. Tixeuil, T. Herman (Eds.), Self-Stabilizing Systems. VIII, 229 pages. 2005.

Vol. 3762: R. Meersman, Z. Tari, P. Herrero (Eds.), On the Move to Meaningful Internet Systems 2005: OTM Workshops. XXXI, 1228 pages. 2005.

Vol. 3761: R. Meersman, Z. Tari (Eds.), On the Move to Meaningful Internet Systems 2005: CoopIS, DOA, and ODBASE, Part II. XXVII, 653 pages. 2005.

Vol. 3760: R. Meersman, Z. Tari (Eds.), On the Move to Meaningful Internet Systems 2005: CoopIS, DOA, and ODBASE, Part I. XXVII, 921 pages. 2005.

Vol. 3759: G. Chen, Y. Pan, M. Guo, J. Lu (Eds.), Parallel and Distributed Processing and Applications - ISPA 2005 Workshops. XIII, 669 pages. 2005.

Vol. 3758: Y. Pan, D. Chen, M. Guo, J. Cao, J. Dongarra (Eds.), Parallel and Distributed Processing and Applications. XXIII, 1162 pages. 2005.

Vol. 3756: J. Cao, W. Nejdl, M. Xu (Eds.), Advanced Parallel Processing Technologies. XIV, 526 pages. 2005.

Vol. 3754: J. Dalmau Royo, G. Hasegawa (Eds.), Management of Multimedia Networks and Services. XII, 384 pages. 2005.

Vol. 3753: O.F. Olsen, L. Florack, A. Kuijper (Eds.), Deep Structure, Singularities, and Computer Vision. X, 259 pages. 2005.

Vol. 3752: N. Paragios, O. Faugeras, T. Chan, C. Schnörr (Eds.), Variational, Geometric, and Level Set Methods in Computer Vision. XI, 369 pages. 2005.

Vol. 3751: T. Magedanz, E.R. M. Madeira, P. Dini (Eds.), Operations and Management in IP-Based Networks. X, 213 pages. 2005.

Vol. 3750: J.S. Duncan, G. Gerig (Eds.), Medical Image Computing and Computer-Assisted Intervention – MICCAI 2005, Part II. XL, 1018 pages. 2005.

Vol. 3749: J.S. Duncan, G. Gerig (Eds.), Medical Image Computing and Computer-Assisted Intervention – MICCAI 2005, Part I. XXXIX, 942 pages. 2005.

Vol. 3747: C.A. Maziero, J.G. Silva, A.M.S. Andrade, F.M.d. Assis Silva (Eds.), Dependable Computing. XV, 267 pages. 2005.

Vol. 3746: P. Bozanis, E.N. Houstis (Eds.), Advances in Informatics. XIX, 879 pages. 2005.

Vol. 3745: J.L. Oliveira, V. Maojo, F. Martin-Sanchez, A.S. Pereira (Eds.), Biological and Medical Data Analysis. XII, 422 pages. 2005. (Subseries LNBI).

Vol. 3744: T. Magedanz, A. Karmouch, S. Pierre, I. Venieris (Eds.), Mobility Aware Technologies and Applications. XIV, 418 pages. 2005.

Vol. 3740: T. Srikanthan, J. Xue, C.-H. Chang (Eds.), Advances in Computer Systems Architecture. XVII, 833 pages. 2005.

Vol. 3739: W. Fan, Z.-h. Wu, J. Yang (Eds.), Advances in Web-Age Information Management. XXIV, 930 pages. 2005.

Vol. 3738: V.R. Syrotiuk, E. Chávez (Eds.), Ad-Hoc, Mobile, and Wireless Networks. XI, 360 pages. 2005.

Vol. 3735: A. Hoffmann, H. Motoda, T. Scheffer (Eds.), Discovery Science. XVI, 400 pages. 2005. (Subseries LNAI).

Vol. 3734: S. Jain, H.U. Simon, E. Tomita (Eds.), Algorithmic Learning Theory. XII, 490 pages. 2005. (Subseries LNAI).

Vol. 3733: P. Yolum, T. Güngör, F. Gürgen, C. Özturan (Eds.), Computer and Information Sciences - ISCIS 2005. XXI, 973 pages. 2005.

Vol. 3731: F. Wang (Ed.), Formal Techniques for Networked and Distributed Systems - FORTE 2005. XII, 558 pages. 2005.

Vol. 3729: Y. Gil, E. Motta, V. R. Benjamins, M.A. Musen (Eds.), The Semantic Web – ISWC 2005. XXIII, 1073 pages. 2005.

Vol. 3728: V. Paliouras, J. Vounckx, D. Verkest (Eds.), Integrated Circuit and System Design. XV, 753 pages. 2005.

Vol. 3726: L.T. Yang, O.F. Rana, B. Di Martino, J. Dongarra (Eds.), High Performance Computing and Communications. XXVI, 1116 pages. 2005.

Vol. 3725: D. Borrione, W. Paul (Eds.), Correct Hardware Design and Verification Methods. XII, 412 pages. 2005.

Vol. 3724: P. Fraigniaud (Ed.), Distributed Computing. XIV, 520 pages. 2005.

Vol. 3723: W. Zhao, S. Gong, X. Tang (Eds.), Analysis and Modelling of Faces and Gestures. XI, 4234 pages. 2005.

Vol. 3722: D. Van Hung, M. Wirsing (Eds.), Theoretical Aspects of Computing – ICTAC 2005. XIV, 614 pages. 2005.

Vol. 3721: A. Jorge, L. Torgo, P.B. Brazdil, R. Camacho, J. Gama (Eds.), Knowledge Discovery in Databases: PKDD 2005. XXIII, 719 pages. 2005. (Subseries LNAI).

Vol. 3720: J. Gama, R. Camacho, P.B. Brazdil, A. Jorge, L. Torgo (Eds.), Machine Learning: ECML 2005. XXIII, 769 pages. 2005. (Subseries LNAI).

Vol. 3719: M. Hobbs, A.M. Goscinski, W. Zhou (Eds.), Distributed and Parallel Computing. XI, 448 pages. 2005.

Vol. 3718: V.G. Ganzha, E.W. Mayr, E.V. Vorozhtsov (Eds.), Computer Algebra in Scientific Computing. XII, 502 pages. 2005.

Vol. 3717: B. Gramlich (Ed.), Frontiers of Combining Systems. X, 321 pages. 2005. (Subseries LNAI).

Vol. 3716: L. Delcambre, C. Kop, H.C. Mayr, J. Mylopoulos, Ó. Pastor (Eds.), Conceptual Modeling – ER 2005. XVI, 498 pages. 2005.

Vol. 3715: E. Dawson, S. Vaudenay (Eds.), Progress in Cryptology – Mycrypt 2005. XI, 329 pages. 2005.

Vol. 3714: H. Obbink, K. Pohl (Eds.), Software Product Lines. XIII, 235 pages. 2005.

Vol. 3713: L.C. Briand, C. Williams (Eds.), Model Driven Engineering Languages and Systems. XV, 722 pages. 2005.

Vol. 3712: R. Reussner, J. Mayer, J.A. Stafford, S. Overhage, S. Becker, P.J. Schroeder (Eds.), Quality of Software Architectures and Software Quality. XIII, 289 pages. 2005.

Vol. 3711: F. Kishino, Y. Kitamura, H. Kato, N. Nagata (Eds.), Entertainment Computing - ICEC 2005. XXIV, 540 pages. 2005.

Vol. 3710: M. Barni, I. Cox, T. Kalker, H.J. Kim (Eds.), Digital Watermarking. XII, 485 pages. 2005.

Vol. 3709: P. van Beek (Ed.), Principles and Practice of Constraint Programming - CP 2005. XX, 887 pages. 2005.

Vol. 3708: J. Blanc-Talon, W. Philips, D.C. Popescu, P. Scheunders (Eds.), Advanced Concepts for Intelligent Vision Systems. XXII, 725 pages. 2005.

Vol. 3707: D.A. Peled, Y.-K. Tsay (Eds.), Automated Technology for Verification and Analysis. XII, 506 pages. 2005.

Vol. 3706: H. Fuks, S. Lukosch, A.C. Salgado (Eds.), Groupware: Design, Implementation, and Use. XII, 378 pages. 2005.

Vol. 3704: M. De Gregorio, V. Di Maio, M. Frucci, C. Musio (Eds.), Brain, Vision, and Artificial Intelligence. XV, 556 pages. 2005.

Vol. 3703: F. Fages, S. Soliman (Eds.), Principles and Practice of Semantic Web Reasoning. VIII, 163 pages. 2005.

Vol. 3702: B. Beckert (Ed.), Automated Reasoning with Analytic Tableaux and Related Methods. XIII, 343 pages. 2005. (Subseries LNAI).

Vol. 3701: M. Coppo, E. Lodi, G. M. Pinna (Eds.), Theoretical Computer Science. XI, 411 pages. 2005.

Vol. 3700: J.F. Peters, A. Skowron (Eds.), Transactions on Rough Sets IV. X, 375 pages. 2005.

Vol. 3699: C.S. Calude, M.J. Dinneen, G. Păun, M. J. Pérez-Jiménez, G. Rozenberg (Eds.), Unconventional Computation. XI, 267 pages. 2005.

Vol. 3698: U. Furbach (Ed.), KI 2005: Advances in Artificial Intelligence. XIII, 409 pages. 2005. (Subseries LNAI).

Vol. 3697: W. Duch, J. Kacprzyk, E. Oja, S. Zadrożny (Eds.), Artificial Neural Networks: Formal Models and Their Applications – ICANN 2005, Part II. XXXII, 1045 pages. 2005.

Vol. 3696: W. Duch, J. Kacprzyk, E. Oja, S. Zadrożny (Eds.), Artificial Neural Networks: Biological Inspirations – ICANN 2005, Part I. XXXI, 703 pages. 2005.

Vol. 3695: M.R. Berthold, R.C. Glen, K. Diederichs, O. Kohlbacher, I. Fischer (Eds.), Computational Life Sciences. XI, 277 pages. 2005. (Subseries LNBI).

Vol. 3694: M. Malek, E. Nett, N. Suri (Eds.), Service Availability. VIII, 213 pages. 2005.

Vol. 3693: A.G. Cohn, D.M. Mark (Eds.), Spatial Information Theory. XII, 493 pages. 2005.

Vol. 3692: R. Casadio, G. Myers (Eds.), Algorithms in Bioinformatics. X, 436 pages. 2005. (Subseries LNBI).

Vol. 3691: A. Gagalowicz, W. Philips (Eds.), Computer Analysis of Images and Patterns. XIX, 865 pages. 2005.

Vol. 3690: M. Pěchouček, P. Petta, L.Z. Varga (Eds.), Multi-Agent Systems and Applications IV. XVII, 667 pages. 2005. (Subseries LNAI).

Vol. 3689: G.G. Lee, A. Yamada, H. Meng, S.H. Myaeng (Eds.), Information Retrieval Technology. XVII, 735 pages. 2005.